LAW
and
THE SOCIAL SCIENCES

The preparation of this volume was sponsored
by the Committee on Law and Social Science
of the Social Science Research Council.

Leon Lipson, Chairman
    Yale University

Phoebe C. Ellsworth
    Stanford University

Lawrence M. Friedman
    Stanford University

Marc Galanter
    University of Wisconsin, Madison

Sally Falk Moore
    Harvard University

Nelson W. Polsby
    University of California, Berkeley

Philip Selznick
    University of California, Berkeley

Stanton Wheeler
    Yale University

STAFF
David L. Sills
    Social Science Research Council

LAW
and
THE SOCIAL SCIENCES

edited by
Leon Lipson and Stanton Wheeler

RUSSELL SAGE FOUNDATION   NEW YORK

The Russell Sage Foundation

The Russell Sage Foundation, one of the oldest of America's general purpose foundations, was established in 1907 by Mrs. Margaret Olivia Sage for "the improvement of social and living conditions in the United States." The Foundation seeks to fulfill this mandate by fostering the development and dissemination of knowledge about the political, social, and economic problems of America. It conducts research in the social sciences and public policy, and publishes books and pamphlets that derive from this research.

The Board of Trustees is responsible for oversight and the general policies of the Foundation, while administrative direction of the program and staff is vested in the President, assisted by the officers and staff. The President bears final responsibility for the decision to publish a manuscript as a Russell Sage Foundation book. In reaching a judgement on the competence, accuracy, and objectivity of each study, the President is advised by the staff and selected expert readers. The conclusions and interpretations in Russell Sage Foundation publications are those of the authors and not of the Foundation, its Trustees, or its staff. Publication by the Foundation, therefore, does not imply endorsement of the contents of the study.

Library of Congress Cataloging-in-Publication Data
Main entry under title:

Law and the social sciences.

Bibliography: p.
Includes index.
1. Sociological jurisprudence. 2. Social sciences—
Research—United States. I. Lipson, Leon. II. Wheeler,
Stanton.
KF379.L36 1986   340'.115   85-62807
ISBN 0-87154-528-4

Cover and text design: Huguette Franco

10 9 8 7 6 5 4 3 2 1

CONTRIBUTORS

Richard L. Abel
  University of California, Los Angeles

Shari Seidman Diamond
  University of Illinois, Chicago

Phoebe C. Ellsworth
  Stanford University

Marc Galanter
  University of Wisconsin, Madison

Julius G. Getman
  Yale University

Jack P. Gibbs
  Vanderbilt University

Jeffrey L. Jowell
  University of London

Edmund W. Kitch
  University of Virginia

Leon Lipson
  Yale University

Stewart Macaulay
  University of Wisconsin, Madison

David R. Mayhew
  Yale University

Sally Falk Moore
  Harvard University

Austin D. Sarat
  Amherst College

Richard D. Schwartz
  Syracuse University

Stanton Wheeler
  Yale University

CONTENTS

INTRODUCTION

Leon Lipson and Stanton Wheeler
Yale University

The Committee on Law and Social Science, appointed in 1974 by the Social Science Research Council, became convinced that the time was at hand for an assessment of research in law and the social sciences.[1] Although the volume is in a formal sense a committee product, in a larger (and we think truer) sense it is the product of a generation of scholars—mostly social scientists and law professors—who believe that the perspectives, data, and methods of the social sciences are essential to a better understanding of the law.

This introduction has three main purposes:

1. to orient the reader to the history of the relationship between law and the social sciences in the United States as organized enterprises, objects of study, academic disciplines, means of social action, and forms of social intervention;

2. to explain the approaches taken by the contributors in this volume, giving a brief notion of the contents of the chapters in the volume and their connections with one another; and

3. to report and hazard some conjectures on some of the principal trends in the law-and-social-science field that may be inferred from the various chapters in the volume.

[1] The members of the committee were Phoebe C. Ellsworth and Lawrence M. Friedman, both of Stanford University; Marc Galanter, University of Wisconsin; Leon Lipson, Yale University (chairman); Sally Falk Moore, Harvard University; Nelson W. Polsby and Philip Selznick, both of the University of California, Berkeley; and Stanton Wheeler, Yale University. David L. Sills served as staff to the committee.

BACKGROUND

The wellsprings of the modern law-and-social-science movement—as its members came to think of it—may be found in two related ideas that were already in evidence by the turn of the twentieth century among some social scientists and academic lawyers.

The first was the growing perception that law is a social phenomenon and that legal doctrine and legal actors are integral parts of the social landscape. Because they are a part of social life, legal phenomena both stimulate changes in other social institutions and are affected by social changes and pressures occurring elsewhere in the society. The law also serves to codify social relations, to make them more explicit, and to impart structure to them. If legal events and actors are thus interwoven with the society, understanding legal phenomena requires examining them not in isolation but in relation to the surrounding social world.

This observation sounds so obvious in the late twentieth century that one wonders how it could ever have seemed otherwise. It is useful, then, to recall the position taken by Christopher Columbus Langdell, professor and dean at Harvard Law School, roughly a century ago. Langdell located the science of law among the other activities of a great university, justified the university as the proper place for the training of lawyers, and had a vision of the subject matter that made the recommended intellectual activity appropriate:

> [It] was indispensable to establish at least two things: first that law is a science; secondly, that all the available materials of that science are contained in printed books. If law be not a science, a university will best consult its own dignity in declining to teach it. . . . If . . . there are other and better means of teaching and learning law than printed books . . . it must be confessed that such means cannot be provided by a university. But if printed books are the ultimate sources of all legal knowledge; if every student who would obtain any mastery of law as a science must resort to these ultimate sources; and if the only assistance which it is possible for the learner to receive is such as can be afforded by teachers who have traveled the same road beforehand,—then a university and a university alone, can furnish every possible facility for teaching and learning law. . . . We have also constantly inculcated the idea that the library is the proper workshop of professors and students alike; that it is to us all that the laboratories of the university are to the chemists and physicists, all that the Museum of Natural History is to the zoologist, all that the botanical garden is to the botanist.

If all the materials for the science of law lay in "printed books," then there would be no need to inquire into other ongoing behavior—of judges, courts, lawyers, juries, or other legal actors—no need, in other words, for the kinds of studies and analyses carried out by participants in the law-and-society movement. And if one used those legal materials primarily to discern legal principles, the capacity of legal life to reflect the nature of the society in which it was located would have remained hidden from view. It was just this capacity that was brilliantly illustrated by Emile Durkheim in his imaginative use of the ratio of civil to penal law in a society as an index of changes in social solidarity.

The second idea underlying the law-and-social-science movement was that legal institutions not only are embedded in social life, but also can be improved by drawing upon the organized wisdom of social experience. Here the pragmatic and the scientific combine to provide a new way of assessing legal doctrine and legal practice. In its less technical form, this view is reflected in the assertion, made by Oliver Wendell Holmes in the 1890s, that the life of law has not been logic but experience. Its most prominent early example among legal materials is the famous "Brandeis Brief" of 1908, which examined dozens of reports of the actual working conditions and experiences of women in factories in a successful effort to help the state of Oregon justify its protective labor legislation in court. The principle that courts, advocates, and scholars should look beyond the cases and the case doctrine to real-life circumstances became one of the cornerstones of the development of legal realism later in the twentieth century.

Later still, a more precise method of organizing certain legal-social experience was worked out for the study of the effect that the enactment of rules by a legislature, or the pronouncement of doctrine and decision by a court, or the promulgation of administrative regulations would have on the behavior of persons and institutions. These "legal impact studies" took on increasing intricacy and formality as policy-makers and scholars learned the importance of attending to desired and undesired effects, to unintended or unforeseen consequences, and to changes that occur as relevant conditions change over the lifetime of a rule.

In its more technical and scientific form, the application of behavioral science to law had equally ardent advocates and detractors. In retrospect, it seems fair to say that many of the advocates were less than fully appreciative of the difficulties encountered in attempting to do relevant and significant social research on legal issues, and thus often claimed more than they could deliver. Manifestoes were eloquent; methodologies, ambitious; results, modest. The advocates often encountered a stridently defensive group of legal academics who were all too ready to pounce on the frailties with professionally specialized acumen as a basis for dismissing the enterprise. Early in the twentieth century, a few American legal scholars built on the work of European social scientists, especially Durkheim and Weber; men like Holmes and Pound recognized the potential of the social sciences for contributing to legal analysis. The rise and decline of legal realism in the United States during the 1920s and 1930s has been well documented and has left some substantive monuments such as the work of Karl N. Llewellyn and E. Adamson Hoebel in legal anthropology. By the end of World War II, the law, science, and policy tradition had had its beginnings at Yale in the collaboration of Harold D. Lasswell and Myres S. McDougal.

The enterprise of law and social science that is reflected in these pages is an outgrowth of the enormous expansion of the social and behavioral sciences that took place in the 1950s and afterward in the United States, building on wartime and postwar research and training. That general movement brought new funding for social research through the establishment of the National Institute of Mental Health and the social-science division of the National Science Foundation. It was also marked by a period in which private philanthropy, most notably the Ford Foundation, made significant grants for large-scale social research (the most prominent result in law-and-society work being the jury studies made by Harry Kalven, Jr., Hans Zeisel, and their colleagues).

The application of behavioral science to law was made easier by three other trends that emerged during this period. First, after World War II major works of European social theory were translated and published in English for the first time, so that the works of Weber, Durkheim, and others became more easily accessible to the American scholarly community. The rebirth of interest in European theory had a second effect: American social scientists moved away from the strong rule-skepticism characterized by the period of legal realism to entertain at least the idea that the study of law could deal with the role of legal principle and legal reasoning in the behavior of legal actors—without becoming in itself an entirely normative enterprise. The result is that many of the studies that have emerged more recently have a joint focus that attends to rules and their interpretation, as well as to the more concrete behaviors of legal actors.

Finally, the singular case of the American caste system and the major Supreme Court decision concerning it, *Brown* v. *Board of Education of Topeka* (1954), highlighted the role, dubious as it was for many, of the social sciences as potential influences on legal policy. Perhaps even more important, the *Brown* case and its aftermath provided a visible, powerful instance of the impact of law on society and in that way stimulated research on law.

Taken together, these developments created a fertile ground for the institutionalization of interdisciplinary work in law and the behavioral sciences. Although the particulars of the developments differed by discipline in ways far too detailed to be recited here, it seems fair to say that something like a "law-and-society" movement was generated during the 1950s and that it grew so much in the 1960s and 1970s that there is by now a large body of findings, propositions, and conjectures worth analyzing in an assessment volume.

There are many signs of the field's institutionalization. There has been a consistent flow of funding specifically for work in law and social science since at least the late 1950s, when the Social Science Research Council—with support from the Ford Foundation—began to give postdoctoral grants for research on American governmental and legal processes. This program ultimately became a responsibility of a new Council Committee on Governmental and Legal Processes (1964–72). In the early 1960s, the Russell Sage Foundation began to devote a major portion of its resources to the law-and-society field. Beginning in the early 1960s and continuing for over a decade, Russell Sage funding provided the principal resources for training and research in law and the social sciences. The funding took three interrelated forms. (1) It provided substantial support to those institutions willing to commit themselves to interdisciplinary programs in law and the social sciences. The first programs were established at the University of California, Berkeley; at the University of Wisconsin; at Northwestern University; and at the University of Denver. Later programs of varying degrees of intensity and duration were established at Yale, Harvard, Stanford, and the University of Pennsylvania. The funding enabled the development of interdisciplinary courses and seminars and support for faculty members and graduate students committed to the enterprise. (2) The Russell Sage Foundation established a fellowship program for a select group of scholars to pursue interdisciplinary training, often at universities that were receiving institutional support. The training, often for two-year periods, enabled the scholars to develop the background that would facilitate a career commitment to interdisciplinary work. (3) The Russell Sage Foundation provided funding for major pieces of sociological research and often published the results of that research. This three-pronged support provided by Russell Sage—for institutions, for individual training, and for research—gave momentum to the law-and-social-science enterprise.

Of special importance in the United States was the development of a new program in law and social science at the National Science Foundation (NSF). The NSF had been funding basic research in the social sciences for many years, but it had never developed a specific program to support research in law and social science. In 1972, such a program was initiated, along the lines of other NSF programs: the screening and selection of research proposals through a system of peer review and the award of research grants to successful applicants. Although the total budget is small (around $1 million a year), it provides a basis for the continuity of research and of research interests. Those receiving awards include anthropologists, economists, political scientists, psychologists, and sociologists, along with those trained primarily in law. Other patterns of support have been institutionalized in a number of European countries: for example, at various Max Planck institutes in Germany and at the Centre for Socio-Legal Studies at Oxford.

The growth of the enterprise is also reflected in the birth of associations and journals devoted specifically to interdisciplinary concerns. In the United States, the Law and Society Association represents a large portion of this interest. The association's annual meetings are attended by lawyers as well as by social scientists. The *Law & Society Review,* the official organ of the association, has been in existence for over fifteen years. A strategically important role was played also in the late 1960s and early 1970s by the Council on Law-Related Studies under the leadership of David F. Cavers, who before moving from Duke to Harvard had been active in founding *Law & Contemporary Problems.*

By the end of the 1970s, many university departments in faculties of arts and sciences had provided recognized home bases for social-science students of law: the sociology of law in departments of sociology, the psychology of law in psychology departments, and so forth. The picture in law schools was different. The law-and-society enterprise once stood pretty much on its own in the law school world; but by now legal history, like law-and-economics, has emerged as a separate program, with its own cast of characters, its own field of application, and its own doctrine. Legal philosophy has had a more diffuse impact in law schools, while the perspective called critical legal theory has gained many adherents. As a consequence of these developments, what was once thought of as the law-and-society enterprise—economics apart—is fighting for space among all the others. The behavioral sciences have remained relatively stable except for beachheads here and there, while the others have grown faster.

THE PLAN OF THIS BOOK

This is at bottom a volume of assessment: it is not a collection of speculative essays and not a set of reports on fresh research. It is designed with attention to three dyads, which in turn are interlocked.

First, the authors of the chapters are about evenly divided between contributors trained and working primarily in law, and those trained and working primarily in one of the social sciences. (One chapter and the introduction are written jointly by different pairs of authors of two different orientations.) Each contributor, however, is conversant with work and problems across the range of relevant disciplines; several of them are formally or informally trained in both law and a social science; most of them hold academic appointments in "well-mixed" faculties or schools; and most are engaged in training and supervising students who attend law schools as well as students who study in faculties of arts and sciences.

Second, the scope of each chapter was fixed not by its supposed disciplinary boundaries but by the importance or interest of the subject and the work done on it, although it will be obvious to the reader that in some cases the topic leans toward one "-ology" more than it does to others.

Third, each chapter contains, in slightly different ratios, both an exposition of the author's point of view and a survey of the pertinent literature—to which, in most cases, the author of the chapter has been a substantial contributor. It ought not to be hard for the reader to make the relevant distinctions.

It would be impossible to summarize the information and opinions presented in the substantive chapters without compressing an already condensed text to an indigestible consistency. We limit ourselves here to some illustrative highlights of their message, reserving the next section for more abstract themes that cut across many of the contributions.

• It has been a commonplace of critics at least since the time of Tocqueville that law spreads to cover ever-more aspects of American life while (or because?) other dimensions of organization such as religion, tradition, community, and fraternity give ground under various current pressures. Sometimes the critics have disagreed, or doubted whether the tendency toward legalization has generally worked for or against equality, for or against participation, for or against justice.

One concomitant of the law's success was that theories about law tended until rather recently to be developed within the legal profession and thus to have a high normative component, no matter whether the theorist's attitude was positive or negative. Social scientists have been exhorted by (academic) lawyers since the 1920s to pay more attention to the law; but the same jurists who thought they welcomed the attention cherished the arcane and thus sometimes forbidding accouterments of the guild. Most law firms probably would have resisted scholarly scrutiny of their part of the legal profession as intrusive, unethical, and irrelevant. In commenting on a proposal that large law firms be studied by legal scholars, an illustrious lawyer once told an illustrious university president, "Let them study the provision of legal services to the poor!" It was not until the 1970s that many academic lawyers accepted as good form the activity of studying law teaching and practice as an enterprise not less respectable than poets writing poems about the writing of poetry or playwrights writing plays about actors or writers. As attention thus came to be focused on the legal profession in the law schools, in part as a result of the interests of scholars engaged in what they termed critical legal theory, observation and analysis were devoted to the possible role of the organization of law school training and lawyering in preserving established hierarchies.

For this reason among others, in the first half of the century the sociology of the legal profession was not a very prominent part of the sociology of the professions: the economics of legal institutions, of lawsuits, and of law firms was not a very favored subject among economists; the anthropology of law did not attract many anthropologists, at least in the field of the law of "advanced" societies; political scientists had and seemed to prefer their own ways of analyzing the state and constitutions.

• One role played by social scientists persisted and has even grown in importance, throughout the changes in the relationship of theoretical perspectives: that of practical applications to the solution of legal problems.

Whatever the views about the wisdom of social science applications in the desegregation arena, it is by now only one of an enormously varied number of applications of social science in trial and appellate courts as well as in legislative and administrative settings. Behavioral-science arguments and evidence have been prominent in many issues concerning evidence and testimony such as the reliability of eyewitness testimony, in cases of race or sex discrimination, in death penalty litigation, in the issues surrounding the location of nuclear energy plants, in questions of jury size and composition, in cases involving natural disasters, as well as in such earlier applications as economic analysis in connection with patent and copyright claims. In some of these areas, the social-science component is neither auxiliary nor ancillary; rather, it lies at the core of the legal claim and the evidence in its behalf. Thus, it is being institutionalized, to some extent, in legal practice, in funding, and in interdisciplinary journals.

Academic lawyers doing "empirical" work may work with or study under social scientists for information and method; the apparent precision of statistical arrays and operations, deceptively implying the possibility of transforming quantity into quality, may have impressed some lawyers or convinced them that judges and juries would be impressed, despite the admonitions of statisticians and social scientists. Law schools sometimes add social scientists to their teaching faculties, encourage law-trained faculty members to add social science training to their skills, and even permit students to take courses elsewhere in the university from lesser breeds.

Social scientists, meanwhile—especially in the recent past—sometimes take advantage of these needs to promote access to legal materials and lawyers for research agendas of their own. Off to one side, the historians have been digging into legal materials, turning up with their spades the messy counterexamples that the past obtrudes on law professors' generalizations.

• Social scientists, trying to blend immanent and external perspectives in looking at law, have recently turned to the settlement of disputes as an object of analysis. Dispute settlement has promised to reward the efforts of anthropologists, historians, communitarians, devotees of critical legal theory, and reformers. Descriptively, the focus on dispute settlement offers a hope of measuring the amount and intensity of certain kinds of claim making and claim adjusting, and thus of getting a handle on litigiousness that goes beyond the observation (itself problematic) of formal litigation. Normatively, it appealed to interests—not always held in common—in cheapness, community, informality, efficiency, and perhaps also in reducing the power and income of lawyers. For some, the very idea of a plurality of dispute-settling institutions, autonomous with regard to the state, would help to retard the growth of Leviathan. Books and articles sported the theme of law without lawyers, law without sanctions, and justice without law. Some of the studies found that some extrajudicial procedures such as commercial arbitration caught on and became established to the extent that they limited or adapted features of the regular legal system. Others suggested that deep and persistent features of American societal development pressed the polity toward a centralizing legal system which, though it might sacrifice some virtues, would help to avert greater vices; to use the language of game theory, this view defended law as a "minimaximizer." At another level of theorizing, some scholars have warned that the focus on dispute settlement should not be taken to imply that the practice of law is limited to representation of clients in disputes.

• One contributor works outside the United States (Jowell), and foreign experience is indirectly reflected in several of the other chapters. Enough is reported to disclose the affirmative and negative forms of the institutional fallacy: that is, the error of supposing that two institutions bearing the same name must serve the same function in two societies, and the error of supposing that a given function cannot be performed in a second society if it lacks an institution by which that function is performed in the first. Unexpected parallels attest the presence of similar difficulties, although not necessarily of comprehensive "convergence": for example, in their domestic businesses, American entrepreneurs and Soviet managers alike often fail to pursue breach-of-contract remedies, theoretically available, because they wish despite the breach to have continuing relationships with the other parties. In one polity, the profit-and-loss statement seems to suffer, in the short run; in the other, the complaint is made that the Plan is distorted by the forbearance of the putative plaintiff; but the businessmen in both polities may well know what they are doing.

• For a profession that prides itself on distrusting large generalizations, the law operates on the basis of implicit tenets whose power is great while they last, although their life may be short. It is true that philosophers of law were not held in great esteem in the United States in the period between the decline of the prestige of Germanic scholarship (about the time of World War I) and the rise of liberal rationalist generalists in the early 1970s. Yet the generalizing enterprise continued under other banners with faint devices on them: rationalizing, harmonizing, promoting uniformity, restating, celebrating the substantive virtues exercised obliquely by procedural nicety, and exalting reverence for constitutions and constitutionalism. More recently, the virtues of economic analysis of legal dynamics have been acclaimed, and the acclamation in turn criticized; some efforts have been made to apply to the law methods used in, or at least reported from, linguistic philosophy, structuralism, and literary criticism; Marxism and other sometimes-critical theories have been brought to bear on the ideological and economic aspects of law work in a contest where the participants recriminate with mutual charges of mystification. Time was when the social sciences found reflection in legal literature chiefly in the form of methodological manifestoes. Now that social science research in law has ramified and deepened, we may be entering a period of declamatory empire building, not by the partisans of law and social science but by advocates of more traditional legal scholarship.

CROSS-CUTTING THEMES AND TRENDS

Although the chapters of the book are focused on various substantive areas and lean primarily on different disciplines, they share several partially overlapping preoccupations. These cross-cutting themes and trends may point in the direction of future research and action.

Power   The chapters on integration and conflict, on private government, on varieties of legal order, on participation, and some of the others refer to instances of continuing tension between private and public ordering of behavior; between diffused and concentrated power; between power in its formal, modern legitimation through the political process and power in its economic and social modes, made partly convertible with other modes through law as well as other processes. Certain activities of all or part of the public are regulated by contractlike arrangements between government and subsets of the people, a development that observers called, with some alarm, the *Kammerstaat* (roughly, corporate state) when they noticed it a generation ago in central Europe. Several chapters—for example, on administration and on private government—deal with the conflicting values of keeping or making public officials accountable and allowing them the discretion without which they cannot do all of their work. In the chapters on deterrence, social science in the courts, and normative issues one can see the contemporary version of venerable arguments over the causes of violation and evasion of the law and, even more problematic, the causes of compliance. The chapters on economic analysis, private government, and varieties of legal order, among others, sketch informal mechanisms for coping and finagling, or (to change the metaphor) social lubricants of the creaky joints in the formal machinery.

Design and Function   These themes are counterpointed against the themes of power. Lawyers are supposed to be specially competent to invent, facilitate, and obstruct connections among purposes, policies, rules, and forms; almost all the chapters give instances of success and failure therein. Accountability versus discretion, mentioned above, is paralleled here by the tension between uniformity of administration and responsiveness to small variation. The neatness of hierarchical organization is counterposed to the flexibility of bargaining and negotiation. In the system in which individuals enter the legal profession, accidents of design and function—which may not be quite accidental—have produced a curious matching stratification of students, law schools, occupational roles, and intellectual perspectives.

Symbolic   Several observers of American law have noticed the conflict between the mystique of legal formality, routine, and language and the pressure for explicitness and candor on the part of courts, legislatures, administrators, and other figures in authority. Sociologists, social psychologists, cultural anthropologists, and social critics have looked at law as ritual, drama, theater, morality play. Students of language and of the legal profession, especially the legal historians, have drawn attention to the changing waves of emphasis between the (inseparable) expressive and instrumental uses of law. Those who wonder at our secular devotion to constitutionalism have linked it both to the historical need for cultural integration and to the philosophical dispute over the immanence of obligation, a connection that leads to the questions about the sources of compliance mentioned above under the theme of power.

Costs   This theme is not an economist's monopoly. In less explicitly pecuniary terms and in other vocabularies, several of the contributors to this volume have taken up the problems of externalities, transaction costs, secondary effects—usually undesired and unplanned—of legal intervention, problematic primary effects (legal impact studies), and occasional secondary gains. The legal system, when measured by most ordinary criteria, seems so obviously inefficient to many that the second-degree revisionists, criticizing the critics and suggesting that the legal system serves to direct resources to their most efficient use by some appropriate standard, feel impelled to meet the charge of paradox.

Institutional   Although the vast literature on legal education is not fully reviewed, some suggestions are made here and there about the duality of law school training and research as partly professional and partly academic. Studies of the interaction between the legal profession and the public raise questions of the degree of penetration of the legal system into lay *mores* and of the degree to which lawyers and jurists have and discharge an ethical obligation to reach the public in disseminating the legal culture. That the legal profession has grown much more attractive, and a little more accessible, as a subject of academic study by social scientists from various disciplines is itself a significant fact of recent legal history.

Dynamic   Lawyers in common-law jurisdictions have long been comfortable, and some have been adept, in analyzing adjudication as a means by which doctrine could be progressively cleansed. In some branches of the law, especially those touched more insistently by history and historians, they have thought about changes over time in the presuppositions of jurisprudence. Now, thanks to the increasing intervention of social scientists or social science in legal research, lawyers' attention is being drawn also to social change; to changes in institutions; to the modification of language over legally relevant intervals of time (control of language through education, caste monopoly of legal vocabulary and professional diction, changes in connotations and currency of terms, changes in style of legal language). The events of administration, legislation, and negotiation are coming more and more to be seen as ordered in a flow, a process of interactive approximation to an end sometimes willed but more often speculatively inferred. Lawyers already have rich informal experience in the workings of organization; now they are being introduced to the more systematic discussions among organization theorists, especially the analysts of bureaucracy, concerning the ways in which organizations not only persist (although the original purposes may obsolesce) but even develop new and invigorating objectives, to which in turn they must be adapted. All of these changes take place at rates which themselves may change; students of law and society have to keep an eye on the primary curve as well as on its derivatives.

Like most collective efforts, the book is less comprehensive and less unified than we should have liked. Some omission was early and deliberate: for example, we decided not to cover the vast field of the administration and substantive doctrine of criminal law (apart from the chapter on deterrence) because so much recent compendia and assessment had been published that more would be only marginally useful. Volumes that themselves consist of secondary evaluation are relatively neglected. The committee regrets that arrangements made for other contributions by scholars from outside the United States did not bear fruit. All the contributors feel that more could well have been said on the details of the practice of law, on the application of economic theories and methods to a wider variety of legal issues, on the language of the law, and on other important subjects that we have ignored or compressed. For all that, we are convinced that the volume gives ample testimony to the vitality of sociolegal research as it has been practiced over the last quarter of a century.

ACKNOWLEDGMENTS

The preparation of the book was supported by a grant to the Social Science Research Council from the Law and Social Sciences Program of the National Science Foundation (SOC 77-11370).

The generous and skillful assistance of three persons is acknowledged with thanks:

David F. Cavers encouraged and, through the Council on Law-Related Studies, took much of the initiative that led to the formation of the Committee on Law and Social Science of the Social Science Research Council.

Ruth Hein Schmitt edited the chapters with a hand laid light or heavy as needed.

David L. Sills, the executive associate of the Social Science Research Council, was indispensably central to the committee. He kept us at work, urged the undertaking on with suggestions, criticism, and tactful exhortation, and lent his encyclopedic knowledge to the editorial task.

❧ 1 ❧

LEGAL SYSTEMS OF THE WORLD

An Introductory Guide to Classifications, Typological Interpretations, and Bibliographical Resources

Sally Falk Moore
Harvard University

INTRODUCTION

All airports of the world look alike. But the political and legal systems of the countries in which they stand have not been similarly amenable to slick homogenization. Nor are they likely to become fully standardized in any foreseeable future, uniform codes notwithstanding.

The fact of legal/cultural heterogeneity, and the consequent possibility of comparison, is a basic resource for research in the social sciences. The intention of this chapter is to encourage more adventure into this field by facilitating entry. It examines some scholarly classifications of legal systems, together with the theoretical assumptions that lie behind them. Because of the author's biases the typologies and theories that touch on anthropological concerns will be commented on more extensively than others. But the more general aim is to compile a brief bibliographical essay that can be used as an introductory guide to existing classifications, comparisons, and descriptions of the legal systems of the world.[1] My intention is to serve as a Baedeker for those who want a glimpse of the territory that could be traveled, offering hints about some places that are scenic even when glimpsed from the library, and warning about others where the academic waters are not always potable.

What are the assumptions that underlie global attempts to compare or to classify? Is there law in all societies? Can legal systems be compared as wholes? Is it possible to

---

[1] This essay was completed in the Spring of 1979. It has been partially updated (in 1984) but time constraints made it impossible to rereview systematically the literature outside the field of anthropology.

compare the social order of a group of hunters and gatherers with law in an industrial society? To what end? What is the purpose of broad comparative studies of legal ideas and practices?

Anthropologists, who have been in the comparison business for a long time, argue that at the very least comparisons unsettle ethnocentric preconceptions of what is natural. A knowledge of other societies makes ours look as constructed as theirs. A dose of comparison also brings to light some constants in the human condition, suggesting the limits of the likely and the boundaries of the possible.

The present objective is much more limited: to make available, even to the timid, a means of entering the vast and jumbled literature on the range of world systems and to point out some issues that have arisen in description and typologizing. Far from being confined to one discipline, the literature includes works by lawyers, historians, political scientists, economists, sociologists, and anthropologists. The very different provenances of the descriptive and analytic work have produced great variety in the treatment of the subject matter. The literature on "other" legal systems includes "problem-oriented" analytic work shaped by the concerns of the social sciences as well as descriptive materials that could easily be the subject matter or raw material of such analysis. The variety of approaches is intimidating, to say nothing of the number of pertinent works. There are no means of being both brief and comprehensive in the face of such a literature. The existence of useful bibliographies and summaries will be noted here to facilitate the task of compression.

The materials in this essay are arranged roughly according to the socio-logic of scale. The largest sociolegal arena, the world, is addressed first, and lesser units follow in descending order of social complexity and cultural heterogeneity. Starting with the international and multinational order, the essay proceeds down the scale of organization to nations that are internally plural in culture and law, next takes up certain legal systems of nation-states academically conceived of as unitary, and closes the review of "types" and "levels" with small-scale societies and "primitive" legal arrangements. This is followed by a final section describing several relatively recent synthesizing works that use comparative materials. Three mount arguments about the direction of legal change but tend to ignore the international and the plural dimensions, with all their conflictual implications. The last emphasizes the deep differences of cultural perspective that lie behind legal traditions in the world today and warns against any easy assumptions about potential consensus.

The term "legal system" is used loosely here, and with some misgivings. "System" is not meant to convey any necessary mechanical or logical consistency or coherence (see discussion in Moore 1978b, "Introduction"). For English speakers, the most familiar referent of "legal system" is that complex aggregation of ideas, practices, principles, institutions, and rules (and ways of making and unmaking them) commonly referred to as "law" in modern American-Anglo-European culture. And by analogic extension the terms "law" and "legal system" are also used (here and in the literature) to refer to ideas and practices in other societies when in function or in form they have some characteristics in common with what is thought of as law, or the domain of the legal in the West.

At first glance, analogic comparisons of this kind seem straightforward enough. But hidden in them are vexing problems of comparability. For example, if a functional definition of law works well for "other" societies, what about applying the same logic to the West itself? Though in the West law is attached to government, in fact, many lawlike functions are performed by "private" organizations. Variations in the division of labor between public government and "private" organizations in the mixed economies of the world and the official absence of the private sector in some socialist countries are only two examples of the many complications arising from cross-cultural definitions that start from Western and formal legal biases. There are many others. One means of overcoming some of these analytical problems is to leave doctrinal definitions aside and to examine the social facts with particular processes clearly in mind. One can ask, for example, to what degree the social fields within the boundaries of any particular nation or region or other entity are operating semi-autonomously, whatever the official definition of the relationship to government and law (Moore 1978b). This gets at the process, the workings, at what is actually operative in the way of superordinate directed control, and reveals what elements of autonomy are retained, and where formal law fits into the picture.

But the literature reviewed here is not itself organized in terms of such questions. What comes into view instead are three major paradigms used for wide-ranging comparisons and classification. One emphasizes the multicultural-plural dimension. A second is strongly centered on comparing the Euro-Anglo institutions and relegates "other" systems to a residual category. The third is fundamentally evolutionary in approach.

The multicultural-plural model is obviously appropriate to international law, to law in nations that were formerly colonial possessions, as well as to the law of certain other multiethnic polities. But the issues raised by the analysis of situations of legal pluralism are not merely polite matters of doctrinal conflict of laws. They impinge on serious political tensions. The U.N. Charter gives peoples the right to self-determination. But in practice, what does that mean? Both in the world as a whole and in nation-states with internally diverse legal systems there are dangerous and volatile questions involved in determining whose legal system shall govern particular situations and considering whether diverse systems can continue side by side. No less stirring are the connected issues of whether certain human and political rights should be universally recognized or to what extent particular groups of persons should have the right to determine the nature of the social order in which they live.

Scholars musing on the future of law in the Western democracies would be short-sighted to ignore the controversies over plural law that preoccupy many of the other countries of the world. Those issues may well spill their explosives into our gardens. Indeed, some related problems are already close to home. The themes of legal pluralism versus universalism and legal diversity versus uniformity, and the questions raised by the dominance of one legal system over another, or the way law differentiates among populations, are everywhere politically controversial in the extreme.

In contrast to the emphasis on diversity and potential conflict in the "legal pluralism" approach, both the Euro-Anglo-centered classification and the evolutionary one tend to treat each legal system as if it were a culturally and politically unitary entity. What I have called the Euro-Anglo-centered form of classification of legal systems is much less political and much more technical in its concerns than the plural one. It embodies the Western lawyers' perspective, which used to make its big distinction between civil-law systems and common-law systems, between systems derived from the Roman law tradition, with its emphasis on codification, and those founded on the common-law tradition of Britain, with its ideological emphasis on the courts and the judiciary. Both of these traditions—civil and common law —have spread throughout the world thanks to the effects of colonial administration, warfare, and economic expansion. Usually added to this basic pair are various other categories: a category for socialist/communist systems, a category for legal systems founded on religion, such as Islamic law, Hindu law, and the like; and a miscellaneous residual "other" category for the indigenous legal systems of those many parts of the world that have not been associated with recently significant political forces.

While the Euro-Anglo-centered classification reflects the scholarly and regional biases of its users, it is not an evolutionary scheme. Humility and internationalism have overcome earlier tendencies in such a direction. The Euro-Anglo-centered scheme has the peculiarity of being founded on the supposed *source* of law in each system. Yet, on close inspection, there are serious questions about the appropriateness of giving such prominence to origins rather than to current sociological reality. The Euro-Anglo-centered classification is not analytically inspiring, but it is an important traditional ordering of material. It comes out of a long heritage of comparative legal scholarship in the West, which has gradually become geographically more comprehensive but not much more focused on social theory.

The third paradigm for broad comparison, the evolutionary, is surely the most fundamental as part of the intellectual heritage of the nineteenth century. (For a brief, lively set of lectures on the background of the subject, see Stein 1980.) Though social evolution has been much argued about since, the nineteenth-century assumptions of Sir Henry Maine, Lewis Henry Morgan, Karl Marx, and Friedrich Engels and, in the early twentieth century, the works of Emile Durkheim and Max Weber still strongly affect the shape of much large-scale comparison in law, whether the new writings are cast to agree or disagree. Questions about the coercive role of the state, about "communitarian" society, about power, privilege, and stratification, and about the rights of the individual were the meat and potatoes of the evolutionists a hundred years ago. In the 1960s there was a powerful revival of these concerns, which is still evident in the literature. Ideas about legal evolution have, for some, become a way of commenting on present politics. In addressing the evolutionary perspective, this essay dwells particularly on classical themes that divide anthropologists in their assessments of "primitive law" and in their approaches to legal ethnography. That section concludes with a synopsis of some of the writings of Roberto M. Unger, Donald Black, Philippe Nonet and Philip Selznick, and Clifford Geertz, all of whom use comparative materials to interpret modern law in very broad terms and to guess at its future.

Are global comparisons really possible? Does any individual have the competence to embrace this vast subject? The very idea is humbling. The quantity of information is monstrous, the amount of detail overwhelming, the linguistic problems considerable. Understandably, those bold few who have tried global comparison, at least nominally, have all used drastic taxonomic measures to reduce the glut of information to manageable proportions. Some of their works are organized around a preconceived and tightly argued thesis. The comparative material then figures essentially as confirming illustration. The alternative is a kind of encyclopedic compendium. The first method, however interesting, has no objectivity. The second, however painstaking, has no analytic force. What follows offers some samples of each approach, along with some other studies and bibliographies (largely limited to those in English) through which the great range of variety of legal systems may be discerned and some current theoretical directions pointed out.

MULTICULTURAL ARENAS AND PLURAL LEGAL SYSTEMS
Some Comparative Approaches to International Law

Karl Llewellyn used to speak of law-government in one breath, virtually as if it were one word—and indeed, for many practical, modern, mundane purposes, this association between law and government is in every way justified (Twining 1973). But it is also obvious that not all the phenomena related to law and not all that are lawlike have their source in government. Recognition of this fact is one of the most prominent characteristics of recent social-science approaches to law. Even in the presence of government the functioning of law depends heavily on nongovernmental economic, social, and political factors.

Anthropologists have long known that some societies operate without government but nevertheless have social order, political organization, and lawlike institutions. In the simplest societies, there is no overarching corporate organization that encompasses and governs the member units (see, for example, Middleton and Tait 1958; Smith 1974). In such acephalous societies, links between member units and systems of common norms are maintained in ways independent of any centralized authoritative organization.

Hierarchical systems, from chiefdoms to modern nations, add "vertical" structures of authority to their many internal "horizontal" interlinkages. By contrast, the modern international arena—a field to which laws pertain and the locus of major political events and the site of enormous international and transnational organizational activity—is, of course, not held together by any world government. There is no corporation of the world, no nation of humankind, though there are international and transnational corporate groups. To the extent that the international field is a political arena without government, it has some formal resemblance to primitive multigroup arenas—a parallel Michael Barkun has noted in his *Law Without Sanctions* (1968). I must admit some reservations about the utility of this analogy.

In *Law Without Sanctions* Barkun approvingly quotes the anthropologist E. A. Hoebel (1954): "International law, so-called, is but primitive law on the world level" (Barkun 1968, p. 32). Hoebel's position derived from his view that the principal progressive characteristic in the evolution of law is the gradual change from primitive "private" enforcement of norms by "interested" parties acting in their own cause to enforcement of norms by impartial "public" authorities. In the modern world, Hoebel predicted, world government would be the culmination of this process, the next evolutionary step. To a great extent he identified the growth of law and order with the growth of centralized government.

This potential for the future development of world government, however, is not the focus of Barkun's argument. The parallel Barkun emphasizes is that, in the absence of central authority, there can nevertheless be structural stability in a system of relations among politically independent social units. In Barkun's view, the point of interest is the process by which this stability is produced among autonomous entities. He contends that the balanced opposition of clusters of military allies operates to maintain the structure both in primitive segmentary lineage systems and in international relations. He also contends that in both contexts, the idea of "jural community" is important and that it is marked by "shared procedures" and "shared perceptual categories" (p. 84).

Barkun used E. E. Evans-Pritchard's description of the pastoral Nuer of the Sudan as the "type" of the segmentary lineage system (Evans-Pritchard 1940). Barkun—the

political scientist committed to systems theory—may have taken too literally an abstraction by Evans-Pritchard—the anthropologist of the ideal way the segmentary lineage
was supposed to work. Barkun uses the idealized version of the Nuer system to stress the
point that, in international relations as in such stateless societies, "[p]reservation of
systemic stability is due to some form of self-regulation rather than to a clearly constituted
superior authority" (p. 32). It is the multicentric, horizontal structure of the two "systems" represented by the Nuer and modern international law—the putative balances
involved and their effects—that Barkun finds striking.

A peculiar distortion is embedded in the logically beautiful but historically improbable
assumption that balanced opposition was the basis of peace in segmentary systems, even if
that idea expresses the native ideological conception of the system rather than Evans-
Pritchard's invention. First, such systems are ethnographically known to have been
characterized by chronic small-scale fighting. A well-known article argues that segmentary lineages are a convenient political form par excellence for predatory expansion
(Sahlins 1961). Furthermore, a balanced opposition is by no means the only way to
maintain temporary stability in multicentric systems. An imbalance produced by clear
advantage, even if temporary, on one side can also keep the peace so long as the weaker
side and its allies do not feel powerful enough to challenge the stronger. Redressing
imbalances, it can be argued, is as likely to engender new fighting as to produce peace
(see Meggitt 1977 on warfare in New Guinea).

The containment of conflict to small-scale fights in segmentary systems may be related
much more closely to the simple economy and rudimentary technology of these societies
than to organizational features. Barkun has taken a particular view of the cold war—the
suspension of large-scale hostilities because of equal power and equal dread—as a durable
systemic balance and made it applicable to certain acephalous primitive systems. But the
analogy may be false, both because segmentary systems probably did not, in fact, operate
as they have sometimes been thought to and because, to whatever extent the localism of
small-scale fighting is an analogous result in tribal and modern conditions, it probably
arises from other causes.

Nor should there be confusion between systemic continuity and peace. There are many
political systems in which the structure has a good deal of durability but in which violent
conflict is endemic (Black-Michaud 1975). The type of patterned relationship, and the
way it is perceived, may remain largely the same, while the dominant persons or groups
may shift from time to time as the result of conflict. This situation has been as true of
segmentary lineage systems, in which control over land or water by particular segments
changed after armed clashes, as it has been of chronic princely rebellions in certain forms
of kingdom. The same obtains in the modern world for many nation-states with unstable
governments. Systemic continuity and peace can be quite different.

Nor are law and warfare absolute opposites that cannot exist in the same social field,
Bohannan to the contrary (Bohannan 1967). Law—or lawlike phenomena, depending
on how law is defined—can have a place in social arenas in which self-serving force is
intermittently used. Not only may certain laws operate at levels of organization other
than the level at which fighting force is regularly deployed (for example, fighting may go
on *between* villages even while orderly forms of inheritance are peacefully adhered to
within villages) but law may also operate in the relations between fighting units during
peaceful interludes between fights.

Stressing common culture and consensus in both international and acephalous systems, Barkun contends that "noncoercive consensus-based supports may be the key to understanding horizontal legal systems in which physical sanctions are, for the most part, structurally impracticable" (p. 65). But were physical sanctions impractical for the bellicose Nuer? And what about war in international relations? Barkun's catchy title, *Law Without Sanctions*, may be an exaggeration of the more peaceful aspects of intermittently conflictual relations, in which those who use force tend to see it as a sanction, while those against whom it is used see the action as wrong. Barkun, like Paul Bohannan (1967), seems to see law and warfare as unmixed opposites, total alternatives as ways of resolving conflicts. But in these unstable multimember arenas, the two are surely part of a single process. The ongoing sorting and resorting of relations takes place in the context of alternating stages of orderly contacts and bursts of violence. The common and competing economic interests—and technological levels—in these social fields would seem to have at least as much to do with the nature of these relations as do the balances of military alliances and the "jural community" of "shared procedures" and "shared categories," to which Barkun gives his principal attention.

The advantage of the systems approach adopted by Barkun—that it abstracts structure from the particulars of context—is also its weakness. In making the structural analogy between primitive acephalous societies and the international arena, the different particulars of milieu that are omitted are, in the end, probably more important for analysis than is the bare systemic likeness. The utility of Barkun's broad comparative perspective is precisely that it raises such questions.

Barkun is obviously committed to continuing comparisons and to the endeavor to account for cultural factors. In 1968, the year *Law Without Sanctions* was published, Barkun was coordinator of a conference at Syracuse University at which Adda B. Bozeman gave a paper, later to grow into a book entitled *The Future of Law in a Multi-Cultural World* (1971). The book's purpose is

> to consider the various meanings carried by law in the actual and normative political systems of the West, the Islamic Middle East, Africa south of Sahara, Indianized Asia and China; with a view to determining whether there are actually any significant points of accord that might justify undifferentiated cross-cultural references to "law" and so be fit to provide a secure foundation for the organization of relations between these realms. [p. 34]

In Bozeman's analysis, "meanings" include practices as well as ideological referents. Though there is talk of "cross-cultural references," Bozeman's conception of meaning emphasizes political action rather than political rhetoric. Her conclusions about the international scope of common elements are far less sanguine than Barkun's. In her argument, the formal definition of states as comparable units in international law is at odds with the political realities. Central governments in much of the non-Western world are inherently unstable from both internal and external causes (pp. 165, 166, 181, 182). Internally, the character of these central governments is determined "mainly by the ambitions, talents and fortunes of a few leading individuals and the close supporters they can organize," thus producing regimes that are "pragmatic and unstable . . . veering everywhere to arbitrary, even despotic rule, and therefore stimulating counterorganizations" that result in "factionalism and intrigue, . . . coups d'état, assassinations, revolutions, and liberation movements directed against 'established' governments" (pp. 165–66). Interventions from outside national boundaries are equally destabilizing, since "real, internationally relevant political power is no longer represented uniformly by officially functioning governments" because it also emanates from "ideologically conceived international parties, mobile military political units, and other dissimilated power centers" that operate "across state boundaries and under the surface of existing governments" (p. 182). Because formal legal concepts do not correspond to these realities, "old distinctions between aggression and defense, civil war and foreign war, and the status of belligerents and that of neutrality are . . . fast becoming blurred if not defunct, leaving vast regions in the throes of chronic strife, guerrilla warfare, insurgency, or counterinsurgency . . . the modern world is being shaped decisively by war" (pp. 183–84). Thus, comparisons lead Bozeman to conclude that what, in a special political sense, she calls the "multicultural" world is too diverse (the character of its diversity being political) to provide a secure foundation for a common international legal order. She has since carried the thesis further and argues that for reasons of cultural difference Western theories and typologies are not adequate to an analysis of conflict and its management in Africa (Bozeman 1976). One may not be comfortable with her approach to Africa, or to politics, yet recognize that the cultural differences are there, and are important.

Bozeman's deeply pessimistic predictions may turn out to be correct. But if they do, there still will be a question of whether the multiplicity of understandings about law were what produced the result. Is there less hope now for international law than there was at some other time in history? Does analytic emphasis on divergent values take too little account of the realities of the world economy? What does the inescapability of worldwide economic interdependence imply for the future of international law? Is the underlying conflictual issue one of multiple legal cultures or one of clashing interests?

What is clear enough is that "the legal" is a domain to be understood neither by itself nor in terms of its official explanations. This holds within social fields that are putatively fully regulated, such as nation-states; and is all the more dramatically apparent in the international arena, where even the claimed domain of the legal is only a small part of the operation of the whole.

A Social-Science Bibliography

A useful, though now somewhat dated, bibliography lists work done in the social sciences related to international law. The two-volume work was published for the American Society of International Law (Gould and Barkun 1970, 1972). The first volume, *International Law and the Social Sciences*, is a discursive, textbooklike essay; the second, *Social Science Literature: A Bibliography for International Law*, is an annotated bibliography. Harold Lasswell, in his introduction to the expository volume, hailed it as "a study that stands somewhere between an innovating treatise and a textbook" (p. xv). The authors describe their own expository volume as follows:

> International Law and the Social Sciences dealt with a representative sample of the more important literature. . . . It undertook to set the sample in a framework of social science concepts that give promise for future developments of international legal studies in harmony with the main currents of social science thought. Conversely, it endeavored to show how social science research itself could take better account of the legal dimension of international relations. [1972, p. 1]

Their conception of the techniques to be used is not far to seek. Surveying the topic of "the utility of social science methods," they see fit to touch on the following: the comparative method; mathematical techniques; factor analysis; communication research; and laboratory experiments, including simulation and gaming. But, as might have been expected given their particular point of view, the authors explain that "[g]eneral systems theory provides, we think, the most promising approach to date for integrating more specialized studies into a general theory" (1972, p. 26).

One may disagree, yet find the scope of the bibliographical volume of interest. The balance and coverage will not satisfy everyone, but much in it continues to be useful. The systems perspective is now applied to the world. It has come to be the mainspring of an important school of thought in the social sciences which considers national states so embroiled in world economy that they can no longer be thought of as independent entities, their legal self-definition to the contrary (Hopkins and Wallerstein 1982).

Legal Pluralism, Cultural Pluralism, and Legal Transplants

The plurality of legal systems in the international arena has a counterpart within many nations. The prospects for plural societies are a key concern in the social sciences (Maybury-Lewis 1984). The world certainly looks as if cultural and political diversity are here to stay. Thus, theoretical studies of legal pluralism and the working accommodation of heterogeneity within larger political systems have much to offer those interested in international relations. *Legal Pluralism* is the title of a major book on the subject by M. B. Hooker (1975), who uses the term to refer to circumstances "in the contemporary world which have resulted from the transfer of whole legal systems across cultural boundaries" (p. 1). In many countries the residue of conquest and colonization has left many racial, cultural, or ethnic groups within the same polity bound by different laws, or affected differently by the same laws. Hooker writes extensively on the impact of colonial government and colonial law. His excellent 78-page bibliography includes J. S. Furnivall on Burma and Netherlands India; J. Duncan Derrett, Bernard S. Cohn, and Marc Galanter on India; G. J. Massell on Soviet Central Asia; A. N. Allott and E. Cotran on Africa; J. N. D. Anderson on Islamic Law; Jerome A. Cohen on contemporary China; and lists hundreds of others.

In many colonies a transplanted metropolitan legal system was not intended to replace all indigenous laws, many of which continued to be in effect. Though the empires and colonies are no more, their complex multiple legal legacy lingers on. Yet it is not only in newly independent countries that distinct laws apply to culturally distinct populations; such differences also exist in some countries long independent and legally autonomous. There is also the obverse situation, in which attempts to homogenize and "modernize" a national legal system by promulgating national laws to apply to the population at large tend, in reality, to produce resistance in the culturally diverse subordinate populations. In this regard, the Soviet Union has had continuing troubles with its Central Asian republics. Hooker's work tries to address all these matters, giving useful references to relevant statutes and to other legal materials as well as to the scholarly literature.

A related issue, the worldwide ethnic revival, frequently has its politicolegal dimensions, and as such it appears in the legal and social-science literature. On the international plane, the ethnic revival may manifest itself as a demand to be allowed to exercise the right to self-determination (for a recent work that reviews some of the issues and literature on self-determination, see Ofuatey-Kodjoe 1977). Within nation-states, the ethnic revival may result in demands for constitutional recognition and specific forms of political autonomy or representation. This is often manifested in appeals to national courts to enforce "customary" rules As a matter of political philosophy and legal policy, the ethnic-rights issue is closely related to questions about the limits of freedom and tolerance (see Bennett 1978). To what extent is it proper for a legal system to be used to impose a way of life on people? In what circumstances and in the service of what ends is such a policy justified? Or, to put it the other way around, to what extent should populations inside a nation-state have the right to follow a way of life of their own choosing, because of tradition, out of religious conviction, or for some other reason? The answers to these questions are far from clear. It is enough to note that those writers who seek to distinguish legally plural societies (in the ethnocultural sense) from others are constructing an analytic type that bears on major questions of policy and practice of our day.

Where the emphasis is on social-science approaches, several productive attempts to clarify the theoretical issues can be found in *Pluralism in Africa* (Kuper and Smith 1969), a set of symposium papers, including important theoretical contributions by the editors. The concerns of the symposium addressed the general consequences of cultural and ethnic diversity in African states, which often involve legal questions. Outrage over the case of South Africa lies in the background of any discussion of pluralism in Africa. Kuper and Smith's theoretical taxonomy obviously has that disturbing empirical referent. But the questions raised by the taxonomy are of much more general relevance. Smith's analytic framework takes account of three dimensions in a polity: the cultural, the social, and the politicolegal. Three questions are asked: are there culturally distinct populations within the polity? (Criteria are provided for measuring cultural distinctiveness.) To what extent do the boundaries of the corporate groups (the formally organized units) in the society correspond to the boundaries of the cultural-ethnic divisions? And are all the cultural-ethnic categories or groups (and/or their members) incorporated into the polity as a whole in a legally equivalent manner? Considering these questions, as applied to various multicultural nations in the contemporary world, Smith has constructed three categories of pluralism in society: (1) in which there is *cultural pluralism* only (institutional diversity without collective social segregation); (2) in which there is *social pluralism* (cultural diversity plus cultural collectivities organized as distinct communities and/or systems of social action as corporate divisions); and (3) the condition of *structural pluralism* (cultural diversity plus distinct social collectivities corresponding to cultural divisions, plus differential political incorporation of these collectivities into the whole common society).

Structural pluralism legally prescribes collective differences of status and of relation to the public domain and, obviously, encompasses the case of South Africa. There can, of course, be de facto ethnocultural inequality in the presence of legal equivalence, and there are many variant forms of the three general types. Instead of types, Leo Kuper proposes dimensions of pluralism that may be found in various degrees and combinations (p. 475). Kuper's variables come closer to accommodating the complexity of reality, while Smith's types tend to reduce that complexity to synthetic units the mind can retain and reflect on.

It is interesting to consider the differences between the Kuper-Smith points of departure and Hooker's legal approach. Kuper and Smith start from the defining situation of cultural diversity within a nation before examining the range of social and political concomitants of that diversity in a series of instances. Hooker starts with a situation in which a whole legal system has been transplanted and ends up by talking about the remarkable persistence of cultural—hence, legal—diversity, despite transplants intended to produce unified legal systems.

In each case, Hooker briefly reviews the historical sequences attendant upon the introduction of the imported legal order; sketches the outlines of the indigenous legal system; gives a valuable introduction to the major statutes and cases under the introduced system; and tries to fill in the definitions, perceptions, and perspectives in each setting. He attempts to cover a vast territory, including: (1) British colonial law and written systems of religious jurisprudence (Hindu, Burmese, Islamic); (2) British colonial law and customary law (African, Malay, Chinese); (3) French colonial law; (4) Dutch colonial law (Indonesia); (5) English law in the White Dominions and in the United States (the legal status of indigenous peoples); (6) the voluntary adoption of Western laws (Turkey, Thailand, Ethiopia); (7) legal pluralism in the Soviet Union. Since Hooker skims this vast material in a mere 600 pages, the sections are quite compressed, but each presents a very clear and useful introduction. The bibliography is extensive and invaluable. It is a pity that Hooker does not seem to have known about the work of Kuper and Smith in time to comment on its framework and perhaps even to incorporate some of its organization into his own approach. Scattered through the descriptive parts of Hooker's book are a number of very interesting interpretations and comments by the author, who has achieved much more than a simple compilation. His preface gives the key to his interest.

> The fact is that, despite political and economic pressures, pluralism has shown an amazing vitality as a working system. It may well be that it—and not some imposed unity—should be the proper goal of a national legal system. Indeed, even within developed nations themselves, there are signs that a plurality of law is no longer regarded with quite the abhorrence common a decade ago. [1975, p. vii]

The far-reaching political implications of such views do raise the question of whether legal pluralism is a stage in a historical process, operating in the direction of unification, or whether the current political salience of cultural separatism will endure, and with it its legal concomitants. The future of legal pluralism in new nations is discussed briefly by Laura Nader and Harry Todd in their editorial introduction to *The Disputing Process: Law in Ten Societies* (1978). Many of the articles in the book, all by Nader's students, concern the choice of a "remedy agent" in situations of dispute. The exercise of choice involves recognition of the substantial differences between the internal legal system of the ethnic group being studied by the anthropologist and the national legal system, strong preferences often being shown by disputants for their indigenous mode of handling things. Nader and Todd argue that there is a case against legal homogenization. They see the homogenization of law as a form of domination, a way of consolidating "power positions." "In a stratified society the ruling elite have much to gain by invoking homogeneity, since it is their culture, or that to which they have adapted, which sets the standard for homogenization" (p. 33). Even accepting the underlying sympathetic intention of this statement "the notion that homogeneity, the state, success and progress, all go hand in hand" should not go unquestioned. There remain serious problems with identifying cultural heterogeneity and legal pluralism with a "better deal for the powerless" (p. 33).

South Africa offers an excellent example of the use of pluralism to enhance stratification. Caste systems represent another form of legal pluralism founded on hierarchy. Hardening ethnic boundaries with the help of plural legal systems does not necessarily benefit those so segregated. "Enclaving" can be a form of exclusion.

Neither legal heterogeneity nor legal homogeneity can be regarded in the abstract as oppressive or benign. The evaluation depends both on the political uses to which the policies are put and on the historical circumstances. Questions of domination and subordination—mixed as they are with regionalism, localism, and pressure for ethnic autonomy—generate considerable heat in the multicultural nations of the world. The headlines of the West not only concern the Kurds and the Baluch but also the bombs of the Basques, the activities of the Scottish separatists, and the burnings of English summer cottages in Wales. These issues will not soon subside. (For some interesting work on the politics of ethnicity and retribalization in modern contexts, see Cohen 1969, 1974a, 1974b.) From the perspective of an approach to law that uses the disciplines of social science, there are ample reasons to identify legal pluralism as a major "type" and to examine the general and special characteristics of the great range of instances in which it has occurred. Hooker's is the major book in the field to date, but the growing recognition of the importance of the topic of legal pluralism is evident. For example, the old *Journal of African Law Studies* has broadened its scope and has been renamed the *Journal of Legal Pluralism*. Edited by Professor John Griffiths of the law faculty of the University of Groningen in the Netherlands, it provides ongoing papers on the subject.

Leo Pospisil (1971) and Lawrence Friedman (1975) employ a much broader conception of the topic, which extends the definition of legal pluralism to include much more than ethnocultural differences. Pospisil thinks of law as always situated in society at a multiplicity of organizational—hence, "legal"—levels. In a somewhat different statement of the matter, Friedman mentions "the existence of distinct legal systems or cultures within a single political community" (p. 196). He identifies three major types—cultural pluralism, political pluralism, and socioeconomic pluralism—subdividing each into two subtypes—"hierarchical" and "horizontal." Thus cultural pluralism is divided into hierarchical colonial systems and horizontal multicultural types. In the latter, the laws of the several ethnic groups in the polity apply to particular cultural communities, without any implication of superiority of one system over another. Political pluralism includes hierarchical legal systems (such as the relation between federal and state governments in the United States) and horizontal federalism (such as the relation of the individual states of the United States to each other). Socioeconomic pluralism includes distinct legal systems for different status groups and de facto distinctions made in the legal system as it is applied to rich and poor (pp. 196–99). Friedman applies the term "pluralism" so broadly that it requires substantial subspecification to clarify each "kind." There can be no argument about words and taxonomy, since each writer can create particular definitions; but readers should be aware that *legal pluralism* does not have the same meaning for everyone.

Quite apart from the question of ethnic separatism, instances in which a whole or partial legal system is transferred from one setting to another can, at the very least, provide social science with a "quasi-experiment" in which one variable is held constant while others change. Alan Watson (1974) argues that subsequent divergences reveal a great deal about the nature of legal development and that the study of comparative law should be confined to "Legal History concerned with relationships between systems" (p. 6). His *Legal Transplants*, which makes the case for a rigorous approach to legal development based on historical evidence, is sharply critical of the use of general evolutionary models to fill in the gaps or to provide interpretations. One can share his preference for hard evidence without finding congenial his limiting definition of comparative law as an academic discipline. Certainly "legal transplants" are a major feature of legal systems around the world, and the study of subsequent developments from the point of view of social science could be extremely fruitful.

In the early days of independence in the Third World, it appeared that studies in "law and development" would provide some important data. The first wave of excitement was overly optimistic and often sociologically naïve (for bibliography and critical comment, see the assessments of law and development studies by Trubek and Galanter 1974; Merryman 1977; Burg 1977). Work in this field was markedly ethnocentric. The unthinking assumption that American models would work anywhere was not infrequently shared by some officials in the receiving countries. John H. Merryman (1977) notes that "[t]he mainstream law and development movement, dominated by the American legal style, was bound to fail and has failed." He offers reasons for this circumstance.

> [I]n third world law and development programs the American actor has neither a reliable "feel" for the local situation nor an explicit theory of law and social change on which to base his proposals. His only recourse is to project what is familiar to him onto the foreign context. [p. 480]

> These characteristics: unfamiliarity with the target culture and society (including its legal system), innocence of theory, artificially privileged access to power, and relative immunity to consequences, have been typical of many law and development proposals and programs for the third world. [p. 481]

Robert B. Seidman (1978) sees the failure of investigations into law and development as a problem of Marxist paradox—"How to use an authoritarian legal order to forge a participatory society?" (p. 470). For those who neither share Seidman's certainties nor have an exaggerated faith in the capacity of laws and legal institutions by themselves to create new societies, much can undoubtedly still be learned from the experience of the developing countries. Legal pluralism, in the sense of both "transplant" and "ethnic separatism," is a significant part of the story, though by no means the whole.

In the social sciences, some major revisions of theory are likely to result once the importance of legal pluralism is more generally acknowledged. For one, evolutionary paradigms of law must be elaborated to take legal pluralism sufficiently into account. At present they usually ignore it as a "type," a "stage," or even a factor, though historically it is a pervasive phenomenon. At best, legal-cultural pluralism seems to be treated as a phase that precedes uniformity—an end that, as noted earlier, is by no means always attained or even desired. Multicultural and multinational legal arenas seem to be here to stay. Second, social science will have to readdress the question whether law is culture-specific, and/or which laws are involved when and for whom. This inquiry is closely connected with the still deeper issue of the forms and conditions by which law can be innovative.

A somewhat gloomy aspect of this question has been addressed in *The Imposition of Law*, edited by S. B. Burman and B. E. Harrell-Bond (1979). The essays deal both with culturally plural and with relatively homogeneous settings. Gamely acknowledging that their title may be misleading, the editors clarify their position by adopting the perspective of one of their contributors, R. L. Kidder, who sees the focus on imposition as the wrong question (p. 296), the right questions being those concerning the "social distance between the lawmakers and governed" and "the layers of intervening organizational complexity." These, he contends, "may be used as a measure of how external a legal system is to the community on which it is enforced" (p. 5). Vilhelm Aubert's contribution makes a similar theoretical argument (pp. 27–43).

Two substantive papers in this lively collection show some of its methodological variety. One, by Leopold Pospisil, titled "Legally Induced Culture Change in New Guinea," relates a sequence of transformations in the Kapauku system that flowed from particular colonial policies. He stresses the differences between the indigenous normative system of the Kapauku and incompatible Dutch and Indonesian rules to which the Kapauku had to adapt (pp. 127–45). In contrast, Richard Abel, in "Western Courts in Non-Western Settings: Patterns of Court Use in Colonial and Neo-Colonial Africa," deals with an entirely different kind of evidence and interprets it by means of a quite different method (pp. 167–200). Abel's evidence consists of aggregate statistics concerning court use. He tries to explain shifts in the figures by using a generalized model of "tribal," as opposed to "modern," society, with concomitant generalized litigant motives and litigant perceptions. Abel uses his models to develop a series of propositions, which he puts forward as hypothetical explanations of variations in the figures. His carefully constructed, lawyerly brief rationalizes a closed body of data in terms of explicit a priori models and assumptions. The conclusions can only be as sound as the very general assumptions, and there may be some alternative explanations, but the clarity and ingenuity of the argument are well worth consideration.

Whatever their differences of data and method, Pospisil's and Abel's papers have in common a focus on historical materials, on change over the years. The interest in legal history rather than in static legal cultures seems to be a powerful trend in comparative work (see, for example, the analysis of the history of crime in Sydney, London, Stockholm, and Calcutta in Gurr, Grabowsky, and Hula 1977). The papers in the collection edited by Burman and Harrell-Bond show that the situation that produces a perceived instance of "imposed" law is most colorful and clear where cultural contrasts between the dominant and the dominated act like labeled radioactive tracers in the body of the receiving culture. It is apparent from the theoretical content of the growing literature on multicultural systems that this is being treated not as a narrow or exotic topic but as one that will eventually have implications for the interpretation of change everywhere.

ANGLO-EURO-CENTERED WORKS AND THE "OTHERS"
National, Religious, and Ethnic Legal Systems

A good deal of the introductory literature on "whole" legal systems that is comparative in intention perforce treats particular legal systems as coherent entities. Some works go even further, to group the historically related systems of several polities into "legal families." In part, no doubt, this practice serves to facilitate the nearly impossible problem of description and compression. But in part, such organization also expresses an idea about the importance of cultural connection, "stylistic" coherence, and historical provenance. A good example is furnished in René David's Les Grands Systèmes de Droit Contemporain, translated and adapted by David and J. E. C. Brierley as Major Legal Systems in the World Today (1978). David and Brierley are very clear about their basis of organization.

What, then, are the major contemporary legal families found in the world today? There would appear to be three at least which occupy an uncontested place of prominence: the Romano-Germanic family, the Common law family, and the family of Socialist law. . . . There are other systems. [p. 21]

Their categorization into European, Anglo-American, and Socialist is evident in the allocation of space. Out of the book's 584 pages, 420 are devoted to the three listed "families." All the "other systems" are compressed into the very short compass of 100 pages. In a section entitled "Other Conceptions of Law and the Social Order," David and Brierley include a chapter on Moslem law; one on the law of India; and another on the laws of the Far East, including China and Japan. The book closes with a chapter on the laws of Africa and Malagasy.

Another summary of the legal systems of the world (also produced under David's editorship) is found in the *International Encyclopedia of Comparative Law*, volume 2, *The Legal Systems of the World, Their Comparison and Unification* (1975). This treatment is more extensive and organized along slightly different lines. Many of the other major figures who appear and reappear in the bibliography of current works of comparison are involved here as well—Konrad Zweigert, Arthur T. von Mehren, E. Cotran, Charles Szladits, J. Duncan Derrett, Tony Weir, G. Sawer, Hessel E. Yntema, and others. The first chapter is titled "The Different Conceptions of Law" and includes Western, Socialist, Moslem, Hindu, Far Eastern (China and Japan), and African models, each article written by a different contributor. Chapter 2, "The Structure and Division of Law," addresses essentially the same array of legal "families" and countries. David contributes chapter 5, "The International Unification of Private Law." Chapters 3 and 4, not yet published, will be titled, respectively, "The Sources of Law" and "Comparative Law." Each contribution ends with a short bibliography of important works. In the introductory book, David and Brierley comment on their basic method of classification into "families."

> This grouping of laws into families, thereby establishing a limited number of types, simplifies the presentation and facilitates an understanding of the world's contemporary laws. There is not, however, agreement as to which element should be considered in setting up these groups, and therefore, what different families should be recognized. [1978, p. 20]

The statement ends with a justification of the authors' choices and criteria. "One cannot aspire to mathematical exactitude in the social sciences"; the conventional comparativist idea of a legal "family" overcomes the inconveniences raised by dealing with the law as the separate systems of many nation-states. It also copes with the historical connections among legal systems, and hence the affinities of content and "style." David's purpose is clearly to make easily accessible a body of information nonspecialists are unlikely to be able to assemble.

The concept of legal families presents a classical solution to a difficult problem of presentation and simplification. But by its own definition, the concept glosses over the great differences that often exist in the actual workings of systems that, for historical reasons, have a formal likeness. A gentle critical comment has emphasized the fact that the classification into legal families, while a convenience to the synthesizing writer, is not an explanatory concept.

> The classical typology explains very little *except* the formal sources of those traits selected as "basic." But the traits are singled out as basic traits precisely because they make a scheme of classification possible. If we know what "family" a country

belongs to, what else do we know about the society? Can we predict anything about its politics, society or economy? Its level of development? [Friedman 1975, p. 202]

In view of the general success of David and Brierley's volume in achieving its introductory purpose, it is perhaps ungrateful to object when in the section on Africa south of the Sahara, the authors note that in these parts of Africa "[o]bedience to custom was generally spontaneous, since it was thought that one was obliged to live as one's ancestors had; the fear of supernatural powers and of group opinion were most often sufficient to assure a respect for the traditional ways of life" (p. 505). This statement repeats, at least by implication, something very firmly embedded in the legal literature about "customary" law—the idea that, more than in other systems, it was obeyed without need for enforcement. There is also an implication that conformity in more complex societies is produced through different processes.

Similar assertions can be found elsewhere in the anthropological literature, all of them misleading in two ways. One, they simply postulate some obvious greater "spontaneity" of obedience and greater conformity in less complex societies than in more complex ones. There is little hard evidence to support such a quantitative statement about incidence. Two, they deliberately ignore such techniques of enforcement as exist in these societies; although these methods are often quite different from those of modern governments, they may nevertheless have effective coercive force. These questions are relevant to more than "customary" law; they bear on the sociological understanding of order and disorder in complex societies, the relationships, incentives, and pressures involved. Nowhere is social order or disorder adequately explained by reference to the strength or weakness of "tradition."

J. Duncan Derrett attacks an analogous and common causal explanation in his editor's preface to *An Introduction to Legal Systems* (1968). Derrett makes his critical point about religion as a basis of law, since his book includes articles on Jewish law, Islamic law, and Hindu law. He writes, "One must avoid the error of supposing that any true law is based on religion or philosophy as such. . . . What is exacted in the name of religion is usually required for other purposes than the religious" (p. viii). He goes on to mention "the rules against usury in Jewish and Islamic law, or the rule in Islamic law that a gift is not completed without a transfer of possession," noting that the conventional idea that these are "derived from religion" dies hard, even if one knows that these rules are due "in the first place to a primitive view of the need for reciprocity in a compact society, and, in the second place, to somewhat primitive canons of evidence" (p. ix). Further, "religion is not a true source of law, but, at most, part of the conceptual framework within which a legal system and legal propositions take their place" (p. xix). Attributing specific legal ideas to types of social relations and the information systems associated with them, Derrett allows no significant causal place to the religious and ideological framework within which these legal ideas are set.

There is substantial evidence to support this view for some matters, and the rules Derrett cites are of that kind. The rules about usury and about the transfer of property are found in many small-scale societies in association with a wide variety of religions. Correlations of this sort or their absence are an excellent advertisement for wide comparisons. But there are other issues to which the particulars of religion and ideology are pertinent. Derrett's generalization seems too broad.

The work Derrett has edited has a scope different from that of the volume by David and Brierley and can be used as a complementary resource. In addition to articles on Jewish, Islamic, and Hindu law, there are chapters on the laws of Rome, China, Africa, and England. "The systems of jurisprudence chosen for treatment in this book were chosen because they are 'historic' " (p. xiii). The strong orientation of David and Brierley's book, on the other hand, is modern and current, though the authors do address the historical roots of the "legal families" they describe. Derrett's anthology, the work of a number of authors with varied interests, has a much less integrated perspective. Pleading strongly for wider comparative knowledge, Derrett offers his book as a contribution in that direction. "One may wonder whether now a man can call himself educated who, having studied, for example, English law for three years goes into the world as a 'lawyer' and has never heard of other systems of law" (p. xiii).

Another nominally global attempt to cover the world's legal systems translated into English—An Introduction to Comparative Law: volume 1, The Framework, and volume 2, The Institutions of Private Law (Zweigert and Kötz 1977)—in fact gives even less space to the "other" legal systems than do David and Brierley. Almost the entire first volume is devoted to the Romanist, Germanic, Anglo-American, and Socialist legal families. A review of this "important contribution to legal scholarship" points out that, although it is entitled "An Introduction . . . the work's remarkable qualities can be fully appreciated only by one with considerable comparative learning" (von Mehren 1979, p. 349). While he has some reservations about the institutions chosen by the authors as typifying particular systems, von Mehren assures his readers that "[t]he book is of great value, not to the neophyte alone, but also to the comparatist and to the student of domestic law who seeks a deeper understanding of the areas of substantive law discussed" (p. 349). Thus, though David and Brierley's Major Legal Systems, Derrett's Introduction to Legal Systems, and Zweigert and Kötz's Introduction to Comparative Law are not "social science" books, all embody a strong sense of the significance of sociocultural differences and their importance to a broad understanding of all law.

Even undergraduate students are now provided with materials to foster a taste for comparisons. Henry W. Ehrmann's Comparative Legal Cultures (1976) is a brief textbook intended to entice students into comparative studies. If the lively comparative interest currently manifested by these publications (and by the many editions through which David's book has gone, including a recent paperback version) develops further, one hopes that other works will appear in which more attention is given to social context, balancing the material on doctrine and institutions. It is noteworthy that one of the declared purposes of these introductions is to make accessible and easily understandable materials that were once the monopoly of the specialist. The same is true of the great proliferation of noncomparative books, all of them introductions to the law of one or another group. A few examples are John H. Merryman on civil law (1969), von der Sprenkel on Manchu China (1962), John A. Crook on Rome and Roman law (1967), A. R. W. Harrison on the law of Athens (1968, 1971), N. J. Coulson on Islamic law (1964), Joseph Schacht on Islamic law (1964), and von Mehren on Japan (1963). These are only a few illustrations of a vast literature of this kind. Anyone interested in new books and articles in English in this field would do well to have a look at Charles Szladits's A Bibliography on Foreign and Comparative Law (1975 to date), an ongoing project that is well arranged, easy to use, and sensibly annotated.

Studies written by legal scholars tend to discuss complex societies with written legal traditions. Anthropologists have tended to avoid these materials, although that attitude may well change. Monographs on the law of lesser-known peoples also abound. A bibliography of some of these works, "The Ethnography of Law: A Bibliographic Survey," was assembled by Laura Nader, Klaus F. Koch, and B. Cox (1966). An even more ambitious bibliographical project, *Introduction Bibliographique à l'Histoire du Droit et à l'Ethnologie Juridique*, under the editorship of John Gilissen, was started in 1963; several volumes have appeared.

Assembling a roster of the legal systems of the world virtually requires a worldwide ethnographic bibliography, a formidable list. As a general rule, the more exotic the society, the more likely it is that its law will be presented as part of a general sociocultural description and that the level of detail will be unsatisfactory. Legal anthropologists account for some notable exceptions to this rule. Lawyers interested in quick access to bibliographic material from anthropology in English that can supply ethnographic examples for comparative purposes will find two resources particularly useful. The *Annual Review of Anthropology*, edited by Bernard Siegel, regularly publishes summary articles reviewing current literature on specialized subjects. Two articles on law and anthropology have been published thus far by Moore (1970) and Jane F. Collier (1975). But many other articles in the *Annual Review* volumes are relevant to law and would be of interest to comparativists; they include articles on kinship, economics, and politics.

The second resource—or rather, pair of resources—are the Human Relations Area Files and the *Ethnographic Atlas*, both brainchildren of G. P. Murdock. Though the files are published in New Haven (dating from the time when Murdock was at Yale), they are subscribed to by a number of major libraries throughout the United States, where replicas are housed. The collection consists of file cards organized according to subject, on which items of information are reproduced verbatim (with attribution) from hundreds of ethnographies. Thus, if one were interested in discovering what forms of land tenure were associated with particular kinds of agriculture, it would be possible to gain a quick overview of the subject by consulting the files, which also provide an initial ethnographic bibliography. Even though it is always necessary to go beyond the files themselves to complete any piece of research, the files are an excellent place to start.

A simpler and more accessible resource is the *Ethnographic Atlas* published in the journal *Ethnology* (edited and published by the University of Pittsburgh since shortly after the time of Professor Murdock's move from Yale to Pittsburgh). Readers are also referred to G. P. Murdock's "Ethnographic Atlas: A Summary" (1967a; see also 1967b; Naroll 1970, 1973). The *Ethnographic Atlas* puts in coded form the key "diagnostic" features of a large sample of societies and cultures, supplying the bibliographical references from which the information was drawn. Thus it is possible to see at a glance the preponderant social forms and the cultural settings in which they occur. Again, since context is essential to interpretation, it is always necessary to go back to the sources, but the *Atlas* can provide an initial guide both to sources and to the worldwide distribution of certain basic characteristics and types. Though law was not one of the central interests of the classifiers, there are nevertheless ways of using these materials for purposes of comparative law.

A recent notable and monumental project that examines particular problems comparatively rather than looking at whole systems suggests by its very existence that things are stirring in the woods and that important new materials are being collected. This enormous, multivolume series, *Access to Justice*, under the general editorship of Mauro Cappelletti and Bryant Garth (1978–79), is a continuation of earlier comparative work on civil litigation and on legal aid (see Cappelletti and Tallon 1973; Cappelletti, Gordley, and Johnson, Jr. 1975). The first volume of *Access to Justice* (in two books) contains twenty-three national reports on the cost of justice and national approaches to problems of access. These are responses to a detailed questionnaire central to the project. The work also includes a general report on the major barriers to effective access and the various reforms that have been attempted. Volume 2, also in two books, is entitled *Promising Reforms and Institutions.* Among other subjects, it gives much attention to the current lively interest in conciliation and mediation as an alternative means of resolving disputes. Volume 3, *Emerging Perspectives and Issues,* assembles a miscellany of papers on a wide variety of topics, most concerning British and American developments, but including one paper on India and one on Africa. The fourth volume, *The Anthropological Perspective,* consists of a rather random collection of descriptive ethnographic articles on disputes in a few villages and small communities in Fiji, Mexico, Tonga, Iran, and Utah and is not comprehensive. The editor's introduction is needlessly mechanical, missing what might have been an opportunity to draw together the general theoretical implications suggested by the volume's title. The scale of the entire *Access to Justice* project is astounding. Few will read the many volumes from start to finish, but there is much that is of interest in each, and the commitment of all those involved both to comparison and to reform is unflagging. It is very much to the credit of the editors that they have tried to reach beyond Anglo-Euro-centered perspectives, even though their attempts to do so are somewhat scattered and uneven.

Given the range of works, the increasing accessibility of an abundant literature on the great variety of legal systems of the world should give rise to further bold and wide-ranging comparative work in the social sciences and in law. A few bibliographic ports of entry have been sketched very briefly to encourage novices on both sides to cross into unfamiliar territory. If enough people make the journey, the nature of the literature itself may well be changed by new questions.

GRAND LEGAL COMPARISONS IN AN EVOLUTIONARY MODE

Classical Themes That Separate Anthropologists

One Person's Custom Is Another Person's Law

Persons reflecting on the evolution of law from its beginnings to the present usually are using such grand overviews to make comments about our own day. The form may be an inquiry into temporal and typological extremes expressed in dualities: then and now, their kind of world and our kind of world, small-scale society and large-scale society; or it may take the shape of a series of types presented on an ascending scale: simple to complex, small-scale to large-scale, and the like. However much these may look like unbiased academic inquiries, such investigations are usually shaped by one of two strong attitudes. Either the writer is trying to demonstrate the extent to which modern legal systems are an improvement over past ways of doing things, or the writer is saying that social life used to be more fair, just, and equitable and is asking when and why things went wrong.

Scholars engaged in social-evolutionary writings today are more likely to focus on how the world came to its present sad condition than they are to celebrate, in one nineteenth-century manner, humankind's remarkable progress. Current evolutionary comment is more likely to be informed by the other nineteenth-century style. The gloomier questions addressed by Marx and Engels often prevail. (See Greenberg and Anderson 1981 on recent Marxisant books on law.) There is little rationalist sunshine. Many continue to idealize the intimate communal world of the past. It is as if the conception of a vanished community were necessary to constitute a convincing critique of the present. For some, all hierarchy and all inequality are evil. The benign conception of government embodied in Hoebel's chapter (1954) about evolutionary growth of law is in sharp contrast with Donald Black's more recent dark vision of the state (1976). A related issue integral to Black's book that blooms academic season after season is one that also occupied the classical social evolutionists: the possibility of a future order without government. Is the story of the growth of law the story of the development of the state? If it is, should the state be interpreted as the bringer of order and peace or as an instrument of oppression?

Like their nineteenth-century forebears, some neo-evolutionist and Marxist anthropologists claim that "primitives" (living in that generic primitive community found only in theoretical writings) have no law. These scholars acknowledge that such societies have order and normative rules. But their lexicon regards as "customs" those rules of stateless societies that carry obligations or prohibitions or constitute enablements. For persons of this doctrinal persuasion there are only two great categories—customary rules and laws of the state. There is also often the intimation that custom is internalized and adhered to voluntarily, while law is imposed, enforced, and oppressive.

For some of these neo-evolutionists, the growth of class inequality and coercion is the major element in human history, all else being subsidiary and distracting. A relatively recent example of this view is represented by Elman R. Service's attempt to redo parts of Lewis Henry Morgan's *Ancient Society* (Service 1975; in a similar vein, see also Fried 1967 and S. Diamond 1971). These writers have had considerable influence in one sector of anthropology and epitomize a view of primitive order that has wide currency outside the field. They take the position that all nonegalitarian orders are ultimately maintained by force and that the main lines of political evolution have been from egalitarian societies without coercive institutions to stratified coercive state systems (Service 1975, pp. 86, 291; Fried 1967, pp. 14–20, 145, 235; S. Diamond 1971, p. 47). Law is perceived as an adjunct of the state and the state as a collection of institutions used to maintain a class structure (Fried 1967, pp. 20, 235). Just as this school emphasizes the authoritative element and inequality in state systems, it stresses the consensual element and equality in prestate systems.

In one section of his book, Service advances the general thesis that in primitive societies custom is effectively internalized by all but deviants and is constantly reinforced by the community through the double inducements of mutual support and good fellowship (1975, p. 83). In this situation exchange and affection are effective substitutes for coercion. But elsewhere in his book Service writes, "It is very common in primitive society that a delinquent's own group will plot to do away with him if all other means fail to control him" (p. 54). Does compliance exist to avert "being done away with" or otherwise punished, or is it to obtain reciprocal favors, love, and esteem? How is one to know? Since both elements are present in all social systems, simple or complex, how is the ethnographer to decide whether the carrot or the stick is operative in a given situation, let alone in that abstraction, the society "taken as a whole"? These neo-evolutionists tend to stress the carrot in prestate systems and the stick in state societies. I would argue that both are universal properties of group social life, which appear in very different forms in different settings. The difference in form is critical, not trivial. But to put the issue as if it were a matter of the simple presence or absence of inequality and hierarchically imposed coercive force is to distort the data egregiously. I agree instead with Eric Wolf (1981, p. 55) when he says, "In contrast to others . . . who tend to see societies built up in the kin-ordered mode as egalitarian, I argue instead that they are replete with real inequalities and plagued by resulting tensions."

The most fundamental inequality in social life, omnipresent in prestate societies as in modern ones, is the asymmetry of power between the individual and the group. The Durkheimian vision of early law, enlarging on this point, imagined that the group would always descend in outrage on any individual who broke the rules, this "criminal" law being the original form of law (1964). The asymmetry between individual and group is undeniably a potentially coercive dimension of group life. But such an analysis disregards one point of major importance in understanding the "law" in many prestate systems— that often subgroups and factions in such societies have competing or conflicting loyalties and interests, and individuals can and do mobilize them in their cause. Knowledge of the way such opposing alignments operate and their importance to law is one of the principal advances in understanding that have developed in social anthropology since the great classical writers on legal evolution began puzzling over "primitives."

Information about such conflicts contributed to legal studies an awareness that disputes in prestate societies are often settled by means that make no claim to being instances of the "application" of rules. Disputes are often pursued and settlements arrived at for political ends. A study of the Shavante Indians of the Brazilian interior notes:

> Among the Shavante . . . all legal "cases" are political issues in the sense that they can only be heard in the men's council, where their resolution depends largely on the relative strengths of the factions. A dispute which does not become a factional matter is not technically a dispute at all. It has a status similar to that of a disagreement which has not been taken to court. [Maybury-Lewis 1974, p. 179]

Norms may be alluded to in such proceedings, and they certainly form part of the cultural background, but such dispute settlement is not the occasion for "norm enforcement" in the modern Western sense. Comaroff and Roberts have addressed the subtle place of rules in one such African system in great detail (1981). There is growing attention to the negotiability of rule and position as fundamental to some social systems (Rosen 1984).

Philip H. Gulliver introduced the first extensive field material on dispute settlements through such processes of "political" contention. The phenomenon, first described in *Social Control in an African Society* (1963), was developed further in *Neighbors and Networks* (1971) and in a number of articles. In the 1963 work, his initial extended statement on the subject, Gulliver tried to distinguish between two major types of dispute settlement. In the *judicial* type, the outcome was determined by third-party, rule-governed decision. In the *political* type, with which his work is largely concerned, the outcome, arrived at through negotiations, was determined by the relative power of the parties and their backers. Gulliver (1979) eventually revised some of his initial definitional categories and expanded the scope of his approach, perhaps partly in response to Moore's critique (1970). Gulliver's original perspectives were instrumental in organizing a subsequent conference of the Association of Social Anthropologists on the relative importance of norms and politics or "power" in dispute settlement in a variety of societies. This conference resulted in a published collection of papers (Hamnett 1977). The theme of the varying place of norms in legal dispute and discourse was further developed by Comaroff and Roberts (1981).

It could be argued that evolutionary and typological issues are implicit in these discussions. Has there been in the course of history a movement from systems predominantly given to managing disputes through "political" means to systems predominantly committed to adjudication? Has there been an overall tendency to move away from situational negotiability in the direction of rule standardization? And do any present-day societies epitomize these types? Although these issues could be said to be implicit in the intellectual tradition that lies behind these anthropological works, neither Gulliver's books, nor the papers in Hamnett's *Social Anthropology and Law*, nor Comaroff's and Rosen's legal/ethnographic writings are directly occupied with large-scale evolutionary comparison. Comparative issues are of necessity library problems, and anthropologists are predominantly field workers. With a few notable exceptions, anthropologists interested in law tended to write ethnographies and to address questions about one people at a time, since that is the normal task of field work. (For other examples in the last decade of single-locality, essentially noncomparative legal ethnography, see Engel 1978 on a provincial Thai court, Starr 1978 on disputes in a Turkish village, Snyder 1981 on legal change in southwestern Senegal, Benda-Beckmann 1979 on the durability of concepts of property in West Sumatra, Moser 1982 on rural Taiwan, Gordon and Meggitt 1985 on the highlands of New Guinea, and Moore 1986 on an African system of "customary" law.)

A good deal of field work is focused on the open-ended exploration of defined problems. Comparative analysis may come afterward; but the stage of comparison is often not reached at all. Laura Nader has sought to overcome this deficiency by trying to persuade her students to concentrate on common problems as they study law in the field in different societies (Nader and Todd 1978). Although comparative in intention, the volume of their papers she edited makes only more evident the seriousness of the problem of comparability. When materials are collected by many different persons with different interests, working in different societies, the results are not comfortably equivalent. No wonder, then, that large-scale comparisons of whole legal systems are seldom attempted.

There has been a recent effort to fill that gap. Katherine S. Newman (1983) has published a revised version of her doctoral dissertation in which she compared legal institutions across more than 60 preindustrial societies. Newman characterizes her interpretation as Marxian or materialist. But, in fact, for all its Marxist nomenclature, the analysis has much in common with G. P. Murdock's correlational studies undertaken in the 1940s and 1950s and with earlier work (Hobhouse, Wheeler, and Ginsberg 1915; Diamond 1971; Murdock 1967a and 1967b). The project is typological rather than historical, and by implication evolutionary. Newman groups "preindustrial societies into seven basic categories according to the level of their forces of production: (1) hunting and gathering, (2) fishing, (3) pastoral, (4) incipient agriculture, (5) extensive agriculture, (6) intensive dry agriculture, and (7) intensive wet agriculture" (p. 111). She then works out a typology of correlated political and legal institutions. There are no great surprises here, factual or theoretical, for those who know the literature. For example, few would doubt that in general "the greater the degree of development of the forces of production, the greater the degree of social stratification" (p. 123). These and other similarly well-established theses (and also, to do her justice, many refinements of them) are examined by Newman as hypotheses. Cross-cultural sampling is used to "test" the hypotheses, in fact, to show the statistical demonstrability of the connections already postulated.

When Newman moves on to discuss the "functions" of legal disputes and legal rules, her thesis is that "legal behavior is oriented toward and straining to accomplish the containment of structurally generated conflict" (pp. 138ff.). Her discussion of the kinds of recurrent disputes and rules associated with particular modes of production is somewhat tautological, but she forges through her preconstructed types undaunted. That law is concerned with hierarchy and unequal access to resources and power wherever these exist is something less than a newly discovered fact and generally implied in the definition of law itself. There are many questions of definitional assumption involved here that could profit from more self-conscious examination. One can plausibly advance a more complex argument, that "law" necessarily is involved both in "structure" and in the "contradictions" in "structure." But everything depends on what is meant by those terms and what sort of dynamic is assumed to link the phenomena to which they allude. The comparative method Newman has used does not leave much space for the examination of such theoretical issues nor for inquiry into historical sequences.

Inherent in the enterprise of comparing whole societies in this wholesale way is a tendency to interpret societies as coherent, logically consistent entities. In any hands, the consequent heuristic simplification into types not only tends to produce ahistorical analyses, but also generates rather flattened synchronic ones. The "type" tends to become a static composite, a construction, removed from actual ethnographic instance. Newman struggles to avoid being misunderstood as simplifying in this way by making many specific allusions to snippets of ethnographies and by making innumerable theoretical disclaimers. Thus, she protests frequently to some unseen critics and says such things as, "This should not be taken to suggest that law has only economic functions; it clearly plays other roles as well. Nevertheless, I am arguing that the regulation of social relations of production is a crucial function of law" (p. 138). There is much more about modes of production in this book than there is about law. Inevitably, in the end, the vast project Newman has designed for herself is very selectively addressed.

In the last decades, two lawyers have also chosen to write on "primitive" law in an evolutionary mode—Simon Roberts (1979) and A. S. Diamond (1971). Diamond's book, a version, revised repeatedly, of earlier works, remains rather old-fashioned, formal, and legalistic. Roberts's approach, while more trendy and socioanthropological, covers a different territory. However, both, like Newman, proceed from a political—economy perspective, classifying "early" law in terms of the kind of society in which it is found, rather than proceeding from particular legal ideas or institutions.

Roberts's book is intended as a textbooklike introduction to the range of premodern societies and their modes of handling conflict. He writes in general terms about ways of maintaining social order and structural continuity before addressing mechanisms for handling conflict. These topics are followed by four brief chapters on nomadic societies, cultivators, stateless societies, and the state. Roberts concludes with chapters on fighting and talking and on rules and power before closing with a very brief discussion of some of the themes in the literature. Roberts eschews statistics and settles for clear prose. The focus throughout is on disputes and their settlement in a variety of political settings.

Roberts does not explicitly use the distinction between custom and law to separate prestate from state systems, but in avoiding the use of the word law when discussing prestate societies, he shows the extent to which his analysis is informed by neo-evolutionary approaches. Giving primacy to bilateral or mediatory resolution of dispute in stateless societies, he concludes that, where such systems involve third-party intervention, the "mode of intervention is restricted" (p. 134). The statement certainly applies to those societies that are politically least complicated and least hierarchical, but it is a contestable generalization when applied to certain chiefdoms. The neo-evolutionist mode of analysis can be most effective when discussion deals with the extremes—the simplest acephalous systems and the fully developed state—but it is seldom subtle enough to account for intermediate types of centralized organization, such as chiefdoms and "segmentary states," tending to give them short shrift. Roberts shares with other neo-evolutionists the notion that, in the absence of a centralized state, "it may be highly misleading to see force as the ultimate incentive towards compliance with socially accepted rules"; like others, he characterizes the withdrawal of social contact and economic reciprocity as "quite the reverse of what we commonly understand as coercive force" (p. 27). He underestimates the effect of such measures. Roberts's limited definition of "coercive force" notwithstanding, it is clear that in most (all?) societies economic costs and penalties can be coercive and, in primitive economic conditions, may even have seriously threatening implications. Indeed, in what society is crude physical force the *principal* incentive toward compliance?

Roberts's book is subtitled "An Introduction to Legal Anthropology," but the author hastens to note on the first page of his preface: "Despite the sub-title, it must be said that this is not a book about law" (p. 9). His entire first chapter is devoted to answering his own question, "Why Not Law?" (pp. 17–29). He replies that to use the "legal model" drawn from our society to analyze others is inappropriate, and he goes on to define that legal model as one whose "point of departure" is a clearly defined corpus of legal rules, which "can provide little help in the study of these groups" (p. 26). Roberts goes even further when he says speculatively that we cannot "be sure that people in another culture will think and speak in terms of 'ought' propositions at all" (p. 26; see also p. 170). (One wonders how children in such imaginary societies might be enculturated?) Roberts has since clarified his position. In *Rules and Processes* (1981) he and the anthropologist John Comaroff have analyzed the complex relationship between norms and actual outcomes in disputes among the Tswana, with considerable attention to the rhetoric involved. Their analysis shows that the "normative repertoire" is clearly present in Tswana thought and speech, but that to understand its pertinence to social life is to go far beyond any simple list of rules.

For some time, there has been growing interest in comparing oral and written literature. Yet only a few of the important differences between oral and written law have been noted. Consequently, it is a matter of no small interest that in Roberts's earlier book (1979) he emphasizes the importance of talking in the resolution of dispute and that he and Comaroff stress the linguistic aspects of Tswana dispute in *Rules and Processes*. There is good reason to consider further the nature of spoken law (see, for example, the limited approach in S. Diamond 1971, pp. 39–48).

A short provocative book on literacy and thought has pertinence to these questions. In Jack Goody's *The Domestication of the Savage Mind* (1977), law is not discussed. Goody's oblique purpose is to show that much of the "grammar of culture" worked out by Claude Lévi-Strauss is a form of cognitive systematization superimposed by the literate anthropologist on the cultural materials of a nonliterate society. It is Goody's contention that the "structuralism" reflects literate habits of thought that do not exist in that form in the cultures analyzed by means of it.

The general discussion is suggestive for theories of law, since it clarifies the difference between applying intellectual capacities to written materials and applying them to living situations. Goody emphasizes three points. First, he notes that the critical analysis of ideas embodied in a corpus of written material is an activity quite different from consideration of ideas bound up in current events. Second, he stresses the cumulative nature of recorded material, opening the possibility of compiling lists and making inventories of information much larger than can be retained by an individual; writing gives permanence—or at least durability—to ideas and information that would be evanescent if carried in an oral tradition only, so that those materials themselves can be studied separately from events. He mentions the contribution of writing to the cumulative growth of knowledge, analysis, and perspective. Third, Goody points out that written materials can constitute a standardized "model for action" for the future, in everything from recipes to the rules and policy directives that make bureaucracies possible.

Inevitably this reflects on ethnography. Anthropologists, who come from a literate tradition, often study peoples living in an oral tradition. The anthropologist imposes a new organization on the gathered data and presents them in a form other than that in which they were observed or heard. This circumstance is as true of the ethnography of law as it is of ethnography in general. Such transformations are not only unavoidable; they are also the essence of analysis. But the systematic understanding the literate form and organization generate may produce a perspective that differs markedly from that of the nonliterate actors whose "legal" activity is analyzed.

Obviously, Simon Roberts is right, as was Paul Bohannan (1957) before him, in stating that nonliterate societies do not have "a clearly defined corpus of rules," if that is understood as the product of a literate tradition. The notion of "corpus" implies an exhaustive list. "Clear definition" requires subdefinition, distinctions, doctrinal commentary, records of case application, and the like. These procedures require writing and record-keeping. By this definition, nonliterate societies cannot have "a clearly defined corpus of rules." Nevertheless, it is not uncommon to find members of nonliterate societies making normative statements, and there are also observable regularities of practice. The challenge for the ethnographer is to find a way to describe these sufficiently processually and contextually so that they are not misunderstood by a literate audience. That is the method the Comaroff-Roberts book (1981) seeks to clarify. The current anthropological interest in this problem is in part a development of sociolinguistics, in part a reaction to the normative style of earlier ethnography, and also to some particularly unproductive examples of the "rule approach."

The work of A. S. Diamond along these lines represents an example of immense scholarly effort impaired by a lack of such sociological understanding. His *Primitive Law Past and Present* (1971) is a revised third edition of a book originally published in 1935. Diamond, having read a great deal in the thirty-odd years between the first and third editions, added much information (and not a little misinformation), but the basic framework remains unchanged in all editions (1935, 1951, 1971). From the start, his interest was in early codes, and his curiosity about the law of nonliterate peoples is a kind of adjunct to the focus on the earliest examples of lists of written laws and their successors. There is nothing ambiguous about his extended typology, based entirely on levels of material culture.

> There is only one time-scale, to call it so, that can be attempted, and that is the economic, using the word in its widest sense—the progression of development of

visible, measurable, material culture. . . . Employing then such a time-scale, our purpose is to find the changes in the growing law that appear at every step in the scale. [1971, p. 4]

His systematic attempt to criticize Maine for relying exclusively on Indo-European materials aimed at going beyond Maine by using a statistical approach to cultural comparison. He did not have Lon Fuller's more experimental turn of mind, in which Maine's thoughts are not taken literally but are treated "as a kind of allegory" (Fuller 1968). Instead, Diamond was trying to reconstruct the evolution of law in a scientific manner through the quantification of cross-cultural variation. He used *The Material Culture and Social Institutions of the Simpler Peoples* (1915) as the typological and temporal framework for his stages of development. The authors—L. T. Hobhouse, G. C. Wheeler, and M. Ginsberg—made a major early attempt at statistical comparison by examining the ethnographic data on 600 societies, classifying them according to the sophistication of the mode of obtaining food, and trying to correlate elements of culture and organization with each type of stage. Diamond sought to fill in the legal dimension of each stage, and to "take up the enquiry where Maine left it" (1935, p. 1; see also pp. 346, 445).

Diamond's purpose was serious, and he worked very hard to achieve it. He arranged his ethnographic information according to a list of topics. Reading his books, it is not difficult to imagine the file cards and their headings. For example, his first chapter, on the lowest level of economic development, starts with a description of the way food gatherers made a living and of the kinds of social units in which they lived (1971, pp. 157–162). This account is peppered with unconnected examples drawn from a wide range of societies. Diamond proceeds by making general statements followed by exceptions or the range of variation. He then discusses the society according to whether it has political offices (p. 162), the nature of its kinship system—groups, who may marry whom, obligations of spouses and affines, divorce, and adoption (pp. 163–64)—the ownership of resources (pp. 164–66), sanctions for wrongful acts (p. 166), the intimations of a boundary between civil and criminal wrongs (p. 167), a list of the kinds of wrongful acts—violence, homicide, and theft (p. 168). He concludes that there is no legal procedure to speak of, noting, "In substance the existence of law is not to be recognized" (p. 170).

Law or no law, a reader will not discover from Diamond's lists the way organized life is carried on in these groups. Diamond is interested in learning only which items from his file of legal topics, drawn from societies with codes, can be found in these simpler ones. The approach might generate interesting comparisons if it were carried out with a broader sense of social context. But a laundry-list approach can never discover material that was not anticipated when the original list was drawn up. For all the hard effort evident in Diamond's work, the product is an aggregate of miscellaneous items more often than it is an effective integration. Both Newman and Roberts attempt less and achieve more. But neither is explicit enough about the changes in anthropological method and theory that have produced quite different kinds of legal ethnography at different periods, and neither sufficiently acknowledges the serious and permanent gaps in the record.

Present anthropological perspectives give much more weight to the colonial or post-colonial circumstances of most field work and to gaps in the record, the variable quality of old ethnography and other problems of evidence, than were formerly thought important. The transformations brought about among subject peoples by the suppression of the indigenous use of force and the removal of autonomy in the colonial period must have been very great. Such measures must have affected precisely those matters regarding enforcement and the workings of the politicolegal system that writers now theorize about so freely. What is known about "social control" in most of the societies anthropologists have studied is limited to information collected in a period of colonial peace. Some few peoples were still in the midst of their traditional forms of warfare and individual fighting at the time they were studied, but those are the exception rather than the rule. Most of the ethnographic material on the use of force, as well as on fighting and warfare, consists of retrospective recollection.

Thus, "the way the system worked" as expounded in evolutionary writings is in important parts conjectural and inferential (for some good modern reports on such evidence as there is, see Meggitt 1977; Strathern 1975 [1971], on New Guinea warfare). From Bronislaw Malinowski's work (1926) on the Trobrianders to Philip Gulliver's work (1963) on the Arusha Masai, the ethnographic study was performed under circumstances quite different from those that had prevailed in precolonial days, but the interpretation was made without much attention to the colonial context. The material is no less interesting and important because of its date. But for an understanding of the social balances involved in the earlier system of using and regulating violence, and the connections of the earlier system with others through trade and warfare, there are necessarily many fundamental gaps in the information. Much that is important about the political dimensions of these precolonial systems will remain permanently uncertain. That circumstance permits moderns to make what they like of them for the purposes of theory, evolutionary or otherwise. As Elizabeth Colson has written, "Those who build theories about the nature of stateless societies have . . . differed profoundly in their view of what life is like under such conditions, a difference which rests upon different assessments of the nature of man" (1975, p. 32).

Dominant Norms and Forms; or, Foxy Manipulators   Not only because what is known about them is usually a "reconstruction," but also because of the distorting pressure of political issues in the present, it is difficult to see nonstate societies as they were. Their law and their social order have come to occupy a polemic place in discussion. In 1973 Elizabeth Colson delivered the Lewis Henry Morgan lectures at Rochester University, later published as *Tradition and Contract* (1975). Fresh from the time of troubles at Berkeley in the 1960s, Colson took as her theme what she saw as the constraints and dangers of life in egalitarian stateless societies, arguing that central governmental authority can bring liberty and security. Clearly reacting negatively to the student vision of "alternative" communities of individuals freely negotiating with each other, she marshaled her knowledge of stateless societies to document the thesis that equality and absence of central authority do not spell freedom from limiting rules nor freedom of expression but that the contrary is the case (p. 51). Arguing that, because people in such societies literally have to fight for their rights and "depend on themselves for ensuring life and property," they live in a state of chronic insecurity (p. 67); she described the price of truce in such settings as involving endemic mutual suspicion and a tense vigilance.

Colson went on to discuss the benefits of centralized government: "we cannot understand . . . the colonial period, or indeed the history of our own time, if we do not understand that people may be prepared to accept authority, even though they find it both threatening and frustrating, because they see it as the guarantor of an overarching security" (p. 67). And of Africans today, who once lived in "small parochial units," she noted, "Whatever their quarrels with government, they want good government rather than less government" (p. 8).

Colson also mentions the desirability of "escaping from those close-knit social networks of village society" (p. 102). Unlike the political evolutionists Morton Fried (1967) and Elman Service (1975), Colson considers the rule of community consensus to be frequently oppressive and requiring an undesirable degree of conformity. For Service and Fried, nonstate societies, whatever their suffocating closeness, are paradise compared with societies that include class stratification, economic inequality, and state coercion. Which side is right? How is one to see legal comparisons clearly, given the present uses of the past?

Colson's argument contains echoes of Sir Henry Maine. Indeed, her introductory remarks (p. 8) allude to the writer who also discussed the tyranny of kinship groups over their members in earlier forms of society and the modern growth of individual liberty. In keeping with the elegant duality of nineteenth-century rhetoric, Maine organized his discussion of legal evolution around two types, ancient law and modern law. He put into a set of succinct oppositions what he saw as the legal significance of the shift from one condition to the other. Most often quoted and most often misunderstood is the movement from status to contract; but more significant to his argument is the change from the family to the individual as the basic social unit. In Maine's usage, "status" meant legal position in a family group, not standing in the modern sociological sense (1861, pp. 126, 169, 170). Related to these shifts were the changes from collective family property to private individual property, from a polity based on the concept of kindred to a polity based on the principle of local contiguity, from inalienable land to salable land, and from intestacy to wills (pp. 270, 131, 260, 268, 195). Maine perceived the prefeudal condition of orderly society as originally organized into corporate patriarchal families that held property in common and whose members were ruled by the male head of the household (p. 311); "the unit of an ancient society was the family, of a modern society the individual" (p. 126). It is interesting that Maine considered the emancipation of women part of the very same historical progression:

> the civilized societies of the West, in steadily enlarging the personal and proprietary independence of women, and even in granting to them political privilege, are only following out still farther a law of development which they have been obeying for many centuries. The society, which once consisted of compact families, has got extremely near to the condition in which it will consist exclusively of individuals, when it has finally and completely assimilated the legal position of women to the legal position of men. [Maine 1880, p. 327]

The certitude with which Maine identified a single process as the mainspring of legal change is remarkable.

How current is this view of legal individualism as social progress? Discussion of some of the issues continues but in a different vein. Alan MacFarlane, an anthropologist-historian, puts forward the argument that individualism in Maine's sense was manifest in English society very early in its history, at least by the thirteenth century; he cites Maine's work in presenting his own in *The Origins of English Individualism* (1978, pp. 186–88, 201). The importance of the date derives from connections made between "individualism" and the origins of capitalism and industrialization, relating individualism also to the origin of the ideology of equality and liberty. "English property relations were at the heart of much that is special about England" (MacFarlane 1978, p. 200). MacFarlane argues that the "individualistic pattern of ownership" was the source of all the central features of English social structure and that, moreover, by putting the date of this phenomenon too late, Karl Marx, Max Weber, and Karl Polanyi were mistaken about the sequence and timing, and hence the cause, of modern capitalist developments. MacFarlane not only contends that England had ceased to be a "peasant" society by the thirteenth century, but also suggests that it may never have been one. He makes his case easier for himself by comparing the complex realities of English history with a simple model of peasant community, but the thesis is nevertheless tantalizing. Prominent among the data he brings forward to support his argument are court records and other materials on the law of real property, particularly documents relating to the forms of tenure, alienation, and inheritance. Law, in turn, is taken to reflect the structure of the family and the place of the individual in it. Today it is plain that some of the themes that occupied Maine are far from dead, but that not only unitary evolutionary typologies but also variations in historical sequences are being brought to bear on these questions.

Maine was limited in his assessment of these matters, not only by the narrow range of ethnographic information available to him but also by his exaggerated preoccupation with what he regarded as the most important and singular feature of modernity—the freedom of the individual as epitomized by his legal capacity to hold private property in land and to make contracts. In *Ancient Law,* Maine paid little attention to developments in the relations between law and formal organizations. He was certainly fully aware of their importance, since he wrote on government in other books. In *The Early History of Institutions* (1880), he referred to two central ideas—"land as an exchangeable commodity" and "the great increase in modern times of the authority of the State"—as the "several great conceptions which lie at the base of our stock of thought" (pp. 86–87). But only the first was the focus of his evolutionary classification of law.

Nearly a century later, Max Gluckman tried to substantiate Maine's principal contentions about ancient law in his field study of the Barotse, a people living in what was then Northern Rhodesia (1955, 1965a, 1965b). But since in 1941, the time of Gluckman's field work, the Barotse were not an "archaic" society but part of a colonial one, Gluckman was "reconstructing" the "tribal" system with full prior knowledge of Maine's model (see Moore 1978a).

Despite Gluckman's respectful declaration of his indebtedness to Maine and his own emphasis on the normative importance of kinship as the model for all obligations in Barotseland, his treatment of these issues and Maine's are quite different. (See Gluckman 1965a and 1965b.) Maine equated kinship with "family"—patriarchal family at that—and saw it as a milieu in which the individual was submerged in the collective so that, except for the patriarch himself, individuals could not act on their own. "In the constitution of primitive society the individual creates for himself few or no rights, and few or no duties" (Maine 1861, p. 311). Gluckman's case analyses simultaneously focus on two aspects; they emphasize certain highly general parameters of mutual obligation lying between persons in such *paired roles* as father-son, brother-brother, and husband-wife; and they clarify the specific manipulative, self-interested activities and negotiated arrangements that actually took place between *particular individuals* in the case histories. The legal question as interpreted by Gluckman is always whether these highly idiosyncratic individual transactions were within the range of cognizable notions of proper behavior in a social role.

In his general evolutionary interpretation, Gluckman postulated that there were two types of relationship, each being the basis of a corresponding type of legal system. The first, characteristic of tribal societies, consists of *multiplex relations*—long-term personal relationships between individuals exhibiting multiple strands of mutual connection; these are connections between the same persons in the economic, political, religious, and social spheres. The second type consisted of *simplex relationships*, single-interest impersonal relationships in which only one strand connects the parties; these may be found, for example, between buyer and seller, employer and employee, and teacher and student. Gluckman never disentangled long-term single-interest relationships from single transactions, though such a distinction might have clarified his analysis. Simplex relationships were held to be characteristic of modern societies.

It was Gluckman's view that in social systems founded on multiplex relationships—such as tribal systems—the law consisted of the general standards of reasonable behavior appropriate to persons in particular roles. He believed that, although some tribal law was expressed in explicit rule statements, its major portion was implicit in role standards. By contrast, he assumed that a modern legal system dominated by simplex relationships had innumerable quite specific and explicit rules referring not to roles but to kinds of transactions and to specific acts. Any lawyer knows that many modern legal standards are related to roles. And a reanalysis of Gluckman's data on Barotse cases reveals very quickly that some Barotse rules also referred to certain acts and transactions *without* reference to the "roles" the parties might occupy. Nevertheless, the contrast Gluckman was mounting lay between a model of social relationships founded on kinship and a model of social relationships founded on commerce. (For Gluckman's general ideas on sociopolitical evolution, see 1965b.) That durable relations—some of them multiplex, some of them "single-interest"—can and do exist in modern society is evident, and Gluckman freely conceded that single-interest transactions do take place in some nonmodern societies. But he was concerned with the *dominant* type and the way it afforded a paradigmatic model for law.

This dual typology has various problems, but what is interesting is not what it is but what it and other work of the period spawned. Gluckman's general interpretations made "tribal" law consonant with a normative, structural-functional model of society, but his case studies suggested the cogency of quite different models (and Gluckman was instrumental in bringing case studies into anthropological respectability). The cases showed particular individuals disputing and often recounting the facts of series of mutual transactions lasting over many years. Gluckman insisted that the outcome of the cases that were tried depended on whether they were thought by the judges to fall within the range of proper behavior in a social role. This suggestion stimulated a great deal of countervailing work to show that often the conduct of individuals could not be accounted for by their "roles" and was much more economically explained by self-interest. In the work of Gluckman's students and colleagues of the "Manchester School"—such as F. Bailey, E. Colson, E. Peters, and V. Turner—and such non-Mancunians as F. Barth, P. H. Gulliver, and L. Nader (and her students), there emerged a picture of People as Finaglers, as competitive and manipulative beings, conscious of norms, not incapable of having ideals, behaving with generosity and even sacrificing for others, but much of the time, when an opportunity exists, acting according to self-interest.

This construct is a marriage of Malinowskian observations of individuals "using" norms and of modern game theory, with some symbolic interactionism thrown in. People as Finaglers have for some years been the stars on the anthropological case-history screen.

They "use" social and cultural institutions. They satisfy the Marxists as well as "the others" with their rapacious materialism, their gamesmanship, their striving for economic and amorous gain. They can be watched on the small scale and observed at the head of governments. They are the Everyman (Every-person) of today, "making it" within the constraints of the social milieu—in some areas, subordinate to the power of others; in their own bailiwick, the makers of momentous minichoices about which anthropologists write books.

This development has led to a changed emphasis in many studies of kinship as-it-works-on-the-ground. And if kin-based systems are not as they once seemed, how is "law" in such systems to be understood? The "old" ethnography tended to record ideal rules of behavior often treating them as prescriptive and mandatory. Current writings tend to stress the fact that even in kin-based systems individuals may nevertheless have strategizing careers. They may play one kinship bond against another or may forge closer ties with some relatives than with others. Kinship is no longer seen as altogether the straitjacket of fixed rules in which genealogy and kinship role tie the hands, but rather a set of classifications and ideas that structure an arena of action within which discretion is exercised, favors and goods are exchanged, reputations are made or broken, and competition is not unusual.

Detail is both the blessing and the bane of these kinds of data, and triviality always a danger. The anthropologist faces the dilemma of attaching the minutiae of these observed "case" situations to larger-scale, longer-term realities while determining what kinds of evidence to use to establish these connections. Legal disputes, legal transactions, and other events involving law are particularly suitable for linking the small-scale to the large-scale, the momentary to the longer-term.

When Maine focused on the capacity of the individual to make contracts and to hold, buy, and sell land, the basic unit was a generic individual who, in his eyes, was the foundation on which the entire structure of modern law was built. The present interactionist perspective on legal disputes concentrates on the experiences of particular individuals in an attempt to understand "the system" from the actor's point of view (Nader and Todd 1978). On the whole, as a result of the interactionist approach, the larger politicoeconomic context is treated the way one might treat the Congo forest or the Arctic ice floes—as an external fact of nature, simply as part of the actor's environment. Individual legal choices of action are "explained" as self-interested or required by the exigencies of the "power structure," but the large-scale background is described rather than "explained."

The neo-evolutionist tends to have a corner on producing large-scale, long-term "explanation." One of the "others," Lloyd Fallers, while joking about Marx and Spencer, grumbled about the evolutionist approach, extolled Talcott Parsons and Weber, and reintroduced the intentional actor at the bottom of it all in his last book, *The Social Anthropology of the Nation-State* (1974). Fallers discussed the unpredictable and non-repeatable aspects of history, concluding that "neither social anthropology nor social science in general can predict the outcome of contemporary nation-states' struggles with their problems" (pp. 121, 140, 143). But he argued that social science might contribute to an "understanding" of those problems, "and hence, perhaps, to the capacity for intelligent self-direction" (p. 143). All of which is rather vague. Fallers's own collection of case studies, *Law Without Precedent* (1969), set in Busoga, Uganda, squarely faces the colonial context of his study and the complexity of the transformation he was witnessing, producing not theoretical synthesis but only an immense amount of detail and some platitudes about legal reasoning. For Fallers, understanding the nation-state meant describing it, supplementing the national aggregate statistics with deeper local material, and taking into account the nature of the leadership. He rejected any argument about historical inevitability—"history is not made up only of the sorts of economic, ecological and sociocultural structures and patterns that social anthropologists and other social scientists may discern. History is also made by men and groups of men, themselves conceptualizing and choosing among the courses of action offered by their situation" (1974, p. 69).

Because his time-scale is much longer and grander, this kind of "historical particularism" usually gives the armchair evolutionist-materialist no trouble. But the ubiquitous Finagler makes problems for the Marxist as field worker. Is the observed choice-making merely an illusion of the actors, whose course of action is really predetermined? Pierre Bourdieu (1977), one of the more reflective of the current crop of widely read Marxist anthropologists, tries to bridge such difficult problems with a new vocabulary—perhaps on the theory that, if contradictory concepts are embraced by a single term, the paradox will vanish from sight. Bourdieu proposes that analytically one should not think of culture as a set of norms. Instead, one should postulate a kind of cultural imprinting of "generative principles" that allow for the Finagler and also for innovation. This cultural frame Bourdieu calls the *habitus* and defines it as the "durably installed generative principle of regulated improvisation" (p. 78). At first sight, there seems an ambiguity about the individual as improviser. The door seems open a crack for creativity and change instituted by individuals. But Bourdieu is too committed a Marxist-determinist for such fluidity.

> Because the habitus is an endless capacity to engender products—thought, perceptions, expressions, actions—whose limits are set by the historically and socially situated conditions of its production, the conditioned and conditional freedom it secures is as remote from a creation of unpredictable novelty as it is from a simple mechanical reproduction of the initial conditionings. [1977, p. 95]

(Someone should have told him long ago that opacity is a bad habitus.) The concept of habitus closely resembles the idea of the internalization of culture. But in defining it as a matter of "generative principle," Bourdieu, like most social anthropologists today, rejects the representation of culture as a list of norms and rules in the old structural-functional or culture-pattern frame. A purely normative mode cannot account for "real" activities— the "practice" of his title, *Outline of a Theory of Practice*, the new focus of field work. Instead of consisting of a list of rigid rules, the habitus gives form to certain capacities, it guides and disposes, and it allows a range of choices to be exercised and a range of improvisations to be generated. But having acknowledged the capacity in the manner of a processual anthropologist, Bourdieu specifies the limits of the capacity in terms of traditional Marxist formulations.

The habitus is intended to explain the operations of "custom" or "prelaw" in Kabylia, where Bourdieu did his field work (p. 16). He describes a general scheme of cultural classification that can be turned to a variety of uses, among them the definition of aggravating or mitigating circumstances. These categories are the generative principles that can be permuted and combined to deal with any case. Bourdieu's conception of modern law is such that he concludes that "the precepts of custom . . . have nothing in common with the transcendent rules of a juridical code" (p. 17). Probably the experience of a civil law system is what leads him to think of law in this way. Bourdieu appears to be saying that the juridical code is to the customary practice what normative anthropology is to the "generative principle of regulated improvisation." He seems not to know too much about comparative law, in practice.

The concept of the habitus tries to encapsulate a paradox, that the culturally determined does not preclude the improvised. (Another analytic scheme has been proposed to deal with these matters; see Moore 1978, pp. 32–53.) Bourdieu has left other paradoxes unresolved. Persons in archaic societies must be materialists like others; but archaic societies often seem to be focused not on economic interest but on symbolic and ritual activities and other apparently "disinterested" works. This fact, according to Bourdieu, is easily accounted for by the phenomenon of institutionalized "misrecognition" (p. 22). Bourdieu considered "the expression of material interests . . . highly censored" in certain types of societies, particularly archaic ones, but contends that this does not mean that the material interests are absent (p. 22). He contrasted the "good faith economy" of archaic societies with the undisguised "self-interest economy" of modern societies, arguing that both kinds of society are really moved by economic interest, but that the archaic economy must "misrecognize" that circumstance (pp. 22, 161, 172). Thus, there is a "systematic emphasis on the symbolic aspect of the activities and relations of production to prevent the economy from being grasped as an economy" (p. 172). As an example he cites gift exchange and its cultural representation by a "sincere fiction of disinterested exchange" (p. 171).

Where the only legitimate form of accumulation is of honor and prestige, these must be regarded as "symbolic capital" (p. 170). Bourdieu argues that in precapitalist societies, just as in capitalist societies, practice never ceases to conform to economic calculation; despite appearances to the contrary, symbolic capital can be accumulated and is ultimately convertible into economic capital (pp. 177, 170). Each of these three terms—habitus, misrecognition, and symbolic capital—embodies an interpretive problem that is troublesome in anthropology for both non-Marxists and Marxists.

Although Bourdieu does not deal at any length with legal anthropology, it is obvious that the explanatory puzzles he addresses are of critical importance to an analysis of "primitive law." Are comparisons to be made on the basis of apparent similarities, or of underlying meanings? And if matters are not as they appear to be, what criteria can be used to determine underlying meaning? One may find Bourdieu's conceptual vocabulary a scholarly form of misrecognition, but he has done much to sharpen the issues. A central problem in anthropology is a problem, not of data, but of meaning. Seeking meaning rather than sociological "laws," some have abandoned the "scientific" perspective as an impossibility in social science and prefer a hermeneutical approach. (For a collection of readings on this general position, see Rabinow and Sullivan 1979; for the argument that law itself is best studied through an "interpretive sociology," see Grace and Wilkinson 1978; and for an eloquent essay on differences of meaning in three legal traditions, see Geertz 1983.)

The interpretive social science people have more to contend with than Marxism, for Marxist anthropologists have no monopoly on economic interpretations of law and legal evolution. From a "free market" political position, Richard Posner produced a comparative article entitled "A Theory of Primitive Society with Special Reference to Law" (1980) that is just as economic in rationale as anything of Bourdieu's. Posner begins by compressing all the major characteristics of primitive or archaic societies into a general-ized "type"—the preliterate or primitive. He goes on to argue that "the theory that law is an instrument for maximizing social wealth or efficiency" may be used as an explanation of many of the distinctive institutions of those societies. In fact, he explains gift-giving, reciprocal exchange, polygamy and bride-price, the size of kinship groups, and "even the value placed on certain personality traits such as generosity and touchiness . . . as direct or indirect adaptations to the high costs of information" (pp. 5, 6). He extends the argument to a number of the specifically "legal" institutions of primitive society.

It is interesting to contrast Posner's and Bourdieu's approaches to the individual. Posner, a lawyer who is not an anthropologist, treats customary institutions. Individuals are in the picture only by implication as typical actors in typical behavior. He is occupied not with individual economizing but with the economic rationality of institutions for the society as a whole. When some ethnographies report an exact schedule of compensations for killing and injuries—for example, forty head of cattle for a homicide—Posner as-sumes that such precise schedules were, in fact, adhered to, and he rationalizes at length why such an arrangement is optimal for primitive societies (pp. 67ff.). Posner is unaware that, even when the rules are stated with exactitude, it is not unusual for negotiation and bargaining to take place about payment; he relies for his anthropological material on Diamond, the scholar of rules.

In contrast, Bourdieu, the anthropologist, like so much of the anthropological commu-nity, focused on People the Finaglers, the choice-making manipulators, the strategizing individuals. Bourdieu's problems arise first in connection with explaining the locus of material interests if people in archaic societies appear to be altruists, and second in explaining choice-making at the individual level while preserving the determinism on a historical level required by a Marxist explanation. He solves these problems with labels; the underlying dilemmas are not resolved. Bourdieu is concerned with states of mind, with symbols, with appearances and misrecognition.

Posner, not concerned with consciousness, notes, "in suggesting that primitive people are economically rational, I am not making any statement about their conscious states. Rational behavior to an economist is a matter of consequences, not states of mind, and in that respect resembles the concept of functionality in anthropology" (1979, p. 78, n. 166). He goes on to cite *Structure and Function in Primitive Society* (Radcliffe-Brown 1952). It is interesting that he should make this analogy by way of legitimation, since in current anthropology there is such widespread awareness of the limited explanatory power of the functional framework. The assumption that everything in society has a function does not necessarily lend rigor to the process of figuring out what that function might be. In good hands, such a method may generate some insights. Radcliffe-Brown conceived of *function* as the contribution made by a custom to the life of the whole society. Thus, in practice, function stressed the interconnection of phenomena. In Radcliffe-Brown's day, social anthropologists answered the question of function by showing the dimension of social relations that attaches to customs and institutions. The function of a ceremony included not merely its declared purpose but also its effects on the social relations of those involved or its apparent fit with some other set of customs and institutions.

Posner is correct in asserting that his approach bears some resemblance to the concept of functionality in anthropology. He postulates that every archaic institution must en-hance social wealth or efficiency or it would not have survived. According to Posner's method, the question follows concerning the particular way in which the institution is economically rational. Sitting at his desk Posner then thinks out the answer. He has no problem providing logically plausible economic rationalizations of the institutions he considers; but his ingenuity is no proof that he is correct. Like reasoning about function, reasoning about economic rationality stresses a putative "effect" of the existence of an institution.

Without any intention of descending into the Althusserian murk, it is useful to consider in this connection Freud's idea (1938) that all major social institutions must be "overdetermined." Freud granted that many "origins" and "causes" may account for the invention of religion beyond his own ideas of an "original" parricide. Since social scientists have abandoned the general search for origins, and since it has become evident that causes are frequently very difficult to isolate, it is often much clearer to talk about consequences, as Posner does. Nevertheless, it could easily be argued that all major social institutions are by definition not only overdetermined but also multiconsequent. Posner is making an inquiry into the economic logic of multiconsequent institutions. That his own version of economic rationality was the only consequence he considered, that his compressed primitive type eliminates the variability that might have tested some of his conclusions, that someone more intimately aware of the ethnographic data might have saved him from some misleading sources—none of these reservations overcomes the stimulus of his challenging argument.

However, as has been noted of a functional approach, "it is of little advantage to know that everything is related to everything else . . . unless it is possible to show the extent to which it is so related" (Goody 1976, p. 119). Just as much interested in material matters as Posner, Jack Goody, in *Production and Reproduction,* used the *Ethnographic Atlas* (coded data on 863 societies) in an effort to show statistically "a positive association" or "a significant trend" of connection among factors relating to inheritance, dowry, and bridewealth (p. 10). His general argument claims that the more intensive the use given to scarce productive resources, the greater the tendency toward retention of these resources within the basic productive and reproductive unit (p. 10). The argument is, in part, a development from an earlier collaborative work on dowry and bridewealth (Goody and Tambiah 1973). There are clear implications for legal history in this work.

Jane Collier has been carrying forward a comparison on a smaller scale of bride "payments" in several societies. She considers the settings in which bride service, equal bridewealth for all brides, or unequal bridewealth is paid in connection with marriage. Following Claude Meillassoux and others, one of her interests is in developing general models of the variety of types of "simple" societies (Collier 1984). Since much of the organization of prestate societies—and, indeed, of many state societies—is kin-based, the controls over women, marriage, reproduction, and production are often closely related. Because matters of kinship and economy are central to understanding the legal order, the subject matter of this line of inquiry will continue to be of high interest to the generalizing comparativist.

The hope for ongoing work is that it will change for the good the cruder classical terms of discussion. (For a variety of current commentaries, see Black 1984.) One hopes for more subtle analyses of observable living societies and more informed speculations about unobservable past societal forms, both infused with more candor about what is not known. The dominant themes of grand interpretation and its certitudes have been the same for a remarkably long time, certainly at least since the nineteenth century; they center on whether the individual knows more security, liberty, equality, and fraternity in primitive conditions and in small self-governing communities than in the smoky cities and rural agribusinesses of modern societies. On such questions as whether the pursuit of rapacious self interest and the use of coercion is more contained in one kind of setting or the other, two extreme camps come to precisely opposite conclusions. Further reiteration of these arguments in the same general terms cannot be very profitable. But there are encouraging signs that in some quarters the content of the discussion is changing.

Three integrating works on modern law by Roberto M. Unger, Donald Black, and Philippe Nonet and Philip Selznick show the unmistakable influence of this long history of debate, and some of their arguments are in a familiar evolutionary mode. But the common preoccupation of these works is clearly a political one—the proper role of the state. In contrast to the 1920s and 1930s, when many American lawyers and social scientists looked with optimism to an increase in the power of government and to legislation and the courts as the source of desirable social reform, the 1960s and 1970s brought skepticism about whether government and legal institutions can carry the burden of such hopes.

After Weber, What? Some Recent Essays on the Grand Scale

Max Weber tried to synthesize the general development of lawmaking and law-finding by outlining a series of developmental stages, with law passing progressively from a high degree of formal and substantive irrationality toward greater and greater rationality. The movement was away from arbitrary and particularistic decisions, and from techniques involving revelation, chance, and the supposed intervention of the supernatural, toward the use of reason, logic, and the systematic application of general rules. Weber hastened to note of his "ideal types" that "the theoretically constructed stages of rationalization have not everywhere followed in the sequence we have just outlined, even if we ignore the world outside the Occident" (Weber 1954, p. 304). His legal evolutionism, which is anything but unilinear, is not focused on a sequence from "collectivism" to "individualism" (see his comments on the latter, pp. 188–89) but rather on other aspects of political and economic organization and what he saw as the corresponding growth of more rational styles of legal thought. Weber's legal training is evident in the large place he gave to professionalism, the development of systems of rules, and the nature of legal formalism and of bureaucratic institutional arrangements. Decidedly a candidate for the position of lawyers' favorite sociologist, Weber felt certain that nothing would ever "stop the continuous growth of the technical element in the law and hence of its character as a specialists' domain" (p. 321). But he returned again and again to the point that, in the manner of substantive content, it is not simply the legal thinking of the specialists but also the political, economic, and ideological contexts of the time and place that are paramount in giving the law its continuously transforming shape. He thought of law as "a rational technical apparatus, which is continually transformable in the light of expediential considerations" (p. 321).

In his *Law in Modern Society* (1976), Roberto Unger bravely tried to "redo" Weber on law and go further. He sought to encompass in one discussion all the world's legal systems of all times and all places and to identify how and why they change, sorting legal systems into a few great types. In a technique borrowed directly from Weber's, Unger argues that the "ideal type" is the most powerful methodological tool for "the reconciliation of generalizing theory and historiography" (p. 45). He extends specifically to law the question to which so much of Weber's work was dedicated—how to account for the uniqueness of modern Western European society and ideas. Also following Weber's script and with the ghost of Marx watching in the wings, Unger is very much concerned with the effects of consciousness, with the way the self-understanding of people in a society affects that society. In Unger's scheme of things, all social change ultimately depends on an aspect of awareness. "The deepest root of all historical change is manifest or latent conflict between the view of the ideal and the experience of actuality" (p. 153).

Since, in Unger's dynamics, social change springs from a dissonance between ideal and real, he must set about defining these for each of the major types of law. He categorizes three such types: customary or interactional law, bureaucratic or regulatory law, and the legal order (pp. 49–85).

Each of Unger's legal types corresponds to a particular kind of society. Thus, customary law is found in tribal society, the bureaucratic order emerges in aristocratic society, and the legal order exists in liberal society. Beyond liberal society, postliberal society is the current phase; Unger named it "modern society." He was careful to note that "[t]he concepts of tribal, liberal, and aristocratic society are meant to be parts of a comparative scheme rather than stages of a universal evolutionary sequence" (p. 137).

Unger's conception of tribal society is a Durkheimian one, in which few groups exist and individuals are joined in strong communal solidarity. The major social distinction is between insiders, who share the "mental experience" of an intense moral communion, and outsiders, with whom "they do not share anything important" (p. 142). "The chief point to grasp is that in tribal societies very different standards of behavior are imposed on relations among insiders and on those between insiders and strangers" (p. 141). Reciprocity is the rule for insiders, while predation is permitted against outsiders.

Law as custom "is neither public nor positive" (p. 50). Unger uses the concept of nonpublic law to indicate that, although customary law is common to the entire society, it is not associated with a central government. He sees a lack of positiveness in the circumstance that custom "is made up of implicit standards of conduct rather than of formulated rules" (p. 50). "Customs are characteristically inarticulate rather than expressed. They apply to narrowly defined categories of persons and relationships rather than to very general classes. And they cannot be reduced to a set of rules" (p. 50).

Unger poses three questions for each of his social types: what is the anatomy of its groups?; what is the nature of the social bond within the society?; and "how will individuals" in such relations "conceive of the place of the ideal in actuality?" (p. 143). Answering these questions for tribal society Unger states that among tribesmen, ideal and actuality are inseparable. They do not have "the experience of moral doubt" and cannot conceive that nature and society might undergo basic change (p. 143; see Needham 1972 for an anthropological view consistent with Unger's on this point). This is an arguable proposition, about which anthropologists are not in agreement.

In Unger's scheme of things, "Each type of society has a focal point of tension, a hidden flaw in its characteristic way of defining the social bond," which becomes the source of its transformation (p. 151). "For tribal society, there is the danger that the community of shared values may fall apart, victim to group conflict" (p. 151). This observation is the very opposite of the primitive scene described by Barkun, Gluckman, Evans-Pritchard, and Sahlins, in which conflict is endemic and the "system" has a continuity to which conflict contributes.

Throughout the theoretical (rather than the descriptive) part of his book, Unger juxtaposes tribal society and liberal society, to accentuate the contrast between them. He goes on to discuss aristocratic society, which he sees as a kind of intermediate type, both historically and logically. The legal order of liberal society is "general and autonomous as well as public and positive." In the legal order, constitutional distinctions separate politics, administration, and adjudication. The law becomes an "autonomous" set of integrated practices and ideas. Rules are applied by a specialized institution, whose main business is adjudication; legal reasoning differs from any other, and a specialized legal profession develops. The legal order emerged with modern European liberal society (p. 52).

In liberal society, every individual belongs to a large number of significant groups. The "association of interests" forms the social bond. The beliefs about the ideal and the experience of the actual a society is said to generate are an ideal of order and an experience of diversity of interests, groups, and ideas. As for the flaw in liberal society, "in its characteristic way of defining the social bond . . . [l]iberal society is vulnerable to the implications of its uniquely unstable system of ranking: some groups in fact have more power than others, yet no group seems entitled to dominate the others. Hence, a continuous struggle takes place between the quest for equality and the need for authority" (pp. 66, 143, 144, 146, 152). Unstable systems of ranking hardly seem the monopoly of liberal society—but Unger's is a schematic representation, not a description of reality.

Two other types are discussed in Unger's scheme—aristocratic society with bureaucratic law, and postliberal society. The latter is the modern society, which gives him his title. He also permits himself some speculations about postmodern society and the possibilities ahead. Unger divides modern society into three types—traditionalist (societies with both a modern and a nonmodern sector, as in developing countries and, in his ordering, Japan), revolutionary-socialist, and postliberal. "The Western capitalist social democracies have become postliberal societies." The reader may be alarmed to learn that in postliberal society the rule of law disintegrates as the boundary between state and society, the public and private spheres, is eroded. "Open-ended standards" come to have a major role in legislation, administration, and adjudication, and there is a shift "from formalistic to purposive or policy-oriented styles of legal reasoning" (pp. 192, 193, 194).

Traditionalist modern societies operate on basically two legal orders: that of the central government and that of the informal system of customary law "that embodies the dominant consciousness of traditionalistic society," but there is also a growth of a "sprawling body of bureaucratic law that mainly regulates the economy" (p. 228). Unger speaks of the underlying tension between "the ideal of hierarchic community, and the experience of social disintegration, bred by life in the modernizing sector" (p. 229). The dilemma of revolutionary socialist society is "its attempt to reconcile industrialism, bureaucratization, and national power with the achievement of an ideal of fraternal or egalitarian community. . . . The society has two kinds of law. There is a law of bureaucratic commands and a law of autonomous self-regulation" in the various communal organizations (pp. 231, 233).

Unger argues that all three types of modern society—traditionalist, revolutionary-socialist, and postliberal—"are obsessed, in different ways, with the reconciliation of freedom and community" (p. 266). He sees two major conflicts to be resolved in the future: the reconciliation of industrialism's need for centralization and specialization with the "longing for community" and the need to define the communitarian ideal in such a way that it strengthens the sense of individual autonomy "to make autonomy compatible with authority" (p. 237).

Law in Modern Society is an attempt to argue for a mode of social analysis while providing an illustrative demonstration of its effectiveness. Unger's thesis is logical within its own terms. It is a closed system. Ideal types are not amenable to criticism, since they are unfalsifiable "types" not representations of reality. Moreover, Unger covers himself by stating that "the differences among the types of law always remain fluid," and he indicates, by way of example, that "a legal order operated against the backdrop of customary and bureaucratic law" (p. 54). Thus, evidence that real societies do not fully conform to the types cannot in any sense invalidate the models. Given these cautions, a critic can at most argue that there may be other, possibly more interesting, questions than those illuminated by this particular way of compressing the data.

What is fascinating about the problems that Unger defines and addresses is that they seem to be so pervasive in a number of disciplines. One set of problems consists of social paradoxes: individual and group, autonomy and authority, freedom and order. The other set is epistemological: paradoxes between subjective and objective, consciousness and reality, determined and contingent, and a whole Pandora's box of problems of communication and understanding and interpretation (see Unger 1975 for an earlier discussion of some of these). His oscillation between specific illustrations and authoritatively stated— never tentatively proposed—general interpretations is a remarkable display. But there are some curious lacunae. For the purposes of his argument, Unger treats societies as completely separate units that are somehow internally unitary, even if he acknowledges that each system contains various parts (for example, the modernizing sector and the "traditional" sector in Third World countries). But where is the interpenetration of national economies? Where is the international arena? Is it possible to speak of any complex society as having a single vision of the ideal or single experience of actuality without falling into some kind of anthropomorphism? It seems, in any case, the reduction of a complex multiplicity to a single coherent representation. But that, of course, is exactly what a "type" is. Unger's logic is not assailable within its own structure, and following its symmetries gives an aesthetic pleasure. The actual is less tidy.

Another intrepid attempt to cut through the comparative problem on a global scale is Donald Black's *The Behavior of Law* (1976). The book consists almost entirely of a series of hypotheses stated as propositions. (For an interesting critique, see Greenberg 1983.) These vary in specificity from the most general—"Across the world law has increased as homogeneous cultures have diversified, and as diverse cultures have homogenized" (p. 78)—to narrower statements about particular societies. The "theory" of law the essay exemplifies is the extended consequence of Black's initial definition of law, which locks him into an inevitably repetitive form of presentation. At the outset, he defines law as "governmental social control": "The quantity of law varies in time and space. It varies across the centuries, decades and years, months and days, even the hours of the day. It varies across societies, regions, communities, neighborhoods, families" (pp. 2, 3). It follows from the definition that, if law is "governmental social control," the amount of governmental control of social life will be found to be variable. Societies without government exercise none; and societies with governments exercise a greater or lesser amount in different social sectors at different times. *The Behavior of Law* attempts to spell out the significance of this finding in a series of statements on covariation. Black's book is not itself a typology of legal systems but rather an essay on what Black sees as the fundamental criteria for distinguishing the "behavior" of law in one social setting from that in another. The covariations have clear typological implications.

Although Black has kind words for quantification, claiming that all his propositions involve measurable variables, he leaves the measuring to future scholars. He merely points out what should be measured, proposing not only the quantity of law but also its "style." In Black's use of the term, "style" is manifested in the measures taken after a law is violated, whether these are penal, compensatory, therapeutic, or conciliatory. "It is possible to formulate propositions that explain the quantity and style of law in every setting. Each of these propositions states a relationship between law and another aspect of social life—stratification, morphology, culture, organization, or social control" (pp. 5, 6).

Black uses these five aspects as chapter headings, proceeding through each topic. His central thesis seems unexceptionable—that the growth of law (government, in his definition) has paralleled the growth of stratification, organization, and centralization in society, as it has been to other aspects of cultural and social elaboration and differentiation. That view has been generally established for a long time. Black's particular choice of approach, however, is informed by a political perspective. The pervasive theme that emerges in Black's analysis is that, in the course of development, law increasingly becomes an instrument of the powerful and the rich; that all things being unequal, law (that is, government social control) "is less likely to serve the needs of the poor and the deviant and more likely to be at the service of the People at the Top . . . the more stratification a society has, the more law it has" (p. 13).

But, in closing, Black speculates on the future and a possible reversal of this postulated trend. He does not believe that society is necessarily destined to get more and more law, and more and more government social control, but welcomes what he interprets as present signs of the erosion of the traditional state. "[I]f the evolution of social life continues on its present course, into the indefinite future, anarchy will return. . . . Anarchy is social life without law, that is, without governmental social control" (pp. 132, 123). In conclusion:

> If all of these trends continue, a new society will come into being, possibly centuries from now, possibly sooner. It will be a society of equals, people specialized and yet interchangeable; a society of nomads, at once close and distant, homogeneous and diverse, organized and autonomous, where reputations and other statuses fluctuate from one day to the next. . . . To some degree . . . anarchy will return. But it will be a new anarchy, as new as society itself, neither communal nor situational, and yet both at once. If these trends continue, then law will decrease. It might even disappear. [1976, p. 137]

A much more proximately reformist position, also concerned with the uses of state powers, is taken by Philippe Nonet and Philip Selznick in *Law and Society in Transition* (1978). These authors also mention a possible "withering away of the state" that may come with the era of "responsive law," and they give it their own redefinition (p. 102). In a footnote, however, they add reassurance. "The idea need not be understood as suggesting the end of all government; it should be interpreted as pointing to a transformation of government away from monolithic and repressive forms of the state" (p. 103). Nonet and Selznick do not buttress their evolutionary discussion with ethnographic materials. They are not concerned with "primitive" societies. Their evolutionary thesis, like Unger's, is constructed in the mode of Weberian ideal types, a similarity they acknowledge (p. 54, fn.).

Law and Society in Transition postulates legal parallels to three types of administrative organization—prebureaucratic, bureaucratic, and postbureaucratic—as repressive law, autonomous law, and responsive law (pp. 22, 16). Though the authors see these types as an evolutionary series, they are careful to note that, while each type has the potential of being transformed into the next, no historical necessity compels this development to happen. Indeed, they speak of their "developmental model" as "a complex dispositional statement. It proposes that certain stages of a system will generate forces leading to specified changes" (p. 23). But they are clear that, though such a model suggests the direction of change, predictions cannot be founded on it, since conditions vary widely, and countervailing forces are frequently at work (p. 23).

In the repressive type, law is the instrument of the powerful; obedience to the rules is exacted from the ruled, but the rulers who make the laws are scarcely bound by them (pp. 29–52). There is "class justice." The conservation of authority is a major preoccupation. Specialized agencies of control, such as police, become independent centers of power. Cultural conformity is enforced, diversity is not tolerated. Archaic states and totalitarian regimes epitomize types of repressive domination, "but the problems that produce it occur, and recur, everywhere" (p. 36).

The cardinal features of autonomous law are the separation of law and politics, the existence of a system of binding rules that places restraints on the exercise of power and limits the obligation of citizens (that is, the acts of the political elite must be legal), and of greatest importance, the development of specialized, relatively autonomous legal institutions (pp. 53–72). Autonomous law bears a strong resemblance to the Anglo-American legal system. "Autonomous law is, in principle, judge-centered and rule-bound." Autonomous law evolves out of the repressive law as "a way of overcoming the arbitrary decision-making of an earlier era." The legal institutions develop "canons of interpretation" and a technical professional expertise, often becoming formalistic and legalistic. "The practitioners of autonomous law are makers and purveyors of 'artificial reason.'" A great emphasis on procedure, as in due process, means that "substantive justice is . . . a hoped-for by-product of impeccable method." The capacity to restrain the authority of the rulers and to limit the obligations of citizens can develop in such a way as to encourage a "posture of criticism" that eventually contributes to the erosion of the rule of law. Advocacy "encourages self-assertion and a searching criticism of received authority. . . . Even in a rule-centered legal order, reasoning must frequently appeal from rule to purpose" (pp. 60, 65, 62, 66, 71, 72, 80).

This attitude sets the stage for the next type, a law of the future. "A vision emerges . . . of a responsive legal order, more open to social influence and more effective in dealing with social problems." Since social purpose, rather than the technical application of rules, is the central consideration of responsive law, purpose becomes a major element in legal reasoning. "With the growth of purposiveness in law it becomes even more difficult to distinguish legal analysis from policy analysis, legal rationality from other forms of systematic decision-making." Arcane language disappears, as does formalism and ritual, depriving jurists of one of their claims to special expertise. To be effective, general purposes must be translated into specific objectives—responsive law is characterized as "result oriented." A much wider range of information must be assessed than is normally taken into account in judicial proceedings, and the potential effects of alternative policies must be projected before a choice is made (pp. 78, 82–83, 84).

Erosion of authority requires increased responsibility on the part of individuals, who become responsible for the foreseeable consequences of all their actions. But the salient virtue of the new civility is respect: "All who share a social space are granted a presumption of legitimacy." Thus, cultural and moral diversity is acknowledged and protected. In a responsive system, crises of public order—such as strikes, demonstrations, and riots—will be solved by negotiation, discussion, and compromise. The objective is the reconstitution of consensus. "Integrative resolutions of crises" should be sought to restore order rather than order being imposed by coercion (pp. 90, 91, 92, 93).

The hallmark of the postbureaucratic organization is decentralization and the broad delegation of authority. In purposive organization, "authority must be open and participatory. . . . The model is the task force organization made up of temporary problem-centered units." What is envisioned is "a loose aggregate of public corporations, each with its own mission and its own public." Risks are also foreseen—a fragmented and impotent polity might result, impervious to direction and leadership, incapable of setting priorities (pp. 99, 103).

The aim is a total transformation of law. "Legal energies should be devoted to diagnosing institutional problems and redesigning institutional arrangements." Regulation, rather than adjudication, becomes the "paradigmatic function" of responsive law. "The diffusion of legal authority and the enlargement of legal participation bring about a 'withering away of the state.' " Nonet and Selznick close with the claim that "responsive law is a precarious ideal whose achievement and desirability are historically contingent" (pp. 102, 106, 108, 116).

Although Nonet and Selznick mention the risks associated with fragmentation and an incapacity to set priorities, the solution to those problems is not really addressed except in the vaguest terms. Still more optimism attends their ideas about demystification. They seem absolutely sanguine about the possibility of abolishing ritual, formality, arcane language, and the like, and they are confident that this change would directly affect issues. They ignore the fact that what can easily happen—and has happened, in many countries with populist ideologists—is that the "new informality" itself acquires a ritual cast and becomes an orthodoxy, possibly even accompanied by an obligatory language. If participation is required by the "system," participation itself can be a ritual performance. If an assembly has to be convened in order to legitimate any decision, the convening of the assembly and eliciting its consent can be routinized, becoming as formal as the wicked authoritative decisions it is meant to replace.

When participation is obligatory, the construction of what I have called ratifying bodies public becomes mandatory, since such bodies are the only admissible source of decision-making legitimacy (Moore 1977). The rule-legitimacy of "autonomous" law is replaced by legitimation by popular consent. But the consent can be as pro forma and as "managed" as the often highly rationalized connection between rules and decisions. There seems little basis for the assumption that participatory assemblies are bound to function as intended by academic idealists. The functioning of participatory organizations in the real world can be treated empirically; there are quite enough of them to study comparatively, and such an investigation may well be worthwhile if the spreading of this style of decision-making is to be anticipated. But in my view, pace Black, and Nonet and Selznick, serious study of the potential withering away of the state in the world in general can safely be postponed.

These four writers recognize but are not troubled by the implications of an existing legal pluralism on the world scale, let alone at the local level. Unger, for one, writes, "modernism creates a basis for the universalization of the human understanding of human affairs" (1976, p. 259). But all that consensualism is for the future. In fact, modernism has not yet produced and may never produce those common understandings Unger thinks possible. Looking out from his Princeton study, the anthropologist Clifford Geertz (1983) sees only irreconcilable diversity. What Geertz argues for is an understanding of cultural heterogeneity and normative dissensus to be achieved through "an hermeneutics of legal pluralism" (pp. 224–35).

To exemplify the point Geertz writes an essay in which he sets out to compare ideas about fact and law in three legal traditions: the Indic, the Islamic, and the Malaysian. He arranges his task with his customary verbal ingenuity. While he appears to be proceeding from the Anglo-American concepts of fact and law, he loses little time in the discussion of that cultural context, and without letting the reader know that he has changed the game, he quickly re-recognizes fact and law as questions of "what is so" and "what is right" (p. 184). And later, without the slightest grinding of gears, he shifts sense again and slides smoothly into an elegant explication of three highly abstract terms in the languages of the three traditions he has chosen: *haqq*, which means "truth"; *dharma*, which means "duty"; and *adat*, which means "practice." All three also mean a great deal more, as Geertz proceeds to explain. These terms give him an opportunity to make general comments on three quite different culturally constructed visions of the world. It also gives him an opportunity to speak for his particular vision of social science. He says that he is "not engaged in a deductive enterprise in which a whole structure of thought and practice is seen to flow . . . from a few general ideas . . . but in a hermeneutic one— one in which ideas are used as a more or less handy way into understanding the social institutions and cultural formulations that surround them and give them meaning" (p. 187). But the essay in question barely gets around to the institutional level, let alone the practical implications for real situations, so the reader is left to muse over the resonant ideas which Geertz presents with his usual art. By no means do all anthropologists find Geertz's "interpretive social science" as broad an avenue to understanding as he does. From the point of view of any lawyer, law would seem to be only tangentially the subject of "Fact and Law in Comparative Perspective." Geertz is using a few legal categories as an entry point for the discussion of different conceptions of the social and moral order. Geertz has a further purpose in linking cultural difference to law. He clearly wants to take some shots at the idea that the world is becoming increasingly homogeneous, and to attack those who interpret it in terms of a materialist-evolutionary social theory. He concludes that differences in the world are increasing, not decreasing. "Things look more like flying apart than coming together" (p. 216). Legal pluralism is florescent. "Agreement about the things that are fundamental . . . is rather spectacularly absent" (p. 224). He wonders about our capacity to live with diversity and sees his own essay as related to the question of "how local knowledge and cosmopolitan intent may comport, or fail to, in the emerging world disorder" (p. 183).

CONCLUSION

Issues that have political currency in one decade are bound to surface eloquently a few years later in the more polemic forms of the comparative literature. One theme apparent in the works reviewed is the debate about government authority versus "self-regulation."

This topic has proved durable and has really become a refrain in some quarters in the Western democracies. Two quite different depictions of the role of law enliven the quarrel. Law is conceived as a potentially benevolent means of shaping and directing society, a useful machine that simply needs some improvements of design; and law is considered at its worst when it directs and at its best when it does no more than establish the external conditions for peaceful (and/or profitable) self-direction.

The latter view often includes arguments either for "free" competition or for participation in decision-making by those affected. That benevolent direction and enlightened self-rule are not real alternatives except on paper must be clear. Compared with any past time, government everywhere now has and uses unprecedented quantities of power, capital, and personnel. (For a short, simple exposition on the role of law in the mixed economies of the Western democracies, see Friedmann 1971; for an interesting essay on law and the state, see Kamenka, Brown, and Tay 1978.) Yet the state, though in some respects overwhelmingly powerful, seems unable to solve many urgent problems in its directive mode. (For an American case study of a failure, see Pressman and Wildavsky 1973.) Lawyers and social scientists are becoming increasingly occupied with the question of how much can or should be done by means of law. It is a mark of the pessimism of this trend that A. N. Allott's book, full of comparative examples, should be entitled *The Limits of Law* and subtitled "The Uses and Uselessness of Law" (1980). Marc Galanter gave one of his articles the title "Legality and Its Discontents" (1979). As some of the literature reviewed here has suggested, the pull toward more centralized authoritative direction and the opposite pull toward more local or special-purpose autonomy are widespread in the world and not confined to the Western democracies (see Galanter 1981). But in the West, given the luxuries of expression afforded by a free press, they take on a particularly public form.

The pervasiveness of these organizational issues provided the logic of the sequence of the materials presented in this article. Vilhelm Aubert is persuasive in stating, "Sociology of law must work closely with theories of organizations, for it is through organizations that modern law primarily becomes effective, if at all" (1979, p. 41; see also Pospisil 1971; Smith 1974). Considered in this framework, the state itself is an aggregation of suborganizations. Hence this essay began with the level that is the most organizationally and culturally diverse and intricate—the international—before moving down the organizational scale to plural societies, proceeding to the level of complex but putatively "culturally unitary" legal systems, next examining primitive systems and simpler societies, also putatively "unitary," and concluding with the grand-scale essays of Unger, Black, Nonet and Selznick, and Geertz who, using comparative examples, try to draw together many of the large questions.

This introduction to the literature on the variety of legal systems in the world suggests that there are a few predominant forms in which the perspectives of social science are manifest in current comparative work. Three general approaches are used in various permutations and combinations.

The first approach begins with a grand paradigm. A range of legal comparisons are then marshaled to illustrate a preconceived interpretive scheme. Systems analysis, the unfolding of legal evolution according to a given pattern, and the assumption that economic rationality can be found at the root of all durable legal rules constitute such paradigms.

A second approach uses a particular type of social (or political, economic, cultural, historical, and the like) context to "explain" or illuminate the operation of a particular legal system. Thus multicultural and plural contexts—or tribal contexts, or socialist governments, or legal "families"—are said to account for certain characteristics of relevant legal systems. The implication of this comparative approach is that if the social or cultural or historical contexts were different, the legal system would also be different. A distinctive organizational or cultural characteristic is used initially to identify the instances to be studied and compared. The social and cultural embeddedness of law is the underlying postulate.

A third approach begins with the assumption of "law as technique" or "law as problem-solving." In this method a particular feature of legal systems is identified and examined across the board in a variety of societies to examine how problems are solved or how the technique works in different places. Thus, the management of dispute, the access of the citizenry to officials, and the treatment of crime have each been compared in this way, as have a myriad of other topics. In this approach, the "problem" solved or the legal technique used is the diagnostic criterion that governs the collection of information. The motive of such comparisons is often declared to be the search for the technique that works best or the better identification of the societal factors that facilitate or obstruct benign solutions. But in this as in both of the other approaches, comparison is as often used to call attention to previously unnoticed regularities or irregularities, thus indirectly testing and repairing the prevalent paradigms of social science itself. This work of redefining social science is at some remove from the direct, practical policy-guiding advice that some agencies solicit, but in the long run this more basic questioning may well be the most useful of all.

The demonstrably increasing interest in studying and comparing the various legal systems of the world is likely to continue to grow. Probably at the top of the list of reasons for this circumstance is the interlocking character of the world economy and the interrelated political fate of all nations and peoples. An increasing number of transactions and organizations, of increasing magnitude and importance, cross national boundaries. Geographically distant events can deeply affect even the largest countries and may penetrate into the affairs of the most remote bush villages.

On the practical side, operating effectively in this multinational arena, or even understanding it as a spectator, requires some understanding of the varieties of legal, political, and social configuration that underlie the formally equivalent national units. Having some knowledge of the legal systems of other societies is useful to anyone who operates professionally or intellectually outside of a parochial milieu—and who will admit to completely parochial interests?

As for the academic discussions about legal evolution that give learned underpinning to current political argument, some comparative knowledge is a considerable defense against being persuaded for the wrong reasons. As a rule, the larger the topic discussed, the more selectively the mass of information must be dealt with, hence, the more dominant the paradigm of the writer. This is true of most discussions of the evolution of law. Selection, speculation, interpretation, and argument can be richly rewarding, but it is an error to call these proofs. Much of what has been written about legal systems as wholes, and about legal evolution in particular, belongs in the category of learned discussion. What Charles Lindblom and David Cohen noted about a wide range of policy-oriented social science applies in this case: "Despite the accepted convention that [social scientists] are engaged in the pursuit of *conclusive* fact and proof, they are instead engaged in producing inconclusive evidence and argument" (Lindblom and Cohen 1979,

p. 81; italics mine). But even these scholars find themselves obliged to concede that professional social inquiry can, on occasion, produce authoritative information.

While much is known, much more authoritative information remains to be garnered about the legal systems of the world and the way they actually operate, and still more is to be learned from the analysis and interpretation of this material. The studies reviewed here suggest that there are encouraging signs of traffic on the academic highways, and that some frequently traveled byways had best be avoided.

Bibliography

Abel, Richard
       1979   "Western Courts in Non-Western Settings: Patterns of Court Use in Colonial and Neo-colonial Africa." In *The Imposition of Law*, edited by S. Burman and B. Harrell-Bond. New York: Academic Press.
Allott, A. N.
       1980   *The Limits of Law*. London: Butterworth.
Aubert, Vilhelm
       1979   "On Methods of Legal Influence." In *The Imposition of Law*, edited by S. Burman and B. Harrell-Bond. New York: Academic Press.
Barkun, Michael
       1968   *Law Without Sanctions*. New Haven: Yale University Press.
Benda-Beckmann, Franz von
       1979   *Property in Social Continuity*. The Hague: Martinus Nijhoff.
Bennett, Gordon
       1978   *Aboriginal Rights in International Law*. London: Royal Anthropological Institute, Occasional Paper no. 37. In association with Survival International.
Black, Donald
       1976   *The Behavior of Law*. New York: Academic Press.

       1984   *Toward a General Theory of Social Control*. 2 vols. Orlando, Fla.: Academic Press.
Black-Michaud, Jacob
       1975   *Cohesive Force: Feud in the Mediterranean and the Middle East*. Oxford: Blackwell.
Bohannan, Paul
       1957   *Justice and Judgment Among the Tiv*. London: Oxford University Press.
Bohannan, Paul, ed.
       1967   *Law and Warfare*. New York: Natural History Press.
Bourdieu, Pierre
       1977   *Outline of a Theory of Practice*. Cambridge: Cambridge University Press.
Bozeman, Adda B.
       1971   *The Future of Law in a Multi-Cultural World*. Princeton, N.J.: Princeton University Press.

       1976   *Conflict in Africa*. Princeton, N.J.: Princeton University Press.
Burg, Elliot M.
       1977   "Law and Development: A Review of the Literature and a Critique of 'Scholars in Self-Estrangement.' " *American Journal of Comparative Law* 25:492–530.
Burman, Sandra B., and Harrell-Bond, Barbara E.
       1979   *The Imposition of Law*. New York: Academic Press.

Cappelletti, Mauro, and Garth, Bryant
    1978–79 *Access to Justice.* 4 vols. Milan: Giuffre.
Cappelletti, Mauro; Gordley, J.; and Johnson, E., Jr.
    1975 *Toward Equal Justice: A Comparative Study of Legal Aid in Modern Societies.* Dobbs Ferry, N.Y.: Oceana.
Cappelletti, Mauro, and Tallon, D.
    1973 *Fundamental Guarantees of the Parties in Civil Litigation.* Dobbs Ferry, N.Y.: Oceana.
Cohen, Abner
    1969 *Custom and Politics in Urban Africa.* London: Routledge & Kegan Paul.
    1974a *Two Dimensional Man.* Berkeley: University of California Press.
Cohen, Abner, ed.
    1974b *Urban Ethnicity.* ASA Monograph no. 12. London: Tavistock Press.
Collier, Jane F.
    1975 "Legal Processes." In *Annual Review of Anthropology,* edited by B. J. Siegel. Palo Alto, Calif.: Annual Reviews.
    1984 "Two Models of Control in Simple Societies." In *Toward a General Theory of Social Control,* 2 vols, edited by Donald Black. Orlando, Fla.: Academic Press.
Colson, Elizabeth
    1975 *Tradition and Contract.* London: Heineman.
Comaroff, John, and Roberts, Simon
    1981 *Rules and Processes.* Chicago: University of Chicago Press.
Coulson, N. J.
    1964 *A History of Islamic Law.* Edinburgh: Edinburgh University Press.
Crook, John A.
    1967 *Law and Life of Rome.* London: Thames and Hudson.
David, René
    1975 *The Legal Systems of the World: Their Comparison and Unification.* International Encyclopedia of Comparative Law, vol. 2. Paris: Mouton.
David, René, and Brierley, J. E. C.
    1978 *Major Legal Systems in the World Today.* 2nd ed. London: Stevens.
Derrett, J. Duncan, ed.
    1968 *An Introduction to Legal Systems.* London: Sweet and Maxwell.
Diamond, A. S.
    1935 *Primitive Law.* London: Longmans Green.
    1951 *The Evolution of Law and Order.* London: Watts.
    1971 *Primitive Law Past and Present.* London: Methuen.
Diamond, Stanley
    1971 "The Rule of Law Versus the Order of Custom." *Social Research* 38(1):42–72.
Durkheim, Emile
    1964 *The Division of Labor in Society.* Translated by G. Simpson. New York: Free Press.
    [1893]
Ehrmann, Henry W.
    1976 *Comparative Legal Cultures.* Englewood Cliffs, N.J.: Prentice-Hall.
Engel, David M.
    1978 *Code and Custom in a Thai Provincial Court.* Tucson: University of Arizona Press.
Evans-Pritchard, E. E.
    1940 *The Nuer.* Oxford: Clarendon Press.
Fallers, Lloyd
    1969 *Law Without Precedent.* Chicago: Aldine.
    1974 *The Social Anthropology of the Nation-State.* Chicago: Aldine.

Felstiner, W. L. F.
  1974   "Influences of Social Organization on Dispute Processing." *Law & Society Review*
            9(1):63–94.
  1975   "Avoidance as Dispute Processing and Elaboration." *Law & Society Review*
            9(4):695–705.
Freud, Sigmund
  1938   *Totem and Taboo.* In *The Basic Writings of Sigmund Freud,* edited and translated by
  [1913]   A. A. Brill. New York: Modern Library.
Fried, Morton
  1967   *The Evolution of Political Society.* New York: Random House.
Friedman, Lawrence
  1975   *The Legal System: A Social Science Perspective.* New York: Russell Sage Foundation.
Friedmann, Wolfgang
  1971   *The State and the Rule of Law in a Mixed Economy.* London: Stevens and Sons.
Fuller, Lon L.
  1968   *The Anatomy of Law.* New York: Praeger.
Galanter, Marc
  1979   "Legality and Its Discontents." In Erhard Blankenburg et al., *Alternative Rechtsfor-
            men und Alternativen zum Recht.* Weisbaden: Westdeutscher Verlag.
  1981   "Justice in Many Rooms: Courts, Private Ordering, and Indigenous Law." *Journal
            of Legal Pluralism* (19):1–47.
Geertz, Clifford
  1983   *Local Knowledge.* New York: Basic Books.
Gilissen, John, ed.
  1963   *Introduction bibliographique à l'histoire du droit et à l'ethnologie juridique.* Bruxelles:
            Université Libre de Bruxelles.
Gluckman, Max
  1955   *The Judicial Process Among the Barotse of Northern Rhodesia.* Manchester: Manches-
            ter University Press.
  1965a   *The Ideas in Barotse Jurisprudence.* New Haven and London: Yale University Press.
  1965b   *Politics, Law and Ritual in Tribal Society.* Chicago: Aldine.
Goody, Jack R.
  1976   *Production and Reproduction.* Cambridge: Cambridge University Press.
  1977   *The Domestication of the Savage Mind.* Cambridge: Cambridge University Press.
Goody, Jack R., and Tambiah, Stanley J.
  1973   *Bridewealth and Dowry.* Cambridge: Cambridge University Press.
Gordon, Robert J., and Meggitt, Mervyn J.
  1985   *Law and Order in the New Guinea Highlands.* Hanover and London: University Press
            of New England.
Gould, Wesley L., and Barkun, Michael
  1970   *International Law and the Social Sciences.* Princeton, N.J.: Princeton University Press.
  1972   *Social Science Literature: A Bibliography for International Law.* Princeton, N.J.:
            Princeton University Press.
Grace, Clive, and Wilkinson, Philip
  1978   *Sociological Inquiry and Legal Phenomena.* London: Collier Macmillan.
Greenberg, David F.
  1983   "Donald Black's Sociology of Law: A Critique." *Law & Society Review* 17(2):337–
            68.
Greenberg, David F., and Anderson, Nancy
  1981   "Recent Marxisant Books on Law: A Review Essay." *Contemporary Crises* 5:293–
            322.

Gulliver, Philip H.
1963   *Social Control in an African Society.* London: Routledge & Kegan Paul.
1971   *Neighbors and Networks.* Berkeley: University of California Press.
1979   *Disputes and Negotiations.* New York: Academic Press.
Gurr, Ted Robert; Grabowsky, Peter N.,; and Hula, Richard C.
1977   *The Politics of Crime and Conflict: A Comparative History of Four Cities.* Beverly Hills, Calif.: Sage.
Hamnett, Ian, ed.
1977   *Social Anthropology and Law.* ASA Monograph no. 14. New York: Academic Press.
Harrison, A. R. W.
1968–71 *The Law of Athens.* 2 vols. Oxford: Clarendon Press.
Hobhouse, L. T.; Wheeler, G. C.; and Ginsberg, M.
1915   *The Material Culture and Social Institutions of the Simpler Peoples.* London: Chapman and Hall.
Hoebel, E. Adamson
1954   *The Law of Primitive Man.* Cambridge, Mass.: Harvard University Press.
Hooker, M. B.
1975   *Legal Pluralism.* Oxford: Clarendon Press.
Hopkins, Terence K., and Wallerstein, Immanuel, eds.
1982   *World Systems Analysis.* Beverly Hills, Calif.: Sage.
Kamenka, Eugene; Brown, Robert; and Erh-Soon Tay, Alice, eds.
1978   *Law and Society: The Crisis in Legal Ideals.* Melbourne, Australia: Edward Arnold.
Kuper, Leo, and Smith, M. G.
1969   *Pluralism in Africa.* Berkeley: University of California Press.
Lindblom, Charles E., and Cohen, David K.
1979   *Usable Knowledge.* New Haven: Yale University Press.
MacFarlane, Alan
1978   *The Origins of English Individualism.* Oxford: Blackwell.
Maine, Sir Henry
1880   *The Early History of Institutions.* New York: Holt.
[1875]
1894   *Ancient Law.* 15th ed. London: John Murray.
[1861]
Malinowski, Bronislaw
1926   *Crime and Custom in Savage Society.* London: Kegan Paul, Trench and Trubner.
Maybury-Lewis, David
1974   *Akwe-Shavante Society.* New York: Oxford University Press.
Maybury-Lewis, David, ed.
1984   *The Prospects for Plural Societies.* Washington, D.C.: American Ethnological Society.
Meggitt, Mervyn
1977   *Blood Is Their Argument: Warfare Among the Mae Enga Tribesmen of the New Guinea Highland.* Palo Alto, Calif.: Mayfield.
Merryman, John H.
1969   *The Civil Law Tradition.* Stanford, Calif.: Stanford University Press.
1977   "Comparative Law and Social Change: On the Origins, Style, Decline and Revival of the Law and Development Movement." *American Journal of Comparative Law* 25:457–91.
Middleton, John, and Tait, David
1958   *Tribes Without Rulers.* London: Routledge & Kegan Paul.

Moore, Sally Falk
    1970   "Politics, Procedures and Norms in Changing Chagga Law." *Africa*, October 1970, pp. 321–44. Reprinted in Moore 1978b.
    1977   "Political Meetings and the Simulation of Unanimity." In *Secular Ritual*, edited by S. Moore and B. Myerhoff. Assen, the Netherlands: Van Gorcum.
    1978a   "Archaic Law and Modern Times on the Zambezi." In *Cross Examinations: Essays in Memory of Max Gluckman*, edited by P. Gulliver. Leiden: Brill.
    1978b   *Law as Process.* London: Routledge & Kegan Paul.
    1986   *Social Facts and Fabrications: Customary Law on Kilimanjaro 1880–1980.* Cambridge: Cambridge University Press.

Moser, Michael J.
    1982   *Law and Social Change in a Chinese Community.* Dobbs Ferry, N.Y.: Oceana.

Murdock, G. P.
    1967a   "Ethnographic Atlas: A Summary." *Ethnology* 6:109–236.
    1967b   *Ethnographic Atlas.* Pittsburgh: University of Pittsburgh Press.

Nader, Laura, ed.
    1969   *Law in Culture and Society.* Chicago: Aldine.

Nader, Laura, and Todd, Harry F., eds.
    1978   *The Disputing Process—Law in Ten Societies.* New York: Columbia University Press.

Nader, Laura; Koch, Klaus F.; and Cox, B.
    1966   "The Ethnography of Law: A Bibliographical Survey." *Current Anthropology* 7(3):267–94.

Naroll, Raoul
    1970   "What Have We Learned from Cross-Cultural Surveys?" *American Anthropologist* 72:1227–88.
    1973   "Galton's Problem." In *A Handbook of Method in Cultural Anthropology*, edited by Raoul Naroll and Ronald Cohen. New York: Columbia University Press.

Needham, Rodney
    1972   *Belief, Language and Experience.* Chicago: University of Chicago Press.

Newman, Katherine S.
    1983   *Law and Economic Organization.* Cambridge: Cambridge University Press.

Nonet, Philippe, and Philip Selznick
    1978   *Law and Society in Transition.* New York: Farrar, Straus and Giroux.

Ofuatey-Kodjoe, W.
    1977   *The Principle of Self-Determination in International Law.* New York: Nellen.

Posner, Richard
    1980   "A Theory of Primitive Society with Special Reference to Primitive Law." *Law and Economics*, XXIII (1):1–53.

Pospisil, Leopold
    1971   *Anthropology of Law.* New York: Harper & Row.
    1979   "Legally Induced Culture Change in New Guinea." In *The Imposition of Law*, edited by S. Burman and B. Harrell-Bond. New York: Academic Press.

Pressman, Jeffrey L., and Wildavsky, Aaron
    1973   *Implementation.* Berkeley: University of California Press.

Rabinow, Paul, and Sullivan, William M.
    1979   *Interpretive Social Science.* Berkeley: University of California Press.

Radcliffe-Brown, A. R.
    1952   *Structure and Function in Primitive Society.* London: Cohen and West.

Roberts, Simon
    1979   *Order and Dispute: An Introduction to Legal Anthropology.* Harmondsworth: Penguin Books.

Rosen, Lawrence
     1984   *Bargaining for Reality.* Chicago: University of Chicago Press.
Sahlins, Marshall
     1961   "The Segmentary Lineage: An Organization of Predatory Expansion." *American Anthropologist* 63:322–45.
Schacht, Joseph
     1964   *An Introduction to Islamic Law.* Oxford: Clarendon Press.
Seidman, Robert B.
     1978   *The State, Law and Development.* London: Croom Helm.
Service, Elman R.
     1975   *Origins of the State and Civilization.* New York: Norton.
Siegel, Bernard J., ed.
     1959–   *Annual Review of Anthropology* [formerly *Biennial Review of Anthropology*]. Palo
     present   Alto, Calif.: Annual Reviews.
Smith, M. G.
     1974   *Corporations and Society.* London: Duckworth.
Snyder, Francis
     1981   *Capitalism and Legal Change.* New York: Academic Press.
Starr, June
     1978   *Dispute and Settlement in Rural Turkey.* Leiden: Brill.
Stein, Peter
     1980   *Legal Evolution: The Story of an Idea.* Cambridge: Cambridge University Press.
Strathern, Andrew
     1975   *The Rope of Moka.* Cambridge: Cambridge University Press.
     [1971]
Szladits, Charles
     1975   *A Bibliography on Foreign and Comparative Law.* Dobbs Ferry, N.Y.: Oceana.
Trubek, D. M., and Galanter, Marc
     1974   "Scholars in Self-Estrangement: Some Reflections on the Crisis in Law and Development Studies in the United States." *Wisconsin Law Review* 1974:1062.
Twining, W. L.
     1973   *Karl Llewellyn and the Realist Movement.* London: Weidenfeld and Nicolson.
Unger, Roberto M.
     1975   *Knowledge and Politics.* New York: Free Press.
     1976   *Law in Modern Society.* New York: Free Press.
Von der Sprenkel, Sybille
     1962   *Legal Institutions in Manchu China.* London: Athlone Press.
von Mehren, Arthur T., ed.
     1963   *Law in Japan: The Legal Order in a Changing Society.* Cambridge, Mass.: Harvard University Press.
     1979   "A Significant Contribution to the Literature of Comparative Law." *Michigan Law Review* 77(3):347–49.
Watson, Alan
     1974   *Legal Transplants: An Approach to Comparative Law.* Edinburgh: Scottish Academic Press.
Weber, Max
     1954   *On Law in Economy and Society.* Translated by E. Shils and M. Rheinstein. New
     [1922]   York: Simon and Schuster.
Wolf, Eric R.
     1981   "The Mills of Inequality: A Marxian Approach." In *Social Inequality*, edited by Gerald D. Berreman. New York: Academic Press.

Zweigert, Konrad, and Kötz, Hein
    1977   *An Introduction to Comparative Law.* 2 vols. Translated by Tony Weir. Amsterdam:
                North Holland.

⌇ 2 ⌇

LAW AND NORMATIVE ORDER

Richard D. Schwartz
College of Law
Syracuse University

INTRODUCTION

Cross-cultural research demonstrates that societies vary dramatically in the extent to which they have an integrated normative order. Folk societies generally adhere to a stable, pervasive, consistent, deeply held set of mores. Complex societies rarely have a comparable degree of normative integration. Law represents a response to the evolutionary decline of normative consensus in complex societies. This paper addresses the following questions: to what extent and in what ways does law interact with norms to maintain, reinforce, or develop normative consensus.

In open societies such as the United States, the integrative capacity of law is especially problematic and the manner in which law contributes to normative integration, when it does at all, is complicated. Law draws on existing norms, adds some norms and principles of its own, and helps sometimes to facilitate an emergent consensus. These processes can be seen emerging as societies become more complex.

The classic model of folk culture (Redfield 1941) emphasizes the pervasiveness and intensity with which normative ideas are shared throughout a society. A normative order

NOTE: In developing this essay, I have received valuable assistance from several law students: Denise Hartman, Mary Kehoe, Maureen Walsh, and Beth Anne Wolfson. All have done valuable service in locating relevant sources and in contributing to the ideas in the paper. An earlier version was reviewed by Leon Lipson, Lawrence Friedman, David Sills, Donald T. Campbell, and Manfred Stanley. Each of them made helpful suggestions. I am grateful to my colleague Sam Donnelly for many good discussions, especially on the thinking of Karl Llewellyn and Lon Fuller. The manuscript was processed with unbelievable efficiency and great good humor by Patricia Marsulá and Cathy Thau.

of that kind has no need for a legal system to promulgate or to enforce behavioral standards. At most, such societies require that someone act as a mediator to help resolve disputes, through agreement between the parties, within the framework of commonly held standards (Schwartz and Miller 1964).

At a slightly more complicated level of social organization, legal authority emerges. In general, legal officials in tribal societies exercise their authority by drawing on, clarifying, and reinforcing the mores. Paul Bohannan has given a plausible account of this process in his concept of "double-institutionalization." Using his experience with the Tiv as illustration, he describes law as a technique for dispute resolution that draws on and reinforces the basic institutional arrangements of the society (Bohannan 1957, 1965). Only when a relationship in those other institutions breaks down is law invoked. On such occasions, third-party intervenors (mediators, arbitrators, or adjudicators) do more than resolve the dispute. They examine the troubled relationship and, in restoring it, enunciate a standard for future conduct.

Such a legal standard tends to differ from the custom or norm in being more sharply defined and somewhat different in content. In the resultant gap between law and custom —which he believes to be inevitable—Bohannan finds a tension that leads to change. Custom and law exert a mutual pull but never fully coincide.

Tension notwithstanding, the content of law in folk societies is deeply affected by custom. Law is fashioned by members of a homogeneous culture who, though legal specialists, are steeped in custom and selected for their knowledge of, commitment to, and exemplification of the mores.

In the further evolution of society, however, a marked change tends to occur in the nature of the mores. There is no need to recount here the story of normative complexity, concomitant with the shift to urban societies based on the economic surplus generated by the agricultural, commercial, and industrial revolutions. As each of these historic economic developments occurs, it facilitates normative change.[1] Characteristically the diversity of normative structure increases.

Faced with growing normative diversity, societies have regularly reacted with cultural reorganizations, revitalization efforts, religious conversions, and other movements aimed at the restoration of normative integration (Wallace 1956). The drive for normative order, taking many forms, is regularly in evidence even as social change creates forces that undercut a simple, uniform set of mores. The pendulum swings unevenly between normative order and chaos—a slow disintegration of consensus, often followed at the extreme of disorder by a sudden movement toward reintegration. Law becomes one of the candidates to supplement or replace a traditional normative order, if not to reintegrate a chaotic one.

Law can react in several possible ways in the face of normative diversity or dissensus. It can selectively absorb norms, pervasive or not, which do exist in the society. It can seek to formulate a new set of behavioral standards, imposing them authoritatively. Or it can facilitate norm formation within the society by creating conditions of interaction in which this process can occur. In fact, it does all of these.

Traditional theorists, as will be seen, have emphasized either legal absorption or legal authority. Another approach is the mutualist position, the point of view taken in this

---

[1] For a comprehensive treatment of these interrelationships following the agricultural revolution, see Turner (1941); no single work known to me comparably covers subsequent societal revolutions.

essay. The mutualist position stresses the mutually reinforcing potential of laws and norms, for attaining that degree of congruence between norms and laws essential for law to function effectively as a regulator of behavior. This can occur through absorption, authority, and the facilitation and reinforcement of norm-forming processes. All three processes are discernable in complex, open societies such as the United States.

One way to attain norm-law congruence is through the absorption in law of normative content that is strongly rooted in the culture. The legal system of the United States provides many channels by which such normative content can influence the promulgation and interpretation of law. Nevertheless, the influence of norms on law is limited by the sparseness of pervasive norms and the prevalence of normative conflict.

Authoritative legal formulations do not necessarily aid in resolving normative differences; to decide between contending parties often exacerbates their antagonism. The invocation of broad principles to justify decisions does not necessarily help to settle conflict. Such principles are often at odds with each other; even when they are consistent, they may not accord with the sense of justice either of the society or of the contending parties.

Procedures that bring together contending parties for "private ordering" of their relations, under conditions that promote bargaining and norm formation, can be cultivated in many areas. Analogous arrangements, which will be called public ordering, involve the establishment by government of norm-forming entities. These activities may contribute to normative order more effectively than do principled decisions, which sometimes leave the parties confused, unsatisfied, at odds with each other, or unpersuaded of the justice or utility of the decisions. Such ordering relationships, and the norms they generate, must however be compatible with and supported by the larger sociolegal framework if they are to be fully effective. Normative integration may ultimately depend on the capacity to bring norms and legal principle into a relationship of mutual support.

This formulation states a point of view that guides the inquiry found in the main portion of this essay. It is a point of view suggested in the work of many scholars, past and present, who have studied the relationship between law and society. Some efforts at studying these questions have also been undertaken in recent years by students of law and society. Eventually, of course, the accuracy and utility of this perspective must be demonstrated through detailed research and application.

Examining the relationship between law and normative order is not the only way to study the interaction between law and society. Two other dimensions of the law-society relationship need to be examined in detail. One is the interrelationship between law and power; another is the interrelationship between law and wealth. Ultimately, a general theory of law and society must deal with all of these interrelationships. At this stage, however, it is helpful to examine each of the three separately.[2] This essay concentrates entirely on law and normative order.

---

[2]Normative order presumably interacts with power and wealth. If law was taken as the dependent variable and the other three as independent variables, the conceptual relationship among the four would be comparable to the models developed by the economists for predicting GNP through simultaneous equation estimations that assume interactions among the independent variables. Models of this type will ultimately prove useful in the study of law and society (Feeley 1976). I assume throughout this essay that law reflects and affects the distribution of power and wealth in society but that normative order constitutes an independent element affecting and affected by law.

PURPOSES OF THIS ESSAY

No subject is more fundamental in the study of law and society than the interrelationship of law and norms. The first purpose of this essay is to show that the topic has been treated, with considerable vitality, by many early scholars. To that end, I briefly discuss diverse classic figures in social science and in jurisprudence, including Eugen Ehrlich, Max Weber, and Henry Sumner Maine in the social sciences[3] and John Austin, Oliver Wendell Holmes, Karl Llewellyn, and Lon Fuller in jurisprudence. All of these scholars concerned themselves in some significant way with the connection between law and norms.

Depending on the reader's disciplinary background, some of these writers may be unfamiliar. John Austin, for example, may not be recognized by social scientists as the nineteenth-century founder of legal positivism, a school of thought that lives in the contemporary work of H. L. A. Hart. Similarly, Eugen Ehrlich, the founder of sociology of law, may be unfamiliar to those whose general approach to law derives from the jurisprudential tradition. Comments on these scholars are inserted to show that important thinkers in both traditions have attended to the law-norm problem.

The second purpose is to show that the subject continues to have significance in contemporary law-and-society thinking. To this end, reference is made to the works of current scholars from both backgrounds, including such contemporary writers as Black, Bohannan, Galanter, Hoebel, Lempert, Macaulay, Mnookin, Moore, Nonet, Ross, and Unger. In this list, it is noteworthy that a division between law and social science is not easily maintained. Contemporary scholars in these fields draw on knowledge of legal and social science disciplines. That these writers attend to norm-law relationships should therefore come as no surprise.

The third purpose is to contribute to theoretical and empirical work on law and norms. This purpose can be served by showing that—in processes that are both general and interesting—law interacts regularly with norms in several ways: by absorbing normative content, by exercising normative influence, and by facilitating the norm-forming process. Much evidence for the existence of these interactions derives from the legal system itself, when examined from the conceptual perspective of law and society.

The analysis of norm-law relationships is general in the sense that it applies to all kinds of law in every society. Laws are defined for purposes of this essay as standards of behavior explicitly enunciated by specialists charged by the society with responsibility for the enforcement of social control. Norms are defined as standards of behavior held as shared attitudes by a society or by a substantial segment of it. Every society that has law in this sense also has norms. Relations between norms and laws, even though varying from mutual support to complete opposition, exist for every area of behavior covered by law.

What makes the topic interesting, that is, a complex problem promising the chance of a solution, is that norm-law relations vary in an orderly way between societies and within societies. Variations between societies reveal in extreme form differences that may be harder to detect within a society. One of the interesting variations concerns the congruence between norms and laws.

When norms and laws do not correspond at all, that is, when they reach an extreme of

---

[3] I omit Durkheim because his position on law and normative order is too complex for brief discussion. His perspective is extremely important, however, and should be dealt with at length. For some discussion of Durkheim's *Division of Labor* (1893), see Schwartz and Cartwright (1973) and Schwartz (1974, 1980).

incongruence, law loses its effectiveness as a regulator of behavior and an integrator of society. This proposition is neither an established generalization nor, at this stage, a readily testable hypothesis. It is presented, rather, as a plausible assertion. If it is true, then research on law-norm relationships assumes great importance for the understanding of complex societies.

The fourth purpose of this paper is to contribute to research efforts in this topical area. To encourage research, more is needed than the demonstration that scholars past and present have shown interest in the problem or that the problem itself is general and interesting. Researchers also want to be assured that something can be done within the area to produce socially significant knowledge. In law-and-society research, the desire for results often involves a search for practical application, with the hope that research can affect the shaping and improvement (somehow defined) of existing legal policy. To this end I explore some of the ways in which law contributes, actually or potentially, to the private and public ordering of relationships and thereby to the formulation of norms potentially more congruent with law.

BACKGROUND IDEAS
Sociology of Law

Selective use of the mores in shaping law has been recognized, one way or another, for a long time. All of the early sociologists of law assume three basic propositions: laws and societal norms are different; societal norms have some influence on law; this influence is not the sole determinant of legal decisions.

Eugen Ehrlich (1936, pp. 26–38) described norms or "living law" as a product of "the inner order of associations." Ehrlich's inner order was, essentially, the social structure of the society. From it came the standards of proper behavior. Ehrlich's main message is that law cannot function effectively unless it adequately takes account of the "living law" derived from the "inner order" of these associations. "[T]he center of gravity of legal development lies not in legislation, nor in juristic science, nor in judicial decisions, but in society itself" (p. xv). This was an exhortation as much as a description. In reality, Ehrlich observed, law usually fails sufficiently to incorporate the norms of "living law." Only in the regulation of commercial behavior does official law closely parallel custom and practice. For this reason, law tends in many other areas to be ignored, evaded, or misused.

Max Weber (1954 [1922], pp. 198–223) also noted the divergence between societal and legal norms. In his discussion of the "honoratiores," he describes ways by which legal officials incorporate into the law some elements of practice and some more abstract concepts from the society. But his emphasis is on the manner in which the legal process goes its separate way. The important requirement of legal decision-making is not that it concur with specific standards of conduct found in the society. It is, rather, that when these standards do not work, the legal process be able to decide authoritatively between disputants. This decision can be made in a variety of ways, including that demonstrated by the khadi, who merely decides particularistically, according to his own religiously informed standards (p. 213, n. 48).

In addition to being authoritative, legal decisions must also be predictable. While in a religious or traditional context, khadi justice may satisfy this criterion, complex societies require a different basis for predictability. To meet the needs of a commercial society, the legal system must develop mechanisms that embody complex norms and rational decision processes (pp. 301–21). As Weber points out, rationality develops quite differently under the civil law of the Continent and the common law of England (pp. 305–21). But in each case, the legal system develops substantive rules and decisional procedures that offer the informed entrepreneur some basis for predicting what will happen if he or she must seek an authoritative judgment from the court. Whatever use the legal system may make of prevailing commercial practice, it does not rely solely on the existing norms. Rather, it develops a set of criteria, including some distinctive and original concepts, that reflect the organization of the legal process at least as much as they draw from the commercial culture.

Of all the scholars who have emphasized the significance of social structure and culture in determining law, Henry Sumner Maine was perhaps the most influential. His *Ancient Law* (1861) traced the manner in which cultural concepts are incorporated into law. Kinship, a basis for privileged social relationships in traditional societies, tends to be used by law for purposes somewhat beyond its original function. The state may, for example, undertake to facilitate the transmission of property or power upon death from the testator to someone other than the kin designated by custom as heir. If such transfers are to be equally effective, they must follow a regular procedure. In the early stages of legal development, they must also be seen to accord with the mores. To attain these two ends, the state invokes the "legal fiction" of adoption. Formal actions specified by law allow the testators to adopt beneficiaries as their own children. In practice, this arrangement legitimizes behavior which, left to the mores alone, would have been subject to challenge. The legal fiction thus provides a device by which the strength of the mores governing kinship can be used to gain acceptance of innovative laws. Although legal fictions continue to be used as law evolves, Maine believed that they become less essential and more transparent (pp. 13–25). With the growth of state power and legal specialization, it becomes increasingly possible for the state to legislate complex arrangements that diverge widely from the mores.

Jurisprudence

A parallel recognition occurred in the field of jurisprudence. That field, the territory of many fine scholars, has been largely ignored by students of law and society because social scientists perceive it as an unclear admixture of *is* and *ought* questions. Ironically, one of the leading figures in jurisprudence, John Austin, took great care in his leading work, *The Province of Jurisprudence Determined,* to draw the line between the *is* of positive morality and positive law and the *ought* of critical morality and natural law. He stressed the importance of looking at law as it is.

Austin's conception of law was so narrow, however, that he left insufficient room for an analysis of the legal system, let alone the normative order. In his concern for precision, he turned the "scientific" study of law into an inquiry on the intellectual consistency of legal decisions. He did not include in his vision the manner in which laws are put into effect or the consequences they produce in the regulation of behavior. It was assumed that laws, properly shaped, would be obeyed. Implicitly, that position is embodied in the dramatic, authoritarian phrase "command of the sovereign," which has become the accepted summary of Austin's position.

Austinian positivism carried another consequence, implied in the same phrase. Law is different from, and not necessarily affected by, the "positive morality" of the society. If custom is sometimes used as a source of law, it must be explicitly adopted by the judges. Once incorporated into the common law, its content remains, even though society and culture change (cf. Fuller 1968a, pp. 44–47). For Austin, the subject matter of law was properly isolated from the rest of society.

Despite the powerful narrowing influence of Austin, jurisprudence has not been constrained by his vision. Particularly in the United States, it has gone far beyond the limits Austin set. Oliver Wendell Holmes (1921) was an important influence in this regard. Associating himself in a way with Austin, he focused on "the prophecies of what the courts will do in fact" as his definition of law (p. 173). Even so, he overstepped the boundaries of Austin's province to question why judges decide as they do. For answers, he looked to history, experience, and socially supported principles. "The felt necessities of the time, the prevalent moral and political theories, institutions of public policy avowed or unconscious, even the prejudices that judges share with their fellow men, have had a good deal more to do than the syllogism in determining the rules by which men should be governed" (Holmes 1881, p. 5). It was entirely proper, Holmes declared, "to regard and study the law as a great anthropological document" (1899, p. 444).

One clear implication of Holmes's position was that law should be examined as a product of society. This orientation found expression in the influential book by John Chipman Gray, *The Nature and Sources of the Law* (1921). In the same tradition, Justice Cardozo (1921) examined the influence on judge-made law of elements outside of the legal process (custom, for example) as well as inside (precedent and statutory construction). In a succinct summary of his views, he wrote:

> My analysis of judicial process comes then to this and little more: logic, and history, and custom, and utility and the accepted standards of right conduct are the forces which singly or in combination shape the progress of the law. Which of these forces shall dominate in any case, must depend largely on the comparative importance or value of social values that will thereby be promoted or impaired. [1947, p. 153]

American legal thought continued to develop this theme: that the normative order influences, but does not exclusively determine, the procedure or substance of law. Two outstanding figures in modern jurisprudence, Karl Llewellyn and Lon Fuller, have made significant contributions to understanding the interaction between law and normative order.

Llewellyn evocatively describes the manner in which the tasks of law—the "law-jobs"—arise from "processes in the general life of the group which first led to the emergence of legal institutions" (Llewellyn and Hoebel 1941, p. 279).[4] Those processes generate claims made in light of emergent standards of rightness. Even in a society without law, such claims and standards promote the creation of law-like processes for dispute resolution. Where formal law exists, social claims and standards provide the "raw material which . . . serves as grist for [legal] institutions" (p. 279). Of particular interest is

---

[4] These quotations are drawn from a chapter in Llewellyn and Hoebel's work on the Cheyenne (1941) and not from a similar article written by Llewellyn in 1940. The perspective of Llewellyn in the article is the same as the corresponding chapter in Llewellyn and Hoebel, the differences being primarily editorial.

the way in which Llewellyn describes the emergence of standards or norms from the processes of social life.

> What comes to be in the way of practice produces in due course its flavor of felt rightness among its practitioners. . . . This line of normation has peculiar interest to matters legal, because it operates so generally, so inescapably. . . . It is . . . a drift in non-legal institutions which then gives off the raw material of expectation and felt rightness out of which a claim can emerge into a conflict-situation, and can emerge with excellent chance of recognition. But that only takes the matter into the legal field. [pp. 280–81]

Llewellyn was deeply concerned with the capacity of legal institutions to recognize and respond to the claims and "normations" of the broader society. Some degree of regularity and predictability is needed, he maintained, if law is to settle claims definitively and to channel or rechannel behavior. Accordingly, he devoted an enormous amount of his energy and creativity to describing, especially in *The Common Law Tradition: Deciding Appeals* (1960), how the legal process reacts with regularity to such claims, once they command legal attention. But he warned that the drive for predictability can get out of hand, producing "the wooden, externalized, graceless, and cumbersome maladaptation which is summed up as legalism" (Llewellyn and Hoebel 1941, p. 288). To avoid this danger, lawyers and judges must not lose touch with the society. They must retain the kind of "situation-sense" that makes it possible for legal decisions to reflect the processes of social relationship and normation constantly recurring and reforming in society. In the Uniform Commercial Code, Llewellyn illustrates the ways in which the normative content arising in commercial relationships can be systematically introduced into legal decision-making.

Lon Fuller showed comparable interest in the relationships between the normative ordering of interpersonal relations and the formal legal decision process. During his last years (1968–75), Fuller focused on the "private ordering" of relationships and their significance for law. In several articles written during this period, he examined the social processes that give rise to customary law, contractual relationships, and dispute resolution by mediation (Fuller 1968a, 1969a, 1969c, 1971). Out of each of these processes may come some "implicit elements" that affect judgment when the formal legal process is invoked. Among these are the shared understandings and normative judgments that emerge out of the process of human interaction.

Fuller saw private ordering as affecting law in several ways. First, in their interpretation of statutes, judges are likely to be affected by the common understandings and normative standards of the general culture. In the example Fuller gives, a judge might have to determine whether a perambulator and a ten-ton truck are "vehicles" under a statute prohibiting the bringing of a vehicle into a park. Fuller makes the point that knowledge of the culture, not a dictionary, is needed and used to achieve a consistent and socially acceptable interpretation of the ordinance (1968a, pp. 58–59). Second, acceptance of the law is likely to be increased if the positive law accords with normative standards emerging from the private orderings. Positive law that conflicts with customary law tends to incur the kinds of problems that impair its "integrity"—the consistency with which it is carried out and the readiness with which it is accepted as legitimate (1969a, pp. 1–13; 1958). Finally, knowledge of the private orderings contributes to restraint on intervention. Where relationships can be worked out among the parties—in contracts for example—the need for legal intervention may be limited to a small proportion of all cases.

Private ordering minimizes the need for third-party intervention. On this important point, Fuller suggests that private ordering works differently, depending on several considerations. The task, he implies, is to determine how well the parties can by themselves work out relationships that optimize their interests without impinging on the broader interests that are the proper concern of the society. His method for exploring this complex subject is to analyze in detail the nature of different forms of private ordering (customary law, contract, and tripartite negotiation), in an effort to determine the characteristic mode and problems of each (1975). Fuller's discussion of the factors affecting the probable success of labor negotiations, with or without the aid of third-party intervention, illustrates his thoughtful and informed analytic procedure at its best (1971).

Thus, in different but complementary ways, Llewellyn and Fuller stress the importance of the normative order as an element in legal decisions. They share a belief that normative content generated in society, while important, is not the only determinant of the law. Each devotes major works to the analysis of the distinctive subculture of the legal process. Each pays close attention to (and applauds) the mechanisms in that subculture that permit the law to absorb, without being overwhelmed by, the normative content generated by the society. They agree that the effectiveness of law as channeler, regulator, controller, or facilitator of human interaction depends on its capacity to absorb and properly use, in appropriate degree, materials derived from the normative order. To what extent do these orientations correspond with the theory and practice of the American legal process?

LEGAL ABSORPTION OF THE MORES

The mechanisms by which the normative order affects law cannot be understood without considering several elements of the legal system. Within each of the branches of government, certain mechanisms offer openings for considering the norms of society or subgroups within it. While this process occurs to some degree in all legal systems, wide variations exist within and among legal systems concerning the nature of the channels, the volume of normative content that can flow through them, and the alternative elements with which societal norms compete in determining the substance and process of law.

Much can be learned on these matters by examining the theory and practice[5] of constitutional government that emerged in England and has developed in the United States. I chose this legal tradition not only because of its familiarity, but also because its commentators and decision-makers often explicitly discuss the processes here being explored. This choice does not imply, however, that other systems of law and government preclude the absorption of mores into the law. Many modern nation-states share the basic features of Anglo-American constitutional government or differ from it in particulars that

---

[5] The term "theory" is used here in the conventional political sense of a set of beliefs about how the system works. In a functioning constitutional system, by definition, substantial correspondence exists between theory and practice, although the correspondence is never perfect. I assume that the practice cannot be fully understood without reference to the theory and that the practice cannot be fully understood only by reference to the theory. The first of these propositions has been underplayed in much sociolegal research as was the second in classical political science. (For a good general introduction to comparative constitutional analysis, see Friedrich 1941.)

do not alter the mechanisms in question. Others that differ fundamentally in the structure of power may well develop functionally equivalent methods for transmitting the mores into the legal decision-making apparatus.

In the Anglo-American constitutional tradition, two desiderata are constantly reiterated: to open government to popular decision and to limit the power of government. These two objectives of constitutional government carry major implications for the selective inclusion of norms into positive law. Each of the branches of government is amenable to some influence by public attitudes but resistant to complete reliance on them, especially when they would infringe on constitutionally protected rights. If the reasons explicitly stated by the courts are assumed to be accurate, there is abundant evidence that the norms enter, albeit selectively, as a consideration in the making, upholding, and implementation of the laws. This is apparent even at the formal level of lawmaking, statutory interpretation, and judicial review.

Sexual mores provide a useful example. Before the so-called sexual revolution of recent years, the conservative strain in American culture manifested itself in legal prohibition of a wide range of socially disapproved sexual conduct. Not only were "crimes against nature" widely prohibited; even the use of contraception was banned in some states. The challenge to the constitutionality of laws prohibiting the sale of contraceptive devices did not succeed until recent years (*Griswold* v. *Connecticut*, 1965).

Rapidly changing moral standards in the sexual area seem to have created a disjunction between law and societal standards.[6] There is plenty of evidence that norms on the use of contraception began to shift well before the legislatures moved toward relaxing the standard (Dienes 1972; National Center for Family Planning Services 1971). Only after changes had occurred in the norms (and, in many states, the law) did the Court find the remaining anticontraception laws to be unconstitutional (*Griswold*, 1965).

This sequence illustrates the tendency of the courts to defer to the legislatures as barometers of public opinion. Courts declare repeatedly that on matters of protecting the public morals (along with the health and well being of the society), the states may use police power to incorporate into law a set of moral standards regarding sexual conduct and to authorize the executive (police and prosecutor) to enforce them.

Judicial deference to the legislature can ensure norm-law congruence if the legislature reflects current public attitudes. Legislatures often imperfectly embody current mores, however, because of cultural lag, pressure group politics, or other considerations. Legislation at variance with the mores creates tension throughout the system. Such laws tend to be erratically enforced because of the diversity of priorities with which police or prosecutors exercise discretion, the difficulty of detection, vice squad cooptation, or even submores (strongly held attitudes of a segment of the population) contrary to the legislation (Kadish 1967). Courts often reflect these tensions by invalidating convictions for "morals" offenses.

There are several bases on which courts may dismiss charges of sexual misconduct, even in the face of legislative action. Such decisions are often justified on due process grounds. For example, the courts might decide that a particular sexual act—such as fellatio or cunnilingus—falls outside the common-law definition of "crimes against na-

---

[6] See, for example, the refusal of the Supreme Court to interfere with the conviction of consenting adult homosexuals for sodomy in private. "It is enough for upholding the legislation to show that the conduct is likely to end in a moral delinquency" (*Doe* v. *Commonwealth's Attorney* 1976).

ture," a term traditionally limited to sodomy and bestiality. If the legislature or state courts did not make clear the broad interpretation of "crimes against nature," the higher court might overturn the conviction, on grounds that the defendant had not received fair warning or that the legislature has failed properly to guide the police and prosecutor in the exercise of their discretion.[7] Such, at least, is the type of formal reasoning favored; it can, of course, be used as a rationalization for intervening in a norm-law conflict.

In cases of this kind, the court typically invalidates the conviction by strictly construing the statute or by declaring the statute itself void because it is vague. In such circumstances, the legislature would, in principle, be able to revise the statute or pass a new one to overcome these problems. Unless the court found other grounds for invalidation, convictions under the revised or new statute could be expected to stand.

In general, the courts defer to the legislatures in permitting them to set standards on behalf of the community. The presumption is that the state is generally empowered to write morality into law, unless some specific constitutionally protected right is impinged. A dramatic instance to the contrary is found in a New York decision that invalidates statutes prohibiting voluntary homosexual practice on the broad ground of a right to be free of unwarranted governmental interference (*People* v. *Onofré*, 1980). This decision appears to be exceptional in the area of sexual behavior (*Fordham Law Review* 1976), although possibly indicative of a trend. For the most part, under the doctrine of separation of powers, the legal system allocates to the legislature the right to decide which of the mores shall be backed with the force of law.

To a lesser extent the court itself may explicitly take account of the mores. An example of explicit judicial use of the norms in statutory interpretation is furnished by a case involving polygamy, *Cleveland* v. *United States* (1946). In the *Cleveland* case, the Supreme Court upheld the conviction for polygamy of a man who had brought some of his wives across state lines to marry them and live with them in accordance with his Fundamentalist Mormon religion. The Court found that the power to convict had been provided by Congress under the Mann Act, the statute passed several decades earlier to attack the practice of "white slavery," in which women were imported into the United States and moved across state lines for "prostitution, debauchery, or any other immoral purpose." In deciding that the Mann Act applied to polygamy, the Court held that marrying plural wives fell into the same category (*ejusdem generis*) as prostitution and debauchery (*Cleveland,* pp. 18, 19). In this instance, deference to the legislature as the agency to decide which mores shall become law is not evident. Rather, the Court decides, in effect, how Congress might have, or should have, treated polygamy if it had taken into consideration traditional and contemporary mores.

The Court characterizes the "establishment or maintenance of polygamous households as a notorious example of promiscuity" (*Cleveland,* p. 19). In a narrow sense, the Court is declaring its conclusion that polygamy falls squarely under the congressional term of "promiscuity." In a larger sense, it seems to be stating that it believes polygamy to be immoral and that this belief is widespread in the society. Under the second interpretation, the Court identifies its own moral judgments and those of the society as congruent.

---

[7] The cases are summarized by Judge Galbreath, dissenting, in *Locke* v. *State* (1973). In that case, the 6th Circuit Court of Appeals overturned a conviction for an act of cunnilingus under a statute prohibiting crimes against nature (*Locke* v. *Rose*, 1975), but it was reversed by the Supreme Court (*Rose* v. *Locke*, 1975).

In effect, the Court relies on the authority of the mores to justify its decision and uses its own authority to reaffirm the mores.

Quite a different role vis-à-vis norm-law congruence is played by the Court when, in constitutional review, it declares a particular law to be beyond the power of governmental regulation. In such cases, the Court is not merely associating itself with pervasive mores. In many instances of constitutional review, strongly held norms rendered into statutory law are found by the Court to be constitutionally impermissible. In that event, the Court finds itself opposing congruence between law and mores or submores. To justify this position, it seeks a principle more general than the specific norms and the laws that embody them.

This situation occurred in recent years when the Court invalidated state laws prohibiting or limiting the mother's right to obtain an abortion during the first trimester of pregnancy (*Roe* v. *Wade*, 1973). In that decision, the Court appears to have contravened some widely held, though not pervasive, moral beliefs.[8] The primary ground on which *Roe* rests is the right to privacy. While the Constitution itself does not contain that phrase, the decision finds such a right in various clauses of the Constitution, in earlier precedents, and in the history of the common law (*Roe* v. *Wade*, 1973, p. 152).

Is the abortion ruling an instance of two mores in conflict, the Supreme Court deciding which shall dominate? One way to look at the process is to find two submores—prolife and prochoice. How large or vocal or powerful a minority must exist before it can be concluded that, instead of a single pervasive more, the society has two divergent submores? On the continuum from mos to submores, the latter predominates when each of the opposing views is advocated openly by organized, politically effective groups. From one point of view, in this stance, the Court has merely taken the side of the prochoice group, using the Constitution to justify its partisan position. In that perspective, its decision embodies one of the submores, which, with judicial help and changing times, might become the mos of the future. In this interpretation, the Court is merely acting as an official arbiter between two political camps.

The Court need not, of course, make a decision between two opposing mores. It can, instead, choose to exercise the "passive virtues," as Alexander Bickel (1962, pp. 111–98) described them (see also Cole 1980). Rather than granting certiorari, for example, the Court might choose not to hear the case. Such a decision decides without deciding: the power of states to limit abortion would be upheld de facto without an explicit decision. This strategy would permit the Court to avoid the choice between the two mores. Again, the Court might take the case but decide the issue on technical or very narrow substantive grounds. Among aficionados of the Supreme Court, such techniques of avoidance are frequently admired as evidence of the highest form of judicial skill.

The Court does not always avoid such choices. In a situation such as abortion, the Court did choose between two standards. It is important to note that the choice appears to be made between principles that are more abstract than the submores immediately at issue.

In effect, when the Supreme Court decides the issue of abortion on demand, it invokes more general principles as a basis for decision. Instead of considering whether it approves

---

[8] Public opinion poll data on attitudes toward abortion do not squarely correspond to the legal decisions. Generally a majority (about 55 percent) opposed abortion on demand but not all abortion. (See Tedrow and Mahoney 1979; Wardle 1980.)

the banning of abortion or permitting abortion on demand, it asks a more general question: Are the state legislatures, in passing this legislation, exceeding their powers under the Constitution by authorizing an impermissible invasion of privacy? In rendering a decision at that level of abstraction, the Court distances itself from two specific norms in conflict. If the submores remain the primary focus, the decision may be very unpopular with those who lose, popular with those who win. If the decision is viewed as merely judicial legislation, a political act reflecting the preferences of the judges or those whom they favor, the stature of the Court may suffer. In cases such as this, the decision may also be carried back into the political arena.

Raising the decision to a more abstract level of principle may alter the public perception of the matter. The chances of such an outcome may well be enhanced if invoked principles already exist in the mores. If, for example, the right to privacy was a revered principle in the culture, could the Supreme Court, in basing its decision on that principle, justify its holding, resolve the political conflict, and enhance its own status? Or might it do the same for a decision holding the opposite, by invoking the principle that accords the states wide discretion under the police power to regulate the health, welfare, and moral standards of the society?

LIMITS TO THE ABSORPTION OF THE MORES

In open societies, the mores are rarely strong enough to determine general legal principles. The reverse process is, if anything, more significant. The enunciation—and widespread adoption—by society of such principles may well depend largely on legal initiative. The principle of privacy, for example, appears to have been shaped as much by the legal process as by cultural history.[9] In a society as diverse as that of the United States, principles of this kind do not emerge spontaneously. Nor do they easily gain pervasive acceptance. When they do, it is often with the help of the legal process. Alternately, the legal process may absorb the content of the mores and redefine, shape, specify, and extend. In either case, moral formulations usually do not become dominant without help from the legal process.

Legal principles may also be invoked in the face of a widespread norm that runs to the contrary. Such appears to have been the situation in the cases concerning the obligation of school children to salute the flag. Although legislatures at every level of government passed such statutes or authorized such rules to be promulgated, the Supreme Court ultimately decided that, when applied to Jehovah's Witnesses, this regulation was unconstitutional under the First Amendment (*West Virginia Board of Education* v. *Barnette*, 1943). The Court thus asserted, in the face of one of the most pervasive mores, that in those circumstances, the law was unconstitutional. Here, the nature of the interaction is clear—a pervasive mos defeated by a constitutional principle. Did this ruling reflect a counter-mos against saluting the flag?

The Jehovah's Witnesses are a small and unpopular sect. If they—together with all

---

[9] This statement merely reflects a general impression. I have in mind a range of compelling statements by legislators, lawyers, and judges such as Pitt (1968), Warren and Brandeis (1890), and William O. Douglas (*Griswold* v. *Connecticut*, 1965, p. 484). While legal formulations may coalesce privacy sentiments, many other factors also enter. Consider, for example, the thesis persuasively advanced by David Potter (1968) that material abundance promoted a degree of privacy in child-rearing, which contributed profoundly to the strength of the value of privacy in American culture.

who personally refused on moral grounds to salute the flag—were added together, the number holding that position would still constitute a small and scattered minority. While the Witnesses' position might be described as part of the mores of a subgroup, this was not one of those situations in which two submores are held by opposing groups of roughly even size or strength. Yet the outcome went against the popularly held standard. Comparable instances can be found in court decisions regarding civil liberties and—regionally, at least—civil rights (Hyman and Sheatsley 1964). Public-opinion polls have found majority, or substantial minority, opposition to free speech for atheists, socialists, and Communists.[10]

In such cases, it is very important to ask how the courts, the "least dangerous branch" of government, decide when to oppose mores as reflected in statutory acts of the legislature. This is one element of the problem discussed at length and with great intensity by the proponents of judicial self-restraint and judicial activism (Berger 1977; Ely 1980; Dworkin 1977; Chayes 1976). Its history as an intellectual problem goes back to *Marbury v. Madison* (1803) and beyond. Its familiarity should not be permitted to obscure its importance in the present context. When the Supreme Court exercises the power of constitutional review, it sometimes prevents strongly held norms, as reflected by legislation, from being accepted as valid law.

The Supreme Court and its commentators recognize that such an act creates tension; Alexander Bickel described it as "the counter-majoritarian difficulty" (1962, pp. 16–23). How can a court, whose members are not popularly elected, thwart the will of elected representatives of the people? Bickel's justification reflects some of the charisma of the sacred-secular institution of the Supreme Court.

> [M]any actions of government have two aspects: their immediate, necessarily intended, practical effects, and their perhaps unintended or unappreciated bearing on values we hold to have more general and permanent interest. It is a premise we deduce not merely from the fact of a written constitution but from the history of the race, and ultimately as a moral judgment of the good society, that government should serve not only what we conceive from time to time to be our immediate material but also certain enduring moral values. This in part is what is meant by government under law. But such values do not present themselves ready-made. They have a past always, to be sure, but they must be continually derived, enunciated, and seen in relevant application. And it remains to ask which institution of our government—if any single one in particular—should be the pronouncer and guardian of such values. [p. 24]

Bickel states as his own view that, because of its detachment, scholarship, and attention to particular cases, the Court provides the most favorable set of conditions for cultivating those larger values (pp. 24–26).

The enunciated and applied values to which Bickel refers, like the principles earlier mentioned, constitute a distinctive and elaborate set of ideas concerning what is right. Though these ideas are not necessarily shared throughout the society, they do constitute a major part of the subculture of the legal profession. They are learned at law school, in a socialization process that is one of the most intense experiences of adult socialization in

---

[10] The most carefully done study of this subject (Stouffer 1955) is now somewhat dated, but I have no satisfactory evidence of a major change on this matter.

American society. They are reinforced through membership and by performance in the profession.

Of particular interest within the legal subculture are those procedural principles described by Lon Fuller in *The Morality of Law* (1969b). The idea of an internal morality first took shape in Fuller's celebrated debate with H. L. A. Hart, in articles published together in the *Harvard Law Review* (1958). The discussion began with Hart's assertion of the positivist thesis—that morality does not always become part of law, and that it should not. If law were isomorphic with morality, claimed Hart, Mill's principle of liberty for all harmless behavior would be infringed. In his response, Fuller did not directly contradict this position; instead, he stated that law itself embodies some moral principles of its own, that is, functional requirements, without which "fidelity to law" would be impossible (Fuller 1958, p. 644). Describing this internal morality, he listed eight procedural attributes. The need for these was derived from the nature of social life—that laws could not succeed in controlling behavior and be accepted as fair unless they were stated generally and publicly in advance of their application. They would also have to be clear, internally consistent, moderate, stable, and administered in a manner that accorded with the stated laws (Fuller 1969b, pp. 46–91). What Fuller described is a set of standards toward which lawyers (attorneys and legislators as well as judges) supposedly aspire.

If Fuller is correct in these observations, law is affected not so much by the society's norms as by the requirements of successful governance, rooted in the structure (rather than the norms) of the society. In meeting those functional needs of society, the legal subculture generates, and to some extent practices, a set of principles. The principles become guides within the system and perhaps for the society beyond (see Selznick 1969; Scheingold 1974).

It is not clear from Fuller's discussion whether he considers this internal morality essential for every society. Elsewhere (1968a), he stresses the variability from one society to another (such as Trobriands and Barotse) in the kinds of relationships that are central and the type of dispute resolution system that works best for different kinds of interaction. His discussion of these variations implies a broad and flexible conception of the optimal mechanisms for social ordering. In his later writings, he clearly sees the significance of social structure as a variable determinant of the normative order, if not also of the legal system (Fuller 1968a, 1969a, 1969c, 1971, 1975).

On this subject a question may be raised concerning the universality of Fuller's prerequisites for law. Societies differ widely on such fundamental process questions as the importance of compromise versus all-or-none outcomes. Such differences might be expected to affect the Fuller requirements, all of which assume the primacy of explicit general rules. Whether societal norms favor Fuller's type of formality, even in American society, should be treated as problematic—a promising and important subject for empirical investigation. If the internal morality of law diverges from societal norms of fairness in significant segments of the society, the legitimacy of law could be undercut, rather than enhanced, by legal adherence to Fuller's internal morality.

Before leaving the concept of the internal morality of law, it should be noted that the legal subculture gets less enthusiastic treatment from many other authors. The idea of a vigorous legal subculture is not novel with Fuller. While descriptions of the legal subculture vary, it is generally recognized as a coherent way of looking at and dealing with the world, different from the society's other subcultures. From that common starting point, however, the observers begin to disagree. While some see law as a way of resolving disputes, others view law and lawyers as creators of chaos. While some applaud legal contributions to equality, others assert that law concentrates privilege. Where some see clarity of thought, others find only confusion.

To what extent can such judgments lend themselves to empirical investigation? Even when stated as hypotheses, propositions of this kind sound primarily exhortative. Yet the questions they raise are worth following. Assuming that all the aforementioned characteristics of the legal culture exist, the interesting questions once again concern the conditions under which they are most likely to occur. The sociology of law need not choose between integrative and conflict models of the legal process; it can learn more by assuming that elements of each exist and by asking when, where, how, and to what degree each functions. The question of which picture is closer to reality bears on the question of how law is affected by the mores and how it, in turn, affects the normative order. If law can be guided by or help to generate pervasive mores or widely accepted principles that might otherwise be lacking, law might minimize conflict and contribute to social integration. If it chooses sides, without persuasively justifying the choice, conflict will be exacerbated.

CONFLICT AND INTEGRATION

The conception of normative integration rests on the premise that the society as a whole can accept common assumptions concerning the society's proper structure and the role of individuals and institutions within it. When such a consensus exists, law can draw on it. In the absence of consensus, law tries to cope through a variety of techniques.

If, for example, the right of property is widely supported, legislatures reinforce that right and courts support it. When, by contrast, the uses of private property arouse a strong reaction from a significant segment of the society, law is challenged to choose between opposing interests.[11] Similarly, if racial discrimination is widely accepted, law has shown its capacity to support it. *Plessy* v. *Ferguson* (1896)—the case that established the legality of "separate but equal accommodations"—is the classic example. When the forces favoring and opposing discrimination become more evenly balanced, the conflict is reflected in the divisions of all branches of government.

The capacity of law to moderate between conflicting norms or principles depends on the perceived legitimacy of the institutions of law and government. When opposing interest groups struggle with each other, their conflict can eventually threaten the stability of the society. Whether this occurs depends on many factors—the power available to each side, the nature and strength of their aspirations, the availability of a mutually acceptable solution, and the capacity of the third-party intervenor to contribute to such a solution.

---

[11] It is easy to illustrate the point if one accepts at face value reasons given in judicial decisions. In *Pennsylvania Coal Co.* v. *Manon* (1922), for example, the Supreme Court upheld a state regulation forbidding the mining of coal in such a way as to cause subsidence of structures even though the coal company had sold land to the plaintiff expressly reserving the right to mine under plaintiff's land. A more recent example is furnished by *Penn Central Transportation Co.* v. *New York City* (1978), wherein the Supreme Court upheld a city regulation prohibiting construction on historical landmarks, affirming an injunction against building an office building on top of Grand Central Station even though the plaintiff owned Grand Central Station. Though opposing interests seem to be at play in these cases, detailed research is needed to estimate the strength of the interests opposed to the assertion of traditional property rights.

As the ultimate recourse in such disputes, the institutions of law and government in stable open societies bear major responsibility for promoting solutions to socially disturbing conflicts. In societies where the mores are strong and pervasive, such challenges tend to be rare. But in a society such as the United States they are frequent enough. Tocqueville pointed out that in America, every political problem became a legal problem (1899).

In the contemporary United States, recourse to the legal process occurs for every kind of problem—social, economic, medical, scientific, and governmental. Such a range of questions, intensely pressed, creates difficulty for law as an integrative mechanism. If disputes are not satisfactorily resolved in the courts, they return unsettled to the legislature, to the administrative agencies, to the institutions in which they originated, or to the streets. As unresolved disputes multiply, they create increasing discontent, conflict, or alienation. If the interests involved in several conflicts coalesce, a split in the society develops, threatening the very structure of the regime. By the time that danger occurs, it may be too late for the institutions of law-government to restore their authority.

The capacity of constitutional government to avoid such instability must be treated as problematic. While great stability exists in Scandinavia, England, most of the British Commonwealth, and the United States, the same has not been true of Latin America or the rest of Europe. Even the stable democracies have shown signs of potential society-wide conflicts. How can the institutions of law-government deal with such conflicts in ways that will strengthen their legitimacy and authority?

The solutions of the past rested to a large extent on a normative consensus regarding the structure of society and the role of law and government. In the United States, the concept of a "land of opportunity" was more than mere ideology: it was supported by demographic realities (Sibley 1953). While mobility was not available to all, enough succeeded, individually or vicariously, in gaining access to wealth and power to minimize discontent. Low-access groups, such as women and racial minorities, were also low in power and, as a result, in expectations. For large segments of the population, a sense of community existed, whether in the small town, the ethnic enclave, the gentlemen's club, the religious congregation, or the political machine. The conflicts that developed (except for the fundamental question of slavery) were managed within the framework of constitutional government. Common law was an acceptable instrument for dealing with crimes of violence, breaches of contract, and personal injuries. The courts and legislatures facilitated in many ways the massive economic development that was widely accepted as paramount in the nineteenth century (Hurst 1960, 1964).

The changing structure of American society in the twentieth century created more difficult problems for the institutions of law and government. Many of the problems took the form of battles between the public and special-interest groups—robber barons, meat packers, political bosses, sweatshop owners. The tendency, starting with the first Roosevelt, was to turn to government for protection against such outrages (Schlesinger 1957). By the time of the second Roosevelt, the New Deal demonstrated that governmental regulation was a politically acceptable method for dealing with a wide range of problems.[12]

---

[12] Roosevelt's overwhelming victory over Landon in 1936, after four years of vigorous regulatory undertakings, is perhaps the best evidence. The regulatory approach continued through Republican as well as Democratic administrations, until the first serious efforts at deregulation under Carter and Reagan.

The role of the courts in this trend merits attention. At first resistant to the extension of government regulatory powers, the Supreme Court gradually accommodated to this development until the final spasm of resistance and acceptance in the mid-1930s. After the Supreme Court accepted the principle of federal regulatory power, Congress assumed command. In that sense, it could be said that a representative body was specifying regulatory policies derived from public sentiments. How well that claim charted the reality is not self-evident. Historical studies in several of these areas suggest that special-interest groups, rather than a broad public consensus, underlay many of these measures (see generally Lowi 1979).

As the evolution continued, however, the connection of governmental regulation with specific norms became increasingly remote. A major shift occurred as Congress and the state legislatures increasingly delegated their authority to regulatory agencies (Waldo 1948). In a generally permissive approach, the courts after 1937 settled for minimal limitations on the power of regulatory agencies. As long as the agencies stayed within the broad mandate accorded by the legislature and applied it in a manner that was not "arbitrary or capricious," their powers were upheld. In case after case, it became clear that the criterion phrase meant the observance of some kind of procedural standards. Recently, even the scope of those court-imposed standards has been limited (*Vermont Yankee Nuclear Power* v. *NRDC*, 1978).

After 1937, the capacity of the Congress to delegate this authority was not called into serious question by the courts.[13] From a constitutional perspective, the powers of Congress were deemed broad enough to encompass every kind of regulation, provided it fell within an appropriate grant of authority, such as the Commerce Clause. In exercising standards against actions that were "arbitrary and capricious" or unsupported by substantial evidence, the courts seem to have felt that they were ensuring the "proper" part of that limitation. As to "necessary," that judgment was left to the legislature.

Within the branches of government then, the courts in effect declined to limit administrative discretion except in extreme or unusual cases. This arrangement, vigorously developed by the New Deal, continued and grew in a wide range of economic, social, and technical areas. The "fourth branch of government" came to be a major mechanism for setting behavioral standards affecting every sphere of life in the society.

Any account of law in modern American society must treat the rules of the administrative agencies as at least *quasi*-legal. They are administered by governmental officials charged by the legislature with responsibility for social control. They are enforced with sanctions administered by the agency, or under agency aegis, by the courts. They are promulgated publicly as general standards. And they are applied in individual instances.

In other regards, agency rules lack some of the typical features of judicially administered law. They are not promulgated by elected representatives, and they are not subject to presidential veto and override. Neither are they a product of common-law evolution. Adjudication under them is not accorded the full protection of procedural due process, although some due process features are sometimes present.[14] Rules of regulatory agencies

---

[13] The leading case, *National Labor Relations Board* v. *Jones & Laughlin Steel Corp.* (1937), broadened and simplified the powers of Congress under the Commerce Clause. The delegative powers of Congress were not seriously discussed thereafter until a recent decision, a concurring opinion by Justice William Rehnquist in the benzene case, *Industrial Union Department, AFL-CIO* v. *American Petroleum Institute* (1980).

[14] See Davis (1972) for a general discussion of due process in administrative proceedings. During the sixties and seventies, Congress and the courts contributed to what has been described as a "due process explosion." For a review, see the discussion and cases in Gellhorn, Byse, and Strauss (1979, pp. 434–515).

are typically applied without practices intended to protect the objectivity of the judge. And they do not utilize anything comparable to the jury of peers.

If regulatory-agency rules are quasi-legal, to what extent do they incorporate the mores of the society? There are some mechanisms by which the agencies can be informed of public opinion. Congress, representing the public, provides a channel by which constituents' views can be heard. Oversight hearings, budgetary hearings, and statutory changes may apprise the agency of public opinion. This channel is remote enough, however, to severely limit its capacity to transmit. Further, the issues of regulatory policy tend to be so technical that a coherent norm rarely emerges. Instead, matters of regulation are likely to be left to "the experts" and to those groups whose interests are manifestly involved and who have the organization and resources to affect the agency, through Congress or directly.[15]

Another channel of influence is available through the rule-making process. By publishing proposed rules in the Federal Register as required under the Administrative Procedure Act (5 U.S.C. 551 et seq., 1981), the agency invites comment from all interested parties. Sometimes the result is supplemented by hearings, by comments on the comments, and by the publication of a revised set of proposed rules before the rules are made final. As with congressional oversight, the populations tapped by these procedures are self-selected from those whose interests are most deeply involved. Even with this selectivity, the two channels hold open the possibility that pervasive mores could affect the final rules.[16]

One reason this outcome does not usually occur is that in the areas in question, the society usually lacks pervasive mores relevant to the rules. In the current heterogeneous society, attitudes and interests are so diverse that a desired policy can rarely be agreed upon. For any given regulation, there are likely to be proponents whose interests are served by the rules and opponents who consider the policy harmful (cf. Jaffe 1954). Although some lobbying groups have purported to represent the public interest, it is difficult to define in a convincing way. The premise that the administrative agencies themselves represent it, once widely accepted, has worn thin (Jaffe 1973).

When opposing interest groups attempt to influence agency policy, neither the process nor the outcome is likely to enhance normative consensus. Agency proceedings are, for the most part, conducted with a minimum of publicity, so that most agency work is unknown, even to the most well-informed outsider. Those whose interests are affected learn of agency actions, if at all, in various undependable ways: sometimes through interest groups to which they belong, sometimes when informed of the rule, sometimes when they are confronted with an instruction to comply, sometimes when they are found in violation. Rarely does this kind of information produce publicity that leads to widespread public awareness (see Boyer 1981).

Furthermore, there is a tendency to assume the expertise of the agency. While this kind of confidence has eroded rapidly in recent years, it has not been replaced by confidence in any alternative. If those affected by the rules are knowledgeable, they are viewed with suspicion because their expertise is combined with vested interest; no one knowledgeable is thought to be objective. If professionals are looked to with some hope,

[15] Davis (1972, pp. 26–52) makes the best justification for such delegation by describing the needs it fulfills.

[16] For a suggestion that the multiplicity of such agencies—charged with sometimes overlapping and conflicting goals—might inhibit the expression of widely held views, see Nader and Seber (1980).

their performance on such matters has been so uneven as to inspire little confidence regarding either expertise or objectivity.

The justification of administrative policy in terms of efficiency does not necessarily invite public support. It may be true, as has often been claimed, that this society favors practical results. Such a value may have created some disposition at the outset toward administrative agencies designed to achieve publicly approved goals. Any such inclination to support regulatory rules has certainly eroded in the face of a widespread belief in bureaucratic inefficiency. So far, movement in Congress to require evaluation of agency policies seems to have produced anecdotal confirmation of the inefficiency theme rather than a serious evaluation of agency efficiency.[17]

Disillusionment with governmental "bureaucracy" may reflect a societal need for something other than efficiency. Criticisms invoked against "Washington" give some clues: waste and inefficiency are included, but so are interference, indifference, and arrogance. Two successive presidents were elected with the help of a promise to "get the government off your backs."

This situation suggests a widespread sentiment that the agencies are delivering the citizens little but a hard time. A popular riddle tells the story:

Q.   "What are the three most frequently told lies?"

A.   "(1) I gave at the office. (2) It's in the mail. (3) I'm from the government and I'm here to help you."

What is involved here is a sense that power is being exercised against the interest of the citizen. A recent study suggests the grounds for such a suspicion. The source of the difficulty is not so much in the initial characteristics of the administrative official as in the nature of bureaucratic organization, the definition of the task, and the criteria of success (Lipsky 1980).

Another criterion on which the agencies score poorly is access. While formal measures have been provided for hearings on rules and decisions (see, for example, Administrative Conference of the U.S. 1981), affected citizens frequently complain that the government simply took over.[18]

An interesting contrast in Washington is found between the offices and corridors of the agencies and the legislative office buildings on the Hill. The House Office Building swarms with people, while the FTC offices are very quiet. Perhaps elected officials attract large numbers of visitors because they welcome their input and their votes—two elements that go hand in hand.

Another consideration, beyond access and input, is a sense of fairness or justice. Many regulatory agencies were originally conceived as instruments for achieving some socially desirable end (see Friedman and Macaulay 1977, pp. 610–20). The widespread belief in inefficiency and indifference undercuts that basis for popular support. In addition, agency decisions are frequently felt to be unfair, taken without consultation, ignoring relevant information, and conceived in ways that do not provide equal treatment or a coherent basis for differentiation.[19]

---

[17] For a thoughtful discussion of the limitations of policy evaluation, see Lindblom and Cohen (1979).

[18] For a collection of such complaints, see *Regulatory Reform: Hearings Before the Senate Committee on the Judiciary* (1979). Manning (1977) suggests that the absence of warning is inevitable given the proliferation of applicable regulations.

[19] For a general review of these problems and some proposed solutions, see Stewart (1975).

All these tendencies suggest that the quasi-legal regulatory agencies are failing to meet criteria deeply imbedded in the constitutional scheme and in the legal subculture. In leaving the field of regulation to them, Congress and the courts may have added unduly to the estrangement of the society from the institutions of law and government.

This is not to suggest that a close correspondence of law and the mores is to be found in a radical restoration to legislatures and courts of the tasks now handled by regulatory agencies. A step toward limiting agency discretion has been repeatedly proposed by Senator Dale Bumpers and has received considerable, though not majority, support calling for judicial review of the agency's interpretation of its delegated authority (Amendment to the Administrative Procedures Act, 1981). A call for reassertion of the power of the courts, in a broad spectrum of rights, has been vigorously advanced (Stewart 1975, Chayes 1976). Whether either trend will substantially develop remains to be seen. Such measures might moderately increase the channels through which public sentiment flows into the lawmaking process, compared with the access provided under agency procedures as they now exist or even as they might (in the interest of "representative bureaucracy") be revised. Unaided proposals of this sort are hardly likely to reconstruct the common-law concept of law as the embodiment of society's normative consensus.

LEGAL IMPACT AND LEGAL CENTRALISM

The discussion thus far suggests the difficulty of attaining norm-law congruence in a pluralistic, anomic society. Neither the courts, the legislatures, nor the administrative agencies provide an easy answer to this problem. Although each of these entities has developed methods for hearing, absorbing, and registering normative consensus—the messages received typically reflect dissensus instead. In these circumstances, law is often called upon for authoritative decisions. Do such decisions contribute to normative consensus?

In general, the answer is no. While the research results are sparse, they do not support the view that law can directly command compliance and directly or indirectly command normative agreement in an open society. Studies of legal impact usually assume that the topic can best be addressed by isolating a law and examining its effects in modifying behavior. The effects characteristically examined in impact analysis are those relating to compliance with the legal standard. To what extent does the implementation of the law decrease violation or increase compliance with that standard?

Thus defined, the inquiry concerning legal impact relates most obviously to law and normative order when law is seen as a device for enforcing legally embodied morality. According to this view, when a law is enforced against a defendant, the judgment serves as a reminder that the legal standard is to be taken seriously. Those who are chastised may modify their subsequent behavior by bringing it into line with the standard. Others, not directly subjected to legal sanctions, learn vicariously to avoid the disapproved behavior. In either case, the effects sometimes achieved, it is argued, include a change in individual attitude and a reinforcement of the societal norm. Through a combination of exhortation and sanction, law may thus lead people to alter their ideas of what is right in conformity with the legal standard.

The conception of law as an effective regulator of behavior is well represented in legal thinking. In criminal law, it does appear to be the dominant view. LaFave and Scott (1972, p. 21), for example, mince no words in presenting this view: "The broad purposes of the criminal law are, of course, to make people do what society regards as desirable and to prevent them from doing what society considers to be undesirable." Packer (1968) acknowledges the centrality of crime control but adds as an equally important purpose the maintenance of due process protections for the accused.

The purposes of the criminal law, written into penal codes and discussed in appellate decisions, include four major objectives—general deterrence, special deterrence, incapacitation, and rehabilitation. Recently retribution has reappeared as an additional acceptable purpose of the criminal law.[20] General deterrence is intended to teach others than the offender to comply with the law. The remaining three purposes represent efforts to prevent the offender from repeating criminal conduct—special deterrence, by inflicting consequences that will lead to subsequent avoidance; incapacitation, by making it impossible (through incarceration, banishment, physical disability, or execution) to act criminally in free society; rehabilitation, by encouraging law-abiding habits. Each of these three is supposed to reduce the frequency with which the violation and other criminal acts occur. Instead, behavior is altered either to inaction or to conduct approved by society. Rehabilitation presumably promotes law-abiding activity in place of crime; special deterrence is expected to inhibit criminal behavior; and incapacitation, for the period of its duration, eliminates the opportunity to commit crimes outside of prison.

Comparable assumptions, less explicitly articulated, are found in legal thinking concerning the law of tort and contract. Personal injuries resulting from a failure to exercise reasonable care are subject to civil sanctions, requiring the negligent person to pay the victim for damages inflicted. Where the tort feasor behaved especially badly (intentionally, deliberately, or maliciously), punitive damages may be imposed. Here, a major part of the explanation is phrased in terms of the effort to require people to behave more carefully, although the element of compensating an innocent victim assumes a prominent place as a parallel objective (see Prosser 1971, p. 9). In contract law, the objectives move even more in the direction of the plaintiff. While the principal aim of contract law is to compensate the plaintiff for losses resulting from breach of contract, the intended effect is also to require that the defendant and similar others be warned of the price they may be forced to bear should they break contracts in the future.[21] For the injured plaintiff, another kind of behavioral effect is envisioned. In effect, the law is saying to the particular plaintiff and to other potential makers of contracts, "Go ahead with a written agreement; the law will see to it that either the agreement is kept or that you will be protected from financial harm." A Comment on the Restatement of Contracts (1932, §329a) puts it in the following terms:

> In awarding compensatory damages, the effort is made to put the injured party in as good a position as that in which he would have been put by full performance of the contract, at the least cost to the defendant and without charging him with harms that he had no sufficient reason to foresee when he made the contract.

[20] In the debate on this issue between Justices Thurgood Marshall and Potter Stewart in *Furman* v. *Georgia* (1972) and *Gregg* v. *Georgia* (1976), Stewart's position favoring retribution as an acceptable legislative purpose seems to have majority support in the Supreme Court. On this matter, *Gregg* runs contrary to earlier dicta, such as that expressed in *Williams* v. *New York* (1949, p. 248): "Retribution is no longer the dominant objective of the criminal law."

[21] For an illuminating discussion of the generality of law as a defining characteristic, see H. L. A. Hart (1961, pp. 18–25).

The residual interest in deterring breaches of contract is evidenced in such concepts as anticipatory breach, under which liability may be imposed on a contracting party who has bargained in bad faith (see Fuller and Eisenberg 1972, pp. 51–57, 759–65).

The accuracy of such assumptions concerning the impact of law on behavior must be questioned. Empirically, there is very little evidence to support them. Despite years of research, social scientists have rarely been able to demonstrate the behavioral impact of a given law, much less its normative effect.

Some of the best-known examples of legal-impact studies support the contrary proposition: that law seems to have a null or negative effect in regulating behavior.[22] The case of Prohibition has often been cited as an instance where criminal law, in this case the Eighteenth Amendment and the Volstead Act, contributed to the opposite of the intended consequences. Not only did Prohibition fail to reduce the amount of alcohol consumption; it added to its production, importation, and use. By subsidizing organized crime, moreover, it contributed to related forms of organized criminal activities. A failure of this magnitude is attributable only in part to the inadequacy with which the Prohibition laws were enforced. The law itself seems to have reflected the views and efforts of a minority of the population. While, by zeal and organization, the temperance movement secured the votes necessary to change the law, it was little help against determined purveyors and consumers of alcohol in getting the law implemented. The failures of prohibition enforcement are attributable in important part to the refusal of the public to support enforcement activities (Sinclair 1962).

On the civil side, manufacturers and suppliers rarely utilize the courts to enforce contracts (Macaulay 1963). They avoid litigation, which would be harmful to their appeal as good business partners, in most instances in which they would have a cause of action. Instead, they make every effort to settle their differences without legal intervention and to maintain the business relationship.

Both these instances, and many more like them, point to the difficulties of the law's regulating behavior in the face of mores running contrary to it. It is this kind of finding that leads a number of scholars to question the accuracy of what has been described as a "legal centralist" view, which supposedly attributes to the agencies of the state the capacity to control behavior throughout the society, without regard to the degree of correspondence between law and the mores.[23]

Recent critiques of legal centralism merit close consideration in this context. While there is a danger that such characterizations can become mere caricature, the efforts of sociolegal scholars in recent years have avoided this temptation. Accordingly, there are available a few statements that soberly seek to describe the prevailing view in the legal subculture of how law and society interrelate. A succinct description of the legal-centralist position is given by Marc Galanter: "Legal scholars and professionals, while accentuating various differences with one another, display a broad agreement about legal phenomena [comprising] adherence, usually tacit, to a set of propositions which, taken

[22] Null effects are found, for example, in Rheinstein's 1972 study of the effects of divorce laws. For an illustration of negative effects, see the studies by Kaplan (1976) and Grinspoon (1977) about legal control of marijuana use.

[23] For a definition and critique of "legal centralism," see Galanter (1977). The extensive description of the "common paradigm" given by Galanter presumably spells out his conception of legal centralism, though the term is not used.

together, provide a cognitive map or paradigm of legal reality" (1977, p. 18). As described by Galanter, this is the common paradigm:

1. Governments are the primary (if not the exclusive) locus of legal controls; that part of the legal process which is governmental is the determinative source of regulation and order in society.

2. The legal rules and institutions within a society form a system in the sense of a naturally cohering set of interrelated parts articulated to one another so that they form a coherent whole, animated by common procedures and purposes.

3. The central and distinctive element of this system is a body of normative learning (consisting, in various versions, of rules, and/or standards, principles, policies) and of procedures for discerning, devising and announcing them.

3A. Purposiveness: rules are (should be) designed to embody principles or effectuate policies.

4. Legal systems are centered around and typified by courts, whose function is to announce, apply, interpret (and sometimes change) rules on the basis of or in accordance with other elements of this normative learning.

4A. The basic, typical, decisive mode of legal action is adjudication (i.e., the application of rules to particular controversies by courts or courtlike institutions in adversarial proceedings).

5. The [body of] rules (authoritative normative learning) represents (reflects, expresses, embodies, refines) general (widely shared, dominant) social preferences (values, norms, interests).

5A. Broad participation in rule-making by adjudication (and by representative government) insures that the rules embody broad social interests.

6. Normative statements, institutions and officials are arranged in hierarchies, whose members have different levels of authority.

6A. "Higher" elements direct (design, evaluate) activity; "lower" ones execute activity.

6B. Higher elements control (guide) lower ones.

7. The behavior of legal actors tends to conform to rules (with some slippage and friction).

7A. Officials are guided by the rules.

7B. The rules control the behavior of the population.

7C. Conformity is the result of assent and the (threat of) application of governmental force.

8. If the above obtain, then

8A. The authoritative normative learning generated at the higher reaches of the system provides a map for understanding it; and

8B. The function of legal scholarship is to cultivate that learning by clarification and criticism; and

8C. Legal scholarship directs itself to remedy imperfections—to bring legal phenomena into conformity with paradigm assumptions. [pp. 18–19]

This useful model can be taken as a substantially accurate description of the prevailing assumptions of the legal subculture. Thus, it helps to explain the behavior of legal actors.

The legal-centralist model can also be used as a set of hypotheses against which to describe the legal process as it functions in the real world. Galanter's view on this matter, shared by many scholars, emphasizes the differences between this model and the actual performances of the legal process.[24] As Galanter states it, "If we look at the legal process in America, we find that as descriptive propositions these assertions do not self-evidently fit the reality very well" (p. 20). I infer from this that Galanter believes the model to be so far from reality that it must be replaced by a substantially different conception of the relation between law and society. Other scholars (including Griffiths 1979; Abel 1973; Black 1972) have joined Galanter in suggesting that patent contradictions of the model are so numerous that only a new model will suffice.

While I would not discourage such efforts, my own inclination is to explore the existing model in order to seek out the changes necessary to make it more realistic. I am drawn to this approach for several reasons. First, there may be substantial truth in widely accepted assumptions. It is important to resist the temptation to assume that whatever explanations people give for their own behavior are inevitably false. While social scientists have generally prided themselves on the discovery of hidden motives and inaccurate perceptions of reality, the enjoyment of the search does not justify the presumption that overt motives and perceptions cannot possibly be substantially accurate. Second, the specific assumptions described in the legal-centralist model seem to me close enough to a realistic description to provide a good starting point. Because it contains much that is correct, it can be especially useful in locating discrepancies from reality. Third, when such inaccuracies are repeatedly discovered, they can be used to correct the model. Galanter asserts that each instance of the gap between the centralist model and the reality tends to be dismissed as an exception—something atypical, peripheral, and transient (1977, p. 20). That response seems to me not inevitable. In fact, the professionals in this field have, over the years, engaged to a surprising degree in major reappraisals of assumptions concerning the legal system. The paradigm described by Galanter is substantially different from what it would have been before Holmes.

The Legal Realists in particular brought about much rethinking—some, though not all, of it reflected in the Galanter model. This does not mean that the basic model has been completely changed. Galanter regrets that "awareness of such discrepancies does not induce professionals (or others) to relinquish their model of the legal system. Rather it spurs them to add ad hoc explanations to account for these irregularities" (1977, p. 20). This dichotomy contains a very important excluded possibility; instead of either ad hoc explanations or total relinquishment, the discrepancies can lead to significant modifications of the model, precluding the need for an entirely new one. Fourth, a model accepted by the professionals in the field, if close to accurate, can be used to encourage members of the profession to think in their own terms about changes in the legal process that they may want to institute. I do not believe that all professions are certain to pursue their individual interests at the expense of broader goals. Given contrasting views of professional commitment to societal service, the attraction of service to the society seems to me a possibility that might be enhanced by the use of an already internalized model, illuminated by empirical reality testing, to show how societal contributions could be increased. Finally, the urgent call to scrap the existing legal-centralist model is unacceptable until a plausible alternative is brought forward to take its place. Those models that have thus far been proposed seem to me either to vary too little from the legal-centralist model to deserve the grand designation of "new paradigm" (Abel 1973) or to have varied

---

[24] For an early expression of this general perspective, see Jerome Frank's *Courts on Trial* (1949).

so much as to have left far behind those empirical findings that accord with, and tend to support, the older model (Black 1976).

I do not mean that the search for new paradigms is unwise. Alternatives are valuable in testing the adequacy of existing models. I do mean that the legal-centralist model as described by Galanter lends itself to use and to constructive modification, especially absent a plausible replacement.

A modified model should begin, however, with a new name, since legal centralism does not accurately describe legal thinking or the legal process. I propose to describe the needed model as "mutualist" rather than "centralist." By mutualist, I refer to an orientation that sees law as (1) affected by the extra-legal norms and structures of the society and as (2) affecting those norms and institutions. A proper use of the term "centralist" denies the influence of society on law. As I read Galanter's description of legal centralism, I think the name is misapplied. His model contains too many assumptions concerning the first type of process to merit the centralist label. His propositions 5 and 5A are especially noteworthy.

> 5.   The [body of] rules (authoritative normative learning) represents (reflects, expresses, embodies, refines) general (widely shared, dominant) social preferences (values, norms, interests).
>
> 5A. Broad participation in rule-making by adjudication (and by representative government) insures that the rules embody broad social interests.

Other models of the legal process seem to me far better described by the centralist label than is Galanter's. Austinian legal positivism, for example, is much more extreme in its centralism. In Austin's view, the command of the sovereign is the starting point of the analysis, and it makes no difference to him whether the sovereign is a king or a legislature, unpopular or popular, reflective of the values of positive morality or not. While Austin acknowledged the possibility that custom could sometimes be converted into judge-made law, he viewed this process as dominated by judicial discretion and discontinuous because custom, once accepted as judge-made law, was converted into positive law and cut off from its origins (Austin 1861, lecture 5; Fuller 1968a, pp. 44–46). H. L. A. Hart (1958, 1961) continues the Austinian approach in stressing the importance of minimizing the transmission of morality into law. Prescriptive implications aside, the Austin-Hart model may be a good description of how law worked in nineteenth-century England (cf. Dicey 1914).

Another highly centralist position is represented in the means-ends orientation. Fully developed by Jeremy Bentham (1948), this type of centralism would guide law by utilitarian considerations, largely determined by the expert lawgiver. Ideas of rightness in the population, to the extent that they differ from the scientific calculus of the greatest pleasure for the greatest number, were to be rejected as wrong (pp. 8–23).

Roscoe Pound's ideas of law as increasingly effective social engineering fit in the same tradition, although tempered by Pound's readiness to include in the calculus the diverse interests (not necessarily rationally justified) of various segments of the population (Pound 1943, p. 39). Despite that development, Pound's approach continues to emphasize the technical decisions of the scientist-engineer: once interests are identified, the prime question becomes one of efficiency rather than normative preference in the population or even in the internal morality of law (Pound 1942, pp. 64–65).

Among the Realists, the same orientation appears in extreme form in the thinking of Walter Wheeler Cook (1927):

> Underlying any scientific study of the law, it is submitted, will lie one fundamental postulate, viz., that human laws are devices, tools which society uses as one of its methods to regulate human conduct and to promote those types of it which are regarded as desirable. If so, it follows that the worth or value to a given rule of law can be determined only by finding out how it works, that is, by ascertaining so far as that can be done, whether it promotes or retards the attainment of desired ends. If this is to be done, quite clearly we must know what at any given period these ends are and also whether the means selected, the given rules of law, are indeed adapted to securing them. [p. 308]

The exclusive concentration on law as an instrument seems to me characteristic of a centralist approach. This view implies that the instrument is available for use by the "sovereign," with or without influence from the population. As Galanter (1977, p. 18) phrases it, in a genuinely centralist part of his model, law-government "is the determinative source of regulation and order in society." In practice, the instrumental approach promotes the role of the expert to determine means-ends relations and of the governmental official to determine priorities and to optimize among conflicting policies. In principle, it calls for input from the public, if at all, to determine only ends, not means. It is government for the people (or the state), but not government by the people.

In the Galanter model, the means-ends orientation is lumped together with principle under the heading of purposiveness—"rules are (should be) designed to embody principles or effectuate policies." This combination blurs an important distinction related to the issue of centralism. Contrary to the means-ends approach in "effectuating policies," the embodiment of principles is not necessarily centralist. Principles enunciated within the legal tradition often correspond to societal morality. Such principles as the right of privacy and free speech connect potentially with pervasive mores; policy calculations, transitory and technical, are less likely to do so. For the current American culture, at least, pragmatic mores are a contradiction in terms.

In this discussion, I am pointing to a distinction that seems to me of fundamental importance for the present topic. The fullest development of legal centralism occurs when the normative orientations of the population are excluded from the processes of law formulation and administration.

In the first part of this essay, considerable attention was paid to the methods by which normative content finds its way into positive law. The occurrence of such normative infusions correspond to propositions 5 and 5A of Galanter's model.

In addition, the legal process sometimes demonstrates a tendency to promote the generation or transmission of societal norms. To the degree that these processes tap normative elements in the society and are not merely reflections of governmental messages being beamed back, the centralist nature of the legal process is further diluted. Often, these processes entail an intertwining of legal and societal elements—an important characteristic of the mutualist model.

Emphasis on these processes is consistently found in the works of Karl Llewellyn and Lon Fuller.[25] Both these scholars were clearly oriented toward the interaction of law and

---

[25] Llewellyn's bibliography was compiled by Twining (1973, pp. 555–61) in his extremely thorough study *Karl Llewellyn and the Realist Movement*. For a bibliography of Fuller, see Bechtler (1978, pp. 223–27).

society and away from legal centralism. In Fuller's work, there is also a strong emphasis on what might be called legal decentralism—an effort to identify those situations of "private ordering" in which governmental intervention is unnecessary or mischievous (Fuller 1969a, 1975).

Considering the influence exercised by these two men, their mutualist orientation indicates that the centralist approach is less dominant than has been suggested. Though it is possible that their positions were not fully understood by the supposed legions of legal centralists, it seems unlikely, in view of the emphasis placed on the mutual approach throughout their work.

I believe that these two scholars gained acclaim not in spite of but because of their commitment to a mutualist perspective, which seems to reach back very deeply into the common-law tradition. It is reflected, for example, in a work thought to epitomize the codification of the common law, Blackstone's commentaries. In a quotation attributed to Blackstone, he resorted to a legal fiction to imply notice of the law: "every man in England is, in judgment of law, party to the making of an act of Parliament, being present thereat by his representatives" (Fuller 1968a, p. 66).

Thus, the statutory act was viewed as witnessed, if not participated in, by the entire population. Depending on its use, such a fiction could promote or reduce attention to the societal norms in the legislative process. While the imperfections of the representative process during this period suggest reduced attention, Edmund Burke's thoughtful observations on the role of the legislator as delegate and as trustee imply the opposite (see, for example, his Speech to the Electors of Bristol). The practice of Lord Mansfield of sharing the bench with merchants in commercial cases also suggests a concern that considerations be given to commercial practice (see Fifoot 1936, p. 93). The pervasive inclusion of the jury in the English and the American tradition further attests to the strength of the mutualist commitment.

The themes developed by Llewellyn and Fuller command attention for a more important reason. Their work constitutes significant progress in trying to locate mechanisms for promoting the integration of norms and law.

Llewellyn's work can be interpreted as a lifelong effort to analyze and shape the mutual interaction of norms and law. His work on the law of sales (1930) paid particular attention to the element of custom in the interpretation of contracts. In developing the Uniform Commercial Code, Llewellyn embodied his general idea that law must be "open-textured" to utilize information from the society (Twining 1973, pp. 302–40). Only by understanding the nature of relationships in the commercial world can legal decisions demonstrate the kind of "situation sense" needed for law to work well. This general philosophy underlies his proposals, implemented in the Uniform Commercial Code (see especially sec. 1-205), to introduce evidence of usage of trade (that is, customary practice) to clarify the intent of a contract.[26]

Similarly, Fuller's work in the study and practice of labor negotiation (1963, 1971) manifests his commitment to the private ordering of social relations. Active in the labor field almost from the beginning of the New Deal, Fuller saw in the labor legislation of the 1930s evidence that statutory law works best when it facilitates the relations between conflicting parties in the society. In the history of American law, there is no more

---

[26]Kirst (1977) contends that Llewellyn's intended role for usage of trade has not been followed by the courts.

dramatic example of the transformation of human interaction, with the aid of a legally generated framework, to promote the private ordering of relationships.[27]

LEGAL FACILITATION OF NORM FORMATION

In the two examples of commercial law and labor law, legal structures provide opportunities for the use of normative content from the society and for the creation of conditions that generate that content. In a society as heterogeneous as the modern United States, the latter process may prove to be extremely important. Lacking pervasive mores and faced with submores in conflict, how can the law contribute to normative order? The following examples—illustrative rather than comprehensive—are intended to emphasize the diverse ways in which such contributions can be made. While the instances are stated in positive terms, it is clear that law can also create conflict and normative disagreement.

1. *Law can equalize the relative power of groups and require them to seek agreement.* In the current society, does legal intervention which equalizes power tend to facilitate the private ordering of relations? That, at least, is a plausible hypothesis. Labor-management relations provide an excellent example. Initially law supported the superordinate position of management by prohibiting, as criminal conspiracy, an effort to organize with the threat of withdrawal of labor (*Commonwealth v. Pullis*, 1806). That tactic, discontinued after Chief Justice Lemuel Shaw's landmark decision in *Commonwealth v. Hunt* (1842), was followed by the use of the injunction, which came to be regularly employed by the courts to prohibit strikes (cf. Frankfurter and Greene 1930). When these efforts failed to reduce labor unrest, a thoroughly different approach was employed. Under the Norris-LaGuardia Act of 1932, the use of the injunction in labor-management disputes was sharply restricted. Three years later, the Wagner Act (National Labor Relations Act of 1935) established provisions for the conduct of representation elections and laid the foundation for collective bargaining between management and the elected union. In effect, this procedure equalized the power relations between the two parties.

The success of this arrangement in reducing labor violence is widely accepted.[28] The outcome appears to have been accomplished by providing each side with an opportunity, within a new framework, to optimize its own interests. It thus facilitated the kind of reciprocity which—in theory, at least—affords a basis for continuing peaceable exchange between parties who had earlier been in conflict. In these circumstances, two kinds of norms seem to have developed—substantive and procedural. Substantively, each of the parties was free to adhere to its own ideas of the proper wages, working conditions, and fringe benefits. It seems fairly clear that there continue to be differences between management and labor on such questions as what constitutes a "fair day's pay for a fair day's work," even though both sides might agree on that verbal formulation.

Closer study than I have seen or done is needed to determine whether an evolution has occurred between labor and management in the acceptance of common standards of

[27] Fuller's focus was on the shaping of law to accord with existing relationships. "For a given social context one form of law may be more appropriate than another, and . . . the attempt to force a form of law upon a social environment uncongenial to it may miscarry with dangerous results" (1969a, p. 27).

[28] I have not been able to locate a rigorous time series which establishes this point (but see Richberg 1954, pp. 112–33, for a knowledgeable account of the decline in unrest on the railroads after the passage in 1926 of the Railway Labor Act, precursor to the Wagner Act).

fairness, and, if so, whether this change is attributable to the sudden introduction in the early 1930s of a new regime in labor-management relations. Attitude may not have followed behavior in these matters. It is an empirical question, potentially an important one, for understanding the norm-forming effects of law.

Norm formation is far clearer at the level of procedure. In this process, the National Labor Relations Board (NLRB), using administrative and judicial support, developed the concept of bargaining in good faith and avoiding unfair labor practices (see Cox 1958). The agency and the courts were clearly affected in their judgment on these matters by the norm-forming processes occurring in bilateral negotiation, mediation, and arbitration. The law, as administered by the NLRB, created multiple opportunities for labor-management interaction, generating a wide range of variation in the relations between the parties. From these variations could evolve the patterns of bargaining and practice that minimized conflict between the two sides, or at least their leaders (Atleson 1973). The selective process included the enunciation of boundaries (unfair labor practices) and the evolution of a prescriptive concept of good-faith bargaining—both important procedural norms generally understood and accepted by management, labor, arbitrators, administrators, and the courts. By now, these norms are perhaps widely enough known and accepted in general terms to have been adopted by the society as a whole. (For an imaginative discussion of the extension of these norms to a campus conflict, see Scheingold 1974, pp. 39–45.)

The example of labor-management suggests that law can create a framework to facilitate private ordering of relations between parties. Detailed study of this example and many others must precede generalizations concerning the conditions under which private ordering occurs and the ways in which law can facilitate these processes. The use of law to equalize power relations may have been only one of the conditions that facilitated the development of procedural and—perhaps—substantive norms shared between originally antagonistic groups. It may also be true that common interests in labor peace, and even a shared sense of equity, contributed to the evolution of these norms. These factors might have existed as background conditions making the new laws more acceptable or providing the motive, once law opened the communication channel, that contributed to more peaceful dispute resolution. If so, the labor-management approach will not necessarily apply to other group conflict situations.

One of the important considerations in the case of labor-management relations is the fact of labor solidarity, or group consciousness, which preexisted the labor reforms of the 1930s (see Daugherty and Parrish 1952). This factor contributed not only to labor violence in the earlier period (see Adamic 1960), but also to the political influence reflected in the labor legislation of the 1930s (Richberg 1954, pp. 125–33). When equalizing legislation is passed, it will not necessarily serve an interest unless the interest group is organized to press its claim. (See Scheingold 1974, pp. 131–48; Sorauf 1976; Handler 1978.) Nor do interest-group politics inevitably guarantee the continued effectiveness of group action in a bargaining or litigation context.

It may be the case that litigation distinctively tends to undercut an interest group by placing the initiative in the hands of lawyers who perceive their task as winning the case. A dramatic instance of the erosion of an interest group during litigation is found in the history of the Contract Buyers League (Fitzgerald 1974). A set of individuals with similar interests may not coalesce because of the weakness of the interest vis-à-vis other concerns, its sporadic nature, or the absence of communication among them. Lawyers are less likely to be available to the isolated individual, the one-shot player, than to the repeat player—especially, of course, if there are differences in the capacity to pay (Galanter 1974). Such barriers to group pursuit of an interest may be diminished by the creation of group interaction, as in labor-management bargaining.

Courts are not the only, or necessarily the most favorable, setting for bringing groups representing opposing interests into interactions that can resolve conflict, channel or rechannel behavior, and facilitate the generation of norms. As an alternative type of setting, labor-management negotiation may be a model from which much can be learned.

2. *Law can foster limited agreements between parties whose basic relationship has disintegrated.* The instance of marital breakdown is the classic case. A careful analysis of time-series data indicates that laws prohibiting or permitting divorce have very little relation to the maintenance of family ties (Rheinstein 1972, pp. 277–307; cf. Glendon 1977). The results point clearly to the dominance of societal norms as a product and reflection of the social forces that have undermined lifelong monogamy.

However, law does have the capacity to contribute to private ordering, even as the marriage dissolves. This process has been described in recent work on child custody. (Mnookin 1975; Mnookin and Kornhauser 1979). The relationships arranged in situations of marital breakdown may be affected by the legal rules and by the expectations of the parties as to what will happen when the rules are applied. The parties are "bargaining in the shadow of the law," using as chips a knowledge of what they may expect if they go to court (Mnookin and Kornhauser 1979). One possible pattern, the norm-centered model, is of particular interest, since the bargaining is governed directly by the legal-norm structure (see Eisenberg 1976).

Thus, if a husband believes he can obtain a binding agreement for visitation rights, he may be prepared to give primary custody to the wife. If such an agreement were subject to invalidation by the court, as proposed (Goldstein, Freud, and Solnit 1979), the husband's willingness to accord the wife primary custody might be diminished (Mnookin and Kornhauser 1979, pp. 968–69). Despite the resounding rejection of this position by the proposers (Goldstein et al. 1979, pp. 185–86), the issue remains an open question, which could benefit from empirical research when jurisdictions adopt the invalidation proposal.

Although Mnookin's work is not directed toward reinforcing the marriage bond, it illustrates ways in which law can affect the process of norm formation. As the parties bargain to settle their postmarital relationships, the legal process may affect the nature of the outcome. In an earlier era, divorce requiring a showing of fault contributed to the open bitterness between the parties. Current research suggests that no-fault divorce has lessened the display of hostility, although the issue is still in doubt as to the destructive effects—as opposed to the cathartic ones—of such open hostility on the range of participants. A careful study in California points to the conclusion that no-fault divorce diminishes overt hostility as well (Weitzman and Dixon 1980).

With the relaxation of fault as a condition for divorce, there is evidence of a growing tendency to treat marital breakdown as an occasion for negotiation to optimize the goals of each partner. Mnookin's analysis suggests that the courts may facilitate the private ordering of relations (1975; Mnookin and Kornhauser 1979). The original position emphasizes the importance of the courts' protecting the stable relationships that emerge, especially as these might affect the child, whose interests may not be adequately represented in the bargain struck between husband and wife (Goldstein, Freud, and Solnit 1979).

The decision as to when and how state intervention is needed depends very much on an analysis of the interactions between the parties, given the nature of their relationship and the objectives they and the society seek to optimize (Fuller 1971). The nature of those interactions as they actually occur must be fully studied to provide a basis on which policies encouraging intervention, abstention, or bargaining can be wisely shaped.

In this example, it should again be noted that the interaction process can generate norms. As divorcing couples struggle with the problem of custody, variations will occur in the conduct of negotiations and in the substantive outcomes. To what extent will these variations contribute to a set of norms as to how these matters should be handled? Will these ideas form into a variety of norms, associated with subgroups in the society, or will a pervasive norm develop? How is this normation process affected by, and responsive to, the economic, demographic, occupational, religious, social, and ideological forces in the society? In what ways can law affect the norm-formation process? What balance can it strike between the facilitation of interaction and the exercise of social control? Does law succeed in accomplishing the jobs of resolving the dispute and channeling or rechanneling the behavior? All these questions and more call for the kind of investigation that can best be carried out by empirical research informed by an understanding of the potential interrelations between law and the normative order.

3. *Law can contribute to norm formation by creating new social entities.* In the above examples, law contributes in various ways to the conduct of interactions; it utilizes entities which, with its earlier support, already exist: a company, a union, a marriage. Law has helped to create these entities through the processes of institutional recognition and support described by J. R. Commons (1924). In addition, the legal process can, for its own purposes, create groups that would not otherwise exist. This situation occurs most clearly when a new law is passed or a new rule is promulgated, setting up a different kind of entity, such as an administrative agency, a port authority, or a regional school district.

A recent example of a law-created entity is the Institutional Review Board (IRB), a group brought into being under rules for the protection of human subjects.[29] The reaction of the academic community—largely one of objection to restraints imposed on the planning and execution of research—expressed a norm on which the researchers substantially agree: autonomy in the planning and execution of research (Katz 1977; Reynolds 1979). Some invoked a broader set of principles, arguing, for example, that the new procedure violated rights protected by the First Amendment (Pool 1980). In the discussion, less attention was paid to the norm-formation potential these regulations created. The IRB typically brought together scholars from a variety of disciplines to deliberate on a case-by-case basis concerning the risk posed to human subjects if a particular research proposal were carried out as planned. These discussions often led to the revision of proposals as a condition for approval; in fact, 30 to 45 percent of all proposals were modified by the IRB (Reynolds 1979, p. 267). Among the most important elements entering these discussions were the magnitude of the risk, the compensating benefit, and

---

[29] See provisions for the Protection of Human Research Subjects in the National Research Act of 1974 (42 U.S.C. 2891). Recent regulations were published in the *Federal Register*, July 27, 1981.

the informed consent of those subject to the risk or those presumed able to consent on their own behalf (Katz 1977, p. 241).

Considerations of this kind derived in part from the statute and in part from the rules promulgated by HEW (now HHS) under the statute. But the application of the rules to particular cases brought about an elaboration of the meaning of the rules similar, in a way, to the process of common-law evolution. Not surprisingly, some variations developed in procedure and substance at different research institutions (Reynolds 1979, p. 261). In the process, norms were produced in each institution as a product of the interactions required by the government. To what extent these emergent norms systematically reflect the local attitudes, activities, personnel, and values is a matter to be investigated. It would be interesting to discover whether local norms differ from one institutional setting to another or whether substantial uniformity is preserved. If there are differences at the local level, on what matters are the differences greatest? How do these differences relate to the preexistent culture and structure of the institution, and to what extent do they penetrate that culture? Does the vesting of this decision-making role in the hands of scholar-teachers—rather than academic administrators or government administrators—facilitate the emergence of standards felt to be more acceptable than they might otherwise be? Has this norm-forming process contributed to the emergence of more general norms among academics regarding the proper measures for protection of human subjects? Has it led to the explicit definition of situations where no such "protection" should even merit consideration if, for example, risk is considered negligible? How do these emergent norms enter into the process by which the Congress, a special commission, and HHS redefine the statute and rules to take into account the emergent ideas of propriety as they emerge from the experience of the IRBs and those affected by it? Are there parallel processes, by which norms reflecting the interests of human research subjects are developed by the subjects themselves or their representatives? Or does the principal source of the opposing interest derive more from the legislators, the press, public opinion, and the courts responding to post-hoc claims of damage?

In the contrast between post-hoc handling of trouble cases—in any of these fora—and preventive measures is found a major difference. Those totally opposed to the IRB often condemn it by invoking the legal principle of opposition to prior constraint (Pool 1980). Those distressed by the danger to human subjects, as revealed in some dramatic examples, protest the absence of effectively enforceable rules. Such opposition might lead to a decision to reject entirely the IRB approach or, alternatively, to compromise the differences. The latter outcome seems reflected in the HHS final rules (Protection of Human Research Subjects, 45 C.F.R. 46, 1981). At all events, for those interested in the process by which law can create new interactions capable of generating norms, the IRB stands as an important example to be researched.

Many other examples of this kind cover a range of phenomena that, when enumerated, sound in other respects utterly incommensurable. I would include on the list of norm-generating entities, created or reinforced by law, such diverse units as draft boards, state endowments for the humanities, the National Conference on Uniform State Laws, professional examination boards, petit juries. An inventory is needed to replace this illustrative list. Research must investigate how such entities generate norms, how these norms interact with the norms of abutting or competing groups, and how the agreements or conflicts between them affect the tasks of dispute resolution. Also, how to channel that research to the institutions of law-government, and how the output from those institutions (such as the law) affects the behavior, attitudes, structure, and process of the norm-generating or private ordering entities (legally created or not) that exist in society.

4. *Law can aggregate the decisions of multiple groups to discern an emergent normative pattern.* In holding capital punishment to be constitutional, the Supreme Court approved a procedure that goes beyond earlier requirements in several ways (*Gregg* v. *Georgia*, 1976). The procedure combines legislative, jury, and judicial roles in a manner to evoke normative citizen judgments to register pervasive patterns if they exist, and to absorb these patterns into law.[30]

In the leading capital-punishment cases (*Furman* v. *Georgia*, 1972, and *Gregg*, 1976), the Supreme Court recognized the significance of public opinion in several ways. The Court agreed that the meaning of "cruel and unusual punishment" is not fixed by its history. Otherwise, that clause would prohibit nothing more than the archaic punishments of the past against which it was originally directed—the rack, the screw, the iron boot, and other penalties designed to inflict intense physical pain. Chief Justice Warren Burger, even though in dissent, expressed the judicial consensus on this point as follows:

> The Eighth Amendment prohibition cannot fairly be limited to those punishments thought excessively cruel and barbarous at the time of adoption of the Eighth Amendment. A punishment is inordinately cruel, in the sense we must deal with it in these cases, chiefly as perceived by the society so characterizing it. The standard of extreme cruelty is not merely descriptive, but necessarily embodies a moral judgment. The standard itself remains the same, but its applicability must change as the basic mores of the society change. [*Furman*, 1972, p. 382]

The justices differed, however, in the method for determining whether the "basic mores of the society" were opposed to capital punishment. Those upholding capital punishment relied on the legislatures to provide the best test of community sentiment. The Court, said the Chief Justice, should overrule legislatures in this area only if there is "unambiguous and compelling evidence of legislative default" (*Furman*, 1972, p. 384)—that is, presumably, a failure of legislatures to register the basic mores.

Between *Furman* and *Gregg*, thirty-five legislatures passed new capital-punishment statutes, providing the majority in *Gregg* with evidence to support their belief that the basic mores were not opposed to the death penalty. Justice Potter Stewart, willing to consider nonlegislative indicators of popular sentiment, found nothing in national public-opinion polls or state referenda (in Massachusetts, Illinois, and California) to counter the inference of public support arising from the new statutes. On this basis, he declared, "American society continues to regard capital punishment as an appropriate and necessary criminal sanction" (*Gregg*, 1976, p. 179). If, in the face of such sentiment, the Court was to declare the death penalty constitutionally impermissible, it would shut off "the ability of the people to express their preference through the normal democratic processes"(*Gregg*, 1976, p. 176).

Justices William Brennan and Thurgood Marshall argued for different criteria. Brennan would have held capital punishment contrary to "the evolving standards of decency that mark the progress of a maturing society," a test for the interpretation of the Eighth

---

[30] For a detailed discussion of the capital punishment cases and their potential for norm formation, see Schwartz (1979).

Amendment enunciated by Chief Justice Earl Warren in *Trop* v. *Dulles* (1958). Capital punishment, Brennan declared, denied one of the most fundamental of those standards of decency—human dignity for all. In his words, "even the vilest criminal remains a human being possessed of common human dignity" (*Furman*, 1972, p. 273). According to Brennan, the Court should give voice to these evolving standards of decency, contributing to the process by which they evolve.

While joining Justice Brennan, Justice Marshall, in a separate concurrence, proposed a different basis for interpreting public sentiment. He would rely on the opinion not of a cross section of the population, but on what the public would think if it was fully informed about the nature and consequences of the death penalty (*Furman*, 1972, pp. 361–62 and n. 145). In *Gregg*, Marshall was able to cite experimental findings by social scientists (Sarat and Vidmar 1976) suggesting that a majority would oppose capital punishment if informed of its ineffectiveness (relative to life imprisonment) in deterring crime (*Gregg*, 1976, p. 232).

In upholding the Georgia statute in *Gregg*, the Court provided several interesting ways in which public sentiment could be expressed regarding the death penalty. It left to the legislatures the power to determine, within limits, whether to authorize capital punishment. It retained, as under the Constitution it must, a role for the jury in determining guilt. Under the Georgia statute, the role of the jury was enhanced in the requirement that it must specifically determine whether aggravating circumstances existed, that it must recommend the death penalty, and that it could do so only if it found aggravating circumstances.

In this use of the jury, the legal process relies on a sample of the population—supposedly, and increasingly, cross-sectional—to express community sentiment on appropriate punishment. In the traditional use of the jury, this function was concatenated and confused with the factual determination of guilt. In developing a bifurcated procedure, where the judgment of guilt is separated from the determination of sentence, the law has helped to disentangle the questions of guilt and punishment. In introducing the concept of aggravating circumstances, the Georgia statute provided a legislative framework within which individual juries can appraise severity, taking into consideration the particular crime and defendant.

The importance of relating severity of the offense to the magnitude of punishment has, of course, long been recognized in criminal statutes. In murder cases, it has typically been handled by allowing the jury to decide on the degree of murder or lesser includable offenses. But this procedure did not permit the jury explicitly to express its sentiments regarding the details of the offense and the characteristics of the offender, as the jury is specifically asked to do under the Georgia statute. In a procedure that requests explicit findings regarding aggravating circumstances, the jury is asked to consider characteristics of the offense and the offender that lead it to recommend the punishment of death.

If these jury findings and recommendations lead to a death sentence, the case, under *Gregg*, must be reviewed by the Georgia Supreme Court. This review is required to determine whether or not the sentence resulted from passion or prejudice and whether or not the evidence supported the specific finding of aggravating circumstances. In addition, the Court is called upon to decide whether or not, in the particular case, the death sentence is "excessive or disproportionate to the penalty imposed in similar cases." This last provision, properly administered, carries the potential of recording the existence of mores, if they exist, or promoting their formation. Operating under this procedure, the

Georgia Court (*Coley*, 1974) and the United States Supreme Court (*Coker*, 1977) found the death penalty for rape too infrequently applied in similar circumstances to meet the test of comparability. From one point of view, these rulings suggest the existence of widespread opinion that rape does not warrant capital punishment. Nevertheless, such a sentiment was not reflected in the penal statutes of Georgia. It is more likely that such a sentiment was inchoate, latent, and beneath the level of general consciousness. It was evoked by a legal procedure which, putting the question in specific form to specific panels of jurors, repeatedly elicited a recommendation against the death penalty in rape cases. The aggregate review, mandated by the statute, calls upon the Court, in effect, to declare the mores. Such a procedure may not only make explicit what has been inchoate; it might also stimulate the evolution of mores by providing a realistic means by which they can emerge.

CONCLUSIONS

The observations of this essay, while presenting a point of view, do not provide a comprehensive conceptual or theoretical formulation. At most, the essay is intended to bring into focus the tasks that emerge from the present perspective.

It states that norms affect law to some extent in varying ways and that law can affect norms not so much by imposing them, as by recognizing their existence and by setting up circumstances to generate them.

A comprehensive formulation developed from this perspective must fulfill several requirements. First, it must specify the processes by which norms affect law. Second, it must specify the processes by which law affects norms. Third, it must locate the circumstances under which each of these effects occur. Finally, it must approach the dynamics by which each process affects the other.

In pursuing these ends, a broad qualitative strategy will probably be valuable. Institutional studies of norm-law interaction over time are likely to be particularly helpful. Some examples of these are already available. For example, a study of workers' compensation law traces the way in which changing legal doctrine of employer liability reflected the cross pressures of employer and employee interests (Friedman and Ladinsky 1967). As doctrinal complexity (such as respondeat superior, fellow-servant rule, and nondelegable functions) multiplied, results became less predictable and less satisfactory to employers as well as employees. The move toward workers' compensation appears to have reflected a combination of economic interest and normative change. When that occurred, however, a new process developed that set a frame within which new norms arose (for a detailed study of the process in California, see Nonet 1969). In that context, it was possible to address several relevant questions concerning the nature of the new norms; how they were affected by group interaction in the new setting; and how they entered social, political, economic, and legal processes.

Institutional historical studies of this kind are important for understanding interactions between laws and norms. They afford an opportunity to search for dynamic processes. In addition, they offer insight into the variations in such interactions in different institutional settings. Institutions may vary widely in their vulnerability to legal impact and in their capacity to affect the law. Labor-management relations seem to have been radically altered by the legal changes of the 1930s, for example, while family changes seem to respond primarily to extra-legal forces. There is a need to establish the nature of such institutional differences and to explore the determinants behind them.

While institutional studies of this kind are crucial, they should be accompanied by research aimed at individual dynamics and societal processes. These interactions are undoubtedly affected by general ideas of morality and legality. Work concerning individual moral development (Piaget 1932; Tapp and Levine 1977) and equity judgments (Adams 1970; Walster et al. 1976) provide valuable knowledge concerning the dispositions carried into institutional settings by their participants. Social psychologists' interaction studies further illuminate the processes of norm formation as affected by group pressures (Asch 1958; Mintz 1958; Sherif 1961) and the resolution of conflicting interests (Kelley and Thibaut 1978). Such processes may have a significant effect—at least indirectly—in determining experience with the law and a propensity to rely on, or to reject, law as legitimate authority or as a functional device for securing the general good.

Work by economists and political scientists at the societal level adds another dimension of importance to the interaction of law and norms. Policy choices reached by voting and by the aggregation of individual preferences transformed on the assumption of transitivity reach contradictory conclusions as a general matter (Arrow 1977). Studies of the Prisoners' Dilemma regularly reach the conclusion that, in most circumstances, collective interests cannot be optimized. Neither of these analyses assumes the existence of motives other than self-interest. In the Prisoners' Dilemma, a solution of value to both parties can, however, be secured if the prisoners have a continuing relationship of trust (Axelrod and Hamilton 1981). Arrow also suggests that the contradictory results of his analysis could be altered in the presence of a compelling normative tradition.

In the end, we are left with a large question. To what extent can the legal system, supported by societal norms, constitute the open society's way of achieving group goals, the equivalent of a traditional belief system and the alternative to totalitarianism for modern societies? That may be the very question on which the future of U.S. society depends. If so, there is every reason to explore it in greater depth, to learn how law-norm interaction works when it does, and to explain how—the society willing—it could be made to work better.

Cases Cited

Cleveland v. United States, 329 U.S. 14 (1946).
Coker v. Georgia, 433 U.S. 584 (1977).
Coley v. State, 204 S.E.2d 612, 231 Ga. 829 (1974).
Commonwealth v. Hunt, 45 Mass. 111 (4 Met. 1842).
Commonwealth v. Pullis, the Cordwainer's Case, Philadelphia Mayor's Court (1806).
Doe v. Commonwealth's Attorney for the City of Richmond, 425 U.S. 901 (1976).
Furman v. Georgia, 408 U.S. 238 (1972).
Gregg v. Georgia, 428 U.S. 153 (1976).
Griswold v. Connecticut, 381 U.S. 479 (1965).
Industrial Union Department, AFL-CIO v. American Petroleum Institute, 448 U.S. 607 (1980).
Locke v. Rose, 514 F.2d 570 (6th Cir. 1975).
Locke v. State, 501 S.W.2d 826 (Tenn. App. 1973).
Marbury v. Madison, 1 Cranch 137, 2 L. Ed. 60 (1803).
National Labor Relations Board v. Jones & Laughlin Steel Corp., 301 U.S. 1(1937).
Penn Central Transportation Co. v. New York City, 438 U.S. 104 (1978).
Pennsylvania Coal Co. v. Manon, 260 U.S. 393 (1922).
People v. Onofré, 51 N.Y.2d 476 (1980) cert. den., U.S. Supreme Court, 451 U.S. 987 (1981).

Plessy v. Ferguson, 163 U.S. 537 (1896).
Roe v. Wade, 410 U.S. 113 (1973).
Rose v. Locke, 423 U.S. 428 (1975).
Trop v. Dulles, 356 U.S. 86 (1958).
Vermont Yankee Nuclear Power v. NRDC, 435 U.S. 519 (1978).
West Virginia Board of Education v. Barrette, 319 U.S. 624 (1943).
Williams v. New York, 337 U.S. 241 (1949).

Bibliography

Abel, Richard L.
     1973   "Law Books and Books About Law." *Stanford Law Review* 26:175–228.
Adamic, Louis
     1960   *Dynamite: The Story of Class Violence in America.* Rev. ed. Gloucester, Mass.: P.
              Smith.
Adams, Stuart
     1970   "The PICO Project." Reprinted in *The Sociology of Punishment,* edited by Norman
              Johnston, Leonard Savitz, and Marvin E. Wolfgang. New York: Wiley.
Administrative Conference of the United States
     1981   *Public Participation in Administrative Hearings.* Code of Federal Regulations. Title I,
              Chapter III, §305.71-6.
Arrow, Kenneth Joseph
     1977   *Social Choice and Individual Values.* 2nd ed. New York: Wiley.
Asch, S. E.
     1958   "Effects of Group Pressure Upon the Modification and Distortion of Judgments." In
              Readings in Social Psychology, 3rd ed., edited by Eleanor E. Maccoby, Theodore M.
              Newcomb, and Eugene L. Hartley. New York: Holt.
Atleson, James B.
     1973   "Work Group Behavior and Wildcat Strikes—Causes and Functions of Civil Dis-
              obedience." *Ohio State Law Journal* 34:750–816.
Austin, John
     1970   *The Province of Jurisprudence Determined.* New York: Burt Franklin.
     [1861]
Axelrod, Robert, and Hamilton, William D.
     1981   "The Evolution of Cooperation." *Science* 211:1390–96.
Bechtler, Thomas W.
     1978   *Law in a Social Context.* Netherlands: Kluwer.
Bentham, Jeremy
     1948   *An Introduction to the Principles of Morals and Legislation.* New York: Harper.
     [1789]
Berger, Raoul
     1977   *Government by Judiciary: The Transformation of the Fourteenth Amendment.* Cam-
              bridge, Mass.: Harvard University Press.
Bickel, Alexander M.
     1962   *The Least Dangerous Branch: The Supreme Court at the Bar of Politics.* Indianapolis:
              Bobbs-Merrill.
Black, Donald
     1972   "The Boundaries of Legal Sociology." *Yale Law Journal* 81:1086–1100.
     1976   *The Behavior of Law.* New York: Academic Press.

Bohannan, Paul J.
  1957   *Justice and Judgment Among the Tiv.* London: Oxford University Press.
  1973   "The Differing Realms of the Law." Reprinted in *The Social Organization of Law,*
  [1965]   edited by Donald Black and Maureen Mileski. New York: Seminar Press.
Boyer, B. B.
  1981   "Funding Public Participation in Agency Proceedings: The Federal Trade Commis-
            sion Experience." *Georgetown Law Review* 70:51–172.
Burke, Edmund
  1960   *The Philosophy of Edmund Burke: A Selection from His Speeches and Writing.* Ann
            Arbor: University of Michigan Press.
Cardozo, Benjamin N.
  1921   *The Nature of the Judicial Process.* New Haven: Yale University Press.
  1947   *Selected Writings,* edited by Margaret E. Hall. New York: Fallon.
Chayes, Abram
  1976   "The Role of the Judge in Public Law Litigation." *Harvard Law Review* 89:1281–
            1316.
Cole, John W.
  1980   "Law and the Accommodating Process." Paper presented at the Symposium on Law
            and Moral Order, Arizona State University, October.
Commons, John R.
  1957   *Legal Foundations of Capitalism.* Madison: University of Wisconsin Press.
  [1924]
Cook, Walter Wheeler
  1927   "Scientific Method and the Law." *American Bar Association Journal* 13:303–8.
Cox, Archibald
  1958   "The Legal Nature of Collective Bargaining Agreements." *Michigan Law Review*
            57:1–36.
Daugherty, Carroll, and Parrish, John B.
  1952   *The Labor Problems of American Society.* Boston: Houghton Mifflin.
Davis, Kenneth Culp
  1969   *Discretionary Justice: A Preliminary Inquiry.* Baton Rouge: Louisiana State Univer-
            sity Press.
  1972   *Administrative Law Text.* St. Paul, Minn.: West, pp. 26–52.
Dicey, Albert V.
  1914   *Lectures on the Relation Between Law and Public Opinion in England in the Nineteenth
            Century.* 2nd ed. London: Macmillan.
Dienes, Thomas C.
  1972   *Law, Politics and Birth Control.* Urbana: University of Illinois Press.
Durkheim, Emile
  1951   *Suicide.* Glencoe, Ill.: Free Press.
  [1897]
  1964   *The Division of Labor in Society.* New York: Free Press.
  [1893]
Dworkin, Ronald
  1977   *Taking Rights Seriously.* Cambridge, Mass.: Harvard University Press.
Ehrlich, Eugen
  1936   *Fundamental Principles of the Sociology of Law.* Cambridge, Mass.: Harvard Univer-
            sity Press.
Eisenberg, Melvin A.
  1976   "Private Ordering Through Negotiation: Dispute Settlement and Rule Making."
            Harvard Law Review 89:637–81.

Ely, John Hart
    1980   *Democracy and Distrust: A Theory of Judicial Review.* Cambridge, Mass.: Harvard University Press

Feeley, Malcolm M.
    1976   "The Concept of Laws in Social Science: A Critique and Notes on an Expanded View." *Law & Society Review* 10:497–523.

Fifoot, Cecil H.S.
    1936   *Lord Mansfield.* Oxford: Clarendon Press.

Fitzgerald, Jeffrey
    1974   "The Contract Buyers League and the Courts: A Case Study of Poverty Litigation." *Law & Society Review* 9:165–94.

Fordham Law Review
    1976   "Note: Constitutionality of Sodomy Statutes." *Fordham Law Review* 45:553–75.

Frank, Jerome
    1949   *Courts on Trial: Myth and Reality in American Justice.* Princeton, N.J.: Princeton University Press.

Frankfurter, Felix, and Greene, Nathan
    1930   *The Labor Injunction.* New York: Macmillan.

Friedman, Lawrence M.
    1965   *Contract Law in America: A Social and Economic Case Study.* Madison: University of Wisconsin Press.

    1975   *The Legal System: A Social Science Perspective.* New York: Russell Sage Foundation.

Friedman, Lawrence M., and Ladinsky, Jack
    1967   "Social Change and the Law of Industrial Accidents." *Columbia Law Review* 67:50–82.

Friedman, Lawrence M., and Macaulay, Stewart
    1977   *Law and the Behavioral Sciences.* 2nd ed. Indianapolis: Bobbs-Merrill.

Friedrich, Carl J.
    1941   *Constitutional Government and Democracy.* Boston: Little, Brown.

Fuller, Lon L.
    1958   "Positivism and Fidelity to Law: A Reply to Professor Hart." *Harvard Law Review* 71:630–72.

    1963   "Collective Bargaining and the Arbitrator." *Wisconsin Law Review* 1963:3–46.

    1968a   *Anatomy of the Law.* New York: Praeger.

    1968b   "Some Observations on the Course in Contracts." *Journal of Legal Education* 20:482–84.

    1969a   "Human Interaction and the Law." *American Journal of Jurisprudence* 14:1–36.

    1969b   *The Morality of Law.* 2nd ed. New Haven: Yale University Press.

    1969c   "Two Principles of Human Association." *Nomos* XI (Voluntary Association), J. Pennock & J. Chapman, eds., pp. 3–23.

    1971   "Mediation—Its Forms and Functions." *Southern California Law Review* 44:305–39.

    1975   "Law as an Instrument of Social Control and Law as a Facilitation of Human Interaction." *Brigham Young University Law Review* 1975:89–96.

Fuller, Lon L., and Eisenberg, Melvin A.
    1972   *Basic Contract Law.* St. Paul, Minn.: West.

Galanter, Marc
    1974   "Why the 'Haves' Come Out Ahead." *Law & Society Review* 9:95–160.

    1977   "Notes on the Future of Social Research in Law." In *Law and the Behavioral Sciences,* 2nd ed., edited by Lawrence M. Friedman and Stewart Macaulay. Indianapolis: Bobbs-Merrill.

1981   "Justice in Many Rooms: Courts, Private Ordering, and Indigenous Law." *Journal of Legal Pluralism* 19:1–47. (Reprint no. 9, Disputes Processing Research Program series, University of Wisconsin, Madison.)

Gellhorn, Walter; Byse, Clark; and Strauss, Peter L.
1979   *Administrative Law: Cases and Comments.* Mineola, N. Y.: Foundation Press.

Glendon, Mary Ann
1977   *State, Law and Family: Family Law in Transition in the United States and Western Europe.* Amsterdam and New York: North-Holland.

Goldstein, Joseph; Freud, Anna; and Solnit, Albert J.
1979   *Beyond the Best Interests of the Child.* New ed. with annotations. New York: Free Press.

Gray, John Chipman
1921   *The Nature and Sources of the Law.* New York: Macmillan.
[1909]

Griffiths, John M.
1979   "The Legal Integration of Minority Groups Set in the Context of Legal Pluralism." Unpublished manuscript.

Grinspoon, Lester
1977   *Marijuana Reconsidered.* 2nd ed. Cambridge, Mass.: Harvard University Press.

Handler, Joel F.
1978   *Social Movements and the Legal System: A Theory of Law and Social Change.* New York: Academic Press.

Hart, H. L. A.
1958   "Positivism and the Separation of Law and Morals." *Harvard Law Review* 71:593–629.

1961   *The Concept of Law.* London: Oxford University Press.

Holmes, Oliver Wendell, Jr.
1881   *The Common Law.* Cambridge, Mass.: Harvard University Press.

1899   "Law in Science and Science in Law." *Harvard Law Review* 12:443–63.

1921   "The Path of the Law." In *Collected Legal Papers.* New York: Harcourt, Brace.

Hurst, James Willard
1960   *Law and Social Process in United States History.* Ann Arbor: University of Michigan Press.

1964   *Law and Economic Growth: The Legal History of the Lumber Industry in Wisconsin, 1836–1915.* Cambridge, Mass.: Belknap Press.

Hyman, Herbert, and Sheatsley, Paul B.
1964   "Attitudes Toward Desegregation." *Scientific American* 211:16–23.

Jaffe, Louis L.
1954   "Effective Limits of the Administration Process: A Reevaluation." *Harvard Law Review* 67:1105–35.

1973   "The Illusion of the Ideal Administration." *Harvard Law Review* 86:1183–99.

Kadish, Sanford
1967   "The Crisis of Overcriminalization." *Annals of the American Academy of Political and Social Science* 374:157.

Kaplan, John
1976   *Marijuana: The New Prohibition.* New York: World.

Katz, Jay
1977   *Informed Consent to Human Experimentation.* Cambridge, Mass.: Ballinger.

Kelley, Harold H., and Thibaut, John W.
1978   *Interpersonal Relations: A Theory of Interdependence.* New York: Wiley.

Kirst, Roger W.
    1977   "Usage of Trade and Course of Dealing: Subversion of the UCC Theory." *University of Illinois Law Forum* 1977:811–71.
LaFave, Wayne R., and Scott, Austin W., Jr.
    1972   *Handbook on Criminal Law*. St. Paul, Minn.: West.
Lempert, Richard
    1972   "Norm-Making in Social Exchange: A Contract Law Model." *Law & Society Review* 7:1–32.
Lindblom, Charles E., and Cohen, David K.
    1979   *Usable Knowledge: Social Science and Social Problem Solving*. New Haven: Yale University Press.
Lipsky, Michael
    1980   *Street Level Bureaucracy: Dilemmas of the Individual in Public Services*. New York: Russell Sage Foundation.
Llewellyn, Karl N.
    1930   *Cases and Materials in the Law of Sales*. Chicago: Callaghan.
    1940   "The Normative, the Legal, and the Law-Jobs: The Problem of Juristic Method." *Yale Law Journal* 49:1355.
    1951   *The Bramble Bush: On Our Law and Its Study*. Dobbs Ferry, N.Y.: Oceana.
    1960   *The Common Law Tradition: Deciding Appeals*. Boston: Little, Brown.
Llewellyn, Karl N., and Hoebel, E. Adamson
    1941   *The Cheyenne Way*. Norman: University of Oklahoma Press, pt. 3.
Lowi, Theodore
    1979   *The End of Liberalism: The Second Republic of the United States*. New York: Norton.
Macaulay, Stewart
    1963   "Non-contractual Relations in Business: A Preliminary Study." *American Sociological Review* 28:55–67.
Maine, Sir Henry Sumner
    1917   *Ancient Law*. London: Dent.
    [1861]
Manning, Bayless
    1977   "Hyperlexis—Our National Disease." *Northwestern Law Review* 71:767–82.
Mintz, Alexander
    1958   "Nonadaptive Group Behavior." In *Readings in Social Psychology*, 3rd ed., edited by Eleanor E. Maccoby, Theodore M. Newcomb, and Eugene L. Hartley. New York: Holt.
Mnookin, Robert H.
    1975   "Child-Custody Adjudication: Judicial Functions in the Face of Indeterminacy." *Law and Contemporary Problems* 39:226–93.
Mnookin, Robert H., and Kornhauser, Lewis
    1979   "Bargaining in the Shadow of the Law: The Case of Divorce." *Yale Law Journal* 88:950–97.
Moore, Sally Falk
    1973   "Law and Social Change: The Semi-autonomous Social Field as an Appropriate Subject of Study." *Law & Society Review* 7:719–46.
Nader, Laura, and Seber, David
    1980   "Power as Process in Regulation." In *The Sociology of Law*, edited by William M. Evan. New York: Free Press.
National Center for Family Planning Services
    1971   "Family Planning, Contraception, and Voluntary Sterilization: An Analysis of Laws and Policies in the United States, Each State and Jurisdiction."

Nonet, Philippe
    1969   *Administrative Justice: Advocacy and Change in Government Agencies.* New York: Russell Sage Foundation.

Packer, Herbert
    1968   *The Limits of the Criminal Sanction.* Stanford, Calif.: Stanford University Press.

Piaget, Jean
    1932   *The Moral Judgment of the Child.* London: Kegan, Paul, Trench, Trubner.

Pitt, William
    1968   Quoted from a speech on the Excise Bill. In *Familiar Quotations,* by John Bartlett.
    [n.d.]   Toronto: Little, Brown.

Pool, Ithiel de Sola
    1980   "The New Censorship of Social Research." *Public Interest* 59:57–66.

Potter, David Morris
    1968   *People of Plenty: Economic Abundance and the American Character.* Chicago: University of Chicago Press.

Pound, Roscoe
    1942   *Social Control Through Law.* New Haven: Yale University Press.
    1943   "A Survey of Social Interests." *Harvard Law Review* 57:1–39.

Prosser, William L.
    1971   *Handbook of the Law of Torts.* St. Paul, Minn.: West.

Redfield, Robert
    1941   *The Folk Culture of the Yucatan.* Chicago: University of Chicago Press.

Reynolds, Paul Davidson
    1979   *Ethical Dilemmas in Social Science Research.* San Francisco: Jossey Bass.

Rheinstein, Max
    1972   *Marriage Stability, Divorce and the Law.* Chicago: University of Chicago Press.

Richberg, Donald
    1954   *My Hero: The Indiscreet Memoirs of an Eventful but Unheroic Life.* New York: Putnam.

Ross, H. Laurence
    1980   *Settled out of Court: The Social Process of Insurance Claims Adjustment.* New York: Aldine.

Sarat, Austin, and Vidmar, Neil
    1976   "Public Opinion, the Death Penalty and the Eighth Amendment: Testing the Marshall Hypothesis." *Wisconsin Law Review* 1976:171–206.

Scheingold, Stuart A.
    1974   *The Politics of Rights: Lawyers, Public Policy, and Political Change.* New Haven: Yale University Press.

Schlesinger, Arthur M., Jr.
    1957   *The Crisis of the Old Order 1919–1933.* Cambridge, Mass.: Riverside Press.

Schwartz, Richard D.
    1974   "Legal Evolution and the Durkheim Hypothesis: A Reply to Professor Baxi." *Law & Society Review* 8:653–68.
    1979   "The Supreme Court and Capital Punishment: A Quest for Balance Between Legal and Societal Morality." *Law & Policy Quarterly* 1:285–355.
    1980   "Mores and the Law: Taking Sumner Seriously." *Behavior Science Research* 15:159–80.

Schwartz, Richard D., and Cartwright, Bliss C.
    1973   "The Invocation of Legal Norms: An Empirical Investigation of Durkheim and Weber." *American Sociological Review* 38:340–54.

Schwartz, Richard D., and Miller, James C.
    1964   "Legal Evolution and Societal Complexity." *American Journal of Sociology* 70:159–69.
Selznick, Philip
    1969   *Law, Society and Industrial Justice.* New York: Russell Sage Foundation.
Sherif, Muzafer; Harvey, O. J.; White, B. J.; Hood, W. R.; and Sherif, Carolyn W.
    1961   *Intergroup Conflict and Cooperation: The Robbers Cave Experiment.* Norman: University of Oklahoma Book Exchange.
Sibley, Elbridge
    1953   "Some Demographic Clues to Stratification." In *Class, Statutes and Power,* edited by Reinhard Bendix and Seymour Martin Lipset. Glencoe, Ill.: Free Press.
Sinclair, Andrew
    1962   *Prohibition: Era of Excess.* Boston: Little, Brown.
Sorauf, Frank J.
    1976   *The Wall of Separation: The Constitutional Politics of Church and State.* Princeton, N.J.: Princeton University Press.
Stewart, Richard B.
    1975   "The Reformation of American Administrative Law." *Harvard Law Review* 88:1667–1813.
Stouffer, Samuel A.
    1955   *Communism, Conformity and Civil Liberties.* Garden City, N.Y.: Doubleday.
Sumner, William Graham
    1906   *Folkways: A Study of the Sociological Importance of Usages, Manners, Customs, and Morals.* Boston: Ginn.
Tapp, June Louin, and Levine, Felice J., eds.
    1977   *Law, Justice, and the Individual in Society: Psychological and Legal Issues.* New York: Holt, Rinehart & Winston.
Tocqueville, Alexis de
    1899   *Democracy in America.* Rev. ed. New York: Colonial Press.
    [1835]
Turner, Ralph E.
    1941   *The Great Cultural Traditions.* Vols. 1 and 2. New York: McGraw-Hill.
Twining, William
    1973   *Karl Llewellyn and the Realist Movement.* London: Weidenfeld and Nicolson.
Unger, Roberto
    1976   *Law in Modern Society: Toward a Criticism of Social Theory.* New York: Free Press.
U.S. Commission on Civil Rights
    1975   *Constitutional Aspects of the Right to Limit Childbearing.* Washington, D.C.: U.S. Government Printing Office.
U.S. Congress, Senate, Committee on the Judiciary
    1979   *Regulatory Reform: Hearings Before the Senate Committee on the Judiciary.* 96th Cong., Serial No. 96-28.
Waldo, Dwight
    1946   *The Administrative State: The Political Theory of Public Administration.* New York: Ronald Press.
Wallace, Anthony F. C.
    1956   "Revitalization Movements." *American Anthropologist* 58:264–81.
Walster, Elaine; Berscheid, Ellen; and Walster, G. William
    1976   "New Directions in Equity Research." In *Equity Theory: Toward a General Theory of Social Interaction,* edited by L. Berkowitz and E. Walster. Advances in Experimental Social Psychology, vol. 9. New York: Academic Press.

Wardle, Lynn D.
    1980   "The 'Gap' Between Law and Moral Order: An Examination of the Legitimacy of
                the Supreme Court Abortion Decision." *Brigham Young University Law Review*
                1980:811–35.
Warren, Samuel B., and Brandeis, Louis D.
    1890   "The Right to Privacy." *Harvard Law Review* 4:193–250.
Weber, Max
    1954   *Law in Economy and Society.* Edited by Max Rheinstein. Cambridge, Mass.: Har-
    [1922]   vard University Press.
    1963   *The Sociology of Religion.* Boston: Beacon Press.
    [1922]
Weitzman, Lenore J., and Dixon, Ruth B.
    1980   "The Alimony Myth: Does No-Fault Divorce Make a Difference?" *Family Law
                Quarterly* 14:141–85.

~ 3 ~

LAW AND THE ECONOMIC ORDER

Edmund W. Kitch
University of Virginia

INTRODUCTION

The subject of law and the economic order can be divided into two questions. First, what is the impact of law upon economic activity? And second, what is the impact of the economy upon the law? The answers to these questions are interrelated, for the ways in which the law affects economic activity will in turn affect the ways in which economic activity creates needs for legal arrangements of one type or another. Indeed, the separation of society into two separate parts—a legal part and an economic part—can be viewed as only a crude metaphor (Cain and Hunt 1979, p. 49). It is convenient for discussion and compatible with the disciplinary divisions of the social sciences, but like any metaphor, it can both illuminate and confuse.

These two questions have been studied separately. The question of the impact of laws upon the economy has been the domain of the applied political economists, from the seminal work of Adam Smith to a contemporary derivative: law and economics. This tradition has tended to see law as a barrier to the operation of the economy, disturbing the operation of the efficient "invisible hand" of the market through harmful regulations (for example, Schultz 1980, p. 649).

The question of the impact of the economy upon law has been the domain of the

NOTE: The assistance of Ruth Booher and the comments, suggestions, and criticisms of Ann Bowler, Lea Brilmayer, Ronald Coase, Jerry Goldman, Ruth Hein, Neil Komesar, Leon Lipson, Henry Monaghan, Richard Posner, Erich Schanze, and the Committee on Law and Social Science of the Social Science Research Council are gratefully acknowledged. Research for this essay was completed in 1981.

sociological-historical tradition inspired by the work of Karl Marx. This tradition has asserted the dominant role of the needs of production in shaping the legal system (Sumner 1979, pp. 246–53; Cain and Hunt 1979, pp. 48–51), a position derived from materialistic determinism.

These two traditions have had little to do with each other. The argument of this essay is that fruitful work will ensue if the political economists take seriously the question implicitly posed by the sociohistorians—does the economy shape the legal system, and if so, how?—and if the sociohistorians apply the methodologies of the political economists—particularly modern analytic price theory—to the interrelationships that have traditionally concerned them. This argument is principally supported by the example of recent works that have—although diverse in origin, style, and conclusion—raised provocative issues about the dynamic of legal development. A central question posed by these works—do formal legal systems embody that set of arrangements which optimizes the productive potential of the social group in which they arise, or, as often put, is law efficient?—provides a unifying theme for the diverse topics surveyed here.[1]

A major theme of the sociohistorical tradition is the importance of ideology and class interest in explaining the structure of legal systems (Sumner 1979, pp. 253–77).[2] Although ideology and class are in the longer run seen as themselves the product of economic forces, in the short run they operate to entrench the position of the dominant class. The rise of a contractarian legal system and its supportive ideology in the nineteenth century—a development greeted with considerable distaste within this tradition[3]—is explained by the needs of the capitalist mode of production and is viewed as a transitory phenomenon. Contractarian ideology is now being displaced by egalitarianism as the capitalist mode of production fades. Thus, a contemporary writer seeking to explain a perceived decline in contractarian legal principles observes that contractarian notions of free choice

> bring with them, inescapably, many other consequences which are today less admired, especially in England. They bring, in particular, the recognition that some individuals are better equipped to exercise free choice than others. . . . And the greater is the scope for the exercise of free choice, the stronger is the tendency for these original inequalities to perpetuate themselves by maintaining or even increasing inequalities. [Atiyah 1979, p. 6]

---

[1] The term "efficiency" is used in this essay as a synonym for that set or sets of arrangements which maximize the productive potential of the social group. Efficiency is not used in a technical, Pareto sense for two reasons: first, to avoid any implication that such a legal system represents a unique equilibrium; and second, to avoid the tautology that since efficiency simply reflects the utilities of the participants in the system, any legal system that arises is likely to be efficient because the participants accept it.

[2] Thus, a leading contemporary example of work in this tradition explains changes in American law during the first half of the nineteenth century as the result of changing conceptions of law. "By 1820 the legal landscape in America bore only the faintest resemblance to what existed forty years earlier. While the words were often the same, the structure of thought had dramatically changed and with it the theory of law. Law was no longer conceived of as an external set of principles expressed in custom and derived from natural law. Nor was it regarded primarily as a body of rules designed to achieve justice only in the individual case. Instead judges came to think of the common law as equally responsible with legislation for governing society and promoting socially desirable conduct. The emphasis on law as an instrument of policy encouraged innovation and allowed judges to formulate legal doctrine with the self-conscious goal of bringing about social change" (Horwitz 1977, p. 30).

[3] As displayed vividly in a work like that of Polanyi (1944) which, written from the perspective of the cataclysmic impact of World War II on Central Europe, argued that nineteenth-century free-market reforms represented a tragic departure from historic and fundamental human arrangements.

The applied political economists have come at the matter from an entirely different direction. It has always seemed obvious to them that the economic needs of mankind were unsatisfied, and that if it were possible to change human institutions to increase the supply of economic goods, then—at least upon careful reflection without regard to narrow and parochial interests—all would join in seeking their reform. To these writers all too much of the law has appeared as a barrier to economic production (for example, Schultz 1980, p. 649). In part because of the strongly reformist spirit of their writings, they have put heavy emphasis on those features of the law that stand in the way of freedom of trade, most notably tariffs. This tradition attacked the mercantilist regulation of eighteenth-century England, inspired important English legal reforms in the nineteenth century, and in the twentieth has been troubled by the advance of contemporary economic and welfare regulation. In recent years these writers have attempted to deploy their principal methodological instrument—self-interest analysis—to account for this perversity in the law (see, for example, Peltzman 1976; Downs 1957).

Given that throughout human history they have been the dominant preoccupation of most people, it would be odd to find that social systems were not responsive to the needs for food and shelter. In modern economics property and contract are seen as having a central role in the operation of efficient markets. But it does not necessarily follow that the productive legal system in all times and all places assigns a central role to property and contract as we know them today. Modern property and contract institutions require a high level of human capital in the form of literacy and organizational and productive know-how that has not been available to all societies. Primitive people can engage in exchange transactions, but a productive contractarian regime requires long-term contract relations of the most subtle and complex sort.

The outcome of extended inquiry along the lines suggested here might be the knowledge necessary to develop a more sophisticated and satisfying theory of the dynamic of legal systems than presently exists. Explanations of differences in legal systems in terms of ideology or power leave unanswered the question of why the particular ideology or form of power. It would be much more satisfactory to link the structure of particular legal systems to exogenous factors such as the conditions of production in the society.[4]

This essay reviews literature relevant to these issues. The universe of potentially relevant literature is vast—much of social science. The discussion will inevitably reflect my perspective. I am trained as a lawyer and industrial-organization economist and have worked within the law-and-economics tradition since 1965. The inquiry is beset with difficulties—the lack of sufficient competence located in a single discipline, the inability to measure the theoretically relevant parameters, the ambiguities of the issues, and the subtlety of the institutions. My principal strategy is to entice by example, to demonstrate that the questions are important and interesting, and to show that the literature gives promise of further advances in understanding.

This essay is divided into three major sections. First is a discussion from a general-equilibrium perspective of what a legal system shaped by the needs of production might look like. It is followed by a summary of the principal findings of the modern American

---

[4]The case for such an approach has been elegantly made (Stigler and Becker 1977). For example, it would be much more satisfactory to link the shifts in the conception of law described by Morton J. Horwitz and discussed above in note 2 to the conditions in the states after the separation of American law from its English origins. The frontier economic conditions of the states may have made maintenance of other than part-time legislatures and an informal and instrumental jurisprudence too costly.

literature in law and economics and consideration of its findings on property, contract, tort, antitrust, and economic regulation in relation to the hypothesis that a legal system is shaped by the needs of economic production. The essay closes with a discussion of the implications of a productivity perspective for the role and structure of government.

GENERAL EQUILIBRIUM: CONCEPTS AND PROBLEMS
Identifying a Legal System Shaped by the Needs of Production

Transaction Costs   In "The Problem of Social Cost" (1960), Ronald Coase introduced a helpful analytic device: examining the effects of law in a world where transaction costs are zero. Transaction costs include all those costs that must be incurred in order to efficiently arrange property and contract affairs among individuals—the costs of acquiring information about the facts, the likelihood of future events, and the tasks and talents of others; the costs of devising suitable and reliable arrangements; the costs of enforcing or responding to breaches of those arrangements when they occur; and so on. The assumption that such costs are zero is both powerful and unrealistic. If true, it would both eliminate the need for a legal system and render irrelevant any existing legal system. All actors in a society of zero transaction costs will have the incentive to agree on arrangements that maximize their joint welfare and will be able to do so costlessly. Any existing legal system becomes irrelevant because in a system that has rules reducing the total welfare, the members will simply make costless, offsetting arrangements that improve welfare. Problems generated in the real world by strategic bargaining maneuvers and enforcement costs are eliminated by the assumption of zero transaction costs.

The insight is suggestive for analysis of the role of law in a society; a legal system will promote production to the extent that it optimizes transaction costs.[5] It is easy to understand some legal rules in this framework. For instance, rules that permit parties to make binding contracts between themselves lower the costs of certain kinds of cooperation. If production is a dominant purpose of legal systems, we would expect them to have a strong tendency to permit contracts to be made and carried out, even in a centrally planned economy. The insight is less tractable when applied to a legal system as a whole because it does not predict the specific rules of any legal system. From such a perspective, the legal system does not simply facilitate agreements—it is the agreement. Just as the theory does not predict the content of contracts between merchants, it does not predict the content of an "optimum-transaction-cost" legal system.

The problem is further complicated if the element of time is introduced. One way to cut the cost of transacting is to make bargains that last over a longer period of time, allowing the costs of transacting to be amortized over more units of activity. If the society operates under constant conditions, the legal system that facilitates production at time one will do so at time two as well. However, if the system experiences such exogenous shocks as changes in technology, climate, or population, productive arrangements at time one will not necessarily be productive at time two. This difficulty could be alleviated

---

[5] Which is different from just reducing transaction costs. In many important situations, the law exploits transaction costs to further productivity. For instance, secrecy exists because of transaction costs and enables firms to gain from investments in information (Kitch 1981a). To use an analogy between friction and transaction costs, an engineer designs machinery employing means to reduce friction (lubrication) and exploiting friction to achieve his ends (braking).

by making the arrangements at time one less costly to change. If change affects wealth distribution, provisions that lower the cost of change will increase resources dedicated to attempts to change the system, shorten the average life of the agreements, and thus raise the costs of transacting for the society per unit of activity. If the costs of making changes in the agreement are raised, the agreement in operation at time two may appear to impede production. However, if its effects through all time periods are taken into account, its effects on production are positive.

The process of change is further complicated by the consideration that the existence of a set of laws at time one will generate responses in the society adaptive to those laws. Those responses will represent investments and will be costly to change. Thus, at time two, with changed circumstances, the optimum legal arrangements will in part be determined by the existing customs and practices generated by the legal system in time one. For instance, if a society accords the vote only to citizens who own property, it will create an incentive for property owners to invest in acquiring the information necessary to make use of the right to vote, and those who anticipate special gains from voting will expend resources to acquire the necessary property. If it is then proposed to void the property qualification for voting, an obvious problem arises from the circumstance that the previously disenfranchised voters have had no incentive to invest in learning how to use the right. Put another way, the path that a society follows to reach a particular position will have a significant impact on what facilitates production in that time period. Two societies otherwise facing the same present conditions may have very different sets of rules, both efficient. The history of any set of legal rules can be expected to have an important role in both determining and explaining their present state.

Private Arrangements   The extent to which private arrangements can offset the impediments to production of legal rules is relevant to the need of the legal system to adapt to changed circumstances. In the theoretical world of no transaction costs, private arrangements are very powerful. No theory exists to predict the relative importance of these forces in the real world. An understanding of the private responses to a rule of law is essential in order to be able to analyze its effects on the society. For instance, it is important in order to understand the effects of such laws as rent control, workmen's compensation, or mandatory minimum-warranty standards that the affected parties— already in a close and continuing bargaining relationship—will readjust their relationship in light of the law. It is plausible that the ability of private arrangements to offset the effects of legal rules increases as the relevant time period increases—that effective transaction costs tend to fall as the time during which a rule is in effect increases. As time passes, the members of a society will learn from experience about the rule's effects. Assuming the absence of exogenous shocks during the period, and assuming that such learning is cumulative and retained and will include learning about the identity of the affected persons and their tastes and abilities, it should be progressively less expensive to make the private arrangements necessary to eliminate the inefficiency. A legal rule can be consistent with the needs of production simply because offsetting private arrangements have made it so.

To take a simple example, the long and well-established rule of contracts that makes unenforceable liquidated damages (damages computed under clauses specifying the damages recoverable in the event of breach) not reasonably related to the actual damages incurred appears to constrain economically productive arrangements (Goetz and Scott

1977; Kronman and Posner 1979, pp. 194–207). If the two contracting parties believed that their welfare would be enhanced by such a clause, there seems no reason to think that they are not correct. There are quite plausible situations in which a contracting party would want to make himself subject to high liquidated damages. For instance, if firms wish to enter an industry where a reputation for reliability is an important asset and entrants have no such reputation, then entrants might compete by offering to be liable for high and easily computed damages if they do not live up to reliability standards—their willingness to do so serving as a substitute for their competitors' reputation. The rule would seem to be an anomaly if law promotes efficiency. Yet if other available devices can serve the purpose equally well, the rule will have no adverse effects on production, and there will be no pressure to change it. Thus, if the entrant can compete by offering lower prices to purchase the needed reputation, funding the purchase through the capital markets, and if this alternative offers entrants an equally effective way to establish themselves, the rule constraining a liquidated-damages clause will not lead to inefficiency in this hypothetical situation. (It may, however, affect the position of particular parties relative to others if there are different comparative advantages in using one strategy as opposed to another.)

It is not known how strong these private forces are, how quickly and at what cost they can overcome impediments to production imposed by law, or how costly it is for a legal system to effectively suppress them—although some systems clearly try from time to time. There is much to suggest that the private forces are very strong, particularly when the legal environment supports the notion of individual freedom of action.

In fact, private arrangements can operate so completely that it becomes difficult to separate the legal system from private custom, as illustrated in the classic example of fine and recovery, where a legal system that constrained the sale of land was converted by the tacit cooperation of conveyancers, advocates, and judges to a system whereby land could be bought and sold through a fraudulent procedure that coopted the officials of the legal system (Plucknett 1956). A contemporary example is furnished by the ownership of radio frequencies under the Federal Communications Act, which provides that station frequencies shall be assigned for three-year periods, to be reallocated at the end of the period "in the public interest" (47 U.S.C. §307). A system that assigns the right to use a frequency for a limited period, subject to an open, public-interest reassignment, impairs the incentive of the holder of the frequency to maximize its long-run value by making investments whose payout period exceeds the three-year period. In fact, however, the broadcast industry and the Federal Communications Commission treat the station licenses as vested property rights; licenses are almost always renewed and they are freely bought and sold. The sophistries and evasions required to square this result with the statute make for interesting logic and occasionally confuse the courts, but the fact is that the result approximates more what efficiency requires than what the legislature contemplated.

In defiance of federal law, settlers in western Wisconsin established a self-enforced system of claims on federal land closed to homesteading (Hurst 1956, pp. 3–6). The story of the legal system generated by the California gold rush to make possible the efficient mining of gold—a system of law built by trespassers on federal land with no standing de jure—is equally dramatic and perhaps better known (McCurdy 1976). It has been suggested that in the more highly regulated and centralized modern environment, the failure of the massive worker-to-retiree transfer in Social Security funding to have a measurable effect on the rate of saving in society may be due to offsetting transfers within families (Barro 1978).[6]

The "Invisible Hand" and Efficient Legal Rules

When they attempt to identify efficient behavior in the marketplace, economists are guided by theory. If the market is competitive and no important externalities are present, behavior of market participants that is persistent over time can be considered efficient; the self-interest of the independent competitive actors generates an "invisible hand" to produce efficient behavior. No such automatic inferences can be made about the institutions that produce law; their differences from the model of the competitive market are too great. Yet it is not implausible that the importance of wealth to every individual in society generates strong and persistent forces toward legal systems that maximize production. It is illuminating to speculate on how those forces might or do operate.

Assuming that such forces are at work in an important way, it nevertheless seems reasonable to assume that there would be substantial time lags in the process by which legal systems tend toward production-enhancing arrangements. It is known in macroeconomics that substantial departures from equilibrium of significant duration can occur. An increase in the supply of money would have no effect in a world of constant equilibrium; if the government doubles the money supply, prices—stated in units of the currency—should also double. This is not, in fact, what happens. Individuals continue to act as if the value of money had not changed while their personal wealth had doubled. They increase their spending, and the economy is stimulated. Only later do they discover that they have been fooled and begin to make adjustments. The system oscillates around an equilibrium, with undershoots and overshoots. Free of shocks, it will tend to settle along a stable trend; but it may take many years for a shock to be fully evened out (Mayer 1968; Hamburger 1974).

The process by which a legal system reaches equilibrium is surely much more complex. It is not at all inconceivable that the periods of the adjustment process frequently exceed the periods between significant exogenous shocks and that legal systems are seldom in equilibrium. This circumstance does not destroy the utility of such a theory as a way of thinking about what is going on in a legal system, but it makes more ambiguous the interpretation of data about a legal system at a particular point in time.

Economists have not inquired into these processes as they have examined the phenomenon of growth. The area of growth could be viewed as one that should be a central preoccupation of the discipline of economics. But the subject of how a society increases its wealth has not yielded easily to inquiry, and work in the field seldom rises above the descriptive except to attain the metaphorical (Rostow 1960). Large elements of the differences in growth rates among different societies are rather easily explained. those who apply a larger stock of capital and effort grow more rapidly—an insight not much more profound than the exhortation to be rich or work harder. While multiple-regression studies of gross national product changes show that such factors account for a large part of the differences in growth rates (Kuznets 1971; Denison 1967), the residual presents an

---

[6]The opposite effect was reported by Martin Feldstein (1974), whose computer program was found to be in error (Leimer and Lesnoy 1980). Feldstein (1980) has reasserted the correctness of his conclusion but not of his program.

unexplained phenomenon. The most popular explanation points to differences in technology, although that explanation leads immediately to the question of the cause of the
differences in technology. One hypothesis that seems worth investigating holds differences in legal systems responsible for differences in growth rates. Legal differences may
not have figured importantly in economists' research because the legal systems of the
countries that have been the principal objects of investigation have not had differences
that are significant for these purposes. To examine a group of advanced countries such as
the Organization for Economic Cooperation and Development group may be simply to
look at a set of countries with similar and economically successful legal systems.

Much informal theory attributes a significant role to legal systems as determinants of
growth rates. The slower rates of socialist countries are often explained by their form of
legal organization, which greatly attenuates the scope of personal property rights and
freedom of contract. The suggestion that underdeveloped countries need strong governments in order to grow is based on the notion that such governments can promulgate
stable legal systems that will encourage the growth of a society. The political settlement
of 1688 in England laid the foundation for the economic dynamism of the eighteenth and
nineteenth centuries (Atiyah 1979). The common-sense notion claims that in order for a
society to turn its energies to growth, it is important to resolve the question of who holds
what rights. On the other hand, a strong government runs the risk that the promulgated
rules will be inappropriate to the situation. To the extent that a government's powers
increase, the nonproductive use of resources dedicated to influencing the uses to which
those powers are put within the society can also be expected to increase.

It has been argued that the relationship between the degree of stability of a legal system
and growth is inverse (Olson 1977). Countries such as the United Kingdom and the
United States, which have long-established, stable governments and legal systems, now
grow at slower rates than do countries that have experienced severe disruptions, such as
West Germany, France, and Italy. It is clear that "too much" law can be bad if it
suppresses the ability of people to rearrange their affairs in ways that benefit them. In the
modern nation-states, it is regulation of various types that has tended to be labeled "too
much law," and these highly sophisticated and intrusive legal regimes require a well-
established legal structure. The observation may simply mean that these countries are
presently out of equilibrium and that it is reasonable to expect that, in these respects,
their legal systems will be reformed.

One plausible strategy for testing the hypothesis that the needs of production shape law
is to examine the records relating to lawmakers' perceptions of their intention. If they
appear to be unconcerned with production, that disclosure would furnish a basis for
rejecting the hypothesis. In fact, materials in the Anglo-American legal culture do not
show a dominant, explicit interest in production; legislators are concerned with electoral
politics and judges with precedent, consistency, and fairness. But such a strategy is
simplistic, because the productivity-enhancing legal system is not necessarily one in
which lawmakers pay dominant attention to the current needs of production. In order for
a legal system to have any impact on a society, it must have stability over time, so that its
rules can become known and people can respond to them. A legal system that focuses
explicitly on current production will have a rhetorical structure of short-run expediency,
making it impossible for members of society to rely on those rules in planning their
actions.

A rhetoric based on precedent and on consistency with that precedent may provide the stability necessary for planning. Similarly, the most productivity-enhancing sources of law may be not explicit preoccupation with production but the implicit rules already present in society's customs, language, and moral codes. To the extent that legal rules can rely on these preexisting cultural phenomena, the problem of social adjustments to the legal rules is simplified and the cost of giving credence and force to the legal rule is reduced.

A central problem with the "invisible hand" hypothesis for a theory of legal development is that there is no mechanism by which the actors can receive information that will signal the path to efficient law. In the price-theory model, market actors whose costs are above the market or who erroneously price their products learn of their error from the market itself; their competitors flourish while they do not. But in the lawmaking process, the law is a monopoly system, and the assignment of property rights is about as imperfect as can be imagined. The judge or legislator receives no benefit equal to the social gain from good law.

Members of the bar tend to become exasperated with the "invisible hand" inquiry into the dynamics of legal reform. American legal professionals have been taught to think of themselves as social artisans, and their enthusiasm for the task obscures its difficulty. How can a legal planner identify a good law without the opportunity to experiment with different approaches? In a market, firms can experiment with various strategies, and successful firms will find their strategies copied by others. The optimum strategy is not discovered through the kind of abstract analysis and interest balancing that is the stock-in-trade of the American lawyer. Nor is it found by formal logical deduction from past practices. Given all the good will in the world, how is a judge or legislator to recognize the optimum path? And if there is no mechanism to guide the jurist, how does the evolution of the legal system amount to more than a set of random events?

Identifiable "Invisible Hand" Mechanisms

The Role of Honor   In spite of the weakness of the responses in the legal system, compared to the highly visible and easily understood reactive processes at work in markets, there are important forces that push toward efficiency. The first of these is similar to the motivation for advances in basic research. The understanding obtained from successful basic research enriches all of mankind, yet the researcher has no property that enables him to capture the benefit. In both cases, in an apparent effort to compensate for the lack of monetary reward, societies confer honors upon the discoverer and the just lawgiver. The successful entrepreneur, who may bestow equally valuable benefits on society, is left with his wealth—which more nearly approximates the value of the benefits he has conferred; the great scientist or lawgiver is accorded a kind of cultural deification. The key figures in the planning and promotion of the American Revolution were well aware of the rewards that would attend a successful venture in lawmaking (Smith 1776, bk. 4, chap. 7, pt. 3). Certain features of lawmaking procedures allow these processes to operate. Even in systems that give high rhetorical service to the concept of citizen governance, law is usually made not through anonymous mass referenda but by identifiable individuals who can receive either public praise or public scorn for the results of their work.

Competing Jurisdictions   Another force that creates incentives for good law is competition among jurisdictions (Tiebout 1956). The importance of this force depends greatly on the geographic scope of a legal system. Accidents of geography and war will produce authorities controlling populations of various size and area, and over time the units of the most successful size will be copied. The need to preserve these competitive forces may explain why well-intentioned calls for world government receive so little favorable response. A federal constitutional system consciously tries to preserve autonomous lawmaking centers within a larger union—an effort that requires complex jurisdictional allocations over subject matter. Even within formally unitary systems, such as the American states, there is a tendency to create different levels of government with different areas of lawmaking competence. The optimum requires a balance between the gains from economies of scale in lawmaking and administration and the losses caused by the reduction in competition between lawmaking authorities and the greater difficulties for a unified system in adapting to nuances of local conditions.

Changes in transportation and communications technology have increased the amount of effective competition in lawmaking, as they have in many product markets. In the United States, even with its elaborate constitutional commitment to federalism (Kitch 1981b), there has been a trend to expansion of the powers of the national government for the last century. It is not clear whether this development represents a shift toward more monopolistic lawmaking or is simply a response to changed technology. For instance, in the 1970s the federal government asserted paramount authority in the areas of environmental regulation and worker safety. It is possible that this development simply reflects technological changes that have increased the geographic range of environmental and safety problems and the strength of international competition, so that the national level has become the desirable level for the exercise of these powers.

From the point of view of someone who disagrees with the outcomes produced by a competitive lawmaking process, the process itself is bad. Thus, advocates of a national minimum wage argued for their cause precisely on the ground that competition among the states would result in a minimum that was too low; proponents of a national incorporation law have argued that competition among the states has resulted in a Delaware incorporation statute that is too permissive (Cary 1974). But the necessary inquiry is more subtle and difficult. It is necessary to determine whether the gains and losses from a particular policy are borne by the authority that makes it or whether the costs of the policy are imposed on others. It is easy to see that a jurisdiction that allows highly noxious polluters to operate on its downwind side does not bear the consequences of its own policy, just as a corrupt sheriff who permits organized criminal gangs to establish bases in his territory to prepare for raids on adjacent jurisdictions is not confronted with the results of their depredations. But where the arrangements being regulated are consensual, it is hard to see how the competition is defective. A state that permits workers to accept contracts for unreasonably low wages faces all the consequences and benefits of that contract. Corporations organized under the laws of Delaware must induce investors to invest voluntarily—an activity in which Delaware corporations have had some small success (Winter 1977, 1978; Dodd and Leftwich 1980).

On a day-to-day basis, emigration and the movement of capital serve as competitive checks on law. Because it is more costly for people to change legal systems than to change toothpaste, the process of adaptation will operate more slowly. But it requires only shifts at the margins to release significant forces. Not everyone must move—only a few people have to change location. Just as I can eschew comparison shopping, secure in the knowledge that the propensity of others to comparison shop will provide some limit on the price I will pay, so, too, can I accept a legal system, secure in the knowledge that the propensity of others to avoid the effects of socially harmful rules will provide some limit to the tyranny I may face.

The people and capital that will respond to differences in legal systems will be those with the lowest costs of doing so. Thus, within a society, the competition may cause emigration most readily among ethnic minorities with cultural ties elsewhere or among groups with foreign-language skills. Their responses generate information and pressures that benefit everyone in the society. To the extent that other factors increase the size of the group with a low marginal cost of emigrating or shifting investment, these pressures are increased. Thus, the opening of the New World to settlement, which increased the advantages of emigration, may explain, in part, the extensive reforms of Western European legal systems during the nineteenth century.

Governments that are losing in this form of competition can resort to restrictions on emigration and capital movements to blunt its effects, just as producers in a failing product market may turn to market price supports or import restrictions. These policies will have their own costs, and in the long run they may be completely ineffective. They can raise the cost of emigration and capital movement, but if at the same time they strengthen the reasons for flight, they will not stop the movement they are designed to affect. In a federal system the national government can limit the use of these strategies by lower-level lawmaking authorities. National citizenship combined with prohibitions on restrictions of the movement of goods, capital, and people will leave those authorities unable to escape this competition (but see Kitch 1981b). A federal system can also employ devices for the effective receivership and reorganization of lawmaking bodies that have failed.

Competing Private Arrangements   If parties who are involved in a long-term, ongoing relationship find that the rules and procedures of the official courts and agencies are not responsive to their needs, they can create their own system of dispute resolution. The most obvious example is contractual provision for arbitration in commercial contracts. Choice-of-law clauses (clauses that state what jurisdiction's law is applicable to the contract) can serve a similar purpose, preventing the application of unfavored law. The ability of parties in many situations to leave the court system puts pressure on the courts to offer rules and procedures acceptable to those parties (Landes and Posner 1979, pp. 242–53).

A government can free-ride on these processes of private lawmaking and adjudication taking place within the society. For instance, if merchants are permitted to arrange delivery terms among themselves and one set of delivery terms proves so convenient and workable that it is widely adopted, in situations where delivery terms have not been agreed upon, the courts can read into the contract the terms that other contracting parties seem so strongly to prefer. Or, to take another example, if private deliberative bodies in corporations, lodges, or political parties develop a common set of procedural rules that seem to facilitate their work, it will make good sense for public bodies to model their rules on these. Again, if a strong social custom develops that people under the age of 18 should not marry because of the harm such marriages can cause to the children and others, the law may refuse to sanction marriage below that age or impose special conditions on it. Thus, even within a unitary legal system, matters can be arranged to allow competition in the development of rules that can then be incorporated into the legal system.

In this process, procedural protections that raise the cost of law enforcement—such as guarantees of trials, provision of counsel, and restrictions on the ability of the government to acquire information—play an important part. These protections raise the cost of enforcing law and make it difficult to impose a legal regime not accepted by significant portions of the population. Because the procedural protections limit the ability of government to impose laws at variance with the needs of the people, the tendency of a legal system to reflect and absorb the practices and customs of the population should be greater in a legal system that recognizes procedural limits on its enforcement strategies.

Courts and Legislatures   There is a large literature comparing lawmaking by courts with lawmaking by legislatures. Frederick Hayek speculated that courts may have an inherent tendency to make law that is superior to that of legislatures (Hayek 1973, pp. 94–144).

If courts make law by following past rules, while legislatures make law by announcing new rules, courts would appear more supportive of productivity than legislatures. Law that follows past rules will have the advantage of compatibility with the private responses generated by those same past rules. If legislatures specialize in situations requiring change, they are working in areas that necessarily will appear less supportive of production than do more stable areas. If, for instance, new technologies of transportation and communication require changes in past rules, new rules will require that parties make adjustments for which they are by definition unprepared.

But such appearances are deceptive. For instance, if modern technology has greatly increased the range of environmental externalities, it may enhance production to create whole new regulatory bodies to deal with them. Adjustment to such new regulatory authorities will necessarily be costly. Viewed from the present, it will be clear that the new legislative initiative is more costly than the old arrangements—a perception that may become confused with the conclusion that making the change is more costly than not making it. Then, too, legislation that has been in place over a long period of time tends to lose its distinctly legislative quality and begins to merge with the larger body of the law; it is easy to lose sight of the fact that the English common law was the product of a long process of interaction between judges and Parliament. In any effort to assess the comparative effects of judges and legislatures, it is necessary to remember past legislative initiatives that have succeeded as well as those that have failed.

Some features of judicial organization more nearly approximate the firm, as that term is used in economics, than the organization of legislatures does. Efforts to model these properties to generate incentives for efficient law seem only to emphasize the missing properties. One model has generated efficient law by the assumption that parties will not relitigate efficient precedents, thus preserving them intact (Rubin 1977; Priest 1977), while another has generated it by assuming that parties will relitigate efficient precedents, thus strengthening them (Goodman 1978). A court can be viewed as a firm composed of judges, and even in an era where courts do not charge fees based on their ability to attract business, a judge's importance and prestige will be enhanced by the fact that the court attracts business of large moment. The importance of this rather trivial incentive will be increased if the arrangements are such that all other aspects of a judge's compensation—his salary, tenure, and amenities—are invariable. Then, at the margin, prestige, honor, or a sense of importance will be the only incentives operating on judges. Judges tend to enjoy long terms, giving them an incentive to invest in enhancing the position of their court.

Concurrent, competing jurisdiction has been a recurrent feature of judicial systems. The common law was the product of judges who faced competition from numerous feudal jurisdictions and from other courts of the king. In the United States, diversity jurisdiction has enabled the federal courts to compete with the state courts across a wide range of law (Landes and Posner 1980). In many cases, geographic competition will also operate. Because plaintiffs seem to have a disproportionate role in the selection of the forum, this competition should generate law biased toward plaintiffs, for instance, rules that lead to larger personal-injury verdicts. However, such procedural devices as the jury and various devices available to defendants to resist jurisdiction—including withdrawing from business in the jurisdiction altogether—may check this tendency.

In the area of lawmaking, judges, unlike legislators, are not able to force acceptance of their rule. The rule made into law by the vote of a coalition of legislators is law and they control the enforcement resources needed to make it meaningful. A rule announced by a court will be law only if it is accepted and followed by other judges. An appellate court has the formal authority to impose new rules on lower-court judges, but it will find that the exercise of its authority contains the seeds of its own destruction. If the appellate court implicitly asserts that it is an appropriate judicial role to depart from precedent and make new rules, it legitimizes the use of this role by all judges. The lower-court judges are then released to find that changed circumstances or more complete arguments justify disregarding the appellate precedent as "badly reasoned," "obsolete," or "unintended." In recent years, the Court of Appeals for the District of Columbia—inspired by the judicial activism of its nominal reviewer, the United States Supreme Court—has become quite skilled at according such treatment to the precedents of its reviewing Court (see, for example, Scalia 1978, pp. 359–75). Consequently, judicial rules must face repeated tests of acceptability in a context where parties adversely and directly affected by them have incentives to produce evidence and argument designed to persuade the court that the rule is misconceived or misguided.

Judges can extend the same treatment to the work of legislatures. And since it is legislatures who provide for courts and give them a role in the enforcement and interpretation of statutes, why should not the legislature get the credit for the work of the courts (Landes and Posner 1975b)? The law is sufficiently complex and interrelated that the task of making significant changes and integrating them with the larger body of the law cannot be completed in a single effort. Surely legislators understand that their product has rough edges and that the courts will smooth them out.

Legislators face the discipline of the vote. Will not legislators who make unsuccessful laws be voted out of office and will not this sanction create as much incentive for legislatures as is created for the judiciary by other forces?[7] It is easy enough to point out that the right to vote for a legislature is so weakly related to the legislative product that few if any citizens have sufficient interest to invest in understanding the issues. After all, the probability that any one vote will affect the outcome is infinitesimal. But the checks

---

[7] Many American judges are elected, and it is widely assumed that the performance of elected judges is inferior to that of unelected judges. This proposition has not been systematically demonstrated.

operating on judges are also weak, and it is not clear which of these incentive structures is weaker.

THE PROPERTIES OF A LEGAL SYSTEM THAT ENHANCE PRODUCTION

The Role of Property and Contract in a Nonmodern Legal System

From a modernist perspective, the keys to a legal system that enhances production are property and contract. If the resources of value to a society are allocated to individuals who, through a system of contract, are given the power to rearrange their rights, markets will operate and the society can move toward an optimum. Much historical work has been done to show that this is, in fact, how legal systems facilitate economic development. James Willard Hurst's classic case study of the lumber industry in Wisconsin documents this process in great detail. The only available way to ship the lumber from any area, for instance, was to float it downstream. The law reinforced a customary system of marks to enable the "shipper" to reclaim his logs at the end of the run (Hurst 1964, pp. 378–80). Similar processes have been documented in primitive legal systems; as a resource becomes scarce, a system of property rights will evolve for the resource (Demsetz 1967).

This vision of property and contract is incomplete. Where large gains result from the uniformity of transactions, those transactions will become uniform and will be incorporated into the legal rules. Just as gains from uniformity will cause form contracts to dominate particular markets in spite of the theoretical power of the parties to vary the form, so, too, will gains from uniformity cause "form" arrangements to become the law. Uniformity makes it unnecessary to retransact the relationships in each time period and saves work in the interpretation and enforcement of relationships so widely followed and understood in the society.

In a society where few variations occur in the economic conditions faced by its members and where the resources available for administration of a legal system are limited, the comparative advantages of form legal relationships may be great. Because the economic conditions of those affected by the rules are virtually identical, identical rules are appropriate to all. Uniform rules reduce the resources that must be used to transmit information about the rules, detect their violation, and enforce them. These advantages would be particularly great prior to the advent of literacy, when the applicable rules and cases can be retained only in the memories of men as stories and moral codes. In such a society the introduction of great diversity in legal relationships could well overwhelm the ability of the legal system to function.

The importance of these effects has been closely documented in the important work of Donald N. McCloskey (1975, 1976; extended and further developed in Dahlman 1980). He studied the phenomenon of the English commons—a system whereby a village cooperatively controlled the public land, known as the commons, under a complex system of regulation and allocation of usage rights.[8] No single member of the peasant

---

[8]The economic regulation of the Middle Ages as it is commonly described in the texts is a challenge, too, under the approach of this article—full of restrictions on the movement of capital, goods, and labor. One wonders how much of the regulation represented an unenforced ideal that did not affect daily economic life. If the current scholarship on the commons proves to be sound, the next challenge will be to understand other economic institutions of the medieval period in welfare terms.

village was allowed to alter the rights the system conferred upon him, although the system did not preclude further transactions relating to the allocated rights. From the fifteenth to the nineteenth centuries, the system slowly eroded, until it was eliminated altogether. In the eyes of the nineteenth-century reformers who advocated the enclosure movement, the commons system was inefficient, the product of superstitious custom. To romantics, it has represented a more cooperative and socially cohesive past. But either view leaves puzzles McCloskey has undertaken to explain. Why did the system display such strong uniformity over such a wide area for such a long period of time? Why did it disappear at different times in different places? His explanation is that, in fact, the system enhanced production under the conditions faced by medieval peasant society; when those conditions changed, the system was changed. The feature most strongly criticized as wasteful—the scattering of an owner's plots—he explains as a response to the need of the members of the village to diversify their crop risk across the different kinds of land in the village. This method of risk diversification arose in a situation where broader markets (which would have enabled saving and purchasing from the inventories of others) did not exist. The commons system disappeared as these markets reached the villages, generally moving inland from areas with access to water transportation. Because the system had enhanced the security of each member of the village and had proven itself across many generations, it became highly standardized—the law of the village. Yet it never precluded retransacting, and McCloskey's strongest evidence for his thesis is that such retransacting did not occur.

More recently, Richard Posner (1980a, 1980b, 1981) has employed an insight of this type to provide an explanation for the highly standardized customs of primitive men in relation to their possessions—customs that seem to mandate donative, nonmaximizing behavior and thus thwart a market economy. Analyzed as a social system, these customs can be seen as devices to reduce individual risk in a world where markets were meager, storage was costly, and survival was problematic.

In the modern setting, those contracts, such as marriage agreements, whose enforcement is largely outside the courts, continue to exhibit a highly standardized character.

The modern system of contracts and property, which is considered so basic to productivity, may, in fact, be a phenomenon closely related to the increased specialization of economic function so evident in industrial society. The gains from specialization generate the resources necessary to support specialized institutions and their accompanying professions at the same time that specialization creates a need for legal arrangements tailored to the needs of each area of economic activity.

The Modern American System

Property and Contract   The modernist, contractarian perspective on the law of property and contracts has generated a considerable and rapidly growing literature on the specific rules of these areas of law. In general, it has been found that the rules of modern Anglo-American property-and-contract law enhance production. A system of property rights presents two central problems.

The first concerns assignment of rights in resources that have no ownership. This question tends to arise when some resource that has previously had no scarcity value for the society acquires value. Examples are the shortage of free land under the pressure of population growth, the scarcity of books to copy in response to printing technology, and the recent positive value of oil deposit on the continental shelf. The most general solution is to confer ownership upon the first possessor. Sometimes a residual-ownership theory finds ownership in the sovereign, but in such instances, the sovereign often uses a first-possession rule to allocate the resource. An alternative allows for competitive bidding, which tends to be used where a rule of first possession would result in severe dissipation of resources in the competition to be first (Barzel 1968).

The second central problem concerns keeping the definitions of property-right boundaries simple enough to prevent the costs of administering the system from becoming excessive. Rules as diverse as the rule against perpetuities (restricting the creation of remote and complex interests in property) and the rule that ideas are not patentable (because it would be impossible to define the limits of a right in an idea) can be understood in this framework.

A principal concern of contracts is to provide easily administered rules for the formation of binding agreements. Such rules as the statute of frauds and the requirement of seals—now abandoned—can be understood in this light. Another concern of contract law is to develop approaches for interpreting agreements in ways that will be responsive to the expectations of the parties.

The Role of the Firm   Analysis of the economic effects of the property-and-contract system usually proceeds on the assumption that the property is owned, or the contracts are made, by individuals. It is an observable fact, however, that property rights are frequently held by firms—partnerships, for-profit or nonprofit corporations, and trusts. This circumstance has on occasion been used to criticize price theory,[9] on the ground that, while individuals may maximize something of human relevance, corporations and other abstract entities clearly cannot. Corporations may, for instance, have no incentive to maximize the value of their property but may have every incentive to maximize the income of their present executives.

The question of which unit to take as the maximizing one is important chiefly because it may affect the power of the theory to explain the economic activity being analyzed. For example, work on the economics of the family has found that much behavior can be explained if the family, not the individual, is treated as the maximizing unit (Becker 1981). The individual has been used as the unit of analysis to explain the emergence of firms, which will emerge to hold and contract in relation to property when that form of the holding optimizes the position of the individuals involved (Coase 1937).

Two schools of thought now dominate economic analysis of corporations. In one, all corporations are efficient because of the discipline that factor markets will place upon the constituents of the entity. If stockholders receive less than a competitive rate of return, the entity will have to pay more for future investment. If management is overcompensated, competition for the management positions will drive the compensation down to the competitive level (Fama 1980). To the other school, the complexities of the corporate structures and positive transaction costs mean that particular arrangements will maximize the value of the firm. These arrangements are thus made a significant area of

---

[9] Price theory is a body of analysis developed by Alfred Marshall and others and now taught as the core subject of economics which derives predictions about the behavior of markets from the assumption that actors in markets act in their own self-interest. The criticism has been that if firms do not maximize their self-interest and are important factors in markets, then markets will not operate as price theory predicts.

study. The details of optimum arrangements will vary, depending upon monitoring technology, the nature of the inputs to the firms, its activities, and the nature of the output (Jensen and Meckling 1976).[10]

The labor union represents a kind of firm closely related in its activities to the business corporation. Traditional analysis has viewed the labor union as a cartel, organizing the labor input to the firm (Posner 1977, p. 527). It has thus been seen as wasteful by raising input costs and restricting the movement of additional labor into areas where it could be used. This theory makes it difficult to explain the seeming stability of modern unions, since the employer could always gain by the expenditure of resources to escape the cartel. Recent work has explored an alternative theory—that labor unions are firms specializing in the provision of high-quality labor inputs (Brown and Medoff 1978; Freeman and Medoff 1979).

Work on property and contracts and the role of the firm has been important for these fields within the professional schools. But it has not presented the theoretical difficulties and challenges involved in work on torts, antitrust, and regulation, where the appropriate approach is far more problematic and difficult.

Torts   The importance of torts rules was highlighted in research on social cost, because it is precisely in the situation where transacting is costly that the rules matter (Coase 1960, pp. 2–6).

In order to illustrate why the legal rules do not matter where transacting costs are low, Ronald Coase took as an example the rights and duties of adjoining landowners. Assuming that one raises livestock and one raises grain, who has the obligation to fence? Coase pointed out that, from an efficiency point of view, it will make no difference where the obligation is placed, as long as the parties can negotiate with each other at negligible cost. Either the responsibility can be put on the owner of the cattle to pay for damage to the grain, or the loss of the grain can be left to the responsibility of the grain owner, who can pay the cattle owner to keep his herds off the cultivated land (or erect a fence, if that proves to be cheaper). At the margin, the incentives of both parties will remain the same.

One property of an efficient rule is that it is clearly communicated to and understood by the members of the society affected by it. A rule with these properties will reduce transaction costs. One way to achieve this goal is to adopt rules consistent with the shared expectations of the culture. If it is widely believed—no matter how irrationally— that when cows eat someone else's crops, the owner of the cows should pay, because "to eat" is an active verb while "to be eaten" is not, then the law can base itself on this expectation. Then, when the adjoining landowners begin negotiations over the problem, they will not be surprised to discover that the law assigns the responsibilities according to their expectations. If liabilities were assigned contrary to the expectations of the society, the friction between "reasonable" expectations and the law would increase costs.

In the case of torts between strangers, transaction costs are high and the content of the controlling legal rule is important. As a result, the most difficult tort problems involve those situations where individual negotiation before the wrong is clearly not feasible. In the case of adjoining landowners, the two owners can identify each other and anticipate

---

[10]The one subject that has generated a significant literature is the market for corporate control (for an introduction, see Posner and Scott 1980, p. 195).

the types of harm in which they are likely to be jointly involved. Indeed, the legal rules that evolve may simply reflect the fact that repeated negotiations have led to the outcome the law incorporates. The same is true of harms arising out of the employment relationship. But in the case of torts between strangers, there is no possibility of negotiation prior to the accident to correct an inefficient rule. The major modern social context in which this problem arises is road accidents. The correct rule has been debated in the literature. Some writers have argued that liability for negligence is the efficient rule in order to make each driver weigh the costs of taking precautions to prevent accidents as against the magnitude of the loss caused by failure to take those precautions. In this view, the negligent driver is the wasteful driver, and the negligence rule reduces the incidence of inefficient conduct (Posner 1972).[11] Other writers, principally Guido Calabresi (1970), have argued that a simple fault system is an inefficient way to assign liabilities from automobile accidents and that liability should be imposed on classes of persons who are the "least cost avoiders." In the common law, the archetype of this approach was the strict liability of blasters for damage to adjacent landowners. No matter how much care the blaster took, he was liable for damage caused by the blasting activity. This put the blaster in a position to weigh whether the gains exceeded the losses before blasting.

This literature is quite abstract, the argument proceeding on the basis of hypotheticals that limit the complexity of the problem. The negligence standard requires the trier of fact to make sophisticated assessments of gains and benefits from particular ways of acting. A strict liability standard that does not admit of contributory negligence as a defense will not work in the almost universal situation where the accident is the joint product of two or more different activities. Such accidents are an example of a joint-cost problem, two or more actors having foregone possible precautions to jointly produce the accident. The only institution that can efficiently solve joint-cost problems is the market —but it is impossible to structure a market for accidents. The available analytic tools cannot handle the problem in its full subtlety.

The difficulty of a direct approach focusing on production in this context may explain why theories based on moral principles or linguistic structure can lead to results congruent with much of the law (Fletcher 1972; Epstein 1973). Given the absence of a "correct" solution assuring efficiency, the efficient solution may be to assign rights and duties and permit the affected parties to adjust to that set of assignments over time. If the assignment process can build on preexisting cultural phenomena, such as the structure of the language or shared moral codes, the assignment can be made more cheaply.

The question remains whether the changes in tort rules that have occurred over time can be explained as responses to changing economic and technological conditions or whether they reflect changes in other cultural values. In this area, a notable phenomenon in the Anglo-American legal world was the rise of a negligence standard in the nineteenth century and its gradual erosion in the twentieth. It is plausible that, if accident-causing technologies are stable over a long period of time, the society will learn through experience the optimum set of rules for the participants in the accident-causing process. This knowledge may express itself in increasingly detailed rules about particular categories and types of activities whose violation would result in liability. The rule that a motorist who does not stop, look, and listen before crossing a railroad track is negligent,

---

[11] This essay argues the case for negligence within the context of nineteenth-century cases and Posner recognizes the problems involved in the use of a negligence system in the context of automobile accidents (Posner 1977, pp. 153–57).

for example, amounts to the rule that any person who violates it is strictly liable for the possible consequences.[12] Any introduction of new accident-causing technologies throws such a system into disarray. The short-run optimum would be to shift to a standard of reasonableness administered in a decentralized way until the society obtained enough experience with the new technology to formulate specific rules applicable to the actors. At that point the system can begin to shift back toward more explicit rules, specifying strict liability. Whether or not there have been significant changes in accident-causing technologies that should have affected the appropriate legal rule, and whether such technological shifts are in fact related to the legal changes that have taken place, are subjects that have barely been investigated.

Antitrust   An intensely studied area has focused on those rules designed to correct real or fancied inefficiencies in the system of property and contracts. In the United States the most notable of these is the Sherman Antitrust Act of 1890, but numerous regulatory schemes also serve the ostensible purpose of improving market operation. The question of whether the Sherman Act was, or could become, a program of market enhancement stimulated the first sustained contemporary effort to use the insights of political economy to illuminate the law (Director and Levi 1956). The literature on the Sherman Act has concluded that the act can and does, in general, promote efficiency. Ironically, the literature has concluded that much economic regulation does not promote efficiency. It was partly the understanding that the rules of the Sherman Act were the product of judicial interpretation, while the regulatory regimes are statutory, that gave currency to the notion that courts make relatively more efficient law.

Sherman Act policy presents two central questions. The first asks whether the system of property and contracts has an inherent tendency to attrition through monopolization; the second addresses the possibility of fashioning a set of legal rules that stop monopolization while permitting production-enhancing forms of competition. The literature has tended to concentrate on the second problem rather than on the first, accepting as given a congressional determination that the problem was of sufficient importance to require a criminal statute. The productivity vision of the Sherman Act is most fully stated by Robert H. Bork (1978). In his view, the Sherman Act is a charter for efficiency, the details having been satisfactorily worked out by the Supreme Court in the early years of the act and tarnished only by more recent judicial and legislative errors.

This view is challenged only by the description of the act as a Jeffersonian charter to preserve independence and autonomy within the economic system. Although this view has clearly had some impact on the decisions of the Supreme Court, it has been in intellectual retreat. Its high point may have been the now discredited opinion of Judge Learned Hand in *United States v. Aluminum Co. of America* (1945), in which competitive success was equated with monopolization.[13] The reason for its retreat is that its advocates

---

[12] This particular rule, announced by Mr. Justice Holmes in *Baltimore & Ohio R.R. v. Goodman* (1927), was made obsolete by changes in automobile technology practically before it was announced, as the Court recognized in *Pokora v. Wabash Ry.* (1934). The rule was applied to an issue of contributory negligence.

[13] Judge Hand denied this, observing that "[a] single producer may be the survivor out of a group of active competitors, merely by virtue of his superior skill, foresight and industry. In such cases a strong argument can be made that, although the result may expose the public to the evils of monopoly, the Act does not mean to condemn the resultant of those very forces which it is its prime object to foster" (*United States v. Aluminum Co. of America*, 1945, p. 430). It is, however, impossible to determine from the opinion what Alcoa did to violate the act other than to plan for competitive success.

have not been able to derive a set of rules that consistently implement its vision. It is difficult to mobilize Jeffersonian antitrust ideology in support of a program that tolerates a corporation such as General Motors. A rule that severely limits the constraints oil companies can place on their independent retail franchisees makes sense only if one is equally willing to limit oil companies' integration forward into retailing. The gains available from modern economic integration are too apparent to make the Jeffersonian vision of the Sherman Act very appealing. And if that vision is applied inconsistently and haphazardly, it becomes a vehicle for obvious unfairness.

The extensive literature on judicial interpretation of the Sherman Act has identified a central flaw in its implementation from a productivity point of view. The courts have tended to confuse forms of vertical integration with constraints on competition. The analysis began in the literature with the patent tie-in cases (see Director and Levi 1956, pp. 291–92; this analysis is fully developed in Bowman 1973). The owner of a patent would license it on condition that the licensee make use of some nonpatented input supplied by the licensor. The courts saw this agreement as an attempt to extend the patent "monopoly" beyond its legal scope and to eliminate competition in the market for the tied product. One famous case involved a requirement imposed by IBM that users of its computers also use punch cards supplied by it (*International Business Machines Corp.* v. *United States*, 1936). The courts' reaction seems sensible until one begins to analyze why IBM might wish to impose such a requirement. The purchaser of the computer is interested in computing services, and if IBM raises the cost of punch cards to the user, it will decrease his demand for the computer. The tie-in does not enable IBM to increase the profitability of its market position in computers. Why, then, might IBM impose such a requirement? One possibility is that IBM can supply punch cards suitable for its computers more efficiently than can others, but, if this is so, IBM would not need to require their purchase, since it would dominate the market anyway. Another possibility is that IBM was in a position to charge monopoly prices on its computers and that the punch cards were being used as a device to meter demand, enabling the company to discriminate in pricing—that is, apply different charges in different markets. However, the effect of price discrimination by a monopolist is to increase his output, contributing to social efficiency. Only if the monopoly is socially undesirable in its origins can a rule prohibiting price discrimination be defended, since price discrimination increases the incentives to engage in such monopolization. But in the patent cases, the monopoly has been treated both by the courts and by commentators as socially desirable.

A related problem is the judicial prohibition of resale-price maintenance agreements. In these cases, a manufacturer has required that distributors of his product sell it for no less than a specified price. The courts have treated such agreements as pacts to eliminate price competition in the markets for distribution services. But again, why does the seller extract such a promise? It would seem that his interest is in lowering, not raising, the selling price. The lower the distribution markup, the greater the demand at the factory. Two explanations have been proffered. One claims that the agreement is not really imposed by the seller but is a response to a cartel of the distributors (Bowman 1955, pp. 826–32). The distributors organize and refuse to handle products unless the manufacturer agrees to accept a minimum markup and enforce it through a resale-price distribution scheme. The other explanation holds that the manufacturer imposes resale-price maintenance because the arrangement is helpful to him in that he wants to create an incentive for the retailers to compete in terms of offering services related to the product rather than in the price of the product itself (Bowman 1955, pp. 840–44; also Telser 1960, pp. 89–96).[14] An easy example in the case of automobiles and appliances is the provision of showroom space and information about the product. If customers can first shop the showroom and then buy from a direct-sale, no-service firm, there will be no incentive for anyone other than the manufacturer to provide this kind of preselling service. Resale-price maintenance will also change the inventory policy of retailers and increase the geographic availability of the product. If consumers know that the retail price is uniform, they will be saved the costs of searching out the most advantageous price.

The literature on antitrust policy toward resale-price maintenance has proceeded largely in terms of abstract price-theory analysis. (For the leading dialogue, see Bork 1966; Gould and Yamey 1967, 1968; Bork 1967; notable exceptions are Bowman 1955; Yamey 1952, 1966). The competing hypotheses could be subjected to more rigorous testing. For instance, it should be possible to determine historically the extent to which distributors did organize effective cartels.[15] Some products have been subjected to resale-price maintenance while others have not, and the competing theories have different implications as to the products to be covered. The cartel theory implies that output would fall as a result of resale-price maintenance. It also implies that all products handled only by stores of the type that successfully organized would be subject to resale-price maintenance and that the intensity of resale-price maintenance would vary from market to market depending on the nature of retail competition in that market. The services theory predicts that resale-price maintenance will cause output to rise, and will be associated with products that require point-of-sale services.

The resale-price maintenance problem is interesting from the point of view of the productivity hypothesis because the law on this point has been unstable in the United States during the twentieth century. After the Supreme Court held that resale-price maintenance violated the Sherman Act (*Dr. Miles Medical Co.* v. *John D. Park & Sons Co.*, 1911), the Congress reversed the rule by a statute that permitted states to provide for resale-price maintenance.[16] Many states chose to permit resale-price maintenance; others did not. Resale-price maintenance expanded during the Depression and contracted during the years after World War II. Only recently, Congress repealed the statute that permitted the states to have resale-price maintenance [Pub. Law 94-145, 89 Stat. 801 (1975)]. Are these changes to be explained as instability in the system or as adaptations to changing conditions? Was the judicial rule wasteful and therefore corrected by Congress? Did the judicial rule become desirable as technological changes greatly reduced the service component of distribution? Or did the ability of retailers to use political power to protect their monopoly position decline as retailing passed into the hands of large and impersonal corporations?

A striking feature of the antitrust area is that the economics literature has had a substantial impact on the legal rules, and the legal cases have had a substantial impact on

---

[14] Telser (1960), influenced by the record in *United States* v. *General Electric Co.* (1926), puts heavy emphasis on a third explanation, the use of resale-price maintenance to assist in the policing of a manufacturer's cartel.

[15] Yamey (1952) found that the impetus came from retailers.

[16] The Miller-Tydings Amendment to the Sherman Act [ch. 690, 50 Stat. 693 (1937)]. When the Supreme Court read the statute in a restrictive fashion in *Schwegmann Bros.* v. *Calvert Distilling Corp.* (1951), Congress immediately responded with the McGuire Act [ch. 745, 66 Stat. 632 (1952)].

the economics literature. The most notable example of legal borrowing from economics is the use of concentration ratio concepts to identify horizontal arrangements that impair competition.[17] The concentration ratio concept was developed by economists as a hypothesis for testing. It ran as follows. Price theory shows that monopolists will have higher profits. It is arguable that industries consisting of few firms will behave like monopolists, because each firm will have an incentive to consider the reactions of its competitors to its pricing and product strategies. If such firms coordinate successfully and behave like monopolists, there should be a systematic correlation between some measure of the number of firms and rates of profitability. The empirical work has yielded confused results (Demsetz 1974; Weiss 1974) and has been bedeviled by serious technical problems. Most important, accounting data are not the same as economic cost data. They may fail to include various assets of real economic value, primarily good will and know-how, or they may incorporate capitalized monopoly returns through past purchase transactions. The courts, however, have adopted the concentration-ratio notion of how to measure anticompetitive effects, with little awareness of its theoretical flaws and empirical weakness.[18] The principal theoretical flaw lies in the circumstance that a product market with even a single seller will not be monopolized as long as there are other sellers who will enter the market when the single seller starts to charge a noncompetitive price. This situation suggests that the real inquiry should concern barriers to entry or concentration measured by potential sellers. A substantial economic literature on barriers to entry exists, but the courts have not made such barriers a central test. Indeed, they have shown a tendency to apply the concentration-ratio notion in a highly inconsistent way, sometimes limiting the market to actual sellers and at other times including potential sellers where necessary to find a transaction illegal. The courts, of course, cannot wait for economics to arrive at consensus tests before proceeding to construe the antitrust laws.

The impact of law on industrial organization has come from the fact that the reported decisions are among the few sources where economists can find detailed descriptions of business behavior. The literature on industrial organization has tended to accept the descriptions and characterizations of the behavior in the opinions (Scherer 1980). Lawyers understand better than do economists that judicial opinions are not scientific reports of the facts involved in the litigation but briefs on behalf of the result that the court has reached. A notable example is the issue of the importance of the strategy of predatory pricing as a tactic to deter competitive entry. The theory has not concluded whether the tactic will work. For many years it was accepted in the economics literature that the Standard Oil case had shown that Standard Oil had systematically and successfully engaged in predatory pricing to deter entry. John McGee (1958), however, showed that when the record was reviewed by a knowledgeable economist, it supported no such finding. This finding raised the question of whether an antitrust rule against predatory pricing was good or bad, since such a rule created the danger that it would be applied to competitive pricing and thus reduce, rather than enhance, competitive pressures.[19] Al-

[17] This approach dominates the Department of Justice merger guidelines, 1 CCH Trade Regulation Reporter ¶4430 (1968).

[18] Richard Posner suggested that the courts use the Herfindahl measure (1969, 1976), an idea adapted from Stigler (1968), in order to better capture the relevant economic variables, particularly the role of potential output expansion by fringe firms. The Herfindahl measure expresses the level of concentration in terms of the sum of the squares of each firm's market share.

[19] The subject has generated a large literature on the theoretically correct test. For recent reviews of this literature, see McGee (1980) and Easterbrook (1981).

though there are other substantial sources of information about business behavior—trade magazines and newspapers, business archives, biographies of business leaders, company histories, and so on—economists have not used these sources to illuminate the problems of industrial organization. Conversely, the historians who have worked with these materials on the whole have had little familiarity with the important economic issues the material might clarify.

The literature on industrial organization is notable for its failure to attempt scientific investigation of the question of whether monopolies and cartels—the central targets of the act—promote or retard efficiency.[20] The only admitted exception to the standard analysis consists of so-called natural monopolies. These are thought of as single-firm industries that emerge because of economies of scale in production that are as large as the market itself. Ever since transportation technologies created national and international markets in many products, these firms have seemed a rather unimportant phenomenon. But cartelization offers other potential gains. One is to organize markets in ways that reduce the buyer's cost of search. Another is to facilitate the exchange of technological information among the members of the industry. What are the effects of cartels that have actually existed? To read the American literature on industrial organization, one would conclude that countries that tolerate cartels have consigned themselves to the scrap heap. Yet a fair number of successful industrial countries tolerate them or have done so in the past.

One particular effect of an anticartel policy is that it restricts the ability of an industry to organize to offset the effects of a rule that impedes production. Where an industry is confronted with rules that cause it to operate inefficiently, one way of overcoming the inefficiency is for the industry to agree on offsetting arrangements. A leading antitrust case that illustrates an agreement of this kind is *Fashion Originators' Guild of America* v. *F.T.C.* (1941). American law has provided no design protection to the fashion industry. This omission has a long and idiosyncratic history, but the economic rationale for affording such protection is as strong as the rationale for extending patents to inventors and copyrights to authors. In *Fashion Originators' Guild*, a group of the fashion industry had voluntarily associated into a system for according protection to dress designs. Member manufacturers agreed to refrain from copying each other's designs, and member retailers agreed to refrain from selling pirated designs. This association provided some protection, although it could be effective only if, over time, the members were able to prevail in fashion market competition with nonmembers. The Supreme Court found that the arrangements violated the antitrust laws, since the members of the association had pledged themselves not to compete with each other in a way that the law recognized as legal.

The extent to which cartels provide important ways for offsetting the effects of legal rules that cause inefficiency is an unexplored question. In my own work, I have identified a stable, pre-Sherman Act cartel that seems to have had precisely that role (Kitch and Bowler 1979). This cartel of elevator operators in Chicago set a uniform rate for the

---

[20] If cartels that do not promote efficiency are unstable, either because they fall apart internally as the result of conflicts among the participants or because their monopoly pricing attracts entry, then the only stable cartels that would be observed would be those that promote efficiency. They would be stable because they are in the interest of all the members and would not attract entry because their efficiency would make entry unprofitable. The issue of what is the actual effect of real cartels can be answered only by close examination of their behavior.

transfer and storage of grain. In effect, the uniform cartel price overcame the effect of a court rule imposed on the railroads that they had to deliver cars to the elevators designated by the shippers. If there were price competition among the elevators, the shippers would have an incentive to exercise this right, impairing the ability of the railroads to handle the trains on a unit basis. Thus, the railroads encouraged the uniform pricing policy of the elevators, their lessees, but they were in a position to capture back from the elevators the profits gained through the rental terms of the leases. Actual cartels have seldom been studied to determine the efficiency effects of their organization.

Economic Regulation   The diverse and complex phenomenon of economic regulation has generated a large literature dedicated to examining its effects on the economy. (For the leading general works on regulation, see Kahn 1971 and Breyer 1982.) Three efficiency rationales have been proffered: natural monopoly, excessive or inadequate competition, and externalities. One nonefficiency explanation has been proffered: redistribution of income. Two other explanations—contracting problems in the transfer of the right to use a government-owned asset and the creation of appropriate incentives for the development of new technology—have not been closely examined.

The natural-monopoly rationale for regulation is as follows. The technology of certain industries dictates that single firms will supply the market. The most prominent natural-monopoly industries are the distribution utilities—telephone, electricity, water, and sewage. The network problems in efficiently arranging the delivery of these services dictate a single system. Yet, because there is a single system, that system, unconstrained, will be able to engage in monopoly pricing. Under this hypothesis, the purpose of regulation is to make a natural-monopoly firm engage in efficient pricing. The problem with this hypothesis is that the imposed regulation has no resemblance to competitive pricing. It has had two features—first, pricing based upon average cost; and second, prohibitions against price discrimination. Competition would force the firm to price at marginal, not average, cost; and in the absence of competition, price discrimination can be used to induce the optimum output from the monopolist.

Regulatory schemes based upon a rationale of excessive or inadequate competition tend to date from the Depression period of the 1930s. This rationale is now discredited. Principal examples of regulation once justified on grounds of excess competition are entry restrictions in airlines, trucking, and long-distance telecommunications and pricing constraints in the field market for natural gas and pipelines and long-distance electricity transmission. More recent examples that seem to be based on the same idea are constraints on petroleum and petroleum-product prices. The argument for these forms of regulation holds that competition in these particular industries is defective, occurring in forms that result either in chronically inadequate or in chronically excessive returns to capital. The problem with this rationale is that no one has been able to explain what makes these industries different from any other industry. The recent moves toward deregulation of the airline, trucking rail, telecommunications, broadcasting, and petroleum industries demonstrate the extent to which these ideas have become discredited.

Nevertheless, closely related ideas have resulted in economy-wide wage-price controls based on the notion that all private firms have a systematic tendency to overprice. The general belief is that the private firms overestimate the propensity of the government to inflate and that wage-price controls are necessary to force them to engage in correct and, hence, efficient pricing. The implementation of such wage and price control programs is accompanied by statements that the government itself has no intention to inflate and that wage-price controls must be imposed because the private sector has erroneously come to believe that the government will, in fact, pursue a policy of inflating the price level.

The recently emerged political and intellectual consensus that regulatory schemes impeding the movement of capital in and out of industries or impeding adjustment in the price level in response to shifts in supply costs or demand schedules are wasteful is not based on new analytic insights. The long-standing opposition of political economists to protective-tariff policies is based on the same ideas. The effect of protective tariffs is to retard the shift of capital within the economy to areas of relative comparative advantage and to overprice imports to the domestic purchaser. Such tariffs are bad for the country in the same way that laws restricting entry and exit or constraining price adjustments are bad.

It is notable that such regulatory regimes tend to arise in the context of atypical shifts in the general price level. During the Depression it was argued that the seemingly continuous tendency of firms to lower prices and eliminate accounting profits, computed in relation to investments carried at book value, reflected a defect in the competitive process of significant and previously unappreciated importance. Only with the benefit of hindsight is it possible to appreciate that the phenomenon was the result of an unprecedented and prolonged contraction in the money supply. Conversely, the present interest in regulation of this type seems to be a perverse response to a shift toward a policy of high expansion in the money supply. Regulation of this type is an embarrassment to the productivity hypothesis. It is so patently wasteful that the hypothesis must be either rejected or limited to courts rather than legislatures, or the regulation must be viewed as a random, accidental error.

It is interesting that this type of regulation has been associated with unusual shifts in the trend of the price level, either up or down. One accomplishment of such regulations is the tendency to increase the visible social harm that flows from these shifts in the price level. If the law tries to hold down prices in the face of rising demand, it will generate queues or complex rationing schemes that consume real social resources. If the law tries to restrain price decreases in the face of falling demand, it will accelerate the fall in volume and increase unemployment and idle capacity. Perhaps these perverse responses are, in fact, the way in which the political system generates opposition to the government's inefficient macro-policies. Absent constraints on price shifts, inflation or deflation would express themselves as shifts in the transaction price level and as shifts in wealth among particular individuals. With price and entry constraints, the disturbances express themselves in much more socially disruptive ways. Are the present movements to eliminate entry restrictions in airlines, trucking, and long-distance telecommunications part of the lagged process of recovering equilibrium after the large shocks generated by the Depression?

A contemporary form of the market-failure rationale has been protective legislation for consumer and worker. This legislation is founded on the assumption that ordinary persons, workers or consumers, are unable to represent their interests in the marketplace effectively because of lack of information. Because the consumer does not understand interest rates, the Truth in Lending Act was passed [15 U.S.C. §1602 et seq. (1976)]. Because the worker does not understand the safety risks of his workplace, the Occupational Health and Safety Administration was established [P.L. 91-596, 29 U.S.C. §651-78 (1976)]. Because warranties are too complicated, the Moss-Magnuson Warranty Act came into being [Pub. Law 93-637, tit. 2, 88 Stat. 2193 (1975)]. The source of the information imbalance is said to be that the firm with which the consumer is dealing has an interest in mastering the subject matter but the consumer, who is in the market infrequently, does not. Or perhaps it is assumed that the firms have the services of high-income people, thought to be intelligent, while they sell to low-income people, thought not to be intelligent. What these arguments generally overlook is the extent to which particular consumers can profit from the market-policing activities of a minority and the extent to which competitive firms will have an incentive to displace high interest rates, worthless warranties, and unsafe working conditions.

One modern form of this regulation that has been much studied and clearly seems inefficient is government restraint on the marketing of new drugs (Peltzman 1973a, 1973b, 1975). This regulation does not simply require the disclosure of relevant information to the consumer; it further demands that the government itself determine whether a drug is suitable, and for what it is suitable, before it is made available. No matter how well informed a particular consumer is, he cannot legally obtain the drug. The government requires proof of safety and efficacy, setting high standards that are inappropriate in many cases. The regulation has raised the cost of introducing new drugs and has therefore reduced their availability. Nevertheless, there is a residual gray market, since those with the means and the will can obtain drugs from foreign countries or seek treatment at medical centers authorized by the Food and Drug Administration to conduct research. It seems odd that consumers should be considered particularly helpless in a setting where, by law, they are required to act with the advice of a specialized professional.

The inability to explain natural-monopoly and market-failure regulation in productivity terms has led to a search for explanations. Regulation can be viewed as a symptom of defects in the organization of political rights. All these explanations face the objection that an efficient solution would give the political system more wealth to allocate than would an inefficient solution. In these models cohesive industrial groups are often thought to have more power than do consumers in general. The point of the regulation is seen to be the transfer of wealth from one group to another in exchange for political support. In this view, trucking and airline regulation transfers wealth from big cities and big shippers to trucking firms, airlines, and small cities and small shippers; banking regulation transfers wealth from small savers to big savers and bankers; telecommunications regulation transfers wealth from users of long-distance service to users of local service; FDA regulation transfers wealth from victims of diseases that would yield only to new drugs to established drug companies; OSHA regulation transfers wealth from small companies to large companies; and so on.

These explanations present several problems. First, the political coalitions they suggest are somewhat odd and inconsistent. Second, there is no reason to think that the regulation generates the wealth to be distributed anywhere. Airline regulation may have held prices up on the dense, low-cost routes, but the principal response of the airlines was to compete those profits away through service competition. Bank regulation holds down interest rates paid to small savers, but the banks compete for these clients through service competition. FDA regulation increases the profitability of old drugs as compared with the profitability that would result if the old drugs faced more rapid obsolescence, but the firms that gain are probably the same firms that would introduce the new drugs if they could. The transfer from long-distance telecommunications users to local users may simply be a transfer from businesses using long-distance telephones to businesses using local telephone service. The third major problem in this theory of economic regulation is its failure to explain why some industries are regulated while others are not. Under this view, all industries are equally good candidates for wealth redistribution.

The literature has accepted externalities as a legitimate reason for regulation. If the legal system is arranged so as to confer benefits or costs of an activity on someone who has either no duty to pay for the benefit or no right to be compensated for the cost, wasteful levels of the activity will occur.

Important modern examples of regulation based on explicit concern with externalities are land-use controls and air and water pollution regulation. The effects of these relatively new and clearly significant forms of regulation have not been closely studied. On their surface, they appear to violate principles of economic efficiency. They restrict the ability of property owners to transact in relation to their property, and they tend to be structured in terms of prohibitions rather than charges proportional to the harm. Yet, the results of these schemes are not really known. There is evidence that an unzoned city is very little different from a zoned city[21]—a fact that may reflect the way in which private parties are able to conduct transactions with the zoning authorities. It may be that zoning increases the relative wealth of those who can influence the zoning authorities—those who are persuasive in administrative proceedings or politically influential—but that they have little impact on the resulting land-use pattern as compared with the pattern that would emerge under an unzoned system. The new, ambitious, and complex pollution-control systems are even less well understood.

It is possible that these systems of regulation are a social response to modern shortages of space, air, and water and that the present systems are part of a process of transition from a system that does not grant property rights in these resources to a system that assigns them.[22] When a primitive tribe encountered a scarcity of hunting space, it is unlikely that the tribe moved instantaneously from a system of open use to a system of defined property rights. In the transition period, there would be efforts to assign hunting areas and to prohibit any hunting activities in violation of the assignments. Only over time would this system come to be understood as a permanent system of rights (Demsetz 1967). Thus, under the modern systems, it is not unlikely that, over time, certain areas will acquire the right to be dirty, and certain areas will acquire the right to be clean, and private property owners within those areas will have the right to transfer the continuing right to engage in similar activity. Then, if there is a system for shifting the allocation of uses at the margins in response to changing technological needs, the resulting systems would seem largely compatible with the needs of production, assuming that the implicit price attached to clean air and water and urban amenity is not too high.

Economists have long argued that a system of charges for polluting will yield superior results because it will permit each firm to equate marginal cost and marginal revenue (Mishan 1971, p. 15). This claim may be valid in the short run, but, unlike a system of standards, a system of charges cannot evolve into a system of property rights.

Two other explanations for government regulatory activity that merit evaluation have barely been considered in the literature. One holds that regulations aim to solve the

---

[21] Bernard H. Siegan intensively studied nonzoning in Houston and was able to detect a few minor differences (Siegan 1970, 1972).

[22] The line of argument here is independently developed and more fully explicated in Maloney and Yandle (1980).

problem of government–private contractual interface; the other would place their origin in the problem of appropriate incentives for technological innovation.

A notable feature of most of the older systems of economic regulation in the United States is that they involve the assignment to private firms of the right to use public property. The classic case is assigning to the distribution utilities the right to use public rights of way. The railroads acquired public lands and the power of eminent domain.

The connection between this problem and regulation was pointed out by Harold Demsetz (1968), who noted that the usual reason given for the regulation of the natural-monopoly distribution of utilities—lack of competition—was in error. Although only a single firm would provide the service, there would be competition among firms for the right to be the one. This competition could take place at the time the franchise was offered. The competition by firms for the franchise would dictate the terms and conditions of service under the franchise.

The difficulties are illuminated by considering the terms and conditions under which the competition will take place. What will the terms of the franchise be? How will the winning competitor be selected? One solution is to allow competitive cash bids for a perpetual-franchise term. The government sells the right to conduct the business to the entity that puts the highest value on the right. But this solution brings its own problems. If the franchise places no constraints on the pricing policies of the franchisee, it will charge monopoly prices. The franchisor will benefit through the franchise fee, but the misallocation effects of the monopoly prices will continue.

The perpetual term presents a problem because it binds all future governments to the assignment. But if governments are to retain their ability to correct errors, it may be important to their structure that subsequent administrations are able to undo the work of their predecessors. Laws are therefore generally subject to repeal, and governments are notoriously unreliable long-term contracting partners. The American Constitution attempted to solve this problem for the states by declaring that no state should pass any law that would impair the obligation of contracts, but the sense that perpetually binding commitments were inappropriate has been so strong that the courts have tended to assist the states in avoiding their contracts. If a renewable term of years is used instead, on the other hand, there are serious incentives to inefficiency as the franchise approaches the end of its term.

The second problem—which arises generally when competitive bidding is involved—is how the government knows how to define the rights and obligations of the franchisee. It is easy enough to see how one might efficiently acquire nails through competitive bidding—but what if the commodity or service is so complex that the government does not have a proper standard for setting the bid specifications? It may be that the very information and know-how essential to set the specifications efficiently is possessed only by the bidders. This problem can be solved by asking the bidders to compete not in terms of cash but in terms of specifications. But then the competition becomes multidimensional and complex to administer. For these reasons, major weapons acquisition programs in the Department of Defense have tended to rely not on purchases on bid but on a form of ongoing relationship closely resembling economic regulation (see the Renegotiation Act of March 23, 1951, 65 Stat. 7, 50 U.S.C. §1211 et seq., not presently in effect).

Another problem with a cash, front-end bid is that it presents the governmental unit with a lump of cash that disrupts regular budget flows and, because of the short time-horizon of politicians, may be dissipated unwisely. However, other forms of payment, such as a per-unit tax, are more disruptive of the marginal revenue equilibrium. Efficiency considerations may therefore account for the frequently adopted solution of noncash competition, which takes place along a range of service parameters, followed by continuing regulation, which places a limit on profitability and attempts to affect the relationship between prices as they affect different customer classes. Although this regulation generates demonstrable inefficiencies in the product or service market, it may nevertheless be less wasteful than a one-time cash competitive auction.

A second explanation for some forms of economic regulation is that they create the correct incentives for development of new technologies. Railroads, electric power, telephones, radio, and aviation were all new and rapidly developing technologies in their time. Part of the investment required in the development of a new technology is the development of the business methods and commercial practices necessary to exploit the invention effectively. These investments tend to be poorly protected by the patent system. The early railroads, electric-power systems, telephone systems, and airlines had to develop in-the-field procedures to identify and meet the needs of their customers. Freedom of entry would have given competitors the opportunity to copy successful methods without bearing their cost. This circumstance suggests a pattern of "infant industry" protection, followed by an easing of entry restrictions as the industry matures. It is possible to understand contemporary airline, broadcast, and telecommunications deregulation in this framework.

In the case of radio regulation, Ronald Coase (1959) has demonstrated that an emerging system of private property rights was disrupted by administrative regulation, and it is now a widely accepted view that a system of property rights in broadcast frequencies would be better for society than the present arrangement. However, examining the problem from the perspective of 1926 leads to the realization that the problem was not simply one of establishing an exclusive right to use as between competing broadcasters in order to minimize frequency interference. There was also a relationship between the frequencies used by various types of broadcasters and the design and improvement of radio receivers. It would assist the designers of the commercial broadcast receivers to know on what frequencies commercial broadcast stations would operate, and it would help commercial broadcasters to know what frequencies the most generally available sets would receive. Purchasers of radios prefer reasonable assurance that their sets will not become obsolete through technological change, so that they can amortize the cost over a longer period. These problems could, of course, all be solved by a system of first-property rights and subsequent negotiations between broadcasters and set manufacturers. But the transaction costs would have been high, the dissipation of resources caused by the first-possession rule might have been considerable, and the instability of the arrangements would have decreased consumers' willingness to invest in the new technology. The radio conferences of the late 1920s, which laid the foundation for the ensuing radio regulation, might well be viewed as an effort to reduce the transaction costs by facilitating communication between the principal parties and eliminating hold-out problems. In such an environment, the short-term license would make sense because there might be the need to correct technological errors. Once the technology's development had slowed and the industry had matured, the system might then be expected to shift toward a system of explicit property rights.

THE STRUCTURE AND SCOPE OF GOVERNMENT

Two issues central to any legal system—the structure of governments and the scope of their activities—have been little examined in work that shares the perspective of this article. Unlike the situation that applies to property, contract, torts, antitrust, and regulation, the connection between these areas of public law and the economy is less apparent. From the perspective of a hypothesis of productivity maximization, however, these subjects are central. For it is the form of the government that will determine how the law reacts to the society. From a contemporary perspective, three major phenomena attract attention: the large expansion of the voting franchise in the Western industrialized nations during the last two centuries; the expansion of the scope of activities carried on by the governments of these countries in the twentieth century (Peltzman 1980); and the emergence of indigenously imposed socialist or anticontractarian legal regimes in numerous countries during the twentieth century (Popkin 1979).[23]

Durability

Some features of the structure of governments such as the elements in legal systems designed to raise the cost of changing legal rules are rather easily explained from a perspective of productivity. While written constitutions make formal provisions along these lines, the tendency is evident on other levels of the legal system as well. Congress will not regularly reconsider difficult and hotly contested matters. The subject of labor relations was considered in 1916, 1935, 1947, and 1959. Civil rights were addressed in 1790, 1869, and 1964. Tax reform bills have a shorter and more regular cycle. A number of institutional features in the judiciary, such as the heavy emphasis on precedent, are designed to increase the permanence of rules. A specialized legal profession increases the continuity and stability of the law.

From a productivity perspective, permanence has a number of advantages. It decreases the incentives for losers under a particular rule to invest in changing that rule. It reduces the frequency of the occasions on which the costs of adapting to changed rules must be incurred. It enables people to plan their affairs with reasonable confidence that the law will not change. And it assures that there will be meaningful experience with a rule before a change is again considered.

Voting Rights

The expansion of the voting franchise may be explicable on economic grounds. In a society where the elimination of conflict is an important welfare priority, it could make sense to give control to the best warriors. To give those warriors incentives to govern well, it could make sense to give them a large stake in the future value of the society, and this could be accomplished through the emergence of a theory of monarchy. But once

---

[23] The existence of these regimes is, of course, a challenge for the thesis of this article (as is the medieval period). Their existence is beyond my competence to explain. It is interesting that they seem to occur around the periphery of the developed world as modern technology comes into contact with primitive or feudal legal systems. The shock of that interaction may lead to a breakdown of customary systems of contract and property and their replacement by centralized systems of command and control. This hypothesis implies the prediction that these regimes will slowly decay back toward a property-and-contract system suitable to modern economic conditions.

installed, the king might find that he can maximize the value of his rights by ceding portions of them to others in order to give them incentives to increase their productivity. The emergence of the mass franchise in the nineteenth century may have been a consequence of the breakdown of a command-and-monitor labor-control system in the face of the production technologies of the Industrial Revolution. (It is interesting that the breakdown of slavery systems occurred during roughly the same period as the expansion of the franchise.)

The new technologies may have required incentive systems and the extension of political rights to place the recipients in a position to protect the property rights thus conferred. At the same time, the opening of national markets by new transportation technologies may have made the actions of national governments of concern to a much greater number of people, and they may have expended resources to acquire the right to influence the decisions of a government newly relevant to them.

Externalities and Economies of Scale

Externalities and economies of scale can explain many government activities. Interrelated examples are national defense and law enforcement. Both activities benefit everyone and can be more efficiently rendered by a single, coordinated entity. Other government services that can be plausibly explained by externality effects include education, transportation, and communications. Services that can be plausibly explained by economies of scale include various kinds of social insurance.

These rationales are indeterminate as to the choice among government provision of the service, government purchase of the service, or the use of specifically tailored property rights. A national-defense force can choose to manufacture its weapons or to purchase them, to provide its own housing or to purchase it, and so on. In those instances where a defense activity has significant potential uses in peacetime, social efficiency will be gained either by buying the services from a private firm (as is done in the United States with the reserve civilian airfleet or the provision of much defense telecommunications) or by permitting the defense component to engage in the peacetime economic activity (as is done with the construction potential of the Army Corps of Engineers). The first choice will contract the size of the government; the second will increase it. The fact that education services may involve externalities does not dictate whether the state should operate the school system directly or provide vouchers enabling families to purchase education.

The use of property rights to overcome problems of externality—once a common feature of British law—is now little considered. Economists have long used the lighthouse as an example of a service that must be provided by the government because of externalities. The beacon helps all passing ships, but none need pay; yet Ronald Coase (1974) has shown how, under the provisions of specially designed franchises, lighthouse services were privately provided in England for over two centuries. Various types of bounties can be used to create private incentives for law enforcement (Landes and Posner 1975b). Where economies of scale are present, the exclusive franchise can be used while, in many of these areas, the government may, alternately, itself provide the service. The electric and natural-gas distribution utilities in the United States tend to be exclusively franchised but privately owned, while the water and sewage distribution utilities are publicly owned. (The difference is, perhaps, accounted for by the fact that the efficient size of the former tends to exceed municipal boundaries, while the efficient size of the latter does not.)

A plausible hypothesis is that changes in the nature of externalities and economies of scale across time and between countries, driven by changes in technology, account for differences in the activities of governments. For instance, the information-handling capabilities of the computer have greatly lowered the costs of transfer payment programs, partly explaining their rapid expansion since World War II. The discussion here will be confined to two topics—the provision of a medium of exchange and the criminal law.

The Medium of Exchange   A medium of exchange need not be supplied by the government. It can be a commodity of convenience and value, such as gold or, as was true in colonial Virginia, tobacco. It can be a credit instrument, such as a bill of exchange or a banknote. Throughout most of recorded history, the medium of exchange emerged, like language, through custom. In the last two centuries, governments have increasingly monopolized the function of providing the medium of exchange. The issue is whether they have done so because they have a comparative advantage in the provision of exchange or simply in order to capture the returns from providing it.

The problem with a medium of exchange generated by convention, such as gold, is that real resources must be used to create the medium of exchange. To be attractive, the substance must have real value in the economy and must therefore be diverted from alternative economic uses. Fiat money, on the other hand, which has little economic value, can more cheaply provide the medium of exchange. But this is a social gain only if the fiat money is as good as the nonfiat money.

In postprimitive economies, the real choices have been between forms of conventional-commodity money and pure fiat money. A system of commodity money can be used as a basis for a system of money created by promises to pay, and in such a system the commodity money may be only a small portion of the total available medium of exchange.

The problem of a conventional-commodity money system has been closely tied to the problems of a fractional reserve banking system. A fractional reserve banking system can generate exchange far in excess of the underlying base. But such a system has tended to be unstable, leading to a complex regulatory regime for banks.

The scholarship on money has not focused on the question of what set of legal arrangements produce the socially optimum form of money or to what extent the numerous changes in the monetary arrangements that have been made reflect either improvements or responses to changing conditions. Instead, it has concentrated on the question of whether monetary policies or budget policies have the most important influence on the course of the national economy. This monetarist-Keynesian debate has tended to treat the question as one about the inherent nature of national economies, never considering that the issue may simply be one of the controlling legal or customary rule. That is, in an economy where the legal rules define money exogenously—that is, by the supply of gold—the government can have neither a monetary nor a fiscal policy. In an economy where the rules require the monetary authorities to stabilize the quantity of money, fiscal policy will be unimportant. In an economy where the monetary authorities are forced to stabilize interest rates, fiscal policy will be important.

Milton Friedman and Anna Schwartz wrote their *Monetary History of the United States* (1963) as a contribution to the monetarist-Keynesian debate. It has been recognized and applauded in this context. What is not generally recognized is that it is a unique example of a study of the effects of changing legal rules over time. The book traces the various American legal arrangements concerning money from 1867 to 1960 and the effects of those changes on measures of the supply of money and upon the gross national product. There is no other area of law where sequential shifts in legal arrangements have been so carefully traced and related to the ensuing economic responses. Only the fragments exist, for example, of a comparable study of the shifting legal policies toward railroads and their effects upon the railroad industry and the economy—to suggest just one topic that might be manageable within the traditional framework of industrial organization (Scharfman 1931–37; MacAvoy 1965; Kolko 1965). Not even this much is available on the changing rules of torts and their impact on accident prevention and accident losses within the economy. It is possible to conceive of monetary policy as directed to a few variables—the quantity of money and the gross national product—while it is much more difficult to describe the output of other legal regimes with concepts that have so limited a number of vectors.

The richness of the insights such a study can provide for a student of law can only be suggested here. The basic legal structure of money in the second half of the nineteenth century was formal and nondiscretionary. Congress set the rules, and the rules determined the supply of money. From 1860 to 1869, the policy was inflationary; from 1869 to 1900, it was deflationary. Perturbations in the gold-based monetary system of the late nineteenth century were introduced by international economic fluctuation. The statutory rule of money creation beginning with the establishment of the Federal Reserve Board in 1911 was highly discretionary, although Friedman and Schwartz are able to reconstruct—from board documents, the record of board actions, and private papers—the actual rules that guided the board and the changes in those rules that took place over time. The study provides a good example of the way in which government bodies that claim to have no rules often in fact do have rules, and how those rules can be reconstructed by subsequent scholarship.

One important aspect of American monetary policy has been control of a fractional reserve banking system, which reduces the cost of producing money but introduces a source of instability into the system. A loss of confidence in the banking system will itself cause a reduction in the supply of money. An important motive for the creation of the Federal Reserve System was to give the private banking system access to a source of additional money during such periods. In the panic of 1907, which precipitated the creation of the Federal Reserve, the monetary contraction was arrested by private agreement among the New York banks to suspend payment (Friedman and Schwartz 1963, pp. 156–68). The agreement violated the banks' deposit contracts, but it worked; the panic passed, and the ensuing depression was sharp but brief. Under the Federal Reserve Act, this option was taken away from the bankers, since it was assumed that they would not need it. In 1929, the option was not available, and no substitute was discovered until President Franklin Roosevelt, in 1933, finally closed the banks.

The Depression of the 1930s is a tragic example of how an economy confronted with a new and untried set of legal arrangements can be seriously harmed. The mechanical monetary systems of the nineteenth century were self-righting. Contraction was counteracted by the international flow of gold. By breaking the link between the domestic monetary system and international reserve assets, the Federal Reserve Act destroyed the self-righting feature. The Federal Reserve System, insensitive to the fact that this feature of the system no longer existed, and misled by the meaning of nominally low interest rates, continued to drain monetary reserves from the system long after the social symptoms had become acute (Friedman and Schwartz 1963, pp. 299–419). Such strong macro-systems, which restrict the ability of private parties to counteract their effects, can do enormous social harm. The rigid and sweeping regulatory programs enacted in the United States during the early 1970s have a similar potential.

On the fiscal side, little work has been done on the institutions that regulate government budgets (Dam 1977). The national budget process was customarily governed by a requirement of balance. This rule fell to the intellectual onslaught of the macroeconomists, who pointed out that the budget could be economically stabilizing only if it was balanced not over the year but over a cycle (Stein 1969). This may be a good example of how an analysis of rules that looks only to their economic effects in the particular market in which they operate can be seriously misleading. The complexity of the cycle-balance rule seems to have overloaded the political controls and brought an era not of cycle balance but of chronic deficits. The problem is that administration of a cycle-balance rule requires identification of the point in the cycle at which a particular budget year is located. Absent clear rules for this determination, the argument can always be made that "this" year appropriately requires a deficit and that the surplus years will be in the future. Unlike the case of a simplistic balanced-budget rule, it is never clear when the cycle-balance rule is being violated.

The Criminal Law   Much of the criminal law can be understood as a system designed to reduce the costs of the property-and-contract system by replacing private enforcement with more efficient public enforcement (Becker 1968; Becker and Landes, 1974). This course has been followed in Anglo-American law for over 200 years. This perspective also explains the intense ambivalence that has attended the use of the criminal sanction in many societies.

A property-and-contract system consumes real resources. Its efficiency requires the owner of property to be secure in the enjoyment of its benefits and his transactions in relation to his property to be voluntary. A property owner will expend resources to protect his holdings; there are reasons to believe that a centralized authority can perform this function more efficiently. Efforts directed at the protection of particular property will benefit all property. Apprehension of a malefactor will reduce the risk of crime to others. There will be substantial economies of scale in patrolling functions and coordinating and exchanging relevant information. These advantages might also be obtained by private agreement among property owners. The government can be viewed as the result of just such an agreement.

Numerous problems arise in connection with the criminal law as a cost-saving device for administration of the property and contract systems. First, errors in its definition and administration—particularly errors of overreach—are not easily corrected. Private parties cannot contract out of criminal liability. Although prosecutors may recognize that aspects of the law are obsolete or inappropriate, they cannot confer immunity, and areas of intermittent enforcement are subject to grave abuse.

Second, the imposition of criminal penalties involves a loss for society. The criminal is removed from productive activities and maintained by the state. An economically optimum criminal-law policy would attempt to make the marginal losses from enforcement of the criminal law equal to the marginal gains. Penalties would be designed so that the marginal social gain from the penalty equals the social marginal loss from imposing it. As in the usual monopoly case, it is possible that welfare can be enhanced by price discrimination. However, it may be impossible for judges and legislators to make the determinations necessary to achieve perfect discrimination. It is impossible to know the social gain that flows from a particular penalty imposed on a particular offender. Discriminations on grosser categories may run afoul of the social consensus necessary to support the criminal law system. For instance, it is likely that the level of penalty necessary to deter rich people is less than the level necessary to deter the poor. Propertied people are subject to the constraints imposed by the system of civil liability, and their own stake in the system makes them less likely to commit crime. The fact that they have high incomes means that the cost of their time is higher. Thus, a shorter criminal sentence may deliver more effective deterrence than will a longer one imposed on an unpropertied person. Yet, such categorization, subject to inherent error in particular cases, runs afoul of basic notions of equal protection.

CONCLUSION

Work in the area of law and the economic order would be enhanced if members of each of the two major traditions were willing to broaden the scope of their inquiry. The political economists have been quick to identify impediments erected by the law to the efficient functioning of the economy. They have seldom considered, however, the ways in which such impediments emerge out of the larger dynamics of legal development. The sociohistorians, on the other hand, have been all too quick to suspend inquiry as soon as they have identified wealth or power or shifts in prevailing ideology, without considering whether wealth and power represent returns to scarce inputs to production and changes in ideology—adaptations to changing circumstances.[24] A fuller consideration of both macro- and micro-perspectives would enrich the work of both.

For those who wish to explore the body of scholarship discussed in this article further, access to the law and economics literature is facilitated by Posner (1977) and by a series of readers: Ackerman (1975), Calvani and Siegfried (1979), Kronman and Posner (1979), Manne (1975), and Posner and Scott (1980). Two scholars, Hicks (1969) and North (1973, 1978), have sketched general theories of history along the lines argued here, but the state of the literature does not permit their effort to be more than suggestive. Good discussions of the problems of methodology and interpretation are to be found in Dahlman (1980, chap. 3) and Popkin (1979, chap. 1).

Cases Cited

Baltimore & Ohio R.R. v. Goodman, 275 U.S. 66 (1927).
Dr. Miles Medical Co. v. John D. Park & Sons, Co., 220 U.S. 373 (1911).
Fashion Originators' Guild of America v. F.T.C., 312 U.S. 457 (1941).

[24] This work would also be improved by attention to elementary price theory, which is often ignored to the detriment of work in this school. Thus, Horwitz (1977) makes numerous elementary errors of inference (see Liebhafsky 1979; Goldberg 1979).

International Business Machines Corp. v. United States, 298 U.S. 131 (1936).
Pokora v. Wabash Ry., 292 U.S. 98 (1934).
Schwegmann Bros. v. Calvert Distilling Corp., 341 U.S. 384 (1951).
United States v. Aluminum Co. of America, 148 F.2d 416 (1945).
United States v. General Electric Co., 272 U.S. 476 (1926).

Bibliography

Ackerman, Bruce
      1975   *Economic Foundations of Property Law.* Boston: Little, Brown.
Atiyah, P. S.
      1979   *The Rise and Fall of Freedom of Contract.* Oxford: Oxford University Press.
Barro, Robert J.
      1978   *The Impact of Social Security on Private Saving.* Washington, D.C.: American Enterprise Institute.
Barzel, Yoram
      1968   "Optimum Timing of Innovations." *Review of Economics and Statistics* 50:348–55.
Becker, Gary S.
      1968   "Crime and Punishment: An Economic Approach." *Journal of Political Economy* 76:169–217. Reprinted in *Essays of the Economics of Crime and Punishment,* edited by Gary S. Becker and William M. Landes. New York: National Bureau of Economic Research (1974).

      1981   *A Treatise on the Family.* Cambridge, Mass.: Harvard University Press.
Becker, Gary S., and Landes, William M., eds.
      1974   *Essays on the Economics of Crime and Punishment.* New York: National Bureau of Economic Research.
Bork, Robert H.
      1966   "The Rule of Reason and the Per Se Concept: Price Fixing and Market Division—Part II." *Yale Law Journal* 75:373–75, 405–52.

      1967   "A Reply to Professors Gould and Yamey." *Yale Law Journal* 76:731–43.

      1968   "Resale Price Maintenance and Consumer Welfare." *Yale Law Journal* 77:950–64.

      1978   *The Antitrust Paradox: A Policy at War with Itself.* New York: Basic Books.
Bowman, Ward S.
      1973   *Patent and Antitrust Law: A Legal and Economic Appraisal.* Chicago: University of Chicago Press.
Bowman, Ward S., Jr.
      1955   "Prerequisites and Effects of Resale Price Maintenance." *University of Chicago Law Review* 22:825–73.
Breyer, Stephen G.
      1982   *Regulation and Its Reform.* Cambridge, Mass.: Harvard University Press.
Brown, Charles, and Medoff, James
      1978   "Trade Unions in the Production Process." *Journal of Political Economy* 86:355–78.
Cain, Maureen, and Hunt, Alan
      1979   *Marx and Engels on Law.* London: Academic Press.
Calabresi, Guido
      1970   *The Costs of Accidents.* New Haven: Yale University Press.

Calvani, Terry, and Siegfried, John
    1979   *Economic Analysis and Antitrust Law.* Boston: Little, Brown.

Cary, William L.
    1974   "Federalism and Corporate Law: Reflections Upon Delaware." *Yale Law Journal* 83:663–705.

Coase, R. H.
    1937   "The Nature of the Firm." *Economica* (n.s.) 4:386–405.
    1959   "The Federal Communications Commission." *Journal of Law and Economics* 2:1–40.
    1960   "The Problem of Social Cost." *Journal of Law and Economics* 3:1–44.
    1974   "The Lighthouse in Economics." *Journal of Law and Economics* 17:357–76.

Dahlman, Carl J.
    1980   *The Open Field System and Beyond.* Cambridge: Cambridge University Press.

Dam, Kenneth W.
    1977   "The American Fiscal Constitution." *University of Chicago Law Review* 44:271–320.

Demsetz, Harold
    1967   "Toward a Theory of Property Rights." *American Economic Review* 57:347–73. Reprinted in *The Economics of Legal Relationships: Readings in the Theory of Property Rights,* edited by Henry G. Manne. St. Paul, Minn.: West (1975).
    1968   "Why Regulate Utilities?" *Journal of Law and Economics* 11:55–65.
    1974   "Two Systems of Belief About Monopoly." In *Industrial Concentration: The New Learning,* edited by Harvey J. Goldschmid, H. Michael Mann, and J. Fred Weston. Boston: Little Brown.

Denison, Edward F.
    1967   *Why Growth Rates Differ, Postwar Experience in Nine Western Countries.* Washington, D.C.: Brookings Institution.

Director, Aaron, and Levi, Edward H.
    1956   "Law and the Future: Trade Regulation." *Northwestern University Law Review* 51:281–96.

Dodd, Peter, and Leftwich, Richard
    1980   "The Market for Corporate Charters: 'Unhealthy Competition' vs. Federal Regulation." *Journal of Business* 53:259–83.

Downs, Anthony
    1957   *An Economic Theory of Democracy.* New York: Harper.

Easterbrook, Frank H.
    1981   "Predatory Strategies and Counterstrategies." *University of Chicago Law Review* 48:263–337.

Epstein, Richard
    1973   "A Theory of Strict Liability." *Journal of Legal Studies* 2:151–204.

Fama, Eugene F.
    1980   "Agency Problems and the Theory of the Firm." *Journal of Political Economy* 88:288–307. Abridged in *Economics of Corporation Law and Securities Regulation,* Richard A. Posner and Kenneth E. Scott. Boston: Little, Brown (1980).

Feldstein, Martin
    1974   "Social Security, Induced Retirement and Aggregate Capital Accumulation." *Journal of Political Economy* 82:905–26.
    1980   "Social Security, Induced Retirement and Aggregate Capital Accumulation: A Correction and Update." National Bureau of Economic Research Working Paper no. 579.

Fletcher, George
    1972   "Fairness and Utility in Tort Theory." *Harvard Law Review* 85:537–73.

Freeman, Richard L., and Medoff, James L.
    1979   "The Two Faces of Unionism." *Public Interest* 57 (Fall):69–93.
Friedman, Milton, and Schwartz, Anna
    1963   *A Monetary History of the United States 1867–1960.* Princeton, N.J.: Princeton
                University Press.
Goetz, Charles J., and Scott, Robert E.
    1977   "Liquidated Damages: Some Notes on an Enforcement Model and a Theory of
                Efficient Breach." *Columbia Law Review* 77:554–94.
Goldberg, Victor P.
    1979   "Review." *Journal of Economic Issues* 13:200–205.
Goldschmid, Harvey J.; Mann, H. Michael; and Weston, J. Fred, eds.
    1974   *Industrial Concentration: The New Learning.* Boston: Little, Brown.
Goodman, John C.
    1978   "An Economic Theory of the Evolution of the Common Law." *Journal of Legal
                Studies* 7:393–406.
Gould, J. R., and Yamey, B. S.
    1967   "Professor Bork on Vertical Price Fixing." *Yale Law Journal* 76:722–30.
    1968   "Professor Bork on Vertical Price Fixing: A Rejoinder." *Yale Law Journal* 77:936–
                49.
Hamburger, Michael J.
    1974   "The Lag in the Effect of Monetary Policy: A Survey of Recent Literature." In
                Monetary Aggregates and Monetary Policy. New York: Federal Reserve Bank.
Hayek, Friedrich A.
    1973   *Rules and Order.* Law, Legislation and Liberty, vol. 1. Chicago: University of
                Chicago Press.
Hicks, John
    1969   *A Theory of Economic History.* Oxford: Oxford University Press.
Horwitz, Morton J.
    1977   *The Transformation of American Law 1780–1860.* Cambridge, Mass.: Harvard Uni-
                versity Press.
Hurst, James Willard
    1956   *Law and Conditions of Freedom in the Nineteenth-Century United States.* Madison:
                University of Wisconsin Press.
    1964   *Law and Economic Growth: The Legal History of the Lumber Industry in Wisconsin:
                1836–1915.* Cambridge, Mass.: Harvard University Press.
Jensen, Michael C., and Meckling, William H.
    1976   "Theory of the Firm: Managerial Behavior, Agency Costs and Ownership Struc-
                ture." *Journal of Financial Economics* 3:305–60. Abridged in *Economics of Corpora-
                tion Law and Securities Regulation,* Richard A. Posner and Kenneth E. Scott. Bos-
                ton: Little, Brown (1980).
Kahn, Alfred E.
    1971   *The Economics of Regulation: Principles and Institutions.* 2 vols. New York:
                Wiley.
Kitch, Edmund W.
    1981a   "The Law and Economics of Rights in Valuable Information." *Journal of Legal
                Studies* 9:683–723.
    1981b   *Regulation, Federalism, and Interstate Commerce.* Cambridge, Mass.: Oelgeschlager,
                Gunn & Hain.
Kitch, Edmund W., and Bowler, Clara Ann
    1979   "The Facts of Munn v. Illinois." *Supreme Court Review* 1978:313–43.
Kolko, Gabriel
    1965   *Railroads and Regulation 1877–1916.* Princeton, N.J.: Princeton University Press.

Kronman, Anthony T., and Posner, Richard A.
   1979   *The Economics of Contract Law.* Boston: Little, Brown.

Kuznets, Simon
   1971   *Economic Growth of Nations: Total Output and Production Structure.* Cambridge, Mass.: Harvard University Press.

Landes, William M., and Posner, Richard A.
   1975a   "The Private Enforcement of Law." *Journal of Legal Studies* 4:1–46.
   1975b   "The Independent Judiciary in an Interest-Group Perspective." *Journal of Law and Economics* 18:875–901.
   1979   "Adjudication as a Private Good." *Journal of Legal Studies* 8:235–84.
   1980   "Legal Change, Judicial Behavior, and the Diversity Jurisdiction." *Journal of Legal Studies* 9:367–97.

Leimer, Dean, and Lesnoy, Selig
   1980   "Social Security and Private Saving: A Reexamination of the Time Series Evidence Using Alternative Social Security Wealth Variables." Unpublished manuscript.

Liebhafsky, H. H.
   1979   "Review." *Journal of Economic Issues* 13:195–200.

MacAvoy, Paul W.
   1965   *The Economic Effects of Regulation: The Trunkline Railroad Cartels and the Interstate Commerce Commission Before 1900.* Cambridge, Mass.: M.I.T. Press.

McCloskey, D. N.
   1975   "The Persistence of English Common Fields" and "The Economics of Enclosure." In W. N. Parker and E. L. Jones, *European Peasants and Their Markets.* Princeton, N.J.: Princeton University Press.
   1976   "English Open Fields as Behavior Towards Risk." In *Research in Economic History: An Annual Compilation*, vol. 1, edited by P. Uselding. Greenwich, Conn.: JAI Press.

McCurdy, Charles W.
   1976   "Stephen J. Field and Public Land Law Development in California, 1850–1866: A Case Study of Judicial Resource Allocation in Nineteenth Century America." *Law and Society Review* 10:235–66.

McGee, John S.
   1958   "Predatory Price Cutting: The Standard Oil (N.J.) Case." *Journal of Law and Economics* 1:137–69.
   1980   "Predatory Pricing Revisited." *Journal of Law and Economics* 23:289–330.

Maloney, M. T., and Yandle, Bruce
   1980   "Rent Seeking and the Evolution of Property Rights in Air Quality." Unpublished manuscript.

Manne, Henry G., ed.
   1975   *The Economics of Legal Relationships: Readings in the Theory of Property Rights.* St. Paul, Minn.: West.

Mayer, Thomas
   1968   *Monetary Policy in the United States.* New York: Random House.

Mishan, E. J.
   1971   "The Postwar Literature on Externalities: An Interpretative Essay." *Journal of Economic Literature* 9:1–28.

North, Douglas
   1973   *The Rise of the Western World.* Cambridge: Cambridge University Press.
   1978   "Structure and Performance: The Task of Economic History." *Journal of Economic Literature* 16:963–78.

Olson, Mancur
   1977   *The Causes and Quality of Southern Growth.* Research Triangle Park, N.C.: Southern Growth Policies Board.

Peltzman, Sam
    1973a   "The Benefits and Costs of New Drug Regulation." In *Regulating New Drugs,* edited by Richard L. Landau. Chicago: University of Chicago Center for Policy Study.
    1973b   "An Evaluation of Consumer Protection Legislation: The 1962 Drug Amendments." *Journal of Political Economy* 81:1049–91.
    1975   "The Diffusion of Pharmaceutical Information." In *Drug Development and Marketing,* edited by Robert B. Helms. Washington, D.C.: American Enterprise Institute.
    1976   "Towards a More General Theory of Regulation." *Journal of Law and Economics* 19:211–40.
    1980   "The Growth of Government." *Journal of Law and Economics* 23:209–287.

Plucknett, Theodore F. T.
    1956   *A Concise History of the Common Law.* 5th ed. Boston: Little, Brown.

Polanyi, Karl
    1975   *The Great Transformation.* New York: Octagon Books.
    [1944]

Popkin, Samuel L.
    1979   *The Rational Peasant: The Political Economy of Rural Society in Vietnam.* Berkeley: University of California Press.

Posner, Richard A.
    1969   "Oligopoly and the Antitrust Laws: A Suggested Approach." *Stanford Law Review* 21:1562–1606.
    1972   "A Theory of Negligence." *Journal of Legal Studies* 1:29–96.
    1976   *Antitrust Law: An Economic Perspective.* Chicago: University of Chicago Press.
    1977   *Economic Analysis of the Law.* 2nd ed. Boston: Little, Brown.
    1980a   "A Theory of Primitive Society, with Special Reference to Law." *Journal of Law and Economics* 23:1–53.
    1980b   "Review Article: Anthropology and Economics." *Journal of Political Economy* 88:608–16.
    1981   *The Economics of Justice.* Cambridge, Mass.: Harvard University Press.

Posner, Richard A., and Scott, Kenneth E.
    1980   *Economics of Corporation Law and Securities Regulation.* Boston: Little, Brown.

Priest, George L.
    1977   "The Common Law Process and the Selection of Efficient Rules." *Journal of Legal Studies* 6:65–82.

Rostow, Walter W.
    1960   *The Stages of Economic Growth: A Non-Communist Manifesto.* Cambridge: Cambridge University Press.

Rubin, Paul H.
    1977   "Why Is the Common Law Efficient?" *Journal of Legal Studies* 6:51–63.

Scalia, Antonin
    1978   "Vermont Yankee: The APA, the D.C. Circuit and the Supreme Court." *Supreme Court Review* 1978:345–409.

Scharfman, I. L.
    1931–37   *The Interstate Commerce Commission: A Study in Administrative Law and Procedure.* New York: Commonwealth Fund.

Scherer, Frederick R.
    1980   *Industrial Market Structure and Economic Performance.* 2nd ed. Chicago: Rand McNally.

Schultz, Theodore
    1980   "Nobel Lecture: The Economics of Being Poor." *Journal of Political Economy* 88:639–51.

Siegan, Bernard H.
    1970   "Non-zoning in Houston." *Journal of Law and Economics* 13:71–147.
    1972   *Land Use Without Zoning.* Lexington, Mass.: Lexington Books.
Smith, Adam
    1976   *An Inquiry into the Nature and Causes of the Wealth of Nations.* Edited by Edwin
    [1776] Cannan. Chicago: University of Chicago Press.
Stein, Herbert
    1969   *The Fiscal Revolution in America.* Chicago: University of Chicago Press.
Stigler, George J.
    1968   "A Theory of Oligopoly." In *The Organization of Industry.* Homewood, Ill.: Irwin.
Stigler, George J., and Becker, Gary S.
    1977   "De Gustibus Non Est Disputandum." *American Economic Review* 67:76.
Sumner, Colin
    1979   *Reading Ideologies: An Investigation into the Marxist Theory of Ideology and Law.*
            London: Academic Press.
Telser, Lester G.
    1960   "Why Should Manufacturers Want Fair Trade?" *Journal of Law and Economics*
            3:86–105.
Tiebout, Charles M.
    1956   "A Pure Theory of Local Expenditures." *Journal of Political Economy* 64:416–24.
Weiss, Leonard
    1974   "The Concentration-Profits Relationship and Antitrust." In *Industrial Concentra-
            tion: The New Learning,* edited by Harvey J. Goldschmid, H. Michael Mann, and J.
            Fred Weston. Boston: Little, Brown.
Winter, Ralph, Jr.
    1977   "State Law, Shareholder Protection, and the Theory of the Corporation." *Journal
            of Legal Studies* 6:251–92. Abridged in *Economics of Corporation Law and Securities
            Regulation,* Richard A. Posner and Kenneth E. Scott. Boston: Little, Brown
            (1980).
    1978   *Government and the Corporation.* Washington, D.C.: American Enterprise Insti-
            tute.
Yamey, B. S.
    1952   "Origins of Resale Price Maintenance." *Economic Journal* 62:522.
    1966   *Resale Price Maintenance.* Chicago: Aldine.

~ 4 ~

ADJUDICATION, LITIGATION, AND RELATED PHENOMENA

Marc Galanter
University of Wisconsin–Madison

Still, litigation is the test; what distinguishes law from other forms of moral culture is the potentiality for measuring actions against its norms through some institutionalized process to determine their legitimacy or illegitimacy. It is with the possibility of litigation in mind that the law user, professional or amateur, thinks and acts.
Fallers 1969, p. 34

It is a strange thing, the authority that is accorded to the intervention of a court of justice by the general opinion of mankind! It clings even to the mere formalities of justice, and gives a bodily influence to the mere shadow of the law.
Tocqueville 1953 [1835], vol. 1, p. 140

But is a blurred concept a concept at all?—Is an indistinct photograph a picture of a person at all? Is it even always an advantage to replace an indistinct picture by a sharp one? Isn't the indistinct one often exactly what we need?
Wittgenstein 1958, §71

LOCATING ADJUDICATION

Adjudication is a blurred concept. Not surprisingly, for it invokes a cultural ideal which exists in several overlapping versions; it also points to a set of behaviors referring to and sometimes approximating this ideal. Ideal and behavior are components of larger systems of regulation and disputing. Much adjudication activity takes place in courts, although these institutions do other things as well. All of this is reflected in the experience and beliefs of varied participants and of wider audiences, popular and elite. This whole configuration of ideals, behavior, institutions, and experience is changing through time.

Thus, the subject matter of this essay resembles a grandiose and ungainly confection composed of distinguishable but interpenetrated irregular rings and layers of behavior, experience, beliefs, ideals, and institutional patterns. The general plan of the essay is as follows. After locating adjudication as a cultural model and a social structure, it proceeds to sketch the wider ecology of dispute processing of which adjudication is a core element. It then moves out through concentric rings to discuss the relation of this model to courts as institutions, to patterns of processing disputes, to personal experience, and to wider social patterns. Finally, it asks how the whole constellation is changing over time.

The primary focus of this essay is on formal governmental dispute institutions in the United States in the recent past. I have insistently if unsystematically sought to illuminate these observations by juxtaposing them with comparisons from other times, other places, and other kinds of legal institutions, both exotic and familiar. The resulting unevenness may have the redeeming value of protecting us from premature closure as well as reminding us how problematic these arrangements are.[1]

The terms "adjudication" and "litigation" overlap in their reference. Both refer to the encounter of "cases" with "courts." But each emphasizes different aspects of the process. Adjudication refers to something the court does—to the process of judging. It conjures up the ceremonious, stately, dignified, solemn, deliberative, authoritative. Litigation, on the other hand, refers to what the adversaries do: their activity may be noble or vindictive or frivolous. Litigation entails the possibility of adjudication, but they may become disassociated, so that there can be litigation without adjudication. They are fused, but the relationship is not invariate. They are two sides of a process, like education and

NOTE: I have been rescued from the worst consequences of my folly in attempting to encompass this topic by the friendly assistance of colleagues who generously commented and helped with sources. Without associating them with the gaps and flaws in this account, I would like to acknowledge the help I received from C. Ronald Ellington, Richard B. Hoffman, J. Willard Hurst, Herbert Jacob, Richard Lempert, Leon Lipson, Stewart Macaulay, Alan Paterson, Austin Sarat, and David Trubek. During its protracted gestation, this essay benefited from the capable research assistance of Susan Bissegger, Mark Lazerson, David Lerman, Joan E. T. Stearns, Reg Stites, Ann Ustad, Gary Wilson, and Laura Woliver. It also benefited from my concurrent involvement in projects supported by the National Endowment for the Humanities and the National Institute of Law Enforcement and Criminal Justice, and from my participation in the National Conference on the Lawyers' Changing Role in Resolving Disputes, held at Harvard Law School in October 1982. The views contained here are my own and should not be attributed to any of these benefactors.

The imperatives of closure oblige me to resist the inclination to incorporate more of the burgeoning literature on litigation, courts, and "alternatives" that has appeared since this essay was cast into its present form in 1983.

[1] The "we" and "us" that populate these pages are a company composed of author and reader. That company does not include the authors of the other essays in this volume or its editors.

school; they each drain meaning from the other. Hence, we can't understand that complex unless we look at both.

Adjudication refers to one of the core phenomena of the legal process. Though not one of the most frequent, it is important not only when it does occur, but also

1. as a potential recourse—a threat or escape;
2. hence, as a source of counters that can be used for bargaining or regulation in other settings;
3. as a model for other processes;
4. as a symbol exemplifying shared or dominant values and hence as a source of legitimacy for norms, offices, acts and so forth. (This aspect is compounded in common-law systems, where adjudication is the primary focus of legal scholarship and holds sway over legal thought vastly disproportionate to its prominence as a source of rules.)

Much of the meaning of other activities in the legal process is expressed in terms of this adjudication core. The making of claims, the arrangement of settlements, the assessment of official action—all these frequently involve reference to adjudication—to actual adjudication or to some imaginary adjudication that could take place.

The Adjudication Matrix

I began by viewing adjudication as a kind of third-party processing of disputes, in which disputants or their representatives present proofs and arguments to an impartial authoritative decision-maker who gives a binding decision, conferring a remedy or award on the basis of a preexisting general rule. I use this not as a set of essential qualities that define adjudication, but because it serves to plunge us in the midst of the set of phenomena to be examined. There is not a single discrete process which can be identified as adjudication. Instead we are addressing a family or cluster of processes that resemble one another and approximate this model in varying ways. Just which are to be accounted adjudication and which are something else is a fruitless question. I shall proceed by constructing a prototype of adjudication, attempting to identify various dimensions in our picture of it and to suggest the range of variation along these dimensions. I shall then attempt to present some instances of current understanding of that variation and of its connection with other aspects of the legal process and with wider social processes.

To identify the structural features and cultural commitments that we regard as adjudication and to understand the affinities and contrasts between different kinds of adjudicative processes, I suggest a series of contrasts or polarities. (These are not meant to indicate dichotomies; rather, they represent points on a set of continua.) In each, the first term is taken as a characteristic of adjudication (or at least of one type) as opposed to other dispute processes. These form a matrix of expectations that I find helpful to describe and explain adjudication and related phenomena.

The matrix is useful because there is a significant clustering among features on the left-hand side of Table 1, but not all these features are present in all real-world instances that we would call adjudication. Indeed, it is unlikely that they would be, in the light of the tensions between some of the characteristics associated with litigation. For example, adjudication involves a simultaneous commitment to decide according to general rules and to handle each case on its individual merits. This suggests that our list (and our

TABLE 1

Some Elements of the Adjudication Prototype

	Elements	Departures
Intake	Individuated	Routine, Random
	Case-by-Case	Programmatic
	Reactive	Proactive
Process	Participative	Nonparticipative
	Forum governance	Disputant Control
	Narrow Relevance	Wide Relevance
Basis of Decision	Formalistic	Result-Oriented
	General Rules	Particularism
	Preexisting Rules	Rule-Making
Decision	Arbitral	Mediative
	Award or Remedy	Therapeutic Reintegration
	All or None	Compromise
	Binding	Advisory
	Final	Continuing Readjustment
Differentiation	Remote	Accessible
	Professional	Lay
	Mediated	Direct Participation
	Recondite	Common Understanding
	Impermeable	Permeable
Connection to Power	Impartial	Allied
	Independent	Dependent
	Governmental	Private
	Coercive	Voluntary

commitments) embraces multiple and perhaps conflicting notions of adjudication. (I would expect even less clustering among the features represented by the right-hand end of each of these dimensions because deviations from adjudication may lie in very different directions. There are more than two kinds of things in the world.)

The items in the left-hand column reflect my sense of the "classical" picture of adjudication in the mid-twentieth century United States imparted to me in my legal education and embellished by subsequent reading and reflection. That this picture fuses descriptive and prescriptive elements is not without advantages. For the matrix enables us to locate competing visions of adjudication as an ideal. Certain of the features listed in the left-hand column are often taken as crucial elements of adjudication, and others as necessary means to achieve them. (Of course, there may be disagreement about which are ends and which are means.) Other observers commend departures from features listed on the left, on the ground that adjudication would be improved by a greater admixture of result orientation, rule-making, wide relevance, mediation, and so forth. Prescriptive visions of adjudication need not be projected to the end points of our continua.

For convenience, I sometimes refer to the locations where adjudication is found as *courts* and the presiding personnel as *judges*, although adjudication takes place at other institutional locations and under the auspices of persons without that title. And, of course, courts and judges in the narrow sense do many other things besides adjudication.

Table 1 lists the dimensions discussed below. To portray the variation along these continua, I give a brief sketch of each of the elements of the prototype and then note *in brackets* some of the departures from the prototype frequently found to be cohabiting with its real-world embodiments.

Individuated, Case-by-Case Treatment

In the adjudication process the units of action are discrete *cases*. The forum addresses delimited controversies between identified persons (or corporate entities) rather than general situations, patterns, problems, or policies. It is obligated to give individuated treatment to each case, not treating cases en masse or on a random or probabilistic basis, but deciding each according to its own merits or qualities.

A case is typically bi-polar. There is a complaining party and one who is the subject of the complaint. Both sides may complain against each other, and each side may be a composite, with disputes among its members. Courts vary in the extent to which they permit a cluster of disputes to be treated as a single case. They also vary in the extent to which they permit whole classes of controversies to be aggregated or decided vicariously and the extent to which general problems may be deliberately packaged in the form of a case in order to address a general condition or to elicit a generalized pronouncement from the forum (for example, the "test case"). And while adhering to bi-polar forms, courts may address complex polycentric disputes (cf. Fuller 1978, p. 394) in which a variety of contenders are arrayed around an issue (cf. Fiss 1979, p. 21).

[Courts develop routines that undermine the individualized response to cases, ignoring their distinctiveness and treating them as fungible (Mather 1973; Sudnow 1965). And courts may depart from case-by-case treatment to adopt a more programmatic focus, in which their response to individual cases reflects concern about a general policy (Galanter et al. 1979). Indeed, commitments to generality, consistency, and publicity may lend a case significance beyond the controversy at hand. Calculated pursuit of such significance—such as deterrence or prevention—pulls against the commitment to individuation.]

Reactive Mobilization of Cases

The adjudicative forum is reactive in the mobilization of its agenda of cases (see Black 1973). The cases are brought to the forum by the initiative of the parties (including institutionalized public accusers); the forum does not reach out proactively to bring cases into itself. Thus a Federal District Court erred in notifying, on its own initiative, potential claimants in a mass accident and inviting them to join the proceedings (*Pam American World Airways* v. *United States District Court*, 1975, pp. 1077–81). [There are historical instances of tribunals with power to initiate cases on their own. Courts may be more closely linked to the initiation of cases. Thus, Haller (1979, p. 274) observes that "[t]hrough the colonial period, the [American] courts generally controlled their caseloads because they issued arrest warrants on complaint of aggrieved citizens and because the rudimentary enforcement officers, such as constables, were generally agents of the courts." Contemporary courts find other ways of encouraging or discouraging particular kinds of cases; some try deliberately to affect the composition of their docket by means ranging from cues to attorneys (Galanter et al. 1979) to lobbying to exclude certain classes of cases from their jurisdiction (see, for example, Burger 1970, p. 933). Reactivity may also be limited by discretionary intake: in the past century, American state supreme courts have gained increasing discretion to choose which cases they hear (Kagan et al. 1978).]

Participation   The disputants participate by presenting proofs and arguments. Often this participation is through expert intermediaries. Participation may be attenuated as, for example, where the forum undertakes responsibility for investigation and proof as is done by the Swedish Public Complaint Board (Eisenstein 1979), or it may approach management of the case by the disputants. [In fact, in a sizable portion of cases in American courts, the defending party is absent and the presentation of proofs and arguments is perfunctory, if not dispensed with entirely.]

Forum Governance   The forum presides over (or consists of) a set of preexisting forms to which it is committed—in contrast, for example, to the Law of the Sea Conference or the Warren Commission. Once initiated, the case proceeds under the control of the forum, according to procedures prescribed by the forum. The forum cannot be dismissed by the parties—as can an arbitrator—nor can they amend its procedures. Important variations in the extent to which the forum delegates control over certain segments of the proceedings to the parties—or to intermediaries certified by the forum to act on their behalf—are discussed below under the rubric of "passive versus active courts."

Narrow Scope of Relevance   The case is defined by claims that specific events, transactions, or relations should be measured by application of some delimited conceptual categories. The forum will hear only matters that are relevant to application of those categories. Frequently its willingness to admit proof and arguments is limited further by other policies—such as those crystallized in rules of evidence, and *res judicata*. Here the forum contrasts with other remedy agents like mediators and counselors who are open to a wide range of matters underlying and connected to the immediate dispute. [Adjudicative fora may have broad rules of relevance, as does the *kuta* of the Lozi of Northern Rhodesia studied by Gluckman (1955). Even the same forum may vary in the scope of relevance: thus, Gluckman (1955, pp. 67, 68) observed that where Barotse disputants were involved in multiplex relationships, the *kuta's* inquiry was broadened to take into account all aspects necessary to reconcile the parties and repair the relationship, while in disputes between strangers the court focused on narrow issues.]

Formal Rationality   The discourse that goes on in connection with adjudication is not open and unbounded. There is a repertoire of legal concepts that is less inclusive than the whole universe of moral discourse or the whole array of sanctioned social norms. The claims of parties are assessed in the light of some bounded body of preexisting authoritative normative learning, to which the forum is committed in advance. Typically, the forum renders a decision by judging the conformance of the parties' claims to established general categories or classificatory concepts (Dibble 1973; Levi 1961; Fallers 1969, p. 32). Application of these general standards precludes response to the unique particularity of the situation or to the external consequences of the decision (cf. Kennedy 1973) and proceeds without a fresh assessment of the wider consequences of the general norm that is being applied. Thus, adjudication approximates to "logically formal rationality" as postulated by Weber (and helpfully explicated by Trubek 1972, pp. 727ff).

[In fact, courts depart from this model of austere formalism in various ways. Appellate judges frame general rules in the hope of producing optimum results (to the dismay of the votaries of "neutral principles" such as Wechsler 1959). Judges at all levels are imbued with a sense that it is their mission to facilitate governmental policies of minimizing drunk driving, prostitution, or pollution (see Galanter et al. 1979). Or—in the style that Weber called "khadi justice"—judges feel impelled to respond to the particular circumstances rather than subsuming cases under general rules (see, for example, Levin 1972).

The inherent ambivalence of general standards requires that judges choose among alternative specifications of norms (cf. Gluckman 1955). In complex legal systems, choice is amplified by the inevitable conflicts and overlaps within a body of norms and among competing bodies—as, for example, in situations of "legal pluralism" (see Tanner 1970; Hooker 1975), where more than one system of legal concepts may be present and available to the disputants and the forum.

At least some adjudication involves parts of the law that are "open-textured," and judges have to choose among variant readings of the existing body of normative learning (Hart 1961; Llewellyn 1960; Levi 1961). Such open-ended rule-making authority may be acknowledged and cultivated or covert and confined. There may be more or less emphasis on the obligation to apply concepts consistently with earlier applications. One dramatic sort of unacknowledged change is the presence of legal fictions, in which fictitious recitals are employed to trigger a desired result without departing from the constraints of authoritative conceptual categories (cf. Fuller 1967).]

Decision and Remedy   Rendering of some authoritative disposition is mandatory: the adjudicator, with her agenda assembled by the parties, is obliged to hear all those cases properly before her. She cannot (as can, for example, the legislature or executive) decline to render a decision. The judge renders her decision on the merits (ascertained in terms of the authoritative learning) rather than arranging an agreement acceptable to the parties. The forum renders an award or remedy to one party rather than engaging in therapeutic reintegration of the parties. The decision is all or none: the forum grants or denies the claim of one party. Indeed, there may be norms against compromise (Coons 1964). The decision is binding rather than advisory. The decision is final. Although there are procedures for trying to reopen it, there are also norms that render readjudication difficult. Typically, the forum cuts its links with the dispute and closes the case rather than undertaking a course of continuing supervision or readjustment of its decree.

[Institutions that are recognizably courts may depart from these features in various ways. In the United States, for example, courts do exercise control over the agenda of cases; there are courts which seek therapeutic reintegration of the parties (see, for example, Foster 1966); compromise decisions and arranged settlements are endemic (see pp. 199–202 below, on settlement); court decisions are often unenforced; continuing supervision and readjustment—traditional in a few areas like railroad reorganization and child custody and support—has expanded in modern "structural" or "public law" or "extended impact" litigation so that judges have undertaken continuing supervision of prisons, mental hospitals, schools, and the like.]

Conversely, courts that avow to reconcile parties and repair relationships may, in fact, act very much like prototypical adjudicators, imposing all-or-none decisions on recalcitrant parties. Starr and Yngvesson (1975, p. 556), reanalyzing Gluckman's material (1955), find that even in cases involving multiplex relations among the disputants, the Barotse court usually "decided in favor of one litigant at the expense of the other, and [made] no further attempt at reconciliation. . . . " Reassessing this and other anthropological work, Starr and Yngvesson stress the need to distinguish the process from the announced goals of the forum, whose notions of compromise and balance may diverge from that of the parties, particularly where there are disparities of power.

Differentiation   Adjudication is differentiated from other activities. (Cf. Bohannon's notion [1965] of law as reinstitutionalization of norms and Hart's notion [1961, p. 78] of law as involving secondary rules.) Abel (1973) provides an elaborate analysis of forum differentiation and its consequences. Typically, adjudication involves special locations, persons, roles, language, postures, costumes, and furniture. Often it involves moving to unfamiliar places and settings, movement that may represent substantial cost or an insurmountable barrier. Many reform schemes aim to dispel this remoteness and lower this cost.

Adjudication is, typically, conducted by professional specialists who have recourse to special forms of knowledge, discontinuous with everyday understandings, and not expressed in everyday language. This specialized learning may be generated in the adjudicative institutions themselves—as in common-law systems where the higher strata of judges produce the doctrinal literature—or there may be, as in contemporary Europe (continuing the Roman tradition), a division between the judge who decides the cases and the legal expert who cultivates and transmits doctrine (Dawson 1960, p. 34; Merryman 1969).

Participation is, typically, indirect and through specialist intermediaries who are attached to the forum or have a monopoly on such intermediation. Enforcement, too, is entrusted to specialized functionaries (bailiffs, jailers) rather than carried out by the parties, their allies, or the community through ostracism or direct physical imposition.

The whole process is insulated from general knowledge about persons and their histories and statuses. Justice is blind; the decision-maker excludes the perceptions and commitments of everyday life to render a decision based solely on those aspects identified as salient by applicable legal categories.

[There are many sorts of departures from this removed, insulated, and impermeable character. Juries, lay assessors, elected judges, short terms of office, and other devices link the process to community concerns and understandings. Permeation by considerations of community standing (Cohn 1959) or political correctness (Lubman 1967) may be deemed proper—or the whole process may be crudely manipulated to external political ends (Kirchheimer 1961). Apart from the deliberate utilization of such bases of decision, the structure of adjudicatory institutions may enable parties to import into the forum their advantages of power, wealth, and experience (Galanter 1974).]

Impartiality and Independence   The forum is impartial. It is not predisposed toward any party. The decision-maker is not an ally of either (set of) disputant(s), but is poised evenly between (or above) them. Unlike the manager or administrator, the adjudicator has nothing of her own at stake in the controversy. Nor is the judge an agent of any entity outside the forum, with responsibility to forward policies other than those crystallized in the applicable legal learning. Impartiality and independence are institutionalized in restrictions on contact with disputants and such devices as tenure and fixed pay to protect the judges against "command influence" and retaliation. [Eagerness to preserve a visibly independent judiciary may induce regimes to remove from regular courts classes of cases thought to require politically responsive judging (Toharia 1975b).]

Attempts to explain patterns of judicial decisions in terms of race or class bias have yielded sparse results (Hagen 1974). Thus, a study of felony dispositions found that little outcome variation could be explained by indicators of overt bias (Eisenstein and Jacob 1977). [However, studies of trial and appellate courts have established that judges give expression to their own policy preferences (for example, Rohde and Spaeth 1976), and their perceptions of public opinion (Gibson 1976). Apart from the carry-over of personal preferences into the judicial role there are structural factors which cut against impartiality. Despite his position as detached umpire, the judge is perforce an agent of the polity, committed to presiding over the administration of various public policies and not uncommonly concerned to effectuate these policies (Galanter et al. 1979; on the pull toward alignment with one of the parties, see the account of Frankel 1976). Governments are often not content with the alignment produced spontaneously, but resolutely enhance it by deploying their powers as employers over appointments, promotions, transfers, and so forth (Bayley 1964, p. 132).]

The forum, as many have observed, tends to develop its own distinctive views, interests, and needs (Starr and Yngvesson 1975; Kidder 1974; Abel 1973; Aubert 1967). The third party becomes another party. Its institutional needs become one of the determinants of the process that transpires there (Balbus 1973; Blumberg 1967). Differentiated and partly autonomous institutions of adjudication are achieved at the price of institutionalizing a distinctive outlook and interest that transforms disputes and colors the application of policy. (And, it should be noted, increasing autonomy and professionalism, typically thought conducive to improved performance, may sometimes be associated with corruption and pursuit of personal ambition [Kagan 1981, pp. 207–8].)

Connection to Organized Power   The prototypical adjudicative institution is an organ of government: it is located in a public building, it is staffed by state officers who apply public norms, and its sanctions are imposed by the compulsory powers of the state. [Historically, the notion that adjudication is a state monopoly is a relatively recent one (Dawson 1960, pp. 5ff.; Weber 1954, pp. 140ff.). In practice, there is an immense amount of adjudication in the private sector—in tribunals embedded in various institutions (churches, universities, labor unions, exchanges, trade associations, and so forth) as well as specialized institutions for arbitration (Mentschikoff 1961). The line between public and private is not a sharp one. Public norms may be applied in private tribunals and enforced by private sanctions; conversely, public tribunals, officials, and sanctions may be utilized to enforce private norms.]

Courts are coercive rather than voluntary. They impose outcomes regardless of the assent of the parties. But, in fact, their decrees are often unenforced. The coercive powers of courts are important even when they are not utilized, for the threat of their use induces settlements between the parties—often, capitulation by one party. The degree of compliance with settlements is higher than with verdicts (Community Service Society 1974; McEwen and Maiman 1984).

Adjudication in the Ecology of Dispute Processing

The adjudication cluster shades off into other kinds of "third-party" decision-making (mediation, arbitration, therapy, administration, political decision-making). All of these third-party processes may be elements in a complex ecology of dispute processes found in most societies. (On the plurality of dispute and remedy processes in all societies, see Abel 1973; Pospisil 1967.) The mapping of this ecology is only beginning and has proven extremely difficult (see Ladinsky et al. 1979). Table 2 provides a simple taxonomy of modes of dispute processing in terms of the basic numerical configuration—a simplification commended for its mnemonic virtues as well as for its (admittedly weak) evocation of the nature of the activity and experience associated with that mode. It is necessary to

TABLE 2

A Taxonomy of Modes of Dispute Processing

Three Parties	Adjudication
	Arbitration
	Fact-Finding
	Mediation
	Therapy
	Administrative Decision-Making
	Political Decision-Making
Intermediate Forms	Champion (e.g., ombudsman)
	Parental Dyad (i.e., one party decides)
Two Parties	Bargaining/Negotiation
	Under threat of resort to third party
	In presence of group norms
	Under threat of exit, or other unilateral action
One Party	Exit
	Avoidance
	Self-help
	Resignation ("lumping it")
No Parties	Failure to Apprehend Remedy
	Claim
	Violation

NOTE: Arranged by the number of principal persons/roles involved in the process of seeking a remedy or resolution. This classification omits various support roles (informer, adviser, advocate, ally, and surrogate) described by Black and Baumgartner 1983.

sketch this larger ecology because adjudication exists not in isolation, but in the context of many other kinds of dispute processing. The kinds of claims and defenses asserted and the arguments used in adjudication may be carried over to other modes. Possible resort to adjudication is an important resource in other arenas; finally, the working of these other modes affects the agenda and substance of the adjudicatory institutions.

Table 2 lists various modes of dispute processing. Each of the terms—arbitration, negotiation, and so on—could be subjected to the same kind of analytic disaggregation as the notion of adjudication. Each refers to a family of arrangements, whose characteristics overlap with members of other families. Since these modes are related along a number of different dimensions, there is no single correct arrangement of these constructs, but I hope that they provide useful landmarks.

Table 2 distinguishes several prominent varieties of third-party dispute processing. Like *adjudication*, each of the others can be thought of as a clustering of the characteristics displayed in Table 1. Thus, *arbitration* refers to a family of processes that share such features as an impartial decision-maker, who enters a binding final award on the basis of proofs and arguments presented by the disputants (or their representatives). It commonly departs from adjudication in that the forum is selected by the parties (either ad hoc, by contractual undertaking, or by adhesion to a standing procedure) and that the forum is nongovernmental. There is also variation as to whether the arbitrator is constrained to decide in accordance with a prefixed body of norms and whether the norms applied are public ones or indigenous to a particular setting. Arbitration may be present in an attenuated form of *fact-finding* in which the parties accept the decisional implications of a finding on the facts and delegate the latter to an agreed upon third party—such as the lumber grader or the patent office. (Fact-finding may have important effects on negotiating positions even where parties have *not* agreed to accept its decisional implications.)

Many kinds and styles of arbitration can exist within a single society. Among the common varieties in the United States are labor arbitration, in which the "law of the shop" is applied (Getman 1979); commercial arbitration in the standing bodies of self-contained trade associations applying norms of the trade; commercial arbitration by ad hoc arbitrators applying some version of governmental law (see Mentschikoff 1961); and the arbitration of tort cases or small claims under the auspices of a court that urges or requires that such cases be diverted to arbitration (Levin 1983).

Mediation refers to a contrasting cluster of dispute processes in which the forum, rather than imposing a binding solution on the parties, arranges a settlement that is agreeable to them. Mediators range from the mere go-between carrying messages, to one who actively devises a solution and persuades the parties to accept it. The mediator may be a specialized standing body or a notable mobilized ad hoc for the purpose (such as the shopping center manager in MacCollum 1967). Mediators may be reactive, or they may be proactive like the mediators in pre-Communist China (Cohen 1966, p. 1217) and Communist China (Lubman 1967, p. 1321). Judges or arbitrators often seek to mediate a dispute, holding in reserve their power of binding decision. Although this mixed form ("med-arb") has been attacked as compromising the integrity of each process (Fuller 1963), it is strikingly prevalent in American dispute processing in settings as varied as labor arbitration, arrangement of consent orders by administrative agencies, plea bargaining in criminal cases, and judicial arrangement of settlements in civil suits.

Mediation shades off into *therapy*—that is, modes of dispute processing that aim not to secure agreement from parties as they are, but to change the parties by giving them insight into their situation or themselves (Gibbs 1967; Golding 1969). Therapy, too, may be mixed with other forms, as in counseling under court auspices (Foster 1966).

Like mediation and therapy, *administrative decision-making* is prospective. But the administrator (for example, the school principal or welfare official) exercises control over the subject matter or parties that extends beyond the immediate dispute; he is responsible for fulfilling the goals of his organization; his aims are not confined to the universe of claims posed by the parties. His inquiry is not restricted by limiting rules of relevance and admissibility; his decision need not apply preexisting general standards (Eckhoff 1966; cf. Fuller 1969, pp. 207ff. on the contrast between legal authority and managerial direction). Of course, agencies with administrative responsibilities may commit themselves to abide by adjudicatory forms.

With *political decision-making* we move away from the impartial and independent decision-maker to one who can be recruited as an ally. The permissible devices of persuasion are enlarged to include exchanges with the decision-maker (support, fealty) as well as proofs and arguments. We move away from the bi-polar case to the polycentric dispute and away from the obligation to decide by reference to a closed stock of preexisting rules to forthright fashioning of new rules—or away from general rules to individual ad hoc decisions. The same subject matters (divorce, incorporation, franchise, territorial dispute) may be handled by political, administrative, or adjudicative decision. Political decision-makers will often act as if they are subject to the constraints of an adjudicator and will engage in mock-adjudicative forms and justifications.

Although the most prestigious and visible third-party processes are governmental in location, sponsorship, personnel, norms, and sanctions, modern societies are honeycombed with third-party processes that are nongovernmental. These range from forums that are relatively independent in all of these respects (for example, religious courts) to those that are closely appended to governmental processes, dependent on them for norms and sanctions. These appended processes include private forums established to forestall governmental intervention in a trade (such as the Motion Picture Code Administration described by Randall 1968) as well as systems of negotiation or mediation that flourish in the anterooms and hallways of official adjudicatory or administrative decision-makers (see, for example, Ross 1970; Macaulay 1966, pp. 153ff.; Woll 1960).

Dispute forums may be separate institutions (a court, the American Arbitration Association, or the like) or embedded within the social setting (workplace, school, church, and so forth) where a dispute occurs. Embedded forums range from those barely distinguishable from the everyday decision-making within the institution to those such as grievance hearings specifically constituted to handle disputes that cannot be resolved by everyday processes.

These three-party processes stand in contrast to *bargaining* or *negotiation* between two disputing parties. Negotiation ranges from that which is indistinguishable from the everyday adjustments that constitute the relationship between the parties to that which is "bracketed" as an emergency or a disruption of that relationship. Negotiations among businessmen (Macaulay 1963), between injury victims and insurers (Ross 1970), among parties to an uncontested divorce (Mnookin and Kornhauser 1979), or in (some styles of) plea bargaining of criminal charges are alike in that no third party is present; but the course of the negotiations is importantly affected by the kind, feasibility, and cost of potential third-party intervention. The ability to invoke a third party of a particular sort may be a crucial element in the bargaining, but such a threat may be insignificant compared with (usually tacit) threats to withdraw from beneficial relations or to cause reputational damage by circulating information to other interested parties. The bargaining parties may themselves have internalized the normative idiom of the third party. (Cf. Barkun's observation [1968, chap. 6] on shared values as effectuating implicit mediation and Eisenberg [1976] on the role of norms in dispute negotiations.)

The contrast between two- and three-party modes is further blurred by the presence of intermediate forms. The *champion*—neither an arbiter with authority to render a binding decision or a mere representative of one party—combines advocacy on behalf of one disputant with an element of investigative judging. The champion is familiar to us in his recent incarnation as the (government) ombudsman (Gellhorn 1966; Anderson 1969; Hill 1976) and in the media ombudsman such as "action line" columns (Palen 1979; Mattice 1980), the complaint bureau, the Better Business Bureau (Eaton 1980), and the elected official who intervenes on behalf of constituents (Mann 1968; Karikas 1980).

The champion is a third party who is something less than a decision-maker. In another intermediate form which I call the *parental dyad* one of the two parties serves as decision-maker as well as disputant. Thus, insurance companies decide the complaints of aggrieved policyholders (Ross 1975); automobile manufacturers decide the warranty claims of car buyers (Whitford 1968); architects serve as both arbitrators and owners' representatives in disputes between owners and building contractors (Johnstone and Hopson 1967, chap. 9). Such decision-makers may be obligated to observe some or many of the requirements ordinarily incumbent on an adjudicator—such as hearing arguments or deciding according to preexisting rules. When we recall administrators disposing of subordinates' complaints and parents deciding (their) disputes with their children, it is evident that the parental dyad is one of the most frequent dispute configurations.

So far I have been discussing modes of disputing that are discursive (what Hirshman 1970 calls "voice"). But there are also unilateral—hence, nondiscursive—modes of processing disputes. These include *exit*—that is, withdrawal from a situation or relationship by moving, resigning, or severing relations, as well as various lesser forms that might better be termed *avoidance* (Hirshman 1970; Felstiner 1974).

Exit and avoidance may be the goal, as well as the sanction, in the dispute process. A disputant may threaten resort to a court in order to effectuate a desired exit (Merry 1979, p. 894). On the other hand, the presence of exit as a credible sanction may be important to the working of other remedies; that is, the threat of resort to exit may create a "bargaining endowment" just as does the threat of resort to adjudication. A remedy for one party may be a sanction to the other, and the threat of sanction may induce remedial action. Exit options are not inherently incompatible with the pursuit of other remedies. The rights-assertion dimension may be usefully distinguished from the exit-versus-remain dimension: an aggrieved party can remain and acquiesce (lump it) or remain and assert his claim; similarly, he may simply leave or he may leave and assert his claim as well (Bruinsma 1979).

Exit and avoidance do not exhaust the possibilities of unilateral dispute processing. *Self-help* includes various forms of direct action—taking or retaining possession of property as well as physical retaliation, overt or covert. Direct physical violence may be the most prominent element in a system of disputing (Hasluck 1954) or it may play an interstitial role (as in the American neighborhood depicted by Merry 1979, p. 912).

Disputants may decline to pursue any of these options and may resign themselves to an unfavorable situation: gains of the available dispute options may appear too low or the cost too high (including opportunity costs, the psychic costs, and physical risks of disputing). Such *resignation* ("lumping it") behavior may be a matter of allowing a single incursion to pass without protest or it may involve acquiescence in continuing predation. Merry (1979, p. 903) describes the frequency of endurance of continuing conflict where the costs of avoidance are too high. Such inaction on the part of individuals has its counterpart among institutions and official disputants such as police, prosecutors, and agencies. (See below, p. 185.)

Resignation—"lumping it"—shades off into *failure to apprehend* a violation or grievance (or underestimation of its seriousness) or the possibility of remedy. Vast numbers of warranty violations, exposures to dangerous substances and conditions, acts of malpractice, and so forth remain undetected. With these cognitive barriers we eliminate the last of the parties and with it the dispute. (The construction of disputes from perceptions of injury is discussed below [pp. 183–186].)

ADJUDICATIVE INSTITUTIONS AND THEIR TRANSFORMATIONS

The first part of this essay portrayed adjudication as a family of dispute mechanisms displaying certain resemblances. Specific members of this family exist as elements in an ecology of mechanisms for constructing, processing, and suppressing disputes. The next part sketched some of these other mechanisms. Adjudication is characteristically located in specialized institutions called courts.[2] Examining these may reveal some of the concomitants of variation in adjudication and may display some of the connections of adjudication to other modes of dispute processing within and outside the courts.

Specialization

Specific adjudicative institutions do not exist in all human societies (Wimberley 1973; in coding a sample drawn from the Human Relations Area Files, he defined courts as "institutions of one or more judges possessing authority to make binding decisions recognized by society," p. 79). Mediation is more widespread and possibly presents an earlier stage in the evolution of legal institutions (Schwartz and Miller 1964). In any event, some adjudication seems to be present in all nation states, and many societies that are not so constituted have institutions in which adjudicative functions are concentrated in separate organs. Such institutions may combine their judicial functions with administrative ones, like the Lozi *kuta* (Gluckman 1955), or may be exclusively judicial, like the Soga court (Fallers 1969). This pairing suggests that a less specialized tribunal is not necessarily less explicit or less elaborate in the performance of its judicial function. Common-law courts have often performed nonadjudicative functions: Dawson (1960, p. 8) describes English local courts of the thirteenth to seventeenth centuries as "mi-

---

[2] Not all such institutions may be called courts in local parlance, and those who preside in them may not enjoy the honorific title bestowed on those who preside over a court. For example, in the United States there are many "courts" located outside the "judicial branch" of government. The status of their officers as "judges" is ambiguous. In 1979, the federal government had a body of "Administrative Law Judges," as Hearing Examiners were renamed in 1972, approximately the size of the judiciary staffing the federal courts (Mans 1979).

crocosms of government organized under judicial forms." Courts may resist the allotment of tasks they view as nonjudicial and observers may fear that institutional integrity is compromised by courts' performance of nonjudicial functions. Nevertheless, most American courts retain an admixture of responsibilities other than adjudication such as naturalization, incorporation, name changes, marriages, and appointment of public officials. (On "the other things that courts do," see Schwartz 1981.)

Courts may not only devote themselves exclusively to adjudicatory functions, but they may specialize in specific sorts of cases. Most courts have jurisdiction over less than all the legal controversies in their societies. Jurisdiction may be limited by territory, by parties (like citizens), by amount or seriousness, or by type of case. The typing may be by some large division such as civil versus criminal, or by finer divisions: courts may be confined to cases involving housing, taxes, domestic relations, claims under government contracts, or the like. Specialized courts tend to occupy the lower reaches of judicial hierarchies, but there may be several tiers of specialized courts, including specialized appellate courts. Higher courts tend to be less specialized, but their jurisdiction is confined in other ways (by foreclosing appeal on many issues, confining review to issues of law rather than fact, and so forth).

Specialized courts may produce different results than do general courts. A study of the United States Court of Customs and Patent Appeals, found evidence that "specialization tends to increase the influence of litigation groups over judicial decisions, and that increased influence may lead to policies that differ significantly from those made by generalist courts" (Baum 1977, p. 846). Assignment to a specialized housing court was found to elicit more programmatic and mission-oriented judicial behavior (Galanter et al. 1979).

Density: The Number of Courts and Judges

Notwithstanding the formidable difficulties of identifying courts and judges for purposes of comparison, the sketchy data available suggest that great disparities exist among societies in the quantitative presence of adjudicative institutions, disparities which have not attracted attempts at systematic explanation. Among industrialized democratic countries, there is a striking variation in the number of judges per million population, as noted in Table 3.

Table 3 displays the dramatic disparities in the presence of judges[3] and the very different ratios of judges to the total number of legal practitioners. Of course, these dramatic contrasts have to be qualified by noting the problem of counting who are judges and what are courts. Similar bodies may be deemed courts in one place and administrative tribunals in another. Are zoning boards and licensing bodies courts? And what of all the counterpart institutions in the private sector—grievance committees, review boards, arbitrators, and the like?

Notwithstanding the vagaries of identification and measurement, Table 3 suggests the presence of important variation. Some of the variance may be associated with differences between civil-law and common-law systems. Common-law adjudication delegates to lawyers tasks performed by the judges themselves in civil-law systems. But the variation

[3] These disparities seem to predate modern conditions. In the eighteenth century the number of royal judges in France was over 5,000, compared with about 15 in England, which had about one quarter the population of France (Dawson 1960, pp. 70–72).

TABLE 3

Judges and Lawyers in Selected Countries

	Judges			Lawyers		
	Year	Number per Million[1]	Source	Year	Number per Million[1]	Source
Australia	1977	41.6	c	1975	911.6[2]	e
Belgium	1975	105.7	d	1972	389.7	b
Canada	1970	59.3[4]	g	1972	890.1[3]	f
Costa Rica	1970	64.8	j	1970	293.1	j
England-Wales	1973	50.9[4]	g	1973	606.4[5,6]	g
France	1973	84.0[4]	g	1973	206.4[5]	g
India	1971	10.9[7]	n	1981	323.6[8]	n
Italy	1973	100.8[4]	g	1973	792.6[5]	g
Japan	1974	22.7	i	1975	91.2[9]	o
				[1982]	[807.1][10]	r
Netherlands	1975	39.8[4]	d	1972	170.8	b
New Zealand	1976	26.8	m	1975	1081.3[11]	l
Norway	c.1977	60.8[12]	o	c.1977	450.0	o
Peru	1970	23.6	j	1970	318.4	j
Poland	1975	93.6[13]	o	1975	92.1	o
Spain	1970	31.0	j	1972	893.4	b
South Korea	1975	14.5	o	1975	23.5[9]	o
Sweden	1973	99.6[4]	g	1973	192.4[5]	g
United States	1980	94.9[14]	a,h,k	1980	2348.7[15]	q
West Germany	1973	213.4[4]	g	1973	417.2[5]	g
Yugoslavia	1979	481.1[16]	p	1979	177.2[17]	p

SOURCES:
[a] Administrative Office of the United States Courts 1980[a]. [b] American Bar Foundation 1973. [c] Barwick 1977, Appendix A. [d] Council of Europe 1975, pp. 33, 114. [e] Disney et al. 1977, p. 79. [f] Egan 1972, p. 384. [g] Johnson et al. 1977. [h] Judicial Conference of the United States 1981, p. 25. [i] McMahon 1974, p. 1379. [j] Merryman and Clark 1978, pp. 486, 497, Tables 7.1, 7.13. [k] National Center for State Courts, 1982. [l] New Zealand Department of Statistics 1976. [m] New Zealand Department of Statistics 1978. [n] Oommen 1983, pp. 19, 20. [o] Rhyne 1978. [p] Savezni Zavod za Statistiku 1981; Tables 103-14, 103-15, 103-16, 103-17, 133-5, 133-9, 133-10, 133-12, 133-13, and 133-14. [q] U.S. Department of Labor, Bureau of Labor Statistics 1982, Table 13-20. [r] Brown 1983, pp. 479, 484.

NOTES:
[1] Unless noted otherwise, all population data taken from *World Population 1979* (Washington, D.C.: U.S. Department of Commerce, Bureau of the Census, 1980).
[2] Disney et al. (1977:78) define lawyers as practicing barristers, principal solicitors in private practice, solicitors employed by principal solicitors, and persons admitted as lawyers who are employed by government, by corporations, or by other private organizations primarily for the purpose of providing legal services. This definition excludes judges, court officials, law professors, and law book publishers.

within each is very large. Numbers may reflect political decisions about the role of courts. Haley (1978) asserts that maintenance of a small judicial plant in Japan reflects a government policy of restricting access to judicial remedies:

> . . . the number of judges in Japan has grown but little for the entire period from 1890 to the present. Thus as the population has grown the ratio of judges to the population has declined from one judge to 21,926 persons in 1890 to . . . one judge to 56,391 persons in 1969. [p. 381]

Haley credits this policy, rather than a cultural aversion to litigation, with the diversion of disputes into mediational modes (see p. 198 below).

The number of courts reflects access in another way, since it affects distance. Analysis of a century of records from a single Chinese district, reveal that "while 60 percent of the civil cases where the plaintiff resided in the city containing the court were litigated to result, only 20 percent of those in which the plaintiff resided 71 to 80 *li* from the city were litigated until the matter was determined" (D. C. Buxbaum 1971, p. 274).

Similarly, the rate at which Zinacantecos took disputes to a ceremonial center was found to be inverse to the distance from that center (Collier 1973, p. 66). Employing size of jurisdiction—the inverse of number of courts—as a surrogate for both costs and absence of familiarity, Abel (1977) found increase in geographic jurisdiction of courts

---

[3] Law Society membership includes retired, nonactive, those in business, government, court officials; some may be members of more than one society.

[4] Johnson et al. (1977) attempt to measure "career judges." They explain that "the functions of a judge vary considerably among the judicial systems embraced in this Study. . . . While part-time judges and 'honorary judges' (generally law assessors) are common in some of . . . [the nations studied], they are rare in the United States. As much as possible, every attempt has been made to control for these particular variations by deleting 'honorary judges' from our manpower totals, and by combining part-time judgeships into equivalent full-time positions."

[5] Johnson et al. delete the judiciary and certain members of the profession not performing an advocacy or representational function, such as government and corporate employees whose possession of a law degree is only incidental. Counted are the private lawyers available to represent clients for a fee, the state prosecutors, salaried lawyers, or private attorneys paid by government to handle criminal cases or to assist individual citizens with noncriminal legal problems.

[6] Includes 27,379 solicitors and 2,485 barristers.

[7] Includes judges and magistrates; unclear whether honorary judges included or not.

[8] India's population in 1981 was 683,810,051, as reported by the preliminary census report, reported in *The Statesman's Yearbook, 1982–83*.

[9] Lawyers registered with the bar association.

[10] The figure in brackets is for all the various legal occupations, as computed by Brown 1983, pp. 479, 484.

[11] Members of New Zealand Law Society holding practicing certificates.

[12] Does not include members of mediation councils, which exist in each municipality. Disputes must be brought before the councils before going to court. Council members are often not lawyers.

[13] Does not include Labor and Social Insurance Courts.

[14] Based on state and federal totals including 354 associate or assistant state judges; does not include 263 part-time federal magistrates, 22 combination federal magistrates, 6,022 part-time state judges and magistrates, and 105 nonjudicial state magistrates. When these judges are included, the figure is 123.25. U.S. Census of 1980 reported a population of 226,504,825.

[15] U.S. Census of 1980 reported a population of 226,504,825.

[16] Includes judges of Ordinary Courts of Law, Economic Courts, and Courts of Associated Labour. When the 54,693 Lay Assessors of the Ordinary Courts and Economic Courts are added, the figure is 2951.6. The total of 5,880 judges of the Associated Courts of Labour is from 1980.

[17] Includes 2,846 lawyers, 210 articled clerks, and 874 "social attorneys of self-management."

inversely related to litigation rates. But the implications of increasing remoteness are not unmixed. If courts are less responsive to everyday disputes, the remoteness from local influence and enhanced accountability to central authority entailed by larger jurisdictions may mean that courts can be used to challenge the locally powerful.

While the number of judges has not been traced over time, there is a hint that, with increasing professionalization, the number of judges has declined. Thus, in France there were from 70,000 to 80,000 judges in the seignorial courts immediately before the revolution (Dawson 1960, p. 79) as opposed to 4,375 in 1973 (Johnson et al. 1977, p. 9–2). It was observed that British rule decreased the number of tribunals available to Indians (Shore 1837, vol. 2, p. 189). The number of judges in Norway doubled in the century and a half after 1814 while the population increased by a factor of four and lawyers by a factor of fifteen (Aubert 1976, pp. 5, 10). In 1925 in Allegheny County, Pennsylvania (population 1.268 million), there were 391 officials with some judicial powers (23 judges, 242 justices of the peace, 46 aldermen, 4 mayors, 68 burgesses, and 8 police magistrates)—that is, one "judge" for every 3,243 residents (Schramm 1928, p. 22) or one judge for every 3,218 if we include the 3 federal judges then sitting in the Western District of Pennsylvania. Fifty years later the population had grown to 1.518 million, but there were only 132 "judges" in the county. This number included 39 active Common Pleas judges, assisted by 4 senior (that is, semiretired) judges, 4 hearing officers, and 1 master; 55 district justices; 8 magistrates; 13 active federal judges assisted by 4 senior judges and 4 magistrates, 2 full time and 2 part time. (The federal court's jurisdiction extended far beyond the county.) [This information is based on telephone interviews conducted by Mark Lazerson.] This otherwise generous count omits the many administrative bodies and officers who perform courtlike functions. The growth of such forums and the increase in full-time positions may have more than offset the observed reduction. Changes in transportation and communication patterns make difficult any conclusion about accessibility of courts. But the point here is that the number of persons exercising regular or ordinary judicial functions has shrunk dramatically. In 1975 there were 11,500 residents per judge, more than three times the ratio in 1925. Whether or not there has been an increase in judicial power, it seems to be concentrated in relatively fewer hands.

The Structure of Courts: Hierarchy and Appeal

Typically, courts are arranged in layers of higher and lower courts, in which the higher courts have greater dignity, wider jurisdiction—territorial, subject matter, seriousness—and exercise some kind of hierarchic control over lower courts. Hierarchy may be rigorous, involving precise delineation of official responsibilities, sharp separation of the office from the incumbent, and rigid differentiation among judges at various levels. On the other hand, positions of superordination and subordination may be less clearly delineated, office and incumbent less clearly separated, and officials at different levels "essentially . . . all homologues with similar authority inherent in their position" (Damaska 1975, p. 510). The hierarchy may be steep, with only a tiny fraction of cases being decided by the highest organs, or it may be flattened out, like the Italian system, where there are no legal limits on appeal to the Court of Cassation, which hears 4,500 civil and 20,000 criminal cases each year (Di Federico 1976, p. 126).

Lower courts may have plenary powers of decision, as in modern common law, or they may make a recommendation to a central and superior decision-maker. Court decisions may be taken to higher courts for correction, as distinct from a rehearing by the same body. The superior court may be staffed by the same body of judges—(as in Roman Catholic matrimonial courts, where the court of one diocese doubles as an appellate court for a neighboring diocese (*Columbia Journal of Law and Social Problems* 1971) or it may be a distinct hierarchic stratum. The second proceeding may be de novo, the entire array of proofs and arguments being explored anew in a fresh proceeding, or like most modern appeals it may be a review limited to examination of alleged errors lodged in the written record of the case. A successful appeal may result in the superior court's decreeing the appropriate outcome or instructing the lower court to do so or returning the case to the lower court for a fresh proceeding. Although the punishment of the erring judge is not the explicit object of appeal, as it once was (Dawson 1960, p. 54), appeals remain a method for the administration of discipline in judicial hierarchies.

In the Anglo-American family of judicial systems hierarchically superior courts are, for the most part, appellate courts, although they may exercise original jurisdiction in restricted categories of cases. The authoritative literature is largely a by-product of this appellate process. Legal propositions enunciated there are binding on lower courts and on subsequent courts under the doctrine of *stare decisis* (see p. 174 below). The learning about the binding authority of decisions may be tacit and conventional or elaborated as a set of formal rules.

Apart from appeal in individual cases, there are other mechanisms to make lower courts accept legal propositions promulgated by superior courts: advisory legal opinions, internal recommendations and circulars (Damaska 1975, p. 496), coupled with inspection and audit procedures, as well as control over assignment and promotion.

Nevertheless in practice lower courts often depart from the pronouncements of superior courts—not only from general prescriptions (Wasby 1970) but also from decrees in specific cases remanded to them (Murphy 1959; *Harvard Law Review* 1954; for a recent review, see Baum 1978). The strictures of hierarchic authority are loosened by a variety of techniques of discretion, interpretation, and evasion which afford courts leeway where they appear bound. On the other hand, inferior judges may strive to emulate their superiors even when they are formally bound to pronounce judgment independently (Di Federico 1976, p. 127).

The Size of Courts: Agreement and Dissent

We may distinguish between "the Court" as an establishment with a certain institutional identity (for example, the Circuit Court of Dane County) and "the court" as the forum in which a particular case is heard. A court in the former sense may consist of an individual judge, but it may also (like most American municipal courts, for example) have dozens of judges of coordinate status. In Anglo-American and many European courts of first instance, each proceeding is heard by a single judge, but some special proceedings may be before panels of judges. Where lay judges sit with professional ones, benches are larger. Two lay assessors along with one professional judge is a typical configuration. (Compare the common-law jury of twelve.)

In the ancient world, courts of far larger size were common: the Courts of the Second Jewish Commonwealth included Sanhedrins of 23 and 71 judges (Mantel 1972); courts of 50 or more were familiar in Rome (Dawson 1960, pp. 17–19). Gluckman's Lozi *kuta* (1955, pp. 9–15) consisted of 20, 30, or more. In India, the traditional *panchayat* nominally consisted of 5 but in practice might include many times that number. Large courts are not unknown in modern settings; in Italy, except in minor cases, judges sit in benches of from 3 to 15 (Di Federico 1976, p. 124).

Judges may be surrounded by other court staff and by auxiliaries to whom fact-finding and decision-making powers may be delegated, either on a standing basis (like probation officers or the judicial magistrates in the American federal courts) or as temporary delegates (special masters, referees, and so forth, see Weinberg 1983; Brazil 1983). There appears to be a recent increase in the size of American court staff and in the use of auxiliaries. For example, growth of staff of the federal judiciary has far outpaced the growth in the number of judges (Clark 1981, pp. 87–88).

Typically, appellate proceedings are before groups of judges—usually, but not always, odd numbers in order to employ majority decision among judges of equal weight. Llewellyn (1960, p. 31) regards sitting in benches as a "steadying factor: stabilizing judicial work, reducing idiosyncrasy and innovation." Compare Di Federico's observation (1976, p. 131) that innovation among Italian judges is greatest in minor courts where they sit alone.

In modern professional courts, multijudge benches typically decide by majority vote. (Some preliminary matters might require a specified minority—for example, four [of nine] justices are required and sufficient to exercise the discretionary appellate jurisdiction of the United States Supreme Court.) Other courts have employed a rule of unanimity (as, with some recent exceptions, the common-law criminal jury) or have assigned different weights to different members. Thus, the Barotse counselors declare themselves in ascending order and the judgment of the senior counselor, as confirmed by the king, is the judgment of the court (Gluckman 1955). Compare the Indian caste panchayat described by Hayden (1981) where later speakers could lower the penalty but not enhance it, an arrangement reminiscent of American military appeals.

For purposes of weighting votes, the judges of modern professional courts are viewed as equals. But courts may contain hierarchic superiors, as the presiding judge of an Italian court, who screens and corrects the work of his colleagues (Di Federico 1976, p. 124). Compare Danelski (1978) on the influence of the chief justice of the United States Supreme Court. Conventions of seniority are common even where formal hierarchy is attenuated—for example, in assignment of opinions, composition of benches, deference, and promotion (see Paterson 1983). In India, departure from a convention of promotion by seniority was widely viewed as a cataclysmic intrusion on the integrity of the judiciary (Gadbois 1982; Dhavan and Jacob 1978).

The deliberations of multijudge courts may be public or secret. (The secrecy may in fact be more or less penetrable, as attested by recent publications on the United States Supreme Court.) On the dynamics of persuasion and bargaining on multijudge courts, see Murphy (1964) and Ulmer (1971). Disagreements may be confined to the interior of these deliberations with the eventual decision an expression of the whole court (as in Italy; Di Federico 1976, p. 124). Or they may be publicly expressed as dissenting votes, in separate opinions, even in opinions dissenting from the judgment of the court.

Dissents may be commonplace: in 1970 there were dissenting votes in 81 percent of all the cases that the United States Supreme Court decided by full opinion (Grossman and Wells 1972, p. 165). On other courts, even courts exercising extensive powers of judicial review, dissents are relatively unusual events: in its first twenty years (1950–70) the Indian Supreme Court decided unanimously all but 7.4 percent of its cases (Dhavan

1977, p. 34). Dissent rates in American state Supreme Courts vary widely, but most have rates lower than 10 percent (Glick and Vines 1973, p. 79). On lower collegial courts (which sit in smaller benches), dissents are even rarer: on California's intermediate appellate courts, dissents were filed in only 1.6 percent of matters disposed of by majority opinion (Wold 1978, p. 64).

The Selection, Recruitment, and Socialization of Judges

The judge may be chosen for the job on the basis of general personal qualities (such as wisdom and integrity) which commend him for the task of resolving disputes—as among the Zapotec (Nader 1969) or in Somalia (Jolowicz 1975, p. 238) or the lay judges still prevalent in many American jurisdictions. (There were 14,000 lay judges in the United States in 1979 [Institute of Judicial Administration 1979, p. 25]. This is many fewer than there had been earlier, but they may be in the process of being reintroduced under other names.) More frequently, judges are selected on the basis of possession of certain special qualifications thought to be acquired by professional training and experience.

Judges may constitute a separate branch of the legal profession with their own distinctive training preceding a career leading from minor to major judicial posts, as in much of the European continent. Such career judges are civil servants and display the typical cautious ambition, concern for job security, and political self-effacement (Luhmann 1976, p. 103). Alternatively, judges may be recruited from within the legal profession—in practice often from an elite segment of it—on the basis of professional distinction. These principles of selection may be mixed, as in India where the higher judiciary combines career judges promoted from the subordinate judiciary and distinguished advocates elevated from the bar.

Where judges are elevated from the legal profession, formal socialization is attenuated and consists mostly of on-the-job training informally administered by fellow judges and lawyers. Because of the threshold of high educational and professional attainments, judges in such a system tend to be recruited from more elite social groups than are other segments of the political elite (Paterson 1983; Schmidhauser 1979; Gadbois 1968–69; Becker 1970, p. 84). Those judiciaries that play a large role in political life and that insert themselves to criticize or overturn governmental policies tend to be staffed by these *honoratiores* judges rather than by civil servant judges.

In the United States a great deal of research has been devoted to the avowed merits of the various formal devices for selection of judges: these include partisan elections, nonpartisan elections, gubernatorial appointment, and initial appointment with subsequent ratification by voters. In spite of heated debate about the effects of these alternatives, selection systems have not been found to be associated with significant differences in the education, legal experience, provenance, or prior experiences of those who occupy the bench. Only minor differences have been found between elected and appointed state supreme courts: neither different role perceptions nor different decisional patterns nor different levels of partisanship have been detected (Flango and Ducat 1979). The work of numerous investigators (reviewed in Ducat and Flango 1975) converges on the conclusion that there is no evidence that formal recruitment procedures have any independent influence on state judicial systems. The absence of findings of difference is rendered less surprising by the fact that selection systems differ far less in practice than on paper: even in elective systems, initial selection is by appointment, elections are rarely contested, and incumbents are almost always retained.

Virtually all of this research has focused on appellate judges who sit on collegial courts. Perhaps greater differences might be discerned among trial judges whose relatively isolated and highly discretionary work situation gives scope for greater impress of their individual characteristics. But it seems doubtful that selection devices operate in isolation from other factors. Analyzing contrasting styles of judging in two cities, Levin (1972, p. 213) argues that different sentencing patterns are the "indirect product of the political systems of their respective cities" which "influence judicial selection, leading to differential patterns of socialization and recruitment that in turn influence judges' views and decision-making processes." He suggests that although selection mechanisms themselves may have little independent explanatory power, they are part of a chain of factors that makes judiciaries reflective of and responsive to local political cultures.

Courts as Bureaucracies

Courts are, of course, bureaucracies in the loose use of that term to describe any organization with a division of labor, some hierarchic direction, and standardized work routines for serving clients or customers according to specified formulas. Many courts also exhibit some features of bureaucracy in a stronger descriptive sense: explicit apportionment of tasks, delimited spheres of responsibility, rules specifying the powers of officeholders related impersonally in a hierarchic grid of offices, centralized administrative control, and so forth. In civil-law systems, the emphasis on career service, explicit hierarchy of posts, precise application of codes, the elaboration of files, and correction and supervision by superiors matches the bureaucratic model fairly closely. But the fit is looser in the common-law judiciaries with their less articulated hierarchy, judges who are not career specialists (but either laymen or lawyers appointed late in life as a reward for professional eminence or political loyalty), who enjoy broad discretion and are subject to little supervision. Nevertheless, bureaucracy is frequently invoked—not unmindfully of the term's pejorative connotations—as a code word to refer to the slide from individualized treatment into stereotyped routines, and from adversary combat to collaborative negotiation. "Bureaucracy" becomes a shorthand expression for the various ways in which other commitments are tempered by the ambitions and fears of incumbents and by the imperatives of institutional maintenance.

The labeling of courts as bureaucracies strikes others as unpersuasive. Jacob (1983) points out that judicial hierarchies lack many of the salient features of bureaucratic control:

> Appellate courts are usually not true hierarchic superiors to trial courts . . . [t]hey may overrule trial court decisions [but t]heir review . . . is initiated by litigants. It is not motivated by a policy focus of the higher court, nor does it constitute a systematic quality control of the work of the trial courts. . . . Supreme courts often promulgate procedural rules that govern trial courts, but they exercise no continuous supervision over day-to-day trial work and almost none over the flow of cases that trial courts process. They almost never hire, transfer, or fire trial judges or other trial courtroom personnel. They have little or no influence over trial court budgets. [p. 193]

As Dill (1977, p. 10) puts it, "courts are loosely connected units enjoying substantial autonomy from each other and from units at higher levels of the system." The judges who preside in the decentralized American court systems that these observers have in mind are invested with personal authority emanating from their offices, not by delegation from the top (Damaska 1975, p. 515).

Nor do individual courts strike observers as conforming to the bureaucratic model. "Courts are networks of organized activities rather than bureaucratically integrated formal organizations" (Heydebrand 1977, p. 765). Larger courts are clusters of parts or courtrooms that each enjoy some autonomy. In spite of the presence of a chief judge and perhaps a professional court administrator, central direction and accountability are attenuated. "Despite its outward appearance of a bureaucracy, the court possesses many of the aspects of a loosely organized feudal order, with an emphasis on fiefs, patronage and personal loyalties" (Sykes 1969, p. 331).

Nor are the individual courtrooms within courts usefully viewed as bureaucracies. The judge is formally superior to the other participants, but they are not his subordinates in the sense that their powers derive from or embody his. He neither supervises their work nor controls their careers. Standard routines and procedures are not imposed by the judge as a hierarchic superior; but emerge from coping by participants (including the judge) who are accountable to principals or constituencies outside the courtroom itself.

This does not imply that courts are in fact separate and autonomous. As one analyst puts it, courts are

> . . . highly enmeshed in a *vertical and horizontal interorganizational network.* For example, courts are *vertically* tied into higher levels of the judicial-professional hierarchy and authority structure, such as appeals courts, judicial councils and conferences, and congressional committees. *Horizontally,* courts are interacting with other trial courts and jurisdictional domains, with police and prosecution, the bar, prisons, probation and parole, and various administrative and social agencies from which cases are received or to which they are transferred, "removed" or "diverted." [Heydebrand 1977, p. 770]

Common-law courts have traditionally lacked many of the formal bureaucratic devices for securing coordination and uniformity. But recently there have been attempts to develop centralized systems of judicial administration separate from the traditional hierarchy of appeals. Such systems involve the formation of judicial conferences, the assignment of "administrative judges," the engagement of professional court administrators, and the application of modern management methods to expedite the flow of business, eliminate idiosyncratic behavior, engage in planning and otherwise increase the effectiveness of the courts (see Gazell 1975; Friesen et al. 1971).

The Court as Decision-Maker

Legal norms frame judicial activity and influence it importantly, but they do not provide single determinate answers to the questions that judges must answer. The multiplicity of norms implies choice among them; their generality requires specification; their ambiguity requires (temporary and partial) resolution. Discretion may be wide or narrow, explicit or implicit. The presence of legal norms and faithful adherence to them does not exclude the operation of other influences on the actions of the judge.

One way of summarizing the judge's responses to the possibilities is in terms of the style or role of being a judge. By this I mean the prescriptions, supplied by the wider legal culture (as embodied in its local variant), that supply the judge with models, methods, and techniques for being a judge, along with standards for assessing judicial activity. The judicial role may include notions of dignified reticence, solemn decorum, passivity and aloofness, responsiveness to community concerns, crusading zeal, and so forth. (Like all such models, it is embodied in practice only imperfectly—much as models of teacher and researcher are.)

Prominent among the components of the judicial role are commitments to certain methods of working with legal materials and combining them with evidentiary and procedural ones. For example, the judge should allow herself to be educated about the contested factual aspects of a case only through certain restricted channels (for example, witnesses) and by materials of certain restricted types, putting to one side both her general knowledge and sources that would be considered reliable in everyday fact-gathering. (These limitations, combined with the supposed superior scope and resources of legislative fact-finding, underlie the argument that American courts lack the capability to assess the complex factual situations in contemporary institutional litigation. On the basis of an interesting comparative analysis of educational reform cases Rebell and Block [1982, p. 209] conclude that courts are "better equipped than legislatures to evaluate social fact evidence systematically and to render analytically reasoned decisions.")

Another common commitment of the judge role is to regard herself as bound to render a decision according to a specified body of legal norms that represents only part of the normative universe. (Other norms that are approved and embraced may be regarded as too unimportant, too delicate, too intricate, or too profound to be fit subjects of legal enforcement.) The judge may be committed to apply this authoritative material in a certain style—for example, by justifying the selection of normative principles in terms of some large general ground, rather than in terms of specific results or consequences that would ensue from their application to the case at hand—or to all similar cases. (Such commitments to formal rationality may carry in their train a tilt toward individualistic substantive norms [Kennedy 1976].)

The normative material recognized as authoritative and binding may include constitutions, decrees, treaties, statutes, customs, and decisions of (hierarchically superior or earlier) courts—as in the common-law principle of *stare decisis*. That principle may be viewed as defining the boundaries of judicial power (as in England where from the late nineteenth century until 1966 the House of Lords regarded itself as without power to overrule its earlier decisions) or as stating a rule of practice from which departures may be justified—as in its American and earlier English variants (Cross 1961, p. 18). Precedent cannot flourish in the absence of recording and communicative apparatus and appropriate cognitive dispositions (Kaplan 1965). But precedent may be influential even where there is little overt communication about binding normative standards (as among the Soga; Fallers 1969, p. 32).

Of course, precedent may count heavily in judicial decision-making even where the judge is not formally obliged to follow it. Thus, continental judges may regard it as a major source for decision-making (Wenner et al. 1978; Wetter 1960; Di Federico 1976). Similarly, the circulation of decisional material that is not formally binding may serve to coordinate responses among scattered decision-makers who are organized not in hierarchies but in looser networks (Shapiro 1971).

"The sharpest role conflicts in American appellate courts" concern the role of judges as lawmakers (Howard 1977, p. 919). The federal appeals judges he studied ranged from enthusiastic innovators to "strict constructionists," with most taking a middle position.

Howard points out that "they differed over issues of degrees within a relatively narrow range of creative opportunities" for most agreed that no more than a tenth of their cases offered any opportunity to fashion new rules.

The formal commitment to precedent enters directly in only a limited segment of judges' decision-making; it applies directly to identification of authoritative rules. In assessing facts, setting calendars, sentencing, and so forth, precedent supplies wide outer limits. Where it applies, the strictures of precedent (like those of hierarchic authority) may be loosened by a variety of techniques of interpretation (ascertaining the rule of the earlier case, characterizing the issues in the present case, drawing analogies) that afford courts considerable leeway to shape doctrine in the course of following it (Llewellyn 1960; Levi 1961). These techniques enable doctrine to change in particulars while the framework remains stable: it is a "moving classification system" (Levi 1961, p. 4; cf. Shapiro 1965, p. 151).

Doctrinal continuity does not rely on the extent to which courts are fettered by formal obligations to adhere to precedent. Lawyers and judges are socialized to a limited range of legitimate techniques of manipulating doctrinal material. They tend to perceive issues in terms of received categories. That appellate courts face issues "already drawn . . . by lawyers, drawn against the background of legal doctrine and procedure, and drawn largely in frozen, printed words . . . tends powerfully both to focus and to limit discussion, thinking, and lines of deciding" (Llewellyn 1960, p. 29). This kind of cognitive channeling is reflected in the courts' decisional output. Shapiro (1965) depicts judicial lawmaking as a series of incremental judgments in which marginal variations from the status quo are selected on the basis of examining a restricted range of factors—in contrast to a rational style in which all relevant data are arrayed to serve systematic pursuit of fully articulated goals. Presumably, judicial decision-making deviates from this incremental prototype more in some fields, more in some phases of the proceedings, and more in some eras.

In his study of appellate judging, Llewellyn (1960) refers to the "period style":

> . . . the general and pervasive manner over the country at large, at any given time, of going about the job, the general outlook, the ways of professional knowhow, the kind of thing the men of law are sensitive to and strive for, the tone and flavor of the working and of the results. [p. 36]

This helpfully alerts us to the fact that the repertoire of legitimate techniques, the thoroughness with which they are internalized, the constancy with which they are adhered to, and the adeptness with which they are employed should be expected to vary from time to time, as well as from field to field, from court to court, and from judge to judge. Wetter (1960) substantiates the dramatic changes over time in an individual court. He sketches the range of styles prevalent in the appellate courts of various industrial societies and the way these reflect the education and career lines, the organization of judiciaries and their relation to organs of government, the kinds of cases the come before them, and so forth. Whether there is a single dominant style of appellate judicial work in a society at any one time is a question that awaits the accumulation of further data. Horwitz (1977, p. 255), for example, observes a "sharp contrast between the utilitarian and instrumentalist character of early nineteenth century private law and the equally emphatic antiutilitarian, formalistic cast of public law." Leaving the realm of appellate courts with their greater visibility, more deliberate pace, orientation to literary sources, and enduring collegial groups, we might expect that variations in style would be even greater in other localities and strata of the judicial system.

Much effort has been expended on attempts to explain the decisions of judges in terms of the propensities they bring to the cases by virtue of their personal histories and characteristics. Great ingenuity has been displayed in the development of measurement techniques to apprehend deep structures of consistency in decision-making viewed as reflecting underlying values or attitudes, or as reflecting various facets of the judges' life experience, and so forth.[4] (Since these techniques rely heavily on the comparison of recorded votes in nonunanimous cases on multijudge courts, most of this literature concerns appellate courts, especially the Supreme Court.) For the most part attitudes and values are inferred from the votes themselves. Since the attitudes are not measured independently of the behavior, the patterns of consistency that are displayed invite rather than supply explanation. In other fields, sustained critical assessment has cast serious doubt on the sufficiency of explanations of actions by attitudes (Wicker 1969; Bentler and Speckart 1981). Where judicial attitude has been measured independently of decisions, a similar dissociation of action and attitude may be found. For example, Gibson (1978) found that neither their political views nor their views about crime had much influence on the sentencing behavior of Iowa trial judges. The influence of attitudes was found to be mediated by the role orientations of the judges.

Attempts to anchor the judge's decisional predispositions in his background or career have not proved very satisfying. The studies concur that for American appellate judges, party affiliation is associated most consistently and strongly with decisional outcomes, age and religion less consistently. But background characteristics are, on the whole, weak predictors of the decisional propensities of judges (Grossman and Tanenhaus 1969, p. 15; Murphy and Tanenhaus 1972, p. 107). Thus, a careful study of nonunanimous decisions of United States Courts of Appeals found that party affiliation, age, religion, candidacy for public office, and previous judicial experience each explained some of the variance in decisions in some categories of cases, but concluded that "the background variables tested . . . cannot account for much of judicial voting behavior" (Goldman 1975, p. 504; cf. Bowen 1965, quoted in Flango and Ducat 1979, p. 34). This study and others suggest that background variables may have more explanatory power in some regions than in others and at some times than at others (Giles and Walker 1975). The tie between background, attitudes, and outcomes is complex. It is mediated by the politics of the court itself, by the persuasion and learning that takes place there (Howard 1968), and by the role conceptions that incline judges to base decisions on specific sectors of their beliefs (Gibson 1978).

In the wake of the rather unsatisfying efforts to explain the decisional propensities of judges in terms of their personal characteristics, a recent and promising line of research seeks to explain decisions in terms of responses to various features of the larger political

---

[4]The literature is vast and has been much discussed elsewhere, so I content myself here with the mere mention of its presence at the periphery of the present inquiry into the adjudication-litigation complex. Pritchett (1948) is accounted the paradigmatic work. Among the many noted studies are those of Schubert (1963, 1964, 1974); Nagel (1961); Ulmer (1960, 1974, 1978); Rohde and Spaeth (1976). Synthesis and assessment can be found in Grossman and Tanenhaus (1969); Murphy and Tanenhaus (1972). A useful selection from research in this tradition, accompanied by helpful analysis, appears in Goldman and Sarat (1978).

environment: judicial decisions are seen as reflecting the local political culture (Levin 1977; Eisenstein and Jacob 1977; Kritzer 1978), currents of public opinion (Cook 1977, 1979; Gibson 1976), and so forth. Unlike the attitude and background research on decision-making, these studies focus on trial courts; typically the dependent variable is sentencing. The portrayal of judges as responding to their perceptions of changing circumstances is akin to the kind of environmental explanation favored by historians (Hurst 1956; Friedman 1973; Horwitz 1977) and to the notion of judges as enmeshed in specific local legal cultures. (See below, pp. 181–182.)

Presiding Over the Process: Passive Versus Active Courts

One durable stereotype depicts the common-law judge as a passive umpire, in contrast to the civil-law judge who actively manages the case before him. In the adversarial common-law system, identification of claims and defenses and presentation of proofs and arguments are controlled by the parties (or their representatives) and the judge presides as impartial umpire. In contrast the inquisitorial system fosters the judge who is "responsible for determining the subject matter of the proceedings, and for securing all evidence needed for ascertainment of the truth. During the proceedings, he not only presides over the taking of proof, but also originates the bulk of questions" (Damaska 1975, p. 525). The contrast is a serviceable one, although contemporary common law and civil law courts hardly represent polar opposites. The spectrum of forum passivity and activity runs from the sort of complete disputant control found in many mediative processes to the total control by the forum familiar in commissions of inquiry (such as the Warren Commission or congressional committees).

The civil-law judge stands at some remove from the pure inquisitor. Like his common-law counterpart, the civil-law judge has power to undertake inquiries on his own, but

> . . . civil law judges seldom exercise this power . . . in the great mass of civil litigation in both traditions the rule is that the parties have considerable power to determine what will take place in the proceedings. Where the civil law judge puts questions to the witness, he does so at the request of counsel, and he ordinarily limits his questions to those submitted by the lawyers. [Merryman 1969, p. 124]

Merryman concludes that ". . . the prevailing system in both the civil law and the common law world is the 'dispositive' system, according to which the determination of what issues to raise, what evidence to introduce and what arguments to make is left almost entirely to the parties" (p. 124). (Cf. Jolowicz 1975, p. 209.) One pair of contemporary observers describe judges in criminal cases in Europe as "more passive and reactive" than their counterparts in the United States (Goldstein and Marcus 1977, p. 282).

Common-law judging lies at some distance from the passive end of the spectrum. The "passive posture of the judge" is, as Damaska (1975) notes, not only "historically novel" but even in theory it is "far from being a general description of the judicial office."

> Instead it applies only to a limited number of procedural contexts and to a restricted class of issues. [In the criminal case] judicial passivity is the rule only during the guilt-determining phase of the trial, and there serves as the norm only with regard to the framing of the subject matter of the proceedings, the collection of evidence, and the presentation of proof. [p. 524]

That other responsibilities curtail or circumscribe judicial passivity is confirmed by the observation of a prominent proceduralist that "the common law tradition is strong that the judge who conducts a trial should play an active part in directing it . . ." (James 1965, p. 5). As one respected American judge (Wright 1962, p. 141) put it: "The administration of justice means administration; a judge has to get into these cases and administer them. The lawyers are likely, in their advocacy, to run off in different directions; it's the judge who shows them where the point of the case is, where the issues are." Or, as Judge Sirica (1979, p. 127) explained, he took the initiative to break through the early resolution of the Watergate break-in arranged by the parties because "I had no intention of sitting on the bench like a nincompoop. . . ."

What is more striking about the common-law judges than their purported passivity is their tendency to delegate and supervise rather than to engage in continuous and detailed work on the case. This is illuminated by Engel and Steele's discussion (1979, p. 311) of "three typical modes of judicial processing [in the American setting], all characterized by substantial de facto delegation of the judge's power of decision and disposition." The first of these is "routine processing with nominal judicial intervention" as in granting relief in default cases or ordering dismissals where the plaintiff has not pursued matters. The second is placing the imprimatur of judicial approval on the actions of the parties, as in confirmation of a typical divorce or plea bargain. Third, where matters move to trial, the judge typically delegates much of the substantive "work and thought" to the lawyers who formulate arguments, prepare orders, and so forth. In each instance there is massive delegation—to clerks, parties, lawyers—who do the work under the supervisory scan of the judge. This tendency for common-law judges to be management rather than production workers is connected with the lower ratio of judges to lawyers (see Table 3), the higher status enjoyed by common-law judges, and their relative freedom from hierarchic control.

The tendency toward a more active judicial role has been noted by various observers (James 1965, p. 7; Chayes 1976; Cappelletti and Garth 1978, pp. 228–29; Galanter et al. 1979; Resnick 1982). Indeed, with their broad powers and weaker hierarchic supervision, common-law judges frequently take far greater initiative in shaping cases and arranging outcomes than the stereotype suggests. Thus, Damaska (1975, p. 525) observes that "in many phases of the criminal process, such as pretrial hearings, *in camera* examinations, and the sentencing stage, passivity and aloofness come to an end. Indeed, at these junctures in the proceedings Anglo-American judges occasionally assume outright inquisitorial postures that are without counterparts in modern continental systems."

Nevertheless, there is a residual loyalty to the ideal of judicial passivity, especially during the trial phase, and particularly likely to be aroused where there is a jury. Thus, the New York Court of Appeals in 1979 reversed two manslaughter convictions on grounds that the "unwarranted, persistent intrusion of the presiding [judge] deprived defendants of [a] . . . fair trial. . . ."

> Not only did the court ask over 1,300 questions of the witnesses, which constituted more than a third of the total number of questions propounded during the entire trial, he also usurped the authority both of the prosecutor and of defense counsel to determine the content, course and manner of their presentations. His elicitation from expert witnesses of extended elaboration of their testimony, his solicitation of objection by the prosecution to interrogation being pursued by defense counsel, and his extraction from a prosecution witness during

cross-examination of a drawing made on the witness stand on the court's instruction and then received in evidence as an exhibit of the People, coupled with the nature and extent of questions addressed to alibi witnesses by way of cross-examination which clearly conveyed the Judge's skepticism as to those witnesses' credibility, compounded the unfairness that marked the judicial proceeding. [*People v. Mees*, 1979, p. 215]

As the dissenting judge pointed out, it was the "incisiveness and not the prejudice of the court's questions" that was the basis of the objection to them (id. 216).

Similarly, judicial initiative in managing case presentation, promoting settlements, devising remedies, and supervising enforcement is familiar in American civil courts. (Judicial embrace of the mediator role is discussed below, pp. 201–202, in connection with the deflection of adjudication into negotiated settlement.) In a pioneering examination of complex public law litigation in federal district courts, Chayes (1976) identifies the emergence of an activist, goal-oriented, "public law style" of judging that moves away from the traditional concept of the trial judge as passive arbiter. Chayes (1976, p. 1284) contrasts "public law" litigation with traditional lawsuits in which there are two discrete and opposed interests, in which the process is party-initiated and party-controlled, in which the judge is a neutral arbiter, and in which the court's involvement ends with the entry of judgment. In the new model, "[t]he judge is the dominant figure in organizing and guiding the case. . . ." Instead of deriving relief from established rights by received formulae, "the trial judge has increasingly become the creator and manager of complex forms of ongoing relief, which have widespread effects on persons not before the court and require the judge's continuing involvement in administration and implementation." (For an analysis which emphasizes the continuities of this style with earlier litigation, see Eisenberg and Yeazell 1980.)

This managerial, goal-oriented style is commonly described as "activist," but reflection suggests that activism is not a single trait but a cluster of kindred styles that can be described on a number of independently measured dimensions. Table 4 summarizes seven dimensions along which judges may (and frequently do) deviate from the prototype of the passive common-law judge.

In the appellate court setting, the "activist" label has referred to judges who are doctrinally innovative and assertive vis-à-vis other decision-makers.[5] Among trial judges

---

[5] This notion of judicial activism is found in the protracted debate among Supreme Court justices and legal scholars over the proper mix of judicial assertiveness with deference to precedent and to other decision-makers. See, for example, *Baker v. Carr* (1961, p. 266; Frankfurter, J., dissenting). Similarly, in the discussion of judicial activism in political science literature, the primary motif is that of assertiveness vis-à-vis other decision-makers. Thus, Abraham (1977, p. 184) defines activism as belief "in a more affirmative, some would say aggressive judicial policy, and [activists] are more ready to say 'No' to governmental enactments and actions. . . . [U]nlike the 'self-retrainers,' the 'activists' would be inclined to 'legislate,' to 'make policy.' " Cf. Shubert's identification (1974, p. 210) of activist decisions as those conflicting with policies of other major decision-makers. Samonte (1969, pp. 157, 172) defines activism as "willingness . . . to decide issues affecting the status, decisions, or activities of the executive, legislative, and administrative branches of government and to uphold . . . and expand judicial power. . . ."

This assertiveness involves the pull of favored policies as well as mere lack of deference. Goldman and Jahnige (1976, p. 206) characterize activism as "the position that courts should not hesitate to foster policies beneficial to society." Restraint, in contrast, is deference to "popularly elected branches of government in *their* determination of suitable public policy." Activism entails a willingness to make a decision where one might be avoided or to decide on broad rather than narrow grounds (1976, p. 112).

In earlier formulations, absence of deference to other decision-makers was clearly linked to what we call

TABLE 4

Some Dimensions of Judicial "Activism"

Precedent-Bound	Doctrinally Innovative
Deferential to Other Decision-Makers	Assertive vis-à-vis Other Decision-Makers
Passive Umpire	Managerial
Arbitral	Mediational
Universalistic	Particularistic (khadi justice)
Formalistic	Mission-Oriented (substantive policy)
Case-Focused	Programmatic

involved with larger "public law" or "extended impact" or "structural" cases, "activism" is likely to include departure from the passive umpire role to participate actively in managing the case, devising the remedy, and so forth. But there are other "activist" styles that are perhaps even more prevalent: the departure from the arbitral stance to aggressive mediation and brokering of settlements (discussed below, p. 201) is perhaps the most common among American judges. Or, the constraint to decide according to general rules may be displaced by a drive to respond to the unique particularities of the case (along the lines of the khadi, in Max Weber's idealization of him; Weber 1958, pp. 216–21). Thus, Martin Levin (1972) describes judges in Pittsburgh as

> typically oriented toward the defendant rather than toward punishment or deterrence. Their decisionmaking is particularistic and pragmatic. . . . Most nonjury trials in Pittsburgh are informal . . . and abbreviated. Most of the judges prefer this arrangement and they also prefer informal procedures for obtaining information concerning defendants. . . .
>
> The Pittsburgh judges' closeness to and empathy with the defendant cause them to stand apart from the law and act as a buffer between it and the people upon whom it is enforced. Most of them act as if they view the law primarily as a constraint within which they have to operate to achieve substantive justice for the defendant. . . .
>
> The Pittsburgh judges tend to reject legalistic criteria in favor of policy considerations derived from criteria of "realism" and "practicality." . . .
>
> They seem often to base their sentencing decisions on frankly extra-legal standards. . . .
>
> Sixteen of the eighteen judges base their sentencing decisions on a very wide range of individual and personal characteristics. . . . They feel that "everything counts"; it is the "whole system" and the "complete picture" that must be considered. They describe their decisionmaking as "intuitive," "impressionistic," "unscientific," and "without rules of thumb." [pp. 192, 203, 210–12]

---

substantive rationality. Thus, Pritchett (1954, p. 198) suggests that the broad, activist view of judicial power flows from a sense of substantive responsibility for the outcome: "For the judicial activist, the *result* is the test of a decision. The validity of formal concepts depends upon whether their use gives the right answer."

Or, pursuit of substantive policy goals may be combined with adoption of a programmatic focus in what has been called the "entrepreneurial" style of judging (Galanter et al. 1979).

There are innumerable possible combinations of these elements of judicial style. Which are accounted as "activist" will depend in large measure on the expectations about judges provided by the local legal culture. Indeed, unbending adherence to legal formality may be accounted "activist" where it departs from shared understandings about the proper mix of formalism with substantive and administrative concerns (Galanter et al. 1979, pp. 728ff.). Such a culture prescribes a set of acceptable styles of being a judge. Some of these local styles, taken as a whole, may be more activist along one or another of the dimensions of activism that have been identified. That is, the modal and accepted style of trial-court judging may be more mission-oriented or managerial in one locality than in another. It is to these patterns of variation among localities that we now turn.

The Persistence of Variation: Local Legal Cultures

Systems of courts are equipped with various devices to minimize idiosyncrasy and to eliminate variation in the way that cases are processed and decided (cf. Shapiro 1980). Yet, local variation in courts remains a striking feature of less centralized systems. In the United States there are multiple bodies of law and the formal institutional arrangement of the tasks, jurisdiction, powers, accountability, and other aspects of courts differs from state to state and often from locality to locality. But there are, in the United States, patterned and persistent differences in what courts do and how they do it that are not attributable either to differences in the substantive law or to differences in the formal structure of courts. Such variation is found between "identical" courts (and agencies) applying the "same" law: uniformity of rules and institutions may be accompanied by significant variation in practice. These persisting and patterned differences may be thought of as giving expression to the "local legal culture"—that is, a set of norms, understandings, concerns, and priorities shared by the community of legal actors and significant audiences. The local legal culture defines the appropriate style of playing legal roles, including that of judge. Thus, it may prescribe the uses of the pretrial conference and the preliminary hearing, the role of the judge in settlement negotiations and in plea bargaining, appropriate dispositions for particular sorts of offenses by particular sorts of offenders, appropriate relations with press and politicians, and so forth (Eisenstein and Jacob 1977; McIntyre and Lippman 1970; Levin 1977; Church et al. 1978; Watson 1975, p. 13). It finds expression in the proclivity of lawyers to file suit, raise certain defenses, invoke procedural forms, speed or delay matters (Jacob 1969a; Zeisel et al. 1959, pp. 223–40). Thus, a study of delay in the courts of twenty-one cities concluded that

> the speed of disposition of civil and criminal litigation in a court cannot be ascribed in any simple sense to the length of its backlog, any more than it can be explained by court size, caseload, or trial rate. Rather, both quantitative and qualitative data generated in this research strongly suggest that both speed and backlog are determined in large part by established expectations, practices, and informal rules of behavior of judges and attorneys. For want of a better term, we have called this cluster of related factors the "local legal culture." Court systems become adapted to a given pace of civil and criminal litigation. That pace has a court backlog of pending cases associated with it. It also has an

accompanying backlog of open files in attorneys' offices. [Church et al. 1978, p. 54]

Comparable local cultures have been found in styles of police work (Wilson 1968) and in the work of other enforcement agencies (Goldstein and Ford 1971). Do all the settings in a locality share in a single coherent legal culture? Church et al. (1978, p. 56) find a strong association between disposition time in state and federal courts in a given locality in spite of their different personnel and different caseloads. We await a thorough description of such a local legal culture. To the extent that they are anchored in and transmitters of the local political culture (Jacob 1969a; Wilson 1968; Levin 1977; Kritzer 1978) we would expect strong common themes and family resemblances among the cultures manifested at various settings in the locality. The presence and tenacity of these local legal cultures means that courts will respond very differently to crises (cf. Balbus 1973) and that general reforms will produce very different results in different settings, often quite contrary to the expectations of those who imposed them (Nimmer 1978).

I do not mean to imply that local legal cultures are independent of and distinct from the authoritative "higher law." Although their substantive concerns include some that are not fully recognized in the "higher law" (such as the exclusion of undesirable neighbors [Babcock 1969] or unwanted sojourners [Foote 1956]), they are better understood as "variant readings" in which elements of the authoritative tradition are reordered in the light of parochial understandings and priorities. Generally, see Matza (1964, pp. 59–67); for some examples, consider the understanding of criminal procedure by the police (Skolnick 1966, pp. 219–29) or of air pollution laws by health departments (Goldstein and Ford 1971, pp. 20–23). These variant cultures can exist with little consciousness of principled divergence from the higher law.

Legal culture does not imply that all actors are unanimous in their judgments, but only that they share a common orientation and a common idiom (cf. Church 1982). Local legal cultures are not monolithic. There may be a range of permissible styles of judging in a single locality or even in the courtrooms of a single court (cf. Galanter et al. 1979). Individual variation is facilitated by the wide discretion accorded the common-law judge and the weak controls over him (compared, for example, to his civil-law counterpart; Damaska 1975).

Variations in style may be situational as well as local or individual. The same court that routinely encourages and assists counsel to "work something out" in the run of cases will shift on occasion to a style of exacting and ceremonious formality (Mohr 1976, p. 639). The local legal culture is not a single style of being a court, but a repertoire of styles and of shared understandings about when it is appropriate to switch from one to another.

PATTERNS OF ADJUDICATION

The most striking research findings about adjudication in contemporary industrial societies can be summed up in the observation that full-blown adjudication is rare, expensive, and avoided assiduously. This may seem paradoxical in the light of current concern about the "litigation explosion" and court overload (for example, Barton 1975; Rosenberg 1972; Manning 1977; but cf. Galanter 1983b). In comparison to many simpler societies, there is relatively little use of full-blown adjudication. Equally striking is the corollary finding that in those instances where adjudicative proceedings are invoked or threatened, there is a gravitation to other forms of dispute processing. The central role of adjudication is mediated and symbolic rather than the direct and authoritative disposition of disputes. In the American setting this pattern of avoidance and diversion is combined with a central symbolic role and a sense that adjudication is omnipresent.

The Mobilization of Disputes

Disputes are not some elemental particles of social life that can be counted and measured. They are not discrete events like births or deaths; they are more like such constructs as illnesses and friendships, composed in part of the perceptions and understandings of those who participate in and observe them. Disputes are drawn from a vast sea of encounters, collisions, rivalries, disappointments, discomforts, and injuries. The span and composition of that sea depend on the broad contours of social life. For example, the introduction of machinery brings increases in nonintentional injuries; higher population densities and cash crops bring raised expectations and rivalry for scarce land (Abel 1979b). Construction of disputes entails the perception of injuries, the identification of persons or institutions responsible for remedying them, location of forums and acceptable presentation to them, investment of appropriate resources and resistance of attempts at diversion. The disputes that arrive at courts can be seen as the survivors of a long and exhausting process by which the dispute has crystallized out of this sea of proto-disputes—a process mediated both by general cultural dispositions and by differential distribution of knowledge, experience, and opportunity among various groups within a society. As part of a larger system of disputing, the institutions of litigation are shaped by this process of construction and selection that provides it with cases. And litigation in turn profoundly affects what happens at other locations in the system by providing cues, symbols, and bargaining counters which actors use in constructing (and dismantling) disputes. To understand what courts do, it is necessary to know about the "earlier" stages of this process.

These early stages may be visualized as the successive layers of a vast and uneven pyramid. Only recently has there been any attempt to examine systematically the lower layers of the pyramid. A pioneering inquiry by Felstiner, Abel, and Sarat (1980–81) provides a useful conceptual map of the lower reaches of the pyramid. They begin, in effect, with all human experience which might be identified as injurious, a starting point that should alert us to the subjective and unstable character of the process, for what is injurious depends on current—and ever-changing—estimations of what enhances or impairs health, happiness, character, and other desired states. Knowledge and ideology constantly send new currents through this vast ocean.

Some of these experiences are perceived to be injurious. (Felstiner et al. call these *perceived injurious experiences.*) Again, there is an ambivalence here—perceived by whom? The temperance worker or safety crusader may have different perceptions than the drinker or the driver—Felstiner et al. apparently confine this category to perceptions by the injured. Among these perceived injurious experiences, some are seen as deserved punishment, assumed risk, or fickle fate; but a subset are viewed as violations of some right or entitlement caused by a human agent (individual or collective) and susceptible of remedy. These, in the terminology of Felstiner et al., are *grievances*. Again, characterization of an event as a grievance will depend on the cognitive repertoire with which society supplies the actor and his idiosyncratic adaptation of it. For example, he may be equipped with ideological lenses to focus blame or to diffuse it. Some of these grievances may be voiced to the offending party. These are *claims*. Many will be granted. Those that are not granted are *disputes*. That is, "a dispute exists when a claim based on a grievance is rejected in whole or in part" (Miller and Sarat 1980–81, p. 527).[6] Using this terminology let me attempt a crude sketch of the lower layers of the pyramid.

First, a very large number of injuries go unperceived. Breaches of product warranties and professional malpractice may be difficult to apprehend and go undiscovered. Or, if the injury is discovered, the injured may not perceive that an entitlement has been violated, the identity of the responsible party, or the presence of the remedy to be pursued.

The perception of grievances requires cognitive resources. Thus, Best and Andreasen (1977, pp. 707, 722–23) find that higher income (and white) households perceive more problems than the poor (and black) with the goods they buy and complain more to both sellers and to third parties. It seems unlikely that this reflects differences in the quality of the goods purchased. Similarly, Curran (1977, p. 126) reports that more educated respondents experience more problems of infringement of their constitutional rights. (On the differential ability to define and evaluate injurious circumstances, see Boyum 1983.)

Where injuries are perceived, one common response is resignation ("lumping it"). In the most comprehensive study[7] available, Miller and Sarat (1980–81) report that over one quarter of those with reported "middle range" (that is, involving the equivalent of $1,000 or more) grievances did not pursue the matter by making a claim. This proportion was fairly uniform across subject matters, with the striking exception of discrimination problems in which almost three quarters did not move from grievance to claim. (Of course, these figures are not measures precisely of lumping it because they may include those who took other forms of unilateral action—like exit or avoidance or self-help.) These estimates for middle-range disputes fit closely with those provided by several studies of consumer problems, mostly smaller. Ladinsky and Susmilch (1985) specifically measured the rate at which Milwaukee consumers with problems "lumped it": they found that roughly a quarter did. This comports with some 28 percent who did not make claims in King and McEvoy's national sample (1976) of consumer problems and 20 percent who did not make claims in Ross and Littlefield's study (1978) of problems with major household appliances. Curiously, the rate is even higher with serious criminal offenses. Ennis (1967) reported that roughly half of those who reported being victimized by index crimes did not make a complaint to the police. Allowing for some admixture of other responses (self-help, complaints to others) this is a rate of lumping it higher than found in "civil" problems. Also, there are some populations with a higher proclivity to lump it: for example, the low-income consumers studied by Caplovitz (1963) made claims in only 40 percent of instances of grievances with their purchases.

---

[6] A slightly different terminology is employed by other researchers: Mather and Yngvesson (1980–81, p. 776) use the term "dispute" to refer to "conflict between two parties (individuals or groups) [that] is asserted publicly—that is, before a third party." (Cf. Gulliver 1979, pp. 75–76; Nader and Todd 1978, p. 15.)

[7] The study analyzes data compiled from a telephone survey of approximately one thousand randomly selected households in each of five federal judicial districts: South Carolina, eastern Pennsylvania, eastern Wisconsin, New Mexico, and central California. Respondents were asked whether their household had experienced any of a long list of problems in the preceding three years. Only "middle-range" problems were recorded—those estimated to involve a value of more than $1,000. This method of starting with a finite list of troubles conventionally associated with civil litigation produces a conservatively biased underestimation of the extent of troubles and grievances (Marks 1971).

"Lumping it" is done not only by naïve victims who lack information about or access to remedies, but by those who knowingly decide that the gain is too low, or the cost too high (including the psychic costs or pursuing the claim). On the contours of inaction, see Macaulay (1963), Ennis (1967), Mayhew and Reiss (1969), Hallauer (1972), Best and Andreasen (1977). Inaction is familiar on the part of official complainers (police, agencies, prosecutors), who have incomplete information about violations, limited resources, policies about *de minimis,* schedules of priorities, and so forth. See Rabin (1972), Miller (1969), Myers and Hagan (1979) (prosecutors); LaFave (1965), and Black (1971) (police).

Exit or avoidance—withdrawal from a situation or relationship by moving, resigning, severing relations, and so forth—are common responses to many kinds of troubles (see Hirshman 1970). Like "lumping it," exit is an alternative to invoking any kind of organized remedy system—although its presence as a sanction may support the working of other remedies. The use of "exit" options depends on the availability of alternative opportunities or partners (and information about them), bearable costs of withdrawal, transfer, relocation, development of new relationships, the pull of loyalty to previous arrangements—and on the availability and cost of other remedies. Felstiner (1974) suggests that the same social developments that enlarge opportunities for exit erode devices for mediation. The inverse association of exit and resort to third parties is neatly displayed in Baumgartner's study (1980) of resort to courts in an American town. Less frequent use of courts in interpersonal disputes by middle class than by lower class residents is explained by the greater mobility of the former, which prevents the accumulation of disputes and provides exit remedies.

Disputes are pursued by various kinds of self-help (physical retaliation, seizure of property, removal of offending objects, and so forth). The extent of self-help in contemporary industrial societies has not been established. But its occurrence is evidently very frequent. Two recent and revealing studies portray self-help as a major component of disputing in American neighborhoods (Merry 1979, p. 912; Buckle and Thomas-Buckle 1981). (Some variables accounting for the amount and forms of self-help are discussed in Black and Baumgartner 1978.) Adjudication and self-help are not mutually exclusive: courts may regulate and authorize self-help (for example, repossession of property).

In the contemporary United States the most typical response to grievances—at least to sizable ones—is to make a claim to the "other party"—the merchant, the other driver (or his insurer), the ex-spouse who has not paid support, and so on. Thus, Miller and Sarat (1980–81) found that over 70 percent of those who experienced "middle-range" grievances made claims for redress. Aggrieved consumers make claims in about the same proportion (Ladinsky and Susmilch 1985; Ross and Littlefield 1978; King and McEvoy 1976). Some claims may be granted outright, but a large number are contested in whole or part. It is this contest that Felstiner et al. label a dispute. Miller and Sarat found that about two thirds of claims lead to disputes. A large portion of disputes are resolved by negotiation between the parties. Almost half of the disputes in the Miller and Sarat survey (1980–81, p. 537) ended in "agreement after difficulty," which I take as indicating the occurrence of negotiation.

Some disputes are abandoned by their initiators. Ladinsky and Susmilch (1982), who coined the term "clumpit" for those who make a claim but don't persist, found that more than one quarter of all consumers with problems abandoned their claims. Similarly, a study of medical malpractice claims found that 43 percent were dropped without claimants receiving any payment (Danzon and Lillard 1982, p. 4).

These data from surveys of individuals (or households) tell us about the grievances, claims, and disputes of individuals. Our picture of patterns of disputing of businesses, organizations, and units of government is even dimmer. A first glimpse of organizational disputing is afforded by the Civil Litigation Research Project (CLRP) study (Trubek et al. 1983, I-95ff.). A sample of 1,516 organizations in CLRP's five localities (17 percent of these organizations were large in the sense of having over 100 employees) were asked about (non–labor-management) disputes with other nongovernmental organizations during the preceding twelve months involving at least $1,000. Only 17.5 percent of these organizations reported having such a dispute, but larger organizations had considerably more: 49 percent of organizations with over 100 employees had disputes, compared with 16 percent of smaller organizations. Interorganizational disputes are larger than those of individuals—44 percent involved more than $10,000. Like the disputes of individuals, most of these organizational disputes were settled bilaterally, without the invocation of a third party.

A dispute may be heard in some "forum" that is part of (and embedded within) the social setting within which the dispute arose—the school principal, the shop steward, the administrator, and so forth. Some "embedded forums" are hardly distinguishable from the everyday decision-making within an institution ("I'd like to see the manager"); others are specially constituted settings—separate from the normal stream of activity in time, place, personnel, formality or applicable norms. We know that a tremendous number of disputes are processed by such forums. We have no count of them, but we do have some idea of the conditions under which they flourish. Resort to embedded forums is encouraged where there are continuing relations between the disputants. Continuing relations raise the cost of exit; they increase the likelihood of some shared norms and they supply opportunities for application of sanctions—for example, by direct withdrawal of beneficial relations or by reputational damage that reduces prospects for beneficial relations.

Such embedded systems of dispute processing may be relatively independent of the official system in norms, sanctions, procedures, and personnel—like those of religious groups (*Columbia Journal of Law and Social Problems* 1970), gangs, the Chinese community in American cities (Doo 1973). Others are normatively and institutionally dependent upon the official system—like the settlement of automobile injuries (Ross 1970) or bad checks (Beutel 1957). This distinction between free-standing and appended remedy systems should not be taken as sharp dichotomy, but as marking points on a continuum (see Galanter 1974, pp. 124ff.). The indigenous regulatory activity of universities and of groups of businessmen (Macaulay 1963; Mentschikoff 1961; Moore 1973) is neither independent of official norms and sanctions nor entirely dependent upon them. Generally the more inclusive and the more enduring the relationship between a set of parties, the more likely it is that their disputes will be regulated in some indigenous forum (see below at pp. 206–8).

The Invocation of Courts

The pyramid imagery imparts to the process of dispute construction and transformation a stability and solidity that are illusory. Changes in perceptions of harm, in attributions of responsibility, in expectations of redress, in readiness to be assertive—all of these affect the number of grievances, claims, and disputes. New activities (based on new technologies) and new knowledge may change notions of causal agency. Some parts of the pyramid are more crystallized. In matters like automobile accident claims and post-divorce disputes, Americans have ample cues on how to perceive the problem; it is "common knowledge" how to proceed; social support for complaining is readily forthcoming; there are occupational specialists ready to receive the matter and pursue it on a routine and standardized basis. Other parts are more shifting and volatile. Over time, we can imagine a moving frontier of perceived grievance. As the span of human control expands so do attempts to extend accountability. Claims of damage from rainfall caused by cloud seeding or "wrongful life" claims are examples of the growing edges of the world of dispute, where the borders between fate, self-blame, and (specific or shared) human responsibility are blurred and disputed. These areas of blurring and contest are eventually resolved. But it should be noted that the area of recognized disputes contracts as well as expands. Claims may become subject to routine reimbursement and removed from disputing. Other sorts of claims may lose their standing—for example, claims to honor or racial superiority, claims to privacy by officials.

As disputes move up the pyramid (and laterally from one forum to another), they undergo many transformations. (Cf. Emerson and Messinger 1977 on the role of third parties in defining and organizing the "trouble.") The disputes that come to courts originate elsewhere and may undergo considerable change in the course of entering and proceeding through the courts. Disputes must be reformulated in applicable legal categories. Such reformulation may entail restriction of their scope: diffuse disputes may become more focused in time and space, narrowed down to a set of discrete incidents involving specified individuals. Or, conversely, the original dispute may grow, becoming the vehicle for consideration of a larger set of events or relationships. The list of parties may grow or shrink; the range of normative claims may narrow or expand; the remedy sought may change; the goals and audiences of the parties may change. In short, the dispute that emerges in the court process may differ significantly from the dispute that arrived there, as well as from disputes in other settings (Engel 1980, p. 434; Mather and Yngvesson 1980–81; Felstiner et al. 1980–81).

Lawyers are often viewed as important agents of this transformation process. They help translate the disputes of clients into applicable legal categories (cf. Cain 1979). But lawyers may also act as gate-keepers, screening out claims that they are disinclined to pursue. Macaulay (1979), studying the dissemination of consumer law to Wisconsin lawyers, found that lawyers tended to defuse consumer claims, diverting them into mediative channels rather than translating them into adversary claims. Just how lawyers perform this translation depends, of course, on the way that the profession is organized. The organization of legal services delivery powerfully affects which disputes come to the attention of lawyers and which get through the filters imposed by the lawyer's case selection process (cf. Mayhew 1975). Thus, Macaulay (1979) found that the organization of legal services in Wisconsin was such as to deliver information about opportunities under consumer legislation to businesses and to wealthy consumers but not to ordinary consumers.

Those disputes that are not resolved by negotiation or in some embedded forum may be taken to a champion or a forum external to the situation. Recourse to any such "third party" is relatively infrequent across the whole range of disputes. In the Milwaukee Mapping Study, Ladinsky and Susmilch (1985) found that only 3 percent of problems were taken to any third party. This is in the same range as Best and Andreasen's finding

(1979, p. 713) that third parties were resorted to in only 1.2 percent of all cases in which consumers perceived problems (3.7 percent of all instances in which they voiced complaints). This included what we have called embedded forums, such as professional associations and the Better Business Bureau; lawyers and courts were only one sixth of the total.

As the stakes increase, so does resort to third parties. In the CLRP study—recall these are grievances involving more than $1,000—23 percent of those with disputes consulted a lawyer (Miller and Sarat 1980–81, p. 537). In two areas the range was much higher: postdivorce disputes, for which involvement with a court was unavoidable; and tort, where the contingent fee system provided ready access. In the interorganizational disputes studied by CLRP (Trubek et al. 1982, I-95ff.) lawyers were used in 35 percent; use increased little in the larger disputes (to 39 percent in disputes involving more than $10,000).

Sixty-four percent of American adults have had at least one professional contact with a lawyer (on matters other than those connected with their business) (Curran 1977, p. 185). (This was not confined to disputes, but included matters like purchasing property and preparing wills.) Slightly more than half of these had used lawyers more than once, with an average of slightly more than two uses per user (1977, p. 190). Use was higher by whites and by the more educated and wealthy. There was a dramatically higher rate of multiple use by those with higher education (1977, p. 193). Yet for a very large portion of the population (47 percent of nonusers, 40 percent of multiple users) the use of lawyers is regarded as a last resort that should not be approached until one has "exhausted every other possible way of solving his problem" (1977, p. 235).

Some of those who consult lawyers (and a few who don't) get to court. Miller and Sarat (1980–81, p. 543) report that about 11 percent of disputants (9 percent when those with postdivorce problems are excluded) took their middle-range disputes to court. This comes to about 7 percent of all households in the survey. In the (mostly smaller) consumer disputes covered by Best and Andreasen (1977) and by Ladinsky and Susmilch (1985), courts virtually disappear from sight. Overall 9 percent of American adults report having had experience in a major civil court and 14 percent in a minor civil court (this includes parties, witnesses, jurors, and observers). Fewer acknowledge experience in criminal courts (major, 6 percent; minor, 9 percent; juvenile, 7 percent) and more with traffic court (26 percent). Only 1 percent report experience with a highest appellate court (Yankelovich, Skelly and White 1978, p. 15). An earlier study found that almost two thirds of North Carolinians claimed personal experience with the courts: 10 percent had brought suit, 7.4 percent had been sued, 25.7 percent had been witnesses, 24 percent had served on juries, and 48.1 percent had been spectators to court proceedings (Walker et al. 1973, pp. 71–72). These scattered data suggest that a sizable minority—probably less than one fifth—of American adults have sometime in their lives been a party to civil litigation.

What is at stake in the cases that get to court? The Civil Litigation Research Project studied a sample of 1,649 cases in five federal courts and state courts of general jurisdiction in five locations: cases involving less than $1,000 were eliminated from the sample. The stakes involved in the median state court case was $4,500. Only a quarter of state cases involved over $10,000. The median federal court case involved $15,000 (Kritzer et al. 1982, p. 82). ("Stakes" was defined as the lawyer's view of what the client would take or give to settle the case; Kritzer et al. 1982, p. 42.)

In the CLRP study of interorganizational disputes (Trubek et al. 1982, I-95ff.), respondents were asked to estimate the percentage of their organization's disputes that went to court: the median estimate was 5 percent but the mean was 17 percent, suggesting that there are a small number of frequent users of the courts. The median response on use of arbitration was two tenths of a percent—about one twenty-third the estimated use of courts. Again, the higher mean response (6 percent) suggests that there are a number of frequent users of this device. But the great preponderance of disputes are dealt with bilaterally, without resort to a third party. The median estimate of no third party involvement was 90 percent. Thirty-one percent of respondents reported that none of their disputes went to court, and 68 percent reported that none went to arbitration.

Even in a society regarded as highly rights-conscious and litigious, there may be very little use of litigation to adjust relations among whole classes of major organizational actors, such as large manufacturing corporations, financial institutions, educational and cultural institutions, and political parties. Macaulay (1963) found manufacturers reluctant to intrude litigation into relationships with their customers and suppliers. Owen (1971, pp. 68, 142) found that in two Georgia counties "opinion leaders and influentials seldom use the court except for economic retrieval." Analyzing patterns of court use, Hurst (1980–81) remarks on

> the absence of sizeable numbers of legal actions in which individuals or firms of substantial or large means appear on both sides of lawsuits. Such potential suitors can afford, and are likely to make extensive use of, skilled professional help to channel their affairs so as to prevent trouble. Similarly, when trouble emerges, they are likely to be equipped to make sophisticated choices of alternatives to litigation to resolve difficulties through bargaining, mediation or arbitration. Apart from these influences of resources available, they are likely to find their own interest deeply engaged in maintaining continuing relations with their potential opponents in litigation, so that the structure of the situation directs them away from the courts. Moreover, the larger the business firm and the more dependent its interests on long-term confident, harmonious relations with a network of others in the community—investors, credit sources, suppliers, customers, elected officials—the more likely that it will shun the publicity that may attend lawsuits. [p. 422]

In some settings, the use of courts has been found to be more frequent among marginal than among central actors (Todd 1978) or among lower-status than among higher-status actors (Baumgartner 1980). These findings comport with the observation that, because the limiting forms of adjudication exclude the deployment of many political resources, courts are particularly attractive forums for those who cannot prevail in more politically responsive forums (Dolbeare 1967, p. 63; Howard 1969, p. 346; McIntosh 1982b; cf. Merry 1982, p. 27).

Like other kinds of remedy-seeking, litigation requires information and skills. Complaints to all third parties come disproportionately from better educated, better informed, and more politically active households (Best and Andreasen 1977; cf. Hill 1976 on the greatly disproportionate rate of complaints by professionals to the New Zealand ombudsman). Those consumers who participated in a massive class action recovery against manufacturers of antibiotics were the responsible, informed nonalienated mainstream (Bartsche et al. 1978). The resources that enable courts to be used may be provided by means other than education and status. Thus, Merry (1979, p. 913), detailing use of a court in an American slum, found that "those who turn to the court generally had some special inside knowledge of court operations, either through a close friend or relative on the police force, or past encounters of kin with arrests and court appearances."

In many American courts, plaintiffs are predominantly businesses or governmental units, while the defendants are overwhelmingly individuals (Galanter 1975, Table 1). Wanner's study (1974, 1975) of civil courts of general jurisdiction in three large American cities found that business and governmental units were plaintiffs in 58 percent of the cases filed in these courts, but defendants in only 33 percent. The modal lawsuit pitted an organizational plaintiff against an individual defendant. A comparable pattern is found in Owen's study (1971) of two county courts (see computation in Galanter 1975, p. 352). The same configuration of organizational plaintiff versus individual defendant is typical in small-claims courts (which handle a substantial proportion—perhaps half [see fn. 8, on p. 193]—of the total civil caseload in the United States. See Yngvesson and Hennessey 1975; Galanter 1975). There is reason to think that this pattern is not uniquely American. An analysis of 489 civil cases in the Amtsgericht (lower civil court) Freiburg (Germany) shows a remarkable resemblance to the American data (Blankenburg et al. 1972). Some fragmentary British data again reveal a similar pattern (Galanter 1975, Table 1).

However, studies of other general jurisdiction courts suggest that the preponderant configuration is individual plaintiff versus individual defendant. In four of the five state courts in the CLRP study individuals were some 75 percent of the plaintiffs. In the Arthur Young & Co. study (1981) of courts of general jurisdiction in five diverse counties, most suits in 1976–77 were by individual plaintiffs against individual defendants. Suits by individuals against businesses (11.4 percent) and businesses against individuals (9.9 percent) were pretty evenly matched. Similarly, McIntosh (1982a) found that, in the most recent period (1940–70), 70 percent of cases in St. Louis Circuit Court were individual versus individual, 17 percent individual versus organization, 4 percent organization versus individual, and 9 percent organization versus organization.

In order to understand the distribution of litigation in a society, it is necessary to go beyond the characteristics of individual parties to consider the relation between them. Are the parties strangers or intimates? Is their relationship episodic or enduring? Is it single-stranded or multiplex? In the American setting, litigation is typically between parties who are strangers. Either they never had any mutually beneficial continuing relationship (as in the typical automobile injury case) or their relationship—marital, commercial, or organizational—is ruptured. In either case, there is no anticipated future relationship (see Merry 1979, p. 895; Sarat 1976). In the American setting, unlike some others, resort to litigation is typically viewed as an irreparable breach of the relationship (see Galanter 1974, p. 113, n. 44).

Black (1971, p. 1097) suggests that invocation of official remedies increases with the relational distance between the parties. This connection between litigation and strangers clearly does not hold for all societies. Morrison (1974) and Kidder (1973) describe to us a pattern of litigation with intimates in India. Consider Morrison's report (1974, p. 57) of the North Indian villagers who "commented scornfully that Netaji [a chronic litigant] would even take a complete stranger to law—proof that his energies were misdirected."

Relations may be so intimate and unbreakable that the built-in sanctions of reciprocity and withdrawal, ordinarily supplied by continuing relations, are neutralized. In such cases intimates may seek outside help. Hence, where parties are locked into relationships, litigation may proceed side-by-side with the continuation of that relationship.

Yeazell (1977, pp. 881–82) describes seventeenth-century English class actions among parson and parishioners, lord and tenants, who were so securely tied to one another that the litigation did not threaten severance. Perhaps this accounts for the immense amount of litigation among inescapable trading partners in the Soviet Union, where it is reported that there were over one million *arbitrazh* cases annually (Loeber 1965). Consider, for example, the earlier report that the Ural Rolling Stock Factory brought 15 cases against the Central Power Equipment Construction Enterprise, which in turn brought 26 cases against it (Bakhchisaraitsky [1937] in Zile 1970, p. 192).

Similarly, the absence of other remedial channels may explain why litigation is more frequent in disputes with geographically distant antagonists than with those near at hand. Engel (1978, p. 143) reports that "at distances where interaction may be presumed most frequent, the rates of litigation are the same as—or even lower than—the rates of litigation at distances where interaction is relatively rare." (Cf. Starr and Pool 1974; Konig 1979, p. 79; Witty 1978, p. 308.) Litigation is also associated with disputes across ethnic lines (Engel 1978, p. 144). Litigation occurs where it is less costly in terms of its disruption of valued relations—particularly multiplex and affective ties. And the absence of such ties makes it less likely that alternative remedies—either mediators or reputational networks with shared norms and sanctions—are available. (Cf. Nelson 1981, pp. 58ff., on the predominance of Quakers as litigants in eighteenth-century New England towns.) But where disputes are about control of irreplaceable resources (land, power, reputation), disputants may be willing to sacrifice valued relationships and pursue the drastic remedies of litigation rather than resort to indigenous remedies (Starr and Yngvesson 1975; Forman 1972; Mendelsohn 1981).

Just as the stakes may affect proclivity to litigate, so the goals of disputants may affect the course the litigation takes. Litigants vary in the extent to which they seek justice or moral vindication instead of, or in addition to, a satisfactory resolution of their immediate discomforts. Although the high rate of litigation has led some observers to characterize Americans as "rights-minded" (Henderson 1968; Hahm 1969), there is evidence that the appetite for justice and vindication in terms of authoritative norms is limited. Thus, Mayhew (1975, p. 413) found that the proportion of respondents reporting serious problems who sought "justice" or legal vindication (as opposed to a satisfactory adjustment) was tiny in all areas other than discrimination: only 4 percent of those with serious problems connected with expensive purchases sought "justice," as did 2 percent of those with neighborhood problems; but 31 percent of those reporting discrimination problems sought "justice."

Another reading of public appetite for justice is provided by Steele's study (1975, p. 1140) of complaints to the Illinois State's Attorney's Consumer Fraud Bureau, which found that the desire for "public-oriented remedies" as opposed to private relief varied directly with income level. Only 4 percent of those with incomes of less than $11,000 requested a public remedy, but 28 percent of those with incomes over $17,000 did so. The complainants to this bureau were isolated individuals. There is some reason to think that individuals complaining in a setting of group activity will be more interested in public-oriented remedies than are unorganized individuals (Mayhew 1968; cf. FitzGerald 1975).

Although disputing in America has a predominantly instrumental character, litigation is sometimes regarded as a vehicle of moral action involving matters of principle over which compromise would be unseemly or unthinkable. (Cf. Aubert's distinction [1963] between conflicts of principle and conflicts of interest.) FitzGerald (1975) portrays the temporary marriage of litigation to an intense moral crusade in the case of the Contract Buyers League, a group of Chicago blacks victimized by a discriminatory system of housing sales. After a period of unsuccessful individual attempts to secure relief, intervention by outsiders precipitated formation of a group which, over a period of several years, engaged in picketing, withholding payments, and resisting attempts at eviction. Fitz-Gerald describes "the intense experience of belonging and acting together," and the "intense feeling of altruism . . . and . . . intense loyalty to those who had joined the group which was 'fighting for justice'" (1975, pp. 184–85). This collective activity generated a powerful sense of communion that "overshadowed their instrumental and economic aim of having the contracts renegotiated" (id., 184) and attracted considerable support from outsiders, including elite lawyers who mounted an innovative and ultimately unsuccessful campaign of litigation on behalf of the League.

The example illuminates by contrast the relatively restrained, narrowly focused, impersonal, and professionalized character of most American litigation. Several very striking accounts of major injury litigation from Japan (Upham 1976; Ino et al. 1975) portray victims, who are ordinarily disinclined to pursue legal remedies in a calculating instrumental fashion, engaging in group litigation which becomes the focus of an all-out struggle of great moral intensity. Consider the following entry from the diary of one of the plaintiffs' lawyers for the Japanese thalidomide children (Ino et al. 1975):

> The ceremony of signing the [settlement] confirmation instrument was held at Prefectural Assembly Hall . . . some 100 people representing 56 families including 30 deformed children were present. The whole function was conducted by the plaintiffs themselves, as the attorneys' team watched the proceedings.
> The senior representative of the group, Mr. Terasaka Kanematsu, in an appeal about the pain shared by the children and parents alike, which wrenched the hearts of those present, pleaded for the defendants' fullest and most sincere execution of the provisions. No applause followed, nor any smiles. President Miyatake [of the offending manufacturer] and the Minister of Health and Welfare, both hanging their heads low, apologized before the children. The Minister pledged that like compensation would be provided for victims who had not brought suit. [p. 185]

It is instructive to compare these examples with the more modulated or segmented struggle of the Buffalo Creek disaster victims. Six hundred victims of a flood caused by the collapse of a faulty mine dam sued the coal company. An intense, and ultimately profitable, *pro bono* effort by a major Washington law firm involved a massive deployment of legal resources, the development of innovative theories of recovery, strenuous and elegant legal maneuver—and ultimately a substantial settlement (Stern 1977, cf. Erikson 1976; Gleser et al. 1981). In spite of the number and proximity of the plaintiffs, there was no direct encounter with their antagonists, or any form of collective action, or any sense that plaintiffs were caught up in a struggle outside the bounds of the lawsuit.

Comparative Incidence of Litigation

The apparently simple inquiry of how much adjudication there is turns out to involve formidable complexities of measurement. Local differences in recording practices and differences in the jurisdiction of courts add to differences in substantive law to make comparison of litigation across societies extremely treacherous. Problems of ascertaining what is a case and who are the participants (Cartwright 1975) are compounded by problems of comparison across time and space. If comparison is facilitated by the formation of a world of cognate institutions (see p. 222–23), it is hampered by the multitude of particular ways in which these institutions are related to their social and political environments. The figures given in Table 5 must be taken with appropriate caution. They suggest great variation in litigation rates. These are rates for the ordinary courts, so the variation they show may be amplified or diminished by controlling for the handling of similar disputes in other forums. To varying degrees, most modern states have curtailed the jurisdiction of ordinary courts, diverting routine and/or sensitive matters into special courts or tribunals (Brand 1971; Toharia 1975b; Haley 1978). Since the proceedings in such tribunals are often analytically indistinguishable from litigation in court, these figures may tell us about the location rather than about the amount of adjudicative disputing in society. At the least we get an indication of the very different uses to which the ordinary courts are put in various societies.

Table 5 also suggests the absence of any gross association of litigation with modernity, wealth, or industrialization. Court figures in industrial societies may be inflated by use of courts to ratify or administer noncontested proceedings like divorces or debt-collection. But adversary contests seem less frequent in industrial societies than in some others. For example, Fallers (1969, p. 22) reports that among the Soga something like one in ten adult males is likely to appear in courts as a principal every year. Dubow (1983) studying another East African society reports that in the Arusha District of Tanzania "about one out of ten adults appeared in court as litigants in a single year." (Cf. Abel 1979b on the decreasing frequency of civil litigation in modern Africa, discussed below, p. 221.) The United States rate of per capita use of the regular civil courts may be roughly estimated at about 44 per thousand[8]—in the same range as England, Australia, Denmark, and New Zealand; somewhat higher than Germany or Sweden; far higher than Japan, Spain, or Italy. It is difficult to know what to make of these rates until we supplement them with data about recording practices and about the other forums and tribunals which handle disputes in each of these societies.

It should be recalled from Table 3 that contrasts in other parts of the legal system are as striking as differences in litigation rates. The United States has many more lawyers than any other country—more than twice as many per capita as its closest rival. And it has a relatively small number of judges. The ratio of lawyers to judges in the United States is

---

[8] The rate given here for the United States is a crude estimate arrived at by the following procedure. The most complete—and admittedly very rough—compilation of data on cases filed in state courts of general jurisdiction (based on data from 44 states) enables us to derive a rate of 21.6 cases per thousand in 1975 (U.S. Dept. of Justice 1979, p. 41). Reassuringly, this rate falls roughly in the middle of range of rates for the counties we know from the surveys of individual scholars (Friedman and Percival 1976; McIntosh 1980–81, 1982a; Daniels, 1981, 1982; Arthur Young et al., 1981). But this figure includes only filings in courts of general jurisdiction. Just how large a portion of all American litigation is in courts of limited jurisdiction is not known, but we can make a guess on the basis of the following computation. For the 14 states for which data are available, the median percentage of the state's total civil caseload handled by courts of limited jurisdiction is 52 percent (Silbey 1979, Table 26). If we assume that roughly half of American state civil litigation is filed in courts of limited jurisdiction, we should double the 21.6 rate to obtain a comprehensive estimate of the rate of civil litigation in state courts. To this we should add the 1975 rate of civil filings in federal courts (0.55 per thousand; U.S. Department of Justice 1977, p. 613). If we do this, the United States rate of per capita use of the regular civil courts in 1975 was just below 44 per thousand. More recent rates for some states with apparently comprehensive data are given in Table 5.

TABLE 5

Case Filings per 1,000 Population[1] in Selected Jurisdictions

	Civil			Criminal		
	Year	Rate	Source	Year	Rate	Source
Australia (Western Australia only)	1975	62.06[2]	c	1975	112.49[3]	c
Canada (Ontario only)	1981–82	46.58[4]	p	1981–82	44.95[5]	p
Chile	1970	12.97[6]	m	1970	12.72[7]	m
Columbia	1970	9.46[6]	m	1970	18.07[7]	m
Costa Rica	1970	24.50[6]	m	1970	28.80[7]	m
Denmark	1971	41.40[8]	d	1970	17.55[8]	d
England/Wales	1973	41.15[9]	i	1973	41.5[9]	i
France	1975	30.67[10]	n	1975	9.31[11]	o
India	1977	4.24[12]	g,l	1977	11.38[13]	g,l
Israel	1978	30.76[14]	b	1978	23.66[15]	b
Italy	1973	9.66[9]	i	1973	65.9[9]	i
Japan	1978	11.68[16]	w	1978	9.40[17]	w
Kenya	1969	4.4[18]	a	1969	23.3[18]	a
New Zealand	1978	53.32[19]	e	1978	35.58[20]	f
Norway	1976	20.32[21]	x	1973	6.16[22]	d

SOURCES:
[a] Abel 1979b. [b] Central Bureau of Statistics 1978, Table Nos. 3 and 5. [c] Commonwealth Bureau of Census and Statistics 1976, Tables 44 and 45. [d] Council of Europe 1975, pp. 33, 114. [e] New Zealand Department of Statistics, 1980a, Tables 4, 29, 58, and 4. [f] New Zealand Department of Statistics, 1980b, Table 22. [g] Dhavan 1978, p. 124. [h] Engel 1978. [i] Johnson et al. 1977. [j] Judicial Council of California 1982, Tables I, VI, XVII, XVII-B, XXX. [k] Judicial Council of Florida 1980, pp. 40, 59. [l] Law Commission of India 1979, pp. 71, 97. [m] Merryman and Clark 1978, pp. 486, 497; Tables 7.1 and 7.13. [n] Ministère de la Justice 1979 [France]. [o] Ministère de la Justice 1978 [France], p. 16 annex II. [p] Ministry of Attorney General [Ontario] 1982. [q] National Bureau of Statistics 1981, Table No. XII-24. [r] Office of State Courts Administrator n.d., Tables Nos. 14 and 15, p. 21. [s] Office of the Chief Court Administrator 1981, pp. B26–27, B31, B32–35, and B41–45. [t] Savezni Zavod za Statistiku 1981, Tables Nos. 103-14, 103-15, 103-16, 103-17, 133-5, 133-9, 133-10, 133-12, 133-13, and 133-14. [u] Starr and Pool 1974. [v] Statistisches Bundesamt 1980, Tables 15.4.1, 15.4.5, 15.7.1, and 15.9. [w] Statistics Bureau, Prime Minister's Office [Japan], 1982, Tables 482–484. [x] Statistik Sentralbyra [Norway], n.d., Table N-10. [y] Supreme Court of Minnesota n.d., Tables 2, B-7, B-8, B-9, B-10, B-13, C-1, C-3, and C-6. [z] Sveriges Officella Statistik 1977, p. 224.

NOTES:
[1] Unless noted otherwise, all population data taken from *World Population 1979* (Washington, D.C.: U.S. Department of Commerce, Bureau of the Census, 1980).
[2] Based on filings in local courts, district court, and first-instance bankruptcy, divorce, and other proceedings filed in the Supreme Court of Western Australia. Western Australia's population in 1975 was 1,146,700, as reported in *Year Book Australia: No. 66, 1982*.
[3] Based on *charges* recorded excluding minor offenses not subject to court process. See note 2 for population data.
[4] Based on filings in the family courts (contentious cases only), county and district courts, small-claims courts, and supreme court. Ontario's population in 1981 was 8,664,600, as reported in *The World Almanac and Book of Facts, 1983*.

TABLE 5

(Continued)

	Civil			Criminal		
	Year	Rate	Source	Year	Rate	Source
Peru (Lima Province only)	1970	25.20[6]	m	1970	3.20[7]	m
South Korea	1978	2.01[23]	q	1978	2.43[23]	q
Spain	1970	3.45[6]	m	1970	8.68[7]	m
Sweden	1973	35.0[24]	i	1974	12.19[24]	z
Thailand (Chiangmai Province only)	1974	.69[25]	h	1974	3.56[25]	h
Turkey (Bodrum District only)	1967	26.20[26]	u	1967	16.40[27]	u
United States						
California	1980–81	69.15[7,8]	j	1980–81	38.05[29]	j
Connecticut	1979–80	57.08[30]	s	1979–80	35.12[31]	s
Florida	1978–79	46.38[32]	k	1978–79	32.01[33]	k
Minnesota	1976	41.54[34]	y	1976	17.48[35]	y
Missouri	1980–81	41.64[36]	r	1980–81	19.53[37]	r
West Germany	1977	23.35[38]	v	1977	9.68[39]	v
Yugoslavia	1980	63.02[40]	t	1979	8.12[41]	t

[5] Based on *charges* received under the criminal code and narcotics code in the provincial courts, cases received in the county courts and cases disposed of in the supreme court. The provincial court data accounts for over 97 percent of the total. See note 4 for population data.

[6] Based on first-instance civil cases filed.

[7] Based on first-instance penal cases filed at the investigative stage.

[8] Based on cases brought before the district courts and high courts as courts of first instance.

[9] Based on judicial filings per 1,000 population.

[10] Based on civil cases, family matters, landlord-tenant cases, garnishments, and orders to pay filed in the tribunaux d'instance and tribunaux de grande instance. France's population in 1975 was 52,655,800, as reported in the *Annuaire statistique de la France, 1981*. Figure based on continental French data only.

[11] Based on cases before the tribunaux correctionnels (418,728) and juridictions d'instruction (investigative judges; 71,253). No separate filing data available for cours d'assises and tribunaux de police. See note 10 for population data.

[12] Based on filings in the district level courts (district/additional judges courts, senior subordinate judges courts, Munsif courts and small cause courts), high courts, and first-instance filings before the supreme court. Because the data for the high court were not separated into first-instance cases and appeals, the rate is somewhat inflated. The high court filings account for 17 percent of the total civil filings.

[13] Based on filings in the sessions courts, magistrate courts, and first-instance cases in the supreme court.

[14] Based on first-instance cases filed in magistrate and district courts, excluding motions.

[15] Based on first-instance cases filed in magistrate and district courts, excluding traffic offenses not resulting in an accident.

[16] Based on ordinary litigation cases, administrative cases, conciliation cases, domestic cases, executions, auctions, bankruptcies, provisional attachments, collection and compromise cases received by the summary and district courts, but does not include nonpenal fines. Including the latter brings the rate to 13.18. Japan's population in 1978 was 114,898,000, as reported in the *Japan Statistical Yearbook, 1982*.

TABLE 5

(Continued)

[17] Based on defendants newly received in the summary and district courts. Because no data for newly received Road Traffic Law cases were available, Road Traffic Law disposals were subtracted from the total of newly received cases. Figure is slightly inflated due to inclusion of appeals from summary courts to district courts, which accounts for about 3 percent of district court total (which itself is 9 percent of total new cases received). See note 16 for population data.

[18] Based on cases filed in primary courts. Kenya's population in 1969 was 10,942,705, as reported by Abel.

[19] Based on cases filed in the magistrate courts, the supreme court as a court of first instance, domestic proceedings, and divorce petitions.

[20] Based on total *charges* excluding traffic summonses.

[21] Based on cases *disposed of* by conciliation boards (71,490) and city and district courts (10,318).

[22] Based on cases brought before the ordinary county and town courts and those same courts functioning as examining and summary courts.

[23] Based on first-instance cases received. South Korea's population in 1978 was 36,969,000, as reported in the *Korea Statistical Yearbook, 1981*.

[24] Based on cases entered in the district courts.

[25] Based on first-instance cases processed in provincial and magistrate courts. Population data provided by provincial office, as reported by Engel.

[26] Based on cases accepted by the district lower civil court and higher civil court. The estimated population of Bodrum District in 1967 was 25,000, as reported by Starr and Pool.

[27] Based on cases accepted by the district lower criminal court and middle criminal court, but does not include the few cases from the district accepted by the regional higher criminal court. See note 26 for population data.

[28] Based on first-instance filings in the supreme court, courts of appeal (usually writs of mandamus), superior courts (including juvenile cases, and excluding probate, guardianship, and mental health cases), and lower courts. California's population in 1980 was 23,668,562, according to the U.S. Census.

[29] Based on first-instance filings in the supreme court, courts of appeal, superior courts, and lower courts, excluding traffic cases. When "Group C" traffic violations—hit-and-run property damage, misdemeanor drunk driving, driving under influence of drugs—are included, the rate is 52.18. See note 28 for population data.

[30] Based on cases added to the superior court's civil division, family division (juvenile and contentious cases only), and housing session dockets. Connecticut's population in 1980 was 3,107,576, according to the U.S. Census.

[31] Based on cases added to the superior court's criminal and housing session—criminal dockets. See note 30 for population data.

[32] Based on filings in the circuit and county courts, including juvenile and excluding probate, incompetency, guardianship, and testamentary trust cases. Florida's population in 1979 was 9,202,000, as reported in the *Twenty-Fifth Annual Report: Judicial Council of Florida*.

[33] Based on felony and misdemeanor filings in the circuit and county courts, excluding traffic cases. See note 32 for population data.

[34] Based on filings in the district courts, municipal courts, county courts (including juvenile cases and excluding probate cases), and conciliation courts (small claims). Minnesota's population in 1976 was about 3,965,000, as reported in the *CBS News Almanac, 1978*.

[35] Based on filings in the district courts, municipal courts, and county courts, excluding traffic cases. See note 34 for population data.

[36] Based on filings in the circuit courts and associate circuit courts, excluding probate cases. Missouri's population in 1980 was 4,917,444, according to the U.S. Census.

[37] Based on filings in the circuit courts and associate circuit courts. See note 36 for population data.

[38] Based on cases received in the municipal, district, and administrative courts. The latter court has jurisdiction over cases with a public authority as defendant.

[39] Based on criminal cases brought to trial, excluding all traffic cases. When serious traffic offenses (hit and run, bodily injury, drunk driving, and so forth) are included, the rate is 14.99.

[40] Based on petitions to "social attorneys of self-management" on violations of self-management rights and social property in 1979 (115,914), cases received by courts of associated labour in 1980 (69,956 including some appeals), administrative litigation in 1980 (31,481 disposals), civil suits (including petitions for order to pay and appeals from those petitions) in 1980 (1,128,000), and cases decided by the economic courts in 1979 (63,378). The Yugoslav Census of 1981 reported a population of 22,354,219.

[41] Based on criminal charges (160,955) and "charge sheets" submitted on "responsible persons" accused of economic violations (20,541). Data are for 1979. Figure is slightly deflated because the population figure used was from 1981 (see note 40).

among the highest anywhere; the private sector of the law industry is very large relative to the public institutional sector. (Perhaps this is connected with the feeling of extreme overload expressed by many American judges.)

FitzGerald's Australian replication (1983) of the Civil Litigation Research Project's household survey—the basis for the analysis of Miller and Sarat (1980–81)—affords a remarkable opportunity to compare the whole dispute pyramid in two societies, not just imponderable litigation rates. FitzGerald asked Australians about the same types of problems and found them to be overall "more frequent perceivers of 'middle range' grievances than their American counterparts" (1983, p. 25). He found an overall similarity in the shape and structure of the disputing pyramids in the two countries—that is, the extent to which different kinds of grievances gave rise to claims, to which claims gave rise to disputes, and disputes to consultation of lawyers (1983, p. 30). Overall, the Australian pyramid was more bottom heavy "with more claims and fewer appeals to the courts per 1000 grievances" (1983, p. 30). In other words, "Australians are substantially more likely to complain about their troubles than are their U.S. counterparts and somewhat more likely to engage in an actual dispute" (1983, p. 30).

But Americans are twice as likely to take these middle-range grievances to court (1983, p. 35). But going to court may mean something different in Australia. From what we have seen about settlement rates in the United States, we know that filing suit is often part of negotiation, the meaning of this difference in filings is not clear. But it at least suggests that the way the negotiation game is played in Australia is different and that lawyers can conduct it without playing the court card. It also may reflect differences in the state of law (more settled), in the organization of the profession (divided), and in fee arrangements (no contingency).

FitzGerald's research reminds us of the disassociation of litigation from other levels of disputing, so that we cannot take the former as representative of the larger whole. It points to the need to explore the way in which grievances are transformed into disputes and lawsuits. It also suggests that these processes are not global and pervasive cultural traits or even characteristics of individual disputants. As in the American study, education, income, occupation, and ethnicity seem to explain little of the variation in grievance rates (1983, p. 28). In both countries "by far the most powerful explanatory factor" for the history of the dispute was the type of grievance involved (1983, p. 39). In other words, what happens depends on institutionalized ways of handling different kinds of disputes, not on broader cultural propensities to dispute.

Cultural Proclivities to Litigate

The construction and mobilization of claims involves shared interpretations of experience. It reflects cultural judgments about offensive behavior, injury, responsibility, the self and its extensions, as well as beliefs and attitudes specifically about remedial procedures. Observed variations in resort to courts may be viewed as reflecting "rights consciousness" or an appetite for seeking vindication in terms of official norms. Thus, Zeisel et al. (1959, chap. 20) attribute striking variations in the rate of making several kinds of tort claims in a number of American localities to differences in the "claims consciousness" of their populations.

The disparagement of litigation and of those who resort to it is found in many cultures. Engel (1978, p. 98) reports that litigation is associated with aggression, self-assertion, overt conflict, and lack of subtlety which are strongly offensive to Thais, whose low estimate of litigation is summed up in the adage that "it is better to eat dogshit than to go to court" (1978, p. 98). An extensive literature on East Asian societies (for example, see Kawashima 1963; Hahm 1969; Cohen 1966) attributes the low rates of litigation in those societies to cultural disapproval of the assertiveness and contentiousness that are associated with litigation.

Attempts to explain use of courts by correspondence with cultural valuation of litigation are unable to exclude structural explanations for wide variations across space and time. Examining the files from a Chinese district from 1789 to 1895, Buxbaum concluded that disinclination to litigate was strongly affected by distance from the court (1971, pp. 274–75). More generally, Haley has argued that the much-cited preference for conciliation in Japan reflects the deliberate constriction of adjudicative alternatives by successive Japanese regimes. Summarizing Henderson's research (1965), Haley (1978) recounts that

> . . . Tokugawa officialdom had constructed a formidable system of procedural barriers to obtaining final judgment in the Shogunate's courts. The litigant was forced each step of the way to exhaust all possibilities of conciliation and compromise and to proceed only at the sufferance of his superiors. . . . Conciliation was coerced . . . not voluntary. Yet . . . litigation still increased. [p. 371]

Modern statutes providing for formal conciliation were not "the product of popular demand for an alternative to litigation more in keeping with Japanese sensitivities." Rather "they reflected a conservative reaction to the rising tide of law suits in the 1920s and early 1930s and a concern on the part of the governing elite that litigation was destructive to a hierarchical social order based upon personal relationships" (Haley 1978, p. 373). Mandatory conciliation brought about not a decrease in litigation, but an even greater increase in the number of cases channeled into the formal process, now enlarged to include additional remedial tracks.

The real check on Japanese litigation is the deliberate limitation of institutional capacity. Courts have limited remedial and sanctioning powers (Haley 1982); the number of courts (see p. 167 above) and advocates is kept small, making litigation protracted and costly. The small number of advocates reflects not an aversion to law, but a severe constriction of opportunities to enter the profession. There is a single institute from which graduates may enter bench, bar, or prosecution. Places are limited to five hundred per year. Haley notes (1978, p. 386) that the number of Japanese taking the judicial examination in 1975 was slightly higher *per capita* than of Americans taking a bar examination; in the United States, 74 percent passed, compared with 1.7 percent in Japan. (The numerous law graduates who are not admitted to the Institute may join one of the various other legal occupations in Japan [Brown 1983].) In sum, the low rate of litigation in Japan evidences not the popular aversion to law but deliberate policy choices by political elites.

In assessing "cultural" explanations for litigation rates, we should recall (from Table 5) that the Dutch, Spanish, and Italian rates may be even lower than Japan's. Few observers have associated Italian society with lack of contentiousness! Litigation rates may reflect public preferences, but these are expressed in a setting of political decisions about the channeling of disputes into forums. Matters may be removed from courts to make recovery certain, limited, and calculable (as with workmen's compensation in the United States; Friedman and Ladinsky 1967). Or they may be removed because of a desire to

have politically sensitive matters handled by tribunals responsive to government directives, while leaving undisturbed the "independence" of the regular courts as in Franco
Spain (Toharia 1975a) or in India during the 1975–77 emergency.

Nor are cultural ideals always reflected in popular behavior. As noted above, where
scarce resources (land, power, reputation) are at stake, violation of norms against conflict
may be seen as a painful necessity. Populations which embrace ideals of harmony and
conciliation may use courts at high rates while disparaging litigation (Kidder 1973;
Morrison 1974; cf. Haley 1978). Lack of fit between the dispute-settlement ideologies of
courts and populace may make courts an arena to be manipulated to serve ambitions and
concerns not contemplated in the formal law (Cohn 1959; Kidder 1973, 1974).

The processes of courts do not necessarily reflect their own institutional ideologies.
Courts that ostensibly repair relationships by effectuating compromises may in practice
impose all-or-none decisions (Starr and Yngvesson 1975). And, as we shall see, courts
which ostensibly produce clear-cut, all-or-none decisions may characteristically bring
about compromise outcomes.

The Litigation Process: Attrition, Routine Processing, Bargaining, and Settlement

In America, the great majority of those disputes that are taken to an adjudicative
forum are disposed of (by abandonment, withdrawal, or settlement) without full-blown
adjudication and often without any authoritative disposition by the court. In fact, of
those cases that do reach a full authoritative disposition by a court, a large portion do not
involve a contest. They are uncontested either because the dispute has been resolved (as
in divorce) or because only one party appears (Cavanagh and Sarat 1980; Friedman and
Percival 1976). Over 30 percent of cases in American courts of general jurisdiction are
not formally contested. The predominance of uncontested matters in American courts is
long-standing (Laurent 1959; McIntosh 1982a; Arthur Young et al. 1981).

Many cases are withdrawn or abandoned because invocation of the court served the
initiator's purpose of harassment, warning, or delay. Police may make an arrest or file
charges for reasons of control with no intention of pursuing prosecution. Similarly, Merry
(1979, p. 902) reports that it is the issuance of the complaint and holding of the
preliminary hearing that are the crucial goals of court use among residents in a poor
neighborhood. The invocation of official adjudicatory institutions does not necessarily
express either a preference or an intention to pursue the dispute in official forums, to
secure the application of official rules, or to obtain an adjudicated outcome. The official
system may be invoked (or invocation may be threatened) in order to punish or harass, to
demonstrate prowess, to force an opponent to settle, or to secure compliance with the
decision of another forum (see below, p. 222).

The master pattern of American disputing is one in which there is invocation (actual
or threatened) of an authoritative decision-maker, countered by a threat of protracted or
hard-fought resistance, leading to negotiated or mediated settlement in the anteroom of
the adjudicative institution. Adversary conflict is replaced by maneuver with an eye to
negotiation; the imposition of arbitral judgment is replaced by mediation.

Plea Bargaining   The best-known instance of this pattern is the processing of
criminal cases in the United States. The term "plea bargaining" is employed popularly

and here to refer to a whole family of patterns of processing criminal cases. These may involve protracted explicit bargaining or tacit reference to established understandings. Feeley (1979) observes that

> discussion of plea bargaining often conjures up images of a Middle Eastern bazaar, in which each transaction appears as a new distinct encounter, unencumbered by precedent or past association. Every interchange involves higgling and haggling anew, in an effort to obtain the best possible deal. The reality of American lower courts is different. They are more akin to modern supermarkets, in which prices for various commodities have been clearly established and labeled in advance. [p. 642]

Compare Ryan and Alfini's description (1979, p. 502) of a setting in which the expectations of participants are grounded in the known upper and lower sentencing limits of the judges.

Agreement may take the form of submission to an abbreviated trial in which formal rules of evidence are suspended and a finding of guilt is foreordained (cf. Mather's "slow plea" [1973, p. 190] and Heumann and Loftin's "walk through" waiver trials [1979, p. 426]). Or, more commonly, it takes the form of an agreement about the charges brought against the accused, about the sentence to be imposed, about subsequent behavior, restitution, or the like. Such patterns have been documented in Canada (Ericson and Baranek 1982; Klein 1976), England (Baldwin and McConville 1979), and Israel (Harnon and Mann 1981), as well as the United States. Goldstein and Marcus (1977, 1978) view the early, simpler, and more lenient disposition of criminal cases in continental European systems through accommodations based on "tacit understandings or patterns of reciprocal expectation" closely analogous to American plea bargaining, a characterization challenged by Langbein and Weinreb (1978).

These nontrial dispositions account for some 80 or 90 percent or more of criminal dispositions in almost every American jurisdiction. Local styles differ as to the stage of the process (McIntyre and Lippman 1970) and the role of the judge. The judge may be passive, merely ratifying deals arranged by the parties; he may actively participate in plea discussions; or he may be dominant, orchestrating the whole process—in effect, imposing the "going rate" as in the Chicago system described by McIntyre (1968). About one quarter of American judges report that their typical role is one of active participation in plea-bargaining discussions. About two thirds report that they do not participate but only ratify dispositions reached outside their presence (Ryan and Alfini 1978, p. 486).

Attempts to eliminate the negotiation element demonstrate the vital role of these processes to the local criminal justice culture. Abolition of the prevalent species of negotiated disposition lead to a shift to others. Thus, Church (1976) describes how a ban on bargaining by prosecutors was followed by a new pattern of sentence discussions with judges. Heumann and Loftin (1979, p. 425) describe how sentence bargaining became common in the wake of a mandatory charging statute.

Where plea bargaining was once viewed as disreputable it has won considerable respectability, because of its perceived contribution to facilitating the work of the courts (cf. Burger 1970). It is also credited with leading to dispositions preferable to the outcomes produced by trial. Thus, the Supreme Court has observed that plea bargaining "can benefit all concerned" (*Blackledge* v. *Allison*, 1976, p. 71). Similarly, judicial participation in the process has become more respectable and there are calls for more judicial supervision to ensure "equal plea bargaining opportunities" (*California Law Review* 1971).

Civil Settlement   Similarly, most civil cases in American courts are settled. That is, they terminate in an outcome agreed upon by the parties, sometimes formally ratified by the court, sometimes only noted as settled, and sometimes (from the court's viewpoint) abandoned. The settlement process may begin and end before filing of suit. A great majority of automobile injury claims, for example, are settled before filing (Ross 1970; Conard et al. 1964; Franklin, Chanin, and Mark 1961). Of claims that become lawsuits, settlement is the prevalent mode of disposition of most commercial cases as well as tort cases (Zeisel, Kalven, and Buchholz 1959, p. 333) and in the overwhelming majority of family cases (although in family cases, the result takes the form of a decree in which one party apparently prevails over the other). Settlement has been the prevalent pattern in the United States for at least half a century (Nims 1950; Clark and Shulman 1937). Similar patterns have prevailed in England: for example, in 1908 only 3 percent of cases in the High Court were tried before either judge or jury (Friedman 1976, pp. 35–36). Similarly, Engel (1978, p. 111) found that in a Thai district most suits alleging private wrongs were settled.

Just as "plea bargaining" on close inspection encompasses a cluster of distinct patterns, the umbrella term "settlement" encompasses a whole family of related but distinct phenomena. It includes bilateral negotiation among the parties (as described by Ross 1970; Stern 1977) before or after filing, more or less articulated to moves in the judicial arena. It also includes participation by third parties—outside mediators, officials, even judges. In recent decades American judges have increasingly accepted the notion that courts should actively promote settlements.

Judges may participate pursuant to a formal judicial responsibility to supervise the settlement (as in class actions, stockholders' derivative suits, bankruptcy reorganization cases, where minors are parties, and so forth). There is a growing body of legal doctrine about the way in which courts are obliged to exercise these responsibilities (*Harvard Law Review* 1976; *Vanderbilt Law Review* 1979). Judges may also participate indirectly where the form of the proceeding requires that the bargain struck by the parties be ratified by the court and embodied in a decree—as in divorce cases (Mnookin and Kornhauser 1979). Judges may also participate in settlement negotiations in the absence of any formal requirement that they supervise the settlement or ratify its results. American trial judges employ a variety of techniques to promote settlement, including voluntary and mandatory conferences, meetings, and consultations with the parties individually, together, and serially. The proffering of settlement formulas and various other techniques of active brokering are utilized by at least some judges.

The participation of American judges in active promotion of settlements is increasing and increasingly respectable. The primary rationalization (like that for endorsement of plea bargaining) is that this departure from the adjudicative model is necessary to preserve the forum from unbearable pressures of caseload. But judges also justify active participation on the ground that such efforts provide greater satisfaction to litigants, repair relations between contesting parties, and avoid untoward results in particular cases. Thus, one federal judge in Pittsburgh, trying a suit that threatened the existence of the Westinghouse corporation, sought to avoid a decision based on contract norms and pressed the parties to settle, explaining:

> The fiscal well-being, possibly the survival of one of the world's corporate giants is in jeopardy. Likewise, the future of thousands of jobs.
>
> Any decision I hand down will hurt somebody and because of that potential damage, I want to make it clear that it will happen only because certain captains of industry could not together work out their problems so that the hurt might have been held to a minimum. [*New York Times*, February 11, 1977, pp. D-1, D-10]
>
> Solomon-like as I want to be, I can't cut this baby in half. [*New York Times*, February 17, 1977, p. 57; quoted in Macaulay 1977, p. 516]

Indeed, many judges accept the notion that settlement promotes more just results than would be produced by full-blown adjudication. Thus, one veteran federal judge told a training session for new federal judges that "one of the fundamental principles of judicial administration is that, in most cases, the absolute result of a trial is not as high a quality of justice as is the freely negotiated, give a little, take a little settlement" (Will in Will et al. 1977, p. 203). The commendation of settlement is connected with the ascendance of a view of the judicial role that departs from that of courtroom arbiter. This is put boldly by another federal judge who counseled new judges: ". . . I urge that you see your role not only as a home plate umpire in the courtroom, calling balls and strikes. Even more important are your functions as mediator and administrator" (Lacey 1977, pp. 4–5).

There appears to be some increase in the portion of cases that are settled, but this is a surmise and remains to be explored, controlling for types of cases. There is no evidence that increased judicial participation in the settlement process brings about more settlements. In their study of state courts of general jurisdiction in twenty-one cities, Church et al. (1978) found that dedicating judicial resources to active participation in settlement neither speeded dispositions nor increased the productivity of judges (measured by the number of cases they disposed of annually). Indeed, a detailed examination of five courts revealed that "the most settlement-intensive courts are the slowest courts" (1978, p. 33). Similarly, studies of federal courts by Gillespie (1976) and Flanders (1978) found no positive relation of settlement involvement with terminations—and some hint of an inverse relation. A controlled experiment on the effect of appellate settlement conferences found no reduction in the number of cases that were to be briefed and argued (Goldman 1979). But we cannot conclude that these judicial efforts do not have other effects. Is it the same cases that get settled? At the same stage? And on comparable terms? With what effects on the currency of endowments or bargaining counters to be used in other cases? And what perceptions of the process by the participants?

This displacement of formal proceedings into mediation and bargaining in the anterooms and corridors is found in the administrative process as well as in the regular courts. The vast majority of matters brought to federal administrative agencies are addressed in "informal administrative hearings" (Woll 1960; cf. Macaulay's description [1966, pp. 153ff.] of the "formal informal settlement system" of the Wisconsin Motor Vehicles Bureau).

Which cases manage to survive the winnowing process and end up being fully adjudicated? (1) Perhaps the single most common type is the case where a party needs the judicial declaration—as in divorce or probate proceedings. In such cases there is typically no contest or, if there was a contest, it has been resolved by the parties before securing judicial ratification.(2) Another very frequent kind of fully adjudicated case is the "cut and dried" case that can be processed cheaply and routinely, as in most collection cases, where frequently the defendant does not appear. In both these types the element of contest is minimal.

Other cases are adjudicated because of a premium placed on having an external agency make the decision. (3) Thus, an insurance company functionary may want to avoid responsibility for a large payout (Ross 1970, p. 72). A prosecutor may prefer that charges against the accused in an infamous crime be dismissed by the court rather than by his office (Newman 1966, p. 72). (4) Or there may be value to an actor in showing some external audience (a creditor or the public) that no stone has been left unturned. (5) Or external decision may be sought where the case is so complex or the outcome so indeterminate that it is too unwieldy or costly to arrange a settlement (cf. Ross 1970, p. 221).

(6) Settlement may be unappealing because the "settlement value" is insufficient. Ross (1970, p. 218) describes the personal injury case in which damages are high but liability sufficiently doubtful to preclude a large settlement. Similarly, criminal accused facing mandatory sentences may find the available bargains unattractive. (7) Even when the bargain is acceptable in itself, it may be spurned because of the effect that accepting it would have on the bargaining credibility of a player in future transactions. A litigant or lawyer may want to display his commitment and thus enhance his credibility as an adversary in future rounds of play (Ross 1970, p. 220; cf. Belli [1957, p. 44]: ". . . I have to maintain my advocacy in court on trial in order to keep up settlement value").

Finally, a party may want to adjudicate in order to affect the state of the law. (8) Some parties—typically recurrent organizational litigants—are willing to invest in securing from a court a declaration of "good law" (or avoiding a declaration of "bad law") even where such a decision costs far more than a settlement in the case at hand (Macaulay 1966; Ross 1970, p. 213; Galanter 1974), since such a declaration will improve its position in series of future controversies. (9) Or parties may seek not furtherance of their interests, but vindication of fundamental value commitments—for example, the organizations which have sponsored much church-state litigation in the United States (Sorauf 1976). Players whose conflict is about value differences rather than about competing interests are less likely to settle. (10) Related to this is the special case of government bodies whose notion of "gain" is often problematic and may seek from courts authoritative interpretations of public policy (that is, redefinitions of their notion of gain) (Galanter 1974, p. 112).

The Elaboration and Decomposition of Adjudication

This prevalence of bargaining and mediation is curiously juxtaposed with a refinement and elaboration of adjudication. Compared with earlier periods, litigation is more complex, more expensive, more protracted. It is more rational in the sense that it is free of antiquated and arbitrary formalities. It is open to evidence of complicated states of fact and responsive to a wider range of argument.

Thus, criminal trials have evolved from rough perfunctory proceedings, in which the accused was summarily tried without benefit of counsel, into an elaborate ballet in which the accused enjoys a guaranteed right to counsel and extensive procedural protections. (See generally, Fleming 1974.) Trials take much longer (cf. Langbein 1979 and Friedman

1979 with Alschuler 1979, p. 239). Not only is the trial itself more elaborate, but it is surrounded by a penumbra of formal proceedings at other stages—arraignments, motions to quash evidence, hearings to determine fitness to stand trial, presentence hearings, and the like.

There is a similar increase in complexity on the civil side. Cases are more complicated. A study of Los Angeles Superior Court found an increase in the number of motions and appearances, a higher proportion of cases utilizing discovery, and longer (though proportionately fewer) trials (Selvin and Ebener 1984, pp. 46, 49). Collateral issues proliferate: there is more formal law and with it a multiplication of decision points which spawn "lawsuits before lawsuits" (Frank 1969, pp. 85ff.)—for example, in proceedings about the composition or notification of a class or about lawyer's fees. With the elaboration of remedial means and procedural safeguards, the original disputes spawn what Damaska (1978, p. 240) calls "companion litigation" which proceeds alongside or supersedes the original substantive controversy.

Contrasted with the serial proceedings of the civil law, the common law has as its centerpiece the presentation of proofs and arguments concentrated in a trial—a single discrete plenary episode at which all the major participants come together. With this burgeoning of "pretrial" and "posttrial" activities—motions, discovery, hearings, conferences, probation reports, reports of special masters, postconviction proceedings, hearings about lawyers' fees, and so on—the trial is no longer the center of gravity of common-law litigation. This diffusion is marked by the fact that an American lawyer might describe himself as a "litigator" in contradistinction to a "trial lawyer" (cf. Grady 1978).

Full-blown adversary adjudication becomes more rare as it becomes more refined and elaborate. In its appointed precincts, we find vast amounts of negotiation "in the shadow of the law," routine administrative processing, abbreviated forms of adjudication (the "trial on the transcript" [Mather 1973], the settlement conference, the "preliminary hearing" [McIntyre 1968], "informal administrative hearings" [Woll 1960]), and active mediation on the part of officials clothed with arbitral powers.

How can we account for the attenuation and abandonment of adjudicative modes? The most prevalent explanation is that these distortions result from massive caseloads that prevent institutions from conducting affairs the way they are supposed to. Plea bargaining then is the result of the immense crush of criminal cases; and settlements of civil and administrative matters are induced by the long delays and high costs.

A series of incisive analyses have demolished the notion that nontrial dispositions in criminal cases are a recent response to pressures of caseload. Heumann (1975) has shown that the proportion of nontrial dispositions has been fairly constant in Connecticut courts since the late years of the nineteenth century. The finding that dispositional practices are not much different in high-volume and low-volume courts (Feeley 1979; Heumann 1975) holds up when controls for available personnel are introduced (Nardulli 1979). A natural quasi-experiment on an occasion when some courts had their workload substantially reduced revealed no shift toward more trials (Heumann 1975).

Of course, caseload pressures may have been connected with the origins of plea bargaining patterns and they certainly affect the process. Heavy caseloads may make it less leisurely in style (Feeley 1979). Caseload pressures made appellate courts write shorter opinions with fewer citations and fewer references to other literature, but were not associated with any significant difference in reversals or in dissents (Kagan et al. 1978, p. 971). And caseload may affect the bargains that are struck. For example, Feeley (1979, p.

254) found heavy caseload strongly related to charge reductions in felony cases. Extremes of congestion may be associated with more lenient disposition (Balbus 1973). Similarly, more crowded dockets and consequent longer delay presumably increase the discounts that defendants can command in settling civil claims.

Caseload may be connected with settlement in another way. A higher volume of transactions creates channels of communication among regular participants. The occurrence of more occasions for establishing trust, exchanging reciprocities, and communicating about what cases are worth and what factors are to be taken into account may rationalize dealings by reducing the amount of learning needed on any single occasion.

A rival explanation attributes the gravitation to settlement to fundamental strategic considerations rather than to temporary institutional conditions. In this "strategic" view, all of the participants, seeking to achieve their goals while avoiding risks, find full-blown adjudication inexpedient. Judges want to achieve "appropriate" dispositions while managing the flow of cases. Most lawyers find trials distasteful: they may bring little financial gain; they disrupt their practice, require extensive preparation, and expose them to risks of losing or revealing lack of expertise (Wessel 1976; Rosenthal 1974, pp. 98–99). If trial offers parties hope of complete victory or vindication, it involves additional cost, protracted delay, and a risk of losing all. For the criminal defendant, choosing trial means more time until resolution and a substantial probability of more severe sentencing (Nardulli 1978, pp. 213ff.; Alschuler 1979). One recent study showed "that individual judges, regardless of sentencing philosophy, systematically sentenced jury defendants more heavily than . . . defendants who had pled guilty or elected a bench trial" (Uhlman and Walker 1980, p. 339). The pull of these strategic inclinations is suggested by the tenacity with which systems of arranged dispositions survive attempts to abolish them (Church 1976; Heumann and Loftin 1979). Where "bargaining" is eliminated (as in Callan 1979) it is by standardizing the terms of arranged disposition, not by increasing the number of trials.

Reports from other settings point to the centrality of the striving of participants to maintain control and avoid untoward risks. Engel (1978, p. 103) depicts the efforts of Thai litigants to retain maximum control over the course and outcome of the lawsuit. This process of control may take very different forms. Kidder (1973) contrasts litigation in India between unspecialized opponents who are locked into permanent multiplex relationships with litigation in America conducted by business specialists in transient single-stranded relationships. In the latter, where the stakes lend themselves to rational calculation and the parties can absorb temporary losses, settlement can be reached by explicit negotiation. In the Indian setting, where the stakes include imponderables like prestige and self-definition, the settlement range is inaccessible through rational calculation and can only be approached tacitly through successive tactical maneuvers.

The decomposition of adjudication into bargaining may be accompanied by the simplification and vulgarization of authoritative legal learning. Refined legal standards are replaced by formulae like "three times specials" (Ross 1970, pp. 107ff.) or by the typifications employed by the criminal court regulars who deal with "heavy hitters," "pros," and "nuisance cases" (Buckle and Thomas-Buckle 1977, p. 158) or with "light" or "dead bang" cases (Mather 1973, pp. 197–98; cf. Sudnow 1965). These typifications of people and events, which cut across legal categories and emphasize qualities relevant to disposition, suggest that bargaining may extend, as well as attenuate, the range of issues considered relevant. Bargaining about criminal dispositions may apply norms about first offenders, youth, seriousness, family responsibility, and so forth, that are institutionalized in the local legal culture, but not in the higher law. Similarly, negotiation in civil cases may take into account a range of norms that are excluded from authoritative decision by the court (Eisenberg 1976).

Changes that make law more elaborate and more "rational" (for example, turning on questions of fact, which can be ascertained by experts or by discovery) require higher investments, create new possibilities of maneuver (using discovery to run up the expenses or disrupt the operations of the other side, for example), and involve new risks. As the cost and complexity of trial increase, the possible outcome of the trial becomes a source of bargaining counters that can be used at other phases of the process. An enlarged right of appeal, for example, is not only a possibility that is encountered at a late stage of the proceedings; it is a source of counters and stratagems throughout the process (Engel and Steele 1979). But as the process becomes more complex, these possibilities can be used effectively only by players who can deploy the resources to play on the requisite scale.

The authoritative legal learning becomes more massive and elaborated. There are more statutes and more administrative regulations and more published judicial decisions. But rules propounded by legislatures, administrative bodies, and appellate courts do not carry a single determinate meaning when "applied" in a host of particular settings. Variant readings are possible in any complex system of general rules. Damaska (1975, p. 528) observes that "there is a point beyond which increased complexity of law, especially in loosely ordered normative systems, objectively increases rather than decreases the decision-maker's freedom. Contradictory views can plausibly be held, and support found for almost any position." (Cf. Feeley 1976, p. 500.) As the authoritative learning produced at the top of the system becomes more complex and refined, decision-makers and other actors are both constrained and supplied with resources for innovative combination. Of course, whether they will use them depends on their other resources.

> [T]he discovery of a unique issue is likely to be a function of the amount of time that lawyers devote to a case, and thus of the amount of money that the client spends on lawyers. If the stakes are high, the problems can become very complex; if the client lacks money, his problems are likely to be routine. [Heinz and Laumann 1978, p. 1117]

Adjudication Outside the Courts

Courts (and other official institutions) are not the only settings in which adjudication (and related modes of disputing) take place. The patterns of litigation in courts that we have examined must be understood in the context of the array of rival and companion institutions in which disputes are processed. Societies are composed of a multitude of partially self-regulating spheres or sectors, organized along spatial, transactional, or ethnic-familial lines, ranging from primary groups in which relations are direct, immediate and diffuse to settings (for example, business networks) in which relations are indirect, mediated, and specialized. Disputes and controls are, for the most part, experienced not in courts (or other forums sponsored by the state) but at the various institutional locations of our activities—home, neighborhood, school, workplace, business deal, and so on—including a variety of specialized remedial settings embedded in these locations. The enunciation of norms and application of sanctions in these settings may be more or less organized, more or less self-conscious, more or less removed (in personnel, location, norms, and so on) from everyday activity. In some of these settings we can recognize counterparts or analogs to the institutions, processes, and intellectual activities that characterize the "big" (national, public, official) legal system. Alongside the "big" legal system are a patchwork of lesser normative orderings which we comprehend by such rubrics as "semi-autonomous social fields" (Moore 1973), "private government" (Macaulay: this volume), or "indigenous law" (Galanter 1981).

There is an immense profusion and variety of such "semi-autonomous social fields." The existing literature includes reports, for example, on self-regulatory activity in a variety of business settings such as shopping centers (MacCollum 1967), trade associations (Mentschikoff 1961), heavy manufacturing (Macaulay 1963), textiles (Bonn 1972a, 1972b), the garment industry (Moore 1973), movie distribution and exhibition (Randall 1968), and auto dealers' relations with manufacturers (Macaulay 1966) and with customers (Whitford 1968). In addition, there are reports on self-regulation within religious groups (for example, *Columbia Journal of Law and Social Problems* 1970) and ethnic communities (Doo 1973), intentional communities (Zablocki 1971), professional associations (Akers 1968), athletics (Cross 1973), and workplaces (Blau 1963).

In these settings are found the range of styles of disputing discussed above (pp. 160–64). Exploration of "indigenous law" should help us to understand why particular styles of disputing emerge at particular locations. For example, it provides a set of observations that enable us to speculate about the dynamics of dyadic and third-party controls. Thus, it might be hypothesized that parties whose roles in a transaction or relationship are complementaries—husband-wife, purchaser-supplier, landlord-tenant—will tend to rely on dyadic processes in which group norms enter without specialized apparatus for announcing or enforcing norms. Precisely because of the mutual dependence of the parties, a capacity to sanction is built into the relationship. On the other hand, parties who stand in a parallel position in a set of transactions, such as airlines or stockbrokers *inter se*, tend to develop remedy systems with norm exposition and sanction application by third parties. This is because the parties have little capacity to sanction the deviant directly. This hypothesis may be regarded as a reformulation of Schwartz's proposition (1954) that formal controls appear where informal controls are ineffective and explains his finding of resort to formal controls on an Israeli moshav (cooperative settlement) but not in a kibbutz (collective settlement). In this instance, the interdependence of the kibbutzniks made informal controls effective, while the "independent" moshav members needed formal controls. This echos Durkheim's notion (1964) of different legal controls corresponding to conditions of organic and mechanical solidarity. A corollary to this is suggested by reanalysis of Mentschikoff's survey (1961) of trade association proclivity to engage in arbitration. Her data indicate that the likelihood of arbitration is strongly associated with the fungibility of goods (her categories are raw, soft, and hard goods). Presumably, dealings in more unique hard goods entail enduring purchaser-supplier relations that equip the parties with sanctions for dyadic dispute-settlement, sanctions which are absent among dealers in fungible goods. Among the latter, sanctions take the form of exclusion from the circle of traders, and it is an organized third party (the trade association) that can best organize this kind of sanction. Similarly, systematic study of indigenous law may reveal to us the conditions under which there are explication of norms; formality of procedure; the development of specialists; reliance on the norms, sanctions, and style of official law; and so forth.

The interconnections between disputing in these indigenous forums and in courts are many. Which disputes get to which forums? Presumably, there are many sorts of disputes that rarely appear in official courts precisely because they are disposed of in these other settings. There may be whole areas of social life which are effectively insulated from the direct involvement of the courts. Thus, in a modern industrial society like Great Britain, a "core" area such as contract law may be formulated and applied primarily by private tribunals (trade group arbitration panels) (Ferguson 1980).

Disputes that do arrive in courts have often been shaped by their transit through other forums: much of the business of courts is acting as a "court of appeal" from the decisions of prison officials, union bodies, stock exchanges, sports commissioners. What courts do or refuse to do in such cases may bestow regulatory powers on these forums. Courts may empower indigenous forums explicitly or implicitly. The possibility of resort to courts may be a doomsday machine inducing acquiescence in indigenous regulation. The flow of influence from public adjudication to indigenous ordering is discussed below.

THE EFFECTS OF ADJUDICATION
Distributive Outcomes

We lack a definitive picture of the immediate results of litigation, but we can assemble a crude sketch. Studies of American courts show that in routine cases courts are overwhelmingly plaintiff's (including prosecutor's) forums. For a period of 150 years in a St. Louis court, defendants consistently won less than 10 percent of civil cases (McIntosh 1978). In two California counties in 1970, plaintiffs won 96 and 97 percent of the cases (Friedman and Percival 1976, p. 287). Similar patterns are found in England (where plaintiffs won over 90 percent of cases for a century [Friedman 1976]) and in Thailand (where defendants won outright in only 2.3 percent of civil cases in a Thai provincial court [Engel 1978]). A similar preponderance is found in criminal cases: only a tiny fraction of defendants are acquitted (see McIntyre and Lipman 1970; Administrative Office of the United States Courts 1984, p. 3). In Thailand there were convictions in 96 percent of the public prosecutions (Engel 1978, p. 51).

This preponderance of plaintiff victories reflects the opportunity of the initiating party to calculate and to screen out unpromising cases. It also reflects a large number of routine cases (especially debt collection) in which the defendant is absent and unable to contest the merits; thus, judgment is by default. Also, in many cases what is in form a plaintiff victory is a ratification of a settlement between the parties. Thus, virtually all plaintiffs in suits for divorce win in form, but typically the decree reflects an arranged settlement between the parties rather than the triumph of plaintiff. To some extent the same is true of criminal proceedings where the court decree ratifies the plea bargain that may not fully reflect the outcome preferred by the victim or the prosecutor. And of course in many cases, plaintiffs who receive favorable judgments are unable to collect money damages, recover property, and so forth. To the extent that plaintiffs (or defendants) seek other direct gains (delay, revenge, vindication, information, credibility with such other actors as stockholders or bankers) the judgment may not be an exact reflection of success. We have no way of measuring these effects in the aggregate.

In the vast majority of cases, the trial court's judgment is the final official pronouncement. Of course, there may be further maneuvers and negotiation between the parties after verdict. A minority of cases are appealed: probably less than 1 percent of the total cases disposed of by state trial courts in the United States (Hurst 1980–81, p. 425). Of the cases that reached American state supreme courts, roughly one third were reversed: the number of reversals rises where appellate courts enjoy discretion in admitting cases for review (Hurst 1980–81, p. 427). But important sectors of trial court activity (such as landlord-tenant disputes) are quite underrepresented in the appellate process. Reversals of trial courts, which loom large as part of the appellate caseload, may be rare occurrences in relation to the total dispositions of trial courts. Davies (1981) reports that in one of California's intermediate appellate courts, only 4.8 percent of cases filed in 1974 were reversed; compared with the appealable trial courts convictions of the previous year, this constituted a reversal rate of 2.6 per thousand convictions. A larger minority of federal cases are appealed. In the late 1960s, about 30 percent of all appealable judgments were taken to the federal Courts of Appeal (roughly a quarter of all contested civil judgments and over half of criminal convictions (Howard 1981, p. 35). The judgment of the trial court was reversed in 21 percent of these appeals—and was otherwise "disturbed" in another 5 percent (Howard 1981, p. 39).

Those who litigate in their business capacity fare better than individuals. Wanner (1975) found that business and government plaintiffs win more often (1975, Table 5) and more quickly (1975, Tables 8, 9) than do individual plaintiffs. Not only are they more successful overall, which might be attributed to differences in the kinds of cases they bring, but they are more successful in almost every one of the heavily litigated categories of cases (Wanner 1975, Table 9). Similarly, in a study of two Georgia courts, Owen (1971) found that individual plaintiffs win less often and individual defendants lose more often than do their organizational counterparts. The Arthur Young et al. (1981, IV-26A) study of courts in five American counties from 1903 to 1977 finds that this pattern of organizational success and individual failure has become accentuated over the course of the century. Organizations are more successful than individuals as defendants as well as when they are plaintiffs. They enjoy greater success against individual antagonists than against other organizations; individuals fare less well contending against organizations than against other individuals.

There is a scatter of evidence to suggest that recurrent organizational litigants fare better not only in courts, but also in other forums such as lobbying (Solomon and Siegfried 1977) and administrative hearings (Kloman 1975). (It may be, however, that the advantages of recurrent play are accentuated by the forms of adjudication: Sarat [1976, p. 366] found that the advantages of repeat litigants were "diluted in the informal, compromise-oriented atmosphere of arbitration.") This pattern of organizational predominance has been found in judicial settings outside the United States (Van Houtte and Langerwerf 1981; Gessner et al. 1978).

If no conclusive explanation of the incidence and outcome of litigation can be teased out of the haphazard collection of data that are at hand, there is enough to provide some suggestive leads. One cluster of hypotheses that is suggested by litigation patterns might be called the party capability theory. By this I refer to the notion that the use and outcome of adjudication reflects the differing capabilities of parties as disputants, capabilities that include the competences of actors and advantages (or disadvantages) conferred by their position in the dispute process.

Party capability includes a range of personal capacities that can be summed up in the term "competence": ability to perceive grievances, ability to obtain information about the availability of remedies, psychic readiness to utilize them, ability to manage claims efficiently, ability to seek and utilize appropriate help, and so forth (see Carlin and Howard 1965; Nonet 1969; Rosenthal 1974). Beyond these personal competences there is a related set of structural factors: the size and organization of the party and its position in the dispute process.

Legal encounters in industrial societies take place, for the most part, between individuals and large organizations. For example, Schuyt et al. (1977, p. 112) found that 63 percent of the legal problems of a stratified sample of Dutch individuals were conflicts with a government agency or a private organization. (Generally, cf. Coleman 1974; Moore 1978, chap. 3.) The contract, lease, grant, license, or other transaction—even the accident—is routine for the organization which has, typically, designed the transaction. If trouble develops, the occasion is one of a kind for the individual. It is an emergency or at least a disruption of routine propelling him into an area of hazard and uncertainty. For the organization (usually a business or government unit), on the other hand, making (or defending against) such claims is typically a routine and recurrent activity conducted by experienced specialists. Such recurrent organizational players ("repeat players") enjoy a set of strategic advantages over infrequent individual players ("one-shotters") (Galanter 1974). Briefly, these include:

- ability to utilize advance intelligence, structure the next transaction, build a record, and so forth.
- ability to develop expertise; ready access to specialists; economies of scale and low start-up costs for any case.
- opportunity to develop facilitative informal relations with institutional incumbents.
- ability to establish and maintain credibility as a combatant. With no bargaining reputation to maintain, the one-time litigant has greater difficulty in convincingly establishing commitments to his bargaining positions (Ross 1970, pp. 156ff.; Schelling 1963, pp. 22ff., 41).
- ability to play the odds. The larger the matter at issue looms for the one-shotter, the more likely he is to avoid risk (that is, minimize the probability of maximum loss). Assuming that the stakes are relatively smaller for recurrent litigants because of their greater size, they can adopt strategies calculated to maximize gain over a long series of cases, even where this involves the risk of maximum loss in some cases.
- ability to play for rules as well as immediate gains. It pays a recurrent litigant to expend resources in influencing the making of the relevant rules by lobbying, and so forth. Recurrent litigants can also play for rules in litigation itself, whereas a one-time litigant is unlikely to do so.

The differences in outcome may be viewed as an artifact of the selection of cases. Organizational parties bring more cases of the kinds that are easiest to win, such as debt collections. The overall pattern then results from their well-selected portfolio rather than from any difference in the rate of return. There seems to be some measure of truth in this, but it does not explain all the observed variation between individuals and organizations. Wanner (1975, Table 9) finds that organizations do better than individuals in almost every kind of frequently litigated case. And organizations do strikingly better not only as plaintiffs, but also as defendants (Wanner 1975, Table 7).

A more refined version of this selection hypothesis would say that organizations not only bring different kinds of cases, but better cases—cases in which the evidence is stronger and the claim is more firmly located within accepted lines of recovery; as defendants, their defenses are more ironclad, and so forth. As plaintiffs, they can avoid bad cases by forbearance to bring suit or by readily accepting a low settlement. As defendants, they settle the more meritorious claims against them—perhaps before filing. To some extent this is a restatement of the party capability cluster. Stronger evidence, more cut-and-dried claims, and unassailable defenses are the result of advance planning and good record-keeping, as well as of the intrinsic merit of the claim. A calculating settlement policy reflects their skill as litigants as much as the virtues of their conduct in the underlying transaction. In good measure, "case merit" is not an alternative explanation, but a specification of one of the ways in which party capability affects the profile of litigation.

Perhaps the differences observed between organizations and individuals are explainable in terms of quantity and quality of legal services. There is evidence (for example, Ross 1970, p. 193) that legal representation makes for a massive difference both in likelihood of recovery and in amount recovered. But much of the difference attributed to legal services is again traceable to difference in party capabilities. When we speak of differences in amount of preventive work, continuity of attention, specialized expertise, economies of scale, shrewd investment in rule development—we are talking about legal services provided to certain kinds of parties. Legal professionals in the United States can be roughly dichotomized into those who service one-shot players on an episodic basis and those who service repeat players on a continuing basis (cf. Heinz and Laumann, 1978). Although there are many exceptions, there is a massive difference in education, skill, and status between these groups. There is also a massive difference in the range and quality of services provided: the profession is organized to provide a wide range of services to organizations and a much narrower range to individuals (Galanter 1983a). FitzGerald's study (1975) of the contract buyers provides a dramatic example of change in the organizational state of parties bringing in its train dramatic changes in the amount, character, and quality of legal services. Organization need not follow from improved legal services, but it seems likely that a broader range of legal services ordinarily will result from organization.

Legal services are surely one vehicle through which differences in party capability have effect. But, for several reasons, I think it useful to retain the broader notion of party capability. First, legal competence is not something supplied exclusively by professionals and entirely separable from the parties. Parties themselves may have different levels of capacity to utilize legal services. For example, Rosenthal (1974) finds superior results obtained by "active" personal injury plaintiffs; Moulton (1969, p. 1662) finds that in a California small claims court in which lawyers are not permitted to appear, businesses that are frequent users "form a class of professional plaintiffs who have significant advantages over the individual." Second, it seems that major distinctions in party competence can exist quite apart from disparities in legal services. The reports of Kidder (1973, 1974) and Morrison (1974) on litigation in India suggest a distinction between the "experienced" or "chronic" litigant and the naïve and casual one that seems to be quite independent of the organization of legal services.

The crucial distinction is between the casual participant for whom the game is an emergency, and the party who is equipped to do it as part of his routine activity. The sailor overboard and the shark are both swimmers, but only one is in the swimming business. The distinction overlaps, at least in the American setting, with two other distinctions—that between individuals and organizations and that between the poor and the wealthy. It is generally organizations that can be repeat players—because in America law is a complex and expensive activity requiring employment of full-time specialists. Organizations can use the law routinely because, given the cost of obtaining or resisting remedies, organizations are the right size—and almost all individuals are too poor to play. And organizations are endowed with a capacity for calculated pursuit of narrow and intense interests that produces pronounced asymmetries in their dealings with natural persons (Coleman 1974). But, as the Indian studies show, in other settings the distinction between habitual and "one-shot" users may be entirely independent of distinctions between organizations and individuals.

The distinction between "repeat players" and "one-shotters" points to an antinomy that strikes me as a fundamental feature of legal life. Presumably, law is corrective and remedial in intent; it is designed to restore or promote a desired balance. But as it becomes differentiated, complex, and mazelike in order to do this with increasing autonomy and precision, the law itself becomes a source of new imbalances. Some users become adept in dealing with it; those with other advantages find that those advantages can be translated into advantages in the legal arena. There arise new differences in access and competence—thus law itself can amplify the imbalances that it set out to correct. The scope and location of these differences in party capability, one expects, would vary with other features of the society.

The party capability theory is a cluster that invites disaggregation in several ways. First, we have to isolate the nature (and composition) of the superior capability enjoyed by some parties. Is it a superior capacity to obtain, store, retrieve, and utilize information? Is it superior ability to employ experts? To coordinate related undertakings? To employ strategies unavailable to other actors? One assumes that these will vary from one class of cases to another, for different parties and at different times and in different social and cultural settings.

Then what are the specific characteristics of the parties which give rise to these superior capabilities? Is it size? Absolute size (measured by personnel or dollars)? Size relative to the other party? Size relative to the claim at stake? Or is it the element of repetition: experience in handling claims? Experience in litigation? In litigation in this forum? In this kind of claim in this forum? In some settings, superior capability may be closely related to being a repeat player in the narrow literal sense. The portrayals of Kidder (1973, 1974) and Morrison (1974) of Indian litigants and Sanders's account (1975) of American drug cases suggest that experience in the forum and adaptation to its exigencies is central to explaining the pattern of results. Other advantages like wealth are mediated through the differential capacities of actors in the immediate setting; these in turn are dependent on familiarity and experience and on tactical options that derive from recurrent play in this forum.

Courts as Sources of Bargaining and Regulatory Endowments

The consequences of adjudication extend beyond the immediate distributive effects on the parties. We have seen that courts resolve by authoritative disposition only a small fraction of all disputes that are brought to their attention. These in turn are only a small fraction of the disputes that might conceivably be brought to courts and an even smaller fraction of the whole universe of disputes. But the observation of the limited role of courts in direct resolution of disputes should not be taken as an assertion that courts are unimportant in the entire matrix of disputing and regulation. The impact of adjudication cannot be equated with the resolution of those disputes that are fully adjudicated. Adjudication provides a background of norms and procedures against which negotiations and regulation in both private and governmental settings takes place. This contribution includes, but is not exhausted by, communication to prospective litigants of what might transpire if one of them sought a judicial resolution. Courts communicate not only the rules that would govern adjudication of the dispute but possible remedies and estimates of the difficulty, certainty, and cost of securing particular outcomes.

The courts (and the law they apply) may thus be said to confer on the parties what Mnookin and Kornhauser (1979) call a "bargaining endowment," that is, a set of "counters" to be used in bargaining between disputants. In the case of divorce, for example,

> . . . [t]he legal rules governing alimony, child support, marital property and custody give each parent certain claims based on what each would get if the case went to trial. In other words, the outcome that the law would impose if no agreement is reached gives each parent certain bargaining chips—an endowment of sorts. [p. 968]

Similarly, the rules of tort law provide bargaining counters which are used in a process of negotiating settlements (Ross 1970). The gravitation to negotiated outcomes in criminal cases is well known. One astute observer concludes that "the actual significance of the sophisticated adversary process before the jury" in American criminal cases is "to set a framework for party negotiations, providing 'bargaining chips'" (Damaska 1978, p. 240). The negotiating dimension is found in the most complex as in the most routine cases: thus, in "extended impact" cases, the involvement of the courts supplies standards and the setting for negotiations among the parties (Diver 1979; Cavanagh and Sarat 1980, pp. 405–7). And, of course, this process is not confined to the United States or to "advanced" societies. The Zinacantecos described by Collier (1973, pp. 70ff.) used the courts infrequently, but predictions of what the court would do significantly affected the settlements produced by local mediators.

The bargaining endowment that courts bestow on the parties includes not only the substantive entitlement conferred by legal rules, but also rules that enable those entitlements to be vindicated—for example, rules requiring production of documents, or rules excluding evidence favorable to the other party or jeopardizing the claim of the other party (for example, contributory negligence). But rules are only one part of the endowment conferred by the forum: the delay, cost, and uncertainty of eliciting a favorable determination also confer bargaining counters on the disputants. Delay, cost, and uncertainty may themselves be the product of rules—for example, a discretionary standard involving balancing of many factors requiring detailed proofs is more costly, time-consuming, and uncertain in application than a mechanical rule. But cost, delay, and uncertainty also result from such nonrule factors as the number and organization of courts and lawyers.

The meaning of the endowment bestowed by the law is of course not fixed and invariable, but depends on the characteristics of the disputants: their preferences, negotiating skill, aversion to risk, ability to respond to deadlines and emergencies, ability to bear costs and delay, and so forth. A different mix of disputant capabilities may make a given endowment take on very different significance.

Bargaining between the parties is not the only kind of "private ordering" that takes place in the law's capacious shadow. We can extend the notion of the bargaining endowment to imagine the courts conferring on disputants a "regulatory endowment" (Galanter 1981). That is, what the courts might do (and the difficulty of getting them to do it) clothes with authorizations and immunities the regulatory activities of the school principal, the union officer, the arbitrator, the commissioner of baseball, and a host of others—regulation which may be exercised through various forms, including adjudicatory ones.

The distinction between negotiation and regulation is a relative one. The continuity between them is displayed, for example, in the continuing relation between a university and its food service contractor, where the process of monitoring performance and negotiating adjustments partakes of (or may be interpreted as) both (Goldberg 1976). Of course, regulation may involve an important element of bargaining—as in agency "notice and comment" rule-making or in the relations of guards to prisoners described by Sykes (1958). Perhaps we should think of bargaining and regulation as the ends of a spectrum, along whose length we can find many intermediate (and alternating) instances.

Courts bestow a regulatory endowment in many ways. First, the courts provide models (norms, procedures, structures, rationalizations) for such regulatory activity. Second, there are explicit authorizations and immunities conferred by the courts (and the law) on an immense variety of regulatory settings—the school teacher and principal, the prison warden, the agricultural cooperative, the baseball league, the union leader. Such authorizations may be explicit rulings about the regulatory activity—as in judicial doctrine about the authority of arbitrators, school officials, and church bodies. Or they may be implicit in rules of jurisdiction, standing, and other procedural doctrine that denies admittance to cases involving certain kinds of regulatory activity.

Finally, there are the implicit authorizations and immunities that flow from the general conditions of overcommitment and passivity. Courts are reactive; they acquire cases not on their own motion, but only upon the initiative of one of the disputants. Thus, there is delegation to the disputants to invoke the intervention of a court. The expense, delay, and cumbersomeness of securing such intervention insulate all regulators by raising barriers to challenging them in the courts. The regulation exercised by hospitals on patients and their families, by landlords on their tenants, by universities on their students, by unions on their members, by manufacturers on their customers are rarely subject to challenge in public forums. By a kind of legal alchemy, the expense and remoteness of the courts (and the overload and lethargy of other agencies) are transformed into regulatory authority which can be exercised by a host of institutions.

The relation of official adjudicatory forums to disputes is multidimensional. Decisive resolution, while important, is not the only link of courts and disputes. Disputes may be prevented by what courts do—for example, by enabling planning to avoid disputes or by normatively disarming a potential disputant. Also, courts may foment and mobilize disputes, as when their declaration of a right arouses and legitimates expectations about the propriety of pursuing a claim; or when changes in rules of standing suggest the possibility of pursuing a claim successfully. Further, courts may displace disputes into various forums and endow these forums with regulatory power. Finally, courts may transform disputes so that the issues addressed are broader or narrower or different from those initially raised by the disputants (see Mather and Yngvesson 1980–81). Thus, courts not only resolve disputes: they prevent them, mobilize them, displace them, and transform them.

The Radiating Effects of Adjudication

By distributing endowments a court may elicit anticipatory compliance or evasive maneuvers, stigmatize or legitimate a line of conduct, encourage or suppress the making of a claim, lower or heighten estimation of conduct or of its regulators. Another way of looking at the radiating influence of judicial action (or inaction) proceeds from a distinction between "special effects" and "general effects." "Special effects" refers to the impact of the forum's action on the specific parties before it. "General effects" are effects of the communication of information by/about the forum's action and of the response to that information.[9] We can isolate (in theory at least) various kinds of effects on the subsequent activity of various actors. For example, I may rob stores less frequently because I am imprisoned and stores are therefore hard to reach (*incapacitation*). On the other hand, I may be placed on probation and as a result subjected to increased *surveillance* by the police, making it difficult to rob stores. Or my chances for breaching contracts may be reduced by the wariness of those who deal with me, wariness that stems from an earlier suit against me. Their reluctance may reflect the stigmatizing effect of sanctions imposed on me by the court, but it may also flow from the ancillary impact of court proceedings on my credit rating, insurability, licensing, business reputation, standing in other forums, and so forth (see Engel and Steele 1979, p. 316). And, of course, such ancillary effects may be produced not only by the substantive decision of the court but by the costs (including benefits forgone) and timing of that decision (or its absence). This example involves elements of surveillance and incapacitation. Alternatively, I might refrain from robbing stores or breaking contracts because I am fearful of being caught and punished again (*special deterrence*). Finally, the experience of being exposed to the law may change my view that it is right to rob stores or break contracts (*reformation*).

If adjudication is a source of moral authority and a locus of struggles for moral vindication, at the same time it harbors tendencies to demoralization. Typically, courts enforce only a delimited part of the whole universe of recognized moral claims, and legal procedures attenuate the connection of litigated claims with the moral environment (Abel 1973). As Fallers (1969, p. 28) observes, the litigant typically "seeks the advantages of the narrow legalism of the forum while claiming the sanction of moral holism." In the American setting at least the promise of moral vindication must be pursued through a

---

[9] This notion of "general effects" takes off from the very helpful discussion of general preventive effects of punishment by Gibbs (1975, chap. 3) as usefully elaborated by Feeley (1976, pp. 517ff.) It is simply a generalization from the illuminating and now familiar (if not entirely serviceable, as Gibbs points out) distinction between special deterrence and general deterrence introduced by Andenaes (1966). Theory about these general effects is still inchoate. In a review of the now sizable literature on deterrence, Gibbs (this volume, chap. 7) observes that since deterrence research has proceeded without controls for other general effects, "all previous reported tests of the deterrence doctrine . . . were really tests of an implicit theory of general preventive effects; and that will remain the case as long as nondeterrent mechanisms are left uncontrolled." Some of the labels used here for the various effects are inspired by, but deviate from, those carefully discussed by Gibbs (1975, chap. 3).

costly, abrasive, and disheartening process in which one must give discounts and accept compromises; the result is less than total vindication. Those with the highest expectations of moral vindication experience the greatest disillusionment in the process—even where they are more successful than more cynical litigants (Crowe 1978).

In addition to (or instead of) changing my disposition toward the underlying transaction (the business deal or the marriage), the experience may change my perceptions and evaluations of the activity of disputing about it, the institutions in which disputes are processed, and myself as a disputant. Thus, debtors who lose collection cases may emerge from the experience with an enhanced sense of political efficacy (Jacob 1969b, p. 264). But winners of injury suits (Danzig 1978, chap. 1) or antidiscrimination cases (Crowe 1978) may be disillusioned with the forum and despair of vindicating their rights. We do not know how participants' experiences affect their ability to perceive and pursue disputes in the future.

Generally, those who prevail are satisfied with their court experience (Ruhnka and Weller 1978, p. 74). But full-blown adjudication may compare unfavorably with other procedures: criminal defendants who are convicted after trial may feel more unfairly treated than those who pled guilty (Casper 1978, pp. 48ff.) Those who experience courts firsthand tend to be less satisfied with them than those who view them from afar (Sarat 1977b, pp. 439, 441). Yankelovich et al. (1978, pp. 11, 18) found that unfavorable evaluations of state courts increased with both knowledge about courts and experience with them. (Cf. Curran 1977, p. 236, on the more critical assessment by multiple users.) Comparable responses have been found in widely different settings. Kidder (1973) reports that Indian litigants were disillusioned with the courts they had encountered

> [but] . . . everyone interviewed believed that the courts above those they had directly experienced would be free of the complications they had found in their own experience. . . . This "grass is greener" phenomenon was as true of recent winners as it was of recent losers and showed up in [experienced] "court birds" as predictably as in the newest novice. [p. 134]

The gap between use and estimation appears even in the Polish community-based Social Conciliation Commission described by Kurczewski and Frieske (1978), where those who think best of the SCC are higher-status groups with little direct experience of its operation.

> The SCC's are favored to a much lesser degree, on *general* criteria, by those who have actually used them as disputants—even though these former SCC users are largely satisfied with, and assess positively, the performance of the SCC in their own particular cases—and these former parties tend to be persons with characteristics of lower status. [p. 328]

Of course, the parties are not the only participants affected by the process of adjudication. The regular participants—lawyers, judges, and others—may be inured to the impact of any single instance, but changed by the cumulative experience. We know little about how being a judge affects judges: some find the experience disillusioning (for example, Forer 1975; Frankel 1980); others respond with complacency, stoicism, creativity. Similarly, little is known about the impact of adjudication on lawyers. Dibble (1973) finds that more experienced lawyers tend to see more issues in their cases. Brazil (1978) suggests that they find litigation demoralizing.

Adjudicative activity affects not only those immediately involved, but others as well. Further effects result from the communication of information about what was (or could be) done by courts. Thus, if I am punished for theft or have to pay damages for breaching a contract, others may reassess the risks and advantages of similar activity. This is *general deterrence*. It neither presumes nor requires any change in their moral evaluation of stealing or breaking contracts, nor does it involve any change in their opportunities to commit these infractions. It stipulates that behavior will be affected by acquisition of more information about the costs and benefits that are likely to attach to the act— information about the certainty, celerity, and severity of punishment, for example. The actor can hold to Hart's "external point of view" (1961, p. 86), treating law as a fact to be taken into account rather than as a normative framework that he is committed to uphold or be guided by. The information that induces the changed estimation of costs and benefits need not be accurate: what the court has done may be inaccurately perceived; indeed the court itself may have inaccurately depicted what it has done.

Courts are not viewed only as mechanisms that display to us the deployment of governmental force. For many of their constituents, at least, courts embody moral authority and their pronouncements induce and reinforce sentiments of moral condemnation and approval. Hence, courts may become battlegrounds of symbolic politics in which condemnation or approval of abortion, unmarried cohabitation, or school prayer are major symbolic prizes testifying to the moral worthiness of various groups in the society (Gusfield 1966). Such symbolic counters may be detached from patterns of actual regulatory behavior. Hence the passionate concern with laws that are only rarely enforced, such as adultery laws and Sunday closing laws.

Perceiving the application of a law may maintain or intensify existing evaluations of conduct—Gibbs (1975) calls this *normative validation*. Or, more dramatically, communication of the existence of a law or its application by a court may change the moral evaluation of an item of conduct by other actors. To the extent that this involves not calculation of the probability of being visited by certain costs and benefits, but a change in moral estimation, we may call this general effect *enculturation*. There is suggestive evidence to indicate that at least some segments of the population are subject to such effects (Berkowitz and Walker 1967; Colombatos 1969). Other studies provide contrasting hypotheses about the conditions under which such enculturation takes place and its relation to the coercive aspects of the law. Thus, Muir (1967) and Dolbeare and Hammond (1971) both examine the reaction of local school boards to decisions of the Supreme Court banning officially sponsored prayer in classrooms. Muir finds substantial compliance and substantial enculturation associated with low perceived coerciveness of the legal setting; Dolbeare and Hammond, finding little compliance, attribute the dissociation of practice from legal doctrine to the absence of coercive pressure.

Adjudication not only validates or changes our evaluation of specific sorts of conduct; it may radiate to wider audiences reassuring messages about the society and its processes (Casey 1973; cf. Edelman 1967). (This is the other side of the tendency, noted above, to estimate remote courts more highly than familiar ones.) The centrality of providing symbolic sustenance is asserted by Becker (1970, p. 12): "The most enduring function of the court—indeed of judicial structure—seems best described as the appeasement of the outrage felt in the soul and mind of man at the instability, tedium, amorphousness, and basic arbitrariness of our natural environment and our mortality." Ball (1975) describes the theatrical "live performance" of courts as dramatic embodiments or presentation of a normative image of legitimate society—dramatizing the seriousness, importance, dignity, rights, and duties of citizens, surrounding them with ceremonious deference. But without further knowledge of the (presumably differentiated) reception process, we cannot specify the policy implications of the insight that courts are important symbolic transmitters.

These do not exhaust the general effects of legal action. There are other radiating effects at the level of disputing as well as at the level of the underlying transaction. The messages of adjudication may be taken neither as facts to be adapted to nor as norms to be adhered to, but as recipes to be followed. Law may be used as a cookbook from which we can learn how to bring about desired results—disposing of property, forming a partnership, securing a subsidy. We may call this effect *facilitation*.

Similarly, litigation may have powerful *mobilization* or *demobilization* effects. It may provide symbols for rallying a group, broadcasting awareness of grievance, and dramatizing challenge to the status quo (*Yale Law Journal* 1970, pp. 1087ff.). On the other hand, concentration on litigation may undermine an organization's ability to employ other political means (Scheingold 1974). Success in litigation may, for example, defuse the drive for wider legislative change. Thus, it is reported that after the Court of Appeals heroically extended the meaning of "unconscionability" in *Williams v. Walker-Thomas Furniture Co.* (1965), the corporation counsel dropped plans to draft consumer legislation for the District of Columbia (Dostert 1968, p. 1186).

The assumption that the authoritative pronouncements of higher courts penetrate automatically—swiftly, costlessly, without distortion—to all corners of the legal world has been challenged by several generations of studies of "the limits of effective legal action" (cf. Pound 1917; Jones 1969). This includes a tradition of "impact studies" which has demonstrated that the penetration of rules is variable and uneven and that the rules undergo significant transformation in the process. (A useful summary of the impact literature is provided by Wasby 1970; see also Becker and Feeley 1973. Some broad generalizations about the conditions conducive to penetration may be found in Grossman 1970, pp. 545ff.; Levine 1970, pp. 599ff. On the limitations of the "impact studies" genre, see Feeley 1976, pp. 498ff.) The impact design curiously echoes the naïve model of perfect penetration by attributing to rules propounded in the lofty setting of the legislature or the appellate court a single determinate meaning when "applied" in a host of particular settings (Feeley 1976, p. 500). But most authoritative norms are ambiguous: variant readings are possible in any complex system of general rules.

The centrifugal perspective adopted here suggests an enlargement of the concerns of the last generation of impact research which started from the doctrinal pronouncements of appellate courts and asked about congruence between that doctrine and the practices of other agencies (lower courts, school boards, police, and the like). In addition to the effects of doctrinal pronouncements, we are interested in the effects of costs, remedies, delay, uncertainty, legitimation, stigma, and all of the other components of the total message transmitted by the courts, including trial courts as well as appellate courts, and including informal mediation and private bargaining as well as adjudication. The product of the court is not doctrine with a mix of impurities, but rather a whole set of messages that can be used as resources in making (or contesting) claims, bargaining (or refusing to bargain), and regulating (or resisting regulation). Effects flow not only from doctrine, but also from patterns of discovery, settlement, cost, and remedy; not only from individual rulings, but from court structures and court routines. And effects flow not only to the behavior that is the subject of judicial pronouncements, but to the attempts of actors to accommodate to the impact of those pronouncements, to the efforts of other actors accommodating those attempts, and so on. Thus, recent studies have charted the impact of the abrogation of the doctrine of charitable immunity on hospital costs (Canon and Jaros 1979; Caldeira 1981–82) as well as on self-regulation within hospitals (Zald and Hair 1972).

Beyond the effects attributed to particular instances of adjudication, cumulative effects are often attributed to institutionalized patterns of adjudication. Thus, the popularization of litigation in sixteenth-century Castile led to a dramatic increase in record-keeping (Kagan 1981, p. 126). More remarkably, courts may be credited with preserving democratic institutions, promoting economic efficiency (Posner 1977), and other salutary results—or with legitimizing oppression, and so forth. The complexities of discerning such effects are illustrated by the debate over whether judicial review by the Supreme Court should be credited with protecting the rights of minorities throughout the course of United States history. Thus, Dahl (1958) and Funston (1975) argue that except in brief transition periods, the Court functions not to protect minorities against dominant political coalitions but instead to legitimate political change. Other observers (Ademany 1973; Casper 1976; Handberg and Hill 1980), using a wider range of data, credit the Court with significant obstruction of the policies of dominant majorities.

In cataloging these various effects, it appears that the impact of adjudication is accomplished primarily through the transmission and reception of information rather than through the direct imposition of controls. Like most other contemporary legal institutions, courts have far more commitments than resources to carry them out. Enforcement agencies cannot possibly enforce all the laws. Nor can individuals enforce all of their rights. In theory courts are open for full adjudicatory hearing of all cases, but in practice their capacity to conduct full-blown adjudications is limited to a fraction of the potential cases. Law is more capacious as a system of cultural and symbolic meanings than as a set of operative controls. It affects us primarily through communication of symbols—by providing threats, promises, models, persuasion, legitimacy, stigma, and so forth. Of course, these radiating effects need not be intended (or perceived) by the forum (or the disputants). The forum may attempt to enhance certain of its effects by cultivating a public image of implacable severity or sage deliberation, by deliberately projecting an image of its general patterns of response, and so forth. Of course, no matter what it tries to project, transmission by the forum is only part of the process. Effects will also depend on the reception side: Who gets which messages? Who can evaluate and process them? Who can use the information? These messages are resources that parties use in envisioning, devising, pursuing, negotiating, and vindicating claims (and in avoiding, defending, and defeating them). Similarly, courts distribute resources by which some parties regulate others (or resist such regulation). The broad pattern of effects of courts will depend on the way these resources are used.

Just how potential disputants and regulators will draw on these resources is powerfully affected by their culture, their capabilities, and their relations with one another. For example, we would expect that the legal endowment would be used differently in bargaining among strangers with no prospect of continuing relations (as in the typical automobile injury claim) than by parties to a long-term relationship; we would expect it to be used differently where disputants shared a normative consensus or where some formidable sanctions were built into their relationship (Macaulay 1963). We would expect it to be used differently where one disputant was dependent on the other. Similarly, we would expect that the regulatory endowment would be used differently in a continuing relation-ship than in an episodic one, and so on.

Messages about what courts do and what they say are mediated through various chan-nels to different audiences with different capacities to receive and evaluate these mes-sages. Audiences may differ, for example, in their ability to make a sophisticated assess-ment of what a court really does—that is, what their bargaining chips really are. Ross (1970, pp. 193ff.) describes the shift in bargaining stances when the knowledgeable lawyer replaces the inexperienced claimant as the bargaining partner. But the lawyer's sophistication may not always be placed at the disposal of the naïve client. Feeley (1979) describes how criminal defendants receive routine offers made to appear as exceptional deals:

> It is the salesman's stock in trade to represent a "going rate" as if it were a special sale price offered only once. The gap between theoretical exposure and the standard rate allows defense attorneys and prosecutors to function in much the same way. Together, prosecutors and defense attorneys operate like discount stores, pointing to the never used high list price and then marketing the product as a "special" at what is in fact the standard price. [pp. 464–65]

Similarly, it has been suggested that the effectiveness of deterrence systems varies with the capabilities of the recipients. While naïve amateurs may generalize the high risk of punishment from one type of crime to another, sophisticated professionals who "make relevant distinctions and . . . put the message into a refined context" will be able to extract more specific and accurate information from the deterrence message. Geerken and Gove (1975) provide this illustration:

> Let us assume, for example, that an armed robber has just been convicted for his crime. A child might receive the message that crime does not pay, a businessman who cheats on his income tax might receive the message that violent or "lower-class" crime does not pay, a burglar might receive a message that armed robbery is too dangerous and an armed robber might receive the message that armed robbery under particular circumstances—a bank for instance—is too risky. [p. 507]

Compare Silbey (1980–81, p. 871) on merchant perceptions of consumer complaint enforcement and Dwyer (1979) on systematic differences in the way in which men and women in southern Morocco perceive law and legal practices and extract support in their ongoing struggle over the subordination of women. Where control is exerted through communication, the system will be powerfully influenced by the information-processing capacities of the recipients—and by the differences in their capacities.

I have used two idioms to discuss the centrifugal flow from the courts: endowments and effects. When discussing courts as sources of bargaining (and regulatory) endowments, the point of view was that of the disputants. In talking of general effects the stance is more detached. The time frame shifts from the strategic present to the retrospective or predictive. Calculations are probabilistic rather than prudential. Judgments are aggregate rather than distributive. The point of view is that of the detached observer or the remote manager of the system, not of a participant interested in specific transactions. What these viewpoints share is a vision of legal action as a centrifugal flow of symbols, radiating beyond the parties immediately involved. Both lead us to focus on the disputants as receivers of this symbolic radiation. And the "endowments" that courts confer depend on the capabilities of actors to receive, store, and use them, capabilities that reflect their skills, resources, and opportunities. The patterns of general effects that we attribute to the courts depend on the endowments that actors extract from the messages that radiate from the courts.

I do not mean to portray these capabilities as immutable qualities intrinsic to the actors, marking the irreducible endpoints of analysis. Disputants' capabilities derive from, and are relative to, structures of communication and structures for organizing action. Capabilities depend, for example, on location on a network that carries information about rights and remedies and on proximity to remedy institutions or "exit" alternatives. The process of distributing and extracting endowments is framed by the larger structures of social life. As these structures undergo change, the character of the centrifugal flow of effects from the courts will change as well. For example, changes in political structures and communication systems may bring in their train a shift from reliance on special effects (impinging directly on disputants) to emphasis on general effects (worked by communication about such impingements). Thus, Abel (1979b, p. 193) suggests that compared with litigation in the tribal setting, modern litigation in Africa involves fewer courts with larger jurisdictions, prosecution of a smaller proportion of wrongs, and imposition of sterner punishments, shifting from the earlier reliance on special deterrence to reliance on general deterrence. This comports with Aubert's observation (1979, p. 30) that the modern state has moved from inexpensive criminal punishments (hanging, whipping) to expensive ones like imprisonment that must be used sparingly. This might imply great reliance on the private sector to deliver sanctions, either by civil damages or by the social and economic cost of entanglement with the legal system.

We might expect the mix and the relative prominence of these radiating effects to vary across space as well as over time. For example, the role of general effects of court action compared with direct effects on the disputants may be greater in the United States, which maintains a relatively small judicial plant but a very large private legal profession, compared with other industrial countries (Table 3).

This centrifugal flow of endowments or effects is rendered even more complex when adjudication (and its kindred processes) is juxtaposed with the uneven but pervasive clusters of patterned norms and sanctions that I have called "indigenous law." The image of "bargaining in the shadow of the law" (Mnookin and Kornhauser 1979) suggests that the law is *there* and the disputants meet in a landscape naked of normative habitation (or in which such structures are subsumed into their "preferences"). Instead we may visualize a landscape overgrown with an uneven tangle of indigenous law. In many settings, the norms and controls of indigenous ordering are palpably *there,* the official law is remote, and its intervention is problematic and transitory. Consider, for example, the businessmen described by Macaulay (1963) or a typical dispute within a university. In such settings the relation might be better depicted as "law in the shadow of indigenous regulatory activity."

The relation of official law to indigenous ordering is not invariably a matter of mutual exclusion (where the former ousts the latter), nor one of hierarchic control (where the latter is conformed to or aligned with the former). Judicial intervention to apply official standards does not necessarily weaken indigenous control. For example, Zald and Hair (1972, p. 66) suggest that the judicial erosion of the doctrine of charitable immunity and the exposure of hospitals to liability for negligence provided enlarged "incentives and sanctions . . . to governmental and private standard-setting bodies such as the Joint Commission [of Accreditation of Hospitals] to induce compliance with standards on the part of hospitals." Similarly, Macaulay (1966) shows that official intervention in the relations between automobile manufacturers and their dealers led to a growth of internal regulation rather than to its attenuation. And Randall's study (1968) of movie censorship reveals how the elaboration of internal controls within the movie industry was a reflection of actual and potential control by the official law. Just as the character of such indigenous regulation is affected in unanticipated ways by developments in the official law, so the presence of indigenous regulation may transform the meaning and effect of the official law.

The complexity of the interface between external and indigenous controls (cf. Katz 1977) is demonstrated in the observation that the official system is frequently used to induce compliance with a decision in an indigenous forum. Thus, Ruffini (1978) describes Sardinian shepherds threatening to complain to officials to force resort to and compliance with the indigenous system of settlement. In the Brazilian squatter settlement described by Santos (1977, p. 79), "the official legal system is presented not as a forum to which a litigant may appeal from an adverse decision under Pasargada law but as a threat aimed at reinforcing the decision of the RA [Residents' Association] under that law." Similar instances in which the cost, delay, aggravation, and risk of being subjected to the official system become a resource of indigenous regulators are found in accounts from India (Meschievitz and Galanter 1982, p. 59), Lebanon (Witty 1978), and Mexico (Collier 1973, p. 263). Thus, official adjudication becomes a means for the enforcement of norms foreign to the official law.

The effects of indigenous tribunals, like those of official courts, are not confined to direct participation in cases. The work of these tribunals may radiate norms, symbols, models, threats, and so forth. In indigenous law, too, the shadow reaches further than its source. What kind of bargaining and regulatory endowments actors extract from the messages depends on their capabilities. Community standing, seniority, reputation for integrity, or formidability may confer capability in the indigenous setting that does not translate into capability in official tribunals. Indeed, indigenous law may be insulated from external controls by its constituents' lack of capability to use official remedies (cf. Doo 1973). Acquisition of capability to use official courts may lead to erosion of indigenous tribunals (cf. Galanter 1968). On the other hand, an equalizing of capabilities in official forums may lead to their abandonment and development of indigenous tribunals, as in the labor-management field.

CHANGES OVER TIME IN PATTERNS AND CHARACTER OF ADJUDICATION

Some long-term changes were noted earlier: the emergence of differentiated judicial institutions and the concentration of judicial power in the hands of smaller, professional judiciaries. These are linked with changes in the character of law. Rationalized systems of secular law, applied by specialized legal institutions forming part of the nation state, consolidated in the industrializing West and spread over most of the world during the nineteenth and twentieth centuries (see Galanter 1966). Changing patterns of adjudication must be seen against the background of this transformation.

Qualitative "before and after" comparisons of litigation across the great divide portray the varied effects of this shift from multiple and sometimes diffuse forums into a system of governmental courts. The arrival of these courts might redistribute power among local groups (as in Thailand; Engel 1978, p. 35). Or their employment by outsiders might disastrously unravel the fabric of local institutions (as in Burma; Furnivall 1948). Or their proceedings might be assimilated into a general atmosphere of didactic conciliation (as in Japan; Henderson 1965). In the Indian case, the one best known to me, there was a shift of disputing from local tribunals (and local notables) to the government's courts which provoked nineteenth-century observers to complain of a flood of litigation. These new tribunals and their strange methods had a powerful allure. Maine (1895, pp. 70–71) speaks of the "revolution of legal ideas" inadvertently produced in the very course of attempting to enforce the usages of the country. This revolution, he found, proceeded from a single innovation—"the mere establishment of local courts of lowest jurisdiction" in every administrative district. These new courts undertook to deal with the merits of a single transaction or offense, isolated from the related disputes among the parties and their supporters. The "fireside equities" and qualifying circumstances known to the indigenous tribunal were excluded from the court's consideration. In accordance with the precept of "equality before the law," the statuses and ties of the parties, matters of moment to an indigenous tribunal, were deliberately ignored. And, unlike the indigenous tribunals which sought compromise or face-saving solutions acceptable to all parties, the government's courts dispensed clear-cut, "all or none" decisions. Decrees were enforced by extra-local force and were not subject to the delays and protracted negotiations which abounded when decisions were enforced by informal pressures. Thus, "larger prizes" were available to successful litigants and these winnings might be grasped independently of the assent of local opinion. The new courts not only created new opportunities for intimidation and harassment and new means for carrying on old disputes, but they also gave rise to a sense of individual right not dependent on opinion or usage and capable of being actively enforced by government, even in opposition to community opinion (Cohn 1959; Rudolph and Rudolph 1965). These "modern" courts have endured in India. Movements to dislodge these Western-style courts in favor of a revival of older indigenous forms of adjudication have enjoyed very limited success in India (Galanter 1972; Baxi and Galanter 1979) as elsewhere (Lev 1972; Takayanagi 1963, p. 31).

If the official government court has flourished in the modern world, it may no longer enjoy the same eminence as the typical and decisive institutional actor in the legal system (Aubert 1969). Courts have been overtaken by the explosive growth of legislative activity and by the exponential increase of administrative agencies and government bureaucracies. Vast areas of disputing and claims have been located away from the regular courts. Individuated treatment based on concepts of fault and contest gives way to generic treatments based on systemic and actuarial solutions. Contest is eliminated and courts, if present at all, act in a highly routinized way or as mere registries, as in workmen's compensation, no-fault auto injury recovery, no-fault divorce, simplified probate.

As courts change there are simultaneous changes in the array of companion and rival institutions that process many comparable claims and disputes. Institutions established to escape judicial formality and to be responsive to substantive policy considerations may become more formal and courtlike. Thus, Nonet (1969) traces the judicialization of the California Industrial Accident Commission. On federal administrative agencies, see Bernstein (1955).

There is a tendency to pay attention to fora during their periods of growth and prosperity. But institutions also undergo decay, displacement, and "downward mobility."

Courts may cease to attract litigants—as in the precipitous decline in caseloads in seventeenth-century Castile (Kagan 1981, pp. 215–16) or eighteenth-century France (Kaiser 1980). Less formal dispute institutions may be deliberately dismantled as a measure of reform (like the elimination of justices of the peace in the United States and the removal of judicial powers from other public officials). But officially sponsored informal tribunals may decline even where they retain political support and their more formal counterparts flourish. Compare the decline of the Schiedesmann in Germany (see Bierbrauer et al. 1978, pp. 48ff.) and the nyaya panchayats in India (Baxi and Galanter 1979).

Where government courts (with regular record-keeping) are established "early" while other aspects of social life remain relatively "traditional," it is possible to trace the change in character of litigation as society undergoes other changes. Thus, Abel has traced changing patterns of litigation from colonial courts in tribal Africa to courts in urbanizing independent African states. He finds that the overall rate of litigation declines (1979b, p. 184), a decrease which reflects a drastic decline in civil litigation combined with a great increase in criminal prosecution.

Industrialism multiplies dealings among strangers and occasions for disputes; new centers of power and increased mobility subvert traditional dispute mechanisms. But eventually the new industrial society produces new valued relationships and new forms of indigenous regulation. Toharia (1975a, p. 57), examining the relations between industrialization and litigation in Spain from 1900 to 1967, finds that the rate of litigation increased during the early stages of industrialization, but leveled off as industrialism matured—even though legal activity (measured neatly in Spain by notarial acts) continues to climb. Evidence that fits this "curvilinear hypothesis" (as Friedman 1976 labels it) has been supplied from Britain (Friedman 1976, p. 34), Sweden and Denmark (Blegvad et al. 1973, p. 104), Belgium (Langerwerf 1978), Japan (Haley 1978), and Italy (Toharia 1975a, p. 57). But compare McIntosh (1982b), who suggests that the process is one of cyclic oscillation.

Changing litigation rates may tell us directly about the location rather than about the amount of adjudicative disputing in society. There are no data from earlier points in American history comparable to contemporary survey evidence, so we have only a dim picture of changes in the lower layers of the dispute pyramid. The number of cases in the regular courts does not disclose the portions of disputes that come before the shifting array of indigenous forums or before other agencies—administrative agencies, zoning boards, licensing bodies, small-claims courts, and others whose number and identity have changed over time. But if they do not tell us about the entire use of third-party dispute institutions, data on litigation may tell us something about changes in the use and practices of the regular courts.

Per capita rates of civil litigation (that is, filings) have increased in the twentieth century in most, but not all, American courts (McIntosh 1980–81, p. 81; Arthur Young et al. 1981; Grossman and Sarat 1975; Daniels 1981; Friedman and Percival 1976). The increase of filings in the federal courts has been more accentuated. These are larger and often more visible cases; a dramatic rise in recent decades is frequently cited as evidence of crushing overload in American courts and feverish litigiousness in American society.[10]

[10] Federal courts handle only a tiny fraction of all the cases filed in the United States. In 1975 approximately 7.27 million cases (civil, criminal, and juvenile) were filed in state courts of general jurisdiction and

But current American litigation rates are not unprecedented. The fragmentary historical record includes instances of sustained higher per capita rates of litigation than now prevail. The litigation rate in the St. Louis Circuit Court in the 1970s is about half of what it was during the early nineteenth century (McIntosh 1980–81; see Daniels 1981). A study of litigation in Los Angeles Superior Court concludes: "The population of Los Angeles County was much more litigious in the 1920s and 1930s and in the late nineteenth century than it is today" (Selvin and Ebener 1984, p. 32).

Scattered evidence from our more remote colonial past suggests even less reluctance to go to court. In Accomack County, Virginia, in 1639 the rate of litigation rate (240 per thousand) was more than four times that in any contemporary American county for which we have data. In a seven-year period, 20 percent of the adult population appeared in court as parties or witnesses five or more times (Curtis 1977, p. 287). In Salem County, Massachusetts, about 11 percent of the adult males were involved in court conflicts during the year 1683; ". . . most men living there had some involvement with the court system and many of them appeared repeatedly" (Konig 1979, p. xii).

As industrialization and urbanization proceed, the subject matter of litigation in the regular courts changes. On the whole, more of it is criminal and less civil. (This is contrary to what might be expected on the basis of Durkheim's hypothesis [1964, p. 132] of the replacement of criminal by civil sanctions as society becomes more intricately differentiated.) A growing portion of the criminal cases are administrative offenses rather than interpersonal crimes (Abel 1979b).

Over the past century there has been a pronounced shift in the make-up of the cases being brought to regular trial courts in the United States. There has been a shift from civil to criminal in the work of these courts, and on the civil side, there has been a shift from cases involving market transactions (contract, property, and debt collection) to family and tort cases (Friedman and Percival 1976; McIntosh 1980–81; Arthur Young et al. 1981, Table 10; Selvin and Ebener 1984, p. 44; Laurent 1959, xxix). Regular civil courts in America are being called on to deal with a very different mix of matters than they used to. These shifts are reflected in the make-up of appellate caseloads. Studies of state supreme courts (Kagan et al. 1977) and of federal Courts of Appeal (Baum et al.

---

about 160,000 in the federal district courts. There has been a dramatic rise in federal court filings in recent decades. Filings in the district courts increased from 68,135 in 1940 to 89,112 in 1960 to 198,710 in 1980 (Administrative Office 1980, p. 3). From 1940 to 1960, the absolute rise barely kept pace with population growth, but from 1960 to 1980 there was a pronounced per capita increase in filings from 0.5 per thousand population to 0.9 per thousand.

Other evidence provides little support for the notion that these are linked with desperate congestion and crushing caseloads. Clark's revealing analysis (1981, p. 81) of federal district court activity from 1900 to 1980 shows a dramatic reduction in the duration of civil cases from about 3.5 at the beginning of the century to 1.16 years in 1980. The number of cases terminated per judge has been steady since World War II and remains considerably lower than it was in the interwar period (Clark 1981, p. 83). Not only has the increase in judges kept up with the caseload, but there has been a massive increase in the support staff. While the average number of cases terminated per judge was approximately the same in 1980 as in 1960, the total employment of the federal judiciary rose during that period from 27.7 per million population to 65.5 per million (Clark 1981, pp. 87–88).

However, there has been a striking growth of appeals in federal courts. The rate at which those eligible to press appeals have exercised that right has risen, especially in criminal cases. The number of appeals filed in the Courts of Appeals almost quintupled from 1960 to 1980, while the number of judges nearly doubled (Howard 1982). Understandably, the Supreme Court, whose filings during this period more than doubled, and the Courts of Appeals are the provenance of much of the imagery of catastrophic overload.

1981–82) trace a parallel movement from business and property cases to tort, criminal law, and public law.

These filing statistics treat all cases filed as equivalent units. But cases are of different sizes and shapes. Some represent hotly contested disputes; others (like most divorce or debt or probate cases) are seeking administrative confirmation of a resolution, a claim, or some action taken. Some represent a major involvement by a court in which a judge actually decides the controversy; others represent little more than registration at the court.

Most cases for the entire span of time in question have been disposed of without a full adversary trial. Voluntary dismissal (presumably a surrogate for settlement) and uncontested judgment have been the most common dispositions recorded in these courts throughout the twentieth century (Arthur Young et al. 1981; Friedman and Percival 1976; McIntosh 1982a). Although the composition of the caseload has changed, and contested cases have become more complex, it appears that a smaller proportion of all cases reach trial. While federal court filings have risen dramatically, the percentage of cases reaching trial has diminished from 15.2 percent in 1940 to 6.5 percent in 1980 (Administrative Office 1940, p. 49; 1980, p. A-26). (Note that this is a measure of trials begun, not trials completed.) A comparison of dispositions in Los Angeles Superior Court between 1915–1940 and 1950–1979 showed a dramatic drop in the percentage tried and a striking increase in the portion settled (Selvin and Ebener 1984, p. 50). Similarly, even in a period of increased filings (and increased jury awards) the number of jury trials actually held fell in both Cook County and in San Francisco County (Shanley and Peterson 1983, pp. 19–20).

Several studies suggest that while litigation rates have risen, there has been a decline in the per capita rate of contested cases (Friedman and Percival 1976; McIntosh 1980–81). In an unpublished study of state trial courts of general jurisdiction in six cities, the late Craig Wanner found that the rate of complete trials or hearings per 1000 of population fell from 12.2 in 1951 to 10.2 in 1981 (Wanner 1983, chap. 6, Table 1). Similarly, there has been a decline in the per capita rate of cases eliciting written opinions from state supreme courts (Kagan et al. 1978, p. 965).

The proportion of cases that runs the full course declines. But for the minority of matters that do run the full course, adjudication is more protracted, more complex, and more expensive. Criminal and civil trials become more elaborate and due process more refined (see p. 203 above) just as full-blown adversary adjudication becomes relatively more rare. As the complexity and cost of full-blown adjudication increase, it becomes a source of counters and signals that permeate the processes of negotiation which occupy and surround the courts.

If full-blown adjudication is relatively less common, absolutely there is more of it. In America, this minority includes a growing component of large and complex cases that involve investments of immense amounts of time, exhaustive investigation and research, lavish deployment of expensive experts, and prodigious use of court resources (see, for example, Tinnin 1973; Stern 1977). It also includes a growing number of what have been called "public law" or "structural" or "extended impact" cases involving public policies and institutions—for example, a prison, mental hospital, or school in which many contending groups are locked together in an enduring relationship. In such cases the traditional format of the lawsuit is stretched in various ways (cf. Chayes 1976; Eisenberg and Yeazell 1980), and this extension of the scope of adjudication is connected with development of an expansive style of judging (Chayes 1976; Fiss 1979; Horowitz 1977). (See p. 179 above.) Litigation on this enlarged scale also reflects the presence of larger aggregations of specialist lawyers with enduring relations to the parties, able to assemble factual materials, coordinate experts, and monitor performance (see Galanter 1983).

In other ways, too, courts are less inclined to shrink from promethean responses. They burst through older ceilings on the scope of remedy: there is an increase by an order of magnitude in the highest awards (Friedman 1980; Peterson and Priest 1982); doctrinal cut-offs that once prevented recovery (charitable immunity, contributory negligence) have been largely effaced.

Judicial willingness to respond to innovative claims is part of a wider shift of legal thought and practice to instrumentalist (result-oriented, consequentialist) modes of decision-making and justification (Friedman 1969, pp. 33ff.; Abel 1973, p. 86; Kennedy 1975). Among professionals, there has been a loss of faith in law as an autonomous scientific undertaking that could discern valid principles of social ordering (Gilmore 1974, 1977; Woodard 1972; Kennedy 1976). Although formal considerations continue to influence outcomes, there is an unmistakable shift away from "internal" decision-making toward decision-making oriented to external goals and consequences. Judges are more inclined to look beyond the corpus of authoritative legal doctrine (Kagan et al. 1978; Friedman 1983). But at the same time that judges are more receptive to substantive rationality, formalism proliferates: forms are used not as a source or guarantor of predictability, but as efficient instruments for processing masses of transactions (Friedman 1966).

Litigation about areas of life previously untouched by the courts mirrors a massive extension of governmental concern into areas of life previously unregulated by the state (as in the great proliferation of environmental, health, safety, and welfare regulation) or where regulation was not closely linked with the application of legal principles. As many activities and relationships not earlier subject to governmental control have become the subject of legislative and administrative concern, they have come before the courts as well. Hurst (1980–81, p. 58) points out that "only limited and episodically selected aspects of these reaches of statute and administrative law come into litigation at all. . . ." Although the judicial role in shaping public policy is overshadowed, there has been extension of judicial oversight and the consequent legalization of whole areas of government activity that were not previously thought to be in need of close articulation with legal principles (Reich 1964). These include large sections of the criminal justice system (Fleming 1974), including police (Haller 1976), prisons, and juvenile justice; and other institutions dealing with dependent clients, such as schools (Kirp 1976), mental hospitals, and welfare agencies (O'Neil 1970).

There has been a parallel extension of judicial supervision over associational life and a concomitant tendency toward the legalization of procedures within organizations and associations. Courts more readily intervene to ensure that various "private governments" conform to the requirements of due process. But the penetration of public adjudication into private associations does not necessarily reduce the amount of indigenous regulatory activity. (See p. 214 above.)

As courts become remote, professional, and expensive, they are less places for individuals to air and resolve everyday disputes and more the province of professionals (that is, those concerned with making and defending claims as part of their ordinary round of activity). Courts become the scene of organizational campaigns to deal with classes of their constituents. Court agendas include large portions of routine administration and supervised bargaining. Courts contribute to dispute settlement less by direct decisive resolution and more by mediation, distributing bargaining counters, and pattern-setting (Lempert 1978; Abel 1979b). Resolutions of particular controversies are eclipsed by the production of wide radiating effects. Severe criminal sanctions (Abel 1979b) and high injury awards (Friedman 1980) become signals and a source of counters used for bargaining and regulation in many other settings.

Over time a smaller proportion of the population are direct participants in contested adjudication. But more Americans have what they perceive to be legal problems and they increasingly use lawyers to deal with them (Avichai 1978). After a period of relative stability, the number of lawyers has increased much faster than the population in the last quarter century (Clark 1981, p. 94) and the portion of national wealth spent on their services has grown dramatically. These lawyers work in larger units with more specialization and coordination than was present earlier (Galanter 1983). But if adjudication declines as part of direct personal experience, it becomes more prominent as a symbolic presence. There is more big-time, major-league litigation involving major institutions and/or pathbreaking claims. There is absolutely (if not proportionately) more law stuff that invites media coverage with its built-in bias toward the dramatic, the novel, the deviant; toward innovation and conflict. There has been a dramatic increase in the amount of media coverage of law and lawyers (apart from the always popular criminal law). While the confidentiality of the lawyer-client relationship remains a central professional norm, commitments to preserve the confidentiality of the interior working of other legal institutions have eroded—as evidenced by "leaks" from and about courts. The cloistered private quality of law practice has declined. Lawyer advertising has accentuated the visibility of lawyers and disseminated information about legal possibilities. A more educated and more informed public is more capable of digesting this richer fare.

We emerge with a paradoxical double vision of adjudication in the contemporary United States, a vision in which adjudication is both more elaborate and more attenuated, more prevalent and more remote. This vision is mirrored in the array of prevalent discontents with the legal process. A significant section of legal, business, and media elites is joined by wider publics in decrying the superabundance of law and the delay, cost, and complexity of litigation (Galanter 1983b). But another cluster of articulate critics (for example, Nader and Singer 1976) assails the lack of access to legal remedies for poor and middle-income individuals and for unorganized citizen interests. Would-be users and their champions complain of lacking remedies (or being forced to yield up inordinate discounts). When courts are available, they are cumbersome and formal, unsuited to dealing with living relationships. At the same time, many judges feel inundated by a flood of litigation and many institutional managers chafe at unwanted exposure to judicial scrutiny. These complaints are articulated by critics who bemoan the "litigation explosion" (Manning 1977) which overloads the courts and injects them into areas for which they are unsuited, distracting them from their proper role, and the arrogation by an "imperial judiciary" of tasks for which courts have neither expertise nor legitimacy (Glazer 1975; Horowitz 1977).

Litigation proliferates. It becomes more complex and refined, but at the same time most of it is truncated, decomposing into bargaining, mediation, or administration. Courts and big cases are more visible. For many in the society, courts occupy a larger part of the symbolic universe (even as their relative position in the whole governmental complex diminishes). Cost and remoteness remove the courts as an option in almost all disputes for almost all individuals. When courts are available, they may be found flawed. Friedman (1971) points out the tendency of constitutional governments to create and recognize new rights even while they relinquish their ability to guarantee and enforce them. The courts join in proliferating symbols of entitlement, enlivening consciousness of rights and heightening our expectations of vindication. As adjudication becomes more elaborated and more prone to decompose into bargaining, the promise of full and decisive vindication that it holds out beckons and recedes before us.

Cases Cited

Baker v. Carr, 369 U.S. 186 (1961).
Blackledge v. Allison, 430 U.S. 63 (1976).
Pan American World Airways v. United States District Court, 523 F.2d 1073 (C.A.9, 1975).
People v. Mees, 240 N.Y.S.2d 214 (1979).
Williams v. Walker-Thomas Furniture Co., 350 F.2d 445 (C.A. D.C., 1965).

Bibliography

Abel, Richard L.
1973   "Law Books and Books About Law." *Stanford Law Review* 26:175–228.
1977   "A Theory of Litigation: Changes in Society, Judicial Institutions and Litigant Behavior in Africa in the Last Half Century." Unpublished manuscript.
1979a   "Socializing the Legal Profession: Can Redistributing Lawyers' Services Achieve Social Justice." *Law & Policy Quarterly* 1:5–31.
1979b   "Western Courts in Non-Western Settings: Patterns of Court Use in Colonial and Neo-Colonial Africa." In *The Imposition of Law*, edited by S. Burman and B. Harrell-Bond. New York: Academic Press.
1981   *The Politics of Informal Justice.* 2 vols. New York: Academic Press.
Abraham, Henry J.
1977   *The Judicial Process: An Introductory Analysis of the Courts of the United States, England and France.* 4th ed. New York: Oxford University Press.
Ademany, David
1973   "Legitimacy, Realigning Elections and the Supreme Court." *Wisconsin Law Review* 13:790–846.
Administrative Office of the United States Courts
1940   *Annual Report of the Director.* Washington, D.C.: U.S. Government Printing Office.
1980a   *Annual Report of the Director.* Washington, D.C.: U.S. Government Printing Office.

1980b   *Management Statistics for the United States Courts.* Washington, D.C.: U.S. Government Printing Office.

1984   *Federal Offenders in the United States Courts: 1983.* Washington, D.C.: U.S. Government Printing Office.

Akers, Ronald L.
1968   "The Professional Association and the Legal Regulation of Practice." *Law & Society Review* 2:462–82.

Alschuler, Albert W.
1979   "Plea Bargaining and Its History." *Law & Society Review* 13:211–45.

American Bar Foundation
1973   *International Directory of Bar Associations.* 3rd ed. Chicago: American Bar Foundation.

Andenaes, Johannes
1966   "The General Preventive Effects of Punishments." *University of Pennsylvania Law Review* 114:949–83.

Anderson, Stanley
1969   *Ombudsman Papers: American Experience and Proposals.* [With a comparative analysis of ombudsmen's offices by Kent M. Weeks.] Berkeley: University of California, Institute of Government Studies.

Arthur Young & Company and Public Sector Research, Inc.
1981   "An Empirical Study of the Judicial Role in Family and Commercial Disputes." Edited by J. J. Pearlstein. U.S. Department of Justice: The Council on the Role of Courts.

Aspin, Leslie
1966   "A Study of Reinstatement Under the National Labor Relations Act." Unpublished doctoral dissertation, Massachusetts Institute of Technology.

Aubert, Vilhelm
1963   "Competition and Dissensus: Two Types of Conflict Resolution." *Journal of Conflict Resolution* 7:26–42.

1967   "Courts and Conflict Resolution." *Journal of Conflict Resolution* 11:40–51.

1969   "Law as a Way of Resolving Conflicts: The Case of a Small Industrialized Society." In *Law in Culture and Society,* edited by L. Nader. Chicago: Aldine.

1976   "The Changing Role of Law and Lawyers in Nineteenth- and Twentieth-Century Norwegian Society." In *Lawyers in Their Social Setting,* edited by D. N. MacCormick. Edinburgh: Green.

1979   "On Methods of Legal Influence." In *The Imposition of Law,* edited by S. B. Burman and B. E. Harrell-Bond. New York: Academic Press.

Avichai, Yacov
1978   "Trends in the Incidence of Legal Problems and in the Use of Lawyers," *American Bar Foundation Research Journal* 1978:289–313.

Babcock, Richard F.
1969   *The Zoning Game: Municipal Practices and Policies.* Madison: University of Wisconsin Press.

Balbus, Isaac
1973   *The Dialectics of Legal Repression: Black Rebels Before American Courts.* New York: Russell Sage Foundation.

Baldwin, John, and McConville, Michael
1979   "Plea Bargaining and Plea Negotiation in England." *Law & Society Review* 13:287–307.

Ball, Milner S.
1975   "The Play's the Thing: An Unscientific Reflection on Courts Under the Rubric of Theater." *Stanford Law Review* 28:81–116.

Barkun, Michael
1968   *Law Without Sanctions: Order in Primitive Societies and the World Community.* New Haven: Yale University Press.

Barton, John H.
1975   "Behind the Legal Explosion." *Stanford Law Review* 27:567–84.

Bartsch, Thomas C.; Boddy, Francis M.; King, Benjamin F.; and Thompson, Peter N.
1978   *A Class-Action Suit That Worked: The Consumer Refund in the Antibiotic Antitrust Litigation.* Lexington, Mass.: Lexington Books.

Barwick, Sir Garfield
1977   "The State of the Australian Judicature." *Australian Law Journal* 51:480, Appendix A.

Baum, Lawrence
1977   "Policy Goals in Judicial Gatekeeping: A Proximity Model of Discretionary Jurisdiction." *American Journal of Political Science* 21:13–37.

1978   "Lower Court Response to Supreme Court Decisions: Reconsidering a Negative Picture." *Justice System Journal* 3:208–19.

Baum, Lawrence; Goldman, Sheldon; and Sarat, Austin
1981–82 "The Evolution of Litigation in the Federal Courts of Appeals, 1895–1975." *Law & Society Review* 16:291–309.

Baumgartner, M. P.
1978   "Law and Social Status in Colonial New Haven, 1639–1665." In *Research in Law and Sociology: An Annual Compilation of Research,* vol. 1, edited by Rita J. Simon. Greenwich: JAI Press.

1980   "Law and the Middle Class: Evidence from a Suburban Town." Paper presented at the annual meeting of the Law and Society Association, Madison, Wisconsin, June.

Baxi, Upendra, and Galanter, Marc
1979   "Panchayat Justice: An Indian Experiment in Legal Access." In *Access to Justice,* vol. 3. *Emerging Issues and Perspectives,* edited by M. Cappelletti and B. Garth. Milan: Giuffre; and Alphen aan den Rijn: Sijthoff and Noordhoff.

Bayley, David
1964   *Public Liberties in the New States.* Chicago: Rand McNally.

Becker, Theodore L.
1970   *Comparative Judicial Politics: The Political Functions of Courts.* Chicago: Rand McNally.

Becker, Theodore L., and Feeley, Malcolm M.
1973   *The Impact of Supreme Court Decisions.* 2nd ed. New York: Oxford University Press.

Belli, Melvin M.
1957   "Pretrial: Aid to the New Advocacy." *Cornell Law Quarterly* 43:34–52.

Bentler, Peter M., and Speckart, George
1981   "Attitudes 'Cause' Behaviors: A Structural Equation Analysis." *Journal of Personality and Social Psychology* 40:226.

Berkowitz, Leonard, and Walker, Nigel
1967   "Laws and Moral Judgments." *Sociometry* 30:410–22.

Bernstein, Marver H.
1955   *Regulating Business by Independent Commission.* Princeton, N.J.: Princeton University Press.

Best, Arthur, and Andreasen, Allan R.
1977   "Consumer Response in Contract Purchases: A Survey of Perceiving Defects, Voicing Complaints, Obtaining Redress." *Law & Society Review* 11: 701–42.

Beutel, Frederick K.
1957   *Some Potentialities of Experimental Jurisprudence as a New Branch of Social Science.* Lincoln: University of Nebraska Press.

Bierbrauer, G.; Falke, J.; and Koch, K. F.
    1978   "Conflict and Its Settlement: An Interdisciplinary Study Concerning the Legal
            Basis, Function and Performance of the Schiedesmann." In *Access to Justice*, vol.
            2. *Promising Institutions*, edited by M. Cappelletti and J. Weisner. Milan: Giuffre;
            and Alphen aan den Rijn: Sijthoff and Noordhoff.

Black, Donald J.
    1971   "The Social Organization of Arrest." *Stanford Law Review* 23:1087–1111.

    1973   "The Mobilization of Law." *Journal of Legal Studies* 2:125–49.

Black, Donald J., and Baumgartner, M. P.
    1978   "On Self-Help in Modern Society." In *The Manners and Customs of Police*, edited
            by D. Black. Orlando, Fla.: Academic Press.

    1983   "Toward a Theory of The Third Party." In *Empirical Theories About Courts*, edited
            by K. Boyum and L. Mather. New York: Longman.

Blankenburg, Erhard; Blankenburg, Viola; and Morasch, Hellmut
    1972   "Der lange Weg in die Berufung." In *Tatsachen Forschung in der Justiz*, edited by
            R. Bender. Tübingen: Mohr.

Blau, Peter
    1963   *The Dynamics of Bureaucracy: A Study of Interpersonal Relations in Two Government
            Agencies.* Rev. ed. Chicago: University of Chicago Press.

Blegvad, Britt-Marie; Bolding, P. O.; Lando, Ole; and Gamst-Nielsen, Kirsten
    1973   *Arbitration as a Means of Solving Conflicts.* Copenhagen: New Social Science Mono-
            graphs E6.

Blumberg, Abraham S.
    1967   "The Practice of Law as a Confidence Game: Organizational Cooptation of a
            Profession." *Law & Society Review* 1:15–39.

Bohannon, Paul
    1965   "The Differing Realms of the Law." *American Anthropologist* 67 No. 6, (pt. 2), pp.
            33–42. Reprinted in *Law and Warfare: Studies in the Anthropology of Conflict*, edited
            by P. Bohannon. Garden City, N.Y.: Natural History Press, 1967, pp. 43–56.

Bolton, Ralph
    1979   "Differential Aggressiveness and Litigiousness: Social Support and Social Status
            Hypotheses." *Aggressive Behavior* 5:233–55.

Bonn, Robert L.
    1972a   "Arbitration: An Alternative System for Handling Contract Related Disputes."
            Administrative Sciences Quarterly 17:254–64.

    1972b   "The Predictability of Nonlegalistic Adjudication." *Law & Society Review* 6:
            563–78.

Boyum, Keith O.
    1983   "The Etiology of Claims: Sketches for a Theoretical Mapping of the Claim-
            Definition Process." In *Empirical Theories About Courts*, edited by K. Boyum and
            L. Mather. New York: Longman.

Brand, George
    1971   "The Avoidance of the Traditional Machinery of Adjudication: A World-Wide
            Trend?" *Social Research* 38:268–97.

Brazil, Wayne D.
    1978   "The Attorney as Victim: Toward More Candor About the Psychological Price Tag
            of Litigation Practice." *Journal of the Legal Profession* 3:107–17.

    1983   "Special Masters in the Pretrial Development of Big Cases: Potential and Prob-
            lems." In *Managing Complex Litigation: A Practical Guide to the Use of Special Mas-
            ters*, by W. Brazil, G. Hazard, and P. Rice. Chicago: American Bar Foundation,
            pp. 1–75.

Brown, Robert
>   1983   "A Lawyer by Any Other Name: Legal Advisors in Japan." In *Legal Aspects of Doing Business in Japan, 1983* (Commercial Law and Practice, Course Handbook Series No. 295). New York: Practising Law Institute, pp. 201–502.

Bruinsma, Freek
>   1979   "The (Non-)Assertion of Welfare Rights—Towards a Critique of the Welfare State." Unpublished manuscript, Florence.

Buckle, Leonard G., and Thomas-Buckle, Suzann R.
>   1977   *Bargaining for Justice: Case Disposition and Reform in the Criminal Courts.* New York: Praeger.

>   1981   "Self-Help Justice: Dispute Processing in Urban American Neighborhoods." Working Paper 85-1, Northeastern University Law, Policy, and Society Program.

Burger, Warren E.
>   1970   "The State of the Judiciary—1970." *American Bar Association Journal* 56:919–34.

>   1976   "Agenda for 2000 A.D.—A Need for Systematic Anticipation." *Federal Rules Decisions* 70:83–96.

>   1977   Remarks of Warren E. Burger . . . American Bar Association Minor Disputes Resolution Conference, Columbia University, New York . . . May 27. Reprinted in 95th Cong., 1st sess., House of Representatives, Committee on the Judiciary, Subcommittee on Courts, Civil Liberties and the Administration of Justice, *State of the Judiciary and Access to Justice.*

>   1982   "Isn't There a Better Way?" *American Bar Association Journal* 68:274–77.

Business Week
>   1977   "The Chilling Impact of Litigation." *Business Week,* June 6, 1977, pp. 58–64.

Buxbaum, David C.
>   1971   "Some Aspects of Civil Procedure and Practice at the Trial Level in Tanshui and Hsinchu from 1789 to 1895." *Journal of Asian Studies* 30:255–79.

Buxbaum, Richard M.
>   1971   "Public Participation in the Enforcement of the Antitrust Laws." *California Law Review* 59:1113–45.

Cain, Maureen
>   1979   "The General Practice Lawyer and the Client: Towards a Radical Conception." *International Journal of the Sociology of Law* 7:331–54.

Caldeira, Gregory A.
>   1981–82 "Changing the Common Law: Effects of the Decline of Charitable Immunity." *Law & Society Review* 16:669–93.

California Law Review
>   1971   "Judicial Supervision over California Plea Bargaining: Regulating the Trade." *California Law Review* 59:962–96.

Callan, Sam W.
>   1979   "An Experience in Justice Without Plea Negotiation." *Law & Society Review* 13:327–47.

Canon, Bradley C., and Jaros, Dean
>   1979   "The Impact of Changes in Judicial Doctrine: The Abrogation of Charitable Immunity." *Law & Society Review* 13:969–86.

Caplovitz, David
>   1963   *The Poor Pay More: Consumer Practices of Low-Income Families.* New York: Free Press.

Cappelletti, Mauro, and Garth, Bryant
>   1978   "Access to Justice: The Newest Wave in the Worldwide Movement to Make Rights Effective." *Buffalo Law Review* 27:181–292.

Carlin, Jerome E., and Howard, Jan
    1965   "Legal Representation and Class Justice." *UCLA Law Review* 12:381–437.
Cartwright, Bliss
    1975   "Afterword: Disputes and Reported Cases." *Law & Society Review* 9:369–84.
Casey, Gregory
    1973   "The Supreme Court and Myth: An Empirical Investigation." *Law & Society Review* 8:385–419.
Casper, Jonathan D.
    1976   "The Supreme Court and National Policy Making." *American Political Science Review* 70:50–63.

    1978   *Criminal Courts: The Defendant's Perspective.* Washington, D.C.: Department of Justice, Law Enforcement Assistance Administration, National Institute of Law Enforcement and Criminal Justice.
Cavanagh, Ralph, and Sarat, Austin
    1980   "Thinking About Courts: Toward and Beyond a Jurisprudence of Judicial Competence." *Law & Society Review* 14:371–420.
Central Bureau of Statistics
    1978   *Judicial Statistics, 1978.* Jerusalem: Central Bureau of Statistics.
Chapman, William
    1981   "Japan: The Land of Few Lawyers," *Washington Post,* April 19, 1981, p. C5.
Chayes, Abram
    1976   "The Role of the Judge in Public Law Litigation." *Harvard Law Review* 89:1281–1316.
Church, Thomas W., Jr.
    1976   "Plea Bargains, Concessions and the Courts: Analysis of a Quasi-experiment." *Law & Society Review* 10:377–401.

    1982   *Examining Local Legal Culture: Practitioner Attitudes in Four Criminal Courts.* Washington, D.C.: National Institute of Justice.
Church, Thomas W., Jr.; Carlson, Alan; Lee, Jo-Lynne; and Tan, Teresa
    1978   *Justice Delayed: The Pace of Litigation in Urban Trial Courts.* Williamsburg, Va.: National Center for State Courts.
Clark, Charles E., and Shulman, Harry
    1937   *A Study of Law Administration in Connecticut: A Report of an Investigation of the Activities of Certain Trial Courts of the State.* New Haven: Yale University Press.
Clark, David S.
    1981   "Adjudication to Administration: A Statistical Analysis of Federal District Courts in the Twentieth Century." *Southern California Law Review* 55:65–152.
Coates, Dan, and Penrod, Steven
    1980–81 "Social Psychology and the Emergence of Disputes." *Law & Society Review* 15:655–80.
Cohen, Jerome A.
    1966   "Chinese Mediation on the Eve of Modernization." *California Law Review* 54:1201–26.
Cohn, Bernard S.
    1959   "Some Notes on Law and Change in North India." *Economic Development and Cultural Change* 8:79–93.
Coleman, James S.
    1974   *Power and the Structure of Society.* New York: Norton.
Collier, Jane
    1973   *Law and Social Change in Zinacantan.* Stanford, Calif.: Stanford University Press.

Colombatos, John
   1969   "Physicians and Medicare: A Before-After Study of the Effects of Legislation on
              Attitudes." *American Sociological Review* 34:318–34.
Columbia Journal of Law and Social Problems
   1970   "Rabbinical Courts: Modern Day Solomons." *Columbia Journal of Law and Social
              Problems* 6:49–75.

   1971   "Roman Catholic Ecclesiastical Courts and the Law of Marriage." *Columbia Journal
              of Law and Social Problems* 7:204–39.
Commonwealth Bureau of Census and Statistics
   1976   *Statistics of Western Australia, Social, 1975.* Canberra: Commonwealth Bureau of
              Census and Statistics, Western Australia Office.
Community Service Society, Department of Public Affairs, Special Committee on Consumer
       Protection
   1974   "Large Grievances About Small Causes: New York City's Small Claims Courts—
              Proposals for Improving the Collection of Judgments." New York: Community Ser-
              vice Society.
Conrad, Alfred F.; Morgan, James N.; Pratt, Jr., Robert W.; Voltz, Charles E.; and Bombaugh,
       Robert L.
   1964   *Automobile Accident Costs and Payments.* Ann Arbor: University of Michigan Press.
Cook, Beverly Blair
   1977   "Public Opinion and Federal Judicial Policy." *American Journal of Political Science*
              21:567–600.

   1979   "Judicial Policy: Change Over Time." *American Journal of Political Science* 23:
              208–14.
Coons, John
   1964   "Approaches to Court Imposed Compromise—The Uses of Doubt and Reason."
              Northwestern Law Review 58:750–94.
Council of Europe
   1975   *Judicial Organization in Europe.* London: Morgan-Grampian.
Cross, Harry M.
   1973   "The College Athlete and the Institution." *Law and Contemporary Problems*
              38:151–71.
Cross, Rupert
   1961   *Precedent in English Law.* Oxford: Oxford University Press.
Crowe, Patricia Ward
   1978   "Complainant Reactions to the Massachusetts Commission Against Discrimina-
              tion." *Law & Society Review* 12:217–35.
Curran, Barbara A.
   1977   *The Legal Needs of the Public: A Final Report of a National Survey.* Chicago: Ameri-
              can Bar Foundation.
Curtis, George B.
   1977   "The Colonial County Court, Social Forum and Legislative Precedent, Accomack
              County, Virginia, 1633–1639." *Virginia Magazine of History and Biography* 85:
              274–87.
Dahl, Robert A.
   1958   "Decision-making in a Democracy: The Supreme Court as a National Policy-
              Maker." *Journal of Public Law* 6:279–95.
Damaska, Mirjan
   1975   "Structures of Authority and Comparative Criminal Procedure." *Yale Law Journal*
              84:480–544.

   1978   "A Foreign Perspective on the American Judicial System." In *State Courts: A*

Blueprint for the Future, edited by T. J. Fetter. Williamsburg, Va.: National Center for State Courts.

Danelski, David S.
1978   "The Influence of the Chief Justice in the Decisional Process of the Supreme Courts." In *American Court Systems: Readings in Judicial Behavior,* edited by S. Goldman and A. Sarat. San Francisco: Freeman.

Danet, Brenda
1980   "Language in the Legal Process." *Law & Society Review* 14:445–564.

Daniels, Stephen
1981   "The Trial Courts of 'Spoon River': Patterns and Changes, 1870 to 1963." Paper presented at the meeting of the Law and Society Association, Amherst, Massachusetts, June 11–14.

1982   "The Civil Business of State Trial Courts: A Rural-Urban Comparison, 1870–1960." Paper presented at the meeting of the Law and Society Association, Toronto, Ontario, June 3–6.

Danzig, Richard
1978   *The Capability Problem in Contract Law: Further Readings on Well-Known Cases.* Mineola, N.Y.: Foundation Press.

Danzon, Patricia M., and Lillard, Lee A.
1982   *The Resolution of Medical Malpractice Claims.* Santa Monica: The Rand Corporation, Institute for Civil Justice.

Davies, Thomas Y.
1981   "Gresham's Law Revisited: Expedited Processing Techniques and the Allocation of Appellate Resources." *Justice System Journal* 6:372–404.

Dawson, John P.
1960   *A History of Lay Judges.* Cambridge, Mass.: Harvard University Press.

Dhavan, Rajeev
1977   *The Supreme Court of India: A Socio-Legal Critique of Its Juristic Techniques.* Bombay: Tripathi.

1978   *The Supreme Court Under Strain: The Challenge of Arrears.* Bombay: Tripathi.

Dhavan, Rajeev, and Jacob, Alice
1978   *Selection and Appointment of Supreme Court Judges: A Case Study.* Bombay: Tripathi.

Dibble, Vernon K.
1973   "What Is and What Ought to Be: A Comparison of Certain Formal Characteristics of the Ideological and Legal Styles of Thought." *American Journal of Sociology* 79:511–49.

Di Federico, Giuseppe
1976   "The Italian Judicial Profession and Its Bureaucratic Setting." In *Lawyers in Their Social Setting,* edited by D. N. MacCormick. Edinburgh: Green.

Dill, Forrest
1977   "Contradictions in Judicial Structure: Law and Bureaucracy in American Criminal Courts." Paper presented at the Conference on Social Science Research in the Courts, Denver, Colo., January 20.

Disney, Julian; Basten, John; Redmond, Paul; and Ross, Stan
1977   *Lawyers.* Sydney: Law Book Company.

Diver, Colin S.
1979   "The Judge as Political Powerbroker: Superintending Structural Change in Public Institutions." *Virginia Law Review* 65:43–106.

Dolbeare, Kenneth M.
1967   *Trial Courts in Urban Politics: State Court Policy Impact and Function in a Local Political System.* New York: Wiley.

Dolbeare, Kenneth M., and Hammond, Phillip E.
1971   *The School Prayer Decisions: From Court Policy to Local Practice.* Chicago: University of Chicago Press.

Doo, Leigh-Wai
1973   "Dispute Settlement in Chinese-American Communities." *American Journal of Comparative Law* 21:627–63.

Dostert, Pierre
1968   "Appellate Restatement of Unconscionability: Civil Legal Aid at Work." *American Bar Association Journal* 54:1183–86.

Dubow, Frederic
1983   "Explaining Litigation Rates in Rural and Urban Tanzania." Paper presented at the annual meeting of the Law and Society Association, Denver, Colo., June 2–5.

Ducat, Craig R., and Flango, Victor Eugene
1975   "In Search of Qualified Judges: An Inquiry into the Relevance of Judicial Selection Research." Paper presented at the annual meeting of the American Political Science Association, San Francisco, September 2–5.

Durkheim, Emile
1964   *The Divison of Labor in Society.* Translated by G. Simpson. Glencoe, Ill.: Free Press.
[1893]

Dwyer, Daisy Hilse
1979   "Law Actual and Perceived: the Sexual Politics of Law in Morocco." *Law & Society Review* 13:739–56.

Eaton, Marian
1980   "The Better Business Bureau: 'The Voice of the People in the Marketplace.'" In *No Access to Law: Alternatives to the American Judicial System,* edited by L. Nader. New York: Academic Press.

Eckhoff, Torstein
1966   "The Mediator, the Judge and the Administrator in Conflict Resolution." *Acta Sociologica* 10:148–72.

Edelman, Murray
1967   *The Symbolic Uses of Politics.* Urbana: University of Illinois Press.

1971   *Politics as Symbolic Action: Mass Arousal and Quiescence.* New York: Academic Press.

Egan, Patricia, ed.
1972   *The Canadian Law List.* Ontario: Canada Law Book.

Eisenberg, Melvin Aron
1976   "Private Ordering Through Negotiation: Dispute-Settlement and Rulemaking." *Harvard Law Review* 89:637–81.

Eisenberg, Theodore, and Yeazell, Stephen C.
1980   "The Ordinary and the Extraordinary in Institutional Litigation." *Harvard Law Review* 93:465.

Eisenstein, James, and Jacob, Herbert
1977   *Felony Justice: An Organizational Analysis of Criminal Courts.* Boston: Little, Brown.

Eisenstein, Martin
1979   "The Swedish Public Complaints Board: Its Vital Role in a System of Consumer Protection." In *Access to Justice,* vol. 2. *Promising Institutions,* edited by M. Cappelletti and J. Weisner. Milan: Giuffre; and Alphen aan den Rijn: Sijthoff and Noordhoff.

Emerson, Robert M., and Messinger, Sheldon L.
1977   "The Micro-Politics of Trouble." *Social Problems* 25:121–34.

Engel, David M.
    1978   *Code and Custom in a Thai Provincial Court: The Interaction of Formal and Informal Systems of Justice.* Tucson: University of Arizona Press.
    1980   "Legal Pluralism in an American Community: Perspectives on a Civil Trial Court." *American Bar Foundation Research Journal* 1980: 425–54.
Engel, David M., and Steele, Eric H.
    1979   "Civil Cases in Society: Legal Process, Social Order, and the Civil Justice System." *American Bar Foundation Research Journal* 2:295–346.
Ennis, Philip H.
    1967   *Criminal Victimization in the United States: A Report of a National Survey.* Washington, D.C.: U.S. Government Printing Office.
Ericson, Richard V., and Baranek, Patricia M.
    1982   *The Ordering of Justice: A Study of Accused Persons as Dependants in the Criminal Process.* Toronto: University of Toronto Press.
Erikson, Kai T.
    1976   *Everything in Its Path: Destruction of Community in the Buffalo Creek Flood.* New York: Simon and Schuster.
Fallers, Lloyd A.
    1969   *Law Without Precedent: Legal Ideas in Action in the Courts of Colonial Busoga.* Chicago: University of Chicago Press.
Feeley, Malcolm M.
    1976   "The Concept of Laws in Social Science: A Critique and Notes on an Expanded View." *Law & Society Review* 10:497–523.
    1979   "Pleading Guilty in Lower Courts." *Law & Society Review* 13:461–66.
Felstiner, William L. F.
    1974   "Influences of Social Organization on Dispute Processing." *Law & Society Review* 9:63–94.
Felstiner, William L. F.; Abel, Richard L.; and Sarat, Austin
    1980–81 "The Emergence and Transformation of Disputes: Naming, Blaming, Claiming . . ." *Law & Society Review* 15:631–54.
Ferguson, R. B.
    1980   "The Adjudication of Commercial Disputes and the Legal System of Modern England." *British Journal of Law and Society* 7:141–57.
Fiss, Owen
    1979   "The Supreme Court, 1978 Term—Foreword: The Forms of Justice." *Harvard Law Review* 93:1–58.
FitzGerald, Jeffrey M.
    1975   "The Contract Buyers League and the Courts: A Case Study of Poverty Litigation." *Law & Society Review* 9:165–95.
    1983   "Patterns of 'Middle Range' Disputing in Australia and the United States." *Law in Context* 1:15–45.
FitzGerald, Jeffrey M., and Dickins, Richard
    1980–81 "Disputing in Legal and Nonlegal Contexts: Some Questions for Sociologists of Law." *Law & Society Review* 15:681.
Flanders, Steven
    1978   "Case Management in Federal Courts: Some Controversies and Some Results." *Justice System Journal* 4:147–65.
Flango, Victor Eugene
    1975   "Court Administration and Judicial Modernization." *Public Administration Review* 35:619–25.

Flango, Victor Eugene, and Ducat, Craig R.
  1979   "What Difference Does Method of Judicial Selection Make? Selection Procedures in State Courts of Last Resort." *Justice System Journal* 5:25–44.

Fleming, Macklin
  1974   *The Price of Perfect Justice.* New York: Basic Books, 1974.

Foote, Caleb
  1956   "Vagrancy-type Law and Its Administration." *University of Pennsylvania Law Review* 104:603–50.

Forer, Lois G.
  1975   *The Death of the Law.* New York: McKay.

Forman, Sylvia
  1972   "Law and Conflict in Rural Highland Ecuador." Unpublished doctoral dissertation, University of California, Berkeley.

Foster, Henry H., Jr.
  1966   "Conciliation and Counseling in the Courts in Family Law Cases." *New York University Law Review* 41:353–81.

Frank, John P.
  1969   *American Law: The Case for Radical Reform.* New York: Macmillan.

Frankel, Marvin E.
  1976   "The Adversary Judge." *Texas Law Review* 54:464–87.

  1980   *Partisan Justice.* New York: Hill and Wang.

Franklin, Marc A.; Chanin, Robert H.; and Mark, Irving
  1961   "Accidents, Money, and the Law: A Study of the Economics of Personal Injury Litigation." *Columbia Law Review* 61:1–39.

Friedman, Lawrence M.
  1966   "On Legal Development." *Rutgers Law Review* 24:11–64.

  1969   "Legal Culture and Social Development." *Law & Society Review* 4:29–44.

  1971   "The Idea of Right as a Social and Legal Concept." *Journal of Social Issues* 27:189–98.

  1973   *A History of American Law.* New York: Simon & Schuster.

  1976   "Trial Courts and Their Work in the Modern World." *Jahrbuch für Rechtssoziologie und Rechtstheorie* 4:25–38.

  1979   "Plea Bargaining in Historical Perspective." *Law & Society Review* 13:247–59.

  1980   "The Six Million Dollar Man: Litigation and Rights Consciousness in Modern America." *Maryland Law Review* 39:661–77.

  1983   "Courts over Time: A Survey of Theories and Research." In *Empirical Theories of Courts,* edited by K. Boyum and L. Mather. New York: Longman.

Friedman, Lawrence M., and Ladinsky, Jack
  1967   "Social Change and the Law of Industrial Accidents." *Columbia Law Review* 67:50–82.

Friedman, Lawrence M., and Percival, Robert V.
  1976   "A Tale of Two Courts: Litigation in Alameda and San Benito Counties." *Law & Society Review* 10:267–301.

Friesen, Ernest C., Jr.; Gallas, Edward C.; and Gallas, Nesta M.
  1971   *Managing the Courts.* Indianapolis: Bobbs-Merrill.

Fuller, Lon L.
  1963   "Collective Bargaining and the Arbitrator." *Wisconsin Law Review* 1963:3–46.

  1967   *Legal Fictions.* Stanford, Calif.: Stanford University Press.

  1969   *The Morality of Law.* Rev. ed. New Haven: Yale University Press.

  1978   "The Forms and Limits of Adjudication." In *American Court Systems,* edited by S. Goldman and A. Sarat. San Francisco: Freeman.

Funston, Richard
  1975   "The Supreme Court and Critical Elections." *American Political Science Review*
            69:793–811.
Furnivall, J. S.
  1948   *Colonial Policy and Practice: A Comparative Study of Burma and Netherlands India.*
            Cambridge: Cambridge University Press.
Gadbois, George H., Jr.
  1968–69 "Indian Supreme Court Judges: A Portrait." *Law & Society Review* 3:317–36.

  1970a   "Indian Judicial Behavior." *Economic and Political Weekly* 5:1–11.
  1970b   "The Supreme Court of India: A Preliminary Report of an Empirical Study."
            Journal of Constitutional and Parliamentary Studies 4:33–54.
  1974   "Supreme Court Decision-Making." *Banaras Law Journal* 10:1–49.
  1977   "The Emergency, Mrs. Gandhi, the Judiciary and the Legal Culture." Mimeo-
            graphed.
  1982   "The Perils of Non-Contextual Analysis: The Contexts of Judicial Appointments
            in India." *Asian Thought and Society* 7:124–43.
Galanter, Marc
  1966   "The Modernization of Law." In *Modernization: The Dynamics of Growth,* edited by
            M. Weiner. New York: Basic Books.
  1968   "The Displacement of Traditional Law in Modern India." *Journal of Social Issues*
            24:65–91.
  1972   "The Aborted Restoration of 'Indigenous' Law in India." *Comparative Studies in
            Society and History* 14:53–70.
  1974   "Why the 'Haves' Come Out Ahead: Speculations on the Limits of Legal Change."
            Law & Society Review 9:95–160.
  1975   "Afterword: Explaining Litigation." *Law & Society Review* 9:346–68.
  1976   "Delivering Legality: Some Proposals for the Direction of Research." *Law & Society
            Review* 11:225–46.
  1981   "Justice in Many Rooms: Courts, Private Ordering, and Indigenous Law." *Journal
            of Legal Pluralism* 19:1–47.
  1983a   "Megalaw and Megalawyering in the Contemporary United States." In *The Sociol-
            ogy of the Professions: Lawyers, Doctors and Others,* edited by R. Dingwall and P.
            Lewis. London: Macmillan.
  1983b   "Reading the Landscape of Disputes: What We Know and Don't Know (and Think
            We Know) about Our Allegedly Contentious and Litigious Society." *UCLA Law
            Review* 31:4–71.
Galanter, Marc; Palen, Frank S.; and Thomas, John M.
  1979   "The Crusading Judge: Judicial Activism in Urban Trial Courts." *Southern Califor-
            nia Law Review* 52:699–741.
Gazell, James A.
  1975   *State Trial Courts as Bureaucracies: A Study in Judicial Management.* New York:
            Dunellen.
Geerken, Michael, and Gove, Walter R.
  1975   "Deterrence: Some Theoretical Considerations." *Law & Society Review* 9:497–513.
Gellhorn, Walter
  1966   *Ombudsmen and Others: Citizens' Protectors in Nine Countries.* Cambridge, Mass.:
            Harvard University Press.
Gessner, Volkmar; Rhode, Barbara; Strate, Gerhard; and Ziegert, Klaus A.
  1978   "Three Functions of Bankruptcy Law: The West German Case." *Law & Society
            Review* 12:499–543.

Getman, Julius G.
    1979   "Labor Arbitration and Dispute Resolution." *Yale Law Journal* 88:916–49.

Gibbs, Jack P.
    1975   *Crime, Punishment and Deterrence.* New York: Elsevier.
    1986   "The Deterrence Doctrine: Theory, Research, and Penal Policy." In *Law and the Social Sciences,* edited by L. Lipson and S. Wheeler. New York: Russell Sage Foundation.

Gibbs, James L., Jr.
    1967   "The Kpelle Moot." *Africa* 33:1–10.

Gibson, James L.
    1976   "Judges as Representatives: Constituency Influence on Trial Courts." Paper presented at the annual meeting of the American Political Science Association, Chicago, Ill., September 2–5.
    1978   "Judges' Role Orientations, Attitudes, and Decisions: An Interactive Model." *American Political Science Review* 72:911–24.

Giles, Michael W., and Walker, Thomas G.
    1975   "Judicial Policy-Making and Southern School Segregation." *Journal of Politics* 37:917–36.

Gillespie, Robert W.
    1976   "The Production of Court Services: An Analysis of Scale Effects and Other Factors." *Journal of Legal Studies* 5:243–65.

Gilmore, Grant
    1974   *The Death of Contract.* Columbus: Ohio State University Press.
    1977   *The Ages of American Law.* New Haven: Yale University Press.

Glazer, Nathan
    1975   "Towards an Imperial Judiciary." *Public Interest* 41:104–23.

Gleser, Goldine C.; Green, Bonnie L.; and Winget, Carolyn
    1981   *Prolonged Psychosocial Effects of Disaster: A Study of Buffalo Creek.* New York: Academic Press.

Glick, Henry Robert, and Vines, Kenneth N.
    1969   "Law-making in the State Judiciary." *Polity* 2:142–59.
    1973   *State Court Systems.* Englewood Cliffs, N.J.: Prentice-Hall.

Global 2000 Report
    1980   *Global 2000 Report to the President.* 2 vols. Washington, D.C.: U.S. Government Printing Office.

Gluckman, Max
    1955   *The Judicial Process Among the Barotse of Northern Rhodesia.* Manchester: Manchester University Press.

Goldberg, Victor P.
    1976   "Regulation and Administered Contracts." *Bell Journal of Economics* 7:426–48.

Golding, Martin P.
    1969   "Preliminaries to the Study of Procedural Justice." In *Law, Reason and Justice,* edited by G. Hughes. New York: New York University Press.

Goldman, Jerry
    1979   "The Preappeal Conference and Effective Justice." *Law and Policy Quarterly* 1: 101–20.

Goldman, Sheldon
    1975   "Voting Behavior on the United States Courts of Appeals Revisited." *American Political Science Review* 69:491–506.

Goldman, Sheldon, and Jahnige, Thomas P.
    1976   *The Federal Courts as a Political System.* 2nd ed. New York: Harper & Row.

Goldman, Sheldon, and Sarat, Austin
     1978   *American Court Systems: Readings in Judicial Process and Behavior.* San Francisco:
               Freeman.
Goldstein, Abraham S., and Marcus, Martin
     1977   "The Myth of Judicial Supervision in Three 'Inquisitional' Systems: France, Italy
               and Germany." *Yale Law Journal* 87:240–83.
     1978   "Comment on *Continental Criminal Procedures.*" *Yale Law Journal* 87:1570–77.
Goldstein, Paul, and Ford, Robert
     1971   "The Management of Air Quality: Legal Structures and Official Behavior." *Buffalo
               Law Review* 21:1–48.
Gordon, Robert W.
     1975   "Introduction: J. Willard Hurst and the Common Law Tradition in American
               Legal Historiography." *Law & Society Review* 10:9–55.
Grady, John F.
     1978   "Trial Lawyers, Litigators and Clients' Costs." *Litigation* 4(3):5–6, 58–59.
Grossman, Joel B.
     1970   "The Supreme Court and Social Change: A Preliminary Inquiry." *American Behavioral Scientist* 13:535–51.
Grossman, Joel B.; Kritzer, Herbert M.; Bumiller, Kristin; and McDougal, Stephen
     1981   "Measuring the Pace of Litigation in Federal and State Trial Courts." *Judicature*
               65:86–113.
Grossman, Joel B., and Sarat, Austin
     1975   "Litigation in the Federal Courts: A Comparative Perspective." *Law & Society
               Review* 9:321–46.
Grossman, Joel B., and Tanenhaus, Joseph, eds., with the assistance of Edward N. Muller
     1969   *Frontiers of Judicial Research.* New York: Wiley.
Grossman, Joel B., and Wells, Richard S.
     1972   *Constitutional Law and Judicial Policy Making.* New York: Wiley.
Gulliver, P. H.
     1973   "Negotiations as a Mode of Dispute Settlement: Towards a General Model." *Law
               & Society Review* 7:667–91.
     1979   *Disputes and Negotiations: A Cross-Cultural Perspective.* New York: Academic Press.
Gusfield, Joseph R.
     1966   *Symbolic Crusade: Status Politics and the American Temperance Movement.* Urbana:
               University of Illinois.
Hagen, John
     1974   "Extra-legal Attributes and Criminal Sentencing: An Assessment of a Sociological
               Viewpoint." *Law & Society Review* 8:357–83.
Hahm, Pyong-Choon
     1969   "The Decision Process in Korea." In *Comparative Judicial Behavior: Cross-Cultural
               Studies of Political Decision-Making in the East and West,* edited by G. Schubert and
               D. Danelski. New York: Oxford University Press.
Haley, John Owen
     1978   "The Myth of the Reluctant Litigant." *Journal of Japanese Studies* 4:359–90.
     1982   "Sheathing the Sword of Justice in Japan: An Essay on Law Without Sanctions."
               Journal of Japanese Studies 8:265–81.
Hallauer, Robert Paul
     1972   "Low Income Laborers as Legal Clients: Use Patterns and Attitudes Toward Lawyers." *Denver Law Journal* 49:169–232.
Haller, Mark H.
     1976   "Historical Roots of Police Behavior: Chicago, 1890–1925." *Law & Society Review*
               10:303–23.

1979   "Plea Bargaining: The Nineteenth Century Context." *Law & Society Review* 13:273–79.

Handberg, Roger, and Hill, Harold F.
1980   "Court Curbing, Court Reversals, and Judicial Review: The Supreme Court Versus Congress." *Law & Society Review* 14:309–22.

Harnon, Eliahu, and Mann, Kenneth
1981   *Plea Bargaining in Israel.* Jerusalem: Alpha Press.

Hart, H. L. A.
1961   *The Concept of Law.* Oxford: Clarendon Press.

Harvard Law Review
1954   "Note: Evasion of Supreme Court Mandates in Cases Remanded to State Courts Since 1941." *Harvard Law Review* 67:1251–59.

1976   "Note: Developments in the Law: Class Actions." *Harvard Law Review* 89:1318.

Haskell, Thomas L.
1978   "Litigation and Social Status in Seventeenth-Century New Haven." *Journal of Legal Studies* 7:219–41.

Hasluck, Margaret
1954   *The Unwritten Law in Albania.* Edited by J. H. Hutton. Cambridge: Cambridge University Press.

Hayden, Robert McBeth
1981   *"No One Is Stronger Than the Caste"—Arguing Dispute Cases in an Indian Caste Panchayat.* Doctoral dissertation, State University of New York at Buffalo.

Heinz, John P., and Laumann, Edward O.
1978   "The Legal Profession: Client Interests, Professional Roles and Social Hierarchies." *Michigan Law Review* 76:1111–42.

Henderson, Dan Fenno
1965   *Conciliation in Japanese Law: Tokugawa and Modern.* 2 vols. Seattle: University of Washington Press.

1968   "Law and Political Modernization in Japan." In *Political Development in Modern Japan,* edited by R. E. Ward. Princeton, N.J.: Princeton University Press.

Heumann, Milton
1975   "A Note on Plea Bargaining and Case Pressure." *Law & Society Review* 9:515–28.

Heumann, Milton, and Loftin, Colin
1979   "Mandatory Sentencing and the Abolition of Plea Bargaining: The Michigan Felony Firearms Statute." *Law & Society Review* 13:393–430.

Heydebrand, Wolf V.
1977   "The Contest of Public Bureaucracies: An Organizational Analysis of Federal District Courts." *Law & Society Review* 11:759–822.

Hill, Larry B.
1976   *The Model Ombudsman: Institutionalizing New Zealand's Democratic Experiment.* Princeton, N.J.: Princeton University Press.

Hirschman, Albert O.
1970   *Exit, Voice and Loyalty: Responses to Decline in Firms, Organizations and States.* Cambridge, Mass.: Harvard University Press.

Hooker, M. B.
1975   *Legal Pluralism: An Introduction to Colonial and Neo-Colonial Laws.* Oxford: Clarendon Press.

Horowitz, Donald
1977   *The Courts and Social Policy.* Washington, D.C.: Brookings Institution.

Horwitz, Morton
1977   *The Transformation of American Law, 1790–1860.* Cambridge, Mass.: Harvard University Press.

Howard, J. Woodford, Jr.

1968   "On the Fluidity of Judicial Choice." *American Political Science Review* 62:43–56.

1969   "Adjudication Considered as a Process of Conflict Resolution: A Variation on Separation of Powers." *Journal of Public Law* 18:339–70.

1977   "Role Perceptions and Behavior in Three U.S. Courts of Appeal." *Journal of Politics* 39:916–38.

1981   *Courts of Appeals in the Federal Judicial System.* Princeton, N.J.: Princeton University Press.

1982   "Query: Are Heavy Caseloads Changing the Nature of Appellate Justice?" *Judicature* 66:57–59, 102 (August).

Hunt, Eva, and Hunt, Robert

1969   "The Role of Courts in Rural Mexico." In *Peasants in the Modern World,* edited by P. Bock. Albuquerque: University of New Mexico Press.

Hurst, James Willard

1953   "Changing Popular Views About Law and Lawyers." *Annals of the American Academy* 287:1–7.

1956   *Law and the Conditions of Freedom in the Nineteenth-Century United States.* Madison: University of Wisconsin Press.

1980–81 "The Functions of Courts in the United States, 1950–1980." *Law & Society Review* 15:401–71.

Ino, Masaru, et al.

1975   "Diary of a Plaintiffs' Attorneys' Team in the Thalidomide Litigation." *Law in Japan* 8:136–87.

Institute of Judicial Administration

1979   *Non-Attorney Justice in the United States: An Empirical Study.* New York: Institute of Judicial Administration.

Jacob, Herbert

1969a   *Debtors in Court: The Consumption of Government Services.* Chicago: Rand McNally.

1969b   "Judicial and Political Efficacy of Litigants: A Preliminary Analysis." In *Frontiers of Judicial Research,* edited by J. Grossman and J. Tanenhaus. New York: Wiley.

1983   "Courts as Organizations." In *Empirical Theories About Courts,* edited by K. Boyum and L. Mather. New York: Longman.

James, Fleming, Jr.

1965   *Civil Procedure.* Boston: Little, Brown.

Johnson, Earl, Jr.

1980–81 "Lawyers' Choice: A Theoretical Appraisal of Litigation Investment Decisions." *Law & Society Review* 15:567–610.

Johnson, Earl, Jr., and Drew, Ann Barthelmes

1978   "This Nation Has Money for Everything: Except Its Courts." *Judges Journal* 17:8–11, 54–56.

Johnson, Earl, Jr., et al.

1977   "Comparative Analysis of the Statistical Dimensions of the Justice Systems of Seven Industrial Democracies." A report submitted to the National Institute for Law Enforcement and Criminal Justice.

Johnstone, Quintin, and Hopson, Dan, Jr.

1967   *Lawyers and Their Work: An Analysis of the Legal Profession in the United States and England.* Indianapolis: Bobbs-Merrill.

Jolowicz, J. A.

1975   "The Active Role of the Court in Civil Litigation." In M. Cappelletti and J. A Jolowicz, *Public Interest Parties and the Active Role of the Judge in Civil Litigation* Milano: Giuffre.

Jones, Harry W.
    1969   *The Efficacy of Law.* Evanston, Ill.: Northwestern University Press.
Judicial Conference of the United States
    1981   *The Federal Magistrates System: Report to the Congress by the Judicial Conference of the United States.*
Judicial Council of California
    1982   *Annual Report of the Administrative Office of the California Courts.* San Francisco: Judicial Council of California.
Judicial Council of Florida
    1980   *Twenty-Fifth Annual Report: Judicial Council of Florida, 1 February, 1980.* Tallahassee: Judicial Council of Florida.
Kagan, Richard L.
    1981   *Lawsuits and Litigants in Castile, 1500–1700.* Chapel Hill: University of North Carolina Press.
Kagan, Robert A.; Cartwright, Bliss; Friedman, Lawrence M.; and Wheeler, Stanton
    1977   "The Business of State Supreme Courts, 1870–1970." *Stanford Law Review* 30: 121–56.
    1978   "The Evolution of State Supreme Courts." *Michigan Law Review* 76:961– 1005.
Kaiser, Colin
    1980   "The Deflation in the Volume of Litigation at Paris in the Eighteenth Century and the Waning of the Old Judicial Order." *European Studies Review* 10:309–36.
Kaplan, Irving
    1965   "Courts as Catalysts of Change: A Chagga Case." *Southwestern Journal of Anthropology* 21:79–96.
Karikas, Angela
    1980   "Solving Problems in Philadelphia: An Ethnography of a Congressional District Office." In *No Access to Law: Alternatives to the American Judicial System,* edited by L. Nader. New York: Academic Press.
Katz, Jack
    1977   "Cover-up and Collective Integrity: On the Natural Antagonisms of Authority Internal and External to Organizations." *Social Problems* 25:3–17.
Kawashima, Takeyoshi
    1963   "Dispute Resolution in Contemporary Japan." In *Law in Japan: The Legal Order in a Changing Society,* edited by A. T. von Mehren. Cambridge, Mass.: Harvard University Press.
Kennedy, Duncan
    1973   "Legal Formality." *Journal of Legal Studies* 2:351–98.
    1975   *"The Rise and Fall of Classical Legal Thought."* Unpublished manuscript.
    1976   "Form and Substance in Private Law Adjudication." *Harvard Law Review* 89:1685– 1778.
Kidder, Robert L.
    1973   "Courts and Conflict in an Indian City: A Study in Legal Impact." *Journal of Commonwealth Political Studies* 11:121–39.
    1974   "Formal Litigation and Professional Insecurity: Legal Entrepreneurship in South India." *Law & Society Review* 9:11–37.
    1980–81 "The End of the Road: Problems in the Analysis of Disputes." *Law & Society Review* 15:717–25.
King, Donald W., and McEvoy, Kathleen A.
    1976   *A National Survey of the Complaint Handling Procedures Used by Consumers.* Rockville, Md.: King Research.

Kirchheimer, Otto
    1961   *Political Justice: The Use of Legal Procedure for Political Ends.* Princeton, N.J.: Princeton University Press.

Kirp, David L.
    1976   "Proceduralism and Bureaucracy: Due Process in the School Setting." *Stanford Law Review* 28:841–77.

Klein, John F.
    1976   *Let's Make a Deal! Negotiating Justice.* Lexington, Mass.: Lexington Books.

Kloman, E. H.
    1975   "Public Participation in Technology Assessment." *Public Administration Review* 35:80–83.

Konig, David Thomas
    1979   *Law and Society in Puritan Massachusetts: Essex County, 1629–1692.* Chapel Hill: University of North Carolina Press.

Kritzer, Herbert M.
    1978   "Political Correlates of the Behavior of Federal District Judges: A 'Best Case' Analysis." *Journal of Politics* 40:25–58.

Kurczewski, Jacek, and Frieske, Kazimierz
    1978   "The Social Conciliatory Commissions in Poland: A Case Study of Nonauthoritative and Conciliatory Dispute Resolution as an Approach to Access to Justice." In *Access to Justice,* vol. 2. *Promising Institutions,* edited by M. Cappelletti and J. Weisner. Milan: Giuffre, and Alphen aan den Rijn: Sijthoff and Noordhoff. 153–427.

Lacey, Hon. Frederick B.
    1977   *The Judge's Role in the Settlement of Civil Suits.* Washington, D.C.: Federal Judicial Center, Education and Training Series.

Ladinsky, Jack; Macaulay, Stewart; and Anderson, Jill
    1979   "The Milwaukee Dispute Mapping Project: A Preliminary Report." Working paper 1979-3. Madison, University of Wisconsin Law School, Disputes Processing Research Program.

Ladinsky, Jack, and Susmilch, Charles
    1985   "Community Factors in the Brokerage of Consumer Product and Services Problems." In *The Challenge of Social Control: Citizenship and Institution Building in Modern Society,* edited by G. Suttles and M. Zald. Norwood, N.J.: Ablex. 193–217.

LaFave, Wayne R.
    1965   *Arrest: The Decision to Take a Suspect into Custody.* Boston: Little, Brown.

Langbein, John H.
    1979   "Understanding the Short History of Plea Bargaining." *Law & Society Review* 13:261–72.

Langbein, John H., and Weinreb, Lloyd L.
    1978   "Continental Criminal Procedure: 'Myth' and Reality." *Yale Law Journal* 87: 1549–69.

Langerwerf, Etienne
    1978   "The Influence of the Industrialization on the Belgian Civil Courts from 1835 to 1970." Paper presented at the 9th World Congress of Sociology, Uppsala, August.

Laurent, Francis
    1959   *The Business of a Trial Court.* Madison: University of Wisconsin Press.

Law Commission of India
    1979   *Seventy-Ninth Report on Delay and Arrears in High Courts and Other Appellate Courts.* Government of India, Ministry of Law, Justice and Company Affairs.

Lempert, Richard O.
1978   "More Tales of Two Courts: Exploring Changes in the Dispute Settlement Function of Trial Courts." *Law & Society Review* 13:91–138.
1980–81 "Grievances and Legitimacy: The Beginnings and End of Dispute Settlement." *Law & Society Review* 15:707.

Lev, Daniel S.
1972   "Judicial Institutions and Legal Culture in Indonesia." In *Culture and Politics in Indonesia,* edited by C. Holt et al. Ithaca, N.Y.: Cornell University Press.

Levi, Edward H.
1961   *An Introduction to Legal Reasoning.* Chicago: University of Chicago Press.

Levin, A. Leo
1983   "Court-Annexed Arbitration." *University of Michigan Journal of Law Reform* 16:537–48.

Levin, Martin A.
1972   "Urban Politics and Judicial Behavior." *Journal of Legal Studies* 1:193–221.
1977   *Urban Politics and the Criminal Courts.* Chicago: University of Chicago Press.

Levine, James P.
1970   "Methodological Concerns in Studying Supreme Court Efficacy." *Law & Society Review* 4:583–611.

Lieberman, Jethro K.
1981   *The Litigious Society.* New York: Basic Books.

Llewellyn, Karl N.
1960   *The Common Law Tradition: Deciding Appeals.* Boston: Little, Brown.

Loeber, Dietrich A.
1965   "Plan and Contract Performance in Soviet Law." In *Law in the Soviet Society,* edited by W. LaFave. Urbana: University of Illinois Press.

Lubman, Stanley
1967   "Mao and Mediation: Politics and Dispute Resolution in Communist China." *California Law Review* 55:1284–1359.

Luhmann, Niklas
1976   "The Legal Profession: Comments on the Situation in the Federal Republic of Germany." In *Lawyers in Their Social Setting,* edited by D. N. MacCormick. Edinburgh: Green.

MacCollum, Spencer
1967   "Dispute Settlement in an American Supermarket." In *Law and Warfare,* edited by P. Bohannon. Garden City, N.Y.: Natural History Press.

McEwen, Craig A., and Maiman, Richard J.
1984   "Mediation in Small Claims Court: Achieving Compliance Through Consent." *Law & Society Review* 18:11–49.

McIntosh, Wayne V.
1978   "Litigation in the St. Louis Trial Courts of General Jurisdiction: The Effects of Socio-Economic Change." Paper presented at the annual meeting of the American Political Science Association, New York.
1980–81 "150 Years of Litigation and Dispute Settlement: A Court Tale." *Law & Society Review* 15:823–48.
1982a   "A Long-Range View of Litigators and Their Demands." Paper presented at the annual meeting of the American Political Science Association, Denver, September 2–5.
1982b   "Private Disputes and Environmental Change: An Aggregate Analysis of Litigation Activity in a State Trial Court." Paper presented at the annual meeting of the Law and Society Association, Toronto, June 3–6.

McIntyre, Donald M.
    1968   "A Study of Judicial Dominance of the Charging Process." *Journal of Criminal Law,
            Criminology and Political Science* 59:463–90.
McIntyre, Donald M., and Lippman, David
    1970   "Prosecutors and Early Disposition of Felony Cases." *American Bar Association
            Journal* 56:1154–59.
McMahon, Margaret May
    1974   "Legal Education in Japan." *American Bar Association Journal* 60:1376–80.
Macaulay, Stewart
    1963   "Non-Contractual Relations in Business: A Preliminary Study." *American Sociolog-
            ical Review* 28:55–67.
    1966   *Law and the Balance of Power: The Automobile Manufacturers and Their Dealers.* New
            York: Russell Sage Foundation.
    1977   "Elegant Models, Empirical Pictures, and the Complexities of Contract." *Law &
            Society Review* 11:507–28.
    1979   "Lawyers and Consumer Protection Laws." *Law & Society Review* 14:115–71.
Maine, Sir Henry
    1895   *Village Communities in the East and West.* London: Murray.
    [1871]
Mann, Dean
    1968   *The Citizen and the Bureaucracy: Complaint Handling Procedures of Three California
            Legislators.* Berkeley: Institute of Governmental Studies, University of California.
Manning, Bayless
    1977   "Hyperlexis: Our National Disease." *Northwestern University Law Review* 71:
            767–82.
Mans, Thomas C.
    1979   "Selecting the 'Hidden Judiciary': How the Merit Process Works in Choosing the
            Administrative Law Judges." *Judicature* 63:60–73, 131–43.
Mantel, Hugo
    1972   "Sanhedrin." *Encyclopedia Judaica* 14:836–39. Jerusalem: Keter.
Marks, F. Raymond
    1971   *The Legal Needs of the Poor: A Critical Analysis.* Chicago: American Bar Founda-
            tion.
Mather, Lynn M.
    1973   "Some Determinants of the Method of Case Disposition: Decision-Making by
            Public Defenders in Los Angeles." *Law & Society Review* 8:187–216.
Mather, Lynn M., and Yngvesson, Barbara
    1980–81 "Language, Audience, and the Transformation of Disputes." *Law & Society Review*
            15:775–821.
Mattice, Michael C.
    1980   "Media in the Middle: A Study of the Mass Media Complaint Managers." In *No
            Access to Law: Alternatives to the American Judicial System,* edited by L. Nader. New
            York: Academic Press.
Matza, David
    1964   *Delinquency and Drift.* New York: Wiley.
Mayhew, Leon H.
    1968   *Law and Equal Opportunity: A Study of the Massachusetts Commission Against Dis-
            crimination.* Cambridge, Mass.: Harvard University Press.
    1975   "Institutions of Representation." *Law & Society Review* 9:401–29.
Mayhew, Leon H., and Reiss, Albert J., Jr.
    1969   "The Social Organization of Legal Contracts." *American Sociological Review*
            34:309–18.

Mendelsohn, Oliver
  1981   "The Pathology of the Indian Legal System." *Modern Asian Studies* 15:823–63.
Mentschikoff, Soia
  1961   "Commercial Arbitration." *Columbia Law Review* 61:846–69.
Merry, Sally Engle
  1979   "Going to Court: Strategies of Dispute Management in an American Urban Neighborhood." *Law & Society Review* 13:891–925.

  1982   "The Social Organization of Mediation in Nonindustrial Societies: Implications for Informal Community Justice in America." In *The Politics of Informal Justice: Comparative Studies*, edited by R. Abel. New York: Academic Press, pp. 17–45.
Merryman, John Henry
  1969   *The Civil Law Tradition: An Introduction to the Legal Systems of Western Europe and Latin America.* Stanford, Calif.: Stanford University Press.
Merryman, John N., and Clark, David S.
  1978   *Comparative Law: Western European and Latin American Legal Systems.* New York: Bobbs-Merrill.
Meschievitz, Catherine, and Galanter, Marc
  1982   "In Search of the Nyaya Panchayats: The Politics of a Moribund Institution." In *The Politics of Informal Justice: Comparative Studies*, edited by R. Abel. New York: Academic Press.
Meyers, Martha, and Hagan, John
  1979   "Private and Public Trouble: Prosecutors and the Allocation of Court Resources." *Social Problems* 26:439–51.
Miller, Richard E., and Sarat, Austin
  1980–81 "Grievances, Claims, and Disputes: Assessing the Adversary Culture." *Law & Society Review* 15:525–65.
Miller, Frank W.
  1969   *Prosecution: The Decision to Charge a Suspect with a Crime.* Boston: Little, Brown.
Ministère de la Justice
  1978   *Compte général 1975: Rapport sur l'administration de la justice criminelle pendant l'année 1975. Tome 1.* Paris: La Documentation Française.

  1979   *Compte général de la justice civile et commerciale, Tome II.* Paris: La Documentation Française.
Ministry of Attorney General
  1982   *Court Statistics Annual Report, Fiscal Year 1981–82.* Toronto: Ministry of Attorney General, Province of Ontario.
Mnookin, Robert H., and Kornhauser, Lewis
  1979   "Bargaining in the Shadow of the Law: The Case of Divorce." *Yale Law Journal* 88:950–97.
Mohr, Lawrence B.
  1976   "Organizations, Decisions and Courts." *Law & Society Review* 10:621–42.
Moore, Sally Falk
  1973   "Law and Social Change: The Semi-Autonomous Social Field as an Appropriate Object of Study." *Law & Society Review* 7:719–46.

  1978   *Law as Process: An Anthropological Approach.* London: Routledge & Kegan Paul.
Morrison, Charles
  1974   "Clerks and Clients: Paraprofessional Roles and Cultural Identities in Indian Litigation." *Law & Society Review* 9:39–61.
Moulton, Beatrice A.
  1969   "The Persecution and Intimidation of the Low-Income Litigant as Performed by the Small Claims Court in California." *Stanford Law Review* 21:1657–84.

Muir, William K., Jr.
    1967   *Prayer in the Public Schools.* Chicago: University of Chicago Press.
Murphy, Walter F.
    1959   "Lower Court Checks on Supreme Court Power." *American Political Science Review*
              53:1017–31.
    1964   *Elements of Judicial Strategy.* Chicago: University of Chicago Press.
Murphy, Walter F., and Tanenhaus, Joseph
    1972   *The Study of Public Law.* New York: Random House.
Nader, Laura
    1965   "The Anthropological Study of Law." In *The Ethnography of Law,* edited by L.
              Nader. *American Anthropologist* 67 (pt. 2):3–32.
    1969   "Styles of Court Procedure: To Make the Balance." In *Law in Culture and Society,*
              edited by L. Nader. Chicago: Aldine.
Nader, Laura, and Singer, Linda A.
    1976   "Law in the Future: What Are the Choices?" *California State Bar Journal* 51:281–
              319.
Nader, Laura, and Todd, Harry F., eds.
    1978   *The Disputing Process—Law in Ten Societies.* New York: Columbia University Press.
Nagel, Stuart S.
    1961   "Political Party Affiliation and Judges' Decisions." *American Political Science Review*
              55:843–50.
    1969   *The Legal Process from a Behavioral Perspective.* Homewood, Ill.: Dorsey Press.
Nardulli, Peter F.
    1978   *The Courtroom Elite: An Organizational Perspective on Criminal Justice.* Cambridge,
              Mass.: Ballinger.
    1979   "The Caseload Controversy and the Study of Criminal Courts." *Journal of Criminal
              Law and Criminology* 70:89–101.
National Bureau of Statistics
    1981   *Korea Statistical Yearbook, 1981.* Seoul: National Bureau of Statistics.
National Court Statistics Project
    1982   *State Court Organization, 1980.* Williamsburg, Va.: National Court Statistics
              Project.
Nelson, William E.
    1981   *Dispute and Conflict Resolution in Plymouth County, Massachusetts, 1725–1825.*
              Chapel Hill: University of North Carolina Press.
New Zealand Department of Statistics
    1976   *New Zealand Official Yearbook 1976.* 81st annual ed. Wellington: Department of
              Statistics.
    1978   *New Zealand Justice Statistics, 1976.* Wellington: Department of Statistics.
    1980a   *New Zealand Justice Statistics, 1977–78 Part A.* Wellington: Department of Statis-
              tics.
    1980b   *New Zealand Justice Statistics, 1977–78, Part B.* Wellington: Department of Statis-
              tics.
Newman, Donald J.
    1966   *Conviction: The Determination of Guilt or Innocence Without Trial.* Boston: Little,
              Brown.
Nimmer, Raymond T.
    1978   "A Slightly Moveable Object: A Case Study in Judicial Reform in the Criminal
              Justice Process—The Omnibus Hearing." *Denver Law Journal* 48:179–210.
Nims, Harry D.
    1950   *Pre-Trial.* New York: Baker, Voorhis.

Nonet, Philippe
   1969   *Administrative Justice: Advocacy and Change in a Government Agency.* New York:
           Russell Sage Foundation.
Office of the Chief Court Administrator
   1981   *Biennial Report of the Connecticut Judicial Department, July 1, 1978–June 30, 1980.*
           Hartford: Office of the Chief Court Administrator.
Office of State Courts Administrator
   n.d.   *Missouri Judicial Report, FY 1980–81.* Jefferson City, Mo.: Office of State Courts
           Administrator.
O'Neil, Robert M.
   1970   "Of Justice Delayed and Justice Denied: The Welfare Prior Hearing Cases." In *The
           Supreme Court Review.* Chicago: University of Chicago Press.
Oommen, T. K.
   1983   "The Legal Profession in India: Some Sociological Perspectives." *Indian Bar Review*
           10:(1),1–46.
Owen, Harold J., Jr.
   1971   *The Role of Trial Courts in the Local Political System: A Comparison of Two Georgia
           Counties.* Doctoral dissertation, University of Georgia.
Palen, Frank S.
   1979   "Media Ombudsmen: A Critical Review." *Law & Society Review* 13:799–850.
Paterson, Alan P.
   1983   "Becoming a Judge." In *The Sociology of the Professions: Lawyers, Doctors and Others,*
           edited by R. Dingwall and P. Lewis. London: Macmillan.
Peterson, Mark A., and Priest, George L.
   1982   *The Civil Jury: Trends in Trials and Verdicts, Cook County, Illinois, 1960–1979.*
           Santa Monica, Calif.: Rand Corporation.
Posner, Richard A.
   1977   *Economic Analysis of Law.* 2nd ed. Boston: Little, Brown.
Pospisil, Leopold
   1967   "Legal Levels and Multiplicity of Legal Systems in Human Societies." *Journal of
           Conflict Resolution* 11:2–26.
Pound, Roscoe
   1917   "The Limits of Effective Legal Action." *International Journal of Ethics* 27:150–
           67.
Pritchett, Charles Herman
   1948   *The Roosevelt Court: A Study in Judicial Politics and Values, 1937–1947.* New York:
           Macmillan.
   1954   *Civil Liberties and the Vinson Court.* Chicago: University of Chicago Press.
Rabin, Robert L.
   1972   "Agency Criminal Referrals in the Federal System: An Empirical Study of Prosecu-
           torial Discretion." *Stanford Law Review* 24:1036–91.
Randall, Richard S.
   1968   *Censorship of the Movies: Social and Political Control of a Mass Medium.* Madison:
           University of Wisconsin Press.
Rebell, Michael A., and Block, Arthur R.
   1982   *Educational Policy Making and the Courts: An Empirical Study of Judicial Activism.*
           Chicago: University of Chicago Press.
Reich, Charles A.
   1964   "The New Property." *Yale Law Journal* 73:733–87.
Resnik, Judith
   1982   "Managerial Judges." *Harvard Law Review* 96:374–448.

Rhyne, Charles S.
    1978   *Law and Judicial Systems of Nations.* Washington, D.C.: World Peace Through Law
            Center.
Rohde, David W., and Spaeth, Harold J.
    1976   *Supreme Court Decision Making.* San Francisco: Freeman.
Rohl, Klaus
    1980   "Dunning Proceedings in West Germany: A German Version of Rubber Stamping
            for Debt Collection." Paper presented at the meeting of the Law and Society
            Association, June 5–8.
Rosenberg, Maurice
    1972   "Let's Everybody Litigate?" *Texas Law Review* 50:1349–68.
Rosenthal, Douglas
    1974   *Lawyer and Client: Who's in Charge?* New York: Russell Sage Foundation.
Ross, H. Laurence
    1970   *Settled Out of Court: The Social Process of Insurance Claims Adjustment.* Chicago:
            Aldine.
    1975   "Insurance Claims Complaints: A Private Appeals Procedure." *Law & Society
            Review* 9:275–92.
Ross, H. Laurence, and Littlefield, Neil O.
    1978   "Complaint as a Problem-Solving Mechanism." *Law & Society Review* 12:199–216.
Rudolph, Lloyd, and Rudolph, Susanne
    1965   "Barristers and Brahmins in India: Legal Cultures and Social Change." *Comparative
            Studies in Society and History* 8:24–29.
Ruffini, Julio L.
    1978   "Disputing over Livestock in Sardinia." In *The Disputing Process—Law in Ten
            Societies,* edited by L. Nader and H. Todd. New York: Columbia University Press.
Ruhnka, John C., and Weller, Steven, with John A. Martin
    1978   *Small Claims Courts: A National Examination.* Williamsburg, Va.: National Center
            for State Courts.
Ryan, John Paul, and Alfini, James J.
    1979   "Trial Judges' Participation in Plea Bargaining: An Empirical Perspective." *Law &
            Society Review* 13:479–507.
Ryan, John Paul; Ashman, Allan; Sales, Bruce D.; and Shane-Dubow, Sandra
    1980   *American Trial Judges: Their Work Styles and Performance.* New York: Free Press.
Samonte, Abelardo G.
    1969   "The Philippine Supreme Court: A Study of Judicial Background Characteristics,
            Attitudes, and Decision-making." In *Comparative Judicial Behavior,* edited by G.
            Schubert and D. J. Danelski. New York: Oxford University Press.
Sander, Frank E. A.
    1976   "Varieties of Dispute Processing." *Federal Rules Decisions* 70:111–34.
Sanders, Clinton R.
    1975   "Caught in the Con-Game: The Young White Drug User's Contact with the Legal
            System." *Law & Society Review* 9:197–217.
Santos, Bonaventura de Sousa
    1977   "The Law of the Oppressed: The Construction and Reproduction of Legality in
            Pasargada." *Law & Society Review* 12:5–126.
Sarat, Austin
    1976   "Alternatives in Dispute Processing: Litigation in a Small Claims Court." *Law &
            Society Review* 10:339–75.
    1977a   "Judging in Trial Courts: An Exploratory Study." *Journal of Politics* 39:368–99.
    1977b   "Studying American Legal Culture: An Assessment of Survey Evidence." *Law &
            Society Review* 11:427–88.

Savezni Zavod za Statistiku
1981   *Statisticki Godisnjak Jugoslavije 1981* (Statistical Yearbook of the Socialist Federal
         Republics of Yugoslavia). Beograd: Savezni Zavod za Statistiku.
Scheingold, Stuart
1974   *The Politics of Rights: Lawyers, Public Policy and Political Change.* New Haven: Yale
         University Press.
Schelling, Thomas C.
1963   *The Strategy of Conflict.* New York: Oxford University Press.
Schmidhauser, John R.
1979   *Judges and Justices: The Federal Appellate Judiciary.* Boston: Little, Brown.
Schramm, Gustav L.
1928   *Piedpoudre Courts: A Study of the Small Claim Litigant in the Pittsburgh District.*
         Pittsburgh: Legal Aid Society.
Schubert, Glendon, ed.
1963   *Judicial Decison-Making.* Glencoe, Ill.: Free Press.
1964   *Judicial Behavior.* Chicago: Rand McNally.
1974   *Judicial Policy Making: The Political Role of the Courts.* Glenview, Ill.: Scott, Fores-
         man.
Schuyt, Kees; Groenendijk, Kees; and Sloot, Ben
1977   "Access to the Legal System and Legal Services Research." *European Yearbook in
         Law and Sociology* 1977:98–120.
Schwartz, Murray
1981   "The Other Things That Courts Do." *UCLA Law Review* 28:438–62.
Schwartz, Richard D.
1954   "Social Factors in the Development of Legal Control: A Case Study of Two Israeli
         Settlements." *Yale Law Journal* 63:471–91.
Schwartz, Richard D., and Miller, James
1964   "Legal Evolution and Societal Complexity." *American Journal of Sociology* 70:
         159–69.
Selvin, Molly, and Ebener, Patricia A.
1984   *Managing the Unmanageable: A History of Civil Delay in the Los Angeles Superior
         Court.* Santa Monica: Rand Corporation, Institute for Civil Justice.
Selznick, Philip
1963   "Legal Institutions and Social Controls." *Vanderbilt Law Review* 17:79–90.
Selznick, Philip, with the collaboration of Philippe Nonet and Howard M. Vollmer
1969   *Law, Society and Industrial Justice.* New York: Russell Sage Foundation.
Shanley, M., and Peterson, M.
1983   *Comparative Justice: Civil Jury Verdicts in San Francisco and Coor Counties, 1959–80.*
         Santa Monica: Rand Corporation, Institute for Civil Justice.
Shapiro, Martin
1965   "Stability and Change in Judicial Decision-Making: Incrementalism or Stare De-
         cisis?" *Law in Transition Quarterly* 2:134–57.
1971   "Impact of the Supreme Court." *Journal of Legal Education* 23:77–105.
1980   "Appeal." *Law & Society Review* 14:629–61.
Shore, Frederick John
1837   *Notes on Indian Affairs.* Vol. 2. London.
Silbey, Susan S.
1979   *What the Lower Courts Do: The Work and Role of Courts of Limited Jurisdiction.*
         Federal Justice Research Program/Office for Improvements in the Administration
         of Justice.

1980–81 "Case Processing: Consumer Protection in an Attorney General's Office." *Law & Society Review* 15:849–81.

Sirica, John J.
1979 *To Set the Record Straight: The Break-In, the Tapes, the Conspirators, the Pardon.* New York: Norton.

Skolnick, Jerome
1966 *Justice Without Trial: Law Enforcement in a Democratic Society.* New York: Wiley.

Solomon, Lester, and Siegfried, John
1977 "Economic Power and Political Influence: The Impact of Industry Structure on Public Policy." *American Political Science Review* 71:1026–43.

Sorauf, Frank J.
1976 *The Wall of Separation: The Constitutional Politics of Church and State.* Princeton, N.J.: Princeton University Press.

Starr, June, and Pool, Jonathan
1974 "The Impact of a Legal Revolution in Rural Turkey." *Law & Society Review* 8: 533–60.

Starr, June, and Yngvesson, Barbara
1975 "Scarcity and Disputing: Zeroing-in on Compromise Decisions." *American Ethnologist* 2:553–66.

Statistisches Bundesamt
1980 *Statistisches Jahrbuch 1980 für die Bundesrepublik Deutschland.* Wiesbaden: Statistisches Bundesamt.

Statistics Bureau, Prime Minister's Office
1982 *Japan Statistics Yearbook, 1982.* Tokyo: Japan Statistical Association.

Statistik Sentralbyra
n.d. *Sivilretts-Statistik 1976* (Civil Judicial Statistics 1976). Oslo: Statistik Sentralbyra.

Steele, Eric H.
1975 "Fraud, Dispute and the Consumer: Responding to Consumer Complaints." *University of Pennsylvania Law Review* 123:1107–86.

Stern, Gerald M.
1977 *The Buffalo Creek Disaster.* New York: Vintage Books.

Stinchcombe, Arthur
1969 "Social Structure and Organizations." In *Handbook of Organizations*, edited by J. G. March. Chicago: Rand McNally.

Sudnow, D.
1965 "Normal Crimes: Sociological Features of the Penal Code in a Public Defender Office." *Social Problems* 12:255–76.

Supreme Court of Minnesota
n.d. *Minnesota State Court Report 1976–77.* Supreme Court of Minnesota.

Sveriges Officiella Statistik
1977 *Rattsstatistik Arsbok, 1975* (Yearbook of Legal Statistics). Stockholm: Sveriges Officiella Statistik (National Central Bureau of Statistics).

Sykes, Gresham M.
1958 *The Society of Captives.* Princeton, N.J.: Princeton University Press.
1969 "Cases, Courts, and Congestion." In *Law in Culture and Society*, edited by L. Nader. Chicago: Aldine.

Takayanagi, K.
1963 "A Century of Innovation: The Development of Japanese Law, 1868–1961." In *Law in Japan: The Legal Order in a Changing Society*, edited by A. T. von Mehren. Cambridge, Mass.: Harvard University Press.

Tanner, Nancy
    1970   "Disputing and the Genesis of Legal Principles: Examples from Minangkabau."
            Southwestern Journal of Anthropology 26:375–401.
Tinnin, David B.
    1973   *Just About Everybody vs. Howard Hughes.* Garden City, N.Y.: Doubleday.
Tocqueville, Alexis de
    1953   *Democracy in America.* New York: Vintage Books.
    [1835]
Todd, Harry F., Jr.
    1978   "Litigious Marginals: Character and Disputing in a Bavarian Village." In *The
            Disputing Process—Law in Ten Societies,* edited by L. Nader and H. Todd. New
            York: Columbia University Press.
Toharia, Jose Juan
    1975a   "Economic Development and Litigation: The Case of Spain." In *Sociology of the
            Judicial Process,* edited by L. M. Friedman and M. Rehbinder. Opladen, West
            Germany: Westdeutscher Verlag.

    1975b   "Judicial Independence in an Authoritarian Regime: The Case of Contemporary
            Spain." *Law & Society Review* 9:475–96.
Trubek, David M.
    1972   "Max Weber on Law and the Rise of Capitalism." *Wisconsin Law Review* 1972:
            720–53.

    1980–81 "The Construction and Deconstruction of a Disputes-Focused Approach: An Af-
            terword." *Law & Society Review* 15:727–47.
Trubek, David M.; Grossman, Joel B.; Felstiner, William L. F.; Kritzer, Herbert M.; and Sarat,
    Austin
    1983   *Civil Litigation Research Project Final Report,* 3 vols. in 2. Madison: Disputes Process-
            ing Research Program, University of Wisconsin Law School.
Uhlman, Thomas M., and Walker, N. Darlene
    1980   "'He Takes Some of My Time; I Take Some of His': An Analysis of Judicial
            Sentencing Patterns in Jury Cases." *Law & Society Review* 14:323–41.
Ulmer, Sidney S.
    1960   "The Analysis of Behavior Patterns on the United States Supreme Court." *Journal
            of Politics* 22:629–53.

    1971   *Courts as Small and Not So Small Groups.* New York: General Learning Press.

    1974   "Dimensionality and Change in Judicial Behavior." In *Mathematical Applications in
            Political Science—VII,* edited by J. F. Herndon and J. L. Bernd. Charlottesville:
            University of Virginia Press.

    1978   "Selecting Cases for Supreme Court Review: An Underdog Model." *American
            Political Science Review* 72:902–10.
Upham, Frank K.
    1976   "Litigation and Moral Consciousness in Japan: An Interpretative Analysis of Four
            Japanese Pollution Suits." *Law & Society Review* 10:579–620.
United States Department of Justice, Law Enforcement Assistance Administration, National
    Criminal Justice Information and Statistics Service
    1977   *Sourcebook of Criminal Justice Statistics—1976.* Washington, D.C.: U.S. Govern-
            ment Printing Office.

    1979   *State Court Caseload Statistics: Annual Report 1975.* Washington, D.C.: U.S. Gov-
            ernment Printing Office.
United States Department of Labor
    1982   *Labor Force Statistics Derived From the Current Population Survey: A Datebook, Vol.
            1.* Washington, D.C.: U.S. Department of Labor, Bureau of Labor Statistics.

Van Houtte, J., and Langerwerf, E.
    1981   "La justice en matière fiscale; le cas de la cour d'appel d'Anvers." *Sociologie du Travail* 23:50–56.

Vanderbilt Law Review
    1979   "Note: The Appealability of District Court Orders Disapproving Settlements in Shareholder Derivative Suits." *Vanderbilt Law Review* 32:985–1001.

Walker, Darlene; Richardson, Richard J.; Denyer, Thomas; Williams, Oliver; and McGaughey, Skip
    1973   "Contact and Support: An Empirical Assessment of Public Attitudes Toward the Police and the Courts." *North Carolina Law Review* 51:43–79.

Wanner, Craig
    1974   "The Public Ordering of Private Relations: Part I: Initiating Civil Cases in Urban Trial Courts." *Law & Society Review* 8:421–40.

    1975   "The Public Ordering of Private Relations: Part II: Winning Civil Court Cases." *Law & Society Review* 9:293–306.

    1983   *The Public Ordering of Private Relations: 30 Years of Civil Litigation in the United States.* Unpublished manuscript [on file with the author].

Wasby, Stephen L.
    1970   *The Impact of the United States Supreme Court: Some Perspectives.* Homewood, Ill.: Dorsey Press.

Watson, Richard A.
    1975   "Staffing the Courts—Where Can We Go From Here?" Paper delivered at the annual meeting of the American Political Science Association, San Francisco, September 2–5.

Weber, Max
    1954   *Max Weber on Law in Economy and Society.* Edited by M. Rheinstein. Cambridge,
    [1922]   Mass.: Harvard University Press.

    1958   *From Max Weber: Essays in Sociology.* Edited by H. H. Gerth and C. W. Mills. New
    [1906–24] York: Oxford University Press.

Wechsler, Herbert
    1959   "Toward Neutral Principles of Constitutional Law." *Harvard Law Review* 73:1–35.

Weinberg, Joanna K.
    1983   "The Judicial Adjunct and Public Law Remedies." *Yale Law and Policy Review* 1:367ff.

Wenner, Manfred W.; Wenner, Lettie M.; and Flango, Victor Eugene
    1978   "Austrian and Swiss Judges: A Comparative Study." *Comparative Politics* 10:499–517.

Wessel, Milton R.
    1976   *The Rule of Reason: A New Approach to Corporate Litigation.* Reading, Mass.: Addison-Wesley.

Wetter, J. Gillis
    1960   *The Styles of Appellate Judicial Opinions: A Case Study in Comparative Law.* Leyden: Sijthoff.

Whitford, William C.
    1968   "Law and Consumer Transaction: A Case Study of the Automobile Warranty." *Wisconsin Law Review* 1968:1006–98.

Wicker, A. W.
    1969   "Attitudes vs. Actions: The Relations of Verbal and Overt Behavioral Responses to Attitudes Objects." *Journal of Social Issues* 25:41–78.

Will, Hubert L.; Merhige, Robert R.; and Rubin, Alvin B.
    1977   "The Role of the Judge in the Settlement Process." *Federal Rules Decisions* 75:203–36.

Wilson, James Q.
 1968   *Varieties of Police Behavior: The Management of Law and Order in Eight Communities.*
         Cambridge, Mass.: Harvard University Press.

Wimberley, Howard
 1973   "Legal Evolution: One Further Step." *American Journal of Sociology* 79:78–83.

Wittgenstein, Ludwig
 1958   *Philosophical Investigations.* Translated by G. E. M. Simpson. New York: Mac-
         millan.

Witty, Cathie J.
 1978   "Disputing Issues in Shehaam, a Multi-religious Village in Lebanon." In *The Dis-
         puting Process—Law in Ten Societies,* edited by L. Nader and H. Todd. New York:
         Columbia University Press.

Wold, John T.
 1978   "Going Through the Motions: The Monotony of Appellate Court Decision-
         Making." *Judicature* 62:58–65.

Woll, Peter
 1960   "Informal Administrative Adjudication: Summary of Findings." *UCLA Law Review*
         7:436–61.

Woodard, Calvin
 1972   "The Limits of Legal Realism: An Historical Perspective." In *New Directions in
         Legal Education,* edited by H. L. Packer and T. Ehrlich. New York: McGraw-
         Hill.

Wright, J. Skelly
 1962   "The Pretrial Conference." *Federal Rules Decisions* 28:141–58.

Yale Law Journal
 1970   "The New Public Interest Lawyers." *Yale Law Journal* 79:1069–1152.

Yankelovich, Skelly and White, Inc.
 1978   *The Public Image of Courts.* Williamsburg, Va.: National Center for State Courts.

Yeazell, Stephen C.
 1977   "Group Litigation and Social Context: Toward a History of the Class Action."
         Columbia Law Review 77:866–96.

Yngvesson, Barbara, and Hennessey, Patricia
 1975   "Small Claims, Complex Disputes: A Review of the Small Claims Literature." *Law
         & Society Review* 9:219–74.

Yngvesson, Barbara, and Mather, Lynn
 1983   "Courts, Moots, and the Disputing Process." In *Empirical Theories About Courts,*
         edited by K. Boyum and L. Mather. New York: Longman.

Zablocki, Benjamin
 1971   *The Joyful Community: An Account of the Bruderhof, a Communal Movement Now in
         Its Third Generation.* Baltimore: Penguin Books.

Zald, Mayer N., and Hair, Feather Davis
 1972   "The Social Control of General Hospitals." In *Organization Research on Health
         Institutions,* edited by B. Georgopoulos. Madison: Institute for Social Research,
         University of Michigan.

Zeisel, Hans; Kalven, Harry, Jr.; and Buchholz, Bernard
 1959   *Delay in Court.* Boston: Little, Brown.

Zile, Zigurds L.
 1970   *Ideas and Forces in Soviet Legal History: Statutes, Decisions and Other Materials on the
         Development and Processes of Soviet Law.* 2nd ed. Madison, Wis.: College Printing
         & Publishing.

～ 5 ～

LEGISLATION

David R. Mayhew

Yale University

Students of governments and of what they do apply both functional and structural typologies. "Rule-making," "rule application," and "rule adjudication" are contemporary terms designating some basic and familiar functions (see Almond and Powell 1966, chap. 6), and of course legislatures, executive or administrative organs, and courts make up a familiar set of structures. An early lesson in most courses in comparative politics teaches that functions do not reside according to any neat one-to-one pattern in structures.

Legislatures, for example, are commonly regarded as the bodies most responsible for rule-making, at least in constitutional states; but in fact they also act in other capacities not readily captured by the basic triad of functions; they commonly deal with citizen grievances, express public opinion, and oversee the administration of laws. General rule-making, the province of legislatures, is also exercised by executive officials, courts, and administrative agencies. In the case of civil rights regulations in the United States, the Supreme Court ordered in the mid-1950s that school systems be desegregated "with all deliberate speed"; the presidency initiated in the enactment of the Public Accommodations Act of 1964 and the Voting Rights Act of 1965; the Equal Employment Opportunity Commission and other administrative units led the development of national rules on affirmative action.

Since institutions evolve, and some new ones are even intentionally created, the question of the functions to be located in each structure is a live and practical one. American regulatory agencies, commonly mandated both to make general rules and to apply them and adjudicate disputes about them, are a multifunctional innovation of the industrial era, variously reshaped decade by decade. The presidency of the French Fifth Republic is an institution rich in functional capacity, designed to perform tasks not very well accomplished by any of the institutions of the Fourth Republic. The elected transnational parliament of the European Economic Community is a new structure in search of consequential functions, in some respects an interesting analogue to the fledgling United States Congress of the 1790s.

Common sense, ancient wisdom, and contemporary scholarship supply at least a number of considerations for any general statement on the appropriate structural location of functions. Within the context of the United States, such considerations turn, for example, on the capacities of legislatures, courts, and administrative agencies as makers of general rules. (For sources for this passage, see Horowitz 1977, chaps. 2, 7; Lorch 1969, chaps. 1, 2; Shapiro 1968, chap. 1; Huntington 1965.) Nine distinctions stand out.

1. In many policy areas, agency personnel are trained as professionals, whereas judges and legislators are not.

2. Agency personnel deal in their policy areas as specialists; so, to an important extent, do many legislatures; except in specialized courts, judges deal as generalists.

3. Bargaining and compromise are routine and legitimate in decision-making among formally equal legislators, but not—or not to a great extent—in agency hierarchies or among judges—though agencies bargain and compromise in dealing with each other, judges participate with other court personnel in plea bargaining, and juries commonly proceed by compromise.

4. Agencies and pertinent sets of legislators often build close relations with outside client groups; courts do not.

5. Agencies give sustained attention to what goes on in their policy areas; legislators, by comparison, give episodic attention; court attention is on an ad hoc basis.

6. Agencies and legislatures are capable of taking the initiative in policy areas; courts wait for cases to be brought.

7. Agencies can generate studies that turn up elaborate social information; legislators can do so as well, although their constructions of reality rely heavily on what they learn from constituents and interest groups; courts ordinarily have before them only the facts of cases, which may supply poor guides to general social realities.

8. Agencies and legislatures commonly set out plans for the future, whereas courts ordinarily render judgments on situations of the past.

9. Most legislatures, like elected executives but unlike agency personnel and judges—in practice, even elected judges—serve in a relation of formal accountability to outside electorates.

In the eye of publics, this last circumstance confers legitimacy on legislators; it also makes them especially interesting to students of democracy and representation. The term "to legislate," it should be noted, is not, in ordinary Western parlance, an exact synonym of the functional term "to make rules." "Legislate" and its noun form "legislation" carry a connotation of structure as well as functions; to legislate is to make rules in a formal process, where one or more of the approving bodies constitute a "legislature" and where at least one of the bodies of the legislature is an elected assembly.

The actual role a legislature plays in legislating may be small or large. The role of the

British Parliament is relatively small; in British lawmaking, cabinet and civil service carry most of the burden. The roles of postwar German and Italian parliaments are somewhat larger, those of the Swedish and Dutch parliaments substantially larger, and those of the United States Congress a great deal larger. These and other legislatures may be arranged along a continuum running from "arenas"—the British case—through "transformative assemblies"—legislatures that do a great deal of instigating on their own, the extreme example being the uniquely influential United States Congress (Polsby 1975; on the British case, see also Walkland 1968).

Congress warrants close inspection. For anyone interested in what happens when a legislature is established to write laws, freed from the obligation of sustaining a government, supplied an electoral base, and accorded considerable influence, the United States Congress furnishes the most rewarding testing ground. Having marshaled nine generalities, I shall proceed by delving into particularities, past and present, of the United States Congress, following what might be called a logic of the best-developed case.

Such logic would lead anyone with an interest in cabinet government to take a close look, covering past and present, at the Westminster model in Britain; those interested in decentralized federalism to inspect Canada; students of "consociational" politics to examine the Netherlands; those concerned with the functions of ombudsmen to track them down in Scandinavia; researchers on the evolution from authoritarian to democratic institutions to examine contemporary Spain; and so on. Studying a best-developed case risks identifying particularities that are no more than idiosyncrasies. Nevertheless, anyone concerned with what happens when a representative national assembly—or, more precisely, a two-part assembly—is allowed to function as a specialized legislative institution should ponder what the United States Congress has done and become over two centuries. (Unless specified otherwise, I shall use the term "Congress" to refer to both national houses—the constitutional and coequal partnership of the Senate and the House of Representatives.)

I shall write about legislation by writing about legislating—the process that generates the product. This course, natural to a political scientist, is, I trust, a useful one. In principle, the product is anything written formally into resolutions or laws—budgetary resolutions, laws authorizing expenditures or appropriating money, regulatory statutes covering corporate or individual behavior, laws prescribing the structure or functions of the branches of government, resolutions declaring judgments on events of the day, laws on pork barrel projects up through important matters of state. All these are formally enactments of Congress, although, of course, in recent decades, the presidency and the agencies have become increasingly important as suppliers of bills and ideas to Capitol Hill.

I shall frame my discussion of congressional process in a fashion that implies answers, or at least shapes speculation about possible answers, to two general questions of interest to students of law and society: What is the nature of whatever ends up on the statute books? How much legitimacy should be assigned to whatever emanates from legislative processes and ends up on the statute books? I shall set out briefly some major kinds of scholarly thinking on what congressional legislating amounts to or ought to amount to and indicate where fuller statements may be found.

The essay is in three parts. First, I shall consider some theories, assertions, accounts, prescriptions, and the like, in which Congress appears as a *passive* institution—a place where the influence of outside individuals, groups, and institutions is felt and recorded.

The second section will offer a consideration of a number of scholarly organizing concepts in which Congress figures as an *active* institution—a set of members who make their own specifiable imprint on the law. Most of the treatments covered in these parts offer at least a grain of truth; it should be noted that the distinction between *active* and *passive* is sometimes blurred. The third part of the article consists of a piece of speculation on a subject insufficiently covered in scholarship—the impact of public opinion on congressional lawmaking.

CONGRESS AS A PASSIVE INSTITUTION

A vast amount of scholarship dealing with the United States Congress during the last century focuses on the outside forces that are said to influence congressional lawmaking, for better or worse, or that might usefully be induced to do so. This concern is not surprising, given that Congress was set up as a representative institution and that the term "representation" ordinarily implies external considerations. Most of the pertinent writing is laced in one way or another with normative notions; views on what the relations of influence are usually underlie views on whether or to what degree congressional lawmaking should be considered legitimate.

The question of what *influence* is—or what *power* is—is a source of unending confusion and controversy in the scholarship. A good state-of-the-art definition of a power relation, which I shall rely on in framing this section, states that a "power relation, actual or potential, is an actual or potential causal relation between the preferences of an actor regarding an outcome and the outcome itself" (Nagel 1975, p. 29).[1]

This definition casts a big enough net to include relations of anticipated reaction—that is, relations in which A has a preference about an outcome and B acts to achieve the outcome because A wants it, but in which A makes no effort to induce B to act and, indeed, may never know that B has acted. Relations of this sort, though in principle detectable, present obvious empirical difficulties of a high order. Still, it is not possible to deal adequately with the subject of influence on legislatures without taking relations of anticipated reaction into account. An example is provided by the hypothetical instance in which a Mississippi congressman voted against a civil rights bill in 1950; hardly anyone back home noticed; nevertheless, people back home almost certainly would have noticed and erupted if he had voted the other way; he knew this and acted so as to minimize the probability of eruption; therefore, the (all white) electorate's preference caused the congressman's action.

Descriptive and prescriptive scholarship identifies four external actors or sets of actors as influencers of congressional activity.

Political Parties

The pertinent writing on parties is prescriptive and could defensibly be situated under either or both of the "active" and "passive" rubrics. I have in mind the "responsible parties" literature, the tradition of writing on Congress that has had the longest life and probably the greatest renown. Its central message is that Congress does not work very well and that it would work a great deal better if cohesive, programmatic, well-organized, electorally competitive, national parties existed and controlled its activities. The argu-

---

[1] Nagel draws no distinction between "power" and "influence," and I shall make no effort to do so either.

ment maintains that the American electorate's preferences are not properly expressed in Congress but that the existence of strong parties could provide such expression. Alternately, the claim is made that the electorate's preferences are not very good anyway, but that better ones would be brought to bear if programmatic parties existed to generate them.

The founder of the tradition was Woodrow Wilson (1956), who discovered what he took to be British party government in the writing of Walter Bagehot and more or less advocated its American adoption in his 1885 work, *Congressional Government*—though without considering that the British electorate of the middle or late nineteenth century encompassed a much narrower stratum of society than did the American electorate. (For a general treatment of Wilson's views on parties, see Ranney 1954, chap. 3.) What Wilson urged—at least implicitly—was no less than an elitist counterrevolution, an abandonment of the Jacksonian mode of politics—with its localism and individualism, its corruption, its incoherence, its messiness, and its explosions of such public sentiment as the anti-Masonic movement, the antibank crusade, Know-Nothingism, abolitionism, the Greenback movement, and the Ku Klux Klan. Better the ritualized combat of a Gladstone and a Disraeli over broad "principles" and overall "programs" than such an unorganized free-for-all.

On the specifics, Wilson urged only a strengthening of parties within Congress itself, but subsequent writers have called for a forging of extraparliamentary party organizations—national and local—capable of keeping members of Congress in line. This recommendation was formalized in the American Political Science Association report, *Toward a More Responsible Party System* (1950), an audacious venture in Anglophilia. (For a retrospective reflection on the committee's statement, see Kirkpatrick 1971.) James MacGregor Burns, one of the leading contemporary exponents of the "responsible parties" cause, has urged a building of more influential extraparliamentary parties. (See, for example, Burns 1963, pp. 325–32.)

But none of this sort of exhortation has ever had much effect. The only American parties with a record of producing voting discipline in assemblies are local machines—such as Chicago's Democratic party organization under Mayor Richard Daley, with its servile board of aldermen. These are hardly the sorts of parties Wilson and his successors have had in mind. Members of Congress remain resolutely individualistic, very little influenced by party leaders inside Congress or by organizations properly called party organizations outside. Party loyalty on roll calls is loose by European standards, and during the twentieth century it has gradually grown looser. Such policy differences as there are between congressional Democrats and Republicans—and the two parties do have their distinctive centers of gravity on many issues—result, for the most part, from differences in personal views or ideologies and in the kinds of electoral constituencies members of either party must satisfy. The combination of Madisonian and Jacksonian traditions probably ruled out a long time ago a building of "party government" at the American national level and thereby ruled out the sort of lawmaking that might flow from it—arguably, a lawmaking more influenced than ours by experts and ideologies, more given to "planning," more abrupt and sweeping in its measures.

Interest Groups

While, in the United States, extraparliamentary parties do not exert much influence, interest groups do. Such groups range from tightly organized trade associations representing single industries through "public interest" groups, such as Common Cause, and mobilization of much of the general public by mail or media, such as the Moral Majority. Organized groups plainly wield a good deal of power in Congress and in lower-level assemblies. A generation ago, this circumstance was a cause of celebration among political scientists. "Group theorists" described and applauded a political world in which all people are free to coalesce in groups to further their interests and in which public policy is legitimately a resultant of group pressures. The classic statement of this brand of pluralism is contained in David B. Truman's *The Governmental Process* (1960). The heady claims of group theory are understandable, given the development of farmers in interest groups, finally, in the 1920s and industrial workers in the 1930s. For a time during the 1940s and 1950s, it seemed to some observers that interest groups, in place of parties, could offer a comprehensive set of linkages between the public and government. But major political problems since 1960 have not been comparably "solved" by the mobilization of interest groups of the farmer or labor kind, and political scientists, like most others, have retreated to a commonplace view of politics. (For a statement of disenchantment with "group theory" pluralism, see Lowi 1969.) This argument holds that some sets of people are better organized than others, that people in general are better organized in some of their roles than in others, and that better organization is likely to win better representation. The claim is certainly true for congressional representation. Minimum wage legislation, for example, a congressional staple, favors unionized adults over unorganized teenagers (whose source of jobs diminishes). Teachers have greater influence on education matters than do students or parents. Unorganized farm workers exercise little influence. In general people are better represented in their roles as producers than in their positions as consumers, as in the case of the tariff over most of American history—although the gap on producer and consumer matters has probably narrowed in the last two decades, with the mushrooming of public-interest groups on and around Capitol Hill.

The marked responsiveness of American legislative assemblies to organized groups raises chronic questions about the adequacy of ordinary lawmaking as a recourse for the relatively unorganized. Often, courts take up the slack, as in the case of general rule-making on racial matters during recent decades.

The scholarship on interest groups is only episodically an improvement on the American muckraking tradition—a genre in which some sets of people accuse other sets of constituting "special interests" (without defining very clearly what the label means), with the allegation that these "interests" get their way by rewarding or punishing politicians. (For an example of this genre, see Green et al. 1972, the flagship book of Ralph Nader's 1972 Congress project.) This scholarship does not cite much evidence or seem to realize that there are other ways of exercising influence—for example, by engaging in one-on-one persuasion and by expending resources to shape public opinion, which thereupon supplies a context in which politicians operate. In surprisingly few instances have scholars looked closely at the actual transactions between interest groups and politicians.[2] Such studies as exist suggest that persuasion—adducing information and making a case in Capitol Hill processes—is a more common means of exerting influence than is the offer of rewards or threats of punishment. Nor are students very sensitive to relations of anticipated reaction; the image of "pressure" is so strong that the influence of groups is

[2] The major study in which these transactions are inspected is Bauer et al. 1963, a study of the making of foreign trade policy in the mid-1950s.

ordinarily thought to be detectable only in actual transactions, though there is no good reason to suppose that a member of Congress from Oklahoma needs to receive any actual message from oil companies in order to be inspired to champion their interests. A final deficiency in the scholarship is its hangover image from the past that interest groups are private-sector organizations making claims on government; in fact, the world of interest groups is increasingly part of the public sector itself, with such organizations as mayors' and teachers' groups cutting a considerable swath on Capitol Hill (Beer 1976).

The President

Presidential influence on Congress is one of the hardiest concerns of American politics and the subject of a great many treatments, both positive and normative. Writing in the former vein—just how much and in what ways do presidents influence Congress—is rife with the problems and considerations inherent in discussing "power." Richard E. Neustadt's *Presidential Power* (1976), the standard analysis on the subject, makes the general case that presidents are most likely to be successful on Capitol Hill in two circumstances. The first is when their standing with the general public is high; members of Congress are then likely to see presidential claims as legitimate or to calculate that they themselves can profit, rather than lose, politically by going along with the White House. The second is when they build good "professional reputations" in the community of Washington politicians—that is, when they have records as forgers of good relations of reciprocal benefit with other political actors. In dealing with legislating, a sensible recourse is to note that president and Congress commonly weigh in at different stages of the process—initiation, information gathering, interest aggregation, and so on. (For a good discussion which picks up earlier scholarship, see Price 1972, chaps. 1, 8.)

Two hundred years of wrestling with the question of the matters on which presidents should exercise influence over Congress yields some clues to the inherent capabilities of representative assemblies. A simple distinction may be helpful. In a role envisioned in the Constitution and first fully exemplified by Lincoln as war leader, a president acts in the manner of a Roman consul—a manager, an executive, a doer of the sorts of tasks that seem to require quick action, centralized information gathering, day-to-day calculation, sometimes secrecy. The obvious examples are foreign policy in all eras of crisis management and economic policy since the mid-1930s—in the latter case, the kind of policy making that requires continuous watching of exchange rates, discount rates, price levels, and unemployment statistics. In playing consul, a president is not, strictly speaking, influencing Congress; rather, he is influencing events. The strengthening or weakening of the presidency as a managerial office—its weakening on foreign-policy matters since the early 1970s, for example—reflects judgments (popular and congressional) on the replacement of ordinary lawmaking processes by managerial processes in specified policy realms.

But many presidents take on a second role, not envisioned in the Constitution and first exemplified by Jackson. In this capacity they act like Roman tribunes. They speak, or claim to speak, for unorganized people not well enough represented in congressional lawmaking—either because too many members of Congress are hostile to what are claimed to be their interests or because congressional processes, for whatever reasons, fail to generate laws promoting what are claimed to be their interests. One thinks of Franklin Roosevelt and his "forgotten men" or Richard Nixon and his "silent majority." In this latter role, presidents do their work by trying to influence what Congress does in passing laws. All welfare-state builders are examples, but so is Ronald Reagan—a striking example, in the early part of his presidency, of a leader acting as tribune, rather than consul, in his all-consuming evocation of public opinion to foster a legislative program.

American views on whether the presidency or Congress should influence events, and on whether or how much presidents should influence congressional lawmaking, are based largely on perceptions of the country's managerial, as opposed to lawmaking, needs and, separately, perceptions of how well the unorganized are represented in Congress. One of the most conspicuous pieces of writing on Congress in recent decades, which argues that Congress should more or less give up trying to pass laws and spend its energies instead on oversight and casework, was written at a high-water mark of cold-war welfare-state liberalism (Huntington 1965).

Public Opinion

A century ago, James Bryce wrote of American legislators, "There is no country whose representatives are more dependent on public opinion, more ready to trim their sails to the last breath of it" (1959, vol. 1, p. 42). It does seem a reasonable assertion that public opinion exerts a greater influence on Congress than any other factor. This is an easier case to believe than to demonstrate, both because the tie between the public and members of Congress is largely (as in the case of the exemplary Mississippi district) a relation of anticipated reactions and because it is hard to decide what counts as a manifestation of public opinion. One study, based on interviews, conducted in the late 1960s in which a sizable number of House members were asked about the influences they felt in voting on a set of important issues, concluded (using some equations) that the perception or anticipation of constituency sentiment far outweighed interest groups, party leaders in Congress, and the presidential administration as an influence on roll call voting (Kingdon 1973, pp. 16–23 and, more generally, chaps. 1, 2).[3] The work's elaborate rendition of interview material makes the case more persuasively than any bare statement of it can. Again, however, the topic of public opinion has been insufficiently explored in the scholarship. It warrants more thinking and more scrutiny.

CONGRESS AS AN ACTIVE INSTITUTION

The next task is to consider Congress as a relatively autonomous institution, to ponder ways in which it makes its own predictable and distinctive imprint on the law. A fruitful approach takes a series of "organizing concepts" often said to capture processes, propensities, or attitudes of the institution or its members. The reason for treating these, once again, is to fuel speculation on the strengths and weaknesses of representative assemblies as generators of laws.

---

[3] Kingdon sets out another equation (p. 20) in which he adds two other causal agents to the four specified here—that is, fellow congressmen (who supply "cues" on how to vote) and staff members (who supply information and advice). The four-variable equation is more interesting than the six-variable, for the reason that the two additional agents could supply a causal relation without its being a "power relation" (in Nagel's sense): we have no decisive reason to suppose that colleagues or staff members care how their cue-receivers vote.

Particularism

There is a well-known legislators' propensity, probably detectable wherever members of assemblies have legislative powers and district roots, to pass out governmental benefits in small packets pleasing to districts or to groups or individuals within them. Such actions can cause—indeed, do cause, in the case of Congress—three kinds of "distortion" in the legislative product and one kind of distortion in members' activity.

Overspending   First, representative assemblies may "overspend" resources on some governmental programs—either rewarding some government programs (particularistic) over others (nonparticularistic) or spending more on some than the private sector would spend (on matters about which private-sector transactions supply a sensible standard). In fostering the Army Engineers' water projects, such as dams, for example, Congress works with a discount rate well under the market rate, thereby supplying more projects than the private market would. (See Ferejohn 1974, chap. 2.)

Inefficiency   Second, assemblies may inspire geographically inefficient allocation of resources within programs. The interesting argument on this matter has recently been set out along with some compelling evidence (Arnold 1979, especially chap. 9). The pertinent point is that for each program, its creators and sustainers—either legislative leaders or the heads of agencies—must earn and keep the support of a majority coalition in Congress. (Agency leaders succeed largely by anticipating the reactions of members of Congress; that is to say, members influence agencies.) On a program offering collections of local goods or services, the way to nurture such a coalition is to spread funds thinly around many districts and states, often creating what can be regarded as inefficiencies. A program to deal with poverty in Appalachia develops over time an extraordinarily broad geographic definition of Appalachia.[4] A Model Cities program designed at the outset as a means of renovating a small set of urban disaster areas ends up as a source of modest and inconsequential funding for no fewer than 151 cities (*Public Interest* 1980). The National Endowments for the Arts and the Humanities start out, unsurprisingly, as patrons of New York City but end up, just as unsurprisingly, as funders of local ventures all over the country (Friedman 1979).

Design Bias   A third kind of "distortion" affects basic program design. Congress seems to prefer programs that offer geographically divisible benefits to other kinds, even if the former are not obviously more efficient. In times of economic downturn, for example, members of Congress reach instinctively for "accelerated public-works programs" rather than other sorts of macroeconomic levers—subsidies to the districts turn up as a way of dealing with water pollution. More generally, Congress prefers categorical grant programs to state and local aid that takes the form of generalized revenue sharing (the elected officials can claim credit for individual grants even if bureaucrats pass them out).

Casework   A fourth "distortion"—in congressional activity rather than directly, in legislative product—occurs in the extraordinary amounts of time and energy members

---

[4] By 1980 nearly 85 percent of the country's population lived in "distressed areas" eligible for federal aid. See *Public Interest* 1980.

spend on casework as a result of inducement from their home electorates (servicing constituents' requests) as compared with actually making laws. Emphasis on casework may reasonably be thought of as a nonstatutory brand of particularism. A survey conducted by the Obey Commission, a panel created by the House in the mid-1970s to study its internal organization, revealed that members of Congress and voters place approximately equal value on the legislative and service roles, that members themselves believe that the former role ought to be far more important than the latter, but that they admit to being induced by constituents' pressure to spend much more time and energy in the latter activity than they think they should (Cavanagh 1978).

These claims should not be taken as a judgment that members of Congress do nothing but build gratuitous dams and chase lost Social Security checks. In fact public-works programs—the old "pork barrel" standbys, with members of Congress retaining substantial discretion over item-by-item allocation—now take up only about 2 percent of the federal budget (Arnold 1978). The major growth in contemporary federal budgets has been in transfer programs—such as Medicare—rather than programs allocating benefits by discretionary or seemingly discretionary decision. And modern congressional offices, bulging with staff members, surely devote more resources to both legislating and casework than did the offices of a generation ago. Nevertheless, particularism is a propensity to watch for and wonder how to correct for.

Specialization

House and Senate members are organized into well over a hundred specialized committees and subcommittees in each house, where most of the essential work of legislating is done.[5] It is probable that no contemporary legislature can make a significant impact on the law without a division of labor to work out adequate methods, and in practice this requires committees. But delegation to committees creates its own sorts of problems, or is thought to do so. Three lines of criticism are worth setting out.

Special Interests   The first argues as follows. For electoral or other reasons, members of Congress ordinarily join committees dealing with programs in which they have a special interest (farm belt members, for example, join the agricultural committees);[6] committees ordinarily carry a great deal of weight on the floor; ergo, the congressional legislative product can come to resemble an unrepresentative collection of committee-centered programs. They may be unrepresentative in the senses both that, if asked, the general public might not approve the enacted individual programs and that, in a hypothetical world where all members of Congress are equally informed and equally influential on all matters, congressional floor majorities might also disapprove. This argument has a ring of truth. Following more or less the same line of reasoning, one scholar posits a budgetary effect—systematic "overspending" on committee programs (Niskanen 1971, chap. 14).

---

[5] For sophisticated treatments of what goes on in sets of House and Senate committees see Fenno 1973 and Price 1972. Fenno covers both chambers but looks more closely at the House. Price concentrates on the Senate. On the building of the House committee system over time, see Polsby 1968.

[6] For a definitive analysis of how Democrats get to be members of committees in the House, see Shepsle 1978. On agriculture in particular, see Jones 1961.

Committee Control   The second critique is a time-specific complaint often lodged by liberals against Congress from the late 1930s through the late 1960s. The argument went as follows: Democrats ordinarily controlled the Congress; committee chairmen (all Democrats) were chosen by seniority; committee chairmen had a great deal of influence; southern Democrats were chairmen in large numbers because they had safe seats and remained in Congress longer than northern Democrats; most southerners were conservatives; ergo, the current form of committee specialization resulted in Congress being controlled by a conservative oligarchy unrepresentative of the membership.

At one time this claim held a slight kernel of truth. Most of the time over these decades, however, the liberals' real problem lay in the fact that they lacked floor majorities, even though they made up a majority of the majority party; in fact, southern committee leaders tended to be fairly representative of cross-party floor majorities in their areas of specialty. But no matter, the argument has become nothing more than historical curiosity now. Congress no longer has a southern tilt.[7]

Division   The third argument makes a persuasive case. Dividing up power among a multitude of committees makes legislating difficult, if not impossible, in the more complicated policy areas. Authorizing dams is easy enough, but arriving at a plan on the order of a congressional "energy policy" is extraordinarily difficult—indeed, more difficult now than it was a generation ago, because of "democratizing" reforms of the 1970s that weakened parent committees and strengthened more than a hundred subcommittees in the House (making the House more like the Senate). (For an account of the reforming of the House in the 1970s, see Dodd and Oppenheimer 1977.) Having legions of cooks stirring around makes for an unusual meal, a late meal, or no meal at all, even if most are working from more or less the same recipe. A few years ago, Jeffrey L. Pressman and Aaron B. Wildavsky wrote a book entitled *Implementation,* in which they pointed out the difficulty of carrying through a federal program that has to survive some seventy "decision points" between its statutory authorization and its final realization (Pressman and Wildavsky 1973). A still unwritten work, *Enactment,* could point out the difficulty of getting out of Congress anything worthy of the name of "energy policy" or anything of the sort, as long as literally scores of committees and subcommittees have a place in its making.

Careerism

Service in an assembly can fit into a lifetime career in many different ways. Members may serve a term or two before withdrawing to private life; this pattern is common in many American city councils and state legislatures. (See Prewitt 1970, pp. 5–17.) Membership in a legislature may be a preface to or a concomitant of holding a higher public position, as in the case of the eighteenth-century British House of Commons, a producer of cabinet members, generals, admirals, and bishops. Municipal and state legislative service may be a part-time occupation, an adjunct to a private career supplying a better and steadier source of income. The typical modern member of Congress, however, is what has been called a fully professionalized legislator, members ordinarily devote full time to their positions, and they aim to pursue lifelong careers on Capitol Hill—

---

[7] That the southern advantage would erode away was evident already in 1965. See Wolfinger and Heifetz 1965.

although, of course, many House members aim to abandon the House and move up to the Senate.[8]

Spending a full career in Congress requires multiple reelection, and this need shapes activities on Capitol Hill. Elsewhere I have argued that members seeking reelection—whatever the length of their term—are induced to engage relentlessly in three specifiable sorts of activity: *advertising*—"any effort to disseminate one's name among constituents in such a fashion as to create a favorable image but in messages having little or no issue content"; *credit claiming*—"acting so as to generate a belief in a relevant political actor (or actors) that one is personally responsible for causing the government, or some unit thereof, to do something that the actor (or actors) considers desirable"; and *position taking*—"the public enunciation of a judgmental statement (which may take the form of a roll call vote) on anything likely to be of interest to political actors" (Mayhew 1974, pp. 49–77). Since members seeking reelection spend much time and energy engaging in these activities, the effects on the legislative product merit consideration.

One set of inferences is obvious. The need to "claim credit" can be expected to generate patterns of particularism. Its further effect of "clientelism"—working to achieve legislative ends in committees under the alert scrutiny of interest groups—has been discussed under "specialization."

Additionally, the politics of position taking has its legislative consequences. (The logic of this is set out in Mayhew 1974, pp. 61–73.) On broad matters, where no single member of Congress can believably claim credit for passing a law or for achieving its effect, the members' sense of craftsmanship or organizational incentives, rather than electoral considerations, must be relied on to yield workable laws. Where the electoral reward is for issue positions rather than programmatic effects, craftsmanship and internal incentives may have limited power. The contrast between the federal tax code and federal statutes regulating industry is illustrative. The tax code presents a history of the painstaking creation of precise, elaborate provisions—"loopholes" to some; this result is what one would expect in a process rife with particularism and clientelism. But regulatory statutes, until the mid-1960s, after which time they were put together by congressional staff members, have been notoriously brief, vague, and studded with internal contradictions. They are best considered as emanations of an amorphous public opinion rather than as exercises in instrumental rationality geared to produce programmatic effects.

The general distinction here is important. Making laws on matters on which members cannot easily claim individual credit can be a breathtakingly haphazard activity. One knowledgeable scholar writes, "Within the Congress words are equated with deeds. Votes represent final acts. There is a concern with administration, but it is focused primarily on those elements which directly affect constituency interests or committee jurisdictions. Legislative proposals seldom are debated from the viewpoint of their administrative feasibility" (Seidman 1970, pp. 65–66).

Coalition Formation

One line of theorizing in contemporary political science gives an arresting answer to the old question of the sort of winning coalitions likely to form where decisions are made by majority rule. William H. Riker has put forth what he calls a size principle, the gist of

---

[8]Congressional service was not always so "professionalized." For a treatment of the evolution toward "professionalization," see Price 1975; and Polsby 1968.

which is that "minimal winning coalitions" are likely to form in assemblies and other settings; people putting together victories will try to make them as narrow as possible (51 percent is the ideal under majority rule) so as to maximize per capita benefits on the winning side (Riker 1962). In a politics of dam building, for example, one might expect outcomes in which narrow majorities of legislators team up to supply dams for their own districts but impose tax burdens on all districts—or, indeed, merely on the districts of excluded minorities. Such a vision is less than edifying, and if members of assemblies routinely behaved as it predicts, it might reasonably be wondered whether assemblies are appropriate bodies for making decisions—or, if they are, whether they ought to make them by majority rule.

The primary objection to this "size principle" theory is that it generates a grotesque misconstruction of congressional reality on matters where it might be thought most directly to apply—that is, on what are often called "distributive" benefits: goods such as dams or block grants, which can be ladled out in piecemeal fashion, district by district. Benefits of this sort do indeed impose diffuse costs on taxpayers everywhere, but they need not of necessity be apportioned in a way that arouses hostility among excluded minorities anywhere. Processes can be arranged so as to allow every district its share of distributive goods at one time or another; impressive evidence suggests that Congress more or less does so arrange them. A statement of a member of the House Public Works Committee of the 1960s renders the spirit of the politics: "Any time any member of the Committee wants something, or wants to get a bill out, we get it out for him. . . . Makes no difference—Republican or Democrat. We are all Americans when it comes to that" (Murphy 1968, p. 23). (For a pertinent treatment of distributive politics on the House Interior Committee of the 1960s, see Fenno 1973, chaps. 3, 4; see also the discussion in Mayhew 1974, pp. 87–91.)

It seems likely that politicians who have to deal with each other over time find it more advantageous to devise long-term, "universalistic" standards of interaction than to exploit each other at the instant. (For a statement of this logic, see Barry 1965, pp. 255–56.) Bureaucrats, too, follow a logic of universalism; on some distributive federal programs, there is decisive evidence that, in doling out benefits so as to build congressional support, the aim of federal agencies is, not to service narrow majorities, but to spread goods around widely enough to silence all opposition (Arnold 1979).

Distributive politics poses its problems, of course, as the earlier discussion of particularism suggests. But injustice or idiosyncrasy brought on by the size principle is scarcely one of them.

It seems more probable that coalition builders try to squeeze out narrow majorities primarily on matters where conflict is unavoidable—on issues where two sides anchored in public opinion do battle on Capitol Hill and where "half a loaf" strategies can supply just enough votes to make one position or another prevail. Surely this happens sometimes (Stephen K. Bailey's classic account [1950] of the passage of the Employment Act of 1946 comes to mind), but how is this situation to be interpreted? Indeed, beyond the familiar ruminations about majority rule and minority rights, what considerations can be brought to bear on any situations in which congressional majorities vote down vocal minorities?

One good question, in line with concerns about coalition building and about the imprints assemblies distinctively make, is whether congressional decision processes tend to exacerbate or to diminish conflict naturally existing in the larger society. A reasonable answer suggests that ordinarily they diminish it. In the language of Capitol Hill, members trying to get a bill passed normally seek to "accommodate" the views of prospective opponents—that is, to shape legislation in ways that will head off objections and, if not to foreclose opposition, at least to reduce its intensity. Ordinarily, accommodation is a tactical necessity. There are in Congress so many dispersed decision points that legislation of any complexity can hardly be passed without it. The Senate, which operates procedurally by "unanimous consent" and where any inflamed Senator can hold up a bill, raises accommodation to a high art.[9] Thus, any image of Congress as a place where majorities routinely and wantonly trample on vocal minorities in passing bills is at variance with reality.

The need for "accommodation" nevertheless raises its own obvious difficulty: blocking bills is easier than passing them. On balance it is probably true that processes on Capitol Hill display a built-in bias for the status quo. Anyone can make up a list of issues on which the public—at least as its views are captured in opinion polls—pushes one way and Congress, by inaction, pushes the other. One such is gun control. Another is national health insurance, a public favorite but so far a congressional casualty to interest-group opposition and the sheer difficulty of maneuvering a bill through. School busing, affirmative action, and school prayer are all matters on which the Supreme Court or any agency handed down rulings that were unpopular with a majority of the public in the 1970s but which Congress did not overturn during that decade. The tendency toward stasis produces a demonstrable effect in the politics of the public sector; federal agencies and programs are hard to create, but once in place and bolstered by clients, they are very difficult to dismantle. (See Wilson 1975 and Kaufman 1976.)

A distinction is in order, however. No public majority or even vocal minority can now be said to be permanently barred from prevailing on Capitol Hill—permanently in the sense that obtained when advocates for blacks' equality were dealt out in the initial constitutional settlement, again in the Compromise of 1877 (giving the Republicans the presidency and the white South autonomy on racial matters, as a settlement of the disputed Hayes-Tilden election), and afterward, until the mid-1960s, by the race-saturated politics of the Senate filibuster. These persisting arrangements between northern and southern whites, embedded in congressional processes, probably belong in a class with the formulas of Dutch and Swiss consociationalism—long-standing quasi-constitutional agreements dividing governmental authority among ethnic, religious, or linguistic segments of the population. Since 1965, many senators of all ideological shades have used the filibuster, but no set of them has presumed to claim—probably none successfully could—that it can legitimately be used over and over again on the same issue. While a bias for the status quo clearly exists, Congress is no longer predictably static on any specifiable issue or set of issues.

And its members do, after all, pass a great number of bills, many of them controversial. A few members dedicated to a goal, fortified by staff work, and capable of shrewd maneuvering can often carry through a piece of legislation; the consumer statutes of the 1960s enacted over industry opposition supply some cases in point. (See, for example, the account in Price 1972, chap. 2.) Indeed, what Robert A. Dahl refers to in another context as a pattern of "minorities rule" is a fair characterization of much congressional

---

[9] Bernard Asbell makes the point with acuity and voluminous evidence in *The Senate Nobody Knows* (1978), a treatment of (among other things) Senate handling of clean air legislation in 1976.

bill passing (Dahl 1963, pp. 131–34). The accommodation required to conform House and Senate bills is also a matter of negotiated compromise.

Deliberation

Lawmakers may be said to be engaging in "deliberation" when the following set of circumstances characterize their activity: (a) they try to change or make up each other's minds about what, if anything, should be enacted into law; (b) they do so by adducing descriptive statements ("facts"), causal statements (for example, "Decontrolling gas prices will reduce demand"), normative statements (such as, "The government shouldn't interfere in people's lives"), or some combination of the three; and (c) the criterion they use, explicitly or implicitly, in arguing whether a bill should become law is whether it would be "good" for some reference group larger than themselves (for example, a district, the farmers, the nation, humanity). In principle, deliberation differs from bargaining—trying to get others to change their positions by making threats or offering inducements, although in practice the two forms of interaction are commonly entangled.

Operating on a premise that legislators register fixed positions or hone them to serve electoral ends, modern scholars have seldom paid much attention to deliberation or taken the process seriously. The oversight is curious, given the earlier emphasis accorded it by the authors of the Federalist papers and by Woodrow Wilson; the prominence of a twentieth-century "problem-solving" scholarship, from John Dewey through Harold Lasswell, that might have, but has not, made it a first-order concern; and the obvious fact that it does indeed take place. One thinks of the losing effort in the Senate in 1970 to confirm the nomination of G. Harrold Carswell to the Supreme Court, in which the arguments in his favor wore thin and in which the salient argument became Senator Roman L. Hruska's that "even if he were mediocre, there are a lot of mediocre judges and people and lawyers, and they are entitled to a little representation, aren't they?" Another illustration is furnished by President Carter's bill allowing election-day registration of voters, which lost its support when critics took a cold look at it and concluded that the potential for fraud was immense (*Congressional Quarterly Weekly* 1977). And there is President Nixon's Family Assistance Plan, impaled on its inconsistencies in the Senate Finance Committee; Senator John Williams adduced elaborate information and apparently persuaded the committee that "work incentives," predicted to be a product of the plan, were a mirage.[10] As a result of the scholarly oversight, political scientists have had little to say on such matters as the televising of congressional floor sessions; whether committee markup sessions (where decisions on particulars are hammered out) should be closed or open; whether treatment of legislative subjects should be scattered around many committees or concentrated in a few;[11] whether hiring of huge legislative staffs makes for

[10] See Bessette 1979, pp. 33–42. For an especially good account of deliberative activity at the committee and subcommittee levels, see Asbell 1978, pp. 10–17, 29–43, 121–27, 131–35, 176–79, 185–89, 198–207, 216–18, 224–28, 328–29, 333–36, 349–64, 371–74, 392–95; these scattered references, if strung together, supply a coherent narrative on the Senate Public Works Committee's handling of clean air legislation in 1976.

[11] See Davidson and Oleszek 1977, an account of the Bolling Committee's effort to make over the House committee system in 1973–74. Discussions among committee members and staff (the latter including some political scientists), reported in chapter 5, display traces of an interest in making committees better deliberative bodies.

better or worse consideration of bills (see Malbin 1977, 1980; Scully 1977); or, in general, what sorts of institutional arrangements make for a proper deliberative setting.

A heterogeneous collection of recent writings, however, offers promise that the topic of deliberation may become an object of scholarly interest. A paper by Joseph M. Bessette (1979) offers a careful probe of its nature.[12] Charles E. Lindblom and David K. Cohen, exemplary of writers in a tradition outside congressional scholarship but relevant to it, have considered how social-scientific knowledge can usefully be inserted into decision-making processes in legislative and other settings (Lindblom and Cohen 1979). Nelson W. Polsby has given thought to the place of deliberation in presidential nominating conventions, settings from which it has virtually disappeared in recent decades as primaries and the mass media have become the realm and instruments of nominating (Polsby 1980). John W. Kingdon and Richard F. Fenno, Jr., both authors of books based on interviews with members of Congress, have told of a practice independent of deliberation but, on close inspection, arguably related to it—the members' standard, time-consuming practice of explaining their Capitol Hill activities, including their votes, to their constituencies (Fenno 1978, chap. 5; Kingdon 1973, pp. 46–53).

Taking positions is not enough: in order to show that they are performing well, members of Congress must travel around their districts and repeatedly make statements— descriptive, causal, and normative—about the legislative issues they deal with in Washington. Knowing that, back home, they will have to cite reasons for their stands on Capitol Hill, they worry and ruminate about how to explain later as they take their stands now. This circumstance, which may not be surprising, suggests the idea of a representative tie of some sophistication. Members can be judged, at least in part, in their home districts according to whether their statements are plausible; the statement making, so judged, is an attenuated form of the sort required in deliberation on Capitol Hill; the more alert constituents, in so judging, are therefore engaging in what amounts to a sampling activity, testing whether their representatives are likely to be much good at deliberating. Fenno argues that, in making explanations and performing the other actions they engage in back home, members of the House try, above all, to create a relation of "trust" with their constituents (Fenno 1978, passim). To carry the argument further, "trust" relations empower members to take part in arcane Washington discussions. It should further be remembered that argument on Capitol Hill, insofar as it is a rehearsal for explanations in the home district—and to some important degree it has this function—imparts popular styles of thinking into Congress's legislative activity.

BACK TO PUBLIC OPINION

The foregoing treatments of influence relations and processes will convey a sense of some of the achievements and difficulties when loosely structured elective assemblies generate laws. But there is a need for a general point of a different sort—one not covered in these treatments, not rooted in available scholarship or easily renderable by standard techniques or scholarship, but important nonetheless for what it suggests about American legislatures, Congress in particular, as distinctively popular institutions.

The point concerns language and style of thinking. As much as any, and probably

[12] For a pertinent earlier offering see Barry 1965, pp. 87–88. Barry sets out seven methods of resolving disagreements, of which "discussion on merits" is one.

more than most, American legislatures are places where ordinary-language, common-sense ways of thinking percolate upward from the public to permeate lawmaking processes and laws. This process can occur either because legislators embody public opinion or because they cater to it—probably as much the former as the latter. Capitol Hill terminology is normally no more complicated than the idiom of journalists or common-law lawyers. Styles of reasoning are ordinary; arguments in the *Congressional Record* are full of references to such images as mares' nests, entering wedges, camels' noses, last-mile walks, cans of worms, Pandora's boxes, stitches in time, golden eggs, roosting chickens, pigs in a poke, forests and trees, babies and bathwater. (See the discussion in Large 1973.)

This commonplace takes on importance with a view toward what the language of lawmaking could be but, at least in the American setting, normally is not—a "scientific" or otherwise inaccessible medium, a language of technical expertise (common, of course, in government agencies), of labyrinthine ideology, or of esoteric ethics.[13] Whatever else may be said about Congress and other American legislatures, they have little in common with task forces of economists or with seminars of Jesuits or Marxists or philosophy professors; their styles of thought and discourse are, by contrast, utterly prosaic.

A way to make this point is to set out some "cognitive grooves," some ordinary-language, common-sense ways of thinking about things, which unquestionably originate in public opinion and which, over and over again, infuse legislative discourse and give shape to American statutory law. I offer ten such "cognitive grooves."

Corrective Measures

"There Ought to Be a Law"
Conjuring up a "scientific" vision of legislating is easy enough; a body of lawmakers settles on some desirable ends and then builds statutes with a vigorous instrumental rationality to achieve them. A law is a "scientific" means to reach an end. But surely lawmaking rooted in public opinion is not likely to take this form, only with important qualifications. In the first place, to the average person, "law" is probably a kind of Mosaic mishmash—a mix of moral command and positive edict. Why pass a law proscribing marijuana or fornication? To set a standard or to abolish a practice? A "scientific" way to reduce air pollution might be to tax factory owners according to the amounts of poison they inject into the air; but this kind of remedy is hard to sell to American publics or their legislators because it appears immoral. If polluting the air is bad, why not simply pass a law stamping it out altogether?

In the second place, legislators rooted in public opinion are somewhat quicker on the draw in framing laws than, I suspect, "scientists" would have them be. They are casual, to say the least, in applying the tenets of instrumental rationality. If something is wrong, "there ought to be a law." The response is reflexive. An example of moralism intertwined with casual thinking is embodied in the Humphrey-Hawkins Act of 1978—an enacted national mandate, barren of instruction on means, to achieve a 4 percent unemployment rate as well as a 3 percent inflation rate by 1983. (See Singer 1978.) It is difficult to characterize such a venture; it can hardly be seen as an exercise in "scientific" lawmaking. The relentless currents of moralism and of quick, reflexive casualness in American lawmaking—at state and local levels in the nineteenth century, but extended to the national in the twentieth—almost certainly rule out a whole brand of economists' thinking

[13] The distinction here is akin to one Bruce A. Ackerman makes between "ordinary" and "scientific" legal language in *Private Property and the Constitution* (1977, chap. 1).

as incompatible with popular democracy: the stark antistatist economics, that is, associated with Milton Friedman. Any collection of American legislators is likely to pass a great many laws in a short time that vigorously free-market economists will find gratuitous or hateful; the public wants them. As long as a century and a half ago, Tocqueville reported on "American legislatures in a state of continual agitation," on the "continual feverish activity of the legislatures," and on the fact that "in America the legislator's activity never slows down" (Tocqueville 1969, pp. 243, 241, 249).

"Regulate It"   The reflexive American response to any malfunction in the private sector—most of the ills of the Industrial Revolution are cases in point—is to call for regulation. Such a recourse is simple, practical, and easily understood. It requires no theory. It flows from a judgment that some practices are good and others are bad.

At the legislative level, regulation is primarily expressed in lists of actions that people or organizations are mandated or forbidden to engage in. During the last two or three decades, when large staffs and "public interest advocates" have become fixtures on Capitol Hill, the lists have grown longer and more detailed. But they still cause despair among all sorts of economists on the ground that their means do not efficiently achieve their ends. (See, for example, the analysis in Ackerman et al. 1974.)

Furthermore, the American "regulatory" recourse has ruled out or taken the place of ways of dealing with the private sector that some would consider more basic or fundamental—for example, the Marxist recourse of "nationalizing the means of production." This is a message of intellectuals, rooted in a complicated body of theory, and it has never had much resonance in the American public or in American legislatures.

"Stamp It Out"   Reflecting public opinion, American lawmakers put a great deal of energy into trying to eliminate easily identifiable evils. Such targets may include slavery, drinking, Communism, drug addiction, vice, unemployment, inflation, pollution, hunger, and poverty.

But while "poverty" can become a fitting statutory target, it is more difficult, if not impossible, for any American legislature to ordain general societal rearrangements in the interest of realizing a complicated ethical theory. John Rawls and Robert Nozick may be captivating in university settings, but their lack of common-sense targets—they attack no manifest evil—makes them unsalable in an American political marketplace. George McGovern's "demogrant" plan of 1972 to give each person $1,000 a year as an incomes policy may have sounded persuasive in Cambridge, but it aroused bafflement and suspicion in the public and, as a result, would almost certainly have been unrealizable on Capitol Hill. Its intended underpinnings were not easy to convey.

"We're in a Crisis"; or, "This Is an Outrage"   There is a common inclination among American legislators, responding to public opinion, to frame measures as a quick reaction to events. One thinks of the "hundred days" legislation in response to the economic crisis of 1933; laws regulating drugs in 1938 and 1962 (the former brought on by a deadly sulfanilamide elixir, the latter by thalidomide) (see Harris 1964, pp. 181–245); the Tonkin Gulf resolution of 1964, giving President Lyndon Johnson what amounted to free rein in Vietnam; mining-safety laws passed in 1941, 1952, and 1969, all inspired by coal-mine disasters (see Lewis-Beck and Alford 1980); the National Defense Education Act of 1958, brought on by Sputnik; the civil-rights laws of 1964 and 1965,

triggered by violence in Birmingham and Selma. No one should be surprised by this reactiveness, of course, or even necessarily dismayed, but it does sometimes yield measures that are not very well thought out in their means or ends.

"Do It Once and for All"   Most of the natural sciences and some of the social sciences proceed by experimentation, either in laboratories or, with suitable application of rules, in real-life settings. Given the chance, therefore, scientists of various sorts might bring an experimental cast of mind to legislating. In many areas of lawmaking, there is no sure way of predicting the effects of a contemplated law. From a scientific standpoint, a reasonable—indeed, an obvious—course on such congressional subjects as campaign finance, minimum wage, water and air pollution, occupational safety, housing, and school busing would be experimentation with different laws in randomly selected parts of the country to observe the results. To be sure, such action would pose constitutional and other kinds of problems. But it is my impression that members of Congress almost never even consider such procedures. My guess is that their view of lawmaking as a substantially *moral* activity—a popularly rooted view—prevents them from contemplating experimentation: if there is a *right* solution to a problem, it must be universally imposed. By an accident of history, American lawmaking was more experimental half a century ago than it is now; fortuitous mixes of state laws on various subjects, at a time when states had greater autonomy, supplied what amounted to "natural experiments"—the individual states serving, in Louis D. Brandeis's phrase, as "laboratories." The current costly recourse at the federal level is, in effect, to try out solutions over time rather than across space.

"Wipe Out Corruption"   Nothing may be easier for people to understand than a charge of "corruption." Hence, a hypersensitivity on the subject has developed among American journalists and lawmakers. As a result, revelations of corruption produce laws; one thinks of the Watergate hearings and the subsequent overhaul of campaign-finance rulings.[14] Further, views on corruption give shape to laws; in important respects, the entire American public sector, with its elaborate civil-service requirements, its auditing arrangements, its reporting and disclosure constraints, its vast paperwork, is a monument to the memory and possibility of corruption. "There are watchdogs who watch watchdogs watching watchdogs." (See, for example, Kaufman 1977, p. 54; more generally pp. 50–56.) Initiative and flexibility can get lost in a quest for palpable honesty; agencies created by American legislatures may not always accomplish whatever else they are supposed to do, but they do manage to spend enormous amounts of money without much of it being illegally misused or stolen.

"Pin the Blame"   The gist of what might be called "blame theories" is that when something goes wrong, someone or a group of someones is intentionally and malevolently causing the situation; there may well be a conspiracy. This strain in American popular thinking has persisted from the beginning, the lineup of villains running from the Illuminati, the Masons, and the Pope up through such modern forces as the "Communist conspiracy," the "military industrial complex," and the Trilateral Commission. (For a

---

[14] For a treatment of the Federal Election Campaign Act of 1974 and its follow-up litigation, see Polsby 1977, pp. 1–43. The act was among other things "a major legacy of [the Nixon] administration" (p. 1).

general treatment, see Hofstadter 1967.) Some blame theories are more sophisticated than others, and some are surely true, but all probably win popular currency by their dealing in blame—one of the simplest of ideas.

A point worth making is that blame theories do not ordinarily achieve as much success in American legislatures as they do among the public; lawmakers seeking explanations, as a preface to writing statutes, are more likely to reach for impersonal causes. Their doing so may offer a good instance (and one that might, in social-science parlance, be "operationalizable"—survive rigorous definition of terms and scrutiny of evidence) of what James Madison expected of congressional representation: that it would "refine and enlarge the public views by passing them through the medium of a chosen body of citizens" (*Federalist Papers* 1961, p. 82).

Nevertheless, at times blame theories do make their mark on Capitol Hill. One thinks of a long line of noisy investigations: the Nye committee of the 1930s, with its theory that munitions makers brought on World War I; the McCarthy hearings and the three-decade run of the House Un-American Activities Committee; more recently, the House Select Committee on Assassinations and its unswerving conviction—evidence or the lack of it notwithstanding—that John F. Kennedy and Martin Luther King, Jr., were both victims of bizarre conspiracies. While such hearings occasionally result in laws, for the most part, the act of investigating in itself—authoritatively assigning the blame—seems to satisfy interested publics.

Anticipatory Measures

"We Need a Program"

"We Need a Program"   The view that, if there is a problem, a government "program" can be created to "solve" it seems to be a twentieth-century idea, perhaps a remnant of the "problem-solving" strain in Progressivism. Sometimes the belief makes good sense; the space program, the Marshall Plan, and the effort of the 1970s to wipe out hunger come to mind. Sometimes it makes less sense; the crash program to wipe out cancer and most of the housing programs since the 1930s are cases in point. But the idea of "having a program" seems deeply ingrained in the popular mind and in politicians' minds. Anyone running for high office is obliged to set forth, for example, a "program for the cities." Consequently, the statute books fill up with plans for programs, whether or not there is good reason to suppose that labeling problems and creating programs to solve them will in fact achieve any intended ends.

"We've Got a Right"

"We've Got a Right"   The notion of rights has always been prominent in American culture, but since the mid-1960s, when southern obstruction of efforts to extend elementary rights to blacks finally gave way in Congress and in the southern state capitals, a new phenomenon has arisen—the persistent, frenetic invention of new rights. (For the treatment of the modern class of rights that amount to entitlements to government largesse, see Reich 1964.) (Of course, the best way to establish a new right is to argue that it is an ancient one currently being traduced.) Some of this invention has been carried on in Congress. The controversy on abortion, which, in principle, could be conducted on utilitarian lines—that is, on the presumed social effects of one policy or another—in fact, took the form of a competitive assertion of rights—as in the politically imaginative declaration of a "right to life" (with its conscious or unconscious appeal to the Declaration of Independence). An excellent current way to bring about large-scale social change is to label a desideratum a "right" by statute, specifying as little as possible about the costs or effects of implementation. In passing the Age Discrimination Act of 1975, for example, Congress "held no public hearings and left behind virtually no legislative history of its intentions to guide the government's policy makers" (Stanfield 1978, p. 2066; for a more extended treatment, see Schuck 1980). The Rehabilitation Act of 1973 included only one sentence barring discrimination against the handicapped in access to public transit; five years later, these few words had cost billions of dollars in public expenditure and filled the *Federal Register* with 51 pages of follow-up regulations (Clark 1973).

A vast potential exists for brief and cloudy laws producing expensive, enduring, and often surprising effects. Declaring "rights" may cause more notable results than creating "programs"; in the case of the handicapped, for example, a program in their behalf—a more traditional recourse—would probably have brought about less actual change. The congressional concern with rights has recently spilled over into foreign policy, where marking up foreign aid bills has sometimes taken the form of list bargaining—my Chile for your Mozambique. Each member has a distinctive list of countries argued to be too wicked on human-rights matters to deserve financial aid. (See Franck and Weisband 1979, chap. 4.)

"Balance the Budget and Stamp Out Waste"   An enduring substratum of public opinion seems to exist in American society that concentrates on money; its tenets are roughly as follows. Government budgets should be balanced. Agencies have an inherent tendency to waste money and should be stopped from doing so. Tax money is, in principle, citizens' property, and the burden is on government to prove it ought to be taken away. Running up a national debt is an improvident and, indeed, immoral act. The Proposition 13 movement in California, and similar initiatives in other states calling for reductions in public spending as a matter of law, have apparently built on a notion that a huge share of public expenditure is simply wasted. (For a good analysis based on national survey data, see Sussman 1978.) A publicly inspired constitutional amendment requiring that federal budgets be balanced may yet be enacted. (See Wildavsky 1980.)

To be sure, such a package of views hardly supplies an accurate prediction any more of what takes place on Capitol Hill: members of Congress, acting in the shadow of Keynesian theory, have not been hesitant to approve deficits and debts. Nevertheless, compared with other governmental organs—certainly the President's Council of Economic Advisers—Congress is a uniquely good reflector of public views on money matters. Decade after decade, the keynote of the House Appropriations Committee's activity has been the stamping out of governmental waste. (See Fenno 1966, especially pp. 98–108.) And deficits notwithstanding, it probably remains the case that no theory of budgeting other than a common-sense balancing theory has ever been decisively sold on Capitol Hill. Congress went along only half-heartedly with the Kennedy-Johnson tax cut of 1964—the first salient Keynesian instrument—and neither the statements nor the actions of its members since that time suggest any firm attachment to notions of counter-cyclicalism. The economic program of the Reagan administration in its early days was a powerful statement of mass opinion on government spending, budget balancing, and waste; but it is interesting that Reagan's macroeconomic proposal that encountered the strongest opposition in Congress was his tax scheme. The administration's Kemp-Roth plan, with its Laffer Curve justification of tax cuts unmatched by spending cuts, aroused suspicion of the sort inspired by the Democrats' Keynesianism of two decades earlier. And the opposition was rooted in public opinion; national surveys supplied evidence that unalloyed budget balancing is the macroeconomics of the mass public.[15] The main problem for economists on Capitol Hill is winning a lasting commitment to any theories at all, budget balancing aside.

These ten categories make my point about public opinion. Anyone examining the product of elective American assemblies, pondering what to make of it and how much to honor it, might consider not only the relations of influence and organizing concepts set out earlier, but also the infusion of raw public opinion into lawmaking. An inspection of congressional behavior on energy matters in the 1970s, for example, certainly warrants a consideration of pressure brought to bear by oil companies, the contemporary status of the presidency, the absence of disciplined national parties, patterns of coalition formation on Capitol Hill, the effects of hyperspecialization in the congressional committee system; but it must also consider the dogged, simultaneous expression on Capitol Hill of the conflicting demands of public opinion: big cars, low gas and oil prices, more investment in energy, more conservation, customary levels of energy consumption, nonintervention abroad, less dependence on imports, less government regulation, and lower taxes.

There is much to be said for the American model of rooting assemblies in public opinion. No doubt, it imparts a signal legitimacy to governmental actions, and it invests legislative enactments with a piecemeal cast of the kind advocated by Karl Popper—consider the "cognitive grooves" having to do with incremental regulation, obvious evils, and reaction to events.

The system also has its costs, however. A summary way of stating them is to cite a contrast drawn by Tocqueville (substituting, with some of the modern European regimes in mind, the phrase "party-centered technocracy" for his "aristocracy"):

> An aristocracy is infinitely more skillful in the science of legislation than the United States democracy ever can be. Being master of itself, it is not subject to transitory impulses; it has far-sighted plans and knows how to let them mature until the favorable opportunity offers. An aristocracy moves forward intelligently; it knows how to make the collective force of all its laws converge on one point at a time. A democracy is not like that; its laws are almost always defective or untimely. [Tocqueville 1969, p. 232]

He continued with a familiar assertion—"the great privilege of the Americans is to be able to make retrievable mistakes."

---

[15] See Samuelson 1978; Clymer 1978; Reinhold 1978. A nationwide election-day survey conducted in 1978 by the Times and CBS News turned up a 3-to-1 voter preference for spending cuts over tax cuts, and a 50 percent to 42 percent rejection of a "large Federal income tax cut, regardless of its effect on prices or government services"—a tendentious but recognizable rendition of Kemp-Roth (Clymer 1978, p. A19). In the same poll, 82 percent of Democratic voters and 86 percent of Republicans said they favored a constitutional amendment requiring federal budgets to be balanced (Reinhold 1978).

Bibliography

Ackerman, Bruce A.
   1977   *Private Property and the Constitution.* New Haven: Yale University Press.
Ackerman, Bruce A., et al.
   1974   *The Uncertain Search for Environmental Quality.* New York: Free Press.
Almond, Gabriel A., and Powell, G. Bingham, Jr.
   1966   *Comparative Politics: A Developmental Approach.* Boston: Little, Brown.
American Political Science Association
   1950   *Toward a More Responsible Party System.* Report of the Committee on Political
             Parties. New York: Rinehart, especially pp. 21–22, 43, 56–65, and 72–73.
Arnold, R. Douglas
   1978   "Legislatures, Overspending and Government Growth." Paper delivered at the
             Conference on the Causes and Consequences of Public Sector Growth, Dorado
             Beach, Puerto Rico.
   1979   *Congress and the Bureaucracy.* New Haven: Yale University Press.
Asbell, Bernard
   1978   *The Senate Nobody Knows.* Garden City, N.Y.: Doubleday.
Bailey, Stephen K.
   1950   *Congress Makes a Law: The Story Behind the Employment Act of 1946.* New York:
             Columbia University Press.
Barry, Brian
   1965   *Political Argument.* London: Routledge & Kegan Paul, pp. 255–56.
Bauer, Raymond A., et al.
   1963   *American Business and Public Policy.* Chicago: Aldine-Atherton.
Beer, Samuel H.
   1976   "The Adoption of General Revenue Sharing: A Case Study of Public Sector Poli-
             tics." *Public Policy* 14:127–95.
Bessette, Joseph M.
   1979   "Deliberation in Congress." Paper presented at the convention of the American
             Political Science Association, Washington, D.C.
Bryce, James
   1959   *The American Commonwealth.* New York: Putnam.
   [1888]
Burns, James MacGregor
   1963   *The Deadlock of Democracy.* Englewood Cliffs, N.J.: Prentice-Hall.
Cavanagh, Thomas E.
   1978   "The Two Arenas of Congress: Electoral and Institutional Incentives for Perform-
             ance." Examination paper, Yale University.
Clark, Timothy B.
   1978   "Access for the Handicapped—A Test of Carter's War on Inflation." *National
             Journal,* October 21, p. 1673.
Clausen, Aage
   1973   *How Congressmen Decide: A Policy Focus.* New York: St. Martin's Press.
Clymer, Adam
   1978   "Most Voters Stay with Democrats But Republicans Make Gains in Governor-
             ships." *New York Times,* November 8, pp. A1, A19.

Congressional Quarterly Weekly
           March 26, 1977, pp. 561–63, 566–67; May 14, 1977, pp. 909–15; May 28, 1977,
           pp. 1034–35; July 23, 1977, p. 1494; September 24, 1977, p. 2052.
Dahl, Robert A.
    1963   A Preface to Democratic Theory. Chicago: University of Chicago Press.
Davidson, Roger H., and Oleszek, Walter J.
    1977   Congress Against Itself. Bloomington: Indiana University Press.
Dodd, Lawrence C., and Oppenheimer, Bruce I.
    1977   "The House in Transition." In Congress Reconsidered, edited by Lawrence C. Dodd
             and Bruce I. Oppenheimer. New York: Praeger.
Fenno, Richard F., Jr.
    1966   The Power of the Purse: Appropriations Politics in Congress. Boston: Little, Brown.
    1973   Congressmen in Committees. Boston: Little, Brown.
    1978   Home Style: House Members in Their Districts. Boston: Little, Brown.
Ferejohn, John A.
    1974   Pork Barrel Politics. Stanford, Calif.: Stanford University Press.
Fiorina, Morris P.
    1977   Congress: Keystone of the Washington Establishment. New Haven: Yale University
             Press.
Fisher, Louis
    1972   President and Congress: Power and Policy. New York: Free Press.
Franck, Thomas M., and Weisband, Edward
    1979   Foreign Policy by Congress. New York: Oxford University Press.
Friedman, John
    1979   "A Populist Shift in Federal Cultural Support." New York Times, May 13, p. D1.
Green, Mark J., et al.
    1972   Who Runs Congress? New York: Grossman.
Harris, Richard
    1964   The Real Voice. New York: Macmillan.
Hayes, Michael T.
    1961   Lobbyists and Legislators: A Theory of Political Markets. New Brunswick, N.J.: Rut-
             gers University Press.
Hofstadter, Richard
    1967   "The Paranoid Style in American Politics." In The Paranoid Style in American
             Politics and Other Essays. New York: Vintage Books.
Horowitz, Donald L.
    1977   The Courts and Social Policy. Washington, D.C.: Brookings Institution.
Huntington, Samuel P.
    1965   "Congressional Responses to the Twentieth Century." In The Congress and
             America's Future, edited by David B. Truman. Englewood Cliffs, N.J.: Prentice-
             Hall.
Jacobson, Gary C.
    1980   Money in Congressional Elections. New Haven: Yale University Press.
Jones, Charles O.
    1961   "Representation in Congress: The Case of the House Agriculture Committee."
             American Political Science Review 55:358–67.
Kaufman, Herbert
    1976   Are Government Organizations Immortal? Washington, D.C.: Brookings Institution.
    1977   Red Tape: Its Origins, Uses, and Abuses. Washington, D.C.: Brookings Institution.
Kingdon, John W.
    1973   Congressmen's Voting Decisions. New York: Harper & Row.

Kirkpatrick, Evron M.
    1971   "Toward a More Responsible Two-Party System: Political Science, Policy Science,
            or Pseudo-Science?" *American Political Science Review* 65:965–90.
Large, Arlen J.
    1973   "Pandora Opens a Can of Worms." *Wall Street Journal*, August 28, p. 10.
Lewis-Beck, Michael S., and Alford, John R.
    1980   "Can Government Regulate Safety? The Coal Mine Example." *American Political
            Science Review* 74:745–56.
Lindblom, Charles E., and Cohen, David K.
    1979   *Usable Knowledge: Social Science and Social Problem Solving.* New Haven: Yale Uni-
            versity Press.
Lorch, Robert S.
    1969   *Democratic Processes and Administrative Law.* Detroit: Wayne State University
            Press.
Lowi, Theodore H.
    1969   *The End of Liberalism.* New York: Norton.
Madison, James, et al.
    1961   *The Federalist Papers.* No. 10. New York: New American Library.
    [1787–88]
Malbin, Michael
    1977   "Congressional Committee Staffs: Who's in Charge Here?" *Public Interest*, Spring,
            pp. 16–40.
    1980   *Unelected Representatives: Congressional Staff and the Future of Representative Govern-
            ment.* New York: Basic Books.
Manley, John F.
    1970   *The Politics of Finance: The House Committee on Ways and Means.* Boston: Little,
            Brown.
Mann, Thomas E.
    1978   *Unsafe at Any Margin: Interpreting Congressional Elections.* Washington, D.C.:
            American Enterprise Institute.
Mann, Thomas E., and Ornstein, Norman J., eds.
    1981   *The New Congress.* Washington, D.C.: American Enterprise Institute.
Mann, Thomas E., and Wolfinger, Raymond E.
    1980   "Candidates and Parties in Congressional Elections." *American Political Science
            Review* 74:617–32.
Matthews, Donald R.
    1960   *U.S. Senators and Their World.* Chapel Hill: University of North Carolina Press.
Mayhew, David R.
    1966   *Party Loyalty Among Congressmen: The Difference Between Democrats and Republi-
            cans, 1947–1962.* Cambridge, Mass.: Harvard University Press.
    1974   *The Electoral Connection.* New Haven: Yale University Press.
Murphy, James T.
    1968   "Partisanship and the House Public Works Committee." Paper presented at the
            annual convention of the American Political Science Association, Washington,
            D.C.
Nagel, Jack H.
    1975   *The Descriptive Analysis of Power.* New Haven: Yale University Press.
Neustadt, Richard E.
    1976   *Presidential Power.* Rev. ed. New York: Wiley.
Niskanen, William A.
    1971   *Bureaucracy and Representative Government.* New York: Aldine-Atherton.

Peabody, Robert L.
    1976   *Leadership in Congress: Stability, Succession and Change.* Boston: Little, Brown.
Peabody, Robert L., and Polsby, Nelson W., eds.
    1977   *New Perspectives on the House of Representatives.* Chicago: Rand McNally.
Polsby, Daniel D.
    1977   "Buckley v. Valeo: The Special Nature of Political Speech." In *The Supreme Court Review,* edited by Philip B. Kurland. Chicago: University of Chicago Press.
Polsby, Nelson W.
    1968   "The Institutionalization of the U.S. House of Representatives." *American Political Science Review* 62:144–68.

    1975   "Legislatures." In *Governmental Institutions and Processes,* edited by Fred I. Greenstein and Nelson W. Polsby. Handbook of Political Science, vol. 5. Reading, Mass.: Addison-Wesley.

    1980   "The News Media as an Alternative to Party in the Presidential Selection Process." In *Political Parties in the Eighties,* edited by Robert A. Goldwin. Washington, D.C.: American Enterprise Institute.
Pressman, Jeffrey L., and Wildavsky, Aaron B.
    1973   *Implementation.* Berkeley: University of California Press.
Prewitt, Kenneth
    1970   "Political Ambitions, Volunteerism, and Electoral Accountability." *American Political Science Review* 64:5–17.
Price, David
    1972   *Who Makes the Laws?* Cambridge, Mass.: Schenkman.
Price, H. Douglas
    1975   "Congress and the Evolution of Legislative 'Professionalism.'" In *Congress in Change,* edited by Norman J. Ornstein. New York: Praeger.
Public Interest
    1980   "Poor America." *Public Interest,* Summer, pp. 148–49.
Ranney, Austin
    1954   *The Doctrine of Responsible Party Government.* Urbana: University of Illinois Press.
Reich, Charles A.
    1964   "The New Property." *Yale Law Journal* 73:733–87.
Reinhold, Robert
    1978   "Poll Indicates Congress Candidates Were More Extreme Than Voters." *New York Times,* November 9, p. A21.
Riker, William H.
    1962   *The Theory of Political Coalitions.* New Haven: Yale University Press.
Samuelson, Robert J.
    1978   "Tax Cut May Come Back to Haunt House Members." *National Journal,* August 5, pp. 1245–47.
Schick, Allen
    1980   *Congress and Money: Budgeting, Spending and Taxing.* Washington, D.C.: Urban Institute.
Schuck, Peter H.
    1980   "The Graying of Civil Rights Law." *Public Interest,* Summer, pp. 69–93.
Scully, Michael A.
    1977   "Reflections of a Senate Aide." *Public Interest,* Spring, pp. 41–48.
Seidman, Harold
    1970   *Politics, Position, and Power: The Dynamics of Federal Organization.* New York: Oxford University Press.
Shapiro, Martin
    1968   *The Supreme Court and Administrative Agencies.* New York: Free Press, chap. 1.

Shepsle, Kenneth A.
1978   *The Giant Jigsaw Puzzle.* Chicago: University of Chicago Press.
Singer, James W.
1978   "It's Not Over Till It's Over." *National Journal,* October 21, p. 1688.
Stanfield, Rochelle L.
1978   "Age Discrimination Regs—They're Turning the Rule Makers Gray." *National Journal,* December 30, p. 2066.
Sussman, Barry
1978   "Waste Angers Taxpayers, Poll Shows." *Los Angeles Times,* October 15, p. IV-2.
Tocqueville, Alexis de
1969   *Democracy in America.* Garden City, N.Y.: Doubleday Anchor.
[1835]
Truman, David B.
1960   *The Governmental Process.* New York: Knopf.
Turner, Julius
1970   *Party and Constituency: Pressures on Congress.* Edition revised by Edward V. Schneier, Jr. Baltimore: Johns Hopkins Press.
Walkland, S. A.
1968   *The Legislative Process in Great Britain.* London: Allen and Unwin.
Wildavsky, Aaron B.
1974   *The Politics of the Budgetary Process.* Boston: Little, Brown.
1980   *How to Limit Government Spending.* Berkeley: University of California Press.
Wilson, James Q.
1975   "The Rise of the Bureaucratic State." *Public Interest,* Fall, pp. 77–103.
Wilson, Woodrow
1956   *Congressional Government.* New York: Meridian, especially pp. 77–82, 91–98, 130–33, 147, 210–14.
Wolfinger, Raymond E., and Heifetz, Joan
1965   "Safe Seats, Seniority, and Power in Congress." *American Political Science Review* 59:337–49.

∿ 6 ∿

IMPLEMENTATION AND ENFORCEMENT OF LAW

Jeffrey L. Jowell
University of London

INTRODUCTION

The legal process is rarely self-initiating. Much law commands obedience and is obeyed. But much still needs to be enforced. A rule does not usually "itself step forward to claim its own instances."[1] Enforcement of law requires action by an individual asserting a right or duty or claiming an obligation or benefit. Some laws (most contracts and torts) rely for their enforcement on private individuals, but many depend upon initiation by public officials.

For example, a law setting a maximum speed limit may of itself induce obedience, but in cases of deviance enforcement is generated by the police. Similarly, laws against racial discrimination may simply through their enactment induce conformity. But in cases of infringement, the individual victim may generate enforcement by complaint to an official agency, which may in turn possess discretion to prosecute enforcement.

As a heuristic device we may employ the illustration below. Law is directed through an administrative agency, which is charged with the enforcement of the law, and emerges at

---

[1] Hart 1961, p. 123.

NOTE: The author would like to thank M. D. A. Freeman and David Noble for their help in the preparation of this essay and David Nelken for his useful comments.

the other end. The ideal of "perfect enforcement" would require its emergence in a straight line. In reality the direction may be refracted.

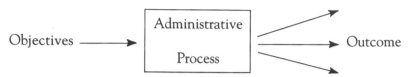

Of course, this illustration is wholly artificial. It assumes that the objective of a law, its purpose or goal, is clear and identifiable in advance. The picture painted by Max Weber of officials enforcing law "without hatred or passion and hence without affection or enthusiasm"[2] gives the impression of a law being clear in its purpose, and thus capable of mechanical enforcement. This view provides a useful ideal-typical construct.

In reality, however, the objectives of a law are often not clear and identifiable in advance. The definition and elaboration of purpose is a crucial issue in the implementation of laws. A law is normally assigned for enforcement in whole or part to a bureaucracy for the express purpose of allowing the bureaucracy to develop and elaborate the law's objectives. One reason for this may be the desire to incorporate community norms, which may change over time. For example, British planning law assigns to local authorities the task of granting or refusing planning permission in accordance with a plan (the Development Plan) and "other material considerations."[3] Fair rental laws may incorporate the concept of a "fair rent" to be decided in accordance with comparable rentals in the neighborhood. These laws invite the enforcers to develop standards, and in so doing to take into account shifting expectations and conditions in society.

Indefiniteness of purpose may have another, political reason, reflecting a compromise between factions in the legislature that could not agree on goals. The administrative arena will then become central to the battle for goals. Consider the possible objectives behind a law against racial discrimination: to persuade the public not to discriminate, to vindicate the rights of individuals who have been the victims of unlawful discrimination, or to equalize opportunities for blacks.[4] Rules about automobile accidents also show a number of differing goals. One goal, that of "justice," is to adjust the consequences of an accident fairly between those involved. Another is to reduce the number and severity of accidents. A further goal is to lower the social costs of accidents, whatever their number, and a fourth is to reduce the cost of administering the system of treatment of accidents.[5]

Again, we must distinguish between the direct objective of a law (the precise behavior commanded or allowed) and the indirect motive. And a distinction must be drawn between instrumental objectives of a law, where the aim is to effect concrete behavior—for example to stop people discriminating or drinking—and symbolic objectives, where the law aims at the public affirmation of social ideals—for example, persuading people that it is *wrong* to discriminate or to drink.[6]

Not only the passing of the law but also the setting up of an administrative structure for enforcement may be instrumental or symbolic. Edelman points out how enforcement

[2] Weber 1947, p. 340.
[3] Town and Country Planning Act, 1971, s.29(1).
[4] Jowell 1975, pp. 169–94.
[5] Calabresi 1970, pp. 24–33.
[6] Friedman 1975, pp. 49–50.

mechanisms may have the function of "symbolic reassurance" and rendering "quiescent" the public who seek the achievement of the law's objectives.[7]

In the "outcome" of the diagram above we confront an equal number of problems. Ideally, the quality of implementation could be tested by matching outcome against objectives. But objectives may be ambiguous, confused, or multifarious. And how do we measure the outcome, or the "impact" of a law? The measurement of impact is notoriously difficult for any public organization. In the absence of an objective, ascertainable, or quantifiable criterion of "success," such as profit margin, ratings, or productivity, organizations are frequently ignorant of how well or badly they are doing (given an identifiable objective). Few police departments can know how much crime and disorder a community would suffer if the police functioned differently, or not at all. Similarly, how do antidiscrimination agencies evaluate the success of their operations? By the number of complaints they receive?[8] By the "strategic" nature of these complaints (insofar as these can be measured)? By the amount of discrimination in the community (insofar as this can be measured)? Even if it can be shown that discrimination is reduced, can we be sure that the cause is the law itself, or the agency's activities? In Britain, for example, it is by no means clear to what extent the massive reduction in smog in big cities was the result of Clean Air laws which forbade the emission of "dark smoke" and the use of certain fuels, or of a general change in the use of fuels (including the widespread introduction of gas and oil-fired central heating to replace coal and wood fires).[9]

Moving now to the black box itself—the administrative process—we locate the bureaucracy (used here not only in reference to Weber's ideal type, but interchangeably with "administration," "administrative agency," or "organization"). In the illustration above the administrative process is the mediating device by which objectives are translated into outcomes.

It is here that the problem of accountability presents itself both to law and to political science. Democratic theory insists that bureaucracy is not a law unto itself, but accountable. Under notions of separation of powers, bureaucracy is an instrument of the legislature. In Britain, a minister is technically responsible to Parliament for the work of his department. Modern government, however, does not in practice permit a high degree of legislative control, and therefore the notion of accountability takes a different form. Accountability to purpose is presented as a modern substitute for traditional constitutional notions. The definition of purpose, according to others, requires more than a mere process of official ratiocination, but also a specific reference to the public interest, defined after taking into account disparate points of view.[10] Echoing this debate is one that argues the respective merits of representative and participatory democracy, and another that identifies competing ideologies in seemingly neutral administrative processes.[11]

Sociolegal studies of implementation mostly avoid the problem of constitutional setting. They content themselves largely with identifying the influences upon bureaucracy in the definition and enforcement of organizational goals. Early studies of the U.S. federal agencies were intrigued with the slack enforcement of regulatory standards.

[7] Edelman 1964.
[8] Wilson 1968, pp. 57–82.
[9] Scarrow 1972, p. 275.
[10] See Stewart (1975, p. 1675).
[11] See McAuslan (1980).

Selznick,[12] Bernstein,[13] and others showed how agencies were "captured" or "co-opted" by the interests they were attempting to regulate.

During the 1950s, the concept of discretion became the focus of interest of legal studies. Federal agencies were asked to define their standards, to reduce their discretion.[14] Concern was expressed at the growth of government "largesse," where individuals received privileges from the state at the mercy of official discretion. Reich favored granting firm "rights" or "entitlement" to recipients under criteria established in advance.[15] In Britain similar arguments were made by groups arguing for "welfare rights,"[16] opposed by Richard Titmuss, who argued that rights can produce a "pathology of legalism" where rules lack responsiveness to human needs and the law creates an "esoteric" and "mystical" atmosphere.[17]

Meanwhile, administrative lawyers were interested largely in judicial review of administrative action and, within that interest, in the rules and standards laid down by the courts to control administrative action. Only recently have they shown interest in some of the wider questions of the control of discretion, largely at the prompting of one of their number, K. C. Davis, to examine techniques at structuring, confining, and checking discretion through rules, open decision-making, and appeals.[18]

Recent work in legal philosophy also bears upon the enforcement process, although not specifically related thereto. Dworkin seeks to delineate the proper role of the judge and denies that the judge "makes" the law.[19] He distinguishes principles from policies, denying judges the right to deal in the latter or the right to exercise discretion in the strong sense of that word.

The recent legal concern with discretion has thus focused attention upon institutional design: the structures and techniques by which the agents of implementation (decision-makers of one kind or another) may be channeled into fidelity to the purpose of the law. The structures include appeals, reviews, and openness. The techniques include rules, principles, and criteria. Where judges are involved, either as agents of implementation or as agents of control (over nonjudicial decision-makers), debate rages over the permissible use of decision referents (policies, principles, or rules).

These purely legal questions are important but leave many questions unanswered that are the concern of the organizational and political theorists, who in turn tend to neglect the legal dimension. The first is that of nonlegal constraints on discretion—the long list of factors which, through various empirical studies, we know influence organizational behavior. These include the constraints of resources, time, professional norms, hierarchy, and incentives. These influencing factors are of interest in understanding the workings of organizations as implementing and enforcing agencies, and they comment also upon institutional design; they may permit the shaping of the structure of an organization in the light of a knowledge of these various constraints.

Recent writings on implementation have examined the exercise of discretion by official

---

[12] Selznick 1949.
[13] Bernstein 1955.
[14] Friendly 1962.
[15] Reich 1964, p. 733; 1965, p. 1245; 1966, p. 1227.
[16] See, for example, Lynes (1969).
[17] Titmuss 1971, p. 113. Compare a recent American contribution on these lines, Mashaw 1983.
[18] See Davis (1969).
[19] Dworkin 1977.

agencies. Mayhew[20] (on antidiscrimination commissions), Nonet[21] (on an industrial accidents commission), and Kagan[22] (on wage- and price-"freeze" legislation) all consider the context of agencies that narrow their wide powers by judicialization of varying degrees (leading in some instances to legalism) and legalization. In these studies organizational and legal theory at last begin to inform each other.

Turning specifically to nonlegal studies of implementation it is noteworthy that Pressman and Wildavsky, seeking studies of implementation, came to the conclusion that little work had been done on that subject.[23] On the other hand, there are a number of works that deal indirectly with implementation and, although rarely expressly identified as such, deal with essentially "legal" problems relating to the use of rules and adjudicative techniques to communicate policy, to solve disputes, and to achieve the broader objectives of accountability and control of discretion.

One of the first works directly from organization theory to speak to implementation is Herbert Simon's *Administrative Behaviour*,[24] which considers how rule-making and control within organizations are achieved through the specification of factual and value premises for subordinates. In this way the discretion of subordinates may be reduced although not entirely eliminated.

This concern to understand the hierarchical control within organizations is shared by lawyers who wish to prevent the distortion of goals by actors within the organizations and who suggest that rules be used as a device to control or to "confine" discretion.

However, a reliance only on rules and a concern only with "top-down" enforcement (implementation through the progressive reduction of discretion) ignore a number of factors operating upon and within an organization, which also influence its outcome.[25] For example, Gouldner[26] shows that rules are secured in a work setting not only by management, but also by labor who attempt to limit the discretionary freedom of their superiors. "Rational management," or control of administrative "distortion," is therefore not the sole function of rules. Others have shown how confining rules of themselves have led to "bureaupathic" behavior. Merton[27] points out how means may be treated as ends, thus both avoiding an organization's objectives and failing to provide the flexibility necessary to achieve the needs of particular clients. Recent studies in industrial relations have shown how an excessive reduction of discretion to the line official (the individual on the "coal face") leads to a low level of commitment to the effective performance of his task.[28]

Studies of organizations thus demonstrate a great deal about implementation and the use of legal techniques to influence outcomes. The question provoking most of them, however, asks why public agencies fail to achieve the goals of public policies and programs. The administrative process is seen as performing the task of "execution." Concern

[20] Mayhew 1968.
[21] Nonet 1969.
[22] Kagan 1978.
[23] See Pressman and Wildavsky (1973, p. 166).
[24] Simon emphasizes the importance of specifying "premises" within organizations for the control of subordinates (1945, pp. 223–24). Compare Dunsire (1979, p. 221).
[25] This point is made very persuasively by Ham and Hill (1984). See also Barrett and Fudge (1981).
[26] Gouldner 1954, p. 232.
[27] Merton 1957, pp. 195–206.
[28] See Fox (1974).

is expressed at the fact that goals are subverted during the process of implementation, causing an "implementation deficit" or "implementation gap."[29] This literature thus focuses largely upon managerial interests, dealing with policy communication, coordination, and control.

We can identify four different organizational "models" derived from different standpoints. The first of these, which Elmore[30] calls the "systems management" model, approximates what has just been described, namely, a model that views implementation as a "top-down" coordination and control. Elmore points out that in this model organizations are assumed to act as units; "policy" is treated as a single identifiable conception, with the process of implementation involving the attempt of the policy-makers and those at the top of the organization to hold subordinates faithful to the policy and accountable for any deviation therefrom.

A second model, the "bureaucratic process"[31] model, represents the sociological view of organizations, including recent research on "street-level" bureaucracy and the implementation of social programs. Studies here deal with routines developed within organizations as a necessary function of specialization and division of tasks and the techniques developed to maintain and enhance positions within the organization, which in turn may subvert original policy goals.

A third model deals with "organizational development" representing recent sociological and psychological theory and has a normative rather than descriptive focus, seeking ways of improving motivation, involvement, and task satisfaction within an organization as a "democratic" alternative to established theories of organization.

These models do point to features of organizations which both inform and correct the excessive concern with control through policy statement from the top-down and with methods of systems management to shape policy-making by hierarchical control. Elmore rightly points out that the second and third models recognize that the process of implementing new policy may begin at the bottom and end at the top, as policy does not exist in any concrete sense until implementers have shaped it and claimed it for their own.[32]

A fourth model, the "conflict and bargaining" model, will be discussed in greater detail below.

This cursory introduction shows from how many perspectives the legal contribution to implementation may be considered. Not all implementation theory is relevant to law, nor is law relevant to all implementation theory. The suggestion here is that more of each is relevant to the other than has been recognized.

It should perhaps be made clear that this essay will not deal with three issues of current concern in most industrial societies. The first relates to broad techniques of economic regulation, the question whether to achieve goals by means of independent agencies, as in the United States, or by means of ownership and control, as with the "nationalized industries" in Europe run by public corporations. The choice of instrument here is dependent upon deep political and economic structures and cultures.

The second issue not considered here relates to the circumstances of nonlegal techniques which are alternative to those employed in traditional administrative regulation

---

[29] Pressman and Wildavsky 1973, pp. xiv, iv; Dunsire 1979, p. 18.
[30] Elmore 1979, p. 601; 1978, p. 185.
[31] Elmore takes this from Allison's model; see Allison (1971).
[32] Elmore 1978, pp. 215–16.

and are exciting increasing interest on both sides of the Atlantic. I refer here to economic-based incentives such as taxes and subsidies as opposed to rule-making, adjudication, and other legal devices.[33]

The third issue not considered here relates to the appropriateness of the *judicial* role in administrative schemes—the role of courts as a check on arbitrary and unreasonable governmental power as opposed to other methods such as executive control or control through instruments such as the U.S. Office of Management and Budget.[34]

LAW IN ORGANIZATIONS

The process of enforcement usually engages the administrator in a choice about his own discretion: whether to keep it wide and open-textured, thus maintaining a variety of options, or to confine it by rule, by a process of *legalization*. This process deals with the substance of the decision: it announces the organizational response to a given situation. The policy to promote safe driving is legalized by the rule requiring a 30-mile-per-hour speed limit on given streets.

The second choice is directed less to the substance of the decision (although this may be affected, too) than to the process of decision-making. This choice relates to *judicialization:* should the decision be taken through some kind of adjudicative process?

Legalization

The argument in favor of legalization is generally based upon the desirability of achieving accountability to purpose, achieved by the announcement of policies. However, the concept of accountability, in the legal literature at least, is not well developed. It is vaguely assumed that the existence of a specific rule will allow a form of redress to an individual who complies with the rule but is nevertheless dealt with as a deviant. An announced speed limit of 35 miles per hour ought to allow redress to a person prosecuted for unsafe driving at 32 miles per hour. Whether redress is possible in practice depends upon a variety of factors relating to the initiation of remedies, proof, and so forth, that will be considered in relation to enforcement. Another meaning of accountability, however, relates to fidelity to purpose. Here the actual process of rule-making is significant. The rule, as the product of that process, becomes the formal operational definition of purpose. There is also a hint in this sense of accountability of an element of *rationality*, a logical and publicized exercise demonstrating the link between powers conferred and consequential action. Although the exercise itself may result in a rule that is arbitrary, or unreasonable, its public aspect opens it to scrutiny and challenge.

These meanings of accountability have a different sense from those advanced by Dicey in his concept of the "rule of law,"[35] which is also directed at accountability, but more at the mistrust of any official discretion, largely on the ground that an affected person must know the rules before being subjected to them ex post facto. Here we have a principle of justice that no one should be condemned without a presumed knowledge of the rule he is alleged to have breached. This assumes a penal law and is understandable in that context where in a world without rules much behavior would involve risky guesses with serious

---

[33] See, generally, Breyer (1982); Breyer and Stewart (1985).
[34] See Mashaw (1983); Ely (1980).
[35] Dicey 1985.

consequences for noncompliance. It is surely fairer to a person prosecuted for dangerous driving to have been made aware of the precise speed limit.

This argument has a slightly different compulsion when dealing not with regulation but with the allocation of resources. Is it fairer to an applicant for a university place to know the precise grades required for entrance? Or an applicant for social welfare benefits to know the precise "entitlement" to a new winter coat? Only recently has an argument been made for "rights" based on ascertainable rules in these areas, which were previously considered "privileges" to be determined at the discretion of the decision-maker.

Legalization is also said to encourage justice—to the extent that rules speak generally and promote uniformity, or the "like" treatment of "like" cases. Regulation of wages or prices, for example, that specifies a certain permissible percentage increase per annum will, if enforced regularly, apply equally to all and be no respecter of particularistic factors. Similarly, welfare benefits specifying a given entitlement should apply to all who qualify, irrespective of their personal merit in the eye of the decision-maker, or factors such as their race, political predilections, or personal connections.

The virtues of legalization as a technique in the implementation process are therefore largely the virtues of legality. These virtues stress congruence to official purpose and distributive justice and accountability, loosely so-called. While none of these virtues speaks directly to substance, they implicitly suggest an adherence to rational decision-making, to purpose, and to the reduction of arbitrariness. This is done by proscribing decision-making criteria that are unrelated to organizational ends or prescribing those that are. As Selznick points out, legalization does not simply allow officials to "congratulate themselves—and await obedience."[36] The rules in themselves may generate scrutiny and appraisal that make them subject to assessment in the light of substantive ends. Legality in itself therefore provides a tendency toward criticism of a law's substance and opens the door to moral debate.

We have thus far considered the principles of legality that are desirable features of any scheme of implementation. To these should be added the advantages to the implementing agent itself of legalization.

Much organization theory tends to assume that implementing agencies oppose legal constraints on their discretion in an effort to maintain and enhance their freedom of action. Legalization also, however, possesses administrative advantages. Rules announce or clarify official policies to affected parties and thus facilitate obedience. They may also allow more efficient handling of cases by allowing routine treatment of cases. A zoning system in planning, a list of features of "substandard" housing, a list of grades for university admission, all allow decisions to be taken more quickly and without constant reappraisal. This in turn reduces the anxiety factor in any administration and conserves the constant energy needed to decide on a case-by-case basis. Max Weber's portrayal of his ideal-typical bureaucrat applying rules *sine ira et studio* alludes to the nonaffective approach of a legalized framework, to the possibility of insulating the decision-maker from the pressure of constant reconsideration. Despite the fact that rules may promote criticism they also, in the short run at least, provide a shield behind which officials may hide, pleading equal and uniform justice in response to criticism.

The virtues of legalization speak largely to the general issues of accountability and administrative dispatch. The general effect is to reduce the personality of both official

[36]Selznick 1949, p. 29.

and affected client in order to promote an "objective" discharge of business. These features are often opposed to another virtue of implementation, namely, that of responsiveness. This tension is seen typically in the rigid "bureaucratic" adherence to a rule in the face of the individual circumstances in a given case. Here we can turn the features mentioned above on their heads and list the virtues as defects. In particular, a virtue from the point of view of the administrator may be seen as a defect from the point of view of the client and vice versa. Uniformity, for example, may be seen also as excusing individualized application. The advantages of routine dispatch of business may preclude a flexible response to a unique situation. The "rational" element in rule-making may produce a result that is not itself easily subject to change and does not itself contain any explanation. Distributive justice may work against individualized justice precisely because cases are not "alike." The administrator's shield may be seen as an unjustified protection from the client's sword.

The competing demands of accountability and responsiveness are echoed in a concern of organization analysts with managerial problems that relate to the implementation of goals. The attempt to devise "rational" procedures for implementation that avoid "distortions" (the refractions referred to in the diagram above) has led to a reliance on the techniques of legalization, setting out routines, procedures, and criteria that are intended to be pursued at various stages of the organizational hierarchy. Commentators have pointed out, however, that these techniques lead in turn to their own distortions and become instances of a bureaucratic pathology, since the ritualistic attachment to these rules is often for the purpose not of advancing organizational goals but of reflecting the status needs of individuals within the organizations.

The essence of the defect of legalization lies in the tendency to legalism. Paradoxically, the search for a reduction of the arbitrary may lead to the legalistic. Arbitrary and legalistic decisions both share the common feature of lack of fidelity to organizational ends. Legalistic enforcement of a traffic law, for example, would prosecute a driver driving through a red light that was stuck, or a doctor driving to an accident on a deserted street at night narrowly exceeding the 30-mile-per-hour limit. Arbitrary enforcement would prosecute only large cars, or blue cars, or bearded drivers. We should note that the mode of enforcement here can be arbitrary (selecting for enforcement by no rational criteria), while the act is nevertheless unlawful (exceeding the speed limit) and the discretion therefore authorized. This differs from a decision that is often said to be arbitrary in the sense of being unauthorized, or unlawful—beyond the powers conferred. An example is the charging of a motorist who in fact did not exceed the speed limit.

Kagan[37] has developed dimensions of modes of rule application which he presents in the dichotomized form shown in Figure 1, which alludes to some of the issues disclosed above. He distinguishes two dimensions of rule application, one that emphasizes adherence to rules and one that emphasizes realization of organizational ends.[38] His "judicial mode" with a high degree of emphasis on each is equivalent to what I have called the legalized decision, and his "legalism" accords with the legalistic decision described above. "Retreatism" is characterized by avoidance of decisions, refusal to take responsibility for any definitive rule application, or cynical manipulation of the rules for the purely personal gain or convenience of the official. "Unauthorized discretion" refers to the deliber-

[37] Kagan 1978, pp. 85–98.
[38] Kagan 1978, p. 95.

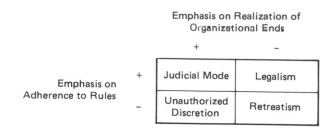

FIGURE 1

Kagan's modes of rule application.

ate ignoring of rules by officials in order to achieve certain outcomes: the policeman who tickets drivers who have broken no legal rule but who seem to him a threat to public safety; the policeman who violates constitutional rules of search and seizure in order to apprehend drivers who the policeman thinks have broken the law in other contexts. Another example would be the welfare department official who circumvents the rules prescribing maximum welfare payments for different classes of recipients in order to provide a recipient with what he—the official—believes is a minimal amount of money to live on decently.

Kagan's distinctions show clearly the different dimensions of the judicial and legalistic decision. His placing of "retreatism" is close to the conventionally "arbitrary" decision (which includes features such as negligence, neglect, and capriciousness). If we were to examine not modes of rule application but modes of legal implementation (the subject of this essay), adjustment could be made to his labeling of "unauthorized" discretion (Figure 2). The perfectly authorized and lawful discretionary decision could stand in its place since that decision, unconfined by a rule, nevertheless allows emphasis on the realization of organizational ends. The unauthorized decision thus falls away as irrelevant for purposes of this revised analysis.

Judicialization

The defects of a fully legalized model of implementation suggest that the discretionary mode has advantages in terms of flexibility of approach yet fidelity to organizational ends. The "discretionary" decision may be formally without structure, for example, leaving to the individual police officer the decision whether or not to prosecute, or it may be structured by any one of a number of forms involving participation or individual justification. The perfectly judicialized decision is one in which proofs and arguments are presented to an "independent" adjudicator.[39] The form of institutionalized participation in itself structures the discretion by exposing the decision-maker to the claims of the interested persons. The independent adjudication role also presumes an unbiased umpire who does not meet with either party in private. Procedural devices such as the right to cross-examination add to the rational intent, which is above all furthered by a reasoned decision, involving justification and the possibility of future criticism.

In addition, adjudication in its perfect form contains a number of functional prerequisites. These flow from the method of institutional participation which requires proofs and

[39] See Fuller (1963, p. 3).

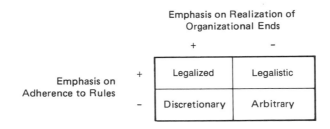

FIGURE 2

Modes of legal implementation.

arguments and therefore requires decision referents to which they can be directed. These referents take the form of rules (of more or less specificity, shading into standards) or of principles.

In his discussion of appropriate adjudicative action in a *judicial* context, Dworkin makes a distinction between principles, to which judges may refer, and policies, to which they may not.[40] Policies involve that kind of standard that sets out a collective goal to be reached. Principles involve standards of justice, fairness, and other dimensions of morality, such as that no man may profit by his own wrong. Arguments of policy justify a political decision by showing that the decision respects or secures some individual or group right.

The distinction between principles and policies is, with his denial of "strong" judicial discretion, central to Dworkin's thesis that judges do not "make" the law. Their task involves weighing of principles, not the application of policy.

This view ties in to Dworkin's view of discretion.[41] He denies that judges possess discretion in his strong sense. Dworkin recognizes judgment (or discretion in the weak sense) where the official is bound by a set of standards (such as the discretion of the sergeant to pick "the five most experienced men" for a patrol). But he denies that judges have discretion in the strong sense (as when the sergeant may pick any five men he chooses for a patrol).

Dworkin's view here is not without some force. For example, the British Supplementary Benefits Commission (SBC) at present grants weekly benefits to applicants according to a catalogue of rules (based on number in family, resources, age, and so forth) and a residual category to cover exceptional needs. These "exceptional needs" payments could be said to be the hole in the doughnut; the area of discretion left open by the surrounding belt of restriction.

A closer look, however, will show that the SBC has discretion only in Dworkin's weak sense. Various policy documents lay down criteria to govern the use of the SBC officer's discretion (one winter coat every four years, for example). It is nevertheless useful to refer to the SBC as exercising discretion, which is defined correctly by K. C. Davis: "A public officer has discretion whenever the effective limits on his power leave him free to make a choice among possible courses of action or inaction."[42] Discretion is the room for decisional maneuver possessed by a decision-maker. It is rarely absent, rarely absolute. It

---

[40] Dworkin 1977, p. 82.
[41] Dworkin 1977, pp. 31–35.
[42] Davis 1969.

ranges along a continuum. When it is low it is usually constrained by rules (such as the rule that a given number of witnesses shall sign a will) and when it is high it is usually governed by standards such as "reasonableness."

It is not necessary here to join the debate as to the appropriate judicial role. The purpose of the present discussion is to indicate constraints on discretion provided by adjudication in the implementation of a law. Here a difference arises between *judicial* and *administrative* enforcement, for in the latter reference to *policy* is not only permissible but frequently the very purpose of the exercise. Policy thus becomes an inevitable decision referent in administrative adjudication. It is often the subject of the adjudication itself.

The application of policy does not, of course, exclude recourse to rules or adjudication. First, as we have noted, a policy may be operationalized by rules. The policy of preventing unsafe driving of vehicles, for example, is legalized as rules (for example, speed limits) are specified. Because of the open texture of language, the rule may still require interpretation (is a pedal car a vehicle?), which gives further scope to adjudicative techniques. In many cases, however, policies are specified not by rules but by less specific standards, general directions (like rules), which require for their implementation a qualitative evaluation. (Is the landlord seeking a "fair rent"? Was the vehicle going at a "reasonable speed"?) This standard may be accommodated over time to shifting practices and values.

If adjudication in an administrative setting allows, and even requires, what, according to Dworkin, is not permitted in a judicial setting, namely, reference to policies, is the process still legitimate to interested persons? Nonet argues that any decision is legitimated by purposive application of laws. One can answer the question more generally by considering the merits and defects of administrative adjudication from the point of view of an affected litigant.

Perhaps the most obvious merits of adjudication for the litigant arise from the fact that it guarantees participation to affected parties. Although they do not make the final decision, the litigants are involved in the decision-making process and are permitted to plead for a decision in their favor and to challenge each other's proofs and arguments. Being immediately involved, they are well placed to advance the strongest case for their proposition. This benefit applies whether the litigant is arguing to principle or to policy.

Rules, as we have seen, are in a sense nonrational. The adjudicator's obligation to reason will provide a check against the use of criteria that are improper, arbitrary, or legalistic, or fail to achieve congruence between the effect of the decision and official objectives. Adjudication contains a desire to give "formal and institutional expression to the influence of reasoned argument in human affairs."[43] The requirement that a decision be justified, and that the justification be published, implies that the justification is open to public criticism. Thus, adjudication normally provides an opportunity for scrutiny and thus for the accountability of the decision-makers to their clientele and to the public.

What strengthens this point is the nature of the justifications embodied in judicialized decisions. Such decisions must be justified by a rule, standard, or principle. Ascriptive or particularistic criteria are illegitimate. Litigants will make their claims as members of a generalized category. In consequence, an appeal to power, private interests, or political expediency will be inappropriate. The adjudicator will in turn be bound to evaluate the claims by means of accepted techniques and by reference to authoritative guides, rather

---

[43] Fuller 1963, p. 13.

than his personal interest in the result or his personal predisposition toward the claimants.

Administrators might also derive benefits from the fact that a reasoned decision was made and openly arrived at with equal participation. The process of adjudication, whatever the decision, might therefore provide administrative action with the gloss of legitimacy.

A final merit of adjudication is the fact that it involves incremental elaboration of laws on a case-by-case basis. Although an organization might feel itself bound by its own decisions, adjudication deals with a specific fact situation, and later cases can be "distinguished" from earlier ones on the basis of the facts. Thus, despite pressures for consistency, which might lead to a rule's ossification, and for the gradual reduction of discretion (features that students of the common law know too well), the case-by-case approach of adjudication allows an administrative body to deal with cases as they arise and to build its commitments gradually, and even to change its mind.

Offsetting these benefits, however, are certain countervailing costs, largely arising from the necessary adversarial structure of the adjudicative format. The adversary structure in itself may be potentially damaging, as it provokes antagonism between the litigants who may need to work together in the future. The adversary-adjudicative situation also places the participants in what game theorists call a "zero-sum" situation. One side must win; the other must lose. The defendant is liable or not liable, guilty or not guilty. Except for the possibility of a flexible settlement out of court, the matter is placed in a clear yes-no, either-or, more-or-less setting. Matters that are suited to compromise, mediation, and accommodation are not best pursued in the structured adversary setting of adjudication.

Rules, as we have seen, may be of benefit to officials as a means of announcing policies to affected parties. Individual application of laws is thus possible without the necessity of administrative intervention. Adjudicative decisions, however, are less possible of communication because they arise in the context of specific dispute situations. The specific dispute orientation of adjudication highlights another defect from the administrative perspective: it concerns individual rights and may thus bear little relation to the primary administrative function, which involves the performance of a particular task. A particular case, for example, may raise questions wider than the question at issue. The adjudicator may deal with the wider questions but is not required to do so, and remarks made on the wider issue are considered strictly *obiter dicta* and thus not binding on future cases. Furthermore, although the specific decision may affect outside parties, the decision-maker is not required to consult or to notify these wider interests.

Institutional Controls on Discretion

Judicialization itself controls discretion to the extent that it influences fidelity to organizational ends or, as put by Nonet, encourages "purposive decisions."[44] It should be repeated that this view adopts what we have seen is a "top-down" approach to organizational decision-making. Ends and purpose are assumed to exist. An alternative "bottom-up" approach would instead see purpose as designed incrementally, carved out of the coal

---

[44] Nonet 1980, p. 263.

face. We shall discuss this later. For the moment organizational ends may be assumed and methods considered that may control administrative discretion to depart from those ends.

Adjudication itself provides a procedural model of control that relies on participation of affected parties. This participatory mode may also be applied outside the adjudicative format. Institutional design may allow the participation of affected persons in a nonadjudicative setting. Nonet[45] presents the models of legitimation that attempt to achieve this. The "pragmatic model" is based upon a principle of "maximum feasible inquiry" leaving it largely to the organization itself to involve the interests involved. The "pluralist model" goes further and builds affected interests into the exercise of organizational powers, thus politicizing the decisions and giving the institution the responsibility to open a forum and manage conflicts within a defined jurisdiction. Echoes of these models are found in British planning law where, moving from an ideology that protects private property and its institutions, two ideologies now compete for recognition, one based upon an ideology of "public interest" (based upon Benthamite principles and relying on public officials to formulate the general interest) and the other based upon an ideology of "public participation" giving a right to all interests—owners of property as well as tenants and neighbors—to a say in all land-use planning decisions.[46]

It might be noted here that participation, in its "pragmatic" or "pluralist" form, does not guarantee a substantive decision that is necessarily faithful to organizational purposes as initially conceived. It is therefore not necessarily a device of accountability. It is, however, a device of responsiveness, an alternative and sometimes competing ideal, which considers acceptability and legitimacy of day-to-day decisions a value in itself.

On the other hand, it is well known that those who involve themselves in participation with an agency may not be representative of the range of interests affected by agency decisions. Representative democracy through periodic election is seen by some for that reason as more democratic, with more possibility of general responsiveness, or less liable to be responsive to sectional interests, than a participatory mode.

Institutionalized participation, in one form or another, is thus a method of controlling discretion through what Davis[47] would call its "structuring"—although he refers here largely to open rule-making procedures and tends to ignore ways of structuring discretion through institutional design that aims at responsiveness through participatory mechanisms. Davis also refers to the "check" on discretion, usually through appeals, not only to courts, but internal administrative review—providing a further look at the decision in question through fresh eyes. To this technique we may add the check on discretion by means of an independent, nonlegal body such as the Ombudsman or, in eastern Europe, by the Prokuratura. In Britain, it is common for decision-making bodies of local authorities to be reviewed by central government, by an inspector at a public inquiry, hearing the matter on behalf of a minister or, increasingly, deciding the issue himself.

In addition to the institutional controls on discretion mentioned, we should add what may be called the general principles of administrative law. These operate in varying degree in different countries and are provided through statute, such as the United States Administrative Procedure Act, or incremental development through a "common law"

---

[45] Nonet 1980, p. 263.
[46] McAuslan 1980.
[47] Davis 1969.

system, as in Britain (although there, too, statute specifies certain procedures before statutory tribunals and inquiries).

A good deal of general administrative law directs the procedures of rule-making and adjudicative bodies and thus informs the content of the legalization and judicialization discussed above. Other rules of administrative law address themselves more broadly to any kind of official decision and thus influence and control discretion (at least to the extent that they are known and acted upon). An example here is the English judicially created doctrine that discretion should not be "fettered" by rule to the extent that a decision-maker must not shut his ears to an application and refuse to listen to anyone with something new to say. An extension of another judicially created doctrine, the right to "natural justice," or a "fair hearing," the "fettering" concept seems to fly in the face of Davis's advice to "confine" discretion wherever possible. Where a decision-maker does so limit his discretion by a rule (for example, that local authorities who spend over 20 percent above their previous year's expenditure will be penalized by losing a proportion of central government grant), the adherents of confining discretion would point up the benefits of specifying the rule about overspending and of limiting a broad discretionary power (to penalize local authorities as the minister "thinks fit"). The rule, however, may in itself cause injustice, or not be fair to the individual case, hence the judicially developed procedure rule requiring the decision-maker who develops such a rule not to fetter his discretion totally, and at least to hear someone who may cast doubt upon the routine application of the rule to that individual case.[48]

ENFORCEMENT OF LAWS
Tasks

Government performs such a variety of regulatory tasks in modern industrialized states that the issues concerning the enforcement or implementation of any one "law" will differ in kind and content from that of another. Clearly there will be great differences in one area of regulation, such as the police enforcement of crime, from another, such as the enforcement of land-use planning controls, consumer protection laws, pollution laws, or the implementation of welfare benefits. Studies that attempt to draw generalized conclusions from any of these areas may be flawed, particularly since even within these areas there may be differences in style, in administrative and legal culture, and in many other factors that force an admission of particularity.

On the other hand, it may also be worth noting those factors which do influence the enforcement process and examining those conditions which may be of general application. We may perhaps begin to aid this process by making a distinction between the various tasks that government does perform. Lowi's policy classification[49] may be helpful here, providing a distinction between (a) distributive policies which have the purpose of creating "public goods"; (b) regulatory policies, both those seeking "public goods," such as antipollution laws, and those seeking to protect specific populations, such as antidiscrimination laws; (c) redistributive policies, such as the provision of welfare benefits.

[48] *Regina* v. *Secretary of State for the Environment* 1982, p. 693.
[49] Lowi 1972, p. 32.

Lowi's fourth category, "constituent policy" (or rules about rules or power), need not concern us now.

It is not suggested here that this classification is completely descriptive of the administrative process. For example, it could be argued that it ignores a vital governmental task, namely, the entrepreneurial task, where government itself through ownership of land or resources performs a managerial task in the public interest. It is suggested that such a classification points up an appreciation of the disparate tasks performed by modern government and introduces a note of caution about generalizing about enforcement and implementation processes across the board.

Levels of Discretion

A further distinction which ought to be made about enforcement refers to the discretionary decision. Most studies of enforcement assume a discretion to implement, or enforce, but fail to distinguish various levels at which that discretion may come into play.

The first level may be that of actual standard-setting. Relevant legislation may provide an open-textured discretion to the enforcement agency to set the standards of deviant or permissible conduct. For example, laws against air pollution in Great Britain allow the enforcement agency, the Alkali Inspectorate, to determine the standard, known as the "best practicable means," for each industrial process. For some processes the standard simply forbids the emission of "dark smoke." Initially this was determined on a case-by-case basis, but subsequently the standard was made more specific by employing grades made available by a diagrammatic chart known as the Ringelmann Chart. Even under the Alkali Inspectorate's wide definition, standards of presumptive limits on the concentration of gases and particles have been set—for example, providing that emissions from cadmium works must contain less than 0.0017 grain per cubic foot. Other standards refer to use of plant, specifying minimum chimney heights, condition and maintenance of kilns, type of fuel, and so on.

The second level of discretion is of a "weaker" kind (in Dworkin's sense) than the first and involves the application of the standard to the conduct. At first sight this might appear to be a question of pure judgment (Was the car driving at a "reasonable speed," or at 30 miles per hour? Did the firm use its "best practicable means" to reduce pollution?). However, where the standard itself is vague, the interpretational question is not one of pure fact. The decisional latitude in itself provides room for maneuver on the part of the decision-maker and allows a variety of external factors to influence the interpretation of the standard. In other words, the term "best practical means" is sufficiently imprecise to allow its definition to be influenced by an assessment of, for example, the costs of the abatement of the pollution to that particular owner, as well as his attitude toward the officials and the problem, taking into account whether he was cooperative or defiant. The standard does not in so many words invite the latter considerations to be taken into account, but in the real world factors that are known to influence the invocation of the enforcement process (such as the attitude of the offender) frequently also influence the interpretation of the standard as applied to the concrete-fact situation and thus influence the definition of the offense itself. In this sense the decision-maker, in practice, has discretion whether or not to take these external factors into account in his definition of the standard.

The third level of discretion applies to the decision to invoke the enforcement process.

Studies of criminal law tend to concentrate here on the decision to arrest or to prosecute, invoking a system that could lead to the deprivation of the offender's liberty, or to penalties such as a fine. Many other enforcement decisions are taken within the criminal system, including whether to grant bail, to caution, or to sentence. In the field of trade regulation or environmental protection the decision to prosecute with a view to penalty is usually taken as a last resort, after attempts to persuade the offender to implement the law have failed. But here, too, the decision whether or not to invoke the enforcement process, even through conciliation, may involve a high degree of discretion.

Influences on Enforcement

In the discussion that follows the distinction between the levels of discretion mentioned above will not always be maintained because all three levels—the establishment of standards, the definition of the offense, and the invocation of the penalty—may be influenced by similar considerations. Another reason, as has been suggested, is that the exercise of any one level may affect the others. For example, the decision not to invoke the prosecution process (say, for dangerous driving) may be expressed as a decision denying the breach of the law (by refusing to label the driving as "dangerous").

The influences on enforcement and implementation are many and will not all be considered here. They vary from the obvious one of financial resources allowing detection and apprehension, to inter-organizational morale of the administration itself. Other factors are more dependent upon the area of enforcement and particular social or cultural factors. For example, La Fave[50] identifies a number of categories or situations where discretion not to arrest is exercised, thus forestalling any possibility of prosecution. These include ambiguous or anachronistic laws, cases where the offender belongs to a minority group among whom the conduct in question is thought to be common, where the victim is unwilling to press charges, or where the prosecution is felt to achieve nothing (he believes cases of domestic violence come into this category). Wilcox's[51] list of reasons why police would not prosecute an offense is longer, taking into account personal factors such as extreme youth, old age, or consequences for a person of otherwise good character. James Q. Wilson stresses the "varieties of police behavior" (in a book of that title)[52] dependent upon organizational arrangements, community attachments, and institutionalized norms governing the daily life of the police and providing its "ethos." Studies of regulation, by contrast, tend to note the power of regulated groups as a factor influencing enforcement.

It is probably not fruitful to attempt, in this essay, to list the various influences on enforcement that may or may not depend on particular circumstances, organizations, and cultures. Instead, three main influences upon enforcement will be noted, relating to the nature of the offense, the nature of the offender, and the officer's perception of the law's purpose. Here, too, it should be stressed, it will be necessary to be relatively selective in the issues covered.

The Offense   A number of studies have noted that a key element in the behavior toward deviance of enforcement agents is the nature of the conduct to be controlled. In

[50] La Fave 1965.
[51] Wilcox 1972, p. 25.
[52] Wilson 1968.

criminal law, what are known as "victimless crimes" (such as drug offenses) may be enforced less rigorously than crimes where a victim has suffered tangible harm. The setting of the deviance may also affect the enforcement process; for example, violence in a family setting is less likely to be prosecuted than that in a public place,[53] and the way the offense was brought to the notice of the enforcement agency may also determine the attitude toward enforcement. It has been noted, for example, that when agencies adopt a "reactive" approach to enforcement, relying on external complaints bringing infringements to their notice, they perceive themselves as having less discretion to enforce or refrain from enforcing than when their approach is "proactive," and the agency makes a positive effort itself to discover breaches of the law.[54]

It has been said that behavior that is normally the subject of regulatory control often differs from behavior traditionally labeled as "criminal" because of a great moral ambivalence surrounding it. Thus, breach of pollution control, for example, is said not to evoke the strong feelings of moral outrage associated with theft, murder, or assault. Kadish considers conduct addressed by regulation as largely "morally neutral."[55] In criminal law a distinction is made between *mala in se* and *mala prohibita,* offenses that are wrong in themselves, without further ado, and those which are prohibited wrongs, requiring further enforcement. The sociologist David Matza uses the word "prohibition" to describe the regulatory as opposed to traditional criminal offense.[56] He considers that prohibitions are still crimes, because they do elicit authorized state intervention, but they differ from other crimes in "failing to self-evidently warrant state intervention." Matza calls the traditional crimes "consensual crimes." Conklin distinguishes acts considered "illegal" from those considered "criminal."[57]

The consequence of the regulatory as opposed to "consensual" crimes is said by these commentators to involve greater discretion to evoke the enforcement process as well as a more conciliatory style of enforcement with a reliance on informal regulating procedures. In short, regulatory offenders have more chance of avoiding any penalty than those who have committed the "consensual" crimes.

This thesis is to a large extent borne out by data. In Britain, the number of court proceedings brought for violation of air pollution regulations is minuscule.[58] The penalties imposed for breach of regulatory laws by courts are often small, and the reasons are not hard to find. Regulatory laws, to a large extent over industrial and commercial practices, aim to control aspects of economic life that themselves have benefits in production and the maintenance of employment. The victims of the "crime" are often not clearly identifiable (Who suffers from an inflationary wage deal or the erection of a building contrary to planning control?). Furthermore, the legislation itself usually expressly allocates discretion to enforce the law, either by providing, as with British land-use planning law, the authority with the power to enforce if it considers it "expedient," or by providing, as with Anglo-American antidiscrimination law, the agency with the power to proceed by way of conciliation rather than direct criminal prosecution as a first step. Contrast this with traditional criminal law, which simply defines the offense. The

[53] See Freeman (1979); Parnas (1967, p. 914).
[54] Reiss 1971; Black and Reiss 1970, p. 63.
[55] Kadish 1963, p. 432.
[56] Matza 1964, pp. 71, 161.
[57] Conklin 1977.
[58] See two recent British studies: Hawkins 1984; Richardson, Ogus, and Burrows 1982.

normal agents of enforcement (police, prosecutors, or attorneys general) then, implicitly, have power to seek sanctions through the courts. Finally, the definition of the regulatory crimes is normally left to the enforcement agency itself. This relates to the different levels of discretion (to define the standard as well as invoke the enforcement process) discussed above. Since the definition of the crime is itself vague, or incorporates the possibility of evasion (such as the "best practicable means" test) or permits a negotiated solution (as with antidiscrimination laws), it is more difficult to associate moral disapprobrium with deviance than with those crimes (such as murder, rape, arson, and theft) that are relatively clearly defined by the legislative process independent of the agency of enforcement.

We ought not to accept the thesis of the less rigorous enforcement of regulatory laws too uncritically, however. Some behavior proscribed by regulatory laws may, after time, become both clearly defined by the incremental elaboration of standards, and also more generally accepted as morally wrong. A case in point might be that of laws against racial and sexual discrimination. Both in Britain and in America these laws were introduced tentatively and with some reservation about interfering with individual and business freedom of choice. The conciliation machinery was introduced partly as a device to give the law the appearance of moral flexibility. However, over time discrimination was no longer considered morally acceptable, and "moral entrepreneurs"[59] presented themselves as advocates of a vigorous approach to the law's more stringent enforcement. Individuals affected by discrimination considered themselves to be victims of deviant behavior and sought to establish their rights against the wrongdoers. In England, so pronounced was this change in attitude to the laws that individuals alleging discrimination were given the right of direct suit against the discriminator through a tort action. Similar examples could be taken from environmental protection laws. At first displaying some moral ambivalence, attitudes changed owing to the progressive definition of standards, public awareness of the harm, and the development of a powerful environmental lobby. The mode of enforcement moved from the proactive to the reactive, with less opportunity for the agency to exercise its discretion not to enforce.

The Offender   There are obvious aspects of the nature and attitude of the offender that will affect individual instances of enforcement, but perhaps less obvious aspects that affect the enforcement process as a whole.

Individual instances may be affected by the two variables postulated by Selznick[60]: danger and authority. Police, having to act quickly in a situation of danger, cultivate "symbolic assailants." Where the victim fits a stereotypical description of that assailant police action is likely to be hostile, affecting vaguely defined areas such as being a "suspicious person" and "loitering with intent." In addition, a number of studies explain differential rates of arrest on the basis of a suspect's cooperation. Police judgment of substantive misconduct is mitigated, according to these studies, by diffidence of the suspect and aggravated by arrogance and defiance.[61]

Expressions of cooperation are also noted as a factor influencing enforcement in the regulatory field. Blau notes that violators in this context were regarded as honest businessmen who had inadvertently engaged in practices that conflicted with some complex

[59] Becker 1963, pp. 147–62.
[60] Selznick 1949, p. 62.
[61] Bottomley 1973, chap. 2.

legal regulations, unless they were willful and repeating offenders.[62] Only the latter were brought into court. In a more recent study three causes of noncompliance are identified, each eliciting a different enforcement strategy. Kagan notes,[63] first, business firms regarded as "amoral calculators," motivated by profit and breaking the law when it is in their interest to do so. In answer to such noncompliance the agency acts aggressively and enforces strictly. Second, the firm is seen as a political citizen whose managers hold strong views as to the nature of proper business conduct. Here noncompliance stems from "principled disagreement" with regulations seen as unreasonable, and the agency attempts to persuade the violator of the rationality of the regulations. Third, the firm may be seen as "organizationally incompetent." In this instance the agency would act so as to advise and assist the violator to comply with the law.

The perception of the offender should also be seen in an organizational and cultural context. Wilson[64] noted the different styles of police enforcement influenced by various factors, including the perception of the offender. His "watchman style," which used discretion to achieve "order-maintenance" rather than law enforcement, was influenced by a "personal" style of a force recruited locally and therefore did not regard violators as alien or hostile. This contrasted with the "legalistic style," where a professional, specialized force stressed their enforcement role. The "service style" departments were again formed in homogeneous (suburban middle class) communities, and they stressed informal sanctioning mechanisms. Maureen Cain's English study[65] of policing resembles Wilson's results; her rural force, in a homogeneous area, shared values and definitions of policing with potential offenders and adopted peace-keeping, service style, as opposed to that of the urban force, where the police adopted a law-enforcement "thief taking" view of their task in the face of a heterogeneous community.

Official Perception of the Law's Purpose   We have seen that enforcement may be influenced by the nature of the offense. Those offenses that are "morally ambivalent," for example, are enforced selectively, and with conciliation rather than prosecution as the main technique. We consider here not the specific nature of the offense and its properties but the aims of the law itself as seen by the enforcement agency or officer.

Any rational application of a discretionary enforcement power contains an appreciation of the purpose behind the exercise. Wilson's "styles" of enforcement are influenced by a variety of factors but also exist to achieve, in their particular environment, a variety of purposes. Bittner[66] comments upon the instrumental use of law on skid row and suggests that the police seek compliance not as an end in itself but as a resource enabling them to achieve some further objective. The point is that the officer's conception of the law's purpose will influence in turn his technique of enforcement.

Returning to our black box into which we saw a law's "purpose" being shone, we may now repeat as simplistic the frequent misconception that that purpose is fixed, defined, and immutable. We raised the possibility that purpose itself may be postponed for definition by the enforcement agency. The process of enforcement as well as standard-setting involves search for purpose.

[62] Blau 1955, especially chap. 9.
[63] Kagan 1979.
[64] Wilson 1968.
[65] Cain 1973.
[66] Bittner 1967, p. 699.

Following the example of the laws controlling pollution, it soon becomes clear to any pollution enforcement agency that both the ultimate purpose of the law and the raison d'être of the agency are not clearly established. A recent study of pollution control in England discovered that officials had three possible purposes of prosecution of violators.[67] The first regarded prosecution as achieving "just deserts," punishing a culpable act in its own right apart from any utilitarian concern with deterrence. This view was held by a minority of enforcement officers, who understood the violation itself to carry with it a notion of culpability and moral condemnation, and the purpose of their task, and that of the law, to punish offenders. A larger proportion of officials however justified prosecution in the interest of deterrence as an encouragement to others to comply. They saw the law's purpose as achieving a broader effect of the reduction of pollution generally.

A more vivid example can be taken from laws against racial discrimination. In a study of their enforcement in Massachusetts,[68] I found three distinct approaches to the enforcement of antidiscrimination laws. These approaches were reflected by three different patterns of results of lodged complaints. The reason lay in the commissioners' different conception of purpose (both the law's and the commission's). The commission's early years were characterized by a "didactic" approach to enforcement. In response to considerable opposition to the enactment of the legislation, the commission was at pains to stress that its purpose was "education and conciliation." At this stage the existence of a law was itself considered to have educational qualities, and the commission was there to conciliate cases, to legitimize the law, and to educate respondents in methods of complying with the law.

The second approach was completely different. This was a tort approach. When pressure from civil rights organizations grew, the law was seen as a device to vindicate the rights of individual complainants. The commission at that point concentrated less on persuading and assisting the respondent to comply than on achieving a remedy for the complainant. In England, too, after the early years of conciliation through an enforcement agency complainants were given the right of direct enforcement against the respondent with the possibility of damages.

The third approach was identified as an equal opportunity approach, where individual cases were seen not primarily to "educate" the respondents nor to vindicate the complainants' rights, but to provide a lever for increased opportunities for blacks and more racial integration in the respondent's firm or housing. "Affirmative action" was seen as the law's main goal.

Clearly, different approaches to purpose can exist as complementary aims. Nonetheless, in some cases the various purposes may be contradictory. They may change over time and exist in any one organization among different officials, as seen in the studies referred to previously. They are not generally considered in most organizational studies that tend to assume fixed purpose, an assumption that may not be justified.

In considering the official construction of purpose we should not ignore the way in which it may be shaped by external constraints such as the necessity for external justification, or the complexity of the enforcement process. We have seen above that the impact of a regulatory law is often not easy to assess. Nevertheless, public enforcement agencies will be called upon to justify their record, usually in their annual reports or

[67] Richardson, Ogus, and Burrows 1982.
[68] Jowell 1975, pp. 169–94.

budgetary claims. The need for justification may in some cases lead the agency to pursue cases that look good on the record, no matter whether they genuinely work to achieve organizational goals (insofar as these are clear).[69] Studies have shown the propensity of enforcement agencies to pursue small violators at the expense of the larger in order to give the appearance of active regulation.[70]

ENFORCEMENT AND THE BARGAINING PROCESS

The discussion about organizational purposes points to a feature of the implementation process that does not accept the view that implementation begins when policy-making ends. Pressman and Wildavsky,[71] for example, define implementation as "starting" when two initial conditions are satisfied, namely, the legitimization of policy through the passage of legislation and the allocation of resources. They consider that the evaluation of implementation must necessarily follow the setting of goals through a formal definitional process.

We have noted how goals may be vague, ill-considered, the result of a compromise, and often left to the agency itself to specify. A "bottom-up" view of implementation and enforcement recognizes that the implementation process and the policy-making process may be linked and that policy is defined in its implementation.

That is not to say that standards are always capable of incremental adjustment. Some laws are clearly set by the legislature. However, the discretion to invoke the enforcement process may then create an opportunity of reflection upon purpose and the possibility of negotiated settlement in the light of competing goals. Assault laws, for example, are relatively clear, but their enforcement in a situation of marital violence may lead to a reluctance to prosecute following, as Parnas[72] has found, from recognition by police that prosecution may exacerbate the poor family situation and lead to a termination of relationships and to deprivation. Here the clear purpose behind the law prohibiting violence is considered secondary to a value that seeks to preserve the well-being of the family unit.

Bargaining is thus an integral part of implementation and enforcement. The Weberian notion of mechanical enforcement rarely occurs. As we have seen, a number of variables influence the stringency of the enforcement, but the possibility of a negotiated settlement is, in most forms of regulation, rarely completely absent. Even in a typically "consensual crime," such as murder or theft, the possibility of negotiation arises even after the invocation of enforcement proceedings in the now well-documented "plea bargain." The opportunity for bargaining, however, exists largely in the area of regulation, for reasons discussed above.

In all situations of enforcement, the bargain arises through an assessment on the part of the law enforcer of the damage costs of the act set against the abatement costs.[73] Thus, in cases of marital violence, we see the damage of the assault set against the costs to the family of enforcement. In pollution regulation the damage to the environment may be measured against the costs of abatement—a firm may be forced out of business or may

---

[69] See Thomas (1982).
[70] Turner 1970.
[71] Pressman and Wildavsky 1973, p. 166.
[72] Freeman 1979; Parnas 1967, p. 914.
[73] See Burrows (1980) and Richardson, Ogus, and Burrows (1982).

locate elsewhere, in both cases causing damage to the local economy and causing unemployment. Or the firm might pass on the costs of abatement to the ultimate consumer.

Underlying this assessment are a number of questions about how both damage and abatement costs are calculated. In water pollution control, it is notoriously difficult to measure the output of polluting effluent or to know its impact.[74] The position of the trader is also difficult to assess and hence the potential damage to society of abatement. Because of these uncertainties regulator and regulatee resort to a certain amount of bluff and counter-bluff, and the process is influenced by the attitudes and approaches mentioned above: whether the trader is a "one-off" violator as opposed to a "amoral calculator." The question of "moral fault" becomes relevant, even where, as in the enforcement of safety legislation by the British factory inspectorate, the law provides for strict liability (without fault).[75]

The setting of regulation particularly attracts a negotiating pattern because of the association of the agency with the regulated, over a period of time. As Hawkins points out,[76] the agency's discretion is "informed by continuity" and "exercised in longitudinal perspective." Compared to penal enforcement, which is normally divorced from a historical context, being based upon what is learned about a specific act or set of acts, regulatory agencies deal with a relatively stable and constant population. Pollution agencies, for example, normally know their firms, their trade, their practices, and their attitudes. Their adaptive stance is therefore largely formed in an effort to achieve cooperation. An approach that seeks sanctions rather than compliance and future cooperation would seem not to be productive. It is here of course that a "symbiotic" relationship may develop and accusations of token enforcement and capture tend to be made.

In this essay, we have been mostly considering enforcement of laws through negative sanction—by crime and regulation. We did consider other kinds of implementation under Lowi's classification, which identifies, for example, distributive and redistributive policies that involve agencies in the provision of services and welfare benefits. Issues of discretion and its legal control also arise here, but is the bargaining model still appropriate?

The general answer to that question is that wherever discretion exists bargaining is likely to be engaged. Even in the distribution of resources through a system of welfare benefits, claimants' organizations and agencies may negotiate for benefit levels. An activity of regulation that is partly distributional is that of land-use planning. Countries differ as to the amount of discretion provided to the decision-makers. A strict zoning system technically provides little discretion, although the variance system, allowing for exceptions to the rules, may introduce a discretionary element. In Britain, the system of development control is highly discretionary; people wishing to carry out land development must apply to local authorities, who are statutorily guided in their response by a "development plan" and the broad standard of "other material considerations."

A "judicial" model of implementation of planning in Britain would see planning permissions being granted or refused in accordance with relatively objective rules and standards. This was the case for some years, the rules being based largely upon fairly specific plans, not unlike zoning maps. In the 1970s, however, I discovered that this

---

[74] See Richardson, Ogus, and Burrows (1982); Hawkins (1984).
[75] Carson 1970, p. 396.
[76] Carson 1970, p. 396.

model was increasingly being abandoned in favor of one based upon contract: applicant and authority negotiated a solution whereby the planning permission would be granted and, in return, the applicant would provide what became known as "planning gain," a benefit to the "community" that was not part of the original application. Thus, for example, instances arose where the applicant for office permission was granted that permission, perhaps at a density higher than the norm. The applicant would, however, on his part agree to dedicate part of the site to the local authority, to be used as a public right of way. Some developers would dedicate buildings for a community center, and even build housing for use as public housing.[77]

This method of bartering for planning permission is very different from that of the normal model of regulation, under which the permission is granted or refused (with or without conditions) in accordance with accepted rules and standards. The contractual model involves the negotiation of standards and a resolution that is agreed, not imposed. In this case it permits the parties to provide conditions (such as the dedication of land or buildings) that would be *ultra vires* if imposed by the regulatory scheme.

Why does this regulatory activity, involving in this case the allocation of a resource (planning permission), also assume, like so much of the enforcement activity that we have considered, a contractual form?

Some answers to that question arise from the particular setting of the activity. As opposed to the typical judicial situation, which has been described by Aubert[78] as "triadic" (the classic triad of plaintiff, defendant, and judge), the planning situation is "dyadic," with only two parties, applicant and decision-maker. Aubert considers the intervention of the institutionalized third party to be the "embryo of the legal phenomenon," developed through third-party intervention to stop blood feuding. The triadic, typically judicial, structure is thus reserved for dissensus, for conflict over facts and values. The dyadic structure, by contrast, tends to be based on bargaining and the avoidance or resolution of conflict.

This explanation is helpful to explain the tendency to bargaining in the planning area, and in other areas of implementation as well. It is, however, doubtful whether the dyadic structure is always sufficient of itself to promote bargaining. A necessary element to induce bargaining into the dyadic relationship is that each side has something to give or something to concede that is of value to the other. Since bargaining is a form of what Lindblom[79] calls "partisan mutual adjustment" it works by each party inducing responses from the other.

The applicant for welfare benefits, for example, is in a suppliant position, with nothing to give in return, and therefore unable to influence his caseworker's decision by reciprocal concessions, adjustments, or unrelated public benefits. (He may offer a private benefit, a bribe, in exchange for the grant, but that issue is not being considered here.)

For this reason, bargaining in planning burgeoned during the "property boom" in England. Planning permissions became extremely profitable. Local authorities began to regard it as legitimate to insist that the profit they had made possible be conceded in part exchange for the planning permission, perhaps in the form of housing or a community center.

[77] See Jowell 1977a, p. 414; 1977b, p. 63.
[78] Aubert 1963, p. 26; 1967, p. 40.
[79] Lindblom 1965.

An additional factor encouraging bargaining is a continuing relationship. Where the parties have to continue living with each other, where they are likely to deal in the future, both sides will be keen to strike a reasonable stance and will be reluctant to "throw the book," or to be regarded as a party with whom one cannot strike a fair deal in an atmosphere of future trust. Even a bad bargain may prove more acceptable than a broken relationship. For this reason bargains were struck in most instances between large developers and local authorities, where a pattern of dealing could be expected in the future.

Given these two factors, then, the dyadic relationship will tend to encourage bargaining. However, other negative features of the judicialized decision that we considered earlier may also lead the participants to prefer a negotiated solution to one that is imposed in a regulatory framework.

Where, as in the English planning system, there is an appeal from the local authority's refusal of permission to the minister, and the appeal will be held under the "triadic" structure of a public local inquiry, there is a risk to either side of an all-or-nothing resolution common, as we have discussed, in the adjudicative format, where one side will win and the other lose. Therefore, bargaining in a dyadic situation will promote what game theorists call the "minimax" principle—minimizing the risk of maximum loss. Other characteristics of the judicialized structure also deter its use—for example, the necessity for relatively precise rules or standards. At a time when planning merits were ill-defined, uncertain, and lacking in consensus, the problem of finding clear authoritative guides for decision-making became acute. The resulting discretion on the part of the decision-maker left a good deal of room for maneuver and allowed extraneous, subjective considerations to be accommodated by a process of negotiation.

The implementation of pay policy, as a further example, has been conducted in Britain over the last few years, not by means of a statutory framework but through informal "guidelines," stipulating a maximum percentage for pay settlements. These guidelines were then used in relations with recipients of government contracts or export credit guarantees. The firms who were said to have made inflationary wage settlements had their grants or contracts withdrawn or refused as a sanction for the breach. Procurement powers have also been used to enforce sex or racial employment policy. Discretionary grants under various industrial aid schemes have been used to achieve wider objectives such as the provision of employment in depressed areas, or increased investment. In a completely different area, Daintith[80] describes how the Labour government decided, in 1974, to secure state participation in the exploitation of North Sea oil. This was done by making the new state oil company, British National Oil Corporation, a co-licensee with existing licensees in any production licence covering a commercially exploitable oilfield. This arrangement was achieved, however, not by legislating rules but by negotiation. Those who were reluctant to concede state participation were apparently threatened with a refusal of a future licence. "Voluntary," "consensual" means were used to achieve the objective.

The Administrative Culture of Bargaining

These examples of a shift to a contractual model of law implementation and enforcement have been cited as selective instances. To some extent each depends on specific

[80]Daintith 1979, p. 41; 1985, pp. 174–97.

structures and features of its particular subject matter, such as the judicialized structure and the available standards. Others may be caused by reasons based on political and economic trends and administrative practices, all of which create a general administrative culture.

One recent feature of Anglo-American public administration, for example, has been a move to a "corporate" approach to government.[81] Essentially, corporate planning intends to communicate the idea that an organization should consider its resources and activities as a systemic whole. It argues that the work of government is seriously hampered by the fragmentation of effort between departments, professions, committees, and other units. Corporate planning tries to bridge organizational gaps, to link common subjects, so that decisions are not taken in isolation without consideration of the system as a whole.

The move to a contractual model is affected by a corporate approach in that official "policy" as seen in its broadest sense, and policies developed in one area (say, the housing department, in relation to council housing) can be achieved in another department (by means of planning powers). Thus, an agreement to construct council housing on the roof of a development is granted in return for planning permission. In a similar fashion "government policy" on pay settlements or racial discrimination may be enforced through powers granted for a separate activity, namely, the placing of contracts or the grant of guarantees or financial assistance.

The deeper structural reasons for bargaining may be more culturally bound. In Britain, Daintith notes the move to bargaining based on the increased state ownership of resources.[82] Instead of ordering individual regulatees to act, the state offers its own resources in return for the objectives it seeks. As the potential dispenser of a benefit in the form of a contract, grant, loan, guarantee, licence, export credit, or permission of one kind or another, government is well placed to exact a benefit for the public interest in return. This kind of manipulation through property ownership is not unlike that detected in the grants of government "largesse" through welfare benefits.

To this feature of British institutional structures may be added a mistrust of litigated solutions, a confidence in the civil service to act benevolently, a fear of judicial sabotage of social welfare objectives, and a suspicion of the "pathology" of law.

Looking further into the structure of modern capitalism, other commentators have noted more deeply rooted economic causes of a general move to discretionary governmental operation. Some have used the term "corporatism" to describe a form of "continuous contract" in which power is shared between the state and large organized groups (such as trade unions and industrial organizations) who bargain with each other to establish mutually acceptable goals.[83] The national legislature establishes wide "framework acts" allocating wide discretionary powers to officials, unwilling to be constrained by rules in order freely to indulge in the bargaining process where policies are struck by largely secret negotiative techniques.

[81] See, for example, the British government report, known as the "Bains Report" (1972) after its chairman, that sought to apply "corporate" management structures to reorganized local authorities.

[82] Daintith 1979, p. 41; 1985.

[83] See Middlemas (1979); Newman (1981). Compare Unger (1976). Unger describes the phenomenon of corporatism in his analysis of the decline of the rule of law in "post-liberal society" and sees corporatism as influencing the breakdown of the traditional distinction between public law and private law. Unger associates the bureaucratization of corporate institutions with their ability to become relatively independent power centers with decisive influence over governmental agencies.

J. T. Winkler,[84] accepting this thesis, considers the process to reflect a state role that he calls directive (rather than supportive). The directive role attempts positively to guide and control the economy to improve national economic performance. The state does this by allowing businesses to remain in private hands, but directs their behavior by attempting to specify or limit their decisions. Examples are general financial powers—to tax, spend, lend, grant, subsidize, borrow, levy, license, issue, purchase, and raise tariffs as well as other financial controls—over prices, incomes, dividends, rents, credits, interest rates, investment, exports and imports, and capital movements.

Any one of these devices of implementation of economic policy may be in use at a particular time. The point made by Winkler is that they are increasingly used, selectively against particular firms, and, for the state to utilize them effectively it must be able to act flexibly. The powers normally granted are therefore discretionary. Thus, in Britain at least, dividend control was used to stimulate industrial reorganization, export credit guarantees to bolster incomes policy, employment subsidies to induce companies into negotiated planning agreements, and state purchasing contracts to encourage racial equality in employment and workers' participation. None of these purposes could have been achieved with rule-bound forms of organization and administration.

CONCLUSION

Implementation and enforcement pose enormous challenges to law and the legal order. For too long the cry "there ought to be a law" was not followed by any attempt to analyze the machinery of enforcement or implementation, the capacity of a law to achieve the desired goals, the consequences of the grant of power to officials, and the manner in which that discretion should be exercised and controlled.

One aspect of the problem has been largely ignored in this essay, namely, the initiation of the remedy by individuals. We have discussed problems surrounding official enforcement, but it should by no means be assumed that aggrieved individuals will have the knowledge, capacity, time, or energy to use laws provided for their benefit, or to challenge what may seem impossible odds. Nor should it be assumed even that officials will necessarily know the general principles or specific rules of administrative law that are meant to guide their behavior.

Until fairly recently, legal contribution to enforcement has been content to deal with questions about a law's sanction, criminal or civil, and the effectiveness of either, with little attention to nonjudicialized remedies or those based upon conciliation. With the growth of interest in administrative justice, attention focused on the capacity of legal techniques to deliver services and to affect the process of enforcement. It is at this point that further and better particulars of the workings of organizations become necessary, and the division of legal and organizational studies becomes a hindrance to a proper understanding of the process of implementation and enforcement.

There are still wider questions to be asked that move away from the traditional concern depicted in the black box diagram with nondistorted implementation of purpose. We have seen how purpose is in any event frequently defined in its implementation. Further, there is a more recent concern with issues of accountability, responsiveness, and the

[84] Winkler 1981, pp. 82–134.

control of discretion that deal not only with the merits and defects of law. They force examination of the administrative culture in which law operates, in the context of given social, political, and economic structures.

Any understanding of implementation and enforcement today must understand not only the micro-legal issues dealing with the day-to-day interaction of official and client and the hierarchical and incentive structure within organizations. It must also attend to the macro-legal issues that treat not only the nature and limits of legal devices, but also the context of law and administration in its wider institutional setting.

Bibliography

Allison, Graham T.
    1971   *Essence of Decision: Explaining the Cuban Missile Crisis.* Boston: Little, Brown.
Aubert, Vilhelm
    1963   "Competition and Dissensus: Two Types of Conflict and Conflict Resolution," *Journal of Conflict Resolution* 7(1).
    1967   "Courts and Conflict Resolution," *Journal of Conflict Resolution* 11(1).
Bains Report
    1972   *The New Local Authorities, Management and Structure.*
Barrett, Susan, and Fudge, Colin, eds.
    1981   *Policy and Action: Essays on the Implementation of Public Policy.* London and New York: Methuen.
Becker, Howard Saul
    1963   *Outsiders: Studies in the Sociology of Deviance.* London and Glencoe, Ill.: Free Press.
Bernstein, Marver H.
    1955   *Regulating Business by Independent Commission.* Princeton, N.J.: Princeton University Press.
Bittner, Egon
    1967   "The Police on Skid Row: A Study of Peace Keeping," *American Sociological Review* 32(5).
Black, Donald J., and Reiss, Albert J.
    1970   "Police Control of Juveniles," *American Sociological Review* 35(1).
Blau, Peter M.
    1955   *The Dynamics of Bureaucracy: A Study of Interpersonal Relations in Two Government Agencies.* Chicago and London: University of Chicago Press.
Bottomley, A. Keith
    1973   *Decisions in the Penal Process.* London: Martin Robertson.
Breyer, Stephen G.
    1982   *Regulation and Its Reform.* Cambridge, Mass.: Harvard University Press.
Breyer, Stephen G., and Stewart, Richard
    1985   *Administrative Law and Regulatory Policy: Problems, Text and Cases.* 2nd ed. Boston: Little, Brown.
Burrows, Paul
    1980   *The Economic Theory of Pollution Control.* Cambridge, Mass.: MIT Press. (First published, London: Martin Robertson, 1980.)

Cain, Maureen Elizabeth
  1973   *Society and the Policeman's Role.* London: Routledge and Kegan Paul.
Calabresi, Guido
  1970   *The Cost of Accidents: Legal and Economic Analysis.* New Haven: Yale University Press.
Carson, W. G.
  1970   "Some Sociological Aspects of Strict Liability and the Enforcement of Factory Legislation," *Modern Law Review* 33(4).
Conklin, John E.
  1977   *'Illegal, but Not Criminal': Business Crime in America.* Englewood Cliffs, N.J.: Prentice-Hall.
Daintith, Terence
  1979   "Regulation by Contract: The New Prerogative," *Current Legal Problems* 32.
  1985   "The Executive Power Today: Bargaining and Economic Control." In *The Changing Constitution,* edited by Jeffrey L. Jowell and A. D. Oliver. Oxford: Clarendon.
David, Kenneth Culp
  1969   *Discretionary Justice.* Baton Rouge: Louisiana State University Press.
Dicey, Albert Venn
  1985   *Introduction to the Study of the Law of the Constitution.* London: Macmillan.
Dunsire, Andrew
  1979   *Implementation in a Bureaucracy.* New York: St. Martin's Press.
Dworkin, Ronald
  1977   *Taking Rights Seriously.* Cambridge, Mass.: Harvard University Press.
Edelman, Murry
  1964   *The Symbolic Uses of Politics.* Urbana: University of Illinois Press.
Elmore, Richard F.
  1978   "Organizational Models of Social Program Implementation," *Public Policy* 26(2).
  1979   "Backward Mapping: Implementation Research and Policy Decisions," *Political Science Quarterly* 94(4).
Ely, John Hart
  1980   *Democracy and Distrust: A Theory of Judicial Review.* Cambridge, Mass., and London: Harvard University Press.
Fox, Alan
  1974   *Beyond Contract: Work, Power and Trust Relations.* London: Faber.
Freeman, Michael David Alan
  1979   *Violence in the Home.* London: Saxon House.
Friedman, Lawrence Meir
  1975   *The Legal System: A Social Science Perspective.* New York: Russell Sage Foundation.
Friendly, Henry J.
  1962   *The Federal Administrative Agencies: The Need for Better Definitions of Standards.* Cambridge, Mass.: Harvard University Press.
Fuller, Lon
  1963   "Collective Bargaining and the Arbitrator," *Wisconsin Law Review* (1).
Gouldner, Alvin Ward
  1954   *Patterns of Industrial Bureaucracy.* Glencoe, Ill.: Free Press.
Ham, Christopher, and Hill, Michael
  1984   *The Policy Process in the Modern Capitalist State.* Brighton: Harvester Press.
Hart, H. L. A.
  1961   *The Concept of Law.* Oxford: Clarendon.
Hawkins, Keith
  1984   *Environment and Enforcement: Regulation and the Social Definition of Pollution.* Oxford: Clarendon; New York: Oxford University Press.

Jowell, Jeffrey L.
    1975   *Law and Bureaucracy: Administrative Discretion and the Limits of Legal Action.* New York: Dunellen.
    1977a   "Bargaining in Development Control," *Journal of Planning and Environmental Law.*
    1977b   "The Limits of Law in Urban Planning [1]," *Current Legal Problems* 30.
Kadish, Sanford H.
    1963   "Some Observations on the Uses of Criminal Sanctions in Enforcing Economic Regulations," *University of Chicago Law Review* 30(3).
Kagan, Robert A.
    1978   *Regulatory Justice: Implementing a Wage-Price Freeze.* New York: Russell Sage Foundation.
    1979   "The Criminology of the Corporation and Regulatory Enforcement Strategies." Unpublished paper, presented at the University of Oldenburg.
La Fave, Wayne R.
    1965   *Arrest: The Decision to Take a Suspect into Custody.* Boston: Little, Brown.
Lindblom, Charles E.
    1965   *The Intelligence of Democracy: Decision Making through Mutual Adjustment.* New York: Free Press.
Lowi, Theodore J.
    1972   "Four Systems of Policy, Politics and Choice," *Public Administration Review* 32(4).
Lynes, Tony
    1969   *Welfare Rights.* London: Fabian Society.
McAuslan, Patrick
    1980   *The Ideologies of Planning Law, Urban and Regional Planning Series,* vol. 22. New York: Pergamon.
Mashaw, Jerry
    1983   *Bureaucratic Justice: Managing Social Security Disability Claims.* New Haven: Yale University Press.
Matza, David
    1964   *Delinquency and Drift: From the Research Program of the Center for the Study of Law and Society* (University of California, Berkeley). New York: Wiley.
Mayhew, Leon H.
    1968   *Law and Equal Opportunity: A Study of the Massachusetts Commission Against Discrimination.* Cambridge, Mass.: Harvard University Press.
Merton, Robert King
    1957   *Social Theory and Social Structure.* Glencoe, Ill.: Free Press.
Middlemas, Keith
    1979   *Politics in Industrial Society: The Experience of the British System Since 1911.* New York: Rowman.
Newman, Otto
    1981   *The Challenge of Corporatism.* London: Macmillan.
Nonet, Philippe
    1969   *Administrative Justice: Advocacy and Change in a Government Agency.* New York: Russell Sage Foundation.
    1980   "The Legitimation of Purposive Decisions," *California Law Review* 68(2).
Parnas, Raymond I.
    1967   "The Police Response to Domestic Disturbance," *Wisconsin Law Review* (4).
Pressman, Jeffrey L., and Wildavsky, Aaron B.
    1973   *Implementation: How Great Expectations in Washington Are Dashed in Oakland; or, Why It's Amazing That Federal Programs Work at All, This Being a Saga of the Economic Development Administration as Told by Two Sympathetic Observers Who*

Seek to Build Morals on a Foundation of Ruined Hopes. Berkeley: University of California Press.

Regina v. Secretary of State for the Environment ex parte London Borough of Brent and others.
　　1982　　*Weekly Law Reports* 2.

Reich, Charles A.
　　1964　　"The New Property," *Yale Law Journal* 73(5).
　　1965　　"Individual Rights and Social Welfare: The Emerging Issues," *Yale Law Journal* 74(7).
　　1966　　"The Law of the Planned Society," *Yale Law Journal* 75(8).

Reiss, Albert J.
　　1971　　*The Police and the Public.* New Haven: Yale University Press.

Richardson, Genevra, Ogus, Anthony, and Burrows, Paul
　　1982　　*Policing Pollution: A Study of Regulation and Enforcement.* Oxford: Clarendon; New York: Oxford University Press.

Scarrow, H.
　　1972　　"The Impact of British Domestic Air Pollution Legislation," *British Journal of Political Science* (July).

Selznick, Philip
　　1949　　*T.V.A. and the Grassroots: A Study in the Sociology of Formal Organization.* Berkeley: University of California Press.

Simon, Herbert Alexander
　　1945　　*Administrative Behaviour: A Study of Decision-Making Processes in Administrative Organization.* London: Collier Macmillan.

Stewart, Richard B.
　　1975　　"The Reformation of American Administrative Law," *Harvard Law Review* 88(8).

Thomas, J.
　　1982　　"The Regulatory Role in the Containment of Corporate Illegality." In *A Research Agenda on White-Collar Crime,* edited by H. Edelhertz and T. D. Overcast. Lexington, Mass.: Lexington Books.

Titmuss, Richard M.
　　1971　　"Welfare 'Rights,' Law and Discretion," *Political Quarterly* 42(2).

Town and Country Planning Act
　　1971　　s.29(1).

Turner, James S.
　　1970　　*The Chemical Feast: Report on the Food and Drug Administration.* New York: Viking.

Unger, Roberto M.
　　1976　　*Law in Modern Society: Toward a Criticism of Social Theory.* New York: Free Press.

Weber, Max
　　1947　　*The Theory of Social and Economic Organization.* Translated by A. M. Henderson
　　[1922]　　and T. Parsons. New York: Oxford University Press.

Wilcox, A. F.
　　1972　　*The Decision to Prosecute.* London: Butterworths.

Wilson, James Q.
　　1968　　*Varieties of Police Behavior: The Management of Law and Order in Eight Communities.* Cambridge, Mass.: Harvard University Press.

Winkler, J. T.
　　1981　　"The Political Economy of Administrative Discretion." In *Discretion and Welfare,* edited by M. Adler and S. Asquith. London: Heinemann Educational.

PUNISHMENT AND DETERRENCE: THEORY, RESEARCH, AND PENAL POLICY

Jack P. Gibbs
Vanderbilt University

The doctrine of deterrence—the argument that legal punishments deter crime—has long been a subject of controversy. Studies carried out in the 1950s, largely limited to the death penalty, indicated that severe legal punishments have no deterrent effects. Toward the end of the 1960s there was a renewal of interest in the subject; and while the research findings did not wholly corroborate the deterrence doctrine, they did suggest that it had been dismissed prematurely in the 1950s. Another turning point may have come about in 1978, when social scientists again began to raise doubts about the doctrine's validity. So, after decades of research, compelling evidence is still wanting. To substantiate or invalidate the deterrence doctrine once and for all, it is necessary to develop research strategies that will solve or avoid several evidential problems.

This essay describes the findings of deterrence studies largely in terms of evidential problems, but the subject transcends the academic. The findings have been duly noted by those who debate penal policy. Thus, the opinions of the Supreme Court pertaining to capital punishment since 1970 show substantial consensus among the Justices that evidence of the deterrent efficacy of legal punishments, the death penalty especially, is simply inconclusive (see Supreme Court Reporter 1976; United States Reports 1973). Perhaps as a result, several of the Justices entertain retribution as a rationale for capital punishment; and several prominent scholars champion a retributive penal policy (notably

Newman 1978; van den Haag 1975; von Hirsch 1976). So, insofar as American criminal justice is governed by any identifiable penal policy, it appears that in one decade the underlying rationale shifted from rehabilitation to retribution; but the seeming demise of the rehabilitative ideal cannot be attributed to the findings of deterrence research.[1] Had the findings conclusively invalidated the deterrence doctrine, they might have furthered the shift to retribution. If both rehabilitation and deterrence are abandoned, retribution becomes the only conspicuous alternative; but the failure of deterrence investigators to solve evidential problems precluded a clear-cut impact on penal policy.

Given the piecemeal character of deterrence studies, their shortcomings are not surprising. The evidential problems are so complicated that their solution may require an intricate division of labor; and without extensive funding of one major project, deterrence research will never encompass all the possibly relevant variables in one design. The allocation by an agency or foundation of a large sum of money for deterrence research will not improve the situation if the money is used to support numerous independent projects, each of limited scope.

SOME QUESTIONS ABOUT LEGAL PUNISHMENTS

Observations on deterrence do not remotely speak to all questions about legal punishment, let alone crime and criminal justice. For that matter, only two seemingly indisputable arguments justify concern with deterrence in the social sciences. First, deterrence periodically becomes a major issue in debates over penal policy, and social scientists can ill afford an indifference to policy issues. Second, judged in terms of amount of research, questions about deterrence have no rival among questions about legal punishment. Both arguments are the principal rationale for the focus of this essay, but more needs to be said about the second argument.

Theories of Punishment

What have come to be recognized as "sociological theories of punishment" have little bearing on deterrence. Rather, the theories ostensibly purport to answer the question: Why does the severity of legal punishments vary over time and among social units? Space limitations alone preclude more than the briefest summary of the answer provided by the theories (for more extensive commentary and references to the literature, see Grabosky 1984).

Emile Durkheim attributed punitiveness to a low degree of division of labor and a postulated concomitant high degree of normative consensus, but he did not provide a coherent argument as to why normative consensus (or a "strong" collective conscience) is supposedly conducive to severe legal punishments. A much more psychological explana-

---

[1] There is a danger in alleging that the rehabilitative ideal has been abandoned, for such a claim could become a self-fulfilling prophecy. Nor is there a basis to assert categorically that rehabilitation programs "do not work." Evidence of the inefficacy of "correctional treatment" in general (notably Lipton et al. 1975) is not denied; but an assessment of that evidence is beyond the scope of this essay, and nothing short of a major research project will be required for that assessment. However, if only in recognition that recent evaluations of rehabilitation programs (again, notably Lipton et al. 1975) appear to have had an enormous impact on opinions in governmental and scholarly circles, some agency or foundation should promote a replication of those evaluations.

tion is offered by the "scapegoat theory," which interprets punitiveness as the sublimation of socially repressed aggressive and sexual urges. The "cultural-consistency" theory is actually a very loose argument that depicts punishment as reflecting general cultural features and conditions of life (where life is harsh, the death penalty is common, for example). From the Marxist perspective (Rusche and Kirchheimer 1939, in particular), punitive legal sanctions stem from fluctuations in the labor market and the efforts of the dominant economic class to maintain exploitative control, with imprisonment supposedly flourishing when the labor market is glutted and capital punishment common when social dissent becomes intense. For Svend Ranulf, punitive legal sanctions are concealed expressions of the moral indignation of the middle class, which is generated by the assiduous conformity required for members of that class to maintain their social position. Finally, Pitirim Sorokin viewed punitive legal sanctions as the manifestation of social ("ethicojuridical") heterogeneity in values and concomitant antagonistic relations along class, ethnic, racial, or religious lines.

Sociological interest in these theories effectively ended long ago, but not from obvious difficulties in bringing evidence to bear on the theories or even apparent exceptions to them. Rather, sociologists are prone to think of social control as "that which contributes to social order"; and, rightly or wrongly, many evidently believe that legal sanctions are not essential for social order. As long as that belief persists, no work on punishment (including deterrence research) is likely to be recognized by sociologists as within the mainstream of their field. Hence, it appears that there is no central question about punishment (legal or otherwise) that truly captures the attention of sociologists, without which there can be no viable "sociology of punishment."

Michel Foucault's work (1977) does have a following among intellectuals and social critics; but it has not given rise to a nomothetic question about legal punishment, nor is it a theory by any conventional standard. Foucault has done nothing more than offer an interpretive description of the transition in Europe from corporal punishment to imprisonment in the period 1750–1850. That transition, widely recognized by penologists long before Foucault, had never been explained in the context of a general theory. Foucault can be said to have explained the transition only if explanation is equated with the use of evocative descriptive terminology, as when he depicts the transition from corporal punishment to imprisonment as a shift in concern with the "body" to a concern with the "soul" (Foucault 1977, p. 16). However intellectually satisfying such description, or "explanation," may be, it is a far cry from a generalization about the sociocultural conditions under which a similar transition should be found outside the European historical context. Further, even if it were granted that Foucault's work is explanatory rather than descriptive, his interpretation throws no light on a subsequent transition in penal measures away from imprisonment nor on a return to imprisonment in the United States during the 1970s.

Whatever the significance of the question as to why the predominant *kind* of legal punishment varies among societies and over time, neither the deterrence doctrine nor most of the six sociological theories (*supra*) bear directly on it. Variation in the predominant kind of punishment (such as corporal as against incarcerative) does not necessarily entail variation in the severity of punishment; and, historical trends in Western countries notwithstanding, there is no obvious reason why there should be an association between bases of penal policy (for example, retribution versus deterrence) and predominant kinds of legal punishment. So variation in the predominant kind of legal punishment poses a distinct question, but it cannot be the central question in the sociology of punishment, since sociologists are not likely to recognize it—any more than they do deterrence research—as within the mainstream of their field.

The Question of Coercion

Unlike questions about deterrence, questions about coercion and social order are central to sociology, primarily because of the long-standing debate between sociologists who subscribe to the Marxist or conflict perspective and those who subscribe to functionalism. One remarkable feature of that debate is the failure of the protagonists to recognize the relevance of deterrence research. Granted that the coercive powers of the state cannot be described fully in terms of legal punishments, the latter is nevertheless a conspicuous manifestation of the former.

Since functionalists emphasize the role of normative consensus in the maintenance of social order, their indifference to questions about the deterrent efficacy of legal punishments is somewhat understandable; but the indifference of Marxist or conflict sociologists borders on a contradiction. Insofar as there is a Marxist theory of criminal law, it tacitly attributes validity to the deterrence doctrine. Legal punishments can be used as a repressive instrument by a dominant class only if the threat of punishment does deter. The curious argument that legal punishments are not really necessary to control dissidents would cast doubt on Marxist ideas about the origin of criminal law. A more cogent argument claims either (1) that legal punishments deter dissidents but not apolitical criminals or (2) that legal punishments prevent crimes through means other than deterrence. There is no rationale for the first claim, which grants limited validity to the deterrence doctrine; and evidence to support the argument will not be forthcoming if Marxists remain indifferent to deterrence research. The alternative (second) claim is justified because punishments may prevent crimes in nine ways other than deterrence (Gibbs 1975); but Marxist writers commonly stress the intimidating character of criminal law, and intimidation is a central notion in the deterrence doctrine. Hence, advocates of the Marxist theory of criminal law cannot pretend that the theory is unrelated, let alone contrary, to the deterrence doctrine. Yet none of the "critical" criminologists emphasize the importance of deterrence research in connection with Marxist theory. The word deterrence does not appear in the subject index of Ian Taylor et al. (1975); and Richard Quinney (1976, p. 415) castigates works on deterrence as "a defense of punishment applied in order to protect a late capitalist social order."

Toward a Central Question

The debate between Marxists and functionalists over social order rests on the dubious presumption that in all societies social order is based on either normative consensus or coercion. Even casual observations suggest that (1) two bases of social order are not mutually exclusive and (2) the predominance of one over the other is a matter of degree, which varies appreciably among societies. The hoary Marxist-functionalist debate should be transformed into this question: In what type of society is social order predominantly based on coercion and in what type of society is social order predominantly based on normative consensus?

While the question may inspire theories, it is far too vague to guide research. The notion of social order defies numerical expression, and coercion appears in such diverse forms that systematic research is possible only by focusing on particular manifestations. While legal punishments are strategic in that regard, it will not do to assert simply that legal punishments reflect a coercive social order. According to that claim, order is coercive in virtually all societies—surely in all literate ones. A much more defensible argument holds that certain properties of legal punishments (for example, their perceived severity, their objective certainty, and their range of application) are indicative of the coerciveness of social order. That argument can be restated as the immediate central question for the sociology of punishment: What properties of legal punishment reflect a coercive social order?

The question will be much more difficult to answer than it may appear. Even if it were possible to express numerically the "severity" of all legal punishments, statutory and/or actual, it would not follow that societies with the most severe punishments are also characterized by the most coercive social order. Durkheim's theory (*supra*) implies that especially severe legal punishments may reflect nothing more than a high degree of normative consensus, but it also implies that in societies with especially severe legal punishments the public favors such severity. By contrast, the Marxist argument appears to be that severe legal punishments reflect the will of a dominant class, and that claim is at least a tacit denial of public support of harsh penal measures.

Perhaps the two arguments can never be resolved because of their nebulous formulations; nonetheless, taken together, they suggest the possibility that social order is coercive to the extent that legal punishments in the society are more severe than the public demands. "Public support" should therefore be treated as a strategic property of legal punishments. While sociologists have done extensive research on preferred penalties (for example, Hamilton and Rytina 1980), the research has not been truly comparative; nor have investigators treated the ratio of severity of legal punishments to the severity demanded by the public as the salient variable.

The statement of a central question for the sociology of punishment need make no reference to deterrence, but legal punishments cannot maintain social order coercively unless they are efficacious to some degree. Accordingly, while the deterrence doctrine may not pose the most important question for the sociology of punishment, it does bear on a central question for sociology as a whole: To what extent can coercion or the threat of it maintain social order?

A BRIEF STATEMENT OF THE DETERRENCE DOCTRINE

Deterrence research has suffered from the seeming belief of investigators that defensible tests of the deterrence doctrine can be conducted without stating it as a systematic theory.[2] Of course exploratory research has a bearing on the doctrine—it may indeed be necessary for the formulation of a theory; but, by itself, exploratory research cannot yield compelling evidence. In any event, from Beccaria and Bentham to the present, the

---

[2] For instances of steps toward the statement of a deterrence theory, see Becker (1968), Zimring and Hawkins (1973), Andenaes (1974), Gibbs (1975), Geerken and Gove (1975), and Blumstein et al. (1978, pp. 3–90). Economists do not recognize any need to state the deterrence doctrine as a systematic theory, evidently because they regard the principles of classical economics as sufficient.

doctrine has remained little more than a collection of vague ideas; consequently, it is grossly oversimplified when reduced to one proposition, such as that certain, swift, and severe legal punishments deter crime. The proposition ignores (inter alia) the point that potential offenders' perceptions of legal punishments are the decisive consideration in deterrence.

Accordingly, it may appear that the deterrence doctrine reduces to this proposition: legal punishments deter crime to the extent that potential offenders perceive them as certain, swift, and severe. But that proposition ignores the "objective" properties of punishment—meaning those that can be described without considering how those punishments are perceived by potential offenders. Unless objective properties of legal punishments (for example, the prescribed maximum prison term for robbery) are treated as components of the deterrence doctrine, it has scarcely any implications for penal policy. Legal officials attempt to promote deterrence largely by manipulating objective properties of legal punishment, with the tacit assumption that such manipulation alters the perception of potential offenders.

In this light, the deterrence doctrine cannot be reduced to one simple proposition; rather, as shown in Figure 1, the doctrine encompasses at least three premises and two corollaries bearing on general deterrence. They are:

Premise I. A direct relationship obtains between the objective properties of punishments and their perceptual properties.

Premise II. A direct relationship obtains between the perceptual properties of punishment and deterrence.

Premise III. An inverse relationship obtains between deterrence and some kind of crime rate.

Therefore:

Corollary I. An inverse relationship obtains between the perceptual properties of punishments and some kind of crime rate.

Corollary II. An inverse relationship obtains between the objective properties of punishments and some kind of crime rate.

Even Figure 1 formulates the doctrine in an oversimplified manner, since it does not

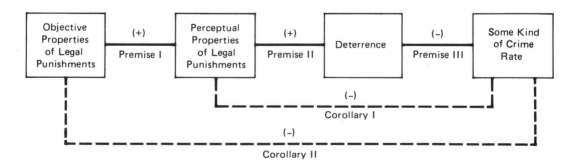

FIGURE 1

Major Components of the Deterrence Doctrine As It Applies to General Deterrence*

*(+) signifies the assertion of a direct relation; (−) signifies the assertion of an inverse relation; ───── signifies an underived proposition; and ---- signifies a derived proposition.

identify particular objective and perceptual properties of punishment that could be relevant. What follows, therefore, bears largely on Premise I, after a brief conceptualization of legal punishment, deterrence, and crime rates.

Legal Punishment

Fortunately, the definition of a "legal punishment" has not been a real issue in debates over the deterrence doctrine. Legal punishment cannot be much further defined than this: it is a punishment prescribed and administered in accordance with law. The vague phrase "in accordance with law" is crucial, for it touches on a criticism that social and behavioral scientists seldom consider. The promotion of deterrence is conducive to the punishment of innocent individuals and falsely publicizing punishments. If the goal is the overall promotion of deterrence, due process becomes secondary to creating the impression that the punishment of alleged offenders is certain, swift, and severe.

The question of the extent to which the pursuit of deterrence leads to violations of due process should draw the attention of specialists in the sociology of law. Deterrence may cease to be advocated as the panacea for the control of crime if it can be shown that its implementation subverts accepted principles of justice.

The simple definition of legal punishment does not clarify the notion of punishment itself; and just as any conceptualization of sanctions (Gibbs 1966) gives rise to problems and issues, so does the conceptualization of punishment. The most pressing problem stems from the recognition of two distinct factors—the intention of those who undertake some punitive action and the perception of the actual or potential objects of that action. An action may be said to be punitive if it is intended to inflict pain or promote fear. The argument against that "narrow" view of punishment is that an action by a legal official may deter if the object of the action perceives it as punitive. So the safest course is to define punishment as an action that (1) is intended to inflict pain on its object or to promote the object's fear of such infliction and/or (2) is perceived by the object as painful or as threatening the infliction of pain.[3] In the case of legal punishments, the actions of officials may take the form of either actual reactions to suspected offenders or the prescription of such reactions (enactment of criminal laws).

Although arrests, indictments, and trials may deter if they are perceived by the accused and by potential offenders as punitive, it would be disputable to identify such actions as legal punishments if the intention of legal officials is the only criterion. Viewed in that context, the definition of legal punishment gives rise to an issue in penal policy—whether officials should employ "procedural punishments" (arrests and the like) to promote deterrence; indeed, the extent to which they actually do so.

Deterrence

As emphasized by Bedau (1970), writers commonly equate deterrence with any way or means by which legal punishments can prevent crimes. Since that practice makes the notion of deterrence a hodgepodge, the proper definition is much more narrow. In a legal context, the term "deterrence" refers to any instance in which an individual contem-

---

[3] Throughout this chapter the word "punishment" is to be understood as referring to legal punishment, but in a few instances the latter term is used for emphasis.

plates a criminal act but refrains entirely from or curtails the commission of such an act because he or she perceives some risk of legal punishment and fears the consequence. Although brief, the definition is consistent with all careful, elaborate conceptualizations of deterrence from Bentham to Bedau because of its emphasis on fear of punishment and perception as the principal factors in deterrence. Granted, so defined, deterrence cannot be observed or measured; therefore, Premises II and III of the deterrence doctrine (Figure 1) cannot be tested directly. But there is no basis to suppose that deterrence ever can be defined so as to make the phenomenon subject to direct observation or measurement.

Types of Deterrence   Although most writers recognize the distinction between specific deterrence—the deterrent impact of punishment on those who have been punished—and general deterrence—the deterrent impact of the threat of punishment on those who have not been punished—two other types should be recognized. In the case of absolute deterrence, the individual has contemplated the crime in question at least once but has refrained each time because of his or her fear of punishment. In the case of restrictive deterrence, an individual contemplates the crime and does not refrain from it because of fear of punishment; he or she does, however, curtail commissions of that crime because of fear of punishment and with a view to reducing the risk and/or severity of the punishment.

Given the conventional general-specific distinction and the additional absolute-restrictive distinction, four types of deterrence can be posited: absolute-general, restrictive-general, absolute-specific, and restrictive-specific. Thus, the deterrence doctrine suggests four distinct theories, each pertaining to only one type of deterrence. The theories are distinct in that evidence for or against one of them will not necessarily be evidence for or against the others.[4] Moreover, the distinctions bear on penal policy.

The deterrence doctrine can bear on penal policy only to the extent that it is empirically valid; but it distorts to argue that deterrence "works" or "does not work," nor is it realistic to think of the doctrine as either true or false. The point is not merely that the deterrent impact of legal punishments may largely be a matter of degree; no less important, the validity of the doctrine may well be related to types of deterrence. Even if all individuals who have been imprisoned for theft, for example, repeat their crime on release, that fact would not preclude substantial restrictive-specific deterrence.

Those who contemplate the policy implications of the doctrine of deterrence should recognize the possibility that legal punishment has the greatest impact on individuals who do commit crimes, perhaps frequently. Moreover, the distinctions bear on attempts to reduce the crime rate by special legal reactions to so-called habitual offenders and professional criminals. Insofar as the goal of those special reactions is deterrence, the consequence is likely to be only restrictive deterrence.

Crime Rates

In testing deterrence propositions, investigators have compared (1) territorial units, such as states; (2) types of crimes within the same territorial unit; or (3) individuals, typically coresidents. In all but the last kind of comparison, the dependent variable has

[4]Nonetheless, some writers (such as Blumstein et al. 1978, pp. 3–63) do not use the term "specific deterrence," and others (Zimring and Hawkins 1973, for example) attach no significance to the notion.

been the CCR (conventional crime rate), where CCR = C/P (100,000), C being the number of instances of a given type of crime reported as having been committed in the unit during some designated period (the average annual number if the period is more than a year), and P being the population size of that unit (for example, number of city residents). The CCR numerator is virtually always an official statistic, such as crimes reported by the police, and the major doubt about any CCR is the reliability of those statistics. Because that doubt amounts to virtual preoccupation, criminologists seldom recognize that, even if all the component statistics were absolutely reliable, the CCR is so uninformative as to render its use virtually indefensible.

If, for example, police records in a city of 50,000 residents report twenty rapes during 1984, the CCR is 40.0; but that rate would reveal very little, not even whether any rapist or victim resided in the city. The police cannot even supply the statistics required to compute a *residential* CCR for offenders, since many investigations fail to identify a suspect. That limitation of the CCR is a serious matter when contemplating a relation between the crime rate of a territorial unit (in the example, a city) and some characteristic of the unit (unemployment rate, racial composition, certainty of legal punishment for crimes, and the like). It is difficult to see how the characteristics of a territorial unit can have the *same* impact on residents and nonresidents, both of whom may enter into the CCR numerator.

Even if the police in the hypothetical city had identified all twenty rapists as residents, it would still not be clear from the CCR whether all rapes were committed by one individual or whether each offense was committed by a different rapist. But the difference is relevant in virtually any study of crime rates. In particular, a determination of twenty rapes by one individual would indicate negligible restrictive deterrence, but absolute deterrence is another matter.

Criminologists should therefore abandon the CCR in favor of special rates. Four such rates are needed in deterrence research, each corresponding to a particular type of deterrence. The impunitive repetitive rate is computed by the formula Ci/Ni, where Ni is the number of members of a population (for example, residents of a city) who have committed the type of crime in question at least once during some stipulated period without having been legally punished before or during the period, and Ci the total number of such crimes committed by the Ni individuals during the period.[5] The impunitive categorical rate is computed by the formula Ni/Ne, where Ne is the total number of members of the population excluding those legally punished at least once before or during the stipulated period. The impunitive repetitive rate is relevant when contemplating restrictive general deterrence, and the categorical rate is relevant when contemplating absolute general deterrence.

With a view to inferences about restrictive specific deterrence, the relevant special rate is the repetitive recidival rate Cu/Na, where Na is the number of members of the population who have been legally punished at least once before or during the stipulated period and who repeated the offense at least once during the stipulated period but after

---

[5] All special rates are described here in only very general terms; but any one of several versions of each rate could be used in research, depending on theoretical interests and resources. Thus, the "stipulated period" could be a particular year or throughout the life of each individual, and "impunity" could be defined so as to exclude punishments for crimes committed outside the jurisdiction in question.

the punishment, and Ca the total number of such offenses committed by Na individuals. Finally, the categorical recidival rate is Na/Np, where Np is the total members of the population who were legally punished before or during the stipulated period.

Special crime rates have been used in only one deterrence study, which found that tests of deterrence propositions are more positive when the crime rate is special rather than conventional (Erickson et al. 1977a). Moreover, special rates have implications beyond the validity of the deterrence doctrine. Any attempt to reduce the high incidence of particular types of crime by policies aimed at so-called habitual offenders or professional criminals is predicated on the assumption that high incidence is largely attributable to a substantial repetitive rate (impunitive or recidival). While that assumption may or may not be valid, the conventional crime rate throws no light on it.

Criminologists have used CCRs almost entirely, scarcely contemplating alternatives. Statistics on previous arrests can be used to compute recidival rates; but since it is ludicrous to suppose that there is a close relation between recidivism and arrest, only data on self-reported crimes are suited for computing the special crime rates in question. Gathering these data entails all manner of problems, resources being only one; and that is all the more the case because the traditional procedure must be expanded to the so-licitation of self-reports of legal punishments. To be sure, there are many reasons for questioning the reliability or validity of such data (see, for example, Hirschi et al. 1980); but self-reported data offer the only opportunity to answer various important policy questions, including the validity of the deterrence doctrine.

The Properties of Punishments

Any attempt to restate the doctrine as a systematic theory should recognize the possible relevance of ten properties of punishments. While a bold theorist may exclude some of them, the choice would have to be based far more on intuition than on research findings. In any event, all of the properties bear on penal policy.

The Presumptive and Perceived Severity of Prescribed Punishments   Some of the various punishments prescribed in a criminal code (statutory penalties) differ only in magnitude, such as a five-year maximum prison term for burglary but twenty years for robbery. While twenty years is obviously greater than five years, potential offenders may not perceive the severity of the former as even approximately four times that of the latter. Hence, the magnitude of a prescribed punishment is an objective property in that it is logically distinct from the perceptions of potential offenders, and it is designated here as the *presumptive severity* of prescribed punishments.[6]

The deterrence doctrine assumes a connection between the presumptive severity of a prescribed punishment and its *perceived severity;* otherwise, the doctrine's implications for penal policy would be considerably diminished. For example, in doubling the maximum statutory prison sentence for a particular type of crime with a view to promoting deterrence, legislators assume that potential offenders will become aware of the change and perceive it as a substantial increase in the severity of the threatened punishment. Again, however, the relation between presumptive severity and perceived severity is an empirical rather than a logical relation.

[6]For a discussion of the appropriate definition of potential offender, see below, p. 346.

The meaning of presumptive severity can be expanded to encompass judgments about the severity of qualitatively different punishments; but such judgments are clearly assumptions about perceptions of severity by potential offenders. Hence, all such judgments (comparing the relative severity of serving one month in jail and paying a $2,000 fine, for example) are much more questionable than judgments of two punishments that can be compared by reference to a given metric (paying a $100 fine versus paying a $200 fine, for example).

Whereas a prescribed punishment's presumptive severity is given by the wording of a statute, its perceived severity can be determined numerically by asking potential offenders a question worded something like this: If 100 represents the amount of pain or discomfort of serving one year in jail, what number would you say represents the pain or discomfort of paying a $10,000 fine? Without going into the technical problems and issues involved in posing perceptual questions, note that any particular punishment could be taken as the standard of comparison. Thus, in the illustrative question the standard for comparison with all other punishments (regardless of kind or metric) could be "execution" rather than "one year in jail."

The distinction between presumptive and perceived severity is all the more important because some punishments, such as a $500 fine and thirty days in jail, cannot be compared as to presumptive severity; and some punishments (the death penalty, for example) have no presumptive severity. Hence, early death-penalty studies (see references in Bedau 1982) were predicated on the implicit assumption that potential offenders perceive execution as more severe than life imprisonment. Without that assumption, the deterrence doctrine does not imply that the murder rate is lower in capital states than in abolitionist states.

In the revival of deterrence research since 1967, attention shifted from prescribed punishments to actual punishments, perhaps as a reaction against the virtual preoccupation in earlier studies with statutory penalties. The slighting of prescribed punishments may. also reflect the implicit judgment that those punishments scarcely play a role in deterrence. Yet when legislators criminalize a particular kind of behavior by stipulating a statutory penalty, that action is surely a threat of punishment. The majority of potential offenders may never learn of the legislative action, but that is only one of many reasons why threatened punishments may not promote deterrence (see Ross 1976). Moreover, if prescribed punishments are not a genuine threat, efforts to publicize them—signs in stores stipulating the penalty for shoplifting, for example—are pointless. Yet the negligible effort devoted to publicizing statutory penalties is a remarkable feature of penal policy in Anglo-American jurisdictions.

Perhaps legislators refrain from widely publicizing statutory punishments because such action would be costly and/or because it would be intimidating to the point of creating a police-state climate. If cost is the consideration, legislators are penny-wise and pound-foolish. As for the distasteful image created by publicizing statutory penalties, it is naïve and politically dangerous to suppose that criminal law can be free of intimidation.

The failure of legislators to publicize prescribed punishments widely is all the more remarkable in that the presumptive severity of prescribed punishments is the only property legislators can manipulate readily. As long as there is judicial discretion in sentencing and parole boards, legislators will not directly control the magnitude of actual punishments. In the United States during the 1970s, legislators responded to the national clamor for "law and order" by increasing statutory prison terms. Such endeavors represent the "cheap" strategy for promoting deterrence. It costs little to threaten punishment; but if prescribed punishments deter only to the extent they are actually applied, then promoting deterrence can be very costly.

Given statutory penalties that can be described in terms of some common metric (a $200 fine, a $1,000 fine, or the like), the relation between presumptive severity and perceived severity is direct but perhaps curvilinear (for example, potential offenders perceive ten years of incarceration as appreciably less than twice as severe as five years). However, the most significant question pertains not to the form of the relation but to the amount of variance among potential offenders in their perception of the severity of a prescribed punishment for a particular type of crime. To the extent that those perceptions vary, the deterrent impact of the punishment is not likely to be even approximately the same for all potential offenders.

Of course, the severity may be such that all potential offenders are deterred. But from Bentham to the present, only fierce retributivists have regarded punishment as other than an evil; and Benthamites argue that punishments should be no more severe or frequent than is required to deter. Even accepting the principle that a prescribed punishment should be so severe as to deter all potential offenders, legislators are not likely to adopt the requisite Draconian criminal code. Should it be known, for example, that the threat of twenty years of imprisonment would deter 95 percent of those who contemplate shoplifting, while the threat of thirty days in jail would deter say 50 percent, the former measure probably would not be adopted. The implementation of a deterrent penal policy forces a consideration of trade-offs. To that end, the central question is not merely the role of the perceived severity of punishments in deterrence, but also the amount of variance among potential offenders as regards those perceptions.

Variance is all the more a problem because statutory penalties in Anglo-American jurisdictions ostensibly apply to all offenders. While there is every reason to suppose that the perceived severity of punishments varies considerably by social class, age, and sex, Anglo-American legislators are not about to make prescribed punishments explicitly contingent on such characteristics of offenders.

American penal policy is a mishmash, a quality reflected in statutory penalties. For most types of crimes, there are alternative penalties—imprisonment or fines—and there is no defensible rationale for not recognizing probation as a punishment. Each alternative penalty is commonly either indefinite or indeterminate—for example, not less than one year of imprisonment nor more than ten years. Such diversity of statutory penalties is necessary for judicial discretion and the "individualization" of criminal justice.

Although judicial discretion determines the presumptive severity of sentences in particular cases, that discretion is consistent with a principle of deterrent penal policy only insofar as the maximum or minimum of any of the statutory penalties for a type of crime presumably promotes as much deterrence as the maximum or minimum of any alternative. Yet in American jurisdictions even maximum fines are so low that the deterrent principle appears violated, although data on perceived severity would be needed to ascertain the extent. Similarly, limiting the length of probation to the maximum possible term of imprisonment violates the principle.

Contrary to conventional wisdom among American legislators, a deterrent penal policy does not require mandatory prison sentences. If the evil of excessive punishment is to be avoided and the cost of punishments reduced, alternative punishments are essential to a deterrent penal policy. Nothing whatever in the deterrence doctrine precludes a fine of not less than $100 nor more than $10,000 for shoplifting rather than a jail sentence of not more than, say, thirty days—provided always that the perceived severity of any amount of one penalty can be roughly equated with a certain amount of the other penalty. Qualitatively different penalties can, however, be equated only in terms of perceived severity.

Such a strategy would pose problems and generate controversy. Legislators could not revise statutory penalties rationally without systematic data on the severity of various kinds of punishments as perceived by a representative sample of potential offenders, but it would be hard to defend the alternative—to continue setting statutory penalties largely by intuition and precedent. Although systematic perceptual data would not reveal the minimum amount of any penalty required for an "acceptable" level of deterrence, that level cannot be identified without those data. In any case, the assumption would not be that all potential offenders can be deterred by the same amount of a particular kind of penalty, such as a $5,000 fine. While there may be, at least for some penalties, a certain level that would deter everyone, applying that punishment in all cases would be intolerably Draconian.

That consideration is precisely the rationale for stipulating a range for each alternative penalty. The strategy requires judicial discretion in sentencing, of course, especially since the imposition of fines implies the capacity to pay. The statutory provision for fines raises the specter of the poor suffering from relative deprivation. However, the purpose of a statutory provision for an enormous range in fines would not be merely to make it possible for the offender to pay, but also to pay money that "smarts." The assumption that the perceived severity of a fine varies inversely with income is another reason for setting statutory penalties by reference to systematic data on the perceived severity of punishments.

The prospect of giving judges enormous discretion in imposing fines may seem dangerous, but less so in light of two arguments. First, judges still have enormous discretion over the liberties of convicted offenders; and, second, their discretion in imposing fines could be limited by requiring them to follow a fixed schedule related to the offenders' estimated annual income.

Of all properties of punishment, the numerical expression of perceived severity poses the most difficult problem. When potential offenders are asked a "magnitude ratio" question, in which they are instructed to compare each of several punishments (five years of imprisonment or execution, for example) with a particular "standard" punishment (such as a one-year jail sentence), the problem is not that respondents are confused by such a question (experience indicates otherwise). However, selecting a standard and assigning a fixed value to it (100 or 1,000, for example) are inherently controversial. There is no truly compelling rationale for selection or assignment, and regardless of the choice it can be argued that the strategy is flawed if respondents differ appreciably in their perceptions of the severity of the standard. For example, if respondent A assigns a value of 50 to five years of probation (relative to 100 for one year in jail, the standard) and respondent B assigns a value of 75 to that term of probation, the difference would be misleading if it were known that B's absolute perception of the severity of such a jail term (the standard) was approximately one half greater than A's perception.

One possible solution is the use of an instrument that enables respondents to express their perceptions of the severity of a designated punishment by the pressure of a "hand squeeze," where the instrument reading for each punishment can be converted to a proportion of the maximum reading for that respondent (that obtained when he or she is instructed, at the outset, to exert maximum force). The use of such an instrument in an extensive survey would not be feasible; but its exploratory use for a small sample of respondents may reveal a very close correlation between values obtained with the physical instrument and those obtained through magnitude questions, thereby justifying those questions.

Objective and Perceived Certainty   There is every reason to assume that the relation between the severity of prescribed punishments for a type of crime and the rate for that crime is contingent on the certainty that those punishments will be applied. The importance of that contingency cannot be grasped without recognizing the distinction between the objective and the perceived certainty of punishment.

Objective certainty can be expressed by the formula Np/Ni, where Ni is the number of instances of a type of crime during a given period and Np the number of such instances that resulted (during or after the period) in the application of the punishment in question. If, for example, 50 out of 200 recorded robberies in a particular city during 1984 eventually result in the imprisonment of an alleged offender, the objective certainty of imprisonment for robbery in that city during 1984 is .25.

Two problems complicate the application of the formula. First, the commonly available figure for Ni is derived from police records; but it has been demonstrated that many crimes (especially victimless crimes) go unreported. Thus, use of police figures is likely to result in an artificially inflated objective-certainty index. Second, arrests and convictions do not necessarily occur within the same year as the commission of the reported crime. For example, it may be 1986 before some offender who committed a burglary in 1984 is imprisoned.

This difficulty may be somewhat alleviated by use of the estimational formula Np_t/Ni_{t-1}, where t denotes a particular year (1984, for example) and $t-1$ the previous year. But even such an estimation does not allow for plea bargaining, whereby offenders are sentenced for a lesser crime.

Whatever procedure is employed for the numerical expression of the objective certainty of punishment, the notion itself is distinct from perceived certainty. The numerical expression of perceived certainty can be realized in a systematic way only by soliciting answers from potential offenders to a question worded something like this: "How many times do you think you could commit [type of crime] in this [city or state] before being sentenced to prison?" The reciprocal of the number given in the answer would represent that respondent's perceived certainty of imprisonment for a particular type of crime, and additional questions would be required to solicit perceptions as to the certainty of other types of punishment (for example, arrest).

It is entirely possible that neither the perceived certainty value for any potential offender nor the average of those values even remotely reflects the objective certainty of punishment for the type of crime in question. That possibility creates a problem when it comes to interpreting Premise I of the deterrence doctrine (Figure 1). Propositions about the relation between particular objective and perceived properties are necessary to assess the empirical validity of Premise I, but the step from that premise to specific propositions entails conjecture. No matter how certain in an objective sense, punishments deter crime only to the extent that they are perceived as certain by potential offenders.[7] Accordingly, if only with a view to policy implications, the deterrence doctrine should be construed as asserting a direct relation among types of crimes or among territorial units between the objective certainty of punishment and average or median certainty of punishment as perceived by potential offenders. If such a relation is found to hold, it will greatly simplify stating the deterrence doctrine as a systematic theory with important policy implications. Legal officials—the police and legislators—will have some justification for anticipating that the crime rate will decline as the result of increase in the objective certainty of punishment.

But even if no relation between objective and perceived certainty can be demonstrated, the demise of the deterrence doctrine, or even the rejection of Premise I, would not follow. A close direct relation seemingly requires that potential offenders have some cognitive basis for assessing the certainty of punishment, which is likely to depend appreciably on the extent to which actual punishments are publicized. It is further possible that perceptions partially reflect the intensity of police surveillance (the frequency of patrols, for example) or other enforcement activities that are distinct from actual punishments (see Lempert 1981–82). So it could be that the relation between objective certainty and perceived certainty is not close, being contingent on publicizing actual punishments and/or on enforcement intensity. If such should prove the case, the only option for stating the deterrence doctrine as a theory[8] will be to recognize the publicizing of punishments and the intensity of law enforcement as objective properties in addition to objective certainty. That procedure will be even more necessary if research findings indicate that both publicizing punishments and enforcement intensity are directly related to perceived certainty, independently of objective certainty. In any case, converting the deterrence doctrine into systematic theories cannot be a simple task.

Even if a close direct relation between objective and perceived certainty holds without controls for publicizing of punishments or enforcement intensity, it would be an illusion to assume that the objective certainty of punishments can be furthered by merely increasing the number of police officers. The research undertaken to date clearly indicates that the relation between objective certainty of arrest and the relative size of the police force is not close by any means (see Wilson and Boland 1978; Riccio and Heaphy 1977).

Objective and Perceived Celerity   Objective celerity (swiftness) is simply the time elapsed between the commission of an offense and the administration of a punishment. While offenders who are punished have some sense of that interval, it would require long experience with criminal justice to appreciate not only the long average time between offenses and the administration of substantive punishments but also the enormous variation from case to case. Systematic data on perceived celerity can be gathered only by

[7] For reasons that are not clear, economists and those who employ the "econometric approach" in the study of deterrence do not emphasize perceptual variables. In contrast, most sociologists treat perception as the central consideration in deterrence (see, especially, Henshel and Silverman 1975).

[8] Here, as elsewhere, it simplifies matters to speak of restating the deterrence doctrine as a single theory; but in fact the doctrine should be restated as four distinct theories, one for each of the four types of deterrence.

soliciting responses of potential offenders to a question worded something like this: "If someone like yourself should commit [designated offense] and be [designation of punishment], what is your guess as to the amount of time between the [designated offense] and the [designation of punishment]?"

It has not been clearly established whether a short interval between an offense and its punishment (commencing with arrest) is necessary, sufficient, or both to establish a "neurological connection" between the events. Moreover, a delay in punishment could heighten the offender's perception of the punishment's severity. In any event, there is little justification for arguing that swift punishment promotes *general* deterrence. When a potential offender learns that someone has received a life sentence for rape one year after commission of the crime, it is not obvious that the potential offender's fear of punishment is lessened by learning of the delay.

Despite these caveats, the conclusion suggested by the literature on experimentation with punishment is entirely consistent with Bentham's argument; for it does appear that in some conditions punishments applied more than a few seconds after a particular behavior do not effectively repress or extinguish that behavior (see Johnston 1972; Van Houten 1983). The symbolic basis of human behavior and the perceived severity of some legal punishments may preclude the extension of the conclusion to specific deterrence in the criminal justice system; but a demonstration that anything remotely approaching that conclusion does apply would have an enormous impact. It would suggest why there is scarcely any systematic evidence of specific deterrence; and it would cast doubts on efforts to promote specific deterrence, since not even a disregard for due process would make the average celerity of legal punishments a matter of hours, let alone seconds.

The Presumptive and Perceived Severity of Actual Punishments   What applies to the properties of prescribed punishments applies equally to the properties of actual punishments, but the distinction between prescribed and actual must be emphasized. To illustrate, if the maximum statutory term of imprisonment for burglary in one jurisdiction, A, is five years, while in another jurisdiction, B, the statutory maximum is ten years, it may be that the average prison term served on a conviction for burglary in jurisdiction A is greater than that actually served in jurisdiction B. Such a seeming inconsistency would have nothing to do with alternative punishments for burglary in the two jurisdictions (such as a greater number of probated sentences for burglary in B than in A); rather, the difference could be due primarily to plea bargaining, judicial discretion in sentencing (which presupposes indefinite or indeterminate prescribed terms of imprisonment), and/or parole policies. In any case, legislators in jurisdiction B would have accomplished little in prescribing ten years for burglary, not only because of the possibility that prescribed punishments alone do not deter but also because legislators do not necessarily control the presumptive severity of *actual* punishments.

Even the elimination of plea bargaining, judicial discretion, and parole boards would not enable legislators to reduce the crime rate by increasing the presumptive severity of prescribed punishments. Granted the distinct possibility that individuals are deterred only by actual punishments, legislators do not control the *perceived* severity of those punishments.

The numerical representation of the perceived severity of punishments, prescribed or actual, for a type of crime is more complicated than it may appear. Those who conduct deterrence research are unlikely to have the resources required to pose two separate questions about perceived severity, one for actual and one for prescribed punishments; nor is there any obvious way to phrase a clearly intelligible survey question about the severity of prescribed punishments as distinct from actual punishments. For that matter, it will not do to speak of "receiving such-and-such sentence of incarceration," for some respondents may think of it as meaning time actually served, while others allow for the possibility of parole.

Even when responses to a single "severity" question are used to assign values to both prescribed and actual punishments for a type of crime, the procedure differs. The illustrative formula for computing the composite value of the perceived severity of prescribed substantive punishment is: $\Sigma Sx + \Sigma Si + \Sigma Sd + \Sigma Sq$, where Sx is the median or mean severity value of the maximum presumptive severity of some prescribed punishment (such as twenty years of imprisonment), Si the value of the minimum presumptive severity of one of the prescribed punishments, Sd the value of the definite presumptive severity of one of the prescribed punishments (a statutory penalty of some particular magnitude, rather than indefinite or indeterminate), and Sq one of the prescribed punishments, if any, that can be described only in qualitative terms (such as execution). Thus, if a jail sentence, a fine, and probation are mutually exclusive statutory penalties for shoplifting, and if each has stipulated maximum-minimum, then six values would enter into the composite value pertaining to the perceived severity of prescribed punishments. By contrast, the formula for arriving at a composite value for actual punishments of a particular type of crime is: $\Sigma(PS)$, where P is the proportion of all actual punishments of a particular kind (including magnitude, if relevant, such as 4.4 years of imprisonment), and S the median or mean perceived severity value of that particular kind of punishment.

Since limited resources may preclude computation of a composite value that represents all prescribed or actual punishments for a type of crime, investigators may have to consider only the maximum or minimum punishment. For that matter, the formulas (*supra*) are only suggestive; and the choice among alternatives is not necessarily dictated by resources, nor is it a purely technical matter. Thus, while it may be true that only *maximum* punishments (prescribed and/or actual) promote general deterrence, such a conclusion should not be assumed uncritically.

Knowledge of Prescribed and Actual Punishments   Individuals will not be deterred by any punishment, prescribed or actual, if they do not know of it; and knowledge of punishments is different from perceptions about certainty and severity. One survey question for potential offenders bears on the "applicability" of a particular kind of prescribed punishment: "Can a person who is found guilty of burglary be sentenced to prison?" A second question, presuming an affirmative answer to the first, pertains to the magnitude of the prescribed punishment: "What is the maximum prison term a person can serve for burglary?" The first corresponding question about *actual* punishments can be: "Do you know of cases during the past five years where persons were sent to prison for burglary?" The second question, presupposing an affirmative answer to the first, asks: "What is your guess of the average amount of time those persons will remain in prison?"

No answer to the foregoing questions would reveal the respondent's perception of the certainty or the severity of imprisonment; but when questions are posed about the certainty or severity of some designated punishment for a designated type of crime, it is assumed that the respondents knew that such a punishment can be or has been applied to the particular type of crime. That consideration gives rise to a problem in attempting to state the deterrence doctrine as a theory—stipulating the logical relation between knowledge of punishments and perceptions of the certainty and severity of punishments.

In stating a deterrence theory, a theorist can ill afford to ignore two issues about knowledge of punishments. The first pertains to what appears to be an indisputable principle: no individual can be deterred by a prescribed or actual punishment without knowing of that punishment. That principle becomes troublesome if a distinction is granted between total ignorance of punishments (not knowing that the behavior in question is subject to any kind of punishment) and incorrect beliefs about the kinds of punishments that apply (or have been applied) to the type of crime in question. Even if potential offenders hold incorrect beliefs about the punishments prescribed for some type of crime, they can be deterred by those beliefs, especially if they perceive those punishments as severe and fairly certain. Accordingly, a deterrence theory may imply that the rate for some type of crime is, *ceteris paribus,* an inverse function of the perceived severity of the punishments that potential offenders believe apply to that type of crime. The beliefs in question can be accurate or inaccurate, but the generalization may be valid even if all the beliefs are incorrect.

Nonetheless, a purely perceptual version of the deterrence doctrine—one that assumes nothing about the accuracy of potential offenders' beliefs and makes no assertions about the relation between objective and perceived properties of punishments—can have no particular implications for penal policy. After all, when legal officials prescribe or administer punishments with a view to promoting general deterrence, they surely assume that numerous potential offenders will come to know of those punishments. Therefore, deterrence theories or tests of them have no obvious policy implications unless they bear on that assumption.

Yet not even a demonstration that the beliefs of potential offenders are totally inaccurate would preclude a deterrence theory that has some policy implications. Even if potential offenders do not know the kind or magnitude of the punishment, appreciable deterrence could be realized by correct beliefs that certain types of behavior are subject to some legal punishment. The argument holds that the functioning of the criminal-justice system as a whole sustains the beliefs. Needless to say, a deterrence theory incorporating that argument would be quite different from one predicated on the assumption that potential offenders have accurate knowledge about kinds and (possibly) magnitudes of punishments, and the policy import of the difference would be enormous. If tests of the two theories should indicate that deterrence is furthered primarily through the functioning of the criminal-justice system as a whole, legislators would be hard pressed to justify attempts at promoting deterrence by prescribing particular magnitudes of punishment to particular types of crimes.

The other issue bears on the very meaning of "accurate knowledge." One of the very few systematic studies of the public's knowledge of punishments in which the findings were interpreted as bearing on the validity of the deterrence doctrine (California Assembly Committee on Criminal Procedure 1968) serves as an illustration. The study surveyed California residents about their knowledge of statutory prison sentences for particular types of crimes. By any reasonable sampling standard, ignorance of those sentences was widespread; but the California investigators' conclusion that the findings invalidate the deterrence doctrine is disputable because the survey was concerned with the public's knowledge of the magnitude of prescribed punishments, not with their applicability. Not to know the maximum prison term for a particular type of crime is a quite different matter from not knowing that some term of imprisonment is possible. The distinction is all the more important if large numbers of potential offenders are deterred by nothing more than knowledge that the crime is subject to *some* term of imprisonment.

In the case of magnitudes of punishments (for example, the maximum prescribed prison term for possession of marijuana), two distinct methods can be used to assess "accuracy" knowledge. The distinction is illustrated by hypothetical figures on four types of crimes, the first figure representing the statutory maximum prison term and the second figure the average "guess" about that maximum by a sample of potential offenders: rape, 25, 32.5; robbery, 20, 26.5; burglary, 10, 8.5; and grand theft, 5, 2.7. Such figures would indicate that the absolute accuracy of knowledge is negligible (especially since the "guesses" are averages and hence underestimate the ignorance of numerous individuals); but when it comes to *proportionate* accuracy, the situation is quite different. The rank-order correlation between actual statutory maximums and the average guesses is +1.00.

A deterrence theory can be predicated on the assumption of substantial proportionate accuracy of knowledge rather than on absolute accuracy—a distinction not emphasized by the California investigators. Of course, even the assumption of proportionate accuracy may turn out to be indefensible; but to the extent the assumption is valid, a theory that incorporates the assumption can justify legislative concern with graduated statutory penalties. For that matter, a theory predicated on certain assumptions about knowledge of the applicability of punishments (not their magnitudes) can have policy implications, especially if any magnitude of the punishments in question (imprisonment, for example) is perceived by potential offenders as severe.

Both the validity and the policy implications of the deterrence doctrine depend on the way the doctrine is stated as a theory. Deterrence theories may differ in many ways, but the contrast in assumptions about potential offenders' knowledge of punishment is likely to be salient.

On the Relations Among Properties of Punishment

An inventory of variables is not a theory, and a defensible deterrence theory cannot be formulated by an uncritical substitution of specific properties of punishment for the designations of generic classes in Figure 1. A theorist may conclude that some of the properties are irrelevant and that the exclusion of some properties would be desirable, if only to simplify the theory; but to date putative tests of the deterrence doctrine do not provide a firm rationale for exclusion.

Whatever properties of punishment are recognized in a deterrence theory, the reduction of Premise I (Figure 1) to specific propositions will be difficult. A deterrence theory is likely to assert a direct relation between the objective certainty and the perceived certainty of punishment, and the same may be said of objective and perceived celerity; but there will be a problem in wording the specific proposition about the relation between the presumptive severity of prescribed or actual punishments and perceived severity. To speak of potential offenders' perception of the severity of a prescribed punishment for a type of crime presupposes that they know of that punishment; and articulating that presupposition in a specific proposition will be complicated. For that matter, whatever the nature of the knowledge variable—whether it pertains to applicability of punishments, their magnitudes, or both—there is no basis for assuming that it is solely a function of any of the objective properties of punishment.[9] Accordingly, while it may be necessary to extend the objective properties of punishment to include the publicizing of actual punishments, the immediate problem is that potential offenders may come to know of prescribed punishments independently of actual punishments. All such problems can be circumvented by stipulating that the theory is to be tested in a condition where all potential offenders have accurate knowledge of the punishments; but since accurate knowledge of all punishments by all potential offenders is unlikely in any jurisdiction, treating knowledge as though it is not problematic would strip the test findings of policy implications.

Even if the issue of knowledge of punishments could be ignored, reducing Premise I to a simple bivariate proposition ignores the distinct possibility that the relation between any objective property of punishment and any perceived property is markedly contingent on one or more conditions (the relation between objective certainty and perceived certainty is contingent on publicizing punishments, for example). The possibility of markedly contingent bivariate relations is no less likely for Corollaries I and II, where some kind of crime rate is the dependent variable. Bentham himself implied that the relation between the severity of punishment and the crime rate is contingent on the certainty of punishment, and there is no basis for arguing that the contingent quality of the relation is peculiar to severity and certainty taken as objective properties. However, Bentham failed to stipulate the exact nature of the contingent relation; and there are at least two possibilities: (1) the relation between the severity of punishment and the crime rate becomes more inverse as the magnitude (level) of certainty increases or (2) the relation becomes more inverse as the *variance* in certainty decreases. Yet a theorist can ill afford to ignore the possibility that the relation between the perceived or objective certainty of punishment and the crime rate is itself contingent on the severity of punishments, with the nature of the contingency also a matter of conjecture.

This litany of complexities is more than a burden for theorists. If a deterrence theory is to have policy implications, the contingent nature of the postulated relation between properties of punishment and the crime rate must be communicated to those who shape policy. The point is well illustrated by the actions of American legislators in reintroducing the death penalty during the 1970s. Ostensibly, these attempts were made in whole or in part to further deterrence; but the mere reintroduction of a statutory penalty does not assure any level of certainty. Moreover, the death penalty may have a lesser deterrent effect than does life imprisonment simply because the objective certainty of execution is substantially less than the objective certainty of imprisonment. Such can be the case even if potential offenders perceive the severity of the death penalty as greater than life imprisonment (see Bedau 1982, p. 110). Yet legislators appear insensitive to the contingent impact of the presumptive severity of prescribed punishments, perhaps because there

---

[9] For an elaborate treatment of the "knowledge problem" and a report of numerous strategic research findings, see Kirk Williams (1977).

is no legislative formula for increasing objective certainty, especially without abandoning a concern for due process.

EVIDENTIAL PROBLEMS PERTAINING TO GENERAL DETERRENCE

There are all manner of alternative methods and kinds of data for the numerical expression of properties of punishment, and the outcome of tests of a deterrence theory is likely to depend on the choice among those methods. Moreover, tests of any deterrence theory may differ as to types of punishment (perhaps only imprisonment), types of crimes (probably those with victims), and types of units of comparison (individuals, territorial units, or types of crime). A theorist may elect to leave the choice in such matters to researchers; but some evidential problems transcend all such considerations, including measurement methods, and a theorist should strive to stipulate a test procedure that avoids those problems.

The Attribution of Assumptions

The immediate evidential problem stems from a common practice in the assessment of social science theories. Rather than test a theory, critics purport to identify the assumptions about human nature or social life underlying the theory. If the putative assumptions are rejected by the critic—that is, they run contrary to the critic's preconceptions—then so much the worse for the theory. The identification of the assumptions of a theory, however, is typically no less disputable than the critics' judgment of them.

The Question of Free Will   One traditional but waning criticism of the deterrence doctrine begins with attributing to it the assumption of free will (see, for example, Schuessler 1952, p. 55). The argument seems to be that the doctrine depicts potential offenders as weighing the risk of punishment against the benefits of the contemplated crime before making a calculated choice. That criticism is mercifully brief, for it does not go beyond the *suggestion* that any theory of human behavior is somehow defective if it assumes free will.

The attribution of the assumption of free will to the deterrence doctrine is strange, if only because the doctrine can be construed as thoroughly deterministic. The following is an oversimplified reduction of the doctrine to one proposition. If in contemplating a crime, the potential offender perceives the legal punishment for that crime as certain, swift, and severe, he/she will refrain from the crime. In what sense does that proposition attribute free will to potential offenders? Even if the proposition suggests that potential offenders experience a choice, that experience cannot be equated with free will. While consistently positive test findings could blunt the particular criticism, demanding such findings is grossly unrealistic, especially in the social sciences. Since no test procedure or outcome can induce critics to cease the attribution of the assumption of free will to the deterrence doctrine, the issue is beyond constructive debate.

The Question of Rationality   A more common criticism attributes the assumption of rationality to the deterrence doctrine. This criticism is truly difficult to assess, if only because "rational human behavior" is a vague notion. Surely the term means more than the simple assertion that human beings commonly engage in behavior with a view to consequences; yet, at least in connection with criminality, it is very difficult to go beyond that idea. If it is claimed that the deterrence doctrine depicts potential offenders as weighing the "costs" of a contemplated crime in terms of punishments against the anticipated benefits, the implied criticism is similar to the argument about free will.

Evidence that some individuals commit crimes without regard to the consequences would not resolve the issue, since the deterrence doctrine does not assert that all individuals consciously contemplate the risk of punishment. The doctrine can be construed as resting on some assumption about accurate knowledge of punishments, but that assumption cannot be equated with the assumption of rationality. Accuracy of knowledge is not even relevant if the deterrence doctrine is stated as a purely perceptual theory, excluding anything akin to Premise I (Figure 1).

Even instances of offenses without prior contemplation of legal consequences would not refute the deterrence doctrine, since it does not reduce to the naïve claim that "punishments prevent crimes through deterrence." Rather, it pertains to *the conditions* in which punishments will deter crime. Surely it is one thing for murderers to kill without previously contemplating the consequences when the objective certainty of the death penalty, or any other punishment, has been, say, 5 percent over several generations; but quite another for them to kill without prior contemplation of legal consequences when the objective certainty of execution has been, say, 90 percent for generations, with all executions widely publicized. Instances of murder in the latter condition would undeniably constitute much more damaging evidence against the deterrence doctrine, but the frequency of "crimes without prior contemplation of legal consequences" may be a function of properties of punishment.

Finally, even if the deterrence doctrine does rest squarely on some assumption about the rationality of criminal behavior, it is not at all clear how that assumption invalidates the doctrine. To deny that human behavior is rational is scarcely more credible than to deny the opposite. The point is that categorical judgments as to the rationality of human behavior (all individuals, behaviors, and situations) are indefensible; and the point is relevant because the deterrence doctrine pertains to criminal behavior, not behavior in general. Accordingly, the fact that human beings have been known to starve rather than eat cattle (a common but ethnocentric illustration of irrational behavior) has no bearing on the deterrence doctrine.

The debate is likely to endure. If critics insist that the deterrence doctrine assumes that criminal behavior is rational and reject that assumption out of hand, there is no assurance that even consistently positive test findings would silence them.

Extralegal Conditions

Defenders of the deterrence doctrine have never claimed that the crime rate is a function of legal punishments only, and that claim is denied explicitly whenever critics present what appears to be contrary evidence. If the robbery rate is appreciably greater in jurisdiction A than in B, despite appreciably greater certainty, celerity, and severity of punishment in A, defenders of the doctrine can argue that A's robbery rate would be even greater if the legal punishments in A did not counteract extralegal conditions that generate robbery in A. The argument thus appears to be simple: properties of legal punishments are *not* the only determinants of the crime rate. While no one questions that argument, acceptance of it gives rise to a horrendous evidential problem. The correlation between properties of punishment and the crime rate is indicative of the deterrent efficacy of legal punishments only if all relevant extralegal conditions (such as, possibly, unemployment) have been controlled. Until relevant extralegal conditions are controlled, therefore, the interpretation of tests of any deterrence theory will be inherently disputable.

Extralegal Generative Conditions   Excluding the deterrence doctrine, no well-known theory of criminality treats legal punishment as a determinant of the crime rate; those theories therefore pertain largely if not exclusively to extralegal conditions. If those theories commanded confidence, a major evidential problem in deterrence research could be circumvented by controlling for variables identified by the theories as determinants of the crime rate. Unfortunately, the theories have never been tested systematically, and they appear untestable.

Recognition that extralegal determinants of criminality cannot be identified defensibly has led some deterrence researchers to examine the relation between properties of legal punishments and the crime rate without introducing controls. That strategy is obviously not a solution, but the alternative strategy—introducing extralegal variables as controls without justification—is hardly more defensible. Yet in examining the relation among states between properties of punishment, numerous investigators have introduced measures of education, income, racial composition, urbanization, and other conditions as control variables without reference to any well-known etiological theory, let alone one that commands confidence. The strategy cannot be defended by pointing to a statistical association between extralegal variables and the crime rate in a particular set of units for a particular time (such as the United States during 1980), since that justification is no more than crude induction. Most of these studies have employed powerful statistical techniques to control for extralegal variables (see, for example, Ehrlich 1975), but it is an illusion to assume that the evidential problem can be solved without reference to an explicit and defensible etiological theory about the type of crime in question.

Extralegal Inhibitory Conditions   The vast majority of well-known theories of criminality purport to identify extralegal conditions that generate crime, and only a few theories postulate particular inhibitory conditions—extralegal conditions that prevent crime. One of those conditions can be identified as *normative* in that it pertains to what is variously identified as the social disapproval, social condemnation, or "seriousness" of criminality. The normative variable is especially relevant because of the distinct possibility that social disapproval of crime varies inversely with the crime rate but directly with the objective certainty and severity of punishment. The argument in the case of the relation with objective certainty is that legal officials invest more resources in the investigation and prosecution of types of crimes that are subject to intense social disapproval. That possibility creates a major evidential problem.

Only recently have deterrence researchers examined the interrelations among measures of social disapproval of crime, the crime rate, and the certainty of punishment—and their findings are disconcerting. Briefly, among types of crimes or delinquencies, there is a substantial negative correlation between the crime rate and the perceived certainty of punishment but a substantial positive correlation between measures of social disapproval and the crime rates. The measures of disapproval are correlated positively with both the perceived and the objective certainty of punishment (Erickson and Gibbs 1978). While the negative correlation between the crime rates and the perceived certainty of punishment is consistent with the deterrence doctrine, the findings suggest that potential offenders perceive the certainty of punishment of particular types of crime in terms of what it should be (that is, the more the social disapproval, the greater the perceived certainty). In any case, the correlation between perceived certainty and the crime rate is negligible when social disapproval of types of crime is controlled. Those findings underscore the reality of the evidential problem.

Policy Implications   If positive tests of deterrence propositions without controls for extralegal conditions prompt those who shape penal policy to manipulate properties of punishment with a view to reducing the crime rate, the outcome can be contrary to expectations in one of two ways. Either the manipulation of properties of punishment (increasing the presumptive severity of prescribed punishments, for example) is not followed by a decline in the crime rate, or it is followed by a negligible decrease in the crime rate. The first outcome is especially likely if the relevant extralegal generative variables vary directly with the properties of punishment, in which case no decline in the crime rate would be misleading. The second outcome would indicate no relation between extralegal generative variables and properties of punishment.

Misleading evidence of deterrence is especially likely to stem from research on the cross-sectional (synchronic) relation between properties of punishment and the crime rate rather than the relation between *change* in the two variables over time (a diachronic relation). Virtually all deterrence research has been limited to cross-sectional comparisons, but those who shape penal policy are not likely to appreciate the distinction. For that matter, the most pernicious myth in social science methodology is that path analysis or so-called causal models justify causal inferences from synchronic statistical relations.

If those who shape penal policy are to be guided by a deterrence theory, they should demand that tests of the theory take the form of diachronic comparisons. However, if such tests exclude controls of extralegal variables that can be justified by reference to theory about the extralegal conditions that generate or inhibit criminality, the findings will simply be inconclusive.

Preventive Mechanisms Other Than Deterrence

Regardless of the thoroughness of controls for extralegal conditions, not even repeated demonstrations of an inverse relation between change in some property of punishment and subsequent change in the crime rate would constitute conclusive evidence of deterrence. That is the case because there are no less than nine ways other than deterrence that punishments can prevent crimes (Gibbs 1975). This survey will restrict itself to a few observations on what appear to be the three most important nondeterrent preventive mechanisms as regards evidential problems and policy implications.

Incapacitation   If the police in a particular metropolitan area arrest a gang of well-organized, active burglars and if those arrests all result in imprisonment, the objective certainty of incarceration for burglary is likely to increase and the burglary rate decrease. Such a temporal relation would appear to be a dramatic manifestation of deterrence, but it is also possible that the decline in the burglary rate reflects only the incapacitation of potential burglars.

No imagination is required to appreciate the argument that some punishments—imprisonment and execution in particular—have an incapacitating effect, but it is less obvious that what appears to be evidence of deterrence may reflect only incapacitation. The most consistent evidence of deterrence has been an inverse relation among states between the objective certainty of imprisonment for a type of crime and the rate of that crime. That relation is consistent with Corollary II (Figure 1) of the deterrence doctrine; however, the conclusion that the relation verifies the premises of the doctrine commits the fallacy of affirming the consequent. The relation can always be deduced from premises that pertain to the incapacitating effects of imprisonment rather than deterrence.

The vast majority of deterrence researchers have recognized the need to control for incapacitation when testing deterrence propositions; but efforts at control confront many problems, some of which transcend the obvious (for example, only execution incapacitates absolutely, and imprisonment for one type of offense may prevent other types of offenses). The less obvious problems stem from recognition that estimates of the incapacitating effects of any kind of punishment entail conjecture.[10] If, for instance, an individual who committed four rapes during 1980 was imprisoned during 1981–84, the suggested conclusion is that his imprisonment prevented sixteen rapes. The conjectural quality of the conclusion is undeniable even if the individual had been convicted for the first rape in 1980 and placed on probation, in which case it could be argued that his three subsequent rapes would not have occurred had his conviction resulted in a long prison sentence. In any event, when attempting to compute an average "incapacitation figure" for a particular set of individuals (such as all persons arrested for rape in Los Angeles during 1980), it is pointless to assume that their previous arrests or convictions even approximate the actual number of previous offenses. Even if arrests or convictions could be equated with the actual number of offenses, an average of those official recidival statistics for particular individuals cannot be justifiably generalized to all offenders. Apprehension may select those who commit the offense frequently and/or those who are inept and are apprehended early in their careers. Nonetheless, in assessing the implications of incapacitation for penal policy, a generalization to *categories* of perpetrators must be entertained.

The only obvious alternative to the use of official recidival statistics is a survey of self-reported crimes, including self-reports of legal reactions (such as arrest, plea bargaining, and substantive punishments). Data from such a survey in only a few metropolitan areas could be used to test deterrence propositions. The immediate use, however, would be to examine the repetitive rates to reach inferences about incapacitation. Generally, to the extent that imprisonment is not selective (and self-reported data provide a systematic basis to examine selectivity), the incapacitating effect of imprisonment on the conventional rate for some type of crime is a direct function of the repetitive rate for that crime.

---

[10]Given the inevitable conjectural quality of estimates of the incapacitating effect of punishments, imprisonment in particular, it is not surprising that investigators have employed divergent methodologies and commonly disagree in their conclusions about the impact of incapacitation on the crime rate (see Cohen 1983).

Both the impunitive repetitive rate and the repetitive recidival rate are crucial in assessing penal policy as it applies to repeaters. In the 1970s legislators increasingly prescribed longer terms of imprisonment for recidivists, but their rationale was not entirely clear. In any case, there is a general issue, one best introduced by the question: "How many instances of each type of crime are committed by recidivists and other repeaters (those who have not been punished)?" The justification of the concern of legal officials with so-called habitual offenders or professional criminals hinges on the answer, but there can be no defensible answer without *unofficial* repetitive and recidival rates.

Until researchers gather unofficial statistics on crimes and legal reactions, controls for incapacitation in tests of deterrence propositions require special strategies. One strategy is to focus on categories of offenses seldom subject to incapacitating punishments. The category of traffic violations is especially strategic, because researchers can employ both official and unofficial incidence figures, the latter from field studies.

Normative Validation   Emile Durkheim's antipathy to utilitarianism (1949 [1893]) led him to emphasize the expressive or symbolic function of legal punishments rather than deterrence. However, because of his inconsistent terminology and garbled arguments, it is not commonly recognized that Durkheim identified a mechanism by which legal punishments may prevent crimes other than through deterrence. That mechanism is designated here as normative validation, and the argument was succinctly illustrated by Sir James Stephens: "The fact that men are hanged for murder is one great reason why murder is considered so dreadful a crime" (quoted in Zimring and Hawkins 1973, p. 80).

Stating the argument more abstractly, legal punishment generates, reinforces, or sustains the condemnation of crime; and individuals are unlikely to commit a type of crime if they intensely disapprove of it. Assuming, for example, that the typical American male condemns rape to the point of never contemplating its commission, it is entirely possible that legal punishments played a part in forming that condemnation and/or in its maintenance. To illustrate another possibility, students may enter a university with a deep-seated condemnation of smoking marijuana; but on coming to know of numerous impunitive reactions to smoking pot, these students engage in the very behavior that they previously deplored.

Some critics reject the distinction between deterrence and normative validation, especially since deterrence researchers commonly do not recognize any nondeterrent preventive mechanism other than incapacitation (see, for example, Blumstein et al. 1978, pp. 3–90). Yet the central notion in deterrence is fear of punishment; and some individuals refrain from committing certain types of crimes, not out of fear of punishment, but ostensibly because they condemn such crimes. Thus, legal punishments could prevent crimes indirectly by maintaining or reinforcing the social condemnation of criminality.

The only reason for ignoring the distinction between normative validation and deterrence is that it creates still another evidential problem. Specifically, since the very properties of punishment that supposedly give rise to deterrence also supposedly promote normative validation, controls for the validating effects will be even more difficult than controls for incapacitating effects. There is no doubt that execution or imprisonment incapacitates to some extent, but whether legal punishments generate, maintain, or reinforce the condemnation of crime is debatable; and no research bears directly on the question, nor is there an obvious research methodology. Even if legal punishments do validate the social condemnation of crime, the extent to which the rate for any type of crime is a function of social condemnation is unknown. Nonetheless, the idea of normative validation is scarcely incredible.

The possibility that legal punishments prevent crimes through normative validation can be taken into account in testing deterrence propositions, providing researchers are willing to employ a limited control strategy not free of conjecture. The conjecture is that the social condemnation of some offenses (such as parking violations) is so negligible that there is "nothing" for legal punishments to sustain, and the punishments are perceived as so mild that they probably do not generate social condemnation.

Stigmatization   Depending on the community and/or social class of offenders, their associates may view a legal punishment as the ultimate criterion of offenders' guilt, and the severity of any punishment symbolizes the enormity of the offense. Such considerations are especially relevant in contemplating what appears to be indisputable—that some crimes result not merely in the legal punishment of alleged offenders but also in their *stigmatization,* as manifested in an offender's loss of friends, spouse, job, license to practice an occupation, reputation, credit, and the like. Some offenders may perceive such extralegal consequences as more painful than the legal punishment itself; and to that extent legal punishments prevent crimes indirectly, through offenders' fear of extralegal correlates.

The distinction between deterrence and stigmatization gives rise to still another evidential problem. As in the case of incapacitation or normative validation, the very properties of legal punishment that supposedly generate deterrence may further stigmatization; and the similarity also extends to methodological questions. There is no obvious general strategy of controls for stigmatization in deterrence research, meaning one that can be applied regardless of the type of crime in question. The only obvious limited strategy is to focus deterrence research on parking violations, the assumption being that potential offenders scarcely anticipate a stigmatizing correlate of the legal punishment.

Controls for stigmatization are necessary only if it is assumed that numerous potential offenders refrain from crime in anticipation of both legal punishment and painful extralegal consequences. But no research findings establish the importance of stigmatization as a preventive mechanism.[11] Nonetheless, when it comes to publicizing legal punishments to promote fear of stigmatization, policy makers should confront the possibility of a counterproductive policy. Briefly, if there is merit to the theory of secondary deviance (Lemert 1972), legal punishments may increase the recidival rate perhaps to an even greater extent than the reductive effect that fear of stigmatization has on the impunitive categorical or repetitive rate.

That result is distinctly possible in regard to the lower class and to certain racial-ethnic minorities. The fear of stigmatization may be negligible in such divisions of the population, for it is a testimonial to the solidarity of the politically powerless that they attach no significance to legal punishments. Nonetheless, while the "have nots" may see no inherent value in their means of livelihood, the deprivation of employment opportunities or

---

[11] Some suggestive findings (see, especially, Tittle 1980, and Zimring and Hawkins 1973, pp. 190–94) do exist, however.

credit as a consequence of a felony conviction could induce them to resort to illegal means.

Evidence that legal punishments have no preventive functions would give rise to wonderment. It is far more plausible to assume that legal punishments both generate and inhibit criminality. When that assumption is seriously entertained, the stigmatization mechanism will receive a more serious hearing than is now the case.

Nondeterrent Preventive Mechanisms and the Target Population   Nondeterrent preventive mechanisms present particularly serious evidential problems in tests of Corollary II of the deterrence doctrine (Figure 1). However, while a demonstrated inverse relation between the objective certainty of imprisonment and the crime rate may reflect incapacitation rather than deterrence, the same cannot be said for the relation between the perceived certainty of imprisonment and the crime rate (which bears on Corollary I of Figure 1), especially if no relation exists between objective certainty and perceived certainty. The latter relation is all the more important since it bears directly on Premise I and gives rise to fewer evidential problems than do tests of corollaries. Yet a test of any propositional version of Premise I or of Corollary I requires surveys of potential offenders about their perceptions of the properties of legal punishments.

The term "potential offenders," used throughout this essay, is ambiguous. Attempts to clarify the term's meaning raise another issue, since there are opposing ideas about the appropriate definition for purposes of deterrence research. The few surveys that have gathered data on perceptual properties of punishment used for their respondents a presumably representative sample of adults or juveniles. That "representative" strategy has been expressly or tacitly rejected by certain critics (see, for example, Cousineau 1973) on the grounds that some individuals are not really potential offenders. The argument is hardly naïve, since most citizens may be so "law-abiding" that they never seriously contemplate certain types of crimes (for example, rape or murder); and individuals can be deterred by the threat of punishment only if they contemplate committing crimes. In strictly logical terms, however, virtually all members of a population above a certain age are potential offenders, especially when the conventional crime rate is the dependent variable in research on general deterrence, for the total population is the denominator of that rate. In any event, it is by no means clear what alternative the critics propose. It will not do to speak of "hard-core offenders" or "professional criminals," since extant definitions of either term are either extremely vague or arbitrary. Moreover, the critics do not indicate how one can justify testing the deterrence doctrine by focusing on those individuals who have been least deterred.

Nonetheless, the identification of "potential offenders" does constitute a serious problem in deterrence research, and it will become even more crucial when researchers attempt to test Premise I and Corollary I (Figure 1). However, the use of the repetitive rate in research on general deterrence may resolve the problem. While its use would avoid the idea that a hard-core or professional class of criminals can be defined and identified, the conclusions would have to be limited to restrictive deterrence. This is not necessarily a crippling restriction, for restrictive deterrence may be the only significant kind of deterrence in American criminal justice. In any case, it is surely pointless to search for evidence of categorical general deterrence among those who obviously have not been deterred.

A Radical Solution of the Mechanism Problem   The only alternative to limited strategies of controls for nondeterrent preventive mechanisms is to abandon all pretense of testing deterrence propositions and to formulate a theory about the general preventive effects of legal punishments. In that light, all previous purported tests of the deterrence doctrine (including the early death penalty studies) are tests of an implicit theory of general preventive effects; and such will remain the case as long as nondeterrent mechanisms are left uncontrolled.

In formulating a theory of general preventive effects, it may be feasible to ignore perceptual properties of punishments because they appear truly crucial only in attempts to distinguish preventive mechanisms. Nonetheless, distinctions as to kinds of preventive mechanisms will remain relevant for penal policy. Should it ever be demonstrated that increases in the certainty and length of imprisonment are the only mechanisms regularly followed by a decrease in the crime rate, then it would surely appear that incapacitation is a major preventive mechanism, since incapacitation operates only through actual punishments. Such a possibility has real import for penal policy. If legal punishments prevent crimes primarily through the incapacitating effects of imprisonment, a substantial reduction of the crime rate will be very costly (see Cohen 1983). Similarly, should it be shown that changes in legal punishment (reintroduction of the death penalty, for example) are followed by changes in the crime rate only some twenty years later (a period effect), the notion of normative validation would become a central consideration in penal policy. Finally, given evidence that the preventive impact of legal punishment is markedly contingent on social class, race, or ethnicity, the notion of stigmatization would warrant more theoretical attention; and those who shape penal policy would be haunted by the incompatibility of democratic principles and "effective" criminal justice.

A BRIEF SURVEY OF RESEARCH FINDINGS ON GENERAL DETERRENCE

The early studies of the death penalty and most studies on deterrence after 1967 supposedly pertained to general deterrence.[12] However, since those studies took the conventional crime rate as the dependent variable, the research designs did not distinguish between general and specific deterrence, nor between restrictive and absolute general deterrence. Additionally, five more obvious defects marred the designs of these studies. First, they were limited to one or two properties of legal punishments—predominantly objective certainty and presumptive severity. Second, the vast majority of researchers considered only one type of substantive punishment—either execution or imprisonment. Third, virtually none of the studies attempted any controls for nondeter-

---

[12] Because of space limitations, this review of research findings and the subsequent review concerning specific deterrence focus primarily on the American literature. Deterrence research currently does not have a large following outside of North America—an unfortunate circumstance for two reasons. First, comparable studies in various countries are needed to ascertain whether the validity of deterrence propositions is contingent on the cultural context; and, second, official crime statistics in several European countries offer greater opportunities for deterrence research than do statistics for the United States. No attempt is made here to improve on Zimring's incisive survey (1978) of experiments in law-enforcement practices (such as the volume and locus of police patrols) in connection with general deterrence. Readers should also look to Ross (especially, 1984) for an extensive treatment of deterrence and traffic violations.

rent preventive mechanisms. Fourth, in the few instances where researchers attempted to control for extralegal conditions, the rationale for the selection of the control variables was obscure and dubious at best. And, fifth, few studies examined the relation between *change* in properties of punishment and *change* in the crime rate.

The Early Death Penalty Studies

Systematic and extensive research on general deterrence commenced with studies in the 1950s of the relation between the death penalty and the criminal homicide rate. With remarkable consistency, it was found that abolitionist states tend to have lower rates than retentionist states and that there is no relation between the abolition or reintroduction of the death penalty and trends in the homicide rate. (For extensive critiques of these studies, see Bailey 1976 and Bedau 1982.)

In recognition of the defects of the early studies on the death penalty—especially failure to consider objective certainty—an investigator conducted an econometric analysis of annual trends in the United States homicide rate between 1932 and 1968 and reached a startling conclusion: "On the average the tradeoff between the execution of an offender and the lives of potential victims it might have saved was of the order of magnitude of 1 for 8 for the period 1933–67 in the United States" (Ehrlich 1975, p. 398).

Despite Ehrlich's introduction of a crucial variable—the estimated objective certainty of execution—his study promptly attracted critics (see the latest review by Forst 1983). For the most part criticism focused on the reliability of Ehrlich's data and his vast array of complex statistical manipulations. Less attention was devoted to the fact that, as in the early studies of the death penalty, Ehrlich's incidence figures pertain to criminal homicide and not to capital murder, raising questions not only about his dependent variable but also about his estimates of the objective certainty of execution. It should also be pointed out that, first, Ehrlich's independent variables did not encompass several possibly relevant properties of punishment, perceptual properties in particular; second, his control for incapacitation was based on an arbitrary estimate of the repetitive murder rate; and, third, he introduced various extralegal variables, such as per capita income, that cannot be justified by reference to a theory. Finally, the most specific and perhaps most telling criticism of Ehrlich's conclusion is suggested by Glaser (1977, p. 244): "The . . . data . . . show a direct relationship between use of the death penalty and homicide rates during 1933–63 . . . and an inverse relation thereafter." Even the nature of the association between the increase in the homicide rate and the decline in the estimated objective certainty of execution in the 1960s (the only period of an obvious inverse relation between the two variables) is disputable. The same increase in the homicide rate took place in states where the death penalty was abolished long before 1960—indeed, even before 1933 (Zeisel 1976).

Policy Implications   Granted that the early studies of the death penalty excluded numerous possibly relevant properties of punishment and rested on the unstated assumption that execution is perceived by potential murderers as a more severe punishment than life imprisonment, those studies are nonetheless more relevant in assessing recent penal policy trends than is Ehrlich's study. The latter is hardly relevant, because legislators have only reinstated execution as a statutory penalty, which in itself assures no objective certainty. By contrast, because the earlier studies were concerned primarily with the association between statutory provision for execution and the criminal homicide rate, the findings of these studies are relevant; and they provide no basis for expecting that the reinstatement of capital punishment will be followed by a decline in the criminal homicide rate.

Even though the findings of deterrence research do not provide answers to several questions about penal policy, they surely suggest an argument American legislators persistently ignore when they reinstate the death penalty to promote deterrence. Briefly, quite apart from any humanitarian objections, the deterrence doctrine in itself supplies an argument against reinstating the death penalty. It is not possible to arrive at a truly defensible estimate of the objective certainty of execution before its de facto or de jure abolition in 1967; but all estimates suggest that it was several times *less* than the objective certainty of imprisonment for murder. Accordingly, granted that some systematic but limited data now show that the public perceives execution as more severe than life imprisonment (Bedau 1982, p. 110), the difference in perceived severity does not remotely approach a conservative estimate of the difference in the objective certainty of the two punishments. The point is all the more relevant since there is no basis for anticipating that the objective certainty of the death penalty will be remotely equal to its estimated level in the 1950s. Thus, while deterrence is a common rationale for reintroducing the death penalty, the deterrence doctrine itself casts doubt on that rationale.

The Objective Certainty of Imprisonment

Since 1967, a series of deterrence studies (for surveys, see Gibbs 1975; Blumstein et al. 1978; Cook 1980; and Tittle 1980) has reported an inverse relation between the objective certainty of imprisonment and the crime rate. The findings, which bear on Corollary II of the deterrence doctrine, are noteworthy in that the relation holds for several types of crimes and among various kinds of territorial units (such as states and counties). Nonetheless, the significance of the findings is disputable.

The most crippling doubt is the possibility of a statistical artifact, stemming from the fact that the relation is between the two ratios (Ni/C) and (C/P), where P is the population size of a territorial unit, C the official number of crimes reported as having occurred in the territorial unit during some period, and Ni the estimated number of such crimes that resulted in the imprisonment of an offender. Since C is the numerator of one ratio (the crime rate) and the denominator of the other (certainty of imprisonment), the argument holds that an inverse relation between the two ratios can be expected on grounds of probability alone (or, a different argument, because of measurement error in C). Considerable attention has been devoted to the problem (Logan 1982, for example), but there appears to be no technique of analysis that can resolve the issue, largely because in such a situation the notion of probability is especially ambiguous.

Several deterrence researchers have raised still another doubt about the relation by suggesting that the causal direction could be opposite to that implied by the deterrence doctrine. According to the "overload model" (Geerken and Gove 1977), a relatively high crime rate exhausts the resources of the criminal justice system for investigation, apprehension, prosecution, and imprisonment; hence, a relatively high crime rate results in relatively low objective certainty of punishment. Treatments of the problem indicate that the findings of deterrence research are likely to be misleading if limited to synchronic analyses (see, for example, Nagin 1978 and Greenberg and Kessler 1982).

While the inverse relation between the objective certainty of imprisonment and the crime rate is statistically significant for several types of crimes (robbery, for example), no study has shown that the certainty of imprisonment explains more than 50 percent of the variance in the rate for any type of crime; and the variance explained for some types of crime is negligible. Perhaps more important, for no type of crime is the relation between the certainty of imprisonment and the rate even approximately uniform over time (for example, 1950, 1960, 1970, 1980), although the same kinds of data, research procedures, and territorial units have varied little over time.

Resolving doubts about the findings will require both diachronic analysis and controls for extralegal variables. However, the suggestion is not that the identification of relevant extralegal variables should be the goal of deterrence research. That identification is the office of criminological theory, and deterrence researchers should concentrate on more immediate doubts about the relation between the objective certainty of imprisonment and the crime rate. Those doubts center primarily on (1) the relevance of punishment properties other than objective certainty, (2) the impact of plea bargaining on estimates of the certainty of imprisonment, (3) the reliability and utility of the conventional crime rate, and (4) the temporal lag between change in the variables (see Chiricos and Waldo 1970 and related commentary by Gibbs 1975, p. 172).

Should future research yield compelling evidence that there is no relation between the objective certainty of punishment (or any other punishment property) and the rate for particular types of crime, a theory of general deterrence would still be feasible. Deterrence theorists should recognize the distinct possibility that legal punishments deter some types of crime much less than others. The argument for recognition of that possibility extends to the assertion that "instrumental-low commitment" types of crimes are more deterrable than "expressive-high commitment" types (Chambliss 1967). Unfortunately, it is doubtful if agreement can be reached in the application of the typology, especially in classifying official types of crimes, such as larceny, rather than particular crimes; and insofar as types of crime can be fitted into the scheme, the findings of deterrence studies do not support the argument (see Gibbs 1975, p. 212).

Policy Implications   Not even proof of a truly close inverse relation between the certainty of imprisonment and the crime rate would have immediate policy implications, for while legislators can readily increase statutory terms of imprisonment, they cannot raise objective certainty in some direct way. Indiscriminate allocation of more resources to the criminal justice system would not assure an increase in the objective certainty of punishment. Given the fact that the specific reasons for the very low certainty of imprisonment (in some United States jurisdictions, as low as 25 percent even for criminal homicide) are not obvious, allocation of more resources to a particular division of the criminal justice system (such as increasing the quality and/or quantity of police officers) may not increase the objective certainty of imprisonment. A substantial increase would require major changes in procedures or practices (those governing plea bargaining, for example) that are somewhat independent of resources. In any event, jurisdictions probably differ as to the locus of the resource shortage in the criminal justice system (understaffed prosecutorial offices in some states, overcrowded prisons in others, and so on). Accordingly, if deterrence studies are to have real policy implications, there is a pressing need for research on alternative strategies for manipulating the objective certainty of punishment.

The ultimate question revolves around the point at which the allocation of resources to the criminal justice system has diminishing returns for any given type of jurisdiction. But the answer, which requires a cost-benefit analysis, bears on a much larger problem. The deterrence doctrine supposedly identifies, albeit vaguely, changes sufficient to reduce the rate for a given type of crime to some specified level. Legislators have yet to stipulate a "tolerable" crime rate and its acceptable cost. A substantial reduction in crime may require an increase in the objective certainty of imprisonment far beyond the resources legislators are willing to allocate to criminal justice. Indeed, it may prove that only a radical abandonment of due process would raise the level of objective certainty to that point.

Controls for extralegal variables are just as essential to assess policy implications as to assess the validity of the deterrence doctrine. In assessing implications, however, regression rather than correlational analysis is needed if those who shape penal policy are to have some idea about the proportional relation between change in the objective certainty of imprisonment and subsequent change in the crime rate. Though the deterrence doctrine will have policy implications even if extralegal conditions cannot be manipulated along with properties of punishment, a defensible estimate of the deterrent efficacy of changes in punishment requires at least statistical controls for extralegal conditions in tests of the doctrine. Such controls are no less important with a view to distinguishing types of crimes as to potential deterrence. If legislators ever undertake a thoughtful application of the deterrence doctrine, it would be strategic to focus on the type of crime that is seemingly most amenable to deterrence. The inability of deterrence theorists to identify that type is unfortunate; and its identification may have to be inductive, making controls for extralegal variables in research all the more essential.

Presumptive Severity: Length of Imprisonment

With remarkable consistency, deterrence researchers have reported no significant inverse relation among states between the average prison sentence served for a type of crime and the rate for that crime (for references, see Gibbs 1975; Blumstein et al. 1978; Cook 1980; and Tittle 1980). True, the vast majority of studies has analyzed only the synchronic relation between the two variables, and inferences from that kind of analysis as to the diachronic relation would be little more than conjecture. Yet the lack of evidence of an inverse relation between change in average sentences served and change in crime rates (Chiricos and Waldo 1970) is all the more puzzling in view of the belief that both deterrence and incapacitation are functions of actual incarcerations.

The most immediate doubts about the evidence stem from unanswered questions concerning the reliability of the official crime rates and the impact of plea bargaining on estimates of the length of prison sentences served. Other doubts about the length of prison sentences served stem from theoretical considerations, one of which is suggested by the deterrence doctrine itself. While there is some evidence that the relation between the presumptive severity of actual punishments and the crime rate may be somehow contingent on the objective certainty of punishment (see commentary in Tittle 1980), it is doubtful if partial correlation can reveal its nature. In some instances, the relation between length of imprisonment and the crime rate is inverse when objective certainty is partialed (that is, subjected to statistical control); but even in those instances the inverse relation is not substantial for any type of crime and absent entirely for other types. The outcome is not really surprising, since partial correlation or any similar statistic cannot reveal a "threshold effect," which would obtain if a substantial inverse relation between severity of punishment and the crime rate appears only when all units of comparison (such as states) exceed a particular level of objective certainty. There is also evidence of a more complex contingency in which the expected inverse relation between length of imprisonment and the crime rate becomes truly substantial only when variance in objective certainty among the units of comparison is literally reduced to a negligible level (Erickson and Gibbs 1973). However, the evidence is limited to criminal homicide and stemmed from an unconventional mode of analysis; therefore, the findings are only suggestive. Since the data required for extensive research on the possibility of a contingent relation are readily available, it is unfortunate that deterrence researchers have slighted the subject.

The other possible explanation of a negligible relation between length of imprisonment and the crime rate pertains to a general principle concerning any behavioral theory: whatever the variables, the relations among them do not hold for extreme values. The principle directs attention to the possibility of a "ceiling effect" in the relation between length of imprisonment and the crime rate—the expected inverse relation may not hold beyond some point in the duration of incarceration. Since prison sentences served for felonies are appreciably greater in the United States than in certain European countries, that possibility is not truly far-fetched, especially since even one year of imprisonment is hardly a slap on the wrist. Long prison sentences supposedly promote general deterrence, specific deterrence, and incapacitation. However, since there are many ways in which prolonged incarceration can offset the specific deterrent impact, if any, of the initial year, it is possible that recidivism is checked more effectively by short prison sentences (see Gibbs 1975, p. 73).

Policy Implications   The lack of evidence of an inverse relation between length of imprisonment and the crime rate casts doubts on recent actions by American legislators to impose mandatory prison sentences without possibility of parole for various types of felonies. While those actions will increase the length of prison sentences actually served, research findings provide no basis whatever for anticipating a subsequent decrease in the crime rate.

If the presumptive severity of actual punishments does have some ceiling effect and if actual prison sentences in the United States have already exceeded that point, further increases will not reduce the crime rate. For that matter, if an increase in the presumptive severity of imprisonment decreases the crime rate only when the objective certainty of imprisonment exceeds some critical level, recent actions of legislators will not decrease the crime rate, because those actions do not assure an increase in the objective certainty of imprisonment.

Individuals as the Units of Comparison

Given the widespread belief that only individual correlations reveal causation, critics are likely to regard tests of the deterrence doctrine at the aggregate level (for example, interstate comparisons) as inadequate. The contrary argument holds that a thorough assessment of the deterrence doctrine requires various kinds of comparisons. In any event, there is now a substantial literature on deterrence research in which individuals have been taken as the units of comparison (see references in Paternoster et al. 1982).

While the data and the procedures of these studies vary considerably from one to the next, certain general shortcomings and merits of deterrence studies at the individual level can be identified. The most conspicuous shortcoming is that virtually all studies have been limited to juveniles or college students and to a few types of crime or delinquency, including status offenses (the exclusion of homicide, robbery, and rape is especially conspicuous). The major merits of the studies are their focus on the perceptual properties of punishment and the use of offense rates based on self-reported delicts (crimes or delinquencies); hence, the studies have expanded the range of evidence beyond that generated by studies at the aggregate level. However, the two kinds of studies (aggregate and individual level) share a shortcoming. Both supposedly bear on general deterrence; but because the data may include individuals who have been punished, the distinction between general and specific deterrence has not been maintained.

On the whole, the findings of studies at the individual level are consistent with deterrence doctrine. Yet the findings are far from consistent when it comes to the relation between perceived severity of punishment and self-reported offenses (compare, for example, Tittle 1980 and Grasmick and Bryjack 1980); and on balance the studies indicate that the relation is insubstantial at best. Moreover, the relation between the perceived certainty of punishment and self-reported offenses at the individual level is far less substantial than is that relation in the few perceptual studies at the aggregate level (Erickson et al. 1977b; Erickson and Gibbs 1978). The familiar explanation—measurement error is less of a problem at the aggregate level—is not informative; hence, another explanation should be entertained—that extralegal conditions are more nearly random at the aggregate level. However, when the social condemnation of crime is controlled (statistically) at the aggregate level, at least in comparing types of crime, there is scarcely any evidence of deterrence (Erickson and Gibbs 1978). By contrast, in numerous comparisons of individuals the control of extralegal variables did not eliminate the inverse relation between perceptual properties of punishment and self-reported offenses, but the relation is much more likely to be eliminated in the case of perceived severity than in the case of perceived certainty. Note, however, that the extralegal variables, whether construed as generative or inhibitory, are no more defensible than the extralegal variables in aggregate studies.

Additional Considerations   The deterrence doctrine cannot be used to reduce the crime rate if the propositions subsumed under Premise I (Figure 1) are falsified. Conventional deterrence studies at the individual level do not bear on the proposition that asserts a direct relation between the objective certainty and the perceived certainty of punishment. The objective certainty of some kind of punishment (such as imprisonment) for

some type of crime (for example, rape) does not vary among coresidents of the same
territorial unit, such as a city or state; rather, the objective certainty of punishment is a
characteristic of a territorial unit (the same for all residents). What has been said of
objective certainty applies to other objective properties; hence, the shift in deterrence
research since about 1975 to comparisons of individuals has reduced the scope of the
evidence and lessened the policy implications.

The deterrence doctrine could be construed as implying that residents of a territorial
unit who do not commit the offense in question perceive the certainty of punishment
more accurately than do residents who do commit the offense. However, the few relevant
findings (for references and commentary, see Gibbs 1975, pp. 207–9; Henshel and
Silverman 1975) indicate that offenders more nearly perceive the objective certainty of
punishment for what it is, while nonoffenders tend to overestimate it grossly. That
difference is consistent with the deterrence doctrine only if the doctrine is construed as
implying that, apart from accuracy of perception, offenders perceive less risk of punishment than do nonoffenders. Yet the argument has no policy implications other than
suggesting that legal officials should conceal the objective certainty of punishment and be
thankful that only offenders perceive it somewhat accurately.

Unfortunately, the findings in question are flawed because they commonly pertain only
to apprehended offenders, whose perceptions may have been influenced by actual punishment. Yet if actually being punished increases perceived certainty, then the perception of
the typical offender and that of the typical nonoffender differ more before the offender's
punishment than after that punishment. Nonetheless, confirmation must await a panel
study commencing prior to the commission of the type of crime in question (for example,
shoplifting) by any individual in the cohort. If such a study were to show that the typical
offender's perception of the certainty of punishment comes to differ from that of the
typical nonoffender only after a first offense, the evidence would be inconsistent with the
deterrence doctrine.

Panel studies are needed all the more because there is now evidence (Paternoster et al.
1983) that the relation among individuals between the perceived certainty of punishment
and self-reported *previous* offenses is substantially influenced by the impact of previous
experience on *present* perceptions. Since that evidence creates doubts about virtually all
findings of deterrence research on individual differences, future research must examine
the relation between perceptions of punishment (whether certainty *or* severity) and
subsequent offenses.

Rare Lines of Research on General Deterrence

Some lines of general deterrence research are so rare that the findings cannot be taken
as even suggestive, let alone conclusive. While space limitations make it necessary to
treat those lines of research only very briefly, there is a special reason for at least
recognizing them. Given all of the evidential problems, conventional lines of research
may prove to be wholly inadequate.

Experimental Work   There are two major possibilities in the way of experimental
research (some kind of nonstatistical control over conditions or variables) on general
deterrence. In one of those the researcher attempts to manipulate perceptions of punish-

ment without (1) changing statutory penalties, (2) altering enforcement practices, or (3) imposing actual punishments. Virtually all such experiments have taken the frequency of some kind of extralegal deviance (for example, cheating in school) as the dependent variable (for some references and commentary, see Gibbs 1975, pp. 190–203), and there have been so few comparable experiments that there is scarcely any basis for a summary of the findings. Moreover, attempts to design punishment experiments such that the findings will have some bearing on the deterrence doctrine (for example, Gray et al. 1982) are discouraged by the reluctance of critics (for example, Pettigrew 1983) even to entertain the possibility.

When statutory penalties or enforcement practices are altered in some conditions but not in others and the incidence of crime is taken as the dependent variable, the research can be characterized as a "policy experiment" (see Zimring 1978). Only a few of the experiments have been designed in a defensible way; and in the best known, the Kansas City experiment (see commentary by Zimring 1978), the manipulation of the patrol intensities in various police beats did not produce significant changes in the official or unofficial crime rate.

Before-and-After Research   Any new statutory penalty, any alteration of enforcement practices, or any actual legal punishment provides an opportunity for testing propositions about general deterrence, though not such that the researchers can create experimental-control conditions. Hence, the research should be designated as before-and-after (or an interrupted time series), because it always entails a comparison of the incidence of crime before and after some change in or event pertaining to criminal law.

Since the early death penalty studies, much of the before-and-after research has focused on a change in statutory penalties for driving while intoxicated (DWI) and/or related enforcement practices (for example, the police commence using a "breatholyzer"). After several very careful studies, the leading researcher, Ross (1984), concluded that in numerous instances an increase in the objective certainty of punishment has reduced the DWI incidence; but the decline is commonly transitory because of a failure to maintain enforcement intensity.

Numerous researchers have interpreted the idea of general deterrence as implying this proposition: shortly before and/or shortly after a severe and widely publicized punishment, the incidence of the related type of crime declines. Virtually all tests of that proposition have considered daily or weekly homicide trends before and after the execution of a convicted murderer (see references in McFarland 1983), and the findings have been markedly divergent. For example, some researchers have reported a decline in homicides just before the execution and an increase just after, while other researchers have reported just the opposite. The most recent researcher (McFarland 1983) reported a significant decline in homicides in conjunction with only one of four U.S. executions; and there is compelling evidence that the decline in the one case—Gary Gilmore's execution—was due to a severe blizzard (an illustration of the complexities of evidential problems, needless to say). So it appears that the deterrent impact, if any, of an execution is contingent on unidentified conditions. Nonetheless, before-and-after research should be continued if only because *negative* evidence (as in McFarland's study) cannot be attributed readily to extralegal conditions; of the major possibilities, only weather appears to change substantially from week to week.

THE DETERRENCE DOCTRINE AS IT APPLIES TO SPECIFIC DETERRENCE

If only because that part of the deterrence doctrine pertaining to specific deterrence has yet to be stated as a systematic theory, all reported evidence on the subject is disputable. Indeed, authors of research reports commonly write as though there is no need to confront this question: What is the basis for expecting that the punishment of an individual for an act will prevent his/her repetition of the act? Nothing less than a theory is needed for a defensible answer, but the formulation of a systematic specific deterrence theory will be difficult. All that can be done here is to introduce some of the possible components of such a theory, as shown in Figure 2.

Particular Components

Virtually all research on specific deterrence has been limited to this propositional version of Corollary II: Among individuals who have been punished for a crime, the frequency of recidivism varies inversely with the presumptive severity of the punishment. An implied illustrative hypothesis (prediction) states: Of all individuals convicted of burglary in a particular jurisdiction and sentenced to varying terms of incarceration, the proportion of those who commit the same crime again after serving less than a year of incarceration will be greater than the proportion committing the crime again after more than five years of incarceration.

Virtually all tests that bear on presumptive severity in connection with Corollary II have been negative. Hence, it appears that one or more of the three premises must be false, although there is no way to identify which one or ones.

Premise I   No tests pertaining to Premise I have been conducted, perhaps because of the difficulty of gathering data on change in the perceptions of punishment (the

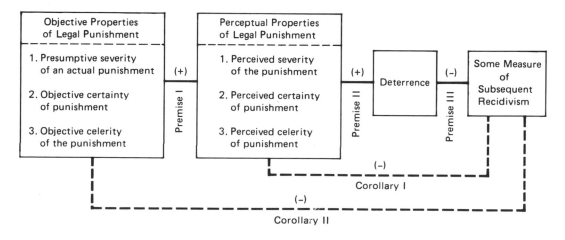

FIGURE 2

Major Components of the Deterrence Doctrine As It Applies to Specific Deterrence*

*(+) signifies the assertion of a subsequent increase; (−) signifies the assertion of a subsequent decrease; ———— signifies an underived proposition; and - - - - signifies a derived proposition.

difference between perception before committing the offense and perception after punishment). Nonetheless, it is pointless to ignore the perceptual character of specific deterrence. The claim that someone refrained from recommitting a crime after punishment because the punishment acted as a deterrent clearly implies that the punishment increased the individual's perception of the certainty and/or severity of punishment.

The problem is that various questions bearing on Premise I are still unanswered. If an individual was ignorant of the prescribed punishment for a type of crime at the time of commission (for example, he or she believed the maximum punishment to be six months in jail, whereas it was actually two years in prison), then an actual punishment could increase that individual's perception of the severity of the risk. Beyond that point, however, the rationale for Premise I is obscure. In particular, while an actual punishment may increase an individual's perception of the *celerity* of punishment, it is not clear how that increase furthers deterrence. Nor can objective certainty be interpreted readily in the context of specific deterrence, for the notion of probability scarcely applies to a single case (the one punishment in question). One interpretation is suggested by the formula: Np/Nc, where Nc is the number of crimes committed by an individual and Np the number of such crimes that resulted in the legal punishment of the individual, including the present punishment.

If the formula is applied only to crimes of a particular type (such as burglary), still another unanswered question is raised: Does punishment for one type of crime deter the offender from other types of crimes, and does avoidance of apprehension for one type of crime lessen deterrence from other types? While it is more feasible to state a specific deterrence theory as though tests of it would be limited to punishments for one particular type of crime, such tests must control for differences among the individuals in question as to additional types of crimes and punishments for them.

Other Components   As long as deterrence itself is not subject to measurement, Premises II and III (Figure 2) cannot be tested directly. Evidence can be brought to bear on the premises through tests of Corollary I; but those tests would require data on each individual's perception of punishment before the crime was committed and after the punishment (in the case of perceived severity, after the punishment has been fully imposed).

The only conspicuous theoretical problem in testing Corollary I is stating a proposition so as to indicate how the perceived celerity is relevant in specific deterrence. The measures of recidivism used to test Corollary II can be used to test Corollary I as well, but there is no defensible rationale other than expediency for basing those measures on official data (such as records of subsequent arrests, subsequent convictions, probation revocations, parole violations). The official figures that have been used in research on specific deterrence are scarcely defensible; and the only viable alternative is a set of rates based on self-reported offenses, especially since self-reports can be used to compute categorical or repetitive recidival rates.

Possible Test Outcomes

An empirical assessment of the validity of specific deterrence theory would require tests of Premise I, Corollary I, and Corollary II. Yet the outcomes of the tests would not have the same implications, either with a view to reformulating the theory or with a view to penal policy.

If credence is placed in past test findings, none of the propositions pertaining to presumptive severity (Corollary II) are likely to be supported. While that outcome would simplify the reformulation of the theory, it would pose a dilemma for those who shape penal policy. It would mean that specific deterrence can be furthered only by increasing the objective certainty of punishment, a goal that is likely to be extremely costly and difficult to realize.

Finally, if the tests support only Corollary I, the theory will become purely perceptual, ceasing to have any particular policy implications. Specific deterrence can then no longer be the rationale for manipulating objective properties of punishment.

A Brief Survey of Evidence

Although numerous investigators have conducted research on specific deterrence, the designs of all those studies are defective in several respects. Briefly, none of the studies considered perceptual properties of punishment, let alone change in such properties; and most of the studies have considered only official figures on recidivism.

Studies with a Particular Conspicuous Design Defect   In one of the earliest and best-known studies, Robert Caldwell (1944) analyzed the recidival rates up to 1943 of individuals who were sentenced in the courts of New Castle County, Delaware, during 1920–39 on conviction for an offense that could have resulted in imprisonment and/or whipping. He reported the recidival rate—percentage subsequently convicted for any type of crime in Delaware or elsewhere—for four categories of offenders: (1) those placed on probation during 1928, 42 percent; (2) those imprisoned but not whipped during 1928, 54 percent; (3) imprisoned and whipped once during 1920–39, 62 percent; and (4) those imprisoned and whipped at least twice during 1920–39, 65 percent. Although Caldwell did not employ measures of perceived severity, the presumptive severity of those punishments appears to form an ordinal scale. Contrary to the idea of specific deterrence, the study shows presumptive severity to vary directly with the categorical *official* recidival rate.

Following Caldwell's study, many studies of specific deterrence were undertaken. Since several surveys of these studies (notably European Committee on Crime Problems 1967; Cramton 1969; Doleschal 1969; Wilkins 1969; Levin 1971; Zimring and Hawkins 1973; Gibbs 1975; Friedman and Macaulay 1977; Moffitt 1983) offer detailed commentary, a few summary observations will suffice. One kind of official recidivism rate or another has been found to be greater for (1) individuals imprisoned, as compared with those placed on probation; (2) individuals who served longer prison sentences; (3) individuals convicted of drunkenness who were incarcerated, as compared with those who were fined; and (4) individuals who received a warning for a traffic offense, as compared with those incarcerated or fined. In all these studies, as in the case of Caldwell's study, the presumptive severity of the punishment appears to vary *directly* with the recidivism rate.

None of the studies employed measures of the perceived severity of punishments or unofficial data on recidivism. Another and perhaps much more crippling defect mars the designs of those studies. Penologists generally agree on two points concerning recidivism and sentencing practices. First, regardless of the punishment (or "correctional treatment"), recidivism appears to be greatest for those individuals who have the "worst record of previous criminality"; and, second, the presumptive severity of sentences tends to be greater for those who have the worst record. Accordingly, since the design of the studies did not incorporate randomization (that is, the selection of the punishment for each individual was not random), it can be argued that the common finding—a direct relation between the presumptive severity of punishment and the recidivism rate—is not compelling.

While the findings indicate that presumptively severe sentences do not overcome all other factors, including previous criminality,[13] the direct relation between previous record of criminality and recidivism scarcely bears on any theory. Yet a criminological theory would be strengthened if it could account for the relation, and the idea of specific deterrence is relevant in that connection. If two individuals have been convicted and imprisoned for the same type of offense, one after the twentieth offense and the other after the second offense, the objective certainty for the "experienced" offender is only 5 percent, while it is 50 percent for the novice. The experienced felon may not perceive the certainty of imprisonment less than does the novice, but the doctrine of deterrence surely suggests that difference. Hence, the exclusion of measures of the certainty of punishment, objective and perceived, has been a major defect in research on specific deterrence.

Research on specific deterrence along the lines suggested requires a panel study of a cohort of potential offenders in which data are gathered at various points over a long period of time on (1) self-reported offenses, (2) self-reported legal punishments of the offenses, (3) perceptions of the certainty of punishment, and (4) perceptions of the severity of punishments. Such a study, though costly and laborious, could yield crucial evidence.

Studies in Which Punishments Have Been Randomized   Given the understandable reluctance of magistrates to randomize punishments, it is not surprising that few studies of specific deterrence have randomized. Again, a few summary observations will suffice to suggest the variety of studies and the preponderant direction of the findings. One kind of official recidivism rate or another has been reported as (1) greater for individuals who were incarcerated, as compared with those placed on probation; (2) not different for individuals who were fined for driving while intoxicated, as compared with those placed on probation; (3) not different for individuals who served a longer prison sentence; and (4) greater for juveniles fined for a traffic offense, as compared with those required to write a paper on traffic safety. The only recent exception (that is, evidence of specific deterrence) is a lower recidivism rate for "domestic assaulters" in Minneapolis who were arrested than for those not arrested (see Sherman and Berk 1984).

The findings of such "superior" studies of specific deterrence are insufficiently compelling for a reason beyond the fact that the randomization of punishments was not always complete (see commentary in Levin 1971). Since none of the studies employed measures

---

[13] It would be misleading to suggest that all studies of specific deterrence have reported negative evidence (see especially, the survey in Moffitt 1983), and the typical negative finding is "no significant relation" between the presumptive severity of punishment and recidivism rather than a significant direct relation. However, the few exceptions (for example, the FBI's "Careers in Crime Program") have been widely criticized for numerous defects in methodology (see Zimring and Hawkins 1973, p. 236), and the negative evidence continues to mount (for example, Klemke 1978).

of the perceived severity of punishment, all judgments of differences in the severity of punishment are questionable except those pertaining to varying lengths of incarceration. But in even one of those exceptions (Berecochea et al. 1973), an approximate six-month difference in length of prison sentence was not sufficient to generate evidence of specific deterrence. True, since the experimental group served 31.5 months and the controls 37.9, the proportionate difference may not appear substantial, and by any reasonable standard the difference in the punishments applied to the control and experimental groups in other studies was even less substantial.

Because randomizing punishments to make them differ markedly in severity would be wholly unjust, the problem appears beyond solution. Worse still, no kind of randomization may be an ideal test. Complete randomization would ostensibly eliminate differences between the experimental and control groups as regards all correlates of recidivism, such as previous offenses, previous punishments, age, employment record, marital status. But consider two groups created by randomized sentences—those who served at least five years in prison and those who were fined the minimum amount prescribed for the felony conviction in question. Surely those who serve at least five years will face greater stigmatization, loss of occupational skills, and disruptions of social relations. Once the punishments have been administered, the extralegal conditions of the experimental and control groups would not be even approximately the same. In view of all these problems, an examination of changes in perceptual properties (both those pertaining to severity and certainty) concomitant with punishment may well turn out to be not merely a desirable feature of research on specific deterrence, but perhaps the only way to arrive at compelling evidence (albeit limited to Premise I).

OCCASION FOR DISBELIEF

This essay has identified little evidence to support the doctrine as it applies to general or specific deterrence, and to question the doctrine's validity is to question not only classical economics but also common sense.[14] After all, virtually all experience demonstrates that some individuals are deterred from some types of crimes in some situations by the threat of some kind of legal punishment. But an informed penal policy requires more than existential propositions.

For those social critics who are determined to defend the deterrence doctrine despite inconclusive evidence, the most effective strategy is to emphasize the defects of research on deterrence. Some defects are debatable and limited to particular studies, such as the exclusion of perceptual properties of punishment. Attention should therefore be directed to two indisputable limitations of deterrence research as a whole. First, for all practical purposes, the distinction between absolute and restrictive deterrence has yet to be recognized in research designs. Second, the same may be said of the distinction between marginal and nonmarginal deterrence.

Elaborating on the second limitation, all deterrence studies have compared either jurisdictions or individuals that differ with regard to some property of punishment (for

---

[14] "Most economists who have given serious thought to the problem of crime immediately come to the conclusion that punishment will indeed deter crime. The reason is perfectly simple: Demand curves slope downward. If you increase the cost of something, less will be consumed. Thus, if you increase the cost of committing a crime, there will be fewer crimes" (Tullock 1974, pp. 104–5).

example, the objective certainty of imprisonment is greater in some jurisdictions than in others); and all such comparisons bear only on marginal deterrence. Evidence of nonmarginal deterrence requires either a comparison of the frequency of some type of act in two jurisdictions—one in which the act is subject to no legal punishment—or a comparison of the criminality of individuals, some of whom have been punished and others who have not been even apprehended. There has never been a study of nonmarginal deterrence, and the findings might sober critics of the deterrence doctrine.

RETRIBUTION AND DETERRENCE

Despite evidence that severe punishments do not further marginal deterrence, they will be defended by an appeal to the doctrine of retribution.[15] That doctrine is enjoying a revival in the United States, one promoted by jurists, legislators, and a few distinguished scholars. Unless future research findings provide more support for the efficacy of deterrence, the drift toward a retributive penal policy may well accelerate.

It has been suggested that the retributive doctrine and the deterrence doctrine are complementary, evidently because both doctrines are interpreted to call for certain and severe legal punishments—that is, both are "punitive" (van den Haag 1975). However, for centuries advocates of retribution have depicted their doctrine as superior on moral or ethical grounds to deterrence. Briefly, they argue that whereas the only end of retribution is justice, the deterrence doctrine uses the individual as a means and is conducive to the punishment of the innocent with a view to promoting general deterrence. The importance of the debate beggars exaggeration.

Some Major Questions, Problems, and Issues

A truly complete and rational penal policy would answer all the questions about legal punishments that now haunt the American criminal justice system. The doctrines of retribution and deterrence are not complementary if they imply different answers to those questions or suggest different bases for seeking answers.

What Is the Appropriate Punishment?   The question calls for a principle that would enable the deduction of the appropriate punishment for any given type of crime. The retributivists have no principle other than "just desert"—at least, none that will bear examination. As a case in point, there is the retributive idea that the severity of the punishment should match the "gravity" of the offense; but a defensible procedure for measuring either variable is wanting. Moreover, even if there were defensible measurement procedures, there is no obvious basis for equating a particular gravity value for a type of crime and a particular severity value of punishment, which is necessary if the punishment is to "match" the offense.[16]

---

[15] For a review of and commentary on the various arguments that may be considered as components of the retributive doctrine, see Fingarette (1977) and Bedau (1978). It is particularly noteworthy that retributivists do not agree as to why "criminals should be punished because they deserve it," but the lack of agreement does not make the retributive doctrine meaningless.

[16] Among contemporary retributivists, Andrew von Hirsch (1976) has most nearly confronted these problems directly; but his strategy is suggestive at best. While von Hirsch eschews the use of the term, he and his colleagues are clearly making an argument for retribution (see commentary by Bedau 1978, p. 602, n. 4).

The alternative strategy of allowing legislators or the public to determine the appropriate punishment for each type of crime is not entirely consistent with the retributivists' tireless concern with justice. When legislators prescribe legal punishments, the political character of crime is glaring; and one must surely wonder how criminal law is "just" if it is enacted by legislators whose cultural background, socioeconomic positions, or ideologies are not representative of those subject to the punishments. Thus, time and again the death penalty has been prescribed by American legislators including not one representative of the black population, whose members have been executed in disproportionate numbers throughout the history of the United States.

While statutory penalties can be determined or guided by some manifestation of public opinion—such as direct voting, referenda, or opinion polls—any proposal along that line gives rise to all manner of problems and issues.[17] One of these bears directly on the retributive doctrine. While the doctrine seems to call for the legal punishment of a crime as an end in itself (criminals are to be punished only because they deserve it), equating retribution with "satisfying the public's demand for vengeance of crimes" is a disputable interpretation. The "lawless" quality of vengeance would make it alien to retributivists' concern with justice. Ordinarily, vengeance is associated with the citizenry's taking the law into its own hands; but allowing public opinion to dictate statutory penalties or judicial rulings is not an altogether different matter. An army of distinguished legal philosophers has argued that criminal law must protect both accused and convicted individuals from the transitory and violent passions of the public. No thoughtful retributivist rejects that argument, but it casts doubt on the proposal to base statutory penalties solely on public opinion. It is therefore hardly surprising that, when speaking to the "appropriate punishment" question, retributivists can say little more than "whatever is the just desert." There is no distinct alternative because from Kant and Hegel to the present it has been recognized that punishments can "resemble" few types of crimes; hence, the *lex talionis* principle has limited applicability, and the death penalty for murder has an ad hoc quality.

Advocates of the deterrence doctrine can approach the question from a quite different perspective. To the extent that the maximum "acceptable" rate for a given type of crime and the maximum "tolerable" cost for realizing that rate are stipulated, it is possible to identify the requisite severity and certainty of punishment. Of course, such an equation is possible only in principle; nonetheless, whereas advocates of the deterrence doctrine can look to empirical findings for an answer to the "appropriate punishment" question, retributivists can do so only if they are willing to abide by the answer to this question: "What does the public want in the way of legal punishments?" Advocates of deterrence will not abide by the answer because public opinion may call for punishments that are more severe than needed to deter (in which case, the punishments would be Bentham's "evil") or far too mild.

---

[17] Most of the problems have to do with feasibility, such as the sheer cost of soliciting public opinion about the appropriate punishment for all types of crime and the frequent alteration of statutory penalties that may be required. However, some of the problems actually give rise to issues, especially in stipulating criteria of "effective consensus." Any criterion is likely to be arbitrary, and it will not do to ignore the distinction between aggregate consensus and structural consensus. To illustrate, even if a substantial simple majority of survey respondents or voters approve of the death penalty, the penalty might be overwhelmingly opposed by some racial-ethnic minorities.

Are More Severe Punishments for Recidivists Justified?   Confronted with the question of increasingly stringent punishment of repeat offenders, contemporary retributivists do not answer in unison (compare, for example, Newman 1978 and von Hirsch 1976). Their divergent opinions are understandable, since recidivism poses a dilemma for anyone who would make justice the central concern in penal policy. Retributivists do agree that criminals should be punished as moral beings fully responsible for their actions; but it is by no means clear how a second offense is any more wrong than a first, especially when the offender has "paid the price" for the first offense.

Unlike retributivists, advocates of deterrence can hope to justify more severe punishments for recidivists on empirical grounds, by attempting to show that specific deterrence requires more severe punishment of repeaters than of first offenders. Advocates of deterrence can regard the question in that light because they view the purpose of punishment as crime prevention, a purpose retributivists do not emphasize. However, the deterrence doctrine is not free of dilemmas. Given evidence that more severe punishments are required for general than for specific deterrence, the decision to employ the more severe punishment would be to use recidivists as means to an end.

Should There Be Judicial Discretion in Sentencing?   It is not surprising that contemporary retributivists admit to dissension in answering the question of judicial discretion (see Newman 1978). No imagination is required to appreciate an offender's feeling of injustice on being punished more severely than someone who was convicted for the same type of crime, especially given a similarity in previous convictions. Yet it is idle to presume that all instances of any type of crime are equally heinous or that types of crimes can be differentiated to assure such homogeneity. Accordingly, if the severity of punishment is to match the gravity of an offense (as the retributive doctrine would have it), exemplary punishments are justified. In that view, the retributive doctrine appears to require judicial discretion in sentencing; but, unlike "individualization of treatment" in efforts at rehabilitation, the sole object of retributive discretion is to equate the gravity of the offense with the severity of punishment.

Two questions remain unanswered—whether an assessment of the gravity of an offense should consider previous offenses and whether such assessments are intolerably subjective. Those questions will haunt the retributive doctrine even if its advocates should all come to endorse judicial discretion in sentencing.

The Essential Difference

The retributive doctrine is an empty formula, since contemporary retributivists either cannot answer specific questions pertaining to penal policy or fail to agree in their answers (for elaboration, see Gibbs 1978 and Bedau 1978). However, it does not follow that the deterrence doctrine is superior, since it, too, fails to provide specific answers to any of the previous questions.

Nonetheless, the argument that the two doctrines are complementary is disputable. Whereas advocates of deterrence appeal primarily to empirical evidence, retributivists clearly base their arguments purely on metaphysical abstractions. Should advocates of deterrence ever be able to provide empirically defensible answers to questions, the difference between the two doctrines may become clearly incompatible. Given evidence that more severe punishments are required for general deterrence than for specific deterrence, advocates of a deterrent penal policy will tend to recommend the more severe punishments (especially given evidence that it would insure even greater specific deterrence), while retributivists, if they are to remain true to Kant and Hegel, will reject that recommendation.

CONCLUSION

While the findings of deterrence research are inconclusive, further research cannot be justified unless conventional research strategies are abandoned. The scope of research must be expanded to encompass all properties of legal punishments, and all manner of evidential problems should be confronted in designing research. An even more immediate need is a sophisticated statement of the deterrence doctrine as a set of systematic and testable theories, each with implications for penal policy.

What is rapidly becoming a popular argument among scholars and those who shape penal policy requires no additional work on the deterrence doctrine to justify an increase in the presumptive severity and the objective certainty of legal punishments. The argument claims, in brief, that even if increases do not promote deterrence, they will at least be consistent with the retributive doctrine. Yet the doctrines of deterrence and retribution are less complementary than they appear to be, as will become obvious if the advocates of the two doctrines are pushed to answer specific questions about penal policy.

Bibliography

Andenaes, Johannes
    1974   *Punishment and Deterrence.* Ann Arbor: University of Michigan Press.
Bailey, William C.
    1976   "Murder and Capital Punishment: Some Further Evidence." In *Capital Punishment in the United States,* edited by Hugo A. Bedau and Chester M. Pierce. New York: AMS Press.
Becker, Gary S.
    1968   "Crime and Punishment: An Economic Approach." *Journal of Political Economy* 76:169–217.
Bedau, Hugo A.
    1970   "Deterrence and the Death Penalty: A Reconsideration." *Journal of Criminal Law, Criminology and Police Science* 61:539–48.
    1978   "Retribution and the Theory of Punishment." *Journal of Philosophy* 75:601–20.
Bedau, Hugo A., ed.
    1982   *The Death Penalty in America.* 3rd ed. New York: Oxford University Press.
Berecochea, John E., et al.
    1973   *Time Served in Prison and Parole Outcome: An Experimental Study.* Report no. 1. Sacramento: Research Division, Department of Corrections, State of California.
Blumstein, Alfred, et al., eds.
    1978   *Deterrence and Incapacitation.* Washington, D.C.: National Academy of Science.

Caldwell, Robert G.
  1944   "The Deterrence Influence of Corporal Punishment Upon Prisoners Who Have
          Been Whipped." *American Sociological Review* 9:171–77.
California Assembly Committee on Criminal Procedure
  1968   *Deterrent Effects of Criminal Sanctions.* Sacramento: Assembly of the State of
          California.
Chambliss, William J.
  1967   "Types of Deviance and the Effectiveness of Legal Sanctions." *Wisconsin Law
          Review* 1967:703–19.
Chiricos, Theodore G., and Waldo, Gordon P.
  1970   "Punishment and Crime: An Examination of Some Empirical Evidence." *Social
          Problems* 18:200–17.
Cohen, Jacqueline
  1983   "Incapacitation as a Strategy for Crime Control." In *Crime and Justice,* vol. 5,
          edited by Michael Tonry and Norval Morris. Chicago: University of Chicago Press.
Cook, Philip J.
  1980   "Research in Criminal Deterrence." In *Crime and Justice,* vol. 2, edited by Norval
          Morris and Michael Tonry. Chicago: University of Chicago Press.
Cousineau, Douglas F.
  1973   "A Critique of the Ecological Approach to the Study of Deterrence." *Social Science
          Quarterly* 54:152–58.
Cramton, Roger C.
  1969   "Driver Behavior and Legal Sanctions: A Study of Deterrence." *Michigan Law
          Review* 67:421–54.
Doleschal, Eugene
  1969   "The Deterrent Effect of Legal Punishment: A Review of the Literature." *Informa-
          tion Review on Crime and Delinquency* 1:1–16.
Durkheim, Emile
  1949   *The Division of Labor in Society.* Translated from the French 1st and 5th editions by
  [1893] George Simpson. New York: Free Press.
Ehrlich, Isaac
  1975   "The Deterrent Effect of Capital Punishment: A Question of Life and Death."
          American Economic Review 65:397–417.
Erickson, Maynard L., et al.
  1977a   "Conventional and Special Crime and Delinquency Rates." *Journal of Criminal Law
          and Criminology* 68:440–53.
  1977b   "The Deterrence Doctrine and the Perceived Certainty of Legal Punishments."
          American Sociological Review 42:305–17.
Erickson, Maynard L., and Gibbs, Jack P.
  1973   "The Deterrence Question: Some Alternative Methods of Analysis." *Social Science
          Quarterly* 54:534–51.
  1978   "Objective and Perceptual Properties of Legal Punishment and the Deterrence
          Doctrine." *Social Problems* 25:253–64.
European Committee on Crime Problems
  1967   *The Effectiveness of Punishment and Other Measures of Treatment.* Strasbourg: Coun-
          cil of Europe.
Fingarette, Herbert
  1977   "Punishment and Suffering." *Proceedings of the American Philosophical Association*
          50:499–525.
Forst, Brian
  1983   "Capital Punishment and Deterrence." *Journal of Criminal Law and Criminology*
          74:927–42.

Foucault, Michel
    1977   *Discipline and Punish.* New York: Pantheon.
Friedman, Lawrence M., and Macaulay, Stewart, eds.
    1977   *Law and the Behavioral Sciences.* 2nd ed. Indianapolis: Bobbs-Merrill.
Geerken, Michael A., and Gove, Walter R.
    1975   "Deterrence: Some Theoretical Considerations." *Law & Society Review* 9:497–513.
    1977   "Deterrence, Overload, and Incapacitation: An Empirical Evaluation." *Social Forces* 56:424–47.
Gibbs, Jack P.
    1966   "Sanctions." *Social Problems* 14:147–59.
    1975   *Crime, Punishment, and Deterrence.* New York: Elsevier.
    1978   "The Death Penalty, Retribution and Penal Policy." *Journal of Criminal Law and Criminology* 69:291–99.
Glaser, Daniel
    1977   "The Realities of Homicide Versus the Assumptions of Economists in Assessing Capital Punishment." *Journal of Behavioral Economics* 6:243–68.
Grabosky, Peter N.
    1984   "The Variability of Punishment." In *Toward a General Theory of Social Control,* vol. 2, edited by Donald Black. New York: Academic Press.
Grasmick, Harold G., and Bryjack, George J.
    1980   "The Deterrent Effect of Perceived Severity of Punishment." *Social Forces* 59:471–91.
Gray, Louis N., et al.
    1982   "A Game Theoretic Analysis of the Components of Punishment." *Social Psychology Quarterly* 45:206–12.
Greenberg, David F., and Kessler, Ronald C.
    1982   "The Effect of Arrest on Crime." *Social Forces* 60:771–90.
Hamilton, V. Lee, and Rytina, Steve
    1980   "Social Consensus on Norms of Justice: Should the Punishment Fit the Crime?" *American Journal of Sociology* 85:1117–44.
Henshel, Richard L., and Silverman, Robert A., eds.
    1975   *Perception in Criminology.* New York: Columbia University Press.
Hirschi, Travis, et al.
    1980   "The Status of Self-Report Measures." In *Handbook of Criminal Justice Evaluation,* edited by Malcolm W. Klein and Katherine S. Teilman. Beverly Hills, Calif.: Sage.
Johnston, James M.
    1972   "The Punishment of Human Behavior." *American Psychologist* 27:1033–54.
Klemke, Lloyd W.
    1978   "Does Apprehension for Shoplifting Amplify or Terminate Shoplifting Activity?" *Law & Society Review* 12:391–403.
Lemert, Edwin M.
    1972   *Human Deviance, Social Problems, and Social Control,* 2nd ed. Englewood Cliffs, N.J.: Prentice-Hall.
Lempert, Richard O.
    1981–82 "Organizing for Deterrence." *Law & Society Review* 16:513–68.
Levin, Martin A.
    1971   "Policy Evaluation and Recidivism." *Law & Society Review* 6:17–46.
Lipton, Douglas, et al.
    1975   *The Effectiveness of Correctional Treatment.* New York: Praeger.
Logan, Charles H.
    1982   "Problems in Ratio Correlation." *Social Forces* 60:791–810.

McFarland, Samuel G.
    1983   "Is Capital Punishment a Short-term Deterrent to Homicide?" *Journal of Criminal Law and Criminology* 74:1014–32.
Moffitt, Terrie E.
    1983   "The Learning Theory Model of Punishment." *Criminal Justice and Behavior* 10:131–58.
Nagin, Daniel
    1978   "Crime Rates, Sanction Levels, and Constraints on Prison Population." *Law & Society Review* 12:341–66.
Newman, Graeme
    1978   *The Punishment Responses.* Philadelphia: Lippincott.
Paternoster, Raymond, et al.
    1982   "Perceived Risk and Deterrence." *Journal of Criminal Law and Criminology* 73:1238–58.
    1983   "Perceived Risk and Social Control." *Law & Society Review* 17:457–79.
Pettigrew, Thomas F.
    1983   "Toward Uniting Social Psychology." *Contemporary Sociology* 12:6–8.
Quinney, Richard
    1976   "Symposium on Wilson's *Thinking About Crime.*" *Contemporary Sociology* 5:414–16.
Riccio, Lucius J., and Heaphy, John F.
    1977   "Apprehension Productivity of Police in Large U.S. Cities." *Journal of Criminal Justice* 5:271–78.
Ross, H. Laurence
    1976   "The Neutralization of Severe Penalties: Some Traffic Law Studies." *Law & Society Review* 10:403–13.
    1984   *Deterring the Drinking Driver.* Lexington, Mass.: Heath.
Rusche, Georg, and Kirchheimer, Otto
    1939   *Punishment and Social Structure.* New York: Russell and Russell.
Schuessler, Karl F.
    1952   "The Deterrent Influence of the Death Penalty." *Annals of the American Academy of Political and Social Science* 284:54–62.
Sherman, Lawrence W., and Berk, Richard A.
    1984   "The Specific Deterrent Effect of Arrest for Domestic Assault." *American Sociological Review* 49:261–72.
Supreme Court Reporter
    1976   *Cases Decided in the Supreme Court of the United States.* St. Paul, Minn.: West.
Taylor, Ian, et al., eds.
    1975   *Critical Criminology.* London: Routledge & Kegan Paul.
Tittle, Charles R.
    1980   *Sanctions and Social Deviance.* New York: Praeger.
Tullock, Gordon
    1974   "Does Punishment Deter Crime?" *Public Interest* 36:103–11.
United States Reports
    1973   *Cases Adjudged in the Supreme Court at October Term, 1971.* Vol. 408. Washington, D.C.: U.S. Government Printing Office.
van den Haag, Ernest
    1975   *Punishing Criminals.* New York: Basic Books.
Van Houten, Ron
    1983   "Punishment." In *The Effects of Punishment on Human Behavior,* edited by Saul Axelrod and Jack Apsche. New York: Academic Press.

von Hirsch, Andrew
    1976   *Doing Justice: The Choice of Punishments.* New York: Hill.
Wilkins, Leslie T.
    1969   *Evaluation of Penal Measures.* New York: Random House.
Williams, Kirk
    1977   "Deterrence and Knowledge of Legal Punishments." Unpublished dissertation,
              University of Arizona.
Wilson, James Q., and Boland, Barbara
    1978   "The Effect of Police on Crime." *Law & Society Review* 12:341–90.
Zeisel, Hans
    1976   "The Deterrent Effect of the Death Penalty: Fact vs. Faiths." *Supreme Court Review*
              1976:317–43.
Zimring, Franklin E.
    1978   "Policy Experiments in General Deterrence: 1970–1975." In *Deterrence and In-
              capacitation,* edited by Alfred Blumstein et al. Washington, D.C.: National Acad-
              emy of Sciences.
Zimring, Franklin E., and Hawkins, Gordon J.
    1973   *Deterrence.* Chicago: University of Chicago Press.

$\backsim$ 8 $\sim$

LAWYERS

Richard L. Abel
University of California, Los Angeles

SOCIOLOGY OF THE PROFESSIONS

The sociology of the professions has been dominated until recently by the structural functionalism of Talcott Parsons (1951, 1954a, 1954b, 1968; Nonet and Carlin 1968; Roth et al. 1973), which simultaneously has furnished the prevailing professional ideol-

NOTE: I am grateful for the editorial suggestions of Lawrence Friedman and Leon Lipson. This chapter was completed in the fall of 1981 and submitted to the editors at that time. It is reasonably comprehensive up to then but necessarily omits anything published subsequently. A number of important books and articles appeared between 1981 and Spring 1985 (when this note was added) on women lawyers (Epstein 1981; Chester 1985; Couric 1984), black lawyers (Segal 1983), entry barriers (Rhode 1985; D. White 1984); legal education (Stevens 1983; Kennedy 1983; Hedegard 1982; Pipkin 1982; Van Alstyne 1982), legal ethics (Luban 1983; Simon 1984; Abbott 1983), the social structure of an urban bar (Heinz and Laumann 1982), rural lawyers (Landon 1982), late nineteenth-century lawyers (Gawalt 1984), a statistical survey of American lawyers (Curran 1985), legal aid (Katz 1982; Cooper 1983; Cappelletti 1981; Garth 1983; Menkel-Meadow 1984; Menkel-Meadow and Meadow 1983; Abel 1985a; Abel 1985b), business lawyers (Gilson 1984), lawyers in the New Deal (Irons 1982), radical lawyers (Gabel and Harris 1982–83; Kinoy 1983), lawyers and doctors (Dingwall and Lewis 1983), large-firm lawyers (Hoffman 1982; Stewart 1983; Nelson 1983), professional associations (Schneyer 1983; Cappell and Halliday 1983; Halliday 1982), the image of lawyers (Mindes and Acock 1982), the regulation of lawyers (Blair and Rubin 1980; Evans and Trebilcock 1982; *Law and Human Behavior* 1983; Rottenberg 1980; Slayton and Trebilcock 1978; Trebilcock, Tuohy, and Wolfson 1979; Nieuwenhuysen and Williams-Wynn 1982; Boreham, Pemberton, and Wilson 1976), English lawyers (Thomas 1982; Flood 1983; Duman 1983; Cocks 1983; Abel 1986; Abel 1987), Australian lawyers (Hetherton 1978; 1981), third-world lawyers (Dias et al. 1981; Lynch 1981; Merryman et al. 1979; Abel 1982), and the comparative sociology of lawyers (Abel 1985c; Abel and Lewis 1987–88).

ogy (Blaustein and Porter 1954; American Bar Association 1974, p. 1c; Royal Commission on Legal Services 1979, vol. 1, pp. 28, 30). In the past decade or so, however, this dominance has been challenged by an empirically grounded critique (Freidson 1970; Johnson 1972, 1977; Roth 1974; *Sociology of Work and Occupations* 1974–date; Berlant 1975; Larson 1977), which offers an alternative theoretical framework for understanding those occupations that claim professional status.

This introduction contrasts functionalism with critical legal theory (Beirne and Quinney 1982; Kairys 1982). Functionalism defines a profession as an occupational category uniquely endowed with a body of theoretical knowledge, the paradigm for which is the natural sciences. This criterion implies that professionals autonomously and progressively elaborate their shared expertise, and it focuses attention on those deviants who lack it and on the threats arising from specialization and routinization. Critical legal theory emphasizes the struggle of occupations to attain professional status and regards theoretical knowledge as a social construct serving to legitimate professional perquisites rather than as the inevitable outgrowth of the cognitive tasks of the occupation. It therefore directs empirical research toward the conditions under which an occupation successfully advances its exclusive claim to such knowledge, the segments within the profession that are active in this campaign, the consequences of the struggle for power relationships within the profession and between it and potential rivals, and subsequent challenges by groups asserting competing bodies of theory (Bucher and Strauss 1961).

Functionalism derives a second professional criterion—formal training—from the centrality of theoretical knowledge. It explains the length of training and the shift from apprenticeship to the university in terms of the quantity and complexity of knowledge to be communicated. A central research issue, then, is the tension between the development and transmission of theoretical principles and training in practical skills (Twining 1967). Critical legal theory hypothesizes, instead, that an occupation institutionalizes and protracts training in order to justify its claim to theoretical knowledge. This condition inevitably creates tension between academics and practitioners (Auerbach 1971) and confers on educational institutions a central role as the gatekeepers allocating entrants to the hierarchy within the profession and justifying that hierarchy.

Functionalism explains professional controls over entry in terms of the need to ensure that entrants receive formal training and acquire essential theoretical knowledge. The empirical question, therefore, addresses the correlation between formal qualifications and competence (Carlson and Werts 1976). Critical legal theory posits market control as the fulcrum for explaining the core of collective occupational behavior (Larson 1977, chap. 2; Abel 1979a). Because it is so difficult for those who sell their services in a market to control the quantity or price of those services or the demand for them, control over the production of producers is the most effective instrument of market control. This conceptualization directs research toward the way in which control is attained and preserved and the efficacy of control, as measured, for example, by the price of professional services.

Functionalism explains the rise of professional associations as an expression of the unique capacity of professionals to maintain technical and ethical standards of performance (Millerson 1964). These associations establish prerequisites for entry, police unauthorized practice, oversee formal training, and promulgate and enforce a code of conduct, performing both prosecutorial and adjudicative functions. The crucial research question is the extent to which any professional association can preserve its autonomy in the face of a double threat—destructive competition fostered by uncontrolled market forces and bureaucratic interference by the state. Critical legal theory sees the professional association as the political instrument through which the occupational category pursues the central goal of market control. Divisions within that category and conflict over how broadly it should be defined initially obstruct the creation of a single association and lead to subsequent fission and external challenges (Kronus 1976). Professionals do not spontaneously eschew competition; they are prevented from engaging in it by the association. And the profession is not autonomous; it is wholly dependent on state authority for its exercise of market control. Research, therefore, concentrates on the extent to which professional segments are able to use state authority to further their parochial self-interest and to disguise that purpose by invoking collective opposition to the market and the state.

Finally, functional theory sees the professional association as the vehicle for mobilizing and expressing altruistic impulses that are claimed to be inescapably associated with the possession of theoretical knowledge. Because functional theory defines altruism as any behavior that lacks an immediate visible material reward, research is directed toward ways of amplifying such behavior. Critical legal theory, by contrast, sees apparently altruistic acts as serving ends that nevertheless are selfish even if the reward may be less obvious (for example, generating future demand by rendering present services at little or no cost) and as legitimating professional privileges (economic, political, and social) by providing symbolic reassurance that their enjoyment is not self-interested. Thus, attention is directed to the ways in which ostensibly altruistic behavior benefits the individual professional and the profession as a whole rather than the client or the public.

This essay will organize recent research on the American legal profession (see Abel 1980), using the framework of critical legal theory. I chose this theoretical paradigm not only because I believe it to be more accurate and powerful, but also because it is consistent with my ethical preference. Functionalism assumes that formal rationality is a superior form of knowledge, entitling those who possess it to exercise domination over others and to enjoy privileges. Critical legal theory asserts that different forms of knowledge cannot be ranked and that the distribution of knowledge can justify neither political, social, or economic inequality nor the abrogation of democracy. Functional theory finds community within the professional association; critical legal theory rejects the possibility of founding community on the domination of others. Functional theory accepts professional paternalism as altruism; critical legal theory insists that altruism can be expressed only between equals.

Given that all definitions are stipulative and that debates over the definition of a profession frequently are little more than ideological smoke screens (Elliott 1972, chap. 1; Habenstein 1963; Office des Professions du Québec 1976, chap. 2), some working concept nevertheless is necessary to limit the phenomenon to be studied, isolate what is theoretically salient, and allow social-structural and temporal comparisons. I will use the notion of a profession to refer to an occupation that produces services for consumption by another and that has attained some degree of control over the market for those services. It is thus a concomitant of the division of labor, which presupposes greater specialization among producers than among consumers (Friedman 1962, p. 143; Johnson 1972, p. 41). Relatively undifferentiated societies may lack most professions, including the legal profession; many tribal societies offer examples (Nagel 1962; Schwartz and Miller 1964), but so does England before Henry II, when litigants represented themselves (Carr-Saunders and Wilson 1933, pp. 30–31). Although the division of labor differentiates producers and consumers, it does not require that the transaction between them involve a sale (Johnson 1972, chap. 3): in premodern Europe, many lawyers were functionaries of the Church (Bouwsma 1973, p. 309); at a later period they were dependents of an aristocratic patron (Larson 1977, chap. 1); under welfare capitalism, legal services may be provided free of charge by lawyers employed by the state.

This definition deliberately makes problematic a number of issues, thereby helping to focus the inquiry. First, what are the services: what has been defined as requiring action by another? The outer boundaries are constituted by the concept of law (itself historically specific)—the formulation, modification, and application of norms (Hart 1962)—but within those limits, there is room for considerable historical variation. Second, who are the producers: what are the categories of the division of labor and the relations within. and between each category? How, and to what extent, have the producers attained market control? Third, who are the consumers of legal services; what are their numbers, characteristics, and organization? Fourth, what is the relationship between producers and consumers: how do they compare in power and status; on what basis is service provided; is the relationship mediated or continuous? Finally, what is the ideological foundation of this entire structure: how is it explained, criticized, and justified by producers, consumers, and others?

I will explore these issues by means of a narrative divided—with inevitable arbitrariness—into three periods: Colonial America (the adaptation of English institutions to the radically different circumstances of the New World); the antebellum period (severance of ties with England, the impact of a new ideology, and the growth of commercial capitalism); and the years before World War I (the triumph of industrial capitalism). By this last date the American legal profession had acquired many of its present characteristics. Later sections detail these qualities as well as subsequent changes, especially those that have occurred since World War II.

HISTORY OF THE AMERICAN LEGAL PROFESSION
Colonial Lawyers

The emergent American legal profession of the seventeenth and eighteenth centuries was necessarily colored by its transatlantic origins (Prest 1981). There was no concept of a *lawyer* in England at that time, much less of a single unified profession. Instead, many occupations specializing in legal affairs struggled—often with little success—to close their ranks to outsiders, resist incursions by competing occupations, and expand their own spheres of operation. At the pinnacle stood the Bar, within which each Inn was self-regulating (Carr-Saunders and Wilson 1933, p. 40); but, by 1750, the Inns possessed little collegial life, offered scant training, and exercised minimal control over entry (Abel-Smith and Stevens 1967, pp. 16–17). Below the Bar was an array of specialties—scriveners, pleaders, conveyancers, proctors in admiralty, doctors of canon law, attorneys, and solicitors (Plucknett 1956, pp. 224–30). Most of these specialists were functionaries of a particular court, by which they were regulated and over which they sought a monopoly. Others were defined by function, such as conveyancing or acting as general agent for an aristocratic household. Qualification for entry to the functional specialties was by apprenticeship; this method was loosely enforced during the seventeenth century and only formalized in 1729, when attorneys and solicitors were given a monopoly by the state and sought an alliance through the Society of Gentlemen Practicers for the purpose of policing it (Carr-Saunders and Wilson 1933, pp. 43–45; Abel-Smith and Stevens 1967, p. 20). The society first discussed formal training through lectures in 1794, and examinations did not begin until the 1830s (Carr-Saunders and Wilson 1933, p. 46; Abel-Smith and Stevens 1967, p. 54). This sequence illustrates a recurrent pattern in the development of professions: state monopoly preceded, and appears to have been a prerequisite for, the creation of a professional association; both antedated formal training, which served, among other purposes, as a post hoc rationalization for the grant of monopoly and the existence of the association.

The English legal occupations, then, offered little for American lawyers to emulate. The Inns of Court could not be reproduced because few colonial judicial institutions played a role as central as that of the Law Courts in London. Nor was there the congeries of specialized courts—the product of a lengthy feudal history—around which occupational subcategories could accrete. Furthermore, local conditions inhibited functional differentiation. There were few legal tasks that the laity could not perform for itself. Because of the largely agricultural economy, the recent origin of title to land (and the plenitude of land), the localized nature of most commerce, and the immaturity of colonial government, American law was less technical than English. Not only were many judges legally untrained, but the laity also had access to and read legal treatises (Boorstin 1958, pp. 197–202). For American lawyers, then, the struggle for professional status was not a competition among occupational subcategories but an effort to convince potential consumers that specialists were useful and should be permitted to represent others (Aumann 1940, pp. 19–26; Day 1973).

The lack of occupational differentiation is demonstrated by the qualifications for entry. Though training for law was generally by apprenticeship, many colonies, especially along the frontier, implemented this requirement laxly, if at all. Only in the larger commercial centers of Massachusetts, New York, Pennsylvania, and Virginia were there the makings of a professional elite, often consisting of graduates of one of the eight pre-Revolutionary American colleges, who then traveled to England to obtain admission to the Inns (Larson 1977, pp. 12–13; Stevens 1971, pp. 408–9; Hurst 1950, p. 266; McKurdy 1976; Klein 1958; Eaton 1951). But these were the exceptions; most lawyers, like most judges, were little differentiated from the laity in terms of origin, training, or even occupation, since many practiced only part-time.

In part, these characteristics of the producers of legal services reflected their market. Consumers were few, geographically dispersed, and relatively unstratified. Outside the cities, few were wealthy, and fees were small. Whatever stratification existed within the profession expressed differences between city and country, officeholders and those without government positions (Day 1973; McKurdy 1972). For similar reasons, lawyers and clients confronted each other as equals in technical expertise and social status; in the cities both tended to be members of the elite, while elsewhere neither was likely to be. Finally, despite the efforts of elite lawyers to raise entry barriers in a few colonies (see, for example, Klein 1958), colonial governments were more likely to remove all barriers or restrict the fees a practitioner might charge (Nolan 1976; 1980, pp. 44–45; see generally Flaherty 1969; Murrin 1971; Nelson 1975; Presser 1976).

Independence to the Civil War

Political separation from England and the consequent internal and external economic adjustments had a considerable impact on American lawyers. After an initial period of disruption, transatlantic trade grew, and English dominance declined. To the ordinary perils of such commerce were added the dangers of the War of 1812. In response to these risks, marine insurance expanded rapidly but bred uncertainties of its own that could be resolved only by litigation. Indeed, litigation generally provided the economic foundation of American lawyers, in much the same way that conveyancing constituted—and still constitutes—the financial base for English solicitors (Abel-Smith and Stevens 1967, p. 23; Royal Commission on Legal Services 1979, vol. 1, chap. 21). The settlement of new territory, land speculation, the absence of good records, and controversies over land seized from Tories all fueled land litigation. Debt collection and, to a much lesser extent, criminal defense were other staples of practice (Bloomfield 1979).

Litigation simultaneously performed other essential roles. Advocacy was its own advertisement. Trials were a popular form of entertainment, not only on the frontier but also in the nation's capital. A reputation for oratorical skills quickly passed by word of mouth, attracting additional business (Friedman 1973, pp. 270, 273; Calhoun 1965). The lawyers' monopoly over courtroom litigation was relatively easy to enforce; encroachments were highly visible, and the regulatory power of the state was immediately available. Litigation also contributed to the development of an American *corpus juris*, assisted by a politically motivated rejection of English law (Nelson 1975). As this body of law became more elaborate and technical (Harris 1972), it transformed the demand for the services of some agent into a market for the services of a legally trained representative. Finally, litigation blurred the distinction between lawyer and client; the professional might purchase the claim to land or the outstanding debt and sue on his own behalf, rather than wait for an uncertain payment from his client (Friedman 1973, p. 269; Hurst 1950, p. 297).

The Revolution directly affected the producers of legal services as well, first by bringing about the departure of significant numbers of Loyalist lawyers (although there is dispute over the exact proportions, which undoubtedly varied from colony to colony) (see Warren 1911; Gawalt 1970; McKurdy 1972; Ely 1973; Nolan 1976). Chance events of this sort—which eliminate a substantial segment of producers, giving those who remain an unprecedented opportunity to gain control of the market as a base for further expansion—played a crucial role in the development of other professions (Kronus 1976). But though those who left were disproportionately officeholders and thus members of the elite (McKurdy 1972), the post-Revolutionary profession was by no means egalitarian. In Massachusetts, the proportion of lawyers with a college education was high and increasing, their social origins were privileged, and many grew wealthy from practice (Gawalt 1969, 1970, 1979; cf. Nash 1965)—though some had to supplement their legal income from other sources. Such stratification was much less pronounced on the frontier, where origins and education meant less and opportunities always beckoned in the next settlement. But even there, by the end of the period, a small number of lawyers had acquired control of a disproportionate amount of business, leaving a mass of marginal practitioners to scramble for what was left (Calhoun 1965, p. 77; Bloomfield 1979; Brown 1970). It therefore is not surprising that Alexis de Tocqueville, visiting the United States in the 1830s, should make his oft-quoted remark:

> In America, there are no nobles or literary men, and the people are apt to mistrust the wealthy; lawyers consequently form the highest political class, and the most cultivated portion of society. . . . If I were asked where I place the American aristocracy, I should reply, without hesitation, that it is not among the rich, who are united by no common tie, but that it occupies the judicial bench and the bar. [1958 (1835), p. 288]

Yet his observation was anachronistic even as he uttered it; the status of the profession rested upon traditional warrants (Larson 1977, pp. 68–69) in the process of being eroded by economic, social, and political change.

This transformation—the Jacksonian attack on privilege—is commonly offered as an explanation for the decline of professions generally, and especially of the legal profession, after 1840. But the effect appears to be exaggerated and the cause misplaced. True, barriers to entering the profession were lowered. The requirement of apprenticeship, which had grown in length between 1760 and 1820 (Barlow 1977, p. 11), was progressively abandoned; 14 out of 19 jurisdictions imposed some such prerequisite in 1800, but only 11 out of 30 did so in 1840 and 9 out of 39 by 1860 (Stevens 1971, pp. 412–13, 417). Attempts to institutionalize legal education in the universities failed, and the dozen private law schools operating in the early 1800s rapidly declined after 1840 (Stevens 1971, pp. 414–15; Reed 1921, p. 132; Hurst 1950, pp. 253–59). Because formal legal education was irrelevant to entry into the profession and inessential for advancement within it, the universities had difficulty attracting students and even more problems keeping them, once they were enrolled. Harvard's three-year degree was shortened to eighteen months; Yale's to two years, with a further reduction for college graduates (Stevens 1971, pp. 418–19, 430). Yet, though the criteria for entry seem lax by contemporary standards, it is not clear that they represented a decline from previous rigor. It has been estimated that the average lawyer in the 1800s received only a primary school education and a legal apprenticeship of 6 to 14 months; and though many states abolished examinations after 1840, those tests had often been a meaningless formality (Hurst 1950, p. 281; Friedman 1973, p. 276; Bloomfield 1971).

What requires explanation, then, is not the deprofessionalization of the bar as a result of the Jacksonian attack but its failure to professionalize until after the Civil War. Yet this may not be a meaningful question. Professionalization is always the result of an active campaign by an occupational category seeking market control, and in this period the prerequisites for such a campaign were lacking. First, the market pressures were relatively weak. Although the number of lawyers was growing much faster than the population— Massachusetts had 15 in 1740 but 640 a hundred years later—the economy was expanding even more rapidly (Barlow 1977, p. 9; Gawalt 1970; Hauser 1976). And the frontier continued to offer an outlet to lawyers who could not make a living in the cities of the eastern seaboard (Harris 1972; Bloomfield 1979).

If the economic impetus to seek market control was absent, so was the institutional foundation necessary to achieve it. The bar associations of this period were local—a heritage of colonial social, economic, and political structures—whereas the market to be controlled and the political apparatus that might control it now were located at the state level. The frontier counterpart of the metropolitan or county bar association was the loose fraternity of lawyers riding the same circuit (Calhoun 1965). In each instance, the functions of the association were essentially social; it was, therefore, incapable of absorbing the large number of new entrants. Finally, there was a failure of leadership. The new elite that succeeded the Tories could not avail itself of the traditional warrants of status, whose legitimacy had been destroyed by the Revolution, and half a century passed before the emergence of new warrants (graduation from an elite school, corporate clients). This last factor may have been critical since, initially, market control always is an elite project. Therefore, after the Revolution, as control over entry passed from bar associations to courts (Friedman 1973, p. 276) and as requirements were eliminated, the associations themselves rapidly atrophied (Stevens 1971, p. 471).

Another prerequisite for market control was a legitimating ideology. As litigators, lawyers displayed oratorical skills that did not differ in kind from those of the ordinary person, though they were more highly developed. Furthermore, lawyers suffered from public opprobrium that had its origins in Puritan suspicion of professionals in general and lawyers in particular (Tabachnik 1976). This suspicion was intensified by the Revolution and its aftermath. If lawyers were prominent in that struggle (Boorstin 1958, p. 205; Surrency 1964; Klein 1974), a number also were visible Tories (McKurdy 1972). The Revolution appears to have imbued some citizens with utopian expectations of a society without lawyers (Nolan 1980, pp. 93–96; Warren 1911, pp. 212–33). The role of lawyers as debt collectors, in a period of economic depression that culminated in Shays' Rebellion, and as advocates for Tories seeking to recover confiscated property aggravated popular hostility (Friedman 1973, p. 265; Gawalt 1970; but see Nolan 1976; Ely 1973). Finally, Jacksonian democracy glorified the ideals of a free market, exemplified in the destruction of the Bank of the United States, as well as direct democracy and egalitarianism, illustrated by the widespread extension of election to, and rotation in, office, including judgeships (Stevens 1971, p. 416). The atmosphere hardly was conducive to the establishment of a professional monopoly.

The Rise of Industrial Capitalism and the Professionalization of Lawyers

The period from the Civil War through World War I saw major changes in all aspects of American society. The professionalization of lawyers proceeded in large part as a response to the emergence of new categories of clients seeking, or capable of purchasing, new kinds of legal services. In the private sector, these were the industrial capitalists (perhaps best exemplified by the railroads) and the financiers on whom they depended (Hurst 1950, pp. 249, 298, 309; Swaine 1946). These new clients needed a distinctive kind of legal service: counseling, planning, and negotiation. Because such services represent an investment for capitalists, whereas litigation is generally a consumable for individuals (cf. Johnson 1977), entrepreneurs were prepared to spend substantial amounts on legal fees. Lawyers were needed to create new forms of business organization and new methods for raising the vast amounts of capital necessary to undertake major projects. State intervention often was necessary to support, protect, and regulate business, or to make loans or grants of land. Since the state can act only through law, it has to be approached, and must respond, through lawyers.

If corporate clients actively sought legal counsel, they also generated a great deal of litigation, defending the numerous lawsuits brought by employees, customers, and others injured by capitalist activity (Hurst 1950, p. 300; Horwitz 1977, chap. 3; Schwartz 1981; Abel 1981a), fighting the battles that accompanied the push toward concentration and monopoly (Hurst 1950, p. 347; Swaine 1946, pp. 461–69), and opposing the formation and activities of labor unions. Therefore, it is not surprising that the contingent-fee system—a uniquely American institution permitting those without resources to initiate litigation (Royal Commission on Legal Services 1979, vol. 1, pp. 176–77)—rapidly expanded during this period (cf. Bloomfield 1979, pp. 269–73).

The public sector also grew, if less quickly, increasing its own use of lawyers and stimulating a reciprocal need in the private sector. The scope and apparatus of social control were transformed: criminal codes lengthened and were rationalized (Alschuler 1979, p. 234), and the personnel of the criminal-justice system was professionalized (Friedman 1979; Haller 1979). Just as a professional judiciary created the need for professional representatives in civil litigation, so professional prosecutors could be opposed effectively only by professional defense counsel. The federal government's legal capacity also expanded: in 1853, the Attorney General had only 3 employees—2 clerks and a messenger—but in 1870 the Department of Justice was created, and by 1897 it had a staff that included the Solicitor General, 4 assistant Attorneys General, 9 assistant attorneys, 3 law clerks, and 44 general clerks (Friedman 1973, p. 561; Eisenstein 1978, pp. 9–13).

Market Control   These changes affected the market for legal services in several ways. Whereas most consumers previously had been individuals or small partnerships, corporations and government now entered the picture, adding heterogeneity and concentrating demand for lawyers in cities, especially the larger commercial and governmental centers. As new markets emerged, old ones were declining or being challenged: collection agencies and finance companies took over debt collection; banks and trust companies invaded estate work; and title-insurance companies displaced lawyers in routine land transactions (Hurst 1950, p. 319; cf. Johnstone and Hopson 1967, chaps. 5–10).

Differentiation among consumers intensified differences between elite and nonelite lawyers. The former developed characteristics that would facilitate the project of market control. They were few in number, they clustered in the major financial capitals, they shared a common background and education, and they served the same clients (Miller 1951; cf. Cain 1976). Because the demand for the services of these lawyers was expanding rapidly, competition did not take seriously antagonistic forms. Their practices generated substantial profits not only because of the wealth and needs of their clients, but also because these lawyers adopted a new form of organization. No longer individual professionals selling their own services, elite lawyers increasingly were capitalists selling the labor of others. Before the Civil War, it was rare for a law firm to have more than two partners, and salaried lawyers remained uncommon until after 1900 (Friedman 1973, pp. 554–55). Although apprentices constituted subordinated labor, there rarely was more than one per lawyer (Hurst 1950, p. 273). In the half-century after the Civil War, however, law firms expanded enormously: the number of partners grew, permitting greater specialization; they began to employ salaried lawyers—associates—many of whom never would become partners. Perhaps most important, the advent of office machines enabled them to replace apprentices, who had spent much of their time copying documents, with low-salaried clerical workers, increasingly women (Hurst 1950, pp. 306–7; Stolz 1972). Finally, elite lawyers transferred their energies from advocacy—where their monopoly was difficult to justify, since "it's only a matter of words" (Morris et al. 1973, p. 310)—to counseling, which offered much greater scope for "technicality" (Jamous and Peloille 1970).

If elite lawyers were well situated to pursue market control, the base of the profession was largely disabled from doing so. The first obstacle was numbers; the 22,000 lawyers of 1850 had increased to 60,000 by 1880 and 114,000 by 1900 (Friedman 1973, p. 549). The second was a high, and growing, level of heterogeneity: class, birthplace, training (Nash 1965), and, after the turn of the century, national origin—though the latter ultimately became a rallying point for a xenophobic campaign to exclude immigrants from the bar (Auerbach 1974). Third, nonelite lawyers were geographically dispersed: they served individuals and small businesses, often located in rural areas and small cities; only with the rapid shift of population from country to city in the twentieth century (Hauser 1976, pp. 20–21) did these lawyers attain a level of concentration that allowed the development of bar associations, and these were more often local organizations than statewide groups (Hurst 1950, p. 314).

Market control in this period, therefore, was an elite project. Only after the elite showed that market control could be achieved and legitimated could subordinate strata emulate the example (Larson 1977, chap. 2). The first step was the creation of bar associations: initially in the major cities—New York in 1870 (Martin 1970), Chicago in 1874 (Kogan 1974)—and then nationwide, with the establishment of the American Bar Association in 1878 (Friedman 1973, pp. 561–62). The last was founded by 75 of the nation's 60,000 lawyers at Saratoga Springs, an exclusive resort, where it continued to meet for the next ten years, thereby ensuring that its membership remained small and homogeneous—1.3 percent of the bar in 1900, 3 percent in 1910, and 9 percent as late as 1920 (Hurst 1950, pp. 287, 289; Friedman 1973, p. 563; Stevens 1971, p. 456). Its functions were as much social as political, and those professional tasks it did undertake—law reform and especially proposals for uniform state laws—are best understood as efforts to legitimate the sudden increase in wealth and influence enjoyed by elite lawyers.

Education   Limitations on the size and membership of the professional elite oc-curred through formal education. At first sight, apprenticeship and professional regula-tion of entry to the bar might seem to provide much more direct ways of exercising power, and the rise of formal education might appear to signify a loss of professional control. But apprenticeship asked too much of the supervising attorney, could not produce enough lawyers to satisfy expanding demand, and was not a cost-efficient source of subordinate labor. It also was too particularistic (cf. Gower and Price 1957, pp. 330–31; Royal Commission on Legal Services 1979, vol. 1, pp. 644–45; vol. 2, pp. 48, 441) in a society that legitimated professional success as an expression of meritocracy (Larson 1977, chap. 8; Bledstein 1976). Finally, since the university alone could elaborate and rationalize the corpus of technical expertise that grounded the claim of American lawyers to constitute a profession, criteria for entry to the bar could only establish minimum standards and were an inadequate means of controlling elite membership.

We still do not know exactly how graduation from an elite university law school became the preferred path for entry to the professional elite during the last quarter of the nineteenth century, but, once established, the dynamic was self-perpetuating. The demand for university legal education allowed the universities to increase the length of the required course. Reversing the trend of the Jacksonian era, Harvard Law School extended its program from eighteen months to two years in 1871 and to three in 1895; other elite schools anticipated or followed its example (Stevens 1971, p. 427). Although only 4 percent of the population of law school age held college degrees (Auerbach 1974, p. 29), by 1896, Harvard required a baccalaureate for admission to its law school; four other schools introduced this requirement by 1921; and still others insisted on several years of college (Stevens 1971, pp. 431–32). The purpose of these prerequisites sometimes was quite explicit: "either a college diploma or an examination including Latin . . . will keep out the little scrubs (German Jew boys mostly) whom the school [Columbia] now promotes from the grocery counter . . . to be 'gentlemen of the Bar'" (Taft 1938, p. 146).

But if elite schools were exclusive, the growth of nonelite law schools had just the opposite effect. Apprenticeship had limited the number and characteristics of those who could aspire to legal careers, since it required both financial sacrifice and good connections (Hurst 1950, p. 256). Nonelite law schools offered an almost unlimited number of places, with few prerequisites and minimal financial demands. Their growth during this period was phenomenal: 21 law schools existed in 1860, 28 in 1870, 61 in 1890, 102 in 1900, and 143 in 1920 (Stevens 1971, pp. 425, 429–30; Woodworth 1973, p. 497). In 1917, Chicago had 9 schools, Washington 8, New York 5, and St. Louis and San Francisco 4 each (Reed 1921, pp. 193–95). Of the 61 law schools operating in 1890, only 18 imposed any requirements for entry, and only 4 of those were as rigorous as most colleges (Hurst 1950, p. 268). Consequently, the number of students grew even more rapidly. There were 345 in 1840; 1,200 in 1860; 4,500 in 1890; 12,500 in 1900; 19,500 in 1910; and 41,400 in 1930 (Stevens 1971, pp. 425, 428–29; Woodworth 1973, p. 497).

Nonelite schools also were financially more accessible: Iowa State University inaugurated public low-tuition legal education in 1868 (Stevens 1971, p. 427), and part-time afternoon and evening schools accepted working men at a tuition as low as $40 a year (First 1976, p. 143). The last category grew most rapidly: 10 such schools enrolled 537 students in 1890; 64 enrolled 10,734 in 1916 (Stevens 1971, p. 429). The proportion of all students in full-time day law schools in New York State fell from 79 percent in 1890 to 15 percent in 1930 (Woodworth 1973, p. 501). The result was the rapid displacement of apprenticeship by law school as a means of qualification: by 1922 only 9 of the 643 students taking the New York bar examination had no law school training (First 1978, p. 361, n. 294).

The reason for this dramatic shift was not pedagogic; apprenticeship had not suddenly become inadequate, and law school indispensable, to transmit essential professional skills. Indeed, law schools devoted relatively little effort to conferring technical competence (Gordon 1980). Rather, the explanation was political; just as law schools had declined during the Jacksonian era as entry to the profession was eased, so they revived as barriers were raised. The proportion of jurisdictions requiring formal training—either law school or apprenticeship—increased from 9 out of 39 in 1860 to 23 out of 49 in 1890 and 36 out of 49 in 1917, of which 28 required 3 years of law school (Stevens 1971, p. 459). In some states, law schools even were able to acquire a "diploma privilege" that automatically entitled their graduates to practice; but the American Bar Association opposed this abdication of control to educators, and the number of schools enjoying it declined after 1908 (Stevens 1971, pp. 457–58). In all other jurisdictions, bar examinations became more rigorous; written tests were introduced in 1876 and became more common after 1900, following the precedent of law school examinations (Hurst 1950, p. 283). Responsibility shifted from the local level to the state; the 4 state boards of bar examiners before 1890 multiplied, until they were found in 37 of the 48 jurisdictions by 1917 (Friedman 1973, p. 564; Stevens 1971, pp. 458–59). This trend was part of a more general movement at the end of the nineteenth century toward occupational licensing, in which the more prestigious occupations often succeeded in securing state sanction for control over entry (Friedman 1965).

But, despite the increased stringency of bar examinations, there was little, if any, reduction in the supply of lawyers. Between 1850 and 1900 their numbers rose much faster than the growth of population (cf. Friedman 1973, p. 549, and Hauser 1976, p. 16)—and the ratio of population to lawyers increased only slightly thereafter—704:1 in 1900, 863:1 in 1920, 764:1 in 1930, and 745:1 in 1940 (Friedman 1973, p. 549; Hurst 1950, p. 314). It is not that lawyers were unconcerned about this trend; as early as 1881, Wisconsin lawyers expressed dismay over the numbers being admitted to the bar (Hurst 1950, p. 314). The proliferation of professional associations attests to the same concern. The 8 state and territorial bar associations in 1878 rose to 20 by 1890, 40 by 1900, and 48 by 1916; in addition, there were nearly 600 other local associations (Hurst 1950, pp. 287–88). But these, like the ABA, remained minority organizations. State bar associations enrolled only 20 percent of all practicing lawyers; state and local groups combined enrolled only 30 percent (Hurst 1950, p. 289). One reason for the continuing failure to control supply may have been the enormous wave of European migration (Hauser 1976, p. 18) with the consequent pressures for routes of upward mobility (see Ben-David 1963–64, pp. 275–77).

Legitimation   The change in the structure of producers during the half-century under consideration affected both the profession's needs for legitimation and the means by which these needs might be satisfied. Legitimation, like market control, was an elite project. First, elite lawyers had to justify their wealth, status, and power, not only in the face of the prevailing egalitarian ethos but also against the jealousy of the mass of the profession, who enjoyed few of those privileges. Second, they had to distance themselves from the clients through whom the privileges had been attained, for the banks, railroads, and other corporations were seen by many as illegitimate—malefactors of great wealth (Berle 1933, p. 341).

Elite lawyers pursued this goal by promoting the concept of legal science (Gordon 1980). First, the ABA created the National Conference of Commissioners on Uniform State Laws and the American Law Institute, both of which fostered the rationalization and unification of substantive and procedural law (Hurst 1950, pp. 362–63; Friedman 1973, pp. 563–64). Second, the ABA supported university legal education, establishing a Section on Legal Education in 1893 and helping to launch the Association of American Law Schools in 1900 (Hurst 1950, p. 362). The appointment to the Harvard faculty of James Barr Ames—the first law teacher who had never practiced—symbolized the new trend (Stevens 1971, p. 455; Seligman 1978a, chap. 2). But if the university carried with it the cachet of science, the price to the profession was some loss of control to a rising professoriate (First 1978; Auerbach 1971). Third, lawyers also legitimate their status through conspicuous public service; for most of the period from the Revolution through 1930, they constituted two thirds of the Senate, one third of the House of Representatives, half to two thirds of all state governors, and a significant proportion of southern state legislators (Hurst 1950, p. 352; cf. Podmore 1977, 1980a). Thus, elite lawyers were active in progressive politics at the national, state, and local levels (Gordon 1980).

Inherent tensions troubled each of these attempts at professional legitimation. One segment of the profession frequently sought to justify itself by delegitimating another (Bucher and Strauss 1961; Podmore 1980b). Meritocracy—the claim that privilege was earned by acquisition of a university degree—necessarily denigrated the competence of those who lacked this credential. Yet, the chasm between the strata could not be acknowledged explicitly; when the Reed Report (1921) recommended recognition of the fact that the two tiers of law schools prepared graduates for two distinct professions, the proposal was vehemently rejected (Stevens 1971, pp. 461–64). Elite participation in progressive politics also accentuated this division, since it was directed largely toward reforming local government by eliminating the political machines through which non-elite ethnic lawyers sought advancement (Hurst 1950, p. 268; Barlow 1979).

Market Control Through Restricting the Supply of Lawyers After World War I

The decades preceding World War I saw the emergence of a legal elite, defined by graduation from certain recognized law schools—which constantly were raising the standards for admission and performance, thus restricting the number and diversity of their students—accompanied by a dramatic expansion of the base of the profession. The most significant change in the postwar period was the reversal of this latter trend. There were fewer law students at the beginning of the 1960s than there had been at the end of the 1920s, despite the fact that the population to be served had increased by nearly half (Hauser 1976, p. 16) and the economy had expanded even more rapidly (cf. Pashigian 1977, p. 72). Limitation was effected by imposing the standards adopted by the elite on nonelite law schools. Although professional associations of law teachers and lawyers were the prime agents in this movement, it ultimately received the backing of the state (First 1978). Yet, these efforts might not have succeeded without the adventitious interruptions in supply caused by the Depression and World War II (cf. Kronus 1976).

Physicians took the lead in market control, as they did in so many phases of the professional project (Larson 1977, chap. 3). When Abraham Flexner began his investigations into medical education in 1900, there were 160 medical schools with a total of 25,213 students. In 1910, mere anticipation of the publication of his study reduced the number of schools to 131 and of students to 21,394. As his recommendations were implemented and the admissions requirements of medical school rose from a high-school diploma (1914) to one year of college (1916) and then to two (1918), the number of schools fell to 85, with 13,798 students, by 1919–20—half what they had been 20 years earlier, although population had increased 40 percent during that period (Stevens 1971, pp. 459–60; Larson 1977, pp. 162–66).

The legal profession had begun moving in the same direction a decade earlier. In 1892, the ABA recommended that all future lawyers receive a minimum of two years of either apprenticeship or law school; by 1897, it urged three years of law school. The Association of American Law Schools, founded by the ABA in 1900, limited its membership to two-year schools and, in 1905, to three-year schools. In 1912, it started to squeeze out night schools by raising standards, and it excluded part-time schools altogether in 1920. Beginning in 1909, the ABA Section on Legal Education and Admission to the Bar proposed a minimum of four years of apprenticeship or three years in a law school and an additional graduate year in a law school or law office; by 1916, it had narrowed this recommendation further to three years of full-time or four years of part-time law school study (Stevens 1971, pp. 453–56).

But these were no more than recommendations. As late as 1917, no state required attendance at a law school. In 1919–20, there were 18 two-year schools and even a one-year school; of the 127 three-year schools, 69 (enrolling 13,318 students) were part-time. Furthermore, in 1916–17, only 7 of the nearly 150 law schools required even three years of college. It is not surprising that the Flexner Report and its aftermath made a strong impression on lawyers. Three years after its publication, the ABA Section on Legal Education expressed interest in a comparable study, and the Carnegie Foundation, which had supported the earlier inquiry, readily agreed to do so again. But the Reed Report (1921; see Stolz 1972) was a grave disappointment to the organized bar. Alfred Z. Reed acknowledged that one- and two-year law schools were fated to disappear, but he maintained openly what everyone acknowledged tacitly—the American legal profession was highly stratified. If the value of elite lawyers was obvious, the base also performed essential functions, satisfying aspirations to social mobility through the attainment of professional status and providing legal services to individuals and small businesses. Different schools with different standards therefore were appropriate (Stevens 1971, pp. 457–59).

The legal profession appeared to accept this situation as unavoidable for the moment and sought to raise the standards for both categories. The Root Committee on Legal Education, established by the ABA in 1921 in response to the unsatisfactory Reed Report, recommended that aspiring lawyers complete at least two years of college and attend law school for four years if they were doing so part-time. The ABA adopted this recommendation and then obtained the endorsement of a conference of state and local bar associations—important political allies, since the 1920s also saw the rise of the integrated bar (McKean 1963), a professional association with compulsory membership, endowed with state authority to control entry. The Association of American Law Schools (AALS) continued to take the lead in differentiating elite institutions (First 1978). It readmitted part-time schools but simultaneously raised the requirements for full-time schools (1922); it imposed a maximum ratio of 100 students to each teacher (1924); it insisted that its members require two years of college (1925); and it added criteria for law school libraries (1927–28). In 1923, the ABA issued its first list of approved schools—39 in Category A and 8 in Category B—and otherwise gradually endorsed the more stringent AALS criteria (Stevens 1971, pp. 461–64, 493–96).

Yet the promulgation of standards by voluntary associations did little more than reaffirm the practices of elite law schools and encourage others that aspired to elite status. The base continued to grow rapidly. Part-time law students outnumbered those in full-time institutions in 1923; four years later, the 106 part-time schools enrolled 57 percent of all law students. Only half the law schools satisfied the ABA requirements, and only one third of the law students attended AALS-approved schools. Only 9 schools required a college degree, and another 9 demanded three years of college; but 32 of the 49 American jurisdictions had no prelegal requirement, and 11 more required only a high school diploma. Finally, although all jurisdictions but Indiana required passage of a bar examination, 9 had no other formal requirements, and only 4 actually required attendance at a law school (Stevens 1971, pp. 496–97).

It was an external event, the Depression, that interrupted this steady growth. Between 1928 and 1931, the number of law students dropped suddenly by 7,000, or 15 percent. This loss was recouped only partly by 1935. The Depression naturally had a different impact on the two major strata of law schools. The aggregate decline of 5,000 students between 1928 and 1935 actually was a composite of a decrease of 10,000 at schools not approved by the ABA and an increase of 5,000 at approved schools; the latter figure is explained only partly by the approval of additional schools. As a result, approved schools expanded their share of the student population from one third to half. Simultaneously, states began to impose the requirements the ABA long had been recommending. Between 1934 and 1936, 11 states instituted a prerequisite of two years of college, and by 1938, 40 of the 48 states had done so. The influence of the ABA increased even more dramatically as states required graduation from the schools it approved.

The consequence of these convergent events was dramatic. In 1938–39, law school enrollment declined by another 3,000 (nearly 10 percent) to 34,539—approximately 12,000 fewer students than before the Depression (a drop of about 25 percent in a decade of rising population). In 1938 alone, 7 schools closed their doors. The upshot was a very substantial extension of the barriers the ABA had sought to impose. In 1938, the 101 schools approved by the Association enrolled 63.7 percent of all law students; 150 law schools required two years of college, and only 30 accepted less. These proportions reversed those of a decade earlier (Stevens 1971, pp. 500–504).

The process was completed by World War II. Law school enrollments fell to a low of 6,422 in 1943–44, a drop of 86 percent from the pre-Depression peak of 1928, and a number of schools failed. The postwar period saw a large influx of students as a result of the imbalance between supply and demand (Pashigian 1977, 1978), the booming economy, and the financial assistance given returning veterans. But of the 51,015 law students in 1947, 36,999 attended full-time ABA-approved schools (73 percent; in 1927, only 43 percent of all students had attended full time), and 86 percent attended ABA-approved schools (compared with 33 percent in 1927). The proportion of students in unapproved schools grew briefly from 14 percent in 1947 to 19 percent in 1949 but then fell to 8 percent (3,502) in 1958. This trend was reflected in, and doubtless largely caused by, state support for ABA control. In 1947, 17 states required graduation from an ABA-approved school, and 2 others gave preferential treatment to such graduates; by 1970, 33 states required graduation from an approved school. Prelegal requirements were also raised. In 1950, ABA-approved schools had to require three years of college; by 1970, 8 states required four years of college, and another 30 demanded three (Stevens 1971, pp. 504–9).

A substantial transformation thus was wrought in little more than 30 years. In 1927, there were 46,384 law students, of whom only a handful were college graduates, more than half attended law school part time, and more than two thirds were enrolled in schools not approved by the ABA. In 1960, there were only 43,695 law students, virtually all of whom were college graduates and attended ABA-approved schools full time (York and Hale 1973, p. 1). If the absolute decline in numbers was slight, it was huge relative to the increase in population and the growth of the economy; the ratio of population to law students rose by 55 percent.

LAWYERS AND CLIENTS IN CONTEMPORARY AMERICAN SOCIETY

The remainder of this essay will present a structural analysis of the current relations between producers and consumers of legal services, the ways in which these relations are mediated by other social institutions, and the means by which the legal profession is legitimated. My focus will be on the methods by which lawyers control, or fail to control, the production *of* producers—that is, their own reproduction—and *by* producers—that is, the supply of legal services (Larson 1977, chap. 4; Abel 1979a). The subsidized redistribution of lawyers' services—simultaneously the principal source of legitimation for lawyers and an increasingly important mechanism for controlling the market by creating and regulating demand—will occupy the following section.

Consumers of Legal Services

The present structure of the demand for legal services is an extrapolation of trends already visible at the turn of the century. In the private sector, the dominant tendency is a radical separation between the markets generated by large corporations (and wealthy individuals) and by individuals (and smaller businesses); in a sample of the Chicago bar, five out of six lawyers worked exclusively for one category or the other (Laumann and Heinz 1979). One reason for this separation is demographic. Lawyers, like other professionals, have been leaving, or failing to settle in, small towns (Blaine 1976), where they served a heterogeneous clientele (Handler 1967; for a novelistic account of small-town practice, see Gardner 1972), in order to concentrate in the largest cities, where the market is segmented (Carlin 1962, 1966; Sikes et al. 1972). By contrast, potential individual clients have been moving away from lawyers—who are located in the center city, near the business district and courthouse—to the suburbs, where lawyers only now are beginning to follow them (Diamond 1981).

Corporations and wealthy individuals dominate this segmented market, consuming approximately half of all the time expended by lawyers (Laumann and Heinz 1979; Pashigian 1978). This dominance obviously is a concomitant of the rise of American capitalism—although the state may play a comparable role in state-capitalist societies (Friedman and Zile 1964; Barry and Berman 1968). It is the product of several convergent factors. First, the size and wealth of the consumer is related to both the quantity of services needed and the continuity of demand; the corporation rationalizes one sector of the market for legal services by aggregating the needs of all actors within the enterprise. Volume and continuity permit lawyers to achieve economies of scale, thereby enhancing their profits. Second, the larger and wealthier the consumers, the more sizable are the transactions in which they engage. The fees that can be charged also are proportionately higher, whether they are related to the value of the transaction—as in corporate finance, estates, and land transactions—or billed by the hour (Hoffman 1973, chap. 3; Royal

Commission on Legal Services 1979, vol. 1, pp. 269–76). Third, only certain categories of consumers need many of the services lawyers offer (Heinz and Laumann 1978). Wealthy individuals seek tax shelters (see, for example, Margolis 1972), large corporations require defense in protracted antitrust litigation—IBM has paid Cravath, Swaine and Moore as much as $10 million a year (Bernstein 1978, p. 106) in a case that began in 1969 and was abandoned by the government only in 1982. Finally, the wealth and status of the client directly correlate with the prestige of a law practice (Laumann and Heinz 1977).

Corporate Consumers   Lawyers seek to control this desirable market in several ways. First, they specialize, not merely, like other professionals, in terms of subject matter—such as tax or patent law—but also, and even primarily, in terms of clients—such as labor unions, insurance companies, and antitrust plaintiffs (Heinz and Laumann 1978; Laumann and Heinz 1979). Although such specialization reduces competition, it simultaneously increases lawyers' dependence on a narrow clientele.

Second, lawyers seek to control the formation and preservation of the lawyer-client relationship. To anticipate a later point, they influence the ways in which individual clients choose lawyers by depriving the public of independent sources of information about the price and quality of legal services and by channeling clients through intermediaries in exchange for favors. By contrast, corporate clients are relatively knowledgeable about the small circle of large firms interested in serving them and are not easily influenced by lay intermediaries. But the large law firm, even more than the sole practitioner, is dependent on a continuous relationship with its corporate clients, both because each client represents a larger proportion of firm income and because large-firm practice entails an extremely high overhead (Hoffman 1973). Major law firms, therefore, take great pains to obtain and retain corporate clients. They hire and reward "rainmakers"—senior partners with close ties to corporate officials (Hoffman 1973; Nelson 1981, pp. 119–23)—a practice that is condemned as fee-splitting when engaged in by nonelite attorneys (ABA 1974, DR 2-107; ABA Commission 1980, Rule 1.6[e]; ABA 1981, Rule 1.5[d]). They encourage partners to accept positions on the boards of directors of clients (cf. Powell 1980), hire the relatives of corporate executives as associates, and place associates who are not made partners in the offices of corporate counsel or in smaller satellite firms that handle overflow business from the corporation (Smigel 1969; Hoffman 1973; Slovak 1980). Decisions to hire an associate and to promote the associate to partner are influenced strongly by the trust the candidate inspires in the firm—and thus will inspire in the client (Baird et al. 1977, pp. 30, 44; Nelson 1981, p. 115). Other mechanisms that also help to preserve the relationship are physical possession of the records of the corporation and accumulated expertise in its affairs, as well as simple proximity—corporation and law firm often are located in the same building (Hoffman 1973). More recently, firms even have established multistate practices in order to follow clients to new jurisdictions (Galanter 1982). As a result, law firms rarely lose major clients and usually do so only because of a change of personnel in client or firm or through a corporate merger (Hoffman 1973).

Law firms thus seek to control the market for corporate consumers by surrendering substantial control to the latter. The sources of lawyer subordination are several. Large though American firms may be compared with law practices in other countries (Royal

Commission on Legal Services 1979, vol. 2, pp. 456–61; Mendelsohn and Lippman 1979; Arthurs et al. 1971), the corporations they serve have hundreds of times their resources, personnel, and influence. Corporations generally spread their legal business among a number of firms, so as not to be overly dependent on any one. They also employ their own in-house lawyers, who serve two functions: they allocate and supervise the work of independent counsel; and, as the fees of outside counsel have grown to nearly twice the cost of in-house lawyering, they perform an increasing amount of the corporation's legal work themselves (Slovak 1979; Nelson 1981, pp. 130–31). By contrast, the ability of the law firm to reduce its dependence on particular clients is limited. It cannot turn down work for an existing client without fear of endangering that relationship; and it is inhibited in accepting new clients by conflict-of-interest rules (ABA 1981, Rules 1.7, 1.9). The cumulative result of these factors is an asymmetrical relationship, in which law firms have gained wealth, status, political influence, and security but at the cost of subordination to their corporate clients (Berle 1933; Stone 1934). This situation is illustrated by recent incidents of unethical behavior (for example, *Securities and Exchange Commission v. National Student Marketing Corp.*, 1977; ABA 1981, pp. 124–40; Galanter 1982; cf. Nelson 1981, pp. 133–34).

Individual Consumers   In many ways, the characteristics of individuals who are not wealthy and of small businesses, as clients of the lawyers who serve them, and of the relationship between the two are the obverse of the situation just described (Heinz and Laumann 1978; Laumann and Heinz 1979). Individual clients, in particular, represent a small, and possibly declining, share of the private sector; one study concluded that only 18 percent of lawyers' efforts are devoted to alleviating the legal problems of individuals (Laumann and Heinz 1979). Such business is not very profitable to lawyers for several reasons. Individuals rarely purchase legal services as an adjunct to capital investment (Johnson 1977); their transactions are relatively small and, therefore, cannot sustain high legal costs (Hunting and Neuwirth 1962; Trubek 1981); most important, they are one-shot affairs (Carlin 1962; Galanter 1974; Curran 1977, pp. 190–94). That individual consumers have remained unorganized is not accidental; the profession has systematically frustrated attempts to rationalize the market by prohibiting advertising (until recently), solicitation, and the use of lay intermediaries (ABA 1974, DR 2-101, 2-102, 2-103). Low and sporadic demand has two consequences. First, lawyers find it difficult to specialize and thereby enhance their market control. Instead, they constantly confront both competition from other occupations, such as banking and real estate—which are unrestrained by professional regulations and thus able to engage in the aggressive pursuit of business (Johnstone and Hopson 1967)—and from consumers who prefer to act for themselves (Ziegler and Hermann 1972; *Yale Law Journal* 1976; but see Tomasic 1978, pp. 22–25). Second, these lawyers must devote considerable energy to obtaining business (Carlin 1962, chap. 3).

Once the lawyer-client relationship is established, however, the lawyer, not the client, is dominant (Reed 1972; Rosenthal 1974; Hosticka 1979; cf. Cain 1979; Medcalf 1978; Danet et al. 1980). The client is expendable because he is unlikely to return. Individual clients have single problems, rather than ongoing needs for legal services; the average American who sees a lawyer at all does so only about twice in a lifetime and probably will take subsequent problems to different lawyers (Curran 1977, pp. 190–91; cf. Royal

Commission on Legal Services in Scotland 1980, vol. 2, pp. 60–63). It is true that the lawyer relies on former clients for future business, since personal referral is the most common means by which prospective clients find lawyers (Ladinsky 1976; Curran 1977, pp. 200–203; Royal Commission on Legal Services 1979, vol. 2, pp. 211–14). But this aspect does not confer significant influence on any individual client—partly because the client cannot evaluate the quality of service. Differences of education, income, social status, gender, and race between lawyer and client also contribute to the dominance of the former (see, for example, Warkov and Zelan 1965; Stevens 1973; Baird 1973; Boyer and Cramton 1974; ABA, Special Committee 1980, p. 26). Most clients consult lawyers involuntarily—in response to such crises as arrest, divorce, and injury—not in order to facilitate a transaction the client has initiated. Even the client who retains a lawyer to draft a will or negotiate the purchase or sale of a home generally enjoys little volition and experiences considerable tension. Whereas the corporate client controls the flow of information to the law firm, the individual client is totally dependent on the lawyer for information about the progress of the case—information the lawyer jealously guards (Rosenthal 1974; Steele and Nimmer 1976).

But if the lawyer has little loyalty toward his client, he is influenced strongly by those with whom he interacts continuously and who are in a position to grant significant favors: administrators (Rast 1978, p. 845; quoted in Macaulay 1979, p. 164); insurance-claims adjusters (Rosenthal 1974; Ross 1970); prosecutors (Blumberg 1967; *Law & Society Review* 1979; cf. Baldwin and McConville 1977); opposing counsel (O'Gorman 1963; *University of Pennsylvania Law Review* 1953); and such other courtroom regulars as clerks, judges, police, and bail bondsmen (Carlin 1962).

Producers of Legal Services

Control over the production of lawyers was largely achieved in the years following World War II. In 1974, only four of the 33,000 people admitted to the bar had received their training through study in a law office (Knauss 1976). Although a few states still admitted graduates of law schools unaccredited by the ABA, only California had a significant number of those schools (Blake 1979). As a consequence, there were fewer law students in 1960 than there had been thirty years earlier, though these were the years of the postwar boom, when corporate demand for legal services was expanding most rapidly. The resulting imbalance between supply and demand (Pashigian 1978) was visible in the starting salaries paid by law firms—which increased more than fivefold between 1965 and 1981—and the decline in discrimination in terms of class, ethnicity, and gender in law firm hiring (Young 1964; Smigel 1969, chap. 3; Hoffman 1973, chap. 8; Fishman and Kaufman 1975, pp. 149–64; Abel 1980, pp. 359–62). Not surprisingly, the response was a rapid rise in the enrollment in ABA-accredited law schools, from 43,695 in 1960 to 110,713 in 1974—more than 250 percent in 15 years (White 1975, p. 202). Yet even this was a controlled expansion of supply; three times as many people took the Law School Aptitude Test in 1973 as were admitted to law school; there were no unfilled seats at ABA schools that year (Ruud and White 1974, p. 344). And it was the base that grew, not the elite schools, which often received ten times as many applications as they had places (York and Hale 1973, pp. 22–25).

Other factors contributed to the attractiveness of law as a career. Many alternative professions became overcrowded; engineering suffered as a result of the overresponse to Sputnik and fluctuations in demand; university teaching posts declined with the passing of the postwar demographic bulge. And law came to be seen as a significant agent for social change, first during the civil-rights movement (Casper 1972a; Council for Public Interest Law 1976, chap. 1) and then with the emergence of the OEO Legal Services Program and public-interest law (*Yale Law Journal* 1970; Johnson 1974; Handler et al. 1978a; Weisbrod et al. 1978; Erlanger 1978). Several commentators have argued that contemporary law students exhibit contradictory motives; many are uncommitted to the practice of law (since the attraction of law as a career is not its content but the fact that it is middle-class); many of those who are committed often harbor the (unconscious) belief that they can be agents for social change while enjoying wealth, power, and status (Nader 1970; Stevens 1973; Erlanger and Klegon 1978; Foster 1981).

Law student bodies have changed in composition as well as size. The virtual monopoly of ABA-accredited schools has meant that admission has grown more competitive even as the entering classes have expanded. Because all ABA-accredited schools now require a college degree for admission, there has been a national standardization of entrance criteria, which virtually are limited to performance in college and on the Law School Admission Test. In consequence, as law schools have abandoned explicit reliance on such ascribed characteristics as race, religion, national origin, and gender, the substitution of college grades and test scores has strengthened other forms of bias under cover of a meritocratic legitimation (Larson 1977), since these indices are highly correlated with socioeconomic status (Warkov and Zelan 1965). This bias is accentuated by the high, and rapidly rising, cost of law school education. Although elite law schools always have been prohibitively expensive for the working class, part-time education provided an alternative route for a majority of entrants to the profession prior to World War II. The great reduction in such opportunities (Kelso 1972; Ruud and White 1974, p. 345) has not been offset fully by the expansion of public university law schools, since the latter generally are full-time institutions. As a result, law students, and especially those at national schools, are from relatively, and increasingly, privileged backgrounds (Stevens 1973, pp. 572–73; Chappell 1980; Zemans and Rosenblum 1981, pp. 32–42; cf. Erlanger 1980).

Before World War II, the legal profession was almost exclusively the domain of white males (cf. Royal Commission on Legal Services 1979, vol. 1, chap. 35). This was, in part, the result of explicit discrimination. Many states would not admit women to the profession until the end of the nineteenth or the beginning of the twentieth century. Law schools also enforced sexist admission policies; Harvard excluded women entirely until 1950 (Auerbach 1974, p. 295; Seligman 1978a, p. 7). It was only during the war, when men were drafted, that a significant number of women attended law school—about 25 percent of the 6,422 law students in 1943–44 were women. But the proportion fell dramatically with the return of the veterans (Stevens 1971, p. 504); consequently, women constituted only 2.8 percent of the profession as late as 1971 (Grossblat and Sikes 1973).

Southern law schools also excluded black students—a policy that was not even challenged until after the war (*Sweatt v. Painter*, 1950)—and few blacks had the educational credentials or financial resources to attend northern schools. Historically, the American Bar Association was openly racist; it responded to the inadvertent admission of three black attorneys in 1912 by requiring all applicants to identify their race and rejecting all blacks until the 1940s (Auerbach 1974, pp. 65–66). This racism was one stimulus for the founding of the National Lawyers Guild (Brown 1938) and the National Bar Association. At the beginning of the 1970s, black, Latino, Asian-American, and Native American lawyers constituted less than 1 percent of the profession (Ramsey 1980, pp. 377–78).

Major changes occurred after 1970 (see Abel 1980, pp. 359–62). Categorical exclusions have been eliminated. Women began attending law schools in larger numbers in the 1970s in one expression of the feminist movement (Epstein 1981). Some schools encouraged ethnic minorities to apply and designed admissions policies that took account both of the need for minority attorneys and of the centuries of political, economic, social, and educational discrimination minorities had suffered (Ramsey 1980). Yet, as recently as 1974, women constituted less than 20 percent of law school enrollments, and the rate of increase was diminishing (White 1975, p. 202; cf. Pipkin 1978). In 1978, ethnic minorities remained grossly underrepresented in law student bodies, compared with their proportions of the population; blacks were 4.3 percent and Latinos 1.7 percent (Ramsey 1980, p. 380; Ramey 1978). Furthermore, these figures stabilized and began to decline. If they are maintained for forty years (the time period necessary to replace the present generation of lawyers), women and minorities still will be underrepresented in the legal profession by about 50 percent.

But even such a modest improvement seems unlikely. Majority law students and alumni and state governments vocally have expressed their suspicions of and resentment toward affirmative-action programs. Faculties generally share these sentiments, although they usually frame their criticism in terms of lower academic preparation and performance, which reduces the likelihood that the student will pursue, or succeed in, a traditional career. The Supreme Court supported these views in *Regents of the University of California* v. *Bakke* (1978), ruling that professional schools must subordinate race to other criteria in admissions decisions. The combined effect of these other criteria—inevitably, college performance and aptitude test scores—together with the high and rising cost of law school, will both reduce the number of minority entrants and ensure that they are from more privileged backgrounds (cf. Zemans and Rosenblum 1981, pp. 32–42).

Not only do law schools have a monopoly over the selection of entrants to the profession; they also control a critical stage of the socialization process (see, generally, Barry and Connelly 1978). In exercising this control, they display a limited autonomy that conceals their fundamental subordination to the profession. The separation of law teachers and practitioners, introduced at Harvard a century ago, is virtually complete; for most faculty, teaching is a full-time, lifetime career, although teachers at less prestigious law schools are likely to practice and those at the elite to consult with, and move between, private practice, professional associations, government, and the judiciary (Fossum 1980a). Faculty members also control their own reproduction. The principal criterion for recruitment—success as a law student—affirms the value of what law teachers do. Yet that qualification generally requires confirmation by the state (a judicial clerkship or a job in the federal executive) or by corporate capitalism (several years as an associate in a law firm). Promotion to tenure and subsequent advancement turn largely on traditional scholarly criteria rather than on skill as a lawyer or in training future lawyers. Yet the hierarchic ranking of subject-matter specializations, headed by corporate and constitutional law, strongly reflects the principal clients the profession serves—

capital and state (Pipkin 1976, 1978). Finally, law school faculties, which had been exclusively male and white, now have hired small numbers of women (Fossum 1980b) and minorities. But professional dominance still is reflected in the range of tolerated political ideologies, which is narrower and more conservative than that found in most university social-science departments.

These tensions between academy and profession also affect the curriculum. Students who enter law school with an image of law as public service (Stevens 1973; Erlanger and Klegon 1978) are greeted with a set of required first-year courses that are at least consistent with such an image, if they also are relevant to later specialization (Zemans and Rosenblum 1981, pp. 144–50). By the second year, however, law students are increasingly subject to influences over which the school has little control—the job market (interviews for summer employment begin at the start of the second year) and the bar examination (almost all students take courses in every subject examined on the bar). As a result, 85 percent of the courses offered at law schools are bar-exam subjects (Seligman 1978b; cf. Bankowski and Mungham 1978). But this narrowing of the curriculum is portrayed as the reflection of market forces (student choice) and faculty autonomy (cf. Auerbach 1970 with Nader 1970) and not as a capitulation to either the profession or the state (but see Zemans and Rosenblum 1981, p. 11).

The conflict between academic autonomy and professional dominance can be seen in the long, and still unresolved, controversy over clinical education. Despite early and eloquent pleas for "lawyer schools" (Frank 1933, 1947), clinical education took root only in the 1960s. At first its growth was rapid—in 1976–77, 139 schools offered 494 programs in 57 fields of law (Gee 1977)—but its status remains tenuous. Traditional law teachers never have been comfortable with clinical education, which threatens their claim to unique mastery of a scientific discipline. Clinical law also tends to be more parochial than clinical medicine; because powerful clients will not entrust their legal problems to inexperienced law students (except those employed by their law firm), such students are limited to handling the legal problems of the poor and disadvantaged. Lawyers also are ambivalent about clinical education. Although they constantly berate law schools for failing to convey essential skills (Baird 1978; Benthall-Nietzel 1975; Zemans and Rosenblum 1981, pp. 34–144), the more elite the lawyers, the more they feel that they acquire these skills in practice (Zemans and Rosenblum 1981, pp. 150–55). Large law firms have strong reasons for retaining control over socialization after law school. Finally, because clinical education requires a low student-teacher ratio and therefore is very expensive, it has depended heavily on government support (Gee 1977). As law schools pursue their elusive academic status, as law firms continue to grow, as government curtails the legal services programs in which students are placed, and as student interest in poverty law declines, clinical education faces a gloomy future (Condlin 1981).

The form as well as the content of legal education reveals professional influence. In virtually all American law schools, the entire first year and much of the other two years are dominated by the "Socratic" dialogue—in which the teacher asks most of the questions and the student is *required* to answer—and the case method—in which analysis is focused principally on appellate cases (Stevens 1971; Gee and Jackson 1975). These pedagogic approaches share several salient characteristics. First, they stress the absolute subordination of student to teacher; the former is exposed as knowing nothing, while the latter hints at omniscience without ever allowing this claim to be tested (Kennedy 1970; Savoy 1970; Stone 1971). This public demonstration of ignorance erodes the self-respect most students bring to law school and accustoms them to the subordinate status they will occupy for several years after graduation. Students simultaneously learn that the only way to gain the respect of their teachers—and, therefore, of their peers—is to accept the school's sole criterion of success and compete for a place in the hierarchy of grades (Turow 1977; Osborn 1979b). The case method permits a level of theoretical abstraction sufficient to differentiate the academy from the profession while still ensuring that the fundamental premises of the legal system are not questioned (Zemans and Rosenblum 1981, pp. 136, 185). Finally, students are required to argue either side of the case at the behest of the teacher. In this way, they become accustomed both to take moral direction from superiors and to value technical dexterity divorced from ethical commitment (Carrington and Conley 1977; Cramton 1978; Hedegard 1979; Katz and Denbaux 1976; Rathjen 1976; Riesman 1957; Scheingold 1974, chap. 10; Shaffer and Redmount 1976; Taylor 1975; see generally Barry and Connelly 1978, but see Erlanger and Klegon 1978; Kay 1978).

Yet the unchallenged dominion of law school is brief. No sooner have matriculates learned to think of themselves as law students (cf. Becker et al. 1961) then they must concern themselves with becoming lawyers. The elite national law schools promise most graduates secure, salaried positions; there is fierce competition for the grades that largely determine the hiring decisions of law firms and corporations (Zemans and Rosenblum 1981, pp. 108–10), but otherwise interest and effort slacken after the first year (Brickman 1978; Pipkin 1976; Stevens 1973). Few students in less prestigious schools can be as confident of employment, and some will have to set up individual practices; consequently, although disillusion with law school is high, energy devoted to schoolwork actually increases (Pipkin 1976). But if the profession penetrates the elite law school by way of career expectations, it influences nonelite law students more immediately. Whereas elite law schools discourage students from term-time work through explicit rules (ABA Special Committee 1980, pp. 34–35, n. 38), class schedules, extracurricular activities, or simple location outside a major metropolis, many students at nonelite law schools work half-time or more after their first year for reasons that combine financial need, training, and career (Zemans and Rosenblum 1981, pp. 44–47, 157). This experience significantly erodes both the educational and the moral influence of law school and simultaneously reduces pressure from both students and practitioners for more professionalized training or formal apprenticeship.

Entry to the Job Market   The profession dominates law students most directly through the impact of the job market as mediated by the placement process. As one first-year student said, "We talk about justice before we come here; we get here and we talk about jobs" (quoted in Foster 1981, p. 243). Where the majority of law school graduates before World War II expected to become independent professionals, today most are anxious to begin their careers as the salaried employees of law firms, corporations, or government, and they expect to remain within similar institutions their entire working lives (Zemans and Rosenblum 1981, pp. 81–84). Large employers have progressively rationalized the labor market. Students rely less on personal contacts and imperfect information (Smigel 1969); instead, law school placement offices collect and exchange hundreds of résumés from both students and potential employers. The placement process also begins earlier. At one time students looked for jobs only after they had passed the bar exam, or at most in their final term. Now the first half of the third year is virtually preoccupied with job seeking, second-year students are obsessed with summer jobs, and even first-year students are affected by employment anxiety. This process is dominated by those employers that hire a substantial cohort of new recruits every year, know their personnel needs far in advance, attract potential employees by offering summer jobs to students (whose productivity does not justify their pay), invest substantial resources in recruitment, and pay high salaries; in other words, large and medium firms and large corporations. And the law school has its own reasons for identifying a successful career with employment in law firms or corporations; such placements confirm the status of the school and produce the graduates who can make future financial contributions. It is not surprising that law students alter their conceptions of what skills and careers are desirable; abandoning criminal justice, poverty law, or active participation in social and political change, they gravitate toward law firm practice (Erlanger and Klegon 1978, pp. 22–26).

If the profession itself is the strongest influence on law schools and law students, the state is another significant factor. First, it is an employer whose importance has grown with the expansion of the regulatory apparatus, to the point where more than one lawyer in ten is a government employee, and more than one law graduate out of every five starts a career with the government (Sikes et al. 1972; Zemans and Rosenblum 1981, pp. 68–69; cf. Royal Commission on Legal Service 1979, vol. 2, pp. 46, 50–51). Because a judicial clerkship has become the most prestigious first job, the criteria for selection shape the behavior of law students; judges, in turn, select students for success and certify their clerks to subsequent employers (cf. Oakley and Thompson 1980).

Second, the state directly regulates legal education. In setting requirements for admission to the bar, the judiciary can and does specify the number of classroom hours a student must complete, the balance between classroom and clinical instruction, and even the particular courses that must be offered and taken (Zemans and Rosenblum 1981, p. 11). The judiciary also has castigated law schools for failing to instill advocacy skills and has threatened to impose additional requirements for litigators (Zemans and Rosenblum 1981, p. 9; Report of the Committee 1979). Sometimes the state even challenges the foundation of professional authority over legal education; for several years the U.S. Department of Education has been investigating the role of the ABA in accrediting law schools, and proprietary schools recently initiated a suit against the ABA to contest the association's blanket refusal to accredit them (Moskowitz 1977; U.S. Department of Health, Education and Welfare 1978; Fossum 1978; Stevens 1980, pp. 249–52). The state also is in a position to influence the norms by which law schools choose their faculty or student bodies or the ethnic or gender composition of each (*Regents of the University of California* v. *Bakke*, 1978).

The third source of state influence—finances—may be all the greater because it is largely invisible. Although legal education has traditionally demanded fewer institutional resources than other forms of professional or graduate training, and sometimes even generates a profit for the university (Stevens 1971; First 1976), this situation is changing under the combined influence of inflation and the growth of both clinical programs and faculty research (especially if the latter is empirical). In response, private institutions have raised tuition—increasing the dependence of their students on government loans—

and sought direct state support. Public institutions, in turn, may have to build a private endowment, increasing their subordination to graduates and thus to the profession.

Thus, control over the production of producers is the result of a complex interplay among law schools, the profession, and the state, illustrated by the changing roles of the bar examination and legal education. Although the bar exam usually is viewed as the paradigmatic licensing provision, it never really performed that function: the few examinations required before the 1890s were mere formalities, and their increasing stringency in the following decades did little more than parallel the growing importance of the law school and its rising admissions standards. For most entrants, acceptance by a law school has been tantamount to entry into the profession. In 1971, for instance, 72 percent of all examinees passed, 80 percent of those taking the bar for the first time did so, and the cumulative pass rate of those who persisted has been estimated at 90 percent (York and Hale 1973, pp. 6–7; cf. Royal Commission on Legal Services 1979, vol. 2, pp. 48–49, 53). Put another way, there is a strong correlation between scores on the Law School Admission Test (which, together with college grades, determines admission to law school), law school grades (which determine graduation), and the probability of passing the bar examination (Carlson and Werts 1976). There is further evidence that the bar examination is less central than law school. Proprietary (profit-making) bar review courses are completely unregulated, although law schools are heavily regulated and proprietary schools are denied accreditation. There are few restrictions on the number of times the bar examination may be taken, although law schools often expel students for academic failure (York and Hale 1973, p. 7). Bar examiners also have been supplanted by law schools as the arbiters of a suitable personality. Whereas character and fitness committees have either become rubber stamps (Association of the Bar 1978) or been prevented from imposing their standards (Cord v. Gibb, 1979), the criteria used to select students for law school (successful completion of sixteen years of formal education) and to determine who graduates from law school are more stringent and appear more universalistic.

Notwithstanding its diminished salience, the bar examination still exerts significant control over entry. First, it remains a major barrier for graduates of law schools not accredited by the ABA. In California—the only state with a significant number of such schools—the relative proportions of graduates of accredited and unaccredited law schools who passed the bar exam between 1974 and 1979 were 76 and 52 percent; for those who were repeating, the percentages were 90 and 73 (Blake 1979). Pass rates for minority applicants, who may be overrepresented in the unaccredited law schools, also are low (Blake 1980). But whereas law schools have been somewhat responsive to charges of cultural bias in the admissions and examination processes and to the need to compensate for prior discrimination (Ramsey 1980), bar examiners generally have rejected such criticisms (Commission to Study the Bar Examination 1975), and courts have upheld them against lawsuits charging discrimination (Antonides 1978).

Second, the bar examination inhibits the geographic mobility of lawyers, although these restrictions are being challenged and relaxed. Many jurisdictions denied noncitizens entry into the profession until the Supreme Court found this exclusion unconstitutional (In re Griffiths, 1973; see also Royal Commission on Legal Services 1979, vol. 1, pp. 495–96). Each state bar, however, continues to exclude the lawyers of other states, and the barriers against out-of-state lawyers are highest in those jurisdictions to which lawyers would most like to migrate—the Sun Belt, for instance (York and Hale 1973, p.

6, n. 26). Yet these controls are diminishing. The multistate bar examination, which most states have adopted in part, is one step toward a common qualification. The requirement of residence prior to the examination, which can impose a significant financial burden on a lawyer practicing in another state, is under attack (*Gordon* v. *Committee on Character and Fitness*, 1979). The rules governing partnerships among lawyers admitted in different states are being liberalized as large firms seek to engage in multistate practice for the convenience of their clients, whether conglomerates or wealthy retirees (Schwartz 1980; Galanter 1982; Becker 1978; cf. ABA 1974, DR 3-103[A], with ABA Commission 1981, pp. 175–78). Here again, as the bar examination becomes less significant as a regulatory device, the elite law schools assume a greater role— recruiting students from, and allocating them to, a national market (but see Zemans and Rosenblum 1981, pp. 47–52).

The profession has lost some control not only over who qualifies as a lawyer and how many do so but also over the practice of law by the unqualified. Every state has rules prohibiting the "unauthorized practice of law" by nonlawyers, and most state and local bar associations have watchdog committees to police infringements of these rules. Their efforts are loosely coordinated by the ABA, which periodically publishes *Unauthorized Practice News*. Yet challenges to the professional monopoly have proliferated in recent years. Businesses offer to help individuals conduct their own divorces, buy and sell real property, fight evictions, form corporations, draft and probate wills, and handle their own small-claims litigation (Abel 1980, pp. 379–82; *Yale Law Journal* 1976). And the state, which created the professional monopoly, now appears less sympathetic to its continuance. The Federal Trade Commission, which has been investigating all service occupations, views professional anticompetitive regulations with the greatest suspicion (*ABA Journal* 1977, 1978). Even the Chief Justice has questioned whether lawyers have a legitimate claim to their monopoly over "minor cases" (Burger 1976, p. 93).

These abridgments of professional control over the supply of legal services appear to be associated with a shift in the locus of regulation from the state to the federal government (cf. Schwartz 1980) and even to the international arena, where there is yet no political entity. This shift reflects the expanded scope of economic activity. Just as local bar associations proved inadequate to the task of regulation in the early nineteenth century, so state bar associations may be increasingly obsolete today. Perhaps this development is the reason why a recent president of the ABA listed "protection of the right of the profession to self-regulation" as one of his highest priorities (Sims 1978, p. 2) and why the ABA has been more active and more effective in the area of demand creation discussed below than have state and local groups. Yet there is reason to think that the efficacy of professional regulation inevitably declines as the scope of the market—and thus the locus of relevant political authority—shifts from locality to state to nation to region, since the political entity becomes more powerful—less subject to influence (cf. Scheiber 1980, pp. 696–707)—and the professional association more bureaucratized, differentiated, and less capable of representing the interests of its increasingly heterogeneous constituency (Orzack 1978, 1980). Some evidence may be found in the fact that only about one half the lawyers in the United States belong to the ABA, whereas two thirds of Chicago practitioners belong to the Chicago Bar Association (Heinz et al. 1976, pp. 769–70); of course, many lawyers belong to the integrated state bars in which membership is compulsory.

Structures of the Profession   If professional control over the supply of lawyers, mediated by the state, has been attenuated, another form is emerging in its place—hierarchic (often bureaucratic) control over subordinates (usually salaried employees) within the unit of production. The law firm is the paradigm, partly because more than half those entering the profession now begin their careers as law firm associates (Zemans and Rosenblum 1981, p. 70). The firm first exercises control through the hiring process, which pervades and increasingly dominates the last two years of law school. Firms scrutinize prospective associates, not only during day-long interviews but also, in the course of summer and part-time employment, throughout one or two years. The flow of information is largely one way; firms deny applicants information about security of employment and the structure of remuneration within the firm but encourage students to feel that they are exercising meaningful career choices by stressing marginal differences of atmosphere (workload, social life, dress code, personalities) and starting salary.

The new associate begins an apprenticeship of five to ten years. There is considerable evidence that significant socialization occurs during this period. Law firms are reluctant to hire mature graduates in their 30s or 40s (who are presumably less malleable), preferring the callow 25-year-old, who has been in school for the previous nineteen years. Fundamental ethical views about professional work are developed during the early years of law practice, under the influence of peers and superiors, rather than in law school (Carlin 1966, chaps. 6, 8); and this socialization process is more intense the larger the firm (Zemans and Rosenblum 1981, pp. 173–87). Several factors combine to enhance the susceptibility of the associate. Because law school has not endowed the fledgling lawyer with practical skills (Zemans and Rosenblum 1981, pp. 135–40, 150–55), the new worker feels grossly incompetent and is dependent on senior associates and partners for the necessary training. Junior associates have virtually no control over their work. The amount is so overwhelming that they constantly feel inadequate, an experience aggravated by competition with other associates (Bazelon 1969, chap. 7; Mayer 1967, pp. 326–38; Hoffman 1973, chap. 8). They have little or no say over the content of the work; although associates can express preferences for particular departments (Nelson 1981, pp. 125–26), those who voice ethical objections to a client or to performing the services a client requests endanger their chances of partnership, or fear that they will do so. The associate simultaneously is denied significant responsibility; contact with clients is limited and mediated by superiors, who assign only sections of problems. But the new associate constantly is subjected to a one-way evaluation by those same superiors, who may never fully disclose the outcome.

Domination in the organization of work is paralleled by domination in the system of remuneration. Associates, as employees, have no control over what they are paid; raises and bonuses arrive as gifts from the partners—or fail to do so (Smigel 1969, p. 81; Hoffman 1973, p. 131). The structure of remuneration within the firm is hidden from associates. Most important, the enormous disparity between partner income and associate salary—often on the order of 5 to 1—restates the hierarchic relationship in the most powerful symbol available to capitalist society. Furthermore, partnership privilege is built on this inequality; partners' incomes are high because associates are paid only a fraction of what they earn for the firm—usually a third—while another third goes to the partners, the remainder being overhead (York and Hale 1973, p. 19; Hoffman 1973, p. 118; Nelson 1981, p. 126; Abel 1981d; but see Liebowitz and Tollison 1978). If associates feel exploited, their only hope of redress is to become partners themselves and exploit others.

The last piece in this structure of control, and the one that holds it together, is the selection of some associates as partners. Although law firms differ, only a fraction of entering associates are made partners—often as few as one or two out of ten (Hoffman 1973, p. 129; Nelson 1981, p. 126). Intense competition among associates is induced by this high degree of selectivity combined with the magnitude of the reward—life-time security, extraordinary income, influence, status, and the domination of new subordinates within the firm (Osborn 1979a). But even those who fail in the struggle for partnership remain subject to the influence of the firm, which helps to place them in smaller, satellite firms, dependent on the parent firm for business, or in the office of legal counsel of the firm's corporate clients (Smigel 1969, pp. 80–90; Slovak 1979, 1980).

This structure of control is far more powerful than the bar examination. When superimposed on the factors that allocate students to primary and secondary school, college, and law school, the process of selecting associates produces an extraordinary homogeneity of class, race, and, until recently, religion and gender (Warkov and Zelan 1965; Smigel 1969, chaps. 3–5; Stevens 1973; Hoffman 1973, chap. 8; Fishman and Kaufman 1975, pp. 149–64; Zemans and Rosenblum 1981, chaps. 3, 5). Because the final stages of recruitment (initial hiring, intermediate promotions, and selection for partnership) are largely invisible and entirely private, they are almost totally unaccountable to public opinion or the courts—although recently there have been a number of lawsuits charging firms with sex and race discrimination (Galvin 1976; ABA Journal 1979, 65:897). Indeed, law firms willingly acknowledge that the capacity to inspire client confidence, sensitivity to client needs, and ability to get along with others in the firm are of the greatest importance when the firm chooses partners (Baird et al. 1977, pp. 30–33, 41; cf. Powell and Carlson 1978). The level of internal control attained through this lengthy and rigorous process of recruitment and socialization is revealed in the capacity of partners to divide partnership earnings, often quite unequally, without overt conflict and to handle the touchy matter of retirement without formal rules (Smigel 1969, chaps. 7–8; Hoffman 1973, chaps. 3–4).

The large law firm is not the only structure that exercises hierarchic control over the production of legal services. Indeed, the single largest unit in the United States is the office of house counsel of AT&T, with 863 lawyers (Schwartz 1980, p. 1275). Offices of house counsel, one of the fastest growing forms of legal practice, increased from 11,000 lawyers in 1951 to 50,000 in 1979 (Schwartz, 1980; Slovak 1979). But the trend may be most dramatic within private law firms. Whereas only 37 firms had more than 50 lawyers in 1959, there were 200 such firms 20 years later, 90 of them with over 100 lawyers; and the 20 largest firms, with a total of 4,681 lawyers, averaged 234 lawyers (Schwartz 1980, p. 1274; Galanter 1982). The proportion of sole practitioners dropped from almost two thirds of the bar 30 years ago to one third today (Schwartz 1980, p. 1274; cf. Sikes et al. 1972) and to 16 percent in a sample of Chicago practitioners (Zemans and Rosenblum 1981, p. 67). Most of the larger firms are also expanding geographically; 19 of the 20 largest had a mean of four branch offices; 15 of these had offices overseas (Galanter 1982). Firms are using more subordinated employees; permanent associates (lawyer employees who never become partners) are reappearing, the ratio of associates to partners in the 50 largest firms grew from 1:1 in 1975 to 1.6:1 in 1979, and the use of paraprofessionals is expanding (Galanter 1982; Brickman 1971; Statsky 1972; W. E. Green 1976;

Nelson 1981; Johnstone and Flood 1980). Finally, the development of office technology has resulted in a substantial increase in fixed capital (Muris and McChesney 1979).

Other structures consisting largely of employees organized hierarchically and bureaucratically have also expanded rapidly. These include legal clinics (Muris and McChesney 1979; Maron 1978), prepaid legal-service plans (Deitch and Weinstein 1976; Pfenningstorf and Kimball 1977), the Legal Services Corporation (Johnson 1974; Handler et al. 1978a; Legal Services Corporation 1975–80), prosecutors and public defenders (Hermann et al. 1977; Eisenstein 1978; Schwartz 1980, p. 1277), and regulatory agencies.

The explanations for and significance of these changes are complex. Economies of scale offer one reason for growth, but some productive units already are reaching, or have surpassed, the size beyond which further expansion produces diseconomies. Increases in the ratio of associates to partners, in the number of paraprofessionals, and in fixed capital all can enhance partners' profits (Siegfried 1976; Bower 1980; Illinois State Bar Association 1975, pp. 88–91). Specialization in response to the greater complexity of private and especially public law is a major factor (Laumann and Heinz 1977, 1979; Mindes 1980; Nelson 1981; Zemans and Rosenblum 1981, pp. 70–80). As clients grow and diversify, law firms must follow suit, especially if they are to satisfy the peak demands created by major litigation (Bernstein 1978). But growth also may have symbolic significance. A firm that is not growing as fast as others may be seen as declining (*American Lawyer*, June 1980), and such an impression can be self-fulfilling. In the absence of clear criteria of quality, size may be the most obvious surrogate (Nelson 1981; cf. Mungham and Thomas 1979).

Size also increases overhead, however, and consequently the dependence of the firm on its clients. A high and predictable volume of work becomes essential; only the larger corporations can pay the fees and furnish the volume; and the expertise necessary to handle such clients, as well as the personal contacts that assure such business, are valuable resources, not lightly squandered. Concentration naturally increases the barriers to entry by new firms. Finally, increased size mandates the progressive displacement of professional self-regulation by bureaucratic controls (Stinchcombe 1959), not so much among partners (Nelson 1981) as by superiors—executive committees, department heads—over inferiors—junior partners, associates, law clerks, and paraprofessionals.

Control over Production by Producers

If professionals control the market for their services mainly through control over the production *of* producers, a subsidiary means is control over production *by* producers (Larson 1977). The latter is more problematic for several reasons. It presupposes the former; it requires reciprocal self-sacrifice, rather than self-interested efforts to exclude competitors; and it is more difficult both to police, since competitive practices by licensed practitioners are less visible than the unauthorized practice of law, and to justify, since it is hard to explain why, in a capitalist society, professionals alone should not compete. Thus, whereas controls over the production *of* producers progressively were strengthened starting shortly after the Civil War, it was not until these were fairly secure—following World War I—that controls over production *by* producers began to be imposed.

Control of Information   The profession has sought to control the information available to potential clients, who must choose among competing producers; indeed, it

often fosters the impression that all producers are equally qualified. The bar examination certifies minimum competence but does not rank those admitted; qualification is for life; and the profession has resisted mandatory continuing education (but see Zemans and Rosenblum 1981, pp. 160–61) and periodic examinations and has rejected responsibility for measuring quality (Carlson 1976; Rosenthal 1976; Steele and Nimmer 1976; Carroll and Gaston 1977; but see Parker 1974).

The lawyer-referral services established by bar associations recommend lawyers to the public at random, refusing to differentiate by quality (Christensen 1970, chap. 5; Berg 1979). Lawyers themselves have defeated and discouraged clients' accusations of incompetence by their conspiracy of silence in malpractice actions (Rothstein 1972; *Yale Law Journal* 1973; Mallen and Levit 1977; Vollmer 1978). A recent incident illustrates the professional attitude. Consumers Union sought to compile a directory of Virginia lawyers that would inform potential clients of qualifications, price, hours, language competency, and the like. But when the organization submitted the preliminary questionnaire to the Virginia State Bar Association, the latter ruled that any attorney responding to it would be subject to disciplinary action (*Consumers Union of United States v. American Bar Association,* 1975).

Yet, though the profession denies clients the means to make independent judgments, lawyers frequently are ranked by other lawyers. Law schools select applicants and grade students—and the law school attended and class standing are the two strongest predictors of career success; law firms hire associates—and there is substantial stability in both type and structure of practice throughout lawyers' careers (Zemans and Rosenblum 1981, pp. 81–87, 114). Elite lawyers assign their acquaintances to categories of competence and financial responsibility in law directories (*Steingold v. Martindale-Hubbell,* 1972). Generalists refer cases to specialists—for a fee (Carlin 1962, pp. 162–63; Rosenthal 1974; pp. 99–101). And bar associations increasingly are seeking control over the inescapable fact of specialization by certifying specialists and allowing only those certified to advertise their expertise (Zemans and Rosenblum 1981, p. 161; Zehnle 1975; *Virginia Law Review* 1975; Hochberg 1976).

A central arena for the struggle to control information about the price and quality of legal services has been advertising. Professional associations did not prohibit advertising until well into the present century. California, for instance, first promulgated such a rule in 1928 and permitted some forms of advertising even later (*Barton v. State Bar,* 1930). The functions of the ban appear to have been twofold—to enhance the image of lawyers as professionals, thereby advancing the project of collective mobility (Larson 1977, chap. 6), and to distribute consumers equally, or at least fairly broadly, among producers, thereby dampening competition. Yet only fifty years after it was imposed, the country-wide prohibition on advertising was lifted (*Bates v. State Bar of Arizona,* 1977; ABA Commission 1980, 1981; cf. Royal Commission on Legal Services 1979, vol. 1, chap. 27; Royal Commission on Legal Services in Scotland 1980, vol. 1, pp. 61–65; *Law Society Journal* [Australia], June 1980, pp. 309–10; ABA 1981, Rules 7.1–7.2).

Several factors contributed to this reversal. The primary legitimation of lawyers has been shifting from professionalism to public service. Although sole practitioners and small firms who had chafed under the ban (Carlin 1962, chap. 5) now opposed liberalization, there was strong pressure from the increasing numbers of younger lawyers (*ABA Journal* 1977)—and half the bar has practiced less than ten years, a third less than five

(Schwartz 1980, p. 1270). Finally, the Supreme Court declared the rule unconstitutional, over strong opposition from the organized profession. This opposition since has been displayed in grudging and incomplete compliance (Cox et al. 1979, chap. 3; Brosnahan and Andrews 1980).

But advertising is not the most important mechanism for informing clients about legal services, and most lawyers have eschewed the opportunities created by the new rules (Cox et al. 1979). Because consumers of personal services generally prefer to rely on the endorsement of someone they know (Ladinsky 1976; Lochner 1975; Curran 1977, pp. 200–203), a direct approach to a potential client, whether by the lawyer or by an intermediary, is more effective. Thus, the ban on solicitation was widely flouted (Carlin 1962), but for purposes of maintaining its image, the organized profession engaged in periodic, highly publicized crackdowns on "ambulance chasing" (Reichstein 1965). And lawyers made a sharp distinction between situations in which they themselves were the intermediaries—house counsel selecting outside counsel (Slovak 1980), law firm "rainmakers" and "finders" attracting corporate and wealthy individual clients (Hoffman 1973, chaps. 4–6; Nelson 1981), generalists referring cases and splitting fees with specialists (Carlin 1962, pp. 162–63; Rosenthal 1974, pp. 99–101)—and situations in which the intermediary was a relatively autonomous layperson who might even seek to control the professional (Carlin 1962, chap. 3). Pressures to relax the ban on solicitation again were resisted by the organized profession, but this time the Supreme Court overruled the bar only in part. It granted constitutional protection to lawyers who offered free services to unrepresented individuals seeking to assert political rights (*In re Primus*, 1978), but not to lawyers motivated by personal gain who solicited paying clients asserting nonconstitutional claims (*Ohralik v. Ohio State Bar Association,* 1978). The profession clearly intends to allow little more solicitation than is constitutionally mandated (cf. ABA Commission 1980, Rule 9.3, with ABA Commission 1981, Rule 713). The reasons for the factual distinction appear to be that the provision of legal services in the first instance enhances the reputation of the profession for public service while posing little threat of competition, whereas, in the second situation, solicitation might detract from the image of professionalism and simultaneously aggravate competition.

Control of Competition   A similar pattern can be perceived in the controversy over prepaid group plans for legal services. These range along a continuum from wholly "open," in which members are entitled to retain any lawyer and be reimbursed for the costs, to wholly "closed," where members are restricted to the services of a single lawyer or law firm (Deitch and Weinstein 1976; Pfenningstorf and Kimball 1977). At both national and state levels, the organized bar sought to promote the former and restrict the latter through discriminatory regulations (ABA 1974, DR 2-102[D] [5]); these organizations were prevented from doing so only by the threat of prosecution by the Justice Department for antitrust violations (Deitch and Weinstein 1976, pp. 21–23). But though open-panel plans appear to leave untouched the existing distribution of business among participating lawyers, client preference for a personal recommendation actually tends to produce concentration in a few practitioners (Marks et al. 1974, pp. 67–70). Furthermore, virtually all the plans that have been established are closed (Deitch and Weinstein 1976, pp. 39–42).

All the practices just described seek to control production by authorized producers in order to limit competition among lawyers. But, of course, the most effective means is price fixing. The organized profession began to set fees as soon as it achieved sufficient control over the production of producers, promulgating minimum schedules and threatening disciplinary action against lawyers who undercut prices. This practice went unchallenged for half a century, until the rise of consumerism stimulated lawsuits that successfully attacked those schedules as violations of the antitrust laws (*Goldfarb* v. *Virginia State Bar*, 1975). But that decision did not prevent lawyers from exchanging information about prices charged, which is what large law firms have been doing for years—subscribing to services offered by firms of accountants, which collect and distribute information on fees charged, hours billed, gross income, partnership shares, associate salaries, and other overhead items (Daniel J. Cantor 1980). This practice affords another instance of the shift from professional to bureaucratic methods of supply control. Yet these new forms of control probably are less effective than those they replaced. At the base of the profession there is competition from nonlawyers, who offer assistance in such matters as uncontested divorces and immigration, and from legal clinics, which cut costs through the economies of scale allowed by advertising, information-processing technology, and use of paraprofessionals (Muris and McChesney 1979). And large law firms have been losing business to in-house counsel, who cost corporations substantially less (Bernstein 1978; Schwartz 1980, pp. 1275–76; Nelson 1981).

A fundamental test of market control is price. Critics of the professions long have contended that control over production of and by producers of services must inflate the cost of those services and thereby reduce their availability (Reed 1921; Carroll and Gaston 1977; cf. Leffler 1978; Shepard 1978; Blair and Rubin 1980). There is considerable evidence to support this view (see, for example, Arnold 1972). It has been estimated that half the income differential between the professions and those occupations that control neither entry nor production is explained by restrictions on supply (Friedman and Kuznets 1945). Others have argued that, though licensing itself does not affect occupational income, difficulty of entry—whether measured by the length of training required (Pfeffer 1974) or the level of restraints on geographic mobility (Holen 1965)—does have such an effect. National time-series data on American lawyers from 1920 to the present show a decline in the ratio of real to equilibrium earnings of lawyers as the supply of lawyers expanded and a rise in that ratio after World War II as a result of the curtailment in supply caused by the Depression, the draft, and the increased stringency of supply controls (Pashigian 1978, pp. 64–67). Large disparities in the fees charged for standardized services by lawyers within the same community (Cox et al. 1979, chap. 5) strongly suggest the absence of vigorous price competition. Finally, inferences can be drawn from the consequences of introducing competition. Differences in the cost of prescription medicine and eye glasses between jurisdictions that allow and prohibit price advertising are striking (*Los Angeles Times*, May 25, 1978, pt. 1, p. 22; *Virginia State Board of Pharmacy* v. *Virginia Citizens Consumer Council, Inc.*, 1976). Conveyancing in South and Western Australia—the two states in which lawyers do not have a professional monopoly—costs one third to one half of the price in the rest of Australia (Basten and Disney 1977, p. 13; Royal Commission on Legal Services 1979, vol. 2, pp. 154–58). And when legal clinics initiated vigorous price competition in the United States, they set fees at half the going rate charged by other lawyers for comparable services (Muris and McChesney 1979; Menkel-Meadow 1979).

Legitimation

As the characteristics, activities, and relationships of producers and consumers of lawyers' services have changed, so have the needs of the profession for legitimation and its means of satisfying them. Legitimation means nothing more arcane than the justification an actor offers for his actions or circumstances. What is felt to require explanation will vary, as will the audience to whom it is directed; the latter may include the actor himself, others similarly situated (in this case, other professionals), clients, and the general public. A number of tensions generate the need to legitimate. The very existence of a category of functional specialists creates tension between the dependence inherent in the division of labor and clients' desires for autonomy (Morris et al. 1973; Curran 1977, pp. 229–32; see, generally, May 1976). Individuals may be responding to this tension when they insist on representing themselves (Haug and Sussman 1969; Torens 1975; *Faretta* v. *California,* 1975; *Yale Law Journal* 1976; but see Tomasic 1978, pp. 22–25). Businesses are reacting to the same dynamic when they seek to keep lawyers out of transactions or to ensure that lawyers will be thoroughly subordinated (Macaulay 1963; Galanter 1982). The equivalent of this interindividual tension at the level of collectivities is the claim by professions that they are self-regulating and thus immune from control by the larger society. Bar associations have maintained that they are exempt from both the First Amendment and antitrust laws, and they even have sought to protect their members from certain criminal sanctions.

A different tension arises out of the conflict between partisanship and neutrality; lawyers vigorously advocate their clients' interests while insisting that lawyers must not be identified with those clients (Curtis 1951; Wasserstrom 1975; Fried 1976; Schwartz 1978; Simon 1978; Luban 1981). The claim to moral unaccountability is not readily accepted, since no other role in society enjoys such a privilege, and lawyer protestations that loyalty to client is moderated by loyalty to the legal system and to society often elicit skepticism and disbelief (*Nebraska Law Review* 1975; Fair and Moskowitz 1975; Waltz 1976). This dilemma is reproduced at the institutional level in the visible identification of the legal profession with clients drawn from a very limited segment of society— primarily corporations and wealthy individuals (Curran 1977, pp. 233–34).

Finally, lawyers cannot escape the tension between the prevailing ideology of egalitarianism and the reality of class and stratification. At the institutional level, the entire legal profession is seen to enjoy privileges of wealth, status, and power (Zemans and Rosenblum 1981, pp. 3–5). Yet from the perspective of the individual lawyer, there are vast differences within the profession among lawyers who practice in different settings, specialize in different subject matters, or serve different clienteles (Carlin 1966, chap. 2; Laumann and Heinz 1977, 1979; Zemans and Rosenblum 1981, chap. 4; Slovak 1980; Nelson 1981). Such intraprofessional stratification is in tension with the underlying assumption of professional equality expressed in the single uniform credential.

Justifications   Several attributes of the legal profession appear to respond to these legitimation problems. The esoteric quality of legal practice and scholarship contributes to the image of law as science, thereby justifying the dependence of clients and the autonomy of the profession. The ideology of meritocracy—mediated by the university, the bar examination, and the job market for law school graduates—justifies both the privileges of the profession as a whole and differential rewards within it. The conspicuous exertions of law students, bar examinees, associates, and even senior lawyers—the strong, often neurotic, intensity of the professional attachment to the work ethic—also serve to argue that lawyers' perquisites are well deserved (Riesman 1951; Bazelon 1969, chap. 7; Turow 1977; Osborn 1979a, 1979b). And indeed, as in all professions, effort (or at least endurance) is rewarded: earnings increase sharply with age (Langer 1978).

A third legitimation has been gaining ground in recent years—the ideology of the market (Abel 1981d). Pressed by the Supreme Court, the Justice Department, and the Federal Trade Commission, the organized profession grudgingly has relaxed restraints on advertising, solicitation, and prepaid legal plans and withdrawn its sanction from price fixing. This trend lends weight to the argument that the market explains the allocation of legal services—their quantity, quality, and price; justifies the moral unaccountability of the lawyer, who works for whoever pays him—an attitude most fully expressed in the "cab-rank" principle of English barristers (Royal Commission on Legal Services 1979, vol. 1, pp. 30–31); and, most important, would be distorted by any kind of external control, which could only detract from optimum efficiency. Yet, like earlier legitimations, this argument, too, is flawed. The market is far from perfect, and there are strong reasons why lawyers' services should not be allocated as though they were simply another commodity (see, for example, *Gideon* v. *Wainwright*, 1963).

Self-Regulation   The two principal legitimations invoked by lawyers, however, are peculiar to the profession—self-regulation and altruism (cf. Fennell 1980). Self-regulation (Blair and Rubin 1980) allays the anxiety of the client who, in a crisis, must depend for vital services on a professional, often a stranger; it justifies the weakness, verging on total absence, of both market and external political controls; it moderates visible partisanship, individual and institutional, with an appearance of neutrality; and it suggests that professional privilege is a concomitant of superior moral worth. If it does not ultimately achieve these goals, it nevertheless contributes to them in a variety of complex ways (Abel 1981b). First, the formal codification of rules of professional conduct conveys the implicit message that whatever is not prohibited or discouraged is approved or at least condoned (cf. Erikson 1966). The decision to represent a client, for instance, is characterized as ethically unproblematic, since the rules offer no guidance. Second, because the rules speak only to the conduct of individual lawyers, they suggest that the ethical dilemmas of the profession are soluble provided the individual behaves properly; structural change is unnecessary. This focus on individual conformity leads readily to an emphasis on education as the means to internalize the rules and inspires periodic revitalization movements. Committees of the American Bar Association proposed revisions of the rules of professional ethics in 1928, 1933, 1937, 1954, and rewrote them in 1970 (ABA 1974, p. i); and yet the ABA once again is engaged in a "comprehensive rethinking of the ethical premises and problems of the profession of law" (ABA Commission 1981, p. i). The primary response to the recent major legitimation crisis, the Watergate scandal, was a requirement by the ABA that students at accredited law schools be instructed in the rules of ethics (ABA Standards for the Approval of Law Schools, § 302[a][iii], August 13, 1974) and the inclusion of ethical questions in state bar examinations. These exercises are largely symbolic. It was known before the reforms that ethical instruction has little effect on attitudes (Carlin 1966, pp. 143–46). Both students and teachers view the courses as unimportant (Pipkin 1979). A number of elite law schools pay only lip service to the ABA requirement (Zemans and Rosenblum 1981, p. 169). And practitioners maintain that law school instruction in professional responsibility has little effect—though they, too, urge that it be continued! (Zemans and Rosenblum 1981, pp. 171–79).

Professional preoccupation with refining the rules and formal education rests on the assumption that the rules will be internalized and thus become self-enforcing. But the assumption is not justified in practice (Carlin 1966, chap. 3). The necessary corrective is an institutional mechanism for sanctioning deviance. As always, such a mechanism introduces the "gap" between the law of the books and the law in action (Abel 1973). One source of dissonance is control over the disciplinary process; there is something inherently suspect in the claim by an occupational category that its members will punish each other for infractions that all find tempting and many commit. *Quis custodiet ipsos custodes?* (Curran 1977, pp. 231–32). The profession responds to the consequent pressure for public accountability in several ways. The organized bar can divest itself of disciplinary responsibility while still ensuring that lawyers remain firmly in control (Powell 1976; Slovak 1981, pp. 170–74). Alternatively, it can coopt lay persons to serve on disciplinary bodies but always in such small numbers that they remain strongly deferential to the professional members (Steele and Nimmer 1976, pp. 923–24; Blake 1978; Arthurs 1981).

Another problem raised by enforcement is the dramatic disjunction between the content of ethical rules and the substance of client grievances—delay, discourtesy, neglect, unresponsiveness, and excessive fees (Marks and Cathcart 1974; Steele and Nimmer 1976, pp. 946–56; Curran 1977, pp. 224–31). This tension, together with the fact that the disciplinary process is wholly reactive, discourages clients from voicing all but an insignificant fraction of their complaints (Steele and Nimmer 1976, pp. 962–63; Royal Commission on Legal Services 1979, vol. 2, p. 252). Lawyers, who are more knowledgeable about both the content of ethical rules and the structure of disciplinary procedures even if they are not as well placed to observe some forms of misconduct, rarely report what they see or even express disapproval (Carlin 1966, chaps. 6, 9; Steele and Nimmer 1976, pp. 973–74).

The disciplinary process itself is extraordinarily lenient; at each successive stage most of the unresolved grievances are disposed of with little or no punishment. Only a trivial number of serious sanctions—lengthy suspension or disbarment—are ever imposed (Carlin 1966, chap. 9; ABA Special Committee 1970; Marks and Cathcart 1974; Steele and Nimmer 1976, pp. 978–99; Association of the Bar 1976; Tisher et al. 1977, chap. 5; cf. Royal Commission on Legal Services 1979, vol. 1, pp. 344–45, 348–49; New South Wales Law Reform Commission 1979, pp. 33–40; Royal Commission on Legal Services in Scotland 1980, vol. 1, chap. 18; Reiter 1978, pt. D).

Finally, self-regulation not only gives the profession a clean bill of health but also justifies intraprofessional stratification. The rules of professional conduct impose on the base of the profession a set of mores—about acquiring business, for instance—that only the elite can observe. At the same time, they permit a degree of loyalty to clients that may be justified at the base of the profession—in criminal defense, for instance—but is not obviously appropriate for elite practitioners lobbying legislatures or opposing regulatory agencies (Abel 1981b). Given this bias in the substance of the rules, an evenhanded application exculpates the elite and stigmatizes the base (Carlin 1966, chap. 10; Shuch-man 1968). Self-regulation thus advances a mythic picture of how lawyers should, and do, behave and what happens to them if they deviate. This picture is becoming ever more anachronistic as professional control is displaced by hierarchic organizations—the law firm, corporation, or state—having far greater influence over practitioners.

Altruism   The last mode of legitimation—public service—is perhaps the most im-portant because it simultaneously can be highly conspicuous while remaining susceptible to professional manipulation. By advertising its altruism, the profession claims that governmental control is unnecessary and that the free operation of market forces could be seriously detrimental to greater representation of the unrepresented. The partisanship of individual lawyers and of the profession as a whole is offset by visible charitable services. And the contribution of time helps to justify the privileges of the entire profession and the unique advantages of its elite.

Lawyers engage in public service through their professional associations and as individ-uals or firms. Professional associations (except, perhaps, those local groups with very homogeneous memberships) are dominated by elite practitioners, and their governing bodies are even more clearly differentiated in terms of the structure of practice, age, class, and ethnic origin (Halliday and Cappell 1979; Powell 1979; Auerbach 1974; Heinz et al. 1976; Carlin 1962, p. 203). Professional associations also are heavily dependent finan-cially on contributions from the corporate clients of these elite lawyers (Halliday and Powell 1977). Nevertheless, they seek to appear to be more representative of the bar by involving prominent legal educators and scholars and, more recently, women and minor-ity lawyers (Halliday and Powell 1977; Halliday and Cappell 1979).

Given this institutional structure, it is not surprising that professional associations engage in those forms of public service that have little explicit political content—education, rationalization of rules (especially those that are more technical and pro-cedural), reorganization of bureaucracies (such as courts and police), review of judicial nominations, and redistribution of legal services (Halliday and Cappell 1979; Slovak 1981). Yet these activities have an indirect payoff. They imbue the professional associa-tion with an aura of selflessness that may help to disguise or distract attention from its self-interested pursuit of other goals, such as market control.

Individually, lawyers engage in two forms of public service. First, they are involved in politics—so involved that they dominate American political life (Melone 1980) and even the politics of other countries, such as Great Britain and Australia, where lawyers generally play a less central role (Podmore 1977, 1980a; Gower and Price 1957; Basten and Disney 1977). Law practice endows lawyers with relevant skills and allows them considerable control over their time. Political activity, in turn, confers visibility and status—thereby attracting new business—and offers new career opportunities. But it is the pro bono publico services that lawyers render without fee or for reduced fees that may be the most controversial manifestation of altruism, at least for the profession itself.

The type and quantity of these services naturally are influenced by the structure of the lawyer's practice. For elite lawyers, pro bono services have the advantage of helping to demonstrate their neutrality and to focus attention on their charitable activities—and away from the energies they devote to paying clients. Thus, it is noteworthy that elite lawyers have transferred some of their efforts from cultural, educational, and other traditional charitable institutions (Smigel 1969, pp. 10–11; Mayer 1967, p. 338) to the environment, the indigent criminal, the tort victim, and the poor in general (*Harvard Law Review* 1970; Marks et al. 1972; Hoffman 1973, chap. 12; Handler et al. 1978a). The emphasis is on the big case, which exploits the skills and resources of the large law firm and simultaneously confirms its importance (see, for example, Stern 1976); only associates handle the routine problems of the unrepresented (Rosenthal et al. 1971; Ashman 1972). This reallocation of resources also made large-firm practice more attractive to the law graduates of the late 1960s and early 1970s (Simon et al. 1973). The nonelite lawyer operates in a very different environment; he is subject to more frequent requests for assistance whose satisfaction would cause him significant financial hardship, and he constantly must strive to secure more paying business. Consequently, he represents those supplicants who are likely to become paying clients in the future or are referred by intermediaries who also channel more remunerative matters; and he disposes of the problem with a minimum of effort (Lochner 1975).

The result is tokenism. Approximately one third of all lawyers do no pro bono work at all; those who do some handle an average of only three cases a year; 60 percent of those cases are disposed in less than ten hours each; and the bar as a whole donates an average of twenty-seven hours per year in charitable services (Maddi and Merrill 1971; Lochner 1975; Handler et al. 1978a, chap. 5). Nor are lawyers any more generous in direct monetary contributions (Rosenthal et al. 1971, p. 168). The differences in the environments and responses of elite and nonelite lawyers inevitably lead to tensions between them, best illustrated by the recent controversy over mandatory pro bono, which the former are advocating and the latter successfully resisting (Christensen 1981; Association of the Bar 1979; cf. ABA Commission 1980, Rule 8.1, with ABA Commission 1981, Rule 6.1; cf. Marks et al. 1972, chap. 14).

Thus, the legal profession draws upon dominant ideologies to give meaning to its structures and behavior and to resolve internal and external tensions. But it also strengthens those ideologies and contributes to the legitimation of basic social institutions.

First, it reinforces the apparent homology among the adversary system, the free market, and liberal pluralism, epitomized in Holmes's notion that the role of the courts is to preserve the "marketplace of ideas" (*Abrams* v. *United States*, 1919). Just as resources are said to be optimally allocated by the market and political decisions best made by electoral competition, so truth and justice are·seen to be ensured by the clash of advocates. By conspicuously championing a few of the unrepresented, the legal profession makes this ideal appear more attainable (Abel 1979b). Second, lawyers depoliticize conflict by legalizing it (Poulantzas 1978, pp. 76–91), thereby detaching individual actors from large aggregates and suggesting that conflict can be resolved without structural change (Scheingold 1974; Abel 1981c, 1982; cf. Handler 1978b). Third, the legal profession exemplifies the meritocratic legitimation of stratification—even more persuasively now that women and minorities have been partly integrated. Fourth, the legal profession reinforces the belief that differences in technical skill compel and justify relations of dominance and subordination, such as those between lawyer and client (Mazor 1968; Wasserstrom 1975; Spiegel 1979; see generally Illich 1977). Indeed, the image of law as a "helping" profession is one of its greatest attractions to potential entrants (Foster 1981; cf. Edelman 1974). Finally, like other professionals, lawyers present one of the few models of meaningful work under capitalism. Where others are cogs in the division of labor, the professional alone can see the whole (cf. Marx 1977, p. 482; Gouldner 1979; Berger and Mohr 1969). Where others experience work as drudgery and shirk it, the professional finds work rewarding, intrinsically and extrinsically, and glories in it (*Work in America* 1973, p. 16). It is not surprising that the activity of professionals—especially doctors and lawyers—is virtually the only work portrayed in fiction, television, or the movies, whether highbrow or lowbrow.

REDISTRIBUTING LEGAL SERVICES

The last two decades have witnessed the beginning of a transformation in the production of legal services that may be as momentous as the rise of the legal profession a century ago. This change, not limited to the United States, is just as marked in the United Kingdom (Abel 1981d; Royal Commission on Legal Services 1979; Royal Commission on Legal Services in Scotland 1980), Canada (Reid 1978), Australia (New South Wales Law Reform Commission 1981), the Netherlands (Schuyt et al. 1977; Griffiths 1977), and other European nations (Cappelletti et al. 1975; Storme and Casman 1978; Zemans 1979; Blankenburg 1980; Garth 1980; Nousiainen 1980) and Third World countries (International Legal Center 1974; Dias et al. 1981). It affects structures and relations of production, the identity of consumers, the role of intermediaries between the two, and the services performed. This transformation can be summarized as the growing importance of demand creation as a strategy of market control.

The need to redistribute legal services has been argued strongly and repeatedly for more than half a century, both in the United States (Smith 1919; Berle 1933; Stone 1934) and in Britain (Leat 1975; Alcock 1976). But until recently, the profession consistently has chosen to minimize the need and to make only the most grudging response (Royal Commission on Legal Services 1979, vol. 1, pp. 101–4). State subsidization of legal services for the poor was denounced as "socialist" in the 1950s (Storey 1951), and most American lawyers remained hostile to the idea as late as the 1970s (Stumpf 1975), although the ABA Board of Governors unanimously supported the founding of the Office of Equal Opportunity Legal Services Program in 1965 (Johnson 1974, p. 63). The situation in the 1980s could not be more different; when Ronald Reagan sought to abolish the Legal Services Corporation in the spring of 1981, virtually every bar association—national, state, and local—strongly opposed his recommendation (*Los Angeles Times*, March 7, 1981, pt. 1, p. 34; *New York Times*, March 11, 1981, pt. 1, p. 14).

Demand Creation

Several factors have converged to produce this explosion of interest in demand creation. First, control over supply, which gradually improved through the 1950s, significantly eroded thereafter. The number of students at ABA accredited law schools increased dramatically—and disproportionately at the base of the status hierarchy (York and Hale 1973, p. 22). Constraints on production by producers—rules concerning advertising, minimum fees, and unauthorized practice—also succumbed to external attack. Demand creation offers both an alternative and a supplement to the constriction of supply as a means of market control, even if it also emerges when supply control is not threatened (Griffiths 1977, p. 262).

Second, the legal profession's need to create demand coincided with new opportunities to do so. The rise of an organized workforce led by union officials interested in negotiating better fringe benefits constituted a category of potential clients who rarely had used lawyers in the past (Mayhew and Reiss 1969; Marks et al. 1974; Deitch and Weinstein 1976). The gradual growth of the welfare state and the emergence of the "new property" (Reich 1964) created myriad rights that lawyers can help to enforce (Leat 1975, p. 167; Schuyt et al. 1977; Royal Commission on Legal Services 1979, vol. 1, chap. 15). The enormous increase in the number of criminal prosecutions (Saari 1979), the progressive legalization of juvenile justice (*In re Gault*, 1967; Lemert 1976; Stapleton and Teitelbaum 1972; Rubinstein 1976; Anderson 1978), and the creation of a constitutional right to legal representation in most criminal cases (*Gideon* v. *Wainwright*, 1963; *Argersinger* v. *Hamlin*, 1972; *Scott* v. *Illinois*, 1979; see, generally, Hermann et al. 1977) have ensured a continuous and expanding demand for lawyers.

Third, demand creation is consistent with the general shift in advanced industrial economies from the production of goods to the production of services (Larson 1977, p. 250; Rothschild 1981). This transformation of productive activity is responsive to two problems. The first is resource scarcity and the resultant need for conservation; the production of services uses far fewer material resources than the production of goods. The other is underconsumption (Sherman 1979); the limits on the consumption of services are more flexible—few people will own more than one washing machine, but the passion for fast food appears insatiable (McKnight 1977). Finally, demand creation allows a more thoroughgoing form of market control, if one that may be more difficult to attain. It specifies not merely who may produce, but also what services will be consumed, by whom, and from whom.

Legal Need   Demand creation is grounded on a reconceptualization of the value of lawyers' services. Studies of "legal need" have played an essential part in this process, comparable to the role performed by sociological jurisprudence in justifying, implementing, and criticizing the New Deal (Glennon 1979; cf. Schlegel 1979). Such studies have proliferated in the last decade, not merely in the United States (Levine and Preston 1970; Curran 1977, especially chap. 1) but also in England (Abel-Smith et al. 1973; Morris et al. 1973; Royal Commission on Legal Services 1979, vol. 2, chap. 8), Scotland (Royal Commission on Legal Services in Scotland 1980, vol. 2, chap. 4), France (Baraquin 1975; Valétas 1976), Germany (Tiemann and Blankenburg 1979), the Netherlands (Schuyt et al. 1977), Australia (Cass and Sackville 1975), and Canada (Colvin et al. 1978). Yet legal need is not a fact but a social construct. Scholars inevitably introduce political values when they assert that people have needs that lawyers can and should fulfill (Lewis 1973; Griffiths 1977, 1980; Marks 1976; Galanter 1976; Mayhew 1975). Whereas, previously, individual lawyers persuaded individual clients to accept proffered services (Rosenthal 1974; Cain 1979; Hosticka 1979), these newer studies allow the profession to act collectively to impute legal needs to entire categories of consumers (Illich 1977).

The studies have identified several barriers to the use of lawyers, which the profession has tried to eliminate or at least lower. The public sector has responded to the claim that lawyers are geographically inaccessible to potential clients (cf. Royal Commission on Legal Services 1979, vol. 1, pp. 46–48) by moving legal aid lawyers from their downtown offices—which are convenient for lawyers who have to make frequent court appearances—to poor neighborhoods, where they have attracted a different clientele (*Harvard Law Review* 1967; Fisher and Ivie 1971). In the private sector, clinics have moved to the suburbs, often locating in chain stores and shopping centers (Diamond 1981); the Royal Commission on Legal Services (1979, vol. 1, pp. 181–82) even urged that the state subsidize loans to lawyers who locate in areas not presently served.

It also is claimed that potential clients are ignorant of the ways in which lawyers can be helpful (Royal Commission on Legal Services 1979, vol. 1, pp. 45–46). Advertising—especially institutional advertising by professional associations (Fennell 1982), often advocating "annual legal checkups"—has been one response (ABA Committee on Professional Ethics, Opinions 179, 205, 227, 307). Prepaid legal services plans are allowed to, and do, offer unsolicited advice to members. Nonprofit legal services offices were exempted from the prohibition on advertising long before the ban was struck down (ABA 1974, DR 2-102[D]). Potential clients also are thought to be deterred by fear of the unknown; there is evidence that once people use a lawyer, the probability of further recourse increases (Curran 1977, pp. 186–94; Marks et al. 1974, pp. 61–64). Pro bono services may help to overcome the initial apprehension and encourage clients to return with matters for which they will pay fees (Lochner 1975).

But the major barrier to the increased use of lawyers generally is thought to be cost (Royal Commission on Legal Services 1979, vol. 1, chaps. 10–16; but see Mayhew 1975). The response has been to transform legal services for the poor from an act of charity to a matter of right (Cappelletti et al. 1975). Yet, though this right has been firmly established in criminal defense, attempts to extend it to civil proceedings have been largely unsuccessful (*Meltzer v. C. Buck LeCraw & Co.*, 1971; *In re Smiley*, 1975; *Lassiter v. Department of Social Services*, 1981; cf. Royal Commission on Legal Services 1979, vol. 1, chaps. 12–15). Instead, the Legal Services Corporation has established a criterion of minimum access—two lawyers for every 10,000 poor people—and, as that goal has been approached, it has shifted its emphasis to the quality of the legal services furnished (Legal Services Corporation 1976–80; 1980, pp. 116–29; Bellow 1977; *Legal Services Corporation News*, October–November 1978; March–April 1979).

In the private sector, the barrier of cost has stimulated a number of responses. Among these are the exclusion from employee income for tax purposes of employer contributions to group legal service plans (Deitch and Weinstein 1976, pp. 29–31) and proposals to allow an income-tax deduction for personal legal expenses, similar to the present deductions for business legal expenses and personal medical expenses (Christensen 1970, pp. 71–73). Many lawyers offer free or below-cost initial consultations, which are now a commonplace in their advertising (cf. Royal Commission on Legal Services 1979, vol. 1, p. 134). Prepaid legal service plans dissociate payment and use. Finally, competition from legal clinics and from other occupations has led to substantial cost reductions.

Redistribution Mechanisms   A brief inventory of mechanisms for redistributing legal services is an essential foundation for comparison and evaluation. They usefully can be categorized by means of two variables—the source of funding and the number of participating lawyers. Government, of course, accounts for the greatest redistribution, acting, for the most part, through employees in the executive branches of federal, state, and local government (Ford et al. 1952; Schrag 1971, 1972)—including prosecutors

(Eisenstein 1978) and public defenders (Silverstein 1965; Etheridge 1970; Hermann et al. 1977; Wice 1978)—and, more recently, legal services lawyers and paraprofessionals. The budget of the latter has grown from less than $5 million before the creation of the OEO Legal Services Program in 1965 (Johnson 1974, p. 39) to more than $300 million at the end of the Carter Administration, when it supported a staff of more than 5,000 lawyers (*Legal Services Corporation News*, July–August 1980). The Reagan Administration, however, seeking to abolish the Legal Services Corporation entirely, succeeded in cutting its 1982 budget by one third (*Poverty Law Today*, Summer 1981). But government also engages in redistribution by reimbursing private lawyers for services they render to the poor. Court-appointed counsel represent accused criminals (Hermann et al. 1977). More recently, experimental judicare programs have begun to pay private lawyers to provide civil legal assistance (Brakel 1974, 1979; Legal Services Corporation 1980).

A second major source of redistribution is charity. Many lawyers do no pro bono work, and those who perform any services tend to provide cursory representation to very small numbers of clients. This philanthropic activity, in which any member of the bar can participate, recently has been supplemented by the emergence of public-interest law firms. Although such firms have antecedents in the ACLU and the NAACP Legal Defense and Education Fund (Casper 1972a; Council for Public Interest Law 1976, chap. 1; Tushnet 1982), which have been in existence for decades, public-interest law experienced a major expansion in the 1970s, as the Ford Foundation and others made substantial investments. At their height in the mid-1970s, there were perhaps 75–100 public-interest law firms, employing more than 500 lawyers, with a total budget in excess of $30 million (Council for Public Interest Law 1976, chap. 2; Handler et al. 1978b). But foundation support began to dwindle toward the end of that decade (Ford Foundation and ABA Special Committee 1976), and other sources of funding remain elusive (*Alyeska Pipeline Service Co.* v. *Wilderness Society* 1975; Settle and Weisbrod 1978).

Finally, some forms of redistribution do not require subsidization by either government or charity, depending instead on lawyers' efforts to reduce the cost of their services and to reach new clienteles (Engel 1977). There are now more than 100 legal clinics, some with dozens of offices (Maron 1978; Bodine 1979). Several million clients also are enrolled in group legal service plans; one study estimated that this figure could reach 10 to 20 million in the 1980s (Deitch and Weinstein 1976, p. 6).

The New Clients   In order to understand the significance of the shift in emphasis from supply control to demand creation, it is useful to pose many of the same questions addressed to earlier historical periods. The first concerns the new clients these services are designed to reach. Several characteristics distinguish them from the clienteles of traditional private-sector lawyers. Perhaps most important, they are almost exclusively individuals, whereas more than half the services of private lawyers are consumed by business associations (Laumann and Heinz 1979). The few exceptions—ethnic, religious, environmental, consumer, neighborhood, and other political groups represented by public-interest law firms (Weisbrod et al. 1978) and more rarely, by legal services offices (Handler et al. 1978a, chap. 3)—only serve to highlight the contrast. Furthermore, they are poorer, less educated, and more likely to belong to ethnic minorities and to be female than are the individual clients served by lawyers in traditional private practice (Fisher and Ivie 1971). This difference is more pronounced in legal services offices, however, than in clinics or group plans, and each delivery system tends to reach the more privileged within the category of potential clients.

These characteristics of clients clearly affect the identities, work, and careers of the lawyers who serve them. Those lawyers are accorded little prestige within the profession. The status of lawyers is determined largely by the status of their clients; poor individuals and major corporations obviously represent polar extremes. The legal problems of the former are defined as unimportant when measured in terms of the monetary value at stake (Katz 1978). Lawyers' status also varies inversely with the degree of involvement in personal problems and with the level of altruism expressed (Laumann and Heinz 1977, p. 180). The mere fact that these lawyers are publicly subsidized often implies—to their clients as well as to others—that they are less well qualified than are lawyers whose services must be bought on the market (Casper 1972b; Morris et al. 1973, p. 311). The income of these lawyers is low (Langer 1978), either because costs must be kept down, as in clinics (Downey 1977b) and group plans, or because public-sector salaries always are relatively depressed. One study estimated that, in 1975, public-interest lawyers earned $9,000 less a year, and legal services lawyers $18,000 less, than they would have made in the private sector (Komesar and Weisbrod 1978); the gap undoubtedly has widened since. Finally, these lawyers carry very heavy caseloads. Legal services attorneys handle 400 to 800 cases a year, compared with 50 to 100 for lawyers in private practice (Handler et al. 1978a, p. 62; cf. Stephens 1980).

Yet, despite their low status and income and difficult working conditions, such jobs are highly coveted. Whereas, before 1965, lawyers who were less qualified or were excluded from other legal careers by race and sex discrimination gravitated toward legal aid offices (Katz 1976), by the 1970s legal services and public-interest lawyers had become fairly representative of the bar as a whole (Erlanger 1978; Handler et al. 1978a, chap. 7). Often, they were better qualified than their counterparts in private practice (Ford Foundation 1973; Johnson 1974, p. 179). Although most were not particularly dedicated to social and political change before working in the public sector, the experience appears to have a radicalizing effect (Erlanger 1978), instilling an ideological commitment (Finman 1971) that keeps lawyers in public-interest jobs when they leave their first position after a few years (Katz 1978; Erlanger 1977; Handler et al. 1978a, chap. 8).

The fact that clients are relatively poor individuals, with isolated problems involving small amounts of money, influences not only careers in law but also the relationship between lawyers and clients. For the majority of lawyers in the private sector who represent businesses or wealthy individuals, relationships with clients tend to endure and to provide a continuous flow of legal work. The acquisition of new clients remains important, but it, too, is performed by lawyers—"rainmakers" in law firms—often through their connections with the general counsel of potential client corporations. By contrast, the market composed of individual clients who are not wealthy is un-rationalized, as was shown in the examination of sole practitioners, who rely heavily on lay intermediaries to channel both fee-generating and pro bono clients. Because the profession always has feared dominance by lay intermediaries, it has prohibited lawyers from paying for their services (ABA 1974, DR 2-103 [b]). But increasing reliance on a strategy of demand creation requires rationalization of the market for individual clients. Thus, large bureaucratic structures serve to aggregate and channel clients; this role is frequently performed by the laity or by lawyers who function more as bureaucrats or entrepreneurs. Examples of such structures include legal services, public defenders, clinics, and group plans (Schwartz 1980). Indeed, the last often is the creation of trade unions (Hapgood 1977). The growing role of intermediaries does much to transform the legal profession from autonomy toward heteronomy (Johnson 1972, chap. 3; Larson 1977, chap. 11).

This tendency toward heteronomy is accentuated by the fact that not only are clients individuals with one-shot problems, but they also are poor and therefore usually require subsidization. The source of the subsidy can exercise significant influence over which clients are served and what services are provided. When lawyers themselves subsidize their clients by rendering pro bono services, they may choose those clients who are likely to generate future paying business; they may seek to please intermediaries who can refer such business (Lochner 1975); they may refuse to render services liable to offend paying clients (Ashman 1972); they may reject clients who are unsympathetic or deviant (Maddi and Merrill 1971); or they may choose to provide a bare minimum of assistance (Lochner 1975; Handler et al. 1978a, chap. 5). When the adversary will bear the cost through court-awarded fees, the lawyer may accept only cases offering a high probability of success (*University of Pennsylvania Law Review* 1974). When it is the employer who subsidizes, through contributions to a union-sponsored group legal services plan, all labor-management disputes may be excluded (Marks et al. 1974; Deitch and Weinstein 1976, pp. 24–25). A group that supports a public-interest law firm may withdraw its funding if the firm engages in activities of which it disapproves (Handler et al. 1978a, pp. 11–12); and foundations always protect their tax-exempt status by insisting that law firms they support follow IRS guidelines and abstain from most political activity (Council for Public Interest Law 1976, p. 65).

Finally and most important, when government itself is paymaster, its control is pervasive. Thus, court-appointed counsel may conduct a relatively perfunctory criminal defense in order to avoid angering the judges who appoint them (but see Hermann et al. 1977, pp. 35–36). Public defenders also may be less than vigorous (Blumberg 1967; Gilboy and Schmidt 1979) from similar considerations. Before 1965, legal aid offices often categorically refused to handle both divorces, of which they disapproved on moral grounds, and bankruptcies, which business donors to the community chest resented (Johnson 1974, p. 10). And a suspicious and often hostile Congress has imposed many substantial restraints on the Legal Services Corporation, prohibiting its attorneys from engaging, or encouraging others to engage, in pickets, boycotts, strikes, or public demonstrations; seeking to influence legislation, initiatives, referenda, or executive orders; engaging in voter registration; representing the "voluntary" poor; representing minors without the consent of their parents; engaging in community organization; offering legal advice with respect to desegregation, abortion, or selective service; filing class actions against government entities; representing aliens; and promoting, defending, or protecting homosexuality (Legal Services Corporation Act of 1974; Legal Services Corporation Act of 1977; *Poverty Law Today*, Summer 1981).

The Professional Dilemma

The shift in strategy from supply control to demand creation aggravates a perennial professional dilemma. Supply control does not directly affect the preexisting market share of authorized producers; it simply precludes nonlawyers from offering those services and impedes entry into the profession. Demand creation, however, tends to result in the creation of demand for the services of particular lawyers, thereby intensifying competition and accelerating concentration. The legal profession as a whole strongly resists this tendency. Thus, it engaged in institutional advertising for years while prohibiting and inveighing against advertising by individual lawyers (ABA 1974, EC 2-2 and nn. 5–7; ABA Journal 1978, p. 1483). It continues to favor open-panel group legal service plans, which spread demand, over closed-panel plans, which concentrate it (Goodman 1979). Both the organized profession and lawyers in the lower strata have opposed the emergence and growth of legal clinics (Downey 1974, 1977a; Menkel-Meadow 1979). The base of the profession long fought the OEO Legal Services Program (Stumpf 1975), and when that battle was lost, it turned its energies toward promoting the concept of judicare (the law's equivalent of medicare). As a result, the Legal Services Corporation (1980) was mandated to study the relative merits of those two delivery systems among others and now is required to fund a program in every state, in which all members of the bar can participate (Poverty Law Today, Summer 1981).

Yet these efforts to inhibit competition, preserve the existing distribution of business, and allocate new business equally largely have failed. Generalized demand creation is ineffective; effective demand creation inevitably concentrates new business. Thus, institutional advertising has been abandoned, and only those lawyers who can invest heavily in individual advertising can profit from it (Cox et al. 1979; Muris and McChesney 1979). The vast majority of group legal service plans is closed—that is, clients are restricted to a single law firm (Deitch and Weinstein 1976, pp. 105–8)—and even those that are formally open channel clients to a relatively few lawyers (Marks et al. 1974, pp. 69–70). Lawyer referral services have begun to inform clients about lawyers' specialization and competence (Berg 1979), perhaps because they have been confronted with competition from private referral agencies (ABA Journal 1978, pp. 1481, 1483). Legal clinics have succeeded beyond anyone's expectations and now are organized into their own trade group, the American Legal Clinic Association. Even within judicare programs, many private lawyers turn down poverty clients (Brakel 1974, pp. 45–49; cf. Royal Commission on Legal Services 1979, vol. 1, pp. 520–21, 529). And judges display favoritism in appointing counsel in criminal and juvenile matters (Hermann et al. 1977, pp. 35–36). The tendency toward aggregation—whether attributable to bureaucratic convenience in the public sector or the desire to achieve economies of scale in the private sector—seems irresistible.

Mechanisms for creating demand also must be compared in terms of the services they render—subject matter, functions performed, and quality—and their cost. It should not be surprising that when cost is lowered—a major barrier to the use of lawyers—patterns of use remain largely unchanged; lawyers continue to offer, and new clients continue to request, the same services that lawyers previously had sold on the market (Mayhew 1975). Thus, traditional legal aid, both in the United States (Johnson 1974, chap. 1) and abroad (Cappelletti et al. 1975, pp. 33–58; Royal Commission on Legal Services 1979, vol. 1, chaps. 10–15), group legal services (Marks et al. 1974; Deitch and Weinstein 1976, pp. 42–45, 169–80), legal clinics (Muris and McChesney 1979; Menkel-Meadow 1979), judicare (Brakel 1974; Legal Services Corporation 1980, pp. 70–79), and pro bono services (Lochner 1975; Handler et al. 1978a, chap. 5), all represent clients in very conventional subjects, principally divorce and other family matters (Legal Services Corporation 1980, pp. 75–78). The functions they perform also are unexceptional. Negotiation is more common than litigation; when lawyers litigate, they rarely appeal adverse judgments (cf. Rathjen 1978); clients are individuals rather than groups; and virtually no effort is devoted to law reform test cases or to impact litigation (Legal Services Corporation 1980, pp. 136–43; Katz 1976; Bellow 1977; but see Cartwright et al. 1980).

Legal services offices, public-interest law firms, and politically committed private firms present a sharp contrast in both respects, handling many more cases dealing with income maintenance, housing, consumer finance, worker health and safety, race and sex discrimination, regulation, and the environment; they also emphasize law reform litigation, legislative lobbying, investigative reporting, organization, and political action (Legal Services Corporation 1980, pp. 75–78, 136–43; Byles and Morris 1977; Handler et al. 1978a, chaps. 3–4 and pp. 112–23; Komesar and Weisbrod 1978; Weisbrod et al. 1978; Abel 1980, pp. 390–91).

Differences in quality and cost are more ambiguous. There is evidence that the several mechanisms for delivering conventional legal services do not vary greatly in quality, whether this criterion is measured objectively, assessed by a panel of experts, or evaluated by the subjective satisfaction of clients (Gutek 1978; Legal Services Corporation 1980, pp. 119–29; Muris and McChesney 1979; Brakel 1974, chap. 7; Etheridge 1970, 1973; Casper 1972b). Rather, the most significant qualitative difference may be that some systems deliver only conventional legal services, whereas others use unconventional means as well, attacking the client's total problem—which may include the legal "solution" (Bellow 1977). The same problem of comparability confuses the issue of relative cost. Several studies have concluded that the cost per case falls within the same general range for each delivery system (Brakel 1974, chap. 8; Legal Services Corporation 1980, pp. 90–104; but see Cole and Greenberger 1973). Yet, if some systems are performing additional services at similar prices, they actually are more cost effective. And the fact that lawyers make a substantial financial sacrifice in working for legal services, public-interest law firms, or politically committed private law firms is further evidence that their services are provided at lower cost.

Legitimation   If the increasing emphasis on demand creation is largely a response to the imperative of market control, it also is part of the efforts of the profession to legitimate itself. All professionals are concerned about image—which, after all, is much of what differentiates them from other occupations. But lawyers seem unusually sensitive; both rank and file and leaders view public opinion as one of the most important problems, often the most important problem, facing the profession (*American Bar Association Journal* 1979, p. 40; Casey 1975; cf. Yankelovich et al. 1978; Sarat 1977). The redistribution of legal services clearly is an important means of legitimation, as witness the virtual unanimity with which lawyers and professional organizations supported the Legal Services Corporation against the attacks of the Reagan Administration. Yet it also introduces new problems for the profession, both external and internal.

The root of the external problem is the difficulty of justifying the redistribution. First, under capitalism, the public sector never has more than tenuous legitimacy (O'Connor 1973), as has been illustrated vividly by both the tax-cutting initiatives and the electoral and legislative victories of fiscal conservatives in the late 1970s and early 1980s. This generic problem is exacerbated by public suspicions of and hostility toward lawyers, whose services are seen as unnecessary at best and probably mischievous (Bloomfield 1980; Curran 1977, pp. 228–29). Just as welfare recipients are stereotyped as chiselers enjoying undeserved luxury, so there is a widespread belief that legal services to the poor are overgenerous, while the legal needs of the middle class go unserved (Cheatham 1963; Christensen 1970; Champagne 1976).

One reason for this critical attitude may be that the poor need legal services in crises that can be read as indicating moral dereliction—divorce, bankruptcy, eviction, criminal charges—whereas the need for medical care, housing, and education is shared with other classes and does not suggest moral turpitude. Evidence of this attitude can be found in the exclusion of felony defense from most group plans (Deitch and Weinstein 1976, p. 45) and of all criminal defense from the jurisdiction of the Legal Services Corporation, as well as in the requirement that the Corporation and other legal assistance programs seek to recover their costs from the recipients (*Poverty Law Today*, Summer 1981).

A related problem is posed by the need to maintain the appearance of political neutrality. The response—a series of restrictions on the Legal Services Corporation, on public-interest law firms, on group plans, and on pro bono services—seriously inhibits what those programs can do for their clients (see Royal Commission on Legal Services 1979, vol. 1, chap. 8).

This situation, in turn, leads to a second dilemma. The redistribution of legal services is both inspired and justified by the liberal ideal of equal justice—making the adversary system work fairly by providing each combatant with a professional ally (Cramton 1975, p. 1342; Royal Commission on Legal Services 1979, vol. 1, p. 51). Yet that ideal cannot be realized under capitalism, and present efforts do not even constitute a serious attempt to do so (see generally Abel 1979b).

Public-sector expenditures on legal services are trivial compared to those in the private sector, which is dominated by corporate clients and by wealthy individuals. At their peaks, the Legal Services Corporation represented approximately 1 percent and public-interest law 0.1 percent of private-sector staff and budgets; and the first two categories are declining, while the last is expanding. Relative resources are dramatically illustrated in another area. In the government's antitrust suit against AT&T, settled in 1982, the Justice Department devoted $12 million to its case, while the company spent $293 million on its defense (*Los Angeles Times*, July 2, 1981, pt. 4, p. 2). Furthermore, subsidized legal services are almost entirely reactive. Lawyers respond to clients' problems after the fact and seek to settle claims, litigating only as a last resort (Katz 1978). Private-sector lawyers, by contrast, spend much of their time counseling clients to anticipate problems and to use the law proactively to pursue their goals. It is inconceivable that government could subsidize lawyers for these latter purposes or that poor individuals could mobilize the law in this fashion (Abel 1979b). Finally, subsidization, whether by the state, charity, or lawyers themselves, imposes substantial constraints on how aggressive and politically active lawyers can be, whereas private-sector lawyers are entirely free from such constraints (see, for example, Goulden 1972; Green 1975). There is evidence that the public is aware of these problems and continues to view both the legal system and the legal profession as biased, notwithstanding the recent highly visible efforts at redistribution (Curran 1977, pp. 227–34; Sarat 1977; cf. Podgorecki et al. 1973).

But if the profession has not been entirely persuasive, it nevertheless has framed the terms of the debate over how equal justice might be attained. Implicit in any redistribution of legal services is the claim that some level of redistribution can achieve the ideal. Such a view is predicated on the beliefs that legal needs are experienced by individuals, not groups; that individuals need advocacy, not counseling; that the creation of rights is primary and enforcement secondary; and that procedural justice can and should be achieved without substantive (that is, social) justice. The focus on the redistribution of legal services distracts attention from the social, economic, and political structures that make redistribution necessary in the first place and that themselves would have to be radically transformed if redistribution were to achieve its proclaimed ends.

Increasing emphasis on demand creation through the redistribution of legal services also generates problems within the profession. First, it aggravates tension between the strata. Elite and base have different reasons for favoring redistribution. Elite lawyers are primarily concerned with legitimation, as shown by their preference for rendering pro bono services in the large, conspicuous case (Marks et al. 1972, chaps. 2–4; Ashman 1972); nonelite lawyers are moved more strongly by market considerations and see demand creation as alleviating the erosion of supply control (cf. Griffiths 1977, p. 268). This tension is visible in the controversies over mandatory pro bono (Association of the Bar 1979) and over advertising and solicitation (ABA Commission 1980, 1981). State subsidization of legal services also has divided the bar. Elite lawyers have enthusiastically supported its contribution to the ideal of equal justice; nonelite lawyers have feared competition, envied the status and security of salaried legal services lawyers, resented their youth and lifestyle, and become insecure about their own competence when confronted with aggressive adversaries, often for the first time (Champagne 1976, pp. 867–70; Stumpf 1975).

Reliance on demand creation introduces additional difficulties. It threatens supply control, which remains essential to the profession and a prerequisite for continuing demand creation. If lawyers create demand, especially by advertising, their professional distinctiveness is significantly diluted; and if they insist on the right of every citizen to legal representation, regardless of means, they no longer easily can reject the offer by nonlawyers to protect that right (Larson 1977, p. 39). Demand creation also intensifies competition within the profession, dividing advertisers from nonadvertisers, clinics and closed-panel group plans from sole practitioners and small firms. Despite professional efforts to establish mechanisms that allocate demand equally, concentration appears inevitable and progressively transforms a professional monopoly of small producers into an oligopoly of bureaucratized entrepreneurs. Finally, demand creation engenders more external regulation and a loss of professional autonomy. Advertising and solicitation are governed by detailed judicial standards; the acceptance of money from foundations subordinates lawyers to both their structures and those of the IRS; the structure of group plans is determined by unions, employers, and government; and state subsidization is accompanied by pervasive control.

The cumulative impact of these changes hardly can be exaggerated. The profession is becoming bifurcated into two unequal branches—lawyers serving business and the wealthy and lawyers serving nonwealthy individuals—that have less and less in common (cf. Reed 1921; Berle 1933; Carlin 1966). The second group is confronted with rising competition from other occupations and from paraprofessionals. Although its members undoubtedly will seek to preserve professional dominance (Green 1976), they are likely to lose substantial business. Lawyers serving individuals increasingly will be employees of large bureaucratic organizations; their work will be routinized; they will retain little autonomy; they will be stigmatized by the low status of their clients and the apparent triviality of the cases; there will be little scope for career advancement, except into the ranks of administration; pay will be low compared with that of lawyers serving business. It is likely that efforts at unionization, already common in the public sector (Kiersh 1979; *Los Angeles Lawyer* 1979; Zenor 1980; cf. Haug and Sussman 1971), will proliferate in response.

Thus, demand creation "solves" the problems of the legal profession only by creating others that appear even more intractable. In seeking to legitimate the redistribution of legal services, demand creation highlights the inescapably political nature of the work of those lawyers who respond to the demand thus stimulated—and by extension, the work of all lawyers. And in striving to strengthen market control, it threatens to deprive many lawyers of the professional status that is essential to such control.

CONCLUSION

Although often portrayed as a timeless phenomenon, the legal profession actually is of very recent origin. Its emergence is inextricably tied to the rise of capitalism and the expansion of the bourgeois state. Lawyers made themselves professionals by perfecting their control over the production of producers. Yet this form of market control—the foundation of the professional project—contains fundamental contradictions. The profession relies on the university to select entrants and to justify its exclusionary policies, but it thereby surrenders significant control over supply to the academy. It invokes a meritocratic ideology to explain the difficulty of entry and the method of allocating lawyers to professional roles and strata; but meritocracy will not persuade those who demand substantive equality, and it is particularly vulnerable to charges of bias concerning class, race, and gender. There appears to be a strong tendency for professions to push supply control too far, to the point where the extraordinary rewards of a professional career motivate aspirants to challenge, surmount, or circumvent the barriers to entry. And though control over the production of producers permits the profession to take the next step and seek to control production by producers, the latter is an internally divisive tactic and extremely difficult to justify publicly.

In recent years, the profession has sought to overcome these contradictions by turning to a second strategy of market control—demand creation. This strategy is permitted and encouraged by an ideological emphasis on individual rights and equality and by the rapid growth of the welfare state. But demand creation also has its costs and dilemmas. It renders lawyers dependent on the intermediaries who organize and channel individual clients and on the source of subsidization—the state or private philanthropy. The low status of clients and the "triviality" of their problems detracts from the respect to which lawyers are accustomed. Efforts to generate and to satisfy demand intensify competition within the profession and promote concentration. They also encourage other occupations—as well as potential clients—to seek to answer "legal needs," both because demand creation heightens awareness of those needs and because the requisite legal tasks are technically simple. Finally, just as there are limits to the control of supply, so there are inherent limits to the stimulation of demand. Individuals simply cannot be convinced that they need significant amounts of legal services; private philanthropy is fickle; and the commitment of the state to subsidizing demand is uncertain but clearly finite.

In order to become and remain professionals, lawyers have had to create, control, and rationalize their markets—first, the market offered by capital (competitive capital, monopoly capital, and the interaction of both with the regulatory state) and, more recently, the market for individual clients, whether or not subsidized by the state. In the process, the production of legal services has been fundamentally restructured. In both the private and the public sectors, productive units have expanded enormously, largely by increasing the numbers of lawyers and paraprofessionals they employ. Externally, these new productive entities are less likely to submit to professional regulation; internally, they are forced to substitute hierarchic and bureaucratic controls for collegial relationships. As a result, the production of legal services is progressively incorporated into capitalist relations of production and begins to display incipient class struggle. But, as the market for legal services is rationalized, it also increasingly is segmented; lawyers who serve capital and those who represent individuals differ in functions, organization, income, status, relations to clients, technical knowledge, and, ultimately, even ideology. As the previously white male profession becomes integrated, it seems probable that differences of race and gender will be superimposed on these lines of segmentation. As a result, a "unified" profession will splinter into distinct groupings, whose interests and perceptions frequently are antagonistic and which, therefore, find it more and more difficult to take concerted action.

These changes in the characteristics of lawyers and clients and their relations to each other have required the profession to develop new legitimations. Lawyers traditionally have presented themselves as autonomous professionals—the basis of their claim that they are morally unaccountable for the actions they take on behalf of clients. But, in fact, lawyers have become increasingly dependent on limited categories of clients—even on individual clients—and consciously have fostered this dependency. Dependence on capital was an essential precondition for the growth of large law firms, the rapid elevation of lawyers' incomes and status, and ultimately for most forms of public service—in government, in professional associations, and in pro bono activities. Dependence on the state has become the prerequisite for the creation and satisfaction of individual demand. Each form of dependence undermines the pretense of professional autonomy; lawyers for capital are too deferential to their clients, and lawyers for individuals are too overbearing and insensitive, or too mindful of the priorities of their paymasters. In order to justify their insulation from market forces and from state control, lawyers also have asserted that they can be, must be, and actually are self-regulating. But self-regulation has become an arena for intraprofessional struggle, often waged by rival professional associations. And professional dependence on capital and state carries with it the threat of greater external regulation, either as an adjunct of state efforts to control capital or as a concomitant of lawyers' reliance on public funds to subsidize service to individuals. Finally, the shift in emphasis from supply restriction to demand creation as a mechanism of market control has been justified by the ideal of equal justice. But that ideal is inconsistent with the commodification of justice under capitalism.

For little more than a century, lawyers have enjoyed an unusual degree of immunity from capitalist relations of production. In the name of professionalism, they have achieved considerable insulation from market forces, dampening competition among themselves and restricting external competition. They thereby have been enabled to take pride in the quality of their work without constantly seeking to maximize profits, and they have avoided the dehumanization associated with either performing wage labor or exploiting the labor of others—at least other lawyers. By successfully resisting state intervention, they have come close to realizing the laissez-faire ideal of liberalism. Yet these privileges are being drastically eroded. The lawyer of today (and perhaps even more of tomorrow) is an entrepreneur selling services in an increasingly competitive market, an employee whose labor is exploited and whose work is routinized and supervised, an employer exploiting subordinates. In each case, the lawyer increasingly is dependent upon state or capital for business and, therefore, increasingly subject to control by either or both. Although the ideal of professionalism undoubtedly will survive as an ever more anachronistic warrant of legitimacy, the profession as an economic, social, and political institution is moribund.

Cases Cited

Abrams v. United States, 250 U.S. 616, 624 (1919) (Holmes, J., dissenting).
Alyeska Pipeline Service Co. v. Wilderness Society, 421 U.S. 240 (1975).
Argersinger v. Hamlin, 407 U.S. 25 (1972).
Barton v. State Bar, 209 Cal. 678 (1930).
Bates v. State Bar of Arizona, 433 U.S. 350 (1977).
Consumers Union of United States v. American Bar Association, Civil Action No. 75-0105 (E.D. Va. 1975).
Cord v. Gibb, 219 Va. 1019 (1979).
Faretta v. California, 422 U.S. 806 (1975).
Gideon v. Wainwright, 372 U.S. 335 (1963).
Goldfarb v. Virginia State Bar, 421 U.S. 773 (1975).
Gordon v. Committee on Character and Fitness, 48 N.Y.2d 266 (1979).
In re Gault, 387 U.S. 1 (1967).
In re Griffiths, 413 U.S. 717 (1973).
In re Primus, 436 U.S. 412 (1978).
In re Smiley, 36 N.Y.2d 433 (1975).
Lassiter v. Department of Social Services, 452 U.S. 18 (1981).
Meltzer v. C. Buck LeCraw & Co., 402 U.S. 954 (1971).
Ohralik v. Ohio State Bar Association, 436 U.S. 447 (1978).
People v. Amor, 12 Cal.3d 20 (1974).
People v. Harrison, 118 Cal. App. 3d Supp. 1 (1981).
Regents of the University of California v. Bakke, 438 U.S. 265 (1978).
Scott v. Illinois, 440 U.S. 367 (1979).
Securities and Exchange Commission v. National Student Marketing Corp. (Commerce Clearing House 1977–78 Transfer Binder) Federal Securities Law Reporter, May 11, 1977, p. 91,598, par. 96,027.
Steingold v. Martindale-Hubbell, Civil Action No. C-72-1469-SW (N.D. Calif. 1972).
Supreme Court of Virginia v. Consumers Union of the United States, 446 U.S. 719 (1980).
Sweatt v. Painter, 339 U.S. 629 (1950).
Virginia State Board of Pharmacy v. Virginia Citizens Consumer Council, Inc., 426 U.S. 748 (1976).

Bibliography

Abbott, Andrew
    1983   "Professional Ethics." *American Journal of Sociology* 88:855–85.
Abel, Richard L.
    1973   "Law Books and Books About Law." *Stanford Law Review* 26:175–228.
    1979a   "The Rise of Professionalism." *British Journal of Law and Society* 6:82–98.
    1979b   "Socializing the Legal Profession: Can Redistributing Lawyers' Services Achieve Social Justice?" *Law & Policy Quarterly* 1:5–51.
    1980   "The Sociology of American Lawyers: A Bibliographic Guide." *Law & Policy Quarterly* 2:355–91.
    1981a   "A Critique of American Tort Law." *British Journal of Law and Society* 8:199–231.
    1981b   "Why Does the American Bar Association Promulgate Ethical Rules?" *Texas Law Review* 59:639–88.
    1981c   "Conservative Conflict and the Reproduction of Capitalism: The Role of Informal Justice." *International Journal of the Sociology of Law* 9:245–67.
    1981d   "Toward a Political Economy of Lawyers." *Wisconsin Law Review* 1981:1117–87.
    1982a   "The Contradictions of Informal Justice." In *The Politics of Informal Justice*, vol. 1: *The American Experience*, edited by Richard L. Abel. New York: Academic Press.
    1982b   "The Underdevelopment of Legal Professions: A Review Article on Third World Lawyers." *American Bar Foundation Research Journal* 1982:871–93.
    1985a   "Law without Politics: Legal Aid under Advanced Capitalism." *UCLA Law Review* 32:474–645.
    1985b   "Lawyers and the Power to Change." *Law & Policy* 7(1) (special issue).
    1985c   "Comparative Sociology of Legal Professions: A Preliminary Essay." *American Bar Foundation Research Journal* 1985:1–75.
    1986   "The Decline of Professionalism." *Modern Law Review* 49:1–41.
    1987   *Sociology of Lawyers in England and Wales.* Oxford: Basil Blackwell.
Abel, Richard L., and Lewis, Philip S.C., eds.
    1987–88 *Lawyers in Society: A Comparative Perspective,* 3 vols. Berkeley: University of California Press.
Abel-Smith, Brian, and Stevens, Robert
    1967   *Lawyers and the Courts: A Sociological Study of the English Legal System 1750–1965.* London: Heinemann.
Abel-Smith, Brian; Zander, Michael; and Brooke, Rosalind
    1973   *Legal Problems and the Citizen: A Study in Three London Boroughs.* London: Heinemann.
Alcock, P. C.
    1976   "Legal Aid: Whose Problem?" *British Journal of Law and Society* 3:151–74.
Alschuler, Albert W.
    1979   "Plea Bargaining and Its History." *Law & Society Review* 13:211–46.
American Bar Association
    1974   *Code of Professional Responsibility and Code of Judicial Conduct.* Chicago: American Bar Association.
American Bar Association, Commission on Evaluation of Professional Standards
    1980   *Model Rules of Professional Conduct* (discussion draft, January 30). Chicago: American Bar Association.
    1981   *Model Rules of Professional Conduct* (proposed final draft, May 30). Chicago: American Bar Association.

American Bar Association, Special Committee on Evaluation of Disciplinary Enforcement
    1970   *Problems and Recommendations in Disciplinary Enforcement* (Clark Report). Chicago:
            American Bar Association.

American Bar Association, Special Committee for a Study of Legal Education
    1980   *Law Schools and Professional Education: Report and Recommendations.* Chicago:
            American Bar Association.

American Bar Association Journal
    1977   "Unauthorized Practice: Trustbusters Eye A.B.A. U.P.L. Opinion." *American Bar
            Association Journal* 63:1702–03.

    1978   "F.T.C. Will Probe Legal Profession." *American Bar Association Journal* 64:33–34.

Anderson, Richard
    1978   *Representation in the Juvenile Court.* London: Routledge & Kegan Paul.

Antonides, John
    1978   "Minorities and the Bar Exam: Color Them Angry." *Juris Doctor,* August-September, pp. 56–59.

Arnould, R. J.
    1972   "Pricing Professional Services: A Case Study of the Legal Service Industry." *Southern Economic Journal* 38:495–507.

Arthurs, Harry W.
    1982   "Public Accountability of the Legal Profession." In *Law in the Balance: Legal Services in the Eighties,* edited by P. A. Thomas. Oxford: Martin Robertson.

Arthurs, H. W.; Willms, J.; and Taman, L.
    1971   "The Toronto Legal Profession: An Exploratory Survey." *University of Toronto Law Journal* 21:498–528.

Ashman, Alan
    1972   *The New Private Practice: A Study of Piper & Marbury's Neighborhood Law Office.*
            Chicago: National Legal Aid and Defender Association.

Association of the Bar of the City of New York
    1979   *Toward a Mandatory Contribution of Public Service Practice by Every Lawyer: Recommendations of a Special Committee on the Lawyer's Pro Bono Obligation.* New York:
            Association of the Bar of the City of New York.

Association of the Bar of the City of New York, Ad Hoc Committee on Grievance Procedures
    1976   *Report on the Grievance System* (Silverman Report). New York: Association of the
            Bar of the City of New York.

Association of the Bar of the City of New York, Special Committee on Professional Education and
    Admissions, and New York State Bar Association, Committee on Legal Education and
    Admission to the Bar
    1978   "The Character and Fitness Committees in New York State." *Record* 33:20–90.

Auerbach, Carl
    1970   "Reply to Mr. Nader." *Minnesota Law Review* 54:497.

Auerbach, Jerold S.
    1971   "Enmity and Amity: Law Teachers and Practitioners, 1900–1922." In *Law in
            American History,* edited by Donald Fleming and Bernard Bailyn. Perspectives in
            American History, vol. 5.

    1974   *Unequal Justice: Lawyers and Social Change in Modern America.* New York: Oxford
            University Press.

Aumann, Francis R.
    1940   *The Changing American Legal System: Some Selected Phases.* Columbus: Ohio State
            University Press.

Baird, Leonard J.
    1973   *The Graduates: A Report of the Characteristics and Plans of College Seniors.* Princeton,
            N.J.: Educational Testing Service.

1978   "A Survey of the Relevance of Legal Training to Law School Graduates." *Journal of Legal Education* 29:265–94.

Baird, Leonard J.; Carlson, Alfred B.; Reilly, Richard R.; and Powell, Ramon J.
1977   *Defining Competence in Legal Practice: The Evaluation of Lawyers in Large Firms and Organizations.* Princeton, N.J.: Educational Testing Service.

Baldwin, John, and McConville, Michael
1977   *Negotiated Justice: Pressures to Plead Guilty.* London: Martin Robertson.

Bankowski, Z., and Mungham, G.
1978   "A Political Economy of Legal Education." *New Universities Quarterly* 32:448–63.

Baraquin, Yves
1975   *Les Français et la justice civile: Enquête psychosociologique auprès des justiciables.* Paris: La Documentation Française.

Barlow, Andrew L.
1977   "Coordination and Control: The Transformation of Legal Education, 1870–1920." Unpublished manuscript.
1979   "Coordination and Control: The Rise of Harvard University: 1825–1910." Doctoral dissertation, Harvard University.

Barry, Donald D., and Berman, Harold J.
1968   "The Soviet Legal Profession." *Harvard Law Review* 82:1–21.

Barry, Kenneth, and Connelly, Patricia A.
1978   "Research on Law Students: An Annotated Bibliography." *American Bar Foundation Research Journal* 1978: 751–804.

Basten, John, and Disney, Julian
1977   "The Australian Legal Profession." Unpublished manuscript.

Bazelon, David T.
1969   *Nothing But a Fine Tooth Comb: Essays in Social Criticism 1944–1969.* New York: Simon and Schuster.

Becker, Howard S.; Geer, Blanche; Hughes, Everett C.; and Strauss, Anselm L.
1961   *Boys in White: Student Culture in Medical School.* Chicago: University of Chicago Press.

Becker, Jay
1978   "Multistatinal Law Firms." *Los Angeles Lawyer,* August, pp. 29, 48–49.

Beirne, Piers, and Quinney, Richard, eds.
1982   *Marxism and Law.* New York: Wiley.

Bellow, Gary
1977   "The Legal Aid Puzzle: Turning Solutions into Problems." *Working Papers for a New Society,* Spring, p. 52. (Also published in *National Legal Aid and Defender Association Briefcase* 34:106.)

Ben-David, J.
1963–64 "Professions in the Class System of Present Day Societies." *Current Sociology* 12:247–330.

Benthall-Nietzel, Deedra
1975   "An Empirical Investigation of the Relationship Between Lawyering Skills and Legal Education." *Kentucky Law Journal* 63:373.

Berg, Constance E.
1979   "Lawyer Referral Services." In *Legal Services for the Middle Class.* Chicago: American Bar Association.

Berger, John, and Mohr, Jean
1969   *A Fortunate Man.* Harmondsworth: Penguin.
[1967]

Berlant, Jeffrey L.
    1975   *Profession and Monopoly: A Study of Medicine in the United States and Great Britain.*
            Berkeley: University of California Press.
Berle, A. A., Jr.
    1933   "Legal Profession and Legal Education: Modern Legal Profession." *Encyclopedia of
            the Social Sciences* 9:340–46.
Bernstein, Peter W.
    1978   "The Wall Street Lawyers Are Thriving on Change." *Fortune*, March 13, pp. 104–
            12.
Blaine, William L.
    1976   *Where to Practice Law in California: Statistics on Lawyers' Work.* Berkeley: Continu-
            ing Legal Education of the Bar.
Blair, Roger D., and Rubin, Stephen, eds.
    1980   *Regulating the Professions: A Public-Policy Symposium.* Lexington, Mass.: Lexington
            Books.
Blake, Gene
    1978   "Lawyer Discipline Process Changes Little: New Lay Members Have Small Effect
            on State Bar System." *Los Angeles Times*, October 8, pt. 2, p. 1.
    1979   "Law Schools May Be Thinned: Bar Plans Move Against Unaccredited Institu-
            tions." *Los Angeles Times*, March 24, pt. 1, p. 26.
    1980   "Minority Group Members Score Lower Than Whites on State Bar Examination."
            Los Angeles Times, March 8, pt. 1, p. 2.
Blankenburg, Erhard, ed.
    1980   *Innovations in the Legal Services.* Königstein, West Germany: Verlag Anton Hain.
Blaustein, Albert P., and Porter, Charles D.
    1954   *The American Lawyer.* Chicago: University of Chicago Press.
Bledstein, Burton J.
    1976   *The Culture of Professionalism: The Middle Class and the Development of Higher
            Education in America.* New York: Norton.
Bloomfield, Maxwell
    1971   "Lawyers and Public Criticism: Challenge and Response in Nineteenth-Century
            America." *American Journal of Legal History* 15:269–77.
    1979   "The Texas Bar in the Nineteenth Century." *Vanderbilt Law Review* 32:261.
    1980   "Law and Lawyers in American Popular Culture." In Maxwell Bloomfield, John P.
            McWilliams, and Carl S. Smith, *Law and American Literature*. Chicago: American
            Bar Association.
Blumberg, Abraham S.
    1967   "The Practice of Law as a Confidence Game: Organizational Cooptation of a
            Profession." *Law & Society Review* 1:15–39.
Bodine, Larry
    1979   "Legal Clinics: The Bargain Bar." *National Law Journal* 1(22):1.
Boorstin, Daniel J.
    1958   *The Americans: The Colonial Experience.* New York: Random House.
Boreham, Paul; Pemberton, Alec; and Wilson, Paul, eds.
    1976   *The Professions in Australia: A Critical Appraisal.* Brisbane: University of Queens-
            land Press.
Bouwsma, William J.
    1973   "Lawyers and Early Modern Culture." *American Historical Review* 78:303–27.
Bower, Ward
    1980   "Law Firm Economics in the 1980's: Bigger—and Better?" *University of Toledo Law
            Review* 11:302–10.

Boyer, Barry, and Cramton, Roger
    1974   "American Legal Education: An Agenda for Research and Reform." *Cornell Law Review* 59:221.
Brakel, Samuel J.
    1974   *Judicare: Public Funds, Private Lawyers, and Poor People.* Chicago: American Bar Foundation.
    1979   "Judicare in West Virginia." *American Bar Association Journal* 65:1346–50.
Brickman, Lester
    1971   "Expansion of the Lawyering Process Through a New Delivery System: The Emergence and State of Legal Paraprofessionalism." *Columbia Law Review* 71:1153–1255.
    1978   "Is Law School a Full Time Enterprise?: Part Time Students and Part Time Teachers." *CLEPR Newsletter* 10(6).
Brosnahan, Roger P., and Andrews, Lori B.
    1980   "Regulation of Lawyer Advertising: In the Public Interest?" *Brooklyn Law Review* 46:423–36.
Brown, Elizabeth Gaspar
    1970   "The Bar on a Frontier: Wayne County, 1796–1836." *American Journal of Legal History* 14:136.
Brown, Esther L.
    1938   *Lawyers and the Promotion of Justice.* New York: Russell Sage Foundation.
Bucher, Rue, and Strauss, Anselm
    1961   "Professions in Process." *American Journal of Sociology* 66:325–34.
Burger, Warren
    1976   "Agenda for 2,000 A.D.—A Need for Systematic Anticipation." *Federal Rules Decisions* 70:79.
Byles, Anthea, and Morris, Pauline
    1977   *Unmet Need: The Case of the Neighbourhood Law Centre.* London: Routledge & Kegan Paul.
Cain, Maureen
    1976   "Necessarily Out of Touch: Thoughts on the Social Organisation of the Bar." In *The Sociology of Law,* edited by Pat Carlen. Keele: University of Keele. Sociological Review Monographs no. 23.
    1979   "The General Practice Lawyer and the Client: Towards a Radical Conception." *International Journal of the Sociology of Law* 7:331–54.
Calhoun, Daniel H.
    1965   "Branding Iron and Retrospect: Lawyers in the Cumberland River Country." In *Professional Lives in America: Structure and Aspiration, 1750–1850.* Cambridge, Mass.: Harvard University Press.
Cappell, Charles L.
    1980   "The Reproduction of Status Hierarchies Within the Legal Profession." Paper presented at the joint meeting of the Law and Society Association and the ISA Research Committee on the Sociology of Law, Madison, Wisconsin, June 5–8.
Cappell, Charles L., and Halliday, Terence C.
    1983   "Professional Projects of Elite Chicago Lawyers, 1950–1974." *American Bar Foundation Research Journal* 1983:291–340.
Cappelletti, Mauro, ed.
    1981   *Access to Justice and the Welfare State.* Alphen aan den Rijn: Sijthoff and Noordhoff.
Cappelletti, Mauro; Gordley, James; and Johnson, Earl, Jr.
    1975   *Toward Equal Justice: A Comparative Study of Legal Aid in Modern Societies.* Milan: Guiffrè; and Dobbs Ferry, N.Y.: Oceana.

Carlin, Jerome E.
  1962   *Lawyers on Their Own: A Study of Individual Practitioners in Chicago.* New Brunswick, N.J.: Rutgers University Press.
  1966   *Lawyers' Ethics: A Survey of the New York City Bar.* New York: Russell Sage Foundation.
Carlson, Alfred B., and Werts, Charles E.
  1976   *Relationship Among Law School Predictors, Law School Performance, and Bar Examination Results.* Princeton, N.J.: Educational Testing Service.
Carlson, Rick J.
  1976   "Measuring the Quality of Legal Services: An Idea Whose Time Has Not Come." *Law & Society Review* 11:287–318.
Carr-Saunders, A. M., and Wilson, P. A.
  1933   *The Professions.* Oxford: Clarendon Press.
Carrington, Paul D., and Conley, John J.
  1977   "The Alienation of Law Students." *Michigan Law Review* 75:887–99.
Carroll, Sidney L., and Gaston, Robert J.
  1977   *Occupational Licensing: Final Report.* Knoxville: University of Tennessee, College of Business Administration.
Cartwright, Bliss; Fiocco, J.; and Wallace, J.
  1980   "Resource Allocation in Legal Aid Lawyering: Re-examining the Hypothesis of Routine Client Services." Paper presented at the joint meeting of the Law and Society Association and the ISA Research Committee on the Sociology of Law, Madison, Wisconsin, June 5–8.
Casey, David S.
  1975   "President's Message: We Have Miles to Go, Much to Do." *California State Bar Journal* 50:455–56.
Casper, Jonathan D.
  1972a   *Lawyers Before the Warren Court: Civil Liberties and Civil Rights.* Urbana: University of Illinois Press.
  1972b   *American Criminal Justice: The Defendant's Perspective.* Englewood Cliffs, N.J.: Prentice-Hall.
Cass, Michael, and Sackville, Ronald
  1975   *Legal Needs of the Poor.* Canberra: Australian Government Publishing Service.
Champagne, Anthony M.
  1976   "Lawyers and Government Funded Legal Services." *Villanova Law Review* 21:860–75.
Cheatham, Eliot E.
  1963   *A Lawyer When Needed.* New York: Columbia University Press.
Chester, Ronald
  1985   *Unequal Access: Women Lawyers in a Changing America.* South Hadley, Mass.: Bergin & Garvey.
Christensen, Barlow F.
  1970   *Lawyers for People of Moderate Means.* Chicago: American Bar Foundation.
  1981   "The Lawyer's Pro Bono Publico Responsibility." *American Bar Foundation Research Journal* 1981:1.
Cocks, Raymond
  1983   *Foundations of the Modern Bar.* London: Sweet & Maxwell.
Cole, George F., and Greenberger, Howard L.
  1973   "Staff Attorneys vs. Judicare: A Cost Analysis." *Journal of Urban Law* 50:705–16.
Colvin, Selma; Stager, David; Taman, Larry; Yale, Janet; and Zemans, Frederick H.
  1978   *The Market for Legal Services, Paraprofessionals and Specialists.* Working paper no. 10. Toronto: Professional Organizations Committee.

Commission to Study the Bar Examination
  1975   "Final Report to the Board of Governors of the State Bar of California." Unpublished manuscript.
Committee to Consider Standards for Admission to Practice in the Federal Courts (Devitt Committee)
  1979   "Report." *Federal Rules Decisions* 79:187.
Condlin, Robert
  1981   "Clinical Legal Education and Instrumental Morality." Paper presented at the Legal Ethics Working Group of the Center for Philosophy and Public Policy, Washington, D.C., January 8–9.
Cooper, Jeremy
  1983   *Public Legal Services: A Comparative Study of Policy, Politics and Practice.* London: Sweet & Maxwell.
Council for Public Interest Law
  1976   *Balancing the Scales of Justice: Financing Public Interest Law.* Washington, D.C.: Council for Public Interest Law.
Couric, Emily, ed.
  1984   *Women Lawyers: Perspectives on Success.* New York: Harcourt Brace Jovanovich.
Cox, Steven R.; Canby, William C., Jr.; and Deserpa, Allan C.
  1979   *Legal Service Pricing and Advertising.* Tempe: Arizona State University.
Cramton, Roger C.
  1975   "The Task Ahead in Legal Services." *American Bar Association Journal* 61:1339.
  1978   "The Ordinary Religion of the Law School Classroom." *Journal of Legal Education* 29:247.
Curran, Barbara A.
  1977   *The Legal Needs of the Public: The Final Report of a National Survey.* Chicago: American Bar Foundation.
  1985   *The 1984 Lawyer Statistical Report.* Chicago: American Bar Foundation.
Curtis, Charles P.
  1951   "The Ethics of Advocacy." *Stanford Law Review* 4:2–23.
Danet, Brenda; Hoffman, Kenneth B.; and Kermish, Nicole C.
  1980   "Obstacles to the Study of Lawyer-Client Interaction: The Biography of a Failure." *Law & Society Review* 14:905–22.
Daniel J. Cantor & Co., Inc.
  1980   *Surveys on Compensation and Economics: 14th Annual for Private Law Firms.* Philadelphia: Daniel J. Canton & Co., Inc.
Day, Alan F.
  1973   "Lawyers in Colonial Maryland, 1660–1715." *American Journal of Legal History* 17:145.
Deitch, Lillian, and Weinstein, David
  1976   *Prepaid Legal Services: Socioeconomic Impacts.* Lexington, Mass.: Lexington Books.
Diamond, S. J.
  1981   "Chain Stores Find Profit in Services: Lawyers, Dentists." *Los Angeles Times,* August 12, pt. 1, p. 1.
Dias, Clarence J.; Luckham, Robin A.; Lynch, Dennis O.; and Paul, James C. N.
  1981   *Lawyers in the Third World: Comparative and Social Perspectives.* Uppsala: Scandinavian Institute of African Studies.
Dingwall, Robert, and Lewis, Philip, eds.
  1983   *The Sociology of the Professions: Lawyers, Doctors and Others.* London: Macmillan.
Downey, Charles E.
  1974   "The Price Is Right—For Everyone But the California Bar." *Juris Doctor,* June, pp. 31–33.

1977a   "Killing Off the Competition." *Juris Doctor*, October, pp. 29–33.

1977b   "Clinics: The State of the Art." *Juris Doctor*, September, pp. 21–25.

Duman, Daniel
1983   *The English and Colonial Bars in the Nineteenth Century.* London: Croom Helm.

Eaton, Clement
1951   "A Mirror of the Southern Lawyer: The Fee Books of Patrick Henry, Thomas Jefferson, and Waightstill Avery." *William and Mary Quarterly* (3rd series) 8:520.

Edelman, Murray
1974   "The Political Language of the Helping Professions." *Politics and Society* 4:295–310.

Eisenstein, James
1978   *Counsel for the United States: U.S. Attorneys in the Political and Legal Systems.* Baltimore: Johns Hopkins University Press.

Elliott, Philip
1972   *The Sociology of the Professions.* New York: Herder and Herder.

Ely, James
1973   "American Independence and the Law: A Study of Post-Revolutionary South Carolina Legislation." *Vanderbilt Law Review* 26:929.

Engel, David M.
1977   "The Standardization of Lawyers' Services." *American Bar Foundation Research Journal* 1977:817–44.

Epstein, Cynthia Fuchs
1981   *Women in Law.* New York: Basic Books.

Erikson, Kai T.
1966   *Wayward Puritans: A Study in the Sociology of Deviance.* New York: Wiley.

Erlanger, Howard S.
1977   "Social Reform Organizations and Subsequent Careers of Participants: A Follow-up Study of Early Participants in the OEO Legal Services Program." *American Sociological Review* 42:233–48.

1978   "Lawyers and Neighborhood Legal Services: Social Background and Impetus for Reform." *Law & Society Review* 12:253–74.

1980   "The Allocation of Status Within Occupations: The Case of the Legal Profession." *Social Forces* 58:882–903.

Erlanger, Howard S., and Klegon, Douglas A.
1978   "Socialization Effects of Professional School: The Law School Experience and Student Orientations to Public Interest Concerns." *Law & Society Review* 13:11–35.

Etheridge, Carolyn E.
1970   "Conflict and Negotiation Processes: The Emergence of the Public Defender Office Within the Legal Profession." Doctoral dissertation, University of Washington.

1973   "Lawyers Versus Indigents: Conflict of Interest in Professional-Client Relations in the Legal Profession." In *The Professions and Their Prospects,* edited by Eliot Freidson. Beverly Hills: Sage.

Evans, Robert G., and Trebilcock, Michael J., eds.
1982   *Lawyers and the Consumer Interest: Regulating the Market for Legal Services.* Toronto: Butterworths.

Fair, Daryl R., and Moskowitz, David H.
1975   "The Lawyer's Role: Watergate as Regularity Rather than Aberration." *Journal of Contemporary Law* 2:75–81.

Fennell, Phil
1980   "Solicitors, Their Markets and Their 'Ignorant Public': The Crisis of the Profes-

sional Ideal." In *Essays in Law and Society*, edited by Zenon Bankowski and Geoff Mungham. London: Routledge & Kegan Paul.

1982   "Advertising: Professional Ethics vs. Public Interest—From Ambulance Chasing to Saatchi & Saatchi." In *Law in the Balance: Legal Services in the Eighties*, edited by P. A. Thomas. Oxford: Martin Robertson.

Finman, Ted
1971   "OEO Legal Services Programs and the Pursuit of Social Change: The Relationship Between Program Ideology and Program Performance." *Wisconsin Law Review* 1971:1101.

First, Harry
1976   "Legal Education and the Law School of the Past: A Single-Firm Study." *University of Toledo Law Review* 8:135–67.

1978   "Competition in the Legal Education Industry (1)." *New York University Law Review* 53:311–401.

Fisher, Kenneth P., and Ivie, Charles C.
1971   *Franchising Justice: The Office of Economic Opportunity Legal Services Program and Traditional Legal Aid*. Chicago: American Bar Foundation.

Fishman, James J., and Kaufman, Anthony S., eds.
1975   *Practicing Law in New York City*. New York: Council of Law Associates.

Flaherty, David H., ed.
1969   *Essays in the History of Early American Law*. Chapel Hill: University of North Carolina Press.

Flood, John A.
1983   *Barristers' Clerks: The Law's Middlemen*. Manchester: Manchester University Press.

Ford, Peyton; Reich, David; and Palmer, Clive W.
1952   *The Government Lawyer: A Survey and Analysis of Lawyers in the Executive Branch of the United States Government*. Englewood Cliffs, N.J.: Prentice-Hall.

Ford Foundation
1973   *The Public Interest Law Firm: New Voices for New Constituencies*. New York: Ford Foundation.

Ford Foundation and American Bar Association Special Committee on Public Interest Practice
1976   *Public Interest Law: Five Years Later*. Chicago: American Bar Association; and New York: Ford Foundation.

Fossum, Donna
1978   "Law School Accreditation Standards and the Structure of American Legal Education." *American Bar Foundation Research Journal* 1978:515–44.

1980a   "Law Professors: A Profile of the Teaching Branch of the Legal Profession." *American Bar Foundation Research Journal* 1980:501–54.

1980b   "Women Law Professors." *American Bar Foundation Research Journal* 1980:903–14.

Foster, James C.
1981   "The 'Cooling Out' of Law Students: Facilitating Market Cooptation of Future Lawyers." *Law & Policy Quarterly* 3:243–56.

Frank, Jerome
1933   "Why Not a Clinical Lawyer School?" *University of Pennsylvania Law Review* 81:907.

1947   "A Plea for Lawyer-Schools." *Yale Law Journal* 56:1303.

Freidson, Eliot
1970   *Profession of Medicine: A Study of the Sociology of Applied Knowledge*. New York: Harper & Row.

Fried, Charles
1976   "The Lawyer as Friend: The Moral Foundations of the Lawyer-Client Relationship." *Yale Law Journal* 85:1060.

Friedman, Lawrence M.
    1965   "Freedom of Contract and Occupational Licensing 1890–1910: A Legal and Social Study." *California Law Review* 53:487–534.
    1973   *A History of American Law.* New York: Simon and Schuster.
    1979   "Plea Bargaining in Historical Perspective." *Law & Society Review* 13:247–60.
Friedman, Lawrence M., and Zile, Zigurd S.
    1964   "The Soviet Legal Profession." *Wisconsin Law Review* 1964:32.
Friedman, Milton
    1962   "Occupational Licensure." In *Capitalism and Freedom.* Chicago: University of Chicago Press.
Friedman, Milton, and Kuznets, Simon
    1945   *Income from Independent Professional Practice.* New York: National Bureau of Economic Research.
Gabel, Peter, and Harris, Paul
    1982–83 "Building Power and Breaking Images: Critical Legal Theory and the Practice of Law." *New York University Review of Law and Social Change* 11:369–411.
Galanter, Marc
    1974   "Why the 'Haves' Come Out Ahead: Speculations on the Limits of Legal Change." *Law & Society Review* 9:95–160.
    1976   "The Duty Not to Deliver Legal Services." *University of Miami Law Review* 30:929.
    1983   "Larger Than Life: Mega-law and Mega-lawyering in the Contemporary United States." In *The Sociology of the Professions: Lawyers, Doctors, and Others,* edited by R. Dingwall and P. S. C. Lewis. London: Macmillan.
Galvin, Dallas
    1976   "Taming the Lions in the Street with Title VII." *Juris Doctor,* September, pp. 8–9.
Gardner, John
    1972   *The Sunlight Dialogues.* New York: Ballantine Books.
Garth, Bryant
    1980   *Neighborhood Law Firms for the Poor: A Comparative Study of Recent Developments in Legal Aid and in the Legal Profession.* Alphen aan den Rijn: Sijthoff & Noordhoff.
Garth, Bryant, ed.
    1983   "Research on Legal Services for the Poor and Disadvantaged: Lessons from the Past and Issues for the Future." Working paper no. 11, Disputes Processing Research Program, University of Wisconsin Law School.
Gawalt, Gerard W.
    1969   "Massachusetts Lawyers: A Historical Analysis of the Process of Professionalization, 1760–1840." Doctoral dissertation, Clark University.
    1970   "Sources of Anti-Lawyer Sentiment in Massachusetts, 1740–1840." *American Journal of Legal History* 14:283–307.
    1979   *The Promise of Power: The Emergence of the Legal Profession in Massachusetts 1760–1840.* Westport, Conn.: Greenwood Press.
    1984   *The New High Priests: Lawyers in Post-Civil War America.* Westport, Conn.: Greenwood Press.
Gee, E. Gordon
    1977   "Trends in Clinical Legal Education: 1970–76." *CLEPR Newsletter* 9(4).
Gee, E. Gordon, and Jackson, Donald W.
    1975   *Following the Leader? The Unexamined Consensus in Law School Curricula.* New York: Council for Legal Education in Professional Responsibility.
Gilboy, Janet A., and Schmidt, John R.
    1979   "Replacing Lawyers: A Case Study of the Sequential Representation of Criminal Defendants." *Journal of Criminal Law and Criminology* 70:1–26.

Gilson, Ronald J.
1984 "Value Creation by Business Lawyers: Legal Skills and Asset Pricing." *Yale Law Journal* 94:239.

Glennon, Robert Jerome
1979 " 'Principles Are What Principles Do': Lawyers in the New Deal." Unpublished manuscript.

Goodman, James T.
1979 "Development of Prepaid Legal Service Plans." In *Legal Services for the Middle Class*. Chicago: American Bar Association.

Gordon, Robert W.
1980 "Legal Thought and Legal Practice in the Age of American Enterprise, 1870–1920: Towards an 'Ideological' Approach to Legal History." Unpublished manuscript.

Goulden, Joseph C.
1972 *The Superlawyers: The Small and Powerful World of the Great Washington Law Firms.* New York: Weybright & Talley.

Gouldner, Alvin W.
1979 *The Future of Intellectuals and the Rise of the New Class.* New York: Seabury Press.

Gower, L. C. B., and Price, Leolin
1957 "The Profession and Practice of Law in England and America." *Modern Law Review* 20:317–46.

Green, Mark J.
1975 *The Other Government: The Unseen Power of Washington Lawyers.* New York: Grossman.
1976 "The ABA as Trade Association." In *Verdicts on Lawyers*, edited by Ralph Nader and Mark Green. New York: Grossman.

Green, Wayne E.
1976 "You've Never Noticed Paralegals? Look Closer." *Juris Doctor*, February, pp. 40–46.

Griffiths, John
1977 "The Distribution of Legal Services in the Netherlands (review of K. Schuyt et al., *De Weg Naar Het Recht*)." *British Journal of Law and Society* 4:260–86.
1980 "A Comment on Research into 'Legal Needs.' " In *Innovations in the Legal Services*, edited by Erhard Blankenburg. Königstein, West Germany: Verlag Anton Hain.

Grossblat, Martha, and Sikes, Bette H., eds.
1973 *Women Lawyers: Supplementary Data to the 1971 Lawyer Statistical Report.* Chicago: American Bar Foundation.

Gutek, Barbara A.
1978 "Strategies for Studying Client Satisfaction." *Journal of Social Issues* 34:44–56.

Habenstein, R. W.
1963 "A Critique of 'Profession' as a Sociological Category." *Sociological Quarterly* 4:291–300.

Haller, Mark H.
1979 "Plea Bargaining: The Nineteenth Century Context." *Law & Society Review* 13:273–80.

Halliday, Terence C.
1982 "The Idiom of Legalism in Bar Politics: Lawyers, McCarthyism, and the Civil Rights Era." *American Bar Foundation Research Journal* 1982:911–88.

Halliday, Terence C., and Cappell, Charles L.
1979 "Indicators of Democracy in Professional Associations: Elite Recruitment, Turnover, and Decision Making in a Metropolitan Bar Association." *American Bar Foundation Research Journal* 1979:697–767.

Halliday, Terence C., and Powell, Michael J.
    1977   "The Legal Association and the Organizational Mediation of Social Change."
            Paper presented at the annual meeting of the American Sociological Association,
            August.
Handler, Joel F.
    1967   *The Lawyer and His Community.* Madison: University of Wisconsin Press.
    1978   *Social Movements and the Legal System.* New York: Academic Press.
Handler, Joel F.; Ginsberg, Betsy; and Snow, Arthur.
    1978a   "The Public Interest Law Industry." In *Public Interest Law: An Economic and Institu-
            tional Analysis,* edited by Burton A. Weisbrod, Joel F. Handler, and Neil K.
            Komesar. Berkeley: University of California Press.
Handler, Joel F.; Hollingsworth, Ellen Jane; and Erlanger, Howard S.
    1978b   *Lawyers and the Pursuit of Legal Rights.* New York: Academic Press.
Hapgood, David
    1977   "Will Prepaid Be Labor's Lost Love?" *Juris Doctor,* July-August, pp. 10–11.
Harris, Michael H.
    1972   "The Frontier Lawyer's Library: Southern Indiana, 1800–1850, as a Test Case."
            American Journal of Legal History 16:239.
Hart, H. L. A.
    1962   *The Concept of Law.* Oxford: Clarendon Press.
Harvard Law Review
    1967   "Note: Neighborhood Law Offices: The New Wave in Legal Services for the Poor."
            Harvard Law Review 80:805.
    1970   "Note: Structuring the Public Service Efforts of Private Law Firms." *Harvard Law
            Review* 84:410.
Haug, Marie R., and Sussman, Marvin B.
    1969   "Professional Autonomy and the Revolt of the Client." *Social Problems* 17:153–61.
    1971   "Professionalization and Unionism: A Jurisdictional Dispute?" In *Professions in
            Contemporary Society,* edited by Eliot Freidson. *American Behavioral Scientist* 14:89–
            104 (special issue).
Hauser, Philip M.
    1976   "Demographic Changes and the Legal System." In *Law and the American Future,*
            edited by Murray L. Schwartz. Englewood Cliffs, N.J.: Prentice-Hall.
Hedegard, James M.
    1979   "The Impact of Legal Education: An In-depth Examination of Career-Relevant
            Interests, Attitudes, and Personality Traits Among First-Year Law Students."
            American Bar Foundation Research Journal 1979:791–868.
    1982   "Causes of Career-Relevant Interest Changes Among First-Year Law Students:
            Some Research Data." *American Bar Foundation Research Journal* 1982:787–867.
Heinz, John P., and Laumann, Edward O.
    1978   "The Legal Profession: Client Interests, Professional Roles, and Social Hierar-
            chies." *Michigan Law Review* 76:1111–42.
    1982   *Chicago Lawyers: The Social Structure of the Bar.* New York: Russell Sage Founda-
            tion; and Chicago: American Bar Foundation.
Heinz, John P.; Laumann, Edward O.; Cappell, Charles L.; Halliday, Terence C.; and Schaal-
    man, Michael H.
    1976   "Diversity, Representation, and Leadership in an Urban Bar: A First Report on a
            Survey of the Chicago Bar." *American Bar Foundation Research Journal* 1976:717.
Hermann, Robert; Single, Eric; and Boston, John
    1977   *Counsel for the Poor: Criminal Defense in Urban America.* Lexington, Mass.: Lexing-
            ton Books.

Hetherton, Margaret
    1978   *Victoria's Lawyers: First Report.* Melbourne: Victoria Law Foundation.
    1981   *Victoria's Lawyers: Second Report.* Melbourne: Victoria Law Foundation.

Hochberg, Jerome A.
    1976   "The Drive to Specialization." In *Verdicts on Lawyers,* edited by Ralph Nader and Mark Green. New York: Crowell.

Hoffman, Paul
    1973   *Lions in the Street: The Inside Story of the Great Wall Street Law Firms.* New York: Saturday Review Press.
    1982   *Lions of the Eighties: The Inside Story of the Powerhouse Law Firms.* Garden City, N.Y.: Doubleday.

Holen, A. S.
    1965   "Effects of Professional Licensing Arrangements on Interstate Labor Mobility and Resource Allocation." *Journal of Political Economy* 73:492–98.

Horwitz, Morton J.
    1977   *The Transformation of American Law, 1780–1860.* Cambridge, Mass.: Harvard University Press.

Hosticka, Carl J.
    1979   "We Don't Care About What Happened, We Only Care About What Is Going to Happen: Lawyer-Client Negotiations of Reality." *Social Problems* 26:599–610.

Hunting, Roger B., and Neuwirth, Gloria S.
    1962   *Who Sues in New York City? A Study of Automobile Accidents.* New York: Columbia University Press.

Hurst, James Willard
    1950   *The Growth of American Law: The Law Makers.* Boston: Little, Brown.

Illich, Ivan
    1977   "Disabling Professions." In Ivan Illich et al., *Disabling Professions.* London: Marion Boyars.

Illinois State Bar Association
    1975   "Economics of Legal Services in Illinois." *Illinois Bar Journal* 1975 (October):73–134.

International Legal Center
    1974   *Legal Aid and World Poverty: A Survey of Asia, Africa, and Latin America.* New York: Praeger.

Irons, Peter H.
    1982   *The New Deal Lawyers.* Princeton, N.J.: Princeton University Press.

Jamous, H., and Peloille, B.
    1970   "Changes in the French University-Hospital System." In *Professions and Professionalization,* edited by J. A. Jackson. Cambridge: Cambridge University Press.

Johnson, Earl, Jr.
    1974   *Justice and Reform: The Formative Years of the OEO Legal Services Program.* New York: Russell Sage Foundation.

Johnson, Terence J.
    1972   *Professions and Power.* London: Macmillan.
    1977   "The Professions in the Class Structure." In *Industrial Society: Class, Cleavage and Control,* edited by Richard Scase. London: George Allen & Unwin.

Johnstone, Quintin, and Flood, John
    1980   "Unadmitted Personnel in English and American Law Offices." Paper presented at the Conference on Legal Services in the 80s, University College, Cardiff, March.

Johnstone, Quintin, and Hopson, Don, Jr.
    1967   *Lawyers and Their Work: An Analysis of the Legal Profession in the United States and England.* Indianapolis: Bobbs-Merrill.

Kairys, David, ed.
    1982   *The Politics of Law.* New York: Pantheon.

Katz, Alan N., and Denbeaux, Mark P.
    1976   "Trust, Cynicism, and Machiavellianism Among Entering First-Year Law Students." *Journal of Urban Law* 53:397.

Katz, Jack
    1976   "Routine and Reform: A Study of Personal and Collective Careers in Legal Aid." Doctoral dissertation, Northwestern University.

    1978   "Lawyers for the Poor in Transition: Involvement, Reform, and the Turnover Problem in the Legal Services Program." *Law & Society Review* 12:275–300.

    1982   *Poor People's Lawyers in Transition.* New Brunswick, N.J.: Rutgers University Press.

Kay, Susan Ann
    1978   "Socializing the Future Elite: The Nonimpact of a Law School." *Social Science Quarterly* 59:347.

Kelso, Charles D.
    1972   *The AALS Study of Part-Time Legal Education.* Washington, D.C.: Association of American Law Schools.

Kennedy, Duncan
    1970   "How the Law School Fails: A Polemic." *Yale Review of Law and Social Action* 1:71.

    1983   *Legal Education and the Reproduction of Hierarchy: A Polemic Against the System.* Cambridge, Mass.: Afar.

Kiersh, Ed
    1979   "Seeking a Better Deal: Why Legal Staffs Are Organizing." *Juris Doctor,* February-March, pp. 26–27.

Kinoy, Arthur
    1983   *Rights on Trial: The Odyssey of a People's Lawyer.* Cambridge, Mass.: Harvard University Press.

Klein, Milton M.
    1958   "The Rise of the New York Bar: The Legal Career of William Livingston." *William and Mary Quarterly* (3rd series) 15:334.

    1974   "New York Lawyers and the Coming of the American Revolution." *New York History* 55:383.

Knauss, Robert L.
    1976   "Developing a Representative Legal Profession." *American Bar Association Journal* 62:591.

Kogan, Herman
    1974   *The First Century: The Chicago Bar Association, 1874–1974.* Chicago: Rand McNally.

Komesar, Neil K., and Weisbrod, Burton A.
    1978   "The Public Interest Law Firm: A Behavioral Analysis." In *Public Interest Law: An Economic and Institutional Analysis,* edited by Burton A. Weisbrod, Joel F. Handler, and Neil K. Komesar. Berkeley: University of California Press.

Kronus, Carol L.
    1976   "The Evolution of Occupational Power: An Historical Study of Task Boundaries Between Physicians and Pharmacists." *Sociology of Work and Occupations* 3(1):3–37.

Ladinsky, Jack
    1976   "The Traffic in Legal Services: Lawyer-Seeking Behavior and the Channeling of Clients." *Law & Society Review* 11:207–24.

Landon, Donald D.
    1982   "Lawyers and Localities: The Interaction of Community Context and Professionalism." *American Bar Foundation Research Journal* 1982:459–85.

Langer, Steven
    1978   "Salary Survey." *Juris Doctor*, August-September, pp. 23–27.

Larson, Magali Sarfatti
    1977   *The Rise of Professionalism: A Sociological Analysis.* Berkeley: University of California Press.

Laumann, Edward O., and Heinz, John P.
    1977   "Specialization and Prestige in the Legal Profession: The Structure of Deference." *American Bar Foundation Research Journal* 1977:155–216.

    1979   "The Organization of Lawyers' Work: Size, Intensity, and Co-Practice of the Fields of Law." *American Bar Foundation Research Journal* 1979:217–46.

Law and Human Behavior
    1983   "Professional Regulation." *Law and Human Behavior* 7(2/3) (special issue).

Law & Society Review
    1979   "Plea Bargaining." *Law & Society Review* 13:189–687 (special issue).

Leat, Diana
    1975   "The Rise and Role of the Poor Man's Lawyer." *British Journal of Law and Society* 2:166–81.

Leffler, Keith B.
    1978   "Physician Licensure: Competition and Monopoly in American Medicine." *Journal of Law and Economics* 21:165–86.

Legal Services Corporation
    1976–80 *Annual Reports.* Washington, D.C.: Legal Services Corporation.

    1980   *The Delivery Systems Study: A Policy Report to the Congress and the President of the United States.* Washington, D.C.: Legal Services Corporation.

Lemert, Edwin
    1976   "Choice and Change in Juvenile Justice." *British Journal of Law and Society* 3:59–75.

Levine, Felice J., and Preston, Elizabeth
    1970   "Community Resource Orientation Among Low Income Groups." *Wisconsin Law Review* 1970:80–113.

Lewis, Philip
    1973   "Unmet Legal Needs." In Pauline Morris, Richard White, and Philip Lewis, *Social Needs and Legal Action.* London: Martin Robertson.

Liebowitz, Arleen, and Tollison, Robert
    1978   "Earning and Learning in Law Firms." *Journal of Legal Studies* 7:65–81.

Lochner, Phillip R., Jr.
    1975   "The No-Fee and Low-Fee Legal Practice of Private Attorneys." *Law & Society Review* 9:431–73.

Los Angeles Lawyer
    1979   "Public Attorneys Sing the Union Song." *Los Angeles Lawyer*, April, p. 10.

Luban, David
    1981   *The Adversary System Excuse.* Working paper LE-1. College Park: University of Maryland, Center for Philosophy and Public Policy.

Luban, David, ed.
    1983   *The Good Lawyer: Lawyers' Roles and Lawyers' Ethics.* Totowa, N.J.: Rowman & Allanheld.

Lynch, Dennis O.
    1981   *Legal Roles in Columbia.* Uppsala: Scandinavian Institute of African Studies; and New York: International Center for Law in Development.

Macaulay, Stewart
    1963   "Non-Contractual Relations in Business: A Preliminary Study." *American Sociological Review* 28:55.

1979   "Lawyers and Consumer Protection Laws." *Law & Society Review* 14:115–51.

McKean, Dayton
1963   *The Integrated Bar.* Boston: Houghton Mifflin.

McKnight, John
1977   "Professionalized Service and Disabling Help." In Ivan Illich et al., *Disabling Professions.* London: Marion Boyars.

McKurdy, Charles R.
1972   "A Bar Divided: The Lawyers of Massachusetts and the American Revolution." *American Journal of Legal History* 16:205.

1976   "Before the Storm: The Working Lawyer in Pre-Revolutionary Massachusetts." *Suffolk University Law Review* 11:46.

Maddi, Dorothy L., and Merrill, Frederic R.
1971   *The Private Practicing Bar and Legal Services for Low-Income People.* Chicago: American Bar Foundation.

Mallen, Ronald E., and Levit, Victor B.
1977   *Legal Malpractice.* St. Paul, Minn.: West.

Margolis, Harry
1972   "The Wonderland of Tax Law." In *The Relevant Lawyers,* edited by Ann Fagan Ginger. New York: Simon and Schuster.

Marks, F. Raymond
1976   "Some Research Perspectives for Looking at Legal Need and Legal Services Delivery Systems: Old Forms or New?" *Law & Society Review* 11:191–205.

Marks, F. Raymond, and Cathcart, Darlene
1974   "Discipline Within the Legal Profession: Is It Self-Regulation?" *Illinois Law Forum* 1974:193.

Marks, F. Raymond; Hallauer, Robert Paul; and Clifton, Richard P.
1974   *The Shreveport Plan: An Experiment in the Delivery of Legal Services.* Chicago: American Bar Foundation.

Marks, F. Raymond; Leswing, Kirk; and Fortinsky, Barbara A.
1972   *The Lawyer, the Public and Professional Responsibility.* Chicago: American Bar Foundation.

Maron, Davida
1978   *Legal Clinics: Analysis and Survey.* 2nd ed. Washington, D.C.: National Resource Center for Consumers of Legal Services.

Martin, George
1970   *Causes and Conflicts: The Centennial History of the Bar Association of the City of New York, 1870–1970.* Boston: Houghton Mifflin.

Marx, Karl
1977   *Capital.* Vol. 1. Translated by Ben Fowkes. New York: Random House.
[1867]

May, Judith V.
1976   *Professionals and Clients: A Constitutional Struggle.* Beverly Hills: Sage.

Mayer, Milton
1967   *The Lawyers.* New York: Harper & Row.

Mayhew, Leon H.
1975   "Institutions of Representation: Civil Justice and the Public." *Law & Society Review* 9:401–30.

Mayhew, Leon H., and Reiss, Albert J.
1969   "The Social Organization of Legal Contacts." *American Journal of Sociology* 34:309.

Mazor, Lester J.
1968   "Power and Responsibility in the Attorney-Client Relationship." *Stanford Law Review* 20:1120.

Medcalf, Linda
    1978   *Law and Identity: Lawyers, Native Americans, and Legal Practice.* Beverly Hills: Sage.
Melone, Albert P.
    1980   "The Rejection of the Lawyer-Dominance Proposition: The Need for Additional Research." *Western Political Quarterly* 33:225–32.
Mendelsohn, Oliver, and Lippman, Matthew
    1979   "The Emergence of the Corporate Law Firm in Australia." *University of New South Wales Law Journal* 3:78–98.
Menkel-Meadow, Carrie
    1979   *The American Bar Association Legal Clinic Experiment: An Evaluation of the 59th Street Legal Clinic, Inc.* Chicago: American Bar Association.
    1984   "Legal Aid in the United States: The Professionalization and Politicization of Legal Services in the 1980's." *Osgoode Hall Law Journal* 22:29–67.
Menkel-Meadow, Carrie, and Meadow, Robert
    1983   "Resource Allocation in Legal Services: Individual Decisions in Work Priorities." *Law & Policy Quarterly* 5:237–56.
Merryman, John; Clark, David; and Friedman, Lawrence
    1979   *Law and Social Change in Mediterranean Europe and Latin America: A Handbook of Legal and Social Indicators for Comparative Study.* Stanford, Calif.: Stanford Law School.
Miller, William
    1951   "American Lawyers in Business and in Politics: Their Social Backgrounds and Early Training." *Yale Law Journal* 60:60–76.
Millerson, Geoffrey
    1964   *The Qualifying Associations: A Study in Professionalisation.* London: Humanities Press.
Mindes, Marvin
    1980   "Proliferation, Specialization and Certification: The Splitting of the Bar." *University of Toledo Law Review* 11:273.
Mindes, Marvin, and Acock, Alan C.
    1982   "Trickster, Hero, Helper: A Report on the Lawyer Image." *American Bar Foundation Research Journal* 1982:177–233.
Morris, Pauline; Cooper, Jenny; and Byles, Anthea
    1973   "Public Attitudes to Problem Defining and Problem Solving: A Pilot Study." *British Journal of Social Work* 3:301.
Moskowitz, Daniel B.
    1977   "Will the ABA Lose Its Accreditation Power? Proprietaries Press Their Case." *Juris Doctor,* November, 27–35.
Mungham, Geoff, and Thomas, Philip A.
    1979   "Advocacy and the Solicitor-Advocate in Magistrates' Courts in England and Wales." *International Journal of the Sociology of Law* 7:169–95.
Muris, Timothy J., and McChesney, Frederick S.
    1979   "Advertising and the Price and Quality of Legal Services: The Case of Legal Clinics." *American Bar Foundation Research Journal* 1979:179–207.
Murrin, John M
    1971   "The Legal Transformation: The Bench and Bar of Eighteenth-Century Massachusetts." In *Colonial America: Essays in Politics and Social Development,* edited by Stanley Katz. Boston: Little, Brown.
Nader, Ralph
    1970   "Law Schools and Law Firms." *Minnesota Law Review* 54:493–96.
Nagel, Stuart
    1962   "Culture Patterns and Judicial Systems." *Vanderbilt Law Review* 16:147.

Nash, Gary B.
    1965   "The Philadelphia Bench and Bar 1800–1861." *Comparative Studies in Society and History* 7:203–20.
Nebraska Law Review
    1975   "Comment: Public and Professional Assessment of the Nebraska Bar." *Nebraska Law Review* 55:57.
Nelson, Robert L.
    1981   "Practice and Privilege: Social Change and the Structure of Large Law Firms." *American Bar Foundation Research Journal* 1981:95–140.
    1983   "The Changing Structure of Opportunity: Recruitment and Careers in Large Law Firms." *American Bar Foundation Research Journal* 1983:109–42.
Nelson, William E.
    1975   *Americanization of the Common Law: The Impact of Legal Change on Massachusetts Society, 1760–1830.* Cambridge, Mass.: Harvard University Press.
New South Wales Law Reform Commission
    1979   *Complaints, Discipline and Professional Standards.* Pt. 1. Legal Profession discussion paper no. 2. Sydney: New South Wales Law Reform Commission.
    1981   *The Structure of the Profession.* 2 pts. Legal Profession discussion papers nos. 4(1) and 4(2). Sydney: New South Wales Law Reform Commission.
Nieuwenhuysen, John, and Williams-Wynn, Marina
    1982   *Professions in the Marketplace: An Australian Study of Lawyers, Doctors, Accountants and Dentists.* Melbourne: Melbourne University Press.
Nolan, Dennis R.
    1976   "The Effect of the Revolution on the Bar: The Maryland Experience." *Virginia Law Review* 62:969.
    1980   *Readings in the History of the American Legal Profession.* Indianapolis: Michie.
Nonet, Philippe, and Carlin, Jerome E.
    1968   "Law: The Legal Profession." *International Encyclopedia of the Social Sciences* 9:66–73.
Nousiainen, Kevat
    1980   "On Legal Expertise and Cost-Free Legal Aid in Finland." *International Journal of the Sociology of Law* 8:165–74.
Oakley, John Bilyeu, and Thompson, Robert S.
    1980   *Law Clerks and the Judicial Process: Perceptions of the Qualities and Functions of Law Clerks in American Courts.* Berkeley: University of California Press.
O'Connor, James
    1973   *The Fiscal Crisis of the State.* New York: St. Martin's Press.
Office des Professions du Québec
    1976   *The Evolution of Professionalism in Quebec.* Québec: Office des Professions du Québec.
O'Gorman, Hubert
    1963   *Lawyers and Matrimonial Cases: A Study of Informal Pressures in Private Practice.* New York: Columbia University Press.
Orzack, Louis H.
    1978   "Professions in Different National Societies." Paper presented at the 9th World Congress on Sociology, Uppsala, August.
    1980   "Educators, Practitioners and Politicians in the European Common Market." *Higher Education* 9:307–23.
Osborn, John Jay, Jr.
    1979a   *The Associates.* Boston: Houghton Mifflin.
    1979b   *The Paper Chase.* New York: Popular Library.

Parker, Douglas H.

1974 "Periodic Recertification of Lawyers: A Comparative Study of Programs for Maintaining Professional Competence." *Utah Law Review* 1974:463–90.

Parsons, Talcott

1951 *Social Structure and Dynamic Processes: The Case of Modern Medical Practice in the Social System.* Glencoe, Ill.: Free Press.

1954a "A Sociologist Looks at the Legal Profession." In *Essays in Sociological Theory.* New York: Free Press.

1954b "The Professions and Social Structure." In *Essays in Sociological Theory.* New York: Free Press.

1968 "Professions." In *International Encyclopedia of the Social Sciences.* Vol. 12. New York: Macmillan.

Pashigian, B. Peter

1977 "The Market for Lawyers: The Determinants of the Demand for and Supply of Lawyers." *Journal of Law and Economics.* 20:53–85.

1978 "The Number and Earnings of Lawyers: Some Recent Findings." *American Bar Foundation Research Journal* 1978:51–82.

Pfeffer, Jeffrey

1974 "Some Evidence on Occupational Licensing and Occupational Incomes." *Social Forces* 53:102–11.

Pfenningstorf, Werner, and Kimball, Spencer L.

1977 *Legal Service Plans: Approaches to Regulation.* Chicago: American Bar Foundation.

Pipkin, Ronald M.

1976 "Legal Education: The Consumer's Perspective." *American Bar Foundation Research Journal* 1976:1161.

1978 "Token Women: An Empirical Test of Kanter's Hypothesis." *American Journal of Sociology* 84:160.

1979 "Law School Instruction in Professional Responsibility: A Curricular Paradox." *American Bar Foundation Research Journal* 1979:247–75.

1982 "Moonlighting in Law School: A Multischool Study of Part-Time Employment of Full-Time Students." *American Bar Foundation Research Journal* 1982:1109–62.

Plucknett, Theodore F. R.

1956 *A Concise History of the Common Law.* 5th ed. Boston: Little, Brown.

Podgórecki, Adam; Kaupen, Wolfgang; Van Houtte, Jean; Vinke, P.; and Kutchinsky, Berl

1973 *Knowledge and Opinion About Law.* London: Martin Robertson.

Podmore, David B. L.

1977 "Lawyers and Politics." *British Journal of Law and Society* 4:155–85.

1980a *Solicitors and the Wider Community.* London: Heinemann.

1980b "Bucher and Strauss Revisited—The Case of the Solicitors' Profession." *British Journal of Law and Society* 7:1–21.

Poulantzas, Nicos

1978 *State, Power, Socialism.* London: New Left Books.

Powell, Michael J.

1976 "Professional Self-Regulation: The Transfer of Control from a Professional Association to an Independent Commission." Paper presented at the annual meeting of the American Sociological Association, New York, August.

1979 "Anatomy of a Counter-Bar Association: The Chicago Council of Lawyers." *American Bar Foundation Research Journal* 1979:501–41.

1980 "Bar Associations in Professional and Societal Context." Paper presented at the joint meeting of the Law and Society Association and the ISA Research Committee on the Sociology of Law. Madison, Wisconsin, June 5–8.

Powell, Ramon J., and Carlson, Alfred B.
    1978   *Defining Competence in Legal Practice: Report of a National Survey of Solo and Small Firm Practitioners.* Princeton, N.J.: Educational Testing Service.

Presser, Stephen B.
    1976   "An Introduction to the Legal History of Colonial New Jersey." *Rutgers-Camden Law Journal* 7:262.

Prest, Wilfrid, ed.
    1981   *Lawyers in Early Modern Europe and America.* London: Croom Helm.

Ramey, F. H.
    1978   "Minority Lawyers in California: A Survey." *Los Angeles Daily Journal Report No. 78-22,* November 17, pp. 4–27.

Ramsey, Henry, Jr.
    1980   "Affirmative Action at American Bar Association Approved Law Schools: 1979–1980." *Journal of Legal Education* 30:377–416.

Rast, L. Edmund
    1978   "What the Chief Executive Looks For in His Corporate Law Department." *Business Lawyer* 33:841.

Rathjen, Gregory J.
    1976   "The Impact of Legal Education on the Beliefs, Attitudes, and Values of Law Students." *Tennessee Law Review* 44:85–116.
    1978   "Lawyers and the Appellate Choice: An Analysis of Factors Affecting the Decision to Appeal." *American Politics Quarterly* 6:387–406.

Reed, Alfred Z.
    1921   *Training for the Public Profession of the Law.* New York: Carnegie Foundation for the Advancement of Teaching.

Reed, J. P.
    1972   "The Lawyer-Client: A Managed Relationship." In *The Social Dimensions of Work,* edited by C. D. Bryant. Englewood Cliffs, N.J.: Prentice-Hall.

Reich, Charles
    1964   "The New Property." *Yale Law Journal* 73:733.

Reichstein, Kenneth J.
    1965   "Ambulance Chasing: A Case Study of Deviation and Control Within the Legal Profession." *Social Problems* 13:3–17.

Reid, Jean-Paul
    1978   *Bibliographie sur l'aide juridique au Canada.* Montreal: Centre National d'Information et de Recherche sur l'Aide Juridique.

Reiter, Barry J.
    1978   *Discipline as a Means of Assuring Continuing Competence in the Professions and Tables of Discipline Activities by Profession: A Study of the Disciplinary Processes in the Professions of Accounting, Architecture, Engineering, and Law in Ontario.* Working paper no. 11. Toronto: Professional Organizations Committee.

Riesman, David
    1951   "Toward an Anthropological Science of Law and the Legal Profession." *American Journal of Sociology* 57:121–35.
    1957   "Law and Sociology: Recruitment, Training and Colleagueship." *Stanford Law Review* 9:643.

Rosenthal, Douglas E.
    1974   *Lawyer and Client: Who's in Charge?* New York: Russell Sage Foundation.
    1976   "Evaluating the Competence of Lawyers." *Law & Society Review* 11:257–86.

Rosenthal, Douglas E.; Kagan, Robert A.; and Quatrone, Deborah
    1971   *Volunteer Attorneys and Legal Services: New York's Community Law Office Program.* New York: Russell Sage Foundation.

Ross, H. Laurence
  1970   *Settled Out of Court: The Social Process of Insurance Claims Adjustment.* Chicago: Aldine.
Roth, Julius A.
  1974   "Professionalism: The Sociologist's Decoy." *Sociology of Work and Occupations* 1:6–23.
Roth, Julius A.; Ruzek, S.; and Daniels, Arlene K.
  1973   "Current State of the Sociology of Occupations." *Sociological Quarterly* 14:309–33.
Rothschild, Emma
  1981   "Reagan and the Real America." *New York Review of Books,* February 5.
Rothstein, Nathaniel
  1972   "Lawyers' Malpractice in Litigation." *Cleveland State Law Review* 22:1–14.
Rottenberg, Simon, ed.
  1980   *Occupational Licensure and Regulation.* Washington, D.C.: American Enterprise Institute.
Royal Commission on Legal Services
  1979   *Final Report.* 2 vols. London: Her Majesty's Stationary Office.
Royal Commission on Legal Services in Scotland
  1980   *Report.* 2 vols. Edinburgh: Her Majesty's Stationary Office.
Rubinstein, Leonard
  1976   "Procedural Due Process and the Limits of the Adversary System." *Harvard Civil Rights-Civil Liberties Law Reporter* 11:48.
Ruud, Millard H., and White, James P.
  1974   "Legal Education and Profession Statistics 1973–1974." *Journal of Legal Education* 25:342.
Saari, David J.
  1979   "The Financial Impacts of the Right to Counsel for Criminal Defense of the Poor." Paper presented at the annual meeting of the Law and Society Association, San Francisco, May 10–12.
Sarat, Austin
  1977   "Studying American Legal Culture: An Assessment of Survey Evidence." *Law & Society Review* 11:427–88.
Savoy, Paul
  1970   "Toward a New Politics of Legal Education." *Yale Law Journal* 79:444.
Scheiber, Harry N.
  1980   "Federalism and Legal Process: Historical and Contemporary Analysis of the American System." *Law & Society Review* 14:663–722.
Scheingold, Stuart A.
  1974   *The Politics of Rights: Lawyers, Public Policy, and Political Change.* New Haven: Yale University Press.
Schlegel, John Henry
  1979   "American Legal Realism and Empirical Social Science: From the Yale Experience." *Buffalo Law Review* 28:459–586.
Schneyer, Theodore J.
  1983   "The Incoherence of the Unified Bar Concept: Generalizing from the Wisconsin Case." *American Bar Foundation Research Journal* 1983:1–108.
Schrag, Philip C.
  1971   "On Her Majesty's Secret Service: Protecting the Consumer in New York City." *Yale Law Journal* 80:1529.
  1972   *Counsel for the Deceived: Case Studies in Consumer Fraud.* New York: Pantheon.

Schuyt, Kees; Groenendijk, Kees; and Sloot, Ben
    1977   "Access to the Legal System and Legal Services Research." *European Yearbook in
              Law and Sociology* 1977:98–120.

Schwartz, Gary T.
    1981   "Tort Law and the Economy in Nineteenth Century America: A Reinterpreta-
              tion." *Yale Law Journal* 91:1717–75.

Schwartz, Murray L.
    1978   "Professionalism and the Accountability of Lawyers." *California Law Review*
              66:669.

    1980   "The Reorganization of the Legal Profession." *Texas Law Review* 58:1269–90.

Schwartz, Richard, and Miller, James
    1964   "Legal Evolution and Societal Complexity." *American Journal of Sociology* 70:159.

Segal, Geraldine R.
    1983   *Blacks in the Law: Philadelphia and the Nation.* Philadelphia: University of Pennsyl-
              vania Press.

Seligman, Joel
    1978a   *The High Citadel: The Influence of Harvard Law School.* Boston: Houghton Mifflin.

    1978b   "Why the Bar Exam Should Be Abolished." *Juris Doctor,* August-September, pp.
              48–55.

Settle, Russell F., and Weisbrod, Burton A.
    1978   "Financing Public Interest Law: An Evaluation of Alternative Financing Arrange-
              ments." In Burton A. Weisbrod, Joel F. Handler, and Neil K. Komesar, *Public Inter-
              est Law: An Economic and Institutional Analysis.* Berkeley: University of California Press.

Shaffer, Thomas L., and Redmount, Robert S.
    1976   "Legal Education: The Classroom Experience." *Notre Dame Lawyer* 52:190.

Shepard, Lawrence
    1978   "Licensing Restrictions and the Cost of Dental Care." *Journal of Law and Economics*
              21:187–202.

Sherman, Howard
    1979   "Inflation, Unemployment and the Contemporary Business Cycle." *Socialist Review*
              44:75.

Shuchman, Philip
    1968   "Ethics and Legal Ethics: The Propriety of the Canons as a Group Moral Code."
              George Washington Law Review 37:244.

Siegfried, John J.
    1976   "The Effect of Firm Size on the Economics of Legal Practice." *Legal Economics*
              2(3):23–29.

Sikes, Bette H.; Carson, Clara N.; and Gorai, Patricia
    1972   *The 1971 Lawyer Statistical Report.* Chicago: American Bar Foundation.

Silverstein, Lee
    1965   *Defense of the Poor in Criminal Cases in American State Courts.* Chicago: American
              Bar Foundation.

Simon, Rita James; Koziol, Frank; and Joslyn, Nancy
    1973   "Have There Been Significant Changes in the Career Aspirations and Occupa-
              tional Choices of Law School Graduates in the 1960s?" *Law & Society Review* 8:95.

Simon, William H.
    1978   "The Ideology of Advocacy: Procedural Justice and Professional Ethics." *Wisconsin
              Law Review* 1978:29–144.

    1984   "Visions of Practice in Legal Thought." *Stanford Law Review* 36:469–507.

Sims, Joe
    1978   "The Future of Self-Regulation in the Legal Profession." Remarks Before the ABA
              National Workshop on Disciplinary Law and Procedure, Chicago, June 2.

Slayton, Philip, and Trebilcock, Michael J., eds.
1978   *The Professions and Public Policy.* Toronto: University of Toronto Press.
Slovak, Jeffrey S.
1979   "Working for Corporate Actors: Social Change and Elite Attorneys in Chicago." *American Bar Foundation Research Journal* 1979:465–500.
1980   "Giving and Getting Respect: Prestige and Stratification in a Legal Elite." *American Bar Foundation Research Journal* 1980:31–68.
1981   "Influence and Issues in the Legal Community: The Role of a Legal Elite." *American Bar Foundation Research Journal* 1981:141–94.
Smigel, Erwin O.
1969   *The Wall Street Lawyer: Professional Organization Man?* New York: New York University Press.
Smith, Reginald Heber
1919   *Justice and the Poor.* New York: Carnegie Foundation.
Sociology of Work and Occupations
1974 to date.
Spiegel, Mark
1979   "Lawyering and Client Decision-making: Informed Consent and the Legal Profession." *University of Pennsylvania Law Review* 128:41.
Stapleton, W. Vaughan, and Teitelbaum, Lee E.
1972   *In Defense of Youth: The Role of Counsel in American Juvenile Courts.* New York: Russell Sage Foundation.
Statsky, William P.
1972   "Paraprofessionals: Expanding the Legal Service Delivery Team." *Journal of Legal Education* 24:397.
Steele, Eric H., and Nimmer, Raymond T.
1976   "Lawyers, Clients, and Professional Regulation." *American Bar Foundation Research Journal* 1976:917–1019.
Stephens, Mike
1980   "The Law Centre Movement: Professionalism and Community Control." In *Essays in Law and Society,* edited by Zenon Bankowski and Geoff Mungham. London: Routledge & Kegan Paul.
Stern, Gerald M.
1976   *The Buffalo Creek Disaster.* New York: Random House.
Stevens, Robert B.
1971   "Two Cheers for 1870: The American Law School." In *Law in American History,* edited by Donald Fleming and Bernard Bailyn. Perspectives in American History, vol. 5.
1973   "Law Schools and Law Students." *Virginia Law Review* 1973:551–707.
1980   "Law Schools and Legal Education, 1879–1979: Lectures in Honor of 100 Years of the Valparaiso Law School." *Valparaiso University Law Review* 14:179–259.
1983   *Law School: Legal Education in America from the 1850s to the 1980s.* Chapel Hill: University of North Carolina Press.
Stewart, James B.
1983   *The Partners: Inside America's Most Powerful Law Firms.* New York: Warner Books.
Stinchcombe, Arthur L.
1959   "Bureaucratic and Craft Administration of Production." *Administrative Science Quarterly* 4:168–87.
Stolz, Preble
1972   "Training for the Public Profession of Law (1921): A Contemporary Review." In *New Directions in Legal Education,* edited by Herbert L. Packer and Thomas Ehrlich. New York: McGraw-Hill.

Stone, Alan A.
    1971   "Legal Education on the Couch." *Harvard Law Review* 85:392.
Stone, Harlan Fiske
    1934   "The Public Influence of the Bar." *Harvard Law Review* 48:1.
Storey, Robert G.
    1951   "The Legal Profession Versus Regimentation: A Program to Counter Socializa-
              tion." *American Bar Association Journal* 37:100.
Storme, M., and Casman, H.
    1978   *Towards Justice with a Human Face.* Antwerp: Deventer.
Stumpf, Harry P.
    1975   *Community Politics and Legal Services: The Other Side of the Law.* Beverly Hills: Sage.
Surrency, Erwin C.
    1964   "The Lawyer and the Revolution." *American Journal of Legal History* 8:125.
Swaine, Robert T.
    1946   *The Cravath Firm and Its Predecessors, 1819–1947.* Vol. 1. New York: Ad Lib Press.
Tabachnik, Leonard
    1976   "Licensing in the Legal and Medical Professions, 1820–1860: A Historical Case
              Study." In *Professions for the People: The Politics of Skill,* edited by Joel Gerstl and
              Glenn Jacobs. New York: Schenkman.
Taft, Henry W.
    1938   *A Century and a Half of the New York Bar.* New York: Author.
Taylor, James B.
    1975   "Law School Stress and the 'Déformation Professionelle.' " *Journal of Legal Educa-
              tion* 27:151.
Thomas, Philip A., ed.
    1982   *Law in the Balance: Legal Services in the Eighties.* Oxford: Martin Robertson.
Tiemann, Fritz, and Blankenburg, Erhard
    1979   *Working Paper on the Evaluation of a Legal Need Survey in West Berlin.* Berlin:
              Wissenschaftszentrum.
Tisher, Sharon; Bernabei, Lynn; and Green, Mark
    1977   *Bringing the Bar to Justice: A Comparative Study of Six Bar Associations.* Washington,
              D.C.: Public Citizen.
Tocqueville, Alexis de
    1958   *Democracy in America.* Vol. 1. New York: Vintage Books.
Tomasic, Roman
    1978   *Lawyers and the Community.* Sydney: Law Foundation of New South Wales and
              George Allen & Unwin.
Torens, Nina
    1975   "Deprofessionalization and Its Sources: A Preliminary Analysis." *Sociology of Work
              and Occupations* 2:323–37.
Trebilcock, Michael J.; Tuohy, Carolyn J.; and Wolfson, Allan D.
    1979   *Professional Regulation: A Staff Study of Accountancy, Architecture, Engineering and
              Law in Ontario.* Toronto: Professional Organizations Committee.
Trubek, David M.
    1981   "Introduction: Studying Courts in Context." *Law & Society Review* 15:584.
Turow, Scott
    1977   *One "L."* New York: Putnam.
Tushnet, Mark
    1982   "Segregated Schools and Legal Strategy: The NAACP's Campaign Against Seg-
              regated Education, 1925–1980." Unpublished manuscript.
Twining, William L.
    1967   "Pericles and the Plumber." *Law Quarterly Review* 83:396.

U.S. Department of Health, Education and Welfare, Office of Education, Bureau of Higher and Continuing Education, Division of Eligibility and Agency Evaluation

1978 *Nationally Recognized Accrediting Agencies and Associations.* Washington, D.C.: Department of Health, Education and Welfare.

University of Pennsylvania Law Review

1953 "Note: The Administration of Divorce: A Philadelphia Study." *University of Pennsylvania Law Review* 101:1204.

1974 "Comment: Court Awarded Attorney's Fees and Equal Access to the Courts." *University of Pennsylvania Law Review* 122:636.

Valétas, Marie-France

1976 *Aide Judiciaire et Accès à la Justice.* Paris: Centre de Recherches pour l'Etude et l'Observation des Conditions de Vie.

Van Alstyne, Scott

1982 "Ranking the Law Schools: The Reality of Illusion?" *American Bar Foundation Research Journal* 1982:649–84.

Virginia Law Review

1975 "Note: Legal Specialization and Certification." *Virginia Law Review* 61:434.

Vollner, Ted

1978 "Lawyer Malpractice Clinic Stirs Anger." *Los Angeles Times,* Pt. 2, May 11, p. 1.

Waltz, Jon R.

1976 "The Unpopularity of Lawyers in America." *Cleveland State Law Review* 25:143–49.

Warkov, Seymour, and Zelan, Joseph

1965 *Lawyers in the Making.* Chicago: Aldine.

Warren, Charles

1911 *A History of the American Bar.* Boston: Little, Brown.

Wasserstrom, Richard

1975 "Lawyers as Professionals: Some Moral Issues." *Human Rights* 5:124.

Weisbrod, Burton A.; Handler, Joel F.; and Komesar, Neil K.

1978 *Public Interest Law: An Economic and Institutional Analysis.* Berkeley: University of California Press.

White, David M.

1984 *The Effects of Coaching, Defective Questions and Cultural Bias on the Validity of the Law School Admissions Test.* Berkeley: Law School Admission Investigation.

White, James P.

1975 "Is That Burgeoning Law School Enrollment Ending?" *American Bar Association Journal* 61:202–04.

Wice, Paul B.

1978 *The Endangered Species: America's Private Criminal Lawyers.* Beverly Hills: Sage.

Woodworth, J. R.

1973 "Some Influences on the Reform of Schools of Law and Medicine, 1890–1930." *Sociological Quarterly* 14:496–516.

Work in America

1973 *Work in America: Report of a Special Task Force to the Secretary of Health, Education and Welfare.* Cambridge, Mass.: MIT Press.

Yale Law Journal

1970 "Comment: The New Public Interest Lawyers." *Yale Law Journal* 79:1069.

1973 "Note: Improving Information on Legal Malpractice." *Yale Law Journal* 82:590.

1976 "Note: Unauthorized Practice of Law and Pro Se Divorce: An Empirical Analysis." *Yale Law Journal* 86:104.

Yankelovich, Skelly and White Inc.
  1978   "Highlights of a National Survey of the General Public, Judges, Lawyers, and
            Community Leaders." In *State Courts: A Blueprint for the Future,* edited by Theo-
            dore J. Fetter. Williamsburg, Va.: National Center for State Courts.
York, John C., and Hale, Rosemary D.
  1973   "Too Many Lawyers? The Legal Services Industry: Its Structure and Outlook."
            Journal of Legal Education 26:1–31.
Young, John A.
  1964   "The Jewish Law Student and New York Jobs—Discriminatory Effects in Law Firm
            Hiring Practices." *Yale Law Journal* 73:625–60.
Zehnle, Richard F.
  1975   *Specialization in the Legal Profession: An Analysis of Current Proposals.* Chicago:
            American Bar Foundation.
Zemans, Frances Kahn, and Rosenblum, Victor G.
  1981   *The Making of a Public Profession.* Chicago: American Bar Foundation.
Zemans, Frederick H., ed.
  1979   *Perspectives on Legal Aid.* London: Frances Pinter.
Zenor, John L.
  1980   "Law Firm Unionization." *Case and Comment* 85(4):8–16.
Ziegler, Donald H., and Hermann, Michele
  1972   "The Invisible Litigant: An Inside View of Pro Se Actions in the Federal Courts."
            New York University Law Review 47:157–257.

℃ 9 ℃

PRIVATE GOVERNMENT

Stewart Macaulay

University of Wisconsin–Madison

Much of what we could call governing is done by groups that are not part of the institutions established by federal and state constitutions. If governing involves making rules, interpreting them, applying them to specific cases, and sanctioning violations, some of all of this is done by such different clusters of people as the Mafia, the National Collegiate Athletic Association, the American Arbitration Association, those who run large shopping centers, neighborhood associations, and even the regulars at Smokey's tavern. It may be necessary to draw a sharp line between public and private governments such as these in order to think about law, but in reality there is no such division. To the contrary, one finds instead interpenetration, overlapping jurisdictions, and opportunities

NOTE: Much of this paper has been shaped by the contributions and critical editing of Dr. Jacqueline R. Macaulay. Other demands on her time made it impossible for her to do any of the writing, and so, at her request, she is not listed as a co-author. My colleague David Trubek read the manuscript critically and offered extensive suggestions. Professors William H. Clune, Marc Galanter, Robert W. Gordon, Willard Hurst, Ellen R. Jordan, Leonard V. Kaplan, Marygold S. Melli, Sally Falk Moore, Theodore Schneyer, and Diane Vaughan read some or part of the drafts of the manuscript and made very helpful comments. A draft was written while I was a visitor at the Centre for Socio-Legal Studies, Wolfson College, Oxford, in 1979, and I benefited greatly from discussions with many people there. I presented part of the text in a paper called "Private Government and Functionalist and Marxist Theories of Law" at Osgoode Hall Law School, York University, Toronto, Ontario, in 1980. Again I benefited from the reactions of those who attended the lecture. The last section was presented at the Conference on Reflexive Law and the Regulatory Crisis, held at the University of Wisconsin–Madison, July 18–21, 1983. I learned a great deal from the responses of the European and North and South American participants. Yet after all of this help, of course, I am still responsible for all errors.

for both harmony and conflict among public and private governments. Formal legal process typically plays a part only indirectly and as a last resort. We are likely to be seriously misled if we assume that there are sharp distinctions between public and private governments and between formal and informal processes. We must recognize that these concepts are only rough generalizations useful for emphasizing aspects of reality rather than accurate descriptions of things existing in the world.

These are not new observations. The concept of private government goes back at least to Ehrlich's theory (1913) of the "living law." However, despite this distinguished lineage, scholars often have failed to see the importance of private social control as it interacts with and affects the formal legal system. Fitzpatrick (1984) points out that even legal realism narrows its focus to formal legal process and doctrine.

> Academic legal knowledge is generated by applying a certain idea of law to the world. This approach cannot extend to social forms which do not find expression in terms of legal process or doctrine. The integrity of "law" is thus obliquely but potently affirmed in areas of scholarship that claim to be fundamentally skeptical of it. [p. 135]

At the same time, far too often, work in law and the behavioral sciences implicitly accepts the distinction between public and private spheres and assumes that one can study the roles played by law in a society by considering only the actors who play official parts. What is needed is a "private government perspective" which both recognizes private associations that affect government and also treats distinctions between public and private spheres as doubtful rather than as given. (Cf. Spitzer 1984.)

At the outset, I will try to give some shape to the amorphous term "private government." While any formal definition would be arbitrary, we need some idea about what we are and are not discussing. Once this is done, we can turn to specific topics in legal studies and consider possible contributions of a private government perspective which emphasizes private rule-making, interpretation, application, and sanctioning as well as the artificiality of drawing any hard line between public and private governing.

PRIVATE GOVERNMENTS AND THEIR RELATIONSHIPS WITH THE PUBLIC LEGAL SYSTEM

What Is a Private Government?

The term "private government" draws an analogy intended to highlight certain features of something that is not a public government. As we shall see, if we put aside for a moment our skepticism about the public/private distinction, we could call many actions of individuals and groups "government" (see Evan 1976, pp. 171–85). The test of any analogy is its usefulness as balanced against the risks of overlooking ways the things being compared differ. Probably those engaged in the social study of law should consider first those private governments that bear some close relationships to public ones.

When might we draw a plausible analogy between private social control and public government? It is easiest to label as a private government a formally defined organization which makes rules, interprets them in the context of specific cases, and imposes sanctions for their violation. The analogy might seem more apt if the organization attempted to mimic the public legal system. For example, at least in the past, "company towns" often sought to govern by using the forms of legal rules, courts, and police—all controlled, however, by a business corporation rather than the citizens.

More typically, however, organizations attempt to take over only some of the functions of public government and mimic only part of the public legal system. Trade associations "legislate" rules of practice and suggest standard forms of agreement (see Leblebici and Salancik 1982); a number of groups "adjudicate" disputes by offering arbitration to their members; corporations establish their own private police to guard against (or engage in) industrial espionage. These groups may borrow some structures and symbols from the public government—for example, private police wear uniforms, badges, and guns; arbitrators may run their hearings by procedures approaching a trial; trade association rule-making may involve established procedures that suggest a legislature and often bring forth political tactics. Even a duel can be viewed as a kind of legal procedure with highly technical rules (cf. Schwartz, Baxter, and Ryan 1984).

Yet we can go beyond these fairly obvious analogies. Any group of people who more or less regularly interact tend to adopt rules, interpret them in light of specific situations, and sanction their violation (see Ford 1983; Schall 1983). If the group has some permanence, and if the actors within it tend to be the same people who value participation, we have what Moore (1978) calls a semi-autonomous social field. These social fields affect the operation of the legal system in many ways. For example, those involved in organized crime have rules that govern buying and selling of illegal goods and services as well as competitive practices and a range of sanctions to support them (see Reuter 1984; Adler and Adler 1983; cf. Cressey 1973). Many of these rules and sanctions serve to make enforcing the law against the group more difficult.

We could call even less formal and temporary relationships private governments if it served any purpose to do so. For example, people are linked in loosely coordinated social networks which may not be as structured, permanent, or valued as a social field (see Hammer 1980; Lee 1980; Nauta 1974). People learn norms and anticipate sanctioning for their violation appropriate to situations such as attending a dinner party with strangers or riding as a passenger on an airplane. We could talk of the legal system of the elevator. There are norms about looking at, talking to, and touching others in such temporary encounters (cf. Taylor and Brooks 1980; Baxter 1984). Sanctions include being ignored, ridiculed, and even threatened with physical violence. Probably these rules and sanctions contribute a great deal to our judgments about the safety of public places; it may be that our greatest demand for the physical embodiment of the criminal law—the uniformed police officer—comes when we see the private government of public places as inadequate. Black (1983) asserts that a "great deal of the conduct labeled and processed as a crime in modern societies . . . is intended as a punishment or other expression of disapproval, whether applied reflectively or impulsively, with coolness or in the heat of passion." He continues,

> most intentional homicide in modern society may be classified as social control, specifically as self-help, even if it is handled by legal officials as crime. From this standpoint, it is apparent that capital punishment is quite common in modern America . . . though it is nearly always a private rather than a public affair. [pp. 35–36]

However, at some point the analogy becomes strained and unsatisfying. There are widely accepted norms about when one should give relatives and friends birthday and

Christmas gifts, and there are sanctions for violating those norms. Nonetheless, most of us probably would be uneasy with the idea of the private government of a friendship or an "illegal" failure to give a Christmas gift (see Caplow 1982).

Another way to define a term is to ask how people have used it. The term "private government" has been used even where there was not a close approximation of public governmental procedures and structures. The most common use of "private government" has been as a rhetorical device in aid of arguing that large corporations ought to be accountable for their actions, somewhat as nations and states are held accountable. Employees, customers, suppliers, and those living in cities who are dependent upon corporate decisions, in this view, ought not be subject to arbitrary action by public or private government; the "citizens" of a corporation ought to have a right to free speech and the like. Whatever the merit of these positions, the argument focuses on amount of power and its impact rather than on the presence or absence of such things as judges in robes, doctrines speaking to the use of power, procedures, and the symbols of legal action.

A number of writers, drawing on anthropological tradition, see us living in a world of legal pluralism, subject to the jurisdictions of overlapping and partially conflicting legal systems (see, for example, Galanter 1981; Fitzpatrick 1984; Nader 1984). In this view, the legal system studied in law schools is but one of many. Here the concept of a legal system is expanded, often implicitly, to cover such things as the norms of the Jewish community living in an area, those of the neighborhood and tenant associations there, those of a particular apartment building and of a particular landlord-tenant relationship, as well as those found in the city's building code and the state laws governing landlord and tenant, property and contract as they are enforced. In this kind of analysis, a great deal of private rule-making and sanctioning is analogized to processes in the formal public legal system; again, usage seems not to demand a particularly close approximation to public government.

The major research on relatively institutionalized social fields is part of a yet unpublished project, "Legal Regulation and Self-Regulation in American Social Settings," by Marc Galanter, a law professor well known for his work in the field of dispute resolution. As part of his study, Galanter collected newspaper articles, accounts from the trade press, magazine stories, and reports of academic research dealing in a wide variety of contexts with what most of us would call governing. Galanter stresses that the relatively institutionalized social fields he has been studying show a much wider range of activities than simple dispute resolution (see, for example, *Harvard Law Review* 1949; Ellickson 1982).

One of the organizations studied by Galanter is the American Institute of Architects (AIA), which has drafted, and continues to revise, an elaborate set of terms and conditions for the construction of buildings. These rules have, effectively, become the law of this industry. While parties could negotiate contracts on some other basis, they seldom do so because it is much easier to use the well-understood and accepted AIA forms, perhaps amending them in one particular or another to cover special situations. For practical purposes, the AIA operates as the legislature in the area of building construction (Havighurst 1961, p. 97); its legislative activity features lobbying and logrolling by various interests, just as we would find at state capitals (Sweet 1978, 1983; cf. Johnstone and Hopson 1967, pp. 329–54). The relationship structured by the AIA standard form contracts is one in which the architect, who is the owner's representative for most purposes, is also the arbitrator of disputes about the meaning of the plans and the quality of work performed. While such a mixed role neglects classical ideas about autonomy as a guarantee of impartiality, it allows a quick and inexpensive way to solve common problems that arise during construction (see Johnstone and Hopson 1967, pp. 315–28). Architects who abuse their role in one contract face problems in future transactions; builders have a number of ways to retaliate for unreasonable decisions; and an architect's reputation is likely to be known within the social field composed of those builders, architects, officials of financial institutions, and others who work together in a particular area. Many other trade associations enforce decisions and impose social control through their power over entry into a field and privileges members would dislike losing (see *Yale Law Journal* 1954). For example, in the international diamond trade, one must be accepted into the group in order to do business at all, and reputations must be carefully guarded in order to continue in the trade (*New York Times* 1984).

The legal pluralism approach shows that in American society the processes of rule-making, dispute avoidance, and resolution take place in a variety of settings apart from public governmental institutions. Even public government itself often participates in semi-autonomous social fields as it attends to its affairs—the Civil Aeronautics Board and the President of the United States interact with an association of airlines operated by private corporations and by national governments in setting international airline fares, for example (see Hannigan 1982; Cain 1983).

Many kinds of groups exercise governmental functions. Some are fairly structured entities which sometimes go to great lengths to mimic the procedures and symbols of public government, while others exhibit only a few of these features. What Galanter calls "mini-governments" vary widely in terms of the formality or informality of their operations, rules, and sanctions; their connection with one or more aspects of social life—some deal with a narrow part of the economy, others with living arrangements, with the family, or with multiple aspects—and their power over their members and their autonomy as against outsiders.

We could plausibly analogize many of these private legal systems to public government if it proved useful to do so. However, we are concerned with studies of the place of law in society and not with writing a dictionary. Thus, we should limit our analogizing to legal-like systems which are relevant to understanding the operations and functions of public government. What, then, are some of the relationships between the public government and these other governments? Which of these relationships seem worthy of attention in the social study of law?

The Relationships and Merging of Public and Private Governments

Often it is important to trace the relationships between public government and groups that carry out functions which are thought to be governmental or which deflect the impact of legal action. However, conceiving the problem this way assumes a distinct entity which we call public government and other distinct entities which operate in its shadow. As we shall see, a private government perspective requires that we both see the amount and nature of private governing and recognize at the same time that public and private governments are interpenetrated rather than distinct entities. First, I will consider some of the relationships, and then I will discuss how distinctions between what is public and what is private are questionable.

There are a number of relationships between public and private governments. Social fields govern in areas where we might expect public government to exercise control. Sills (1968) notes that

> [it] is difficult to overstate . . . the part played by voluntary associations in the actual business of governing the United States, in the sense of making decisions on policy and of providing services to citizens. . . . In large cities, voluntary associations seem to serve largely as important pressure groups; in medium-sized cities they virtually run the municipal government. . . . In small towns the decision-making role is filled by families and cliques, leaving to voluntary associations such service tasks as raising funds for the library, decorating the plaza, and maintaining the cemeteries. [p. 375]

Professional groups, for example, practice "self-regulation" in order to ward off public regulation. At times this is done totally apart from public government. At other times, however, a profession or an occupational group "captures" a public agency and exercises self-regulation in the guise of public regulation. Many state statutes, for example, facilitate self-government by organized occupational groups. Often members of state boards that license occupations or professions must be members of these groups.

Large corporations may assume functions usually thought of as governmental when they want control and little accountability. Many organizations have their own private police forces which offer everything from crowd control to protection of executives in foreign countries (see Livingstone 1981). O'Toole (1978) reports that

> General Motors has a force of 4200 plant guards, which makes its corporate police force larger than the municipal police departments of all but five American cities. And the Ford Motor Company has twenty-four ex-FBI agents on its payroll to counter threats ranging from dishonest employees to industrial spies. The business world seems to believe that law enforcement is too important a matter to be left to the police. [p. 42]

(See also Ghezzi 1983; Kakalik and Wildhorn 1977; Shearing and Stenning 1983; Stenning and Shearing 1979.) Spitzer and Scull (1977) note that private police can seek to deter or gain restitution rather than gather evidence for criminal trials, and they can use more sophisticated, scientifically advanced, technical equipment than most law enforcement agencies could afford or would be allowed to use under rules specifying constitutionally acceptable evidence.

Large corporations often handle theft, embezzlement, and appropriation of trade secrets by employees by what has been called the "second criminal law system" (Cole 1978). Employees suspected of criminal activity are demoted or fired, and sometimes they are forced to make restitution. Procedures and standards of evidence differ sharply from those found in the public criminal law system in its formal operations; the mere appearance of wrongdoing may be enough to cost an employee his or her job or prompt a transfer to a less desirable position; the employer does not worry about proof beyond a reasonable doubt or the hearsay rule. Indeed, in this process the "facts" may never be established. The employer may have only strong suspicions. The employee may admit nothing or the employee may never be confronted with a charge of wrongdoing and may never be sure why he or she was transferred, demoted, or fired.

In the 1970s, failure to prosecute white-collar crime became a political issue in the

United States. However, few who took stands against soft treatment for such criminals recognized the existence and operation of the second criminal justice system. It may be that both "defendants" and "prosecutors" in this system are better off than had cases been tried before courts. Employees accept this resolution of the situation in exchange for a promise not to initiate prosecution in the public criminal process or to make public their wrongdoing. The corporation, by using the second criminal justice system, may avoid damage to its reputation since a public prosecution might bring into question the adequacy of its supervision of its employees, and an accused employee might make countercharges of wrongdoing directed at other corporate officers. On the other hand, the second criminal justice system has costs as well as benefits. Those wrongly suspected may have no opportunity to establish their innocence. Those rightfully suspected may be free to move elsewhere and embezzle or steal company secrets again, unless the story is passed on by a gossip network.

Unionized employees who appear in a grievance procedure before a labor arbitrator could, perhaps, be said to participate in a third criminal justice system. Arbitrators may consider past alleged misconduct such as pilferage on the job, illegally obtained evidence, and information gained by wiretapping (see Fleming 1961, 1962), none of which could be used in a public criminal proceeding on the question of guilt or innocence. Again, this means that some of the values entailed in the public criminal justice system will not be implemented in this private proceeding.

Public government can attempt to facilitate the growth and operation of particular social fields in order to serve some public end. For example, during the Carter Administration, many saw the legal system as failing to cope with disputes within the family; in neighborhoods, workplaces, and retail markets; and in the landlord-tenant relationship. Accordingly, in the 1970s, a number of neighborhood justice centers were established with support from the Law Enforcement Assistance Administration of the Department of Justice and from some private foundations. Members of a community were to bring their disputes before trained mediators for help in resolving them. Evaluation studies indicate that the programs had only modest success (see, for example, Felstiner and Williams 1978, 1979; Snyder 1978; Tomasic and Feeley 1982). Generally, people did not voluntarily bring cases to these centers. Many of the cases handled came to the centers when prosecutors, clerks of court, or judges diverted criminal charges to mediation. For example, a husband might be charged with beating his wife. When faced with the choice of a neighborhood justice center or a criminal trial, both husband and wife often preferred the less formal setting. However, when there was no outside coercive force pushing everyone inside the doors, those with power to settle scores on their own terms had little reason to play. Landlords, creditors, and retailers, for example, tended to be satisfied with existing structures for the exercise of their power.

Often where delegalized dispute settlement has been successful in the United States, it has been tied to groups viewed as culturally distinct from mainstream American society and subject to discrimination because of bias. Chinese-American, Native-American, and Jewish groups all have mediation systems. It is difficult to leave these communities without paying a high price in lost relationships. Thus, the groups are able to induce their members to participate and accept decisions. In short, one cannot create a community by creating a court. Public government can foster existing social fields and institutions, but if new ones are to be created, there must be incentives to participate in them.

Relationships between public and private governments also may involve partial or total conflict, more or less openly recognized. At one extreme stands the crusading prosecutor heading a strike force attempting to battle organized crime or the British government seeking to control the "Provisional Wing of the Irish Republican Army" (see Burton 1976). Colonial powers long imposed a version of the common law or a civil code on top of "native law." While, in theory, there were principles to coordinate the two systems, often the reality was legal pluralism and competition. In many countries today there are internal colonies wherein national and indigenous governments exist in a variable relationship of conflict and cooperation.

Religious groups, too, may have practices that violate the law of the state, with varying outcomes. The state tried to stamp out polygamy among the Mormons, but special exemptions to formal laws have been carved out to relieve the Amish from the requirements of compulsory education. Sometimes the official law is stated as applicable to everyone, but it is not enforced against members of particular religious groups or is enforced only in response to a complaint from an outsider with power.

Another mixed relationship can be seen between public government and trade associations. While self-regulation by professionals long has been accepted as offering certain values (see Barber 1978), those championing the interests of consumers complain that self-regulation often discourages competition by erecting barriers to entry and fixing prices for services. During the 1970s, various units of the United States government challenged a number of trade associations in the name of competition. One such challenge won lawyers the right to advertise, although the risk of losing professional reputation keeps many from engaging in this kind of competition for clients (see Macaulay 1985).

In addition to these areas of conflict, there are others in which private organizations act counter to official policy (see Biersteker 1980). When American labor unions refuse to unload ships carrying cargo from Communist countries, it makes it difficult for the State Department to implement a policy of increasing trade with eastern European nations in order to lessen the dependence of those nations on the Soviet Union (see Bilder 1970; Friedmann 1957; Miller 1960). This kind of conflict occurs also in less recognizable forms. For example, in the late 1960s, when official United States policy imposed a boycott on Cuba, the Ford Foundation sent a number of Third World scholars and government officials to visit Havana. The foundation could do "privately" what the United States government did not wish to do publicly. However, such action may have furthered United States interests (see Arnove 1977), and so the conflict may have been more apparent than real.

Another kind of conflict between public and private governments may be prompted when members of an organization turn to the legal system seeking to change the balance of power which works to their disadvantage. On the one hand, there are battles before courts and legislatures for rules which, it is hoped, will benefit the less powerful. On the other hand, rules are not self-implementing, and often a battle to vindicate any rights gained is waged before courts and administrative agencies. For example, a faction of a religious group may seek to oust those in control; courts have been asked to arbitrate conflicting versions of the true faith in disputes about control of church property.

While it is important for many purposes to chart relationships between public and private governments, this schematic statement of the task can be misleading. Implicit in the idea of "relationships" between public and private sectors is the idea that they are separate and distinct. Sometimes this is the case, but often it is not. The American legal system has relatively open borders even in its formal description: jurors drawn from the community act as triers of fact; judges and prosecutors often are elected; critically important roles are played by lawyers who typically are thought of as private professionals serving as officers of the courts (see Schmidhauser 1979). The rules of law themselves often are justified as the will of the people or as the product of a pluralistic bargaining process.

"Backstage" one finds even greater penetration of the public sector by the private. "Power elite" theories seek to establish links between private centers of economic power and governmental officeholders and activities (see, for example, Mills 1956; Dye 1978; Hopkins 1978; Kerbo and Della Fave 1983; Milward and Francisco 1983; Useem 1983). Effectiveness of reform legislation often turns on the existence of face-to-face sanctions in a social field that encompasses both governmental officials and private leaders of various kinds. (Cf. the work of Lindblom 1977; see Tilman 1983 on reactions to Lindblom's work.) The effective boundaries of social fields are unsettled and often are the focus of struggle and change (Weyrauch 1969, 1971). Some people are leading actors in a social field, while others are bit players. Yet this relationship can change gradually or rapidly.

Semi-autonomous social fields are likely to be found at the margins of public government itself. For example, American courts are faced with many cases involving personal injuries caused by automobiles. Litigation has grown since the early days of motoring, and there has been the parallel development of insurance to cover liability. This has prompted the growth of professional insurance adjusters who determine what the company is willing to offer in settlement, plaintiffs' lawyers who work for contingent fees and bargain or litigate to increase the amount paid, specialized insurance defense lawyers who come forward when litigation threatens, and experts of many kinds who sell their opinions about the condition of products and patients. All of these actors find themselves in a continuing relationship mediated by judges and clerks of court, governed by a loose system of rules and sanctions (see Ross 1970), and so they are "repeat players," interested in the impact of what they do in today's case on next year's transactions (Galanter 1974). As a result, the vast majority of cases are settled out of court by these specialists, whose moves are governed both by rules enforced through powerful though informal sanctions and by explicit or tacit threats to file a complaint and litigate in court.

Within the criminal justice system, a similar field involves those who regularly prosecute and defend criminal cases. Assistant prosecuting attorneys and defense counsel play leading roles. Other important actors include trial judges, clerks of court, police officers and officials of the department, the public defender's office, and even newspaper reporters and editors (see Carter 1974; Pritchard 1985). In a corrupt city, one might also include the leaders of organized crime and key political officials (see Block and Thomas 1984). Any of these people can look forward to sanctions from some of the others if they make work in the social field more difficult. All find their tasks easier to carry out if they can count on cooperation and favors from the others. Mileski (1971) comments:

> One attorney . . . noted that whenever he obtained an "unreasonable" acquittal, the prosecutor penalized him by not calling his cases until the end of the day's session. This "penalty" would last about a week after the disapproved disposition. Not only the lawyer but also his client, then, must sometimes sit all day in court

for reasons irrelevant to the substance of the cases at hand. Ordinarily, clients with attorneys have their cases scheduled for very early or very late in the day's session. The court thus allows the attorneys to salvage most of each day for out-of-court matters. Defendants without attorneys are told the day, but not the time, of their court appearances. This favor may add to the court's leverage in coaxing attorneys toward routine cooperation. [p. 489]

Generally, those who interact repeatedly over time will find themselves in a semi-autonomous social field with rules and sanctions which reflect some balance of the long-term interests of all the actors in that field. Often this balance is not totally congruent with the official definition of roles (see Mechanic 1962). Many studies have shown that agencies charged with enforcing a law may try to mediate, educate, or persuade the targets of the regulation to comply with some part of the law or with its spirit, rather than going to court to seek sanctions for violations. Wherever this kind of "soft" law enforcement exists, there is reason to look for a social field with rules and sanctions of its own that apply both to the targets of regulation and to the regulators.

Anyone familiar with the social study of law will see the relevance of many of these examples of nongovernmental governing to concerns in the field. This review of the relationships between the legal system and various kinds of organizations and social fields which are formally outside the boundaries of government suggests that we must be concerned not only with private associations which mimic the structures and symbols of public government but also with those social fields closely related to the legal system which affect its operations. Ultimately, however, judgments about what the label "private government" requires turn on the usefulness of the analogy. This calls for the consideration of several problems in the field, asking what would be gained by a focus on various kinds of associations that do some of the work of the formal legal system or affect its operations.

PRIVATE GOVERNMENT AND TOPICS IN THE SOCIAL STUDY OF LAW

A private government perspective could improve work in a number of areas of law and the behavioral sciences. I will consider three major examples: (a) private government and the limits of effective legal action; (b) social fields, the legal system, and stability and change in society; and (c) the autonomy and accountability of private associations.

Private Government and the Limits of Effective Legal Action

At least since Pound's essay in 1917, "the limits of effective legal action" has been a classic problem, but one lacking classic answers. Much of the writing assumes a state issuing commands to individuals who, acting alone, choose to comply or evade in view of the benefits of crime and the costs of punishment considered in light of the risks of being caught. However, Moore (1978, p. 58) suggests that the limited success and unintended and unwanted side effects of innovative social legislation can be explained partly because "new laws are thrust upon going social arrangements in which there are complexes of binding obligations already in existence. Legislation is often passed with the intention of altering the going social arrangements in specified ways. The social arrangements are often effectively stronger than the new laws."

Developing this suggestion, I shall consider the functions of informal, relatively unstructured social networks, more permanent social fields, and then structured private governments of some complexity. Finally, I will examine implementation of regulations calling for affirmative action to hire and tenure women in universities as an example showing how structure and social fields involving both regulators and regulated interact to blunt the impact of laws seen as of questionable legitimacy by many of those affected.

The Impact of Increasing Degrees of Structure   Relatively unstructured *informal networks* can serve as gatekeepers, rationing access both to illegal goods and services and to government services and benefits. In both instances, such networks affect the impact of law. Those who sell illegal goods and services seldom can operate at a fixed address with a sign over the door inviting the public to trade nor can they advertise in the newspapers or in the Yellow Pages. Loosely structured social networks of people channel customers to those who can supply what is wanted, filter out unwanted individuals such as police officers pretending to be customers, and serve to insulate most levels of criminal organization from detection and punishment. For example, a visitor to a city can ask a hotel employee, a cab driver, or a bartender for aid in finding prohibited drugs, gambling, or a prostitute. If the visitor has selected the right person, he or she will be sent to one or more people guarding access to the illegal goods or services. Those experienced in finding illegal items will be able to read hints, body language, and situations to minimize difficulty in making links with suppliers. Each person in the network usually can screen out unwanted customers and possible police officers. Those participants at street level are easiest to find, but they know only what they need to know in order to minimize the risks to others in the criminal network. There is a system of rewards and punishments to hold the system together. Those who channel wanted customers can make money; those who tell police too much can be injured or killed.

Such networks sometimes can be used by law enforcement officials, with more or less success, as leverage points for applying the law against major entrepreneurs as well as the street-level sales force. Officers posing as potential customers buy the illegal goods or services and arrest those involved. Prosecutors then sometimes are able to trade a favorable plea bargain for information or testimony against those higher up in the chain of distribution. This works, of course, only when the value of the plea bargain outweighs the danger of retaliation from those who control the criminal network.

Similar networks can ration access to government services. Elected public officials at all levels do "casework" for their constituents (see Lineberry and Watson 1980; Abney and Lauth 1982). Sometimes this involves sending people to the right official with the necessary information. In a close case, at least, it is easier for an administrator to say yes than to reject a claim and explain the denial to a mayor, a representative, or a senator. Union shop stewards, religious leaders, and community leaders also perform such brokerage roles, sending people to the right place and exerting what influence they have on the decision that is made. Friends at school, at the workplace, or at the playground or laundry also can offer more or less accurate information on how to cope with government systems—where to go, whom to see, and what to say to gain access (see Nelson 1980). (Cf. the situation in the Soviet Union. See Simis 1982; Di Franceisco and Gitelman 1984.)

This rationing of access to public services often has impact on the effectiveness of reform law. Those who lack information and endorsements may be at a disadvantage:

they fail to ask for services to which they are entitled or their claims may get lost in bureaucratic procedures, prompting them to give up. Moreover, there is reason to expect that the well-connected who can use endorsements from various kinds of leaders to affect administrative decisions will come from some groups in the society rather than others. Some officials are bribed to produce favorable decisions, but bribery costs money. Some will have more opportunity than others to influence action this way (see Deysine 1980). Thus, laws that purport to apply equally to those entitled to their benefits will serve some and not others. Furthermore, some benefits are granted only if certain conditions are met; this is done to influence behavior. Insofar as lawmakers attempt to regulate in this manner, they will be only partially effective to the extent that gatekeepers channel services to some people and keep them from others. Those left out will have little incentive to modify their behavior in the desired direction.

Finally, those who serve as brokers of information and access may tell their clients how to comply with the form and not the substance of the law or how to hide the fact that they are not entitled to licenses or benefits. Here, too, brokerage systems may influence the impact of law. For example, a particular office of a state motor vehicle department may have an informal policy of failing teenage males unless they pass three "rule-of-thumb" tests which the inspectors think demonstrate respect for traffic laws. A group of friends at school may tell X, who is reckless and has great contempt for traffic laws, about these tests. X carefully complies and passes the three tests when he seeks his driver's license. X may pass and be licensed, but his recklessness and contempt may even be encouraged since he has beaten the system.

Lawyers sometimes serve the same function, telling clients how to comply in form but not in substance. Even if few lawyers show clients how to avoid having crimes detected, there is at least anecdotal evidence that many clients think lawyers will provide such service. Lawyers, then, may be hired to serve as substitutes for the gatekeepers involved in informal social networks, offering information about the operation of government agencies and, in some cases, influence over the content of decisions (see *Vanderbilt Law Review* 1984).

The kind of *social field* discussed by Moore as "often effectively stronger than the new laws" usually is more structured and permanent than the informal networks considered so far. Social fields can serve most of the functions of informal networks but their structure and permanence allow them additional means of warding off the influence of legal commands. There are a number of examples of social fields playing this part: Moore's own work considers an elite in an African nation attempting to implement a socialist program in the face of resistance from village and tribal units. In our country the closest analogy to the situation described by Moore might be a religious group that withdraws from ordinary society in order to continue a religious practice deemed illegal by state or federal law. Governments and religious groups have battled, with mixed results, over sending children to secular schools, polygamy, and the use of drugs in ceremonies.

Social fields need not be as structured, permanent, or distinct as a settled community to succeed in warding off regulation by the state. For example, those who work together or who are regulars at a bar may deal in stolen goods. Employees of a lumber yard may offer good bargains on stolen building materials to the group (see Henry 1981). Those who work in restaurants may help each other minimize their income tax burden by devising and sharing strategies for reporting as little income as possible on tax returns. It might look suspicious for a waitress to report no tips, but she may welcome help in determining how little she can report safely. Those who identify themselves as professional criminals may form a fairly structured network to aid their activities. One of the functions of a prison is that of a center for developing and reinforcing criminal networks. For example, safecrackers can share techniques and information about good places to rob, and those in the business are identified so that they may be contacted when ex-inmates resume their criminal careers and need help.

Social fields serve to undercut the impact of law in a variety of ways. A group can delegitimate compliance and make violation seem ordinary and acceptable. Those who would comply or even suggest doing so may be the subject of ridicule, ostracism, or even violence. In such a case, if membership in the group is valued, one has to consider risking loss of his or her position before complying openly. Alternatively, evasion can be legitimated in a number of ways. The definition of a situation can be transformed so that members can deny that they are violating a legal norm. For example, those who take goods from their employer can argue that it is not really stealing but a customary right and part of their compensation (see Tersine and Russell 1981). Or if members of the group have to acknowledge they are violating the law, violation can be rationalized, and this rationalization can be repeated so that it becomes part of the common sense of the field. For example, those who work in restaurants and receive tips justify not reporting all of them on their tax return because of all of the loopholes in the tax system benefiting the rich, the general unfairness of the tax system, or the senseless way in which governments spend money.

Members of the group also can teach techniques of evasion which minimize the risk of detection. Those interested in stealing by subverting the computers that control so much of modern business can share the latest techniques and ways to counter safeguards against tampering. If members of a social field regularly meet for legitimate purposes, this serves to cover their discussions of plans for breaking the law. For example, parents who attend the same church may plan on how to initiate prayers in their local school despite rulings of the Supreme Court. If they are all tied to the community, those who might object and try to blow the whistle could be subject to many powerful sanctions. Their children might be subject to ridicule and ostracism, their businesses might be boycotted, or their homes vandalized. In a small city, no one might be free to object to prayers in the local schools.

Moore's position stresses the power of social fields to resist unwanted regulation. Nonetheless, one wonders how far these groups can ward off the larger society when those who hold power are offended by or fear the social field. The Federal Bureau of Investigation had great success in undermining the Communist party during the 1950s; it had less success in similar attempts against groups in the civil rights and antiwar movements of the 1960s and 1970s. The Brazilian and Uruguayan governments seem to have defeated urban guerrilla movements which were well organized private governments seeking to overthrow public authority, but the British government has not been able to overcome the Provisional Wing of the Irish Republican Army. It seems unlikely that an adequate explanation of these differences can be found in the structures or processes of the revolutionary groups in the various countries—indeed, the processes and structures of most contemporary revolutionary groups draw on a common literature, including, importantly, the writings of the Brazilian Carlos Marighela (1971). At least part of the explanation for the different degrees of success in repressing guerrilla movements might involve the unwillingness of the British to use all of the tactics that the military regimes found acceptable. Probably public governments can overcome most, if not all, social fields if it is worth the price. However, undercover work attempting to infiltrate the group, harass-ment, and manipulation of public opinion to turn the group into a pariah require skill and money. They also cost valued privacy and freedom of association. More repressive mea-sures carry a higher price.

Social fields also may act in ways apparently serving to implement the operation of the legal process. Groups can support those seeking to enforce their rights under existing laws or to change the rules. A group may supply money and access to lawyers and others who know how to litigate, negotiate, and lobby. It also may serve as an audience, applauding appropriate behavior. If, as often is the case, lawmaking and law enforcement must be triggered by complaints, a group can provide not only resources but a shield against retaliation. In fact, one who speaks out may find it hard to back down and settle or drop the matter if the group defines this as selling out. Of course, all these valuable functions will be supplied only for a price. Groups will not support those they oppose, they will not campaign for legal action against their interests, and they may focus retaliation against the one seeking legal action that offends other members. As a result, individuals may be given powerful incentives to transform their desires and translate them into a vocabulary approved by whatever groups are available. In this way, for example, labor unions can limit the effectiveness of laws designed to give rights to individual union members against union leaders; an American Association of University Professors chapter on a campus can help insulate the administration from challenges by faculty members denied tenure or contract renewal and frustrate laws designed to affect such decisions.

When we turn from informal networks and social fields to what we more comfortably can call *private governments*—formally structured complex organizations such as business corporations, universities, and major charitable foundations—we find still additional barriers to effective legal action. Organizational structure and process itself is an impor-tant variable in attempts to control behavior, as a number of writers are beginning to recognize. I will begin by viewing the deviance of business corporations from a private government perspective, generalize this analysis by applying it to universities, and then attempt to show that complex organizations such as corporations and universities cannot always be viewed as something distinct from public government. Social fields often cut across organizational boundaries with important consequences for the impact of law.

Corporations are subject to a wide variety of direct legal controls in all Western societies. However, in the past few decades many have become concerned about the limited effectiveness of rules designed to protect the market, the environment, consum-ers, or the political system. Apparently, business organizations have a good deal of power to deflect what reformers think is or ought to be the law.

Public government also attempts to induce large organizations to implement certain policies less directly. An enforcement agency may pursue a policy of "soft" law enforce-ment, seeking to persuade large organizations to comply with agency directives. The threat of legal action may serve as part of the agencies' negotiating power, but this threat is often limited by obvious difficulties in applying sanctions. Also, if an agency can succeed in getting a large business corporation to agree to change practices, it, in effect, gains the use of the private organization's internal communication and sanction system to change the way things are done in local offices and places of business throughout the country. Governments also deal with private organizations by using contracts. By using the benefits of holding a government contract as an incentive, an agency can often gain agreement to carry out social policies more or less related to the transaction. For example, federal contractors must pay certain minimum wages and offer their workers certain conditions of employment. Despite these techniques, however, reformers worry that corporate deviance or mere token compliance is unacceptably high (*New York Times* 1985).

Several authors have stressed the effects of structure and process in studies seeking to understand unlawful organizational behavior and to fashion innovative and more effective sanctions. Coffee (1981) and Vaughan (1982, 1983) draw on sociological theories about the functioning of organizations, while Braithwaite (1982), Fisse (1981), and Fisse and Braithwaite (1984) base their analyses on an empirical research project in which over 200 senior executives of 50 transnational corporations, as well as many government officials, have been interviewed. I will first describe this group of studies, and then I will offer some additional considerations.

Vaughan argues that the environment in which organizations operate and their own processes generate incentives for individuals working within them to engage in deviant activity. Following Merton (1957a, 1957b), she argues that the goal of organizational success is so highly valued that the importance of attaining it outweighs concern about the means used. Businesses seek economic success measured in ways such as market share or the price of the corporate stock. Great efforts have been made in modern business corporations to create decentralized structures and sophisticated accounting systems so that those responsible for profit and loss can be rewarded or punished. At the same time, normative support for succeeding only through legal means has been progressively lessened.

For example, the definition of deviance usually is doubtful. Reforms will not be perceived as sensible and right if they make it harder for managers to gain rewards and avoid punishments within the organization. While reformers may see programs that minimize environmental pollution as highly beneficial, a manager may see only that they increase the costs of operation making it harder to reach the target for return on investment. Also, since it is costly and difficult to prosecute a large corporation quite able to defend itself, government agencies frequently resort to negotiations and informal proceedings. Those who violate the law are seldom sanctioned severely, and, as a result, only a few examples of wrongdoing are publicized. The fact that deals are made may suggest that the subject is not an important issue of right and wrong. Coffee points out that a sanction severe enough to outweigh the benefits of violation would have to be so great as to threaten the existence of the corporation. As a result, sanctions tend to be mere tokens; they are more like fines for overtime parking than punishment for truly wrongful behavior. Since government so often cannot enforce the law, managers evade and achieve success. Thus, illegal action becomes accepted within an organization as just the way things are done. Managers who attempted to comply with the law would face a serious handicap when compared with those who cut corners to get results.

Vaughan recognizes that her structural incentive argument fails to explain the behavior of all corporate actors. Many, if not most, business people do not violate the law. Others violate it but are not aware they are doing so because they do not know the rule or they misunderstand what it commands. She cites with approval Coffee's explanation for illegal behavior which rests on an interaction between psychological and structural factors. Coffee notes that modern corporations tend to be multidivisional and decentralized. Top management allocates funds to managers of profitable divisions and disciplines those who fail to meet targeted goals for return on investment. Thus, the manager responsible for operational decisions is increasingly separated by organizational structure, language, goals, and experience from the financial managers who plan for the future and decide on rewards and punishments. Coffee argues that this means that "the locus of corporate crime is predominantly at the lower to middle management level" (p. 397). He explains that

> [t]he middle manager is acutely aware that he can be easily replaced; he knows that if he cannot achieve a quick fix, another manager is in the wings, eager to assume operational control over a division. The results of such a structure are predictable: When pressure is intensified, illegal or irresponsible means become attractive to a desperate middle manager who has no recourse against a stern but myopic notion of accountability that looks only to the bottom line of the income statement. [p. 398]

Vaughan recognizes that incentives to violate laws are not a sufficient explanation for corporate crime; there must be opportunities for unlawful conduct as well. In large complex organizations unlawful behavior may be both encouraged and hidden from insiders at other levels as well as from outsiders. Officials of subunits are likely to defend their domain whatever the claims of other units or outsiders. Control over subunits largely rests on accounting systems which disclose the consequences of various practices but obscure other things. In Coffee's terms, this allows senior managers to "piously express shock at their subordinates' actions while still demanding strict 'accountability' on the part of such managers for short-term operating results" (p. 410).

The analysis in these articles could be carried further. Vaughan notes that corporate managers may have ties outside the corporation that provide incentives to comply with the law or not to get caught violating it. She says that "[a]lternative skills, alternative sources of income, and alternative validating social roles reduce financial and social dependence on the firm. Consequently, external rewards and punishments may reduce the organization's ability to mobilize individual efforts in its behalf, despite processes that produce a normative environment supporting unlawful conduct" (p. 1392). Obviously, corporate managers, like the rest of us, have acquired complex attitudes about following rules from family, neighborhood groups, schools, mass media, and experience. On the one hand, there are general messages indicating that we should obey the law. On the other hand, we often learn in school, and particularly from competitive athletics, that we may cheat for a good cause. From newspapers and television we learn that respected figures break rules in all kinds of social games. Corporate life can be seen as a game where winning is the only goal.

At the same time, social fields and organizations such as business corporations may reward compliance with the law. In at least some corporations there are ways to avoid the kinds of pressures described by Vaughan and Coffee. For example, one may be able to use members of the legal staff as a way to support compliance rather than violation. Lawyers can be blamed for increasing costs by fashioning procedures in response to new regulations, and a manager may be able to bring his or her department's activities to the attention of the general counsel's office so that he or she will appear to be forced to comply. The legal staff may welcome a chance to symbolize respect for the law since the techniques of compliance are within its domain, and the need to respond to regulation enhances its power within the organization. A manager may be able to dress an ethical stance in prudential garb: complying with the law can be justified in terms of the negative consequences of the likely bad publicity if the firm was caught violating a regulation.

This is not to say that Vaughan and Coffee are wrong in stressing the pressures to evade the law, but more emphasis on possible offsetting pressures supporting compliance would seem warranted. We know little about when the balance falls one way or the other. Furthermore, corporations that have suffered serious blows to their reputations as the result of publicity surrounding getting caught violating the law may modify their incentive systems to ease the pressures for deviance—at least temporarily. Of course, as Coffee stresses, while the formal message from a corporate president's office may call for compliance, the real message communicated may be, rather, "don't get caught."

Coffee's argument that the locus of corporate crime is middle management seems only partially true. Undoubtedly, in many cases the pressures he describes are real. Nonetheless, some kinds of corporate crime must involve the participation of top management. For example, decisions to sponsor a military coup to overthrow the government of a nation which has threatened corporate interests, to bribe high governmental officials, to continue participation in international cartels during wartime with corporations based in enemy nations, and the like are not usually within the power of middle management to make or implement. Certain multinational corporations, moreover, interact with governments, pursuing what could be viewed as their own foreign policies. Lowenthal (1978) observes that

> [in] a curious sense, it is much easier for the [United States] government to manage its relations with the Soviet Union or China than with Chile or Peru. Latin American and Caribbean countries are very strongly influenced by decisions taken by Exxon, the American Smelting and Refining Co. (ASARCO), United Brands, Citibank, Manufacturers' Hanover Trust, or Chase Manhattan, to name just a few examples. And some of the main problems in inter-American relations—especially access to capital and technology—are issues over which the U.S. government has considerably less influence than non-governmental actors. [p. 122]

For example, during the Carter Administration, it was United States foreign policy, reinforced by legislation, not to supply arms to nations that repressed the human rights of their citizens. However, American corporations could evade government policy by channeling sales through their foreign subsidiaries. It seems likely that the decisions to make such sales were made at the upper levels of management.

A Case Study: Affirmative Action for Women in Universities   Finally, the discussion in these articles draws a rather sharp distinction between public and private spheres and fails to cover social fields that include both the regulators and regulated. We will turn to an extended example—affirmative action for women at universities—to stress that the structure of a large private government and the existence of social networks cutting across formal boundaries can work together to blunt the effectiveness of regulation. In other words, we will use a private government perspective to analyze the limited impact of a legal reform. We will stress both the relationships between public and private spheres and the interpenetrations of the two areas. The example also will make clear that much of the analysis in the articles just considered is not limited to business corporations but applies to other complex organizations as well.

Women have faced barriers to becoming and remaining university professors throughout the history of higher education in this country because of conscious policy or circumstance (Bernard 1964). By 1972, there were three bodies of law designed to eliminate discrimination against women and members of minority groups by large academic institutions. First, Title VII of the Civil Rights Act of 1964 was extended to universities and colleges, allowing academic women who saw themselves as victims of discrimination in hiring, promotion, or tenure to sue for court orders directing that they be granted the position to which they were entitled, damages, or both. Groups of women also could form a class and sue on behalf of themselves and others, seeking judgments placing a university under judicial supervision to ensure the abolition of discrimination. While there were some notable victories, courts have been hesitant to substitute their judgment for those of professionals about the quality of teaching and scholarship. Second, under the Equal Pay Act academic institutions may not pay different salaries to men and women with substantially equal qualifications who occupy substantially equal positions.

Finally, under Executive Order 11375 universities which receive large federal contracts must submit a plan to take affirmative action to overcome the effects of past discrimination against women (see, generally, Prager 1982). Employers must analyze their work force and the pool of qualified potential employees and establish goals so that the composition of a work force eventually will reflect the percentages of women in the pool. This is not a quota system nor a requirement that women less qualified than available men be hired. Rather, the federal contractor must show some progress as a result of good faith efforts in meeting goals when required reports are made.

Generally, this regulation of academic hiring received mixed reviews from the regulated. University professors and administrators did not object to the Equal Pay Act, and few had difficulty with the idea that a woman who had suffered discrimination ought to have a remedy. However, most of them expected almost no valid claims because they believed that universities, with but few exceptions, hire, promote, and grant tenure on the basis of merit. Some were concerned with the potential burden of defending a discrimination claim even when it lacked merit. Most senior professors and administrators saw affirmative action as unsuited to a university.

In the 1970s, women's organizations, along with minority and handicapped groups, sued the federal agencies charged with enforcing the requirement of affirmative action and negotiated promises that the law would be enforced. Nonetheless after more than a decade, members of these organizations remain dissatisfied with the amount of compliance with affirmative action laws by universities while federal grants and contracts continue to flow to them (see, for example, Abramson 1977; Hornig 1980; McKenna and Denmark 1975; Page 1978; Vladeck and Young 1978).

A sketch of the process involved in attempts at enforcement over a decade at a major campus of a state university—called State University at Fillmore for purposes of this study—will illustrate the complex and multileveled interactions when a private government is reluctant to carry out the demands of public government (see J. Macaulay 1980). In 1970, after complaints of nonenforcement of the law were made by national women's groups, representatives of the Office of Civil Rights (OCR) of the Department of Health, Education and Welfare visited State University at Fillmore. They told university administrators that they saw a pattern of underutilization of women and of salary discrimination. The 1970 campus affirmative action plan was found to be inadequate, and campus officials signed an agreement to produce an acceptable one, update it annually, and submit the plan and the reports to OCR. The OCR staff announced that it planned a follow-up visit to the campus in January 1971.

The president of State University then issued a directive to all campuses in the system, including the one at Fillmore, to appoint an affirmative action officer (AAO) and a Committee on the Status of Women. This was done at Fillmore, and the AAO and the committee gained a measure of power from the threat to federal contracts and grants posed by the OCR visit and planned return. Salaries were investigated, and a number of extreme cases of discrimination were uncovered. Deans and department chairpersons were told to grant raises to remedy these inequities. A number of women were discovered teaching a major course load without permanent positions and at low pay. Many of these women were promoted to tenure track positions or given tenure in recognition of their long service and the unfairness of their past treatment by the university. A utilization analysis was done, and it revealed a pattern of underrepresentation of women in the majority of departments at the campus.

Once these steps were taken, however, a pattern developed which was to be repeated throughout the decade. The AAO would work on an affirmative action plan and write reports with data on the hiring, promotion, and tenuring of women. Field personnel of the various federal agencies which successively were given enforcement responsibility over universities would write or visit the campus. Members of a social field composed of women with some connection to the university who were dissatisfied with progress on affirmative action would meet with the federal personnel and point out defects in the plan and statistics. The field personnel would recommend that the Fillmore campus be required to take certain steps or have contracts and grants disapproved. But then the threatening clouds would blow away and officials in Washington would pronounce the Fillmore campus still approved to receive contracts and grants although it never produced the kind of plan or data which would seem to be required in order to comply with the letter or purposes of the law.

Moreover, although the number of women hired increased, the proportion of those with permanent tenured positions rose very little. Women's promotion chances remained low, and departments that never employed women in proportion to their availability continued always to fall short of their goals. One year a state civil rights agency found probable cause to believe that a university department had discriminated against a woman when it refused to grant her tenure; another year a state commission on women found the university's efforts in affirmative action to be inadequate. Women, and members of minority groups, continued to point to figures showing that the university was falling far short of its announced goals. Still the university kept saying that it was fully complying with all laws and regulations, and federal agencies took no action against it.

Four explanations stand out for the success of State University at Fillmore in warding off the impact of these laws: affirmative action lacked legitimacy; the structure and process of the university diffused responsibility and made it hard to find reliable data; social networks that included both regulators and the regulated had the power to deflect enforcement; and the consequences of cutting off contracts and grants to a great research university were unacceptable. They will be examined in turn.

Affirmative action for women at universities progressively lost legitimacy in the eyes of those with the power to make decisions. The academic community can be viewed as a loosely coordinated social field, and its culture operated to undercut the legitimacy of this program. Affirmative action was sharply attacked in a number of books and articles written by professors (see, for example, Lester 1974; Posner 1979; Sowell 1976). This literature tended to paint an idealized picture of university life, glorifying an unselfish pursuit of truth, devotion to students, and decision based on merit—the academy was pictured as something like a religious community, fundamentally different from factories and business offices where affirmative action might make some sense. Affirmative action regulations were labeled "reverse discrimination," as the title of one book put it (Glazer 1975). Whatever the merits of the arguments presented, these books and articles helped professors and administrators justify evading or minimally complying with the letter of the law (cf. Lipset 1982).

In addition to questionable legitimacy in the eyes of those making hiring, promotion, and tenure decisions, government officials charged with enforcing affirmative action regulations faced problems of structure and process. Most prestigious universities have a complex structure characterized by a tension between the powers of those who administer and those who teach and do research. Formally, usually a university is run by a governing board which delegates power to a chief executive officer. This administrator, in turn, appoints deans to administer various subunits. Within these divisions, there are departments charged with teaching and research in their own area. In theory, deans and chairpersons administer while the faculty makes policy within boundaries set by statutes or a charter and the decisions of the governing board. In practice, however, professors are "street level bureaucrats" (cf. Prottas 1978; Carter 1974) who operate relatively autonomously with little direct supervision. The faculty claims, and often has, power to decide who is to be hired, promoted, and given tenure. Those higher up the chain of command have veto power, but custom demands that it be used only sparingly. Obviously, there is great opportunity for negotiation and politics within the formal decision-making process.

Just as Vaughan and Coffee suggest, this decentralization of power had important consequences for the enforcement of affirmative action requirements. It was hard to detect violations and noncompliance as long as those in the departments making the hiring and tenuring decisions knew enough not to post signs saying "no women need apply" and to make gestures such as advertising positions and interviewing at least a few women along with the men being considered in the usual course of recruiting.

Government officials exerted pressure for affirmative action at higher administrative levels. Professors usually learn about affirmative action regulations not by reading the law but from directives coming down from above. Those who wrote the directives at Fillmore tended to simplify and pass on interpretations which would not upset traditional practices very much. Professors also learned about the rules from atrocity stories passed along by deans and chairpersons that told of the costs and burdens of red tape and bureaucratic procedures. These stories may well have undercut any impulse to make significant changes in departmental recruiting and decision-making.

Since most important hiring and tenure decisions take place in the departments, administrators were able to close their eyes to evasion as long as they could find some apparent or symbolic compliance. The day-to-day burden of dealing with affirmative action usually is placed on an assistant to the university head. Such assistants have had relatively little power unless the president or chancellor wanted to push for compliance. Assistants who want to keep their jobs are likely to negotiate for gestures and proceed cautiously (see Liss 1977). They have little incentive, from the standpoint of their careers, to make available information that might embarrass the university. Rather, all the incentives are to interpret the data as showing progress in hiring women. (Cf. Weiss and Gruber 1984.) If this proved difficult, assistants could at least make a case for good faith effort to comply in the face of adverse economic conditions, budget constraints, and less hiring and tenuring.

In addition to the questionable legitimacy of affirmative action and structural characteristics of the university, there is also a social field comprising those who are supposed to enforce these laws and those university professors and administrators who are the targets of regulation. For example, State University at Fillmore had acquired a reputation as a leader in affirmative action for women because of its early efforts to correct clear-cut examples of discrimination. As a result, in 1974 its AAO became a consultant to the Department of Health, Education and Welfare. Her role was reflected in a memorandum written in February of that year. She reported that she was "spending almost half of every week in Washington, D.C., trying to win a modification or deletion" of rules such as those requiring the compilation of data about employees. Without these data complete statistical analyses for evidence of underutilization of or discrimination against women could never be done. Moreover, she described her plan to go only so far in complying with the letter of the affirmative action regulations as to be able to comply fully within ninety days if and when the federal government ever insisted that the Fillmore campus meet them; her constant contact with officials in Washington apparently enabled her to judge when it would be necessary to begin to compile a precise plan and detailed and accurate statistics.

The AAO was a member of the faculty of a department at Fillmore, an officer of the campus administration, and a consultant to the federal government's enforcement agency. Her role crossed formal organizational boundaries. The consequences for the impact of the law were shown by events in November and December of 1974. In November, an assistant to the president of State University wrote HEW's director of the Higher Education Division, asking how the affirmative action plans of various campuses of State University should be submitted for approval by HEW. The director and the AAO of the Fillmore campus were well acquainted as a result of all the consulting and lobbying in Washington. On December 3, the director telephoned the AAO at home in the evening after working hours. The AAO's memorandum concerning the conversation states:

> [The director] indicated to me that the agency did not wish to engage in general institution-wide compliance reviews while the standards and procedures . . . [then in effect] are still extant. She further indicated that to the best of her knowledge and belief no major university could be today found in compliance if . . . [these] standards are applied. Consequently, she stated she believed that an on-site review at this time, as required by Revised Order 14 for approval of an affirmative action plan, would find many or all . . . system schools out of compliance, without regard to any excellence or lack of it in real progress in affirmative action. She expressed the further belief that the target of such reviews

would automatically become the . . . [State University at Fillmore] . . . and that we were very likely therefore to go to fund cut-off.

She indicated that she felt such compliance reviews in the present circumstances would be very destructive, supportive neither of affirmative action nor of educational goals. But, she noted, in view of the currently pending suit in which NOW, WEAL and others have charged HEW with nonenforcement, she was not at liberty to instruct . . . [the assistant to the President of the University] . . . in writing not to submit the plans.

In view of all these circumstances she asked me if I could insure that the plans were not submitted.

The AAO's solution to this problem was to "draft a tentative letter" for the HEW director to send to the assistant to the president "indicating that the plans *could* be submitted but that the agency maintained a reviewing schedule to which, absent some pressing necessity, it preferred to adhere." The letter was written, the Fillmore campus plan was not submitted, and this threat to the flow of federal money passed.

This was not the only instance of informal contacts designed to blunt compliance with the letter of the regulations. Whenever the threat looked serious, administrators of the Fillmore campus and influential professors were able to go over the head of the field investigators and the regional offices and take their case to top officials in Washington. Those at the top of the chain of command in the agencies charged with enforcing affirmative action regulations are part of the higher education social field. Whatever formal organization charts might indicate, these cabinet officers, top level administrators, and their staffs often were former university professors, foundation executives, or others who held graduate degrees and were sympathetic to the traditions of higher education and who were often linked by friendship or long association with officials in national educational associations if not directly with those who ran the Fillmore campus. These federal officials were not "captured" by the university administrators; they just understood one another and shared similar attitudes and values. Often, during the 1970s, those ultimately responsible were former academics temporarily serving as cabinet officers or administrators. As the Fillmore campus chancellor's lawyer told a group of law students, when a contract or grant was held up because of questions about affirmative action at this campus, administrators, professors, and representatives of higher education organizations in Washington "have been able to find the people who are ultimately responsible for whatever the regional office is off on and help to get them back on the track."

Finally, we have to look to the consequences of enforcing the affirmative action regulations to the letter. If the federal government had cut off all grants and contracts to State University at Fillmore, it would have crippled a major research and teaching center. Both public and private universities are dependent on federal funds. Moreover, if administrators and professors at Fillmore had been forced to comply with the federal regulations as they were written, traditional hiring practices would have been overturned and many members of the faculty would have been antagonized. Yet this price did not have to be paid because affirmative action for women did not have great public support, and those who ran State University at Fillmore had friends with important positions in the legislative and executive branches of the federal government. In short, it was far easier to have symbolic but unenforced regulations than to pay the price for implementing them.

Social Fields, the Legal System, and Stability and Change in Society

Those writing broad social theories often see a need to account for law and legal institutions. One interested in the social study of law frequently finds these accounts unsatisfying because the theorist posits a formal picture of law. When one adds private governments, social fields, and networks to a sociological view of law, much found in these broader social theories seems inadequate if not wrong. Of course, turning from normative claims or theoretical statements about the functions of legal systems to a description of law in operation makes neat theories messy and complex, but oversimplification seldom is a virtue.

While this is not the place to describe and distinguish the variety of existing social theories and their accounts of the role of law, I will consider elements common to many of them and then discuss how concern with private governments, social fields, and networks might add to or question these theories. I am not offering a worked-out picture of society that accounts for the parts played by law and the legal system, but rather examples that suggest some of the things that any theory must deal with if it is to be useful to those concerned with the place of law.

The Roles Played by Law in Various Social Theories

Before one can question the treatment of law in a social theory, it is necessary to sketch the way in which it deals with it. Here I will describe briefly and generally the account of law in structural-functional, conflict, and Marxist-derived theories. In the next section, I will consider how elements in these theories might be questioned if a broader view of the place of law were taken.

Many social theorists have offered what are called *structural-functional theories*. Here the focus is on social structure—the more or less enduring patterns of the ways people interact. Social phenomena are seen as interdependent as in a biological system. Action taken in one social unit affects the functioning of others. For example, economic and legal systems affect each other: an impoverished society cannot afford complex legal institutions, but modern industrialized nations have developed legal institutions where police, judges, lawyers, and regulatory agencies importantly affect the way business is conducted.

In most social theories, a major problem is the explanation of social order and the operation and continuation of societies. Most structural-functionalists see law as an important factor in such an explanation (see, for example, Bredemeier 1962; Grace and Wilkinson 1978; Koch 1980; Lamo de Espinosa 1980; Mishra 1982; Parsons 1962; Wilkinson 1981). They draw pictures of a relatively harmonious and stable society with the legal system playing a key role at its margin. People have expectations about the behavior of others and how others expect them to behave. Thus, one can rely on what others will do and pattern one's own conduct in order to fit in. People learn how to act in particular situations, and the norms governing social behavior become part of their psychological make-up. Most obligations are fulfilled naturally, and external sanctions play only a secondary, and often indirect, role. While there is much normative regulation, law is only an objective and visible part of a pyramid of habits, customs, norms, rules, and law.

Compliance with social norms may be enforced by sanctions inherent in reciprocal relationships, which exist in great numbers in any society. One has friends, interacts in groups for recreation, and repeatedly engages in business dealings with the same people.

One who complies with the expectations of others in these relationships will continue to receive whatever benefits are involved, which may range from love or esteem to profitable business opportunities. One who disappoints the expectations of those in continuing relationships risks being subject to a range of sanctions: one's partners may frown, use sarcasm or ridicule, discontinue the relationship, or retaliate by using violence. (Cf. Griffiths' 1984 comments on gossip systems.) Only in extreme situations will one's partners call the police or file a lawsuit.

Those disputes that occur despite internalized norms and relational sanctions will be the product of ambiguity in the application of generally held values to particular situations. This creates a need for arbiters who can impose, or threaten to impose, sanctions so that their decisions about the proper interpretation of the norms will be carried out. In this way, legal activity serves the function of social integration by aiding the coordination or unification of various parts of the society.

Adjudication clarifies values in light of changing situations. In most instances, the decision of a court or arbiter will be accepted and does not have to be imposed. However, the legal system must be related to the state so that its monopoly of the legitimate use of force ensures that legal norms override any inconsistent social norms. In a few rare cases, a display of force may be needed to assert the priority of legal norms over all others by sanctioning those deviants who are not contained by other means of social control. Sanctions can be imposed only when permitted by the rule of law: one may be arrested, tried, convicted, and imprisoned for robbery only when the elements of the crime are present. If sanctions could be imposed apart from the rules, they would lose some or all of their normative force.

Some particularly important social values will be institutionalized as special legal agencies are created to protect them (Mayhew 1968). Certain kinds of equality are at least symbolized when a government creates an Equal Employment Opportunities Commission; certain patterns of coping with labor disputes are institutionalized by the creation of a National Labor Relations Board. These agencies must then have access to the people who violate the norms being protected. This means that those aggrieved must have incentives to participate in bringing problems to them.

When important disputes do come to the legal system as complaints, causes of action, or pleas for services, the system can then serve other functions which also carry out social integration. Disputes signal policy-makers and the interpreters of norms that there is need for an adjustment so that similar disputes or claims do not arise in the future.

Many theorists also see actual decisions as serving to legitimate society, the legal system, and the particular judgment in a case in a number of ways. The norms selected for application are seen as appropriate, and their application is consistent with the expectations of those observing the legal process. The legal system itself may have enough prestige so that members of the public will see any norms applied or interpreted by it as just, simply because they are crystallized in legal doctrine. Acceptance flows from at least two sources. First, the legal system is viewed as autonomous and not dependent on other centers of power. It can make and enforce its decisions impartially. Second, legal officials are selected in ways that most members of the society see as appropriate—they are experts who are selected in recognition of their skill, they have long practical experience, they are elected by the people, or they are appointed by those who symbolize the society. Finally, legal action promotes legitimacy because the legal system is perceived as having enough effectiveness to implement the norms it serves; it is more than idle rhetoric and pious preaching in the face of reality.

Conflict theories attack structural-functionalism, but, generally, this perspective tends to criticize ideas about the functions of law in society rather than offer a complete theory of its own (see, for example, Chambliss and Seidman 1971; Chambliss 1973, 1979; Quinney 1975). Conflict theorists see society not as harmonious and stable but held together by the use or threats of force. Law legitimates police violence and other uses of power to undercut attacks on the system. The reality of law is a police officer with a club or a SWAT team with automatic weapons attacking any group that threatens the stability of the existing order. Law supports the structures of property and exploitation. Under a system of division of labor, people are not self-sufficient, and they need cash to buy their needs. This means that they must have jobs and keep them. However, one's claim to a job under the law is always questionable. Those who challenge their employers risk being fired and gaining a reputation as troublemakers so that substitute employment will be difficult to find. These threats, rather than a general normative consensus, dampen open dissent and explain the persistence of societies in which few of the people share most of the benefits.

Conflict theorists turn structural-functionalism on its head. Instead of normative consensus, they say there is a great deal of dissensus and cynical knowledge. Instead of seeing the society, its legal system, and particular decisions as legitimate, they see cheating, manipulation, or simple resignation as the ways to cope with an unjust system which cannot be confronted directly. People at the bottom of the distribution of wealth and status do not accept their place as part of the natural order of things or as their just reward for lack of effort or skill. They see people at the top of the society as having gained their position illegitimately or as descendants of such people. Business executives cheat on their taxes, bribe American and foreign government officials, and foist shoddy products on the public. Elaborate rationalizations are fabricated by those at all levels for violating official norms.

Conflict theory tells us that, contrary to the claim of the structural-functionalists, the legal system and particular decisions seldom yield legitimacy. People do not see law as salient to their lives; at best, it is a background factor with limited impact. While the daily operation of law possibly might reflect common sense, people hear only about extraordinary cases. The acquittal of the man who attempted to assassinate President Reagan did not create legitimacy for either the criminal justice system or the insanity defense (see Hans and Slater 1983). Indeed, those decisions which are publicized are likely to provoke anger and dissensus. One need mention only the opinions of the Supreme Court concerning school prayers, abortion, and racial integration of the public schools as examples. People suspect that legal decisions often turn on wealth and connections rather than on apolitical, rational norms applied by an autonomous body of experts. Awareness of institutions such as plea bargaining and the settlement of personal injury cases would seem to reinforce such a view. Legal procedures do not reassure most people that the game is fair. Rather, they appear to be ploys in a game benefiting the economic interests of the legal profession and those who can pay the best lawyers to play for their side.

Austin Turk (1976) points out that, even when it is not corrupt, the legal system may promote conflict rather than social integration. Control of the system, for example, is a prize about which groups can fight—the power to appoint judges and administrators is one of the things gained by winning elections. Moreover, the chance to mobilize whatever power courts possess can be an incentive to abandon acceptance of the status quo. *Brown v. Board of Education* (the school desegregation case) was one of many factors provoking the civil rights movement and conflict in an effort to change traditional ways in the South (see Harding 1975). The chance of victories before courts and legislatures may undercut compromise, generating more conflict rather than stabilizing the society.

Marxist-derived theories show a different view of the functions of the law in postcapitalist societies. (For reviews of this literature, see Greenberg and Anderson 1981; Jessop 1980.) Most of these theorists, rather like the structural-functionalists, see society as composed of a number of subsystems and structures. While in a Marxist-inspired theory, the economic system and class relations will be central, the state and law are seen as necessary or useful in attempting to cope with contradictions, inconsistencies, and imperfections in the interest of the dominant class. Koch (1980, p. 6), in an essay highly critical of Marxist-derived theories, finds that they typically see the state and law fulfilling functions such as "the guarantee of legal relations, especially the relations of private property, the provision of general material conditions for production activity (the 'infrastructure'), the regulation of the conflict between wage-labour and capital and the defence and expansion of total national capital on the capitalist world market."

Many of these theorists see traditional bourgeois law as undercutting the possibility of effective class struggle, as working toward the acceptance of exploitation through mystification. In liberal states, individuals are formally equal before the law and are bearers of rights. Balbus (1977), in an often-cited article, argues that capitalist legal systems make people into citizens, abstracted from their personality and actual social situation. In this way they can be made to appear equal, despite all the real differences in status and power between the dominant and dominated classes. This militates against the formation of class consciousness. "[T]he 'community' produced by the legal form contributes decisively to the reproduction of the very capitalist mode of production which makes genuine community impossible" (p. 580).

Related theories see law as part of the battle for common sense (see Femia 1983). Except in times of stress, all classes accept a world view in which the existing order is seen as natural and proper. However, this view advances the interests of only the dominant class. Traditional intellectuals rationalize concepts of social order as the material basis of the dominant class's power change. Law and legal intellectuals are but part of this larger picture. For example, as economic crisis during the depression of the 1930s began to prompt greater governmental regulation of the economy, economists and law professors in sympathy with the New Deal fashioned a rationalization for action which previously had been thought unconstitutional. Simplified versions of the new ideology were passed along and ultimately became part of the vocabulary of both major American political parties. When economic conditions changed and New Deal regulation inconvenienced business, another generation of economists and law professors appeared ready to champion efficiency, free markets, and other symbols of a capitalist world view.

Adding Private Governments, Social Fields, and Networks to Social Theory
None of these theoretical pictures adequately incorporates the roles played by private governments, social fields, and networks and their complex relationships with the formal

legal system. In particular settings some writers recognize that theories must be expanded to cover individuals acting in groups (cf. Zimring 1981; Gottlieb 1983; Nader 1984). However, this has been the exception rather than the rule. I will consider a number of instances where the theories seem to assume a state or legal system on one side confronting an isolated individual on the other. I will note where social groups have been added to the analysis. Finally, I will suggest what might be added to these theories if a broader perspective were used consistently.

"Legal" Functions Are Played by Private Systems. At the outset, recall that the state and the legal systems often face competition from private governments which perform some or almost all of their functions. In talking about the effectiveness of law, I noted that corporations may be able to socialize employees to internalize norms different from those of the larger society, and they may be able to sanction noncompliance with corporate norms. If the public law calls for measures to protect the environment, but the cost of these measures threatens the economic health of the corporation, officials must cope with this conflicting set of signals. On the one hand, these officials can comply with the law but seek to influence elections so that new legislators, governors, and presidents will change the rules or enforcement practices. On the other hand, they can try to evade the command of the law, and often do so with great skill.

Other forms of competition with public government were noted earlier. Private governments such as corporations, churches, and labor unions can pursue their own foreign policies, in concert with or in opposition to official policy (see, for example, Kowalewski and Leitko 1983; Teulings 1982). Nations may form alliances with large multinational corporations or such corporations may seek to overthrow governments. Churches may battle nations about human rights, seeking to affect what is called world public opinion. Labor unions may boycott goods from certain nations. Private governments often take over what we think of as state functions. Corporations often provide their own police when the public police seem inadequate to serve their interests, and I have already noted how white-collar crime is often handled privately. Trade associations often make rules governing members, devise standard forms to facilitate making contracts, and arbitrate or mediate disputes.

In short, a social theory cannot assume that public government has a monopoly on those functions the theory assigns to "the legal system" (see Greenberg 1976). Of course, a theorist can escape this problem by expanding the term "legal system" to include whatever agency, public or private, performs what the theorist wishes to call legal functions. However, such a move glosses over whether it makes a difference if a particular function is performed publicly or privately. It seems likely that the more private and decentralized the structures for performing a social function with broad impact, the greater the problems of coordination and integration.

Channeling and Filtering Matters In and Out of the Legal System. Not all problems, disputes, claims, and the like existing in society come before legal officials, and many of those that do are not handled in ways that these theorists assume. Thus, functions assigned to the legal system by many of these theories become questionable. Here I will consider the consequences for these theories of two aspects of social fields and networks: the filtering and channeling done by gatekeepers to the legal system and the coping with recurrent legal problems that takes place on the margins of law.

There has been extensive study of dispute processing during the past decade. Relying on some of this work, Luhmann (1981) expands structural-functional theory to show that whether or how the legal system will play an integrative role is uncertain. He offers a theory of "thematization thresholds" as a barrier to transforming problems into legal questions. While law can stabilize people's expectations in interaction as these theories assume, for this to happen legal norms must be made into the theme of discussion between the parties—concrete situations must be "thematized" as legal questions: a buyer's dissatisfaction with the quality of a new car, for example, could be discussed with the dealer in terms of warranty and the remedy limitation in their form contract rather than in terms of other kinds of norms. However, in many situations there are good reasons to avoid invoking legal norms. By openly confronting another with the question of whether she is acting legally, one shatters the comfortable consensus that is normally assumed in a social relationship. Legal themes introduce the possibility of disagreement about interpretation of norms or the history of the situation and tend to force discussion into a dichotomy of right and wrong. Assertion of legal right is an attempt at coercion, and it may be a challenge to fight to defend one's honor. Interaction is moved from the domain of family life, a continuing economic relationship involving trust, and the like. In these domains what is given up now is likely to be rewarded by benefits that come later. It is difficult to threaten divorce and still keep a marriage alive; it is hard to contest issues in a divorce proceeding and continue to interact afterward.

Whether or not one will cross this thematization threshold is determined, Luhmann says, in large part by the prospects of social support in case conflict should arise. Turning to law usually means withdrawing from the relationship in question, and often one needs support to replace the benefits of the situation rejected. A legal discussion may initiate a chain of events with an unpredictable outcome, and the more uncertain the future, the more support is needed.

FitzGerald, Hickman, and Dickins (1980) see members of relevant social fields and networks serving not only as supporters but also as audiences, reality-testers, and defusers when disputes arise. For example, the group at the bar separates likely combatants; networks of friends and relatives repair defective products so the buyer does not have to confront a seller and demand a remedy; the women watching over small children at a playground work out potential neighborhood disputes. People in social fields can suppress disputes by making fun of one who voices a complaint or by reacting in such a way as to communicate that an asserted claim of right shows weakness and a lack of self-reliance (see Engel 1984). Baumgartner (1985) suggests that middle-class people may be less willing to use the legal system than those lower on the social scale. The threat of disapproval by one's peers may serve a gatekeeping function. At times those in a social field can act as champions or mediators, offering ways to communicate with the other party in the dispute, suggesting solutions, or adding their own power to press for resolution (see Eisenstadt and Roniger 1980). Significant others, on the other hand, can pour gasoline on the fire and raise consciousness—one can be told to fight and how to do it. Such an audience, moreover, may make it difficult to back down and compromise or withdraw without a loss of face.

Who plays these roles? Members of social fields or networks centered in the workplace or neighborhood may be called on. Ethnic or religious communities may be invoked when members do not view themselves as autonomous. However, Ladinsky and Susmilch (1983) find that in consumer disputes people tend not to contact third parties but to act alone. It may be that people have a repertoire of disputing techniques in certain areas but not others (see Sharp 1980). It may be that Americans, at least, face a complex of norms about "not airing dirty linen in public" and "what will the neighbors think."

Rather than ignoring a problem, acting alone, or consulting acquaintances, some Americans go, or are sent, to lawyers. Social fields and networks may still play a part in dealing with the dispute. Usually, the client is buying access to the social field in which the lawyer acts. The lawyer has contacts and can get things done; the lawyer can act as mediator or go-between; the lawyer can suppress a dispute, encourage the client to fight, or attempt to work out a settlement (see Macaulay 1979).

Most social theories ignore the activities of lawyers and officials and deal with law in its most formal aspect. Law tends to be seen as adjudication or a supreme court giving meaning to guarantees of equal protection. Yet adjudication and the interpretation of norms are only part of a larger process involving negotiation, bargaining, and the assertion of power. Probably the key finding of nearly three decades of the social study of law is that a descriptive model of the legal process in the criminal area involves plea bargaining with trials and appeals operating at the margin as factors to consider during negotiations. On the civil side, insurance adjusters meet injured victims or their lawyers and work out settlements in which the chance of trials and appeals affects what is offered and accepted. This kind of patterned dispute processing frequently is carried on by private governments, social fields, and networks where there are identifiable roles, rules, and sanctions. In some bargaining arenas recurrent problems are dealt with by a relatively fixed cast of characters. For example, those who prosecute and defend criminal cases play defined roles but so do police officers, social workers, and others who are regularly involved. In these arenas the problems of individuals tend to be channeled into limited repertoires of solutions which have been developed by specialists who are influenced as much by their own goals and those of the institution as by the needs of disputants. In such arenas facts are not established beyond a reasonable doubt and rights are not vindicated. Rather, rights and facts are only factors in reaching a deal in which the interests and power of all participants will be reflected.

Even when we find adjudication in its more formal dress, we cannot assume that particular decisions solve the problems and define the rights once and for all (cf. Lindgren 1983). A particular appellate opinion may be but a battle in a larger war. For example, retail gasoline dealers battled the large oil companies for about forty years, seeking to enlarge and redefine their rights. The relationships were structured by lawyers for the large companies so that the dealers would have few, if any, rights. Individual dealers first sued, offering novel legal theories backed by atrocity stories to justify a change in the balance of power. Generally they lost. Eventually their trade associations mobilized and directed resources into a long battle. They also sought relief from administrative agencies. While they often failed to gain a change in the rules, they did gain the services of agency staffs as coercive mediators. Finally, the organized dealers turned to both state and federal legislatures. Here they won what appeared to be major victories. Under some of the statutes that were passed dealers could not be canceled except for cause; under others a requirement of good faith was imposed. However, the war was not over. The large oil companies went to court seeking interpretations of the statutes and challenging them on constitutional grounds.

During the whole course of this legal warfare, the oil companies used their economic power to shape relationships with their dealers. The chance that dealers might win rights from courts and legislatures may have affected the companies' actions, but neither this chance nor the rights ultimately won put dealers in control. The cases and statutes were battles in a war rather than authoritative interpretations of ambiguities in values. Social theories that neglect the impact of legal decisions on bargaining position or fail to see that bargaining power rests on far more than legal rights explain almost nothing.

These social theories tend to identify law's role with conflict. However, much of law in any social system is facilitative. Do we drive on the right-hand or the left-hand side of the street? Can people act in groups with limited liability? Is there a way to notify others about my claims to your property? Can my less tangible claims serve as security for loans? Can we drink the water and milk and eat the lettuce with reasonable assurance that we will not be ill tomorrow? Will there be roads and bridges, and will the snow be cleared from them so we can transport our products to market? Will the conditions exist for a workable system of insurance? Will there be schools, hospitals, libraries, and parks? Private governments, social fields, and networks all draw upon these facilitative resources provided by the public legal system, and often legal regulation provides a focus for the formation or continuation of a relatively private group. In short, social theories must deal with interactions between and interpenetrations of public and private units.

Legitimacy and Mystification as Mediated by Social Groups. Social fields and networks also qualify in other ways some of the social theories we have considered. For example, both structural-functional and Marxist-derived theories tend to assume that societies are held together, at least in part, by a consensus about values. Of course, in one theory the writer talks of legitimacy while in the other the consensus is the product of false consciousness. Law is supposed to serve social integration by *clarifying* values so that disputes will be avoided and expectations realized. However, it is possible that *ambiguity* in the interpretation of generally accepted social norms and inconsistency in their application may in fact aid in holding societies together (Mills 1983). As Galanter (1979, p. 17) points out, modern society is "a world of loosely overlapping partial or fragmentary communities." Americans, at least, tend to be spatially and ideologically segregated. Certain ethnic and religious groups maintain a separate identity, more or less willingly. Those who live in upper-income suburbs see themselves as distinct from factory workers, who distinguish themselves from the poor who inhabit inner cities. People also form distinct but partial communities based on lifestyle. One way all of these communities can coexist in relative harmony is by the overestimation of consensus on values as well as by a fair amount of physical and cultural isolation.

Sometimes members of a society share allegiances to values at a high level of abstraction, but differ about interpretations. Sometimes our values may have contradictory implications so that people are free to draw their own conclusions without renouncing the value. For example, all Americans might agree that they favor equality, free speech, and constitutional government. However, members of one group may stress equality of opportunity while those belonging to another group advocate affirmative action to offset past discrimination. Some will tolerate freedom for the thought they hate while others distinguish free speech from treason or from pornography that incites violence against women. Some stress the rights of the accused while others remind us of the rights of victims and potential victims.

When matters can be left ambiguous, the members of each social field can support the general norm and be comforted by an interpretation favoring their interests or point of view. As the conflict theorists remind us, an authoritative interpretation through the process of adjudication and appeal may only provoke anger and division rather than integration. Sometimes some of the strain may be reduced by discretionary enforcement. In theory, an authoritative interpretation by a court of last resort settles matters. In practice, those who must enforce the law may hesitate to force groups whose members feel intensely about the matter to comply with a law that affronts them (see Macaulay and Macaulay 1978). Moreover, normative ambiguity allows regulators and the regulated to evade the authoritative interpretation and rationalize their action in terms of fundamental values. They do not have to see themselves as outlaws. Those advocating the official interpretation may be dismayed by what they see as hypocrisy, but those responsible may be unwilling to pay the price of coercing a sizable minority into compliance (cf. Hagen, Silva, and Simpson 1977).

Some writers have turned to social fields to explain deviance. If, following structural-functional theories, one sees social order as resting on internalized norms, perhaps reinforced by sanctions based in reciprocal relationships, how then can crime be explained? Many have found the explanation in deviant subcultures which promote norms counter to the official ones. For example, one can point to adolescent gangs in large cities where one proves courage and gains status by a willingness to engage in violent conduct and to risk arrest. For these people, law provides an official norm to violate, and the police and the rest of the criminal justice system provide the opportunity to display skill in evading, manipulating, or coping with the demands of authority.

There are a number of distinct subcultural theories. Some writers see younger people as surrounded by those who transmit conventional social norms and others who transmit procriminal norms. The ratio of these associations determines whether younger people learn one or the other pattern (Sutherland and Cressey 1978). Other writers stress social learning in interactions with those who can reinforce or punish and offer models of conventional or criminal behavior (see, for example, Burgess and Akers 1966; Akers 1977). Many theorists emphasize more material factors, such as accepting conventional goals of success and material rewards but rejecting conventional limitations on the means of attaining such ends. When people find their access to legitimate opportunities blocked by discrimination or class barriers, they are likely to discover illegitimate opportunities (see, for example, Cloward and Ohlin 1960; Cohen 1955). Instead of gaining a Cadillac by business success in conventional terms, one becomes, for example, a narcotics dealer.

Other scholars have objected to these explanations for deviance as oversimplified. On the one hand, while gangs of poor youths do exist, there is a political dimension to emphasizing deviant subcultures. These theories stress threats to the social order from the poor and invite segregation and various types of social control measures, ranging from crackdowns on gang activity to being drafted into the armed forces. The theories tend to overlook crime committed by members of the middle and upper classes who, presumably, are part of the dominant majority culture. Many of their crimes are committed secretly and not as a group activity—one seldom embezzles, for example, as a way to show off one's courage to other corporate officers or one's associates at the country club.

On the other hand, available empirical evidence does not support the existence of delinquent subcultures standing apart from the main body of society. Delinquents and criminals say they do not approve of their own illegal conduct, such subcultures as one can find do not contain a coherent set of inverse values, and delinquents tend to affirm much of conventional morality (Elliot and Voss 1974; Kornhauser 1978; Regoli and Poole 1978). Some suggest that it may be more profitable to abandon subcultural explanations and turn to theories stressing weakness of social control and increasing opportunity to commit crimes in modern society (see, for example, Cohen and Felson 1979).

Nonetheless, any complete theory of criminal behavior must note that social fields may facilitate if not cause some kinds of violations of the law (see Ekland-Olson 1982). Even if they do not constitute true rival cultures to mainstream society, those who use cocaine often are part of a social field which can help rationalize violating the law. One may be motivated to steal for any number of reasons which may or may not include exposure to a deviant subculture. However, if one who steals is part of a gang of those who also steal, he or she may be provided with a vocabulary with which to derogate the victim and justify the act. Moreover, those who use illegal drugs or crack safes also can pass along information on how to gain access to drugs or offset the latest countermeasures of safe manufacturers. Beginners may learn from professionals techniques of minimizing the chances of arrest, conviction, or a harsh sentence. Group communications may serve to magnify both the amount and success of criminal activity on the part of those who were insiders. In other words, the advantages of considering social fields when theorizing still exist even when the role played by groups fails to provide a complete explanation for behavior.

Many of the social theories we considered see law as playing a part in establishing legitimacy, symbolic satisfactions, or a false consciousness through mystification. These ideas are plausible and undoubtedly contain more than a little truth, but they are unclear about how the process of communication and persuasion is supposed to take place. There is reason to think that any messages broadcast by the legal system are mediated through social fields and networks which may transform and distort them. Moreover, any complete theory must deal with the countermessages which rivals of the state and the public legal system attempt to transmit with varying effect. It is useful to distinguish, and discuss separately, two versions of the impact of law on attitudes which seem to be implicit in these social theories: law and things legal are said to legitimate or mystify the nature of the legal system and liberal society in the eyes of *citizens in general.* Whatever the merits of that assertion, law and things legal may have an impact on the perceptions of *those who seek to enter the legal arena* and must play by its rules.

Many theorists have posited that legality serves to legitimate liberal societies, or some part of their processes, but they are unclear about how this occurs. The public is supposed to have faith because of the relative autonomy of legal officials, formal procedures, and the rule of law. For example, some drew the lesson from the Watergate scandal that "the system works," because the Supreme Court held that President Nixon was bound by the law and could not hide behind a vague "executive privilege."

There are several difficulties with these claims. Schools teach the conventional view of the legal system and mass media communicate a great deal about certain features of it, but people still know little about the legal process in operation and what they know is often distorted (Albrecht and Green 1977; Casey 1976; Cortese 1966; Hearst Corp. 1983; *Michigan Law Review* 1973; National Center for State Courts 1978; Williams and Hall 1972). Perhaps it is enough to sense in some vague and imprecise way that a good legal system is out there. Indeed, there is evidence that those who have the least contact with the American legal system are the most satisfied with it (National Center for State Courts

1978). Nonetheless, vague and distorted pictures of lawyers, judges, police, and administrators would not seem enough to foster a reliable faith or sense of legitimacy. We might suspect that dissonance between the normative claims of American law and an introduction to the realities of plea bargaining, personal injury settlement, and bureaucratic routine would disenchant those who had to confront reality.

Moreover, social fields and networks are not defenseless against messages sent by the legal system. The *Dred Scott* decision, overturning the Missouri Compromise and denying standing to former slaves who had fled to the North, did not change the view of abolitionists about the morality of slavery. The decisions of the Supreme Court of the past few decades dealing with desegregation, school prayers, abortion, and contraception have not legitimated the positions taken by the Court in the eyes of many citizens. Instead, in such instances law has provoked counterreactions and has served as the focus for rallying opposition. Fundamentalist religious leaders and conservative politicians have formed an uneasy alliance to decry the loss of morality symbolized by these decisions. A loose social network has arisen around these issues (Watts 1983). Such groups have targeted elected officials whom they saw as holding the wrong views on one or more of these issues and swung elections against them. Members of the Congress who respond to such views have sought to overturn or undercut many of these Supreme Court decisions with varying success, through withdrawing jurisdiction of the Supreme Court over school prayers, cutting off federal funds to states which provide abortions to welfare recipients, and influencing judicial and administrative appointments. Perhaps in the long run the Supreme Court decisions that prompted all this conflict will become the conventional wisdom of most citizens. However, at least in the short run, instead of enhancing legitimacy they have provoked some measure of conflict and disintegration.

If we recognize that few people in any society ever read legal opinions, legislative committee reports, or statutes in the full original text, we should be prompted to turn to another social field important in the process of promoting legitimacy or provoking outrage— the mass media. Messages about legal action are conveyed to the public by journalists, television reporters, script writers, and novelists. Perhaps some of these people are influenced by law professors and others who can claim expert standing to comment on legal action in light of conventional theories of law. These communicators, however, tend to be at least skeptical if not cynical about the normative claims of legal actors because they see too much of what goes on backstage. Their task, moreover, is to capture public attention and so they are attracted to what is provocative rather than the typical. Accounts of the legal system operating by the book which might reassure readers or viewers seldom are front-page news. On the other hand, for many reasons, news tends to be muckraking rather than revolutionary; bad people rather than the system tend to be blamed.

The chains through which messages about the legal system pass undoubtedly are complex, distorting, and not well understood. Moreover, while it is fairly easy to study what is sent out by the mass media, films, or novels, it is much harder to learn just what different kinds of people receive from such messages. Individuals may reinterpret a report of a distinguished law professor's views about a Supreme Court decision to suit their own world view, and perhaps this is more likely to happen when they are part of a social network with a stake in another view. Some honor civil libertarians but others call them friends of criminals and enemies of the nation. Supreme Court opinions may be seen as upholding basic values or as idealistic but unrealistic. The rule that a defendant is presumed innocent until proved guilty, for example, is seen by members of many groups as an unwarranted attack on the competence of the police.

Perhaps, over time, subtle messages which are repeated on news broadcasts and entertainment programs affect attitudes despite the conservative efforts of fundamentalist churches, organized interest groups, or the regulars at the tavern. However, we must remember the great skill members of many groups possess to reinterpret or reject ideas that offend them. In short, it is clear that if a social theory tells us that law affects attitudes and no more, the theory is, at best, incomplete. To be meaningful, the theory also must describe in a plausible fashion the process by which those whose attitudes are reinforced or changed learn about legal action and what they make of what they learn.

Similar objections can be raised to Marxist-derived theories of law that talk of false consciousness and mystification. Hunt's statement (1976) is typical:

> Legal norms . . . have the role of moulding and inducing acceptance of the power differentials that are encapsulated within them. . . . The concept of citizenship, formal equality of participation in the public affairs of society, is transposed in the field of law through the "rule of law" and associated concepts. Thus the assertion of the legitimacy of law is a celebration of social unity facilitated by the formal universalism of its symbolic content. [pp. 40–41]

The criteria for judging such assertions are a matter of dispute. On the one hand, some Marxist theorists would deny that their writing can be judged by non-Marxist social science. If correct theory tells a scholar that bourgeois law mystifies and helps produce false consciousness, all that is necessary is to find examples. "Data are important in terms of how well they describe the 'actualization of the objective role' played by events and concepts, and they are irrelevant otherwise" (Marenin 1981, p. 10). On the other hand, analyses such as that by Balbus (1977) in the *Law & Society Review*, apparently rest on observation of capitalist legal systems. Therefore, it seems appropriate to ask how much such theories would be altered if the roles played by social fields and networks were considered. As will be seen, such a move both challenges and supports parts of Marxist-derived analyses.

Balbus says that citizenship is a "substitute gratification which compensates for the misery of reality," and the "absence of communal relationships within . . . everyday existence" (p. 580). Without a good deal of qualification, it seems implausible that abstract citizenship is a substitute for community in the minds of many people in capitalist society. Citizenship has meaning only through those partial communities that exist in such nations. One usually votes as part of an undifferentiated mass, and, except in the rare case of an extremely close election, it would not matter if one stayed home and neglected to participate. However, one discusses politics with the regulars at the tavern, the lunch group at the office, neighbors, and the like, and it is here in these partial communities that one's views, vote, and being a citizen gain meaning. At least in the past, some have felt obligations of citizenship called for volunteering to join the armed forces. During World Wars I and II, this won approval from one's social network. One's family members shared in the display of citizenship by putting a banner with a blue star in the window of their home, an act designed to gain approval from an audience of those whose opinions mattered. Finally, we can point out that those for whom reality is the most miserable are least likely to vote and most likely to view political activity with cynicism.

Theorists of the left often see capitalist society as characterized by what they see as a lack of "genuine" community. However, people acting in social fields and networks often feel some sense of community, and, at times, the legal system provides a focus for that sense. For example, a study of older black and white women who had incomes below the government's definition of poverty found that

> Black women made greater use of alternative medical systems, had larger networks of family and friends, participated at greater rates in institutional support systems, and rated themselves higher with respect to health and happiness than did White women. These differences were attributed to the closely cooperative life styles of Black women. These patterns of mutual support were thought to be a highly sophisticated cultural adaptation to historic and economic circumstances. [Curran 1978, p. 39]

The legal system was a focus for cooperative activity within these networks of black women; they had to help each other cope with systems providing government benefits, and, particularly because of their membership in churches, they were organized to do so. We can debate whether this was a *genuine* community, but it is clear that while one should not romanticize their situation, picturing these women as alienated and isolated would be a distortion of their strength. Moreover, it seems unlikely that the lack of a cooperative lifestyle of the older white women studied by Curran is a result of their status as abstract citizens with rights, or their false consciousness about the nature of society and its legal system. At the least, to be convincing Marxist-derived theories must trace the linkages between an ideological picture of legal persons developed by theorists and such matters as the apparent alienation of these older white women.

Another theme related to law as mystification concerns the impact of capitalist ideology on family relationships. The "bourgeois family of liberal capitalism," it has been said, "was privatized and offered a refuge, an emotional haven, from the cold harshness and impersonal competition of the outside reality" (Hearn 1980, p. 131). However, the family in postcapitalist society is losing "its capacity to provide its members with a private space" and is turning into an association which focuses "more on output than on warmth and shared concern." Perhaps theorists such as Balbus have this in mind when they tell us that "the 'community' produced by the legal form contributes *decisively* to the reproduction of the very capitalist mode of production which makes genuine community impossible" (p. 580).

Whatever the problems of the modern family, it is unclear how legal ideology affects the sense of community in family-living arrangements. Furthermore, other social networks—the fellows at the club or tavern, the members of the bowling league, or the women who gather regularly to talk and drink coffee—also may offer some refuge from "the cold harshness and impersonal competition of the outside reality" (see Bissonette 1977; Genovese 1980; Schoenberg 1980). Such social fields and networks often carry some norms of altruism and community, whatever their success in implementing them.

There is little evidence, nor even much of a plausible theory, connecting the attitudes and values of the worker standing with his friends at the bar in a tavern with the logic of the legal system at the doctrinal level. Indeed, there is evidence that people think it wrong to invoke the law within one's social fields. One keeps one's word, for example, rather than finding loopholes in the language of contracts with family and friends (see Engel 1984). Moreover, any theory of mystification by legal concepts must take into account many workers' sophistication and cynical knowledge about power and privilege in their society (see Stack 1978).

People in social fields regularly help each other cope with legal norms. They help each other comply. However, they may legitimate evasions of the law and teach each other how to evade successfully, often redefining legal norms to their own advantage. Port workers, for example, accept the idea that one should not steal, but they do not see taking damaged cargo as stealing (Hoekema 1975). Networks of employees often take, as of right, reasonable amounts of supplies from their employer, viewing this as just part of their compensation. Breaking what are deemed as foolish laws can become a game: even as loosely structured a group as Japanese commuters share their schemes to cheat the national railways by riding without paying the full fare (Noguchi 1979). In short, "[s]ocial relations in capitalism often deceive in appearance, but their observers are not always deceived because 'they have minds of their own,' minds which sometimes accurately reflect contradictory class interests" (Sumner 1979, p. 265).

Another problem with assertions about the legal system's contributions to legitimacy or mystification is that legality may more effectively shape attitudes and conduct of members of some groups than among others. It has been argued that "it is typically the case that subordinate classes do *not* believe (share, accept) the dominant ideology which has far more significance for the integration and control of the dominant class itself." This is true because "the apparatuses of transmission of belief are not very efficient in reaching the subordinate classes" (Abercrombie and Turner 1978, pp. 153, 159). Similarly, Ray (1978, p. 155) asserts that "it is not entirely clear that the market and the economic subsystem perform legitimation functions for the *whole* of liberal capitalist society, rather, this is restricted to the bourgeois class, which must convince *itself* that it no longer rules—hence its development of universal ethics and natural law."

Some support for this idea can be found in a study of the Massachusetts Commission Against Discrimination, which found that compromises and settlements involving small amounts of money were much more common than vindications of rights. Working-class complainants tended to be satisfied with what they received because they did not expect to gain much from a legal agency. In contrast, middle-class complainants, who had the highest percentage of favorable outcomes, tended to be the least satisfied because they thought they had rights and expected the system to vindicate them. "For many, a major cost of filing is the discovery that the legal system does not operate the way it is supposed to" (Crowe 1978, p. 234; cf. Baumgartner 1985). This was not news to the poor and working-class complainants; their social networks and experiences carry that message loudly and clearly.

Of course, it is not clear that even all of the most privileged groups in society believe in the rule of law, the autonomy of the legal system, and the like. Those who seek to capture regulatory agencies, influence the course of legislation, and affect appointments to judicial and administrative posts by making campaign contributions, bribes, and similar exercises of influence seem unlikely to be innocent believers in official rhetoric. Perhaps the few at the top and the many at the bottom, then, share cynical knowledge about how things are done.

Having said all this, it is still possible that legal forms do contribute something to legitimacy or mystification. People often act as if they did believe in the power of law. Legal symbols and rhetoric are appropriated selectively by those in social fields on many occasions to rationalize action. Members of these social fields may also attempt to introduce legal ideas as a limitation on the power of those who dominate the field. For example, private police look like the public police—they wear uniforms with badges, carry guns, and use what we think of as police equipment. Given the multiple and overlapping police forces in the United States, it is easy to confuse private with public officers. Private arbitration panels often meet in courtrooms or other public places which have the architecture of authority, and at least some of their discourse uses the language of legal rights. Employees of private universities and business corporations have increasingly claimed that administration and management must give reasons for decisions, and in American culture such justifications tend to have legal or constitutional overtones. Those who want to curb the power of those in charge often speak of due process and free speech; those who hold power often talk of property and contract rights. Private groups often select leaders and take positions by holding elections. One does not have to sit through too many meetings of governing boards of private organizations to gain a healthy respect for the mystificatory power of Robert's Rules of Order in the hands of a master at the game.

Law also can be a cultural resource, selectively drawn upon to aid in the operation of social fields. Santos (1977) studied a squatter settlement in Rio de Janeiro which he called Pasargada. Under Brazilian law, the entire settlement was illegal because it was built without authorization on land belonging to the government. Yet, the settlers of Pasargada held what they saw as property interests in their houses. They established a private government—the Residents' Association—to deal with disputes and to create a structure under which their homes could be leased, bought, and sold. The Residents' Association borrowed and adapted Brazilian legal concepts and procedures to carry out these transactions. Much of the procedure carried out the evidentiary, channeling, and cautionary functions of legal formality (see Fuller 1941). To effect a transfer, the parties came before the *Presidente* of the Residents' Association. He questioned them to determine whether they understood the transaction, much as a notary does in many civil-law systems. A typed contract or lease was produced which was a powerful formality in a community where typewritten documents are not an everyday matter and literacy cannot be assumed. The signed or marked leases and conveyances were filed at the office of the Residents' Association, and filing itself was an important ceremony, giving the transaction legitimacy much as the recording of a legal document might in public legal systems.

Such legal ritual probably lessened conflict by offering symbols of the transfer of property and increasing the awareness of the parties about the nature of their transaction. It also probably served to assert the authority of the Residents' Association and to clothe it with some legitimacy. Squatter law must be appropriate since it is "just like" the law used by the rich in those parts of Brazil where the streets are paved (which the residents of Pasargada called "the law of the asphalt"). It also was hoped that the legal concepts and procedures used would help defend the autonomy of the settlement against the Brazilian government. Transfers purported to deal only with interests in the houses and made no claim to the land on which they stood. The Residents' Association mediated disputes between residents. Santos observes that "[b]y providing Pasargadians with peaceful means of dispute prevention and settlement Pasargada law neutralizes potential violence, enhances the possibility of orderly life, and thus instills a respect for law and order that may carry out when Pasargadians go into town and interact with official society" (p. 90). This, too, may have protected the settlement. There was always a risk that public authority would send in bulldozers and destroy the settlement, but there was hope that the more self-contained and trouble-free the settlement, the less likely it would be to attract the unwanted attention of governmental authorities.

Santos shows that the legitimating or mystifying power of legal form and rhetoric is a weapon which can be appropriated by both the dominant and the dominated under certain conditions. Of course, groups with wealth can make better use of this weapon and use it in more situations. Moreover, the success of the Residents' Association in Pasargada probably turned on many factors in addition to its adaptation of the forms and vocabulary of Brazilian law. If the land on which the settlement was built was needed for a project which the Brazilian government saw as critically important for the development of the country, we can wonder whether legality would stop the bulldozers.

Whatever the impact of the ideological structure of liberal legal systems on general public opinion, those who use these systems for their own purposes, or who find that they must cope with them, face the necessity of transforming their position into the language of tort, contract, property, due process, free speech, or the like. To what extent, if at all, do such transformations mystify those who want to or must use the legal system?

Groups seeking some degree of social change, or the alteration of the balance of power within a social field or network, seldom are thwarted in seeking favorable readings of basic norms because of the law's emphasis on formal equality, individual rights, and fair procedures. Many of the theorists appear to know little of the reality of modern legal doctrine. Often they credit it with far too much coherence. There are counterprinciples that call for protection of people because of the disadvantaged position of their group. Even where the legal process requires claims to be stated in terms of legal rights, groups can be mobilized around what, in form, is stated as an individual claim. On its face, *Brown v. Board of Education* (the school desegregation case) appeared to be a dispute between Linda Brown and the school system in Topeka, Kansas. It is safe to say that few were misled and failed to see that any decision would speak broadly to the position of blacks in American society.

However, Trubek (1980–81) points out that the law itself is one of the filters that determine what disputes will emerge and what forms conflicts will take. He suggests that the entire behavioral system relating to processing particular types of disputes—including the relevant legal doctrine—"not only transforms the various individual conflicts: in so doing it 'transforms,' so to speak, a raw conflict of interest into a social process with limited possibilities. The disputes that do emerge are those in which basic economic relationships are not challenged: all other possibilities are filtered out" (p. 743). For example, I have mentioned the long-term struggle between retail gasoline dealers and the major oil companies about the nature of their relationship. The arguments of the dealers' lawyers were framed in terms consistent with one strain of classical notions of property and contract. One could imagine claims for much broader protections for the dealers which their lawyers would have been foolish to assert in an American court—for example, the dealers might benefit if a court were to appoint a receiver to supervise the relationships between, say, Mobil Oil and all its dealers; few lawyers would ask for anything so broad for fear of prejudicing their chance of getting anything at all.

One might view this kind of transformation and judgment about what kinds of claims are likely to sell before American judges as mystification. On the other hand, it is possible that no one involved in the gasoline dealers' battles was fooled in the slightest. Everyone may have accurately appraised the amount of power dealers could bring to bear and decided that a slight extension of contract and property ideas was the most that could be hoped for at the moment in question. Either way, Trubek's point holds—American judges and legislators are unlikely to redistribute wealth and power other than incrementally. Few with any experience in the system would expect them to. Indeed, many who have never considered the matter, if asked, might prefer a legal system whose output was incremental to revolutionary change. Those who are, or would be, suspicious of revolutionary change might be wrong, but they are not necessarily mystified.

If we focus on legislation rather than adjudication, we can find an area in which some mystification may take place as Marxist-derived theories suggest. The rhetoric heard in the legislative process is similar to that heard before the courts, but it is not the same. Those claiming to represent farmers, organized labor, small businesses, consumers, the unemployed, and the like typically try to relate the claims of their groups to the interests of the nation as a whole. They claim the need for regulation to alter the balance of power in certain relationships in the society. The lawmaking process usually involves a degree of pluralistic bargaining among certain interests. Seldom will claims be made in the name of the working class in a Marxist sense; seldom will legislation be passed which purports to redistribute wealth more than marginally. More often groups win legislation creating rights for individuals who, for example, have been the victims of discrimination or bad faith.

However, such legislative victories may be more symbolic than real. If rights are to be more than words in a statute book, lawyers usually are needed to represent those who think they have been wronged. Sometimes statutes give complainants a reasonable chance of winning a considerable amount of money, but more often these new rights can be protected only by injunctions that courts hesitate to grant, the damages that can be proved are likely to be low, and establishing a cause of action requires difficult and costly legal research and expert testimony.

It is difficult to mobilize groups to raise funds necessary to bring successful cases to vindicate individual rights. After the statute is passed, sympathetic groups may turn their attention elsewhere or just fade away, believing that the war is won. Private lawyers may donate services, but the supply of those able and willing to do this is low. Given these problems, a reform law may at best create a weak bargaining entitlement, setting the stage for negotiation rather than vindication. It would be fair to say that members of groups that win the passage of statutes creating individual rights without providing an adequate means of vindication have been mystified into thinking they had won a war when they had only won an initial battle. Of course, the failure of a particular statute to affect behavior can be the focus for another legislative battle, but fashions in reform change and it may be difficult to argue for the creation of an administrative agency when deregulation is the cause of the moment or for government-paid legal services when those programs displease powerful interests.

When we consider various social theories and their accounts of the roles played by the legal system, and then add private governments, social fields, and networks, we see that whether law plays the parts assigned is unproved. Many social theorists seem to have accepted the view of the centrality of law championed by legal scholars, but an expanded perspective shows that in many, or most, instances law and the legal system may be irrelevant or appear briefly in a walk-on part. While, on occasion, law may be in the spotlight center stage, the task is to account for when law and legal actors play major parts and when these roles are played by others.

Of course, it is possible—but difficult to establish—that legal norms and legal practices play an important background role so that social interaction would be very different if they were not present. People act on the basis of many tacit assumptions about the present and future and things legal may be one of the factors providing the reassurance necessary for social interaction. We assume, in most instances, that we are safe walking the streets during the day, that criminals will be arrested, and that contracts will be performed. When we lose this faith, as in time of civil war or a repressive takeover by a military government, our behavior changes. It would be difficult to show the part played by law in our tacit assumptions as compared with customs, experiences, and the like. Yet it seems plausible that it is there. Moreover, legal norms and procedures are a potential resource which always might be mobilized by one group or another, and the chance that this could happen may affect official behavior, perhaps in subtle ways. Police, mayors, governors, regulatory agency personnel, and legislators know that if they affront the beliefs and interests of groups of people, they might mobilize and retaliate by voting the rascals out or by bringing a suit in the courts.

If law fails to play the roles it is assigned in various social theories, there may be costs unless its parts are well played by other associations and groups. Luhmann (1981) sees the filtering done by social fields and networks as potentially harmful.

> As a conflict-regulating system that is always belatedly set in motion, i.e. only when called upon, the legal system very seldom takes the initiative. . . . Excessive inhibition of the thematization of law may, therefore, lead to a kind of drying up of the legal system, and so leave the regulation of conflict to other mechanisms—e.g. morality, ignorance, class structure, or the use of force outside the law—whose social structural compatibility may be problematic. [p. 247]

Luhmann, thus, seems to believe that there is a function best performed by the public legal system. If disputes, claims, and the like are the basis for the perception of problems by legal institutions, the filtering and channeling done by social fields and networks are likely to offer a distorted view to lawmakers. Cases before agencies and the courts and bills being lobbied before legislatures are a biased sample of problems in the society (cf. Galanter 1983, p. 70).

If we were to look closely at the roles played by private governments, social fields, and networks, we might see an important problem of legitimacy, undeveloped in the theories we have considered. Hurst (1960, pp. 518–19) tells us that throughout American legal history, "we sought to make all secular power responsible to power outside itself, for ends which it alone did not define." Unger (1976) sees the recognition of the power of private associations as bringing into question the legitimacy of the liberal state. He asserts that

> the increasing recognition of the power these organizations exercise, in a quasi-public manner, over the lives of their members makes it even harder to maintain the distinction between state action and private conduct. Finally, the social law of institutions is a law compounded of state-authored rules and of privately sponsored regulations or practices; its two elements are less and less capable of

being separated. All these movements, which tend to destroy the public character of law, carry forward a process that begins in the failure of liberal society to
keep its promise of concentrating all significant power in government. [pp.
201–2]

The parts played in society by private governments, social fields, and networks are far
more diverse and complex than the roles envisioned in the social theories discussed.
Individuals are subject to a web of norms and sanctions, only some of which are imposed
by the state. If, in Hurst's words, "secular power [is not] responsible to power outside
itself, for ends which it alone did not define," we can expect those subject to the
jurisdiction of such private governments and more structured social fields to challenge
their autonomy. Moreover, some response from public government may be needed to
preserve its own legitimacy. I will now turn to such questions.

The Autonomy and Accountability of Private Associations

In the United States, relationships between government and various kinds of associations are complex and uncertain. While much of our earlier disquiet about regulation has
been overcome, private associations ranging from the family to multinational corporations still have large claims to autonomy. Advocates of greater accountability tend to find
the threat to individual liberty, efficiency, or other values coming from powerful private
associations as well as the state. Tocqueville (1835) saw equality in the new democracies
leading to control by the bureaucratic state. However, he thought that voluntary associations would serve to restrain the power of the state and, indeed, the power of other
associations. Durkheim (1950), on the other hand, saw individual liberty as threatened
both by private associations and by the state. Liberty required the balancing of both the
power of secondary groups which surround the individual on all sides and that of the
nation-state so that "collective particularism" is held in check. "And it is out of this
conflict of social forces that individual liberties are born" (p. 63).

There is a sprawling normative and descriptive literature about regulation (see Tomasic
1984). It deals with such things as its justification in terms of market failure, capture of
regulatory agencies by those supposedly regulated, the new regulation gained by the
reforms in the 1960s and 1970s, and the deregulation movement of the 1970s and 1980s.
In order to make the discussion in this section more manageable, I will narrow my focus
to attempts by individuals or groups *within* a private association to gain action by the legal
system to affect the balance of power inside the group. I will take as an example the
claims of employees and those who hold franchises against employers and franchisors.
The area is important and provides good examples, and much of what is said would apply
also to factional struggles in churches, political parties, athletic organizations, and similar
associations.

Much of this discussion also will be relevant to the adequacy of structural-functionalist
conflict, and Marxist-derived theories considered in the last section. However, in addition I have had an opportunity to consider neo-evolutionary theory in the sociology of
law. Teubner (1983, 1984a, 1984b), in a synthesis of several theoretical works, sees legal
systems in Western societies moving from what Weber called a formally rational style to a
substantively rational one with the rise of the welfare state. However, recent crises may
prompt what Teubner calls "reflexive rationality," as the public legal system more and

more seeks to gain substantive goals by working through private associations. However, when we look at concrete examples of the process about which Teubner writes, we will see that reflexive rationality may produce consequences that some would challenge.

First, I will sketch the claims for autonomy and for accountability of private associations and will consider their applications to the employment relationship. Second, I will consider Teubner's synthesis of a number of major evolutionary theories and his description of reflexive rationality. Finally, I will consider challenges to the corporatism implicit in reflexive rationality.

Accountability and Autonomy in the Employment Relationship   When we look at the legal response to claims by members of groups against those in control, usually we find plausible theories calling for accountability being matched against norms justifying autonomy from outside authority. This may reflect, to a large degree, the decay of older views which drew a sharp line between public and private spheres of life. Public action was seen as constrained by the rule of law; private interaction within groups was simply a matter of free contract and choice. By the 1980s, if not long before, the purity of such distinctions had been lost. To use Unger's words (1976, p. 193), in postliberal society there is only a "general approximation of state and society, of public and private sphere."

The original theory, which still has a good deal of rhetorical power, saw public governments as holding a monopoly on the legitimate use of force. However, this power to constrain liberty had to be limited. Public officials thus acted only under the rule of law. Citizens were protected from governmental action by a Bill of Rights. Government control rested on elections, and power was constrained by checks and balances, federalism, or both. Private activity, including a right of association, was left free of restraint, subject only to the boundaries set by the law of property, contract, tort, crimes and similar legal categories. Counterbalancing associations offset the power of any particular group. One dissatisfied with a particular club, church, or business organization could go elsewhere, and this threat of exit and competition supplied all the regulation needed. Indeed, an important part of American history involves accounts of groups breaking away from religious organizations and forming new sects to pursue the true faith. This threat of exit constrains leaders to temper their actions.

Of course, the limitations of the rule of law, separation of powers, and federalism on public government and the freedom from state regulation enjoyed by private associations probably always have been less effective than claimed. Government officials probably have acted first and hoped to rationalize what was done later; discretion has long been a major part of our legal system. Private associations have always had to cope with some regulatory elements inherent in contract, property, tort, and criminal law. Nonetheless, one who would rationalize discretion of public officials or regulation of private associations has had the burden of persuasion.

Economic crises and social struggles have prompted the growth of the modern welfare state, which increasingly has attempted to regulate private associations. Instead of a sharp line between public and private purposes, governments promise to take whatever measures are needed to promote the success of the economy, to guarantee equality, and to deal with foreign threats of one kind or another. Instead of applying formal rules through classic procedures, modern governments increasingly rely on those who claim expert status and exercise discretion in the pursuit of these substantive goals. Also, instead of regulating conduct, government officials often bargain with various interests. Government may attempt to affect social conditions by trying to influence the action of the private sector in many ways, ranging from controlling the supply of money to setting terms for government contracting. At the same time, private associations have grown in power and significance and assume what are seen as public functions (see Nachmias and Greer 1982). Business corporations may wield critical influence over the future of employees, customers, suppliers, and the communities or regions in which they operate. Those dependent on them cannot exit easily. If a stable or expanding economy is seen as a public function, the operations of these large business organizations seem to many to be more than mere private action. Moreover, many corporations develop and supply transportation, communication, and weaponry viewed as essential to the national interest. When bad judgments, accidents, or world economic conditions threaten large organizations engaged in such important functions, it has been seen as a matter for public concern and government action.

Kennedy (1982) sees six stages in the decline of the public/private distinction. First, there are hard cases with large stakes—we manipulate the distinction and analyze it. Second, intermediate terms develop—we recognize that some situations are neither one thing nor another but share the characteristics of each. Third, the distinction collapses— we realize that however one tries to apply it, one ends up in a situation of hopeless contradiction. Property and contract, for example, can be viewed as examples of delegated state power since they are supported by cops and courts. Fourth, rather than abolish the distinction, we see matters along a continuum from polar cases of public and private action. Institutions in the middle seem to need rules which are a mixture of those appropriate to public and private modes. One balances factors that cut one way or another. Fifth, we see that questions about where an instance fits on the continuum involve manipulation of balanced pro/con policy arguments that come in matched pairs. Finally, at times the ends of the continuum may seem closer together than either end does to the middle. Kennedy calls this "loopification." Parents act more like judges, legislators, and police than officials of very large corporations; yet the family and legal officials would seem to be at opposite poles of the public/private continuum. When this stage is reached, it is hard to take seriously the distinction between what is public and what is private as a justification for treating one situation differently from another.

We can see something of the process Kennedy describes in the attacks on the claim of what, traditionally, were seen as private associations to autonomy from regulation. While some earlier works questioned this autonomy (see, for example, Hale 1920), attention was focused on the issue by Berle and Means (1932), who argued that there had been a separation of ownership from control of the large publicly held business corporation. The majority of shareholders lacked information and ability to mobilize their voting rights in all but extreme situations. Corporate executives, thus, were free to govern in the light of their own interests, subject only to whatever discipline might be found in the various markets in which the corporation dealt. Since corporate democracy was but an empty form and competitive pressures but an uncertain check, public regulation and control were justified.

Then during the early 1950s, a number of writers saw large business corporations as "private governments," exercising powers similar to those of states unchecked by the market, the rule of law, or the Bill of Rights (see, for example, Friedmann 1957; Hansloe 1961; Schwartz 1960; Wltz 1957). Eells (1962, p. 278) observed that "private government is no imaginary construct of academic minds, but is now widely accepted wherever men come to grips with the facts of political life. The corporation of the future is certain to be assessed not only as an element in the economy but also as a contributor—or as a deterrent—to freedom and order." Berle (1952, p. 942) found an emerging principle holding that the "corporation, itself a creation of the state, is as subject to constitutional limitations which limit action as is the state itself."

While separation of ownership from control and private government theories can be challenged on a number of grounds, both became part of the American political and legal culture. (For a modern version of the argument, see Ewing 1977.) One finds traces of each one in many battles before courts and legislatures about the autonomy or accountability of private associations. As Hanslowe (1961, p. 104) notes, during the 1940s and 1950s, "in labor relations, at least, quasi-governmental powers . . . [were] . . . being circumscribed by . . . quasi-constitutional restraints." These kinds of arguments seem to fall somewhere in the middle of Kennedy's six stages. Private government, for example, is an analogy. General motors is both like and unlike the state of Wisconsin. As a result, a matched set of predictable arguments fall into place—one calls for GM employees to be protected by guarantees of due process and free speech while the other argument stresses that, unlike a true government, GM's powers over its employees do not extend to the right to imprison or keep them from seeking work elsewhere. Logically, starting from the public/private premise as it has developed, the case is a tie.

By the 1930s, it was difficult to predict when private associations would be seen as autonomous and which form of regulation, if any, would be imposed. Chafee (1930, p. 1021) said that judicial competence to settle disputes within associations rests on a balance of four normative factors which "may be called, for the sake of vividness, the Strangle-hold Policy, the Dismal Swamp Policy, the Hot Potato Policy and the Living Tree Policy. The first favors relief; the last three oppose relief." The strangle-hold policy involves a judgment about the seriousness of the consequences of expulsion or other injury done to a member: "some associations have a strangle-hold upon their members through their control of an occupation or of property which can be ill spared." The dismal swamp policy reflects the difficulty a court would face in learning enough to decide the case. For example, judicial review of "the highest tribunal of the church is really an appeal from a learned body to an unlearned body." Attempts at judicial control of the internal affairs of a powerful association which commands the devoted adherence of its members might cause great resentment and have small chance of success. Courts will hesitate to pick up such a hot potato. Finally, the value of autonomy itself may induce courts to leave associations alone. Chafee argues that

> [t]he health of society will usually be promoted if the groups within it which serve the industrial, mental and spiritual needs of citizens are genuinely alive. Like individuals, they will usually do most for the community if they are free to determine their own lives for the present and the future. A due regard for the corresponding interests of others is desirable, but must be somewhat enforced by public opinion. Legal supervision must often be withheld for fear that it may do more harm than good . . . [for example, freedom] is desirable for schools and colleges. . . . The courts, like the legislatures, can hardly profess to be better

> qualified to decide how teaching shall be carried on than are the teachers and
> their administrative associates. [pp. 1027, 1028–29]

Views about this living tree policy may have changed somewhat since Chafee wrote, but
the policy still commands respect.

About thirty years later, the editors of the *Harvard Law Review* (1963) recast Chafee's
policy considerations as (1) interest in group autonomy, (2) practical limitations on
judicial inquiry, (3) harm caused the individual and society by autonomy, (4) alternative
methods of control, (5) extent of monopoly power, and (6) determination of whether a
governmental grant of rights or powers imposes, by implication, corresponding duties. Of
course, whatever its other functions jurisprudential writing that talks of weighing and
balancing such factors is only generally descriptive or predictive. There is no scale on
which to place these factors one by one and no dial on which to read their weights in
grams or pounds. In most cases contrasting but equally plausible cases for autonomy and
for accountability could be made. Indeed, after 117 pages of analysis, the *Harvard Law
Review* tells us that judicial control of the conduct of private associations is "an area
where few legal principles seem to have emerged" (p. 1100). We face all the problems of
Kennedy's fourth stage—what he calls "continuumization." (See also, Ellman 1981;
Fuller 1969; *Harvard Law Review* 1962; *Yale Law Journal* 1963.)

Klare (1981, p. 465) observed that liberal theory faces a difficult problem in rationalizing regulation of a supposedly private economy. "The core of the problem is to find a
justification for public regulation which does not in logic lead to the notion that *all*
economic decisions of societal consequence (e.g., all investment decisions by the 'top
500' corporations) should be subject to public control." As we shall see, legal decision-
makers often are concerned about this slippery slope.

We can see many of the difficulties with the distinction between public and private by
examining the legal treatment of the employment relationship and its close relative, the
franchise. These relationships are social fields and sometimes structured private governments. Throughout the twentieth century, employees have sought to alter the balance of
power between them and their employers, and they have enjoyed some success. In this
section I will first paint, with very broad strokes, a rough history of the legal response to
the claims for intervention in employment relationships in the United States in this
century. Second, I will look at some of the factors affecting the actual balance of power in
that relationship, including all of the legal activity. The discussion suggests an important
question yet to be addressed adequately in the social study of law: why and when do
people turn to the formal public legal system rather than some form of private government? I will also set the stage for considering evolutionary theories concerning the parts
played by legal systems as the role of the state has changed in capitalist societies.

The starting point for considering legal reaction to the employment relationship in this
century is the classic position that the matter is simply one of free contract. Regulation is
not needed because if a job is, for example, more dangerous, employees will be paid more
to take the risks. In theory, those employees who held contracts for specific terms held
rights and were subject to duties determined by voluntary agreement. However, courts
almost never would grant specific performance of an employment contract and force
people into a distasteful close personal relationship. In most instances, an aggrieved party
was left to seek damages. If an employer breached the contract, an employee usually
would have to be paid the balance of the salary that would have been earned less any

income the employee received from a substitute job taken after being fired. If an employee breached by leaving the job, the employer's damages usually were worth so little that a suit would not be brought. As might be expected, if an employee left taking trade secrets or valuable skills to use in direct competition with the employer, courts might enjoin this attack on property.

However, at the turn of the century as today, most employees did not hold contracts for fixed terms but worked under an employment-at-will. In theory, equality is preserved. The employer is free to discharge the employee, and the employee is free to leave for good, bad, or no reason. However, in times of labor surplus, the employee is at a disadvantage. For example, in *Comerford v. International Harvester* (1938), the Supreme Court of Alabama held that a worker who had alleged that he was fired after his wife refused the sexual advances of his boss had failed to state a cause of action. It explained that the employer "could have well decided that it would be in the interest of good management not to have both plaintiff and the guilty assistant sales manager working together under the circumstances. It could have concluded that the services of the sales manager were preferable and retained him without in the least ratifying or condoning his conduct toward the plaintiff." In short, employees-at-will must please the boss or look for work elsewhere.

In the early decades of the century, reformers sought to gain statutes regulating certain aspects of the employment relationship. Legislation was passed in a number of states attempting to govern wages, hours, and working conditions. Of course, this led to the great constitutional battles concerning liberty of contract and substantive due process. Not until the 1930s was it clear that such legislation was constitutional.

The legal response to labor unions and strikes was hostile. Such activity could be attacked as tortious or as criminal conspiracy. Police and sheriffs used force to remove strikers from their employer's property, and union organizers were attacked by law enforcement officers with both legal and illegal means. Moreover, courts would enjoin union activity and strikes and enforce promises by employees not to join unions—"yellow dog contracts."

As part of the reforms of the New Deal, the American legal system took a very different stance. Collective bargaining was symbolically legitimated in terms of union democracy, a collective contract, and private adjudication through arbitration. The government supported and attempted to influence a private legal system. Employees in a bargaining unit could vote to determine whether they wanted to be represented by a union, and, if so, by which one. Once a union was certified by the National Labor Relations Board as the bargaining representative, the employer had a duty to bargain in good faith. The result of this process would be a contract governing wages and conditions of employment for a fixed term, which had to be ratified by the individual workers. The contract typically is interpreted and applied to specific problems through a grievance procedure. There are a number of steps, usually beginning with a complaint to a foreman and ending with arbitration. The courts, particularly since World War II, have supported arbitration in a number of ways and have sharply limited challenges to an arbitrator's power. Unions, in turn, have been subjected increasingly to a duty of fair representation in the grievance procedure. On the other hand, during the life of a collective bargain, employees lose the right to strike and wildcat strikes can be enjoined. All parties, as well as the public, are deemed to have an interest in continuing production. Displeasure with the grievance process can be expressed legitimately only by seeking a new arbitrator for future disputes, by collective bargaining when the current contract expires, or by voting for new union officers or a new union.

Over half of the American labor force continues to work under only an employment-at-will, and there have been a number of developments over the last thirty years indicating an increasing willingness to cut away at the autonomy of the employment relationship. For example, franchisees have battled franchisors before courts, legislatures, and administrative agencies. Their successes influenced attempts of employees-at-will to gain rights.

Before the changes in the law that occurred from the 1950s through the 1970s, those holding franchises to sell nationally advertised products and services were in form independent business people but in substance they resembled employees. Franchisors create a nationally known product and a trademark. They plan how retailing is to be conducted and often select the location of each place of business. The franchisee contributes capital and management to the particular outlet and will share in the profit or loss generated there. However, a franchise was a highly dependent relationship. The franchisor could cancel at any time without having to show justification. If a franchisee had invested in the business and had built up a local reputation tied to the franchisor's trademark, the franchisee had a great deal to lose. Thus, there were real incentives to please the franchisor's supervisors in charge of the particular location. Franchisees often complained of a contradiction between the symbols used by the franchisors and the reality of the relationship—franchisees were supposed to be independent business people, but the form contracts drafted by Wall Street lawyers gave the franchisees few, if any, rights and reserved all power to a not always benevolent authoritarian ruler. While franchisees often look like small capitalists, before statutes offered some protection, their franchises could be terminated without cause. While franchisees may appear to be "running their own business," they actually occupy a position hard to distinguish from that of an employee-at-will. Franchisees, however, often can afford to organize and lobby for legislation while employees-at-will have been limited to individual appeals for help from the courts.

While there were some victories by franchisees before the courts, generally their decisions favored the large corporations that created the relationships. With some exceptions, the courts protected a property interest in the product or service and the trademark (see Jordan 1978). It was just a matter of free contract. Franchisees were held to have taken the risk when they accepted the standard form contract as the blueprint for the relationship.

Then automobile dealers and retail gasoline dealers gained statutes, both at the state and federal levels (see *Minnesota Law Review* 1975). These statutes were thought to affect the balance of power within the private governments of franchising. The symbols found in this legislation tend to involve due process, the use of a franchisor's power in good faith, or the existence of reasonable cause for its use after an opportunity to cure defaults by the dealer. However, the rights gained by the automobile and gasoline dealers were limited and subject to performance of duties. It seems clear that the legislators accepted the case offered by the lobbyists for the dealers but were concerned, as well, with what they saw as the franchisors' legitimate interests and the rights of the public. The statutes and their legislative histories exhibit great concern that there not be too great an invasion of private decision-making.

Another example of our willingness to whittle down the autonomy of the employment relationship can be found in the results of the civil rights struggles during the 1950s and 1960s. Legal protections against discrimination based on race, sex, and age are now widespread. Such laws may have the greatest impact on employees-at-will who lack union or contract protection against unfair treatment by their employers. Cases such as the *Comerford* decision, involving an employee fired because his wife rejected the sexual advances of his supervisor, likely are no longer the law.

During the 1970s, the employment-at-will doctrine was subject to challenge in many states, with very mixed results. Many states continued to uphold the older view. The Supreme Court of Alabama, for example, refused to find a cause of action when an employee of a hospital alleged she had been fired because she refused to falsify medical records as part of a fraudulent scheme. The court remarked that to rule otherwise would "abrogate the inherent right of contract between employer and employee." Any change had to be left to the legislature.

However, other state courts created causes of action for employees-at-will (see *Harvard Law Review* 1980). Cases have involved discharges for such reasons as refusing to respond to sexual advances, being absent from work to serve on a jury, blowing the whistle on illegal activity within a corporation, and making insurance claims which would affect the rates paid by the employer. The theories used to justify intervening in the employment relationship have varied widely, and, typically, the nature of the cause of action is left extremely uncertain. Some courts found an implied obligation of good faith inherent in any contract, but the requirements of that duty were left to case-by-case definition. Others appraised the reason an employee was fired to see if it violated public policy. The California courts recognize a tort cause of action for wrongful discharge that carries with it the possibility of punitive damages.

However, many courts which recognized some right of action also seemed concerned about making it too hard to discharge incompetent workers and prompting nuisance settlements when there was any doubt about the propriety of a termination. In *Pierce v. Ortho Pharmaceutical Corp.*, the Supreme Court of New Jersey required a "clear mandate of public policy" to be violated in the discharge before relief would be given. Such policy could be found in "legislation; administrative rules, regulations or decision; and judicial decisions," and in "certain instances, a professional code of ethics." An employee's own ethical objections to an employer's practices were not enough to justify a refusal to work on a project, and so firing the employee did not violate public policy. Employment still remains more private than public; employers still have a claim to autonomy, and accountability, so far, is reserved for cases involving atrocity stories (see Lopatka 1984).

Reflexive Rationality: The Legal System Working Through Private Associations to Achieve Substantive Goals   We have seen that the relationship between the public legal system and private associations is uncertain and there is conflict among normative claims concerning autonomy and accountability. Teubner (1983, 1984a, 1984b) sees legal thought evolving through a number of stages to one where dispute resolution and social integration will be decentralized and handled within various private associations. Law will play a role at the margin, influencing outcomes by demanding procedures and new forms of participation rather than prescribing substantive results. We will consider his evolutionary theory in light of our discussion of the employment and franchise relationships and attempts to influence the balance of power within them. Finally, we will consider Klare's challenge (1981, 1982) that such reflexive approaches only mask the exercise of power and stand in the way of further development of real decentralization of power and control to the level of individuals and small groups.

Teubner looks at neo-evolutionary theories about the place of law in society fashioned by Nonet and Selznick (1978), Luhmann (1982), and Habermas (1979) and offers a synthesis which predicts the direction development of legal thought is likely to take. All of these writers argue that while law is affected by social change, there are limitations on its adaptability. External needs and demands are selectively filtered into the legal system and adapted in light of the logic of normative development. This process, however, can lead to crisis. Legal structures may not provide the conceptual resources nor the effective regulation needed for maintenance of the overall social system. Moreover, legal action may be seen as illegitimate if legal norms are out of phase with social ones. There was such a crisis when the legal approach appropriate to early capitalism confronted its later development. We may face another today as the legal approach appropriate to the welfare state is under attack in many Western nations.

In the nineteenth and early twentieth centuries, capitalism was facilitated by what Max Weber (1954) called *formal rationality*. Internally, law was rationalized by rule-oriented reasoning, which was manipulated by professionals who shared a legal culture. The justification for this style of law rested on its contributions to individualism and autonomy from government control. Externally, this style of law facilitated private ordering by guaranteeing a framework within which substantive judgments could be made by individuals. In this manner, it contributed to mobilizing and allocating resources, and it appeared neutral and autonomous from political and economic power. With the rise of the regulatory welfare state in the mid-twentieth century, Western legal thought evolved to a style which, in Weberian terms, was *substantively rational*. Law lost most of its formal characteristics. Internally, law was then rationalized in terms of achieving substantive ends—law was an instrument and not an end in itself. It was justified in terms of the perceived need for collective regulation of social life because of the failures of the market. Externally, this style of law is the main instrument by which the state affects market-determined patterns of behavior. It is seen as legitimate when it works to provide full employment, end discrimination, assure consumers that they will get a certain level of quality, and the like. Formal rationality was primarily a judicial style; substantive rationality was a tool of legislatures and administrative agencies, although some courts followed legal realism in this direction.

Increasingly in the 1970s and 1980s, substantive rationality is caught in the crisis of the regulatory welfare state. (Cf. Tomasic 1984.) On the one hand, social processes and economic arrangements seem too complex to be governed by the kinds of regulatory arrangements that can be fashioned within our traditions. On the other hand, the regulatory welfare state has been losing legitimacy. Insofar as it was justified by its claims to gain substantively valued ends, to a great degree it just has not worked. For example, despite the claim that the economic system would be managed, inflation has cut real income and unemployment has become a significant problem in many Western nations. Despite promises to desegregate American society, race, class, sex, and ethnicity still affect one's life chances significantly apart from talent and effort. The substantive style of legal and political rhetoric loses its power to convince those who listen to it, particularly in light of the claims of traditional formal rationality. Substantive rationality does not seem to be "law"; rather, the ends sought and the methods used can be labeled as the preferences of those who have captured power. In short, formal rationality can be turned against substantive rationality to delegitimate it.

One response to this crisis is to call for a return to formal rationality, deregulation, and governmental retreat. The public sector will withdraw and the private sphere will produce efficiency and freedom once again. There is reason to doubt whether such a strategy could succeed. Too many are interested in at least some of the benefits of the welfare state to allow a recreation of the governmental system of 1900—the cry often seems to be, "cut the budget for your programs but not mine." Moreover, even if such a recreation of what we think was the past could work, the transition from governmental systems of, say, the 1960s to a passive and neutral state likely would produce socially unacceptable burdens.

Teubner suggests, rather, that the next stage of legal evolution will be from substantive rationality to what he calls *reflexive rationality*. Here, the legal system would regulate self-regulation. Law would seek to facilitate rather than endanger self-regulatory processes, organizations, and the distribution of rights. Teubner (1984) notes that the model of social reality found in substantive rationality is

> rather primitive in comparison with the complicated self-referential structure of the various social subsystems. . . . Taking self-reference seriously means that we have to give up conceptions of direct regulatory action. Instead, we have to speak of an external stimulation of internal self-regulating processes which, in principle, cannot be controlled from the outside. [p. 298]

Law would not take responsibility for outcomes, seeing such an effort as often beyond its capabilities. The justification for this style of law would be success in coordinating forms of social cooperation. It would not be a return to formal rationality, merely adapting to or supporting what were seen as "natural" social orders. It would attempt to guide human interaction by redefining and redistributing property rights. Externally, reflexive law would structure and reform semi-autonomous social systems, by shaping both their procedures of internal discourse and their methods of relating to other social systems. The major goal would be neither power-equalization nor participatory democracy. It would be the design of organizational structures which made institutions such as corporations, semi-public associations, mass media, and educational institutions sensitive to the outside effects of their attempts to maximize their own goals.

He offers examples to lend some empirical support to his theory. "Labor law . . . is, with respect to collective bargaining, characterized to some degree by a more abstract control technique in which we can recognize a 'reflexive' potential." Teubner recognizes that a strategy of decentralization will fail if asymmetries of power and information successfully resist attempts at equalization through law. He suggests that the legal system can operate reflexively by imposing standards of good faith and public policy in order to prompt processes of social self-regulation in semi-autonomous social systems. Also private associations could be commanded to develop constitutions which require them to operate in harmony with the requirements of other social institutions. He concedes that the adequacy of such approaches is unclear. However, reflexive rationality is an attempt to gain many of the benefits of both formal and substantive rationality with fewer of the costs of each. Whatever its normative status, one can find examples of this approach in modern law.

Teubner is unclear about how he thinks legal thought influences activity in other subsystems. Other subsystems may incorporate conceptions of legal rights and duties, transformed to meet their requirements, into their expectations and procedures. Legal thought may make issues salient and may affect background assumptions about what is natural or proper. Those acting within other subsystems may respond to the threat of the application of power to implement legal thought. However, there are many kinds of legal power. At one extreme, legal thought can be crystallized in a judgment which various state officials may enforce. People can be put in jail, property can be seized, licenses can be granted or revoked, and these orders may be enforced by agents of the state armed with weapons. At the other extreme, even the suspicion that another might commence legal action may affect behavior. Tacit and explicit threats to sue or seek new legislation or regulation may force the one threatened to examine legal arguments, the costs of defending a position in the process, and the impact on reputation of being challenged. The one threatened may decide to surrender, fight, or attempt to negotiate a settlement. Some legal agencies, such as higher appellate courts, often are relatively autonomous from direct applications of political and economic power. (However, one must recall the great contrast in views between judges appointed to the United States courts of appeal by Presidents Carter and Reagan.) Other legal agencies, such as administrative agencies and legislative committees, are influenced in varying degree by legal, moral, and political ideas as well as power and privilege. This, too, affects decisions about how to respond to actual or potential assertions of legal power.

We can only speculate about how Teubner would fit a description of the way legality is delivered into his theory. As we will see, it is easier to make the case for possible influence on self-regulation than for social integration. Many of the attempts to regulate employment and franchise relationships might be examples of what we could call indirect reflexive rationality. Even the chance that formal or substantive rationality might be exercised within the legal system may affect procedures and the balance of power within private associations. Whether such changes, in fact, serve to integrate the functioning of these associations with that of other social structures is hard to establish, but the possibility is present. I will look at the impact of some of the legislation and other legal activity dealing with, first, franchises, and, second, employment-at-will. Finally, I will turn to collective-bargaining law and the possibility that decentralized activity may prompt social integration at the price of the interests of individual workers.

The threat of lawmaking and negative public relations affected self-regulation in the area of automobile dealer franchises in the United States. The publicity given the hearings before a committee of the United States Senate and the challenging questioning of the top officials of the automobile manufacturers provoked a response that was more beneficial to the dealers than the statute that finally was passed (Macaulay 1966). After being embarrassed by testimony about the past practices of General Motors, its president sought to take the public relations initiative. During the hearings he announced a revised franchise contract which gave General Motors dealers a number of valuable rights. Moreover, dealers' representatives would meet regularly with the top officials of the company in a setting in which they could raise questions, offer suggestions, and learn of the reasons for future plans. Furthermore, decisions to terminate a dealer could be reviewed through a process ending with a decision by a retired Justice of the Supreme Court. Other manufacturers followed suit, defining rights and duties in some detail, and creating different types of systems of review. Ford's revised contract with its dealers even looked like an elaborate statute, with definitional sections and a detailed index.

In several states, the dealers' association or the administrative agency regulating manufacturer-dealer relationships began mediating disputes. One important part of such mediation was bringing new representatives of the manufacturer into the transaction. Instead of a fight between a dealer and a zone or area supervisor who is judged by the rate of sales in the territory, dispute processing now involved the dealer, the zone or area supervisor, a representative of the manufacturer from the home office, and someone from the state agency or trade association. Instead of acting as the final authority, the zone or area supervisor's decision and past actions were now subject to review. It seems likely that the possibility of such review would have a deterrent effect. Before supervisors acted, now there would be a real incentive to get their facts straight and to build a file justifying terminating the dealer or taking other action. Moreover, bias, nepotism, and similar factors that are unrelated to the goals of the manufacturer but often play a role in dependent relationships also were likely to be deterred.

Of course, a number of cases were brought before the courts under the federal and state statutes by dealers against manufacturers. The dealers rarely won. Yet the flow of litigation itself may have had some impact on large bureaucratic organizations such as the automobile manufacturers. Lawyers and executives much more senior than those normally involved in day-to-day contact with dealers had reason to establish policies and see that they were implemented so that the manufacturers could defend themselves in litigation. Again, this was likely to restrain the discretion of area or zone supervisors who were directly responsible for decisions concerning dealers. In order to structure practice so that an automobile manufacturer was ready to cope with a flow of litigation involving its relationship with dealers, it would want evidence that the dealer had had the opportunity to retail the best-selling models and that the dealer had failed to do as well as other similarly situated dealers. Such record-keeping likely added to the objectivity of judgments about terminating dealerships.

> All of these private systems have far more meaning for most dealers than lawsuits for damages under the [federal] Good Faith Act or proceedings under [state] administrative-licensing statutes to revoke licenses of factory representatives. The major significance of these formal legal proceedings is that they support the private other-than-legal ways of dealing with problems. [Macaulay 1966, pp. 204–5]

The various civil rights statutes and the cases creating some remedies for employees-at-will may have a similar impact. There is some risk of legal challenge if an employer passes over for promotion or fires a member of a racial minority, a woman, a handicapped person, or anyone over forty. Drucker (1980) comments that "[i]t's getting harder to dismiss any employee except for 'cause.'" He continues:

> Standards and review will, paradoxically, be forced on employers in the United States by the abandonment of fixed-age retirement. For companies to be able to dismiss even the most senile and decrepit oldster, they will have to develop

> impersonal standards of performance and systematic personnel procedures for employees of all ages. [p. 18]

Such procedures, of course, will limit the powers of supervisors and constitutionalize more and more employment relationships. As Selznick (1968, 1969) has argued, once reasons must be given to justify action, those reasons are open to examination and challenge. At least in close cases, many supervisors are likely to avoid the burden of persuasion and give an employee a second chance to meet defined standards of performance.

The relatively few cases involving employment-at-will in which employees have gained some measure of victory have prompted a great deal of writing in business publications such as *Fortune*, the *Harvard Business Review*, and the *Wall Street Journal*, as well as the law reviews. A number of major corporations have created some type of internal review system governing discipline, failure to promote, and discharge of such employees. The cases and the writing may have made the matter salient to those in charge of personnel. Seminars and training sessions about coping with the new employee-at-will cases have been sold to personnel managers and corporate lawyers. Many consulting firms offer to create informal dispute resolution processes to deal with the rights and duties of such employees. Part of the reason for the interest in such programs may have been an attempt to show courts that new rights need not be recognized; part may have been an attempt to offset claims of unfairness in case firms were sued by an employee. The informal dispute resolution procedure adopted may be more or less elaborate, but most call for review by people without a personal stake in the case. Whatever the difficulties facing an employee claiming to have been treated unfairly before such an internal body, the chance that a supervisor's decisions might be reviewed by those who could affect the supervisor's career again could serve some deterrent function. Supervisors ought to be prompted to create files on employees which could withstand review. Of course, crafty supervisors could manipulate such files, and those who conducted the review might tend to back up supervisors automatically and distrust employees. Nonetheless, the need to be able to make a case should serve as some limitation on arbitrary power.

These may be examples of reflexive rationality. Certainly, legal action affected procedures of internal discourse, and we could say that property rights had been redefined and redistributed in the franchise and employment cases. However, Teubner stresses that reflexive rationality is neither power-equalization nor participatory democracy. In addition, this kind of rationality must affect the ways semi-autonomous social systems relate to other social systems. On the one hand, it may be that the cumulative effect of all the increases in the rights of employees and franchisees will be to raise costs and make it harder to discipline and discharge the lazy and incompetent. As a result of this factor and others, American products could cost more and become more shoddy. In turn, cheaper and higher quality foreign products could enter American markets, ultimately prompting unemployment and economic crisis. On the other hand, perhaps fair procedures, a measure of job security, and the accountability of supervisors diminish the price paid for the effects of arbitrary action by supervisors. Moreover, the systems described may aid supervisors to better target and deal with the truly incompetent or inefficient since responsibility and performance ought to be better identified and evaluated. Changes in a social institution such as employment probably will affect other institutions such as the family or the economy as a whole.

Teubner sees "reflexive potential" in the "abstract control technique" used in labor law. Here, public government fosters a private legislative and adjudicatory system for the social end of promoting labor peace while redistributing wealth and affording workers some influence over working conditions. Klare (1981, 1982a, 1982b) criticizes what he calls liberal collective-bargaining theory by showing that its inner logic "deflects and demoralizes popular participation and, through cooptation of popular struggle, ultimately reinforces the institutional infrastructure of capitalism" (1981, p. 482). Klare's argument enables us to consider Teubner's reflexive rationality in more detail.

Klare argues that liberal collective-bargaining law theory ultimately rests on a delegation of power to make socially important decisions to corporations and large, bureaucratically run labor unions. This delegation results in management decision-making about what is critically important and gives it the power of command in the workplace. Essentially, of course, this is the private government argument. However, Klare stresses that liberal theory actively promotes workers' rights in certain limited and carefully defined contexts. Our collective-bargaining law has engendered some democratic participation of employees in workplace governance. Unions do protect employees from some unilateral and arbitrary dictates of management. The grievance procedure is the most important source of whatever due process Americans have on the job. Unions can be a context within which workers form and express aspirations and experience the dignity that comes with having some influence on decisions governing one's life. Nonetheless, Klare argues that the accepted theory of collective bargaining defines for workers, for union leaders, and for the public what is possible and desirable in the workplace. It stands in the way of progress toward freedom there and toward gaining for workers a dominant voice respecting the organization and purposes of work and the disposition of the products of labor.

Liberal collective-bargaining theory uses a legislative and private government metaphor to serve a number of key rhetorical purposes. Workers vote for union representatives who negotiate a collective bargain in light of the power to strike. The bargain will concern wages and conditions of employment. However, management will not surrender control over such things as whether to open new plants or close old ones, or whether to adopt new basic manufacturing techniques. Management, for example, designs a new model automobile, plans the organization of the factory and the division of labor among people and machines, and then employs unionized workers who are governed by a bureaucratic chain of command within which decisions of importance often are made far removed from anyone at the local level. Collective bargaining can influence, but not control, this process.

Once a collective bargain, usually published as a small book written in legal language, is ratified by the membership, workers then lose their right to strike during the life of the contract. Workers, management, and the public are deemed to share an interest in continuing production or providing services. In place of a strike, during the life of the contract the exclusive remedy for disputes is the grievance process which leads, ultimately, to arbitration. But unions also become large bureaucracies removed from their membership. They are held responsible for the compliance of their members with the contract. Union officials develop their own interests which are not always congruent with those of the workers at a particular plant or in smaller work groups. Their role becomes political, involving manipulation of both managers and workers. Almost inevitably, some groups of workers will be favored over others.

Liberal collective-bargaining theory presents grievance arbitration as a technical and apolitical matter of contract interpretation. Collective bargains are seen as contracts which, as other contracts, primarily concern the parties. The role of public law is limited to enforcing a bargain, and since the agreement provided an institutionalized, private internal dispute resolution process, arbitration will be enforced. This helps vindicate a limited role of government in supporting the grievance arbitration process while still continuing to recognize a private character of industrial decision-making. The end result is that procedure is separated from substance so that the quality of working life and fairness of compensation turn on bargaining power rather than norms of substantive justice. The workers have only the form of industrial due process rather than democratic self-governance. They must surrender control of their disputes to union officials and ultimately to labor lawyers who transform them into grievances phrased as interpretations of the collective bargain. The process itself involves a multilayered series of stages, hearings, and legal forms which ensure that decisions are delayed. Arbitration may resolve the dispute as so transformed but leave the real problem untouched. Decision-makers, though deemed expert, may understand little of life in a particular plant or the experience of workers in general. Labor lawyers and law professors who serve as arbitrators seldom have experience of life in the workplace or the impact of layoffs and unemployment.

Moreover, workers often face disincentives at many plants to bringing a grievance and pursuing it. Whyte (1956, p. 13) reports that "[w]orkers don't like to be considered 'trouble-makers.' It isn't a case of the worker thinking, if I pass on this grievance, I will be fired; nothing as crude as that, but rather an uneasy feeling that if I put this in the grievance procedure, management will not forget and maybe somewhere along the line I will not get the breaks that I am entitled to." At one time, union officials also filtered out grievances that they thought unwarranted or tactically unwise to push in light of positions to be taken at the next collective-bargaining negotiating session. While the expanding definition of the duty of fair representation may inhibit the more open forms of gatekeeping, union officials cannot be expected to support fully what they see as unwarranted or unwise claims (see Weir 1976).

When workers see a major portion of their lives under the control of management and union officials and see collective-bargaining and grievance procedures as largely meaningless rituals, they may exercise what power they still retain (see Farrell 1983). When economic conditions are such that jobs are not scarce prizes, often they can slow down the pace of the work; do passable but not high-quality work; engage in horseplay and foolishness to confront boredom; take, sometimes as of right, goods and materials from the employer; or engage in an illegal wildcat strike (see Atleson 1973). They can also turn to factional fights within their unions. Such practices can damage the reputation of their company's products, subjecting the firm to competitive pressure. On the one hand, this may provoke new and better forms of work organization, but it may also provoke company demands for concessions from unions or spur decisions to use more industrial robots and high technology to eliminate the need for many workers.

Klare and Teubner differ in their appraisal of reflexive rationality. To a great extent, they are seeking different ends. Klare (1981, p. 456) sees the philosophy of collective-bargaining law as "an important effort to conceptualize, justify and legitimate the modern, regulatory state in the period of advanced industrial capitalism." Unions and large corporations are seen as engaging in *private lawmaking,* "although their *de facto* power rivals or even supersedes that of public agencies and although their actions are of societal consequence." Welfare-state social democracy, acting in support of collective bargaining, loses sight of the ideal that "the highest aspiration of democratic culture should be to generate and nurture in all people the capacity for individual and collective *self-*governance and *self-*realization of their potentials" (1982a, p. 83).

Teubner, on the other hand, does not see the main goal of reflexive rationality as "power-equalization nor an increase of individual participation in the emphatic sense of 'participatory democracy' " (p. 440). He tells us that, rather, "law must act at the subsystem-specific level to install, correct, and redefine democratic self-regulatory mechanisms. Law's role is to decide about decisions, regulate regulations, and establish structural premises for future decisions in terms of organization, procedure, and competencies" (p. 437). The goal is "to create the structural premises for a decentralized integration of society by supporting integrative mechanisms within autonomous social subsystems" (p. 417). Integration requires that corporations, semi-public associations, mass media, and educational institutions be sensitive to the outside effects of their attempts to maximize internal rationality (cf. Cohen 1983). Teubner would like to have both social integration by decentralized means and power equalization in self-regulatory processes. However, he recognizes the danger that reflexive rationality could be "perverted easily into a sheer moralistic appeal" (p. 439).

Whatever our views about social integration and increasing individual control of one's own life, there is a tension between self-regulation and social integration. This suggests that while the law may be evolving toward some version of reflexive rationality, the process may not solve all problems and avoid crises. It may be that the legal system is doomed to make a succession of vain efforts to offset the contradictions of late capitalism and late socialism as it is practiced in the Soviet Union and eastern Europe today (see Bowers 1982; Sabel and Stark 1982; Simis 1982).

Moreover, we can note that both Teubner and Klare seem curiously apolitical. Klare writes as if those who worked to gain the rights for workers to organize and collectively bargain were free to write any program they pleased. Teubner writes about evolution from formal to substantive to reflexive rationality. Evolution in a biological sense implies that things just happen, perhaps by a cumulative series of accidents and a process of natural selection. In social science, evolution seems to connote a systematic and almost inevitable progression following an inner logic. Taken either way, there is some plausibility to the idea of evolution from one legal style to another. However, we may be disquieted by the absence from the picture of those who attempt to plan changes or individuals and groups struggling for advantage and power. (Cf. Ray's criticism [1983] of Luhmann's theory, a theory that serves as part of the foundation for Teubner's position.) In Joerges' words (1983, p. 29), "the Achilles' heel of reflexive rationality . . . is that a requirement [that affected groups] . . . renegotiate does not change the balance of power which determines the outcome of the negotiations." (Cf. Hearn 1984.)

Insofar as we accept the idea of an evolutionary tide as the product of natural forces, however, there is no reason to assume that evolution will stop with reflexive rationality. This is particularly true as long as we continue to have difficulty distinguishing public from private action. Reflexive rationality would seem only to postpone the day of reckoning for a distinction that Kennedy (1982) tells us is hard to take seriously.

Teubner's progression assumes a legal system with sufficient autonomy to control other social systems so that they will be integrated into a total collective unit. However, if an empirical picture of modern societies shows interchanges between and interpenetration among legal and other systems, major questions remain unanswered. It is easy to imagine legal agencies delegating self-regulatory power to various social units; it is harder to see how reflexive law would enable legal officials to coordinate and resolve conflicting claims in light of the powers of private governments and social fields and networks to influence legal outcomes and evade commands.

If Klare clears away the mystifications of liberal collective-bargaining theory, he seems to assume that the way will be open for "democratic self-management of the workplace by workers; [for] . . . giving a dominant voice respecting the organization and purposes of work and the disposition of the products of labor to those who perform work . . ." (1981, p. 451). However, the abandonment of "industrial democracy" might lead to a kind of corporatism or state socialism where workers had less power rather than more. The experience of those who have attacked liberal institutions in the name of lifting false consciousness is not reassuring.

On the other hand, due process, rights, and bureaucratic structures often break down into bargaining in the shadow of the law. Henry (1982) reports that a number of legal measures in Great Britain during the 1970s prompted management to formalize rules and procedures to deal with the disciplining of individual workers for acts such as theft of company property. In a sense, this was another example of reflexive rationality. However, as Klare might have predicted, Henry reported that the procedures functioned to give management a legitimate method of dismissing workers without being subject to question. Henry found, however, that many employers had moved from formal internal procedures to reliance on automatic employee self-discipline, often reinforced by a trade union. This

> was especially apparent where work was structured into small teams or gangs, working for pooled bonuses. Under such circumstances, said one employer, "employees wish to be seen contributing to their working groups and are reluctant to disrupt the normal pattern" since, as another pointed out, "equal effort is required by gang members." Here there can be "pressure from other workers on slackers" or "sanctions on people whom the team don't feel are pulling their weight." This pressure can be informal, "from colleagues to the offending employee" or more formally by "shop stewards who make points cautioning members who break company rules" and whom they "get to toe the line" by either having a "quiet word" or in extreme cases, "advising local district officers of the union." [p. 374]

Henry sees the possibility that, as suggested by Abel (1981) and Santos (1980), "participatory disciplinary technology becomes the ultimate form of capitalist control" (cf. Scraton and South 1984). However, participation of this type may also bring with it some limited autonomy and self-confidence. This could bring about the "penultimate stage of the process whereby the existing relations of production are undermined and replaced." Perhaps this is the road an evolution to reflexive rationality will take, and perhaps it will prompt the next evolution (cf. Derber and Schwartz 1983; Feldberg and Glenn 1983).

I doubt that those capitalists who now benefit by the distinction between public and private spheres and the delegation of power justified by it will be content to sit and watch the "natural" evolution to worker control. Indeed, Blankenburg (1984) points out that instead of an evolution from stage to stage in the style of legal thought, all forms of rationality may exist at once. Substantive rationality did not end the claims of formal rationality, and reflexive rationality is unlikely to erase formal or substantive rationality from the minds of those concerned with legal thought. Distinguished jurists often use inconsistent styles of legal thought. They serve as ideological ploys rationalizing shifting positions about autonomy and accountability of private social control. They reflect the power of those who control associations and those affected by them.

CONCLUSION

As we have seen, viewing society as involving relationships between only the state and individuals presents major difficulties for the social study of law. Theories about the state or society tend to overlook the remarkable ability of individuals to cope with attempted regulation by evasion, manipulation, conscious ignorance of the law, and bargaining in the light of more or less plausible legal arguments. Yet a picture of law confronting or confronted by isolated individuals also is too simple to capture enough of reality for many purposes. We live in a world of legal pluralism. Private governments, social fields, and networks administer their own rules and apply their own sanctions to those who come under their jurisdiction. Sometimes individuals are insulated from public governmental activity by social fields; sometimes public government officials are members of social fields which cut across formal boundaries of the public and the private.

These complicated interrelationships are important for the social study of law. An article in the *New York Times* (1982), for example, reported that those who supply and those who use cocaine constitute an integrated social field. In return for access to the drug, lawyers provide information on changes in the narcotics law, and on the doctrine of search and seizure, and keep track of arrest warrants. From these lawyers, dealers have learned to use occupied buildings because police need a warrant before they can enter. Often the process of obtaining a warrant will prompt a warning so that drug operations can be moved. Plumbers who use cocaine convert the pipes in a building so that drugs can be sent in tubes to other rooms quickly. Telephone repair people and others with experience in electronics make their contribution by installing sophisticated equipment so that conversations in other rooms can be monitored. Electricians install doors that can be opened only by remote control. Scanners are used to listen to police radio calls, and communications equipment helps alert people on upper floors that unwelcome visitors are entering the building. Of course, police officers, too, can become users of cocaine, and they are in a position to make valuable contributions to the maintenance of the network.

Clearly, this report suggests some of the limits on effectiveness of drug laws. However, it also suggests some of the difficulties with theories that see people as so socialized to comply with law that it is part of their personality. We can question whether the story describes a true deviant subculture or just a social network in which commonly held values other than complying with the law are stressed. Americans are socialized to gratify their desires. They learn to win at games, and clever shading of the rules is a matter for amusement rather than horror. Law enforcement officials commented that many in the middle class no longer thought of cocaine use as against the law.

Many involved in the cocaine trade learn and use entrepreneurial skills which they, because of class or race, could not learn or use in legal occupations. A large part of underemphasized American history involves ill-gotten gains serving as the base for the next generation of a family or a group moving into mainstream society. We can view participation as a form of rebellion and taking control of one's life, or we can see it as exploiting the weaknesses of one's fellows for personal gain. Undoubtedly, the illegality of the cocaine trade has prompted the creation of deviant norms within the group of users and suppliers as well as the use of swift and severe sanctions for even suspected deviation. I wonder whether Teubner would want to find "elements of reflexive rationality" in this decentralized system of private lawmaking. Do networks distributing illegal drugs contribute to social integration or disintegration? All in all, the example is a good one with which to test the kinds of theories about law and society which have been discussed in this paper.

The relationships between the state, individuals, and various human associations ranging from the family to multinational corporations are as poorly described in the law-and-society literature as they are difficult to evaluate. It is often assumed that there has been a great loss of community in modern industrial societies. Novelists and playwrights dramatize these themes. In this view, people are but cogs in an industrial machine who live rootlessly in interchangeable neighborhoods, unencumbered by real ties to family, friends, those who share their job skills or their tastes in recreation, or those who share religious observances. This picture undoubtedly shows some of the reality of modern life, but it is an overstatement, more applicable to some people than others.

Even at the bottom of the economic and status ladder, one often finds strong family ties, a religious-based system of coping with problems, and associations functioning to provide recreation and self-defense. Irving (1977, p. 879), after studying people in urban settings in England and the United States, concluded that social networks "remained close-knit in a surprising variety of urban situations, and they continue, even in this mobile age, to remain substantially rooted in the residential locality." Galanter (1979) reminds us that the

> survival and proliferation of indigenous law in the contemporary United States remains concealed from those who are looking for an inclusive and self-contained *gemeinschaft*, unsullied by formal organization, which enfolds individuals and integrates their whole life experience. What we find instead is a multitude of associations and networks, overlapping and interpenetrating, more fragmentary and less inclusive. . . .
>
> Such partial communities, linked by informal communications and sometimes by formal communications devices as well, provide much of the texture of our lives in family and kinship, at work and in business dealings, in neighborhood, sports, religion, and politics. There are varying degrees of self-conscious regulation and varying degrees of congruity with the official law. This is a realm of interdependence, regulated by tacit norms of reciprocity and sometimes by more explicit codes. The range of shared meanings is limited but the cost of exit is substantial. If we have lost the experience of an all-encompassing, inclusive community, it is not to a world of arm's length dealings with strangers, but in large measure to a world of loosely joined and partly overlapping partial or fragmentary communities. In this sense our exposure to indigenous law has increased at the same time that official regulation has multiplied. [pp. 16–17]

Ferguson (1983, p. 51) says that "[t]he standard anarchist recommendations for post-revolutionary society—workers' collectives, producers' and consumers' cooperatives, neighborhood councils—are all attempts to provide . . . [an open public] . . . space, where the ideas and goals of diverse individuals could come together and form the direction for collective action." She continues to say that "[i]n an open public situation, with full participation by all members, power need not be seen as the ability of some to make others do that which they would not otherwise have done. Instead, power could become the capacity to shape the collective situation—a positive force enabling individuals to do together that which they cannot do separately." However, Ferguson recognizes that anarchism cannot eliminate all coercion and all law. The pressure of one's peers is not the most innocent kind of coercion. In contrast to Kennedy, she concludes that "[t]he members of the collective must continually establish and reestablish the boundary between public and private acts, and not try to either erase the boundary or fix it once and for all."

Those who have been frustrated by the mindless operation of bureaucratic formal rationality can see much to admire in the anarchist vision. Yet there are two matched classic objections. Frug (1980, p. 1070) tells us that "[w]hat makes the concept of popular participation so unrealistic to us is not only its frightening unfamiliarity, but also our conviction that all decision-making requires specialization, expertise, and a chain of command." We can imagine a chaotic attempt to design a new automobile or stereo receiver and produce it by popular participation or an attempt of a major symphony orchestra to produce a work of the stature of a Beethoven concerto by a collective participatory process. Efficiency, our civil religion, seems to demand supporting hierarchies by deeming an area to be private, by leaving matters to the logic of property and contract. Yet the benefits of a division of labor do not establish that present chains of command are natural or inevitable. Ferguson mentions the second concern. All collective action is a threat to the individual who does not agree, who promotes an alternative view, or who just wants to be left alone. One speaking with the authority of the collective may act against such individuals for the good of the group or for the official's own self-interest. Given all the difficulties in asserting rights successfully—the cost barriers to litigation, the contradictory nature of our theories of rights, and the power of those with whom one has long-term relationships to retaliate later—rights are a feeble defense against power. Yet until we think of a way to achieve what now looks to be a utopia where all power is neatly equalized and balanced, rights may be all we have. As Kennedy (1981, p. 506) observed, "[e]mbedded in the rights notion is a liberating accomplishment of our culture: the affirmation of free human subjectivity against the constraints of group life, along with the paradoxical countervision of a group life that creates and nurtures individuals capable of freedom." These normative contradictions help explain the problematic relationships between the larger public government, private governments, social fields, and networks.

An appreciation of the role of private governments, social fields, and networks, as we have seen, is critical for the development of many of the classic topics of the social study of law. The relationship of public and private normative orderings tells us much about the place of law in society and the fate of attempted reforms. Lurking in all of these concerns are great questions about freedom and control of individuals and their associations, the autonomy of centers of power and their integration into a functioning society, and problems of the interrelationships and interpenetration of public governments and private associations. Our present understanding of more and less institutionalized social fields and their connections with the larger legal system is, to say the least, underdeveloped and in need of attention. Articles surveying fields often end by calling for either more research or more theory. Here, I can safely do both. In addition, we ought not forget what we already know. Private government performs many of the functions commonly associated with public government, and it is likely that the more decentralized the structures for carrying out a social function, the greater the problems of coordination and integration. At the same time, the public/private distinction is suspect. While it may be useful or vital to carve out areas of activity and put them beyond public control, reifying public and private governments and seeing them as distinct entities only obscures reality. In Zimring's words (1981):

> It is sometimes possible both to know something important and to ignore that knowledge. To do this is to generate the phenomenon of the well-known secret, an obvious fact we ignore. When Edgar Allan Poe suggested that the best location to hide something is the most obvious place, he was teaching applied law and social science. [p. 867]

Cases Cited

Brown v. Board of Education, 347 U.S. 483 (1954).
Comerford v. International Harvester, 235 Ala. 376, 178 So. 894 (1938).
Dred Scott v. Sandford, 60 U.S. (19 How.) 393 (1857).
Pierce v. Ortho Pharmaceutical Corp., 84 N.J. 58, 417 A.2d 505 (1980).

Bibliography

Abel, Richard L.
     1981   "Conservative Conflict and the Reproduction of Capitalism: The Role of Informal Justice." *International Journal of the Sociology of Law* 9:245–67.
Abercrombie, Nicholas, and Turner, Bryan S.
     1978   "The Dominant Ideology Thesis." *British Journal of Sociology* 29:149–67.
Abney, Glenn, and Lauth, Thomas P.
     1982   "Councilmanic Intervention in Municipal Administration." *Administration and Society* 13:435–56.
Abramson, Joan
     1977   "Measuring Success or, Whatever Happened to Affirmative Action?" *Civil Rights Digest* 9:15–27.

Adler, Patricia A., and Adler, Peter
    1983   "Relationships Between Dealers: the Social Organization of Illicit Drug Transactions." *Sociology and Social Research* 67:260–78.
Akers, Ronald L.
    1977   *Deviant Behavior: A Social Learning Approach.* Belmont, Calif.: Wadsworth.
Albrecht, Stan L., and Green, Miles
    1977   "Cognitive Barriers to Equal Justice Before the Law." *Journal of Research in Crime and Delinquency* 14:206–21.
Arnove, Robert F.
    1970   "The Ford Foundation and 'Competence Building' Overseas: Assumptions, Approaches, and Outcomes." *Studies in Comparative International Development* 12:100–126.
Atleson, James B.
    1973   "Work Group Behavior and Wildcat Strikes: The Causes and Functions of Industrial Civil Disobedience." *Ohio State Law Journal* 34:751–816.
Balbus, Isaac D.
    1977   "Commodity Form and Legal Form: An Essay on the 'Relative Autonomy' of the Law." *Law & Society Review* 11:546–88.
Barber, Bernard
    1978   "Control and Responsibility in the Powerful Professions." *Political Science Quarterly* 93:599–615.
Baumgartner, M. P.
    1985   "Law and the Middle Class: Evidence from a Suburban Town." *Law and Human Behavior* 9:3–24.
Baxter, Leslie A.
    1984   "An Investigation of Compliance-Gaining as Politeness." *Human Communication Research* 10:427–56.
Berle, Adolph A., and Means, Gardner C.
    1932   *The Modern Corporation and Private Property.* New York: Macmillan.
Berle, Adolph A., Jr.
    1952   "Constitutional Limitations on Corporate Activity: Protection of Personal Rights from Invasion Through Economic Power." *University of Pennsylvania Law Review* 100:933–55.
Bernard, Jesse
    1964   *Academic Women.* State College: Pennsylvania State University Press.
Biersteker, Thomas J.
    1980   "The Illusion of State Power: Transnational Corporations and the Neutralization of Host-Country Legislation." *Journal of Peace Research* 17:207–21.
Bilder, Richard B.
    1970   "East-West Trade Boycotts: A Study in Private, Labor Union, State, and Local Interference with Foreign Policy." *University of Pennsylvania Law Review* 118:841–938.
Bissonette, R.
    1977   "The Bartender as a Mental Health Service Gatekeeper: A Role Analysis." *Community Mental Health Journal* 13:92–99.
Black, Donald
    1976   *The Behavior of Law.* New York: Academic Press.
    1983   "Crime as Social Control." *American Sociological Review* 48:34–45.
Blankenburg, Erhard
    1984   "The Poverty of Evolutionism: A Critique of Teubner's Case for 'Reflexive Law.'" *Law & Society Review* 18:273–89.

Block, Alan A., and Thomas, Philip A.
    1984   "Beyond the Courtroom Door." *Australian Journal of Law and Society* 2:110–28.
Bowers, Stephen R.
    1982   "Law and Lawlessness in a Socialist Society: The Potential Impact of Crime in East Germany." *World Affairs* 145:152–76.
Braithwaite, John
    1982   "Enforced Self-Regulation: A New Strategy for Corporate Crime Control." *Michigan Law Review* 80:1466–1502.
Bredemeier, Harry C.
    1962   "Law as an Integrative Mechanism." In *Law and Sociology,* edited by William Evan. New York: Free Press.
Burgess, Robert L., and Akers, Ronald L.
    1966   "A Differential Association-Reinforcement Theory of Criminal Behavior." *Social Problems* 14:128–47.
Burton, Frank
    1976   "The Irish Republican Army and Its Community: A Struggle for Legitimacy." In *The Sociology of Law,* edited by Pat Carlen. Keele: University of Keele.
Cain, Maureen
    1983   "Introduction: Towards an Understanding of the International State." *International Journal of the Sociology of Law* 11:1–10.
Caplow, Theodore
    1982   "Christmas Gifts and Kin Networks." *American Sociological Review* 47:383–92.
Carter, Lief II.
    1974   *The Limits of Order.* Lexington, Mass.: Lexington Books.
Casey, Gregory
    1976   "Popular Perceptions of Supreme Court Rulings." *American Politics Quarterly* 4:3–45.
Chafee, Zechariah, Jr.
    1930   "The Internal Affairs of Associations Not for Profit." *Harvard Law Review* 43:993–1029.
Chambliss, William J.
    1973   "Functional and Conflict Theories of Crime." *MSS Modular Publications* 17:1–23.
    1979   "Contradictions and Conflicts in Law Creation." In *Research in Law and Sociology,* vol. 2, edited by Rita J. Simon and Steven Spitzer. Greenwich, Conn.: JAI Press.
Chambliss, William J., and Seidman, Robert
    1971   *Law, Order and Power.* Reading, Mass.: Addison-Wesley.
Cloward, Richard A., and Ohlin, Lloyd E.
    1960   *Delinquency and Opportunity.* Glencoe, Ill.: Free Press.
Coffee, John C., Jr.
    1981   " 'No Soul to Damn: No Body to Kick': An Unscandalized Inquiry into the Problem of Corporate Punishment." *Michigan Law Review* 79:386–459.
Cohen, Albert K.
    1955   *Delinquent Boys.* Glencoe, Ill.: Free Press.
Cohen, Lawrence E., and Felson, M.
    1979   "Social Change and Crime Rate Trends: A Routine Activity Approach." *American Sociological Review.* 44:588–608.
Cohen, Steven R.
    1983   "From Industrial Democracy to Professional Adjustment." *Theory and Society* 12:47–67.
Cole, Richard B.
    1978   "The Second Criminal Justice System." *S.A.M. [Society of Advanced Management] Management Journal* 43:17–23.

Cortese, Charles F.
      1966   "A Study in Knowledge and Attitudes Toward the Law: The Legal Knowledge
                Inventory." *Rocky Mountain Social Science Journal* 3:192–204.
Cressey, Donald R.
      1973   "Advanced Notice and Government by Law Within Criminal Confederations."
                International Journal of Criminology and Penology 1:55–67.
Crowe, Patricia Ward
      1978   "Complainant Reactions to the Massachusetts Commission Against Discrimina-
                tion." *Law & Society Review* 12:217–35.
Curran, Barbara W.
      1978   "Getting By with a Little Help from My Friends: Informal Networks Among Older
                Black and White Urban Women Below the Poverty Line." *Dissertation Abstracts
                International* 39(4-A).
Derber, Charles, and Schwartz, William
      1983   "Toward a Theory of Worker Participation." *Sociological Inquiry* 53:61–78.
Deysine, Anne
      1980   "Political Corruption: A Review of the Literature." *European Journal of Political
                Research* 8:447–62.
Di Franceisco, Wayne, and Gitelman, Zvi
      1984   "Soviet Political Culture and 'Covert Participation' in Policy Implementation."
                American Political Science Review 78:603–20.
Drucker, Peter F.
      1980   "The Job as Property Right." *Wall Street Journal* September 25, 1979, p. 20.
Durkheim, Emile
      1958   *Professional Ethics and Civic Morals.* Glencoe, Ill.: Free Press.
Dye, Thomas R.
      1978   "Oligarchic Tendencies in National Policy-Making: the Role of the Private Policy-
                Planning Organizations." *Journal of Politics* 40:309–31.
Eells, Richard
      1962   *The Government of Corporations.* Glencoe, Ill.: Free Press.
Ehrlich, Eugen
      1936   *Fundamental Principles of the Sociology of Law.* Translated by Walter L. Moll with an
                introduction by Roscoe Pound. Cambridge, Mass.: Harvard University Press.
Eisenstadt, S. N., and Roniger, Louis
      1980   "Patron-Client Relations as a Model of Structuring Social Exchange." *Comparative
                Studies in Society and History* 22:42–77.
Ekland-Olson, Sheldon
      1982   "Deviance, Social Control and Social Networks." In *Research in Law, Deviance and
                Social Control,* vol. 4, edited by Steven Spitzer and Rita J. Simon. Greenwich,
                Conn.: JAI Press.
Ellickson, Robert C.
      1982   "Cities and Homeowners Associations." *University of Pennsylvania Law Review*
                130:1519–80.
Elliot, Delbert S., and Voss, Harwin L.
      1974   *Delinquency and Dropout.* Lexington, Mass.: Lexington Books.
Ellman, Ira Mark
      1981   "Driven from the Tribunal: Judicial Resolution of Internal Church Disputes."
                California Law Review 69:1378–1444.
Engel, David M.
      1984   "The Oven Bird's Song: Insiders, Outsiders, and Personal Injuries in an American
                Community." *Law & Society Review* 18:549–79.

Evan, William
 1976 *Organizational Theory: Structures, Systems, and Environments.* New York: Wiley.
Ewing, David W.
 1977 *Freedom Inside the Corporation: Bringing Civil Liberties to the Workplace.* New York: Dutton.
Farrell, Dan
 1983 "Exit, Voice, Loyalty, and Neglect as Responses to Job Dissatisfaction: A Multidimensional Scaling Study." *Academy of Management Journal* 26:596–607.
Feldberg, Roslyn L., and Glenn, Evelyn Nakano
 1983 "Incipient Workplace Democracy among United States Clerical Workers." *Economic and Industrial Democracy* 4:47–67.
Felstiner, William L. F., and Williams, Lynne A.
 1978 "Mediation as an Alternative to Criminal Prosecution: Ideology and Limitations." *Law and Human Behavior* 2:223–44.
 1979 *Community Mediation in Dorchester, Massachusetts: Alternatives to Adjudication. An International Study.* Los Angeles: Program for Dispute Systems Research, University of Southern California.
Femia, Joseph V.
 1983 "Review Article: Gramsci's Patrimony." *British Journal of Political Science* 13:327–64.
Ferguson, Kathy E.
 1983 "Toward a New Anarchism." *Contemporary Crises* 7:39–57.
Fisse, Brent
 1981 "Community Service as a Sanction Against Corporations." *Wisconsin Law Review* 1981: 970–1017.
Fisse, Brent, and Braithwaite, John
 1984 "Sanctions Against Corporations: Dissolving the Monopoly of Fines." In *Business Regulation in Australia,* edited by Roman Tomasic. North Ryde, N.S.W.: CCH Australia Limited.
FitzGerald, Jeffrey M.; Hickman, David C.; and Dickins, Richard L.
 1980 "A Preliminary Discussion of the Definitional Phase of the Dispute Process." Paper presented at the Law and Society Association Conference, Madison, Wisconsin, June.
Fitzpatrick, Peter
 1984 "Law and Societies." *Osgoode Hall Law Journal* 22:115–38.
Fleming, R. W.
 1961 "Some Problems of Due Process and Fair Procedure in Labor Arbitration." *Stanford Law Review* 13:235–51.
 1962 "Some Problems of Evidence Before the Labor Arbitrator." *Michigan Law Review* 60:133–68.
Ford, Frederick R.
 1983 "Rules: The Invisible Family." *Family Process* 22:135–45.
Friedmann, Wolfgang G.
 1957 "Corporate Power, Government by Private Groups, and the Law." *Columbia Law Review* 57:155–86.
Frug, Gerald
 1980 "The City as a Legal Concept." *Harvard Law Review* 93:1057–1154.
Fuller, Lon L.
 1941 "Consideration and Form." *Columbia Law Review* 41:799–824.
 1969 "Two Principles of Human Association." In *Voluntary Associations,* edited by J. Roland Pennock and John W. Chapman. New York: Atherton Press.

Galanter, Marc
    1974   "Why the 'Haves' Come Out Ahead: Speculations on the Limits of Legal Change."
            Law & Society Review 9:95–160.

    1979   "Beyond Legal Representation: Dispute Processing, Non-judicial Alternatives and
            the 'Third Wave' in the Access-to-Justice Movement." Paper presented at the
            Colloquium on Access to Justice After the Publication of the Florence Project
            Series: Prospects for Future Action, Florence, Italy, October 15–18.

    1981   "Justice in Many Rooms: Courts, Private Ordering, and Indigenous Law." *Journal
            of Legal Pluralism* 19:1–47.

    1983   "Reading the Landscape of Disputes: What We Know and Don't Know (and Think
            We Know) About Our Allegedly Contentious and Litigious Society." *UCLA Law
            Review* 31:4–71.

Genovese, Rosalie G.
    1980   "A Women's Self-Help Network as a Response to Service Needs in the Suburbs."
            Signs: Journal of Women in Culture and Society 5:S248–56.

Ghezzi, Susan Guarino
    1983   "A Private Network of Social Control: Insurance Investigation Units." *Social Prob-
            lems* 30:521–31.

Glazer, Nathan
    1975   *Affirmative Discrimination: Ethnic Inequality and Public Policy.* New York: Basic
            Books.

Gottlieb, Gidon
    1983   "Relationalism: Legal Theory for a Relational Society." *University of Chicago Law
            Review* 50:567–612.

Grace, Clive, and Wilkinson, Philip
    1978   *Sociological Inquiry and Legal Phenomena.* London: Collier Macmillan.

Greenberg, David F.
    1976   "On One-Dimensional Marxist Criminology." *Theory and Society* 3:611–21.

Greenberg, David F., and Anderson, Nancy
    1981   "Recent Marxisant Books on Law: A Review Essay." *Contemporary Crises* 5:293–
            322.

Griffiths, John
    1984   "Village Justice in the Netherlands." *Journal of Legal Pluralism* 22:17–42.

Habermas, Jurgen
    1979   *Communication and the Evolution of Society.* Boston: Beacon Press.

Hagen, John; Silva, Edward T.; and Simpson, John H.
    1977   "Conflict and Consensus in the Designation of Deviance." *Social Forces* 56:320–
            40.

Hale, Robert L.
    1920   "Law Making by Unofficial Minorities." *Columbia Law Review* 20:451–56.

Hammer, Muriel
    1980   "Social Access and the Clustering of Personal Connections." *Social Networks*
            2:305–25.

Hannigan, John A.
    1982   "Unfriendly Skies: The Decline of the World Aviation Cartel." *Pacific Sociological
            Review* 25:107–36.

Hans, Valerie P., and Slater, Dan
    1983   "John Hinckley, Jr. and the Insanity Defense: The Public's Verdict." *Public Opinion
            Quarterly* 47:202–12.

Hanslowe, Kurt L.
    1961   "Regulation by Visible Public and Invisible Private Government." *Texas Law Re-
            view* 40:88–135.

Harding, Vincent
  1975   "The Black Wedge in America: Struggle, Crisis and Hope, 1955–1975." *Black Scholar* 7:28–30, 35–46.

Harvard Law Review
  1949   "Private Lawmaking by Trade Associations." *Harvard Law Review* 62:1346–70.
  1962   "Judicial Intervention in Disputes over the Use of Church Property." *Harvard Law Review* 75:1142–86.
  1963   "Judicial Control of Actions of Private Associations." *Harvard Law Review* 76:983–1100.
  1980   "Protecting at Will Employees Against Wrongful Discharge." *Harvard Law Review* 93:1818–44.

Havighurst, Harold C.
  1961   *The Nature of Private Contract.* Evanston, Ill.: Northwestern University Press.

Hearn, Frances
  1980   "Adaptive Narcissism and the Crisis of Legitimacy." *Contemporary Crises* 4:117–40.

Hearn, Frank
  1984   "State Autonomy and Corporatism." *Contemporary Crises* 8:125–45.

Hearst Corporation
  1983   *The American Public, the Media and the Judicial System: A National Survey on Public Awareness and Personal Experience.* New York: Hearst Corporation.

Henry, Stuart
  1981   "Decentralized Justice: Private v. Democratic Informality." In *Informal Institutions: Alternative Networks in the Corporate State,* edited by Stuart Henry. New York: St. Martin's Press.
  1982   "Factory Law: The Changing Disciplinary Technology of Industrial Social Control." *International Journal of the Sociology of Law* 10:365–83.

Hoekema, Andre
  1975   "Confidence in Justice and Law Among Port Workers." *Sociologia Neerlandia* 11:128–43.

Hopkins, Raymond F.
  1978   "Global Management Networks: The Internationalization of Domestic Bureaucracies." *International Social Science Journal* 30:31–46.

Hornig, Lilli S.
  1980   "Untenured and Tenuous: The Status of Women Faculty." *Annals, AAPSS* 448:115–25.

Hunt, Alan
  1976   "Perspectives in the Sociology of Law." In *The Sociology of Law,* edited by Pat Carlen. Keele: University of Keele.

Hurst, James Willard
  1960   "The Law in United States History." *Proceedings of the American Philosophical Society* 104:518–26.

Irving, Henry W.
  1977   "Social Networks in the Modern City." *Social Forces* 55:867–80.

Jaffee, Louis L.
  1937   "Law Making by Private Groups." *Harvard Law Review* 51:201–53.

Jessop, Bob
  1980   "On Recent Marxist Theories of Law, the State, and Juridico-Political Ideology." *International Journal of the Sociology of Law* 8:339–68.

Joerges, Christian
  1983   "Regulatory Law, Private Government and Self-Regulation: A Comment on Stewart Macaulay." Paper presented at the Conference on Reflexive Law and the Regulatory Crisis, Madison, Wisconsin, July 18–21.

Johnstone, Quintin, and Hopson, Dan, Jr.
    1967   *Lawyers and Their Work.* Indianapolis, Ind.: Bobbs-Merrill.
Jordan, Ellen R.
    1978   "Unconscionability at the Gas Station." *Minnesota Law Review* 62:813–56.
Kakalik, James S., and Wildhorn, Sorrel
    1977   *The Private Police: Security and Danger.* New York: Crane, Russak.
Kennedy, Duncan
    1981   "Critical Labor Law Theory: A Comment." *Industrial Relations Law Journal* 4:503–
            6.
    1982   "The Status of the Decline of the Public/Private Distinction." *University of Pennsylvania Law Review* 130:1349–57.
Kerbo, Harold R., and Della Fave, L. Richard
    1983   "Corporate Linkage and Control of the Corporate Economy: New Evidence and a
            Reinterpretation." *Sociological Quarterly* 24:201–18.
Klare, Karl E.
    1981   "Labor Law as Ideology: Toward a New Historiography of Collective Bargaining
            Law." *Industrial Relations Law Journal* 4:450–82.
    1982a   "Critical Theory and Labor Relations Law." In *The Politics of Law: A Progressive
            Critique,* edited by David Kairys. New York: Pantheon Books.
    1982b   "The Public/Private Distinction in Labor Law. *University of Pennsylvania Law Review* 130:1358–1422.
Koch, Koen
    1980   "The New Marxist Theory of the State or the Rediscovery of the Limitations
            of a Structural-Functionalist Paradigm." *Netherlands Journal of Sociology* 16:1–
            19.
Kornhauser, Ruth R.
    1978   *Social Sources of Delinquency.* Chicago: University of Chicago Press.
Kowalewski, David, and Leitko, Thomas A.
    1983   "Transnational Corporations and Intergovernmental Organizations: The Trilateral
            Commission Case." *Journal of Political and Military Sociology* 11:93–107.
Ladinsky, Jack, and Susmilch, Charles
    1983   "Community Factors in the Brokerage of Consumer Product and Service Problems." Working paper no. 14, Disputes Processing Research Program, University of
            Wisconsin Law School.
Lamo De Espinosa, Emilio
    1980   "Social and Legal Order in Sociological Functionalism." *Contemporary Crises* 4:43–
            76.
Leblebici, Huseyin, and Salancik, Gerald R.
    1982   "Stability in Interorganizational Exchanges: Rulemaking Processes of the Chicago
            Board of Trade." *Administrative Science Quarterly* 27:227–42.
Lee, Trevor R.
    1980   "The Resilience of Social Networks to Changes in Mobility and Propinquity."
            Social Networks 2:423–35.
Lester, Richard A.
    1974   *Antibias Regulations of Universities: Faculty Problems and Their Solutions.* New York:
            McGraw-Hill.
Lindblom, Charles
    1977   *Politics and Markets.* New York: Basic Books.
Lindgren, Janet S.
    1983   "Beyond Cases: Reconsidering Judicial Review." *Wisconsin Law Review* 1983:583–
            638.

Lineberry, Robert L., and Watson, Sharon M.
    1980   "Neighborhoods, Politics, and Public Services: The Case of Chicago." *Urban Interest* 2:11–18.

Lipset, Seymour Martin
    1982   "The Academic Mind at the Top: The Political Behavior and Values of Faculty Elites." *Public Opinion Quarterly* 46:143–68.

Liss, Lora J.
    1977   "Affirmative Action Officers: Are They Change Agents?" *Educational Record* 58:418–28.

Livingstone, Neil C.
    1981   "Fighting Terrorism: The Private Sector." *Conflict* 3:177–219.

Lopatka, Kenneth T.
    1984   "The Emerging Law of Wrongful Discharge—A Quadrennial Assessment of the Labor Law Issue of the 80s." *Business Lawyer* 40:1–32.

Lowenthal, Abraham F.
    1978   "Latin America: A Not-So-Special Relationship." *Foreign Policy* 32:107–26.

Luhmann, Niklas
    1981   "Communication About Law." In *Advances in Social Theory and Methodology*, edited by K. Knorr-Cetina and A. V. Circourel. Boston: Routledge & Kegan Paul.
    1982   *The Differentiation of Society*. New York: Columbia University Press.

Macaulay, Jacqueline
    1980   "The Failure of Affirmative Action: A Case Study." In *Rocking the Boat: Academic Women and the Academic Process*, edited by G. DeSole and L. Hoffman. New York: Modern Language Association.

Macaulay, Jacqueline, and Macaulay, Stewart
    1978   "Adoption for Black Children: A Case Study of Expert Discretion." In *Research in Law and Sociology*, vol. 1, edited by Rita J. Simon. Greenwich, Conn.: JAI Press.

Macaulay, Stewart
    1963   "Non-Contractual Relations in Business: A Preliminary Study." *American Sociological Review* 28:55–67.
    1966   *Law and the Balance of Power*. New York: Russell Sage Foundation.
    1979   "Lawyers and Consumer Protection Laws." *Law & Society Review* 14:115–71.
    1985   "Lawyer Advertising: 'Yes, but . . .'." Forthcoming. (Louvain, Belgium: European Workshop on Consumer Law.)

McKenna, Wendy B., and Denmark, Florence L.
    1975   "Women and the University." *International Journal of Group Tensions* 5:226–34.

Marenin, Otwin
    1981   "Essence and Empiricism in African Politics." *Journal of Modern African Studies* 19:1–30.

Marighela, Carlos
    1971   *For the Liberation of Brazil*. New York: Penguin Books.

Mayhew, Leon H.
    1968   *Law & Equal Opportunity: A Study of the Massachusetts Commission Against Discrimination*. Cambridge, Mass.: Harvard University Press.

Mechanic, David
    1962   "Sources of Power of Lower Participants in Complex Organizations." *Administrative Science Quarterly* 7:349–64.

Merton, Robert K.
    1957a   "Social Structure and Anomie." In *Social Theory and Social Structure*. Rev. ed. Glencoe, Ill.: Free Press.
    1957b   "Continuities in the Theory of Social Structure and Anomie." In *Social Theory and Social Structure*. Rev. ed. Glencoe, Ill.: Free Press.

Michigan Law Review
    1973   "Legal Knowledge of Michigan Citizens." *Michigan Law Review* 71:1463–86.
Mileski, Maureen
    1971   "Courtroom Encounters: An Observational Study of a Lower Criminal Court." *Law & Society Review* 5:473–538.
Miller, Arthur S.
    1960   "The Corporation as a Private Government in the World Community." *Virginia Law Review* 46:1539–72.
Mills, C. Wright
    1956   *The Power Elite.* Oxford: Oxford University Press.
Mills, Edgar W., Jr.
    1983   "Sociological Ambivalence and Social Order: The Constructive Uses of Normative Dissonance." *Sociology and Social Research* 67:279–87.
Milward, H. Brinton, and Francisco, Ronald A.
    1983   "Subsystem Politics and Corporatism in the United States." *Policy and Politics* 11:273–93.
Minnesota Law Review
    1975   "Regulation of Franchising." *Minnesota Law Review* 59:1027–63.
Mishra, Ramesh
    1982   "System Integration, Social Action and Change: Some Problems in Sociological Analysis." *Sociological Review* 30:5–22.
Moore, Sally Falk
    1978   *Law as Process: An Anthropological Approach.* London, Henley, and Boston: Routledge & Kegan Paul.
Nachmias, David, and Greer, Ann Lennarson
    1982   "Governance Dilemmas in an Age of Ambiguous Authority." *Policy Sciences* 14:105–16.
Nader, Laura
    1984   "The Recurrent Dialectic Between Legality and Its Alternatives: The Limitations of Binary Thinking." *Pennsylvania Law Review* 132:621–45.
National Center for State Courts
    1978   *State Courts: A Blueprint for the Future.* Williamsburg, Va.: National Center for State Courts.
Nauta, A. P. N.
    1974   "Social Control and Norm Restrictiveness: Some Results of an Inquiry into Neighbor Relationships." *Sociologia Neerlandia* 10:233–43.
Nelson, Barbara J.
    1980   "Help-Seeking from Public Authorities: Who Arrives at the Agency Door?" *Policy Sciences* 12:175–92.
New York Times
    1982   "Cocaine Use by Middle Class Called Widely Accepted in the New York Area." *New York Times*, December 13, p. 15.
    1984   "A Diamond Maverick's Clash with the Club on 47th Street." *New York Times*, November 13, §iv, p. 5.
    1985   "White Collar Crime: Booming Again." *New York Times*, June 9, §3, pp. 1, 6.
Noguchi, Paul H.
    1979   "Law, Custom, and Morality in Japan: The Culture of Cheating on the Japanese National Railways." *Anthropological Quarterly* 52:165–77.
Nonet, Philippe, and Selznick, Philip
    1978   *Law and Society in Transition: Toward Responsive Law.* New York: Harper.

O'Toole, George
  1978   *The Private Sector: Rent-a-Cops, Private Spies and the Police-Industrial Complex.* New York: Norton.
Page, Barbara
  1978   "The Assault on Affirmative Action." *Politics & Education* 1:31–38.
Parsons, Talcott
  1962   "Law and Social Control." In *Law and Sociology,* edited by William Evan. New York: Free Press.
Posner, Richard A.
  1979   "The *Bakke* Case and the Future of 'Affirmative Action.' " *California Law Review* 67:171–89.
Pound, Roscoe
  1917   "The Limits of Effective Legal Action." *American Bar Association Journal* 3:55–70.
Prager, Jeffrey
  1982   "Equal Opportunity and Affirmative Action: The Rise of New Understandings." In *Research in Law, Deviance and Social Control,* vol. 4, edited by Steven Spitzer and Rita J. Simon. Greenwich, Conn.: JAI Press.
Pritchard, David
  1985   "Homicide and Consensual Justice: The Agenda-Setting Effect of Crime News on Prosecutors." Unpublished manuscript.
Prottas, Jeffrey Manditch
  1978   "The Power of the Street-Level Bureaucrat in Public Service Bureaucracies." *Urban Affairs Quarterly* 13:285–311.
Quinney, Richard
  1975   "Crime Control in Capitalist Society: A Critical Philosophy." In *Critical Criminology,* edited by Ian Taylor, Paul Walton, and Jock Young. London: Routledge & Kegan Paul.
Ray, Lawrence J.
  1978   "Habermas, Legitimation, and the State." *Journal for the Theory of Social Behaviour* 8:149–63.
  1983   "Review Essay: Systematic Functionalism Revisited." *Journal for the Theory of Social Behaviour* 13:231–41.
Regoli, Robert M., and Poole, Eric D.
  1978   "The Commitment of Delinquents to Their Misdeeds: A Re-Examination." *Journal of Criminal Justice* 3:3–28.
Reuter, Peter
  1984   "Social Control in Illegal Markets." In *Toward a General Theory of Social Control,* edited by Donald Black. New York: Academic Press.
Robbins, James J., and Heckscher, Gunnar
  1941   "The Constitutional Theory of Autonomous Groups." *Journal of Politics* 3:3–28.
Ross, H. Laurence
  1970   *Settled Out of Court: The Social Process of Insurance Claims Adjustments.* Chicago: Aldine.
Sabel, Charles F., and Stark, David
  1982   "Planning, Politics, and Shop-Floor Power: Hidden Forms of Bargaining in Soviet-Imposed State-Socialist Societies." *Politics & Society* 11:439–75.
Santos, Bonaventura de Sousa
  1977   "The Law of the Oppressed: The Construction and Reproduction of Legality in Pasargada." *Law & Society Review* 12:5–105.
  1980   "Law and Community: The Changing Nature of State Power in Late Capitalism." *International Journal of the Sociology of Law* 8:379–97.

Schall, Maryan S.
   1983   "A Communication-Rules Approach to Organizational Culture." *Administrative Science Quarterly* 28:557–81.
Schmidhauser, John R.
   1979   *Judges and Justices: The Federal Appellate Judiciary.* Boston: Little, Brown.
Schoenberg, Sandra Perlman
   1980   "Some Trends in Community Participation of Women in Their Neighborhoods." *Signs: Journal of Women in Culture and Society* 5:S261–68.
Schwartz, Louis B.
   1960   "Institutional Size and Individual Liberty: Authoritarian Aspects of Big Business." *Northwestern University Law Review* 55:4–53.
Schwartz, Warren F.; Baxter, Keith; and Ryan, David
   1984   "The Duel: Can These Gentlemen Be Acting Efficiently?" *Journal of Legal Studies* 13:321–55.
Scraton, Phil, and South, Nigel
   1984   "The Ideological Construction of the Hidden Economy: Private Justice and Work-Related Crime." *Contemporary Crises* 8:1–18.
Selznick, Philip
   1968   "The Sociology of Law." In *International Encyclopedia of Social Sciences,* vol. 9, edited by David L. Sills. New York: Macmillan and Free Press.
   1969   *Law, Society, and Industrial Justice.* New York: Russell Sage Foundation.
Sharp, Elaine B.
   1980   "Citizen Perceptions of Channels for Urban Service Advocacy." *Public Opinion Quarterly* 44:362–76.
Shearing, Clifford D., and Stenning, Philip C.
   1983   "Private Security: Implications for Social Control." *Social Problems* 30:493–506.
Sills, David L.
   1968   "Voluntary Associations: Sociological Aspects." In *International Encyclopedia of the Social Sciences,* vol. 16, edited by David L. Sills. New York: Macmillan.
Simis, Konstantin
   1982   *USSR: The Corrupt Society—The Secret World of Soviet Capitalism.* New York: Simon and Schuster.
Snyder, Frederick E.
   1978   "Crime and Community Mediation—The Boston Experience: A Preliminary Report on the Dorchester Urban Court Program." *Wisconsin Law Review* 1978:737–91.
Sowell, Thomas
   1976   " 'Affirmative Action' Reconsidered." *Public Interest* 42:47–65.
Spitzer, Steven
   1984   "The Embeddedness of Law: Reflections on Lukes and Scull's *Durkheim and the Law.*" *ABF Research Journal* 1984:859–68.
Spitzer, Steven, and Scull, Andrew T.
   1977   "Privatization and Capitalist Development: The Case of the Private Police." *Social Problems* 25:18–29.
Stack, Steven
   1978   "Ideological Beliefs on the American Distribution of Opportunity, Power, and Rewards." *Sociological Focus* 11:221–33.
Stenning, Philip, and Shearing, Clifford
   1979   "Private Security and Private Justice." *British Journal of Law and Society* 6:261–71.
Sumner, Colin
   1979   *Reading Ideologies: An Investigation into the Marxist Theory of Ideology and Law.* New York: Academic Press.

Sutherland, Edwin H., and Cressey, Donald R.
1978   *Criminology.* 10th ed. Philadelphia: Lippincott.

Sweet, Justin
1978   "Lawmaking by Standard Forms: A Study of AIA Contract Documents." Unpublished manuscript.

1983   "The Architectural Profession Responds to Construction Management and Design-Build: The Spotlight on AIA Documents." *Law & Contemporary Problems* 46:69–82.

Taylor, Ralph B., and Brooks, Debra Kaye
1980   "Temporary Territories?: Responses to Intrusions in a Public Setting." *Population and Environment* 3:135–45.

Tersine, Richard J., and Russell, Roberta S.
1981   "Internal Theft: The Multi-Billion-Dollar Disappearing Act." *Business Horizons* 24:11–20.

Teubner, Gunther
1983   "Substantive and Reflexive Elements in Modern Law." *Law & Society Review* 17:401–46.

1984a   "Autopoiesis in Law and Society: A Rejoinder to Blankenburg." *Law & Society Review* 18:291–301.

1984b   "After Legal Instrumentalism? Strategic Models of Post-regulatory Law." *International Journal of the Sociology of Law* 12:375–400.

Teulings, Ad
1982   "Interlocking Interests and Collaboration with the Enemy: Corporate Behaviour in the Second World War." *Organizational Studies* 3(2):99–118.

Tilman, Rick
1983   "Social Value Theory, Corporate Power, and Political Elites: Appraisals of Lindblom's *Politics and Markets.*" *Journal of Economic Issues* 17:115–31.

Tocqueville, Alexis de
1945   *Democracy in America.* 2 vols. Translated by Henry Reeve, revised by Francis
[1835] Bowen, and edited by Phillips Bradley. New York: Knopf.

Tomasic, Roman
1984   "Business Regulation and the Administrative State." In *Business Regulation in Australia,* edited by Roman Tomasic. North Ryde, N.S.W.: CCH Australia Limited.

Tomasic, Roman, and Feeley, Malcolm M.
1982   *Neighborhood Justice: Assessment of an Emerging Idea.* New York: Longman.

Trubek, David M.
1980–81 "The Construction and Deconstruction of a Disputes-Focused Approach: An Afterword." *Law & Society Review* 15:727–47.

Turk, Austin
1976   "Law as a Weapon in Social Conflict." *Social Problems* 23:276–91.

Unger, Roberto Mangabeira
1976   *Law in Modern Society: Toward a Criticism of Social Theory.* New York: Free Press.

Useem, Michael
1983   "Business and Politics in the United States and United Kingdom: The Origins of Heightened Political Activity of Large Corporations." *Theory and Society* 12:281–308.

Vanderbilt Law Review
1984   "Self-Help: Extrajudicial Rights, Privileges and Remedies in Contemporary American Society." *Vanderbilt Law Review* 37:845–1045.

Vaughan, Diane
1982   "Toward Understanding Unlawful Organizational Behavior." *Michigan Law Review* 80:1377–1402.

1983   *Controlling Unlawful Organizational Behavior: Social Structure and Corporate Miscon-duct.* Chicago: University of Chicago Press.

Vladeck, Judith P., and Young, Margaret M.
    1978   "Sex Discrimination in Higher Education: It's Not Academic." *Women's Rights Law Reporter* 4:59–78.

Watts, Jerry
    1983   "The Socialist as Ostrich: The Unwillingness of the Left to Confront Modernity." *Social Research* 50:3–56.

Weber, Max
    1954   *Max Weber on Law in Economy and Society.* Edited, with an introduction and
    [1922]   annotations by Max Rheinstein. Cambridge, Mass.: Harvard University Press.

Weir, Stanley L.
    1976   "Book Review of Carl Gersuny, Punishment and Redress in a Modern Factory." *Contemporary Sociology* 5:631–33.

Weiss, Janet A., and Gruber, Judith E.
    1984   "Deterring Discrimination with Data." *Policy Sciences* 17:49–66.

Weyrauch, Walter O.
    1969   "Governance Within Institutions." *Stanford Law Review* 22:141–53.

    1971   "The 'Basic Law' or 'Constitution' of a Small Group." *Journal of Social Issues* 27:49–63.

Whyte, William F.
    1956   "The Grievance Procedure and Plant Society." In *The Grievance Process.* East Lansing: Michigan State University Labor and Industrial Relations Center.

Wilkinson, Philip J.
    1981   "The Potential of Functionalism for the Sociological Analysis of Law." In *Sociological Approaches to Law,* edited by Adam Podgorecki and Christopher Whelan. New York: St. Martin's Press.

Williams, Martha, and Hall, Jay
    1972   "Knowledge of the Law in Texas: Socioeconomic and Ethnic Differences." *Law & Society Review* 7:99–118.

Wirtz, W. Willard
    1952   "Government by Private Groups." *Louisiana Law Review* 13:440–75.

Yale Law Journal
    1954   "The American Medical Association: Power, Purpose, and Politics in Organized Medicine." *Yale Law Journal* 63:937–1022.

    1963   "Private Government on the Campus—Judicial Review of University Expulsions." *Yale Law Journal* 72:1362–1410.

Zimring, Franklin E.
    1981   "Kids, Groups and Crime: Some Implications of a Well-Known Secret." *Journal of Criminal Law & Criminology* 72:867–85.

ᦞ 10 ᦞ

ACCESS TO JUSTICE:
CITIZEN PARTICIPATION
AND THE AMERICAN LEGAL ORDER

Austin D. Sarat
Amherst College

INTRODUCTION

The study of citizen participation in the legal system has yet to achieve the status accorded the analysis of participation in the overtly political institutions of constitutional democracies (see Verba and Nie 1972; Dahl 1961; Arendt 1959). Whereas the latter has a long-standing tradition and addresses a fairly coherent set of questions, the study of participation in the legal system is not a well-defined subject matter.[1] There are few clearly recognized research traditions or theories that take participation in the legal order as a central focus or locate it in a coherent body of theory.[2] Nevertheless, there is now available a wide-ranging literature in the sociology of law which discusses, albeit often

---

NOTE: I would like to acknowledge helpful comments made by Sheldon Goldman, Sally Merry, J. J. Perlstein, Philip Selznick, and Martin Shapiro.

[1] Indeed some would suggest that the subject of participation in the legal order is too diverse and elusive to be comprehensible in a single treatment. They question whether participation is, or is yet, a subject. "There may be less intellectual substance than meets the eye: a fashion pretending to intellectual substance. Reality may take its revenge on such moral forwardness. Or, to the contrary, we may be seeing the beginning of a tendency that will grow larger and more urgent and therefore call for a lot of good thought: conceptual as well as historical analysis" [Kateb 1975, pp. 89–90; see also Braybrooke 1975].

[2] The study of disputes and disputing may be an exception (Trubek 1980–81). Yet, most research on disputing is concerned with the analysis of different types of dispute processing institutions rather than the behavior of disputants (for exceptions, see Miller and Sarat 1980–81; Ladinsky and Susmilch 1983; Merry and Silbey 1984).

indirectly, the nature, extent, antecedents, and consequences of citizen participation in the legal order. That literature highlights the social organization of citizen participation, its significance in liberal legal orders, and the dilemmas and contradictions of citizen participation in legal institutions.

It is, of course, very difficult to define precisely and to limit clearly the idea of citizen participation in the legal system. Most treatments of the subject present no definitions. They present themselves not as studies of participation in general but rather as studies of particular, discrete, well-defined forms of participation such as litigation or complaining. Alternatively, discussions of citizen participation are often presented as part of a broader concern with access to justice. Where that is the case, the definitional problem is further compounded.

Lawrence Friedman (1978, p. 5) points out that "when people talk about 'access to justice' they may mean many different things. But every discussion assumes a goal called 'justice' and assumes further that some group or type of person . . . finds the door to justice closed, or at least too stiff to move on its hinges." Access to justice is typically and uncritically taken to mean access to legal justice. Moreover, while discussions of access pose empirical questions, the concept of "access to justice" has no empirical referent (Griffiths 1977, p. 280). The concept refers only to the freedom to bring a nearly infinite range of issues and problems to the attention of legal officials. In this sense access to justice and citizen participation are treated as equivalent concepts. Where this is the case, it is possible to avoid

> the error that writers in the "access" tradition continually fall prey to: treating as an empirical notion their idea that people (especially the poor) ought to be using legal services more than they do. One would also avoid the mistake of confusing the political problem of unequal access with the empirical fact of unequal use. [Griffiths 1977, pp. 281–82]

While the equation of access and participation may help solve the problem of equating *is* and *ought,* it does not solve the conceptual problem of bounding the behaviors to be observed and interpreted. Ultimately no resolution will be fully satisfactory. Following Nie and Verba (1975, p. 1), I use participation in the legal system to refer to legal activities by which private citizens, acting individually or in organized groups, seek to influence the actions of officials charged with administering, enforcing, or interpreting the law. Participatory activities include those through which citizens seek to enlist the state to help remedy some individual problem or achieve some individual goal as well as those that seek to shape public policies through judicial or administrative action (see Scaff 1975). This conception of citizen participation in the legal system thus covers a broad range of both activities and institutions.

Modes of participation in the legal order vary in terms of what political theorist Carl Cohen (1971) calls their "breadth," "depth," and "range." Breadth refers to the number of people who actually participate in the legal process. Here sociologists of law have attempted, for example, to calculate litigation rates as a portion of potential legal problems (Miller and Sarat 1980–81). A fully participatory legal order would be one in which all citizens seeking to use legal institutions to deal with their problems had the opportunity, in fact as well as in theory, to do so. A fully participatory legal order would be one in which all citizens affected by a decision may and do participate in determining it (Mayo 1960). While such an ideal is, in practice, unachievable, the degree of participation in the legal system can be ascertained by determining "the proportion of those in a community affected by a decision who do or may participate in the making of it" (Cohen 1971, p. 8).

The second dimension of participation is its depth. Participation is deep to the extent that participants are involved in activities "to identify issues, formulate proposals, weigh evidence in argument on all sides, express convictions and explain their grounds . . . and in general to foster and strengthen deliberation" (Cohen 1971, pp. 17, 18). The deeper the participation provided, the more "democratic" is the process in which that participation occurs—presuming always that the opportunity for and extent of citizen participation are already fairly broad. The deep participation of a few is no substitute for the participation of the many. Voting, on the other hand, is the clearest example of participation that may be relatively broad but is rarely very deep.

The discussion of the depth of participation also raises the empirical question of what exactly constitutes participation. To file a lawsuit, for example, one does not necessarily, or even usually, have to engage in deliberation or in the process of reasoned argument. Filing may be a purely formal act, whose real importance has little or nothing to do with adjudication or any other legal process. There is some evidence that filing may be a symbolic act, a way of "letting off steam" not meant to initiate legal proceedings (Sarat 1976). Most contacts with legal institutions do not lead to prolonged engagement in deliberative activities but are intended and serve only to facilitate processes of private bargaining or interaction in which the role of law is purposely minimized (Mnookin and Kornhauser 1979; Michelman 1973; Steadman and Rosenstein 1973; Black 1971). Insofar as the sociology of law has attempted to quantify access to justice and to measure citizen participation, it has generally treated each type of contact with legal institutions as of equal weight and importance. Variation in the intensity, duration, or depth of involvement is rarely considered.

Another important aspect of participation in legal processes is its "range" (Cohen 1971, p. 22). Range refers to the scope of the questions on which citizens' involvement is welcome. Once it is known how many people can and do participate and how deeply they are involved with the legal system, it becomes possible to ask about the range of issues and concerns they become involved with. The greater the range of participation, the more democratic is the legal order. A fully democratic legal order would, in theory, open most if not all questions to citizen input and would respond to most if not all the types of problems citizens encounter and desire to bring to it. Legal orders and specific legal institutions establish rules and procedures to provide the framework and the limits within which participation can occur. These rules screen out particular types of issues owing to the limited competence or capacity of particular institutions (Cavanagh and Sarat 1980) or to protect decision-makers from the pressure of citizen demand (Scott 1973). Variation in the strictness of such rules reflects tensions and contradictory impulses, toward autonomy and responsiveness, built into a liberal legal order.[3]

---

[3] Perhaps the most important and controversial of the rules governing the range of participation are those affecting standing to sue in the federal courts. These rules are a general derivation of the case-and-controversy provision of the Constitution which, as interpreted by the federal courts, requires that citizen participation in the courts be limited to matters on which there are genuinely adverse positions—that is, matters on which there is some substantial opposition of interest between or among the parties—as reflected in an actual and ongoing dispute amenable to judicial remedy. While the constitutional provision defines what is a case and limits the decision-making activities of courts to the resolution of cases (see Sedler 1972),

Although my consideration of participation includes many elements, five principal exclusions should be noted. The first is involuntary forms of contact between the citizen and the state—contacts growing out of the use of the state's coercive power. Although criminal defendants have contact with the legal process, the idea that they participate in it in the same sense that a voter or a plaintiff in a civil case participates makes little sense.

---

rules of standing refer to the characteristics of the parties seeking to litigate particular cases. Standing should be viewed

> as involving problems of the nature and sufficiency of the litigant's concern with the subject matter of the litigation, as distinguished from problems of justiciability—that is, the fitness for adjudication—of the legal question which he tenders for decision. . . . More precisely stated, the question of standing . . . is the question of whether the litigant has a sufficient personal interest in getting the relief he seeks, or is a sufficiently appropriate representative of other interested persons, to warrant recognizing him as entitled to invoke the court's decision on the issue of illegality. [Hart and Wechsler 1953, p. 174; see also *Warth* v. *Seldin* 1975]

The core of the standing doctrine, which the courts have derived from the Constitution itself, is that citizens will be allowed to litigate only if they have demonstrated a personal interest in the outcome of the matter they bring to court and if the interest asserted by the plaintiff amounts to a legal right arguably within the boundaries of common law, statutes, or the Constitution (Vining 1978). The courts have, however, added meaning and interpretations to this core in an uncertain, sometimes contradictory, and complex line of cases. Such cases led former Justice William O. Douglas to suggest that "generalizations about the standing to sue are largely worthless as such" (*Association of Data Processing Service Organizations Inc.* v. *Camp* 1970).

In recent years, the range of participation allowed under rules of standing has been most in question with respect to issues involving public law and the actions of the state (see Jaffe 1965, 1968; Berger 1969; Albert 1974; Stewart 1975). The controversy centers on the conditions under which individuals or groups will be allowed access to challenge the actions of administrative agencies or other public bodies. The difficulties of establishing the range of participation in this area are great, since it is difficult, if not impossible, to determine the nature, if any, of injuries resulting from public actions or the identity of people affected (see Kalven and Rosenfield 1941; Zacharias 1978).

While the general movement has been toward an expansion of the range of participation through the liberalization of standing (see *Flast* v. *Cohen* 1968; *Association of Data Processing Service Organizations Inc.* v. *Camp* 1970; *Sierra Club* v. *Morton* 1972; *U.S.* v. *Scrap* 1973; *Duke Power* v. *Carolina Environmental Study Group* 1978; Davis 1970; Hasl 1973), that movement has not been uniform and consistent. For example, in 1973 the Supreme Court ruled that standing requires not only that the plaintiff demonstrate a concrete injury, but that the injury be "directly" related to the claim and action subject to adjudication. Thus, an unwed mother was not allowed to sue a district attorney for failing to prosecute the father for nonsupport; the plaintiff could not show that her failure to receive support payments resulted from the failure to prosecute (*Linda R. S.* v. *Richard D.* 1973). In 1975, the Court denied standing to a coalition of individuals and organizations that tried to challenge a zoning ordinance on the grounds that it unconstitutionally discriminated against low-income individuals by restricting the range and availability of affordable housing. In deciding that the rules of standing require demonstration that the asserted injury was the consequence of the actions of the defendant and that the relief desired would remedy the alleged harm, the Court argued that the plaintiffs had failed to meet those tests and that it was insufficient to "rely on little more than the remote possibility . . . that [the plaintiffs'] situation might have been better had [the defendants] acted otherwise and might improve were the Court to accord relief" (*Warth* v. *Seldin* 1975; see also *Simon* v. *Eastern Kentucky Welfare Rights Organization* 1976).

The uncertain path of decisions affecting the rights of citizens and organized groups to litigate claims against the government reflects the uncertain relationship between autonomy and responsiveness in the American legal order. In essence, the rules of standing are a "legal fiction" used by the courts to control the amount and kinds of citizen participation. While they have some foundation in the Constitution, they are for the most part simply "prudential" (Cavanagh 1979). The regulation of standing also regulates the fora in which participation and conflicts are allowed. The liberalization of standing allows relatively weak or loosely organized groups to contest the actions of better-organized and more powerful social groups able to exert their influence in the legislative and administrative process. Thus, when environmentalists sue the Atomic Energy Commission, they are carrying into the courts a dispute with a public utility that they were unable to win in or through private or other public action (*Calvert Cliffs Coordinating Committee* v. *A.E.C.* 1971). As a result, expanding the range of participation in the judicial process serves to increase the responsiveness of the legal order at the same time that it protects a pluralist system of group representation and social life (Lowi 1979).

Even a juror has, in effect, the prerogative of refusing the state's invitation to serve. No such option is open to the criminal defendant (contrast Ross and Littlefield 1978; Casper 1978). Coercion is antithetical to participation.

The second and closely related exclusion involves what might be called "ceremonial" participation (Nie and Verba 1975, p. 2)—activities in which citizens take part in organized expressions of support for the authorities. While every act of participation carries with it some component of support, participation is, at its core, a demand activity (Easton 1964). Participation is a form of behavior through which citizens influence the legal process, through which they make claims on each other and on the state, and in which interests are expressed (Milbrath 1965; Pennock 1979; D. Thompson 1970). Citizen participation can be contrasted with the activities of political mobilization in which the state overtly organizes demonstrations or ritualistic, noncompetitive elections to support or sustain its claims to legitimacy and through which citizen activities and energies are directed toward the achievement of purposes defined by and for the state (Edelman 1971; Nettle 1967). Thus, following my definition, much of what is called participation in nondemocratic nations would not be so labeled.

A third exclusion concerns the standard forms of electoral participation and the activities associated with them, activities through which the "directive" officials of a constitutional democracy are selected (Cohen 1971). This is not to say that such activities are unimportant or even unrelated to participation in the administration and enforcement of the law. One unexplored area of inquiry involves the relationship between political and legal participation. It may be that the two are linked through feelings of efficacy (Jacob 1969) or that they occur sequentially; individuals resort to litigation, for example, when legislative or executive institutions prove impenetrable or unresponsive (Dolbeare 1967; Kluger 1976). Alternatively, legal participation may provide a stimulus to a broadened interest in, or ability to take part in, the activities through which majority rule operates (Scheingold 1974). The distinction between activities through which the majority exercises its directive influence and activities through which citizens and groups vindicate claims to rights is used by some to differentiate political and legal participation (Commager 1941).

My definition begins by referring to "legal activities"—that is, activities permitted or sanctioned by the legal system itself. This qualification eliminates from treatment a wide range of activities—for example, riots and violent demonstrations—that citizens may use to press their claims on legal institutions. These admittedly important activities constitute a separate topic. It may be that nonconventional participation is crucial in shaping the context for more conventional activities and the functions of the legal order. Placed under the stress of civil disorder, institutions may be forced to take demands seriously that would otherwise be ignored (Piven and Cloward 1972) or to breach normal procedures (Balbus 1974). The threat of activity in the streets puts pressure on legal institutions and may lead them to be more responsive to demands of a more conventional nature (Lipsky 1968, 1970).[4]

---

[4]In this framework, how can civil disobedience be classified? In a constitutional democracy, is it participation of a conventional kind or is it unacceptable behavior? These questions are the very stuff of which entire jurisprudential theories can be woven (see Dworkin 1978). By definition, civil disobedience is a refusal to obey the law. Generally it is thought to refer to (1) a deliberate violation of a valid law, (2) committed as a form of protest and is (3) nonrevolutionary, (4) public, (5) nonviolent, and (6) designed to educate or persuade either majority sentiment or specific legal officials (Bedau 1969). Civil disobedience may

Last I exclude from consideration jury service. This exclusion is, in many ways, the most serious. As jurors, citizens become decision-makers; their participation is deep and highly significant. Nevertheless, I exclude jury service because it is virtually unique as an example of such participation and because its inclusion would carry us far afield from the main body of sociolegal work on citizen participation.[5]

---

be thought to be conventional in that the civil disobedient typically acknowledges the legitimacy of the legal order. It is not a repudiation of public values. "Practitioners of civil disobedience maintain an allegiant perspective, at least to the extent of not repudiating totally the authority of political officials, or of the regime and its self-proclaimed values. . . . [T]hey indicate to the regime their willingness to carry on the conflict in a fashion which presumably permits the regime to respond in an equally civil manner" (Zashin 1972, p. 115; see also Cohen 1964; Keeton 1965). The nonviolent character of civil disobedience is what makes it civil and what makes a civil response possible. Thus, it is a further acknowledgment of the legitimacy of the legal order.

But is civil disobedience within the boundaries of conventional citizen participation? Surely it is not usual. No claim has been made that civil disobedience is or ought to be the regular fare of citizens or of the society. Some argue that civil disobedience is outside the boundaries of conventional participation because it represents an assertion by particular groups that they stand above the law. Such critics argue that civil disobedience represents a significant threat to a society of consent and to the avenues through which individuals participate in the administration and/or enforcement of the law. When particular groups appear to establish themselves as the ultimate judges of the validity of law, participation is threatened by a challenge to the rules governing participation and the responsibilities and duties citizens assume in any participatory legal and social order (Rostow 1971).

Others contend either that civil disobedience is a form of normal citizen participation or that it contains within it all the constituent elements of participation, properly understood. It has been suggested that, under strict conditions, civil disobedience may be considered an aspect of constitutional litigation (Fortas 1968). The most important of these conditions is that those employing civil disobedience accept punishment for their violations of law and only violate laws they intend to challenge. Abe Fortas argues that, by breaking the law and submitting to punishment—or, more accurately, arrest—the civil disobedient forces the courts to adjudicate his claim that the violated law is invalid. Employing litigation to settle the rightness of claims is a characteristic form of legal participation. No less a scholar than Alexander Bickel (1965) contends that the kind of "testing" civil disobedience engenders is within the boundaries of acceptable participation in a constitutional democracy. Civil disobedience is "an appeal—almost in the technical-legal sense—to higher lawmaking institutions, which the system provides. In such a system some flouting of the local law, aimed at provoking action by the higher sovereignty, is virtually invited" (p. 79).

More generally, civil disobedience may be considered compatible with citizen participation in a constitutional democracy because it is closely analogous to other forms of conventional participation (Zashin 1972, p. 117). Civil disobedience may be a particularly dramatic technique of persuasion, but its effectiveness depends on convincing others of the dissonance between particular laws and basic and widely shared values. "Acts of civil disobedience seek . . . to call public attention to the view that a principle of moral importance is held to be violated by a law or policy sanctioned by public authorities" (Bay 1966). Civil disobedience is political communication directed at both citizens and public officials. In a constitutional democracy, civil disobedience presumes that public officials will be tolerant and restrained enough to differentiate it from civil disorder (Gurr 1976).

Those who accept civil disobedience as a legitimate form of citizen participation in a constitutional democracy view it as a highly principled response to the inability to vindicate claims or win reforms through other forms of participation (Spitz 1954; Wasserstrom 1961). Civil disobedience "seems to arise out of a sense that the system is not really open to . . . change or to certain conceptions of the good society. . . . It emerges from the experience of repeated failure to achieve more than gradual reform despite an abnormally large amount of . . . conventional political action" (Zashin 1972, p. 319). Nevertheless, the effect and effectiveness of civil disobedience can be assessed only in particular cases and with reference to particular circumstances. Its overall place in an understanding of citizen participation in the legal order remains in contention.

[5] Research on citizen participation and the jury is distinctive in its variety and its concern for uniting empirical and normative questions. Given the prohibition against penetrating the jury room, research on jurors has had to rely heavily on post hoc reconstruction and even more heavily on simulation (Kessler 1975; Thibaut et al. 1972; O'Mara 1972). Typical research presents a college student with a hypothetical, or

CITIZEN PARTICIPATION AND THE DILEMMAS OF LIBERAL LEGALISM

Citizen participation, no matter how it is defined, occupies an ambiguous and contradictory position in liberal legal theory and in liberal legal orders. Liberalism, because it is inexorably linked to the idea of limited government (Hayek 1960; Corwin 1948), limits popular sovereignty by prescribing the means through which it may be exercised and proscribing its exercise in entire portions of the state apparatus. While citizens are invited to play a part in the selection of legislators and even, in some jurisdictions, of judges, they are not, with rare exceptions, expected to play a directive role in decisions about the application, enforcement, or interpretation of legal norms. Instead, those functions are, in liberal theory, to be performed autonomously by courts or administrative agencies. Here liberal legalism requires a separation between law and politics, with citizen participation, in its fullest sense, relegated to the realm of the political. Judicial and administrative decisions are made according to rules (Fuller 1971b; Lowi 1979, chap. 11); discretion is to be limited; the pressure of citizen demands, majority sentiments, or interest group activity is deemed to be out of place. Fair procedure, the morality of the game, rather than responsiveness, is seen as the key to legal justice (Resnick 1977; Kennedy 1973).

Law is elevated "above" politics; that is, the positive law is held to embody standards that public consent, authenticated by tradition or by constitutional

---

perhaps filmed, case and manipulates the subject to test comprehension, bias, or deliberative characteristics (see, for example, Lawson 1970). Perhaps even more characteristic of jury research is its attention to the relationship between the actual operation of juries and certain normative standards, most often derived from the law governing the selection, structure, and decision-making of juries (Erlanger 1970). Jury research has placed empirical inquiry at the service of evaluation, demonstrating the way in which prescriptive or normative premises can guide empirical investigation. To this extent, it may not contribute to a cross-culturally valid theory of the behavior of law (Black 1976), but it does test the compatibility of legal rules and legal behavior.

Among the subjects covered by jury research are the effects of size and rules governing unanimity on jury decisions (Zeisel and Diamond 1974; Walbert 1971); the frequency of jury "nullification" (Myers 1979; Howe 1939); and the prevalence of racial, sexual, class, or personal biases in jury decisions (Hoffman and Brodley 1952; Boehm 1968; Landy and Aronson 1969; Levine and Schweber-Koren 1976). From the perspective of concern with participation, the most important issues in jury research are jury representativeness and jury competence. These two issues address the breadth and depth of citizen participation in serving the legal order.

From its beginnings, the legitimacy of the jury has been based, at least in part, on the claim that juries represent the voice of the community (Wells 1911). Defining the boundaries and nature of the communities from which legal juries are to be drawn has been persistently difficult, but the ideal of fairly accurate reflection of community sentiment remains strong. Thus representativeness deals with the breadth of participation achieved in the jury system.

The introduction of nonprofessionals into the legal system has, however, often been questioned. Criticism has focused on the ability of juries to effectively discharge decision-making responsibilities (Redmount 1971; R. Simon 1967, 1975; Kalven and Zeisel 1966). Since the mid-nineteenth century, juries in America have been limited to considering questions of fact (*Yale Law Journal* 1964); a competent jury is one that does not judge the applicability or fairness of the law (for another perspective, see Kadish and Kadish 1973). In addition, juries are supposed to decide cases on the basis of the evidence presented to them, without any form of prejudice. Given the complex and technical nature of legal procedures, many scholars wonder "whether uninitiated laymen are . . . able to comprehend the evidence and . . . instructions, and whether court procedure is not so organized as to diminish rather than increase the possibilities of a rational judgment of the facts" (Erlanger 1970; see also Strawn and Buchanan 1976).

process, has removed from political controversy. The authority to interpret this
legal heritage must therefore be kept insulated from the struggle for power and
uncontaminated by political influence. In interpreting and applying the law,
jurists . . . have a claim to the last word because their judgments are thought to
obey an external will and not their own. [Nonet and Selznick 1978, p. 57]

Liberal legalism derives its claims to legitimacy, in large part, from this sense that law is
autonomous, that it is above the play of politics.[6] As a result, the role of citizen participation must be limited. In an autonomous legal order the business of law is "technical." At
issue are questions about the meaning and applicability of legal rules. Decisions must be
made in a disinterested and impartial manner. There is, in the United States, a long-
standing suspicion of the capacity of citizens to display the restraint necessary to allow for
such impartial judgment (Tocqueville 1863; Redford 1969). Citizen participation designed to pressure legal officials threatens their capacity to make legally correct decisions
and the legitimacy of any decisions they make.

Liberal legalism portrays citizens as self-regulating and independent and the role of law
as residual. Citizens are allowed to mobilize the law through carefully defined channels.
Rules of standing, which govern access to courts and other legal institutions, require
individuals to demonstrate that they have suffered a "real injury" before they are allowed
to present their case (see Jaffe 1968; Scott 1973). Citizen participation in the legal order
is, thus, instrumental and defensive. The legal culture "assumes that each citizen will
voluntarily and rationally pursue his own interests, with the greatest legal good of the
greatest number presumptively arising from the selfish enterprises of the atomized mass"
(Black 1973, p. 138). When citizens participate, they do so individually, and the legal
system proceeds case by case. Responsibility for broad-based social decisions is assigned to
legislative bodies presumably directly responsive to popular sentiment (Hayek 1973).

Moreover, even where participation is encouraged, liberal theory stresses the limits of
citizen competence. Participation is facilitated by the intervention of a trained legal
specialist (Simon 1978). Lawyers speak the language of the law, and it is their responsibility to serve each client by exercising professional judgment and responding to particular problems (Freedman 1975; Hazard 1978). The lawyer mediates between the citizen
and legal order, acting as gatekeeper and partisan advocate for a limited cause (Casper
1972).

Citizen participation is, in liberal legalism, not, however, completely denigrated. One
need only note the importance of the jury in Anglo-American legal theory to recognize
that that theory is not perfectly consistent in its attitude toward citizen participation.
Indeed, rhetorically, the jury receives far more than its due as a domesticator of state
power and an avenue for direct citizen involvement. While jury service is one of the most
intensive, and remarkable, forms of citizen participation, it is clearly anomalous, the
exception rather than a model from which generalizations can be drawn in understanding
the role of citizens in a liberal legal order.

Citizen participation is, in general, neither as extensive nor as decisive as it is when
citizens take on the mantle of juror. In the usual pattern participation is limited to the

---

[6] As Roberto Unger (1975, 1976) has argued, autonomy is a quite recent legal norm, which developed
with the emergence of liberal culture and social institutions. Its viability is linked to the viability of that
culture and those institutions.

activities associated with the initiation of the legal process, the mobilization of law enforcement, or the presentation of facts and arguments before a competent tribunal. Participation becomes litigation, complaint, petition, on the one hand, and a highly ritualized form of discourse, generally carried out by paid intermediaries—lawyers—on the other. In this sense, citizen participation in the legal order is typically limited and indirect. (It is on these most typical patterns that this chapter focuses.) Due process not popular sovereignty is the governing ethos.

The rules of due process themselves provide a formula for participation in the legal process (Fuller 1978). Although it does not require citizens to select those who will judge them, due process does require that individuals be heard by those who sit in judgment and be allowed to take part in a contest of reason and argument. "It confers on the affected parties a particular form of participation . . . that of presenting proofs and reasoned arguments for a decision in their favor" (Fuller 1978, p. 45; see also *Mullane* v. *Central Hanover Bank & Trust Company* 1950). While liberal legal theory guarantees citizens a role as plaintiff, complainant, defendant, or respondent in procedures in which their lives, liberties, or property are at stake, the precise contours of such participation—what it requires and when it must be made available—are by no means fixed or clear (Kadish 1957). Recent expansion of the scope of due process to include more of the implementation and enforcement of the law is thus both an acknowledgment by the state of the expanded reach of its powers and a provision for an expanded opportunity to participate in the exercise of those powers (Rubenstein 1976; Currie and Goodman 1975; Miller 1977; Davis 1970).

By treating citizen participation in the legal system as an aspect of due process, liberal theory transforms the claims of participation into arguments for access to justice. In the American legal tradition access to justice and due process of law are inseparable and both are considered to be minimum prerequisites of justice itself (Scanlon 1977; Simon 1978). The right to one's day in court, the right to be heard, the right to take part in procedures through which one's fate is determined all provide the basic substance of due process, which is, in turn, at the heart of our conceptions of fairness and justice (*Boddie* v. *Connecticut* 1971; *Goldberg* v. *Kelly* 1970; see also Abram 1978). Moreover, in liberal legal theory access to justice not only is essential in insuring fairness to individuals but is portrayed as necessary in domesticating the exercise of power. Citizen initiative, complaint, and involvement provide an opportunity to check and oppose the arbitrary use of state power. The image of a public official or agency called to account by a citizen before an independent, impartial court of law occupies a central place in contemporary liberal thought (see, for example, Ackerman 1984 and Ely 1980). As Justice John Marshall Harlan put it,

> Perhaps no characteristic of an organized and cohesive society is more fundamental than its erection and enforcement of a system of rules defining the various rights and duties of the members enabling them to govern their affairs and definitively settle their differences in an orderly, predictable manner. . . . It is to courts . . . that we ultimately look for the implementation of a regularized, orderly process of dispute settlement. . . . [Yet] without due process of law, the state's monopoly over techniques for binding conflict resolution could hardly be said to be acceptable under our scheme of things. Only by providing that the social enforcement mechanism must function strictly within these bounds can we

hope to maintain an ordered society that is also just. [*Boddie* v. *Connecticut* 1971, pp. 374–75]

Along with the right to vote, the right to participate in the legal process is fundamental to liberal theory. It is both through elections and through appeals to autonomous legal institutions, especially the courts, that citizens preserve all their other rights (Michelman 1974). The general anticipation of accessible legal justice and being able to participate in the legal order transforms, according to that theory, all social relationships and shapes the way individuals experience the meaning of citizenship. "This anticipation matters both on account of its deterrent effects on the behavior of those who must contemplate being voted on or sued and on account of its effects on the potential participant's own understanding of society and his or her place in it" (Michelman 1974, p. 536; see also Dam 1975).

Moreover, by making legal justice accessible, the legal order invites citizens to participate in rituals of affirmation. By accepting the invitation to employ legal processes, citizens in effect affirm their faith in legal norms and their belief in the relevance of those norms to the social order (Grossman and Sarat 1981). When citizens bring their grievances to legal institutions they express a hope, if not a belief, that their status as rights holders will be recognized by law, that their legal rights, once recognized, will be realized in practice and that that realization will, in fact, make a difference in their lives (Scheingold 1974).

Access to justice and citizen participation help to legitimate the legal order by making law appear open, available, and responsive to those with significant grievances and needs. Of course, not all grievances and needs are legally cognizable (Vining 1978), but paradoxically the law, precisely by limiting access, is able to strengthen the perceived boundary between law and politics as well as the perceived subservience of legal decision-makers to the model of rules (see *Harvard Law Review* 1976). The legitimacy of liberal legalism thus depends in important ways on maintaining the precarious balance between justice accessible according to rules and justice available on demand. This is a balance that, in any liberal legal order, moves and changes over time. Law both encourages demands for increased access by recognizing new rights and responds to social conflict by recognizing or restricting rights. The history of citizen participation in the legal order is, as a result, a history not of even and predictable progress but instead a history of reform and resistance.

Access to justice and citizen participation are not, however, uniformly aids to the legitimacy of law. Indeed, they may pose threats to that legitimacy in several ways. First, to the extent that a liberal legal order coexists with democratic, or representative, political institutions, citizen participation in the legal system may appear inadequate by comparison. What has, in other contexts (see Ely 1980; Edelman 1984), been called the "majoritarian dilemma" works in the legal order to push for an expanded role for citizens. Restrictions on access, no matter how well justified in liberal theory, will, in the context of the majoritarian presumption, always appear suspicious and unjustified. Democratic participation establishes a standard and an expectation against which the rather limited forms of participation available in the legal order may appear inadequate. This tension requires apologists for liberal legalism to work hard to maintain the distinction between politics, where participation is acknowledged to be more fully appropriate, and law, in which impartiality, neutrality, objectivity, and reason provide the essence of decision (see Fuller 1978 and Fiss 1982). Acknowledgment of the limits of impartiality and reason in legal decisions (see Singer 1984) would legitimate and encourage demands for greater and more extensive participation than a liberal legal order could easily accommodate. Thus, participation, demanding as it does greater citizen involvement and responsiveness on the part of legal institutions, threatens the very legitimacy it helps to establish.

The contradictory relationship between participation and legitimacy is seen in yet another way in demands that access to justice be made available more widely and more equally. Arguments about access to justice typically begin with the observation that access is unevenly and unequally distributed throughout the population (see Carlin et al. 1967; Cappelletti and Garth 1970). The recognition of unequal access threatens the legitimacy of liberal legalism by pointing to gaps and inadequacies in the fulfillment of its own self-proclaimed commitment to equal justice under the law. Discovery of systematic inequality in the ability and opportunity to use legal institutions and resources thus undermines our faith in the capacity of law to treat all citizens with dignity and to serve all who merit its service. At the same time, those arguments typically call for reforms in legal rules and practices or in the provision of legal services, which have the effect of suggesting that law itself can overcome this defect and that the problems of those without adequate access can be properly addressed through legal change. Demands for equalizing access to justice ultimately

> communicate a symbolic message . . . that formal justice can be attained within a capitalist legal system and, once attained, will produce substantive justice. They define the problem as a "gap" . . . between the promise of redistributing lawyers' services and the peformance. The proximate goal of closing the gap is thereby substituted for the ultimate goal of justice. In place of questions about the capacity of legal reform to effect fundamental change in political, economic and social institutions, we are directed back to the legal system conceived as an autonomous entity, to be evaluated by the unique standards of formal justice. [Abel 1979c, p. 40]

Here critique turns into affirmation, and threats to legal legitimacy turn into support.

A third element of citizen participation that may challenge the legitimacy of law arises when contact with the legal system has the effect of disillusioning or disappointing citizens. To the extent that citizen participation in the legal system acquaints citizens with the "reality" of the day-to-day operation of the legal system, it may have the effect of diminishing respect for and belief in the idealized visions of law which people may possess (see, for example, Casey 1974; Sarat 1977). On the other hand, where citizens come to see the gap between the law's ideals and practices, legal legitimacy may not be damaged if citizens revise their expectations and develop a more pragmatic approach to law (see Merry 1985) or if they blame failures on officials or incumbents while continuing to credit and endorse the legal order's aspirations. In any case, citizen participation holds the potential for undermining the claims of liberal legalism even as it appears to signify acceptance of them.

There is, of course, more to citizen participation than its impact on legal legitimacy. It has, for both the legal order and the citizens who use it, instrumental effects which, like those associated with legitimacy, are contradictory. At the level of the legal order itself, access to justice and citizen participation play an important role in keeping law in touch with the social order in which it is embedded. This is not to say that citizen participation is the only vehicle through which legal institutions can learn about their environment. Every legal system relies upon a mix of "reactive" and "proactive" intelligence-gathering mechanisms (Black 1973, p. 128).

The balance between proactive and reactive elements found in a legal order varies over time in response to specific problems (Nonet and Selznick 1970). The more reactive a legal order, the more it depends on citizens to detect the problems, articulate the disputes, or uncover the violations upon which legal policy can be based. The limits of legal policy are effectively set by citizens (Pennock and Chapman 1975). The legal system that relies on reactive methods is unable to act on matters that "citizens are unable to see, fail to notice, or choose to ignore" (Black 1973, p. 130).

Such a legal order can regulate how much it "knows" about social problems by raising or lowering barriers to citizen participation. Citizens may want to bring matters to the attention of legal officials in order to demand redress or explanation, but they may be unable to meet the qualifications or standards the law establishes (Vining 1978). Alternatively, their intentions may be diverted by lawyers who serve as the major channeling and linking devices for citizen participation in the legal order (Parsons 1954). Yet the greatest barriers to participation undoubtedly reside in the articulation and linkage of the prevailing legal ideology and the social relations in which potential legal problems arise (Bumiller 1984). In America today, despite the frequent complaints about excessive legalization (see, for example, Ehrlich 1976), "the reluctance of citizens to mobilize the law is so widespread . . . that it may be appropriate to view legal inaction as the dominant pattern of empirical legal life" (Black 1973, p. 133; see also Miller and Sarat 1980–81).

The greater the reliance on reactive methods of citizen participation, the more the legal system will reflect the biases, prejudices, and moral diversity of the society in which it is embedded. The legal order participates in a pattern of selective enforcement determined by the citizenry. "Each citizen determines for himself what within his private world is the law's business and what is not; each becomes a kind of legislator beneath the formal surface of legal life" (Black 1973, p. 142). Seen in this light, the decision not to participate is in itself a form of participation, an important determinant of the reach, scope, and capacity of legal control (Cobb and Elder 1972).

The refusal of citizens to bring problems to the attention of legal officials may result from the internalization of an ideology of self-blame (Sennett 1980), a predominant cultural preference for private resolution (Sarat and Grossman 1975), doubts about the efficacy of legal intervention, individual cost/benefit calculations (Johnson 1978a), and/or a crisis of legitimacy in which the appropriateness of the entire structure of legal control is questioned (Nisbet 1975; Wolin 1980).[7] In addition, citizens may avoid invoking legal processes because those processes are relatively predictable, so citizens feel that they can surmise what the legal decision would be and act in light of that prediction. The refusal to bring problems to law, no matter what their cause, sets the effective boundaries of law, the extent to which legal institutions have the chance to respond to social problems.

---

[7] The question of what constitutes such a crisis of legitimacy is recurring and unanswered (J. Freedman 1978). Refusal to take part is itself a form of withdrawal of consent, but what level or threshold must this reach before there is a crisis of legitimacy?

When people turn to law, when they seek to participate in the legal process, their participation has the effect of extending or reinforcing the reach of legal norms. Participation is, in this sense, as necessary in determining the penetration of law as it is in shaping the structure of legal intelligence. Citizen participation in the legal order involves the attempt to apply officially recognized legal norms to regulate social behavior (Lempert 1976, p. 173), to bring those norms to bear in situations where their previous presence was insufficient to protect rights or secure redress for injury, or to use them in preference to informal, private, customary canons of behavior (see Fitzpatrick 1985; Bohannan 1967). Law is used not to displace those canons of behavior but rather to complement them.

In any society, however, the invocation of law is one measure of its social significance and centrality in the total system of normative ordering. This is not to say that the penetration of law and legal norms can be fully understood by measuring the level of citizen participation. Surely that is not the case. The relevance of legal norms is seen in the way those norms are incorporated into the culture and come to order social relations. This incorporation, what some have called "the living law" (Ehrlich 1975) and others "hegemony" (Gramsci 1971), is the true measure of the law's influence. But that influence is unlikely to endure very long without the regular mobilization and application of legal norms to particular cases that citizen participation may engender.

Here again the status of citizen participation in a liberal legal order is contradictory. Just as participation may be said to increase the range of legal intelligence and the penetration of legal norms, so too may it strain the institutional capacity of legal institutions and challenge the authority of existing legal norms. Too much participation or participation that is too intense threatens the ability of a liberal legal order to function effectively (Huntington 1975). Legal institutions do not, or so the argument goes, possess the institutional resources or capacity to deal with a high volume and wide range of citizen demands. Typical is the complaint of former Judge Simon Rifkind (1976, p. 5) concerning the so-called litigation explosion. "The courts," Rikfind argues, "are being asked to solve problems for which they are not institutionally equipped or not as well equipped as other available institutions."

Discussions of the capacity of legal institutions, like courts, assume that they display a set of relatively fixed attributes and modes of decision-making and that these attributes generate inherent limitations on the volume and kinds of issues and problems that such institutions can reasonably be expected to manage effectively. Institutional capacity refers to the fit between what these institutions are and what they do, and the way in which their resources, expertise, and procedures bear on their ability to provide effective service. Some issues and problems cannot be dealt with by liberal legal institutions. A too insistent participation, or justice that is too accessible, by bringing such matters forward threatens to precipitate a crisis of institutional capacity (compare Horowitz 1977 and Cavanagh and Sarat 1980).

Participation, even as it informs and extends the reach of legal norms, restricts the ability of legal institutions to satisfy the demands made upon them. The capacity of the legal order to function effectively depends on an imbalance between rights proclaimed and rights actually claimed (Friedman 1971). Because not all citizens can or will seek to vindicate the full range of rights available to them (Miller and Sarat 1980–81), the legal order can be more generous in its recognition of rights. A legal order in which the full range of recognized rights is in fact realized by the entire citizenry is inconceivable. The appropriate balance of participation and nonparticipation, and the appropriate intensity of participation, cannot perhaps be determined empirically; nevertheless, the mainte-nance of such a balance is an important condition to effective legal control. Too much participation, and the institutions of law are overwhelmed; too little, and they are isolated (Keim 1975).

The spirit of participation in a liberal legal order partakes of the spirit of criticism and challenge. Citizen participation frequently requires legal institutions to examine and revise legal rules and to scrutinize the rules and procedures of other parts of the state apparatus. The universal promises and commitments of a polity committed to the rule of law provide a standard against which its performance can be measured. Citizens disem-powered in the political process arc thus enabled to employ legal institutions as arenas of struggle (Thompson 1975; Santos 1977). That participation may involve a demand that the interests served by liberal legalism live up to their legitimating ideology and an attempt to use that ideology in political struggles against prevailing structures of power. Thus it is now widely recognized that "law," as Samuel Johnson observed (Boswell 1969, p. 498), "supplies the weak with adventitious strength."

These tensions and dilemmas of citizen participation lead in the United States today to the simultaneous, and contradictory, claims that law is at once insufficiently accessible (Nader 1980) and overwhelmed by the demands made upon it (Tribe 1979). These claims have given rise to two different social movements, a movement for "access to justice" (Cappelletti and Garth 1978) and a movement for delegalization, deregulation, and the development of alternatives to legal institutions (Harrington 1982). While there are points at which these movements are linked, they thrive on two different impulses, impulses that pull at our legal order in different ways and pull it in different directions.

Over the past two decades arguments for making legal justice more accessible have covered the entire range of forms of legal participation. Those arguments have been classified into "three waves," each with a different conception of the meaning of access and the proper reach of citizen participation in the legal system (Cappelletti and Garth 1978). The first wave was embodied in the legal-aid approach, which takes for granted that access to justice requires an equal opportunity for all citizens, regardless of socioeco-nomic status, to obtain the services of a lawyer. Participation was understood to be individual and remedial, as well as rather formal. The ability of particular classes of people to act within the traditional avenues made available by the liberal legal order was put in question. The solution for problems of access was generally believed to be govern-mentally subsidized legal services (Carlin and Howard 1965; Cappelletti and Gordley 1972; Johnson 1974). If the technical expertise needed to make justice comprehensible and accessible could be more broadly diffused, the problem of unequal access could be overcome.

The second wave of access-to-justice arguments begins with the proposition that indi-viduals as such are not disadvantaged. Rather, the growth of modern, complex, bureau-cratic institutions inflicts injustices and problems on whole classes of people without common connection or organizational affiliation. These problems of mass injury raise classic "public goods" and "free rider" problems (see Olson 1971; Trubek 1978a), in which no single individual may have the knowledge, ability, or incentive to act for the entire affected "diffuse interest" (Cappelletti and Garth 1978). Access and participation are considered to be group-based and more than remedial. The argument calls for "radical" rethinking of traditional legal notions, including concepts of standing, fair procedure, and legal representation itself (Cappelletti et al. 1975). Expanded class action rules (*Harvard Law Review* 1976), altered standing rules that allow private groups to act in courts and before administrative agencies for the public interest (Jaffe 1968), and the growth of public-interest law (Handler et al. 1978; Rabin 1976) promote the growth of "social advocacy" as a model for access and participation.

The first two waves of the movement share a concern with "finding effective legal representation for interests otherwise unrepresented or underrepresented" in the legal process (Cappelletti and Garth 1978, p. 222). In its third wave, the access-to-justice movement comes together with the movement for delegalization to support the development of a range of institutions and procedures outside the formal legal order, the function of which would be to provide access to justice instead of access to *legal* justice. In this wave, the access movement seeks to move beyond and to supplement previous advances in equalizing legal representation and providing avenues for redress of mass injuries by expanding the range of quasi-legal institutions through which justice is provided (Sander 1976; McGillis and Mullen 1977; Galanter 1976; Johnson 1978b; Danzig 1973). The creation of new fora, such as Neighborhood Justice Centers, was an attempt to expand the range of issues and people on which and for whom justice might be provided. It was an attempt to stimulate citizen participation by providing arenas for participation that are both informal and more clearly geared to providing services tailored to the characteristics of disputes and disputants (see Harrington 1984).

New fora in theory provide the vehicles through which citizens and groups can enforce rights. New fora may even affect the motivation of citizens and groups whose problems are possibly amenable to legal redress. Limited available evidence suggests, however, that such expectations may be exaggerated (Buckle and Thomas-Buckle 1981) and that the price of this expansion of fora is to expand the social control capacity of the state without subjecting that capacity to legal procedures, to neutralize and defuse potentially significant political conflict, and to take pressure off legal institutions (Abel 1982; Blomberg 1977). Recently, in fact, efforts have been made to roll back the earlier waves of the access movement (Sarat 1981) while encouraging the proliferation of nonlegal alternatives.

The delegalization movement supports such a development not out of a concern to expand the range of citizen participation but out of a desire to minimize the costs and inefficiencies associated with the kind of formality and procedure demanded by law (Tribe 1979) and in order to preserve and protect the allegedly limited capacity of existing legal institutions (Council on the Role of Courts 1984). Here the overriding concern is with efficiency in the dispute resolution and social control tasks peformed by legal institutions (Abel 1979a). Whereas the access-to-justice movement seeks to resolve the tensions posed by citizen participation in a liberal legal order by furthering democratizing law, the response of the delegalization movement is technocratic and managerial. That movement seeks to use nonlegal alternatives not to supplement but to replace expanded access and to resolve the dilemmas of citizen participation by limiting and diverting it.

The divergent impulses of the access-to-justice and delegalization movements indicate the depth of the dilemma of participation in the American legal system. The contradictions embodied in these movements display in sharp relief the fundamental contradictions of liberal legalism. The tension created by simultaneous pulls toward greater and lesser accessibility provides the frame for understanding the role of citizen participation in the American legal order. This tension has existed throughout United States history (Purcell 1973). How it is resolved at any time—that is, how much and what kind of participation is allowed and occurs—goes far in tracing the development of the legal order, its self-confidence, and its effectiveness.

CITIZEN PARTICIPATION AND THE SOCIOLOGY OF LAW

As we move to consider what is known about participation in the sociology of law, we move away from its contradictory connections to the legal order and toward a concern for its determinants and consequences at the level of individual participants. Sociological research, given its predominantly pluralistic and positivistic orientation (Trubek 1984), has concentrated on explaining why citizens do or do not participate and has given little attention to the problem of tracing the linkages between participation and the status of liberal legalism (for an exception, see Abel 1979b). It has surveyed a wide range of modes of participation and has recognized that participation may arise as the isolated behavior of individuals seeking specific redress for an injury or as the actions of voluntary associations and bureaucratic organizations, as well as by diffuse classes or groups, seeking to give legal form to their shared position. Sociological research demonstrates that participation helps shape the law in action and may help to change the law on the books. Remedies for past offenses become vehicles for the creation of new public norms or reinterpretation of old ones.

Out of all the recognized diversity of access and participation, two distinct patterns emerge in the sociological literature. The first arises from the interested behavior of discrete and identifiable actors who participate in the legal process for themselves and who mobilize the law for remedy, redress, or vindication. This is legal participation as remedy-seeking behavior. The second involves the activities of advocates for diffuse interests—for example, consumers and environmentalists—who involve themselves in adjudication and administration to represent those interests affirmatively as well as defensively. Here participation moves beyond remedy to reform; here participants are as interested in changing rules or practices as they are in winning particular cases.

The separation of remedial and reform-oriented participation is, of course, in actuality never quite that neat. Particular participants may play for the rules in any form of legal participation. Reform goals often begin with the recognition of, and the desire to remedy, a pattern of discrete but related injuries. Moreover, this separation should not be taken as an implicit endorsement of the law/politics distinction. Indeed, quite the opposite is intended. By including reform-oriented participation under the rubric of citizen participation in the legal order and by noting continuities between remedy-seeking and reform-oriented participation I intend to suggest that it is possible to read the literature on citizen participation to show how legal processes are used purposively and instrumentally and how those processes are employed as part of ongoing political struggles (Nonet and Selznick 1978; for specific examples, see Thompson 1975; Kluger 1976; Sarat 1982).

Participation as Remedy-Seeking Behavior

One of the most common images in the sociology of law is the image of the troubled case, of the dispute, disruption, or disorder. In this image citizens come to law to get help in dealing with social problems. Legal institutions are described as performing remedial work when the normal patterns of social cohesion are broken (for an interesting criticism of this perspective, see Engel 1980). They are portrayed as but one of a variety of mechanisms that function to deal with human troubles and disputes (Sarat and Grossman 1975; Engel and Steele 1979). Citizens participate by choosing law either as a complement to or instead of another of those mechanisms for processing or resolving their grievances.

Citizen participation, in this image, results from two kinds of failures. The first is the failure of citizens to avoid, or autonomously manage, social problems. The mobilization of law or the invocation of any third-party process is indeed a request for authoritative intervention. Autonomy is relinquished, at least in some part of one's life; authority is appealed to. The turn to law thus represents an acknowledgment of the limits of individual self-regulation. The second failure is the failure of informal, embedded mechanisms of social control. Here the literature that treats participation as remedy-seeking displays a powerful preference for social order. Conflict, disruption, disorder are treated as a kind of social disease. The job of law is, in this view, to repair the fabric of social relations such that conflict can be avoided or repressed.

The first interest in research on remedy-seeking is with the question why some events are perceived as troubling while others are not, or why some people are more grievance-prone than others. There has been almost no empirical research on these questions (for an exception, see Bumiller 1984). Yet, remedial participation begins with the perception that something needs to be remedied, and it becomes possible when that matter is translated into a form for which the law can provide a remedy (Felstiner, Abel, and Sarat 1980–81).

While virtually every problem can be framed as a legal grievance and therefore can enable the mobilization of law, sociolegal research talks about a wide range of alternative mechanisms that might be used to obtain redress. In so doing, sociologists of law have unwittingly exaggerated the availability and use of private remedies by discussing them in such abstract terms as "mediation" or "arbitration." In any specific case, however, finding mediation or arbitration may be quite difficult (Nader 1979). While the aggregate of private and public alternatives to law may be sizable, such alternatives will rarely be able or willing to deal with more than a narrow range of problems. Furthermore, the movement of problems between and among private remedy agents and between the private and the public realm has yet to be mapped.

No reliable evidence exists on the variety of paths particular disputes might take or on the conditions governing their routing. It is not known how much of the entire range of society's remedial activity takes place in and through legal institutions. However, research on everyday, intrapersonal disputes indicates that most are managed through one or another variety of "self-help" without any explicit form of legal intervention (see Buckle and Thomas-Buckle 1981, 1982; Engel 1984; Baumgartner 1984; Berk et al. 1984). A recent study of a broader array of civil disputes found that approximately 10 percent led to litigation (Miller and Sarat 1980–81). To consider remedial participation in the legal system as a whole, it is necessary to imagine a measure by which such activity can be indexed against all the events individuals perceive as needing remedy (Lempert 1979). Decision-making behavior must be imagined in which participants decide where and how to carry on activities designed to resolve their problems.

Explaining Remedy-Seeking

Traditionally, when sociologists of law have examined access to justice in the context of remedy-seeking behavior, they have described individuals and groups making choices on how to handle problems among a wide variety of known alternatives, each of which varies in its procedures and, most important, in the associated costs and benefits (Johnson et al. 1978; Carlin et al. 1967; Sarat 1976). Some have even attempted to describe access to justice as analogous to consumption decisions (Jacob 1969).

It has recently been suggested that remedy-seeking can be better understood as investment behavior, in which individuals invest time and money in various activities designed to facilitate remedy and redress (Trubek 1979; Ordover 1978). In this view, the activities or remedial participation are carried out under conditions of imperfect information and uncertainty. Participants, unaware of all the possible alternatives open to them, cannot regularly and reliably anticipate the outcome of participation in one or another activity carried out in any dispute-processing institution (Komesar 1979). The investment approach sees costs "created" in and through the process of participation. Time and money are expended within precise contours determined by the participants. The monetary costs of litigation, for example, may be allocated among lawyers' fees and court costs; more appropriately, they may be thought of as the result of specific activities, such as seeking information through discovery. Thus the time and money invested in participation represent a dependent variable that requires explanation, rather than an independent variable that can itself be used to explain patterns of participation.[8]

The investment analogy suggests that citizens participate in legal processes to maximize the likelihood of obtaining maximum redress (for a similar argument, see Riker and Ordeshook 1968; Landes and Posner 1979). They calculate an "expected value" for each decision they must make in structuring their participation. That calculus is a function of the participant's perception of the best outcome of his or her activities, of the probability of obtaining that outcome, and of the time and money required to do so. Since expected values are calculated under conditions of imperfect information, participants may discount their calculations in accordance with their faith in the reliability, accuracy, and completeness of the information at their disposal (Shapiro 1969).

---

[8]This is not to suggest that monetary costs may not act as a barrier to participation. Such costs can and do limit access. Since so many forms of participation in the legal process require the assistance of trained legal counsel, the monetary costs of participation are particularly important. While few systematic descriptive data are available on the costs of various types of participation, some suggest that legal fees for handling even such relatively simple matters as uncontested divorces may be beyond the means of middle-class citizens (Johnson 1978b, pp. 921–22). Obviously, the costs of using a lawyer's services vary greatly (Trubek et al. 1983; Kritzer et al. 1984). What matters is that particular kinds of people are effectively barred from participation simply because they cannot afford its economic costs. Government-subsidized legal services and contingent-fee arrangements cannot entirely eliminate this barrier. Furthermore, the cost means that "litigation by persons of any income level will be effectively foreclosed when the stakes are rather modest. In many cases, a disputant would incur more expenses in participating in the lawsuit than he stands to gain or save from winning. Moreover, the uncertainty inherent in most litigation means that the stakes must exceed the costs by a substantial margin before it is rational to file or defend a claim in courts" (Johnson 1978b, p. 9).

An understanding of remedy-seeking from this rational choice perspective requires that the expected-value calculus for any participatory activity must be explained. Four basic factors, in this view, affect remedy-seeking participation: they are party capability, participant goals, the perceived characteristics of alternative means of obtaining redress, and the capability of intermediaries or agents such as lawyers. All these factors presume that the opportunity to participate in the full range of desirable legal and private processes is open, that is, that the rules under which these processes operate permit the kind of participation envisioned in any particular case. This simplifying assumption is generally made in empirical studies of remedy-seeking. Yet, even within the confines of such a simplification, it is striking how little is known about each of the factors.[9]

Party Capability   The phrase "party capability" was first made popular in the sociology of law by Marc Galanter (1974), who argued that participation in legal processes, litigation in particular, can be understood in terms of the differential abilities of litigants to employ legal institutions. The participation of any party is a function of that party's ability and willingness to participate. "Party capability" thus refers to individual resources and dispositions. If remedy-seeking behavior in legal institutions is unevenly distributed throughout the population, it is because party capability is itself unevenly distributed (see Carlin et al. 1967).

The resources necessary for remedy-seeking behavior are time, money, and skill. Different forms of participation may require each of the three to a different degree and in a different mix. Little attention has been devoted to the first of the resources, since conceptualizing and measuring time is very difficult and the time requirements for different forms of participation vary greatly. Yet, it is widely recognized that time affects participation.

Many studies of small-claims courts, for example, suggest that individuals' failure to bring or prosecute cases is in no small way a function of the "opportunity costs" associated with these courts (Steadman and Rosenstein 1973; Moulton 1969; Yngvesson and Hennessey 1975). Furthermore, the difficulties encountered by such newly developed informal tribunals as Neighborhood Justice Centers in attracting participants to some extent may be attributed to the time-intense nature of the proceedings they conduct (Institute for Social Analysis 1979). Paradoxically, more informal procedures, such as mediation, may be less attractive and accessible to citizens than their advocates believe because they require participants to engage in an extended sequence of discussions and bargaining (Felstiner and Williams 1979; Sarat 1984). The reduction of economic costs and even the minimization of delay may not compensate for the relatively intense and direct involvement.

The most intense use of time is required in those forms of participation in the legal

---

[9]The limits of empirical inquiry become all the more striking if participation in legal processes is seen as both dynamic and interactive. Few, if any, empirical studies have traced the development and continuity of remedy-seeking behavior or have systematically examined the way remedy-seeking begins and changes (for useful theoretical work, see Vidmar 1979; Felstiner, Abel, and Sarat 1980–81; Mather and Yngvesson 1980–81). Finally, little or no empirical work in this area attempts to understand participation in the context of the interactions that occur between and among the various parties engaged in remedy-seeking. These facts should caution against too heavy a reliance on available empirical work and suggest the outlines of one avenue of future research on citizen participation and remedy-seeking in and through the legal process (Trubek 1979).

system that are "deep." The clearest example is, of course, jury duty. The juror must sacrifice substantial amounts of time, most of which will be consumed in waiting or participating in the rituals through which juries are actually empaneled (Ashby 1978; Richert 1977; Vanderzell 1966).

The most common explanations for variations in remedy-seeking focus not on time investment but rather on some measurement of position in systems of social stratification. Socioeconomic status provides a summary concept that includes both money and skill. The money, or income dimension, is rather obvious. Skill refers to knowledge, experience, or facility in the kinds of activities that compose remedy-seeking. Indicators of skill include education, information or knowledge about law and the legal system, and prior experience with it. When monetary resources and skill, considered as expertise and experience, are considered, the most significant source of variation in remedy-seeking is, in the view of some, not socioeconomic status differences between or among individuals but the difference between individuals, typically "one shotters," and organizations, usually "repeat players" (Galanter 1974).

Some data support the hypothesis that organizations are more frequent users of courts than are individuals; "figures from a variety of courts suggest that plaintiffs are predominantly business or government units while defendants are overwhelmingly individuals" (Galanter 1975, p. 348). Such organizations command the resources to participate in courts and the expertise and experience to do so effectively. They are able to exploit those abilities to the fullest extent when they are opposed by single individuals. According to research by Wanner (1975), "business and governmental plaintiffs win more often and more quickly than do individual plaintiffs. Not only are they more successful overall . . . but they are more successful in almost every one of the heavily litigated categories of cases" (cited by Galanter 1975, p. 357). Wanner's research (1974) further documents the pattern of litigation in which organizations are more frequent users of courts. In the three courts he studied he found business and governmental units to be plaintiffs in almost 60 percent of the cases. While other research in other courts is equally supportive of Galanter's hypothesis (Pagter et al. 1964; Dolbeare 1967; Hollingsworth et al. 1973; Kagan et al. 1977), recent studies of state and federal trial courts of general jurisdiction show considerable variation in the pattern and configuration of participation (Grossman et al. 1982; Trubek et al. 1983; see also Vidmar 1984).

There is little doubt that organizations as participants are advantaged by certain institutional factors. Because they are often "repeat players" (Galanter 1974, p. 97), they are able, for example, to develop expertise as well as informal relations with decision-makers, and to structure rules over a series of contacts with legal institutions. Thus when participation involves a contest between such organizations and individuals, it raises questions about equal justice of a kind not ordinarily recognized as within the scope of equal protection.

Nevertheless, there are important problems with this argument. First, the concept of organization is itself too diffuse and inclusive to have much analytic utility. The category of organizations includes everything from the neighborhood grocery store and the Boy Scouts of America to General Motors and the United States Department of Justice. The claim that organizations are more capable remedy-seekers hides considerable variation within that category even while it suggests that the legal system is itself structured in such a way as to respond to bureaucratic rationality and economies of scale.

It is not known whether the higher levels of organizational remedy-seeking indicated by litigation rates hold across all fora or in other legal processes. Indeed, it may be that those levels of participation are a simple function of the frequency with which organizations are involved in disputes. There is some evidence that particular types of organizations will go to considerable effort to avoid the escalation of problems into the kinds of disputes that require the mobilization of law (Ross and Littlefield 1978). Given the high costs of most legal processes, organizations, especially commercial enterprises, have taken steps to encourage the development of extrajudicial, nonlegal techniques for dealing with disputes that do arise (Bonn 1972; Stern 1968). Little is known about the behavior of different kinds of organizations when they encounter potential legal problems. This fact highlights the need to examine the behavior of organizations in terms of their relative involvement with legal problems and to disaggregate the category of organizations to provide for more appropriate comparative units.

In the case of individuals, income and skill are consistently associated with higher levels of citizen participation in remedy-seeking behavior. Whether the particular form of participation is litigation (Hunting and Neuwirth 1962; Rockwell 1968), recourse to lawyers (Curran 1977; Griffiths 1977; Mayhew 1975; Sykes 1969), calling the police (Jacob 1971; Skogan 1976; Dodge et al. 1976), or registering complaints with administrative agencies (Crowe 1978; Steele 1975; Nader 1979; Best and Andreasen 1977; Lehnen 1975; Jowell 1975), participation is more frequent among those with higher incomes, higher education, and more extensive knowledge of the law (but see Miller and Sarat 1980–81).

Party capability is an important indicator of the fit between legal processes and systems of social stratification. The institutions of liberal legality are organized and established to regulate and serve private property—or, more accurately, wealth in the form of private property. Ownership of, or connection to, property facilitates access more readily than mere disposable income. Property provides the occasion for contact with the legal system, which in turn contributes to the development of skill and expertise in remedy-seeking (Mayhew and Reiss 1969). With the exception of domestic relations, individuals are most likely to have dealings with lawyers in making arrangements for the acquisition or transfer of real property (Curran 1977).

> [T]he association between income and legal contacts is in part an organizational effect. The legal profession is organized to service business and property interests. The social organization of business and property is highly legalized. Out of this convergence emerges a pattern of citizen contact with attorneys that is heavily oriented to property. [Mayhew and Reiss 1969, p. 313; see also Silberman 1979]

Research on participation has, to this point, paid too little attention to such relationships. The embeddedness of patterns of participation in the fit between legality and particular, dominant social groups may be important, perhaps more important than any other single factor, in explaining why and how legal institutions are used in society (Bumiller 1984; Abel 1979b, 1982).

Capability to participate also includes an ideological or normative dimension, which may operate to inhibit participation for those otherwise seemingly capable of participating. Whether and how people participate and use legal processes results, in large measure, from the way law is represented in and through cultural systems in which citizens are embedded. By recognizing the fit between legal organization and the interests of particular groups or classes we can begin to understand why subordinate social groups display an ideology of avoidance or pragmatic and skeptical involvement (Doo 1973; Merry 1979, 1985; Bumiller 1984). Moreover, despite the widespread perception of litigiousness (Barton 1975; for a contrary view, see Galanter 1983), there are significant cultural and ideological barriers built into liberalism and liberal legalism that act to discourage remedy-seeking participation (see Katz 1973).

Bringing problems to law, no matter what its outcome, may create greater problems than would be the case if private troubles were kept private. To enter a legal claim for redress involves a social declaration of trouble, a declaration that, in many ways, results in considerable social disorganization and disruption. One need only consider the situation of the employee who begins to perceive herself to be the victim of gender discrimination. For her the declaration of trouble, the making of a claim, is trouble itself.

Even in less complex situations, seeking remedies through law entails numerous risks, from breaching public presumptions of order to indicating and acknowledging in a public way that one's life is troubled, risks that may deter potential claims. Notions of civility encourage people to ignore trouble. Given these notions, alleging trouble almost always brings some trouble on the self, making it uncomfortable work to be avoided (see Katz 1973).

In addition to the risks associated with breaching public presumptions of civility and decorum, one who alleges that another has caused trouble may confront problems from admitting his or her own involvement. To publicly acknowledge that there is trouble in one's life, as participation in legal institutions requires, is to run the risk of being stigmatized, gossiped about, or ostracized, because claimants may be held causally or morally responsible for not having done something to prevent or avoid the trouble in the first place. Blaming the victim is, indeed, a common cultural preoccupation.

A known trouble may be less troubling than what results when the lid is off. The revelation of additional grievances, of counterclaims, or of long-suffering that may come to light in the wake of socially acknowledged trouble gives but one indication of the value of the effort to endure without complaint (see Katz 1973; Bumiller 1984). While the social declaration of trouble always has the potential to restore order and harmony, such declarations almost inevitably open the floodgates for recrimination and retribution. The burden of raising a claim and invoking the law is the fear of opening a Pandora's box of retribution.

At the level of explaining individual participation these cultural and ideological barriers result in a set of attitudes, norms, and dispositions referred to as "legal competence" (Carlin et al. 1967). To engage in remedy-seeking through legal processes, an individual must

> see the law as a resource for developing, furthering and protecting his interests. This is partly a matter of knowledge. The competent subject will be aware of the relation between the realization of his interests and the machinery of law-making and administration. He will know how to use this machinery and when to use it. Moreover, he will see assertion of his interests through legal channels as desirable and appropriate. . . . The legally competent person has a sense of himself as a possessor of rights and he sees the legal system as a resource for vindication of those rights. He knows when and how to seek vindication. [Carlin et al. 1967, pp. 62–63]

This description specifies both "rights consciousness" and a belief that it is appropriate and effective to assert rights through legal processes as the crucial ideological requisites to citizen participation.

Participant Goals   A second major factor emphasized in studies of citizen participation involves the goals of the participants. The literature suggests that individuals consider the nature of their problems, their precise needs, and the fit between problem and available procedures. Where legal institutions seem inappropriate to their specific problem, citizens seek out private alternatives or simply endure the problem (Merry 1979; Engel 1983).

The range of participant goals identified as relevant covers both monetary and nonmonetary, direct and indirect objectives (Trubek 1979; Sarat and Grossman 1975). Direct goals pertain to the specific injury or problem that engenders remedy-seeking. Indirect goals pertain to the parties themselves or to their social situation rather than to the injury or problem. Thus individuals mobilize the law to try to harass or intimidate (Merry 1979; Sarat 1976), to obtain revenge, or simply to be spiteful (Leff 1970). They invoke legal processes to try to structure relations with other parties or establish conditions favorable to their long-term interests (Ross 1970). Alternatively, participation in legal processes is avoided when citizens are involved in long-term or multiplex relationships which they desire to maintain. Adversarial processes typically focus narrowly on the specific instance of trouble they are called upon to resolve; they treat relationships as if they had no context beyond the problem itself. They escalate trouble in ongoing relationships by dealing with only one aspect of the social interaction from which it arises.

Relatively little empirical research has assessed the structure of participant goals and their impact on access to justice. What research there is has focused almost exclusively on the maintenance of relationships as a goal. Studies of litigation (Merry 1979; Sarat 1976) as well as studies of police–citizen contact (Black 1971; Gottfredson and Hindelang 1979) support the hypothesis that those with continuing relations will, in general, seek to avoid the legal process to remedy their problems. While a substantial proportion of the cases that make their way into lower criminal courts arise out of ongoing relations (Vera Institute of Justice 1977), given a choice of alternatives, those seeking to maintain relationships seem inclined to avoid remedy-seeking through legal processes (for contrary evidence from another culture, see Kidder 1974; Morrison 1974). Individuals who have known each other for a long time prior to their disputes and who anticipate continuing their relationship are much more likely to seek remedies through informal procedures than are those without such a past or anticipated future. "Of the cases involving parties who had known each other a long time prior to the dispute and who expected to continue their relationship, approximately 7 percent were decided by adjudication as opposed to 58.8 percent of those in which the parties had no prior or anticipated future relationship" (Sarat 1976, p. 358). While long, involved, ongoing relationships cause difficulties for effective resolution of grievances, it is the future of relationships that most strongly influences participant behavior.

> A relationship with a long past has little binding power if the participants expect that they will never see each other again. Conversely, even a relationship of relatively short duration may have considerable force if the participants realize that they will have to deal with one another for a long period of time in the

future. A limited future changes the calculation of costs and gains, making confrontation cheaper. [Merry 1979, p. 920]

The impact of relational goals on remedy-seeking has also been talked about in terms of
the nature of the transactions in which problems emerge (Williamson 1979). Two major
types, routine and idiosyncratic, have been identified. Routine transactions involve
goods or values readily available in the community. Should the transactions between two
parties cease, neither would have great difficulty replacing the goods or the value that
would be lost. In a market context, there are enough sellers and buyers to match any
buyer with any seller without creating much difficulty or loss. In such a situation,
continuing relationships have little value and are unlikely to exert much influence on
remedy-seeking behavior (Williamson 1979).

Idiosyncratic transactions involve goods or values that are specialized or rare—or, to
use market terms, for which there are relatively few sellers and buyers. The rarity of the
good or value involved in a relationship imposes a high cost for substituting a comparable
good or value. When relationships involve such goods or values, remedy-seeking behavior will be structured to minimize the chance of disruption (Williamson et al. 1975).
Such reconceptualization of party relationships avoids the simplifying assumptions that
the past or future governs participation. Instead, it focuses attention on the specifics of
situations out of which such participation and remedy-seeking arise.

Even if participant goals are thus reconceptualized, little is known about the relative
importance of maintaining a relationship as against other goals. One study compared
the explanatory power of relational history with that of participant dispositions, prior
remedy-seeking behavior, and the presence of lawyers in explaining remedy-seeking
behavior in a small claims context, and found that relational history was most useful in
explaining such behavior (Sarat 1976). Other studies of participation in other contexts
(Gottfredson and Hindelang 1979) argue that the goal of preserving relationships is a less
important factor. Calling the police, for example, is more often a function of the
seriousness of the victimization individuals experience than of their relation with the
offender (see also Bercal 1970).

In the end, here as elsewhere, the nature of the problem seems to structure remedy-
seeking (Gottfredson and Hindelang 1979, p. 16; Silbey and Merry 1984). Remedy-
seeking behavior thus appears influenced by the particular characteristics of individual
problems as much as by the general goals or identity of participants (Curran 1977; Marks
1971). Studies of legal participation and access to justice, therefore, may have to become
more problem-specific than they have been in the past. Remedy-seeking is structured by
the availability of remedies and the forms of procedures tailored to particular problems.
Generalization is hindered because remedy-seeking is reactive; what initiates such activity is as important as the characteristics of those engaging in it.

Perceived Characteristics of Legal Processes   Since remedies can be pursued in
many ways, individuals assess the expected value of participation against the characteristics of the institutions and procedures open to them. Explanations of patterns of participation must take account of participants' perceptions. Sociologists of law have catalogued
a wide range of dimensions along which it is possible to characterize dispute-processing
institutions (Nader and Todd 1978; Abel 1973; Felstiner 1974). There has, however,

been little or no empirical assessment of the attractiveness of particular elements, either generally or in the context of specific problems.

Several elements may be important in structuring remedy-seeking. First is time—both the participant's time and the length of time from the initiation of a process to its termination. While considerable attention has been devoted to the problem of "delay" in explaining the operation of courts (Zeisel et al. 1959; Levin 1975; Church 1978), little comparative study has assessed case-processing time among legal institutions (for an exception, see Institute for Social Analysis 1979; see also Trubek et al. 1984). Almost no empirical attention has been given to the question of how delay affects the behavior of individuals as participants in the legal system. While it has been generally assumed that litigants, for example, want rapid determination of their claims, such a desire is far from universal (Sarat 1978). Individuals who use legal processes to harass or intimidate others involved in disputes have no incentive to desire rapid disposition of their claims. Moreover, those seeking to advance or promote private negotiations may find delay positively desirable (Mnookin and Kornhauser 1979; Eisenberg 1976), to say nothing about the incentive of defendants who choose to prolong or exploit delay in legal processes.

Other important institutional characteristics of the legal process are the degree of "expertise" in the particular matters of concern for potential participants and the ability to produce desired outcomes. Perceptions of the inability of the police, for example, to solve many common types of crime is an important explanation for the rarity with which some types of victimization are reported (Ennis 1967). The visibility or publicity of remedial processes also influences rates of participation for particular classes of people with particular kinds of problems (Sarat 1976). The extent to which such processes are adversarial is also significant, especially concerning problems in ongoing relationships. A final determinant is the extent to which different processes lead to decisions on the basis of preexisting norms and to precedents that can be used to structure future transactions. The fit between the characteristics of institutions and the goals of participants governs the form of remedy-seeking behavior in particular situations (Zemans 1983). The precise relationship depends, however, on the information individuals have or can obtain. Limited information may lead to decisions that are inappropriate to particular goals. Most often, the advice of lawyers both structures the way in which institutional characteristics are perceived and shapes the modes of citizen participation (Lempert 1976; Macaulay 1979; Sarat and Felstiner 1986).

Lawyers as Intermediaries   The discussion thus far has assumed that participation in remedy-seeking involves individual citizens interacting with each other and acting directly in the legal system. But, in much remedy-seeking behavior, one, or both, of the parties has a lawyer and acts through the lawyer as an intermediary and agent. Participation is indirect, and the lawyer's skill and advice determine how citizens participate and how effective that participation will be. The lawyer plays an important role in structuring the information upon which decisions about remedy-seeking are based. His or her estimates become the basis for the expected value calculus that forms the core of those decisions (Rosenthal 1974; Macaulay 1979). Whether legal services actually improve the quality of access and participation cannot, of course, be known. But, given current procedures, legal representation is thought to be a minimum prerequisite for access to justice.

The first wave of the movement for access began, as I noted above, with the assumption that legal representation was unavailable to poor people, that is, that its maldistribution reinforced the social effects of poverty (Cahn and Cahn 1964). It was assumed that the poor suffered from a variety of needs and problems for which law could provide effective remedies (Carlin et al. 1967). Empirical research has been undertaken to ascertain the extent of these needs and problems and the extent to which poor people were able to obtain legal services. This tradition of research dates back to the mid-1930s when Charles Clark and Emma Corstvet undertook a small survey in New Haven, Connecticut. They presented respondents with a series of thirty-eight problems and asked whether each had been encountered in the previous year and, if so, whether the respondent had consulted a lawyer. About one half of those interviewed had encountered one or another of the problems, but over three-quarters of these were handled without lawyers (Clark and Corstvet 1938, p. 1276). The authors concluded that a substantial amount of "undone legal business" was found among people of low or moderate income. Other surveys document the limited role played by lawyers in dealing with the problems of such people (Missouri Bar 1963; Rockwell 1968; Levine and Preston 1970; Curran and Clarke 1970).

> Notwithstanding what appears to be a highly active and varied problem-solving style, when it comes to relating problems and problem solution to the legal process the view of the legal process held by the poor is narrow and rigid. What the poor call legal problems are only those problems . . . for which remedies have been previously demanded and secured. The poor do not view the law as relating to their unique life problems. . . . This view necessarily means that the poor understate their legal needs and, further, that they under-utilize the legal system. The consequences have been brought on by the past failure of the legal system to allocate sufficient legal services to the poor and by the past pattern of allocating all available services only to those needs articulated by the poor. [Marks 1971, pp. 10–11]

In all, approximately two-thirds of the adult population has, at one time or another, had contact with lawyers (Curran 1977; see also Mayhew and Reiss 1969; Stolz 1968). While the precise meaning of "contact" is uncertain, it is clear that recourse to a lawyer is usually concentrated on a rather narrow range of matters involving the acquisition or transfer of property or problems arising in domestic relations. Indeed, if the data are correct, with the exception of buying and selling property, middle-income individuals are not much more likely to seek legal assistance than are people with lower incomes (Mayhew and Reiss 1969). In part this situation reflects the fact that, on the whole, people do not encounter most of the types of problems lawyers are equipped to handle (Miller and Sarat 1980–81). Outside of property and family problems, consumer problems—many of which are of little monetary consequence—appear to be the most common problems encountered in the population (Curran 1977, p. 35).

Given the apparent reluctance or inability of people to bring most problems to lawyers, it is not to be expected that remedy-seeking behavior will frequently lead individuals into deeper kinds of legal participation. One of the things that prevent or inhibit movement toward lawyers and the legal system is the absence of a structure of intermediaries and referral sources that might direct them there (Ladinsky 1976; Frank 1976; Lochner 1975). Legal services are provided through an "imperfect market," in which information is highly skewed and not easily available (Ladinsky 1976). Sources of information tend either to be informal and unstructured or to have difficulty penetrating the social networks that govern decisions about remedy-seeking. More and better information about the operation of those social networks and the way they work in different cultural settings and for different types of potential legal problems is needed (see Ladinsky and Susmilch 1983).

From Clark and Corstvet to Curran, the measurement of the use of legal services began with the idea that there are unmet legal needs for which such services could or should be provided. Despite some empirical evidence of a rising demand for legal services throughout the population (Avichai 1978) and the widespread sense that law is ever more implicated in the lives of citizens, the legal profession seems anxious to increase its share of the social business that, given the range of legal remedies, might be brought to it. Surveys of legal needs, which are little more than sophisticated forms of market research, have recently been subjected to important criticism, concerning both the validity of the data they generate (Marks 1976) and the political biases their approach reveals (Griffiths 1977).

Measuring the breadth of legal needs and their translation into demands for services is indeed quite complex. Empirically, it is difficult to know what to count. If access to justice is seen to require the use of a lawyer, for example, there is the question of what using a lawyer means. And even if the concept of access to justice can be operationalized with respect to specific legal institutions, it is still problematic to ask individuals about their participation. Are questions directed to all instances of participation, or is the focus problem-specific? Even if most problems can be overcome, what would remain is the comparison of individuals in their private lives and as members of organizations in a business or professional capacity. It is fair to say that the sociology of law has been less successful than one might expect in accounting for citizen participation, at least in part because of an inability to overcome these substantial problems of measurement (for suggested new techniques, see Felstiner, Abel, and Sarat 1980–81).

Measurement problems are compounded when "need" is examined against some preconceived, static list of problems defined as eligible for legal remedies. Such an approach "has elements of a legal intelligence test when taken to its logical conclusion. . . . It carries with it the possibility that those who did not take problems to lawyers will not admit to having had the problem" (Marks 1976, p. 195). The list of static problems fails to incorporate the dynamic elements of legal participation, assuming that legal needs exist and can be identified when, in fact, much of the work of law and the thrust of remedy-seeking behavior is creative (Mather and Yngvesson 1980–81). Interpretations previously ignored or remedies previously unused become themselves the subject of participation and debate. Thus, "the static list approach is likely to miss problems that require creative legal services or the application of emerging legal doctrines" (Lempert 1976, p. 177). The legal-needs approach implies or assumes that legal participation ought to be a normal response to the occurrence of problems for which law provides a remedy. Yet, the legal system could not meet all the demands that would be put upon it if such were indeed the case, nor would such a society be worth living in.

The substitution of other concepts or units for legal need, although obviously desirable in studying the use of lawyers, may prove equally problematic. Are grievances or disputes the appropriate concept against which to measure legal participation? Is there anything comparable to the idea of criminal victimization that can be used in exploring civil justice? In the area of crime, the correspondence between what the law recognizes as criminal behavior and what people, in fact, experience as criminal victimization is much closer. Furthermore, the dynamic element of law creation, which is very much part of remedy-seeking behavior in civil matters, is largely absent on the criminal side. Problems analogous to those in studies of legal need can themselves be found in research on criminal victimization (Sparks et al. 1977), but the essential difficulties of developing a measure against which citizen participation can be indexed seem particularly acute in studies of "lawyer-seeking" behavior (Ladinsky 1976).

Once individuals engage lawyers, the extent and nature of their active involvement and participation are highly varied. Although little empirical work on the extent of client participation has been carried out (for exceptions, see Cain 1979; Rosenthal 1974; Hosticka 1979), two general tendencies have been noted. In the first, participation stops in the lawyer's office. Clients trust the independent professional judgment of their lawyers, whom they engage precisely because they are unable, on their own, to deal with their problems or to obtain redress from legal institutions. The price of obtaining effective access to justice is clients' abandonment of their directive role. Lawyers assume, generally uncritically, the interests of the client or substitute their own; thus, "the passive client's delegation of responsibility and control detaches him from the problem-solving process. . . . The competent professional is able to see what is in the best interests of his client—and to make those interests his own" (Rosenthal 1974, pp. 15, 22).

In contrast to the traditional model stands the "participatory" model. Within this framework the lawyer never takes the problem away from the client but encourages the client to be active and informed, cautioning against delegating decision-making and insisting that the client retain rights of consultation and final authority. Law and legal problems are understood to be flexible, open, and defined by the individuals experiencing them. The lawyer is consultant, general and technical adviser, and, within the limits of professional ethics, implementer of the client's wishes. The participatory model assumes no conflict between effective access to justice and client participation (Appel and Van Atta 1969; Brill 1973; Cain 1979).

Under the traditional model, citizen participation is vicarious at best. Under the participatory model, an effort is made to ensure that the client's legal citizenship is realized in all its dimensions. While Rosenthal (1974) developed his models in the context of traditional, individualistic, remedial participation, they seem no less applicable in determining who is, in fact, participating in the legal process when what is at stake is reform rather than remedy (see Burke 1979). The potential for conflict between lawyer and client is as great, if not greater, in such cases. Clients may desire individualized remedies, and lawyers may have a personal or ideological interest in broad-based reform. The ability of clients to participate meaningfully may be less apparent, since they frequently come from disadvantaged backgrounds. The ability of the client to control the lawyer is removed when legal services are paid for through government subsidy or the contributions of private groups. But the issue remains the same: who participates—lawyer or client—who gains access to justice, and at what price.

Moreover, once individuals engage lawyers, the advice and information they obtain are critical in determining if or how they will participate in legal processes. Relatively few empirical studies of lawyer–client interaction describe or analyze lawyers' performance in this shaping function (Rosenthal 1974; Macaulay 1979; Cain 1979). The ethics of legal practice make such research extremely difficult (see Danet et al. 1981; but see Sarat and Felstiner 1986). What is known indicates that the lawyer is very much in charge (Rosenthal 1974; Hunting and Neuwirth 1962) in even the most straightforward and traditional legal matters. The more complex the problem, the more the client is passive (Burke 1979; Laumann and Heinz 1977). In fact, lawyers tend to become the effective participant in matters involving any representational activity. Presumably, variation in client participation in and control over lawyers' decision-making generally follows the outlines of variation for other kinds of participation, except that the importance of such personality factors as self-confidence and assertiveness is increased. But these are, at best, untested hypotheses.

The uncontrolled lawyer is able to substitute his own interest and his desire to maintain his professional reputation, or some refined perception of the client's interest for the client's clearly expressed interest. The uncontrolled lawyer may develop his own sense of the case, redirecting remedy-seeking behavior to suit it. Such is clearly the case with lawyers who handle product-quality complaints (Macaulay 1979). Most often, they act to "cool out" individuals who come to them seeking an aggressive confrontation with the seller of the defective goods. The lawyer channels remedy-seeking away from legal processes and often tries to convince the client that no remedy is either possible or justifiable. Indeed, clients who remain active participants often pursue different strategies, with better results (Rosenthal 1974). Three-quarters of such clients receive what they call satisfactory outcomes from their remedy-seeking behavior in personal injury cases, as compared with only 40 percent of those who effectively turn their claims over to an attorney. Citizen participation through lawyers defines legal participation. Its quality and results depend upon the interaction of lawyers and clients and the skills and dispositions each brings to that interaction.

Each of the factors discussed above plays an important role in structuring remedy-seeking behavior. Each captures part of the process through which individuals perceive and respond to needs, problems, grievances, and disputes. Each helps to explain when and why legal institutions are employed. Yet, any analytic scheme at least partly falsifies the social aspects as well as the personal dynamics controlling choices and decisions. Empirical studies of remedy-seeking are relatively rare, and the state of the art is relatively primitive. Moreover, there is a tendency in such empirical work to isolate and treat separately characteristics of individuals, of problems, and of the operation of the legal institutions. Research on participation and remedy-seeking behavior needs both greater theoretical sophistication and integration of individual, social, and institutional perspectives.

Effects of Remedial Participation

Citizens go to law not merely to take part in a ritual or to identify themselves with particular symbols of authority but also to achieve particular outcomes. At the most basic level, they participate in legal processes to obtain some benefit for themselves and for others or to avoid some undesirable event or occurrence in their lives. In many instances, however, it is not possible to assess the outcome of any single act of participation for the person involved. Complex chains of causality, as well as the passage of time, blur the relationship of participation and decision. There are, nevertheless, instances in which that relation is fairly direct. Most of these occur when citizens seek to use the legal process to obtain specific redress or vindicate a particular claim. Participation can then be assessed in terms of the success of the participants in accomplishing their goals (Kritzer et al. 1985).

Discussion can also focus on the effect of participation on citizens' attitudes toward law and the legal system. Do those who take part feel more or less respect for and confidence in the legal process? Do they have higher or lower opinions of legal efficacy? Are they more or less likely to equate law and justice (Walker et al. 1972; Richardson et al. 1972; Mahoney et al. 1978; Sarat 1977; Sarat and Felstiner 1985)? To the uninitiated citizen, legal processes may seem distant and formal. When, and if, that distance and that formality are penetrated, citizens may come to appreciate the real genius of the law or may, on the other hand, become cynical about its procedures (Casey 1974). Does participation stimulate a desire to participate? Obviously, there are those who become "repeat players" by necessity if not choice; but there are occasions on which access to justice and participation in the legal process may be but one available alternative. In such situations, the real impact of participation becomes visible.

There is at least one other level on which to examine the effect of participation—private citizenship. As Fuller (1971a, 1978) suggests, the legal order seeks, at least in theory, to establish reason and judgment as the optimum method for carrying out the affairs of society.[10] In the ideology of liberal legalism law seeks to establish that men and women can transcend the world of interests simply understood; that they can govern their affairs in terms of articulated and articulable principles, norms, and rules; and that they can dispassionately judge the affairs of others. Citizenship thus is said to offer a moral opportunity as well as a moral duty (Tussman 1970). Tocqueville (1863), for example, spoke about that opportunity in the context of citizen participation on civil juries. While the participation about which he spoke is anomalous, his argument is that jury service has a transforming influence on the people involved and an uplifting impact on the community.

> The jury . . . serves to communicate the spirit of the judges to the minds of all the citizens; and this spirit, with the habits which attend it, is the soundest preparation for free institutions. It imbues all classes with a respect for the thing judged and with the notion of right. If these two elements be removed the love of independence becomes a merely destructive passion. It teaches men to practice equity; every man learns to judge his neighbor as he himself would be judged . . . the jury teaches every man not to recoil before the responsibility of his own actions and impresses upon him with that . . . confidence without which no political virtue can exist. It invests each citizen with a kind of majesty; it makes them all feel the duties which they are bound to discharge toward society. . . . By obliging men to turn their attention to other affairs than their own it rubs off that private selfishness which is the rust of society. [p. 364]

In addition, the threat of seeking access to legal justice is explicit or implicit in almost all private bargaining and negotiation, inevitably producing a new incentive and provid-

---

[10] This model is, of course, rarely upheld by the law itself. Studies of lower criminal courts, for example, hardly portray them as places of reason and dispassionate judgment (Feeley 1979).

ing private interaction with a normative cast (Eisenberg 1976). In its social context, access rarely takes the form of access to legal justice (Miller and Sarat 1980–81). Nevertheless, that potential serves to set the style of access to other kinds of justice. Law establishes a model for society; the due process of law becomes an important force in the due process of private life (Selznick 1969; Kirp 1976). A last resort when private justice proves unsatisfactory, access to legal justice is a vehicle for establishing the context in which private justice is carried out (Mnookin and Kornhauser 1979; see also Zemans 1983). In some circumstances, access to legal justice is socially intolerable, even when the law—or such legal forms as contracts—is used initially to structure a private transaction (Macaulay 1963). The numerous and complex effects of legal participation or the threat of legal participation on private affairs have yet to be charted. Yet recent theoretical work in the sociology of law has acknowledged the primacy of the private impact of public justice (Galanter 1979; Jacob 1969).

> [C]ourts function as a potential sanction by intimidating one's opponent. . . . Courts are used extralegally, not as a form for adjudicating disputes according to shared legal principles, but as a weapon marshaled by disputants to enhance their power and influence. Disputes taken to court are not adjudicated, but are in Gulliver's terms, "negotiated." . . . The disputant's ability to appeal to court and the probability of success in that arena influence his or her relative power to "negotiate" a settlement. [Merry 1979, p. 919]

The interaction between private and public ordering is the centerpiece in the study of civil justice. The significance of citizen participation in the legal order cannot be fully understood without acknowledgment of that interaction. At least from the point of view of individual citizens, the success of law might be said to vary inversely with its utilization.

And, what about the effect of participation on citizen attitudes toward the legal system itself? Here substantial evidence indicates that participation does not breed confidence in or respect for legal institutions. Instead, it seems associated with disillusionment and diminished respect (Rhunka and Weller 1978; Yankelovich, Skelly, and White 1978; Jacob 1971; McIntyre 1967; Richardson et al. 1972; Sarat 1975). The more people know about legal processes, the less they like and respect them. Participation turns citizens into critics. Citizens' myths about law and the wisdom and fairness of legal institutions (Tapp 1974) are almost inevitably disappointed in the face of overcrowded, less than majestic, courts and administrative agencies (Tyler 1984).

Furthermore, citizen involvement with the legal system is frequently traumatic, arising in response to difficult, often injurious, events. Often the law can neither repair nor resolve the injury (Bureau of Social Science Research 1967; Ennis 1967; Skogan 1976; Gellhorn 1972; Rosenblum 1974; Nader 1979). Participation may discourage further involvement in the legal process or may encourage utilization of private means for dealing with problems that might otherwise have found their way to the legal system. For example, victims of automobile accidents involving significant property damage or personal injury are significantly less likely to litigate if they have previously been party to litigation (Hunting and Neuwirth 1962).

Some believe that the most important effect of remedy-seeking behavior is that it transforms and alters the problems or disputes for which legal remedies are sought

(Mather and Yngvesson 1980 –81). In this process conflicts are narrowed and de-politicized; grievants are led to see their grievances as individual and idiosyncratic remedy-seeking. Participation in liberal legal institutions, thus, is said to produce a form of self- and social alienation (Abel 1982). However, other forms of participation attempt to break out of the individual, remedial mode. They are both more collective and more explicitly political. It is these forms which, because they challenge the usual legal form, may pose the greatest challenges to liberal legalism.

Participation as Reform

To talk about these other types of participation is to talk in two different ways. First, what I call reform-oriented participation is oriented toward using the administrative and/or judicial processes for the purpose of trying to change/reform the law itself. In this sense reform-oriented participation indicates the weakness of the law/politics (implementation versus policy-making) distinction which is at the heart of liberal legalism. Indeed, reform-oriented participation shows the extent to which instrumentalism is an accepted and appropriate view of the legal process. By such participation, courts and other legal institutions are subject to the same "logic of purpose" that governs lawmaking institutions. Purposiveness

> calls for inquiry into (1) substantive outcome and (2) what is factually needed for effective discharge of institutional responsibilities. In other words, purposive law is result oriented, thus departing sharply from the classic image of justice blind to consequence. . . . The concern is with legislative rather than adjudicative facts, with factual patterns and with the systematic effect of alternative policies, rather than with particular outcomes. [Nonet and Selznick 1978, p. 84]

The second way of talking about reform-oriented participation focuses on litigation or administrative action as a way of changing social relationships. It is here that the legal process may become an arena for struggle in which the disadvantaged mobilize legal norms as a political tool.[11]

While both uses of reform-oriented participation are undoubtedly always a part of liberal legalism, it has only been since the late 1950s that groups interested in social reform have consistently and regularly turned their energies to the processes of administration and adjudication (see, for example, Kluger 1976). Such interest was, to some extent, stimulated by tendencies toward judicial activism, yet it also reinforced them

---

[11] While there seems little doubt that reform-oriented participation has extended the range of issues on which citizens or citizen groups have a right to participate, there is little evidence about the quality or frequency of reform-oriented participation (Williams 1972). Formal rights are no guarantee of actual participation. Some data, however, document reform-oriented participation in the area of environmental protection.

In the first five-and-a-half years of its existence, the Michigan Environmental Protection Act was the subject of 117 lawsuits or administrative hearings (Haynes 1976); interestingly, ad hoc rather than established environmental groups were most active (DiMento 1977; Sax and DiMento 1974). Citizen suits brought under the National Environmental Protection Act are much more prevalent than their state counterparts. In the first three years following its enactment, approximately 250 NEPA suits were filed in federal courts (Crampton and Boyer 1972). The number of citizen suits or the amount of public intervention in the administrative processes cannot be compared meaningfully with data on the various forms of remedy-seeking. Given the nature of such reform-oriented participation, one would expect it to be more limited, but perhaps no less significant in its impact.

(Glazer 1975). The receptivity of the courts invited social reform litigation which, in turn, encouraged innovativeness in judicial decision-making. It was to some extent encouraged by legislative action creating new rights or providing new responsibilities for administrative agencies (Rodgers and Bullock 1972; Dienes 1970). Yet, activity for social reform, in and through courts and administrative agencies, was also prompted by the failure of legislatures to extend such rights or to respond adequately to impulses for social change (Scheingold 1974).

At the same time, over the last three decades a strikingly greater number of lawyers and lawyers' organizations have been interested in using courts as administrative agencies to change law and to reform society. Beginning about 1970, the public-interest law movement became an important ally of and tool for social reform groups (see James 1973; Weisbrod 1978; Handler et al. 1978). Finally, the last three decades have witnessed a proliferation of client groups turning to lawyers and to courts to carry out their political activities.

The key impetus in this recent upsurge of reform-oriented participation was, of course, the movement for black civil rights. Its "success" in winning concessions and establishing new rights interested others, such as environmentalists, women, consumers, who had a broad range of concerns. Participation in and through courts and administrative agencies, aimed at securing social reform through law reform, grew by imitation. Often the same leaders and lawyers moved from one issue to another, bringing enthusiasm and knowledge of techniques to newly emerging groups or movements (Handler 1979).

The first element that distinguishes participation as a vehicle for reform from remedy-seeking behavior is its group base. Reform-oriented groups generally represent collections of individuals united by interests not involving production or work-related activities, and typically focus on ideological rather than material concerns (Jaffe 1968). Furthermore, while in remedy-seeking behavior participants usually seek to mobilize the law in order to protect or vindicate their own rights with little concern for the effect or impact on others, reform participation is designed to produce legal decisions as statements of policy affecting the conditions of whole classes or groups of people (Scheingold 1974).

The distinction between remedy-seeking and reform-oriented participation is, in practice, rarely clear. What looks like remedy-seeking may be the first move in a social-reform strategy; an activist court or judge may use a narrow legal action to make a decision with consequences well beyond those understood or intended by the original participants. The legal action may begin as remedial but may be "taken over" by participants with reform goals (Sorauf 1976; Vose 1972; Epstein 1985). Yet, the extent and scope of reform-oriented participation is itself significant in indicating the range of responsiveness of legal institutions and the dilemmas of liberal legalism.

Reform-oriented participation is most often directed against the policies of the state. It aims to shape and reshape those policies by subjecting them to the scrutiny of new ideas and to the discipline of new interpretations of old values. Yet, at the same time, reform-oriented participation allows expansion of the competence and capacity of courts and administrative agencies, as well as a broadening legal impact. By letting groups, or advocates for groups, register claims on behalf of the public or of particular classes of interested citizens, the legal system expands its intelligence-gathering abilities and the range of individuals formally subject to its decisions. Again, the duality of participation and institutional capacity must be noted. Reform-oriented participation subjects the legal system to increased pressure to produce substantive justice, to enter the domain of policy implementation, and to find innovative ways to respond to modern mass injuries (Hazard 1976; Handler 1976).

From Remedy to Reform   Such participation frequently begins in the remedial mode. Particular individuals suffer real injuries, which are similar to those suffered by others by virtue of common identification or membership in a social group (Kluger 1976). However, because the legal system treats injuries on a case-by-case basis, it is difficult to establish patterns and connections between injuries and group membership. The first wave of the modern era's reform-oriented participation sought, as an overriding goal, to force legal institutions to recognize and come to terms with such patterns, acknowledging widely dispersed inequalities associated with racial differences.

The model for such participation is provided by the activities of the NAACP Legal Defense Fund. This organization, originally established as an adjunct to the NAACP, began in the 1930s to use litigation as an affirmative tool in the quest for black civil rights. Prior to that time, the NAACP had engaged in constitutional litigation on an ad hoc basis (Greenberg 1974). Until relatively recently, the Legal Defense Fund received support from the parent organization and other private sources. From its beginnings it maintained a modest professional staff and a network of cooperating attorneys. Its major focus has been both the defense of individuals engaged in civil rights activities and the establishment of litigation strategy for marshaling major challenges to existing laws. Furthermore, its efforts and strategy have been consistently and singularly given over to the goal of equality through law.

Reform-oriented participation often proceeds through the litigation of "test cases," to which the constitutional principle rather than the individual grievance is crucial (Casper 1972). In order to pursue a test-case approach, a group must choose carefully the cases it promotes. The right configuration of facts must be found to provide the maximum opportunity for a favorable, precedent-setting decision; "priorities are established that emphasize taking cases with the broadest potential impact" (Rabin 1976, p. 223). In this sense, the litigating group is "proactive" in its strategy, seeking to use the lawsuit as a vehicle for the recognition of new rights and the reshaping of public policy.

> The process of constitutional litigation has become intensely political. Most of the cases come not as individual suits for remedy but as well-organized pursuits of favorable constitutional rulings. . . . And in varying degrees most of the actors and institutions in the judicial process recognized them as cases that not only raised important constitutional questions but that also were bound to affect bitterly opposed issues of public policy. [Sorauf 1976, pp. 342–45]

The use of test cases focuses reform-oriented participation on the courts. While judicial rulings are assumed to provide both direction and leverage for political and social change, the object of such participation is essentially negative. Reform is achieved when past practices of discrimination, for example, are halted. In addition, test-case reform activity has usually been carried out within the context of recognized legal principles rather than trying to forge new ones. It is used by groups identified with discrete and identifiable classes of individuals who experience relatively clear-cut injuries and grievances (see Olson 1984).

Mass Injury, Diffuse Interests, and the Premises of Pluralism   Much contemporary reform-oriented participation begins not as part of the ongoing activity of identifiable groups; it is initiated instead in response to broad and intangible injuries and is carried on in the name of a diffuse class of individuals without perceived common identity (Trubek 1978a). Such participation has, over time, become increasingly focused on administrative processes (Stewart 1975). Court decisions and litigation have been used as vehicles to open up that process to participation by groups and interests previously unable to secure access. Court decisions and the threat of litigation provide the leverage to induce administrative agencies to take seriously the interests of consumers, environmentalists, and others seeking to identify themselves with the public interest (Sax 1971). The courts require that administrative agencies allow such groups to take part in agency policy, rule-making, and adjudication. One form of participation in the legal process, litigation, is used to open up new avenues of participation in other parts of the legal process (Jaffe 1968). Litigation and participation before administrative agencies are thus reciprocal and interactive strategies of reform (Handler 1979). When agencies refuse to recognize the interests of diffuse groups, courts will often require them to do so.

Two conditions encourage the growth of reform-oriented participation aimed at the administrative process. First, the complexity and interdependence characteristic of advanced industrialism ensure that when injuries occur they will be felt by large segments of the society. Threats to the quality of the environment on a mass scale affect everyone but no single individual standing alone; "more and more frequently the complexity of modern societies generates situations in which a single human action can be beneficial or prejudicial to large numbers of people, thus making entirely inadequate the traditional scheme of litigation as merely a two-party affair" (Cappelletti 1978b, p. 519).

Second, administration and regulation grow as responses to modern imperfections in the economic market, which prevent private remedies from adequately compensating for mass injuries. Much has been written about the reasons for the growth of public regulation and its function (see, for example, Kolko 1963; Bernstein 1953), and it is now commonplace to acknowledge the immense power and scope of regulatory processes. Critics, arguing that regulation has failed to protect the public from mass injuries or to respond adequately to those that occur (Trubek 1978a; Lowi 1979), suggest that agencies typically succumb to the pressures of the regulated; because of their dependence for information and expertise on those whom they regulate, they are relatively easily captured and become, in effect, defenders.

The twin phenomena of mass injury and the extension of the administrative state emphasize the importance of groups as participatory units. Agencies respond to organization. Yet, since the injuries which may give rise to reform-oriented participation are widely shared, it is difficult for diffuse interests to act collectively and effectively.

> A diffuse group . . . refers to a large number of individuals who share a common interest in a specific public policy. If government effectively controls the prices charged by an industry . . . any benefits accruing to consumers of the industry's product will be enjoyed by all those who purchase its goods or services. So these consumers are a "group" in this very general sense. But this group is diffuse because it is not an organized entity. . . . [T]hey lack a mechanism by which they can pool their resources to provide sustained advocacy for such policies. [Trubek 1978b, p. 460]

The dilemmas and difficulties of organizing diffuse interests into effective participant groups provide a continuing theme in the literature on reform-oriented participation (Stewart 1975; Handler 1979; Rhode 1982). The costs of organizing such interests are immense. They are neither geographically nor socially contiguous, nor does the shared interest occupy a substantial part of their lives (Trubek 1978b). Moreover, since the products of any participation on behalf of diffuse interests are quite clearly "public goods" (Olson 1971), individuals have no incentive to either register a claim or support a group acting on their behalf (Cappelletti 1978a).

Despite these difficulties the participation of diffuse interests has increased. This has been helped by a loosening of rules of standing and other access-regulating devices. This loosening indicates a willingness of the legal order to respond to claims in behalf of social as well as individual rights. It also acknowledges the imperfections, imbalances, or biases in the operation of interest representation in the administrative process.

In the traditional model of autonomous, expert, public-interested administrative decision-making (Stewart 1975), agencies were portrayed as having limited amounts of discretion, which they were to use in accordance with their authorizing legislation. They were believed to be dealing with complex technical questions of policy implementation rather than policy choice, and their decisions were assumed to be justifiable in terms of the need to protect the public interest. Agencies were thus understood to be subject to the governance of legislatures and the supervision of courts (Stewart 1975; Lazarus 1974). The traditional model breaks down under the weight of evidence that agencies use their discretion for the benefit of the groups and interests they are intended to regulate. The abuse of discretion and the capture of administrative agencies by private groups is a function of the relative weakness of those agencies vis-à-vis the interests with which they must deal. "Limited agency resources imply that agencies must depend on outside sources of information, policy development and political support. This outside input comes primarily from organized interests, such as regulated firms, that have a substantial stake in the substance of agency policy and the resources to provide such input" (Stewart 1975, pp. 1685–86). Rules limiting agency discretion do little to address this tendency, and it, in turn, seems to threaten the claims of administrative agencies to legitimacy (J. Freedman 1978).

Those claims are based in large part on the theory of normative pluralism (Trubek 1978b), which has gained increasing acceptance. According to this theory, all affected interests can and should participate in the decision-making of administrative agencies and, through their participation, influence the implementation of legal rules (Dahl 1956).

> Normative pluralists contend that if citizens are free to organize groups to represent their collective interests, if all such groups are able to participate in policy debates, and if decision-makers are constrained to take into account the interests of various groups in their own deliberations, the political system will give equal weight to each individual's interest, and the views of the majority of citizens, as expressed by their organized representatives, will ultimately prevail. [Trubek 1978b, p. 462]

The absence of equal access and equal consideration of interests is a bias in pluralism generated from flaws in the dynamics of group development and representation (Connolly 1969; Kariel 1961)—a bias those concerned with access to justice and participation seek to correct (Bonfield 1969; Lazarus and Onek 1971).

Arguments in favor of expanding opportunities for reform-oriented participation diagnose the bias of pluralism and the failures of regulation to operate to protect the public interest as a problem of access, thus reinforcing the tendency of liberal legalism to portray law as self-correcting as well as autonomous. Accepting the premise of normative pluralism that access breeds influence, they seek to correct the imperfections of the pluralist model by recognizing new interests and devising forms of representation to articulate them. The critique of normative pluralism, which is a foundation for much of the push for reform-oriented participation, accepts that pluralism is or can be a reasonably accurate description of the processes through which legal rules are implemented and that responsive, participatory administrative processes are a useful vehicle for social reform.

Acceptance of the premises of pluralism can be seen in three interrelated doctrinal developments responsive to and reflective of the growth of reform-oriented participation (Stewart 1975, p. 1716). The first is the expansion of due process rights and a recognition of new interests in liberty and property, seen in several Supreme Court cases (*Goldberg v. Kelly* 1970; *Bell* v. *Burson* 1971, and *Goss* v. *Lopez* 1975) in which the Court required administrative agencies or public schools to provide notice and hearing before the termination of benefits or the deprivation of rights. These cases have developed new concepts of property and liberty, which accord rights of participation in agency proceedings to welfare recipients, occupants of public housing, and students (O'Neil 1970). While the expansion of due process seems more clearly to provide new opportunities for remedy-seeking, the abandonment of traditional concepts of liberty and property it has brought is rooted "in the decline of legal formalism based on a close-knit structure of discrete rights and counterpart official duties, and in the struggle to adapt legal controls to expanded government authority" (Stewart 1975, p. 722).

The second development is the growth in the types of interests entitled to judicial review of administrative agency decisions. This doctrinal development in the law of standing has opened up access to courts and provided greater openness in the administrative process. Most of the "new standing" allows diffuse interests and their representatives the right to challenge decisions when agencies have failed to allow them to participate in formal proceedings or when agencies fail to pay serious attention to their expression of interest (*University of Pennsylvania Law Review* 1972; Albert 1974; Trubek 1978b; Homburger 1973). Rights of participation have been accorded to groups seeking to represent themselves and their members as well as to groups seeking to vindicate the public interest. As a result, "the number of persons with a legally protected stake in any agency decision has multiplied, and standing has been liberally granted to allow judicial enforcement of the requirement that agencies consider all such effected interests" (Stewart 1975, p. 1723).

Finally, there has been expansion of opportunities to intervene in proceedings initiated by others and to require agencies to initiate and employ formal proceedings in arriving at their decisions (D. Shapiro 1968; Crampton 1972; Gellhorn 1972). Rights to intervene have become coextensive with standing rights (see *Office of Communication of the United Church of Christ* v. *F.C.C.* 1966). The courts have also recognized the rights of parties affected by agency decisions to demand that those decisions be made in and through formal proceedings, in which that party and others with an interest in the decision may participate (see *Environmental Defense Fund, Inc.* v. *Ruckelshaus* 1971).

Representation and Reform-Oriented Participation   Doctrinal developments embody a judicial recognition of the demise of the traditional model of autonomy in the enforcement and implementation of law and a formal recognition of the need for expanded representation of interests. Reform-oriented participation, however, continues to face the dilemma of who is to represent diffuse interests and how they are to be represented (Crampton 1974; Rhode 1982). The question remains of who is participating when groups seek to use the legal system for purposes of social reform. Who is, in fact, gaining access to justice when groups sponsor or act for individuals (see Wilson 1973; Gronemeier 1974; Sabatier 1975)?

A study of church–state litigation suggests that group sponsorship often comes at the price of group takeover (Sorauf 1976). Individuals are rarely able to afford participation beyond, or indeed up to, trial in such cases. In order to press their claims on appeal—or, in some cases, to persist to the trial phase—they need the expertise and assistance of groups with a continuing interest in church–state issues. Such groups are not, however, willing or able to provide aid to all who desire it. As a result, they must decide which clients and cases they will support. Typically, that decision and the involvement of particular groups and their attorneys tend to refine and redefine cases they accept. Issues that may have been of direct interest to the individual initiating the case may be dropped; new dimensions of the claim, which may or may not be important to the main party, are developed. Group sponsorship may be necessary in order to afford individuals realistic and reasonable chances of winning particular kinds of cases, but the case that is won often bears little resemblance to the issue that originally motivated it (Felstiner, Abel, and Sarat 1981; Mather and Yngvesson 1980–81). Group participation does not necessarily make individual participation more meaningful.

> Most individual members of the class of interests assertedly represented will probably be completely unaware of the participation on their behalf. Alternatively, such individuals may see no tangible connection between their interests and the litigation. . . . Whatever vicarious participation they may enjoy is a far remove from the model of Athenian democracy which underlies much of the rhetoric of public interest representation. [Stewart 1975, p. 1767]

The dilemmas of representation have led courts to impose rather strict requirements of prior notice on class actions (see *Eisen v. Carlisle and Jacquelin* 1974). Groups seeking to participate on behalf of or for others have been required to demonstrate some direct and concrete stake in the subject of their participation (*Sierra Club v. Morton* 1972). How much private advocacy has been hindered or limited by such restrictions is unknown. Nevertheless, class actions and public interest litigation remain important vehicles through which reform-oriented participation may be carried out (Homburger 1973; Cappelletti 1978b; Aaronson 1975).

Another, comparable concern with the question of who is being represented and who is participating arises in discussions of public-interest lawyers (Cahn and Cahn 1970; Bell 1975; Riley 1970; Burke 1979). Supported largely by private foundations, these lawyers direct their activities to law reform (Handler 1976). The practice of public-interest law has many variants, ranging from individual pro bono work to full-time practice in group law offices (Handler 1978).

While concerns of public-interest law have been as broad as its organizational forms, several themes are common to all its expressions. First, the practice of public-interest law is largely concerned with ensuring access to governmental decisions for interests previously unrepresented (Rabin 1976; see also Leone 1972). Public-interest lawyers seek to bring into the judicial and administrative processes the interests of environmentalists, consumers, and other diffuse interests. In addition, "underlying the currency of 'public interest law' is a newly emergent and valid understanding of the need to protect all members of society and in their relatively passive capacity as citizens who consume not only material goods and services but also government policies and programs" (Cahn and Cahn 1970, p. 1006). Second, in contrast to the activities of the Legal Defense Fund and other "traditional" law reform groups, public-interest lawyers have focused on the procedural adequacy and substantive justice of administrative procedures rather than on the interpretation and application of recognized constitutional principles through litigation. They have sought "effective access in a broad range of fora rather than pursuing implementation of identifiable constitutional values" (Rabin 1976, p. 241). Third, public-interest lawyers have been proactive in identifying necessary reforms and then finding clients to represent in an action to effect such reform (Cahn and Cahn 1970). Some public-interest law firms have been closely tied to particular reform groups, which have helped to establish their agendas, but more typically they have been independent and have ranged over a wide spectrum of issues. Taking it upon themselves to ensure the responsiveness of legal processes, they employ advocacy skills for avowedly political purposes.

Because of that independence and their proactive orientation toward reform, public-interest lawyers have threatened the traditional model of client service and client control, as well as traditional conceptions of the relation of law and politics (Mazor 1968).

> The public-interest lawyer is a man with commitments which precede and define the client; and the nature of his client, his activities and his source of funds often allows him the freedom to assert personal values in his professional work. . . . In terms of the traditional theory of legal representation the involvements of a lawyer's personal values in a particular cause threaten the paramount concern of the lawyer–client relationship, the idea of total devotion to the client's interests as the client sees them. [*Yale Law Journal* 1970, pp. 1120–22]

Many public-interest lawyers see themselves as representing constituencies rather than clients, even when that stance requires some sacrifice of the advantages of the main client (Casper 1972); indeed, some public-interest lawyers are "clientless lawyers."

Even when there is a relatively discrete and identifiable client, the public-interest lawyer is likely to be in a position of control and authority greater than that permitted under the theory of "lawyer as agent" (Burke 1979). Choices of strategy and goals may provide as much conflict between client and lawyer in social reform activities as they do in remedy-seeking (Bell 1975). Clients are generally in a weak position to assert their interests against public-interest lawyers. Often, the client interest begins only after the lawyer has defined the problem. The client, who is frequently drawn from the socially disadvantaged or legally unsophisticated (Harrison and Jaffe 1972), can easily be replaced. Since the lawyer's source of support comes from foundations, the client is also deprived of monetary controls over the lawyer's behavior (Brill 1973). Nevertheless, since it is as often the case that clients and public-interest lawyers share ideological commitments and motivations, they avoid the tension between the desire for specific and individual remedies and the drive to achieve precedent-setting decisions (Burke 1979, p. 11).

Absent the usual mechanisms for or guarantee of accountability, the issue becomes the compatibility of public-interest law and the ideals of participation and access it advocates (Cahn and Cahn 1970). Critics are suspicious of upper-middle-class professionals defining and protecting the public interest. While there is some evidence that the new populism represented by public-interest law extends participation and makes participation and access to justice more meaningful and real (Lazarus 1974), the pattern is highly varied. Some see public-interest lawyers as taking the heart out of reform-oriented participation and creating dependency on a new class (Hunt 1979). Others believe that public-interest law adds force to reform-oriented participation (Cappelletti 1978b; Trubek 1978b; McLachlan 1971). It is, however, hard to deny that questions of representation remain unanswered. Public-interest makes participation meaningful by transforming the locus from individuals to groups. It seeks to redefine legal representation to encompass political advocacy and to legitimize that redefinition in terms of the unique skills and perspectives of legal professionals in a liberal legal order (Lazarus and Onek 1971). The price of democratizing the legal process and opening access to diffuse interests is greater power for the legal profession and, perhaps, greater passivity for individual citizens as well as renewed strength for the "myth of rights" (Scheingold 1974).

The Effectiveness of Participation as a Vehicle for Reform   The first, and perhaps most important, effect of reform-oriented participation is to diminish the distinction between law and politics; such participation represents, reflects, or produces a movement away from autonomy in the implementation and administration of legal norms. The activities of social-reform groups and public-interest lawyers are themselves political, whether they are addressed to legislatures, courts, or administrative agencies. The Supreme Court has explicitly accepted the legitimacy of the politicization of litigation and administrative processes. "In the context of NAACP objectives, litigation is not a technique for resolving private differences: it is a means for achieving the lawful objectives of equality of treatment by all government . . . for members of the Negro community in this country. It is thus a form of political expression" (*NAACP* v. *Button* 1963). The recognition of the political nature of group-sponsored litigation and other types of reform-oriented participation alters the basis on which legal institutions justify their actions. The burdens of justification become ever more difficult to discharge and the conflict engendered by legal decisions becomes ever more intense (Nonet and Selznick 1978).

The object of reform-oriented participation is, in the first instance, to secure rights of participation and to formalize the procedures through which administrative decisions are made. When this process is successful, formality replaces informality; rules replace discretion. Formality, however, brings added costs, both to participant groups and to law-enforcement agencies (Manning 1977). Formal procedures are expensive and time-consuming. Requiring skills and expertise in advocacy and legal rules, they are ill-suited to flexible fact-finding and problem-solving. Rather, they narrow and limit the scope of inquiry and view social problems in the context of ritualized procedures. Formality breeds passivity in those charged with making decisions and focuses decision-making on particular cases. "The complex scientific, technological, social and economic issues presented in so much of current administration are often ill-suited for resolution by adjudicatory procedures that produce gargantuan records whose size varies inversely with [their] usefulness" (Stewart 1975, p. 1773; see also Boyer 1972; Jowell 1969). Formality, however, also counters imbalances in power and puts greater accountability on decision-makers (Abel 1982). To this extent, reform-oriented participation seeks to justify the exercise of power in accordance with preexisting legal norms.

Perhaps most important, new rights in administrative processes and new opportunities for judicial review of decisions provide citizen groups with an important resource in their efforts to obtain recognition of their interests in informal agency procedures. Potential lawsuits that will delay and complicate administrative action provide these groups with a kind of influence not provided by their expertise or organizational ability (Stewart 1975, p. 1771). Furthermore, regular participation may allow such groups to derive the bargaining advantages that normally accrue to repeat players (Galanter 1974). As with remedy-seeking, the real importance of access for reform-oriented citizen groups is not revealed by actual rates of participation. The accessibility of judicial processes and the threat of involving them transform the structure of pluralist relationships within which agencies operate—another example of the often neglected relationship between legal rights and political power (Trubek 1974).

Of all the questions about reform-oriented participation, the most obvious concerns its effectiveness in securing changes in legal rules and translating those changes into meaningful reform. In one view, the attempt to achieve social reform in and through participation in the legal system is seldom successful and often dysfunctional, participation being a tribute to the strength of "the myth of rights"—the ideology of liberal legalism that stresses the accessibility of law, its responsiveness, and the efficacy of legal rules as resources for social change. Legal rules are but one available tool, whose real significance depends on the political power of those seeking reform.

> [D]irect deployment of legal rights in the implementation of public policy will not work very well given any significant opposition. . . . Using courts to make things happen in the real world ultimately pits the victorious litigant with a court order against those who are inclined to resist. . . . [T]he impact is restricted by post-judgment power relations. [Scheingold 1974, pp. 13, 117; see also Dolbeare and Hammond 1971; Rodgers and Bullock 1972]

The real significance of reform-oriented participation in the legal system may be that it helps to activate and stimulate political action. The recognition of rights legitimizes group grievances; it may give a sense of shared identity to otherwise amorphous groups (Piven and Cloward 1972). Reform-oriented participation alters the configuration of forces concerned with and able to exert influence on reform issues (Trubek 1974). Whether it transforms that configuration enough to secure genuine reform, however, ultimately depends on a variety of factors beyond the control of legal officials.

Handler (1979) has examined the conditions under which reform-oriented participation would be effective in the areas of environmental litigation, consumer and civil rights, and social welfare. He identified five factors: characteristics of the participating groups, the relationship of costs and expected benefits, the nature of the implementation process required to enforce legal rights, the nature of the remedies available, and the structure of the law-reform community. His case studies suggest that the key to effective reform-oriented participation is found in the interaction of group characteristics and the nature of the implementation process. Participation fails to achieve meaningful reform when the implementation of new legal rights is decentralized and lengthy and when reform groups lack the "staying power" to monitor implementation and keep pressure on the implementers (Handler 1979, chap. 6). The lack of staying power is, in turn, a function of the free-rider problem, the financial and resource constraints on reform groups, and their lack of significant political resources.

Law-reform efforts fail because of the difficulty of translating rights or policies into new patterns of behavior by public officials and private opponents. While the call for "public advocacy" (Trubek 1978b; Murphy and Hoffman 1976) may alleviate some of the resource constraints that limit reform, there is no evidence that even publicly supported advocates are able to translate rights into social reform. In the final analysis, however, reform-oriented participation contributes to changing legal processes by forcing legal officials to attend to interests they would otherwise ignore and by opening up new avenues and providing encouragement to remedy-seeking by individuals who might otherwise lack recourse.

This democratization of the legal process is not without its enemies, who believe that we have gone too far in the name of equality and responsiveness (see Hunt 1979). The 1980s have brought a broad-scale attack on those who demanded or facilitated reform-oriented participation. This attack came at a time when it appeared that that type of participation was becoming institutionalized and widely accepted (see Lewis 1981). Although the attack's final outcome is by no means certain, much can be learned about access to justice and reform-oriented participation by attending to it.

Liberal legalism is caught in an unresolvable tension (Shklar 1964). It encourages the belief in law as a vehicle for social change, and in so doing strengthens its claims to legitimacy; it tolerates and supports modes of participation that use legal means in innovative ways; it advertises the significance of rights and remedies. Yet, when participation promises to become generally effective—to work out the logic of democratization in liberal societies—support is withdrawn. At the point when the precarious balance of legitimation benefits and instrumental costs tilts too heavily toward the latter, the state itself is enlisted in the effort to withdraw or limit the forms and frequency of reform-oriented participation.

The sociological study of that form of participation has barely begun. Few empirical studies of it exist. For the most part, work in this area has been doctrinal or normative, largely ignoring motivations, strategies, and impacts. Moreover, the interaction of remedy-seeking and reform-oriented participation, on the one hand, and that participation and the structure of bargaining inside and outside legal processes, on the other, require greater attention than either has received. Ultimately, however, work in this sector must take seriously the politics of participation and must contribute to an understanding of the dynamics of that participation and the liberal legal order in which it occurs.

CONCLUSION

How much is known about citizen participation in the legal system? Does it constitute a coherent subject or simply a loosely bounded area of concern? It is important to recognize that the empirical study of access to justice and citizen participation is a relatively new enterprise. Yet there is little doubt that over the past twenty years empirical work in the sociology of law has made a substantial contribution to our knowledge about and understanding of citizen participation in the legal system. Nevertheless, there are important areas of incompleteness and bias which need to be addressed.

The most important area of incompleteness is seen in the study of what I have called reform-oriented participation. In comparison to work that focuses on remedy-seeking, the study of reform-oriented participation seems sorely lacking. We know relatively little about its causes, about the conditions under which it emerges, about its patterns or its impact. There has been much speculation about the transforming impact of group participation, but little is actually known about the relationship of participation and the process of social reform through legal institutions. The relationship of reform-oriented participation in the administrative process and similar participation in courts and legislatures needs to be charted. In the end, however, it is the relative play of private power that determines the efficacy of political or legal reform, and therefore the impact of private power on reform-oriented participation must be described and analyzed.

These gaps in knowledge are explicable when one considers the very great difficulty of identifying and charting reform-oriented participation. But more is at issue here than an operational problem. The neglect of reform-oriented participation indicates the extent to which legal sociologists themselves are at home with, and accept, the law/politics distinction, the extent to which legal sociologists consign reform-oriented participation to political scientists or others whose normal subject is power or pressure. Legal sociology does not make available theoretical categories or research traditions into which reform-oriented participation can be fit. Thus the great bulk of research on participation focuses on its remedy-seeking, dispute-resolving variety.

The study of remedy-seeking participation fits quite well into a long-standing and well-intended tradition in anthropology. There the focus is on the troubled case and its resolution. Critics (see Kidder 1980–81; Cain and Kulscar 1981–82) contend that the influence of the anthropological tradition supports, in the study of remedy-seeking, strong presumptions of "equality, case discreteness and individualism" (Kidder 1980–81, p. 719). These presumptions, according to this view, go very nicely with the assumptions of liberal legalism and have led researchers to ignore the possibility that remedy-seeking may arise not out of discrete injustices but in response to "systematic inequities, [and] institutionalized asymmetrical developments in society's relationships" (Kidder 1980–81, p. 719).

The treatment of participation as remedy-seeking behavior tends, according to this argument, also to participate in the liberal tradition of individualism. The dominant paradigm looks at participation as a species of individual cost/benefit calculations in which particular persons choose among a variety of means for managing their problems. Social context is treated not as itself an object of dispute or trouble but merely as an influence on individual choices. Participation as remedy-seeking is seldom seen "as an element in shifting relationships between groups, as battlegrounds in strategic maneuvering to reorder power relationships and upset disadvantageous 'balances'" (Kidder 1980–81, p. 700). The problem is not simply that individuals may not be the right units of analysis but that researchers have accepted that the subject of the participation as it is presented according to the requirements of legal institutions, for example, *Smith/tenant* v.

Brown/landlord, is the real subject. This tendency reflects an embrace of the assumptions of liberal legalism itself, an embrace, albeit implicitly, of a pluralist conception of social and political organization and the absence of a theory that might connect particular instances of participation with broader, more systematic social injustices (Cain and Kulscar 1981–82).

The study of participation as remedy-seeking has to this point been almost completely ahistorical (for an exception, see Abel 1979b). As a result, participation is treated not as a conditioned response to particular social conditions but as a species of relatively unconstrained individual choices. Historical work would serve to show how participation changes in response to changing configurations of power and practice within social and legal systems. The absence of historical research means that we do not know how patterns of participation or nonparticipation get established and how they change. It means that we have no baselines against which to determine whether current patterns indicate a growth or decline in the involvement of legal institutions in social life, that we do not know how existing norms concerning citizen participation evolve from previous norms and behaviors and how those norms serve to establish, maintain, or challenge social advantages. Finally, the ahistorical quality of the study of participation hinders our ability to know whether complaints about the lack of access to justice reflect a chronic state necessitated by the internal logic of liberal legalism or whether they respond to conditions developed and maintained by particular groups who benefit from limited citizen participation (Kidder 1980–81, p. 724).

Finally, critics contend that studies of participation in general, and remedy-seeking participation in particular, treat inequalities in opportunity, willingness, and ability to participate as noncumulative and unidimensional (Cain and Kulscar 1981–82). Differences in wealth, knowledge, culture, and ideology, each of which may be correlated with differences in participation, are rarely correlated with each other. Thus, as Cain and Kulscar argue, research on participation fits in

> directly . . . [with] pluralist conflict theory, according to which participants may differ in power or in strategic skills . . . but only along a single dimension. . . . The differences in power are capable of being equalized: more money, more knowledge, more organization, even more experience, may be given to the weaker party, and then the difference would disappear. [Cain and Kulscar 1981–82, p. 380]

The assumption that differences are noncumulative and can be remedied is itself one way in which studies of participation support liberal legal theory even as they illuminate its tensions and contradictions.

But the state of research on citizen participation is not all incompleteness and bias. That research reminds us that participation, even in a flawed and imperfect legal order, serves to advance important values. As described in an argument for expanding opportunities for litigation, these values are several.

> *Dignity values* reflect concern for the humiliation or loss of self-respect which a person might suffer if deprived of an opportunity to litigate. *Participation values*

reflect an appreciation of litigation as one of the modes in which persons exert influence, or have their wills "counted" in societal decisions they care about. *Deterrence values* recognize the instrumentality of litigation as a mechanism for influencing or constraining individual behavior in ways thought socially desirable. *Effectuation values* see litigation as an important means through which persons are enabled to get, or are given assurance of having, whatever we are pleased to regard as rightfully theirs. [Michelman 1973, pp. 1172–73]

These values, the argument continues, can and should be used to recognize the importance of litigation and other forms of participation even where its outcomes and consequences for the legal system are uncertain.

Recognition of the inherently contradictory qualities of citizen participation in liberal legal orders provides a beginning point for future inquiry. That inquiry should treat citizen participation as an important indicator of the responsiveness, or at least the openness, of legal processes. As participation varies, it shapes the way those processes are perceived and the way they in fact function. Yet, that variation is itself manipulable by the legal order. Thus, the subject of access to justice and citizen participation brings together micro-perspectives and macro-perspectives in the sociology of law. With few exceptions (see, for example, Nonet and Selznick 1978), research and analysis have avoided the linkage issues raised by citizen participation. It is now appropriate to attend to them, so that an assessment of access to justice and participation can become an assessment of the nature and health of the legal order itself.

Cases Cited

Association of Data Processing Service Organizations Inc. v. Camp, 397 U.S. 150 (1970).
Bell v. Burson, 402 U.S. 535 (1971).
Boddie v. Connecticut, 401 U.S. 371 (1971).
Calvert Cliffs Coordinating Committee v. A.E.C., 449 F.2d 1109 (1971).
Duke Power v. Carolina Environmental Study Group, 438 U.S. 59 (1978).
Eisen v. Carlisle and Jacquelin, 417 U.S. 156 (1974).
Environmental Defense Fund, Inc. v. Ruckelshaus, 439 F.2d 584 (1971).
Flast v. Cohen, 392 U.S. 83 (1968).
Goldberg v. Kelly, 397 U.S. 254 (1970).
Goss v. Lopez, 419 U.S. 565 (1975).
Linda R. S. v. Richard D., 410 U.S. 614 (1973).
Mullane v. Central Hanover Bank & Trust Company, 339 U.S. 306 (1950).
NAACP v. Button, 371 U.S. 415, 429 (1963).
Office of Communication of the United Church of Christ v. F.C.C., 359 F.2d 994 (1966).
Sierra Club v. Morton, 405 U.S. 727 (1972).
Simon v. Eastern Kentucky Welfare Rights Organization, 426 U.S. 26 (1976).
U.S. v. Scrap, 412 U.S. 669 (1973).
Warth v. Seldin, 422 U.S. 490 (1975).

Bibliography

Aaronson, Mark
    1975   "Welfare Litigation as a Political Strategy." Paper presented at the meeting of the
             American Political Science Association, San Francisco.
Abel, Richard
    1973   "A Comparative Theory of Dispute Institutions in Society." *Law & Society Review*
             8:217.
    1979a   "Delegalization." In *Alternative Rechtsformen und Alternativen zum Recht*, Erhard
             Blankenburg et al., eds. Opladen: Westdeutscher Verlag.
    1979b   "The Rise of Capitalism and the Transformation of Disputing." *UCLA Law Review*
             27:223.
    1979c   "Socializing the Legal Profession." *Law and Policy Quarterly* 5.
    1982   "The Contradictions of Informal Justice." In *The Politics of Informal Justice*, Richard
             Abel, ed. New York: Academic Press.
Abram, Morris
    1978   "Access to the Judicial Process." *Georgia Law Review* 6:247.
Ackerman, Bruce
    1984   *Reconstructing American Law*. Cambridge, Mass.: Harvard University Press.
Adamany, David, and Dubois, Philip
    1976   "Electing State Judges." *Wisconsin Law Review* 1976:731.
Albert, Lee
    1974   "Standing to Challenge Administrative Action." *Yale Law Journal* 83:425.
Appel, Victor, and Van Atta, Ralph
    1969   "The Attorney–Client Dyad." *Oklahoma Law Review* 22:243.
Arendt, Hannah
    1959   *The Human Condition*. Chicago: University of Chicago Press.
Ashby, John
    1978   "Juror Selection and the Sixth Amendment Right to an Impartial Jury." *Creighton
             Law Review* 11:1137.
Avichai, Yakov
    1978   "Trends in the Incidence of Legal Problems and the Use of Lawyers." *American Bar
             Foundation Research Journal* 1978:289.
Balbus, Isaac
    1974   *The Dialectics of Legal Repression*. New York: Russell Sage Foundation.
Barton, John
    1975   "Behind the Legal Explosion." *Stanford University Law Review* 27:567.
Baumgartner, M. P.
    1984   "Social Control in Suburbia." In *Toward a General Theory of Social Control*, Donald
             Black, ed. New York: Academic Press.
Bay, Christian
    1966   "Civil Disobedience: Prerequisite for Democracy in Mass Democracy." Paper
             presented at the meeting of the American Political Science Association, New
             York.
Bedau, Hugo
    1969   *Civil Disobedience*. New York: Pegasus.
Bell, Derrick
    1975   "Serving Two Masters: Integration Ideals and Client Interests in School Desegrega-
             tion Litigation." *Yale Law Journal* 85:470.

Bercal, Thomas
  1970   "Calls for Police Assistance." *American Behavioral Scientist* 13:681.
Berger, Raoul
  1969   "Standing to Sue in Public Actions." *Yale Law Journal* 78:816.
Berk, Richard, et al.
  1984   "Cops on Call." *Law & Society Review* 18:479.
Bernstein, Marver
  1953   *Regulating Business by Independent Commissions.* Princeton, N.J.: Princeton University Press.
Best, Arthur, and Andreasen, Alan
  1977   "Consumer Responses to Unsatisfactory Purchases." *Law & Society Review* 11:701.
Bickel, Alexander
  1965   "Civil Rights and Civil Disobedience." In *Politics and the Warren Court.* Alexander Bickel, ed. New York: Harper & Row.
Black, Donald
  1971   "The Social Organization of Arrest." *Stanford Law Review* 23:1087.
  1973   "The Mobilization of Law." *Journal of Legal Studies* 2:128.
  1976   *The Behavior of Law.* New York: Academic Press.
Blomberg, Thomas
  1977   "Diversion and Accelerated Social Control." *Journal of Criminal Law and Criminology* 68:224.
Boehm, Virginia
  1968   "Mr. Prejudice, Miss Sympathy and the Authoritarian Personality: An Application of Psychological Measuring Techniques to the Problem of Jury Bias." *Wisconsin Law Review* 1968:734.
Bohannan, Paul
  1967   "The Differing Realms of Law." In *Law and Warfare,* Paul Bohannan, ed. New York: Natural History Press.
Bonfield, Arthur
  1969   "Representation of the Poor in Federal Rulemaking." *Michigan Law Review* 67:511.
Bonn, Robert
  1972   "Arbitration: An Alternative System for Handling Contract Related Disputes." *Administrative Science Quarterly* 17:254.
Boswell, James
  1969   *The Life of Samuel Johnson.* London: Oxford University Press.
Boyer, Barry
  1972   "Alternatives to Administrative Trial Type Hearings for Resolving Complex Scientific, Economic and Social Issues." *Michigan Law Review* 71:111.
Braybrooke, David
  1975   "The Meaning of Participation and of Demands for It." In *Participation in Politics,* J. Roland Pennock and John Chapman, eds. New York: Lieber-Atherton.
Brill, Harry
  1973   "The Uses and Abuses of Legal Assistance." *Public Interest* 31:38.
Buckle, Leonard, and Thomas-Buckle, Suzann R.
  1981   "Self Help Justice in Three Urban Neighborhoods." Paper presented at the annual meeting of the Law and Society Association, Amherst, Mass.
  1982   "Varieties of Informal Dispute Processing in American Neighborhoods." Unpublished manuscript.
Bumiller, Kristin
  1984   "Anti-Discrimination Law and the Enslavement of the Victim." Unpublished manuscript.

Bureau of Social Science Research
    1967   *Report of a Pilot Study in the District of Columbia on Victimization and Attitudes Toward Law Enforcement.* Washington, D.C.: U. S. Government Printing Office.

Burke, Susan
    1979   "Client Participation: Another Look at Who's in Charge." Paper presented at the meeting of the Law and Society Association, San Francisco.

Cahn, Edgar, and Cahn, Jean
    1964   "The War on Poverty." *Yale Law Journal* 73:1317.
    1970   "Power to the People or the Profession." *Yale Law Journal* 79:1005.

Cain, Maureen
    1979   "The General Practice Lawyer and the Client." Paper presented at the Conference of Lawyers and the Sociology of the Professions, Oxford, England.

Cain, Maureen, and Kulscar, Kalman
    1981–82 "Thinking Disputes." *Law & Society Review* 16:375.

Cappelletti, Mauro
    1978a   "Governmental and Private Advocates for the Public Interest in Civil Litigation." In *Access to Justice,* vol. 2, Mauro Cappelletti and Bryant Garth, eds. Amsterdam: Sijthoff & Noordhoff.

    1978b   "Vindicating the Public Interest Through the Courts." In *Access to Justice,* vol. 3, Mauro Cappelletti and Bryant Garth, eds. Amsterdam: Sijthoff & Noordhoff.

Cappelletti, Mauro, et al.
    1975   *Toward Equal Justice.* Dobbs Ferry, N.Y.: Oceana.

Cappelletti, Mauro, and Garth, Bryant
    1978   "Access to Justice: The Newest Wave in the Worldwide Movement to Make Rights Effective." *Buffalo Law Review* 27:181.

Cappelletti, Mauro, and Gordley, James
    1972   "Legal Aid: Modern Themes and Variations." *Stanford Law Review* 24:347.

Carlin, Jerome, et al.
    1967   *Civil Justice and the Poor.* New York: Russell Sage Foundation.

Carlin, Jerome, and Howard, Jan
    1965   "Legal Representation and Class Justice." *UCLA Law Review* 12:381.

Casey, Gregory
    1974   "The Supreme Court and Myth." *Law & Society Review* 8:385.

Casper, Jonathan
    1972   *Lawyers Before the Warren Court.* Urbana: University of Illinois Press.
    1978   "Having Their Day in Court." *Law & Society Review* 12:237.

Cavanagh, Ralph
    1979   "Zones of Interest and Injuries in Fact." Unpublished manuscript.

Cavanagh, Ralph, and Sarat, Austin
    1980   "Thinking About Courts: Toward and Beyond a Jurisprudence of Judicial Competence." *Law & Society Review* 14:372.

Church, Thomas
    1978   *Justice Delayed.* Williamsburg, Va.: National Center for State Courts.

Clark, Charles, and Corstvet, Emma
    1938   "The Lawyer and the Public." *Yale Law Journal* 47:1272.

Cobb, Roger, and Elder, Charles
    1972   *Participation in American Politics.* Baltimore: Johns Hopkins University Press.

Cohen, Carl
    1964   "The Essence and Ethics of Civil Disobedience." *Nation* 198:257.
    1971   *Democracy.* New York: Free Press.

Commager, Henry Steele
    1941   *Majority Rule and Minority Rights.* Gloucester, Mass.: Smith.
Connolly, William, ed.
    1969   *The Bias of Pluralism.* New York: Atherton.
Corwin, Edwin
    1948   *Liberty Against Government.* Baton Rouge: Louisiana State University Press.
Council on the Role of Courts
    1984   *The Role of Courts in American Society.* St. Paul, Minn.: West Publishing.
Cover, Robert
    1979   "Dispute Resolution: A Foreword." *Yale Law Journal* 88:910.
Crampton, Roger
    1972   "The Why, Where and How of Broadened Public Participation in the Administrative Process." *Georgia Law Journal* 60:525.
    1974   "Panel I: What Is the Public Interest? Who Represents It? *Administrative Law Review* 26:385.
Crampton, Roger, and Boyer, Barry
    1972   "Citizen Suits in the Environmental Field." *Ecology Law Quarterly* 2:407.
Crowe, Patricia Ward
    1978   "Complainant Reactions to the Massachusetts Commission Against Discrimination." *Law & Society Review* 12:217.
Curran, Barbara
    1977   *The Legal Needs of the Public.* Chicago: American Bar Foundation.
Curran, Barbara, and Clarke, Sherry
    1970   *Use of Lawyers' Services by Low Income Persons.* Chicago: American Bar Foundation.
Currie, David, and Goodman, Frank
    1975   "Judicial Review of Federal Administrative Action." *Columbia Law Review* 75:1.
Dahl, Robert
    1956   *A Preface to Democratic Theory.* Chicago: University of Chicago Press.
    1961   *Who Governs?* New Haven, Conn.: Yale University Press.
Dam, Kenneth
    1975   "Class Actions: Efficiency, Compensation, Deterrence and Conflict of Interest." *Journal of Legal Studies* 4:47.
Danet, Brenda; Hoffman, Kenneth; and Kermish, Nicole
    1981   "Obstacles to the Study of Lawyer–Client Interaction: The Biography of a Failure." *Law & Society Review* 14:905.
Danzig, Richard
    1973   "Toward the Creation of a Complementary Decentralized System of Criminal Justice." *Stanford University Law Review* 26:1.
Davis, Kenneth Culp
    1970   "The Liberalized Law of Standing." *University of Chicago Law Review* 37:450.
Dienes, C. Thomas
    1970   "Judges, Legislators and Social Change." *American Behavioral Scientist* 13:511.
DiMento, Joseph
    1977   "Citizen Environmental Legislation and the Administrative Process: Empirical Findings." *Duke Law Journal* 1977:409.
Dodge, Richard et al.
    1976   "Crime in the United States." In *Sample Surveys of the Victims of Crime,* Wesley Skogan, ed. Cambridge, Mass.: Ballinger.
Dolbeare, Kenneth
    1967   *Trial Courts in Urban Politics.* New York: Wiley.

Dolbeare, Kenneth, and Hammond, Phillip
    1971   The School Prayer Decisions: From Court Policy to Local Practice. Chicago: University
              of Chicago Press.
Doo, Leigh-Wai
    1973   "Dispute Settlement in Chinese-American Communities." American Journal of
              Comparative Law 21:637.
Dworkin, Ronald
    1978   Taking Rights Seriously. Cambridge, Mass.: Harvard University Press.
Easton, David
    1964   Systems Analysis of Political Life. New York: Wiley.
Edelman, Martin
    1984   Democratic Theories and the Constitution. Albany: State University of New York
              Press.
Edelman, Murray
    1971   Politics as Symbolic Action. Chicago: Markham.
Ehrlich, Eugen
    1975   Fundamental Principles of the Sociology of Law. New York: Arno.
Ehrlich, Thomas
    1976   "Legal Pollution." New York Times Sunday Magazine, February 8, 1976, p. 17.
Eisenberg, Melvin
    1976   "Private Ordering Through Negotiation." Harvard Law Review 89:637.
Ely, John
    1980   Democracy and Distrust. Cambridge, Mass.: Harvard University Press.
Engel, David
    1980   "Legal Pluralism in an American Community." American Bar Foundation Research
              Journal 1980:425.
    1983   "Cases, Conflict and Accommodation." American Bar Foundation Research Journal
              1983:803.
    1984   "Oven Bird's Song." Law & Society Review 18:551.
Engel, David, and Steele, Eric
    1979   "Civil Cases and Society." American Bar Foundation Research Journal 1979:295.
Ennis, Philip
    1967   Criminal Victimization in the United States. Washington, D.C.: U.S. Government
              Printing Office.
Epstein, Lee
    1985   Conservatives in Court. Knoxville: University of Tennessee Press.
Erlanger, Howard
    1970   "Jury Research in America." Law & Society Review 3:345.
Feeley, Malcolm
    1979   The Process Is the Punishment. New York: Russell Sage Foundation.
Felstiner, William
    1974   "Influences of Social Organization on Dispute Processing." Law & Society Review
              9:63.
Felstiner, William; Abel, Richard; and Sarat, Austin
    1980–81 "The Emergence and Transformation of Disputes: Naming, Blaming, Claiming."
              Law & Society Review 15:631.
Felstiner, William, and Williams, Lynne
    1979   "Mediation as an Alternative to Criminal Prosecution." Law and Human Behavior
              2:223.
Fiss, Owen
    1982   "Objectivity and Interpretation." Stanford Law Review 34:739.

Fitzpatrick, Peter
  1985   "Law and Societies." Unpublished paper.
Fortas, Abe
  1968   *Concerning Dissent and Civil Disobedience*. New York: Signet Books.
Frank, John
  1976   "Legal Services for Citizens of Moderate Income." In *Law and the American Future*, Murray Schwartz, ed. Englewood Cliffs, N. J.: Prentice-Hall.
Freedman, James
  1978   *Crisis and Legitimacy*. Cambridge: Cambridge University Press.
Freedman, Monroe
  1975   *Lawyers' Ethics in an Adversary System*. Indianapolis: Bobbs-Merrill.
Friedman, Lawrence
  1971   "The Idea of Right as a Social and Legal Concept." *Journal of Social Issues* 27:189.
  1978   "Access to Justice: Social and Historical Context." In *Access to Justice*, vol. 2, Mauro Cappelletti and Bryant Garth, eds. Amsterdam: Sijthoff & Noordhoff.
Fuller, Lon
  1971a   "Human Interaction and the Law." In *The Rule of Law*, R. P. Wolff, ed. New York: Simon & Schuster.
  1971b   *The Morality of Law*. New Haven, Conn.: Yale University Press.
  1978   "The Forms and Limits of Adjudication." In *American Court Systems*, Sheldon Goldman and Austin Sarat, eds. San Francisco: Freeman.
Galanter, Marc
  1974   "Why the 'Haves' Come Out Ahead." *Law & Society Review* 9:95.
  1975   "Afterword: Explaining Litigation." *Law & Society Review* 9:347.
  1976   "The Duty Not to Deliver Legal Services." *University of Miami Law Review* 30:929.
  1979   "Justice in Many Rooms." Dispute Processing Research Program, University of Wisconsin. Working paper.
  1983   "Reading the Landscape of Disputes." *UCLA Law Review* 31:4.
Gellhorn, Ernest
  1972   "Public Participation in Administrative Proceedings." *Yale Law Journal* 81:359.
Glazer, Nathan
  1975   "Towards an Imperial Judiciary." *Public Interest* 41:104.
Gottfredson, Michael, and Hindelang, Michael
  1979   "A Study of the Behavior of Law." *American Sociological Review* 44:3.
Gramsci, Antonio
  1971   *Selections from the Prison Notebooks*. New York: International Publishers.
Greenberg, Jack
  1974   "Litigation for Social Change." *Record of the New York City Bar Association* 29:320.
Griffiths, John
  1977   "Review of the Distribution of Legal Services in the Netherlands." *British Journal of Law and Society* 4:260.
Gronemeier, Dale
  1974   "From Net to Sword: Organizational Representatives Litigating Their Members' Claims." *University of Illinois Law Forum* 1974:663.
Grossman, Joel, et al.
  1982   "Dimensions of Institutional Participation: Who Uses the Courts, and How?" *Journal of Politics* 44:86.
Grossman, Joel, and Sarat, Austin
  1981   "Access to Justice and the Limits of Law." *Law and Policy Quarterly* 3:125.
Gurr, Ted
  1976   *Rogues, Rebels and Reformers*. Beverly Hills, Calif.: Sage.

Handler, Joel
    1976   "Public Interest Law: Problems and Prospects." In *Law and the American Future*, Murray Schwartz, ed. Englewood Cliffs, N. J.: Prentice-Hall.
    1978   "Public Interest Law Firms in the United States." In *Access to Justice*, vol. 3, Mauro Cappelletti and Bryant Garth, eds. Amsterdam: Sijthoff & Noordhoff.
    1979   *Social Movements and the Legal System: A Theory of Law Reform and Social Change*. New York: Academic Press.

Handler, Joel, et al.
    1978   *Lawyers and the Pursuit of Legal Rights*. New York: Academic Press.

Harrington, Christine
    1982   "Delegalization Reform Movements." In *The Politics of Informal Justice*, Richard Abel, ed. New York: Academic Press.
    1984   "The Politics of Participation and Nonparticipation in Dispute Processes." *Law and Policy Quarterly* 6:203.

Harrison, Gordon, and Jaffe, Sanford
    1972   "Public Interest Law Firms." *American Bar Association Journal* 58:459.

Hart, Henry, and Wechsler, Herbert
    1953   *The Federal Courts and the Federal System*. New York: Foundation Press.

Harvard Law Review
    1976   "Developments in the Law—Class Actions." *Harvard Law Review* 89:1318.

Hasl, Rudolph
    1973   "Standing Revisited: The Aftermath of Data Processing." *St. Louis University Law Journal* 18:12.

Hayek, Friedrich
    1960   *The Constitution of Liberty*. Chicago: University of Chicago Press.
    1973   *Law, Liberty and Legislation*. Chicago: University of Chicago Press.

Haynes, Jeffrey
    1976   "Michigan's EPA in Its Sixth Year." *Journal of Urban Law* 53:589.

Hazard, Geoffrey
    1976   "Representation in Rule Making." In *Law and the American Future*, Murray Schwartz, ed. Englewood Cliffs, N. J.: Prentice-Hall.
    1978   *Ethics in the Practice of Law*. New Haven, Conn.: Yale University Press.

Hoffman, H. M., and Brodley, J.
    1952   "Jurors on Trial." *Missouri Law Review* 17:235.

Hollingsworth, Robert, et al.
    1973   "The Ohio Small Claims Court." *University of Cincinnati Law Review* 42:469.

Homburger, Adolf
    1973   "Private Suits in the Public Interest in the United States of America." *Buffalo Law Review* 23:343.

Horowitz, Donald
    1977   *Courts and Social Policy*. Washington, D.C.: Brookings Institution.

Hosticka, Carl
    1979   "We Don't Care About What Happened, We Only Care About What Is Going to Happen." *Social Problems* 26:599.

Howe, Mark
    1939   "Juries as Judges of Criminal Law." *Harvard Law Review* 52:582.

Hunt, Franklin
    1979   "The Lawyers' War Against Democracy." *Commentary* 68:45.

Hunting, Roger, and Neuwirth, Gloria
    1962   *Who Sues in New York City?* New York: Columbia University Press.

Huntington, Samuel
    1975   "The Democratic Distemper." *Public Interest* 41:9.
Institute for Social Analysis
    1979   *National Evaluation of the Neighborhood Justice Centers Field Test.* Washington,
             D.C.: National Institute of Law Enforcement and Criminal Justice.
Jacob, Herbert
    1969   *Debtors in Court.* Chicago: Rand McNally.
    1971   "Black and White Perceptions of Justice in the City." *Law & Society Review* 6:69.
Jaffe, Louis
    1965   *Judicial Control of Administrative Action.* Boston: Little, Brown.
    1968   "The Citizen as Litigant in Public Actions." *University of Pennsylvania Law Review*
             116:1033.
James, Marlise
    1973   *The People's Lawyers.* New York: Holt.
Johnson, Earl
    1974   *Justice and Reform.* New York: Russell Sage Foundation.
    1978a   "Courts and the Community." In *State Courts: A Blueprint for the Future,* Theodore
             Fedder, ed. Williamsburg, Va.: National Center for State Courts.
    1978b   "Promising Institutions." In *Access to Justice,* vol. 2, Mauro Cappelletti and Bryant
             Garth, eds. Amsterdam: Sijthoff & Noordhoff.
Jowell, Jeffrey
    1969   "The Limits of the Public Hearing as a Tool of Public Planning." *Administrative
             Law Review* 21:123.
    1975   *Law and Bureaucracy.* Port Washington, N.Y.: Dunellen.
Kadish, Mortimer, and Kadish, Sanford
    1973   *Discretion to Disobey.* Stanford, Calif.: Stanford University Press.
Kadish, Sanford
    1957   "Methodology and Criteria in Due Process Adjudication." *Yale Law Journal* 66:319.
Kagan, Robert, et al.
    1977   "The Business of State Supreme Courts, 1870–1970." *Stanford Law Review* 30:121.
Kalven, Harry, and Rosenfield, Maurice
    1941   "The Contemporary Function of the Class Suit." *University of Chicago Law Review*
             8:684.
Kalven, Harry, and Zeisel, Hans
    1966   *The American Jury.* Boston: Little, Brown.
Kariel, Henry
    1961   *The Decline of American Pluralism.* Stanford, Calif.: Stanford University Press.
    1969   *Open Systems.* Itasca, Ill.: Peacock.
Kateb, George
    1975   "Comments on David Braybrooke's 'The Meaning of Participation and of Demands
             for It.'" In *Participation in Politics,* J. Roland Pennock and John Chapman, eds.
             New York: Lieber-Atherton.
Katz, Jack
    1973   "Settlement Procedures and the Social Form of Trouble." Unpublished manu-
             script.
Keeton, Morris
    1965   "The Morality of Civil Disobedience." *Texas Law Review* 43:507.
Keim, Donald
    1975   "Participation in Contemporary Democratic Theories." In *Participation in Politics,*
             J. Roland Pennock and John Chapman, eds. New York: Lieber-Atherton.

Kennedy, Duncan
    1973   "Legal Formality." *Journal of Legal Studies* 2:351.
Kessler, John
    1975   "The Social Psychology of Jury Deliberations." In *The Jury System in America*, Rita
            Simon, ed. Beverly Hills, Calif.: Sage.
Kidder, Robert
    1974   "Formal Litigation and Professional Insecurity." *Law & Society Review* 9:11.
    1980–81 "The End of the Road? Problems in the Analysis of Disputes." *Law & Society
            Review* 15:717.
Kirp, David
    1976   "Proceduralism and Bureaucracy." *Stanford Law Review* 28:841.
Kluger, Richard
    1976   *Simple Justice.* New York: Knopf.
Kolko, Gabriel
    1963   *The Triumph of Conservatism.* Chicago: Quadrangle.
Komesar, Neil
    1979   "Notes Toward a Theory of Conflict Choice." Paper presented at the meeting of
            the Law and Society Association, San Francisco.
Kritzer, Herbert, et al.
    1984   "Understanding the Costs of Litigation." *American Bar Foundation Research Journal*
            1984:559.
    1985   "Winners and Losers in Litigation." Unpublished manuscript.
Ladinsky, Jack
    1976   "The Traffic in Legal Services." *Law & Society Review* 11:207.
Ladinsky, Jack, and Susmilch, Charles
    1983   "Community Factors in the Brokerage of Consumer Product and Service Prob-
            lems." Unpublished manuscript.
Landes, William, and Posner, Richard
    1979   "Adjudication as a Private Good." *Journal of Legal Studies* 8:235.
Landy, D., and Aronson, E.
    1969   "The Influence of the Character of the Criminal and His Victim on the Decisions
            of Simulated Jurors." *Journal of Experimental Social Psychology* 5:141.
Laumann, Edward, and Heinz, John
    1977   "Specialization and Prestige in the Legal Profession." *American Bar Foundation
            Research Journal* 1977:155.
Lawson, Richard
    1970   "Relative Effectiveness of One-Sided and Two-Sided Communications in Court-
            room Persuasion." *Journal of General Psychology* 82:3.
Lazarus, Simon
    1974   *The Genteel Populists.* New York: Holt.
Lazarus, Simon, and Onek, Joseph
    1971   "The Regulators and the People." *Virginia Law Review* 57:1069.
Leff, Arthur
    1970   "Ignorance, Injury and Spite." *Yale Law Journal* 80:1.
Lehnen, Robert
    1975   "Citizen Interaction with Public Agencies." Paper presented at the meeting of the
            American Political Science Association, San Francisco.
Lempert, Richard
    1976   "Mobilizing Private Law." *Law & Society Review* 11:173.
    1979   "More Tales of Two Courts." *Law & Society Review* 13:91.

Leone, R. C.
1972   "Public Interest Advocacy and the Regulatory Process." *Annals of the American Academy of Political Science* 400:46.
Levin, Martin
1975   "Delay in Five Criminal Courts." *Journal of Legal Studies* 4:83.
Levine, Adeline, and Schweber-Koren, Claudine
1976   "Jury Selection in Erie County." *Law & Society Review* 11:43.
Levine, Felice, and Preston, Elizabeth
1970   "Community Resource Orientation Among Low Income Groups." *Wisconsin Law Review* 1970:80.
Lewis, Anthony
1981   "Conserving the Society." *New York Times*, April 16, p. A31.
Lipsky, Michael
1968   "Protest as a Political Resource." *American Political Science Review* 62:1144.
1970   *Protest in City Politics.* Chicago: Rand McNally.
Lochner, Philip
1975   "The No Fee and Low Fee Legal Practice of Private Attorneys." *Law & Society Review* 9:431.
Lowi, Theodore
1979   *The End of Liberalism*, 2nd ed. New York: Norton.
Macaulay, Stewart
1963   "Non-Contractual Relations in Business." *American Sociological Review* 28:55.
1979   "Lawyers and Consumer Protection Laws." Dispute Processing Research Program, University of Wisconsin. Working paper.
McGillis, Daniel, and Mullen, Joan
1977   *Neighborhood Justice Centers.* Washington, D.C.: Office of Development, Dissemination and Testing, National Institute of Law Enforcement and Criminal Justice.
McIntyre, Jennie
1967   "Public Attitudes Toward Crime and Law Enforcement." *Annals of the American Academy of Political Science* 374:34.
McLachlan, Michael
1971   "Democratizing the Administrative Process: Toward Increased Responsiveness." *Arizona Law Review* 13:835.
Mahoney, Barry, et al.
1978   "The Public and the Courts." In *State Courts: A Blueprint for the Future,* Theodore Fedder, ed. Williamsburg, Va.: National Center for State Courts.
Manning, Bayless
1977   "Hyperlexis." *Northwestern University Law Review* 71:767.
Marks, F. Raymond
1971   *The Legal Needs of the Poor.* Chicago: American Bar Foundation.
1976   "Some Research Perspectives for Looking at Legal Needs and Legal Services Delivery Systems." *Law & Society Review* 11:191.
Mather, Lynn, and Yngvesson, Barbara
1980–81 "Language, Audience and the Transformation of Disputes." *Law & Society Review* 15:775.
Mayhew, Leon
1975   "Institutions of Representation: Civil Justice and the Public." *Law & Society Review* 9:401.
Mayhew, Leon, and Reiss, Albert
1969   "The Social Organization of Legal Contacts." *American Sociological Review* 34:309.

Mayo, Henry
    1960   *An Introduction to Democratic Theory.* New York: Oxford University Press.
Mazor, Lester
    1968   "Power and Responsibility in the Attorney–Client Relationship." *Stanford University Law Review* 20:1120.
Merry, Sally
    1979   "Going to Court." *Law & Society Review* 13:891.
    1985   "Concepts of Law and Justice Among Working Class Americans." *Legal Studies Forum* 9:59.
Merry, Sally, and Silbey, Susan
    1984   "What Do Plaintiffs Want?" *Justice System Journal* 9:151.
Michelman, Frank
    1973   "The Supreme Court and Litigation Access Fees—I." *Duke Law Journal* 1973:1153.
    1974   "The Supreme Court and Litigation Access Fees—II." *Duke Law Journal* 1974: 527.
Milbrath, Lester
    1965   *Political Participation.* Chicago: Rand McNally.
Miller, Charles
    1977   "The Forest of Due Process of Law." In *Due Process,* J. Roland Pennock and John Chapman, eds. New York: New York University Press.
Miller, Richard, and Sarat, Austin
    1980–81 "Grievance, Claims and Disputes: Assessing the Adversary Culture." *Law & Society Review* 15:525.
Missouri Bar
    1963   *A Motivational Study of Public Attitudes and Law Office Management.* Jefferson City, Mo.: Missouri Bar.
Mnookin, Robert, and Kornhauser, Lewis
    1979   "Bargaining in the Shadow of the Law." *Yale Law Journal* 88:950.
Morrison, Charles
    1974   "Clerks and Clients." *Law & Society Review* 9:39.
Moulton, Beatrice
    1969   "The Persecution and Intimidation of the Low Income Litigant as Performed by the Small Claims Court in California." *Stanford Law Review* 21:1657.
Murphy, Terrence, and Hoffman, Joel
    1976   "Current Models for Improving Public Representation in the Administrative Process." *Administrative Law Review* 28:391.
Myers, Martha
    1979   "Rule Departures and Making Law: Juries and Their Verdicts." *Law & Society Review* 13:781.
Nader, Laura
    1979   "Disputing Without the Force of Law." *Yale Law Journal* 88:998.
    1980   *No Access to Law.* New York: Academic Press.
Nader, Laura, and Todd, Harry, eds.
    1978   *The Disputing Process.* New York: Columbia University Press.
Nettle, John
    1967   *Political Mobilization.* London: Faber.
Nie, Norman, and Verba, Sidney
    1975   "Political Participation." In *Handbook of Political Science,* Nelson Polsby and Fred Greenstein, eds. Reading, Mass.: Addison-Wesley.
Nisbet, Robert
    1975   *The Twilight of Authority.* New York: Oxford University Press.

Nonet, Philippe, and Selznick, Philip
   1978   *Law and Society in Transition*. New York: Harper & Row.
Olson, Mancur
   1971   *The Logic of Collective Action*. Cambridge, Mass.: Harvard University Press.
Olson, Susan
   1984   *Clients and Lawyers*. Westport, Conn.: Greenwood.
O'Mara, J. J.
   1972   "The Courts, Standard Jury Charges—Findings of a Pilot Project." *Pennsylvania Bar Journal* 120:166.
O'Neil, Robert
   1970   "Of Justice Delayed and Justice Denied." In *Supreme Court Review*, Philip Kurland, ed. Chicago: University of Chicago Press.
Ordover, Janusz
   1978   "Costly Litigation in the Model of Single Activity Accidents." *Journal of Legal Studies* 7:243.
Pagter, Carl, et al.
   1964   "The California Small Claims Court." *California Law Review* 52:876.
Parsons, Talcott
   1954   "A Sociologist Looks at the Legal Profession." In *Essays in Sociological Theory*, Talcott Parsons, ed. New York: Free Press.
Pennock, J. Roland
   1979   *Democratic Theory*. Princeton, N.J.: Princeton University Press.
Pennock, J. Roland, and Chapman, John
   1975   *Participation in Politics*. New York: Lieber-Atherton.
Piven, Frances Fox, and Cloward, Richard
   1972   *Regulating the Poor*. New York: Vintage Books.
Purcell, Edward
   1973   *The Crisis of Democratic Theory*. Lexington: University of Kentucky Press.
Rabin, Richard
   1976   "Lawyers for Social Change." *Stanford University Law Review* 28:207.
Redford, Emmette
   1969   *Democracy and the Administrative State*. New York: Oxford University Press.
Resnick, David
   1977   "Due Process and Procedural Justice." In *Due Process*, J. Roland Pennock and John Chapman, eds. New York: New York University Press.
Rhode, Deborah
   1982   "Class Conflicts in Class Actions." *Stanford Law Review* 34:1183.
Rhunka, John, and Weller, Steven
   1978   *Small Claims Courts*. Williamsburg, Va.: National Center for State Courts.
Richardson, Richard, et al.
   1972   *Perspectives on the Legal Justice System*. Chapel Hill, N.C.: Institute for Research in Social Science.
Richert, John
   1977   "Jurors' Attitudes Toward Jury Service." *Justice Systems Journal* 2:233.
Rifkind, Simon
   1976   "Are We Asking Too Much of Our Courts?" *Federal Rules Decisions* 70:96.
Riker, William, and Ordeshook, Peter
   1968   "A Theory of the Calculus of Voting." *American Political Science Review* 62:24.
Riley, David
   1970   "The Challenge of the New Lawyers." *George Washington Law Review* 38: 547.

Rockwell, Richard
    1968   *A Study of Law and the Poor in Cambridge, Massachusetts.* Cambridge, Mass.: Community Legal Assistance Office.
Rodgers, Harrell, and Bullock, Charles
    1972   *Law and Social Change.* New York: McGraw-Hill.
Rosenblum, Victor
    1974   "Handling Citizen Initiated Complaints." *Administrative Law Review* 26:1.
Rosenthal, Douglas
    1974   *Lawyer and Client: Who's in Charge?* New York: Russell Sage Foundation.
Ross, H. Lawrence
    1970   *Settled Out of Court.* Chicago: Aldine.
Ross, H. Lawrence, and Littlefield, Neil
    1978   "Complaint as a Problem Solving Mechanism." *Law & Society Review* 12:199.
Rostow, Eugene
    1971   "Civil Disobedience." In *Is Law Dead?* Eugene Rostow, ed. New York: Simon & Schuster.
Rubenstein, Leonard
    1976   "Procedural Due Process and the Limits of the Adversary System." *Harvard Civil Rights-Civil Liberties Law Review* 11:49.
Sabatier, Paul
    1975   "Social Movements and Regulatory Agencies." *Policy Sciences* 6:301.
Sander, Frank
    1976   "Varieties of Dispute Processing." *Federal Rules Decisions* 70:111.
Santos, Bonaventuro de Sousa
    1977   "The Law of the Oppressed." *Law & Society Review* 12:5.
Sarat, Austin
    1975   "Support for the Legal System." *American Politics Quarterly* 3:1.
    1976   "Alternatives in Dispute Processing." *Law & Society Review* 10:339.
    1977   "Studying American Legal Culture." *Law & Society Review* 11:427.
    1978   "Understanding Trial Courts." *Judicature* 61:318.
    1981   "Review of *Access to Justice.*" *Harvard Law Review* 94:1911.
    1982   "Abortion and the Courts." In *American Politics and Public Policy,* Allan Sindler, ed. Washington: Congressional Quarterly.
    1984   "The Emergence of Disputes." In *A Study of the Barriers to the Use of Alternative Methods of Dispute Resolution.* South Royalton, Vt.: Vermont Law School.
Sarat, Austin, and Felstiner, William
    1985   "Law Talk in the Divorce Lawyer's Office." Unpublished manuscript.
    1986   "Law and Strategy in the Divorce Lawyer's Office." *Law & Society Review* 20-93.
Sarat, Austin, and Grossman, Joel B.
    1975   "Courts and Conflict Resolution." *American Political Science Review* 69:1200.
Sax, Joseph
    1971   *Defending the Environment.* New York: Knopf.
Sax, Joseph, and DiMento, Joseph
    1974   "Environmental Citizen Suits." *Ecology Law Quarterly* 4:1.
Scaff, Lawrence
    1975   "Two Concepts of Political Participation." *Western Political Quarterly* 28:447.
Scanlon, T. M.
    1977   "Due Process." In *Due Process,* J. Roland Pennock and John Chapman, eds. New York: New York University Press.

Scheingold, Stuart
 1974 *The Politics of Rights.* New Haven, Conn.: Yale University Press.
Scott, Kenneth
 1973 "Standing in the Supreme Court—A Functional Analysis." *Harvard Law Review* 86:645.
Sedler, Robert
 1972 "Standing, Justiciability and All That." *Vanderbilt Law Review* 25:479.
Selznick, Philip
 1969 *Law, Society and Industrial Justice.* New York: Russell Sage Foundation.
Sennett, Richard
 1980 *Authority.* New York: Vintage Books.
Shapiro, David
 1968 "Some Thoughts on Intervention Before Courts, Agencies and Arbitrators." *Harvard Law Review* 81:721.
Shapiro, Michael
 1969 "Rational Political Man." *American Political Science Review* 63:1106.
Shklar, Judith
 1964 *Legalism.* Cambridge, Mass.: Harvard University Press.
Silberman, Matthew
 1979 "The Effect of Opportunity Structures on the Use of Lawyers." Paper presented at the meeting of the Law and Society Association, San Francisco.
Silbey, Susan, and Merry, Sally
 1984 "The Problems Shape the Process." Unpublished manuscript.
Simon, Rita
 1967 *The Jury and the Defense of Insanity.* Boston: Little, Brown.
 1975 "Introduction." In *The Jury System in America,* Rita Simon, ed. Beverly Hills, Calif.: Sage.
Simon, William
 1978 "The Ideology of Advocacy." *Wisconsin Law Review* 1978:29.
Singer, William
 1984 "The Player and the Cards." *Yale Law Journal* 94:1.
Skogan, Wesley
 1976 "Citizen Reporting of Crime." *Criminology* 13:535.
Sorauf, Frank
 1976 *The Wall of Separation.* Princeton, N.J.: Princeton University Press.
Sparks, Richard, et al.
 1977 *Surveying Victims.* New York: Wiley.
Spitz, David
 1954 "Democracy and the Problem of Civil Disobedience." *American Political Science Review* 48:386.
Steadman, John, and Rosenstein, Richard
 1973 "Small Claims Consumer Plaintiffs in Philadelphia Municipal Court." *University of Pennsylvania Law Review* 121:1309.
Steele, Eric
 1975 "Fraud, Disputes and the Consumer." *University of Pennsylvania Law Review* 123:1107.
Stern, James
 1968 "Alternative Dispute Settlement Procedures." *Wisconsin Law Review* 1968:1100.
Stewart, Richard
 1975 "The Reformation of American Administrative Law." *Harvard Law Review* 88:1669.

Stolz, Preble
     1968   "The Legal Needs of the Public: A Survey Analysis." Research Contributions of
               the American Bar Foundation, no. 4.
Strawn, D. U., and Buchanan, Raymond
     1976   "Jury Confusion: A Threat to Justice." *Judicature* 59:478.
Sykes, Gresham
     1969   "Legal Needs of the Poor in the City of Denver." *Law & Society Review* 4:255.
Tapp, June
     1974   "Legal Socialization." *Stanford University Law Review* 27:1.
Thibaut, Joseph, et al.
     1972   "Adversary Presentation and Bias in Legal Decision Making." *Harvard Law Review*
               86:386.
Thompson, Dennis
     1970   *The Democratic Citizen.* Cambridge: Cambridge University Press.
Thompson, E. P.
     1975   *Whigs and Hunters.* London: Penguin.
Tocqueville, Alexis de
     1863   *Democracy in America.* Vol. 1. Translated by Francis Bowen. Cambridge: Seyer.
     [1835]
Tribe, Laurence
     1979   "Too Much Law, Too Little Justice." *Atlantic Monthly* 244:25.
Trubek, David
     1974   "Notes on the Relationship Between Litigation and Political Power." Unpublished
               manuscript.
     1978a   "Environmental Defense." In *Public Interest Law,* Burton Weisbrod, ed. Berkeley:
               University of California Press.
     1978b   "Public Advocacy: Administrative Government and the Representation of Diffuse
               Interests." In *Access to Justice,* vol. 3, Mauro Cappelletti and Bryant Garth, eds.
               Amsterdam: Sijthoff & Noordhoff.
     1979   "Interim Project Summary." Civil Litigation Research Project, University of Wis-
               consin.
     1980–81   "Introduction: Studying Courts in Context." *Law & Society Review* 15:485.
     1984   "Where the Action Is." *Stanford Law Review* 36:575.
Trubek, David, et al.
     1983   "The Costs of Ordinary Justice." *UCLA Law Review* 31:72.
     1984   "Costs, Processes and Outcomes." Unpublished manuscript.
Tussman, Joseph
     1970   *Obligation and the Body Politic.* New York: Oxford University Press.
Tyler, Tom
     1984   "The Role of Perceived Injustice in Defendants' Evaluations of Their Courtroom
               Experience." *Law & Society Review* 18:51.
Unger, Roberto
     1975   *Knowledge and Politics.* New York: Free Press.
     1976   *Law in Modern Society.* New York: Free Press.
University of Pennsylvania Law Review
     1972   "Public Participation in Federal Administrative Agency Proceedings."
Vanderzell, J. H.
     1966   "The Jury as a Community Cross Section." *Western Political Quarterly* 19:136.
Vera Institute of Justice
     1977   *Felony Arrests.* New York: Vera Institute of Justice.

Verba, Sidney, and Nie, Norman
    1972   *Participation in American Politics.* New York: Harper & Row.

Vidmar, Neil
    1979   "Social Psychological Aspects of Disputes and Their Transformation in a Small Claims Court." Paper presented at the meeting of the Law and Society Association, San Francisco.
    1984   "The Small Claims Court." *Law & Society Review* 18:515.

Vining, Joseph
    1978   *Legal Identity.* New Haven, Conn.: Yale University Press.

Vose, Clement
    1972   *Constitutional Change.* Lexington, Mass.: Heath.

Walbert, D. F.
    1971   "The Effect of Jury Size on the Probability of Conviction." *Case Western Reserve Law Review* 22:529.

Walker, Darlene, et al.
    1972   "Contact and Support." *North Carolina Law Review* 51:43.

Wanner, Craig
    1974   "The Public Ordering of Private Relations, Part I." *Law & Society Review* 8:421.
    1975   "The Public Ordering of Private Relations, Part II." *Law & Society Review* 9:293.

Wasserstrom, Richard
    1961   "Disobeying the Law." *Journal of Philosophy* 58:641.

Weisbrod, Burton, ed.
    1978   *Public Interest Law.* Berkeley: University of California Press.

Wells, Charles
    1911   "The Origins of the Petty Jury." *Law Quarterly Review* 27:347.

Williams, Jerre
    1972   "An Evaluation of Public Participation." *Administrative Law Review* 24:49.

Williams, Martha, and Hall, Jay
    1972   "Knowledge of the Law in Texas." *Law & Society Review* 7:99.

Williamson, Oliver
    1979   "Governance Structures and Contractual Relations." Unpublished manuscript.

Williamson, Oliver, et al.
    1975   "Understanding the Employment Relations: The Analysis of Idiosyncratic Exchange." *Bell Journal of Economics* 6:250.

Wilson, James Q.
    1973   *Political Organizations.* New York: Basic Books.

Wolin, Sheldon
    1980   "Reagan Country." *New York Review of Books,* December 18, p. 9.

Yale Law Journal
    1964   "The Changing Role of the Jury in the Nineteenth Century." *Yale Law Journal* 74:170.
    1970   "The New Public Interest Lawyers." *Yale Law Journal* 79:1069.

Yankelovich, Skelly, and White, Inc.
    1978   *The Public Image of the Courts.* Williamsburg, Va.: National Center for State Courts.

Yngvesson, Barbara, and Hennessey, Patricia
    1975   "Small Claims, Complex Disputes." *Law & Society Review* 9:219.

Zacharias, Fred
    1978   "Standing of Public Interest Litigating Groups to Sue on Behalf of Their Members." *University of Pittsburgh Law Review* 39:453.

Zashin, Elliot
    1972   *Civil Disobedience and Democracy.* New York: Free Press.
Zeisel, Hans, et al.
    1959   *Delay in Court.* Boston: Little, Brown.
Zeisel, Hans, and Diamond, Sheri
    1974   "Convincing Empirical Evidence on the Six-Member Jury." *University of Chicago Law Review* 41:281.
Zemans, Frances
    1983   "Legal Mobilization." *American Political Science Review* 77:690.
Zinn, Howard
    1971   "The Conspiracy of Law." In *The Rule of Law,* R. P. Wolff, ed. New York: Simon & Schuster.

SOCIAL SCIENCE
IN LEGAL DECISION-MAKING

Phoebe C. Ellsworth
Stanford University

Julius G. Getman
Yale University

The ways in which social science data are used in legal decision-making have rarely been systematically studied. We do not know how frequently courts refer to social science research or how often it is used by legislatures. When social science data are cited, it is extremely difficult to determine whether they helped to shape the outcome or whether they were used to provide a scholarly justification for decisions reached on other grounds. When social science has influenced the law, it is often impossible to say whether it has served to make rules more just or procedures more efficient.

The literature on the application of social science research in the legal process has focused on the role of research in shaping legal rules—particularly in important constitutional cases—and in forming major social policies. In thus restricting their attention to a few pinnacles, most analysts have necessarily ignored the vast terrain that spreads out below. This is understandable, as the terrain is largely uncharted, and not even the boundaries are well delineated. Faced with this indefinite territory, we hope to suggest the range of settings in which social scientists are consulted by legal actors or social science research is used to inform their decisions.[1]

---

[1] There are a number of important areas that we shall *not* cover. The use of social science in policy-making has been reviewed and assessed elsewhere, as has the burgeoning use of social science in evaluation research (see, for example, Struening and Guttentag 1975), and in many cases these do not involve decision-making that is specifically legal. The uses of specific data from specific disciplines within the social sciences, particularly economics, which we know little about, are addressed in other chapters of this volume. Although the legislatures of the larger states and the United States frequently call upon social scientists to testify at hearings, those who have analyzed the process have generally concluded that an honest desire for information is not a major motive, and that intracommittee negotiations and ideological predispositions play a more important role in the outcome (cf. Lochner 1973). The use of social science data by administrative agencies is an important topic and deserves better treatment than it has received, here or elsewhere.

The first section of this chapter will describe the use of social science data at various levels of decision-making, ranging from the assessment of the legal status of individuals to the delineation of major general principles. First, we will examine the ways in which social scientists and their tools directly affect the fate of particular individuals who become embroiled in the legal system, either at the trial-court level or outside of formal litigation. Then we will move to a recent development in individual assessment that has raised particularly difficult and controversial issues—the situation when social scientists do not examine the participants in the specific case at all but contribute their general expertise, based on aggregate data, to the decision of a particular individual's fate. We will then move from the assessment of individuals to the assessment of groups or organizations and to one of the apparent triumphs of social science—the evaluation of representativeness or equality of treatment. This successful application of social science methods will be compared with the inconsistent success of the application of social science concepts in the definition of general legal standards. From there we will move to a consideration of the use of general social science data and theory in the trial court, and only then will we move on to the level where substantial bodies of data are brought to bear on large abstract legal decisions, typically in the appellate courts and the legislatures.

The second section examines two specific branches of law—labor law and criminal law—in an attempt to understand why the use of social science data in the first is so slight and in the second so common. In labor law, the use of social science data is infrequent and unsophisticated; decision-makers seem reluctant to employ available data. In criminal law, decision-makers are frequently willing, and sometimes eager, to use available data, but the value of this endeavor has turned out to be highly controversial.

Finally, the third section discusses some general epistemological issues that may underlie the difficulties of fruitful collaboration and the pessimism of previous writers—in particular, the advantages and disadvantages of the adversary system as a method for determining scientific truth.

VARIETIES OF SOCIAL SCIENCE INFORMATION

In focusing on high-level interactions, such as the use of social science research in establishing constitutional doctrine, the existing literature about law and social science tends to neglect the significant interactions that take place through the testimony of social scientists (or others who deal professionally with social science concepts or methods) concerning the decisions of particular cases. It is important to recognize that social science information may enter the legal system in many different guises. The image of empirical data riding up through the courts in full panoply, to achieve their own footnote in *Brown v. Board of Education,* though dear to the hearts of social scientists, is memorable in part because it was, and still is, unusual. Infinitely more common are the routine day-to-day assessments of obscure individuals with problems by obscure individuals with power over them: of prisoners by parole officers, of suspects by lie-detection experts, of unfortunate children by social workers, and so on. No general principle is enunciated, no aspect of the legal system is changed; only an individual person or family is affected. Between these extremes, social scientists may participate at all levels—as evaluators of particular reforms or programs, as expert witnesses providing assessments of particular instances or general states of affairs, as lobbyists or authors of amicus briefs.

Least susceptible to analysis, but perhaps most important, is the influence of social science theory and research on the intellectual climate of the general culture.

Although we will examine these various influences of social science separately, they are clearly not independent. The social worker and the prison psychologist use tests developed by basic researchers and theoreticians and, in turn, their dissatisfaction with these tests may lead, directly or indirectly, to changes in both the theories that generated them and the laws that ratified their use. The testimony of an expert witness is more likely to be accepted, and more likely to be influential, when the underlying theory has already diffused into the general consciousness of the intellectual community, so that it strikes the audience as a slightly more scientific version of common sense.

Individual Case Assessments

One of the most common uses of social science information in the legal system is the evaluation of particular people, usually by means of psychological tests and clinical interviews. Many judgments that were formerly based on the intuitions of lay persons (judges and jurors)—especially in criminal law, family law, and juvenile law—have been redefined as matters requiring scientific expertise.

Theories of individual adjustment and development are largely the domain of psychology and psychiatry, and although some may argue that psychiatry is not a social science, it would make no sense for our purposes to discuss the one without the other. Theories of normal and abnormal child development, for example, have been generated within both disciplines and have traveled so quickly across the boundaries between the disciplines that it would be fruitless and artificial to try to disentangle them. Likewise, members of both disciplines have developed methods of clinical assessment. The Rorschach test, invented by a psychiatrist, and the Thematic Apperception Test (TAT), devised by a psychologist, are both based on the theoretical notion that responses to ambiguous stimuli may reveal underlying personality dynamics, and in practice the two instruments are often used interchangeably. Sociologists and anthropologists may also be called upon to play a role in individual assessments—the former, for example, in delinquency cases, and the latter in cases involving members of special subcultures, such as Native American groups. But the field has been dominated by the research and theories of psychologists and psychiatrists, and in relation to their participation in the legal system distinctions between them have largely been drawn along lines of status rather than of substance.

In addition to our choice of a definition of social science broad enough to include psychiatry, for the purposes of this section, we would like to extend our definition of the term "social scientist" or "social science expert" to include people who have some training in social science and who routinely use the products of social science in making or influencing decisions that have legal consequences, but who do not participate in advancing the science itself. Individual assessments, particularly in nonlitigated cases, are rarely made by people who conduct basic research or develop social science theory. Rather, they are made by parole board members, social workers, and other practitioners who apply the tools and theories developed by social scientists. Often, these applications become widespread and firmly established without the scrutiny, and sometimes even without the knowledge, of the original scholars or their successors. While it may be unfair to blame social scientists for the uses and misuses of their ideas in these contexts, it would be foolish to ignore an influence that is so pervasive and consequential.

Assessments Made by Experts and Ratified by Courts — COMMITMENT —
The involuntary civil commitment of individuals to mental hospitals is probably the area
in which nonlegal experts first created an indispensable role for themselves. Up until the
mid-nineteenth century, civil commitment took place without any formal procedures or
legislative restraints whatsoever; friends, relatives, courts, police, or people charged with
managing the poor could commit a troublesome individual to a mental hospital or, if the
person was indigent, to a poorhouse (Deutsch 1949). Beginning about mid-century,
however, some knowledge of the abuses of this system began to seep into the public
consciousness, partly as a manifestation of the increasing reform ethos of the time and
partly in response to a number of dramatic real and fictional accounts of normal people
wrongfully locked away in asylums by dastardly relatives or colleagues. According to
Deutsch, "the plight of the perfectly sane individual 'railroaded' to a 'madhouse' by
relatives, friends, or business associates scheming to separate him from his fortune or his
sweetheart" (p. 418) became a popular theme in the press and literature of the period.

Courts and legislatures moved with the times by articulating both medical and legal
standards designed to prevent the indiscriminate incarceration of the unfortunate. In
1845, the Massachusetts Supreme Court laid down the first rule requiring medical
justification for involuntary commitment, stating that a patient could be restrained in an
institution only as long as such "restraint is necessary for his restoration, or will be
conducive thereto" (*Matter of Josiah Oakes*, 1845), thereby requiring an explicitly therapeutic justification for civil commitment. As this kind of justification became more
widespread, the opportunity for physicians to assume an important regulatory role expanded.

In the meantime, during the 1860s and 1870s, legal restrictions on civil commitment
developed rapidly. Rights to notice and to some form of hearing were extended in many
jurisdictions, and some states even instituted mandatory jury trials. However, the court's
responsibility for the actual scrutiny of the civil commitment process was short-lived.
Prominent members of the medical profession's progressive association of neurologists
argued that the formal legal procedures were likely to confound therapeutic objectives.
Their own response to the public clamor was to advocate, and eventually to achieve,
permanent state commissions on lunacy. Initially founded in the 1870s, these commissions—which were frequently dominated by physicians—increased in number, and their
power expanded markedly over the next quarter-century.

The medical view began to dominate the legal view. By the late 1890s, many of the
formal procedures designed to protect the rights of those committed to mental hospitals
had been relaxed, a relaxation considerably facilitated by the creation of the categories of
"voluntary" and "temporary" commitments involving a minimum of judicial process
(Deutsch 1949).

By the turn of the century, physicians had gained substantial control over the civil
commitment process, and throughout the first half of the twentieth century, they continued to press for easier and more informal "humane" civil commitment procedures,
occasionally achieving their goals through statutory changes, more frequently
through failure of the courts to enforce laws that remained on the books (such as the
right to jury trial). Physicians were considered uniquely qualified to diagnose and treat
the mentally ill, and for years they continued to do so unhampered and generally un-
examined by the law. Research psychologists performed an important ancillary role in

developing test instruments for the measurement of various types of mental disorders, but when it came to actually deciding whether or not to confine a particular person, an M.D. degree was the main criterion for expertise. Until quite recently, the diagnosis of mental disorder for the purposes of civil commitment was the prerogative of physicians, regardless of their training in psychology or psychiatry, and the medical profession exercised almost complete discretion over the freedom of persons suspected of mental illness. In many jurisdictions, a surgeon or dermatologist was allowed to commit a person to a mental hospital, while a psychologist was not.

The situation was such that mistakes and abuses were nearly invisible: neither the physicians nor the family members who committed a person were likely to raise questions about the discretion involved in civil commitment proceedings. Any patient's claim that the commitment decision was erroneous or malicious would tend to be taken as a predictable delusional symptom—in the rare cases where it was heard at all beyond the walls of the asylum. The law ratified the discretionary powers of the experts and allowed the system to develop without substantial intervention; few cases were brought for consideration, largely because the patient was too weak an adversary to make use of the adversary system. Not until the 1960s did members of the legal profession resume significant efforts to alter this approach, advocating and in many jurisdictions eventually achieving the right to a judicial hearing for persons involuntarily committed to mental hospitals, for example.

ADOPTION — The development of adoption standards involving enormous discretionary powers in the hands of experts parallels the example of civil commitment in many respects. In this instance, however, the experts were social workers, a far less prestigious guild than the physicians.

Homeless children had long been recognized as an important problem by crusading amateurs, in line with the ethos of general social reform of the late nineteenth century. In fact, these amateurs exercised considerable power before they were successfully challenged in the 1920s. Through intensive lobbying, social workers managed to achieve discretion over these children as great as that exercised by physicians over civil commitment cases. The social workers successfully promoted legislation requiring a decisive role for their expert opinion in the adoption process (Macaulay and Macaulay 1978). By the mid-1930s, most states had laws requiring a recommendation by a recognized child-placement agency; some required that the agency specifically approve the adopting family, but even when the recommendation was not binding, judges almost invariably accepted an agency-approved home (Gallagher 1936; Doss and Doss 1957). In several states it became a criminal violation for any intermediary not working for such an agency to place a child for adoption (Doss and Doss 1957), despite the total lack of evidence that independent, nonprofessional placements were any more harmful to children than were agency placements (Macaulay and Macaulay 1978).

Thus, as with civil commitment, there was little legal scrutiny of adoption decisions; the law simply handed over the power to the social workers and remained ignorant of the consequences. Again, there was no strong adversary to challenge the system. Those who suffered were either children or would-be parents who had been judged unsuitable by the adoption agencies. The courts, ignorant of child psychology themselves, would be unlikely to decide that a parental hopeful who was rejected on the basis of a clinical interview with a trained social worker knew more than the expert about the best interests of children.

That social science experts have exercised enormous power at this level is indisputable. Some may argue that this power is not an example of a "use of social science by the legal system" because the social scientists are operating quite independently of the legal system. It is true that, until recently, these issues have not been raised in court and the law has not addressed them. But the fact that the law has not exercised significant independent discretion in these areas, while it has in conceptually similar areas (such as juvenile status offenses and cases of child deprivation and neglect), is the best evidence of the power of the social scientists. Furthermore, the power wielded by the social scientists in these areas has not been independent of the legal system: it has been explicitly handed over and sanctioned by the law. The law has delegated to physicians (for example, members of mental health commissions, which evolved from the early commissions on lunacy) the power to set standards and decide on legal issues of confinement and deprivation of civil liberties for people who are believed to be mentally ill. Similarly, adoption agencies were given temporary legal custody of certain children and explicitly granted the power to designate their "legal guardians." That these issues seem somehow less "legal" than those that are regularly or spectacularly contested in the courts should be taken as a demonstration of the success of social science.

Another argument, more basic and more telling, is that these issues are not germane because, in fact, social science research and data are not used by the practitioners. While the power of the experts in these areas may demonstrate the success of social scientists, it is not clear that it says anything about the power of social science theory and research. When an expert's discretion is unlimited, his power is the power of person, of status, and his decisions are only weakened by documentation. The data probably affect the expert's judgment, and thus influence legal decisions, but the connection cannot be traced with a clear, straight line.

Nonetheless, the disdain that eminent social scientists may feel for the practices of social workers and of admitting physicians at mental hospitals does not erase the power these individuals exercise in the name of social science. Classifying these practices as "not social science" may assuage wounded vanity, but it leaves the real problems untouched. It seems inevitable that the major impact of social science research and theory on decisions about particular individuals will be made by people whose knowledge is dated and haphazard. In assessing the impact of social science, it is important to take account of the distortions introduced as the information passes from its origins to its practical applications.

Social Scientists in Court   Much more visibly, individual assessments by social scientists have become common at the level of the trial court in certain kinds of cases. Cases involving children who are mistreated or who mistreat other people and cases involving the mentally ill are rarely tried without making use of the opinions of nonlegal experts, and criminal cases make frequent use of the reports of probation officers. Psychiatric or psychological testimony is essential when the issue of competency to stand trial is raised. The role of the social scientist—usually, but not exclusively, a psychiatrist, psychologist, or social worker—has expanded during this century as the rehabilitative ideal came to encompass new categories of people. Throughout most of the nineteenth century, decisions about the relative fitness of parents in child-custody cases, the moral promise of juvenile offenders, and perhaps even the sanity of criminal defendants were made by judges (or juries, where an insanity defense was presented) on the basis of experience, the arguments of counsel, and observation of the courtroom proceedings. When the focus of the law in certain areas changed from past criminal behavior to the future potential of the individual, the courts did not immediately feel a corresponding need for expert assessment of individual potential. Most people, and perhaps an even greater proportion of judges, regard themselves as fairly good judges of character.

The medical expert testifying about mental disorders was an early exception to this rule. The prestige of physicians, coupled with the mysteriousness of mental disease, removed assessments of insanity from the realm of unaided lay or judicial judgment rather early. By 1875, mental illness was clearly defined as a medical problem, and although relatives, acquaintances, and clergymen still commonly testified about the mental condition of criminal defendants, the testimony of medical doctors was regarded as considerably more competent and credible. The trial of President Garfield's assassin in 1881, for example, included not only a parade of highly credentialed superintendents of asylums, neurologists, and "alienists," but also a gynecologist, a few general practitioners, and (for the defense) nonmedical acquaintances who had concluded that the defendant was deranged (Rosenberg 1968). Gradually, the psychiatrist, and to a lesser extent the psychologist (*Jenkins* v. *U.S.*, 1962), came to exercise almost exclusive domain over these assessments.

It took longer for the law to come to believe that special expertise might also be required for evaluating individuals in situations where severe mental pathology was not an issue. Two interrelated factors that probably contributed to the transition from lay to professional "expertise" were the expansion of the classes of cases requiring individual assessment and the expansion of the social sciences, and consequently of the class of experts. Juvenile crime became a growing social problem, and sociologists and psychologists offered a growing number of explanations. Likewise, the number of contested child-custody decisions grew rapidly as the divorce rate climbed. Eventually, expert assessments became a common, if not necessarily influential, feature of these cases.

Although the role—and the power—of the expert in a trial court varies considerably, it ordinarily follows one of two patterns: that of adversarial witness or that of court technician. The adversarial-witness arrangement typically involves two experts, one enlisted by each of the parties; the court-technician arrangement generally relies on one expert, employed in a branch of the legal system (for example, a probation department) or some other government agency (such as a welfare office).

The performance of social scientists as adversarial witnesses in the assessment of individual cases has not heaped honors upon their heads. Rather, it is generally regarded as lamentable or ridiculous, depending on the perceiver's own professional identification. The example of opposing psychiatrists in a case involving an insanity defense is the most notorious: the image of the psychiatrist who will make any diagnosis if the price is right was as commonplace in the newspaper coverage of the trial of Garfield's assassin as it is today, and as worrisome to the medical establishment (Rosenberg 1968).

This attitude of skepticism has had negative effects that extend far beyond any particular pair of contradictory experts to a general mistrust of psychiatric expertise (see Bazelon

1974) and of the legitimacy of the insanity defense. In several recent polls, a majority of respondents have agreed with the statement that "the insanity defense is a loophole allowing too many guilty people to go free" (Louis Harris 1971; see also Fitzgerald and Ellsworth 1984). The level of credibility gradually built up by physicians in defining mental disorders as a problem requiring medical expertise is largely dissipated in the courtroom by the apparent ease with which qualified experts are able to reach opposite conclusions about the same person, and it is highly likely that jurors often revert to their own common sense in assessing a defendant's mental state. Only in cases of organic mental disorders—such as psychomotor epilepsy, severe retardation, or traumatic brain injury—are psychiatric experts still held in the same high esteem as other medical experts (Ellsworth et al. 1984), probably because people believe that in cases of this sort psychiatrists are like "real doctors"—able to make determinations approximating the kind of either/or judgments the law requires.

The same sort of "battle of the experts" occurs in contested child-custody cases, where each embittered parent enlists a psychiatrist to show that the other parent is hopelessly unfit or irrevocably estranged from the affection of the child. The difficulties and the problems of credibility in court are quite similar. That conflicting testimony by experts in custody cases has not become a matter of common knowledge and contempt may be because the parties involved rarely achieve the fame of an insane homicidal recidivist or a Patricia Hearst.

Movement from Individual Assessment to the Use of Aggregate Data

We have argued that one of the most pervasive (and least visible) uses of social science expertise is in the assessment of the fitness, dangerousness, sanity, truthfulness, or emotional well-being of individuals. In many areas, social scientists (especially psychologists) and social science technicians have become indispensable cogs in the machinery of routine legal procedures. But recently, perhaps in part because of a conscientious realization of their own influence, theorists, clinicians, and basic researchers in psychology have begun to reevaluate their own ability to make accurate individual assessments. In one area after another, they have arrived at the same gloomy conclusions: there is very little reason to believe that their predictions are more accurate than chance and very good reason to believe that they are worse than predictions based on purely actuarial considerations, or even than predictions based on a combination of actuarial data and clinical assessment (Meehl 1973; Dawes 1971; Shah 1969). Contrary to their earlier confident claims, psychologists are now loudly denying their power to make valid individual predictions about the dangerousness of parolees or mental patients (Monahan 1978; Wexler 1976); the fitness of parents (Ellsworth and Levy 1969; Goldstein, Freud, and Solnit 1973); the likelihood that a particular individual will benefit from psychotherapy or any particular treatment program (Wexler 1976; Ennis and Litwack 1974); or success on a job, on parole, or even in graduate school (Dawes 1971; Meehl 1973; Mischel 1968).

Had the social scientists simply come forward with a humble admission that their earlier claims were false, that their ability to perform their allotted task in the legal decision-making process was severely limited, the issue probably would not have occasioned a major controversy. It would have been possible simply to reply that, despite weaknesses and flaws, their evaluations were still the best available means of arriving at essential legal judgments; they should work to improve their techniques, of course, but in the meantime, they should continue as they had been. But the social scientists now claim that their clinical evaluations are not the best available means of arriving at such judgments—that, in fact, there is a more accurate technique: the prediction of the individual's behavior from aggregate statistical data on others in the same position.

In areas like these, where the social science technician has become essential to the working of some part of the legal system, and then more esteemed and renowned social scientists deny the validity of the techniques, the social scientists are in a particularly good position to push through reforms based on more general social science data and theory. Having made their contribution necessary, they are able to command attention when they want to restructure the nature of that contribution. Two of the areas in which social science has had the greatest influence in recent years provide examples of just this sort of foot-in-the-door phenomenon: parole decision-making and child custody.

Clinical Flexibility versus Standardized Criteria — PAROLE DECISIONS — By the mid-1960s, it had become clear that the individualized evaluations that supposedly characterized decisions about eligibility for parole led to large and irrational disparities in the treatment of similar cases. At the same time, social science was discovering that individualized clinical judgments were highly unreliable in a variety of contexts and less accurate than predictions made on the basis of actuarial tables (Meehl 1973; Dawes 1971). Even when the factors entering into the actuarial tables are derived solely on the basis of the factors used by groups of people making individualized judgments, the tables outperform the people (Dawes 1971, 1979).

In this intellectual context, a large-scale study of parole decision-making was launched in 1972. Funded by the Law Enforcement Assistance Administration, it was conducted by the Research Center of the National Council on Crime and Delinquency in collaboration with the Federal Parole Board and a group of advisers from the social sciences. The goal of the project was to "provide objective, relevant information for individual case decisions; to summarize experience with parole, as an aid to improved policy decisions; and to aid paroling authorities in more rational decision-making for increased effectiveness of prison release procedures" (Gottfredson et al. 1973). The study resulted in a set of guidelines consisting of a scale of offense severity and a "salient factor score" designed to predict success during parole and based largely on the individual's prior record of crime and parole violations. Using base-rate actuarial expectancies, the guidelines indicate a range of months to be served for each combination of offense and offender characteristics.

The parole guidelines represent the single most important instance of a system designed by social scientists with a particular legal context in mind and adopted for use in a routine administrative way by a branch of the criminal-justice system. They are also important in that they epitomize the controversy generated over actuarial predictors in deciding the fate of individuals.

The guidelines (1977 revision) are diagrammed in Table 1. The categories of offense severity are ranged along the vertical axis. Parole boards are given detailed lists of examples of the offenses falling into each category—for example, possession of stolen property valued at less than $1,000 is a "low severity" offense, possession of less than $20,000 in counterfeit currency is a "moderate severity" offense, theft of a motor vehicle

TABLE 1

Guidelines for Parole Decision-Making, Customary Total Time (in Months)
to Be Served Before Release (Including Jail Time)

| Offense Characteristics: Severity of Offense | Offender Characteristics: Parole Prognosis (Salient Factor Score) | | | |
	Very Good (11 to 9)	Good (8 to 5)	Fair (5 to 4)	Poor (3 to 0)
Greatest II	Greater than below, specific ranges not given			
Greatest I	40–55 mos.	55–70 mos.	70–85 mos.	85–110 mos.
Very High	26–36	36–48	48–60	60–72
High	16–20	20–26	26–34	34–44
Moderate	12–16	16–20	20–24	24–32
Low moderate	8–12	12–16	16–20	20–28
Low	6–10	8–12	10–14	12–18

for resale is a "high severity" offense, and rape is a "greatest severity" offense (Level I). The categories of salient factor score ratings appear on the horizontal axis. Of the eleven possible salient factor points, nine are related to the inmate's prior record; points are given for a career free of prior convictions, incarcerations, parole violations, car thefts, and forgeries, and for having reached the age of 18 (1 point) or 26 (2 points) by the time of the first commitment. The other two points are for prior history of opiate or heroin dependence (loss of 1 point) and employment or school attendance for at least six months out of the last two years prior to conviction (gain of 1 point) (Gottfredson, Wilkins, and Hoffman 1978).

The data-based parole guidelines have been quite influential. During the period from October 1974 to September 1975, the Parole Commission stated that 84 percent of the decisions were within the guidelines (Hoffman and Stone-Meierhoefer 1977). There is no way to tell whether this high percentage represents a slavish adherence to the guidelines, since no one knows how many of the 84 percent would have been decided differently without them. The guidelines were formally adopted for use in federal parole decisions, and there is some evidence that the use of the salient factor scoring system is also becoming common at the sentencing stage (Coffee 1978).

In some ways, the impact of the parole guidelines is greater and in some ways less than its architects might have hoped. It is greater in that the very existence of an apparently easy method for assessing risk may invite its use in situations for which it was not designed. The use of the salient factor score as a means of evaluating offenders at the sentencing stage is a good example, since there has been no research on the validity of this instrument in predicting the behavior of a noninmate population (Coffee 1978). On the other hand, the effectiveness of the guidelines is limited, in that some of the better predictors of parole success—such as age, education, and family ties—were ultimately dropped from the salient factor scoring system because they are not in the control of the individual (see Underwood 1979), and thus their use might constitute a denial of equal protection. The remaining socioeconomic factor—recent employment or school attendance—has also been criticized as resulting in "punishment based on status" (Coffee 1978). In some cases, compromise predictors, such as whether the crime was a car theft— highly correlated with age but presumably involving a free decision on the part of the individual—could be substituted; in other cases, some of the better predictors simply had to be discarded without replacement. Thus, the social science influence is limited in that the law has chosen to sacrifice predictive power for other considerations, explicitly choosing a set of guidelines known to be less accurate than the best available.

In addition, the influence of social science in this area may be temporary in that, even though the recommended reforms were adopted (with modifications), early enthusiasm has diminished and has been replaced by a great deal of controversy. The reform itself may not survive or may not spread very far beyond the federal system; with the recent resurgence of retribution as an acceptable goal of punishment, some states have reinstated determinate sentencing, and in some jurisdictions there is strong pressure to abolish parole altogether. The liberals' traditional protests against determinate sentencing have been muted by their discomfort at the use of status-sensitive variables (Coffee 1978).

Because the Federal Parole Guidelines were based on careful research and several validation studies, because they have been adopted for routine use by a major federal criminal-justice agency, and because their history has been so well documented, they have had an important influence in making explicit the moral and epistemological issues surrounding the use of aggregate data. The dilemma raised by the consideration of data averaged over many individuals in determining the fate of a particular person is a real one, and one on which it will be very difficult for legal and scientific thinkers to reach agreement. Some legal thinkers have argued that the most accurate method of prediction may be unfair because it is "inconsistent with respect for the autonomous individual" (Underwood 1979, p. 1409; see also Coffee 1978). More utilitarian legal theoreticians and many social scientists find it difficult to understand how a predictive method that makes more mistakes can be fairer. They contend that this fairness is only apparent, that it is a veneer masking the injustice done to those who are misclassified as "bad risks" on the basis of inaccurate clinical judgment or a compromise formula.

The critics' focus on the unfairness of specific factors beyond the control of the individual may actually represent a more general concern about any sort of categorical, aggregate data-based system of prediction. It has been argued, for example, that educational history should not be used, since it overlaps with race and is thus a "status-sensitive" variable (Coffee 1978). But, of course, the "prior convictions" variable overlaps with race as well. Neither Coffee nor the researchers for the Federal Parole Commission report which of these is more highly correlated with race, nor do they present any empirical evidence as to the relative autonomy of individuals who drop out of school in the tenth grade as compared with those who get arrested, charged, and convicted of an offense. The assumption that a prior conviction is the result of a free decision on the part of the individual, while school nonattendance is the result of social status, is highly questionable, to say the least. In addition, both John Coffee and Barbara Underwood feel that one danger of such predictive methods as the parole guidelines is that they tend to minimize the importance of nonquantifiable, "soft" variables related to the mental state of the offender. Thus, the issue comes full circle: it was the very unreliability and potential for nonquantifiable unfairness and racial overlap in these inexplicit clinical variables that motivated the guideline system in the first place. It seems to be the idea of deciding the fate of individuals on the basis of data drawn from large samples of other people that most fundamentally disturbs the critics.

And this concern is a legitimate one; even staying within the bounds of their traditional realm of accuracy, the social scientist must admit that, in fact, aggregate statistics can only predict aggregate behavior. They cannot predict the individual case. As Sherlock Holmes put it:

> While the individual man is an insoluble puzzle, in the aggregate he becomes a mathematical certainty. You can, for example, never foretell what any one man will be up to, but you can say with precision what an average number will be up to. Individuals vary, but percentages remain constant. [Doyle 1974, p. 91]

This is true in principle, and it is also true in practice; methods similar to the Federal Parole Guidelines have been shown to be quite inaccurate—like other methods, they tend to overpredict violence (Monahan 1978; Rector 1973; Resnick 1979). The social scientist can safely claim only that actuarial methods are better than clinical intuition: better because they are more accurate, and better because the factors are explicit, allowing less room for such clearly illegitimate factors as racial prejudice to operate systematically and in secret.

The issue is not one of the permissibility of probabilistic judgments in prediction. All prediction involves probabilistic judgments, as do assessments of the likelihood of uncertain past events, such as the guilt of a defendant. The social scientists have not introduced probabilistic thinking into the legal system but have made the probabilities explicit. The law shows extreme fastidiousness about open discussion of quantified probabilities. An expert witness who conducts three tests, describes their construction and reliability in detail, and makes a quantified judgment may fare less well in court than one who uses the same three tests—or only two, or one, or none—and makes a confident, unquantified judgment based on his or her general expertise.

Probability judgments are not the issue, if we accept that the goal is prediction. Prediction itself is the issue. To what extent *is* the goal prediction? Judgments about deterrence and judgments about rehabilitation seem necessarily to involve prediction, whereas judgments about retribution or "justice" do not, although the factors that are used may have predictive power and may even overlap considerably with those used for prediction. Uncertainty about the role of prediction may well underlie many of the issues that are so hotly contested. If prediction is the goal, then it seems self-evident that the best and most accurate method should be used. The problem is that, typically, prediction is only one of several goals or values and that it does not coexist very comfortably with other values such as autonomy and the appearance of fairness. The usual solution of satisfying these other values by using an inferior method of prediction strikes no one as a very happy compromise.

CHILD CUSTODY DECISIONS   —   Similar issues involving the merits of moving from individualized assessment to more efficient general guidelines for decision-making have also surfaced in relation to child custody, although the controversy in the literature has been less heated and more sporadic. The arguments against individualized assessment and for alternative, less subjective standards (see Ellsworth and Levy 1969; Goldstein, Freud, and Solnit 1973) resemble the arguments involved in the case of parole, with the additional problem that the time taken to make such assessments may cause greater damage to the child than will a "wrong" decision. Assuming no flagrant abuse or neglect, recommended guidelines are based on parental agreement and continuity, an arbitrary choice being dictated in contested cases in which the two parents have equally continuous contact.

The transition from individual assessment to the application of guidelines based on aggregate data appears to have been smoother and less controversial in the case of child custody than in the case of parole. There are several possible reasons that this might be so. It may be that in child-custody decisions, no real transition has taken place. Judges and family-relations officers can find authority in the literature (Goldstein, Freud, and Solnit 1973) for exercising exactly the same kind of intuitive individualized clinical judgment they exercised before. These authors' controversial and rather amorphous concept of the "psychological parent," to designate a parent with whom the child has a continuous trusting relationship, may not place any real constraints on the choice of caretaker. The decision-makers may simply have replaced the term "fit parent" with the term "psychological parent" without otherwise changing their behavior. Or it may be that the behavior of decision-makers has, in fact, become more standardized but that they complain less because they feel as though they are still making individually tailored judgments.

Since the mid-1970s, more than 25 states have enacted laws providing for joint custody, in which legal and often physical custody of the children after divorce is shared by both parents. In some states there is even a presumption in favor of joint custody. This rapid proliferation of a new form of custody is not based on new empirical research. The old empirical arguments in favor of continuity, formerly used to justify the swift and permanent assignment of the child to the parent who had had more pre-divorce continuity of contact with the child, are now being used to justify joint custody, which presumably permits continuity of the relationship to both parents. What little research there was on joint custody per se was methodologically so weak that no conclusions could be drawn about whether joint custody promoted or undermined the best interests of the child. Yet the best interests standard remains, and joint custody decisions become more common every year—not because of any new empirical knowledge, but probably because they please the parents and seem to give the judge a compromise way out of an agonizing decision (Reppucci 1984).

CAPITAL SENTENCING DECISIONS   —   The difficulty in finding an acceptable compromise between standardized criteria and clinical flexibility is nowhere more obvious than in the Supreme Court's recent series of decisions on discretion in capital sentencing, in which the Court has attempted to arrive at a standard that would permit individualized consideration without permitting unjustifiable discrimination. In 1972, basing their decision in part on empirical evidence of the bias and unreliability of standardless jury decision-making, the Court overturned existing death-penalty laws on the grounds that the unbridled discretion allowed to juries by current practice resulted in life-or-death decisions that were arbitrary and capricious, and possibly severely discriminatory (*Furman* v. *Georgia*, 1972). In 1976, the Court rejected mandatory death sentences on the grounds that they did not allow individualized consideration (*Woodson* v. *North Carolina*, 1976) and permitted what was essentially a guideline system of aggravating and mitigating factors to allow discretion properly bridled (*Gregg* v. *Georgia*, 1976). There was disagreement on the Court on how binding the guidelines were, but certainly there was no requirement that they be empirically based. For example, the Court found acceptable the Texas requirement that the jury estimate whether the defendant would probably be a continuing threat to society (*Jurek* v. *Texas*, 1976; *Barefoot* v. *Estelle*, 1983)—a type of estimate that has an unmitigated record of failure among professionals (Monahan 1978). In 1978, the Court astonishingly attempted to distinguish acceptable discretion from unacceptable discretion by requiring unbridled discretion for mitigating factors but not for aggravating factors (*Lockett* v. *Ohio*, 1978). Since discretionary mitigating factors include all those that are logically the opposites of the impermissibly discretionary aggravating factors (defendant is white, middle-class, charming, handsome, and so on), it is hard to see what is gained by this formulation.

"Exact" Probability Estimates   Lawyers and statisticians are generally agreed that the use of combinatorial statistical methods to estimate the probability that a defendant committed a particular act is impermissible in a criminal trial (see, for example, Finkelstein and Fairley 1970; Tribe 1971), but their reasons differ. The statisticians believe that correct application of statistical methods is extremely difficult, if not impossible. First, estimates of the population frequency of the individual attributes to be combined (for example, the percentage of men with beards, of green-and-gold T-shirts) are likely to be quite inaccurate. Second, the assumption of statistical independence is almost certain to be violated, and assessments of the degree of nonindependence are also likely to be inaccurate (how much more or less likely is a bearded man to wear a green-and-gold T-shirt than anyone else?). Finally, even when they are based on adequate measures, statistics can only permit the conclusion that an event is extremely unlikely; they cannot guarantee that it is unique. That is, they cannot tell whether the defendant in question is the only person who fits the damning description or whether there is one other such person. And, of course, if there could easily be one other person, then (in the absence of other evidence linking the defendant to the crime) the statistical identification of the defendant drops toward a 50 percent probability—in theory, nowhere near certainty beyond a reasonable doubt.

Some lawyers, on the other hand, seem more concerned with the persuasive power of the numbers. They fear, for example, that the numbers will carry the day (Tribe 1971), so that jurors will be unable to give the nonquantifiable factors their due. This is, of course, an empirical question, and the scanty data that exist indicate that, if anything, people *underestimate* the relevance of base-rate statistical data (Kahneman and Tversky 1973).

The lines of this debate have not yet been clearly drawn, nor have the underlying concerns been explicitly stated. Blood typing and even fingerprint identification, which involve probabilistic, statistical judgments, do not—or at least not any longer—arouse the same uneasiness. Thus, it is possible that the social scientists' and lawyers' concerns are the same simple doubts about the accuracy of statistical methods of identification on the basis of combined probability estimates. But there may also be more fundamental, ill-specified moral and emotional issues, vaguely embarrassing because they seem predicated on the desirability of ignorance. However, at this time, the statistical methods are so ill-equipped for the task that the essential epistemological confrontation is not likely to come about in the near future.

Finally, it should be remembered that a probability estimate is always derived and interpreted by a person with values. A number may seem inordinately high or comfortably low, depending on the decision-maker's perception of the consequences of a wrong decision. For example, W. B. Fairley (1977), in an excellent article on the difficulties of estimating low-probability events, using as his example the prediction of a catastrophic accident from the marine transportation of natural gas, develops a series of analytical guidelines, which if properly applied, would generally indicate that the probabilities are not nearly as tiny as they appear to be. Two examples of these guidelines are that "estimates of 'the' probability of an accident must include contributions from all the possible sources of the accident" (p. 349); and that "the widest related base of potential accident experience . . . should be surveyed" (p. 350), with particular attention to those factors that might increase the danger of an accident. The underlying value in applying these guidelines is the belief that such an accident would be so disastrous that it is imperative to make sure that the statistics are not manipulated to create a false sense of security. But if these same guidelines were used for the prediction of dangerousness in mental patients or parolees, the problem of overprediction would be even further exaggerated, resulting in the confinement of even larger numbers of harmless people. Here the competing value of the rights of those confined is salient, and guidelines that seem neutral, sensible, and valuable in one context seem paranoid and illegitimate in the other. In the end, the meaning of a probability estimate is in the eye of the beholder, and it is likely that the vision is far more influential than the number viewed.

Assessment of Groups and Organizations: Representativeness and Equality of Treatment

In addition to the assessment of particular individuals, social scientists and social science methods may be used to assess discrimination in particular collectivities or organizations. Social scientists tend to consider this kind of application of their skills more creditable and exciting than the assessment of individuals; it is also far less frequent. Tests of representativeness and tests of equality of treatment are fundamentally questions of fairness and equal protection, and in both cases the legal question seems to be formally very similar to the kinds of question basic statistical tests were designed to answer: Is this sample representative of the larger population? Does the apparent difference between these two groups reflect systematic differences in the treatment they are receiving, or could a difference of this size occur by chance, given equal treatment?

The Role of Social Scientists in Assessing Jury-Pool Representativeness
Perhaps the simplest example of the use of social science in testing representativeness involves the jury. More than a century ago, the Supreme Court, holding that a statute limiting the venire to white males violated the equal protection clause of the Fourteenth Amendment, enunciated the more general principle that the exclusion of any identifiable demo-

graphic group "having the same legal status in society as that which [the defendant] holds" would threaten the essential nature of the jury as a tribunal embodying a broad democratic ideal (*Strauder* v. *West Virginia*, 1880, p. 308). Although the consistency with which the Supreme Court Justices endorsed this general proposition over the next half-century considerably exceeded the consistency with which they applied it, since 1940 they have become increasingly firm and articulate in insisting that venire lists be made up of a representative cross-section of the community (among others, *Smith* v. *Texas*, 1940; *Taylor* v. *Louisiana*, 1975).

Initially the Court was concerned with intentional exclusion, and the cases involved efforts to establish illegitimate motives or intentions. Attempts to define unfair selection procedures on these bases have largely been replaced by definitions based on consequences: if the composition of the pool of jurors differs substantially from that of the community, it is by definition unrepresentative, regardless of the motives of the jury commissioner (*Duren* v. *Missouri*, 1979).

At first, judges used intuitive, subjective judgments to decide whether a difference between the composition of the venire and that of the population from which it should have been drawn was large enough to conclude that the venire was unrepresentative; many may still do so. But because simple statistical tests allow calculation of the exact probability that such a discrepancy could occur with a fair (random) method of drawing the venire, social scientists versed in statistics are increasingly called upon to make such assessments. This development undoubtedly makes challenges to the composition of jury panels much easier; given passable census data on the community, the comparison between the community and the venire is both extremely simple and perfectly precise. As a consequence, challenges to the representativeness of the venire, although still not common, have become more frequent (Kairys, Schulman, and Harring 1975). In addition, the very knowledge that a workable criterion for assessing representativeness exists undoubtedly inspires self-correction and reform even in jurisdictions where jury-selection procedures have not yet been challenged; the impact of the social science contribution is therefore far wider than the actual use of the technique in court.

Estimating the impact of the statistical definition of representativeness on the legal concept of discrimination is more difficult, and necessarily inconclusive. On the one hand, it can be argued that the use of statistical methods in determining representativeness is simply that—the use of a method. No new social science data or theories have influenced the definition of the issues or the procedures for selecting jury panels. Rather, the criminal-justice system has simply adopted a tool that allows more precise measurement of something it had always considered important to measure. One scholar argues that in racial-exclusion cases decided between 1935 and 1960, the Supreme Court Justices' unformulated, nonquantitative criterion for a substantial discrepancy corresponded quite closely to the .05 probability level conventionally accepted by social scientists as the definition of a "significant difference" (Ulmer 1962). According to this pessimistic argument, no new general principles have emerged from the use of statistical methods. For example, the Court has not declared any general method of jury panel selection—such as the use of voter-registration lists—unconstitutional per se because it implicitly excludes certain segments of the population. Instead, a new challenge and a new statistical analysis must be carried out for each questionable venire. Like the assessment of individuals, the assessment of the representativeness of jury pools is ad hoc.

On the other hand, the fact that the ideals of jury representativeness and fair selection procedures were defined by the law with little explicit reference to social science should not obscure the importance of the social science contribution. In the first place, a vague abstract standard is much less valuable than a standard that allows for precise measurement of the degree to which it is matched or approximated in the situations it was designed to test. Statistical methods have turned an ideal into a criterion that is precise and easily workable.

Second, despite the Court's long history of endorsement of the principle of representativeness, in practice the Justices' reliance on representativeness as the central issue in jury composition has increased substantially, and their definition of representativeness has also changed and sharpened over the last century. (It should also be noted that because some of these developments have occurred in nonracial cases and in cases decided since 1960, they are not reflected in Ulmer's 1962 analysis.) In *Strauder,* the Court's decision was based primarily on its view of the Fourteenth Amendment as a vehicle for extending basic civil rights to black citizens, and the issue of representativeness was a secondary one. Over the years, the Court gradually narrowed in on a concept of representativeness more closely approximating the statistical concept. The Justices dropped the requirement that the defendant be a member of the excluded class (see *Yale Law Journal* 1965, p. 920, n. 10; *Taylor v. Louisiana,* 1975). They moved from a focus on cases involving de jure exclusion (such as *Strauder*) through cases involving almost complete de facto exclusion (for example, *Norris v. Alabama,* 1935) to cases in which groups were included but underrepresented relative to their numbers in the community (*Taylor v. Louisiana,* 1975; *Duren v. Missouri,* 1979; see also *Ballew v. Georgia,* 1978). They also moved from a focus on discriminatory intent to a focus on discriminatory consequences (*Taylor v. Louisiana,* 1975; *Duren v. Missouri,* 1979).

Although the relationship is difficult to document, it seems quite likely that the Court's changing perspective was affected by its awareness of the technology for assessing and assuring representativeness and by the increasingly accepted sociological and psychological argument that prejudice and discrimination can manifest themselves in a variety of subtle and insidious ways in situations where the perpetrators deny any discriminatory intent. A truly random sampling procedure, of course, would eliminate all biases, intentional and unintentional; in *Duren,* the Court explicitly defined bias as the product of a nonrandom system of jury selection.

Even less easy to specify empirically is the Court's gradual move toward a definition of an illegitimately excluded group as one with a distinctive attitudinal perspective. In *Ballard v. U.S.* (1946), the Court stated for the first time that it was not necessary to show that an excluded class of jurors would actually behave differently from those included, only that they would bring a distinctive outlook to the jury. In *Ballew v. Georgia* (1978), this time relying on social science data on group decision-making, the Court concluded that a particularly important reason for guaranteeing jury representativeness is that "the counterbalancing of various biases is critical to the accurate application of the common sense of the community to the facts of any given case" (p. 234).

Finally, the reliance on statistical methods for decisions about the constitutionality of jury selection procedures may have a more general symbolic significance. The acceptance of such methods in one context means that ultimately legal scholars and practitioners will have to consider explicitly the uses for which such methods are and are not appropriate, and develop criteria. The fact that statistical assessment of venire representativeness has drawn no substantial criticism from legal or social-scientific sources (as compared, for example, with the application of social science techniques during voir dire) makes such assessments a useful baseline against which to measure other uses of statistics, so that lawyers and social scientists may intelligently ask, "Is this usage different from that one, and if so, why?"

The Role of Social Scientists in Employment-Discrimination Cases   Another task for which the help of social scientists is frequently solicited is the assessment of fair hiring practices. It is useful to examine the similarities and differences between the employment situation and the simpler task of assessing venire representativeness. In litigating whether or not a firm or institution has been guilty of discrimination in hiring, promotions, or rates of pay, it is common to ask social scientists to carry out a statistical analysis of the existing situation, comparing it with what might be expected to result from a color-blind or sex-blind procedure, and to estimate the possibility that any apparent difference resulted by chance.

The process by which the courts and the litigants have come to rely so heavily on social scientists is an interesting one—not guided or shaped by any major systematic effort by social scientists. As in the case of jury representativeness, it developed out of the limitations of traditional legal methods of proof to establish patterns of discrimination and through the courts' realization that racial discrimination was a systematic problem. The development of the law under Title VII of the 1964 Civil Rights Act has increasingly recognized and encouraged the use of statistical analysis of employment data as the result of a significant conceptual change in the definition of discrimination. Title VII made it unlawful for an employer:

> 1. to fail or refuse to hire or to discharge any individual or otherwise discriminate against any individual because of such individual's race, color, religion, sex or national origin. [Civil Rights Act of 1964, §703(2)]

This language suggests that illegality requires the intentional application of different standards to employees or job applicants on the basis of race, sex, or religion. This standard, which was generally assumed to have been the one enacted, implies an investigation into the motive of an alleged offender (see Fiss 1971). But as the law developed, the courts came to define discrimination to include the use of hiring or employment standards that have a disparate negative impact on protected groups, regardless of the employer's state of mind, unless such standards can be justified on the basis of business necessity.

The leading decision was *Griggs v. Duke Power and Light Company* (1971), in which the Court held that the use of employment tests and the requirement of a high-school diploma were both discriminatory practices because they operated "to disqualify Negroes at a substantially higher rate than white applicants" where "neither standard is shown to be significantly related to successful job performance." Rejecting the employer's argument that it was not guilty of violating the law because it did not adopt these standards with a view to their racial impact, the Court stated, "Absence of discriminatory intent does not redeem employment procedures or testing mechanisms that operate as 'built in headwinds' for minority groups and are unrelated to measuring job capability." The standard thus enunciated suggested the necessity for two different but related empirical investigations. The plaintiff must show that the employment practice in fact "operated as a built in headwind"—that is, that it disqualified minority candidates at a disproportionate rate—while in response the employer could seek to justify the practice on the ground that it was "significantly related to successful job performance." Social scientists were routinely employed by both sides to carry out the investigations (Copeis 1977).

Although the question of intentionally different treatment did not easily lend itself to proof through statistical analysis, statistical analysis is the obvious way to establish disparate impact. It has turned out to be virtually the only acceptable way to establish the validity of claimed justification.

In developing the Court's definition of discrimination, it is not easy to trace the impact of social science data or analysis. Social scientists' criticism of the reliability of employment tests and other criteria helped to convince the courts that important business purposes were not necessarily served through their use and that such tests were biased against minorities (see Brief for Petitioner in *Griggs* v. *Duke Power*, 1971). It seems likely, however, that the same conclusions would have been reached even without the help of social scientists. The scope of employment discrimination was and is common knowledge, and testimony about the hiring record of those institutions involved in the early cases provided obvious proof of racial discrimination, even to the most unsophisticated observer. Moreover, the Court was not presented with scientific testimony about the scope of discrimination nor about the need for generalized remedies, and the Court's rejection of employment testing was similar to its rejection of other hiring standards; it was based on the Court's broad reading of the statute. As the Court stated in *Griggs*, "the objective of Congress . . . was to achieve equality of employment opportunities and to remove barriers which have appeared in the past to favor . . . white employees" (*Griggs*, 1971). The Court was, in part, influenced by the guidelines on employment set out by the Equal Employment Opportunities Commission (EEOC). The EEOC's determination that tests and other hiring standards violated Title VII seems to have been based on data demonstrating that such standards tend to eliminate a higher percentage of blacks than whites. The standards the EEOC developed to determine when a prima facie case of discrimination was made and the documentation necessary to establish a business-necessity standard were developed with the aid of social scientists. In general, the standards made it easy to establish a prima facie case and extremely difficult to refute one (EEOC Guidelines on Employer Selection Procedure 1970).

In sum, social science has played an important role in developing and enforcing standards in the area of employment discrimination, but here, too, the impact has been achieved piecemeal, through individual contributions aimed at establishing specific points about the reliability of individual tests rather than through work aimed at defining the dimensions and nature of discrimination. The situation in employment discrimination is more complicated than that of the jury pool, because employers were told that they could continue to employ a test that disqualified a disproportionate number of blacks and women if they could establish its correlation with job performance. Although *Duren* explicitly leaves open the possibility that a jury may be chosen from a panel that systematically departs from a fair cross-section if "there is adequate justification for this infringement [of the defendant's interest in a fair jury]" (1979, p. 368), in fact there has been no successful attempt to demonstrate adequate justification. Establishing a correlation between test scores and job performance raised the difficulty that such a correlation could only be demonstrated by measuring the performance of minorities and comparing it with test results, but since the agency assumed differential validity—so that tests might be valid for whites but not for blacks—overall validity could normally be demonstrated only after substantial numbers of women or minority employees were hired. Employers also faced a heavy burden in seeking to establish that the number of blacks or women in the hiring pool was significantly smaller than their proportion in the population. The ease with which a prima facie case of discrimination could be made out was, and is, in sharp contrast to the enormous statistical hurdles involved in demonstrating that disparities are in fact legitimate.

Social science method was employed as a weapon in the fight against discrimination, and in that capacity it certainly appeared powerful to most observers. Whether this state of affairs will long continue is not clear. The increasing use of statistical analysis in Title VII cases has revealed certain weaknesses, which are probably inherent in the attempt to use scientific measurement to determine whether a legal standard has been met. The statistical issues have become more and more complex as plaintiffs have developed new theories and defendants have hired economists and mathematicians to demonstrate that disparities in hiring or pay can be explained on the basis of such nonracial criteria as education, experience, or job performance. Complexity has inevitable consequences. It creates delays; it favors the more affluent institutional plaintiff and the wealthy defendant, who can enlist the aid of experts; and it lessens predictability, with the result that courts will be confused and the effective decisional criteria will be hidden, blurring the moral principle allegedly vindicated through the process. These developments are likely to lead to pressure for change, so that the standard of decision becomes one more easily applied by courts.

For example, in a case arbitrated by one of the authors, a claim was made that a community college in California discriminated against blacks in hiring faculty. The university had an affirmative-action office and offered a program of courses in Black Studies. The plaintiff was a black woman who was a few credits short of her master's degree.

The case presented a series of extremely complex questions. In accepting the master's degree criterion, the size of the applicant pool had to be considered. This meant defining arbitrarily the geographic area from which it was reasonable to assume that people were available and estimating how many blacks with master's degrees were in that area. In determining the validity of the master's degree requirement, it had to be made clear whether it was business-related and whether it served to disqualify blacks at a higher rate than whites. A determination had to be made whether the appropriate ratio was the number of minority applicants hired to the number of openings or the number of blacks in the work force to the number of whites. Further, should the Black Studies program be treated separately from other hiring for these purposes? If one looked separately at the general hiring program, would a one- or a two-tailed test be a more appropriate measure of significance? Was it permissible to vest final discretionary authority in the provost, a white male?

None of these are questions that regular legal processes are likely to deal with very well. The factual issues are extremely difficult to resolve without considerable research, the legal questions cannot be addressed without knowing a great deal about how academic institutions operate, and the moral implications are complicated. Considerable pressure might therefore be expected for standards that are more easily justified and applied. The issues involved in such cases represent a clash of legitimate values rather than the vindication of a clear moral principle. Thus, the sense of outrage that fueled the earlier decisions has been replaced by the sort of calculation about precedent and meaning characteristic of most areas of the law.

Over time, the Supreme Court grew less receptive to EEOC standards (see *Teamsters v. U.S.*, 1977), employer representatives became increasingly sophisticated in the use of statistical method to demonstrate that factors other than race or sex can explain apparent differences in promotional or hiring policies, and some concern was expressed that the focus on systemic questions has tended to bypass potential plaintiffs with a particularized claim of invidious treatment. Nevertheless, despite its weaknesses, the use of social science techniques in the area has permitted a field of law originally described as a "poor imperfected thing" to have a major impact on hiring practices across the country.

As is the case with venire representativeness, challenges to employment practices are relatively easy to prepare, and the very existence of the method has greatly increased the frequency with which jury commissioners and employers can expect to be challenged. Social science has given real meaning to what were formerly vague standards, permitting their general application. In addition, in both areas the challenges have, on the whole, been successful, and the perception of the likelihood of a successful challenge may well lead more and more jury officials and companies to change their practices before they are questioned.

Two Examples of the Explicit Use of Social Science to Define General Standards: Treatment and Insanity

Venire representativeness and employment discrimination are examples of the use of social science methods to decide legal issues. We have argued, however, that concepts are affected by the methods available for measuring them. The use of statistical methods is not simply the adoption of a superior instrument for estimating a quantity the legal system has always considered important; like many measuring instruments, its use has helped to shape conceptual changes in the legal meaning of representativeness.

This contribution has been implicit, not formally acknowledged by courts or legislatures. However, in other situations, social science expertise, if not social science research and methodology, has had an explicit role in provoking the enunciation of new legal standards that apply to whole classes of cases. A good example of this kind of participation is evaluation of institutions for the mentally ill or retarded.

The Definition of Adequate Treatment   In *Wyatt v. Stickney* (1971, 1974) and *Heiderman v. Pennhurst State School and Hospital* (1979), psychiatrists and psychologists testified to the adequacy of the hospital facilities to achieve their goals. In *Wyatt v. Stickney*, the question involved the ability of the hospital to discharge its duty to provide treatment for mental patients; in the *Pennhurst* case, similar issues were raised specifically with respect to mentally retarded patients. The influence of current psychological thinking in these and related decisions (for example, *O'Connor v. Donaldson*, 1975) was twofold: first, an informal, implicit influence contributed to the elevation of the idea of "treatment" to a criterion for permissible long-term civil commitment; second, the criteria for adequate treatment were formally defined. Since the late 1950s, criticism from both legal activists and psychologists has led to the perception of the mental hospital as a "restrictive" or "drastic" alternative, jeopardizing not only the patients' civil rights, but often their mental health as well (Wexler 1976). The legal formulations shifted and came, at least tentatively, to accept the proposition that, since the purpose of segregating the nondangerous mentally ill was to provide rehabilitative treatment, under the equal protection clause, the justification for their incarceration depended on the treatment (Ennis and Emery 1978; Wexler 1976). If the "treatment" failed to measure up to minimally adequate standards, the justification for confinement would vanish, and the patients should be released. Given this formulation, the decision in any particular case required an expert evaluation of the quality of care in the institution.

Obviously, the social scientists' role in answering a question like this is much less constrained than it is in the application of a statistical test to the venire. In *Wyatt* v. *Stickney* and in *Pennhurst*, psychologists and psychiatrists testified on a wide range of questions related to treatment, including education, rehabilitation, training, staffing, facilities, restraints, abuse, the therapeutic value of various drugs, and the availability and suitability of alternative types of care. In deciding whether the particular institutions met the minimum requirements, it was inevitable that the social scientists should make an effort to specify what the minimum requirements were and not surprising that in accepting the social scientists' decision on the adequacy of the particular institution, the legal system would also accept their general definition of adequacy. In cases such as these, therefore, the assessment of a particular organization may have fairly direct and immediate general implications.

Although it may be too early to evaluate the success of social science in drafting a workable definition of adequate treatment, the attempt so far seems promising. But early promise has not always been fulfilled when lawyers and mental-health professionals have collaborated in constructing definitions. The attempt to use social-scientific and medical expertise to draft a formal legal standard of insanity was famously promising at the start, but later became a notorious disappointment.

The Definition of Insanity   For years, both the psychiatric and legal literatures criticized the legal standard for insanity because it made no sense in psychiatric terms. The charge was frequently made that the legal definition of insanity based on the defendant's inability to distinguish between right and wrong required the law to differentiate among people whose mental states were medically indistinguishable. A great deal of concern was expressed about this unfortunate and nonscientific standard, and various efforts were made to amend the legal definition of insanity to lend it greater psychiatric validity, a goal which turned out to be difficult to achieve. Finally, in what was initially hailed as a major breakthrough, the District of Columbia Court of Appeals adopted the Durham rule (*Durham* v. *U.S.*, 1954), which held that the hallmark of insanity was the diagnosis of a mental disease as that concept is used by the psychiatric community. However, once promulgated, the Durham rule elicited even more criticism than the original M'Naghten "right and wrong" test.

Critics pointed out that the legal and medical definitions are directed to different issues. There is no reason for the question of punishment to turn on the desirability of treatment. Moreover, many psychiatrists and psychologists began to question the basic concept of mental illness just at the time the courts adopted it. Courts and legal scholars have largely drawn back in disarray, with a general consensus that the effort to adopt the scientific standard was a major blunder. In short, the law turned out to be more resistant to change than many scholars assumed it would be, because the behavioral assumptions addressed by scientific research turned out, in retrospect, not to have been crucial to the existing rule.

It should be noted that, for all the controversy it generated, there is little evidence that the change to the Durham rule had much effect on the behavior of juries. Rita Simon's research (1967) suggests that juries given the M'Naghten instructions were slightly less likely to acquit by reason of insanity than juries given either the Durham rule or no instructions on the legal definition of insanity, the latter two groups not differing from each other. The differences she found may have been attenuated by the fact that individual jurors often enunciated a right-wrong standard when it was not included in the instructions, presumably on the basis of their previous experience or reading, and they may have persuaded other jurors to adopt it. In general, remarkably little research was devoted to the actual consequences of the use of different definitions of insanity; the controversy was mainly spurred by theoretical and conceptual differences between legal and psychological purposes and points of view.

One of the most fundamental assumptions of psychiatry, for example, is that mental illness is a continuous variable, permitting rational judgments of "more" or "less," but in many cases allowing only the most arbitrary judgments of "present" or "absent." The judgment of guilt or innocence requires that insanity be considered not as a continuous but as a dichotomous variable. Unless this basic difference can be resolved, there can be no mutually compatible definition at the higher levels, and since the dividing line is arbitrary, there will be plenty of room for contradictory expert testimony at trial court.

But surely it could be argued that adequacy of treatment is a continuous variable as well; the line between adequacy and inadequacy is as arbitrary as the line between sanity and insanity. Although, so far, the law's need for a dichotomous judgment has not raised problems in this area, it is possible that conflicts will arise in the future. It is notable that most of the cases that have been decided in favor of patients and against mental institutions resemble the early employment-discrimination cases in that the institutions fell so far short of minimal standards that a simple description of the conditions could well have persuaded a layman, without the addition of any social science theory about standards of adequate treatment.

Nevertheless, the task of defining adequacy of treatment is probably easier than the task of defining sanity (or insanity). The actual standards laid down involve minimal standards of adequacy, acknowledging both the continuous nature of the variable and the possibility of defining a consensually validated threshold. It would probably not be possible, from a medical point of view, to arrive at a set of minimal standards for sanity (in fact, it could be argued that M'Naghten attempted to do just that). Insanity is not only a continuum, it is many continua: it is multivariate. For any set of clear workable minimal standards that can be devised, it is possible to envision some subset of universally recognizable lunatics who could meet those standards. While it may be possible to define necessary standards for sanity, it is much more difficult—and probably impossible, at present—to define sufficient standards (or, alternatively, to define necessary conditions for insanity). Most elements will be diagnostic only in combination with many other elements.

Further, given the articulation of minimally acceptable standards, the tribunal may be in a position to make more sensitive, differentiated judgments in the treatment case than in the insanity case. The law's dichotomous judgment may be less absolute in the former case, because it is possible to estimate the size of the discrepancy between acceptable practices and the actual practices of a given institution and to tailor the remedies accordingly. One institution may fall short because the number of doctors fails to reach the quota specified by the definition of an acceptable patient-staff ratio, while another falls short on ten other dimensions as well. Perceived blameworthiness is likely to be a function of such differences in size of discrepancy.

Judgments of insanity ordinarily do not permit such sensitive consideration of degrees of mental disturbance or of the range of possible remedies. The tribunal is given no opportunity to consider the whole range of mental states between normal and insane at the same time, to place the defendant at the appropriate place on this continuum, and to recommend remedies accordingly. For all intents and purposes, the insanity defense still requires a dichotomous judgment between guilty and innocent—a judgment of enormous symbolic significance.

The Use of General Social Science Data and Theory in the Trial Court

The use of general aggregate data at the level of the trial courts has expanded into many new areas since *Brown v. Board of Education* (1954). Social scientists have testified on such diverse areas as the effects of prison environments, the reliability of eyewitness identification, the effects of bilingualism on school children, community perceptions of obscenity, issues relating to jury composition (for example, motions for change of venue based on widespread community prejudice, the conviction-proneness of juries empowered to decide capital cases), and a host of factors believed to exert strong but subtle influences on juror perceptions, ranging from pretrial publicity to the clothing of the participants (prison or police uniforms, for instance).

The example of eyewitness identification will serve as a useful illustration. Although psychological testimony on factors that impair eyewitness accuracy dates from the turn of the century, such testimony was seldom attempted and still more seldom accepted until the 1970s; since then, its use has burgeoned. In most such cases, the expert testifies to basic, well-established research findings about individual and situational factors that impair a person's ability to remember events clearly; these factors include the passage of time, the complexity of the event, emotional arousal, social expectations and stereotypes, perceptual biases, events occurring between the original perception and the witness's report, and the form in which the question is asked (see Loftus 1979; Wells and Loftus 1984). In most of these cases, the expert does not examine the eyewitness but rather testifies to basic factors known to affect perception and memory. It is then up to the jury to decide which of these factors were present and important in the case before them and how much the jurors should modify their belief in the witness on the basis of their new general knowledge. The expert may also warn them that certain plausible factors are not useful in assessing the witness's credibility—for example, by referring to the frequently replicated finding that the confidence of the witness is not related to his or her accuracy (see, for example, Wells, Lindsay, and Ferguson 1979).

Until recently, the admissibility of such testimony was highly unsettled. In 1974, for example, when one of the authors testified on eyewitness accuracy in a trial court, the testimony was accepted subject to a motion to strike. As the result of a hung jury, however, the case was retried before a different judge, who accepted the motion to exclude the testimony as speculative and irrelevant. (In neither instance did the judge ask for an outline of the testimony before deciding whether to let the witness take the stand.) Although general testimony on eyewitness accuracy is increasingly accepted, its admissibility is still up to the discretion of the trial-court judge and varies from one jurisdiction to another. Quite recently, general legal recommendations designed to introduce a greater skepticism about the testimony of eyewitnesses have been made. For example, in a 1976 report to the House of Commons, Lord Devlin stated:

> We do however wish to insure that in ordinary cases prosecutions are not brought on eyewitness evidence only and that, if brought, they will fail. We think that they ought to fail, since in our opinion, it is only in exceptional cases that identification evidence is by itself sufficiently reliable to exclude a reasonable doubt about guilt. [Devlin 1976]

And in the United States, lower-court judges' discretionary decisions to exclude expert testimony concerning the reliability of eyewitness identifications have been overturned in several recent appellate court cases (*State v. Chapple*, 1983; *People v. McDonald*, 1984; *U.S. v. Downing*, 1985). In this area, at least, the trend has been toward recognition of the relevance of *general* psychological theory and data to particular cases.

It is likely that social scientists' growing concern with the application of research on perception and memory to the courtroom setting helped to stimulate this development and that the law's prior and independent concern with the power of the eyewitness increased judicial and legislative receptivity to the social science data; the two are undoubtedly so organically and circularly connected that attempts to demonstrate a unidirectional influence, here as elsewhere in the relationship between social science data and legal thinking, must prove fruitless.

The Generalized Use of Social Science in Shaping the Law

In the legislatures and higher appellate courts, where the aim is to establish general rules and principles, the uneasiness and uncertainty about the application of aggregate-level data to the individual case largely disappears. Here, at last, the decision-makers and the data gatherers are dealing at the same level of abstraction: the decision-makers want to establish general laws and principles of justice that will apply not just to one situation, but to a defined universe of situations; and the social scientists can offer general principles of behavior and data based on the behavior of many individuals or groups. The decision-makers may, of course, decide that the data are not germane or not trustworthy, and, as has been shown in regard to the insanity defense, there may be numerous other obstacles to fruitful collaboration. But with the disappearance of the individual, the awful question of specific applicability and fairness is no longer an issue.

Whether it is this sort of epistemological compatibility that appeals to them or whether it is simply the perceived importance is an open question, but social scientists tend to focus primarily on these abstract upper levels in their discussions of "the uses of social science data in the legal system" (see Lindblom and Cohen 1979). It is a common fantasy of social scientists that the Congress or the Supreme Court make a major policy change, explicitly giving the credit to their research. This almost never happens, of course, and there is a tendency among social scientists to underestimate the use of social science data because they define *use* as "exclusive reliance on social-science data in major decisions" (see Weiss 1979). Just as simplistically, there may be a tendency on the part of the social scientists, exhilarated by the unfamiliar atmosphere of the adversary system, to equate *use* with *victory*.

The Influence of Social Science Data in the Appellate Courts   Gauging the degree of actual use of social science data since the first major attempt and symbolic victory in *Brown* v. *Board of Education* is not easy. In an examination of all United States Supreme Court cases in 1954, 1959, 1964, 1969, and 1974, Victor Rosenblum and his colleagues concluded that the frequency with which social-scientific works are cited is increasing, but that the same cannot be said for reliance on social science—that is, for the importance of the data to the point at issue, or the importance of the empirical point for the outcome of the case (Rosenblum et al. 1978). So far, the Court has used social science mainly for unimportant issues, although Rosenblum feels that there is some indication that this situation had begun to change by 1974.

Although the technique of examining all the cases in a sample of years is, in principle, the most accurate way of assessing trends in judicial reliance on a given form of evidence, in practice it is very risky when the sample is small. Many of the major examples of the use of social science data in the twenty-year period covered by Rosenblum's research—the cases concerning jury size and unanimity, those concerning the death penalty, the cases extending the rights of juvenile delinquents, and the eyewitness-identification cases, among others—happened to be decided in years that were not sampled.

Although the case study method used by Donald Horowitz (1977) cannot provide any reliable indication of such trends, it does, through salient counterexamples, suggest important qualifications to Rosenblum's general conclusion that social science, even when cited, is relatively uninfluential. Horowitz argues, for example, that in certain cases (such as *Hobson* v. *Hansen*, 1969, 1971, and *In re Gault*, 1967), the appellate courts gave too much weight to social science, handing down decisions that went far beyond the evidence cited.

It is difficult to reach any but the most tentative conclusions on the general use of social science data by the appellate courts because the phenomenon itself is so diverse. First, there is huge variability in the quality of available data across issues. High-quality, relevant empirical data exist for very few issues of the sort the courts consider. Depending on the particular issue, there may be important empirical questions with little or no relevant data, unrecognized empirical questions with a respectable body of data, empirical questions on which the data are mixed either in quality or in implications for the outcome, or both, and even fundamentally nonempirical issues to which a litigant will attempt to apply empirical data. Appellate-court judges are not in a very good position to distinguish among these possibilities.

The Ways in Which Social Science Data Reach the Appellate Courts   Even when there is consensus on the empirical nature of the question, there seems to be little consistency in the ways in which social scientists become involved in studying empirical issues potentially related to major legislation or test cases, in the degree of their collaboration on the case itself, or in the ways in which the data come to the attention of the legislatures or the Supreme Court. The long-term adversarial method, foreshadowed by *Brown* v. *Board of Education,* involving years of planning and collaboration between lawyers and social scientists in the definition of the empirical propositions and the collection of new data or organization of old data, all with the same degree of care as is lavished on the legal preparation, is exceedingly rare and likely to be feasible only for institutional litigants. The capital-punishment cases of the 1970s brought, like *Brown* v. *Board of Education,* by the NAACP Legal Defense and Educational Fund were of this type, as were certain children's rights cases (for example, *Parham* v. *J.R.*, 1979). In these cases, the briefs presented by the parties or by amici curiae contained comprehensive summaries of the available data, compiled or overseen by social scientists. (In both instances, the Court seems to have decided that nonempirical issues were more important than empirical ones.)

Quite a different model is represented by the Court's use of increasingly sophisticated social science data in the series of cases on jury size and unanimity. In these, the social scientists were not involved in the preparation of the arguments, and, in fact, very little social science research was presented in the briefs. And yet, in *Williams* v. *Florida* (1970), the Supreme Court held that six-member juries were constitutional, concluding that there was "no discernible difference in the performance of six and twelve member juries" in accuracy of verdicts, ratios of convictions to acquittals, representativeness, or the minority's ability to resist majority pressure. The Court cited "experiments" in support of some of these contentions and relied on intuition for others. Sometimes the "experiments" consisted of rather flimsy anecdotal reports; at other times the Court apparently based its opinion on studies that could only support the opposite conclusion. For example, they argued that a 5-to-1 split and a 10-to-2 split would put identical pressure on the minority, whereas the classic, well-replicated finding in the study they cited (Asch 1952) is that a minority of two is much less likely to conform than a lone dissenter, regardless of the size of the majority.

Later, in *Colgrove* v. *Battin* (1973) the Court cited more recent studies as having established the correctness of its earlier conclusion. Their use in the Court opinion appeared to give to the studies cited both decisiveness and permanence, which their hopelessly flawed designs did not merit (Zeisel and Diamond 1974; Saks 1977). In the unanimity decisions (*Apodaca* v. *Oregon,* 1972; *Johnson* v. *Louisiana,* 1972), as with the issue of representativeness in *Williams,* the majority rejected the empirical data mentioned by the dissenters and simply relied on intuition, deciding that juries would behave in the same thorough, conscientious manner whether or not a unanimous decision was required.

Many social scientists were disturbed by these decisions: those whose data were not used, those whose data were used (or misused, as they saw it), and several who simply felt that, if the question was to be phrased empirically, the best available empirical data should be used in the most careful way possible. Leading experts on jury research challenged the Court's conclusion and pointed out that the early research studies cited by the Court were not experiments and that the later studies were designed so poorly that their results were uninterpretable.

The number of studies on jury size and unanimity grew enormously during the 1970s. But for most purposes, of course, the timing was wrong. One of the problems with the use of social science data by the courts is that a court may have to (or may choose to) decide an issue before adequate data exist, and typically the decision cannot easily be changed should the data cast it into question. Despite the power of the argument against its position on six- and twelve-person juries, it would be difficult for the Supreme Court to change now. Constitutional principles cannot be changed back and forth with the ebb and flow of scholarly debate about the reliability and validity of various studies without doing damage to the sense of stability inherent in the idea of a rule of law. Thus, it appeared that the wealth of research on the relative risks and disadvantages of six-member juries would simply sit there, mute and embarrassing.

Much of this research was used, however, in *Ballew* v. *Georgia* (1978), when the Court reviewed all or most of the data on six- and twelve-member juries and used it to decide that five-person juries were unconstitutional. Again, social scientists did not collaborate in writing the briefs, and in fact the briefs do not include many references to empirical research on juries. Nonetheless, the Court made *Ballew* a major test case on jury size, and it may well represent the most extensive and sophisticated use of social science research to date in a majority opinion, the one real difficulty being that all the data pertain to the differences between six- and twelve-person juries and do not speak to the differences between the unconstitutional five-member jury and the constitutional six-member jury. Finally, in *Burch* v. *Louisiana* (1979), the Court, citing the *Ballew* opinion, held that unanimity was required in six-person juries. No social science research was mentioned in this opinion.

The cases concerning jury size and unanimity, like some of those discussed by Horowitz (1977), illustrate the dangers of the introduction of empirical social science issues at the appellate-court level: the search for relevant data is often incomplete and haphazard, and the time available to reach a binding decision is short. In almost all cases, the Court does reach a decision, sometimes basing it on the limited empirical evidence that happens to have come to its attention, sometimes rejecting the evidence as inconclusive and deciding the case on other grounds. Although this state of affairs has been widely criticized (see Horowitz 1977), it has generally been accepted as inevitable. A social scientist, it is argued, faced with inadequate evidence, has the luxury of postponing a final decision until better evidence has been collected; this option is not available to appellate-court judges.

"Temporary" versus "Permanent" Empirical Decisions   That the courts' decisions are constrained by the requirement of finality is largely a matter of faith, however; no one has really systematically considered the presumed evils that would follow from the Court's reaching a decision based on the evidence before it but explicitly raising the possibility that new empirical evidence would compel a different decision. Thus, the decision in *Williams*, rather than concluding that six-person juries were definitely no different from twelve-person juries, might have held that, since the available evidence was insufficient to demonstrate a difference, for the time being none would be assumed; six-person juries would be permissible, but this decision might be changed if a substantial and convincing body of new evidence were to be produced.

There is at least one precedent for such a decision. In *Witherspoon* v. *Illinois* (1968), the petitioner presented sketchy evidence based on three unpublished studies indicating that because juries that were empowered to decide capital cases were "death qualified" by excluding opponents of capital punishment such juries were more likely to convict than other juries. Witherspoon contended that he had therefore been tried by a tribunal that was "less than neutral" on the question of guilt or innocence. The Court rejected the empirical data as "too tentative and fragmentary" to demonstrate a bias toward conviction, and it held that a modified form of death qualification, excluding only the most adamant opponents of the death penalty, was still permissible. However, it also acknowledged that the question was an empirical one, and that although present data were insufficient to answer it, future data might demonstrate that Witherspoon's claims were correct.

Social scientists eventually responded to this encouragement by conducting a variety of methodologically superior studies of the effects of death qualification. Unlike most social science research considered by the courts, many of these studies were designed with the specific, legally relevant empirical questions in mind, in direct response to the *Witherspoon* opinion. As recommended by Thomas Pettigrew in another context, the social scientists were "in on the case from the beginning to shape its form towards issues that social science can address competently" (1979, p. 26). Along with the previous research, their studies were introduced in an evidentiary hearing at the trial-court level, and later in appellate-court litigation in the California Supreme Court. The testimony at the hearing included extensive discussion of all the old and new research, as well as general testimony on such methodological issues as statistical significance, procedures for controlling extraneous variables, and the types of generalization that can be made on the basis of different types of study.

The California Supreme Court's decision in *Hovey v. Superior Court* (1980) analyzes this record in detail and shows an unusually strong grasp of the empirical and methodological issues. The decision goes far beyond *Witherspoon,* accepting the social science data on every point raised. But, like *Witherspoon,* it concludes that there is at least one unanswered empirical question that must still be dealt with before a final decision can be reached.

The *Hovey* decision is notable not only for the fact that it drew the "social scientific" conclusion of "not proven," rather than going on to make a binding conclusion of "not true"; it is also an excellent example of the analysis of social science evidence by an appellate court.

> The opinion contains a discussion of empirical social scientific data that is far more extensive and knowledgeable than any that has ever appeared in a published opinion by an American court. All of the objections that are commonly raised to the use of social science in litigation are addressed and overruled. Indeed, the factual issue that is reserved as unresolved is carefully defined as an empirical issue on which further scientific research is needed. [Gross 1980, p. 22]

The unresolved factual issue involved the possible counterbalancing effect of excluding jurors who would *always* vote for the death penalty; subsequent research demonstrated that this group is far too small to outweigh the effects of the *Witherspoon* exclusion (Kadane 1984). In 1985, the Eighth Circuit, on the basis of the entire empirical record including the new evidence, held that the practice of death qualification is unconstitutional because it biases capital juries against the defendant in determining guilt and innocence and because it impairs the representativeness of the jury (*Grigsby v. Mabry,*

1985). However, the Fourth Circuit, on the basis of the same record, held that the practice is constitutional, and that empirical social science evidence should not be considered in deciding the constitutional question (*Keeten* v. *Garrison*, 1984). The U.S. Supreme Court largely followed *Keeten*. It criticized the studies in ways that indicated an unfamiliarity with scientific method as well as with the research in the record, but then held that a bias toward quality verdicts in capital cases was constitutionally permissible in any case (*Lockhart* v. *McCree*, 1986).

The plan of research and litigation on death qualification, like that leading up to *Brown* v. *Board of Education*, represents a carefully planned effort in which lawyers and social scientists educated each other so that the research would be relevant to the legal issues and its presentation to the courts would be comprehensive and accurate. The cases on jury size and unanimity embody the opposite extreme—the reliance on social science data in the Supreme Court opinions, especially *Ballew*, coming as a complete surprise, not only to the social science community, but to the litigants themselves. Between these two extremes there is room for a wide range of major and minor roles for social scientists and social science. Perhaps the most frequent influence is the one least susceptible to documentation—the absorption of social science thinking through the general intellectual climate, so that judgments that would have required authority thirty or fifty years ago now seem to be based on common sense. When social-scientific and legal views coincide, progress is likely to be rapid. The move toward deinstitutionalization, for example, was spurred on the one hand by legal activists' increasing concern about depriving innocent people of their liberty and, on the other, by social scientists' increasingly well-documented belief in the harmful effects of institutionalization (Wexler 1976).

RECEPTIVITY TO SOCIAL SCIENCE DATA IN DIFFERENT AREAS OF LAW

Although similar problems of design and use arise whenever efforts are made to influence the law by means of evidence from the social sciences, certain legal realms seem to have been more receptive to social science data than others. Many of our examples have been drawn from criminal law, family law, and mental-health law. In part, this is a consequence of our own familiarity with the literature (economic data are regularly used in antitrust cases, for example), but in part the differences are real. The significant role social science has played in developing criminal-justice procedures, for example, is in sharp contrast to its limited role in discussions of the procedures used to settle disputes in labor relations. It has long been recognized that the procedures used to determine rights and resolve disputes and the remedies employed to correct misconduct will have a powerful effect on the fairness and efficiency of American labor law. A rich literature exists, dating back to Frankfurter and Green's significant and effective analysis of the labor injunction (1930). But influential empirical research is scarce. Only a few studies have attempted to measure the success of existing programs or to examine their operation. Changes in procedure have rarely, if ever, arisen in response to scientific data, although labor relations have furnished an area of considerable procedural development during the past few decades. We will examine labor law in an attempt to understand why social science is seldom used in this area. We will then briefly consider the use of social science in criminal law and examine the similarities and differences between the two fields.

Labor Law[2]

There are several reasons to expect labor relations to be in the vanguard of successful collaboration between law and social science. One of the first important cases in which the Supreme Court acknowledged the relevance of empirical data was *Muller v. Oregon* (1908), which involved the right of the state to limit hours of work for women. The brief in that case, filed by Louis Brandeis, became renowned for its effective marshaling of social facts to persuade the court that women were entitled to special legislative protection. To this day, the term "Brandeis brief" is sometimes used to describe a brief focusing on data rather than doctrinal analysis. The development of information about labor relations pursued by scholars in many fields is the primary focus of the entire discipline known as industrial relations. Scholars of industrial relations include economists, sociologists, organizational behaviorists, and lawyers. In passing the National Labor Relations Act, Congress further established a specialized agency, with the expectation that it would become familiar with the realities of labor relations through personal experience and scholarship. Serious legislative efforts to amend the labor law are frequently made, and scholars are often asked to testify.

Despite the rich potential collaboration, the law of labor relations has not been significantly shaped by what has been called professional social inquiry (Lindblom and Cohen 1979). This situation is not due to unwillingness by decision-makers to consider the views of academics. On the contrary, the development of labor law has been importantly influenced by the ideas of law professors—ideas frequently derived from their personal experiences. For example, in a highly significant series of decisions, the Supreme Court overruled earlier precedent to make encouragement of labor arbitration a major goal of national labor policy.[3] The leading opinions derive their picture of labor arbitration from a series of lectures by Harry Shulman, then dean of the Yale Law School. Shulman (1956) based the lectures on his own experience as Chief Umpire for the Ford Motor Company and the United Auto Workers. The Court ignored the few published efforts to systematically study the topic. Many labor-relations experts have since pointed out that Shulman's description of arbitration is idiosyncratic and not generally applicable. Similarly, the Supreme Court based its most important decision defining the duty to

---

[2] This section is primarily concerned with the use of social science in labor law adjudication, rather than in legislation. While social scientists are frequently asked to testify about the wisdom of proposed legislation, and social scientists have been advisers to legislators, social science research has not played a major role either in shaping labor-relations legislation or in setting the legislative agenda. The basic structure of United States labor-relations law represents a balance of powerful political forces. Any effort at change perceived to be favorable to either side creates enormous counterpressure. In the course of political battle, lines are drawn on the basis of commitments, ideology, and voter pressure. The implications of empirical research rarely surface among such powerful forces; nor does such research spur Congress to initiate legislation. Typically, labor legislation is initiated and managed by organized labor or by management groups on the basis of their own political agenda. The evidence also suggests that, at least for the present, empirical research does not play a major role in establishing the political agenda of the parties. Thus, despite studies indicating their lack of importance as a practical matter, both labor and management have committed considerable resources to the struggle over so-called right-to-work laws.

[3] In 1960, the Supreme Court decided three cases in a single day, establishing national policy concerning arbitration. The cases are known as "the Steelworkers Trilogy" or "the Trilogy." They are *United Steelworkers of America v. American Manufacturing Company*, *United Steelworkers of America v. Warrior and Gulf Navigation Company*, and *United Steelworkers of America v. Enterprise Wheel and Car Corporation*.

bargain in good faith on writings by Professor Archibald Cox while overlooking systematic studies of bargaining.[4]

Despite its claim to specialized effective decisions, the National Labor Relations Board (NLRB) rarely shows familiarity with studies of industrial relations. When social science research is referred to, it is usually to confer authority. The overwhelming body of decisions is based on technical manipulation of doctrine rooted in statutory analysis and questionable behavioral assumptions; the Court's decisions sometimes show exasperation with the Board's processes, but judical decisions reflect the same difficulties.

To the extent that there is sporadic use of empirical research, it is naïve. Legislative debate—on the state, local, or federal level—is, if anything, less well informed, and rarely does enacted legislation contain anything even suggesting a meaningful impact of social science.

The limited role of social science in shaping policy can be explained by many factors, none of which is confined to labor law.

The Absence of Directly Relevant Research   Problems in designing relevant research are pertinent to the situation. In general, all the following circumstances have contributed to the relative paucity of directly relevant research.

1. The complex nature of the legal rules as well as the fact that behavioral assumptions are rarely stated have made it difficult for social scientists to identify legally relevant research topics. By contrast, problems in the criminal-justice system are highly publicized and more likely to come to the attention of social scientists. Legal scholars seldom have the expertise or time to design social science research in either area. Even scholars who are capable of identifying behavioral assumptions are rarely capable of designing research projects to test them.

2. The sensitive nature of labor relations has impeded field studies. It accounts for the absence of cooperation from necessary parties and the desire of the NLRB itself to protect its process.

3. The types of research questions presented by legal assumptions in labor law are rarely central to the concerns or questions that interest social scientists.

4. Social scientists do not readily appreciate the institutional constraints under which the legal system operates, so that proposals for change can rarely be easily implemented.

5. The complexity of the issues almost always precludes the possibility of resolving by research all the factual questions to which answers would be needed for intelligent guidance of public policy.

The Limited Use of Available Data   Despite the paucity of field research geared to legal issues, a fair amount of data collected by social scientists could be utilized in establishing or changing legal rules. There are essentially three types of study: research directly aimed at testing the validity or desirability of legal or administrative rules; industrial relations research with implications for legal rules; and data collected in other areas with implications for labor relations, such as studies of conflict resolution, bargaining, and mediation in other contexts, and studies of group dynamics.

---

[4] See *National Labor Relations Board* v. *Insurance Agents International Union AFL-CIO* (1960), citing Cox (1958).

None of these has been utilized effectively or systematically, for reasons that are both general and particular to the type of research. The problems involved in using social-scientific research to change the basic direction of an area of law are suggested by the experience of one of the authors in investigating the wisdom of NLRB regulations of union organizing campaigns.

At the heart of the American system of industrial relations is the process by which employees vote for or against union representation in elections conducted and regulated by the NLRB. The stakes are high. If the majority of employees vote for representation, the union selected becomes the representative of all the employees in the voting unit, even though some might bitterly oppose it. The employer may not then deal with individual employees or with any other group, and he may not take unilateral action with regard to wages, hours, or working conditions before bargaining with the union. If a majority votes against representation, the union has no official standing and may not bargain, even for its members (*J. I. Case Co.* v. *National Labor Relations Board*, 1944; *National Labor Relations Board* v. *Katz*, 1962). Before the election, both union and employers typically conduct campaigns attempting to convince the employees to vote either for or against representation. On the authority of general statutory language forbidding employers to interfere with, or unions to use coercion against, the right to organize, the NLRB has developed an elaborate system of rules to govern campaign tactics. The Board has defined its regulatory purpose to be "to provide a laboratory in which an experiment may be conducted under conditions as nearly ideal as possible to determine the uninhibited desires of the employees. . . . Where, for any reason, the standard falls too low, the Board will set aside the elections and direct a new one" (*General Shoe Corporation*, 1948, pp. 124, 126).

The NLRB's scheme of regulation rests on certain assumptions about employees' voting behavior. It assumes that employees are attentive to the campaign, that free choice is fragile, and that employees' votes can easily be manipulated by nuances of retaliation coming from employers or through misrepresentations from unions. The Board assumes that employees will interpret employers' ambiguous statements as threats of reprisal and will be coerced thereby into voting against representation (Getman, Goldberg, and Herman 1975).

For some time, scholars had questioned the Board's assumptions. In particular, in a famous article, Derek Bok pointed out that many were inconsistent with the findings of voter studies in political elections (Bok 1970). A major study was undertaken to test the validity of the Board's assumptions (Getman, Goldberg, and Herman 1975).[5] For the six-year study, completed in 1975, the authors examined thirty-one elections, interviewing a panel of employee voters both before and after each election. An effort was made to contrast voter behavior in those elections in which the employer's campaign was thought to interfere with employee rights under the Act and those elections in which the employer's conduct was unobjectionable under the Board's standards. In each case, data were collected from the parties concerning the tactics they used, and the determination

---

[5] The Board refused to cooperate with the study until it was required by court order to turn over to the investigators the names and addresses of voters in its elections. The opinion by the Court of Appeals castigated the board for its refusal to cooperate and its hostility to a carefully designed, potentially valuable study.

as to legality was made by one of the NLRB's eminent administrative-law judges. In roughly two thirds of the studied elections, some illegal behavior took place, and roughly half of these involved illegality serious enough to warrant a substantial remedial order.

The study's basic finding was that conduct assumed by the Board to interfere with freedom of choice does not, in fact, affect employee voting behavior. The study also indicated that unions encounter significantly greater difficulty than do employers in communicating their message. The authors suggested massive changes in the NLRB's regulatory system, urging much greater freedom of speech for employees and greater access to employees for unions (Getman, Goldberg, and Herman 1976).

The study received considerable scholarly attention. Social scientists generally found its methodology careful and its findings compelling (Goetz and Wike 1977; Kochan 1977). Lawyers were more critical, and commentators raised questions from the perspective of labor and management (Miller 1976; Eames 1976). The vast majority of the comments were favorable, although many reviews challenged some aspect of the research designs, the findings, or the recommendations. The response from the Board itself in deciding whether to pay serious attention to the study was revealing.

In *Shopping Kart Food Market, Inc.* (1977), the majority of the Board relied in part on the study in deciding that it would no longer overturn elections based on campaign misrepresentation. The previous highly controversial doctrine had been under attack from within the Board for some time. The majority in *Shopping Kart* made clear, however, that it did not intend to adopt the study's suggested approach generally. "We shall, of course, continue our policy of overseeing other campaign conducts which interfere with employees free choice outside the area of misrepresentation." The minority sharply attacked the study and its conclusion. It accused the majority of preparing to drop the NLRB's traditional approach, and it rejected the study's general conclusion on the grounds that "forty-three years of conducting elections convinces us . . . that employees are influenced by certain union and employer campaign statements." The level of debate between the majority and minority was highly unsophisticated. As David Shapiro of the Harvard Law School pointed out, "On the one hand, the majority simply referred to the study without any consideration of its strengths and weaknesses. The dissenters, on the other hand, tried only to score debators' points against it without any pretense of objectivity" (1977, p. 1593).

Although the *Shopping Kart* decision was hailed as proof of the potential impact of social science on legal doctrine (Roomkin and Abrams 1977), the Board did not address itself to further changes on the basis of the study, and a short time later, with the change of a single Board member, it overturned the *Shopping Kart* decision. After criticizing the study's methodology, the Board majority commented:

> Even if this particular study was clearly supportive of all the author's conclusions, however, we would still not find it an adequate grounds for rejecting a rule which has been established for fifteen years. While we welcome research from the behavioral sciences, one study of only thirty-one elections in one area of the country is not sufficient to disprove the assumptions upon which the Board has regulated election conduct. . . . [*General Knit of California, Inc.*, 1978, p. 622]

Therefore, the Board continued to apply its traditional assumptions, almost totally ignoring the study.

Judicial response has been similarly limited. Even though a few courts have noted that the study casts doubts on the validity of the Board's assumption, the courts are bound by the statutory scheme to defer to the Board's officially proclaimed expertise.

The study was referred to extensively in the debate on the Labor Reform Act of 1977 (H.R. Report No. 95-637, 1977, pp. 24–35, 38–39; S. Report No. 411-22, 1977, pp. 144–261), but that act was not passed, and the study played only a minor role in a debate which was heavily political. Political currents in labor relations were far more influential than the findings of any scholarly work in shaping the bill's contours and its final fate. Nor has the study been followed by significant additional field work, although the desirability of such research has been noted many times.

Both the high cost of field work and the desire of research-funding agencies to commit their resources to path-breaking studies have militated against replication in this area. With regard to this study and other empirical work, the Board's willingness and ability to respond adequately have been limited by the fact that the NLRB and its staff are lawyers neither familiar with nor adept at dealing with social science data.

Where research supports intuitive assumptions, it may be referred to without critical consideration of the techniques by which it is gathered. Data that are counterintuitive are certain to be viewed suspiciously, little personal or institutional competence being available to evaluate their reliability. The suspicion is inevitable to the extent that the data suggest that the Board and its employees have devoted their effort to a meaningless or harmful process of regulation. Nor is the Board able to determine the extent to which it is safe to generalize on the basis of the limited data available. Because the field is a sensitive and adversarial one, and the issues are so complex that there has been no research, any research which concludes that significant change is desirable will inevitably be subject to hostile criticism.

Research in which the implications are spelled out and the researcher takes a forthright position on changes the Board should make becomes suspect as unduly adversarial. If the implications of research are not spelled out, they are likely to be misunderstood. Since in the field of labor relations the interest groups are extremely well organized, efforts to refute any significant research will be encouraged by whichever side feels aggrieved by it. To some considerable extent, both the law and its interpretation reflect the existing political balance between labor and management. Any potential effect of social science research on the law might disturb the balance and embroil the agency in bitter political controversy. This situation would obtain regardless of whether the data were favorable or opposed to union activity.

Moreover, almost by definition, significant change is likely to run counter to the ideological convictions of a majority of the Board. The existing system is shaped by legislative policy decisions reflected in statutory language and by a venerable line of decisions committing the agency to various points of view. A healthy sense of institutional modesty will mediate against substantial change in response to research findings when the implications and the generalizations which may be drawn from them are not easily determined.

Attitudes about the underlying realities of labor relations are frequently strongly held; they are based on a combination of political ideology, personal experience, and widely shared assumptions. Faced with a choice between such strong, widely shared beliefs and even carefully documented research findings, supported by regression analysis and matrices and mathematical formulas which they do not understand, decision-makers will, not surprisingly, opt for the former, particularly when the latter have been challenged by opposing data or have been subjected to critical attacks by other social scientists. Thus, counterintuitive data have rarely been embraced in a direct fashion. Empirical work may, of course, help to change general attitudes, and thus to precipitate change, but such an effect is difficult to predict. It requires a wide range of complementary work tied together by a general theory or model that gains acceptance, such as the general notion that administrative regulation generally fails to achieve its objectives.

Thus, experience with labor law suggests that, in an area lacking a substantial amount of research resulting in fairly clear policy implications, counterintuitive or controversial social science research findings are unlikely to effect changes in the law. On the other hand, the notion that empirical research is effective only when consistent with the intuitive knowledge of decision-makers is disturbing, suggesting both that research is rarely likely to make a difference to the basic approach which the law takes in an area and that its primary function will be conservative, confirming the behavioral basis for existing approaches, and suggesting interstitial improvement.

General Limitations on the Use of Social Science in Labor Law   A limited role for social science is likely to deter legal scholars or others concerned with reforming the system from undertaking complex empirical work. Such a situation requires that significant effort be expended to produce minor change. Traditional legal scholarship offers potentially greater impact for less effort. By discussing whether decisions are consistent with generally accepted doctrine, legislative history, or the researcher's own assumptions, traditional legal scholars have made a significant impact on the system of labor laws.[6] Nor does the prospect of a minor impact on legal rules appear to have much appeal to social scientists. Only a small fraction of industrial-relations research is therefore aimed at, or significantly shaped directly by, legal rules.

Thus, both the supply and the impact of social science research directly geared to legal rules are predictably limited. The use of other types of social science data offers some advantages but also introduces additional problems. Since other types of data are not explicitly designed to address issues arising in labor law, they have the advantage of appearing neither as prolabor nor as promanagement or even as having a scholarly ax to grind. Thus, the aura of scientific impartiality is more easily maintained, but the applicability of the data to specific labor-law relations is always questionable. For example, the dynamics of political elections, which have been widely studied, may or may not be applicable to NLRB elections, which have not been thoroughly studied. The Board has consistently ignored or depreciated the applicability of studies in contexts other than labor, on the assumption that the employees' economic dependence on the employer creates a unique situation. Similar studies of bargaining in other contexts have not been viewed as significant in shaping the employer's bargaining obligation under §8 (2) (5) of the NLRA, probably because they have not addressed the complex type of ongoing multifaceted relationships involved in collective bargaining.

[6]Thus, for example, Professor Archibald Cox has helped to shape the law dealing with the obligation to bargain in good faith (see text accompanying note 4, above) and the relationship between unions and members in the processing of grievances without any systematic investigation of the existing relations between grievants and stewards on how they would be affected by various possible approaches.

In addition, even if applicability was assumed, the implication of general studies on other contexts of labor-law rules is unlikely to be clear. Furthermore, the more general the data, the wider the field from which competing data may be selected, partly because the applicability, interrelations, and selection are involved in applying social science. The usefulness will, in part, turn on the sophistication of judges and of the lawyers who appear before them. Sophisticated use of empirical research by lawyers is hampered by the fact that only rarely will lawyers be tempted to deal with social science in a manner related to the likelihood of its utilization by courts. For most lawyers in routine cases, the start-up cost of investigating social science phenomena is not worth the effort. Studies are referred to in briefs only in important cases. The lack of familiarity increases the likelihood that when the lawyers and the courts do use social science data, they will do so badly.

The misuse of social science data is at least as old as *Muller* v. *Oregon,* the case that first sustained differentiation on the basis of gender. The brief in that case by Louis Brandeis reflects all the problems of adversarial nonscientific use of data and the result has created a myriad of obstacles for those seeking gender equality under the Constitution. Justice Brandeis is commonly recognized as one of the great legal minds of all time, but his brief is embarrassing in the way it links data of various types (Babcock et al. 1973, pp. 35–37). That it helped to lead the court to a questionable willingness to permit sexual differentiation has been noted several times. Given these considerations, it is not surprising that social science research is rarely used intelligently by courts or agencies to shape the law of labor relations. Moreover, none of the difficulties referred to are unique to labor relations.

However, the analysis does not exclude effective use of research in other cases or in other ways. Indeed, the balance of powerful political forces that tends to overwhelm social science data as a source is not always present. Several circumstances can be identified in which social science has played or is likely to play a significant role in the judicial process. When the law is uncertain or is in a state of flux and the behavioral assumptions upon which previous doctrine has rested become widely challenged, empirical data can play a role in either negating or reinforcing the assumptions on which previous doctrine rested. One explanation of the famous Footnote 11 in *Brown,* dealing with the findings of social scientists about the inherent inequality of "separate but equal" schools, is that it helped to complete the rejection of the behavioral assumptions underlying *Plessy* v. *Ferguson* (1896). Once social science comes to play a significant role in such areas, it is possible to assume that its use will increase because lawyers and judges in the field will become more familiar with it.

Reasons for Use and Nonuse The NLRB's failure to rely on empirical research is not typical of all administrative agencies. Since the use of empirical research by administrative agencies has not been systematically studied, however, it is impossible to obtain a precise picture of specific differences in various agencies. Such data as are available suggest that the Board is at one end of a very broad continuum, in that it does not conduct, authorize, or utilize social science research in formulating either rules or enforcement policies. Other agencies use social science research to a much greater extent (*Administrative Law Review* 1980). The Federal Trade Commission (FTC), for example, uses such materials in determining which cases to pursue in developing proof of the impact of conduct thought to be misleading to consumers and in evaluating the economic consequences of mergers and other actions deemed to be unfair (see, for example, Stanton 1980; Federal Trade Commission 1980). Social-welfare agencies frequently employ social science to determine the size and composition of groups entitled to benefits. The Environmental Protection Agency (EPA) has used it to determine the best strategy to use in eliminating pollutants (Ackerman and Hassler 1981). The variety of reasons why the Board lags behind other agencies in the use of social science is instructive about the factors that promote or retard an agency's receptivity to more traditional materials.

The Board has developed its doctrines entirely through adjudication rather than by rule-making. It is probable that the adjudicatory format is less favorable than is rule-making to the presentation or evaluation of sophisticated social science materials (Shapiro 1977, p. 1543).

The Board's professional staff is heavily weighted with lawyers. Lawyer field examiners are likely to investigate charges. In dubious cases, the decision on whether the charge is meritorious is submitted to a panel of lawyers. The final decision is made by the regional attorney and the regional director, who is almost certain to be a lawyer. This decision is appealed to other lawyers. If the matter is litigated, it is heard by administrative-law judges, who are lawyers. It may be appealed to the Board, whose members are almost exclusively lawyers, themselves supported by sizable staffs composed of lawyers. Failure to comply with the Board's order will trigger enforcement action by another group of attorneys.

As the result of a historical quirk, the Board is not authorized "to appoint individuals for the purpose of conciliation or mediation or for economic analysis" [National Labor Relations Act, 1947, §4(2)]. The limitation against the use of economists has prevented the Board from developing sophisticated familiarity with the area of social science currently most often related to legal decision-making.

The Board has no authority to initiate proceedings—only the parties have that privilege. Probably as a consequence, the NLRB has never developed a strategy for allocating its resources in certain areas or industries. The need to allocate resources has motivated such agencies as the EEOC and the FTC to employ social science methodology to estimate the areas where need and/or opportunity are greatest. The Board's constituencies are politically powerful, and the Board can generally play the role of impartial adjudicator rather than that of advocate. Since the Board does not have responsibility for allocating resources, it does not need to have an accurate profile of the groups utilizing its resources.

The Board's failure to employ social science has not made it notably less able than other agencies—such as the FTC and EPA—to carry out its mission. Indeed, studies of the FTC have been sharply critical; its use of social science has not prevented knowledgeable commentators from criticizing its basic policies and its allocation of resources. Scholars have similarly criticized other agencies, such as the EPA, which utilize social scientists much more than does the NLRB.

Nor has the absence of guidance from social scientists prevented labor and management from developing innovative quasi-legal institutions. The establishment of labor arbitration as a private system of justice has been one of the few acknowledged successes in dispute resolution in our time. It arose as a complement to the bargaining process, with little participation by the government and almost none by social scientists interested in labor relations specifically or dispute resolution generally. This process holds a significant cautionary message for social scientists, suggesting that complementary private interaction may be the key to attaining fair procedure, and when that occurs the system is likely to develop spontaneously.

Criminal Law

If problems of labor law exemplify the difficulties of stimulating pertinent research and persuading decision-makers to use it, the field of criminal law reveals that it is possible to develop considerable interaction, although neither lawyers nor social scientists view it as altogether successful. Social science has affected such questions as the standards for insanity, the constitutionality of the death penalty, the desirability of incarceration, and the proper strategy to be used in sentencing.

It is not easy to explain why the interaction is so much greater in criminal law. It is true that criminology has developed as a branch of research directly bearing on questions of public policy in criminal law; but there has been a great deal of field research in labor relations, which also exists as a special academic discipline.

Both as a result and as a cause of the interaction, criminological research is more frequently directed specifically to improving the legal system than is labor-relations research. When scholars know their work may have an impact, they are likely to address the legal questions. When courts and legislatures are aware that such research exists, and that it has been utilized in the past, they are more likely to take it into account.

The courts' willingness to consider social science research in dealing with criminal law probably reflects the general perception that the American system of criminal justice is a failure and that new ideas and approaches are called for. There is probably less willingness to be experimental about labor law because there is a general sense that the current approach is adequate and because the general public is much less aware of the issues, and therefore much less likely to complain. Moreover, suggestions for revision arise naturally from the interaction between political parties.

The existence of data and their use by courts and legislatures have not led to a general feeling of success. There may be more dissatisfaction about the role of social science in criminal law than in any other area, even including race relations. The sense of failure seems to derive from four major sources.

First, the proliferation of data has not answered the basic factual questions to which scholars have addressed themselves. Different studies point to different conclusions about such issues as the deterrent effect of punishment, whether imprisonment decreases crime, whether rehabilitation is possible, and the impact of shorter sentences. Second, there is a developing realization that policy issues are more complex than was once realized and that data collection and interpretation are at most only a first step toward their resolution. Third, even if the answers to substantive questions were known, they would not readily lead to the establishment of public policy because there is widespread disagreement about such fundamental issues as the goals of criminal laws and the criteria for characterizing conduct as criminal.

Finally, disappointment with the contribution of social science to criminal justice is almost surely related to general disappointment with the criminal-justice system. It has not stemmed the growth of crime. It is seen as having neither deterred nor rehabilitated and as failing to mete out appropriate punishment. The system is perceived to dispense justice unequally, the poor and members of minority groups singled out for harsher treatment in a variety of ways.

Dissatisfaction with social science based on its inability to make the United States system of justice more effective may ultimately reflect a misconception about what the law can accomplish. If problems of crime and inequality are ever resolved, it will be through major changes in the way society is organized, not through changes in legal rules or procedures.

THE EVALUATION OF SOCIAL SCIENCE DATA

Along with many others, we have suggested that social science data are much more readily assimilated in legal decision-making when they agree with the decision-maker's intuition, with common sense, or with the prevalent intellectual culture. Often a general point of view is assimilated, rather than any specific data. The drawbacks of relying on common sense are that it may be false and that its sources, because implicit, are not easy to discredit. In theory, this represents a major difference between the use of particular bodies of social science research and the use of vague current notions originally inspired by social science. In practice, a social scientist may draw false conclusions from an empirical study, and the research itself may not be easy to discredit. Not all research is good research; some is worthless, and some is worthless for reasons not easily grasped by the layman (Campbell and Stanley 1966; Cook and Campbell 1979). Ideally, the law should rely on valuable, methodologically impeccable research and should reject studies that have fatal flaws; but how are legal decision-makers to know the difference?

For deciding other kinds of facts and ascertaining the validity of the statements of other kinds of witnesses, the law has relied on the adversary system; this process is also favored by many lawyers and appellate-court judges as the appropriate method for evaluating social science research. As Justice Lewis Powell stated in his concurring opinion in *Ballew* v. *Georgia:*

> I have reservations as to the wisdom—as well as the necessity—of Mr. Justice Blackmun's heavy reliance on numerology derived from statistical studies. Moreover, neither the validity nor the methodology covered by the studies cited was subjected to the traditional testing mechanisms of the adversary process. The studies relied on merely represent unexamined findings of persons interested in the jury system. [p. 246]

There are several difficulties. Even at the appellate-court level, where the judges can study written arguments at their leisure, their competence may be insufficient to address or even comprehend the opposing arguments. This was undoubtedly the case when an econometric model of the deterrent efficacy of executions was presented in the United States' brief in the death-penalty case of *Fowler* v. *North Carolina* (1976) and was rebutted with alternative models by petitioner. How is the court to choose in an argument involving the adequacy of the data base, the significance of regression coefficients, and the choice of appropriate control analyses? In a situation like this, one party may, in fact, have the stronger arguments, but the court can only conclude—as apparently the Supreme Court did on the issue of deterrence—that experts disagree. But disagreement among experts should not be grounds for disregarding the empirical issues entirely.

Instances of complete unanimity among the social science community are extremely rare, and it would be unfortunate if the Court were to insist on a standard of absolute agreement before accepting social science data. To consider the weight of evidence evenly balanced whenever there is any disagreement is to ignore all the degrees of probability between a fifty-fifty chance and certainty.

In general, the series of death penalty cases that began in the 1960s provides a good example of the difficulties in presenting empirical data to be considered in the decision of a constitutional question and in assessing the impact of these data after the fact. The briefs in these cases contained exhaustive analyses of the discriminatory application of the laws, the deterrent impact of capital punishment, long-term trends in public opinion, and other empirical issues. The Supreme Court's response to these areas of research has been tentative. In each case the court initially emphasized the importance of research and then drew back. The reasons for the hesitation are complex. It reflects, in part, the difficulty of assessing the merits of sophisticated research; in part, the conflict between social science data and general community attitudes toward deterrence; and in part, the fact that values not directly addressed by the empirical research are also implicated in consideration of the death penalty.

With regard to the discriminatory impact of the death penalty, the Court's position may be explained not by doubts about the research, but by the difficulty of responding to it. Almost any scheme for the imposition of capital punishment is likely to have discriminatory implications. While this circumstance argues against capital punishment, its ramifications are wider. The criminal-justice system is so constructed that minority groups and the poor are most likely to be apprehended, most likely to be charged with serious crimes, least likely to be acquitted, and most likely to be given heavy sentences. Discriminatory impact is endemic and difficult to overcome. In the end, the argument turns on the empirically obvious but legally ambiguous proposition that "death is different." Thus, the existence of a great deal of research may force the appellate courts to consider social science, but the interaction has so far produced disappointing results in terms of developing new, more effective, or fairer legal standards.

Justice Powell argues that this confusion about the reliability of social science data is produced by their belated presentation at the appellate-court level, that the way to decide these issues is to introduce them in the trial courts, so that they will be subject to the traditional testing mechanisms, the adversary process (see also Rosenblum et al. 1978).

The "battle of the experts" in insanity cases and other cases involving individual assessment suggests that the traditional testing mechanisms may be flawed. In such cases expert testimony by opposing adversarial witnesses probably has a negligible influence on the outcome of the case. When an expert's statements are flatly denied by another expert, neither seems very credible. If two social scientists, under oath, contradict each other, the jury can only conclude that one or both are perjuring themselves; that the truth is so complex and so elusive, and the social science so crude and fumbling, that the honest best guesses of the experts are hardly better than anyone else's; or that one expert is right and the other is wrong. The third possibility is the one ideally assumed by the adversarial system: there is a knowable truth, witnesses are honest, and judges or jurors will decide which witnesses are more credible on the basis of the witnesses' real knowledge of the facts. Undoubtedly there are many cases in which one expert does appear to be much more credible than the other and in which the outcome is influenced by expert testimony. But there is no reason to believe that the appearance of credibility has any relation to the actual expertise or honesty of the expert; the more persuasive social scientist may carry the day, but the more respectable social science theory, knowledge, and data may receive no particular favor.

Having listened to expert testimony, and having testified ourselves, we are by no means convinced that the trial court is an appropriate forum for evaluating scientific data. First, important information may be omitted. The questions other informed critical scientists would think of may simply never be asked; and if a question is not asked, the question-and-answer format of the courtroom makes it difficult, if not impossible, for the scientists to provide the information. The assumption is that one adversary or another is interested in every relevant piece of information, but it may be a very dubious assumption indeed, if the witness wants, for example, to explain the meaning of statistical significance to the court. The first problem with this assumption is that neither lawyer may know enough about social science research to know what information he or she should be interested in. The second is that, especially in a jury trial, both lawyers may have an interest in keeping the testimony simple, and many studies simply cannot be adequately evaluated if the record omits a detailed description of the research methods and statistical analyses.

Thus, one problem with the introduction of social science evidence at the trial-court level, in order to be sure that it has been subjected to the "traditional testing mechanisms" by the time it reaches the appellate courts, is that the functions of the two tribunals are not the same. The concerns of the trial-court judge and jury are local, sharply focused on the particulars of the individual case before them; the appellate courts are more interested in identifying and rectifying general patterns of injustice. The data the appellate courts need to assess general phenomena may often be considered too general, too unrelated to the specific case, to be presented in the trial court. In tailoring cases to the trial-court judge and jury, the most effective legal strategy may be to omit a substantial proportion of the general information that may be critical at the appellate-court level. An attorney who has his eye on the appellate courts and who is using the trial court primarily as a forum for introducing the data into the record may be willing to bring forward all the relevant social science information on a given topic, but his comprehensive and beautifully prepared case may still be stymied by the trial-court judge. The judge may decide that data collected in other jurisdictions or general methodological testimony are not germane to the case at hand and may reject the introduction of important and relevant social-scientific studies on the grounds that they are hearsay, common sense, or mere speculation. Thus, the record may include expert opinions by witnesses without including the research on which those opinions are based and by which they may be evaluated.

Some of the problems are illustrated by the school-desegregation cases, in which the NAACP Legal Defense and Educational Fund actively sought respected social scientists as experts on two major lines of argument. First, they were called to testify that, in fact, the black schools in a particular jurisdiction were inferior to white schools; second, and more basic, they were asked to use general, aggregate data and theory to testify that the separation itself inevitably created inequalities that discriminated against the blacks both educationally and psychologically. The use of such aggregate-level data was unusual at the time, and it is clear that the lawyers felt quite uncertain about its acceptability at the trial-court level. Although some of their witnesses testified solely on the basis of general data on the negative effects of segregation, the lawyers felt that it was very important that at least one witness replicate his research by administering tests to a few children in the actual school districts involved in the controversy. It seems that this caution was justified; a frequent technique of the attorneys for the school boards was to demonstrate that the expert—often someone from a different part of the country—knew very little about the particular district and the particular litigants, to emphasize repeatedly that the findings were not based on tests of local children, and to argue that the testimony was thus inapplicable to the particular case at hand (see Kluger 1976).

Another problem with the introduction of social science evidence at the trial-court level is that there is no reason to believe that the skill of effective courtroom testimony is highly correlated with the skill of scientific expertise, and there is every reason to believe that a trial attorney, if forced to choose, will prefer the better witness to the better scientist. Even an excellent scientist is likely to be less than perfectly coherent, and perhaps less than perfectly honest, on the witness stand. Unable to anticipate questions, to prepare answers in advance, or to offer full explanations; threatened by contemptuous attacks with no opportunity for rebuttal; restricted by a good cross-examiner to yes and no answers—the scientists are not apt to appear at their best. A facile dogmatism may sound better—and read better in the record—than a more hesitant and more accurate response. The mode of presentation and the kinds of questions asked are often so foreign to the professional experience of most research scientists that it is difficult to believe that the answers given in this context could possibly be the best account of the research or that the interchange could provide a valid text for deciding what is scientifically true and what is not.

If opposing experts were given free rein to argue the issue between each other in the courtroom, without the lawyers or judges determining what to ask or what to criticize, the record would probably be a much better representation of the scientifically important issues. But of course one of the experts might admit to being persuaded, which would not be at all fair to his "side."

The use of competing experts is only one aspect of the problem of maintaining scientific neutrality in an adversary process. In many contexts, expert witnesses may experience various forms of pressure to shape their testimony or research to make it most favorable to the side employing them. The most obvious pressure is in the fact that the expert's fee will be determined by how much he is asked to do, and thus in turn will depend upon how potentially favorable his testimony and research appear to be. The expert is typically informed either directly or indirectly about what is desired, and payment at a per diem rate is offered. The number of days employed generally vary directly with the perceived usefulness of the testimony as that emerges from preliminary discussions and follow-up meetings. In short, to some extent the expert can control the fee by offering a maximum amount of support. Beyond such narrow self-interest there is the inevitable desire to return something of value for payment received, which may often be substantial.

Potential experts may also be flattered and told how valuable their testimony will be. Further, the case will be described from a partisan perspective, making it easy to believe that the lawyers who are seeking help have both fairness and legal precedent on their side. Even without contradicting professional beliefs, an expert witness motivated to be helpful is often in a position to phrase the testimony in a way that will help the employing side. Similarly, expert witnesses who are asked to collect and/or to analyze data may construct their analyses in a way favorable to the side they are supporting.

In rare cases, some of the problems of the adversarial use of experts have been creatively circumvented by innovative methods of preparing the witnesses and introducing their testimony. For example, in a California school-desegregation case, a compromise between the use of adversarial and court-appointed experts was achieved. The judge appointed eight experts with various skills and perspectives to study and report on desegregation in Los Angeles. The experts were given questions in advance and asked to prepare written responses independently and at their leisure. Thus, they had the opportunity to be as comprehensive, accurate, and responsive as possible with regard to the specific issues raised and, if they felt it important, to raise additional issues. They were also allowed to consult with one another, so that they could resolve those differences that were more apparent than real, educate one another about relevant research, and divide up the task according to their separate competencies. Objections by the lawyers for the parties involved led to a decision that the experts would not communicate directly with the judge but would deal with the various parties and with the court-appointed referee (Pettigrew 1979). It may be that the introduction of such alternative mechanisms for presenting general social science evidence will help to avoid the demeaning and uninformative battles of the experts that often result from traditional procedures.

Questions about the adversarial use of social science have also been raised with regard to research sponsored by groups hoping to use the research to shape legal doctrine in a particular fashion. Presumably the sponsoring group—be it a religious organization, a group established to protect the interests of minorities or women, an industry, or a single-issue political lobby—is less interested in scientific discovery than it is in generating supportive evidence for conclusions already reached.

The problem can be broken into three issues: the choice of studies to be undertaken, the quality of the research itself, and the link between the empirical data and the legal conclusions. Sponsoring organizations clearly have an influence on the choice of research topics; to return to an earlier example, many foundations have had a special interest in criminal justice, few have been concerned with labor law. A more serious problem for judicial decision-makers is that the sponsoring organization will also look for research that is likely to produce results favorable to its point of view. Studies that appear risky or unpromising may not be attempted. Unless other parties or other researchers are interested in the same general topic, the available research may be an incomplete or biased sample of the universe of possible studies that might be done in an area. Of course, unsponsored investigators also choose to pursue some ideas and abandon others, but it is generally assumed that their goal is to satisfy curiosity rather than to muster support for a desirable conclusion. According to the adversary system, obvious gaps in the research program will be discovered and pointed out by opposing experts. This safeguard may not always work, however, particularly if the party introducing the research has energy, preparation, and surprise on its side. Even if the two adversaries are prepared for the contest, there is still the more basic problem of the adversary presentation of scientific research: the courts' inability in dealing with technical data to distinguish sound criticism from frivolous attacks.

The quality of sponsored research can range from excellent to laughable; its range is the same as that of any research. Protection against biased or inferior studies is slightly easier to achieve than protection against an incomplete research program. By requiring full disclosure of the research design, the measures, the sample, and the procedures, the courts can assure that they and the opposing experts will have all the information they need to assess the validity of the presented research. It is easier to judge the validity of a set of studies presented in evidence than it is to judge the outcome and impact of an unspecified set of studies that might have been done but were not. Although still a very difficult task, it is probably no more difficult in relation to sponsored research than to any other kind. If anything, adversaries are likely to be unusually thorough in their scrutiny of the methodology of sponsored research. Anticipation of this kind of painstaking examination by hostile parties may, in some cases, even improve the quality of sponsored research; a researcher who expects to be subjected to cross-examination may be more attentive to detail than one who does not.

The link between a body of research and a legal conclusion is often more obvious when the research is sponsored by an organization with legal goals, since the legal strategy and the research strategy may be developed together. Regardless of where the research funding comes from, collaboration between lawyers and social scientists is very helpful in assuring that the research addresses the legal issues. When the experts are on the witness stand, of course, the lawyers who recruited them may press them to go beyond the data to address more general legal issues, but the judges are much more capable of dealing with this kind of exaggeration than they are in assessing the research itself, and we have not noticed any instances where they have been swayed by an expert's legal conclusions.

In sum, the main problem with sponsored research is that only certain studies may be carried out, while other plausible studies are avoided. Once a study is performed, however, the research and the conclusions drawn from it can be judged on their merits, and the problems are no more or less formidable than those presented by any social science research.

The neutrality of any social science research—even when it is not sponsored—has also been questioned, on the grounds that the selection of research projects inevitably reflects the political and social biases of social scientists. Since social scientists tend to be political liberals, the argument goes, their research tends to be structured in such a way as to advance liberal causes and to bypass research thought and felt to have antiliberal implications. Even if this process does not take place, the questions chosen for investigation will reflect the liberal agenda. Questions such as the effect of poverty and social conditions on crime rates came to be investigated, but the relationship between crime rates and racial integration of neighborhoods did not.

It is difficult to evaluate the accuracy of this criticism, particularly in terms of its implications for the law. Currently, economics is the social science with greatest impact on the law, and it is simply not true that the field of law and economics is dominated by liberals. Conservative groups concerned with social issues are well organized and often well funded. On many questions, such as the effectiveness of regulation on the value of social programs, research has not reflected the supposed liberal bias. Thus, this criticism raises another of the many interesting but basically unexplored questions about the interaction between law and social science.

Some Tentative Generalizations

In preparing this chapter, we have been struck by the diversity and flexibility of the relationships between law and social science. Some areas of law have been powerfully affected by social science thinking, while others have been largely immune. It is difficult to explain these differences in terms of the importance of the legal issues or of the types of public policy being pursued. Indeed, as our discussion of labor law demonstrates, even the existence of a field of social research closely allied to the area of legal regulation does not assure legal decision-makers' receptivity to social science data and reasoning.

The willingness of courts and agencies to pay attention to social science is most affected by the types of determination they are asked to make prior to arriving at their decision. In resolving disputes, courts traditionally perform two functions. They make findings of fact about the behavior of the parties, and they determine which legal rules should be applied to the fact as found. Sometimes, when none of the existing rules seem appropriate, a new rule is established for the case at hand. This is the routine legal business of the courts. The rules themselves are based on legislation, precedents, generally accepted concepts of justice, and widely shared factual assumptions.

The law seems most receptive to social science when legal outcomes turn upon individual predictions or assessments, as is the case in such areas as parole, civil commitment, adoption, custody disputes, and application of laws regarding sexual deviance. In all these areas, in order to decide the case before it, the court must consider how to classify the individual in terms of preexisting legal categories or the likely impact of its decision on the behavior of the people it affects. Is the person who might be paroled likely to commit violent crimes? Will the person whose mental health is being adjudicated be able to live a self-sufficient life outside an institution? Is the alleged psychopath likely to commit crimes of a sexual nature? Which parent is likely to be better able to care for the needs of the child? Questions like these cannot be resolved by fact-finding of the traditional sort, nor does the outcome turn on the court's ability to find the proper legal standard to be applied. It is interesting to note that the use of social science experts became much more widespread in custody disputes as the law moved from judging past behavior and relying on a general standard (favoring maternal control) to comparative predictions.

It seems natural for the courts to consider social science in making such evaluations; identifying variables that predict behavior and measuring their impact is a central concern of social science. Nevertheless, the process of using social science to aid legal prediction in legal contexts has been far from smooth. Several significant institutional features make it difficult to incorporate social science in the procedures involving individual assessments.

First, because most of these cases involve no great principle or issue, highly regarded social scientists are unlikely to become directly involved. Clinical practitioners in allied fields are most easily and inexpensively available, and perhaps the most willing to shape their testimony to the desires of the lawyers who call upon them. Further, the very lack of judicial expertise that makes the use of social science desirable also makes it difficult to establish adequate guidelines about suitable credentials; thus, it is frequently the case that the people who attempt to base their testimony on social science research and theory have only a passing familiarity with the field.

Second, the questions with respect to which prediction is sought are typically not questions that social science has addressed directly, nor are they questions that are regularly dealt with by clinicians. Thus, there is no reason to assume that clinical experience is necessarily valuable in addressing them. Clinical psychologists are trained to make diagnoses of various degrees of psychological maladjustment, but the value of such diagnosis for the prediction of specific forms of future behavior, such as violence and parental cruelty, has so far proven highly dubious. In addition, clinicians are rarely trained to make comparative judgments. Complex behaviors like criminality or child-rearing are obviously the product of the interaction of a large number of situational and individual factors. In extreme cases, the individualized diagnoses of the quasi-experts probably do not make much difference to the judgments that would have been rendered anyway; in the large gray area of borderline or "middling" cases, the use of such diagnoses probably serves to make a speculative enterprise slightly more rational and standardized, but not necessarily more accurate.

Third, the processes by which experts are recruited, prepared, and questioned is calculated to make their presentation more adversarial than scientific, and the circumstances by which experts learn the facts are sometimes highly suspect. They are frequently called upon to testify on the basis of clinical criteria, without having examined the party about whose characteristics they are testifying. Much of the literature on the use of expert witnesses has therefore focused on the weaknesses of the process.

Fourth, problems connected with the use of clinical evaluation have led to efforts to achieve greater accuracy through the use of general standards derived from aggregate data in such areas as parole and bail proceedings. But judging the individual case in terms of statistical generalities also presents problems. The use of aggregate data makes it more difficult to take into account possibly significant idiosyncratic circumstances. Moreover, certain standards based on aggregate data—such as education or family background—are so closely related to race, ethnic background, or poverty that their use raises substantial constitutional issues and jurisprudential questions.

Social science is also frequently used in situations where the law is prepared to withhold or modify its judgment depending on an evaluation of the defendant's mental condition. Such issues as fitness for trial, the insanity defense, and diminished responsibility are of this type. Most of the problems relevant to the legal use of clinical experts apply in adjudging mental states in these areas as much as they do when the question is primarily one of prediction. The adversarial nature of the proceedings, the difficulty of obtaining valid data, and the weakness of the experts' scholarly credentials continue to be problems. This sort of assessment differs from prediction, however, in that the legal questions involved in judging mental states appear to be closely related to the clinical questions frequently addressed in determining a course of treatment; indeed, there is a substantial overlap in terminology. The similarities between the legal and clinical issues have turned out to be deceptive, however, and the differences are greater than earlier legal commentators recognized. Even though similar characterizations are used, when notions of insanity and mental illness are used for different purposes—such as punishment and treatment—they generally turn out to have different content. Use of the same label can mask the fundamental differences in the questions addressed, resulting in a fair amount of confusion. The problem is compounded by the fact that legal standards seeking to incorporate scientific judgment may become outdated by changes in science; thus, the law embraced the medical concept of mental illness just when scientists came to distrust it. The law must presume a definable difference between the mentally insane and the morally reprehensible, while scientists assume that similar elements of compulsion and choice are present in a wide range of conduct usually treated as criminal. As it turns out, the determination of mental status creates many of the same problems as does prediction, with the additional problem of distinguishing between legal and clinical judgments.

The great majority of interactions between law and social science involve neither high-level social science nor high-level law. They involve people at the margins of both disciplines; sometimes, people who are not lawyers consider recommendations or evidence from people who are not social scientists. Thus, the changes in the legal system brought about by social science are in the main likely to be gradual, slowly proliferating as changes in both disciplines reach to the lower-level practitioners. It is for this reason, among others, that the general climate of informed opinion is much more likely to lead to significant changes in the operation of the legal system than is innovative research aimed at changing legal standards, especially when the conclusions of that research are unexpected.

Occasionally the legal goals and the social-scientific capacities are well suited to each other, and where this occurs progress may be rapid. Although originally defined as a fundamental goal by the law, the concept of the representative jury developed and changed partly in response to the recognition of the capacity of social science to measure it. The case of jury representativeness is perhaps the simplest (and most successful) example of the assessment of unequal treatment by means of blind statistical definitions of equality, and the consequent clarification of the legal concept of inequality. Similar attempts in other areas have become common, and show promise, but they have rarely worked out quite so simply.

In comparison with other questions about legal substance or procedure that social scientists might be asked, it is striking how frequently they have been asked to measure or define, justify or condemn unequal treatment in domains as diverse as those of *Muller* v. *Oregon, Brown* v. *Board of Education,* and *Furman* v. *Georgia.* In labor law, the Congress has referred to social science findings to determine whether unions and employers have equal opportunity to get their messages heard. It is a hallmark of our period that claims to equal treatment are more frequently made and, once made, are treated more seriously than they were in the past. Thus, the need to assess differences and the task of defining equality arise repeatedly in different contexts. Because, almost by definition, social science investigation is concerned with the existence of differences between groups of subjects, its use in responding to legal questions involving equality of treatment is not surprising.

The role of social science in addressing questions of equality suggests both its appeal and its limitations. Questions arising out of efforts to enlist the law on behalf of claims for equal treatment almost always include an empirically testable component. Do certain hiring standards tend to disqualify more blacks than whites? Do unions have an opportunity equivalent to the employers' to get their message to the employees during an organizing campaign? Are blacks more likely than whites to receive the death penalty? Are prison terms equal for men and women? Do men and women differ in their ability to endure long hours of work? Does racial segregation improve the quality of education? Is it likely to have negative emotional consequences for pupils?

None of these questions is easily answered empirically, but in all cases, strategies have been developed to help address the legal question. In most cases the cost of collecting the data has been great, but since these questions are of considerable importance, they have all been addressed, and the work has received recognition from courts or legislatures. The quality and quantity of data available to respond to these questions have, however, frequently been unsatisfactory. Where the establishment or reversal of legal rules is involved—particularly constitutional doctrine, which is likely to be relatively permanent—it is dangerous to proceed unless the data are powerful or unless they support the rule that would be employed in their absence. The use by courts and legislatures of such data has frequently been unsophisticated.

Moreover, in none of these cases does resolution of the empirical question necessarily resolve the legal question. Behind the empirical question are always questions of public policy; sometimes, these are brought into sharper relief, but sometimes they are obscured by the availability of data. The relationship between the policy question and the empirical question is crucial in determining the influence of the data. In the case of employment discrimination the policy questions were answered in a way that made the data of great importance. In school-segregation cases, it is difficult to be sure, but the policy questions seem to have been answered in such a way as to make the social science data largely irrelevant. With regard to union access to employers' policy, intuitive judgments have thus far outweighed the impact of the data.

The evidence suggests that the role of social science in defining the major goals of the legal system is necessarily limited but that it can help to give more precise meaning to existing standards. Social science methodology can also help to determine which of a number of procedures can best achieve a desired goal. Such a limited role does not mean that the contribution of social science to the legal system will be a modest one. The impact of such collaboration has been highly significant in such areas as employment discrimination and jury representativeness. The use of social science techniques made an important legal standard workable, and in so doing, it clarified and modified the standard itself.

Social science rarely shapes the legal rules applied to judge conduct, but when it has, it has often been in areas of constitutional principles involving major questions of national policy, such as the death penalty or the legality of segregated education. In each of these areas—as is typically true when social science data are used—they were first employed for the relatively simple task of challenging the underpinnings of a rule of law, the validity of which was already in doubt. But in areas of great importance and controversy, the use of social science for limited purposes has generated more sophisticated data and analyses, casting doubt upon the validity of the data or analyses originally relied upon by the courts. The resulting attempts to come to grips with large amounts of contradictory data and analyses have not been notably successful. Characteristically, the law has become committed to one body of scientific data before the scientific debate has crystallized; with the advent of new information, it has had either to create additional distinctions—as in the areas of jury size and unanimity—or to ignore data—such as those bearing on the problems of white flight to avoid integration. Where social science data are not addressed to topics of major national debate, as was true of the study of union representation, unless the issue is controversial enough to generate a great body of legally oriented research, the existing system is likely to remain intact and the impact of social science to be merely interstitial and minor.

The fact that social science has largely played an interstitial role in shaping general rules of law should be neither surprising nor even depressing. Most important legal decisions involve empirical questions; questions of values, often competing values; political questions; and, in the case of the judiciary, questions of precedent and statutory interpretation.

Of those questions that are empirical, many may not have been addressed by social scientists, and many may only have been addressed in ways that have dubious relevance to the question in its legal context. Thus, while empirical data may be very important in the consideration of some of the questions raised in any of a large variety of legal decisions, few such decisions are restricted to empirical questions. Typically, the empirical issues coexist with a variety of nonempirical issues, and in such cases the appropriate role of social science data is a partial one.

In focusing on social science, we, like our predecessors, have found that the empirical data are subject to abuse and neglect at every level, from the assessments of individuals to the interpretation of constitutional principles. But these problems are not unique to social science. The task of working out general rules and achieving satisfactory resolutions of complex controversies is extremely difficult and complicated, and it is not at all clear that the use of social science is any more haphazard or convoluted than the use of any other type of information. Had we chosen to write on the role of lawmakers' values, or legal scholarship, or political considerations, or judicial precedent in legal decision-making, we doubt that our conclusions would have been simpler or more straightforward.

Thus, the interstitial use of social science data is not the problem, and the confused and often contradictory uses are not unique to social science data. The problem is that the relevant considerations are rarely spelled out in advance or even explicitly delineated in retrospect. The legal question is seldom parsed in a way that clearly identifies the empirical issues and separates them from the moral issues or the political issues, and almost never is any direct statement made about how much weight should be given to each of these classes of information. If social scientists knew which empirical questions lawmakers were likely to care about, and how much influence persuasive data on such questions would have, they could make informed choices about which interstices they wanted to try to fill. Instead, they are in the position of everyone else who wants to influence the law and must proceed on hope and guesswork.

Cases Cited

Apodaca v. Oregon, 406 U.S. 408 (1972).
Ballard v. U.S., 329 U.S. 187 (1946).
Ballew v. Georgia, 435 U.S. 223 (1978).
Barefoot v. Estelle, 463 U.S. 880 (1983).

Brown v. Board of Education of Topeka, 347 U.S. 483 (1954).
Burch v. Louisiana, 441 U.S. 130 (1979).
J. I. Case Company v. National Labor Relations Board, 321 U.S. 332 (1944).
Colgrove v. Battin, 413 U.S. 149 (1973).
Duren v. Missouri, 439 U.S. 357 (1979).
Durham v. U.S., F. Rptr., 214, 2d series (1954).
Fowler v. North Carolina, 428 U.S. 904 (1976).
Furman v. Georgia, 408 U.S. 238 (1972).
Gault, In re 387 U.S. 1 (1967).
General Knit of California, Inc., 239 NLRB 619 (1978).
General Shoe Corporation, 77 NLRB (1948).
Gregg v. Georgia, 428 U.S. 153 (1976).
Griggs v. Duke Power and Light Company, 401 U.S. 424 (1971).
Grigsby v. Mabry, 758 F.2d 226 (8th Cir. 1985).
Heiderman v. Pennhurst State School and Hospital, 446 F.Supp. 1295 (1979).
Hobson v. Hansen, 269 F.Supp. 401 (1969) and 327 F.Supp. 844 (1971).
Hovey v. Superior Court, 28 Cal.3d 1 (1980); 616 P.2d 1301.
Jenkins v. U.S., 113 C.A., D.C. 300 (1962).
Johnson v. Louisiana, 406 U.S. 356 (1972).
Jurek v. Texas, 428 U.S. 262 (1976).
Keeten v. Garrison, 742 F.2d 129 (4th Cir. 1984).
Lockett v. Ohio, 438 U.S. 586 (1978).
Lockhart v. McCree, 90 L. Ed. 2d. 37 (1986).
Muller v. Oregon, 208 U.S. 412 (1908). Brief of Amicus Curiae for the National Consumers
    League in Muller v. Oregon.
National Labor Relations Board v. Insurance Agents International Union AFL-CIO, 361 U.S.
    477 (1960).
National Labor Relations Board v. Katz, 369 U.S. 736 (1962).
Norris v. Alabama, 294 U.S. 587 (1935).
Matter of Josiah Oakes, 8 Law Rptr., Mass. S.Ct. (1845).
O'Connor v. Donaldson, 422 U.S. 563 (1975).
Parham v. J.R., 442 U.S. 584 (1979).
People v. McDonald, 33 Cal. 3d 351 (1984).
Plessy v. Ferguson, 163 U.S. 537 (1896).
Shopping Kart Food Market, Inc., 228 NLRB 1311 (1977).
Smith v. Texas, 311 U.S. 128 (1940).
State v. Chapple, 660 P.2d 1208 (Ariz. 1983).
Strauder v. West Virginia, 100 U.S. 303 (1880).
Taylor v. Louisiana, 419 U.S. 522 (1975).
Teamsters v. U.S., 431 U.S. 324 (1977).
U.S. v. Downing, 753 F.2d 1224 (3d Cir. 1985).
United Steelworkers of America v. American Manufacturing Company, 363 U.S. 564
    (1960).
United Steelworkers of America v. Enterprise Wheel and Car Corporation, 363 U.S. 593
    (1960).
United Steelworkers of America v. Warrior and Gulf Navigation Company, 363 U.S. 574
    (1960).
Williams v. Florida, 399 U.S. 78 (1970).
Witherspoon v. Illinois, 391 U.S. 510 (1968).
Woodson v. North Carolina, 428 U.S. 280 (1976).
Wyatt v. Stickney, 334 F.Supp. 1341 (M.D. Ala. 1971) aff'd sub. nom. Wyatt v. Aderholt, 503
    F.2d 1305 (5th Cir. 1974).

Bibliography

Ackerman, B. A., and Hassler, W. T.
  1981   *Clean Coal, Dirty Air.* New Haven: Yale University Press.
Administrative Law Review
  1980   "Symposium on Empirical Research in Administrative Law, Part II." *Administrative Law Review,* Winter.
Asch, S. E.
  1952   "Effects of Group Pressure Upon the Modification and Distortion of Judgments." In *Readings in Social Psychology,* edited by G. E. Swanson, T. M. Newcomb, and E. L. Hartley. New York: Holt.
Babcock, B.; Freedman, A.; Norton, E. H.; and Ross, S. C.
  1973   *Sex Discrimination and the Law.* Boston: Little, Brown.
Bazelon, D.
  1974   "Psychiatry and the Adversary Process." *Scientific American,* June 1974, 18–23.
Bok, D.
  1970   "The Regulation of Campaign Tactics in Representation Elections Under the National Labor Relations Act." *Harvard Law Review* 78:38.
Campbell, D. T., and Stanley, J. C.
  1966   *Experimental and Quasi-Experimental Designs for Research.* Chicago: Rand McNally.
Coffee, J. C., Jr.
  1978   "The Repressed Issues of Sentencing: Accountability, Predictability, and Equality in the Era of the Sentencing Commission." *Georgetown Law Journal* 66:975–1107.
Cook, T. D., and Campbell, D. T.
  1979   *Quasi-Experimentation: Design and Analysis Issues for Field Settings.* Chicago: Rand McNally.
Copeis, D.
  1977   "The Numbers Game Is the Only Game in Town." *Howard Law Journal* 20:374.
Cox, A.
  1958   "The Duty to Bargain in Good Faith." *Harvard Law Review* 71:1401.
Dawes, R.
  1971   "A Case Study of Graduate Admissions: Application of Three Principles of Human Decision Making." *American Psychologist* 26:180–88.
  1979   "The Robust Beauty of Improper Linear Models in Decision Making." *American Psychologist* 34:571–82.
Deutsch, A.
  1949   *The Mentally Ill in America: A History of Their Care and Treatment from Colonial Times.* 2nd ed. New York: Columbia University Press.
Devlin, Rt. Hon. Lord Patrick
  1976   *Report to the Secretary of State for the House Department of the Departmental Committee on Evidence of Identification in Criminal Cases.* House of Commons, April 26. London: Her Majesty's Stationery Office.
Doss C., and Doss, H.
  1957   *If You Adopt a Child.* New York: Holt.
Doyle, A. C.
  1974   "The Sign of the Four." In *Tales of Sherlock Holmes.* New York: Ballantine Books.
Eames, P.
  1976   "An Analysis of the Union Voting Study from a Trade Unionist Point of View." *Stanford Law Review* 28:1181.

Ellsworth, P. C.; Bukaty, R. M.; Cowan, C. L.; and Thompson, W. C.
1984   "The Death-Qualified Jury and the Defense of Insanity." *Law and Human Behavior* 8:81–93.

Ellsworth, P.C., and Levy, R. J.
1969   "Legislative Reform of Child Custody Adjudication: An Effort to Rely on Social Science Data in Formulating Legal Policies." *Law & Society Review* 4:167–233.

Ennis, B. J., and Emery, R. O.
1978   *The Rights of Mental Patients.* New York: Avon Books.

Ennis, B. J., and Litwack, C.
1974   "Psychiatry and the Presumption of Expertise: Flipping Coins in the Courtroom." *California Law Review* 62:693–752.

Equal Employment Opportunities Commission
1970   "Guidelines on Employee Selection Procedure." *Federal Register* 35(149), August 1.

Fairley, W. B.
1977   "Evaluating the 'Small' Probability of a Catastrophic Accident from the Marine Transportation of Liquefied Natural Gas." In *Statistics and Public Policy,* edited by W. B. Fairley and F. Mosteller. Reading, Mass.: Addison-Wesley.

Federal Trade Commission
1980   Staff Memo: "Industrywide Enforcement Policy Session."

Finkelstein, M. O., and Fairley, W. B.
1970   "A Bayesian Approach to Identification Evidence." *Harvard Law Review* 83:489–517.

Fiss, O. M.
1971   "A Theory of Fair Employment Laws." *University of Chicago Law Review* 38:235–314.

Fitzgerald, R., and Ellsworth, P. C.
1984   "Due Process vs. Crime Control: Death Qualification and Jury Attitudes." *Law and Human Behavior* 8:31–52.

Frankfurter, F., and Green, N.
1930   *The Labor Injunction.* New York: Macmillan.

Gallagher, E. G.
1936   *The Adopted Child.* New York: Reynal & Hitchcock.

Getman, J. G.; Goldberg, S. B.; and Herman, J. B.
1975   "NLRB Regulation of Campaign Tactics: The Behavioral Assumptions on Which the Board Regulates." *Stanford Law Review* 27:1465.

1976   *Union Representation Elections: Law and Reality.* New York: Russell Sage Foundation.

Goetz, R., and Wike, E. L.
1977   Book Review. *Kansas Law Review* 25:375.

Goldstein, J.; Freud, A.; and Solnit, A. J.
1973   *Beyond the Best Interests of the Child.* New York: Free Press.

Gottfredson, D. M.; Wilkins, L. T.; and Hoffman, P.
1978   *Parole and Sentencing Guidelines.* Lexington, Mass.: Lexington Books.

Gottfredson, D. M.; Wilkins, L. T.; Hoffman, P.; and Singer, S. M.
1973   *The Utilization of Experience in Parole Decision Making: A Progress Report.* Washington, D.C.: U.S. Department of Justice.

Gross, S. R.
1980   "Social Science and the Law: Educating the Judiciary and the Limits of Prescience." Paper presented at the annual convention of the American Psychological Association, Montreal.

Hoffman, P., and Stone-Meierhofer, B.
    1977   "Application of Guidelines to Sentencing." *Law and Psychology Review* 3:53–60.
Horowitz, D. L.
    1977   *The Courts and Social Policy.* Washington, D.C.: Brookings Institution.
Kadane, J. B.
    1984   "After *Hovey*: A Note Taking into Account Automatic Death Penalty Jurors." *Law and Human Behavior* 8:115–20.
Kahneman, D., and Tversky, A.
    1973   "On the Psychology of Prediction." *Psychological Review* 80:237–51.
Kairys, D.; Schulman, J.; and Harring, S., eds.
    1975   *The Jury System: New Methods for Reducing Prejudice.* Philadelphia: National Lawyers Guild.
Kalven, H., Jr.
    1968   "The Quest for the Middle Range: Empirical Inquiry and Legal Policy." In *Law in a Changing America,* edited by G. C. Hazard, Jr. Englewood Cliffs, N.J.: Prentice-Hall.
Kluger, R.
    1976   *Simple Justice.* New York: Knopf.
Kochan, T.
    1977   "Legal Nonsense, Empirical Examination, and Policy Evaluation." *Stanford Law Review* 29:1115.
Lindblom, C. E., and Cohen, D. K.
    1979   *Usable Knowledge: Social Science and Social Problem Solving.* New Haven: Yale University Press.
Lochner, P. R., Jr.
    1973   "Some Limits on the Application of Social Science Research in the Legal Process." *Law and the Social Order (Arizona State University Law Journal)* 1973:815–48.
Loftus, E.
    1979   *Eyewitness Testimony.* Cambridge, Mass.: Harvard University Press.
Louis Harris and Associates, Inc.
    1971   *Study No. 2016.*
Macaulay, J., and Macaulay, S.
    1978   "Adoption for Black Children: A Case Study of Expert Discretion." *Research in Law and Sociology* 1:265–318.
Meehl, P. E.
    1973   *Psychodiagnosis: Selected Papers.* New York: Norton.
Miller, E.
    1976   "The Getman Goldberg Herman Questions." *Stanford Law Review* 28:1163.
Mischel, W.
    1968   *Personality and Assessment.* New York: Wiley.
Monahan, J.
    1978   "The Prediction of Violent Criminal Behavior: A Methodological Critique and Prospectus." In *Deterrence and Incapacitation: Estimating the Effects of Criminal Sanctions on Crime Rates,* edited by A. Blumstein, J. Cohen, and D. Nagin. Washington, D.C.: National Academy of Science.
Pettigrew, T. F.
    1979   "Tension Between the Law and Social Science: An Expert Witness's View." In *Desegregation. Schools and the Courts,* vol. 1, edited by J. Greenberg et al. Eugene, Ore.: ERIC Clearinghouse on Educational Management, University of Oregon.
Rector, M.
    1973   "Who Are the Dangerous?" *Bulletin of the American Academy of Psychiatry and the Law* 1:186–88.

Reppucci, N. D.
  1984   "The Wisdom of Solomon: Issues in Child Custody Determination." In *Children, Mental Health, and the Law,* edited by N. D. Reppucci, L. A. Weithorn, E. P. Mulvey, and J. Monahan. Beverly Hills: Sage Publications.

Resnick, A.
  1979   "The Federal Parole System and Decision-Making Guidelines: Criticisms of a Response to Criticism." Unpublished manuscript, UCLA Law School.

Roomkin, M., and Abrams, R.
  1977   "Using Behavioral Evidence in NLRB Regulation: A Proposal." *Harvard Law Review* 90:441.

Rosenberg, C. E.
  1968   *The Trial of the Assassin Guiteau.* Chicago: University of Chicago Press.

Rosenblum, V.; Phillips, C.; Phillips, S. H.; and Merrick, H.
  1978   "Report on the Uses of Social Sciences in Judicial Decision Making." Draft report to the National Science Foundation, Northwestern University.

Saks, M.
  1977   *Jury Verdicts.* Lexington, Mass.: Heath.

Shah, S.
  1969   "Crime and Mental Illness: Some Problems in Defining and Labelling Deviant Behavior." *Mental Hygiene* 53:21–33.

Shapiro, D.
  1977   "Why Do Voters Vote?" *Yale Law Journal* 86:1532.

Shulman, H. S.
  1956   "Reason, Contract, and Law in Labor Relations." *Harvard Law Review* 68:999.

Simon, R. J.
  1967   *The Jury and the Defense of Insanity.* Boston: Little, Brown.

Stanton, T.
  1980   "The Ethnography of Government-Industry Relations: The Federal Agency and Its Environment." Paper presented at the 79th annual meeting of the American Anthropological Association, Washington, D.C., December.

Struening, E. L., and Guttentag, M., eds.
  1975   *Handbook of Evaluation Research.* Beverly Hills, Calif.: Sage.

Tribe, L. H.
  1971   "Trial by Mathematics: Precision and Ritual in the Legal Process." *Harvard Law Review* 84:1329–93.

Ulmer, S.S.
  1962   "Supreme Court Behavior in Racial Exclusion Cases: 1935–1960." *American Political Science Review* 56:325–30.

Underwood, B. D.
  1979   "Law and the Crystal Ball: Predicting Behavior with Statistical Inference and Individualized Judgment." *Yale Law Review* 88:1408–48.

U.S. Congress, House
  1977   *Report of Committee on Education and Labor on H.R. 8410.* H.R. Report No. 95-637, 95th Cong., 1st sess.

U.S. Congress, Senate
  1977   *Report of Committee on Human Resources on S. 2467.* S. Report No. 411-22, 95th Cong., 1st sess.

Weiss, J. A.
  1979   "Access to Influence: Some Effects of Policy Sector on the Use of Social Science." *American Behavioral Scientist* 22:437–58.

Wells, G. L.; Lindsay, R. C. L.; and Ferguson, T. J.
    1979   "Accuracy, Confidence, and Juror Perceptions in Eyewitness Identification." *Journal of Applied Psychology* 64:440–48.
Wells, G. L., and Loftus, E. F., eds.
    1984   *Eyewitness Testimony: Psychological Perspectives.* Cambridge: Cambridge University Press.
Wexler, D. B.
    1976   *Criminal Commitments and Dangerous Mental Patients: Legal Issues of Confinement, Treatment, and Release.* Washington, D.C.: National Institute of Mental Health.
Yale Law Journal
    1965   Note: "The Defendants' Challenge to a Racial Criterion in Jury Selection: A Study in Standing." *Yale Law Journal* 74:919–35.
Zeisel, H., and Diamond, S. S.
    1974   "Convincing Empirical Evidence on the Six-Member Jury." *University of Chicago Law Review* 41:281–95.

ᵔᴖ 12 ᴖᵔ

METHODS FOR THE EMPIRICAL
STUDY OF LAW

Shari Seidman Diamond
University of Illinois, Chicago

Scientific study of the behavior of law uses some of the same methods that law itself employs. Both build on comparison (Levi 1949), draw from experience with human behavior, and attempt to provide rules that will govern future observations. Refutations of both legal and scientific theory occur when the theory is shown to be internally inconsistent. In legal theory, however, refutation also takes place when a court rejects the proposed legal theory. In contrast, a social scientific theory or hypothesis makes predictions that must be testable (or falsifiable; see Popper 1959) by patterns of behavior, rather than by authoritative decision. The data need not be immediately available, as when a scientific theory predicts that if law A is passed, behaviors X, Y, and Z will follow. It must be possible, however, to anticipate an arrangement of events that will either support the hypothesis or provide grounds for its rejection, based on observed behavior.

My primary emphasis in this essay is on problems encountered in testing scientific theories and hypotheses about law. Like most inductive processes, the development of theory is difficult to chart, and I will make only a few methodological points about exploratory analysis that may stimulate new theory. Yet the emphasis on theory-testing methods is not a reflection of the unimportance of theory development. Indeed, if the scientific theories about law were less fragmentary and underdeveloped, many methodological difficulties would dissipate. A theory that makes clear predictions is perhaps the best guide for a researcher in choosing the most appropriate research design and analytic techniques. Although the focus is on theory-testing and research design, it is important to acknowledge that valuable exploratory work may use little of either, at least in its early stages. Before specific research questions take form, it may be necessary to become well acquainted with the environment. A rigid plan for data-collecting may not help, simply because it is difficult to anticipate where the data will come from and what form they will take. Since methodological concerns with the reliability and validity of data are critical at every stage of research, the discussion of these topics will be applicable to research on law both at exploratory and at later stages. The material on research design is most useful at the stage when questions have already taken shape. After some introductory observations on distinctive features of law that have implications for methodology, I shall discuss methods in four major categories under which research in law is being done. Finally, I will mention certain special problems of measurement.

DISTINCTIVE FEATURES OF LAW WITH IMPLICATIONS FOR METHODOLOGY

Most of the characteristics of law and legal institutions that have implications for methodology are not, as individual qualities, unique to the study of law. As a group, however, they form a distinctive collection that exerts a powerful influence on the contours of research possible in this area. Some of these features of law and legal systems—such as multiple separate but interacting system components and the low frequency of some legal events—consistently create problems of method. Other features—such as the partially public nature of legal activity and the existence of various jurisdictions with differing legal structures—both impose special difficulties and provide unusual opportunities for the researcher.

Boundaries and Apparent Boundaries

The legal system is made up of a variety of separate but interacting organizations. The apparent quasi-independence of law-enforcement activities from adjudication and of adjudication from postadjudication treatment of offenders in criminal justice has led researchers to focus on only one of the three institutions—police, courts, or corrections. Such a "slice-and-chop" approach ignores important sources of influence on the behavior to be explained. Police officers' actions may be influenced by what they expect of the courts; court sentences may be responsive to jail conditions as well as to characteristics of the probation and parole systems. Moreover, a change in one part of the system may not affect a particular outcome because other parts in the system compensate for the change. Thus, a legislative increase in a minimum penalty may have no effect on sentencing if prosecutors adjust to the legislative change by altering their charging policies. These interlocking relationships create problems of method because the researcher cannot confine research to a readily identifiable self-contained group of actors and yet understand what determines and what is affected by a targeted behavior.

The borders between legal and nonlegal activities create a similar need to extend the usual boundaries of research on the behavior of law. Since law is both socially formed and designed to socially influence, the interpenetration of legal behaviors and institutions with nonlegal activities is ubiquitous and inevitable. Thus, the legal relationship between the union steward and the contractor in the better-dress business (Moore 1973) both shapes and is influenced by the contractual relationship between the union and the employer; the characteristics of a court may affect the way disputing individuals press claims in nonlegal settings (Yngvesson and Hennessey 1975); the characteristics of community mental-health facilities and civil commitment procedures employed to deal with disturbed persons may affect police and court behavior in the criminal-justice system; and, most broadly, the legal culture (Friedman 1977) that encompasses all citizens may affect and be affected by the way laws are implemented, the way they operate, and the way they change. If a major purpose of the scientific study of law is to explain variation in legal phenomena (Gibbs 1968), the absence of clear channels of influence is a major obstacle. Because of the multiple sources and receivers of legal influence, there is a dangerous potential that important influences will be neglected or missed. The result is a continuing methodological problem of how to extend the research focus far enough so that the behavior at hand may be fully understood.

The Leaky Funnel of Legal Activity

A funnel has sometimes been used as a metaphor for the way the legal system processes cases. A leaky funnel is probably a more accurate image, because numerous holes allow a case to escape before it reaches the spout at the bottom. On the civil side, only a portion of arguments result in complaints; complaints may be filed and then dropped; and only a tiny percentage of filed complaints are tried. The appeal system extends the winnowing process even further. On the criminal side, surveys of victimization indicate that many offenses are never reported to the police. Those reported may or may not result in arrest. Arrest may or may not be followed by indictment, and retained cases may or may not be followed by trial.

This pattern of activity creates several related methodological difficulties. If the interest is in a particular decision-maker—for example, the prosecutor—the cases actually brought to the prosecutor will form only a partial set. The police may not bring some cases to the prosecutor because they know these cases will not be pursued. The omitted cases can only be examined if police screening procedures are studied directly, since cases not actually brought to the prosecutor have escaped the funnel at that earlier stage. Because each decision-maker can terminate activity of some cases and these cases have no continued identity in the legal system, the only way to obtain a full picture of case processing is to begin with the earliest stage and to follow the cases through completion. This procedure is extraordinarily expensive; in addition, the independent record-keeping methods of the agencies at the various stages may make complete tracings almost impossible.

Low Frequency of Some Events

In part because of the leaky-funnel effect, the low frequency of some legal events is likely to make research costly and time-consuming. A sample of 3,000 civil cases found only 27 appeals and 9 overturned verdicts (Rosenberg 1964). The number of cases that actually go to trial is a tiny fraction of all cases filed. A study of jury behavior in a large urban United States District Court that had the cooperation of three federal judges took a year and a half to obtain a sample of 13 criminal jury cases (Diamond and Zeisel 1974; Zeisel and Diamond 1978). Only two cases were lost to this study because of attorney objection; the majority resulted in pleas, a few in trials before the judge when a jury was waived at the last moment, and one in a successful motion to suppress. A sample of decisions to arrest can be gathered only by observing police during long time periods when no behavior occurs that is likely to lead to arrest. Prison riots, hijackings, and major antitrust and water-pollution cases are happily rare; but this circumstance may prove frustrating to the researcher interested in observing and studying them.

All-or-None Judgments

Many legal decisions are naturally dichotomous—arrest or no arrest, contest or plead guilty, find guilty or find not guilty, find for plaintiff or find for defendant. Even among more complex decisions, the basic initial question may be dichotomous. In sentencing, the primary decision is whether to incarcerate or to release, and only secondarily how long should the period of incarceration be.

The most commonly used statistical tools of social science—such as multiple regression and analysis of variance—are most appropriate and powerful with continuous measures as dependent variables. Newer models, such as log-linear analysis, are designed to handle dichotomous independent and dependent variables, but require larger samples for analysis. When the loss of power associated with dichotomous legal decisions is combined with the case loss brought about by the leaky-funnel effect, the problems of analyzing such low-frequency events as appeal outcomes are magnified.[1]

Multiple Varying Jurisdictions

The wide natural variation in laws and legal environments across different legal jurisdictions creates both advantages and disadvantages for research. Even within the United States there are 51 separate jurisdictions at the state level, and the variation in laws and legal institutions is tremendous. For example, 44 states employ lay judges (Silberman 1979); in some cases these are elected, in others they are appointed by the governor, in still others they are selected by local government officials or by the chief judge of a superior court. While most states allow lay court judges to sit alone, in Vermont they sit with attorney judges. In 40 of the 44 states, some form of training is provided, and in 25 it is required. Training programs vary from three days or less (Indiana) to seven weeks (Florida). In some jurisdictions, lay judges can exercise civil jurisdiction to a $200 monetary limit (Georgia), while in others the upper limit is $5,000 (North Carolina); lay judges in Texas are not permitted to impose prison sentences, while those in New Hampshire can sentence up to a year.

If the search extends beyond the borders of the United States, the variety is even greater. Lay judges preside over the bulk of criminal-trial practice in England, sitting in panels of three, assisted by a legally trained clerk who advises them during the proceedings but does not deliberate with them. Socialist countries use lay judges extensively. Other countries employ mixed tribunals, in which laymen sit with professional judges; in

---

[1] *Multiple regression* and *analysis of variance* are both statistical techniques that can be used to analyze the relationship between a dependent or outcome variable and a set of independent or predictor variables. Both techniques assume that the outcome variable is a random variable with a certain probability distribution. When used with a dichotomous outcome measure, this assumption is violated. *Log-linear techniques* permit the researcher to test directly the interaction effects of more than one independent dichotomous variable on a dichotomous dependent variable. *Power* is the ability of a test to detect effects or differences when the effects or differences actually exist. Many statistical tests make assumptions about the behavior and characteristics of the measures on which they are used (see Berk 1980). When these assumptions are incorrect, the power of the test is reduced.

such situations the laymen may be advisory (in some African countries) or able to outvote their professional colleagues (the French mixed bench includes three professionals and nine laymen, with eight votes needed for conviction).

The example of practices governing lay judges shows marked variation within a relatively small area of legal behavior. In a larger conceptual framework—for example, practices in different cultures governing the use of third parties to settle disputes—the range expands much further.

This heterogeneity, which provides a rich arena for exploring the sources and effects of legal variation, also means that research results obtained in a single legal setting may not apply in another context. For example, supplying counsel for youthful offenders in Zenith produced better outcomes for those clients, while in Gotham counsel apparently had no effect (Stapleton and Teitelbaum 1972). A probable explanation for the difference appeared to be the different court organizations. In Zenith, the juvenile-court judges were relatively new to the bench; a state's attorney was present at each stage; arraignment, adjudication, and disposition were separate, with time provided for attorney preparation; and transcripts were made of court proceedings. In Gotham, experienced judges held a traditional view of the juvenile court; no prosecutor was present at hearings, the stages of processing were combined, and transcripts to facilitate appeal were not made. The study suggests that Gotham, less accustomed to defense counsel, discounted their presence and reduced their ability to be effective. But even this hypothesis is tentative, for it may be that only one of the observed differences between Gotham and Zenith was crucial, or even that some unnoticed difference was responsible. Thus, variety, a rich source for hypotheses, may also hinder attempts to generalize.

The Partially Public Nature of Legal Activity

Finally, and perhaps most significantly, a distinguishing characteristic of the legal system is its partially public nature. Some centers of legal activity, including most courtrooms and many legislative sessions, can be entered with unusual ease by both the casual observer and the serious researcher. Appellate court opinions and legislative votes are systematically reported, providing voluminous materials to document the behavior of law. Indeed, it can be argued that the ease of access in large measure explains the extensive research on judicial behavior. Studies focusing on appellate courts, whose decisions and opinions can be scrutinized in any major library, avoid most of the financial and logistic problems of ordinary field research and laboratory experiments.

But the greater part of legal activities is less public. The criminal history of offenders, internal police documents, and jury deliberations are but a few of the areas to which access is either limited or forbidden by law. Only in Switzerland do panels of judges debate and reach their verdicts in public. The interaction of attorneys and clients, settlement conferences between attorneys and clients, settlement conferences between attorneys, and the invocation of legal norms and threats to sue in disputes between neighbors or businessmen, all occur at the edges of the formal legal apparatus and are often viewed only indirectly, if at all, through retrospective interviews with the participants.

Other aspects of the systems are also difficult to trace. As much as one third of the money expended in the criminal-justice system may go to private police and protection.

Since some states require only one license for a firm of private investigators, which can then hire an unlimited number of operatives, it is difficult even to know how many private police are active (Scott and McPherson 1971).

Finally, perhaps the most troublesome problem of accessibility arises because law is a system of social control, with a central focus on deviant behavior. Deviants typically take great pains to shield their activities from both official and unofficial observation. Some behaviors, such as burglary and assault, can be indirectly assessed, but only insofar as victims report them. Other behaviors, such as income-tax violation and much white-collar crime, may be known only to the violator himself. Patterns of invisible deviance encourage researchers to accent the relatively more visible crimes, and this factor may partially account for both the steady flow of studies of driving violations (for example, Feest 1968; Robertson 1976; Ross 1973) and the general dearth of empirical research on white-collar crime.

Not all police departments and judges' chambers are equally inaccessible to the researchers. When research requires the cooperation of police, judges, attorneys, or violators, the difficulty may be not whether access is permitted but who permits it. One study of pretrial settlement met with refusals by 14 jurisdictions before it could be implemented. Reasons for refusing to participate ranged from case overload through the view that it was inappropriate for a judge to take a role in plea discussions to prosecutorial objection to what was considered an invasion of executive function (Kerstetter and Heinz 1979). The methodological questions are whether and to what extent findings obtained in settings willing to permit research can validly apply to contexts where the actors are more recalcitrant.

When access can be obtained, the researcher interested in legal phenomena can often unearth records of behavior extending back in time that would turn researchers in mental health or family structure green with envy. Tax accounts, land sales, marital unions and dissolutions, the names of disputing parties, and the nature of legal disputes have all been recorded more or less regularly in most literate societies. Unfortunately, all too often the precise kind of information needed to test a critical hypothesis was not viewed as important by earlier clerks and recorders. The vote of a hung jury, for example, may not appear in the court file; no effort was made to keep track of whether court-ordered recoveries were paid (Yngvesson and Hennessey 1975), and testimony was not recorded in arbitration (Sarat 1976) or in small-claims courts. Parole boards may not record the reasons for their decisions (O'Leary and Nuffield 1972), and no record, apart from the final decision, is kept of sentence review in Massachusetts and Connecticut (Zeisel and Diamond 1977). Because, as a rule, prosecutors in criminal cases cannot appeal, few transcripts are available for cases ending in not guilty verdicts; in civil cases, transcripts for cases not worth appealing are not available. Even where some attempt has been made at regular record-keeping, omissions and other sources of both biased and unreliable measurement are common.

The public quality of some legal records is precisely the characteristic that contributes to their weakness for some research purposes. Because the records and decisions are public, they may be designed in part for audience effect. Police departments, for example, justify their budgets on the basis of their crime statistics; because offense categorization requires substantial judgment and the arrest decision is subject to wide discretion, crime and enforcement patterns are particularly susceptible to police organizational pressures.

Prosecutors, looking toward election, typically include guilty pleas in their conviction tally and exclude dismissals from the base of their conviction rates. Other legal participants also have the regular responsibility of publicly justifying each of their decisions. Much can be learned from the reason provided by a judge, for example, in his public explanation (Llewellyn 1960), but such a reasoned justification is not necessarily a complete picture of the construction of a decision.

Increasingly in recent years researchers have been finding creative ways to take advantage of public access and to overcome barriers to access and weaknesses of available data. Schwartz and Orleans (1967) were able to obtain aggregate information on groups of income tax returns, thus avoiding objections to the release of individual data. Carroll (see Carroll and Payne 1977) and Wilkins and his colleagues (see, for example, Gottfredson et al. 1975) have successfully conducted research on decision-making by parole boards, an area long closed to public view. They observed parole hearings and analyzed justifications, but in addition devised information searches and judgment tasks as well. Surveys of victimization (U.S. Department of Justice 1975) have helped to overcome local idiosyncrasies in official crime reporting.

Each of these strategies solves some of the problems associated with other techniques of data collection. Yet each is subject to its own limitations, and no one approach is likely to be without problems. Surveys of crime victimization, for example, face inherent limitations from memory decay in their respondents (National Academy of Sciences 1976).

The real methodological benefit of the partially public nature of law is that, for any question, a variety of data-collecting methods is likely to be available. Thus, law is an area in which it is eminently possible to use a variety of different measures and approaches to study the same problem. This multimethod strategy allows weaknesses in one design to be corrected by strengths in another. When outcomes from different methods converge, greater confidence in the research findings is the result (Feigl 1958).

In the range of research approaches to law explored below, the tensions imposed by these qualities recur: public–confidential; record richness–record unreliability; boundaries–overlap; heterogeneity–ability to generalize. The tensions cannot be completely resolved, but acknowledging them may help to shape more self-conscious research decisions.

For this discussion, research on law has been divided into four major categories. Studies within each category show similar methodological problems. The first category of research focuses on the emergence and change of law and legal institutions and traces changes in legal behavior, treating law and legal behavior as dependent variables at the societal or group level. The second category, which takes the individual as the unit of interest, explores the emergence of legal problems and legal knowledge and attitudes— more generally, legal culture. The third studies the operation of law and legal institutions; research on the ways courts conduct their business and how judges are selected falls into this group. The final category, which deals with studies on the impact of law and legal change, treats laws and legal arrangements as independent variables in causal analyses.

Some studies will not fall neatly into a single category. For example, comparative studies often focus on both operation and impact. The general research questions posed in each category, however, tend to share methodological obstacles; the groupings used for discussion are made with that focus in mind.

EMERGENCE AND CHANGE OF LAW
AND LEGAL INSTITUTIONS

Emergence and change are perhaps the most difficult social processes to assess, since a law or legal institution may command interest only after it is in place or has undergone alteration. Typically, therefore, historical questions (for example, how did the regulation of energy sources develop? what produced the current structure of the criminal code?) are explored by cross-sectional research techniques.

Tracing Emergence and Change

Investigators often interview informants who recount how matters were handled in earlier days and who report their beliefs about how changes came about. To the extent that time dims and interests distort these responses, materials based on retrospection may be limited or misleading. In some cases, of course, such sources are the only ones available. In societies with an oral tradition, the past may be almost totally inaccessible except through informants willing to reconstruct it (Nader 1969; Nader and Todd 1978). Careful cross-checking of responses from several sources and attempts to identify informants with different vested interests can help to reduce reporting bias (see Richardson, Dohrenwend, and Klein 1965 for an excellent discussion of interviewing techniques), and the result may significantly contribute to knowledge about the past.

This approach has many limitations. It presumes that informants originally absorbed the material that the researcher wishes to uncover, that they remember it, and that they are willing to share it with the interviewer. Social scientists tend to be skeptical of respondents' reports even on current events; the passage of time only increases most of the distortions associated with such data. Legal anthropologists (for example, Allott, Epstein, and Gluckman 1969) have been sensitive to the many problems of reconstructing events by using informants, and they have suggested some strategies to reduce the impact of those problems (see, for example, Black and Metzger 1965; Epstein 1967).

It is easy to criticize almost any research tool; a crucial issue is whether other methods are available with fewer or different flaws. Often it is possible to supplement interview data in reconstructing past events. For example, a study of changes and sources of change in California criminal legislation during the turbulent period from 1955 to 1971 began in 1971 with a substantially qualitative analysis based primarily on interviews with legislators and members of special-interest groups active during that period. The report examined eleven selected legislative sessions, identifying major bills and trends observed in party shifts, partisanship changes, and lobby activities. To the interview data were added materials from newspapers, interest-group propaganda, committee transcripts, and a variety of secondary sources (Berk, Brackman, and Lesser 1977, p. 24). Even so, as the authors pointed out, the data base represented a purposive sample, constrained by feasibility (organized lobbies may leave substantial paper, for example, but may have little impact). Moreover, because it is difficult to explain the process of transforming these voluminous primary-source materials into an analytic product, the traditional methodological requirement that the reader be informed about how a study, or at least an analysis, may be replicated is not met.

In sharp contrast to the chapter that reports this qualitative effort is the quantitative analysis that followed. Examining the manifest legislative intent of almost seven hundred revisions in the California Penal Code, the authors attempted to detect trends in the code by systematically analyzing a wide range of changes. Most of these were unlikely to cause repercussions detectable, and therefore susceptible to report, by system participants, but small alterations can have overall effects that may be observed by using a systematic quantitative approach. The results indicate the value of the quantitative analysis. The qualitative chapter implied that the interests of civil-liberties advocates and of law-enforcement professionals were in straightforward competition, so that what one lost the other gained. Successful years for those on one side were remembered as disheartening by those on the other. But the quantitative analysis indicated that this picture of a zero-sum game was too simple. Because law-enforcement advocates concentrated on criminalization and penalties while, at least in the early 1960s, the civil-liberties lobby focused primarily on issues of due process, both sides could achieve success through the same legislation.

In addition to coding legislation, the authors developed quantitative measures of partisanship, lobby influence, and newspaper coverage for the same period and identified data on crime rates and public opinion from other sources. Using these additional measures, they explored various causal models that might explain changes in the Penal Code. Although this aspect of the study is relatively weak, in part because of the short time series and some unavoidable weaknesses in particular indices, the work provides a useful model of the potential sources of data available over time in a literate society that can be used to trace legal functioning.

I have discussed this example in considerable detail to show that researchers can often take advantage of the pervasive documentation of legal behavior to obtain a check on the subjectivity of informants and observers. Since qualitative data will generally be richer in detail and may be a fruitful source of hypotheses, mixing the two research approaches is a natural resource for the study of legal behavior.

Many attempts to investigate legal change over time have focused on courts. Even though regularity in the recording activities of these institutions eases some of the difficulties of answering longitudinal questions, obstacles are by no means absent. One study, which recorded the number and type of civil cases filed in two California Superior trial courts in 1890, 1910, 1930, 1950, and 1970, reports that changes in the distribution of cases support the hypothesis that the function of trial courts has shifted away from dispute settlement toward routine administrative tasks (Friedman and Percival 1976). Testing the hypothesis in the Superior Court was complicated by changes in the jurisdiction of the Court during that period. For example, the jurisdictional floor of the Superior Court went up from $300 to $3,000 during the period between 1890 and 1970. Even after corrections for inflation, a "real" increase in jurisdictional amount apparently occurred (Lempert 1978, pp. 113–14, n. 22). Because this research, which sought to test a hypothesis about changes in court usage over time, was confined to the superior-court level, an alternative explanation for the pattern shifts cannot be dismissed—cases may have been diverted to other courts. But if the study had attempted to examine inferiorcourt cases as well, it would have faced additional problems: the records of the lower courts, particularly for early periods, tend to be incomplete (Friedman and Percival 1976, p. 277). Under such circumstances, another strategy—examining the data on the superior courts immediately before and after changes in the jurisdictional amount— would have allowed the researchers to test the effect of the jurisdictional change. By confining the observations to twenty-year intervals, the opportunity to make this test was missed.

The choice of interval has a major effect on the ability to detect trends over time. One study (Grossman and Sarat 1975) examined litigation rates in American federal courts at ten-year intervals, from 1902 through 1972. Changes from decade to decade are portrayed in Figure 1. Had a twenty-year interval been selected for this study, the change in rates would have appeared as in Figure 2 if 1902 had been the first year chosen for analysis, suggesting a slow, steady increase in rate, or as in Figure 3 if the starting year had been 1912, suggesting a more erratic pattern. The difference between these figures makes the clearest case for attempting to increase data points and to decrease gaps between them when research is aimed at detecting patterns over time. A ten-year interval, of course, is not necessarily ideal. Had the authors collected their data at intervals of five years, two years, or one year, still different patterns might have emerged.

With limited resources, there will always be a tradeoff between the stability of estimates at given points—a function of the number of cases sampled at each point—and the identification of actual trends—facilitated by increasing the number of data points. If the cost of data collection is held constant, increasing the number of data points over time usually forces a reduction in the total sample size as well as a reduction in the sample size at each time point. It is more expensive to sample ten cases every fifth year than to sample twenty cases every tenth year, because the researcher using the smaller interval must work through twice as many files to draw a sample of the same size as must the researcher using the larger interval. The smaller interval may introduce still additional costs because of the difficulty of locating extra files housed in different storage locations over time (different filing cabinets, storerooms, basements, and warehouses across town).

The balance between intervals and the number of cases at each time point must

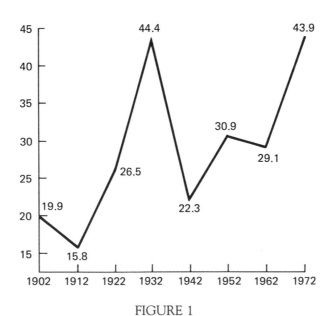

FIGURE 1

Federal civil cases per 100,000 population, 1902–72
(adapted from Grossman and Sarat 1975, Figure 3).

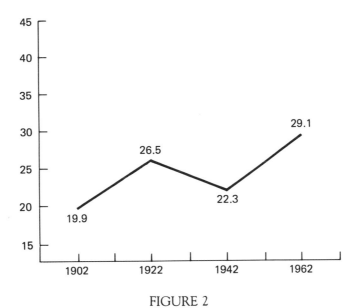

FIGURE 2

Federal civil cases per 100,000 population, 1902–62
(adapted from Grossman and Sarat 1975, Figure 3).

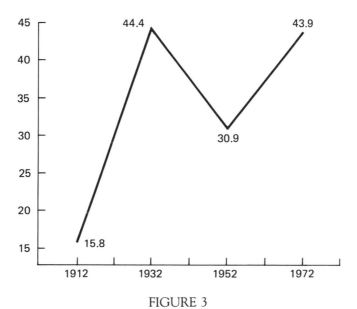

FIGURE 3

Federal civil cases per 100,000 population, 1912–72
(adapted from Grossman and Sarat 1975, Figure 3).

ultimately be struck according to what is most essential to the hypothesis of interest. It is not possible simultaneously to maximize detailed breakdowns both at given points in time and over time. Where prior research or good theory suggests stability over time or homogeneity at given points, sampling decisions can emphasize the more important source of variance. When neither prior research nor theory provide clear signposts, it may be useful to collect pilot data, sampling to gauge variations within and across years on major variables, before the final sampling framework is established.

Anticipating Change

In each of the three research examples just discussed, it has been assumed that the investigator was forced to ask a retrospective question. Yet legal change may often be anticipated. Part of the extensive literature on Africa and India reflects the recognition that the transition from colony to independent nation and the confrontation between customary and externally imposed legal systems are fertile arenas for legal change. Modernization in general is associated with the restructuring of societies and their legal systems. Anthropologists have been alert to these opportunities (for example, Baxi and Galanter 1979; Collier 1976), but they and other social scientists have rarely taken advantage of the opportunity to anticipate and study legal emergence and change in the United States.

For example, advanced computer technology means that new crimes must be defined, and the laws of privacy may undergo alteration. When New Jersey proposed new gambling activities, the state created a plausible research opportunity for those interested in the emergence of a new scheme of legal control. Discoveries in the areas of recombinant DNA and the catastrophe at the Three Mile Island nuclear plant have raised concerns that are likely to generate legal responses. The enormous problems of energy sources and supplies may promote new or altered mechanisms of legal control.

The difficulty in studying any emerging or changing area is that the time frames over which important changes will occur are less predictable than in most other subjects of research. Neither researchers nor their granting agencies will readily accept a gestation period that cannot be estimated and a research strategy that must remain consistently malleable and potentially mobile. Yet the research problem may call for such flexibility and patience. Not surprisingly, the passage of time is helpful in answering longitudinal questions. To realize its advantages may require a "technology" of funding research and a method of distributing tenure and other awards more akin to the lifetime studies of public health and epidemiology than to the short-range studies that characterize most social-scientific research.

TRACING LEGAL DEVELOPMENT IN THE INDIVIDUAL
Legal Socialization

How people come to understand and develop attitudes toward law and legal institutions has been the focus of research deriving from two traditions—psychological interest in moral development and studies of political socialization from political science (Tapp and Levine 1977). As is true for other kinds of studies of emergence, questions concerning legal socialization are basically longitudinal. Retrospective attempts to answer such questions have serious inherent weaknesses. Interviews with adults are unlikely to identify sources of their beliefs and attitudes, if only because few are aware when or where they accumulated their ideas about the law. However, four types of studies of legal socialization attempt to cope with these difficulties.

Correlational Studies   The first approach is through correlational studies comparing the attitudes or knowledge about law of individuals known to come from different backgrounds. If the attitudes and knowledge differ among groups, the difference is attributed to the background variable. For example, to the extent that children of educated parents have greater knowledge about law or more consistently adhere to legal principles of free speech than do those born to parents with less education, the proposition that parental instruction is a source of legal socialization receives some support.

As is true for all correlational research, the objection to such an inference is the possibility that the obtained correlation is spurious, the result of a third—unknown— variable, such as parental intelligence or income, which affects parents' education and exerts a separate effect on the child's legal socialization. The likelihood of spurious relationships is particularly high in the literature on legal socialization, because many reported results are limited to zero-order correlations between single potential causes and the measure of legal attitude or knowledge. Although they do not provide a complete cure, multivariate methods (Blalock 1972) offer some improvement by providing a simultaneous test of various potential influences on legal socialization. The degree of improvement depends upon (a) how well potential influences are identified and measured and (b) the extent to which they are uncorrelated with one another.

Cross-Sectional Studies   A second approach, the cross-sectional "developmental" research design (Cutler 1977), attempts to identify the points at which individuals undergo changes in legal knowledge and attitudes by testing individuals of different ages. Its value hinges on the assumption that sampling and test materials do not differ across age levels. When applied to some comparisons, this assumption may be plausible. For example, fifth, seventh, ninth, and twelfth graders were studied for their reactions to laws that present potential intrusions on individual freedoms (Gallatin and Adelson 1971). The four age groups in the American sample were all drawn from the same midwestern suburb, and the subjects were largely middle-class, suggesting that the rate of high-school dropouts in the sample was likely to be small. Differences across age level were therefore not likely to be due to the selective loss of students in the higher grades. By contrast, a purportedly developmental study that compared responses of high-school students with those of college students would be ignoring the fact that not all high-school students go to college. The attitudes of the college students might differ from those of the high-school students because the groups contained different types of individuals and not because they differed only in maturation or educational experience. Such concern is more than speculative; it has been found that college-bound high-school students are more tolerant than those who are not college-bound (Langton and Jennings 1968), and others have reported that college attendance is a good predictor of adult support for civil liberties (see, for example, Key 1961; Stouffer 1955).

Other kinds of socialization studies raise the same selection question. One study of judicial socialization divided 128 Florida judges into three groups—those who had been on the bench 5 years or less, those who had been judges between 6 and 15 years, and those who had served for more than 15 years. Differences in response among the three groups were attributed to a combination of agency and judicial socialization (Alpert, Atkins, and Ziller 1979). But the explanation may, in fact, reflect the pattern of decisions to leave the bench. The authors suggest that 4.5 to 5 years as a judge represents a critical point at which to decide to make judging a career. Judges still on the bench, policemen still on the force, or guards still employed in a prison after 15 years all may differ from judges or policemen or guards who leave their positions after a shorter period of time. An assessment of attrition rates in the proposed research setting will help the researcher to evaluate how much of a threat selection poses to a developmental explanation of differences, but as a general rule, the larger the interval in age or experience, the greater will be attrition and the consequent danger of a selection artifact.

Other methodological difficulties arise in the cross-sectional developmental design. Even assuming zero attrition, "the older may differ from the young at any given point in time due to maturational factors, or because they are members of different cohorts and were raised in differing sets of social and political circumstances" (Cutler 1977, p. 295). In a study of the magnitude of age and cohort effects (Nesselroade and Baltes 1974), the effect of age was evaluated by comparing the attitudes of 14-year-old high-school students (in their freshman year) with attitudes of students from the same class during the following year, when they were 15 years old. The cohort effect was evaluated by comparing the attitudes of 14-year-olds in the first year with the attitudes of the new cohort of 14-year-olds in the following year. These two 14-year-old classes were thus the same age when tested but had been born (and raised) on the average of one year apart. The researchers showed that the cohort difference was as large as the age effect, suggesting that generational differences can be as powerful as developmental effects.

The Cohort Approach   A third major type of study design for legal socialization, the cohort approach, requires multiple cross-sectional samples collected at more than one point in time for different groupings stratified by age, year in school, or time in office, to help distinguish age, cohort, and time-of-measurement effects (Schaie 1965). For example, a finding that the attitudes toward law of 18-year-old boys differed from those of 14-year-old boys in 1968 might arise because the particular political turbulence of that year influenced 18-year-olds, while leaving 14-year-olds unaffected. An alternative explanation is that a general developmental trend changed the attitudes of 14-year-olds by the time they became 18. An additional cross-sectional survey of 14-year-olds and 18-year-olds in another year would test these alternate explanations. If a generational explanation is not responsible for the difference found in 1968, the same difference should appear in comparisons between the same age groups tested in 1966, 1970, and 1976 (see Mason et al. 1973 and Glenn 1976 for discussions of the statistical analysis of cohort designs).

The need for a test of generational effects will, of course, depend upon the probable difference in the relevant experience of different cohorts. For example, a cohort or generational explanation for differences observed in 1953 between 14-year-olds and 15-year-olds (born in 1939 and 1938, respectively) would be less plausible than a generational explanation for the difference in 1968 between 14-year-olds and 18-year-olds. The life experience of the 14- and 15-year-olds would be closer because of the smaller age gap.

More importantly, the year 1953 was unlikely to have different legal implications for children of 14 and 15. Unlike the 18-year-olds, neither group could vote or be drafted.

The Panel Design Unlike the other three methods, the fourth method for the study of legal socialization traces changes in the same set of respondents over time. When the original sample includes respondents at different stages of development, the so-called panel design (Lazarsfeld and Fiske 1938), like the cohort design, provides the opportunity to distinguish developmental trends from age-specific historical effects. In addition, because the same respondents are tested several times, the direct tracing of attitudinal change is facilitated. The researchers not only learn that 54 percent of the sample, for example, distrust attorneys, as compared with 49 percent of the sample measured two years earlier, but they can also identify the 15 percent who became more trusting and the 20 percent who became less trusting. The backgrounds and recent experiences of the respondents who switched can be examined for clues about the source of their changed attitudes.

Panel designs are costly both in terms of researchers' time and in the extra effort entailed in relocating respondents who have moved, disappeared, or simply grown tired of contributing data. In addition, the possibility always exists that response content will be influenced by prior testing (Campbell 1957). A small cross-sectional sample of new respondents in each wave of the panel can be examined to gauge the extent of shifts attributable to prior testing, however, and the multicohort panel remains the strongest source of interview data on legal socialization.

Emergence of a Legal Problem

Nader, writing about dispute settlement among the Zapotec of Mexico, noted that "it is obvious that no case (or only the very rare one) begins and ends in the courtroom" (1969, p. 71). Although legal problems tend to be examined only after the problem has formally emerged with the filing of a complaint, legal problems begin much earlier. Tracing the development of legal problems and identifying the types of conflicts that do and do not lead to legal action require a method to identify a population of potential sources of conflict. Studies that begin with filed court cases can investigate directly only the types of cases most likely to be settled after that point (see, for example, Wanner 1975). Because those that are winnowed away before filing cannot be systematically traced, data are lacking on the circumstances that lead to avoidance—limiting or withdrawing from the relationship with another disputant to such an extent that the dispute no longer remains salient (Felstiner 1974). Little information exists about the process or incidence of claiming legal rights when the formal enforcement of these rights turns out to be unnecessary. A study of complainants to the Massachusetts Commission Against Discrimination—which found that social class was directly related to greater participation in the complaint process and to better outcomes from it—did not investigate whether class was a predictor of willingness to initiate the complaint process (Crowe 1978). Similarly, one attempt to explain why certain conflicts in the textile industry were brought to commercial arbitration was hampered because it examined only those conflicts that were in fact arbitrated. The conclusion that sellers "do not arbitrate cases which are weak or cases against buyers with whom they enjoy good business relations" is supported by interviews with attorneys and parties in the arbitrated cases (Bonn 1972, p. 577). Yet, such a claim can be directly validated only by examining a sample of conflicts, tracking those that are brought to arbitration and noting those that are abandoned.

There is a logical problem in developing causal structures to explain litigation—"we have somehow to define the total population of law-relevant conflicts and legal needs in order to operationalize the question, which factors determine the portion that is finally taken to court," which cannot be done without normative assumptions defining "legal needs" (Blankenburg 1975, p. 316). As a preliminary approach to this problem, Blankenburg selected a population of conflicts for which legal action is no doubt a possible outcome and one that requires an early decision: he examined those litigants who, having lost in court, must decide whether to appeal. This population of defeated parties defines a somewhat limited, and perhaps idiosyncratic, set of conflicts. It is, of course, more time-consuming and costly to follow conflicts defined at the pre-judicial stage, for the life of a conflict may be long.

Other studies suggest deeper historical probes. It is often possible to identify a class of potential complainants or a population of possible disputants. One telephone survey questioned consumers about their experience with thirty-four typical products. This approach enabled the researchers to gauge rates of reported complaints and efforts to obtain redress. They could also identify those who reported having experienced problems but did not attempt formal action, and, within the limits of the survey technique, they could distinguish the characteristics of successful complainers from those who were unsuccessful or who failed to complain (Best and Andreasen 1977). In another study a sample of TV and washing machine purchases was drawn from the files of a cooperative appliance company. The researchers questioned the customers on their experiences with the purchased item and on whether and how they lodged complaints. In addition, field observations of sales, delivery, and service were conducted, and complaint letters to the company and the Better Business Bureau were analyzed (Ross and Littlefield 1978). Even this design, however, is somewhat incomplete; as the authors pointed out, the data do not indicate the correspondence between "objective" defects (potential sources of action) and subjectively defined problems. Such an extension could be handled with an inspection of a sample of merchandize, which would then be traced to the consumers who purchased each. These consumers would, in turn, be questioned in a longitudinal design.

In each of these consumer studies, the population of purchasers formed the universe of individuals who could potentially generate complaints. Other kinds of conflicts are likely under specifiable circumstances—the signing of a lease opens the door to possible land-lord–tenant disputes; a condominium conversion may stimulate legal conflict among neighbors. The cost of tracing the development of legal conflict will be reduced if the researcher can take advantage of knowledge about the contexts in which conflict is likely to occur and can draw the sample accordingly. At the very least, it is possible to define the total population of potential complainants or disputants who can become involved in a particular kind of legal dispute.

Two basic strategies can be used. In the first, a subgroup is identified that has a particularly high probability of becoming legally entangled. For example, individuals who previously have been divorced are more likely to become divorced again than those who have never been divorced. The researcher will accumulate divorces at a higher rate from a sample of these divorced individuals than when data collection proceeds from a random sample of all adults. The potential cost of this strategy is the possibility that the previously divorced may have unique patterns of marital conflict and resolution and may use the legal system differently than do their counterparts in first marriages.

An alternate strategy identifies all individuals who can potentially become involved in the legal conflict under scrutiny. Thus, for divorce, the total potential group of parties is the married population (and, as Rich Lempert pointed out to me, at current rates of divorce, simply tracing all marital outcomes may result in a substantial proportion of contemplated and completed divorce). Of course, not all target outcomes are highly probable; and the tradeoff between representativeness and required initial sample size will depend on the research question. An optimum solution may be a stratified sample, in which the researcher oversamples from subgroups known to end up with high rates of legal action.

It may be possible to reduce the costs of longitudinal research by identifying a population retrospectively and using archival data sources to trace changes over time. One study, for example, traced the officially recorded criminal careers of the birth cohort of nearly 10,000 males born in 1945 in Philadelphia who resided in the city from their 10th to their 18th birthdays (Wolfgang, Figlio, and Sellin 1972). Research did not begin until 1964, but school records and selective service lists enabled the researchers to identify the group retrospectively; official records on encounters with the law from police, courts, and correctional agencies were used to trace dealings with the criminal-justice system. School records also offered a wealth of information on such items as race, intelligence scores, achievement measures, and attendance. Moreover, because income correlates highly with other measures of socioeconomic status and school files include residential location, an estimate of socioeconomic status could be coaxed from the available data. The researchers were able to examine the correlations between these measures and police records in their efforts to identify precursors of formal contact with the legal system. Greater interest in the regular recording of social indicators as well as computer capability for data storage may make such research more feasible in the future.[2]

THE OPERATION OF LAW AND LEGAL INSTITUTIONS

Since the legal system is a product and source of public activity, it may appear surprising that so little is known about the range of its daily activities and the criteria it uses in arriving at decisions. Yet the amount of primarily descriptive research reported in the literature—for example, characteristics of cases brought by civil courts (Wanner 1974); the charging process by prosecutors (Neubauer 1974); jury-selection procedures (Levine and Schweber-Korea 1976); reduced-fee work by attorneys (Lochner 1975); misdemeanor trial court proceedings (Mileski 1971)—testifies to an absence of basic information. This lack may be due, in part, to the relatively recent history of systematic empirical investigation by social scientists on the operation of legal institutions. The fact that law is not fully open to scrutiny is another potential explanation. Finally, the tremendous variety of laws

[2]There are, however, countervailing trends that seek to limit such data accumulation. Concern with privacy and protection of subjects suggest to many that data collection should be limited (see Katz 1972; Capron 1975).

and legal organizations and activities may inhibit the descriptive work required to order the legal universe and stimulate the development of theory.[3]

Some Current Approaches and Their Limitations

The primary methodological obstacles to description involve sampling problems, limits on access within a setting, and bias in records and respondents. When the research purpose extends beyond simple description, additional difficulties arise. The researcher concerned with explaining the activities of the legal institution under examination must consider the interdependent nature of the legal system—acknowledging, for example, that decision-making on the part of public defenders may influence and be influenced by prosecutorial practices and that both may influence and be influenced by the local trial bench. With respect to studies of litigation, for example, there are "difficulties in analyzing the flow of business in a single forum that is part of a larger complex" (Galanter 1975, p. 365). Contextual effects similarly inhibit attempts to simulate adequately the operation of a legal institution extracted from its normal environment.

The approaches widely used to study legal operations include case studies, participant surveys, samples of official production records, and, less often, simulations.

The Case Study   The case study typically focuses on one small part of the universe. At some level, nearly every research project represents a kind of case study. Apart from national probability surveys, all these efforts focus on a small, nonrandom subgroup of settings—a nonprobability sample of respondents or institutions. Even national probability samples, except for multiwave ones, may be viewed as case studies of a single time period. Typically, however, the term "case study" applies to an examination of one location and one set of interacting participants. Thus, a case study can concentrate on a single prison (Jacobs 1977), a single parole agency (McCleary 1978), a group of delinquent high-school-age boys (Chambliss 1973), a mechanism for dispute resolution in a small African village (Gibbs 1963), or even a single trial (Zeisel and Diamond 1976).

A good case study closely scrutinizes the context of the behaviors it examines with an intensity not generally possible in other research designs. Because legal and illegal organizations and activities often have quite distinct public and private faces, intensive extended observation of a group of actors may be necessary to dig beneath the surface. The case study can, therefore, be an especially revealing tool in sociolegal research.

The research plan of a case study is typically more flexible than are other research strategies, precisely because the researcher does not know in advance exactly what information will be most useful and where the best sources of data will lie. Perhaps this crucial flexibility is why case studies are among both the most and the least illuminating pieces of research.

The intensive case study of legal behavior is probably most productive in situations where very little is known about the general type of legal behavior in question. At the extreme, study of unfamiliar dispute-settlement procedures in China by Westerners might begin with an exploratory case study in this unknown territory. Similarly, case studies of

---

[3] Although theory jumps ahead of description and provides a structure for further observation (Popper 1963), a framework of familiarity with the range of character of legal activity, rather than a census of its behavior, seems necessary to promote the most powerful theorizing.

Neighborhood Dispute Centers (see, for example, Buckle and Thomas-Buckle 1980) have laid critical foundations for subsequent, more tightly structured examinations of the Centers' impact on disputes.

The case study may also be usefully employed when the terrain is well known but investigation deals with an unusual instance. For example, when John Mitchell and Maurice Stans were acquitted of conspiracy to impede the investigation of Robert Vesco, a fugitive financier, a *New York Times* reporter interviewed the jurors in the case, who reported that their first vote had been 8 to 4 in favor of conviction. It was known that jury verdicts generally reflect the majority view on the first ballot, particularly when the majority has as many as eight members (Kalven and Zeisel 1966; Penrod and Hastie 1979); this trial provided an opportunity to investigate the reasons why a majority would alter its choice of verdict. The results provided a clue: the single juror who was a college graduate began in favor of acquittal. A bank vice president, he arranged to have movies and other entertainment provided to the jurors during their sequestration; during the deliberations, he apparently drafted requests to have portions of the testimony reread. The verdict and reports from his fellow jurors indicate that his influence on the ultimate group decision was strong.

Perhaps more than almost any other research design, the value of case studies depends on the conclusions drawn from them. An attempt to generalize about the legal landscape from an examination of a tiny corner can be entirely misleading. Law is quite different from the natural sciences, where sampling concerns pose limited threats to the ability to generalize because there is little variability among the units being studied—such as metal bars or beakers of sulfuric acid—with respect to the properties being investigated. In the social sciences, and particularly in studies of legal institutions, variety is both rampant and important, since it may directly relate to and affect the behavior of interest. For example, as a result of the Mitchell-Stans case study, it can be hypothesized that a minority juror's social class and educational background can cause a significant increase in the persuasiveness of the minority position. This hypothesis may not be an accurate explanation for the particular verdict. Even if it is correct, it may hold only in cases where the defendants and witnesses are prominent and themselves well educated, when the trial receives substantial publicity, when the jury is sequestered, or when the more educated juror has provided the jury with concrete benefits.

The case study is often criticized as a research method because its results may lack external validity—that is, it is not clear that insights obtained from the particular sample of behavior can be applied to other settings, to other subjects, and the like. The challenge is to integrate the potentially rich yield of the case study with other kinds of research to build theory by sensitive comparisons and to generate new hypotheses that can be systematically tested.

The Participant Survey   The survey is popular with scholars interested in the social-scientific study of law. Since it is often easy to sample respondents with information about the law, legal problems, or the legal system (for example, a questionnaire can be mailed to every tenth lawyer listed in the Martindale-Hubbell Directory), the survey appears to avoid many of the weaknesses of the case study. Surveys were the primary data collection instrument in more than half the sample of research proposals I reviewed as a panelist for the Law and Social Science Program of the National Science Foundation.

This romance with the survey is of relatively recent vintage, and there has been a tendency for its new acquaintances to hit every legal topic with this methodological hammer. Thus, members of the general public have been asked about their support for the police and their fear of crime (Block 1971), their experience as crime victims (Ennis 1967, among others), and their attitudes toward civil liberties (Wilson 1975). Consumers have been questioned on their complaint behavior (Best and Andreasen 1977). Defendants have been respondents in studies of perceived fairness in treatment (Casper 1978). Judges have responded to surveys covering a wide range of topics, from their perceptions of the roles they occupy (Ungs and Baas 1972) to the way they reach decisions on sentencing and bail (Hogarth 1971; Konečni and Ebbesen 1979).

One problem with many legal surveys, not inherent in the survey method itself, is particularly likely to arise in studies of law. Because there are so many legal jurisdictions, actors, and communities, definitions of common terms may vary dramatically across potential respondents. A survey that does not determine in advance how respondents define key terms may discover too late—or not at all—that respondents have been inconsistent in their interpretation of questions. For example, a survey of prosecutors across the country might ask how often plea bargaining occurs in their court.

> Some prosecutors will tell you that in their jurisdictions no "plea bargaining" goes on, but readily admit that many cases are "settled" before trial. Some judges . . . deny that any "plea negotiations" go on in their courts. They are right: . . . defendants are simply informed that . . . they can either "plead guilty and get mercy or go to trial and get justice." Some prosecutors, defense counsel, and law professors share the view that such an arrangement is not plea bargaining. [McDonald 1979, p. 385]

The investigator whose pilot work discloses such variation can define or avoid ambiguous terms in the survey, thus reducing the probability that respondents are answering what are, in effect, different questions.

A survey of citizens, lawyers, judges, clerks, or litigants may provide fascinating data on the perceptions of these legal participants. But when the research question asks, "How does a law or legal institution operate?" the survey is likely to be only partially successful in providing answers. Some instances of potential distortion are clear: the defendant claims his guilty plea was the result of external pressure (Blumberg 1967) or judges deny that lawmaking is a judicial activity of any frequency or importance (Ungs and Baas 1972).

Other instances of potential error are less obvious. Lochner (1975) was interested in learning how private attorneys came in contact with no-fee and low-fee clients, why they helped them, the age and ethnic composition of the clients, and the kind and caliber of legal work performed for them. Attorney–client privilege would preclude any sampling of case files in an attorney's office, and since these cases infrequently result in official court action, court files would provide little relevant data. Lochner conducted a survey of attorneys to obtain his answers. Yet, even assuming the best intentions on the part of the attorneys, it is questionable how accurate attorneys are likely to be when asked to summarize the demographic characteristics of part of their practice or how much attorneys can tell us about the caliber of the legal services they provide.

Sampling Official Records   When descriptions of legal operations are based on samples of officially produced records, fewer questions are raised about their accuracy. The usual rationale is that figures collected by an organization for its own use in the course of its regular activities are not subject to presentational distortions. However, motivation to manipulate regularly collected measures also exists whenever the figures are used to justify resource allocations or to reflect on the skill or industry of those responsible for producing them. For example, until 1973, larceny under $50 was not included in the FBI Crime Index; larceny above $50 was included. Since the classification of an offense as an index or nonindex crime depended on a police evaluation of the lost property, there was ample opportunity for police to affect index larceny rates before 1973. Change in property evaluation by police may be the real explanation for an apparent drop in index larceny rates following the enactment of Nixon's anticrime program and the installation of a new police chief in Washington (Seidman and Couzens 1974). To the extent that an organization's records are the object of outside attention, they should be viewed with some skepticism.

At least two organizational clues signal potential bias in archival data. The first is the distance of the record-keeping portion of an organization from its operating activities. The Administrative Office of the United States courts, for example, is organizationally separated from the activities of the various courts. In contrast, until recently, the Federal Bureau of Investigation had responsibility both for law enforcement and for keeping national crime statistics; the new separate department of Criminal Statistics in the Justice Department was formed in large measure to create an independent archive; some interesting research waits to be done evaluating the impact of this separation on federal crime statistics.

Second, national reporting systems may foster inaccuracy of information. They invite "invidious comparisons among information producing units" (Reiss 1980, p. 370). As a result, strictly local reports may be more reliable.

It is difficult to provide many useful specific guidelines to uncover bias and unreliability in archival data. The best counsel is to check for consistency among different sources of data. For example, a study of homicides by police officers compared homicide figures from two data sources—local and state police department reports and coroners' death certificates (Sherman and Langworthy 1979). The assumption motivating the comparison was that the coroners' figures would be more accurate and that the police figures would produce an undercount. In fact, 50 percent fewer homicides were listed in coroners' data than in police reports. According to interviews with coroners, this surprising result was apparently due to the dependence of coroners on police for information in nearly all homicide cases and the reluctance of coroners to alienate the police by homicide classifications. This example does not contradict the general principle that vested interest can strongly affect record-keeping; it does indicate that sources of self-interest are not always obvious.

As with survey data, definitions in archival data can fluctuate—over time, and across institutions. Homicide, for example, has a different meaning in Vital Statistics than in FBI data. A formal complaint to an antidiscrimination agency in one state may be classified as an informal action in another. Researchers may also come to records with definitions that differ from the understandings of those who did the recording. Nevertheless, because of their comparatively easy availability and generally low reactivity,[4] compared with most other data sources, legal records can provide valuable information about legal life. The meaning of an entry should not routinely be taken at face value; it is itself a research question.

Simulations and the Problem of Context   In their attempts to avoid being swamped by the complex context of legal behaviors, researchers may temporarily ignore or hold constant some of the forces that normally impinge on the behavior of interest. Simulations of legal institutions and activities offer a potential for control unavailable in the typical legal setting. At their best, they permit a microscopic examination of processes usually layered with a confusing set of extraneous influences, and sometimes they permit a kind of access to activities shielded from direct observation. Jury simulation is a popular example of this type of research. Investigators, typically psychologists (such as Landy and Aronson 1969; Mitchell and Byrne 1973), expose subjects to information on an offense and offender or a dispute between parties. The "jurors" are then asked to respond to a set of questions about the material they have viewed or to deliberate with other respondents to reach a decision in the simulated case. A goal of this research is to disclose the way juries process information and reach their verdicts.

Greater control and narrow focus have their costs, however. The magnification they allow sometimes results in distortion. A jury simulation using a section of a trial that dwells heavily on the character of the defendant, for example, may produce findings that mistakenly suggest a heavy weighting on defendant characteristics in jury deliberations. The omission of voir dire and judicial instructions from most jury simulations neglects the role of these mechanisms in channeling jury decisions. In addition, experimental subjects, aware that their decision will have no consequences for the parties in the case, may decide cases differently than do real juries (Diamond and Zeisel 1974; Wilson and Donnerstein 1977).

Additional difficulties occur when an attempt is made to simulate the operation of legal activity in the system as a whole. The ambitious simulation research program of Thibaut and Walker and their colleagues (Thibaut and Walker 1975; Lind, Thibaut, and Walker 1973) has attempted to compare the operation of adversarial and inquisitorial systems for the resolution of disputes. In one study law students were asked to play the role of attorneys in one of two systems (actually four systems, but two of them are not relevant to this discussion). In the adversarial system, the outcomes were to be contingent on how successful each subject was in representing their client's interests. In the inquisitorial system, the subject-attorneys were responsible to the court, and their outcomes were to be determined not by the result in the case but by their ability in helping the judge arrive at "as fair and accurate a decision as possible" (Thibaut and Walker 1975, p. 31). After reading a description of the trial case, the subjects had five opportunities apiece to spend points to buy facts that might help prepare their cases. Since the number of points at the end of the experiment would in part determine the outcome for the subject, there was some incentive to buy as few facts as possible. The facts available for purchase were varied, so that as the subject-attorneys purchased facts, they might find that 25 percent,

---

[4] *Reactivity* refers to a change in behavior produced because the person or organization being measured is aware that his behavior is being monitored.

50 percent, or 75 percent of the facts favored their client. The results of this study showed that client-centered (adversary system) attorneys purchased more facts than did court-centered (inquisitorial system) attorneys only when the distribution of facts appeared unfavorable to the attorney's client. The authors conclude that "the adversary system apparently . . . does instigate significantly more thorough investigation by advocates initially confronted with plainly unfavorable evidence" (Thibaut and Walker 1975, p. 40).

Perhaps the conclusion is correct, but advocate behavior embedded in a single case context is rare indeed. The decision is generally not whether or not to invest time and effort in an attempt to win a lone case, but how to allocate time and effort among cases that have greater or smaller promise in an attempt to optimize outcomes across a number of clients. When confronted with an unfavorable initial assessment in the presence of additional pressures and choices, the adversary outside the laboratory may be even more likely to terminate his investigation and settle or plead without further information search. The question in this simulation, as in all legal simulations, is whether the behavioral influences are so basic that they can be generalized to apply to real attorneys or other legal actors in real legal settings.

Contextual problems are particularly noticeable in simulations because the researcher must construct each source of potential influence (such as additional cases on the subject-attorney's caseload). Similar problems, however, occur outside the laboratory and off the computer as well. One response has been to focus inward and avoid the spillover and feedback influences of the environment in which a legal activity or organization operates. A study of the distribution of civil cases in two California counties shows that the percentage of family and tort cases among all cases filed has increased over time (Friedman and Percival 1976). The authors suggest that this change in the mix of cases supports the hypothesis that the courts have come to function less as dispute resolvers and more as ratifiers of decisions already reached by the parties. The use of the court's total caseload as the base against which changes are assessed, however, assumes a peculiarly insular use of the term *function* (Lempert 1978). To be sure, the Friedman-Percival analysis describes what the courts do, but it does not address the more interesting question of what function, or changing function, they occupy in society.

To answer this second question requires a larger view, one that extends beyond the boundaries of the court's behavior and examines the court's role in resolving disputes as a proportion of the disputes arising in the population. There is, of course, no direct way to count the number of disputes a court might be asked to settle, and certainly no way to obtain this figure for various times in history. It is, however, possible to obtain a reasonable proxy by using the adult population figures for the two counties. A reanalysis of the data using this population base illustrates the consequences of extending the research on function beyond the court docket; one of the two counties shows no evidence of reduced dispute settlement by the court, even though the percentage of cases reaching trial or hearing has dropped. The court has simply come to play a greater role in other areas (Lempert 1978).

The discussion of the Friedman-Percival study illustrates a general problem that arises in much descriptive research on law—a lack of attention to the context of the behavior under scrutiny. The frequency of civil jury trials in a jurisdiction, for example, may be conditioned by the court calendar's backlog and a preference for criminal cases. Rates of settlement without reference to such organizational constraints are of limited value in understanding litigant preferences. Descriptive research need not be insensitive to context, for researchers can usually collect the necessary background information; it is simply that they rarely do.

Comparisons That Increase the Yield from Description

The form and yield of descriptive research on the operation of law are conditioned by three important characteristics of legal behavior. The first is the great variety across settings of legal behavior and organizations. This variability requires replication across settings to ensure that results are not idiosyncratic to a single tested site. A second critical characteristic of legal settings is the presence of numerous partisans with different loyalties. Partisanship can be employed to advantage by using the multiple perspectives of the various actors in a legal setting to test the validity of descriptions obtained from each group. Finally, a third characteristic of law important for descriptive yield is the frequent availability of several different types of data sources—for example, archival as well as interview—in each setting. Multiple data sources produce a more rounded picture when the results of the multiple measures can be compared.

Replication   The question, "Would this finding hold true with other subjects, in other settings, at other times?" can be answered directly only by explicitly replicating research in varying contexts. Yet, the variety of different types of sites and subjects makes replication across all potential sites and subjects impractical—and impossible across all possible points in time. The certainty that specific findings are generalizable—have external validity (Campbell and Stanley 1963)—is always logically questionable. The probability that results will apply generally, however, varies markedly from investigation to investigation. If, for example, the site of a case study is chosen because a progressive police administrator is willing to invite research scrutiny, and other police organizations that have been approached have decided not to participate in the research, the studied organization is probably atypical in other respects as well. The value of such a case study as a general description of police organizational behavior will be limited. But it is not only the obvious distinctiveness of this setting that undermines this case study as a general description; it is rare that *any* single case study of legal behavior can provide a picture of operations that will apply to most other nominally similar organizations. The variability across legal settings is too great.

The sampling approaches discussed below are presented in large measure as methods for extending the single-site descriptive study. It is important to note, however, that single-site impact studies also need replication to test the real possibility that causal impact of the treatment was conditioned by the environment of the research.

When description is the goal, the ideal research strategy uses both sampling and intensive study of a wide variety of sites and respondents, obtaining a large enough group to reflect the texture and heterogeneity of legal systems or prosecutors' offices or traffic courts in the population of interest. Because of the costs entailed in comprehensive sampling, it is rarely the preferred approach. If a researcher did draw a large sample from the population of all potential sites, the compromise with other aspects of the design would usually be so great as to destroy the value of the enterprise. For example, a mailed survey of a random sample, or even a full census, of all United States state prosecutors' offices could be conducted, instead of a detailed series of case studies of a few offices. The survey would permit collection of some limited information on all offices willing to respond to the questionnaire, but it would provide a view of office functioning only through the (perhaps defensive) eyes of the respondents. The gain in breadth would be at a great sacrifice in depth. If the researcher is interested only in the number of lawyers employed in the typical prosecutor's office, the survey strategy is sensible. But if the information being sought is less readily available or more sensitive, such a superficial though comprehensive sampling strategy is a poor choice.

An alternate approach that capitalizes on the contributions of both extensive and intensive investigation selects a small number of sites specifically chosen to reflect the range of possible variation. This strategy usually involves choosing characteristics that, for theoretical reasons, are expected to be associated with variation in the behavior under study (such as crime rate or caseload pressure if the study deals with plea bargaining). Most often the number of potentially important characteristics will generate a series of types of settings, and the researcher must select from among them. Two guides may be useful. First, the full list of possible sites should be compared with the generated types, so that representatives of the modal category or categories can be included. Thus, research that attempts to characterize plea-bargaining practices in the United States would select one or more urban courts, where the bulk of criminal indictments occur. Second, an attempt can be made to maximize the heterogeneity of selected sites. If the research discloses that plea bargaining takes a similar form in a large urban court with a heavy caseload and in a small rural court with a small flow of business, replication across these extremes increases the probability that courts more moderate in character share analogous practices. Of course, sites at the tails of the distribution may not behave in the same way as do sites near the center. For example, in both extremely long, complex civil trials and in short, clear-cut cases, judges may be more likely to blame counsel for not settling than they would in moderately ambiguous, medium-sized cases. Both theory and available evidence are critical in evaluating the benefits of adding another site or case in light of the obvious increase in costs.

In addition to requiring some theory of relevant variation in the phenomena under study, site selection also requires some knowledge of the distribution of actual variation in possible sites. For this latter purpose, a survey may be necessary, but official records can often be used for an adequate approximation of cases handled, offenders incarcerated, housing-market characteristics, and the like.

While the absence of theory, data, or time and money may prohibit the study of multiple instances, the addition of a single second site, however selected, provides a substantial boost to the reliability of descriptive, or any other, research. If the findings can be replicated in a second site, they cannot be dismissed as idiosyncratic. It was found, for example, that neither the Massachusetts nor the Connecticut sentencing review divisions changed more than 3 percent of all sentences eligible for review (Zeisel and Diamond 1977). Though it can be argued that the explanation for this low rate of change lies in procedures shared by the two states—such as informal proceedings conducted by a panel of trial judges who at other times accepted pleas, tried cases, and sentenced offenders—the low rate cannot logically be attributed to characteristics that the two states do not share. For example, Connecticut's division gave reasons for its decisions, while in Massachusetts no reasons were given. The similar results in the two states eliminated presence or absence of reason-giving as a factor crucial to the observed results.

If replication does not lead to parallel results, the differences can be used to enrich description and restructure theory. It is important to note, however, that explanations resulting from nonreplication give rise to new hypotheses rather than test old ones. If plea bargaining is found to be extensive in city A (urban, high crime rate, heavy caseload) and rare in city B (rural, low crime rate, low caseload), it can mean that some or all of these three selection criteria explain the difference in response, or that some unmeasured characteristic is responsible.

While comparisons within the same research project usually have the advantage of general comparability in methods of design, data collection, and analysis, external validity can also be extended by comparisons with research conducted by other investigators. For example, Laura Nader and her students attempted to coordinate their ethnographic research on the disputing process in different cultures by agreeing in advance on "what data they would collect and within what framework the collection of data would be collected" (Nader and Todd 1978, p. xi); all researchers examined choices among the same seven procedural modes for dealing with grievances, conflicts, or disputes. While some substantial variation did occur in the ultimate products, the approach clearly facilitated the intended cumulative impact.

More commonly, comparisons must be drawn across independent studies. Ross and Littlefield (1978) compared their findings on complaint handlings with the results of previous surveys by Best and Andreasen (1977) and King and McEvoy (1976). All three studies showed a positive correlation between socioeconomic status and the frequency of complaints, despite different samples and different measuring instruments. The replication solidified confidence in the relationship and, in fact, gained added strength from the methodological heterogeneity of the three studies.

Failures to replicate are less directly illuminating. Both the Ross-Littlefield and Best-Andreasen studies revealed dissatisfactions among approximately 20 percent of the purchasers of television sets and appliances, strengthening confidence in the figure. King and McEvoy, however, found complaints among 32.4 percent of their respondents. Ross and Littlefield suggest that the disparity can be explained by the fact that the King-McEvoy study included a variety of consumer problems experienced in the course of a year. The difficulty is that, whenever different results occur across studies, methodological as well as substantive candidates for explaining those differences arise. These must be explored, and it is not always possible to decide among them.

If the exercise of comparing across studies is to produce some cumulative effect, it is critical that methodological choices in sample sites and measurement operations be specified as clearly as possible. To the extent that subsequent researchers can identify such differences in approach, probable explanations can be tested in further research.

Sometimes comparisons across settings and subjects are implicit rather than explicit. Such studies assume a standard of behavior in one setting and contrast the results obtained from a study conducted in another setting. A study of Korean dispute resolution, for example, suggests that Korean tradition is alegal and that, in contrast to Western tradition, a declaration of intention to resort to law is tantamount to a declaration of war. As evidence, the author cites a survey of Korean respondents who were asked, "When you are involved in a quarrel or a dispute with another person and he declares to you, 'I am going to settle this legally,' how would you feel?" (Hahm 1969, p. 24). The choices of response were *Bad, Indifferent, Good, Other,* and *No Response;* 56

percent of the Korean sample chose *Bad*. The study presumes that a Western sample would respond otherwise, showing greater indifference to or relish for a legal settlement. Yet, when I asked a haphazard sample of twenty Chicago adults the same question, half of them also chose *Bad*. While the sample selection in my informal study can be questioned, the results do suggest some of the dangers in relying on a presumed but untested standard of comparison. Explicit testing across relevant settings is the obvious cure.

Comparative testing is not easy. Much has been written in particular on the linguistic and contextual difficulties of parallel testing across cultures. Nonetheless, the difficulties cannot be circumvented by flatly assuming responses in an untested setting.

Utilizing Partisanship　　　Participants in the legal system, more than those in other arenas, are commonly placed in partisan roles—lawyers, defendants, plaintiffs. This series of potential respondents with varying viewpoints creates an opportunity for researchers to examine their subject through these various filters; partisanship can create perils for those who are content to rely on the perspective of a single group of partisans. One study, for example, set out to evaluate the degree to which jury verdicts in criminal cases in Birmingham, England, were consistent with the evidence presented to the jury (Baldwin and McConville 1979a, 1979b). Since legal restrictions prohibited direct access to jurors or jury deliberations, the researchers interviewed the judge, the prosecution and defense solicitors,[5] and the police officer in each of the sampled cases. There was considerable disagreement among the groups of respondents. While no doubt was raised by anyone in one third of the acquittals, acquittal was seen as doubtful by only one of four possible respondents in 27 percent of the cases. Moreover, the distribution of evaluations by type of respondent was generally consistent with partisanship: defense solicitors saw acquittals as justified most often—83 percent of the time; police officers saw them as justified least often—48 percent of the time.

These results pinpoint two values of partisanship. First, because the direction of bias for particular respondents is often patently clear, it can provide a kind of ceiling or floor on the true value. A project that studied pro se divorce, for example, sent questionnaires to a sample of lawyers who handled divorce cases (*Yale Law Journal* 1976). One half the attorneys reported that they spent an average of twenty minutes or less preparing the complaint in an uncontested case; none reported spending more than an hour. Since it is socially desirable to appear to be spending more rather than less time on a case, these figures can probably be viewed as a kind of maximum estimate for the activity. Similarly, an interview survey of Oregon adults found that one in four admitted to some form of income tax evasion (Mason and Calvin 1978). While some respondents may have invented evasion out of bravado, it is probable that 25 percent represents a floor for the actual, but directly inaccessible, figure.

With the addition of a second partisan view, the other research value of partisanship emerges. That is, it is possible to get both an upper and a lower limit for some estimates. Thus, police officers in the Baldwin-McConville study saw acquittals as unjustified in 52 percent of the cases. Defense solicitors found them unjustified in 17 percent of the cases. The combination of these results suggests that in somewhere between 17 percent and 52 percent of these cases there were grounds to characterize the acquittal as unjustified.

---

[5] They attempted to interview the barristers in these cases as well but were unable to obtain the requisite permission.

When the responses of partisans are available, a further opportunity arises to categorize the observations as clear or conflicted. Thus, Baldwin and McConville classified a jury acquittal as questionable only when both the trial judge and one other respondent viewed it as doubtful. Of course, the way to combine such data may be open to dispute—for example, should a verdict be viewed as questionable only if both the police officer or prosecutor and defense solicitor agree?—but the availability of sources with conflicting perspectives offers a set of clues missing when a single source is employed.

Multiple Data Sources   Bias and error are not confined to survey measures. A strength of research on law is its frequent ability to take advantage of other available data sources to cross-check results, both within method—such as resorting to two different archival sources—and across method—such as combining observation and self-report.

Legal behavior is studied and counted by numerous groups, providing a variety of unexpected sources (see Gottfredson and Gottfredson 1980 for a useful sampling). For example, data on thefts can be found in Interstate Commerce Commission files, which include these figures as a cause of loss and damage claims paid to common carriers of freight. While different agencies may use different definitions and independent data collection by all agencies cannot be assumed, multiple archives can provide an important check on consistency. The study of homicides by police described on p. 657 (Sherman and Langworthy 1979) is one example of this approach. A second is a study of the 1969 FBI Uniform Crime Reports section on Careers in Crime (Zeisel 1973). The FBI's follow-up study of offenders released from the federal law-enforcement system in 1963 showed a 92 percent rearrest rate in 1969 for those who had been acquitted or had their charges dismissed. Since this figure was surprisingly close to 100 percent and was much higher than the 65 percent average for all offenders in the group, the author became suspicious. The FBI had a clear interest in suggesting a high rearrest rate for this group—the agency was at the same time arguing that the courts were being too soft on crime and were dismissing cases and acquitting people highly likely to commit new crimes.

Figures from the Administrative Office of the United States Courts provided the needed check. These totals revealed that the offenders included in the FBI data base were only two thirds of the offenders counted by the Administrative Office. Moreover, the FBI sample was clearly biased: it included only one fourth of the persons in the dismissed or acquitted category.

The researcher's comparison of the distribution of offense charges in the FBI sample with the Administrative Office census showed that charges associated with high rearrest rates, such as auto theft and burglary, were greatly overrepresented in the FBI sample, while charges associated with lower rearrest rates, such as fraud, were underrepresented. He was thus able to prove that the FBI sample was nonrandom in a way that inflated rearrest rates.

Comparing results obtained by different data-collection techniques extends the strategy of cross-checking for consistency. Interview data from prostitutes who report that all of their clients are "important" people may be suspect. Such reports, however, could be supported by the researcher's own observations: "Of some fifty persons seen going to prostitutes' rooms in apartment houses, only one was dressed in anything more casual than a business suit" (Chambliss 1971, p. 1153).

Sociolegal researchers rarely take advantage of the available multiple sources for data.

Two studies of parole-board decision-making are notable exceptions. Parole-board members were asked to evaluate experimental cases in tightly controlled simulations, where their use of information in reaching decisions could be directly monitored. In addition, archival data on actual parole decisions were analyzed (Gottfredson et al. 1975; Carroll and Payne 1977).

There is, of course, the possibility that a widened net of measurements will reveal inconsistency. In such cases, the researcher or reader must reserve judgment or decide which data source carries greater weight. One study of judicial sentencing found that judges' reports showed the use of criteria different from those that were revealed by simulated studies of their sentencing judgments; results from the latter method also differed from results obtained from archival analysis of actual sentencing judgments and case characteristics (Konečni and Ebbesen 1979). The researchers suggest that the actual case-file results are most trustworthy, but there are good grounds on which to question that conclusion. Case-file results suffer from problems associated with multicollinearity—high intercorrelations among the case characteristics—and the results may also be distorted by influential, but unmeasured variables.

Each method, of course, has its weaknesses; tentative resolution of inconsistent results from different methods will depend on the particular research problem and what is already known about the behavior under study. Interview data inspire less confidence when the questions are sensitive; simulation tasks requiring expert decision-makers to make judgments similar to those they make daily are probably more trustworthy than those that use tasks unfamiliar to the subjects. The payoff from the use of multiple methods arises because consistency in results builds a comprehensive picture and even inconsistency provides a starting point for correcting method-specific conclusions.

THE IMPACT OF LAW AND LEGAL CHANGE

Research on law has been criticized for its general focus on effects and its pervasive treatment of law as an independent variable (Gibbs 1968; Feeley 1976). While the literature shows increasing attention to issues of emergence and operation, interest in legal impact is likely to remain strong. Since legal change is a primary approach to social control, both policy-makers and basic researchers continue to be interested in the limits of and possibilities for effecting change through law. Moreover, as dissatisfaction with existent legal structure appears to be increasing, so, too, are attempts to alter and improve it (such as Neighborhood Justice Centers and attempts to eliminate plea bargaining); researchers are participating in the evaluation of these planned modifications and alternatives.

"Does a change in law (or legal arrangement) A produce a change in behaviors B, C, and/or D?" is a causal question. Drawing heavily on the work of John Stuart Mill, Cook and Campbell (1979) list three criteria important for inferring cause. It must be shown that (1) covariation, or correlation, exists between A, the presumed cause, and B, the effect; (2) the change in A precedes the change in B; and (3) no plausible alternatives can explain the variation in B. On the surface, it may appear that these criteria are easily met and that most causal research attends to them. In fact, causality is difficult to demonstrate, and the requisite criteria are often dismissed or ignored in studies attempting to gauge the effects of law. A review of the weaknesses of some designs commonly used to assess the effects of legal change, with particular attention to alternative causal explanations or threats to internal validity, will illustrate the difficulties. Much of the terminology and the notation are drawn from Campbell and Stanley (1963); the interested reader is referred to Campbell and Stanley and the more recent Cook and Campbell (1979) for more complete discussions of concerns with validity in causal research and to Lempert (1966) for a discussion of how Campbell and Stanley's approach applies specifically to research on legal-impact research.

The present discussion focuses on the issues that most commonly create problems of inference for studies of legal change. One important issue of measurement logically precedes discussion of particular research designs in legal-impact research. Research of this kind generally assumes that the independent variable—legal change—has been implemented as planned. Researchers focus their attention on whether the dependent variables targeted by the research have been affected by the presumed change. Yet, in legal innovation, the slippage between design and enactment is likely to be great (Diamond 1981a). Treatments may not be implemented, may be implemented in a dramatically modified form, or may be implemented but not reach their intended audience; for example, a penalty for a particular offense is made more severe, but potential violators are not aware of the change. Researchers studying the impact of law may prematurely conclude that a legal change is ineffective, or they may adduce incorrect reasons for concluding that it is effective.

In laboratory research, it is standard practice to measure the "take" of the independent variable as well as the response in the dependent variable. If the independent variable is not manipulated successfully, no real test of its impact is presumed to occur. Researchers studying the effects of law in field settings can reduce the ambiguity of their results by taking a cue from their laboratory colleagues and measuring the extent to which their manipulations have taken place.

Preexperimental Designs

The case study used to assess cause-effect relations focuses on a situation in which the presumed cause is present and determines whether the predicted effect can also be found. A study of the effect of California's Lanterman-Petris-Short Act observed the petition hearings of 100 persons who filed writs of habeas corpus after being committed involuntarily to mental hospitals. In the language of the study, "it is important to assess the impact of the Act on the processing of mentally disordered individuals," since the "Act has been widely heralded as a vital step toward curbing unnecessary commitment while retaining some institutional control over the severely disturbed individual" (Warren 1977, p. 631). The comparative standard implicit in these statements, as in all causal studies, is the behavior that would have occurred if the presumed cause—in this case, the Lanterman-Petris-Short Act—had been absent. Yet Warren's data provide no such standard; all the observations took place after the effective date of the act. Thus, if X represents the act—or any presumed cause or treatment—and O represents the outcome measures for the cases before the court (or posttest observations for any individuals, organizations, or subjects whose behavior is being monitored), the design reads

$$\underline{X \qquad O}$$

where time advances from left to right. In Warren's study, the data simply reveal that the statutory criteria "were not strictly applied" in the examined cases. The handling of these cases may in fact have represented an improvement over past practice and may have signaled a real change attributable to the passage of the act. This research design cannot make that assessment. Nor can it prove that the act did not change matters for the worse. The analysis does contain one alternate standard—the act's criteria of mental disorder, dangerousness, and grave disablement. The research is an interesting evaluation of the extent to which behavior reflects the normative standard of the new law, and thus it adds to the literature of law on the books versus law in action. In this sense, the research is more properly categorized as a descriptive study of operation and is not a causal study at all.

The absence of a comparative no-X or other-X standard is partially handled by a second commonly used design, in which a pretest is added before X, the legal measure of interest, is introduced:

$$\overline{O_1 \; X \; O_2}$$

Differences between behaviors measured before and after the change are attributed to the intervention in this so-called before-after design. But legal changes evaluated by this method may erroneously appear effective because factors other than the legal change of interest are responsible for the O_1-O_2 shift.

Legal changes are frequently enacted against a background of demonstrated extraordinary needs. A sharp rise in crime leads to crime-prevention legislation; a sudden increase in traffic fatalities evokes an announced crackdown on speeders (Campbell and Ross 1968); signs prohibiting parking appear the winter following a blizzard that produced streets clogged with snow and stranded automobiles. A comparison of prechange behavior with postchange behavior discloses a drop in crime rate, a reduction in fatalities, an improvement in traffic flow that coincide with the legislative or enforcement change. The question remains whether the change would have occurred in the absence of the treatment. In all these examples, the preintervention level of performance—crime rate, traffic fatalities, street congestion—was unusual, perhaps because of weather or some other chance factor. Behavior fluctuates over time, deviating above or below its mean occurrence. If it is unusually high at one reading, it will generally be lower at the next; if it is unusually low on one occasion, the next measurement is likely to be higher. This statistical regression toward the mean may be mistaken for an effect of the treatment when the timing of a change or its allocation to particular individuals is determined by the extremity or deviance of the preintervention scores. Thus, any program for treating delinquency can appear to reduce recidivism when the participants are selected for the magnitude of their prior criminal records and a simple before-after design is used to evaluate the program (Maltz 1978).

Since legal changes occur frequently, identifying X as the treatment to be evaluated does not ensure that the legal system will remain constant in all other important respects. One study of the change from twelve-member to six-member juries in Michigan civil trials was interested in evaluating the effect of jury size on verdicts (Mills 1973). Accordingly, it compared the percentage of plaintiff verdicts and the size of awards before and after the jury size was reduced. Unfortunately, this legal change coincided with a series of other changes that could also explain any changes or constancies in the pattern of verdicts shown in the data. A mediation board was instituted, and procedural rules were modified to allow discovery of the limits of insurance policies. The study was unusual in that the researcher searched for and uncovered a number of these rival explanations, but he was unable to identify their impact on verdicts and awards.

History—the set of events apart from X that occur between O_1 and O_2—poses a pervasive threat to causal inference in the before-after design. Such events are less likely if O_1 and O_2 are close in time, but because multiple simultaneous legal changes are common, the difficulty of distinguishing their separate effects may be substantial.

The comparison between O_1 and O_2 assumes that the measurement procedures are identical at the two time points. If changes occur, instrumentation or instrument decay may cause the false appearance of a treatment effect. Just as crime rates can be affected by a change in the monetary evaluation of stolen property by police, rates can also change when adjustments are made in the name of improvement. Until 1969, the Federal Bureau of Narcotics and Dangerous Drugs assumed that all addicts were known to hospitals or to the police and that, therefore, the total addict population was represented in the agency's register. In 1970, the estimate was subjected to the new assumption that only one addict in five was known. Therefore, the addict population suddenly quintupled (Epstein 1977). A treatment introduced between 1969 and 1970 would have looked remarkably addictive in the absence of information about this accounting change.[6]

Concurrent measurement of the two groups of subjects (cases, individuals, organizations, jurisdictions)—those who have and those who have not been subjected to the legal change—can control for some, but not all, of the deficiencies of the single posttest and before-after designs:

In this design, two (or more) groups who have received different treatments are compared by measuring all groups at the same time. An enormous amount of research on legal change has used this nonequivalent control group design. The research has generally taken one of two forms. In the first, the groups represent different jurisdictions that have enacted different laws or made available different legal arrangements, such as the death penalty (Sellin 1959). In the second form the treated cases consist of those who have voluntarily selected to receive or apply X, while the untreated cases consist of those who have rejected it or chosen an alternate treatment, such as the six-person rather than a twelve-person jury (Bermant and Coppock 1973) or attorney- rather than self-representation (Sarat 1976).

While this design avoids some of the threats to validity faced by the before-after approach, a major competing explanation for differences between the groups remains: selection differences may have produced the variation in posttest performance. An early study on the death penalty, which compared the rate of homicides in states that had the death penalty with the rate in states without the death penalty, found no evidence for a

---

[6]In fact, the apparent jump in addiction was used by the Nixon Administration to justify its crusade against heroin.

deterrent effect on homicide (Sellin 1959). The use of adjacent states, however, did not guarantee that the states compared were similar in all relevant characteristics apart from their death-penalty statutes. Such unchecked differences can affect homicide rates and the deterrence hypothesis cannot be rejected solely on the basis of this original design.[7]

Investigators using the design often examine factors that characterized the two groups before the treatment—for example, unemployment rates and percentage of population aged 15–24 in death-penalty and non–death-penalty states (Baldus and Cole 1975). This analysis takes place either before one group actually receives the treatment or, more commonly, retrospectively. In either case, equivalence on the pretreatment measures is used to support the inference that they were equivalent before the time of treatment in other important respects—an inference always open to serious question.

The probability that an unidentified cause lurks in the background is particularly high when the treatment condition is determined by the choices of those who are being treated. A study of the New Jersey optional six-member jury system demonstrates the principle. Verdicts in civil cases when a six-member jury decided the case were compared with verdicts in cases when one of the parties requested and thereby received a twelve-member jury (Institute for Judicial Administration 1972). The results were used to test the causal question whether jury size affects verdicts. There was good reason to wonder why a party would request twelve jurors, since the decision would produce a higher jury fee and could be viewed by the court as imposing an additional burden. The data on case characteristics reveal the wisdom of this concern; twelve-member jury cases were more complex, led to higher average settlement levels as well as verdict sizes, and involved longer trial times apart from deliberations. These differences alone, and not jury size, could explain any pattern of results obtained from the posttest verdict comparisons (see Zeisel and Diamond 1974 for a more complete discussion).

A similar alternate set of explanations arises in studies that attempt to gauge the effect of legal representation on case outcomes by comparing plaintiff verdicts in cases with and without counsel (such as Hollingsworth, Feldman, and Clark 1973; Steadman and Rosenstein 1973). Attorneys are likely to be hired not only by plaintiffs who can afford their services but also by plaintiffs who believe the investment will pay off and whose cases may, in fact, be stronger.

The three research designs just discussed have been termed preexperimental (Campbell and Stanley 1963). Their general weakness in not ruling out alternative causal explanations or threats to internal validity typically leaves the investigator with questionable support for conclusions about impact. The designs can be valuable where well-grounded theory or supplementary data can rule out competing causal explanations. In the absence of such additional information, however, the lack of control can be fatal to valid inference.

In contrast, two other kinds of research designs avoid or can repair most, or at least many, of the weaknesses of these designs by their structural arrangements. They are controlled or randomized experiments and quasi-experiments.

---

[7] Subsequent studies (Bowers 1974; Sellin 1967; Zeisel 1976; and others) have combined this control-group design with time-series data before and after abolition; the similar results from these analyses make the original conclusions considerably stronger.

Randomized Experiments

In randomized experiments, units are assigned to treatment groups according to an intentionally arbitrary or random schedule. Pretest measures may or may not be used, but because group membership is determined by the roll of a die or a random number table, each unit has the same probability as any other unit of being assigned to a particular group.

Issues of Design   Randomized experimental designs can be diagramed (R signifying randomization):

$$\begin{array}{ccc} \overline{R \; X \; O} & & \overline{R \; O \; X \; O} \\ R \quad\;\; O & \text{or} & R O \quad O \\ \hline \end{array}$$

These designs ensure that, within the limits of sampling error, the groups will be equivalent at the time of the pretest, so that any differences that appear at the posttest can be attributed at a specified level of confidence to events that took place after assignment to conditions. The difference between the two designs is the absence or presence of a pretest.

Pretests are attractive because they increase the chance that a true difference between treatment groups will be detected at the posttest. Because pretest and posttest measures on the same variable tend to be highly correlated, the pretest can be used to control statistically for error variance due to individual variation, making systematic variation— treatment impact—more visible. The main disadvantage of the pretest is that it may be reactive: pretesting may affect the subject's response to the treatment. While pretests were once viewed as powerful sensitizers, however, there is little evidence for their impact outside the laboratory (Cook and Campbell 1979), and pretests are generally desirable, particularly in field research where their impact in reducing error variance is often crucial.

The difficulty with pretests for much research on law is that it often makes no sense to measure subjects before treatment on the major dependent variable. One randomized experiment studied the effect of court-supervised appellate conferences on settlement rates (Goldman 1978). Cases were randomly assigned the offer of a conference or no such offer; the rates of settled cases (and other outcome measures) for the two groups were compared after all cases were closed by court decision or settlement. In another study, delinquents were randomly sentenced to the usual probationary treatment or assignment to a new rehabilitative program; the recidivism rates of the two groups were then compared to test the program's effectiveness (Empey and Erickson 1972). If a treatment is expected to affect the recidivism, case dispositions, or criminal sentences of a specified group of treatment recipients, no pretest measure of these variables exists.

Alternative strategies to control error variance when pretests are unavailable include matching or blocking on other relevant characteristics before assignment to treatment conditions and using alternative measures expected to correlate with the dependent measure as proxy pretests (see Keppel 1973, chap. 23, for a good description of these approaches). Researchers studying the behavior of law generally face substantial variability in the particular population; strategies for controlling that variation can form an important tool of their research, reducing the likelihood that a real difference will be overlooked.

The pretest equivalence produced by random assignment procedures rules out nearly all the threats to internal validity that hold for preexperimental designs. Regression would not be mistakenly identified as a treatment effect, since the pretest performance of both treated and untreated groups should be equivalent, and even if both groups are selected for their extreme scores—for example, high rate of reported drug use—regression between the pretest and posttest should be equivalent in both groups. External historical changes, apart from the treatment—administrative procedures affecting appellate court cases, for example—by affecting all cases could not account for group differences at the posttest.

Instrumentation changes, like regression and history, would be the same across groups for most studies. An exception may occur, however, if record-keeping is not constant across groups. In some correctional programs, the information on the criminal violations of program participants may be greater than that for controls, because the program has more frequent and intensive contact with the treatment group (for example, Lerman 1975; Long 1979). One solution is to use an independently derived count, when it can be obtained, for an even-handed outcome measure (Long 1979). Even if the result is an undercount, the loss of information should affect all groups equally and will not distort the comparison between treatment groups.

No comparable solution is available when the different measurement across groups affects actual outcomes. Thus, if the experimental treatment is intensive supervision of parole cases and if intensive supervision means extensive surveillance resulting in a higher rate of parole violation for members of the experimental group, no outside measurement source can equalize the treatment and control groups. It may not, however, be appropriate to label this difficulty a problem of instrumentation. While the surveillance effect subverts the integrity of the original outcome measure as a reflection of actual criminal behavior, the difference in the rate of violation is a genuine effect of the treatment on the outcomes for such offenders.

Selection can account for posttest differences through differential attrition across experimental conditions. For example, if a residential treatment program for delinquents keeps them available to researchers for posttest measurement while some control-group members moved away, or if a less desirable treatment condition leads some of those assigned to it to drop out before posttest measures can be taken, researchers face differential composition of their groups at the posttest. Nonetheless, the differential dropout is an effect of the treatment and may in itself be of interest. Moreover, in many studies of legal impact, archival dependent measures—case outcomes, recidivism rates, and the like—are available and attrition by individuals, in the sense of unavailability for posttesting, may not be at issue.

Issues of Feasibility   There is little argument about the general methodological superiority of randomized experiments for causal inference. But there is considerable controversy over the general feasibility of this strategy when the effectiveness of laws or administrative procedures is being tested.[8] Problems of morality as well as feasibility are

---

[8] In laboratory settings randomized experiments are used almost exclusively to test causal propositions. The weakness of such research arrangements hinges not on the question of internal validity but on the question of external validity or generalizability.

acute when the direct or indirect allocator of treatments is a representative of government. Ethical questions are then raised, informed by normative standards of due process and equal protection.

The arguments against random assignments hinge on the ethical and legal permissibility of withholding potentially beneficial treatments, such as a rehabilitation program or a pretrial conference, from some or of imposing potentially harmful treatments, such as a long prison term, or a work requirement associated with welfare payments, on only a portion of those eligible for them. The equal-protection clause generally requires that governmental classifications be reasonable rather than arbitrary and that they have a rational relationship to a legitimate government purpose.[9] A citizen who, as a result of experimental allocation, is subjected to a deprivation or a hardship that does not fall equally on all who are in similar circumstances can argue that the difference in treatment is not rationally related to a legitimate purpose. Where experimental deprivations or benefits are at issue, the legal question has never been resolved definitely, but the sense of required fairness underlying the Fifth and Fourteenth Amendments has influenced many decisions about the kinds of experiments with which the government can cooperate. It has also affected the designs of various experiments to allow potential subjects to opt out, so that randomization is applied only to those who remain. This method, of course, leads to questions about the extent to which the findings can be assumed to apply to those unwilling to participate.

Several responses can be made to arguments against randomized legal experiments that mandate participation. The first focuses attention on the allocation of treatment rather than the treatment itself. In fact, random assignment is designed specifically to ensure the identical opportunity to receive a particular treatment for all similarly situated individuals; this equality of opportunity therefore meets the standards of the equal-protection provision.

A second response is that evaluation of the impact of a proposed legal change constitutes a legitimate governmental purpose. Experiments are conducted only when the effect of a proposed treatment is not clear and the alternatives to systematic controlled experimentation are to (1) implement an untested policy on the total eligible population; (2) attempt no policy change; or (3) implement the policy on a trial basis on part of those eligible, but with unsystematic distribution, so that the groups are not strictly comparable. To the extent that the treatment in (3) is not reasonably related to the classification criteria, such uncontrolled trials may raise objections on grounds of equal protection, and for that reason unsystematic allocation is less defensible than is the controlled experiment that offers the greater promise of improved knowledge.[10]

The value and permissibility of the experimental allocation of treatments in legal contexts has received some federal court support. Approving a New York Welfare Service experiment in which 25 percent of those eligible were required to participate in a work program, the Court concluded that

---

[9] The Equal Protection Clause of the Fourteenth Amendment is aimed only at state action and does not extend to acts carried out under federal authority. The Fifth Amendment, however, contains a due-process clause, binding on the federal government, guaranteeing all citizens equal protection of the laws.

[10] This logic has a closer apparent link with applied research on law than with more basic research, but the long-term value of information about legal systems and their effects should constitute a similarly justifiable purpose.

a purpose to determine whether and how improvements can be made in the welfare system is as "legitimate" or "appropriate" as anything can be. This purpose is "suitably furthered" by controlled experiment, a method long used in medical science which has its application in the social sciences as well . . . the Equal Protection Clause should not be held to prevent a state from conducting an experiment designed for the good of all, including the participants, on less than a statewide basis. [*Aguayo v. Richardson* 1973, p. 1109]

Apart from this case, little direct legal commentary addresses the acceptable limits of controlled experimentation in law. Some standards have been suggested, however, in an attempt to avoid legal and ethical conflict. When fundamental rights are involved, a controlled experiment must withstand the test of strict scrutiny demanding that the classification not only be reasonable but also serve a compelling governmental interest (*Massachusetts Board of Retirement v. Murgia* 1976).[11] Fundamental rights include the right to vote, the right to interstate travel, and rights guaranteed by the First Amendment. Since the list is quite modest (Gunther 1972), it will not substantially inhibit legal experimentation. Moreover, legal experimentation aimed at these rights is unlikely, since no policy change would be permitted to eliminate them (Zeisel, Kalven, and Buchholz 1959).

Morris (1966) has argued that even in an area as ethically loaded as the punishment of offenders, experiments using random assignment can be permitted if they follow two principles. The first is the principle of "less severity": "the new treatment being studied should not be one that is regarded in the mind of the criminal subjected to it, or of the people imposing the new punishment, or the community at large, as more severe than the traditional treatment against which it is being compared" (Morris 1966, pp. 648–49). This standard is not altogether clear in many settings, because the status quo may not be an appropriate reference when the policy choice is between the experimental introduction of new treatment X for some and a general shift to X for all. Theoretically, then, the standard should be what the individual would have received in the absence of an experiment; operationally, that criterion will be difficult to determine in many cases.

Morris's second principle holds that experimentation must take place at an administrative, not the judicial, stage. The present penal system is so full of irrational and unfair disparities that an experiment, which in the long run is expected to reduce irrelevant disparity, simply structures what is already rampant (Morris 1966, p. 653). This standard would presumably be applicable in any legal setting in which discretion is exercised without clear evidence that the decisions relate systematically to permissible criteria. The argument is not that the randomized experiment is desirable in an absolute sense, but that it introduces no greater variability than present practice at the administrative level and offers the promise of increased knowledge.

One basic dilemma must be addressed in any experimental effort—how to balance the severity of the problem and the promise of the proposed treatment, on the one hand, against the relative potential hardship in degree and duration associated with research participation, on the other. Even when constitutional arguments against experimentation are not raised, it is necessary to consider these factors, particularly in legal experi-

[11] But see *Pointer v. Texas*, 380 U.S. 400, 413 (1965) (concurring opinion, Goldberg, J.), in which it is maintained that fundamental rights may not be withdrawn for purposes of experiment.

ments. In law, more than in other social systems, the appearance of justice is critical. The tension between these factors has led some researchers to suggest that experiments should minimize differences between experimental treatments (Green 1976). If extreme contrasts are avoided, however, modest treatment effects may go undetected.

While the courts provide only limited support for the legality of randomized experiments on legal questions, other evidence shows that such studies are permitted—they have been carried out. Randomized experiments have examined the impact of bail on appearances for trial (Botein 1964–65); the effect of pretrial conferences on settlement rates in civil cases (Rosenberg 1964); the impact of counsel on outcomes for juvenile offenders (Stapleton and Teitelbaum 1972); the role of a pretrial conference to which victim, defendant, and police officer are invited in affecting the outcomes of criminal indictments (Kerstetter and Heinz 1979); the contrasting effects of mandatory milieu therapy for delinquents and traditional probationary supervision (Empey and Erickson 1972); and the extent to which gate money on release from prison can reduce recidivism (Lenihan 1977).

Clearly, randomization is a feasible approach in sociolegal research, but it is equally clear that some circumstances will be more congenial to experimental resource allocation than others. If there is general agreement among constituencies that a proposed experimental treatment is likely to have few or no detrimental side effects and that it may provide a novel benefit to those treated, experimentation of any kind is more likely to be favorably perceived. In the Manhattan Bail Project arrestees were categorized as promising or unpromising candidates for bail on the basis of a background check of family ties and other qualities believed to be associated with good bail risks. The names of a random half of those rated acceptable were then given to the judge, who was free to use or ignore this information in his bail decision. The study revealed that judges granted bail more often for the recommended cases, but the recommendation appeared to have no effect on whether or not the arrestee appeared in court at the appointed time. Moreover, those who were recommended for bail—the experimental group—were less likely to be convicted and received lighter sentences than the control group of the good but unrecommended candidates (Botein 1964–65). These results support the perception that the experimental treatment offered, if anything, a favorable opportunity for a random half of the sample.

A similar, if less frequent, sequence arises when treatments of similar desirability are compared. Court-supervised conferences between opposing counsel may be viewed as advantageous or as an additional burden to appellants who are asked to participate in them (Goldman 1978). In such an instance, therefore, it is not clear until after completion of the study whether the experimental group has been inconvenienced or has benefited, and it is hard to argue that randomization imposes unequal risks.

Legal treatments can sometimes be imposed simultaneously on all possible parties—for instance, a change to no-fault divorce or a raise in the guaranteed minimum wage. Often, however, it is simply not possible to implement a change in such a way as to include all eligibles. Legislatures will be willing to expend only limited funds for an untested change, or trained personnel and technological equipment may be in short supply when an innovation is first put in place. Random assignment of, for example, space in public housing (Greely 1977) may be viewed as an equitable solution to the allocation of scarce resources among equally deserving potential recipients.

Even when involuntary assignment is ruled out, it is often possible to introduce a voluntary component without great loss in interpretability. Juvenile defendants could not be forced to accept a free attorney—they could only be offered the service (Stapleton and Teitelbaum 1972). Nor were these defendants prevented from obtaining outside legal services. The random assignment controlled the offer of a no-fee attorney. As a result, in city A, 82 percent of the cases in the experimental condition had counsel representation, while only 39 percent of the control cases were represented by counsel. The corresponding figures for city B were 83 and 11 percent. Even though the actual treatments received by experimental and control cases were made more similar by the voluntary design, outcome differences between treatment conditions were detected for city A; these differences could be attributed directly to the effects of attorney representation.

In other voluntary experiments, the contrasts have not been as well preserved. Counseling services were made available to a random half of a group of high-school-age women whose earlier performance and behavior in school had suggested that they might become delinquent (Meyer, Borgatta, and Jones 1965). Because many of the girls who were offered counseling made minimal or no use of the offer, it was not clear whether the treatment was ineffective: the two groups did not receive very different treatments.

The original design to test the effect of pretrial conferences on civil cases in New Jersey called for random assignment of cases to a pretrial conference or to a control condition without such a conference (Rosenberg 1964). Because New Jersey had previously required a pretrial conference in all personal-injury cases filed in the state's major courts, the judiciary was opposed to denying a random half of all cases access to what they believed to be a beneficial mechanism to which litigants were entitled. A compromise made the pretrial conference mandatory for half of all cases and optional for all others. One half of the defendants for whom the pretrial conference was not required elected and received one. Because one half of the control group actually received the treatment, the comparison was considerably watered down. The study's finding that conferences have no effect must properly read, "There is no effect of a required pretrial conference on settlement rates and outcomes." The study as implemented could not determine the effects of denying a conference to those who thought it desirable.

Voluntary treatment appears to have the greatest chance of preserving the intended experimental contrast when the offered treatment is perceived as more desirable than is a control condition. Only in that instance is it likely that subjects will voluntarily choose the offered treatment in large enough numbers to provide a strong test of impact.

The clear advantages of randomized experimental designs for inferring cause suggest that the boundaries imposed by legal, ethical, and political constraints should be pushed as far as possible by researchers attempting to assess legal impact. When randomization is not possible, however, a number of other designs can rule out many, if not most, alternative causal explanations or threats to internal validity. Such designs are called *quasi-experimental* (Campbell and Stanley 1963).

Quasi-Experiments

Time Series   The interrupted time-series quasi-experiment is a natural choice for researchers interested in the compact of law (Lempert 1966). Behavior is charted over time according to the following basic design:

$$O_1\ O_2\ O_3\ O_4\ O_5\ X\ O_6\ O_7\ O_8\ O_9\ O_{10}$$

A series of measures are taken at regular intervals before the legal treatment and after the treatment is implemented. An interrupted time-series was used to study the impact of Britain's 1967 Road Safety Act on traffic deaths and accidents (Ross 1973). Examining the monthly fatality and accident rates from 1961 through 1970, the study demonstrated that the passage of the act, which imposed tests of driver intoxication through breath analysis and imposed severe penalties for drunk driving, was associated with a significant drop in traffic fatalities and in accidents involving serious injuries.

Though similar to the $O_1 \, X \, O_2$ preexperimental design, the time-series is able to rule out regression as an alternative explanation for change, since the stability of the pretreatment level can be directly assessed. Moreover, the ordinary seasonal variations that accompany some litigation rates, crime levels, accident frequencies, and other measures are also unlikely to be mistaken for changes caused by treatment. The effects of regularly occurring cyclical variation can be statistically removed in the analysis of time-series designs by expressing the series of measures as deviations from the expected cyclical pattern (Box and Jenkins 1976; McCain and McCleary 1979).

A time-series experiment can be examined for several different kinds of effects. The first is a change in level (or intercept), such as would occur, for example, if a determinate sentencing bill raised the duration of prison sentences in one jurisdiction an average of one year. The $O_1 \, X \, O_2$ design can be used to detect this effect, but it will not identify a second potential product of legal innovation, a change in trend (drift or slope). This effect would occur if, for example, prison sentences had been increasing on the average of one month every year until the new sentencing bill, after which the process speeded up so as to increase by two months each year. A third effect would be a change in the variation around the mean level. In this sentencing example, researchers might make entirely opposite predictions, some arguing that determinate sentencing will produce less variation in time served, because prisoners are less at the mercy and whim of the parole board, others suggesting that indeterminate sentencing allows the parole board to moderate the disparity produced by the varying sentencing practices of different judges, and that determinate sentencing will, therefore, lead to greater variation in prison sentences.

One of the clearest attractions of time-series analysis is its ability to test the persistence of change. An analysis of the effects of Nebraska's 1972 no-fault divorce law that studied divorce rates for various groups showed that the rate for black, but not white, couples increased significantly after the introduction of no-fault legislation, over and above the earlier pattern of an increasing rate (Mazur-Hart and Berman 1977). It further showed that the rate change for blacks gave no sign of returning to its earlier level. Since race and socioeconomic status tend to be correlated, this finding was consistent with the intended effect of making divorce more available to people of low socioeconomic status by reducing the cost. In contrast, an observed rate increase among persons over 50 was short-lived, suggesting that no-fault provisions relieved a backlog of potential divorces among older persons by changing the cost-benefit ratio sufficiently for them to seek divorces (p. 310).

Some of the weaknesses inherent in the $O_1 \, X \, O_2$ design also mar the simple interrupted-time series, despite its obvious strengths. Other historical events can coincide with the treatment and can offer competing explanations for change; particularly when politically sensitive results are at issue, instrumentation changes may occur (see discussions in Seidman and Couzens 1974; Epstein 1977). In addition, most discussions of time-series recommend 50 or more data points for analysis; researchers must therefore rely largely on the existence of archival measures collected for other purposes. Many regularly collected figures are available in long series, but two problems are frequent—available figures are often recorded only at yearly or more widely spaced intervals, and some figures are missing and must be estimated.

Time-series experiments must also confront questions about the timing of the treatment and the appearance of effects. Not all interventions, even legal mandates, represent abrupt changes from which immediate effects can be expected. For example, in 1967, the Supreme Court guaranteed juveniles the right to representation by counsel when they are involved in proceedings that can result in a finding of delinquency and consequent incarceration (*In re Gault*). Yet research conducted in three jurisdictions after *Gault* went into effect (Lefstein, Stapleton, and Teitelbaum 1969) disclosed that the juveniles covered in *Gault* were fully advised of their right to counsel in only 56, 3, and 0 percent, respectively, of the cases observed. If a study of the effect of *Gault* were designed to examine the court outcomes for juveniles before and after the *Gault* decision, it is difficult to say when the post-*Gault* observation period should begin. When gradual diffusion occurs, time-series analyses must attempt to model that diffusion process (Cook and Campbell 1979, pp. 226–27).

Delayed causation creates similar difficulties, particularly when the lag in treatment effects is unknown. For example, how much time must pass before a regulation affecting the purchase of guns can be expected to affect their use in criminal violence? "Once the time-series data have been plotted, it is remarkably easy to generate plausible causal rationale for belated shifts in the series" (Cook and Campbell 1979, p. 228); it also becomes more likely that alternate explanations are responsible.

While such questions of timing weaken the time-series quasi-experiment, they lurk in the background of all causal designs. A single posttest administered when implementation has not yet fully occurred or when effects have not yet appeared (or have already disappeared) leads to a conclusion of "no difference." Because the time-series remains one of the most promising approaches for analyzing the impact of legal change, it is being used with increasing frequency. As in all research that depends on data collected regularly over an extended period, the growth in time-series research is being aided by the interest in social indicators, and the future looks more promising than the past, since one can plan on acquiring the relevant data at theoretically appropriate intervals.

Nonequivalent Control-Group Designs   The combination of a control group with a pretest produces the following basic nonequivalent control group design:

$$\begin{array}{c}\underline{O \ X \ O} \\ \cdots\cdots\cdots \\ \underline{O \qquad O}\end{array}$$

This design is used frequently in research on legal impact, often in situations that could otherwise result in use of the similar, but less interpretable, preexperimental design , in which pretests are absent. While the pretest data introduce significant improvement, several cautions are in order. First, even if the nonequivalent groups do not differ on their pretest averages, they may differ in other ways that affect their posttest scores. Second, the available statistical techniques often used to adjust for pretest nonequivalence generally cannot completely control for initial differences. While their fallibility is most likely to result in underadjustment of differences at the pretest because of error in random measurement, overadjustment can also occur, so that even the direction of bias cannot always be specified. The third caution associated with the nonequivalent control-group design is that the interpretability of the results from such an experiment will depend on the pattern of the outcome data.

A study of the effect on traffic fatalities of laws requiring motorcyclists to wear helmets illustrates some of these issues (Robertson 1976). The research compared the rate of fatal motorcycle crashes per 10,000 registered motorcycles per year in eight states that enacted laws mandating the use of helmets and eight matched states that did not. The analysis covered a three-year period, including the year before enactment, the year of enactment, and the year after enactment.

Suppose that the fatality rates were higher at the pretest in the legislating states and dropped to the same level as those in the control states by the time of the posttest. Differential statistical regression could reasonably account for the result if legislation is passed in a state when figures for the previous year are particularly shocking. If the rates in legislating states dropped significantly below those in the control states, regression would offer a less plausible explanation. This comparison illustrates how the interpretability of such designs depends on outcomes (for a more complete review, see Cook and Campbell 1979, chap. 3).

The data did not, in fact, reveal any significant difference in the preenactment fatality rates of the two sets of states, leading the researcher to conclude that the significant difference obtained after enactment was due to the legislation introduced in half the states. Unfortunately, pretest equivalence does not necessarily reflect general equivalence across the treated and untreated groups. The two may still differ in other variables that affect the posttest scores. To the extent that state environmental factors affecting fatality rates in motorcycle accidents also affect the introduction of legislation, such underlying nonequivalence can be expected; for instance, legislatures enacting helmet laws may also spend money on road improvements.

A variety of alternative analytic techniques can be used on nonequivalent control-group designs—such as analysis of variance, analysis of covariance, and analysis of variance with matching or with gain scores (for a review, see Reichardt 1979)—but reports of results must be tempered. "With the present state of the art in the social sciences, any one of these statistical methods could be biased enough so that a useful treatment might look harmful and a harmful treatment might look benign or even beneficial" (Reichardt 1979, p. 197; see also Lord 1967; Cochran and Rubin 1973).

More elaborate versions of the nonequivalent control-group design can introduce some additional controls to increase its interpretability (see Cook and Campbell 1979). One variation promising for research on legal impact is the regression-discontinuity design.

In some cases, nonequivalence is a result of explicit selection procedures. For example, the poor with incomes below a specified level may be entitled to free health services or free legal counsel. Research may be aimed at testing the extent to which this legally mandated treatment affects outcomes. Those who do and those who do not receive the treatment, such as free counsel, may be different in other ways that will affect their case outcomes, so that income may be expected to correlate with outcome even in the absence of treatment (Figure 4). If those below level X receive a treatment that improves their performance, the graph of outcomes may be altered as shown in Figure 5. By comparing

FIGURE 4

the success predicted at income level A based on treated individuals, and success predicted at A based on untreated individuals (by using the two regression equations), the plot of scores can be tested for the discontinuity that would be predicted if the provision of free counsel affected outcomes.

The allocation according to presumed need or desert frequently presents a satisfactory alternative to administrators or legislators who oppose random assignment. This design is not, however, without weaknesses. When the shape of the distribution is not linear, the researcher must examine more complicated models. Furthermore, the tails of a distribution are particularly likely to show behavior that does not closely fit a regression line, even in the absence of a treatment. Thus, when the treatment cutting point is near the edge of the range of the pretest, such as a poverty-level income might be, it will be difficult to estimate the shape of the distribution of scores on the short side of the cutting point.

A more practical problem can also arise. If the exact location of a cutting point is known, it can be manipulated so that, for example, income levels have a greater tendency to be reported at just below the cutting point than just above it; in such a situation,

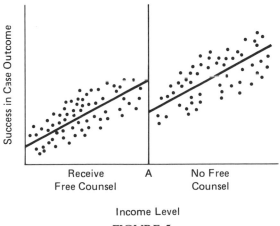

FIGURE 5

the borderline case is more likely to become eligible for desirable treatment. While it is possible to examine for inaccurate reporting or to base estimates on a range around the cutting point rather than on a single cutting score, a clear, rather than a fuzzy, cutting point will produce the most sensitive test of a treatment effect by this useful but under-used design.

Combining Control Groups and Time-Series   Because designs using either inter-rupted time-series or nonequivalent control groups have different weaknesses, combining them into a single design often enables the researcher to rule out competing explanations that neither design could handle alone. For example, traffic fatality rates in Connecticut were studied before and after a crackdown on speeding (Campbell and Ross 1968). The analysis also examined the pattern of traffic fatalities during the same period for neigh-boring states. The time-series allowed a check for regression and cyclical variation, while the control states permitted a test of whether fatality patterns based on some shared historical event, such as a particularly hard winter, could be responsible for a drop in Connecticut's fatality rate. (In fact, no clear effect of the new enforcement policy could be detected.)

The risk of a change in instrumentation was not controlled in this study, since states keep their own highway records.[12] In other cases, however, it may sometimes be possible to identify a control group that should be subject to the same adjustments of data as the group being treated. The study of the British Road Safety Act predicted that fatality rates from drunk driving should be affected only during those hours when the pubs were open; the fatality rate when pubs were closed was the control time-series (Ross 1973). The absence of change in the rate of the control series suggested that neither instrumentation nor shared historical influences could be responsible for the drop in fatalities that oc-curred during the hours that the pubs were open. While such nonequivalent control groups may be difficult to identify, the search pays off in one of the strongest available tests of legal impact.

Nonexperimental Methods

Because the behaviors that law attempts to affect are the products of a variety of nonlegal influences, ruling out selection and historical threats to internal validity is critical in the quasi-experimental test of legal effect. Purely statistical, rather than design, controls can also be used to unravel competing causal explanations. Such multivariate tools as multiple regression (Blalock 1972; Draper and Smith 1966), log-linear analysis (Bishop, Fienberg, and Holland 1975; Goodman 1970, 1972, 1975), path analysis (Dun-can 1966, 1975), and structural equations (Goldberger 1972; Goldberger and Duncan 1973), when used to infer causality, represent a marked improvement over the simple correlational preexperimental design. At bottom, however, they share its basic weakness; they measure the strength of the relationship between independent and dependent vari-ables and conclude that a causal relationship exists based on the correlational evidence. To the extent that the researcher has been able to identify and adequately measure all other variables that may explain the relationship, this method can be successful. Unfor-

---

[12] Actually a selection-instrumentation interaction (Campbell and Stanley 1963).

tunately, theories about legal behavior have generally not yet achieved such ability to specify causal models (for a good discussion of these and other problems in the literature on deterrence, see Fisher and Nagin 1978), and to the extent that variables are unidentified or are crudely or unreliably assessed, inaccurate conclusions about causal relations will be drawn.

Multiple regression is generally used to explain variation in an interval-level variable, such as the length of a prison term, by examining the correlation between that variable and a series of independent variables, such as severity of crime or criminal record. When the independent variables are known to precede the dependent variable in time, such methods can predict or forecast the value of the dependent variable from information about the levels of the independent variables. Thus, the offender's personal characteristics as well as characteristics of the crime may be used to help predict the length of a prison sentence a given offender will receive. If R^2—the amount of variation in the length of the sentence accounted for by the predictor characteristics—approaches 1 (100 percent), the prediction will approach perfect accuracy. In practice, prediction is usually far from perfect. For example, most studies have been able to explain only half the variation in criminal sentence levels (see, for example, Wilkins et al. 1976; Diamond 1981b).

It is, of course, useful to improve chance level predictions by 50 percent, but such results—or even the hypothetical 100 percent explanation results—do not necessarily disclose the causal structure of the criminal sentence. If psychiatric prognosis is a strong predictor of sentence when such other factors as prior criminal record are controlled, its predictive value may arise because prior employment stability—an unmeasured variable—affects both psychiatric prognosis and sentence. The omission or poor measurement of critical causal variables not only tends to reduce R^2, it can also create the appearance or disappearance of relationships between the measured independent variables and the dependent variable.

In research on legal decisions, the false identification of variables as causes, as opposed to predictors, may have important value overtones. If some independent variables, such as race, affected legal decisions, they would show unacceptable discriminatory behavior by legal decision-makers. But race tends to correlate highly with other variables viewed as permissible determinants of such decisions—employment record, for example—and this covariation will make attribution about the real causes of the decision questionable.

Multiple regression techniques assume that the dependent variable is quantitative. In much research on law, however, the outcome variable is more properly seen as dichotomous and qualitative: the parole board grants or does not grant parole, the plaintiff collects damages or does not. Multiple regression can still be applied by treating the regression coefficient as a change in the probability of being granted parole or collecting damages, but some statistical problems may arise. Heteroscedasticity[13] can be handled by reweighting, but predicted probabilities outside of the 1–0 range may require alternative estimation procedures (Berk 1980). Alternate models like probit, logit, and discriminant function analysis (see Finney 1971; Namboodiri, Carter, and Blalock 1975) were

---

[13] *Heteroscedasticity* occurs when errors of prediction have different variances at different levels of the independent variable.

specifically designed to handle data with dichotomous dependent variables and avoid the problems of range associated with multiple regression.

The dependent variable in sociolegal research is often a mixture of dichotomous (for example, incarceration or none) and quantitative (for example, length of incarceration). A modification of probit analysis, called a Tobit model, can be used to deal with the common legal situation in which the dependent variable is truncated in this fashion. (See Berk 1980 for a useful discussion of the strength and weaknesses of multiple-regression techniques and their alternatives in criminal-justice evaluation research.)

These analytic techniques all use some continuous data, either as independent or as dependent variables. Yet available data may often be intrinsically categorical—sex, type of plea—or may only be available in categorical form—aged 18 and over, versus under 18. When both independent and dependent variables are categorical, log-linear techniques are preferable to multiple-regression techniques and their derivatives, particularly since they permit direct testing for nonlinear effects.

Path analysis moves beyond simple stepwise regression to investigate the alternate underlying models that can produce causal relationships. Thus, it can be used to investigate, for example, whether the correlation between prior record and the sentence recommended by a probation officer is more likely to be the result of the record's direct influence on sentence, the record's effect on the probation officer's prediction of the prospects for successful adjustment on probation which in turn affects sentence, or the operation of both causal paths (Hagan 1975). While this approach can force explicit consideration of the variety of complex causal paths that the real world can include, the use of path analysis to quantify specific causal contributions assumes, like regression models, not only complete specification—all relevant variables are measured—but also that each variable is measured reliably so that a path will not be rejected or given too little weight because of measurement error. The difficulty in meeting these assumptions is acknowledged in textbooks (for example, Duncan 1975, p. 50; Greenberg 1979, p. 53) but is often ignored in more substantive writing.

Research on law is particularly susceptible to problems associated with missing variables and unreliability of measurement. Apparently fertile archives are replete with unreliable data or with gaps in the data, and it may often be necessary to code some variables rather crudely (see Carroll and Mondrick 1976; Cartwright 1975; Church 1976). For example, measuring the seriousness of offenses by using the maximum sentence permitted under the criminal code (Hagan 1975) is likely to result in an evaluation that only approximately reflects the seriousness of the particular offense being scored (Greenberg 1979). Some direct support for this observation comes from the finding that the severity of sentences in a federal New York court was higher for drug offenses than for other offenses, even when maximum possible penalty was controlled for (Diamond 1981b). If the drug-offense variable had not been included, the variance it explained might have been attributed to some other variable with which it was correlated, such as race.

In other cases, it will not be possible to measure a potentially important set of variables adequately. A study of parole decisions did not code information on education, marital status, and occupation, although those data were available, because the information was judged too unreliable (Carroll and Mondrick 1976). The researchers were also unable to gain access to letters written to the parole board by such interested parties as wives—another variable that may have affected parole decisions.

The choice between experimental approaches and the nonexperimental or passive observational techniques (Cook and Campbell 1979) for assessing cause in studies of legal effects—the choice, that is, between design and statistical control of alternate causal hypotheses—tends to follow the disciplinary boundaries of the particular researchers. Psychologists typically favor the manipulation of experimental or quasi-experimental work, while economists more often rely on passive measurement. Sociologists and political scientists have traditionally done little experimental work, but there appears to be some evidence that the situation is changing. The strength of experimental methods lies in the fact that the active variation of the independent variable requires fewer assumptions, thereby facilitating causal inference. The benefits of experimental research can be garnered, however, only if the researcher can control events or is able to take advantage of natural experiments. These occasions will always be less frequent than occasions for passive observation.

Fortunately, legal change often creates opportunities to investigate theoretically important relationships. In 1966, in *Baxstrom* v. *Harold,* the Supreme Court held that equal protection of the law was denied any individual who was detained longer than the maximum sentence in an institution for the criminally insane without a new hearing to determine current dangerousness. This ruling, which resulted in the transfer of nearly one thousand reputedly dangerous mental patients in New York to civil mental hospitals, provided an opportunity to evaluate the validity of the predictions that had been used to justify extended detention (Monahan 1978). A subsequent similar ruling in Pennsylvania (*Dixon* v. *Pennsylvania,* 1971) released a number of mentally disordered offenders outright. Studies revealed relatively low rates of violence in the civil mental hospitals (Steadman and Cocozza 1974) and among those who were released (Thornberry and Jacoby 1974). Similarly, police strikes potentially create an opportunity to assess the effect of certainty of punishment on crime rate (but see Greenberg 1979 on reciprocal causation). Finally, Baldus and Cole (1975) have argued that on even a widely measured and analyzed policy such as the death penalty, the quasi-experimental time-series comparisons between abolitionist and death-penalty states before and after the introduction of the death penalty (Sellin 1967) have produced more reliable and convincing data than the multiple-regression approach (for example, Ehrlich 1975). In explaining their greater confidence in the use of the time-series, Baldus and Cole comment, "There are many questions which, because of inadequacies of data or theory, are best studied by simpler methods" (p. 173). The simplicity of control through design can often avoid weaknesses that statistical sophistication cannot eliminate.

SOME SPECIAL MEASUREMENT PROBLEMS AND OPPORTUNITIES FOR RESEARCH ON LAW

Several issues of measurement, which cut across the substantive and design categories, present special problems and opportunities for reliable and valid measurement of behavior related to law. They include access to confidential and sensitive information, some special weaknesses of legal archives, and the use of systematic observational techniques in research on law.

Confidential and Sensitive Information

Individuals often view their dealings with the law or the legal system as sensitive and personal. Reports of such dealings are highly vulnerable to distortion.

> The most common method of sociological research, the interview, usually misses the goal of getting valid data on norm-relevant behavior: the interviewees either do not admit how often they break a norm or they brag about actions they would never dare to perform. They try to evade an answer by giving an opinion: they tell the interviewer what should be done, not what they do in fact. Interviews are very good if we want to know something about attitudes or opinions, but it is always dangerous to make inferences about actual behavior from such data. [Blankenburg 1966, p. 113]

Even when noncriminal acts are under investigation, legal dealings are viewed as confidential, posing problems of access for the researcher. Moreover, the promise of confidentiality usually made by social scientists to their respondents cannot always be honestly given for studies of legal behavior. As is the case for reporters but not for lawyers, researchers' data can be subpoenaed. In the New Jersey Negative Income Tax experiment, experimental subjects were given guaranteed annual incomes; the Mercer County grand jury wanted to learn whether some of these same people were also illegally on welfare rolls (Kershaw and Small 1972). An out-of-court settlement was probably the only measure that prevented a court order to turn over the names of the experimental subjects. Whatever rules may come to prevail in the future, only National Institute of Justice grants can promise researchers and their respondents real protection from government attention at present.

Despite the obvious weaknesses of self-reports, they are often the only direct source of information on certain topics, such as victimizations unreported to the police or officially undetected drug use. Fortunately, some new techniques can increase the validity of interview and questionnaire data by providing a genuine guarantee of anonymity to respondents. One is the randomized-response approach. (See Fox and Tracy 1980 for a review of the growing literature on this method.) Using this method, respondents privately toss a coin to determine which of two questions they will answer. One question is the sensitive one of interest to the research. The other is a benign question, whose answer has a known distribution in the tested population. While no single answer can be tied to any particular respondent, the researcher can use probability models to obtain a true picture of the pattern of response among the subjects. The cost lies in the requirement of larger samples to achieve equally reliable results, but the potential for increased validity may warrant the higher cost.

Problems of access may also arise when data files are involved. Records containing sensitive information about individuals and their legal histories may be shielded by government agencies, making it difficult for researchers to obtain them. With appropriate arrangements to limit the reporting of information so that individuals cannot be identified, such access can often be arranged, at least in some form. Requesting aggregate tax-return data on groups of individuals avoided the objection that would have been raised had data on individual tax returns been called for (Schwartz and Orleans 1967). A similar objection to the release of background descriptions for individual jurors was overcome by the use of aggregate profiles instead (Zeisel and Diamond 1976).

Difficulties of access also arise because of systematic differences between those respondents who are willing and those who refuse to share their legal histories and experiences, between police departments or administrative agencies who welcome researchers and those who do not. It is difficult to document patterns of access to organizations because, while researchers commonly report their response rates in surveys of individuals, organizations' response rates are rarely reported. The probable magnitude of the problem of access to organizations could be gauged more readily if researchers reported their efforts at negotiation—failures as well as successes (for an example, see Kerstetter and Heinz 1979).

Legal Archives

As part of its daily operation, the legal system records information about the cases it processes. In view of the interplay among subsystems, the available archival data are a reasonable source for tracing the progress of cases through the system and learning how the legal system handles people and cases. While sensible, however, the approach can involve considerable difficulty. A discussion of efforts to identify and follow parties in a study of state supreme courts provides a revealing list of ways in which disputes can lose and gain parties as they are decided, appealed, remanded, and the like (Cartwright 1975, writing of his research with Friedman, Kagan, and Wheeler). In addition to deaths and disappearances there are, among other changes, unions and banks who intervene, judges who become respondents, subsets of plaintiffs and defendants who become joint appellants. "Legal disputes join disparate parties into temporary social units ('forced marriages') whose identity through time is always problematic" (Cartwright 1975, p. 372). Complex coding schemes are required to maintain order in the data, and reliable tracing will usually be possible only at the cost of substantial redundancy in the coding at each stage.

Similar difficulties may arise in tracing an individual through the criminal-justice system. Police and court identification numbers are often different. Individuals use aliases, and a criminal career may not be conveniently confined to a single jurisdiction.

Tracing changes in patterns—for example, whether cases are more likely to be dismissed under a new statute—can be done by using archival data, but several problems are common. The first is a substantial lag between the time a case is filed, even within a particular court or with a single agency, and the time it is closed. If cases opened during a particular calendar year are examined for outcomes that occur through the end of the following year, the cases opened early in the year will have a better chance of having been disposed of than those opened near the end of the year. The remedy for a study interested in changes in case processing over time is to keep the time constant across cases, even if that method means considering some early cases as still open when in fact they are closed. Thus, a case filed on January 3, 1988, can be coded according to its status—disposed of by dismissal, plea, and the like, or still open—on January 3, 1989, while a case filed on September 20, 1988, will be coded according to its status on September 20, 1989. This practice will keep lags more or less constant over time—but not completely, because equal time periods may not be equal in all important respects. Staffing changes, for example, may mean that a case opened on January 3, 1988, receives less official attention over the subsequent year than does a case opened on September 10, 1988.

The label given a case in its first formal contact with the legal system—such as the arrest charge—may not exclusively, exhaustively, or accurately describe a set of similar cases. The sample of cases may thus change over time if the formal label is relied on to define the set of cases, simply because the use of the label has changed. Ample evidence exists of the legal system's flexibility in processing similar behaviors differently. The British Road Safety Act was associated with a rise in drinking and driving charges. Yet careful investigation of police arrests on other charges—"dangerous driving" and "careless driving"—showed that the act, "contrary to popular impression, did not greatly increase the likelihood of police action in the event of drinking and driving. Rather, it changed the form of the action" (Ross 1973, p. 48).

Similarly, when the provision in the United States Code relating to the importation of drugs was changed in 1971, the range of penalties for heroin convictions was reduced from 5–20 years to 0–15 years. A study tracing sentences resulting from heroin indictments in San Diego found no change in sentence level after the change in law. A procedural effect on plea bargaining set in, however; 79 percent of guilty pleas under the old drug statute were to a statute with a lower sentence frame—such as crimes involving tax payments with respect to the drugs—while under the new law, only 19 percent involved a charge reduction. Thus, while earlier it had been necessary to use another statute to obtain a sentence of less than five years, after the legal change this device was no longer necessary (Nimmer 1977). Though the legal change produced an alteration in the name of the charge conviction, sentence level apparently remained stable. Both these examples suggest how critical it is to examine legal processing for spillover and compensatory effects, tracing both direct and indirect patterns of influence.

Despite these gaps, omissions, and coding nightmares, one of the greatest advantages the legal system offers the researcher is its proliferation of detailed records. As researchers gain experience in tapping the information maintained in legal files, and as the regular recording activities of legal organizations are more often computerized, retrieval of archival data can increasingly supply researchers with rich opportunities to analyze a wide range of legal activities.

Systematic Observation

The quasi-public nature of much legal activity suggests that much greater use can be made of systematic observational techniques as an additional tool in studying the behavior of law. For example, research on the processing of cases in a lower court used observational techniques to provide a detailed picture of arraignments and dispositions in that court (Mileski 1971; see Weick 1969 and Reiss 1980 for discussions of systematic observational techniques). Although this approach examines public behaviors while only partisan participants will be privy to behind-the-scenes activities, the systematic record-keeping of the public face of a case by a trained observer without a vested interest is an important source of information about legal institutions. Partisan participants may not be willing or able to make such observations, and archives will not record all the detailed information that observation can provide. Each method has its weaknesses, of course; a rounded description of behavior is most likely when multiple individual perspectives and measurement approaches—such as surveys, archival data, and observations—are used in the same study.

Sociolegal research uses research methods employed in other areas of empirical inquiry. But the characteristics of law and the state of theorizing about law and legal institutions create special difficulties and opportunities in the application of available methods. In this discussion, I have tried to alert the reader to those special characteristics that have the most important methodological implications for law.

The history of systematic empirical investigation of the behavior of law is relatively recent. While some of the qualities of legal behavior and records reviewed here create obstacles for research, it is likely that the coming years will see substantial growth of research on law. The value of the research will depend heavily on the ability of investigators to overcome these obstacles—for example, unreliability and change in the sources of measurement, to make use of the special possibilities of law for research—such as multiple-data sources with varying biases and limitations, and to make wider use of stronger methodological approaches, such as longitudinal study, randomized experiments, and time-series designs. Much remains to be done, but with sharpened tools, the future promises significant growth in our knowledge about the behavior of law. Certainly our first steps indicate that pursuit of that knowledge will be lively.

Cases Cited

Aguayo v. Richardson, 473 F.2d 1090 (2d Cir. 1973).
Baxstrom v. Harold, 383 U.S. 107 (1966).
Dixon v. Attorney General of the Commonwealth of Pennsylvania, 325 F. Sp. Supp. 966 (1971).
In re Gault, 387 U.S. 1 (1967).
Massachusetts Board of Retirement v. Murgla, 427 U.S. 307 (1976).
Pointer v. Texas, 380 U.S. 400 (1965).

Bibliography

Allott, A. N.; Epstein, A. L.; and Gluckman, M.
    1969   Introduction. In *Ideas and Procedures in African Customary Law*, edited by M. Gluckman. London: Oxford University Press.
Alpert, L.; Atkins, B.; and Ziller, R.
    1979   "Becoming a Judge: The Transition from Advocate to Arbiter." *Judicature* 62:325–36.
Baldus, D. C., and Cole, J. W. L.
    1975   "A Comparison of the Work of Thorsten Sellin and Isaac Ehrlich on the Deterrent Effect of Capital Punishment." *Yale Law Journal* 85:170–86.

Baldwin, J., and McConville, M.
    1979a   *Jury Trials.* London: Oxford University Press.
    1979b   "Trial by Jury: Some Empirical Evidence on Contested Criminal Cases in Eng-
             land." *Law & Society Review* 13:861–90.
Baxi, U., and Galanter, M.
    1979   "Panchayat Justice: An Indian Experiment in Legal Access." In *Access to Justice,*
            vol. 3, edited by M. Cappelletti and B. Garth. Alphen aan den Rijn: Sijthoff and
            Noordhoff.
Berk, R. A.
    1980   "Recent Statistical Developments: Implications for Criminal Justice Evaluations."
            In *Handbook of Criminal Justice Evaluation,* edited by M. W. Klein and K. S.
            Teilmann. Beverly Hills, Calif.: Sage.
Berk, R.; Brackman, H.; and Lesser, S.
    1977   *A Measure of Justice.* New York: Academic Press.
Bermant, G., and Coppock, R.
    1973   "Outcomes of Six and Twelve Member Jury Trials: An Analysis of 128 Civil Cases
            in the State of Washington." *Washington Law Review* 48:593–96.
Best, A., and Andreasen, A. R.
    1977   "Consumer Response to Unsatisfactory Purchases: A Survey of Perceiving Defects,
            Voicing Complaints, and Obtaining Redress." *Law & Society Review* 11:702–42.
Bishop, Y.; Fienberg, S.; and Holland, P.
    1975   *Discrete Multivariate Analysis: Theory and Practice.* Cambridge, Mass.: MIT Press.
Black, M., and Metzger, D.
    1965   "Ethnographic Description and the Study of Law." *American Anthropologist* 67:
            141–65.
Blalock, H. M.
    1972   *Social Statistics.* New York: McGraw-Hill.
Blankenburg, E.
    1966   "The Selectivity of Legal Sanctions: An Empirical Investigation of Shoplifting."
            Law & Society Review 2:109–30.
    1975   "Studying the Frequency of Civil Litigation in Germany." *Law & Society Review*
            9:307–19.
Block, R. L.
    1971   "Fear of Crime and Fear of the Police." *Social Problems* 19:91–101.
Blumberg, A. S.
    1967   "The Practice of Law as Confidence Game." *Law & Society Review* 1:15–39.
Bonn, R. L.
    1972   "The Predictability of Nonlegalistic Adjudication." *Law & Society Review* 6:563–
            78.
Botein, B.
    1964–65 "The Manhattan Bail Project: Its Impact on Criminology and the Criminal Law
            Processes." *Texas Law Review* 43:319–31.
Bowers, W. J.
    1974   *Executions in America.* Toronto: Heath.
Box, G., and Jenkins, G.
    1976   *Time Series Analysis: Forecasting and Control.* San Francisco: Holden-Day.
Buckle, L. G., and Thomas-Buckle, S. R.
    1980   "Bringing Justice Home." Paper presented at the annual meeting of the Law and
            Society Association, Madison, Wisconsin, June.
Campbell, D. T.
    1957   "Factors Relevant to the Validity of Experiments in Social Settings." *Psychological
            Bulletin* 54:297–312.

Campbell, D. T., and Ross, H. L.
  1968   "The Connecticut Crackdown on Speeding: Time Series Analysis." *Law & Society Review* 3:33–54.
Campbell, D. T., and Stanley, J.
  1963   *Experimental and Quasi-Experimental Designs for Research.* Chicago: Rand McNally.
Capron, A. M.
  1975   "Social Experimentation and the Law." In *Ethical and Legal Issues of Social Experimentation,* edited by A. M. Rivlin and P. M. Thomas. Washington, D.C.: Brookings Institution.
Carroll, J. S., and Payne, J. W.
  1977   "Judgments About Crime and the Criminal: A Model and a Method for Investigating Parole Decisions." In *Perspectives in Law and Psychology: The Criminal Justice System,* vol. 1, edited by B. D. Sales. New York: Plenum.
Carroll, L., and Mondrick, M. E.
  1976   "Racial Bias in Decision to Grant Parole." *Law & Society Review* 11:93–107.
Cartwright, B.
  1975   "Conclusion: Disputes and Reported Cases." *Law & Society Review* 9:369–84.
Casper, J. I.
  1978   "Having Their Day in Court: Defendant Evaluations of the Fairness Treatment." *Law & Society Review* 12:237–51.
Chambliss, W.
  1971   "Vice, Corruption, Bureaucracy, and Power." *Wisconsin Law Review* 1971:1130–55.
  1973   "The Saints and the Roughnecks." *Society* 11:24–31.
Church, T.
  1976   "Plea Bargains, Concessions, and the Courts: Analysis of a Quasi-experiment." *Law & Society Review* 10:378–413.
Cochran, W., and Rubin, D.
  1973   "Controlling Bias in Observational Studies: A Review." *Sankhya* (series A) 35:417–46.
Collier, J. F.
  1976   "Political Leadership and Legal Change in Zinacantan." *Law & Society Review* 11:131–63.
Cook, T. D., and Campbell, D. T.
  1979   *Quasi-Experimentation: Design and Analysis Issues for Field Settings.* Chicago: Rand McNally.
Crowe, P. W.
  1978   "Complaint Reactions to the Massachusetts Commission Against Discrimination." *Law & Society Review* 12:217–35.
Cutler, N. E.
  1977   "Political Socialization Research as a Generational Analysis: The Cohort Approach Versus the Lineage Approach." In *Handbook of Political Socialization,* edited by S. A. Renshon. New York: Free Press.
Diamond, S.S.
  1981a   "The Effects of Legal Change and Their Detection: Some Recurring Obstacles." In *Applied Social Psychology Annual 2,* edited by L. Bickman. Beverly Hills, Calif.: Sage.
  1981b   "Exploring Sources of Sentence Disparity." In *Perspectives in Law and Psychology: The Trial Process,* vol. 2, edited by B. D. Sales. New York: Plenum.
Diamond, S. S., and Zeisel, H.
  1974   "A Courtroom Experiment on Jury Selection and Decision Making." *Personality and Social Psychology Bulletin* 1:276–77.

Draper, N. R., and Smith, H.
    1966   *Applied Regression Analysis.* New York: Wiley.

Duncan, O. D.
    1966   "Path Analysis: Sociological Examples." *American Journal of Sociology* 72:1–16.
    1975   *Introduction to Structural Equation Models.* New York: Academic Press.

Ehrlich, I.
    1975   "The Deterrent Effect of Capital Punishment: A Question of Life and Death." *American Economic Review* 65:397–417.

Empey, L. T., and Erickson, M. L.
    1972   *The Provo Experiment: Evaluating Community Control of Delinquency.* Lexington, Mass.: Lexington Books.

Ennis, P. H.
    1967   *Crime Victimization in the United States: A Report of a National Survey.* Report of the U.S. President's Commission of Law Enforcement and Administration of Justice.

Epstein, A. L.
    1967   "The Case Method in the Field of Law." In *The Craft of Social Anthropology,* edited by A. L. Epstein. London: Tavistock.

Epstein, E. J.
    1977   *Agency of Fear.* New York: Putnam.

Feeley, M.
    1976   "The Concept of Laws in Social Science: A Critique and Expanded View." *Law & Society Review* 10:497–523.

Feest, J.
    1968   "Compliance with Legal Regulations: Stop Sign Behavior." *Law & Society Review* 2:447–61.

Feigl, H.
    1958   "The Mental and the Physical." In *Minnesota Studies in the Philosophy of Science,* vol. 2, edited by H. Feigl, M. Scriven, and G. Maxwell. Minneapolis: University of Minnesota Press.

Felstiner, W.
    1974   "Influence of Social Organization on Dispute Processing." *Law & Society Review* 9:63–94.

Finney, D. J.
    1971   *Probit Analysis.* 3rd ed. Cambridge: Cambridge University Press.

Fisher, F., and Nagin, D.
    1978   "On the Feasibility of Identifying the Crime Function in a Simultaneous Model of Crime Rates and Sanction Levels. In *Deterrence and Incapacitation: Estimating the Effect of Criminal Sanctions on Crime Rates,* edited by A. Blumstein, J. Cohen, and D. Nagin. Washington, D.C.: National Academy of Sciences.

Fox, J. A., and Tracy, P. E.
    1980   "The Randomized Response Approach: Applicability to Criminal Justice Research and Evaluation." *Evaluation Review* 4:601–22.

Friedman, L. J., and Percival, R. U.
    1976   "A Tale of Two Courts: Litigation in Alameda and San Benito Counties." *Law & Society Review* 10:267–301.

Friedman, L. M.
    1977   *Law & Society.* Englewood Cliffs, N. J.: Prentice-Hall.

Galanter, M.
    1975   "Afterword: Explaining Litigation." *Law & Society Review* 9:347–68.

Gallatin, J., and Adelson, J.
    1971   "Legal Guarantees of Individual Freedom: A Cross-national Study of the Development of Political Thought." *Journal of Social Issues* 27:93–108.

Gibbs, J. L.
  1963   "The Kpelle Moot: A Therapeutic Model for the Informal Settlement of Disputes."
          Africa 33:1–11.
Gibbs, J. P.
  1968   "Definitions of Law and Empirical Questions." *Law & Society Review* 2:429–46.
Glenn, N. D.
  1976   "Cohort Analyst's Futile Quest: Statistical Attempts to Separate Age, Period, and
          Cohort Effects." *American Sociological Review* 41:900–904.
Goldberger, A. S.
  1972   "Structural Equation Methods in the Social Sciences." *Econometrics* 40:979–1001.
Goldberger, A. S., and Duncan, O. D., eds.
  1973   *Structural Equation Models in the Social Sciences.* New York: Seminar Press.
Goldman, J.
  1978   "Experimenting with Appellate Reform: The Second Circuit Experience." Pa-
          per presented at the meeting of the Law and Society Association, Minneapolis,
          May.
Goodman, L.
  1970   "The Multivariate Analysis of Qualitative Data: Interactions Among Multiple
          Classifications." *Journal of American Statistical Association* 65:226–56.
  1972   "A Modified Multiple Regression Approach to the Analysis of Dichotomous Vari-
          ables." *American Sociological Review* 37:28–46.
  1975   "The Relationship Between Modified and Usual Multiple Regression Approaches
          to the Analysis of Dichotomous Variables." In *Sociological Methodology,* edited by
          D. R. Heise. San Francisco: Jossey-Bass.
Gottfredson, D. M., and Gottfredson, M. R.
  1980   "Data for Criminal Justice Evaluation: Some Resources and Pitfalls." In *Handbook
          of Criminal Justice Evaluation,* edited by M. W. Klein and K. S. Teilmann. Beverly
          Hills, Calif.: Sage.
Gottfredson, D. M.; Hoffman, P.; Sigler, M.; and Wilkins, L.
  1975   "Making Paroling Policy Explicit." *Crime and Delinquency* 21:4–44.
Greely, H.
  1977   "The Equality of Allocation by Lot." *Harvard Civil Rights-Civil Liberties Law Review*
          12:113–41.
Green, B. H.
  1976   "Applying the Controlled Experiment to Penal Reform." *Cornell Law Review*
          2:158–76.
Greenberg, D.
  1979   *Mathematical Criminology.* New Brunswick, N.J.: Rutgers University Press.
Grossman, J. B., and Sarat, A.
  1975   "Litigation in the Federal Courts: A Comparative Perspective." *Law & Society
          Review* 9:321–46.
Gunther, G.
  1972   "In Search of Evolving Doctrine on a Changing Court: A Model for a Newer Equal
          Protection." *Harvard Law Review* 86:1–48.
Hagan, J.
  1975   "The Social and Legal Construction of Criminal Justice: A Study of the Pre-
          sentencing Process." *Social Problems* 22:620–77.
Hahm, P. C.
  1969   "The Decision Process in Korea." In *Comparative Judicial Behavior,* edited by G.
          Schubert and D. Danielski. New York: Oxford University Press.
Hogarth, J.
  1971   *Sentencing as a Human Process.* Toronto: University of Toronto Press.

Hollingsworth, E.; Feldman, W. B.; and Clark, D. C.
    1973   "The Ohio Small Claims Court: An Empirical Study." *Cincinnati Law Review*
              42:469–527.
Institute for Judicial Administration
    1972   *A Comparison of Six- and Twelve-member Juries in New Jersey Superior and County
              Courts.* New York: Institute for Judicial Administration.
Jacobs, J.
    1977   *Stateville: The Penitentiary in Mass Society.* Chicago: University of Chicago Press.
Kalven, H., and Zeisel, H.
    1966   *The American Jury.* Chicago: University of Chicago Press.
Katz, J.
    1972   *Experimentation with Human Beings.* New York: Russell Sage Foundation.
Keppel, G.
    1973   *Design and Analysis: A Researcher's Handbook.* Englewood Cliffs, N.J.: Prentice-Hall.
Kershaw, D. N., and Small, J. C.
    1972   "Data Confidentiality and Privacy: Lessons from the New Jersey Negative Income
              Tax Experiment." *Public Policy* 20:257–80.
Kerstetter, W., and Heinz, A.
    1979   *Pretrial Settlement Conference: An Evaluation.* Washington, D.C.: U.S. Govern-
              ment Printing Office.
Key, V. O., Jr.
    1961   *Public Opinion and American Democracy.* New York: Knopf.
King, D., and McEvoy, K.
    1976   *A National Survey of the Complaint Handling Procedures Used by Consumers.* Rock-
              ville, Md.: King Research.
Koneçni, V., and Ebbesen, E.
    1979   "External Validity of Research in Legal Psychology." *Law and Human Behavior*
              3:39–70.
Landy, P., and Aronson, E.
    1969   "The Influence of the Character of the Criminal and His Victim on the Decisions
              of Simulated Jurors." *Journal of Experimental Social Psychology* 5:141–52.
Langton, K., and Jennings, M.
    1968   "Political Socialization and the High School Civics Curriculum in the United
              States." *American Political Science Review* 62:852–67.
Lazarsfeld, P. F., and Fiske, M.
    1938   "The Panel as a New Tool for Measuring Opinion." *Public Opinion Quarterly* 2:
              596–612.
Lefstein, N.; Stapleton, V.; and Teitelbaum, L.
    1969   "In Search of Juvenile Justice: Gault and Its Implementation." *Law & Society
              Review* 3:491–562.
Lempert, R. O.
    1966   "Strategies of Research Design in the Legal Impact Study: The Control of Plausible
              Rival Hypotheses." *Law & Society Review* 1:111–32.
    1978   "More Tales of Two Courts: Exploring Changes in the 'Dispute Settlement Func-
              tion' of Trial Courts." *Law & Society Review* 13:91–138.
Lenihan, K.
    1977   "Unlocking the Second Gate." *Research and Development Monograph of the U.S.
              Department of Labor.*
Lerman, P.
    1975   *Community Treatment and Social Control: A Critical Analysis of Juvenile Correctional
              Policy.* Chicago: University of Chicago Press.

Levi, E.
1949   *An Introduction to Legal Reasoning.* Chicago: University of Chicago Press.

Levine, A. G., and Schweber-Korea, C.
1976   "Jury Selection in Erie County: Changes in Sexist Systems." *Law & Society Review* 11:44–55.

Lind, A.; Thibaut, J.; and Walker, L.
1973   "Discovery and Presentation of Evidence in Adversary and Nonadversary Proceedings." *Michigan Law Review* 71:1129–44.

Llewellyn, K. N.
1960   *The Common Law Tradition: Deciding Appeals.* Boston: Little, Brown.

Lochner, P. R., Jr.
1975   "The No Fee and Low Fee Legal Practice of Private Attorneys." *Law & Society Review* 9:431–73.

Long, S. B.
1979   *Rehabilitating Criminals: Is It Treatment or Our Evaluation Methods Which Have Failed?* University of Washington and Bureau of Social Science Research.

Lord, F.
1967   "A Paradox in the Interpretation of Group Comparisons." *Psychological Bulletin* 68:304–5.

McCain, L., and McCleary, R.
1979   "The Statistical Analysis of the Simple Interrupted Time Series Quasi-experiment." In *Quasi-Experimentation: Design and Analysis Issues for Field Settings,* edited by T. Cook and D. Campbell. Chicago: Rand McNally.

McCleary, R.
1978   *Dangerous Men: The Sociology of Parole.* Beverly Hills, Calif.: Sage.

McDonald, W. F.
1979   "From Plea Negotiation to Coercive Justice: Notes on the Respecification of a Concept." *Law & Society Review* 13:385–92.

Maltz, M. D.
1978   *Why Before-After Comparisons of Criminal Activity Should Not be Used to Evaluate Delinquency Programs.* Report of the Center for Research in Criminal Justice, University of Illinois, Chicago.

Mason, D.; Mason, W.; Winsborough, H. H.; and Poole, W. K.
1973   "Some Methodological Issues in Cohort Analysis of Archival Data." *American Sociological Review* 38:242–58.

Mason, R., and Calvin, L.
1978   "A Study of Admitted Income Tax Evasion." *Law & Society Review* 13:73–90.

Mazur-Hart, S., and Berman, J.
1977   "Changing from Fault to No-Fault Divorce: An Interrupted Time Series Analysis." *Journal of Applied Psychology* 7:300–312.

Meyer, H. J.; Borgatta, E. F.; and Jones, W. C.
1965   *Girls at Vocational High.* New York: Russell Sage Foundation.

Mileski, M.
1971   "Courtroom Encounters: An Observation Study of a Lower Criminal Court." *Law & Society Review.* 5:473–538.

Mills, L.
1973   "Six-Member and Twelve-Member Juries: An Empirical Study of Trial Results." *University of Michigan Journal of Law Reform* 6:617–711.

Mitchell, H. E., and Byrne, D.
1973   "The Defendant's Dilemma: Effects of Jurors' Attitudes and Authoritarianism." *Journal of Personality and Social Psychology* 25:123–29.

Monahan, J.
  1978   "The Prediction of Violent Criminal Behavior: A Methodological Critique and Prospectus." In *Deterrence and Incapacitation,* edited by A. Blumstein, J. Cohen, and D. Nagin. Washington, D.C.: National Academy of Sciences.

Moore, S. F.
  1973   "Law and Social Change: The Semi-Autonomous Social Field as an Appropriate Subject of Study." *Law & Society Review* 1:719–46.

Morris, N.
  1966   "Impediments to Penal Reform." *University of Chicago Law Review* 33:627–56.

Nader, L.
  1969   "Styles of Court Procedure: To Make the Balance." In *Law in Culture and Society,* edited by L. Nader. Chicago: Aldine.

Nader, L., and Todd, H., eds.
  1978   *The Disputing Process-Law in Ten Societies.* New York: Columbia University Press.

Namboodiri, H.; Carter, L.; and Blalock, H.
  1975   *Applied Multivariate Analysis and Experimental Design.* New York: McGraw-Hill.

National Academy of Sciences
  1976   *Surveying Crime: A Report of the Panel for the Evaluation of Crime Surveys.* Washington, D.C.: National Research Council.

Nesselroade, J. R., and Baltes, P. B.
  1974   "Adolescent Personality Development and Historical Change: 1970–1972." *Monographs of the Society for Research in Child Development* 39 (l, serial no. 154).

Neubauer, D.
  1974   "After the Arrest: The Changing Decision in Prairie City." *Law & Society Review* 8:495–518.

Nimmer, R.
  1977   "The System Impact of Criminal Justice Reforms." In *Law, Justice, and the Individual in Society,* edited by J. Tapp and F. Levine. New York: Holt, Rinehart & Winston.

O'Leary, V., and Nuffield, J.
  1972   "Parole Decision Making Characteristics." *Criminal Law Bulletin* 8:651–81.

Penrod, S., and Hastie, R.
  1979   "Models of Jury Decision Making: A Critical Review." *Psychological Bulletin* 86:462–92.

Popper, K.
  1959   *The Logic of Scientific Discovery.* London: Hutchinson.
  1963   *Conjectures and Refutations: The Growth of Scientific Knowledge.* London: Routledge & Kegan Paul.

Reichardt, C.
  1979   "The Design and Analysis of the Nonequivalent Group Quasi-experiment." Doctoral dissertation, Northwestern University.

Reiss, A. J., Jr.
  1971   "Systematic Social Observation of Natural Social Phenomena." In *Sociological Methodology,* edited by H. Costner. San Francisco: Jossey-Bass.
  1980   "Variation in Criminal Justice Research Designs." In *Handbook of Criminal Justice Evaluation,* edited by M. W. Klein and K. S. Teilmann. Beverly Hills, Calif.: Sage.

Richardson, S. A.; Dohrenwend, B. S.; and Klein, D.
  1965   *Interviewing: Its Forms and Functions.* New York: Basic Books.

Robertson, L. S.
  1976   "An Instance of Effective Legal Legislation: Motorcyclist Helmet and Daytime Headlamp Laws." *Law & Society Review* 10:467–77.

Rosenberg, M.
  1964   *The Pretrial Conference and Effective Justice.* New York: Columbia University Press.
Ross, H. L.
  1973   "Law, Science and Accidents: The British Road Safety Act of 1967." *Journal of Legal Studies* 11:1–78.
Ross, H. L., and Littlefield, N. O.
  1978   "Complaint as a Problem-Solving Mechanism." *Law & Society Review* 12:199–216.
Sarat, A.
  1976   "Alternatives in Dispute Processing: Litigation in Small Claims Court." *Law & Society Review* 10:339–75.
Schaie, K. W.
  1965   "A General Model for the Study of Developmental Problems." *Psychological Bulletin* 64:92–107.
Schwartz, R., and Orleans, S.
  1967   "On Legal Sanctions." *University of Chicago Law Review* 34:274–300.
Scott, T., and McPherson, M.
  1971   "The Development of the Private Sector of the Criminal Justice System." *Law & Society Review* 6:267–88.
Seidman, D., and Couzens, M.
  1974   "Getting the Crime Rate Down: Political Pressure and Crime Reporting." *Law & Society Review* 8:457–93.
Sellin, T.
  1959   *The Death Penalty.* Philadelphia: American Law Institute.
  1967   *Capital Punishment.* New York: Harper & Row.
Shapiro, A. E.
  1976   "Law in the Kibbutz: A Reappraisal." *Law & Society Review* 10:415–38.
Sherman, L. W., and Langworthy, R. H.
  1979   "Measuring Homicide by Police Officers." *Journal of Criminal Law and Criminology* 70:546–60.
Silberman, L.
  1979   *Non-Attorney Justice in the United States: An Empirical Study.* New York: Institute of Judicial Administration.
Stapleton, W. V., and Teitelbaum, L. E.
  1972   *In Defense of Youth.* New York: Russell Sage Foundation.
Steadman, H., and Cocozza, J.
  1974   *Careers of the Criminally Insane.* Lexington, Mass.: Lexington Books.
Steadman, J. M., and Rosenstein, R. S.
  1973   " 'Small Claims' Consumer Plaintiffs in the Philadelphia Municipal Court: An Empirical Study." *University of Pennsylvania Law Review* 121:1309–61.
Stouffer, S.
  1955   *Communism, Conformity, and Civil Liberties.* New York: Doubleday.
Tapp, J. L., and Levine, F.
  1977   "Reflections and Redirections." In *Law, Justice and the Individual in Society: Psychological and Legal Issues,* edited by J. Tapp and F. Levine. New York: Holt, Rinehart & Winston.
Thibaut, J., and Walker, L.
  1975   *Procedural Justice: A Psychological Analysis.* Hillsdale, N.J.: Erlbaum.
Thornberry, T., and Jacoby, J.
  1974   "The Uses of Discretion in a Maximum Security Mental Hospital: The Dixon Case." Paper presented at the annual meeting of the American Society of Criminology, Chicago.

Ungs, T., and Baas, L.
    1972   "Judicial Role Perceptions: A Q-Technique Study of Ohio Judges." *Law & Society Review* 6:343–66.

U.S. Department of Justice
    1975   *Crime Victimization Surveys in 13 American Cities.* Washington, D.C.: U.S. Government Printing Office.

Wanner, C.
    1974   "The Public Ordering of Private Relations, Part One: Initiating Civil Cases in Urban Trial Courts." *Law & Society Review* 8:421–40.
    1975   "The Public Ordering of Private Relations, Part Two: Winning Civil Court Cases." *Law & Society Review* 9:293–306.

Warren, C. A. B.
    1977   "Involuntary Commitment for Mental Disorder: The Application of California's Lanterman-Petris-Short Act." *Law & Society Review* 11:628–49.

Weick, K. E.
    1969   "Systematic Observational Methods." In *Handbook of Social Psychology*, 2nd ed., vol. 3, edited by G. Lindsay and E. Aronson. Reading, Mass.: Addison-Wesley.

Wilkins, L. T.; Kress, J. M.; Gottfredson, D. M.; Kalpin, J. C.; and Gelman, A. M.
    1976   *Sentencing Guidelines: Structuring Judicial Discretion.* Washington, D.C.: U.S. Government Printing Office.

Wilson, D., and Donnerstein, E.
    1977   "Guilty or Not Guilty? A Look at the 'Simulated' Jury Paradigm." *Journal of Applied Social Psychology* 7:175–90.

Wilson, W. C.
    1975   "Belief in Freedom of Speech and Press." *Journal of Social Issues* 31:69–76.

Wolfgang, M. E.; Figlio, R. M.; and Sellin, T.
    1972   *Delinquency in a Birth Cohort.* Chicago: University of Chicago Press.

Yale Law Journal
    1976   "The Unauthorized Practice of Law and Pro Se Divorce: An Empirical Analysis." *Yale Law Journal* 86:104–84.

Yngvesson, B., and Hennessey, P.
    1975   "Small Claims, Complex Disputes: A Review of the Small Claims Literature." *Law & Society Review* 9:219–74.

Zeisel, H.
    1973   "The FBI's Biased Sampling." *Bulletin of the Atomic Scientists* 39:38–42.
    1976   "The Deterrent Effect of the Death Penalty: Facts v. Faiths." *Supreme Court Review* 1976:317–43.

Zeisel, H., and Diamond, S. S.
    1974   " 'Convincing Empirical Evidence' on the Six-Member Jury." *University of Chicago Law Review* 41:281–95.
    1976   "The Jury Selection in the Mitchell-Stans Conspiracy Trial." *American Bar Foundation Research Journal* 1:151–74.
    1977   "Search for Sentencing Equity: Sentence Review in Massachusetts and Connecticut." *American Bar Foundation Research Journal* 4:881–940.
    1978   "The Effect of Peremptory Challenges on Jury and Verdict: An Experiment in a Federal District Court." *Stanford Law Review* 30:491–531.

Zeisel, H.; Kalven, H.; and Buchholz, B.
    1959   *Delay in the Court.* Boston: Little, Brown.

INDEX OF NAMES

INDEX OF CASES

INDEX OF SUBJECTS

OUT OF THIS
CENTURY

OUT OF THIS CENTURY

Confessions of an Art Addict

Peggy Guggenheim

Foreword by Gore Vidal

Introduction by Alfred H. Barr, Jr.

UNIVERSE BOOKS
New York

Published in the United States of America in 1979
by Universe Books
381 Park Avenue South, New York, N.Y. 10016

© 1946, 1960, 1979 by Peggy Guggenheim
Foreword © 1979 by Gore Vidal
"Venice" © 1962 by Ugo Mursia Editore

Book and jacket designed by Harry Chester Associates

Printed in the United States of America

79 80 81 82 83/10 9 8 7 6 5 4 3 2 1

NOTE: Only one person who is still alive and whose real identity the author and publisher prefer not to reveal is given a pseudonym in this book: Llewellyn.

Library of Congress Cataloging in Publication Data

Guggenheim, Marguerite, 1898-
Out of this century.

Autobiographical.
Updated and combined ed. of the author's Out of this
century and Confessions of an art addict, with new
material added.
Includes index.
1. Guggenheim, Marguerite, 1898-   2.   Art
patrons—United States—Biography. I.   Guggenheim,
Marguerite, 1898-   Confessions of an art addict.
II.   Title.
N5220.G886A36   1979   704'.7 [B]   78-68475
ISBN 0-87663-337-8

To James Johnson Sweeney

Apropos of the dedication of this book the following telephone conversation occurred:

Peggy Guggenheim: Sweeney, I have something very embarrassing to ask you. Would you mind if I dedicated my memoirs to you?

James Johnson Sweeney: On the contrary, I would be flattered and delighted.

Peggy Guggenheim: I hope you will not live to regret it.

James Johnson Sweeney: I hope you mean I'll live but not regret it.

Contents

List of Illustrations

Foreword by Gore Vidal

In the winter of 1945–46 I was a Warrant Officer in the Army of the United States, stationed at Mitchell Field, Long Island. I had just finished a first novel, *Williwaw,* based on my experiences as the first mate of an army freight supply ship in the Aleutians. Before I enlisted in the army at seventeen, I had lived in Washington, D.C. My family was political-military. I give these little personal facts to set the scene for my first meeting with Peggy Guggenheim.

In the early part of that winter I had met Anaïs Nin. I was twenty. She was forty-two. Our long and arduous relationship, or Relationship, began in the cold, as the sweet singer of Camelot would say. Anaïs was a shining figure who looked younger than she was; spoke in a soft curiously accented voice; told lies which for sheer beauty and strangeness were even better than the books she wrote—perhaps because what she wrote was always truthful if not true while what she said was intended only to please—herself as well as others.

"I shall take you to a party, *chéri,*" she announced. We were in the five-floor Greenwich Village walk-up where she lived with her husband (a banker who made movies and engravings and helped

Anaïs play at being a starving Bohemian). Anaïs always called me
"chéri" with a slightly droll inflection. Since I had not yet read
Colette, it was several years before I got the joke. But then she did
not get all my jokes either. So "chéri" and Anaïs went to Peggy
Guggenheim's house (described on page 259) and "chéri" has never
forgotten a single detail of that bright, magical (a word often used
in those days) occasion. In a sense, like the character in *Le Grand
Meaulnes,* I still think that somewhere, even now, in a side street
of New York City, that party is still going on and Anaïs is still
alive and young and "chéri" is very young indeed, and James Agee
is drinking too much and Laurence Vail is showing off some
bottles that he has painted having first emptied them into himself
as part of the creative process and André Breton is magisterial and
Léger looks as if he himself could have made one of those bits of
machinery that he liked to paint; and a world of color and humor
is still going on—could be entered again if only one had not
mislaid the address. Recently I came across an old telephone book.
I looked up Anaïs's number of thirty-five years ago. Watkins
something-or-other. I rang the number; half-expected her to
answer. If she had, I'd have asked her if it was still 1945 and she
would say, Of course. What year did I think it was? And I'd say,
No, it's 1979, and you're dead. ("*Chéri*" was never noted for his
tact.) And she would laugh and say, Not yet.

Not yet. Well, "yet" is here. And so is Peggy Guggenheim.
When I first saw her she was smiling—a bit sleepily. I remember
something odd hanging about her neck . . . . Barbarous jewelry?
My memory's less perfect than I thought. Actually, I remember
Agee's red-rimmed drinker's eyes and Vail's white streaming hair
rather more vividly than I do Peggy, who drifted effortlessly
through her own party, more like a guest than a hostess.

There. I am getting, as it were (as Henry James would say),
*some*thing of Peggy's aura then and now. Although she gave
parties and collected pictures and people, there was—and is—
something cool and impenetrable about her. She does not fuss.
She is capable of silence, a rare gift. She listens, an even rarer
gift. She is a master of the one-liner that deflates some notion or
trait of character or person. As I write this, I am trying to think of
a brilliant example; and fail. So perhaps it is simply the dry tone—
the brevity with which she delivers her epitaphs—that one
remembers with pleasure.

Peggy never liked Anaïs. For some reason, to this day, I have never asked her why. Last year, shortly before Peggy's eightieth birthday, we were sitting in the *salone* of her *palazzo* on Venice's Grand Canal (writing that sentence I begin to see Peggy Guggenheim as the last of Henry James's transatlantic heroines, Daisy Miller with rather more balls), and Peggy suddenly said, "Anaïs was very stupid, wasn't she?" It is the artful making of statements in the form of a question that sets apart Peggy's generation from the present age where there are no questions, only thundering self-serving assertions.

"No," I said. "She was shrewd. And she got exactly what she wanted. She set out to be a legendary figure." Legend was a word that Anaïs always used with reverence. "And she lived long enough to see herself a sort of heroine to the women's liberation movement."

"That may be shrewd," said Peggy—in the late afternoon light the sleepy narrow eyes suddenly shone like cats' eyes—"but it seems a stupid thing to want to be."

Now Peggy has been transformed by time (with a bit of help from her own shrewd nature) into a legend of the very same variety that Anaïs had in mind, a high romantic Murgeresque mind. Yet, at eighty, the legendary Peggy keeps a sharp eye on a world that is declining rather more rapidly than she is. After all, Venice is sinking, literally, beneath her unfinished white *palazzo*. If the ultimate dream of the solipsist is to take the world with him when he dies, Peggy may very well end by taking Venice out of this world and into her own world where that party still goes on and everyone is making something new and art smells not of the museum but of the maker's studio.

Last summer I asked, "How are you?" Polite but real question: she'd been in considerable pain with some disturbance of the arteries. "Oh," she said, "for someone dying, not bad."

It seems to me that these two memoirs—artful rather than artless, though the unknowing will not get the point to the art—reflect a world as lost now as the Watkins number that did not ring for lack of a digit. But since the prose in this volume is all Peggy's own, something has been salvaged. One hears in these lines the brisk yet drawling voice; sees the sudden swift side-long glance that often accompanies her swift judgments; takes pleasure if not in her actual self, in its shadow upon the page.

I last saw Peggy looking very shadowy on Italian television. Venice was celebrating her eightieth birthday; or at least that part of Venice which has not sunk into sloth as opposed to the Adriatic.

The camera came in for a very close shot of Peggy's handsome head. An off-camera voice asked her what she thought of today's Italian painters. The eyes shifted toward the unseen questioner; the half smile increased by a fraction. "Oh," she said, "they're very bad." Then always the Jamesian heroine, she added, "Aren't they?"

Consternation throughout Italy. The heroine of *The Golden Bowl* had shattered the bowl—and prevailed once again.

Introduction by Alfred H. Barr, Jr.

Courage and vision, generosity and humility, money and time, a strong sense of historical significance, as well as of esthetic quality—these are factors of circumstance and character which have made Peggy Guggenheim an extraordinary patron of twentieth-century art. On ground rocked by factionalism, she has stood firm, taking no sides, partisan only of the valuable revolution. Consequently we find in her collection works which are diametrically opposed in spirit and form, even though they may seem to be alike in their radical strangeness.

The collection is Peggy Guggenheim's most durable achievement as an art patron, but it is quite possibly not her most important. I have used the threadbare and somewhat pompous word "patron" with some misgivings. Yet it is precise. For a patron is not simply a collector who gathers works of art for his own pleasure or a philanthropist who helps artists or founds a public museum, but a person who feels responsibility toward both art and the artist together and has the means and will to act upon this feeling.

Peggy Guggenheim had no early interest in modern art. In fact, she loved and studied Italian Renaissance painting, particularly that of Venice. Berenson's books were her guide, and perhaps they confirmed that sense for the history of art which she carried into the twentieth century, the very point in time and taste at which her mentor stopped.

Then in the late 1930s, largely as an amateur's diversion, she opened an *avant-garde* gallery in London. Marcel Duchamp was her chief adviser (the same who in New York twenty years before had counseled Katherine Dreier in her creation of the pioneering *Société Anonyme*). Guggenheim Jeune, as she humorously called the enterprise, gave several excellent exhibitions, among them England's first one-man shows of Kandinsky, the first abstract expressionist, and Yves Tanguy, the surrealist painter. At the same time, the gallery gave their first exhibitions to young artists such as John Tunnard, the best of the new English abstract painters of the period. Yet these achievements seemed to her too impermanent.

Early in 1939 Peggy Guggenheim "had the idea of opening a modern museum in London," a project which must have seemed urgent, the director of the Tate Gallery having not long before declared for customs purposes that sculptures by Calder, Arp, Pevsner and others, which Guggenheim Jeune was importing for a show, were not works of art at all.

With her usual flair for enlisting the ablest help, she asked Herbert Read, later Sir Herbert, to become the director of this projected museum. Read, generally considered the leading English authority on modern art, was persuaded to resign his editorship of the highly respectable *Burlington Magazine* in order to assume his new and adventurous position. The patron and the director drew up an ideal list of works of art for the new museum—a list which was also to serve as the basis for the opening exhibition. A building was found, but before the lease could be signed World War II began and the dream faded, or better, was suspended.

In Paris during the winter of the "phony war" Peggy Guggenheim, only a little daunted, kept on adding to the collection, "buying a picture a day" with the advice of her friends Duchamp, Howard Putzel and Nellie van Doesburg. She even rented space for a gallery in the Place Vendôme, but meanwhile the cool war turned hot. The Brancusi *Bird in Space* was bought as the Germans were nearing Paris.

During the first year of the German occupation the collection was safeguarded in the Grenoble museum; but it was not shown there because the director feared the reprisals of the collaborationist Vichy régime. Finally, in the spring of 1941, the collection and its owner reached New York.

Thanks largely to the influx of refugee artists and writers from Europe, New York during the war supplanted occupied Paris as the art center of the Western world. Later, most of the Europeans returned, particularly to France; yet, in the postwar world, Paris seems clearly less preeminent and New York remained a contestant partly because of the rise of the most internationally respected group of painters so far produced in the United States. In their development, Peggy Guggenheim, as patron, played an important, and in some cases a crucial, role.

She had been frustrated in London, in Paris and in Grenoble, but in New York, thanks to its distance from the conflict, she was able temporarily to realize her vision. With the advice of the Surrealist painter Max Ernst and the poet André Breton, she continued to add to her collection and published a brilliant catalogue, *Art of This Century*, the title she also gave to her new gallery.

Art of This Century immediately became the center of the vanguard. Under the influence of Duchamp, Ernst and Breton, the surrealist tradition was strong but never exclusive. The great abstract painter, Piet Mondrian, was also welcome and took an active part as a member of the juries which chose the recurrent group shows of young American artists.

In the first "Spring Salon," 1943, three young painters stood out: William Baziotes, Robert Motherwell and Jackson Pollock. Within a year all three were launched by the gallery with one-man shows. Pollock's exhibition, with an enthusiastic catalogue preface by James Johnson Sweeney, won special admiration. Then, again with remarkable prescience, Art of This Century gave shows to Mark Rothko, Clyfford Still and others. I say prescience because although their work had not come to full maturity at that time, Rothko, Still, Baziotes, Motherwell, Pollock and two or three others are now recognized in the United States and increasingly in Europe as the chief pillars of the formidable new American school.

Early pictures by these painters, bought by Peggy Guggenheim out of their shows in the 1940s, may be seen in her collection today. Jackson Pollock, the most renowned of them, is represented by several works, though not by his largest, a mural commissioned by his patron for the lobby of her New York residence. Pollock she also helped financially, and when in 1947 Art of This Century closed she helped to place the artists in other galleries.

Today, in Venice, Peggy Guggenheim, her collection and her exhibition gallery continue to work. Visitors who study the collection with the sounds of the Grand Canal in their ears should know something of the history of the collector as patron—particularly Americans, who owe a special debt to their countrywoman, Peggy Guggenheim.

OUT OF THIS CENTURY

Chapter 1

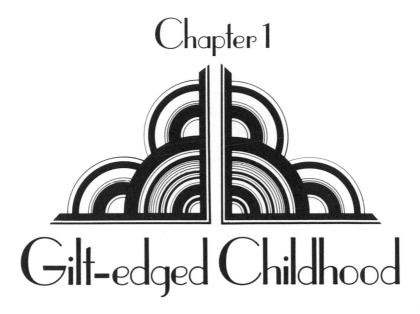

Gilt-edged Childhood

I have no memory. I always say to my friends, "Don't tell me anything you don't want repeated. I just can't remember not to." Invariably I forget and I repeat everything.

In 1923 I began to write my memoirs. They began like this: "I come from two of the best Jewish families. One of my grandfathers was born in a stable like Jesus Christ or, rather, over a stable in Bavaria, and my other grandfather was a peddler." I don't seem to have gotten very far with this book. Maybe I had nothing to say, or possibly I was too young for the task which I had set myself. Now I feel I am ripe for it. By waiting too long I may forget everything I have somehow managed to remember.

If my grandfathers started life modestly they ended it sumptuously. My stable-born grandfather, Mr. Seligman, came to America in steerage, with forty dollars in his pocket and contracted smallpox on board ship. He began his fortune by being a roof shingler and later by making uniforms for the Union Army in the Civil War. Later he became a renowned banker and president of Temple Emanu-El. Socially he got way beyond my other grandfather, Mr. Guggenheim the peddler, who was born in Lengnau in German Switzerland. Mr. Guggenheim far surpassed

Mr. Seligman in amassing an enormous fortune and buying up most of the copper mines of the world, but he never succeeded in attaining Mr. Seligman's social distinction. In fact, when my mother married Benjamin Guggenheim the Seligmans considered it a *mésalliance*. To explain that she was marrying into the well known smelting family, they sent a cable to their kin in Europe saying, "Florette engaged Guggenheim smelter." This became a great family joke, as the cable misread "Guggenheim smelt her."

By the time I was born the Seligmans and the Guggenheims were extremely rich. At least the Guggenheims were, and the Seligmans hadn't done so badly. My grandfather, James Seligman, was a very modest man who refused to spend money on himself and underfed his trained nurse. He lived sparsely and gave everything to his children and grandchildren. He remembered all our birthdays and, although he did not die until ninety-three, he never failed to make out a check on these occasions. The checks were innumerable, as he had eleven children and fifteen grandchildren.

Most of his children were peculiar, if not mad. That was because of the bad inheritance they received from my grandmother. My grandfather finally had to leave her. She must have been objectionable. My mother told me that she could never invite young men to her home without a scene from her mother. My grandmother went around to shopkeepers and, as she leaned over the counter, asked them confidentially, "When do you think my husband last slept with me?"

My mother's brothers and sisters were very eccentric. One of my favorite aunts was an incurable soprano. If you happened to meet her on the corner of Fifth Avenue while waiting for a bus, she would open her mouth wide and sing scales trying to make you do as much. She wore her hat hanging off the back of her head or tilted over one ear. A rose was always stuck in her hair. Long hatpins emerged dangerously, not from her hat, but from her hair. Her trailing dresses swept up the dust of the streets. She invariably wore a feather boa. She was an excellent cook and made beautiful tomato jelly. Whenever she wasn't at the piano, she could be found in the kitchen or reading the ticker-tape. She was an inveterate gambler. She had a strange complex about germs and was forever wiping her furniture with Lysol. But she had such extraordinary charm that I really loved her. I cannot say her husband felt as much. After he had fought with her for over thirty years, he tried to kill her and one of her sons by hitting them with a golf club. Not succeeding, he rushed to the reservoir where he drowned himself with heavy weights tied to his feet.

Another aunt, who resembled an elephant more than a human being, at a late age in life conceived the idea that she had had a love affair with an apothecary. Although this was completely imaginary, she felt so much remorse that she became melancholic and had to be put in a nursing home.

My most attractive uncle was a very distinguished gentleman of the old school. Being separated from his wife who was as rich as he, he decided to live in great simplicity in two small rooms and spend all his money on fur coats, which he gave away to girls. Almost any girl could have one for the asking. He wore the *Légion d'honneur* but would never tell us why he had been decorated.

Another uncle lived on charcoal which he had been eating for many years, and as a result his teeth were black. In a zinc-lined pocket he carried pieces of cracked ice which he sucked all the time. He drank whiskey before breakfast and ate almost no food. He gambled heavily, as did most of my aunts and uncles, and when he was without funds he threatened to commit suicide to get more money out of my grandfather. He had a mistress whom he concealed in his room. No one was allowed to visit him until he finally shot himself, and then he could no longer keep the family out. At the funeral my grandfather greatly shocked his children by walking up the aisle with his dead son's mistress on his arm. They all said, "How can Pa do that?"

There was one miserly uncle who never spent a cent. He arrived in the middle of meals saying he didn't want a thing and then ate everything in sight. After dinner he put on a frightening act for his nieces. It was called "the snake." It terrified and delighted us. By placing lots of chairs together in a row and then wriggling along them on his stomach he really produced the illusion. The other two uncles were nearly normal. One of them spent all his time washing himself and the other one wrote plays that were never produced. The latter was a darling and my favorite.

My other grandfather, Meyer Guggenheim, lived happily with his stepmother's daughter to whom he was married. They brought up an even larger, if less eccentric, family than the Seligmans.

There were seven brothers and three sisters. They produced twenty-three grandchildren When my grandmother died my grandfather was looked after by his cook. She must have been his mistress. I remember seeing her weep copious tears because my grandfather vomited. My one recollection of this gentleman is of his driving around New York in a sleigh with horses. He was unaccompanied and wore a coat with a sealskin collar and a cap to match. He died when I was very young.

I was born in New York City on West Sixty-ninth Street. I don't remember anything about this. My mother told me that while the nurse was filling her hot water bottle, I rushed into the world with my usual speed and screamed like a cat. I was preceded by one sister, Benita, who was almost three years older than I. She was the great love of my early life, in fact of my entire immature life. But maybe that has never ended.

We soon moved to a house on East Seventy-second Street near the entrance to the Park. Our neighbors were the Stillmans and the Rockefellers. Opposite us lived President Grant's widow. My father remodeled this house and made it very elegant. Here my second sister Hazel was born when I was almost five. I was fiendishly jealous of her.

There is nothing about this house that does not still arouse my most poignant memories. In fact for years I dreamed about it. To enter our new domain you had to pass not one but two glass doors with a vestibule in between. Then you found yourself in a little marble entrance with a fountain. On the wall was a stuffed eagle with chains. My father had shot it himself, though it was a legal offense. He had done this in the Adirondacks, where we had a camp and went in the late summer.

Behind this hallway, which had a marble staircase, there was a door which led to the elevator. In 1941, when I returned to New York after an absence of many years, I went back to this house to visit an aunt who lived there. When we were in the elevator my daughter of sixteen, who was accompanying me, suddenly burst out with, "Mama, you lived in this house when you were a little girl?" I modestly replied "Yes," and to convince her added, "This is where Hazel was born." My daughter gave me a surprised look and concluded with this statement: "Mama, how you have come down in the world." From then on the butler, who was ushering us upstairs, looked upon me with suspicion and rarely admitted

me to the house. However, my memories alone warranted my
admission.

On the reception floor there was a high-ceilinged dining room
with panels and six indifferent tapestries. In the back was a little
conservatory filled with plants. In the center of this floor was a
reception room with a huge tapestry of Alexander the Great
entering Rome in triumph. In front of it was a double-trayed tea
table with a monstrous silver tea set. It was in this room that my
mother gave a weekly tea party to the most boring ladies of the
haute Jewish bourgeoisie, which I was forced reluctantly to
attend.

In the front of the house was our Louis Seize parlor with huge
mirrors, tapestries on the wall and tapestried furniture. On the
floor was a bearskin rug which had an enormous red mouth and a
red tongue. Sometimes the tongue broke loose, and, when it was
detached, it had the most revolting appearance. The animal's
teeth were forever being mended as they also came out. There was
also a grand piano. One night I remember hiding under this piano
and weeping in the dark. My father had banished me from the
table because, at the tender age of seven, I had said to him, "Papa,
you must have a mistress as you stay out so many nights."

The center of the house was surmounted by a glass dome that
admitted the daylight. At night it was lit by a suspended lamp.
Around this was a large circular winding staircase. It commenced
on the reception floor and ended on the fourth floor where I lived.
I recall the exact tune which my father had invented and which
he whistled to lure me when he came home at night and ascended
the stairs on foot. I adored my father and rushed to meet him.

The third floor belonged to my parents. In the front was a
library with red velvet paneled walls and large glass bookcases that
contained the classics. Here there was another fur rug, a tiger
skin. On the walls were portraits of my four grandparents. This
room, as well as every room in the house, had cream colored lace
curtains at the windows.

It was in this room that I sat at a large Louis Quinze table with
a glass top and was fed by a maid whose sole duty at that time was
to see that I ate. I never had any appetite. When my tears were of
no avail, I protested by vomiting and the feeding came to an end.

In the back of the house my mother had her room. It was
preceded by a little alcove containing cupboards, which space she

needed for her large wardrobe. The bedroom was covered with pink silk and had twin beds. The furniture was mahogany with brass incrustations. On her bureau, which was much too high for her to use as a dressing table, was a set of silver brushes and bottles. There was a long cheval glass, in front of which my mother sat to have her hair brushed by her French maid or by a special hairbrusher who came in for that purpose. This was the hour that I was allowed to play in my mother's room. Behind her room was my father's dressing room.

Upstairs my sisters and I had a whole floor to ourselves until my grandfather Seligman came to live with us. My room was next to a steep and dark staircase that led up to the servants' quarters. It frightened me and I had nightmares about it.

I also have poignant memories of the servants' quarters which were less than adequate, and seemed to be distinctly in contrast to our elegant rooms. The men-servants' rooms were the worst of all. They were not on the top floor, which was bad enough: they were in the back of the house on queer little landings along the servants' back stairs. The kitchen was below the ground floor and, in consequence, very dark.

My mother gave many dinner parties and I remember on one of these occasions the nurse rushed downstairs to call my mother away from the table. She had heard a baby cry in the kitchen-maid's room and upon investigating the matter she had found a newly born infant hidden in a trunk, strangled in its own navel cord. The girl had come to our house only a few days before to take refuge. She had given birth alone and then murdered her illegitimate offspring. Our family doctor declared her insane to save her from prison.

My childhood was excessively unhappy: I have no pleasant memories of any kind. It seems to me now that it was one long protracted agony. When I was very young I had no friends. I didn't go to school until I was fifteen. Instead I studied under private tutors at home. There was one period when I took lessons with a girl called Dulcie Sulzberger. She had two brothers who fascinated me, one in particular, Marion.

My father insisted that his children be well-educated and saw to it that we acquired "good taste." He himself was keen on art and bought a lot of paintings. In Munich he had us painted by

Lenbach but since I was only four at the time I do not remember anything about it now. My memory goes back only to Hazel's birth. Lenbach painted me in a Vandyck costume and, for some strange reason, gave me brown eyes instead of green, and red hair instead of chestnut. With Benita he was less fanciful. Perhaps because she was so beautiful, he portrayed her as she really was, with brown hair and brown eyes. I have two portraits, one of myself, and the other one of Benita and me, in which I appear with golden hair. These are the greatest treasures of my past.

The only toys I can remember were a rocking horse with an enormous rump and a doll's house containing bearskin rugs and beautiful crystal chandeliers. The doll's house must have left me with a fearful nostalgia, because for years I tried to reproduce it for my daughter. I spent months papering walls and buying objects to furnish her house. In fact I still can't resist buying toys. I immediately give them away to children but I must buy them for my own delight. I also remember a glass cabinet filled with tiny hand-carved ivory and silver furniture, which had an old-fashioned sculptured brass key. I kept the cabinet locked and allowed no one to touch my treasures.

My strongest memories are of Central Park. When I was very young my mother used to take me driving there in an electric brougham. There was a certain rock on the East Drive that resembled a panther about to spring. I called it "the cat," and whenever we passed it, I pretended to telephone to it to say hello or to warn it of our arrival. For a telephone I used the speaking tube of our brougham. Later I rode in the Park in a little foot-pedaled automobile. The Mall was the perfect place for this. In the Ramble I climbed rocks all by myself, while my governess waited below. In the winter I was forced to go ice skating, which caused me to suffer agonies. My ankles were too weak and my circulation much too bad. I shall never forget the excruciating pain I felt from the thawing of my toes, when returning from the lake I clung to a stove which was in a little cabin intended for skaters.

All this left me with such painful memories that I have carefully avoided the Park ever since. In fact I refused to visit it when I came back to New York in the early 1940s. However, one hot summer night Alfred Barr insisted on taking me there. I tried to find all the haunts of my childhood, but everything was changed. Only the Ramble with its old castle remained, true to my childhood memories.

Not only was my childhood excessively lonely and sad, but it was also filled with torments. I once had a nurse who threatened to cut out my tongue if I dared to repeat to my mother the foul things she said to me. In desperation and fear I told my mother and the nurse was dismissed at once. Also I was not at all strong and my parents were perpetually fussing about my health. They imagined I had all sorts of illnesses and were forever taking me to doctors. At one period of my life, when I was about ten, they decided I had some intestinal disturbance and found a doctor who ordered me to have colonic irrigations. These were administered by Hazel's nurse and, as she was quite unqualified for her task, the result was catastrophic. I got an acute attack of appendicitis and was rushed off to the hospital at midnight and operated on. For days I was kept in ignorance of the operation, since they thought I was too young to be told. However, I did not believe their silly stories and insisted that my stomach had been cut open.

Soon after this, my sister Benita developed the whooping cough and we had to be separated lest I catch it and cough open my newly healed, and let me add, enormous wound. My mother took a house in Lakewood, New Jersey, for herself and Benita, and I was sent to a hotel with a trained nurse. Needless to say I passed a lonely winter and only occasionally was I permitted to speak to Benita on the street and from a great distance. My mother had several nieces who were marriageable and she was perpetually giving house parties for them while she shut poor Benita up in a wing of the house. As a result Benita became melancholic. I must have been very precocious and spoiled, since I was allowed to visit my mother and entertain her visitors. I fell in love with one of them. His name was Max Rossbach and he taught me to play pool.

Not long after this I had a bad accident while riding in Central Park. As I passed under a bridge some boys on roller skates overhead made such a noise that my horse bolted. My lady riding teacher was as incapable as I of stopping the beast. I lost my seat, fell to the ground and was dragged for quite a distance. I could not disengage my foot from the stirrup and my skirt caught on the pommel. Had I been riding astride this never would have occurred. I not only hurt my foot but I seriously injured my mouth. My jaw was broken in two places and I lost a front tooth. A policeman, finding the tooth in the mud, returned it to me in a letter, and the next day the dentist, after disinfecting it, pushed it up into its original position. This did not end my troubles. My jaw had to be set. During the operation a great battle took place among the attending surgeons. Finally, one of them triumphed over the other and shook my poor jaw into shape. The vanquished dentist, who was called Buxbaum, never got over this. He felt he had superior rights over my mouth, as he had been straightening my teeth for years. The only good that came out of all this was that it put an end to the agonies I had been suffering in the process of being beautified. Now that had to end. The first danger incurred was the possibility of being blood-poisoned. When that passed, the only risk I ran was of getting hit in the mouth and losing my tooth again before it was firmly implanted. In those days my sole opponents were tennis balls, so that when I played tennis I conceived the bright idea of tying a tea strainer in front of my mouth. Anyone seeing me must have thought I had hydrophobia. When it was all over, my father received a bill for seven thousand five hundred dollars from the dentist who had never admitted his defeat. My father persuaded this gentleman reluctantly to accept two thousand.

In spite of all the trouble I went through to preserve the tooth, I knew it could not remain with me for more than ten years, after which time its root would be completely absorbed and the tooth would have to be replaced with a porcelain one. I was prophetic in gauging its life, may I say, almost to the day. After ten years I made an appointment to have it replaced before it fell out, which it did exactly two days before the dentist expected me.

One of my first great passions was for the actor William Gillette. I went to all his matinées and virtually screamed to warn him when I thought he was going to be shot by an enemy in the play *Secret Service*.

I had taken to riding again as soon as I was allowed to after my accident, but this time I took no chances. Not only did I have a male teacher but I also learned to ride astride. At fourteen I fell in love with my riding teacher. He was a fascinating Irishman who flirted with all of his pupils.

Benita was the only companion of my childhood and I therefore developed a great love for her. We were perpetually chaperoned by

French governesses, but they were always changing, so that I can barely remember them. Hazel, being so much younger, had a nurse and lived a distinctly separate life. I don't remember my mother at all at this age.

When I was five or six my father began to have mistresses. A certain trained nurse lived in our house in order to massage my father's head, since he suffered from neuralgia. According to my mother, this nurse was the cause of all her troubles in life as she somehow influenced my father for the bad, without actually ever having been his mistress. It took my mother years to rid herself of the poisonous presence of this woman in our household, for my father depended on her so much for the massage. However, we finally got rid of her, but it was too late. From then on my father had a whole series of mistresses. My mother took it as a great offense that my aunts remained friendly with this nurse and had long feuds with them for befriending her. All this affected my childhood. I was perpetually being dragged into my parents' troubles and it made me precocious.

My father always called me Maggie; only much later did I become Peggy. He had beautiful jewelry made for us which he designed himself. In honor of my name, Marguerite, he once presented me with a little bracelet that looked like a daisy chain, made of pearls and diamonds. My mother received more substantial presents, among them a magnificent string of pearls.

I adored my father because he was fascinating and handsome, and because he loved me. But I suffered very much as he made my mother unhappy, and sometimes I fought with him over it. Every summer he took us to Europe. We went to Paris and to London where my mother visited hundreds of French and English Seligmans. We also went to fashionable watering places. My mother was very mean about tipping and on one occasion I remember to my great embarrassment seeing all our luggage chalked with crosses. When we were leaving Trouville the hotel porters had marked them as a sign of warning to the porters of the next hotel, our future victims.

My father engaged a lady called Mrs. Hartman to teach us art. We brought her to Europe with us and it was her duty to make us cultured. She took us to the Louvre, to the Carnavalet and to the châteaux of the Loire. She taught us French history and also introduced us to Dickens, Thackeray, Scott and George Eliot. She also gave us a complete course in Wagner's operas. I am sure Mrs. Hartman did her best to stimulate our imaginations, but personally, at that time, I was more interested in other things. For one, I was infatuated with my father's friend Rudi. He was a typical roué and I can't imagine now why he fascinated me. I was so much enamored of him that I wrote mad letters about my passion, in which I said my body was nailed to the fire of the cross. When Rudi married one of my cousins whom my mother had brought to Europe with her, and whose unfortunate marriage I fear she and my father arranged, I wept bitter tears and felt completely let down. I complained, saying he had no right to trifle with the affections of two women at once. At this time I must have been about eleven.

Besides this exalted life which I seem to have led, I had a hobby for something much more material—I collected elegant little wax models and dressed them in the most fashionable of clothes, which I created and executed myself. This was inspired by the fact that we were summering in Trouville where all the ladies and the courtesans were so chic.

One day when I was having tea with Benita and my governess at Rumpelmeyer's in Paris, I found myself fascinated by a woman at the next table. I could not take my eyes off her. She seemed to react in the same way to us. Months later, after I had been tormenting my governess to tell me who my father's mistress was, she finally said, "You know her." Like a flash the face of the woman at Rumpelmeyer's came to my mind and when questioned my governess admitted I was right.

This woman was called the Countess Taverny. She was neither pretty nor young. I never understood my father's infatuation for her. But she had the same agreeable quality (maybe sensuous) of his trained nurse. The Countess was dark and resembled a monkey. She had ugly teeth which my mother used to refer to with contempt as "black." We met this woman everywhere in Paris. It was most awkward. One day at the dressmaker Lanvin, my mother, accompanied by Benita and me, walked into a room where Countess Taverny was seated. My mother rushed out of the room and we followed her. The Lanvin staff, with correct French understanding, gave us another *salle* to ourselves.

The Countess, as we used to call her, or C.T. as my father referred to her for short, meaning Countess Taverny, wore the most elegant clothes. She had one suit which was made entirely of baby lamb fur. One day when we were taking our morning walk in the Bois on the Avenue des Acacias, we met the Countess wearing this costume. My mother protested to my father regarding his extravagance. To console her he gave her money to have the same suit made for herself. Being a good business woman she accepted the money but instead she invested it in stocks and bonds.

Countess Taverny had been preceded by another lady. This lady, whom I never saw, nearly succeeded in marrying my father. In fact my mother had come to the point of divorcing him. But the whole Guggenheim family came in groups and individually, begging her to reconsider her decision. We had streams of visitors all day long. Their one idea was to avoid this catastrophe. Finally my mother gave in. I don't know when the affair ended, but I do know that the disappointed mistress received a large consolation prize and for many years part of my income went to her regularly, twice a year.

Countess Taverny did not last long and was followed by a young blond singer. She was with my father when he was drowned on the *Titanic* in 1912 and was among the survivors brought back to New York.

In 1911 my father had more or less freed himself from us. He had left his brothers' business and had his own in Paris. This was a move he doubtless made to be able to live a freer life, but its consequences were more far-reaching than he ever realized. By leaving his brothers and starting his own business, he forfeited his claims to an enormous fortune. He had an apartment in Paris and was interested in or owned a concern which built the elevators for the Eiffel Tower. In the spring of 1912 he was finally to return to us after an eight months absence. He had a passage on some steamship which was canceled because of a strike of the stokers. By this mere accident of fate he was to lose his life: he booked a place on the ill-fated *Titanic*.

On April 14th, as people came out of the Metropolitan Opera House, they were greeted with shouts of "Extra!" announcing the dramatic sinking of this gigantic liner on her maiden voyage. In order to make a record trip for the White Star Line, Bruce Ismay, the president of the company, who was himself on board, and the captain ignored the warning of icebergs and forged their way ahead completely disregarding the danger. The *Titanic* rushed to her doom. The first iceberg she encountered ripped her bottom open. Within an hour she sank, stern and bow going under together after a terrific explosion which split her in two. There were only enough life boats for a quarter of the people on board. Others who could swim were frozen in the icy water before Captain Rostrom of the S.S. *Carpathia* could come to their rescue. Seven hundred people were saved out of twenty-eight hundred. The world was shaken by this disaster. Everyone waited breathlessly for the *Carpathia* to dock to find out who were the lucky survivors. We wired Captain Rostrom to find out if my father was on his ship. He wired back, "No." For some reason I was told this while my mother was kept in ignorance until the last minute. Then two of my cousins went down to meet the survivors. They met my father's mistress.

With my father there died a lovely young Egyptian, Victor Giglio, who was his secretary. He had had a hard time in the past and was happy to have been engaged by my father, thinking his troubles were ended. I was attracted to this beautiful boy, but my father did not approve of my ardor. A steward of the *Titanic,* a survivor, came to see us to deliver a message from my father. He said that my father and his secretary had dressed in evening clothes to meet their death. They had wanted to die as gentlemen, which they certainly did, by gallantly giving their places to women and children.

My father's body was never recovered and was therefore not buried in Halifax with those that the sea washed up. Many other well-known men were lost on the *Titanic,* among them Harry Elkins Widener, John B. Thayer, John Jacob Astor, Edgar Meyer, and Isidor Straus with his wife who refused to leave him. In those days before World War I and before the sinking of the *Lusitania,* the sinking of the *Titanic* was considered a worldwide tragedy. Naturally there was an inquest, but the captain had committed suicide, or rather he had had the decency to go down with his boat. From then on we avoided the White Star Line like the plague.

At the time of my father's death we were living in the St. Regis Hotel—we had rented our house to one of my aunts—where we had enormous apartments. In those days the St. Regis Hotel was the stronghold of the Guggenheim family. My uncle Daniel had a whole floor beneath us. Every Friday evening there was a family reunion, when my uncles would get together to talk business while my aunts retired to a corner to discuss clothes. Needless to say they had plenty to recount on this score, since they all went to the most expensive dressmakers in New York.

After my father's death I became religious. I attended the services in Temple Emanu-El regularly, and took great dramatic pleasure in standing up for the *Kaddish* (the service for the dead). My father's death affected me greatly. It took me months to get over the terrible nightmare of the *Titanic,* and years to get over the loss of my father. In a sense I really have never recovered, as I suppose I have been searching for a father ever since.

When my father died, he left his business affairs in an awful muddle. Not only had he lost a vast fortune by discontinuing his partnership with his brothers, but the money he should have had, some eight million dollars, he had lost in Paris. The small amount that was left was tied up in stocks that were yielding no interest and were at such a low ebb that they could not be sold. However, my mother did not know this and we continued living on the same scale. My uncles, the Guggenheims, very gallantly advanced us any funds we needed, keeping us in supreme ignorance. Finally my mother discovered the truth and took drastic steps to end the false situation. To begin with she started spending her own personal fortune. We moved to a cheaper apartment with fewer servants. She sold her paintings, her tapestries and her jewelry. She managed very well, and although we were never poor, from that time on I had a complex about no longer being a real Guggenheim. I felt like a poor relative and suffered great humiliation thinking how inferior I was to the rest of the family. My grandfather Seligman died four years after my father, and then my mother inherited a small fortune from him. We immediately reimbursed my father's brothers. After seven years my uncles settled my father's estate. They had finally put things into such shape that by advancing their own money my sisters and I each inherited four hundred and fifty thousand dollars and my mother slightly more. Half of what I received was placed in trust and my uncles insisted that I voluntarily do the same with the other half.

Of course we went into mourning. I felt important and self-conscious in black. In the summer, to my great relief, I was allowed to wear white. We went to Allenhurst on the New Jersey coast, which was the summer resort of most of the Jewish families we knew. Not actually Allenhurst but the places next to it, Deal Beach, Elberon and West End, were all built up with the homes of the Jewish bourgeoisie. It was the ugliest place in the world. Not one tree or bush grew on this barren coast. The only flowers I remember were rambler roses, nasturtiums and hydrangeas, and since then I have not been able to endure them. My grandfather had a family mansion in West End, in which all his children were born, including my mother, the youngest. It was in this hideous Victorian house that my grandfather, at the age of ninety-three, died during World War I.

My Guggenheim uncles all owned the most magnificent houses on this coast. One uncle had an Alsatian wife and with her French taste they built a house which was an exact copy of the Petit Trianon at Versailles. Another uncle had a magnificent Italian villa with marble Pompeian inner courts and beautiful grottoes and sunken gardens. Compared to these my grandfather Seligman's house was a modest affair. It was completely surrounded by two porches, one on each floor. The porches were covered with rocking chairs where the entire family sat and rocked all day. It was so ugly in its Victorian perfection that it was fascinating. The culminating point was the family portraits. My mother and her two sisters and five brothers had all been painted as children, in costumes of the period made of black velvet with white lace collars. In their hands they carried birds, Bibles or hoops. They looked so heavy-eyed in these portraits that they were unmistakably Semitic.

As most of this coast was inhabited by Jewish families, it became a sort of ghetto. In Allenhurst, which was anti-Semitic, there was a hotel opposite us that would not admit Jews. During the summer, to our great delight, it burned down while we stood watching. Every summer that we did not spend in Europe we spent on this horrible coast. We bathed in the Atlantic in the wild breakers and played tennis and rode horses. However, I much preferred Europe and the next year, 1913, we persuaded my mother to take us back.

When war broke out in 1914 we were again in England, visiting one of my mother's cousins, Sir Charles Seligman. I remember shocking him very much by my careless and extravagant appetite. He was worried about the lack of food that would result from the war, and I had asked for some more beef to finish up my mustard.

Chapter 2

Virginity

During my sixteenth summer I became conscious of sex. It was very upsetting and frightening. It began pleasantly when I fell in love with Freddy Singer, a nephew of the Singer Sewing Machine people. We were all living in a hotel in Ascot. His brother fell in love with Benita, so we had great fun dancing and playing tennis together. But after that I had a disagreeable fright about sex. I was visiting one of my Seligman grand-aunts in Kent. In her household was a young medical student from Munich, who was an American by birth and therefore not interned. I felt he wanted to seduce me and I think he was amused by my fear and played up to the role of seducer. I have never been so terrified in my life. Later when I met him in New York he resumed his role again, but this time he wanted to marry me. I convinced him to marry my cousin instead. She was my best friend and he seemed to be in love with both of us. I was then in school and my cousin was a mature woman fifteen years older than our suitor. The marriage was successful and they had lovely twin daughters.

During the war I finally was sent to school. The Jacoby School was a private school on the West Side for young Jewish girls, and I would walk there every day through Central Park, since we lived in an apartment on Fifth Avenue and Fifty-eighth Street. But after a few weeks I developed whooping cough and bronchitis, and had to spend the winter in bed. I was lonely and neglected, as it was the year of Benita's début, and my mother was very busy with her. Somehow I managed to do all my homework alone and kept up with the school course and passed all my exams. I am not at all intellectual and it was a great effort. But I did like reading, and I read constantly in those days. I read Ibsen, Hardy, Turgenev, Chekhov, Oscar Wilde, Tolstoy, Strindberg, Barrie, George Meredith and Bernard Shaw.

My second year at school was slightly more fortunate than my first. I managed to attend regularly, with the exception of a short period when I contracted the measles. We had a busy winter preparing to produce *Little Women* as our graduation play. Mrs. Quaife, our wonderful dramatic teacher, conceived a life-long affection for me, introduced me to Browning's poems and gave me the rôle of Amy in the play. When I left school I renounced the idea of going to college. This was due to Benita's influence. She talked me out of it, she said I had done the same to her. For years I regretted it.

During my second school year I began to have a social life. I organized a little dance club with my schoolmates and some other girls. To cover the expenses of a monthly ball, we all contributed money. We were permitted to invite one or two boys to come and dance with us. We made a list of the desirable young men in our Jewish circles and then I held a mock auction sale and auctioned them off to the highest bidder, who then had the privilege of inviting him. These parties were gay and really not at all stuffy.

About the time I graduated from school I began a great friendship with a beautiful girl called Fay Lewisohn. She resembled Geraldine Farrar, which was most appropriate, as her home was the center of gatherings of the Metropolitan Opera Company. My feeling for Fay was much greater than hers for me and I now think that mine was unconsciously of the order of *Mädchen in Uniform*. Maybe Fay suspected this. In any case she was interested in young men.

Fay's mother, Mrs. Adele Lewisohn, and her grandmother, Mrs. Randolph Guggenheimer, were charming hostesses. They entertained lavishly not only singers, but also all the intellectuals of New York. Unfortunately Fay and I were too young to take

part. Or rather, Fay hated this as much as I hated being dragged
into my mother's social life. They lived on Fifth Avenue in a
house with a strange balcony on the top floor bearing stone figures
of women resembling caryatids. Mrs. Lewisohn admired me, as I
did her; and years later when I met her in Paris she told me how
suitable a friend she had considered me for Fay and regretted that
her daughter did not appreciate me as much as she did. She
considered me a serious-minded girl compared with Fay who loved
only pleasure.

During the summer of 1915, I received my first kiss. It was
from a young man who took me out driving every night in my
mother's car. He invariably borrowed our automobile to drive
home afterward and would bring it back every morning at seven on
his way to the station, when he went to New York to his job. My
mother disapproved of my suitor because he had no money. She
controlled herself until the night when he kissed me for the first
and last time. We were in the garage and as he leaned over me, by
mistake he put his arm on the horn. This awoke my mother. She
greeted us with a storm of abuse and screamed at us, "Does he
think my car is a taxi?" Needless to say, I never saw the young
man again. My mother felt triumphant, but several years later
Fate proved her, according to her standards, entirely in the
wrong, as this young man fell heir to a million dollars.

After graduating from school I was rather at a loose end. I
continued reading with my voracious appetite and studied courses
in history, economics and Italian. I had one teacher called Lucile
Kohn, who had a stronger influence over me than any other
woman has ever had. In fact, because of her, my life took a
completely new turn. It didn't happen suddenly; it was a gradual
process. She had a passion for bettering the world. I became
radical and finally emerged from the stifling atmosphere in which
I had been raised. It took me a long time to liberate myself, and
although it was not for several years that anything occurred, the
seeds that she sowed sprouted, branching out in directions that
even she never dreamed of. Her interests were entirely political
and economic. She had complete faith in Woodrow Wilson. But
when she was disappointed by his inability to carry through his
program she joined the labor movement. I did not follow her,
being by then in Europe, but I sent her vast sums of money. Later
she told me that I had altered her life, too, by sending her this

money. She acquired an important standing in the labor movement and worked fervently for it after that time.

During the war I learned to knit. Once I started, I never stopped. I took my knitting everywhere with me, to the table, to concerts, even to bed. I became so adept I could make a sock in one day. I remember my Grandfather Seligman greatly disapproving of my speed, which he claimed made me spend too much money on wool. I fear his parsimoniousness surpassed his patriotism.

As we could not go to Europe during the war, my mother took us up to Canada one summer. We motored all the way. During the entire trip I knitted and missed most of the beautiful scenery. However, I managed to look up occasionally and felt well recompensed for my sacrifice. In Canada we made great friends with the Canadian soldiers who were stationed near Quebec. Benita and our friend, Ethel Frank, and I had great fun with them. On the way home we were politely but firmly turned out of a hotel in Vermont for being Jewish. As the state law forbids hotel keepers to refuse lodgings overnight, we were allowed to remain until morning and then we were informed that our rooms were rented. This gave me a new inferiority complex.

Later I went to a business school to learn stenography and typing. I thought I might get a war job. However, I was too stupid to keep up with the girls who were all of the working class and who made me feel like a rank outsider. I soon gave it up.

In 1916 I made my début. I gave a big afternoon Leap Year party in the Ritz Tent Room. From then on I went to many parties and was taken out in the evening by young men. I found this sort of life idiotic, though I was a good dancer and loved dancing. The whole thing seemed to me artificial and I never met anyone I could talk to seriously.

Eventually, we moved to 270 Park Avenue. My mother permitted me to choose furniture for my bedroom, and I was allowed to charge it to her. But unfortunately I disobeyed her and went shopping on the sacred Day of Atonement, the great Jewish holiday *Yom Kippur*. I had been expressly warned not to do this and I was heavily punished for my sin. As a result my mother refused to pay for the furniture. I was left stranded with this large debt which I had to take out of my allowance. Benita came to my rescue and supported me for weeks. Among many other things, I remember going for a beauty treatment to Elizabeth Arden's at Benita's expense.

Ever since my earliest childhood every day at twelve sharp a sad old lady with a lisp called Mrs. Mack came to our house. She was a shopper and had a little book in which she would note any object that was required in our household. One day it was three yards of lace, a bottle of glue or six pairs of stockings. Another day it might be a box of soap, sewing silk or a green feather for a hat. At Christmas time she was most occupied when she came with a much larger notebook and found out confidentially, in turn, what each of my sisters and I would like for presents from Mrs. Dan, Mrs. Sol, Mrs. Simon, Mrs. Murray, etc., as she called my Guggenheim aunts. Then she proceeded to the shops where she had charge accounts and received ten percent discount on her purchases. As she invariably bought everything wrong, most of her life was spent in exchanging things. When we shopped for ourselves we did much better and she benefited just the same because we charged everything to her.

In 1918, I took a war job. I sat at a desk and tried to help our newly-made officers buy uniforms and other things at reduced rates. I had to give advice and write out many cards of introduction. I shared this job with my friend Ethel Frank, who had been my most intimate school companion. When she fell sick, I did all her work and mine, and the long hours proved too strenuous for me. I collapsed. It began by my not sleeping. Then I stopped eating. I got thinner and thinner and more and more nervous, I went to a psychologist and asked him if he thought I was losing my mind. He replied, "Are you sure you have a mind to lose?" Funny as his reply was, I think my question was quite legitimate. I used to pick up every match I found and stayed awake at night worrying about the houses that would burn because I had neglected to pick up some particular match. Let me add that all these had been lit, but I feared there might be one virgin among them. In despair my mother engaged Miss Holbrook, my dead grandfather's nurse, to look after me. She accompanied me everywhere. I wandered around, revolving in my brain all the problems of Raskolnikov, thinking how much I resembled this hero of Dostoevsky's *Crime and Punishment*. Finally Miss Holbrook, by sheer force of will, made me think of other things. Little by little I became normal again. During this period I was engaged to a flying officer who was still in this country. I had several fiancés during the war as we were always entertaining soldiers and sailors.

In the spring of 1919 Benita married Edward Mayer, a young American aviator who had just come back from Italy. The whole thing was most unfortunate. Since 1914 she had been in love with a Russian baron she had met in Europe. For some reason or other, which I could never make out, this Russian, although he seemed to love her, never came to the point of actually proposing to her. During the war he was attached to his legation in Washington and we saw him often in New York.

However, in a moment of weak-mindedness, she married the flier because he threatened to commit suicide if she didn't. Peggy, our best friend, and I were witnesses at City Hall. As soon as the marriage was over we came back and told my mother. She was all for having it annulled, and Benita seemed to agree. But in the end she went off with the aviator on a honeymoon and they settled down together. To me he was completely unworthy of her. He was handsome in a flashy way, but superficial with no depths of passion. He was melodramatic. I was madly jealous and unhappy. I missed her presence in our house beyond words, and I was left alone with my mother, for Hazel was at boarding school. My mother's one idea was to sacrifice her life to her children and she had done nothing else since the death of my father. We wished that she had married again instead.

In the summer of 1919, I came into my fortune. I was an heiress and I was independent. My mother was greatly upset. She could no longer control me. The first thing I did was to make an extensive trip all over the United States. I invited my brother-in-law's cousin to chaperon me. We went from Niagara Falls to Chicago and from there to Yellowstone Park, all through California, down to Mexico, up the coast to the Canadian Rockies. At that time Hollywood was just born. It was so small that it was almost nonexistent. I had a cousin there who introduced me to some movie people. They all seemed quite mad. On the way home we visited the Grand Canyon. Then we returned to Chicago, where I was met by my aviator fiancé; who had been demobilized. He introduced me to his family, who were all Chicagoans, but I did not make a hit. I complained too much about the provincialism of Chicago. As I was leaving on the Twentieth Century, he told me it was all off. I was very unhappy because I thought I was in love with him and was patiently waiting for him to make a fortune in the loose-leaf paper business so that he could marry me. His name was Harold Wessel.

In the winter of 1920, being very bored, I could think of nothing better to do than have an operation performed on my nose to change its shape. It was ugly, but after the operation it was undoubtedly worse. I went to Cincinnati where there was a surgeon who specialized in these beauty operations. He made you choose a plaster model of the nose you preferred. He never was able to give me what I wanted, a nose "tip-tilted like a flower," something I had read about in Tennyson. During the operation (performed under a local anesthetic), when I was suffering the tortures of the damned, surrounded by five nurses in white masks, the doctor suddenly asked me to choose again. He could not do what he had planned. It was all so painful I told him to stop and leave things as they were. As a result of the operation my nose was painfully swollen for a long time and I didn't dare set foot in New York. I hid in the Middle West waiting for the swelling to go down. Every time it rained I knew it beforehand, because my nose became a sort of barometer and would swell up in bad weather. I went to French Lick, Indiana, with a friend and gambled away nearly another thousand dollars, the operation having cost as much.

A short time later Margaret Anderson came to me and asked me if I would give her some money for *The Little Review*, and an introduction to one of my uncles. She said that if people believed in preventing wars the best possible thing to do was to subscribe to the arts. Being young and innocent, I hoped I had put off the next World War for several years by contributing five hundred dollars to *The Little Review*. I sent Margaret to my fur coat uncle and if she did not succeed in getting five hundred dollars out of him (I can't recall now) I trust at least that she got a fur coat.

If Lucile Kohn was responsible for my radical beliefs, my actual liberation came about quite differently from any manner she might have foreseen. One day when I was at my dentist's, I found him in a predicament. His nurse was ill and he was doing all his work alone. I offered to replace the nurse as best I could. He accepted my help, for which he paid me $2.35 a day. I opened the door and answered the telephone. I held instruments for him and boiled them. I also learned which of my acquaintances had false teeth. Of course I was recognized by the patients, who asked Dr. Scoby in great surprise if it wasn't Miss Guggenheim who admitted them into the office. All this soon came to an end when the real nurse returned.

I now felt in need of a job so I offered my services to my cousin, Harold Loeb. He had a little radical bookshop near Grand Central Station. I became a clerk and spent my afternoons on the balcony writing out checks and doing various boring jobs. I was permitted downstairs only at noon, when I had to replace the people who went to lunch, at which time I sold books. When I complained of my fate to Gilbert Cannan, who came often and sat for hours in the bookshop, he said to me, "Never mind, Lady Hamilton started out as a kitchenmaid."

Though I was only a clerk, I swept into the bookshop daily, highly perfumed, and wearing little pearls and a magnificent taupe coat. My mother disapproved of my working and came often to see what I was up to and to bring me rubbers if it was raining. This was embarrassing. My rich aunts also came and literally bought books by the yard to fill their bookcases. We had to bring out a tape measure to be sure the measurements coincided with their bookshelves.

In the bookshop I met many celebrities and writers and painters, among them Marsden Hartley and my future husband, Laurence Vail, as well as Leon Fleischman and his wife Helen, who later married James Joyce's son.

Although I received no salary in the Sunwise Turn Book Shop, Harold Loeb and his partner, Mary Mowbray Clarke, allowed me a ten percent reduction on all the books I bought. In order to have the illusion of receiving a big salary, I bought many books of modern literature and read them all with my usual voracity.

The people I met in the Sunwise Turn fascinated me. They were so real, so alive, so human. All their values were different from mine. I loved Mary Mowbray Clarke. She became a sort of goddess for me. Eventually she sold the bookshop to Doubleday Doran, having bought out Harold Loeb long before.

Marsden Hartley impressed and terrified me. So did Gilbert Cannan. I was much less afraid of Laurence. He was about twenty-eight at this time, and to me he appeared like someone out of another world. He was the first man I knew who never wore a hat. His beautiful, streaky golden hair streamed all over as the wind caught it. I was shocked by his freedom but fascinated at the same time. He had lived all his life in France and he had a French accent and rolled his r's. He was like a wild creature. He never seemed to care what people thought. I felt when I walked down the street with him that he might suddenly fly away—he had so little connection with ordinary behavior.

The Fleischmans became my great friends. They practically adopted me. I was so unhappy about Benita that I was delighted to have a new home. I fell in love with Leon, who to me looked like a Greek God, but Helen didn't mind. They were so free.

One day Leon took me to see Alfred Stieglitz. They put the first abstract painting I had ever seen in my hands. It was painted by Georgia O'Keeffe. I turned it around four times before I decided which way to look at it. They were delighted. I didn't see Stieglitz again until twenty-five years later, and when I talked to him I felt as though there had been no interval. We took up where we left off.

Soon after, I went to Europe. I didn't realize at the time that I was going to remain there for twenty-one years, but that wouldn't have stopped me. My mother went with me and she brought my Aunt Irene Guggenheim's cousin, Valerie Dreyfus, to help look after me. I was already too much of a handful and my mother knew she couldn't keep up with me. As much as I could, I dragged these two ladies all over Europe with my usual speed and my usual enthusiasm. Soon my mother got tired and handed me over to Valerie. *She* could keep up with me. In fact she encouraged me. She was a wonderful guide, had been everywhere before and was a very smart traveler. We went to Holland, Belgium, Spain and Italy. With my mother we had already been to Scotland, all over England and through the Loire country.

In those days my desire for seeing everything was very much in contrast to my lack of feeling for anything. That was born, however, as a result of my other frenzy. I soon knew where every painting in Europe could be found, and I managed to get there, even if I had to spend hours going to a little country town to see only one. I had as a great friend Armand Lowengard, the nephew of Sir Joseph (later Lord) Duveen. He was a fanatic about Italian painting. Seeing what a good subject I was, he egged me on to study art. He told me that I would never be able to understand

Berenson's criticism. This remark served its purpose. I immediately bought and digested seven volumes of that great critic. After that I was forever going around looking for Berenson's seven points. If I could find a painting with tactile value I was thrilled. Armand had been wounded in the war and was rather badly done in. My vitality nearly killed him and though he was fascinated by me, in the end he had to renounce me, as I was entirely too much for him.

I had another boyfriend, Pierre. He was a sort of cousin of my mother's. I felt wicked because I kissed both him and Armand on the same day. He wanted to marry me but I merely wanted to have as many suitors as I could collect. Soon I wanted more than that. I had a great friend, Fira Benenson, a Russian girl. We lived in the Crillon Hotel in Paris and tried to outdo each other in collecting proposals. We dressed in the most elegant French fashions and I am sure we were idiotic.

I didn't see the Fleischmans again until I returned to America for a brief visit in the spring to attend Hazel's wedding to Siggy Kempner. I then persuaded the Fleischmans to come and live in Paris. As they had a child and little money, Leon having resigned as a director of Boni and Liveright's publishing house, it was all very complicated. But they came. It changed their life as much as they had changed, and were still to change, mine.

Through the Fleischmans I again met Laurence Vail. Helen Fleischman was a friend of Laurence's. She was having a little affair with him into which Leon had pushed her. It excited him. She told me that she wanted me to come to dinner with Laurence and then she told Laurence not to pay too much attention to me because Leon would be offended. I think Leon must have been, as Laurence and I got quite friendly.

A few days later Laurence took me out for a walk. We went to the tomb of the Unknown Soldier and then we walked along the Seine. I was wearing an elegant costume trimmed with kolinsky fur that I had designed for myself. He took me into a bistro and asked me what I wanted. I asked for a porto flip thinking I was in the kind of bar I was used to. In those days I led only the most expensive sort of life and had never set foot in an ordinary café and had no idea what to order.

At this time I was worried about my virginity. I was twenty-three and I found it burdensome. All my boy friends were disposed to marry me, but they were so respectable they would not rape me. I had a collection of photographs of frescos I had seen at Pompeii. They depicted people making love in various positions, and of course I was very curious and wanted to try them all out myself. It soon occurred to me that I could make use of Laurence for this purpose.

Laurence lived with his mother and his sister Clotilde in a very bourgeois apartment near the Bois. When his father was not in a sanatorium having a *crise de nerfs*, he was living at home upsetting his entire family. Laurence's mother was an aristocratic New England lady. His father was a painter of Breton ancestry, half French, half American. He had been neurasthenic for years and his family had no idea what to do about him. They had tried everything but he was the world's great incurable neurotic.

Laurence wanted to get away from home again. His mother gave him a small allowance of one hundred dollars a month and, considering her income was ten thousand dollars a year, she wasn't over-generous. But she preferred to spend it on her husband, whose capital had long since vanished paying doctor's bills. He had been in every sanatorium in Europe. Laurence might have taken a job but he didn't like working. He was a writer of considerable talent but as yet unknown.

He now told me he was about to take a little apartment, and I asked if I could pay half the rent and share it, hoping by this maneuver to get somewhere. He said yes, but soon changed his mind. The next time I saw him he told me he had taken a hotel room in the Rue de Verneuil on the left bank, in the Latin Quarter. He came to see me at the Plaza-Athénée Hôtel where I was living and started to make love to me. When he pulled me toward him, I acquiesced so quickly that he was surprised by my lack of resistance. However I told him that we could not do anything there as my mother might return at any moment. He said we would go to his hotel room sometime. I immediately rushed to put on my hat, and he took me to the Rue de Verneuil. I am sure he had not meant to. That was how I lost my virginity. It was as simple as that. I think Laurence had a pretty tough time because I demanded everything I had seen depicted in the Pompeian frescoes. I went home and dined with my mother and a friend gloating over my secret and wondering what they would think of it if they knew.

Chapter 3

Marriage

Laurence was considered the King of Bohemia. He knew all the American writers and painters and a lot of French ones too. In those days they met at the Café de la Rotonde in Montparnasse. But Laurence had a row with a waiter or the manager of that café and he made everybody move opposite to the Dôme. After that they never returned to the Rotonde. Laurence gave wonderful parties in his mother's apartment. The first one I went to was very wild. I took with me a bourgeois French playwright, and in order to make him feel at home in the midst of Bohemia, I sat on his lap most of the evening. Later I received a proposal (I can hardly say of marriage) from Thelma Wood, the girl who was to become the well-known Robin of *Nightwood.* She got down on her knees in front of me. Strange things were happening everywhere. Laurence's father was at home and was very annoyed by the confusion the party caused. In desperation he retired to the toilet where he found two delicate young men weeping. He retired to another bathroom where he disturbed two giggling girls. He liked to be the center of attraction. If there was anything going on he wanted to be the star himself. After he had made a scene he felt better. Even if no one else paid much attention to him, at least his wife must have.

I soon met two great friends of Laurence: Mary Reynolds and
Djuna Barnes. They had both been his mistresses. They were
very beautiful women. They had the kind of nose I had gone all
the way to Cincinnati for in vain. Mary was dark with a beautiful
figure. She was tall and elegant and had soft eyes. Her widow's
peak was her great attraction. She was the only person in Bohemia
with any money, and yet she was always broke because she lent it
or gave it all away the minute it arrived from America. She was a
war widow. She was waiting for some man called Norman to join
her in Paris, but first he had to disentangle himself from his wife.

Djuna was quite different. She was already a well-known
writer. Leon had borrowed a hundred dollars from me to help pay
her passage to Europe. Later she did journalistic jobs. She rushed
around Europe interviewing famous people. She wrote articles
about celebrities for which she received enormous prices. At this
time she was not rich.

Helen Fleischman told me to give Djuna some underwear. A
disagreeable scandal ensued as the underwear I gave was Kayser
silk and it was darned. I had three distinct categories of
underwear: the best, which I had decorated with real French lace
and which I was saving for my trousseau; my second best that was
new, but unadorned, and that which I sent to Djuna. After she
complained, I sent her the second best sets. I went to visit her.
She was sitting at the typewriter wearing the second best
underwear. She looked handsome with her white skin, her
magnificent red hair and her beautiful body. She was very much
embarrassed to be caught wearing the underwear after all the
rows that had been made. Anyhow I apologized about the first lot I
had sent her, and she forgave me. When Helen gave Djuna
presents she just opened her cupboards and said, "Help yourself."
I felt I should be less mean, so I gave Djuna my favorite russet
cape and my favorite hat. It was adorned with a cock's tail
feathers and when she wore it she looked like an Italian soldier.

One day I took Djuna to the Musée du Louvre and gave her a
lecture on French art. I think she was bored. We met Mary
Reynolds there and all three of us went to lunch. All through the
meal I could not talk to them. I had a lot of homework to prepare.
In those days I was studying Russian because I did not like Fira
Benenson to have secrets from me. All her friends were Russian

and I felt left out of their conversations, so I decided to study their language.

When Laurence told Helen about our affair she took it very well. But Leon was furious. Anyhow that ended Laurence's affair with Helen and from then on he belonged to me. I decided really to go in for my love affair in a big way, so I convinced my mother to go on a little trip to Rome with one of her nieces. She left Valerie Dreyfus behind to chaperon me. Poor Valerie had no idea what was going on, but she took a room in the Hôtel Plaza-Athénée where I was living and tried to look after me. Laurence came nearly every day.

One day Laurence took me to the top of the Eiffel Tower and when we were gazing at Paris he asked me if I would like to marry him. I said "Yes" at once. I thought it was a fine idea. As soon as he had asked me, he regretted it. In fact, from then on he kept changing his mind. Every time I saw him look as though he were trying to swallow his Adam's apple I knew he was regretting his proposal. He got more and more nervous about our future and one day he ran away to Rouen to think matters over. Laurence's mother, Mrs. Vail, insisted on sending Mary Reynolds with him (she even paid her train fare), hoping that this would cause sufficient trouble to end the engagement. But when they got to Rouen they did nothing but fight, and soon Laurence wired that he still wanted to marry me.

As we were more or less engaged I decided to warn my mother. She came rushing back from Rome to stop the marriage. She thought she should get references of Laurence's. She asked him who would give any. Laurence had a wide circle of acquaintances and at St. Moritz he had once met the King of Greece, so to tease my mother he gave the king's name. My mother carried a little notebook and inscribed names in it. She was quite puzzled and even asked me how she could communicate with the King of Greece. Of course no one thought that we should marry. Leon went to my mother and told her how much of a catastrophe it would be, and Marion, an old friend, the brother of Dulcie Sulzberger, begged me to give up the project. He said, "Do anything, come and live with me as a sister, but don't marry Laurence." Of course I did marry him. It was all the fault of a lawyer called Charlie Loeb. We went to him to find out how it could be done and before we knew it he got all the papers and posted the bans and drew up a *séparation des biens* to protect my rights.

After the bans were posted I began to think we might really marry, but suddenly Laurence decided to go to Capri with his sister Clotilde and postpone the wedding. I was to return to New York, where he would join me in May if we still felt like marrying. One afternoon, when he was all packed, he went to buy the tickets for his trip. My mother, Mrs. Vail and I sat in the Hôtel Plaza-Athénée, each with her private feelings about the future. Suddenly Laurence appeared in the doorway, looking as pale as a ghost and said, "Peggy, will you marry me tomorrow?" Of course I said, "Yes." After that I was still not at all sure that Laurence would not run away, so I decided not to buy a dress for the wedding. I bought a hat instead.

The morning of the wedding Laurence's mother phoned me to say, "He's off." I thought she meant Laurence had run away. He hadn't. She merely meant that he was on his way to fetch me. We went in a tramcar to the Mairie of the Seizième Arrondissement at Avenue Henri-Martin, where the ceremony was to take place.

We had all invited lots of friends. There were four distinct elements among the guests. First of all, Laurence had invited all his Bohemian friends, but as he was rather ashamed of marrying me, he had written them *petit bleu* notes briefly asking them to be present, as though he were asking them to a party, and he did not even mention who the bride was to be. My mother invited all her French Seligman cousins who lived in Paris, and all her bourgeois friends. Laurence's mother invited the American Colony, of which she was herself a well known hostess. I invited all my friends. They were very mixed at that time. They were writers and painters, mostly from a very respectable milieu, and of course there was Boris Dembo, my Russian friend, who came to the wedding and wept because I wasn't marrying him. Helen Fleischman was my witness and Laurence's sister was his. My mother nearly cried because she was not asked to sign the register, so we had to let her add her name to the others. We made her provide lots of champagne and she gave us a big party at the Plaza-Athénée after the ceremony.

When we had all drunk a lot of champagne and danced for hours, someone suggested that Laurence take me away on a honeymoon. We were going to Italy in three days but Laurence did not seem to be in the slightest hurry about ending the wedding party. He was tied up with his sister and hated leaving her. He felt that his marriage in some way would break up his relationship with her. To console him I said she could join us in Capri, where we were going on our honeymoon. I then asked my Russian teacher, Jacques Schiffrin, to come too, but Laurence objected, and I had to disinvite him. Finally Betty Humes, a friend of Laurence who was in the consulate service, persuaded him to take his bride away. We went to a hotel on the Rue de Rivoli and then to bed. We soon got up, however, as we had invited many of our friends to come to a second wedding party at the little Boeuf sur le Toit in the Rue Boissy d'Anglas. On the way there we went to Prunier's and ate a lot of oysters.

The next morning my doctor came to administer a *piqûre*, as I was recovering from the flu. He was Proust's doctor and had looked after him all that winter, when he was dying. He now seemed elated by my marriage and told me I was entering into a marvelous new life. I was surprised as I felt depressed and said, "Do you really think so? I don't."

As soon as I found myself married, I felt extremely let down. Then, for the first time, I had a moment to think about whether or not I really desired the marriage. Up to the last minute Laurence had been in such a state of uncertainty that I had been kept in suspense and never questioned my own feelings. Now that I had achieved what I thought so desirable, I no longer valued it so much.

We went to have lunch with my mother. She was curious about what she imagined was my introduction to love and I was boastfully apologetic about the smell of Lysol which I was carrying around with me. My mother, thinking she would catch me, asked, "How often did you use it?" I was disgusted with her indiscretion and refused to answer her question. All the waiters in the Pláza-Athénée looked at me as though they too were curious.

Two days later we went off to Rome. My mother came to the station with an emergency passport for me bearing my new name, Marguerite Guggenheim Vail, in case I felt the need of running away from Laurence, as I was now on his passport.

In Rome we looked up my cousin Harold Loeb, who was publishing *Broom* magazine with Kitty Cannell. Harold was shocked by Laurence's sockless feet in sandals. I wanted to retain my independence so I looked up my former beaux in Rome, and Laurence found some former girl friends. I still felt distinctly let down by my marriage and somehow thought it ought to be much more exciting.

Laurence chose an ideal place to take me for our honeymoon. He had lived in Capri before and while I had spent a few brief hours there with Valerie on one of our hasty trips, I had no idea what it was like. I had merely visited the Blue Grotto in a boat. Now we settled down and rented a villa on the Tiberius side of the island, very high up. As we walked down to the sea every day for our swim we found the climb back very trying in the heat. We swam at different beaches but our favorite one was the Piccola Marina. At the Grande Marina we rented little boats called sandolas which were manipulated with a double oar. First you used it on one side and then on the other. We rowed out to meet the steamboat that came from Naples every day. It was all exciting and new to me. I had never been in such a natural place and the beauty of this simple life delighted me.

Capri itself is like an enchanted island. Once you have come there it is very difficult to leave. Most of the inhabitants are *queer* but the beauty of the place and its marvelous setting in the blue Bay of Naples are too good to be true. It is a small rocky island that rises high out of the sea. Above is another town called Anacapri, and below are little fishing villages. The main town, Capri, is the center and has its intense social life on the piazza like all Italian towns. There was a café called Morgano's where one met and made friends. The walks around Capri are extremely beautiful and in parts the vegetation resembles the moors of Scotland.

There were no cars on the island and very few carriages. There was a funicular which took people up from the boat landing to Capri. One's life depended more or less on the supplies brought over by the boat. For days one could be cut off from the mainland by the rough seas. One had absolutely no sense of responsibility, the whole atmosphere reminding one of an *opéra bouffe*. The following year I was to fathom the depths of intrigue here and then I really got to know Capri much better. But that comes later.

We had many strange neighbors. Our nearest one was a Swedish count who lived a mile farther up our road on the way to the ruins of Tiberius's villa. The count, who was a descendant of Marie Antoinette's faithful lover Fersen, lived with a goatherd he had adopted. In order to hold him, he first had him educated, and then he taught him to smoke opium. They were a handsome young couple. Capri was full of such people.

There was one old lady who sold coral in the streets. She was reported to be the ex-mistress of the Queen of Sweden.

Krupp had built himself a magnificent villa here with his war profits. Mrs. Compton Mackenzie had a wonderful villa overlooking the rocks called the Faraglioni, while Mackenzie had built a little stone hut up in the heath at the very top. The year before I came, the Marchesa Casati roamed about the island with a leopard.

I soon found that I had married into a strange family. My mother-in-law was fussy but she was a fine woman of the old school. She was a D.A.R. and behaved like one. Even though she had not approved of the marriage, once it was accomplished she accepted me wholeheartedly. I think she really liked me, and she was the first person I ever met who admired my looks. I had been brought up to believe that I was ugly, because my sisters were great beauties. It had given me an inferiority complex. When Mrs. Vail met Benita and Hazel, she claimed that I was better looking than either of them. Imagine how this surprised and pleased me. Mrs. Vail accepted me as a daughter-in-law, but she never permitted me to call her "Mother."

If Mrs. Vail accepted me, I cannot say the same for her daughter Clotilde. She was the thorn in my marriage. She adored her brother with a passion one could not fail to admire and which he reciprocated. (They gave one the feeling that they were made for incest; and by not indulging in it they augmented their frustrated passion.) Everything was "my brother" with Clotilde. She did not relinquish one inch of him to me. She always made me feel that I had stepped by mistake into a room that had long since been occupied by another tenant, and that I should either hide in a corner or back out politely. She was a very strong character and I soon found her trying to run my household. My life was doubly complicated by the fact that she was excessively attractive, and was perpetually having love affairs. At first I was shocked, but later I outgrew my puritanical prejudices. Every time she had a new lover Laurence became wildly jealous and, as I was his whipping boy, I suffered very much from it all. Clotilde was three or four years older than I, and completely mature while I was a baby. That also put me at a disadvantage. She had a very beautiful mezzo-soprano voice and had been studying for years to be a singer. Clotilde had long blond hair the color of Laurence's. They looked exactly alike as they both had their mother's beaky Roman nose. But Clotilde was small.

As soon as we were settled in Capri, or rather after three weeks, Clotilde joined us. She did allow us to be alone for that short period. She brought with her an Italian friend called Elaine Le Bourg, which helped a lot, but when Laurence and Clotilde stalked together on the Piazza at the hour when everyone collected, I was made to feel nonexistent.

I did not have any responsibilities in Capri because our house was run by four Italian sluts, who made love every night with soldiers in our garden. Teresina, the mother of an illegitimate baby, and her three little sisters looked after us. Their salary was minute and only two of them were paid, but they made up for it by cheating us outrageously when shopping and by taking home half of the food. In Italy this was more or less taken for granted by Americans, and when Elaine, as a good Italian woman, wanted to put a stop to it Laurence as a foreigner would not hear of it. The sluts were charming. They sang Neapolitan songs for us all day long and they even brushed and combed my hair which was too long for me to cope with. They served good meals and we considered ourselves lucky to have them in our household.

Laurence was snobbish about my family. He did not like the Guggenheims, and was perpetually making fun of them. One day after my Aunt Rose had arrived at our house riding a mule, as she could not walk up the hill, he told me that it was extremely appropriate, since it appeared to be quite in keeping with the Old Testament. Another day he told me he would like to throw all my uncles over the cliff where Tiberius had killed his enemies. I was so offended I burst into tears.

In the late summer we left Capri for St. Moritz. We motored through Italy and stopped in Arezzo and San Sepolcro to see the Piero della Francesca frescoes. I enraged Laurence by looking for Berenson's seven points instead of enjoying the paintings for themselves. We went to Venice, Florence and Milan and finally ended up in a little train that zigzagged up to the Engadine.

I had never been to St. Moritz before and was much impressed by the social life there; not that we took much part in it. As a matter of fact we led a quiet family life with Mrs. Vail and Clotilde and a few friends of mine from England and New York who showed up. Laurence and I played a lot of tennis and we won a tournament. We played well together for he was very strong at the net and I backed him up. I accepted his directions and never let him down.

In the fall I went to New York to see Benita. I had planned this trip long before my marriage and nothing in the world could interfere with it. Laurence went off with Clotilde to the Basque country on a motorbike that Benita had given him for a wedding present.

Benita had settled down with her husband and they seemed quite happy. There was still terrible jealousy between him and me, and Benita was like a rose between two thorns. Before I left New York I signed a contract with a publisher who wanted to publish a novel that Laurence had written long before.

After a short time I realized that I was going to have a baby. I was quite sick but very happy, and I wired Laurence in order to warn him. My beautiful aunt, Irene Guggenhcim, took me back to Europe with her in her stateroom, because I was so sick and she wanted to look after me. I was in bed for the whole trip. Laurence met us at Southampton, and we were very happy to be together again.

We had to plan our future about the birth of our child. We immediately called him Gawd Guggenheim Vail and decided he must be born in London. We did not want him to be a French citizen, which he would be if he were born in Paris. Both Laurence and his father had been born there and the third generation would be claimed by the French and forced to do military service. Laurence had an American passport and had served as a liaison officer in the American Army with the heavy artillery in the last war.

Aunt Irene's daughter Eleanor, who had married the Earl of Castle Stewart, a psychoanalyst, took me to her doctor in London. She had just had a baby and she was very pleased with Dr. Hadley's care. He told me when to expect the birth of Gawd and we decided to go back to France for the winter and return to London in May.

We went down to Sussex to visit Eleanor and I remember her husband telling me what an exciting life I was going to have with Laurence, instead of the dull one Eleanor was leading with him. I don't know why everyone thought my future was to be so thrilling. It certainly was, but I wonder how they all knew it before I did.

Laurence was a dynamic person. He had an amazing personality and he was handsome. He had great charm which he was forever turning on people successfully. He always made me feel inferior. I was inexperienced when I met him and I felt like an awful baby in his (what I considered at the time) sophisticated world. Laurence was always bursting with ideas. He had so many he never achieved them because he was forever rushing on to others. He just tossed them off the way most people toss off clichés. It was extraordinary. His vitality was fantastic. He could stay up three nights running. I could never do without my sleep, and when I lay in bed waiting for him to come home, knowing he was drunk and apt to be in trouble, I had no rest. He brought me into an entirely new world and taught me a completely new way of life. It was all thrilling, often too thrilling.

It is difficult to remember now how Laurence and I began fighting. We had one quarrel before we were married, in the Plaza-Athénée Hôtel, caused, I think, by something Valerie Dreyfus said. Laurence made a scene and stalked out in a fury. However, it never dawned on me that this was a sample of what I might expect perpetually in the future. Laurence was very violent and he liked to show off. He was an exhibitionist, so that most of his scenes were made in public. He also enjoyed breaking up everything in the house. He particularly liked throwing my shoes out of the window, breaking crockery and smashing mirrors and attacking chandeliers. Fights went on for hours, sometimes days, once even for two weeks. I should have fought back. He wanted me to, but all I did was weep. That annoyed him more than anything. When our fights worked up to a grand finale he would rub jam in my hair. But what I hated most was being knocked down in the streets, or having things thrown in restaurants. Once he held me down under water in the bathtub until I felt I was going to drown. I am sure I was very irritating but Laurence was used to making scenes, and he had had Clotilde as an audience for years. She always reacted immediately if there was going to be a fight. She got nervous and frightened, and that was what

Laurence wanted. Someone should have told him not to be such an ass. Djuna tried it once in Weber's restaurant and it worked like magic. He immediately renounced the grand act he was about to put on. As a result of these displays of anger he got into an awful lot of trouble with the public authorities and was often arrested. One of the first big fights I can remember was in a theatre when we went to Raymond Roussel's play, *Locus Solus*. Everybody was hissing it and of course Laurence was for it. He made a demonstration and a royal battle followed, and being pregnant I did not want to be involved. Laurence's opponents were numerous and they got him down on the floor. The *Commissaire de Police* was sent for and came to his rescue. Later he gave us his box so that we might see the rest of the play in safety.

The next big fight I remember was in the Hôtel Lutétia. It was brought on entirely by my lack of tact. I had resumed my Russian lessons with Jacques Schiffrin, and I announced to Laurence that I was in love with my teacher. Laurence picked up an ink-pot and hurled it at the wall. It broke the telephone and spattered the room with ink. The room had to be repapered. To remove the spots on the floor I found a miraculous little deaf man who came every day for weeks. He squatted on the floor bringing out from a bag an array of bottles which he applied one by one until the spots completely vanished. Schiffrin, in the meantime, borrowed money from me to pay his printing bill. He was launching his *Editions de la Pléiade* and ran short of funds. In return he gave me six hundred copies of his first beautiful book, *La Dame de Pique*. I went to all the book shops of Paris to dispose of my six hundred volumes. I was not very successful as a saleswoman and soon Schiffrin, who was well on the way to success, bought them back from me.

Because of my money I enjoyed a certain superiority over Laurence and I used it in a dreadful way, by telling him it was mine and he couldn't have it to dispose of freely. To revenge himself he tried to increase my sense of inferiority. He told me that I was fortunate to be accepted in Bohemia and that, since all I had to offer was my money, I should lend it to the brilliant people I met and whom I was allowed to frequent.

When we started living in Paris I was quite sick because of my pregnancy and I took some medicine every day. Bob Coates, having no idea what was wrong with me, and as he himself was suffering from some stomach disturbance, insisted on trying my medicine. At that time he was a young writer living a Bohemian life in Paris and he was one of our best friends.

Laurence loved big parties and we never missed a chance to give one. He liked me to dress extravagantly and he took me to Paul Poiret and made me buy elegant clothes, but my fast advancing waistline was not very attractive and I did not look very chic in these wonderful costumes. Hazel joined us in Paris. She was already divorced and that winter she married Milton Waldman.

In the middle of the winter we went down to the Riviera. We found a little villa at Le Trayas and rented it for two months. One of my cousins in the automobile business sold me an old second-hand Gaubron, whose cut-out was perpetually open and it made a terrible noise. We hired a chauffeur and Laurence learned to drive the car. Our life here was very simple. We had only one maid, and we stayed in the villa most of the time. But Laurence bathed in the sea all winter and went to the markets to bring home food. Since I was ill I spent weeks reading all of Dostoevsky. Of course we had our fights to pass the time. What we fought about in Le Trayas and what took up two weeks of our time before we finally signed a truce was the fact that Bob Coates wanted to borrow $200 from Laurence in order to go back to America. For some reason I took this badly and would not let Laurence have the money. He had to refuse it to Bob. Finally Clotilde came down to visit us, and we ended our battle.

In March Benita came to Europe for she wanted to be with me for the birth of Gawd. When she discovered my Bohemian life, she was shocked and was much against it. Benita was extremely conventional and her husband made her more so. It was difficult for her to make a bridge between two such different ways of life.

At the end of April I went to London with Fira Benenson to look for a house. Laurence was to follow with the new car we had just bought, a Lorraine Dietrich. The Gaubron had collapsed. I looked as if Brancusi's egg had been superimposed on my slender person.

I rented a beautiful house with a garden in Kensington up on Campden Hill. We were very comfortable and there was plenty of room for guests and nurses when the moment arrived. Mary Reynolds stayed with us for a while but left to join Norman when

he finally came from America. Benita and her husband were living
at the Ritz, with my mother. We did not want my mother to know
when Gawd was expected. She fussed so much it was nerve-
racking. We had managed to keep her in ignorance of his
existence for a long time. Now she thought he was much younger
than he was.

Actually, on the night of his birth, there was none of my family
about. I had left Benita at seven o'clock in town and I was not
feeling too well, but I came home to a dinner party Laurence and I
were giving. Our guests were Mary Reynolds and Norman, and
Tommy Earp and his wife, and an old friend of Laurence from his
Oxford days and his wife, and Bob McAlmon. During the dinner
we drank the health of someone under the table, meaning Gawd.
Tommy Earp, who had no suspicions, began looking for a dog.
Soon after dinner the wife of Laurence's Oxford friend threw a
pillow at me and that seemed to have an immediate effect. To my
great embarrassment the waters broke and I retired upstairs.
Mary got hysterical and wanted to put me to bed. Laurence
rushed off in the car with Earp to fetch the nurse. She had been
actually engaged for that day, but was waiting to be called. When
she arrived she took everything in hand and made me do the right
things. All I can remember is the most dreadful pain that came in
waves and that got worse and worse. Each time I felt as though I
could not endure any more. Mary sat on the steps with Laurence.
Finally the nurse allowed him to go and fetch Dr. Hadley. When
he arrived I was suffering the most excruciating pain. He asked
me if I wanted an anesthetist and by then naturally I said "Yes." I
felt as though wild horses were dragging me apart, and I had come
to the end of my strength. When the second gentleman in a top
hat, who took ages to put on his white spats, arrived, my troubles
ended but the doctor's didn't. The chloroform worked so well that
Gawd refused to budge and had to be taken by forceps. He arrived
at eight in the morning just in time for breakfast, and Mary and
Laurence saw him before I did, for which I never forgave her.
When I came to and was told I had a boy I felt embarrassed to
think that I had harbored a male creature inside my being for so
long.

Laurence phoned my mother. She thought it was a joke and she
would not believe that she had a grandchild. We had fooled her so
well that she did not appear until the evening, and then was

completely surprised to learn that Gawd was really there. He was born on May 15, the anniversary of Benita's wedding and the day after Mrs. Vail's birthday. We named him Michael Cedric Sindbad Vail. Mary named him Cedric in honor of Cedric Morris, a great friend of hers, a painter. Sindbad (from the Arabian Nights) was Laurence's choice; mine was Michael. He was darling, but very ugly. He had a wrinkled little red face, a lot of black hair, enormous protruding ears, and heavenly feet and hands. The day nurse was a sort of dragon, but the night nurse was an angel. So we postponed all our fun until the night.

I nursed Sindbad for one month. After that I had no milk. Nursing was painful and for some reason I was an unnatural mother and could never give my breast to my children without the assistance of a nurse. If the babies had had to depend on me they would have starved. Dr. Hadley made me stay in bed three weeks. I was bored and read George Moore and Henry James to amuse myself.

It was at this time that Peggy came to stay with us. I don't know what else to call her throughout this book, for she changed her name so often. She first came into my life at school, but as she was one class ahead of me, I never knew her well. Then she married my cousin Edwin Loeb. That didn't work, and Benita and I made her get a divorce. When she came to London she was just recovering from her divorce. She had not as yet got into any further trouble. Laurence loved her, and I was delighted as she was my oldest friend. She is hard to describe, because she was so elusive. If you ever pinned her down to anything you would find out the next day that she had told someone else the exact opposite of what she had told you. She saw around and into everything, and therefore had no *parti pris;* consequently we always called her double-faced. But she was the only really intelligent woman I have ever met. She had the logical brain of a man. She looked like a Cheshire cat because she had an enormous mouth which was perpetually grinning. She was extremely stubborn. She seemed to know what she wanted in life, but she didn't at all really know what was good for her. For some strange reason she always had the wrong husband, and she had three of them. As a mother she was a great success, and had lots of pleasure from her three children. However, at this stage she had no children. Peggy never failed to appear at the crucial moments in my life. I felt all I had

to do was to bring out my Aladdin's lamp and Peggy would pop up
and help me.

We all went back to Paris for the fourteenth of July as
Laurence always celebrated that festival by dancing in the streets
for three nights. I couldn't keep up with him.

After Paris we went to Villerville in Normandy and rented a
place for the summer. It was a hideous old house, with a bathtub
in the cellar; it greatly resembled my grandfather's house, but this
one had a beautiful garden with a studio where we all painted,
even I. Clotilde and Peggy were with us, and Mina Loy. Louis
Aragon, who was Clotilde's boyfriend at the time, came for a visit.
So did Harold Loeb and Kitty Cannell and Man Ray and his
remarkable hand-painted Kiki. One day James Joyce and Nora
walked in. They were looking for their daughter who was in a
boarding school somewhere on the coast.

Benita had gone back to America and I was unhappy without
her again. I watched the French Line steamships go out to sea
from Le Havre, past our house, and wished I were leaving too.

In the fall we went back to Capri. Peggy and Mary and Clotilde
were with us. This time we stayed in a little hotel in the center of
town. My cousin Eleanor Castle Stewart had found me a nurse
called Lilly, whom we had brought back to the continent with us.
She was so dark that she looked more like a foreigner than like an
English girl. Men were always running after her. She was
completely innocent and unsophisticated and excited about traveling. Lilly took good care of Sindbad as she had been trained in a
hospital, and she was naturally conscientious.

Soon after we were in Capri Laurence got into trouble. He was
jealous of a new lover of Clotilde's. This little Italian, whenever
he spent the night away from his wife, pretended he had been to
the Caccia or to shoot little birds up on the heath. We used to
tease Clotilde and ask her if she had been to the Caccia when she
spent the night with him. She did not like the fact that Captain
Patuni, as he was called, refused to be seen in public with her.
Because of his wife he had to hide Clotilde. One night at dinner
she complained bitterly about this and got Laurence, who was
drunk, all worked up. He rushed into a private club where
Captain Patuni was playing cards with some men and threw all
the cards he could seize into Captain Patuni's face. A battle
followed. A policeman had his thumb broken. Laurence was put

In chains and lay on a table waiting to be carried off to jail. He had as an enemy the *sindaco* of Capri, whom he had once mocked, and as a result this man was his sworn enemy. Laurence was forced to spend ten days in jail awaiting trial. He was in a damp cell, and we were told to send him meals from the hotel. We also sent him wine and whiskey and lots of books. He was guarded by a wonderful jailer who had lost his job temporarily for allowing his prisoners out every night. When they were out they went on with their profession and brought their booty back to jail. He was reinstated but without salary.

This jailer accompanied the judge, who was blind, on his walks to and from the courthouse. He told me that he had the judge's consent for me to go to the prison to visit Laurence, but that I should get the permission myself. I went to the judge and fell on my knees, pleading my baby's ill health as an excuse to talk to my husband. I even wept. The judge was noncommittal, but soon after that the jailer came to see me. He told me to wear black and to come to a certain corner of the road where a big black dog would be waiting for me and would conduct me to the prison. I was terrified, and if Clotilde hadn't forced me to go, I would certainly have backed out. When I got to the prison, where I soon went every night, I fell asleep, exhausted by my worries and my attempts to rescue Laurence. Everyone on the island had a new scheme to free him. All the schemes involved enormous bribes, and they seemed dangerous and uncertain.

Finally Mary found the solution. She was picked up by a lawyer, Signor Tirelli, who had come from Rome for the day and who thought she was Clotilde. Having heard about the scandal he offered his services, which we accepted. Mary went with him to Rome to see the American Consul-General, who was a great friend of the Vails, hoping he would help us, but all he said referring to Laurence was, "That boy was always crazy." Signor Tirelli was the lawyer of the American Consulate. He was a clever old thing, and came over one day to prepare the case, the date of the trial finally having been set. He went around the island and collected enough witnesses to prove that Laurence was drunk and had meant no harm. When the trial came up on the tenth day, the barman of the Quisiana Hotel, where we had started out our evening, testified that we had not only had eight cocktails, but that they were gin, which in Italy is not usual, and that after dinner we had drunk large quantities of Veuve Clicquot champagne. Captain Patuni was called as a witness, but refused to appear. He was forcibly brought by two soldiers and had nothing unpleasant to say against Laurence. The policeman was bribed to be silent. Laurence was released and we left Capri that day on Tirelli's yacht for Amalfi. I insisted on this. Laurence did not like it, but I made him go. Before leaving he stalked around the piazza with Clotilde to show that he was not beaten. Tirelli charged us the modest sum of one thousand dollars, the voyage on his yacht thrown in. After that he charged us another five hundred to have Laurence's name removed from the records of crime.

I was rather ashamed to think that my husband had been in prison, and whenever the matter came up I tried to explain quickly what the offense had been.

When we said goodbye to the jailer, who had become our dear friend, we gave him a large tip. He immediately lost it or said he had, and had to be given another. He told Laurence his only desire in life would be to serve someone like him by guarding his fortune. He said he would have liked to sit and watch a large pile of money which should be placed on the floor in a room, and which would be safe with him.

Amalfi was as beautiful as Capri, but in quite a different way. It did not have the charm of an island. We took walks in the sloping countryside which was covered with vineyards. There were also several towns in this vicinity and we had to drive to get to them. One was a long way off and very high up. It was called Ravello and had a most beautiful twelfth-century building with cloisters covered in Virginia creeper. I wanted to buy the house, which was called Casa Rodolfo, but I could not produce the sum necessary because all my money was tied up in trust.

After Amalfi we decided to go to Egypt for the winter, but Clotilde and Peggy went back to Paris. Our dragoman took us everywhere, and saw to it that we bought everything. It wasn't difficult because Laurence and I were fascinated by the souks of Cairo. We found wonderful earrings for virtually nothing, and bought dozens of them to take back to Paris, since Clotilde, Mary and I were all frantic collectors. We also bought materials and Laurence had suits made with Egyptian cloths of all colors. He bought me perfumes, little coats and a cape from the Sudan, and he bought himself the oddest little rag dolls, beautiful Persian

prints and a water pipe. We ate only in Arab restaurants where
the chief food is lamb. There was one restaurant where we ate
out-of-doors, but it was an ordeal, because during the meals,
whole streams of beggars and vendors of food solicited us in turn.
It would have been possible to buy our entire meal from these
passers-by. The Arabs called me "Princess" to flatter me, thus
hoping to get larger *bakshish*. I have never seen such shameless
people. They were just like flies. One brushed them away merely
to have them return the next minute.

We were admitted to the mosques, but not at the sacred hour of
prayer when the male Arabs would squat in the courtyards around
fountains washing their private parts and urinating before they
turned their faces toward Mecca and the setting sun to invoke
Muhammad.

We spent days in the souks shopping and drinking Turkish
coffee, the thickest and sweetest coffee in the world. It is served
to you by all the shopkeepers if they have hopes of selling you
something expensive. One could never buy anything immediately.
Shopping in Cairo involved days and days of bargaining. It just
had to be done in the traditional way, tiresome as it was.

In the evenings we went to the Arab quarter. This was
considered low and incorrect for foreigners, especially for ladies.
Laurence went everywhere he saw a sign, "Out of bounds for
British officers and soldiers." I remember a beautiful Nubian girl
who did a *danse de ventre*. She so much resembled Hazel, in spite
of being as black as could be, that I called her my sister. Laurence
was fascinated by her and I decided to give him an evening off to
be with her. At that time we were living in the desert in Mena
House, next to the Pyramids of Giza. One evening, when we had
been shopping in Cairo, I left Laurence and went back alone to
Mena House. Considering my sacrifice he might have been nicer
to me. When he put me on the bus he purposely threw all my
packages about or dropped them in order to embarrass me, for he
was annoyed at having had to carry them all afternoon. He
returned late that night, and by chance I followed him into the
bathroom and saw that something was wrong. He had to admit the
truth. Suddenly I was angry when I thought what I might have
been exposed to, and refused to make love to him for days. He told
me that the girl wore white underwear and had a very high bed.
When he could not climb up to it she took him under the armpits
and lifted him up like a doll.

The next day we went camping in the desert. This is not at all what it sounds like. Nothing could be more luxurious. It entails a complete caravan of camels and attendants, a cook and tents and furniture and food all being brought along. It was certainly worth it because it is the only way to see the desert.

The desert is a vast sea of sand which rolls in all directions and in all shapes. It is mountainous and sometimes rocky. Occasionally there is a mirage or an oasis and often you meet other caravans. Otherwise you would feel completely lost. Nothing is more uncomfortable than riding a camel. The jerking and swaying motions drive you mad and exhaust you. You can't rise in a trot or gallop. You just sit in agony. Later I took to riding donkeys instead, and that turned out to be marvelous fun. They have a wonderful little gait, almost better than that of a horse.

We decided to take a trip up the Nile and all the dragomen of Cairo began running after us trying to rent us a *dahabeah*. We were invited to the home of one dragoman in the desert where he gave us a sumptuous meal of thirteen courses. Finally in desperation we ran away to Luxor where we rented a modest boat that depended entirely on the whimsical moods of the Nile winds and on a crew of eight to pull us if necessary. When the winds failed the crew got out and walked on the shore and drew the boat along by ropes. Laurence and I became so impatient that often we got out and walked along the banks, waiting for the boat to catch up with us.

Geographically Egypt is a strange country. It depends entirely on the Nile for its existence; otherwise it would merely be desert. Egypt varies much in width. At its widest point it covers many miles (as in the Delta land) and at other places it shrinks to about one foot. Its cultivated land exists only where the Nile has watered it. Along the banks a system of irrigation is in continuous motion. The lovely singing noise of the revolving wheel that turns as a camel walks in circles to propel it, greets one at regular distances. Buckets of water are attached to this wheel, and as they come out of the Nile full they disgorge their contents into a trough which feeds the channels dug for irrigation. Sometimes there were no camels and human energy replaced them with a simple hand derrick.

All along the banks were little villages of mud huts. The women of the town would come down to the water's edge carrying pitchers on their heads to fetch the water. Laurence insisted on bathing in the Nile, in spite of the dangers of crocodiles and germs, and one day he frightened away a whole bevy of women who screamed as he emerged naked from the water.

The people of Egypt are mostly Arabs, and they are very poor. We tried to learn their language from the dragoman who came on the *dahabeah* with us but he spoke perfect English. He drank a bottle of whiskey a day. The captain was very handsome and I conceived a slight passion for him. He played Arab music for us on a tom-tom.

Once you get on the Nile, you must give up all sense of time, but I couldn't. I became so impatient that I almost went mad. Laurence spent hours below in a cabin writing a book. He had a Puritan conscience, and he was a writer. Sindbad and Lilly were left behind in the hotel in Aswan at the First Cataract. I got bored, and to amuse myself I bought a pregnant goat. I had hoped to see it give birth. However, it fooled me by choosing the one short hour I was absent, visiting some friends on a Cook's steamboat. The captain sent a sailor to fetch me, but it was too late. Soon after that the whole boat reeked of goat smells and we could not endure it. I gave it to the captain. We also had two sheep on board. They were affectionate and sat on our laps. Eventually we were supposed to eat them, since all our food consisted of mutton courses. Sometimes we had as many as five in one meal, all prepared in different fashion. But I could not bear to think of eating the sweet sheep, so we gave them to the captain, too.

We went right up to the Second Cataract of the Nile at Wadi Halfa. We thus saw all the best temples as well as the Valley of the Kings with its gigantic twin statues. It was just before Tutankhamun's tomb was opened. The strongest impressions I have of Egypt proper have nothing to do with the Arabs and their civilization. What the Egyptians stood for was something so cruel, so subtle and so dignified. The carvings of the Egyptians on all the tombs were exquisite and the temples so overwhelming in size that one felt like a midget. Some of the temples were under water at this time because of the machinations of the dam at Aswan. We went in a rowboat through the courtyard of Kimombo Temple which was half under water and we saw only the top half of the Phalaes Temple.

At Wadi Halfa we were entertained by the governor. It was rare that people got that far on a *dahabeah* and he wanted to honor us. The British ruling class were pretty awful in their colonies. We did not relish this visit.

On the way back we picked up a steamboat and were tugged part of the way. It was strange seeing Egypt fly past in the moonlight instead of having it unroll itself like a slow-motion film in the sunlight. It was also exciting to recognize all the spots we had passed before.

When we left the boat after three or four weeks, the men expected a tip. We didn't know what to give them. I suggested a pound each, but they were not very pleased. Then we added another pound to each and they were very happy and cheered us. In those days I was very mean, and Laurence had a hard time arranging things with my money as I always tried to interfere. Finally he tipped the dragoman with his own money. Much later I told Benita how badly I behaved to Laurence and she wept for him.

When we got back to Cairo we left Sindbad and Lilly in Mena House and went to Jerusalem. For the first time in my life I felt ashamed to have married outside my faith. The Jews of Jerusalem looked upon me askance. Palestine was a young country in those days in spite of its extreme age. It was in its infancy as it had just been given back to the Jews. It didn't seem to be working any too well. There were terrible fights among the Muslims, the Jews and the Christians. They all wanted to own the key to the Holy Sepulchre. Jerusalem itself was little built up. Most of the activities were concentrated on farming. The only thing that really impressed us was the Wailing Wall. It mortified me to belong to my people. The nauseating sight of my compatriots publicly groaning and moaning and going into physical contortions was more than I could bear, and I was glad to leave the Jews again.

We returned by a different steamship line, disembarked at Genoa and from there we took a night train to Paris. As soon as we arrived I dispatched Laurence and Lilly and Sinbad, and decided to face the customs on my own. Everything we had bought in Cairo was concealed between my dresses in my Innovation trunk. It was very ingenious because not only were there innumerable Sudanese clothes for Clotilde, Mary and me, but also an odd collection of embroidered tablecloths and pillow slips. The worst offense was the Turkish tobacco that we were bringing into France. This was not allowed. At the last minute Laurence ripped open an enormous rag doll that he had bought and filled it with about four hundred cigarettes. Nothing was found and I retired with my booty. When I got to the Hôtel Lutétia and began to unpack I could hardly believe my eyes. I felt as if I were a magician bringing things out of a hat. We gave a cocktail party every Sunday and showed our wonderful Arab treasures to our guests.

The rooms in the Lutétia were not big enough for us now that we had Sindbad, so we took an apartment on the Boulevard Saint-Germain for six months. It was Proustian and we did our best to make it cozy. We horrified the Vicomte de Cambon, our landlord, by buying rustic French furniture and installing it in the place of his *Louis Seize meubles,* which we hid in the backroom. We brought all of Laurence's library here and had all the books I had received as wedding presents from my family in America. When we moved from the apartment we caused a scandal on the Boulevard Saint-Germain by throwing all our books out the window and catching them in sheets below in order to remove them.

We gave fantastic Bohemian parties in this flat. Laurence made me buy a cloth-of-gold evening dress ·at Poiret's. Now I was so thin again it suited me perfectly. I also wore a headdress made by a Russian lady who was Stravinsky's fiancée. It was a tight net gold band that made my skull look like Tutankhamun's. Man Ray photographed me in this costume with a long cigarette-holder in my mouth. It was sensational. In those days I never drank, and I was bored at these parties where everybody got tight. I hated people being sick in my house, and I especially hated people making love on my bed. Once a lady left her corsets behind and called for them later. After the guests would leave I went around, like my aunt, with a bottle of Lysol. I was so afraid of getting a venereal disease.

To one of these parties I invited one of my mother's nieces who happened to be in Paris on her honeymoon with her second husband, after she had got rid of the roué whom I resented her marrying over my head at the age of eleven. When she arrived at this party she was fascinated by a couple of beautiful young men who were dancing closely, locked in each other's arms. I made her

sit and guard the silver all evening, telling her that I had no idea
who half of my guests were as Laurence picked up odd people in
bars when he was tight and invited them all to our house. We kept
open house every Sunday evening. At another one of these parties,
Kiki, Man Ray's mistress, hit him in the face and called him a
dirty Jew. My mother was present and was outraged. She told Kiki
what she thought of her.

My mother was much more conventional than I, and she was
forever inviting Laurence and me to the Ritz to her parties. On
the other hand, she seemed to enjoy our Bohemian parties as well.
She had made great friends with Mrs. Vail and was dragged into
the American Women's Club which was Mrs. Vail's stronghold.
My mother was probably at her best at this time, because she
could at last have a life of her own. She was no longer tormented
by father's infidelities, and all her children were married. But she
never actually relinquished her daughters. She used to phone me
every morning and tell me it was cold or raining and that I should
wear a warm coat or rubbers, as the case might be. This drove me
frantic, but what I hated most of all were the conventional parties
at the Ritz and being perpetually told that I led the wrong kind of
life. Anyone who was not rich she referred to as a beggar, and any
woman who had a lover she called N. G., meaning no good. She
was greatly disappointed that I had not married a Jewish
millionaire. Nevertheless, she liked Laurence because he flirted
with her. She herself had had various proposals, which she turned
down. One was from a Sicilian duke, who wrote to ask her to lend
him a return ticket to America, at the same time lamenting the
fact that although he would like to marry her he regretted that he
was not rich enough "to keep her in her usual luxury stand." She
was, I am afraid, a one-man woman and, after the bad luck she
had encountered with my father, she put all her energies into
making matches for other people.

She had a strange habit of repeating everything three times.
Once when we were dining with her at the Ritz, Laurence tickled
her leg under the table; her only comment to this was, "Shush,
Peggy will see, Peggy will see, Peggy will see." Once when she
went to a milliner to order a hat with a feather, she said, "I want a
feather, feather, feather." She is reported to have received a hat
that bore three feathers. In New York when finally at the age of
fifty she learned to drive a car, she was stopped by a policeman in

a one-way street for going against the traffic. Her reply, if inconsistent, was correct. She said, "I am only driving one way, one way, one way." She not only repeated everything three times, but she also always carried three coats with her which she was perpetually changing. In a heat wave she wore two silver foxes and fanned herself to keep cool. She always carried three watches, one was a wristwatch, one she wore around her neck as a necklace, and the third one formed part of a lorgnon. The latter she could not use as she could see only with the lorgnon. Therefore it was impossible to benefit by this double arrangement. She was very generous to her children although she had a phobia about spending money. She gave me a fur coat or an automobile every year and was forever putting money in trust for me, but when it came to tipping everything went wrong, and one had to be perpetually on the lookout or be frightfully embarrassed. She was an inveterate gambler and very secretive about the size of her income.

During the course of this winter Mary, who also wore a Poiret evening dress I had ordered for her, led a wild life. She usually ended up in bed in this dress with several people. One night she lost her key and she went home with Marcel Duchamp. That started what one might designate as the Hundred Years' War. The next morning she came to us for taxi fare to go home because she was scared to ask Marcel for more than ten francs. At that time she lived near the Eiffel Tower in a little apartment she had made beautiful with maps she pasted on the walls and with earrings hung as décor instead of paintings.

Marcel was much sought after. It was very difficult to attach him, and in any case he disapproved of the mad life Mary led in the Boeuf sur le Toit with homosexuals. Her great friend was Moises who gave her credit in his nightclub, and as a result she spent fortunes there.

Marcel was a mysterious man. He hadn't painted since 1911, the days of the *Nude Descending a Staircase*. That had made him famous. Now he only played chess, and was on the French chess team. He also bought and sold Brancusis. Marcel was a handsome Norman and looked like a crusader. Every woman in Paris wanted to sleep with him. His particular vice was ugly mistresses. Mary was really much too beautiful for him, but in the end she managed to get him anyhow. It took years, but that probably made it more exciting. He was forever coming and going. At one time he even married a hideous heiress to please Picabia. It was during a period when Mary and he were not on speaking terms, but immediately after the wedding he went to find Mary and they had a reconciliation. Marcel soon divorced his wife.

In the spring of 1924, Comte Etienne de Beaumont organized and financed the *Soirées de Paris*. He rented the Cigale, a famous music hall in Montmartre, and engaged all the best talent of Paris to write music, dance and paint scenery for him. Stravinsky and *Les Six* composed music, Lifar, Riabouchinska, Lopokova, Borovansky, Toumanova, Massine, Danilova and other famous stars danced. Picasso, Ernst, Picabia, Chirico and Miró did décors for him. It was all very exciting because the artists collaborated with the Comte de Beaumont instead of just accepting orders as was the case with the Russian Ballet.

This also was the beginning of the social aspect of the ballet. It became very chi-chi and between acts we went into the bar where we met all our friends. It was, incidentally, the last good ballet ever produced.

This was a pleasant change and quite an improvement on our usual routine of life. We generally spent every night in cafés in Montparnasse. If I were to add up the hours I have whiled away at the Café du Dôme, La Cupole, the Select, the Dingo and the Deux Magots (in the Saint-Germain quarter) and the Boeuf sur le Toit, I am sure it would amount to years.

There were not only ballets but plays. Cocteau wrote *Roméo et Juliette* and Tristan Tzara wrote *Le Mouchoir de Nuage*.

During the winter I got the idea of bobbing my hair. Clotilde and I were the only women left in our world with long hair. Laurence adored it that way, but I was awfully sick of the struggles I had with brushing and combing it, and from the headaches it gave me. I must say it was beautiful. It was chestnut colored and very long and wavy. One day I went and had it cut off. When I came home I did not dare face Laurence. I tried to hide my head under a hat. When he finally caught me he was so furious he threw me under the dressing table. I conserved my mane, but I could no longer consider it part of myself.

In the spring Benita and her husband came to Europe again. She was more shocked than ever by our wild Bohemian parties. Benita and her husband left for Italy and my mother and I without

Laurence Joined them in Venice. I considered myself an efficient guide, since this was my fourth visit to Venice, and I knew where all the churches and paintings were. I did not yet know Venice on foot, but I was soon to learn that, too. Laurence had given me an inkling of the existence of another life in Venice, when he had taken me for walks on a few of the best known highways of communication that zigzagged around Venice. But when we were there it was too hot to do much walking and we had spent our few days bathing at the Lido. He had initiated me in the use of the steamboat, called a *vaporetto,* which replaced the tramcars of other cities. Before that, I had traveled only in gondolas, like the idle rich and tourists, who never really get to know Venice. The following fall I was to learn every inch of my adored city for we were to live there for three months. But that comes later.

When I left Benita I promised to spend the summer with her in St. Moritz. Laurence was a faithful husband, but during my absence in Venice he had had an affair with a beautiful girl called Katherine Murphy: The affair ended as soon as I came back, but nine months later I went with Laurence to see Katherine's baby. We never knew if it was Laurence's, Katherine's husband's or Bob McAlmon's.

One night Bob McAlmon, who was one of our best friends, gave a big party in a restaurant in the Champs Elysées. He had as guests Louise Bryant and her husband William Bullitt, who was later our ambassador to France. We happened to be sitting at the next table, and Bob, finding himself short of funds, asked us to cash a check so that he might pay his bill. I was annoyed that he should have left us out of this party, and told Laurence not to help Bob in any way. Laurence was furious with me and when we got back to Mrs. Vail's flat where we were staying at the time, we had a dreadful row. In the middle of it Clotilde, who was in the room next door, overheard us and came in to take Laurence's part. I told her it was none of her business and that she should keep out of married people's fights. Clotilde told me to leave the apartment and I was so upset I began rushing around the flat as I was, quite naked. Mrs. Vail took the situation in hand and said to me, "This is my apartment, not Clotilde's, and you are not going to leave." She really was always a good mother-in-law to me.

In the summer we set out for Karesee in the Austrian Tyrol. We drove there over the Stelvio, the highest pass over the Alps and which was used by the Italians for auto races. The road zigzags in hairpin bends up to eleven thousand feet. At every corner we had to stop and back-up our car and turn, for the chassis was much too long for this road which had been built for little racing cars. It was terrifying as we thought each time we might go over the side and drop into the valley below. Our engine couldn't stand the strain of going up in first gear and the water boiled over. We discovered a little mountain stream and carried water back in our bathing caps. When we got to Bolzano we found only one room. Clotilde was with us and Sindbad was to follow with Lilly, by train. We spent a miserable night, Laurence making scenes without end because I wanted to join Benita for the summer and he did not want to go to St. Moritz where we were to meet her, since she would not come to Karesee. Clotilde and I were exhausted by morning, but we continued our trip.

The Austrian Tyrol is the loveliest country in Europe. It doesn't frighten one like the Engadine. Its scenery is less imposing and much more acceptable. Laurence did a lot of rock-climbing with guides. He was good at this and had been brought up to walk on glaciers and climb the highest mountains of Europe. Mrs. Vail was one of the first women mountain-climbers of the Alps. Personally I hated even walking uphill and was terrified the only time that the Vails took me on a glacier, the Diavolezza, near St. Moritz. I thought we would fall into every crevasse, and we came pretty near being killed at one moment, but that, it seems, is part of the excitement required to spur people on to this unnatural sport. They claim that when they reach the top of a mountain some thousands of feet high and see the sun rise they are recompensed for all the hours of hard work and danger they have put into it. They certainly deserve their reward.

In the end Laurence gave in and took me to St. Moritz. I don't think he liked being with my family, but I was always with his. After St. Moritz we went to Lake Como with Benita and her husband and stayed at Tremezzo. Mrs. Vail and Clotilde were with us too. We swam in the lake, we played tennis and I tried to learn to play golf to keep up with the Vails. I was so bad that I felt I had killed my teacher as he soon died, and I gave up this sport forever. Benita and her husband taught us to play Mah Jong. It became a vice. In the evenings we danced.

By this time Sindbad could walk and talk, and he had become

very beautiful. His black hair had turned into thick blond curls
and he had quite a few teeth and wonderful rosy cheeks. I was
quite mad about him, as were all the members of my family.
Benita adored him too as she had no child of her own, having had
many miscarriages. Laurence hadn't wanted a baby, but once
Sindbad arrived he was crazy about him. He really wished to have
a girl, so I promised him I would give him one. I said I would
never stop until I had produced one. So we tried to make a
daughter. In the beginning we couldn't make anything. We were
disappointed for three months. At that time Sindbad was eighteen
months old.

Benita and her husband returned to America, and Laurence
and I remained with his family in Tremezzo for the late summer.
Even Mr. Vail was with us for a while, but he soon went back into
a sanatorium.

We went down to Milan where Clotilde was to join an opera
company. She was to sing in the provinces somewhere in Italy.
Laurence and I left her to go to Venice where we settled down for
three months. We took rooms in a depressing old-fashioned hotel
on the Riva, which was modest in price. Up to then I had lived
only in the more elegant hotels. Laurence had a workroom with a
large stove. The smell that emerged from it was so disagreeable
that he couldn't work. Finally we investigated and found it was
packed with French letters. After the burning rubber was
removed he was able to continue the novel he was writing.

Mary was with us. She loved Italy and spent several months out
of each year in an old castle at Anticoli, near Rome. She was
almost a native by now, and felt great sympathy with the people.
She conversed with everyone in rather good Italian. My Italian
became more fluent after awhile. I had studied the language for
years but it had never seemed real till I lived in Italy. Reading
D'Annunzio's plays and novels in New York was most unreal.

Laurence found an old friend, Favai, in Venice. He was an
Italian Jew, who looked like an El Greco, with his long face and
black beard. His profession was to make false old masters, which
were sold to the unsuspecting public. He gave up his job
temporarily to help us buy the antique furniture with which I had
decided to furnish our home. Not that we had a home, but I knew
that if we bought the furniture we would eventually have one.

Shopping in Italy was almost as tiresome as shopping in Cairo. The question of bargaining was the all-important thing. It became dreadfully boring to have to go back to the same shop six or seven times in order to reduce the price asked to something normal. Favai discovered some wonderful objects that really should have been in museums. Then there was the added trouble of getting them out of Italy, since export of real antiques was prohibited by the government. We found a beautiful fifteenth-century oak buffet which required four men to carry. It looked Spanish as it had once been decorated with red velvet, and little bits of this remained around its metal incrustations. In an attic in Treviso, Favai discovered a beautiful thirteenth-century chest. It had wonderful carvings depicting a baptism and a woman fainting. Of course we bought it, and later I found its sister in the Victoria and Albert Museum in London. We found eleven three-legged oak chairs, all with different carvings. The astute shopkeeper told us that he could have a twelfth one made for us. After ordering it we found dozens of these chairs at many of the other antique dealers.

It was a lot of fun, but what I enjoyed most was getting acquainted with Venice on foot. Laurence had lived there as a child for his father had always gone there in the autumn to paint. Laurence knew every stone, every church, every painting in Venice; in fact he was its second Ruskin. He walked me all over this horseless and autoless city and I developed for it a lifelong passion. Everything in Venice is not only beautiful but surprising. It is very small, but so complicated because of the S-shaped Grand Canal that you are forever getting lost in its little streets. You always come out eventually on the Grand Canal, but not at all where you expect. Nothing is more tiring than these promenades, however, because they involve walking over endless bridges with steps.

The Piazza San Marco with its wonderful soap-bubble-domed Byzantine cathedral and its seventeenth-century arcades is one of the most beautiful squares in the world. It would be pleasant to walk there because there are no automobiles or horses, but the tourists are almost as objectionable. Sitting in cafés around the side or listening to music produced by a brass band in the evening is less dreary. What I really preferred were all the other piazzas that I discovered on my walks about the town. These are unknown to all but the Venetians, as tourists never get any farther than the Piazza San Marco. However, every parish of Venice has its piazza.

It is unnecessary to go into the foul odors of Venice. They fade away or become unimportant compared with the overwhelming beauty of a city that still bears the architecture of ten centuries. Needless to say I wanted to buy a *palazzo*, but I was again handicapped by the foresight of my uncles who had made me put all my money in trust.

While we were in Venice, Lilly got pneumonia and I looked after Sindbad every day instead of on Thursdays, as was my habit. I got so tired carrying around this enormous child, who did not like crossing the bridges with all their steps, that I engaged a little maid to help me. To my great shame she turned out to be about fourteen years of age, and not much bigger than Sindbad, but I presume she was used to looking after a large family of younger brothers and sisters. We often used to take him to the Piazza where he sat and fed the pigeons.

In the winter, there were no tourists to feed the pigeons and they were virtually starving. We felt it incumbent on us to supplement the rations allowed them by the municipality of Venice. Every day at noon we arrived in the Piazza with our five kilo bags of grain. The flutterings of the hungry creatures were alarming, and the wind caused by their flight almost blew us away.

Because of Laurence's exhibitionism he dressed rather eccentrically. Besides never wearing a hat and having golden hair streaming over his face, he attracted attention in various other ways. He wore white, azure blue, terracotta or beige overcoats. His shirts were made from the materials that were designed for entirely different purposes. They were of all colors, but what he liked best was to find an odd material, intended for drapes or furniture covering, at Liberty's in London. These gay, sometimes flowered patterns, he took to the most conservative shirtmakers on Half Moon Street and insisted (to their surprise) on having them made into shirts. He wore sandals rather than shoes. His feet turned in like a pigeon's. I believe he had some kind of a shoe complex because every time he went into a shoe shop he became hysterical and made a scene which often ended by his rushing out without buying anything. His jackets and trousers were a rare assortment. He wore the most conspicuous trousers he could find. They too were of all colors. At one time he had a brown corduroy suit made by one of the smartest tailors in London, but later he preferred to wear ordinary French workingman's blue-velvet trousers that he found in the markets of Toulon. In addition, he had a large collection of weird ties.

In Venice Laurence got the silly idea that he wanted me to have a sable cap made for him to protect his ears from the cold while driving. I think it represented a symbol of power. I refused to gratify this very extravagant wish. Instead, after many fights, I had made to order for him an Italian officer's black cloth cape with a velvet collar. At first he did not like it, but soon he realized how handsome he looked in it with his beautiful blond hair, and from then on he favored it.

When the rainy season finally drove us out of Venice we went to Rapallo. There at least we had sun, but we paid for it. What a horrible dull little town it was! We met Ezra Pound there and joined his tennis club and played every day. Ezra was a good player, but he crowed like a rooster whenever he made a good stroke. Later when I met him in Paris and told him how much I hated his beloved Rapallo, he said, "Maybe you have unpleasant personal memories of it." There was every reason why I should have. Besides my being very bored there, Laurence upset life considerably by terrible rows.

On New Year's Eve we attended a party in a private nightclub. Laurence got jealous of a man who asked me to dance, and went over to his table and insulted him. A big fight ensued. I was taken by the shoulders and hurled against the wall. I did not in the least relish this treatment because I was pregnant again. In the end we were forcibly evicted from the night club and were looked at askance in the tennis club.

One night Laurence and I had a bad private fight. It started by his calling Benita a bore, and to retaliate I said Clotilde was a whore. This so infuriated Laurence that he smashed to pieces a new tortoise-shell dressing-table set I had bought that very day, after months of bargaining in the Italian fashion. He knew just what this meant to me. I had a complex about toilet sets ever since I had regarded with horror my mother's silver brushes and combs. As a child I had spent all my savings on collecting a set of twenty-three ivory pieces in Paris on the Boulevard Haussmann to decorate my dressing table. It was a sort of fetish and I had had "Peggy" engraved on each piece. Ever since I had gone to Italy with Valerie I had dreams of acquiring a tortoise-shell set to replace this ivory one, which had long since vanished.

Laurence's destruction of it was to me more than painful. After he did it he dragged me down to the sea where, though it was a cold night, he rushed in with all his clothes on. After that he insisted on taking me to the cinema where he sat shivering in his wet clothes. No wonder Ezra thought my memories of Rapallo may possibly have been unpleasant.

We motored along the coast and on our way to Paris we found ourselves in an enchanting place called Le Canadel. It was little known at that time and quite unexploited. It was half way between St. Raphael and Toulon on the Côte des Maures. There was a long unpeopled sand beach edged by a forest of pine trees. We stayed at a very dull *petit bourgeois* hotel, but down below was the café and inn of Mme Octobon. It was primitive, but the food was delicious, and people drove there for meals from miles away. We decided to live in this part of the world and began to ask if there were any houses for sale. We were told there was one about a mile away. It was an inn called La Croix Fleurie, where Cocteau stayed every winter with Raymond Radiguet. It was just above the sea and had its own beach extending about a mile toward Cap Nègre. This beach was the first place the American troops landed in 1944, in their invasion of the south of France.

The house itself was not inviting but it was a nice little white plaster building in the Provençal style. It had a double exterior staircase ascending to a balcony which gave access to three spacious rooms. There were another three rooms and a bath in the back. Since this house was so small the owner had added a wing, which made the place not only possible but attractive. The wing consisted of one large room with a huge fireplace and three French windows that reached to the high ceiling and gave out on a lovely terrace with orange trees and palms, forty feet above the sea. There was a kitchen with a primitive coal stove and two other rooms and a toilet on the ground floor. There was neither telephone nor electric light. But there was plenty of sun and pine trees and the sea with a private beach. What more could one want? On the other side of the road there was a double garage with three servant's rooms. About three-quarters of an acre of land went with the house. It was uncultivated and was covered with pine trees to the left of the house, and in this tiny forest was a green wooden cabin.

We bought the house and immediately, as the French do, our landlord clinched the affair by producing the *notaire* from Cogolin, who happened to be present, and we signed a promisory document.

However, when I got home and considered my rash act I regretted it. Not that I did not like the place, I loved it; but I realized how much too much we had offered to pay for it, not only offered but actually agreed in writing in the presence of a *notaire*. I consulted with Laurence, and we decided to go back and tell them that we had cabled to America for the money and that it was not forthcoming, as it was all in trust. We said we were going to New York in a few months, and that we would do our best to raise some funds. The landlord was so scared that he reduced the price by one third, which approached what he should have asked in the beginning, and in order to save his face he declared that, since we were not intending to use it as a hotel and were relinquishing those rights, we were entitled to a reduction. We thereby forfeited forever the privilege of calling our villa by the charming name of La Croix Fleurie and we found ourselves in the position of not being allowed ever to make a hotel on these premises or to sell them as such.

We were not to take possession of our new home until the summer. We expected the birth of our daughter in August, so we knew we would not live there until the fall. We now signed the real *acte de vente* at Cogolin, the official head of the *commune,* and celebrated with a bottle of champagne. Then we found some local builders, and Laurence ordered a little house to be built for him as a studio on the other side of the road.

After that we left for America, but not to raise the funds, because I did have just the amount necessary. I went, of course, to see Benita. At the last minute Laurence came with me, although he hadn't meant to. He was writing a novel, and did not want to do any more traveling.

We arrived in March, and Laurence chose as our residence the Brevoort Hotel. Sindbad was a year and ten months old; he had had a great success with everyone on the boat, the *France.* But not as much success as a wonderful conversationalist named Esther

Murphy (later Mrs. Chester Arthur III), who held everyone spellbound for a week by her endless and fascinating talk. She seemed never to stop, and I wondered how anyone could know so much and sleep so little.

Mina Loy, who was not only a poetess and a painter, was always inventing something new by which she hoped to make her fortune. She had just created a new, or old, form of *papier collé*— flower cut-outs which she framed in beautiful old Louis Philippe frames she bought in the flea market. She asked me to take these to New York for her and sell them. Laurence gave them the wonderful title Jaded Blossoms. I arranged to have an exhibition in a decorator's on Madison Avenue. They were to take one-third commission, which is normal, but I provided all the clients. When it came to hanging them Laurence assisted us. He was so Bohemian and temperamental that the lady in charge of the shop wanted me to send him away, but when I explained that he was my husband she could not refuse his help. The exhibition was a great success, and I sold the Jaded Blossoms everywhere. Benita bought two which she offered to the Metropolitan Museum, but they were refused. I looked up all my old friends, hoping to sell them Jaded Blossoms. I became so obsessed by this that I went all over New York carrying them on my fast-growing stomach. My poor daughter was perpetually buried under them.

When I felt I had sold enough, Laurence and I began to look for a house for the summer. We had no idea as yet where Pegeen was to be born. We got more and more depressed at the prospect of a summer in America, and finally in desperation went back to France on the *Aquitania,* with my mother. We thought we had fooled her again about the date of the birth of our daughter, but one day she walked into the bathroom when I was having a bath and informed me that surely I had made a mistake.

In order to avoid giving another soldier to France we decided to go to Switzerland just in case Pegeen turned out to be a boy. So at the end of July we went to Ouchy on Lake Geneva just below Lausanne. Mrs. Vail found us a doctor. As her husband knew almost every neurologist and psychologist in Switzerland this was easy. The doctor said Pegeen would be born between the first and eighteenth of August. I decided not to have chloroform this time, and a midwife was engaged to look after me. She came on the first of August and we added another room to our suite in the enormous Beau Rivage Hôtel. The nurse turned out to be handsome. She resembled a Leonardo da Vinci Madonna, and I was greatly attracted to her. She became bored with nothing to do and every time she said good-night, she begged me to give birth before dawn. After two weeks I began to lose faith in ever giving birth again in my life. There was a head-waiter in the hotel whose wife was also expecting a child, and every day we politely inquired about each other's future prospects. On the seventeenth day of August Laurence pulled a terrific scene in the dining room. I have no idea now what it was all about, but I remember his throwing a whole dish of beans in my lap and then later rushing around in our apartment, throwing all the furniture about and breaking a chair. Maybe this stirred Pegeen because the next day I began to feel queer. The midwife sent me on a long walk with Laurence along the lake. It was extremely painful and we had to stop every now and then when the birth pains became too awful. Toward evening we took out Sindbad's cot and dressed it up in curtains. That of course settled it for my mother. She had the tact to pretend that she had not noticed it, but she sat up all night with a paper upside down in her hands in an adjoining room with Clotilde. About ten o'clock we sent for the doctor. This time Laurence was very happy for he was not banned from the room, as he had been in England at the birth of Sindbad. In fact he was permitted to hold one of my legs. As the pains got more and more unendurable I regretted my decision not to take chloroform. When I felt the wild horses dragging me apart I begged for a few whiffs. The midwife had some ready and every time the pain started she held it to my face. All I remember is her saying to me, *"Poussez, madame!"* And in the end evidently I did not do my bit and just as they were about to take Pegeen with forceps she relented and came by herself at eleven-thirty.

The whole performance was so quiet that our neighbor in the hotel could not believe a baby had been born. I never screamed once. I held a handkerchief in my hand throughout the entire birth. In some strange way it must have given me a feeling of safety. When the pains got too bad I dug my nails into my palms hoping to vary the agony. I also clutched onto the railings of the brass bedstead.

This time I had made Lilly promise that no one would see my baby before I did. The minute she was born Lilly hid her and waited for me to come to before showing her. She was brought to me in a towel. Instead of being covered with blood as I had expected, Pegeen was covered with what seemed to be cold cream. She was all white. She looked exactly the way Sindbad had looked in every other respect. She had black hair and blue eyes. As she was a girl I knew then that I would never have another child. I had kept my promise to Laurence.

The afterbirth pains lasted for days. On the eighth day I was put on a chaise longue and soon after I was allowed to get up. One day when the midwife was out and I was alone with Pegeen, she began to cry. I could hardly walk across the room to her and I felt as if all my insides would fall out. I nursed her for a month and then I couldn't any more. It happened this way.

Laurence and I decided we had endured Ouchy long enough and we wanted to go to our new home in the south of France. Laurence started ahead in the car, and I went by train with the two babies, Lilly and the midwife. When we arrived in Lyons we were told we had three-quarters of an hour to wait. I rushed out with Lilly and Sindbad in order to get them some lunch. When we got back to the train it had left. Pegeen and the midwife and all the luggage had disappeared. I was quite frantic as I thought I would never see my baby again. The midwife had no idea where we were going and had never traveled before. Instead of losing my head, I had the presence of mind to go to the *chef de gare*. He immediately wired to the next station the train was to stop at and asked that the midwife and Pegeen and the fifteen suitcases be taken off the train. Then Lilly and Sindbad and I were put on another train. We remained at the next station for only about two minutes, but just time enough to recover Pegeen, the nurse and the suitcases. As a result of the shock I lost my milk. Luckily we had some powdered milk with us, for Pegeen was already getting one bottle a day.

Our new home was in a place called Pramousquier. My mother always mispronounced it Promiscuous. It wasn't a village or a town. It merely possessed a railway station and a few houses. A little train passed eight times a day, four going from St. Raphael to Toulon and four from Toulon to St. Raphael. It took about four hours to get to these destinations, so we naturally preferred our car. Once when there was a strike on this line Laurence suggested that I give the strikers a thousand dollars to keep them

going. He preferred this to Lucile Kohn's causes, where a lot of
my money went. As a result of my gift we were the only people
who were served on the line during the strike, and we continued
to receive ice and other packages. When the strike was won we
were allowed to ride free on the railroad. We used this little train
to go to the neighboring village of Cavalière, where there was a
small shop, and to Le Canadel where we drank Pernod at Mme
Octobon's. However, most of my life was not spent on this little
train, which looked like a toy and made a noise like an express,
but was spent in a Citroën car chasing around the coast buying
food. I raced this little train for many years, carefully avoiding it
at the most dangerous crossings where people were often killed.
Our house painter had lost his son in this way. He was run down
on his motorbike. The painter received my condolences with tears
at the same time, and in the true French manner he tried to sell
me the motorbike.

We had no electricity for years, and at first we had no
telephone. We had an old ice-box and we received our ice by the
train every morning. It was thrown off on the railway line, and
often I had to chase to Cavalière where it got thrown off by
mistake. The country was grassless, cowless, and therefore
milkless. Our nearest real town was Le Lavandou. It had a post
office from which the postman came on a bicycle every day. I am
surprised he brought us our mail because we had a wild sheep dog
who leaped on and bit anyone in a uniform. She had been left one
day by Gabrielle Picabia. We found Lola tied to an orange tree,
and although she was ferocious, we could not do other than accept
her as a gift. Anyway, she was very sweet to everyone not in
uniform. All my frustrated desires to witness a birth were satisfied
finally by Lola, who gave birth on our couch in the sitting room.
She was completely unconscious of the fact that she was about to
be a mother, and her surprise was touching. I forced her to accept
and look after her babies. We kept three or four of them and they
became ferocious. They rushed about the countryside with Lola,
eating all the chickens. We were perpetually having to pay fines
for chickens killed, and even once for those that might have been
born. Later we had nine cats whose kittens the dogs sometimes
ate at birth.

We had an Italian gardener called Joseph. With the help of
Laurence he laid out beautiful gardens, but the dogs were forever

tearing them up, and Joseph wanted to be rid of them. In order to encourage us to give them·away he used to collect all their *merde* every morning with a shovel and place it on the terrace around our breakfast table. We were puzzled for months wondering why the dogs chose this spot for their convenience until it finally occurred to me that Joseph had plotted this himself.

All our maids were Italian, and as a result our kitchen and larder were filthy. It is a miracle we did not all get poisoned from the rotting of food in the heat and the excessive filth. By degrees we made ourselves a comfortable existence, or rather Laurence did. We furnished our house with all the beautiful Venetian furniture, but Laurence insisted on buying some comfortable sofas and chairs. He rebuilt the house and made a lovely little library. After that he ordered a big studio over the garage for Clotilde. In the end we had four houses, for we had another one built on the extreme end of our property for Bob and Elsa Coates.

Pramousquier was a real home and it grew perpetually in every way. We really felt we belonged to the country. Laurence being almost French we were rooted there. By degrees more and more people came to visit us.

One of our first guests was Mina Loy, who came with her daughters, Joella and Faby. Mina painted a fresco in her bedroom. She conceived lobsters and mermaids with sunshades tied to their tails. We had good food finally by engaging *cordon bleu* cooks in Paris and buying a whole set of copper pans to bribe one to stay with us. We had a wine cellar and Laurence saw to it that it was well filled. However, in the early stages I remember one maid pouring all the wine left in bottles together. The only discrimination she had made was between red and white.

That winter we went up to Wengen to ski. Laurence loved this sport but I never dared to try it, my sense of balance being as weak as my ankles. Since my painful experiences in my childhood I carefully avoided anything that I knew would be unpleasant. Naturally I got bored waiting all day alone in the hotel with the babies. One day I took Sindbad out on a sled and cracked a rib. I decided to go to Paris and leave Laurence with Clotilde. I intended secretly to lead a wild life, and enjoy my freedom of ten days.

I gave a big cocktail party in Laurence's studio. It was a dirty old workshop in an *impasse* or *cul de sac* but ideal for Bohemian parties. This was the first party I had given without Laurence in Bohemia, and I was very pleased with myself.

After this party I found what I wanted, but I was excessively tight and was almost unconscious of it. When Laurence came back he sensed at once that I had been up to something, but it was so harmless that he need not have taken it so badly. The night he arrived without any warning I was with my friend Boris Dembo. That certainly was perfectly innocent, but Boris left at once because Laurence was in a state of frenzy. He immediately proceeded to give a demonstration in the Hôtel Lutétia where I was living. He rushed around tearing up the whole place and throwing all my clothes in the middle of the room. My shoes went out the window. Then he tried to get into the babies' room. Fortunately our new nurse, who had just replaced Lilly, had locked herself in, and she did not have the pleasure of seeing him in this state. Laurence then found my hair which I had so carefully conserved in a drawer and taking it with him, kissing it, he rushed out, only to return in a few hours to begin the scene all over again.

This was not the end. It went on for days and it ended up by producing an unknown husband for Clotilde. I admitted to Laurence that I had been untrue to him, but I lied about who it was. He suspected some nonexistent person who lived on Avenue de la Bourdonnée. One night when we were having dinner in a little bar in Montparnasse, Laurence, who was still chafing over my infidelity, suddenly arose and hurled four bottles into the corner just over the heads of four Frenchmen who were peacefully eating their dinner. Naturally they took this very badly, and the police came and removed Laurence in a pushcart. I fainted on the bar, and when I came to, Laurence was in prison.

Clotilde, who was with us, suggested that we go and get Marcel Duchamp to help us out of our troubles. He told Clotilde immediately to get the four Frenchmen to withdraw their complaints. They all agreed except one, and another one fell in love with Clotilde and later married her. He was a handsome Vendéen and although completely out of our world, belonging to an old French military family, he managed to enjoy himself in our midst. If he started off this way he certainly could stand anything.

Marcel and I wandered around Paris all night longing to go to bed together, but we did not consider it an appropriate moment to add to the general confusion.

The next morning I went to the police and escorted Laurence to the *Commissaire*. Laurence was covered in blood and wore no tie, and we were guarded on this walk through the streets by several policemen. It was very romantic. Then Laurence was freed and he thought his troubles were over, but they were not.

The fight continued, and one night when Laurence and I were still at it, he dragged me to the Gare de l'Est and said we were going to Provence overnight. We sat in a double-decker train waiting for it to leave when he suddenly changed his mind and took me out. Then we walked in the streets and to my great surprise, offering me a glass of beer, he pushed me through an unknown door. To my amazement fifteen naked girls greeted us, begging us each to choose one of them as a partner. I was so surprised I chose the ugliest one. We sat and talked and Laurence's choice, who was quite pretty, told him she knew who he was. She had read about his goings-on in the paper and had recognized him from the description. This was not my first admittance to a brothel. I had been to one in Venice, but this time the girl seemed to want to continue the friendship. I gave her my address. One day much later she appeared in a car at Pramous-quier. She waited at the gate, uncertain as to whether I would admit her. She was on her yearly holiday with a girl friend, and when I saw her with clothes on I did not immediately recognize her. Finally I invited her in and she bored us for an hour with a very commercial conversation and departed.

I think this must have been the year that the British coal miners went on strike. I was greatly moved by their struggle and when the affair reached the point of becoming a national issue I decided to make a large donation. I cabled my bank in New York to sell the last ten thousand dollars of stock I had left from my grandfather's inheritance. This caused a lot of trouble, because my uncle who gave fur coats to girls disapproved and interfered. He asked the bank if I thought I were the Prince of Wales. I finally managed to get the money but just too late. By the time it reached England the strike was over. Laurence consoled me by saying, "Never mind. There will be just enough for every miner to have a glass of beer."

While I was in Paris Berenice Abbott had asked me to lend her five thousand francs to buy a camera. She said she wanted to start photography on her own. To pay me back she came to Pramousquier and took the most beautiful photographs of Sindbad and Pegeen and me. I certainly was well reimbursed.

About this time Mina Loy and I embarked on a great business venture. With her usual genius she had invented three new forms of lampshade. One was a globe of the world with a light inside it. One was a shade with boats whose sails were in relief. They were fixed on separately and gave the illusion of old schooners sailing in the wind. Her third invention was a double-cellophane shade with paper cut-outs in between, which cast beautiful shadows. I had set her up in a shop on the Rue du Colisée, and she had a workshop next to Laurence's studio on the Avenue du Maine where she employed a lot of girls. I ran the shop and she and Joella, her daughter, ran the workshop. When I went to America I took with me fifty or so of these shades with strict instructions from Mina where not to sell them. I am afraid I disregarded her instructions for I had not paid much attention to them.

For the opening of the shop in the Rue du Colisée we allowed my mother to invite her *lingère* to exhibit some underwear at the same time, as we then thought to make some money; this upset Mina so much that she refused to be present at the *vernissage*. We also sold some hand-painted slippers made by Clotilde, and later we gave Laurence an exhibition of his paintings. They were very decorative, but quite childish. The best one was called *Women and Children*. It portrayed factory women with their children at their breasts and horrible smug factory owners looking on, smirking, with cigars in their mouths. Laurence had not been influenced by the Surrealists who came to Le Lavandou in summer in large bands and wandered in and out of our house in their vague way with their artificial wives. André Masson and Gaston Louis Roux lived very near us and they were good friends of ours.

The lampshade shop was very successful, once I got rid of the underwear. Laurence's uncle was horrified when he heard that I worked there myself. He asked Mrs. Vail if I even accepted money. The Vails were very snobbish and had an awful shock when their cousin, a Rhinelander, married a Negress in New York.

In the summer we took a trip to the Pyrenees and landed in

Font Romeu at midnight. When we drove up to the door of the elegant hotel we surprised the *concierge* by handing out a package that contained a sleeping child, Sindbad. The *concierge* had hardly recovered from his shock when we fished on the floor of the car and handed him a second one, Pegeen. We left the nurse Doris and the children here and drove on to Andorra, the smallest republic in the world. There we found the president raking in hay. It was as democratic a country as it was tiny. From there we went to Barcelona.

We spent hours walking on the Ramblas and hours fighting in our room. Every time we sat in a café a shoe-shine boy appeared and offered his services. The dust underfoot certainly warranted this operation being made every few minutes. The strange thing was that every time my shoes were cleaned they came out a different color; once they were silver, once rose, and once green. Wherever we looked we saw signs that read Gomez Ideales. On the way back we passed the monastery of Montserrat, but the road was so bad we did not dare ascend to its heights.

During the winter Laurence completed his novel, *Murder! Murder!* It was a sort of satire of our life together and, although it was extremely funny, I took offense at several things he said about me. He was so upset that he seized the manuscript and burned it in the stove of his studio. That day Pauline Turkel was coming from Nice to type it. Laurence had to dictate a rough draft of it from memory. This time he was kinder to me.

We had a wonderful life in Pramousquier. We had perpetual sun and therefore needed no heat in the house. We merely burned a big log in the living room in the evening. Laurence swam all the year round. I didn't. All one had to do was jump out of bed, slip on a bathing suit and run down to the beach. I spent hours there reading and sun-bathing. I usually got up at nine or ten, had breakfast on the terrace, then did my daily shopping for bread and ice or went milk hunting, or for whatever else was necessary. The shops delivered the rest of the food from Le Lavandou and Hyères. After that I went down to the beach. About two o'clock we ate lunch on another terrace, which was much cooler in summer as it was sheltered by trees and built on an overhanging cliff that was swept by pleasant breezes. We always drank so much wine, even if it was only the wine of the countryside or Muscadet which came from Clotilde's future family estate, that in summer we took a siesta every afternoon. We lunched out-of-doors all the year round.

In winter we ate on our large terrace overlooking the sea. It was covered with palm trees that blossomed in March, and with orange trees that gave forth the most delicious perfume in the early winter when the orange blossoms flowered. The whole countryside was covered with mimosa which abounded in our garden, and for months everything seemed to have turned yellow. Besides the pine trees the country was covered with olive and cork trees; in fact cork was the great industry of the south. There was a little factory back in the hills at a place called Collobrières. The corks were cut on a machine which one woman manipulated by hand, the process being nearly medieval. At Collobrières there was an inn where we enjoyed wonderful six-course meals for eight francs. Another place we drove to was the Forêt du Dom where wild boars were hunted. Here we had equally good meals of boar, for the same modest prices.

In the afternoon Laurence took us in large groups (consisting mostly of women) for a walk in the country. We had only two directions to walk in. One we named *du côté de chez Swann* and the other *le côté de Guermantes*. There were several variations, however, and we went back into the country and over the hills. Sometimes Laurence went on longer walks right over the top of these hills, called Les Maures after the Moors who had once inhabited this coast. The countryside was covered with towers the Gauls had built to keep a lookout for the greatly feared return of the Moors.

Toward evening we always had our second swim. Sometimes we would vary our life, which was completely directed by Laurence, by going to Le Canadel and having Pernod at Mme Octobon's before lunch or before dinner.

Mme Octobon was a solid Belgian woman. Her husband was a fiery Frenchman who often attacked her with a carving knife, but because of their business they could not separate. They led a sort of Dance of Death. Wherever we went we were accompanied by our four dogs who were most unpopular in the neighborhood. Lola was always my favorite, but Laurence took a great fancy to Lulu, her eldest daughter, who greatly resembled a crocodile. In fact, he insisted on having both these animals share our bed. Lulu grew so enormous there was hardly room for me.

Laurence developed a passion for the game of *boules*. He instituted serious games on the terrace. Joseph the gardener was a great champion. He and Laurence laid out an orchard in front of Laurence's studio. They also raised tomatoes which were delicious when eaten raw and hot. At one period we had a wonderful pig called Chuto, who used to follow Joseph around with the devotion of a dog. It was painful to have to kill and eat Chuto and see his blood turned into black sausages. A specialist came from Le Lavandou to perform this operation in our kitchen. Chuto was so fat after Joseph had wined and dined him for months that we should have had enough ham for years. Unfortunately we had to take all the meat to Paris with us on a trip, and it turned green en route from the cold. We also had a chicken farm, but we spent so much money on grain to induce the birth of a few eggs that in the end we gave it up.

In the winter we suffered from the *mistral*. It lasted for days on end, filling the house with sand, breaking all the windows and obstructing the roads with fallen trees.

After Sindbad was a few years old he accompanied us everywhere, but Pegeen, who was still too young, was left behind with Doris. I think unconsciously she developed the feeling of being not wanted by us and became extremely attached to Doris. Laurence was full of vitality and drove us all over the country, sometimes to Nice and back overnight without our stopping to sleep. Once we went to visit Evelyn Scott at Cassis, arriving at four in the morning. We often went to Toulon to shop for delicacies and to spend a gay evening, or to St. Tropez to dine. Our nearest large town was Hyères but that was so dull and full of English retired civil servants that we went there only to shop. In the evenings if we remained at home we always had guests whom we served the most delicious food and wine. We were rarely alone. Either we had house guests or invited people who lived in the neighborhood. We went to Paris for the rainy season which started in November and lasted two months; and every summer in the middle of August we went to the mountains for three weeks to avoid the terrific heat.

Laurence loved traveling and especially driving. He drove as though the furies were in pursuit of him. Once he took me to Paris in nineteen hours without stopping to sleep. We stopped only now and then to drink enough to keep going. As he drank an awful lot, I was very nervous. I never knew what was going to happen at such moments in the car. He would never let me drive. For years we never set foot in a train. We went everywhere in our Lorraine Dietrich and later in our Hispano. Of course I drove my little Citroën myself.

In the winter of '27 we went again to New York on the *Aquitania,* this time taking with us two babies and two girls. One was Doris, our new English nurse, sent by Hazel to replace Lilly's successor who had gone back to England with boils. Doris was very pretty. She was hospital trained, but she looked more like a Gaiety girl than a nurse. By the time she came to Pramousquier life was quite gay. She soon got herself a beau and Lilly greatly regretted her rash behavior in going back to England when Pramousquier bored her, but then it was too late. The other girl was one of our handsome Italian maids. They both had great success wherever they went, and enjoyed New York immensely.

This time I arrived with fifty lampshades and fifty lamps. Mina had collected Louis Philippe bottles in the flea market, and Laurence had also suggested using the southern glass wine-bottles that we found at Le Lavandou as bases for the wonderful shades. They cost a few cents and I sold them for twenty-five dollars. Mina also used silver, blue and green witch balls for lamps. I became efficient and soon found myself selling everything to all the shops Mina had told me to avoid as well as to all the others. I had to mount the shades myself because I could not find anyone to do it for me. I sold five hundred dollars worth, and sent Mina a check, but she was furious because I had not obeyed her instructions. She was afraid her invention would be cheapened by the department stores. Finally in Paris all her ideas were stolen, and although she had copyrights she had to give up her business. It was impossible for her to conduct it without a businessman and a lot more capital.

When I arrived in New York, Benita told me that she was going to have a baby in August at about the time of my birthday. This was her fifth attempt. She had lost all the others in the early months and greatly desired to have a child, especially for her husband. This time she had great hopes of going through with it for she was already past the dangerous month when she had lost all the others.

Benita looked more beautiful than ever. Her pregnancy did not in the least unbecome her. Her long slender neck seemed even more graceful and accentuated as it rose from her rather more mature form. She had one dress that was black with a pink front. I used to tease her and tell her the black part was herself and the pink was the baby. She was shy and embarrassed by this joke. Her face looked exactly the same as it did when Lenbach painted her twenty-four years before. Her brown eyes and hair, her tiny nose and olive skin and her beautiful hands with tapering fingers never seemed to change. She was calm and happy in her pregnancy and seemed quite content to drive with me all over New York, while her Swedish chauffeur helped me to deliver and carry Mina's bottles and lampshades.

Of course I never wanted to leave her but Laurence insisted on going up to Connecticut to finish his book *Murder! Murder!* We stayed in the house where Hart Crane boarded. I don't see now how Hart endured us with our noisy babies and Doris and the maid, but he seemed to enjoy having us and was very cordial. He lived an extremely monastic life up there, seeing nobody for months on end. In winter he nearly went mad from ennui and once threw his typewriter out of the window into the snow. He had a collection of strange records, one of the best being Cuban music.

Soon I left and went back to Benita for a short while, but Laurence again tore me away from her. This was much more tragic as I wanted to be with her for the birth of her child.

Regretfully I allowed Laurence to take me back to Europe. I promised Benita I would return alone in September after her baby was born.

When we got to Paris Laurence found a court summons. He had been tried in his absence and condemned to six months' imprisonment for throwing the bottles at the four gentlemen in the restaurant. One of them had not withdrawn his complaint. This was very serious and had to be dealt with at once. Clotilde's fiancé produced one of the best lawyers in France, Maître Henri Robert. He was a *batonnier* and therefore qualified to plead in court. Laurence was told to take him fifteen thousand francs in bank notes, as he was not supposed to accept any money for his services. When he saw Laurence's embarrassment at being unable to offer the money, he tapped on the table with French practical sense saying, *"Mettez ça là."* The trial took place in the Palais de

Justice and was very impressive but the result was not satisfactory. The noble name of Lafayette, who was a friend of Laurence's grandfather, was brought up, and a novel of Laurence's, which had been published in America, was produced. Laurence was let off his prison term but given a *sursis,* which meant that if he ever had another offense, six months would be added to his sentence.

Soon after this I met Isadora Duncan who was then living in the Hôtel Lutétia in great straits, but nevertheless she gave us champagne. I am sure she hoped I would help her out of her difficulties, but I am afraid I didn't. She came to visit us at Pramousquier with the little Bugatti car she was so soon to meet her death in. Isadora had bright red hair and a wonderful purple and rose costume. She objected to my being called Mrs. Vail and named me Guggie Peggleheim. She said, "Never use the word wife." She was vital and colorful even at this late stage of her life, although she seemed to be rather demoralized. The news of her death upset me considerably.

In the summer of '27 Mary Butts came to stay with us and brought her daughter Camilla, a charming child but neglected by her mother, who was always up in the clouds. One day she got a sunstroke and was very ill. Doris and I had to look after her. Mary took a whole tube of aspirin in one day when her opium gave out. She believed in black magic and was perpetually trying to initiate Laurence into her mysteries. He loved the atmosphere she produced and she was extremely clever at flattering him.

In the middle of all this one day I opened by mistake a cable that was addressed to Laurence. It told him to break the news to me that Benita had died in childbirth. It was such a shock that I did not realize it. I was like the man who was cut in half by a very sharp sword and who laughed at his murderer. Whereupon the murderer said, "Get up and shake yourself." When he did as he was bid he fell in two. I pretended nothing had happened. I went right on doing some accounts I was in the middle of. When I got up, I felt virtually as though I had been cut in two. I seemed to have lost part of my physical being My first thought was that I had deserted Benita. I could not forgive myself for having come back to Europe with Laurence. I started to cry and couldn't stop for weeks. All I wanted was flowers. Clotilde and Laurence went to Toulon and brought back all they could find and put them everywhere. Clotilde was very nice and for once she really said the right thing to me; she knew what I felt because of her love for Laurence. I couldn't look at my children for days. I felt I had no right to have any.

Benita's baby was born dead. It was a case of placenta previa, the most dangerous thing in childbirth. It causes a hemorrhage which is usually fatal. The doctors, to cover themselves, pretended it had no connection with her miscarriages, but of course she never should have been allowed to have this child.

Laurence was painfully jealous of my suffering and kept insisting that I still had him in the world. That of course was not what I was thinking about at the time. It so much deranged him that he made dreadful scenes. After that I never felt the same toward him again and I blamed him for having separated me from Benita for all those years.

I received many condolence letters and began writing mad replies. I was slightly off my head. My greatest consolations were listening to the Kreutzer Sonata on the phonograph and the letters that Mary Loeb wrote me. She was Benita's closest friend and was suffering as much as I was. If only we could have been together at this time it would have helped. Peggy suddenly arrived from America with her husband and her daughter who was Pegeen's age. She was actually on the sea at the time of Benita's death and did not know of it. We went to Toulon to meet her and I drank lots of brandy to give myself the courage to break the news to her.

Every summer we had to leave Pramousquier for three weeks to avoid the terrible heat of the Midi which was very bad for the children. This time Laurence drove all of us to a little mountain hut he had found way up in the Alps behind Barcelonnette. He loved the high mountains where he went climbing. We took Peggy and Doris and the three children. Peggy's husband did not come with us. He had gone to Paris on business. I was so miserable I could not eat or sleep. All I did was cry. Doris thought I was going to die. She fed me to prevent my losing any more weight. Laurence kept making scenes all the time. He stopped Peggy from talking to me about Benita by telling her I did not like it. I couldn't understand why she withheld from me my only consolation, and I remained alone in my grief. After weeks we discovered what Laurence had done through his jealousy.

The following year as a result of all this was an unusually

stormy one and finally broke up my marriage. A fortune teller in Paris said to me, "You will meet a man in the south of France who will be your next husband." I laughed at her and replied, "I never see any men in the south of France except our neighbor, an old farmer." But she was right. On the twenty-first of July, 1928, the first anniversary of Benita's death, I met the man who was to give me a new life.

As a result of Benita's death I decided never again to go to America. I inherited a lot of money but I could not bear the thought of spending her money so I gave it all away. Of all the consolations I was offered from everyone the one that impressed me most was from the *chefesse de gare* at Le Canadel. She was a warm, southern type and always helped me out of my difficulties. Living in such an out-of-the-way place, they were numerous. She was supposed to be the whore of the countryside, but she certainly had a very philosophical point of view. When she heard of Benita's death she said, *"Nous ne sommes tous que passagers sur cette terre."* In view of the fact that she lived in a railway station it was most appropriate.

When we returned from the mountains Laurence's friend, Betty Humes, came to visit us, with her friend Dr. Carlozza, a Roman Rosicrucian. He tried to help me in my grief by teaching me his religion. He read my palm and he also predicted another husband for me. This so much enraged Laurence that he made a dreadful scene in Toulon one night. He threw me down on the Boulevard de Strasborg and then he burned a hundred-franc note. He was taken to the police and Peggy and I went to rescue him. When I protested at their interference in what I considered my affair, the police claimed he had a right to knock down his wife if he wanted to, but that he had no right to burn a banknote, as it was an insult to the Banque de France. An hour later he was released in spite of the Banque de France.

In the fall my mother arrived from America. Laurence drove me right across France to Cherbourg to meet her. It was the weekend of the Jours des Morts and of All Saints' Day, and wherever we drove we encountered hundreds of mourners carrying chry santhemums to their relatives' graves.

The children came up to Paris to see my mother and I placed them in a kindergarten where they immediately got whooping cough. I was worried that we would be put out of the hotel, but

the manager pretended not to notice it, and only when we left sent
me a bill for disinfection of the rooms.

Laurence went to Mégève, a little mountain resort, at the time
quite unknown, to ski with Clotilde. He broke a rib and was laid
up for a short while. I remained alone in Paris with the children,
still absorbed by my grief. I was glad to be rid of Laurence as he
was making terribly jealous scenes over Benita. One night he tore
up the photographs I had had enlarged from snapshots taken of
her years before. My room was full of them and he hated their
being there.

During that winter I met Emma Goldman and Alexander
(Sasha) Berkman. They were glamorous revolutionary figures and
one expected them to be quite different. They were frightfully
human. Emma was very vain and it took me years to see through
her. First I worshiped her and when later I was disillusioned she
did not like it and she revenged herself by leaving me out of her
memoirs.

My mother had given us another car, this time a wonderful
Hispano. We bought the chassis and then we ordered a silver-
colored open body for it. Laurence always insisted on lots of air.
By mistake the body turned out to be sky-blue instead of silver and
had to be painted all over. When we finally got it we left for the
south, taking Emma Goldman with us. She took to the Hispano as
though it were the most natural thing in the world for her to be
driving in it.

Unfortunately the Hispano began to limp. It was ridiculous to
have such a magnificent car that would barely move at ten miles
an hour. It kept stopping all the time. Finally we were forced to
remain overnight at Châlons and have the tank cleaned out. Then
it flew like a bird. Emma was disgusted with the whole
performance.

Very soon after we built the house for Bob and Elsa Coates at
Pramousquier Bob decided to go back to America. Elsa remained a
year without him and then she followed him. She offered her
house to Kitty Cannell and Roger Vitrac. They came to live with
us and we had a nice life with them. In the evenings we read
Montaigne aloud and had delightful talks. One night we went to a
brothel in Marseilles to see a special film. Afterward Kitty, who
was unwell, fainted. The whores were very sweet to her and
looked after her with great kindness. During this brief moment

Benita and Peggy Guggenheim as painted by Franz von Lenbach, 1903

Myself in 1908

Peggy, Hazel and Benita Guggenheim
in Lucerne, 1908

My sister Benita looked more
beautiful than ever. Her long
slender neck seemed even more
graceful. Her brown eyes and
hair, her tiny nose and olive skin
and her beautiful hands with
tapering fingers never seemed to
change.

Myself in 1912

Myself in 1913

My Jacoby School graduating class. I
am at the extreme left in the top row.

The King of Bohemia, 1922　　　　　　　　　In Egypt, 1923

Laurence Vail

On our honeymoon in Capri, 1922

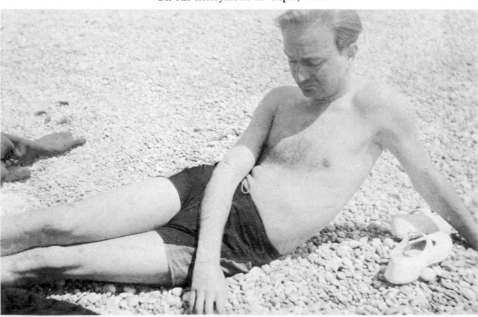

Myself in my cloth-of-
gold evening dress by
Poiret, with a headdress
by Vera Stravinsky, 1924

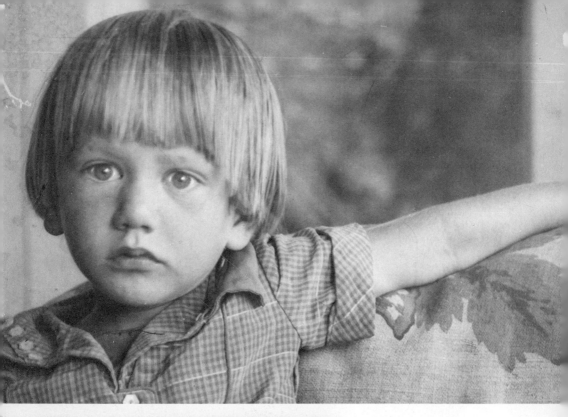

Berenice Abbott asked
me to lend her five
thousand francs to buy a
camera. She said she
wanted to start
photography on her own.
To pay me back she took
the most beautiful
photographs of Sinbad
and Pegeen. I certainly
was well reimbursed.

Vitrac borrowed a hundred francs from Laurence and rushed upstairs. He got back before Kitty was revived and she was never any the wiser.

But of course we got restless and decided to travel again. Laurence and I put the Hispano on a boat at Marseilles and disembarked at Algiers. This was not the most interesting town of North Africa by any means, it was too Europeanized. I much preferred Tangiers where I had been with Valerie. From there we motored in the desert to Biskra, Bou Saida and right down to Kairouan. At Kairouan we were offered the spectacle of the sword-eaters, but we refused to have this religious ecstasy performed artificially for our benefit.

In the desert we passed a broken-down Ford. An Arab squatted patiently by its side awaiting help, and twenty-four hours later he was in the same position with the same degree of patience. I really believe these people have no sense of time. Once we were arrested for giving a lift to two Arab boys who turned out to be running away from home. When we paid their return fare we were allowed our freedom. We also gave a lift to two English missionary ladies. I am sure they regretted it, because one of them became ill from the fumes of the Hispano and nearly fainted. We had a windscreen that kept out the air so efficiently that no one could bear to be in the back of the car.

Then we went to Constantine and Carthage and ended up at Tunis. Everywhere I bought fantastic earrings to add to my collection. It was all very much like Egypt, except that we had the new experience of driving through the desert.

Early in the following summer I invited Eleanor Fitzgerald, otherwise known as Fitzi, to come to Europe. She was much overworked by her theater activities and needed a holiday. Because of the death of her lover she was extremely unhappy, and as I was still unhappy about Benita, we tried to comfort each other. Fitzi was a great friend of Emma Goldman.

Chapter 4

End of My Life with Laurence Vail

In the summer of 1928 Emma Goldman was living at St. Tropez in a charming little house I had given her. She was engaged in writing her memoirs. We had finally convinced her that she must do this, and a fund had been raised to give her the wherewithal to live during this period. I headed it and continued to add to it whenever necessary. She had for a secretary, as she herself couldn't put two words into readable English, a mad American girl called Emily Coleman. Emily, unlike most people who are mad, did not hide it. On the whole it was a pleasant quality because it manifested itself in terrific enthusiasms and beliefs which my cynical entourage would never do more than sneer at. She shared with Blake the persuasion that all things are possible if you have faith. She was passionately interested in people and in literature and life.

Emily looked like a little boy, although she was twenty-nine, and she had a son a few months younger than Sindbad. Even though I liked her at once it never occurred to me what a role she was to assume in my life. Emily insisted that she was a writer herself and was merely helping Emma out in her dilemma. She was, in other words, not Emma Goldman's secretary. Emma adored her and mothered her and spoiled her, and in return, without receiving any salary, Emily lived in Emma's house and knocked her tremendous manuscript into shape.

Poor Emma much preferred anything to writing. She was a woman of action, and was delighted if we motored over to spend an evening with her, when she would give up her work for the day and make us a marvelous meal. She was a Jewish *cordon bleu* and her gefilte fish was her *pièce de résistance.* Laurence thought she ought to write a cookbook instead of her memoirs.

Emily had a nice husband. He was a businessman in the advertising world who had also written a book on psychology. Emily had left him to stay with Emma because she needed this climate for her health. It was the beginning of the end of their marriage, although then she did not know it. At this time she was in love with an Englishman whom she had met at St. Tropez. She was constantly with him and his wife, and produced them in the way she always produced everything she thought she had discovered—with the delight a magician manifests in bringing something out of a hat. And indeed they were miraculous. Their names were John and Dorothy Holms.

When I first met John Holms I was impressed by his elastic quality. Physically, he seemed barely to be knit together. You felt as if he might fall apart anywhere. When you danced with him it was even more apparent, because he could move every muscle of his body without its being noticeable and without the usual jerks one suffers in such cases. He was very tall, over six feet in height. He had a magnificent physique, enormous broad shoulders and small hips and a fine chest. He wore a small red beard and looked very much like Jesus Christ. His hair was wavy, thick and auburn red. His skin was white, but from the southern sun it had turned pink. His eyes were deep brown and he wore glasses; he had a classical straight nose. His mouth was small and sensuous and seemed to be pursed up under his moustache. Like all Englishmen he was proud of his ancestors but he hated his father, who was Scotch by descent and had been governor-general of the United Provinces of India.

John was born in India and when he was a few years old he was separated from his parents and sent to boarding school with his sister in England. He loved his mother, a beautiful Irishwoman descended from Nicholas Ferrar, the founder of Little Gidding.

He rarely saw his family, who were living in retirement at
Cheltenham. He found all contact with them difficult because he
belonged to a different world. He knew much too much about
theirs, and they knew much too little about his. His father had
wanted him to enter the diplomatic service, but when the war
broke out he was a student at Sandhurst Military College and
joined up at the age of seventeen. At that time, he was as strong as
a bull and had killed four Germans by hammering them on the
head when he had surprised them breakfasting under a tree. For
this, to his great shame, he was given the Military Cross. After
six months of war on the Somme in the light infantry, he had
been taken prisoner in a night patrol, and had spent the rest of the
war (two years) in a German prison camp. In prison he met Hugh
Kingsmill, who became a lifelong friend. His other great friend
was Edwin Muir.

In the prison, because he was an officer, he had been pretty
well treated and was unfortunately allowed to have all the liquor
he wanted to buy. This undoubtedly had done him much harm,
for his capacity for drink was greater than anyone's I have ever
known. He drank about five drinks to other people's one and yet
he never seemed to be affected by it until about three in the
morning when he looked peculiar, with his eyes half shutting.
However, he never behaved badly in any way. Drink made him
talk, and he talked like Socrates. All his varied education and
knowledge of people and life, which should have been expressed in
writing, came out in conversation. He held people spellbound for
hours. He seemed to have everything at his fingertips, as though
he had been in contact with everything, had seen everything and
thought about everything. He was like a very old soul that nothing
could surprise. This gave him a detached quality and I was greatly
astonished much later when I discovered what passion lurked
under this indifferent exterior. I always thought of him as a ghost.
He was definitely a frustrated writer, although at one period in his
life he had had a great success in London writing criticism, and he
still received letters begging him to write articles. He could not get
himself to write at all any more. And though he needed money
very badly because he received only a meager allowance from his
father, he preferred to live in the greatest simplicity at St. Tropez
rather than go back to England. He had lived all over Europe since
the war, in Ragusa, in Salzburg, in Dresden, in Forte de Marme,

in Cagnes, in Zagreb and in Paris. He had been with his wife Dorothy for nine years, and she had traveled nearly everywhere with him. Now, however, they were more like brother and sister, their sexual life being over. They had led a very stormy existence. He had taken her away from a man called Peacock and had gone through months of hell, while she wavered between them. He had carried a pistol constantly, with the idea of killing himself if she did not remain with him. Dorothy at this time was very much absorbed in a book she was writing about Peacock; it was an extraordinary and beautiful book. She adored John and claimed that she was writing it for him. I am sure it was true. She must have been created by him, for no woman could live with him that long and not be entirely reborn.

Dorothy complained all the time about John, even though she loved him. She said she was a governess to a baby and had to do everything for him and could never leave him. She complained because they were so poor. She complained because he would not write. She complained because they did not live in England and because he no longer desired her sexually and she complained because he had never married her. She belonged to a middle-class family and felt inferior because of this. She was attractive and handsome and also, strangely enough, had red hair. But her eyes were not like John's. They were green and cat-like. She had a beautiful white skin and a nice figure, but she was seven years older than John, who was nearly thirty, and that worried her. She was also sad because she had no children. This was also a cause of complaint. They were a strange couple and I was fascinated by them.

The first evening I met John was the anniversary of Benita's death and I did not feel very happy. Laurence insisted on going to St. Tropez to dance in the bistros. In the end I went too. My melancholy turned into a kind of desperation and I remember getting quite wild and dancing on the table. This must have made an impression on John Holms, but all I remember now is that he took me to a tower and kissed me. That certainly made an impression on *me,* and I can attribute everything that followed to that simple little kiss.

Later I asked the Holmses to come to visit us at Pramousquier. They came overnight and we went in bathing at midnight, quite naked. John and I found ourselves alone on the beach and we

made love. He talked to me very seriously and asked me what I
liked in literature, and for some mad reason all I could think of
was May Sinclair. After that I did not see him for a long time,
because Laurence and I took the children, Fitzie and Clotilde,
Hazel and Milton Waldman to Maloja for a month to avoid the
summer heat of the Midi. I did not forget John Holms, and I am
certain that I was unconsciously postponing him for my future
because the minute I got back, I went to find him.

As I say, the first thing I did when I got back to the Midi was to
look for the Holmses. They had left their house, and I did not
know where they were. I went to the post office and, when I
found out their new residence, I walked in on them. They were
surprised and, I think, pleased. John took me for a walk on the
hill behind his house. The landscape greatly resembled the
English moors. Then he took me swimming at Ramatuelle. I was
very happy with him and we got on very well. They had finally
decided to go back to England, so that John could make some
money writing and live again in the intellectual world from which
he had fled. I invited them to come and stay with us at
Pramousquier. At first they were reluctant, but when I offered
them Elsa Coates's little house next to ours, they said they would
think about it. Dorothy wanted peace and quiet to finish her book.
In the end John made Dorothy come. She always did everything
he wanted her to do. I liked her very much at this time and she
liked me. I found her conversation fascinating. Soon she felt
uncomfortable in my presence and began gently liquidating me,
but that was when she suspected I was becoming a danger to her.

The day before I went to get them I felt a certainty about my
future. I was living in the exciting expectancy of one about to
enter into a new love affair. I really only acted from a blind force
which drove me on and on. I could not live with Laurence any
more as our scenes were becoming more horrible. In Maloja we
had had another dreadful evening in a café, when he had thrown
everything about, and in St. Tropez, after we got back, he had
tried one night in a bistro to tear off all my clothes because he was
upset by Clotilde's making a spectacle of herself dancing with her
skirts up to her thighs, and because he was suspicious of John.
Alexander Berkman had to come to my rescue. He stopped
Laurence from making me quite nude in public, and then

Laurence slapped me so hard in the face that, although I must have been quite drunk, I became sober.

By this time I had had enough, and I wanted to leave Laurence, but I was afraid to go off on my own. Once Emma Goldman had asked me how I could lead this kind of life. I told her that I could not leave the children and that I did not want to talk about it. But finally I decided things were too bad to continue. A few months before, Laurence had thrown me down the steps of his studio, and then burned up my sweater, and walked on my stomach four times in the same evening. I told Laurence, sort of vaguely and jokingly, that when we separated I would give him Sindbad and I would take Pegeen. I imagine when John Holms kissed me I unconsciously decided I would use him to make my escape.

In the beginning I was not in love with John, but one night when he disappeared for an hour, I got quite frantic. Then, for the first time, I knew I loved him. We used to go out into the country together and make love. Sometimes we went down to the rocks under his house. The minute Laurence went up to his studio and I saw his light lit, I ran over to John's house to fetch him. That was our hour. Soon John began getting difficult about Laurence and asked me to discontinue my matrimonial relations. I found this hard to do. It was all getting too much and I wanted John to take me away, but he couldn't make up his mind. He lived in a perpetual state of paralysis of will, and he hated to give up Dorothy. Dorothy didn't think I was a serious person, but John realized what he could do to me and he was fascinated by the idea of remolding me. He knew I was half trivial and half extremely passionate, and he hoped to be able to eliminate my trivial side.

John and I wanted to be alone, if only for one night. Laurence had asked us all to go to Toulon on a sort of spree. John and I connived very carefully to avoid going on this party. In fact, John was so clever that even up to the last minute I myself did not know if he were remaining with me or not. However, he did. Dorothy went off to Toulon with the others and at last we were free to do whatever we wanted. We went to a real bed for the first time, but got up in the middle of the night, fearing the others would return. We sat in the sitting room for hours awaiting their return, all the time thinking we might have remained in bed. Laurence came home very late. He had left Dorothy in Toulon because she had drunk too much and was sick. The next day we all went back to fetch her. She was hysterical, but still not suspicious of me.

A few weeks of living under this strain was enough for me, and unconsciously I arranged to bring things to a head if John wouldn't. One evening, knowing that Laurence was about and not in his studio, which was the only time we were safe, I went over to John's house and kissed him. Laurence followed me and caught us, which I suppose was what I wanted, but what I had not foreseen took place: a terrible battle from which a death might easily have resulted. John was much stronger than Laurence, but he did not want to hurt him, and when Laurence attacked him, he merely tried to hold Laurence down until I went to get someone to intervene. I lost my head and went to get Dorothy, who was in the bathtub at my house. She took so long to get out, they might have been killed ten times. Finally we got the gardener to come to the rescue, and at the moment he entered the house, John was about to knock out Laurence in desperation because Laurence wanted to hit him with a heavy pewter candlestick. The gardener went to Laurence's rescue as he was his master.

Laurence told Joseph not to interfere, but at least that ended the deadly battle. Both were completely shattered. Laurence went back to our house and I went with him. He told me that he would not stand having the Holmses at Pramousquier any longer and that I was to get rid of them. Dorothy came in during the middle of the conversation and Laurence told her that John and I were lovers. She told Laurence that he was mad, but she looked distraught. Laurence went back to their house and told John that he would kill him on sight if he ever met him again. I was out of my wits, and I immediately arranged to have the Holmses leave by a little back path and take refuge in Mme Octobon's bistro. While escaping, Dorothy injured her leg on the barbed-wire fence. Laurence went to the bistro to look for John, but Mme Octobon hid the Holmses and would not let Laurence see them. Then I knew it was all over, and I planned for everybody's escape. I bribed the gardener to take a note to the Holmses. I sent them some money and told them where to meet me. The Holmses got off to Hyères that night, and I was to join them the following day at Avignon.

It is very strange after living with a man for seven years to know that you are spending your last night with him. In the morning I asked Laurence if he would mind if I went to London for a few weeks to visit Peggy. Of course he thought this peculiar. When he said he would not like it I did not insist. I sent him to Hyères to the bank to cash a check, and when I kissed him goodbye, I wept. I can't imagine why he wasn't suspicious.

We had a very nice, primitive sort of girl staying in the house with us, Clotilde's sister-in-law. She was in love with Laurence and I was always urging him to make love to her, which he did. I hoped that after I left he would marry her, which he didn't. I took her part of the way with me so that she might bring back the car, and I also gave her a talk about Laurence and told her I was leaving him and that I hoped she would look after him. She was shocked and surprised for she had had no idea that was my intention. I kept quiet until the last minute before the train pulled out of St. Raphael, when I left her with a note of farewell for Laurence.

John and Dorothy spent the night in Hyères, and they were still there the next morning when Laurence went to the bank. Dorothy was terrified of Laurence. She thought he was a madman, and when she saw him in the street she made John climb up a water-pipe to hide in their room before Laurence killed him, which she believed Laurence had expressly come to Hyères to do. It was all very humiliating.

Chapter 5

My Life with John Holms

When I arrived in Avignon and found John and Dorothy Holms, the first thing I did was to throw away my wedding ring. I was standing on a balcony, and I threw it into the street below.

Though this was a symbolic gesture, I have regretted it ever since. It was such a nice little ring, and I have found myself so often in need of one. Dorothy was very much upset because her leg had become infected escaping over the barbed-wire fence. She still did not know that John was really in love with me, as he had not had the courage to tell her. He always put off everything. We somehow still managed to make love without her suspecting it. But I don't think that would have worried her so much as the fact that we intended to live together.

We wanted to go to London, but Dorothy made me send for my lawyer, who met us in Dijon, which was half-way to Paris. When he saw John and Dorothy he warned me I was jumping from the frying pan into the fire. Unfortunately, he was also Laurence's mother's lawyer, and that caused a lot of trouble as they felt I had stolen a march on them. I only wanted a legal separation, but he talked me into a divorce. I gave him a note for Laurence as the lawyer forbade my writing him. Worst of all he never delivered this note. He told Laurence of my intentions by phone, for which Laurence naturally never forgave me. The lawyer sent me home at once, telling me I had put myself in the worst possible position by leaving my domicile. After we had been in Dijon for a few days we left for the South.

The first night we got back we went to fetch Emma Goldman and Emily Coleman, and we all went to Fréjus for the night to talk about the divorce. Emma wanted to put in her word with Laurence so she wrote him a letter that made him furious. She told him to be big and to give me the children. I was still so afraid of Laurence that when I went home the lawyer suggested having me guarded by two thugs, but I declined such protection. When we broke all this news to Emily, she was rather upset because she was in love with John herself, and I think that only then did Dorothy realize what it was all about. Anyhow, I left John and Dorothy in a hotel in Grimaud and returned home. When I got there I found Pegeen alone with Doris. Doris told me that Laurence had gone to Paris with Sindbad and the girl Papi, who had taken wonderful care of him and had not let him out of her sight during all those terrible hours when he realized I had run away.

Laurence and I soon reached a deadlock about the children. I was willing to let Sindbad live with Laurence and I keep Pegeen, but I wanted to be guardian of them both. He would not consent to my being guardian of both of them. In the end he sent down our mutual friend Peggy, who tried to fix things up. Finally, after keeping a lawyer waiting for three weeks at St. Tropez, we came to some agreement, and a document was drawn up to protect Laurence. His lawyer insisted on it before we filed petition for the divorce. I wanted very much to live with John Holms, and only if I renounced him could I have stuck to my point and been guardian of both children. However, I did not think it fair to take everything away from Laurence, and also I had no idea how to bring up a boy. At that time I did not know that John Holms would be with me for so many years. I also felt compassionate about Laurence and did not have any idea that he would rearrange his life as quickly as he did.

The agreement about the children made me guardian of Pegeen, and Laurence of Sindbad. It was stipulated that I was to have Sindbad live with me sixty days a year. No condition was

made about Pegeen living with Laurence. The divorce was then
filed and asked for on the grounds of desertion of me by Laurence.
It had to be brought up in Draguignan, the capital of the Var, the
department Pramousquier was in. In three months, we would
have to have a *conciliation*. In other words, Laurence and I would
have to appear in court together and refuse for the last time to live
together again.

Finally, before Christmas, John and I went away together.
Dorothy had left for Paris. We motored all over the Bouches-du-
Rhône and the Var. It was freezing cold, as only the Midi can be
in winter after the sun has set, and I was suffering from sciatica,
which I must have contracted in the woods making love with John
when we had no other place to go. So the trip was not very
successful.

Then we went to London where we did not remain for long. I
had to live in Pramousquier, because of the divorce, and I thought
I had to hide John, so he spent the winter in the Pardigon Hotel,
ten miles away, and I motored over to see him every evening,
returning home at four in the morning. Later Laurence told me
that Kitty Cannell's sister had reported seeing us together in the
hotel, so all my efforts at hiding were useless. In any case this
would not have interfered with the divorce once Laurence had
agreed to it.

Dorothy had left with the understanding that John and I would
try it out for six months. She went to Paris and was unutterably
miserable, and secretly hoped that John would come back to her.

In January I had to go to the *conciliation* at Draguignan. The
South was covered with snow for the first time in twenty years.
Trees were down, and the roads were almost impassable. John,
whom I had taught to drive, drove me there. I left him in a café a
few miles outside of Draguignan.

It was painful and embarrassing to meet Laurence again. It was
the first time I had seen him since I had run away. For his
birthday I had knitted him a beautiful sweater and for a divorce
present he had sent me a pair of earrings. It was awkward coming
face to face with him. He was very bitter, and when we met on
the landing of the steps, waiting to be admitted to the judge,
Laurence made sarcastic remarks to me.

When we went before the judge I had no idea how to reply to
his questions and I kept asking Laurence what to say. I think that

prejudiced the judge. He was a Presbyterian schoolmaster and decided that this was only another case of collusion. He could not understand why I was willing to give Sindbad to Laurence. After the *conciliation* Laurence and I had a drink and I wept. Finally I left him and went back to John, who was waiting in the café. He was in a state of anguish because he thought I had decided to return to Laurence.

The divorce actually took another two years to be granted, and then only on the grounds of cruelty. Doris and Peggy and the café-keeper of St. Tropez, all of whom had witnessed the scenes, had to appear in court to prove Laurence's cruelty. For all this I had to pay my lawyer ten thousand dollars (he said he never handled a divorce for less) and two thousand dollars to Laurence's lawyer. It certainly wasn't worth it but I only discovered what it would all come to long after I was in it.

When this was over we were more or less free and were able to start out on our travels. It seems to me that John Holms and I did nothing but travel for two years. We must have gone to at least twenty countries and covered ten million miles of ground. We wanted to go to Vienna. We arrived there on the last train, after all the others were stopped because of the blizzards, and found ourselves the only people in the *wagons-lits.* The Danube was frozen and it was impossible to remain out-of-doors for more than a few minutes at a time. Even then one had to be covered from top to toe. We remained indoors, most of the time in bed. I had never led such a wonderful life before. John opened up a whole new world of the senses to me, a world I had never dreamed of. He loved me because to him I was a real woman. I refused to listen to him talk, and he was delighted that I loved him as a man.

Although in the beginning I refused to listen to him talk and fell asleep at night while he was holding forth to me, little by little I opened my ears, and gradually, during the five years that I lived with him, I began to learn everything I know today. When I first met him I was like a baby in kindergarten, but by degrees he taught me everything and sowed the seeds in me that sprouted after he was no longer there to guide me.

I am sure that during the first two years of our life I was purely interested in making love, but when that lost its intensity I began to concentrate on all the other things that John could give me. I could pick at leisure from this great store of wealth. It never occurred to me that it would suddenly come to an end. He held me in the palm of his hand and from the time I once belonged to him to the day he died he directed my every move, my every thought. He always told me that people never got what they expected from a relationship. I certainly never dreamed of what I was to get from him. In fact, I never knew that anyone like John existed in the world. I don't know what he expected from me, but I don't think he was disappointed. His chief desire was to remold me, and he felt in me the possibilities that he was later to achieve, although he admitted that he got many other things he did not expect.

When I first met John, not only was I ignorant of all human motives, but, worst of all, completely ignorant of myself. I lived in a repressed, unconscious world. In five years he taught me what life was all about. He interpreted my dreams and analyzed me and made me realize that I was good and evil, and made me overcome the evil.

John not only loved women: he understood them. He knew what they felt. He always said, "Poor women," as though he meant they deserved extra pity for being born of the wrong sex. He was so conscious of everybody's thoughts that it was painful for him to be in a room with discordant elements. Therefore he was supremely careful whom he chose to invite together. He had a wonderful gift of bringing out people's best qualities. He spent most of his time reading, and his criticism was of a quality that I had never before encountered. He was a great help to his writer friends, who accepted his opinions and criticisms without reserve. He never took anything for granted. He saw the underlying meanings of everything. He knew why everybody wrote as they did, made the kind of films they made or painted the kind of pictures they painted. To be in his company was equivalent to living in sort of undreamed of fifth dimension. It had never occurred to me that the things he thought about existed. He was the only person I have ever met who could give me a satisfactory reply to any question. He never said, "I don't know." He always did know. Since no one else shared his extraordinary mental capacity, he was exceedingly bored when talking to most people. As a result, he was very lonely. He knew what gifts he had and felt wicked for not using them. Not being able to write, he was unhappy, which caused him to drink more and more. All the time that I was with him I was shocked by his paralysis of will power.

It seemed to grow steadily, and in the end he could hardly force himself to do the simplest things.

When I first met John he dressed badly. He wore his beard much too long, and had a broken front tooth from diving into a rock. After I had succeeded in arousing his vanity he remedied all these things by degrees and began to look quite different. In the beginning I cut his hair for him but later I forced him to go regularly to the barber, which for him was an ordeal. In London he bought some English clothes. He was always at his best in gray flannel trousers with a tweed jacket. He never wore a hat but always had a scarf of some sort which he perpetually left behind in bars when he was tight.

After we had spent six days in deserted Vienna, where all the restaurants were empty and where everyone was dying without coal, we went on to Berlin. Berlin was horrible, like what I imagine Chicago must have been at that time. I walked all over the city and saw nothing to justify my curiosity. We went to the opera and to some night clubs full of gay boys, but it was all very dreary. I was delighted to get home again.

Soon after this we went to Corsica in a new Citroën we had bought, and made a complete tour of the island. John said the scenery reminded him of Donegal in Ireland, where he had spent his childhood. It rained most of the time, but what a beautiful, rugged and savage country it was. The food was not good and the hotels were bad, with the exception of a few English chi-chi places which had been built in the last few years. The land skirting the sea was rather like Italy. It was rarely flat and the roads were very winding where the sea had made deep inlets. We saw Napoleon's birthplace, and the home of the original anise from which Pernod is made.

After we got back John had to pay his yearly visit to his family. Of course he could not take me with him, and although his family thought he was married to Dorothy, she had never been to see them either. Actually, he had always put off legalizing his union with her, and after living with her so long there seemed to be no hurry to go through all the red tape of getting married. Only an extreme crisis could have made him take this step.

When he came back from England I met him in Marseilles, and we went at once on another trip, this time to the island of Porquerolles. It is one of the three islands opposite the mainland

of the country we lived in, and could be reached by sailing-boat
from Giens. It was tropical and wild, and reminded me of islands
in the Pacific, although I had never seen any. There was one little
port, and many swimming beaches, and a primitive hotel set in a
jungle. We took many walks and, as we were so happy to be
together again, it did not matter much where we were.

It wasn't long before Dorothy began to take our love affair
seriously. She had spent six months without John in Paris, and of
course she hated me. She went about saying the wildest things,
and writing John terrible letters against me. I had only seen her
once in the interval, and that was entirely by mistake. When on
our way back from London we stopped at Paris. John had told her
where he was staying on the Quai Voltaire, but did not have the
courage to tell her that I was with him. She arrived early one
morning and found us in bed. A dreadful scene took place. She
beat my feet and told me I was a wicked woman, and she had to be
removed by the *valet de chambre*. I was so ashamed afterward that
I left the hotel secretly, and allowed John to announce our
departure.

Her hostility only egged me on. I must say I was pleased that
she was not really John's wife, for that would have put me in a
much worse position. But suddenly, in the spring, she decided
John had to marry her because she had resolved to return to
England. She claimed everyone had believed for years that she
was Mrs. Holms and she would be in a false light if people found
out she wasn't, especially since she felt like a deserted wife. John
said he did not want to marry her. Naturally he would rather
marry me if he married anybody, but I was still in the throes of
divorce. Finally, she was so unhappy and became so insistent that
John went up to Paris and married her.

I was looking after Pegeen at this time for Doris was on her
yearly holiday. Pegeen was very much attached to Doris, and
became even more so after the divorce, as she felt quite lost and
insecure in all the confusion. When she was left alone with me
for a month she clung to me like ivy to the oak and would not let
me out of her sight. She was the most beautiful thing I have ever
seen at this age. Her hair was platinum blond, and her skin was
like fresh fruit. She was still under four years of age, and living
under these uncertain conditions upset her considerably. She
liked John very much, but was surprised to meet him again. It was

the first time she had seen him since he had been forced to leave Pramousquier. Pegeen never showed any signs of jealousy toward John; she just never wanted me to be out of her sight, and when once I tried to leave her in Paris for a few days with Peggy and her children, who were Pegeen's friends, she went on strike and I had to take her with me. She felt abandoned and frightened.

Peggy introduced us to Jed Harris in Paris. He wanted to rent our house in Pramousquier, so we went back to put it in order for him. He came down and stayed at Mme Octobon's at Le Canadel and appeared every day making new demands, as he did not think he would be sufficiently comfortable. We put in mosquito-screens for him and painted a room and did various other things to please him. Finally he lost his courage and ran away, sending me a check for five thousand francs indemnity. It was most generous, and later I rented the house to an American princess called Murat, who appreciated my home more than Jed Harris had.

In Paris I saw Sindbad for the first time since the breakup. It was a painful experience and released all the suppressed agony I felt over losing him. Sindbad was then living with his grandmother, but Laurence would not let me see him alone so we all went together to some park. The meeting was unnatural with Laurence present as a spy. Sindbad wore a little white sailor-suit with long trousers and seemed very strange. Although I never actually lost him, I imagine I came pretty near it. Laurence did everything in his power during those first years to separate me from my child. Laurence's behavior was caused partly by revenge and partly through fear that I would take Sindbad back. The divorce had not yet been granted, and the settlement that his lawyer had made was not really valid until it was incorporated in the divorce papers. Though I did not know it at the time, Laurence was living with a woman called Kay Boyle whom he had allowed to take him in hand during his great misery and she was already giving him a child.

Kay and Laurence did everything they could to separate me from Sindbad. Fortunately they never succeeded, because the bond between Sindbad and me was too strong for anyone to break. Laurence was always threatening to take him away, and once he even suggested going to live in Russia. Finally John intervened and made me write the kind of letters to Laurence that would give him confidence in me, and he finally abandoned his suspicions that I was trying to get the child away from him. He more or less came to terms with me. But he never allowed me to have Sindbad for more than sixty days a year to the minute that the letter of the law allowed. The first years of my life with John were completely poisoned, as I was extremely miserable without Sindbad, whom I adored. My only consolation was that Kay was a very good stepmother.

We decided to make an extensive tour of northern Europe in our new Citroën car. There was just room for Pegeen, Doris and my dog Lola. I went south to settle the house, which had been rented for the summer, and to fetch Doris and Pegeen. It was awkward breaking the news to Doris about John. However, if she had any scruples about my living in sin the thought of a trip to Norway and Sweden must have consoled her. We drove up to Paris to pick up John who had been in London for a few days. Then we started on our grand tour.

We motored all through Belgium and Holland, cut through Germany, crossed the Kiel Canal and went to Hamburg. One of my strongest recollections of this part of the trip was my spending a whole day with tears streaming down my cheeks because I had had a terrible dream about my separation from Sindbad; the dream seemed to release all my repressed feelings, and I could no longer control them. By the time we arrived in Sweden, sometime later, I was so upset that I wanted to go back to Laurence. I felt I could no longer endure my life without Sindbad. John said Laurence would not take me back, and that he must have felt great relief (in spite of his first misery) from the fact that the tension which had once existed between us was over.

We went from Germany to Copenhagen, a provincial, dull and Nordic city, and I hated it. I have never been able to get used to the North. It always frightens and chills me. I had felt the same way about Edinburgh years before, although I considered it a beautiful city. Then we went to Oslo, which I liked better than Copenhagen, but I really feel happy only in southern towns, or at least in Latin ones. After Copenhagen we traveled everywhere by boat and took our car with us. It was terrifying to drive it over the two little lopsided planks which were provided for its entrance and exit to boats. Sometimes, the car was picked up in the air by derricks and put on the boat. I once saw a Norwegian pony suffer the same fate, and I felt sorry for it when I saw its legs dangling in midair. Between boats we raced from one ferry to another driving over terrible roads, and perpetually getting out of the car to open and shut gates that enclosed cattle.

It rained every day in Norway and we could barely see the magnificent fjords except for a half-hour a day, between four and four-thirty, when the sun came out like clockwork. We were too late for the midnight sun, but in any case we weren't far enough north to encounter it. We went only as far as Trondheim, which is the most barren town I have ever seen, and certainly as far north as I have ever been.

Lola became pregnant in Trondheim and, since there was barely room for her in the car anyway, her increasing size made life more and more awkward. She and Pegeen shared a sort of bunk, and as Lola got fatter and fatter, Pegeen had to fight for her rights to maintain her place. Twenty minutes before we reached home Lola gave birth to her first puppy in the car, just behind John's neck. We named this offspring Trondjen, which is how we pronounced Trondheim.

We crossed the frontier high up in a part of Sweden that resembled Scotland. It was wild and moorlike, and one could travel hours without seeing a soul. Once we found a lone house with a tree growing out of its roof. We motored for miles through pine forests, with lakes, and as there were no towns anywhere we lost our way in the dark. We finally reached Stockholm at four in the morning. It looked so beautiful in the white night, I was bitterly disappointed when I beheld it in the daylight, all changed. We found the people most amiable and the food wonderful, especially the smorgasbord. Thirty or more dishes spread out for you at every meal! There was plenty of schnapps, but the pubs were open only at certain hours. We had no desire to remain long in this barren country without civilization, so we motored back through Germany just in time to spend a beautiful Indian summer in the Austrian Tyrol in September—what a contrast that was to the gloom of the North; and what a relief to have no more rain. On the way we drove to Weimar and saw Goethe's birthplace, through Thuringia's wonderful forests, and passed several days in Munich. From Munich we went to Bad Reichenhall.

Because of John's chronic mental paralysis, he put off writing to Dorothy all summer, although he carried her manuscript with him everywhere. He was supposed to revise it and return it to her.

I was horrified by what seemed to me to be his callousness, never dreaming how much he himself was suffering from his neglect of her and his inability to do anything about it. Later he told me that he constantly had the feeling that a wolf was tearing at his breast. When we got to Trondheim he finally spent several days on her book and returned it to her. By one of those awful accidents of fate one of the pink feathers from my negligee got into the manuscript while I was reading it. This, when she finally received it, upset Dorothy considerably. She was miserable, for she had hoped that when John married her it meant that he would return to her, but by now she realized this was not the case.

I think one reason John was so attracted to me was because I was just the opposite of Dorothy. I took life rather less seriously and never fussed. I joked about everything and he brought out my unconscious wit; he even enjoyed being a foil for it. I was completely irresponsible and had so much vitality that I am sure I was quite a new experience to him. I was light and Dorothy was heavy. She was always sick and my health was marvelous. Both she and John suffered from insomnia. He would lie awake reading all night while I slept like a baby. Dorothy was dowdy and dressed with no taste. She had piano legs while mine were just the opposite. In fact John named me "Bird Bones." He didn't even mind my strange nose and, in honor of it, called me "Dog Nose." The peculiar thing was that Dorothy and I had the same beautifully shaped cranium and in that one respect we resembled each other.

When we got to Bad Reichenhall in Bavaria, a few miles from the Austrian Tyrol, we decided to remain there for the month of September. John wanted to write an article he had promised to some English paper, but of course he never did it.

The Austrian Tyrol is the country I love most in Europe. I adore the rocky mountains with the trees growing straight up into the air as rigid as telegraph poles. I love the soft-spoken Austrians and the wonderful atmosphere of relaxation they produce. Of course, this was before the Anschluss. Besides the lake that D. H. Lawrence describes in *The Captain's Doll*, there were many others just as beautiful, one with an old monastery in the center. We went to Hitler's future home, Berchtesgaden, without realizing what that name was to mean in a few years, and from there to Salzburg, although we were too late for the music festival. John had lived there at one time and had strange memories of Stefan Zweig whom he had met there.

I think this was one of the happiest times of our life. We had made friends with an Englishman and his Danish wife, and they had a daughter Pegeen's age, so we all had company. Bad Reichenhall itself is a horrid sort of "cure place," where you take baths for your health, but we remained there very little as we were perpetually motoring around the vicinity.

In Munich, we had bought a phonograph and lots of records, and that was the beginning of a real enjoyment of music which John aroused in me. He was horrified by my bad taste. No wonder. In those days I liked Rubinstein's *Melody in F* and Schumann's *Träumerei* better than anything else. Soon he made me appreciate Mozart, Bach, Beethoven, Schubert, Brahms, Haydn, Handel and later Stravinsky and "The Six." After I was once initiated, I sat for hours listening to music, but I always preferred to hear it at home. Occasionally John took me to concerts and to Mozart's operas.

We went back to Pramousquier at the beginning of October, and as I said before, we arrived just twenty minutes too late for Lola, who had already given birth to one puppy in the car. They were very beautiful babies, but the southern climate did not suit them, probably because of their northern heritage, and Trondjen died of distemper.

We soon got restless, and went to Paris to live. At first we had no home other than the Hôtel de Bourgogne et Montana near the Place du Palais Bourbon. I had decided to sell the house at Pramousquier and give Laurence the proceeds, as I really considered it his property, having long since made him a present of the house which was actually in my name. So I sent for all the furniture and divided it with Laurence. My share I placed in storage. I had already given him the Hispano-Suiza, to sell for his divorce expenses.

Laurence was very secretive about his life, but soon I discovered, by chance, that he was a father again. He had had a little daughter and I asked him to let me see her. I felt badly, as I had had an operation performed in a convent by a wonderful Russian doctor called Popoff. The nuns were strict and dirty and had no idea why I was there. However, they tried to take care of me, and on Sunday morning woke me up at six to put a thermometer in my mouth which they never came back to remove. When I remonstrated they excused themselves on the grounds of being at prayer. Dr. Popoff, who was supposed to have been the *accoucheur* of the Grand Duchesses of Russia, admitted one to this convent for needing a *curetage,* and then was credited with saying suddenly, in the middle of the operation: *"Tiens, tiens, cette femme est enceinte."*

When I went south to settle Pramousquier I brought back my darling dog Lola. She had never lived in a big town before, and the first morning the maid took her out she got frightened and escaped. We had wild hopes of recovering her by searching in the lost dog's home, otherwise known as the *fourière,* and for months we went there daily. Finally we reduced our visits to two or three a week. Never have I seen a more heartrending and upsetting sight. The *fourière* was full of lost creatures who set up the most horrible howls to attract attention the minute anyone entered. Every day there were new homeless beasts, but never Lola. The dogs must have thought we had come to claim them, or rather they hoped that their masters were about to rescue them. In the end, we had to give it up. Someone else must have wanted Lola as much as we did, or they would have brought her back to us because we placed a touching ad in the *Paris-Midi,* offering a big reward.

During this period I was slightly more friendly with Laurence, and he allowed me to see Sindbad every Thursday for the entire day, but would never let him sleep in my house. Soon after that he moved to the Marne; I used to meet him half-way, take Sindbad back to Paris for a short time and bring him back in the evening. This proved so tiring for the child that I motored down to La Fierte, where he lived, and tried to find places to go with him. Of course it didn't work. One day Laurence made a terrible scene when I brought Sindbad back, so I postponed my visits, expecting to have the child live with me for part of the summer.

Emily Coleman was in Paris, and we saw her quite often. We took Sindbad and Johnnie out together on Thursdays, and thus started a lifelong friendship between the two boys, who were almost the same age. One night, when we were in a café, I left Emily and John and went to join Laurence at another table, little dreaming of the effect it would have on John. It seems he nearly went off his head, and Emily had to walk him up and down the street to calm him. The next day she warned me that I was playing with fire; and for the first time I realized what a passionate person John Holms was underneath his calm exterior.

We had rented a furnished flat with a studio in the Rue Campagne Première and, as it was leased under my married name, John used to be called Vail, which annoyed Laurence considerably. I therefore resumed the name Guggenheim to avoid trouble.

I took John to meet Helen Fleischman and Giorgio Joyce. We saw quite a lot of them and often with his parents, James Joyce and Nora. They lived an intense family life and it surprised John, who was so anti-family, that Giorgio should be so tied up with his parents. Lucia Joyce, Giorgio's sister, was often with them too. She was a sweet girl who was studying dancing. Giorgio had a good bass voice and used to sing for us, frequently with his father, who was a tenor. John enjoyed talking to Joyce but, since he never could have been one of Joyce's sycophants, the relationship was casual. They had both lived in Trieste, and I remember their reminiscing about the Bora wind, Trieste's worst evil. While it blew (and sometimes it lasted for days) ropes were put up in the streets to help people circulate.

Suddenly my mother arrived from America. I hadn't seen her since my separation from Laurence, and although she approved of that, she thought I was mad to give him Sindbad and she never forgave me for it. She had no idea about John, and it was difficult to initiate her. Fortunately, when she arrived Edwin Muir and his wife were in Paris, and when she came to see me she met them at my house. It was a good beginning. She would not believe that I was living with John, and that I wasn't going to marry him. She always called him Mr. Holms and treated him formally. She never liked him; she thought he was a terrible man for having married Dorothy, and because he didn't work. I tried to impress her a little bit by his family. She wrote down in her notebook "Governor of the United Provinces of India." After she had made several inquiries, she came back and told me I was wrong, that his name should have been Lord Reading. However, she had to accept John as she knew I would not see her otherwise. One day when the Muirs were in my house Dorothy came to the door and made a terrible scene saying they had no right to befriend me.

I liked Edwin Muir from the very beginning. He was frail and timid, and so sensitive and pure that you could not do otherwise than like him. You felt his talents, even though he was shy and never acclaimed himself. Muir reminded me of a man who has been asleep in front of a fire too long and could not recover from his drowsiness. They had had a hard life and had struggled painfully to keep alive by doing translations. They were almost better known as the translators of *Jüd Suss* than as anything else. They had translated Kafka, and thus introduced him to the English-speaking world. Muir always consulted John before publishing his own books, and once, when he hadn't, John said the book was a catastrophe. Muir adored John and after his death, when I asked him to write something about him, this is what he sent me. He enlarged on it and used it himself in his own autobiography, *The Story and the Fable*.

I first met John Holms one Sunday morning in Glasgow in the summer of 1919. Hugh Kingsmill arrived at my lodgings with him as I was starting out for a walk in the country: when I opened the door I heard their English voices echoing up the stairs. Hugh had to go on to Bridge of Allan, and Holms agreed to come with me. It was a still, warm day. We wandered about the moorlands to the south of Glasgow, ate in a little tearoom and returned in the evening, meeting a two-mile-long line of courting couples as we approached Glasgow. Holms was in the uniform of a Scottish regiment, glengarry, khaki tunic and tartan trews. I cannot remember much about that day except that we had an argument about Pater, and later discussed the merits of windy and calm weather: Holms hated bracing winds and I, being then an admirer of Nietzsche, was in favour of them. As we were returning he began to quote Donne, whom I did not know at the time, and we stood leaning against a gate with the scent of hay in our nostrils while he mildly intoned:

> And while our souls negotiate there,
>   We like sepulchral statues lay,
> All day the same our postures were,
>   And we said nothing, all the day.

Then he recited the opening verse of "The Relic," stopping with delight at "the last busy day" and the picture of the resurrected visitor waiting by the lover's grave to make "a little stay." These lines seemed to be in keeping with the rounded haycocks in the field and the long line of couples passing like a millennial procession in the evening light.

The first thing that struck me about Holms was a still watchfulness which set me thinking of the Old Testament, never far from a Scotsman's mind. By the end of the day the watchfulness had turned into a watchful benevolence, which was characteristic of Holms if he liked anyone. The next time we met was in London after my marriage, and I saw a great deal of him later in Dresden, Forte dei Marmi and the south of France, where we both chanced to be living; and afterwards in London.

Holms gave me a greater feeling of genius than any other man I have met, and I think he must have been one of the most remarkable men of his time, or indeed of any time. There was a strange contrast between his instinctive certainty and grace as a physical being, and the painful creaking of his will. In his movements he was like a powerful cat: he loved to climb trees or anything that could be climbed, and he had all sorts of odd accomplishments: he could scuttle on all fours at a great speed without bending his knees: walking bored him. He had the immobility of a cat too, and could sit for a long time without stirring; but then he seemed to be filled with a boundless dejection; it was as if he were a captive imprisoned far within himself, beyond rescue. His body seemed to fit him for every enjoyment, and his will for every suffering. He had constantly the struggle which Wordsworth noted in Coleridge: "the amazing effort which it was to him to will anything was indescribable." The act of writing was itself an enormous obstacle to him, although his one ambition was to be a writer. His knowledge of his weakness, and his fear that in spite of his gifts, which he never doubted, he would not succeed in producing anything, intensified his stationary combat and reduced him to shaking impotence. He was persecuted by dreadful dreams and nightmares.

His mind had a majestic clarity and order, and when turned on anything was like a spell which made objects assume their true shape and appear as they were, in their original relation to one another, as on the day of creation. He once had the idea of writing a poem describing the evolution of the species, pictorially, showing all the various animal forms developing from an archetype by an enormous foreshortening of time; and his talk often gave the same impression. It had no surface brilliance; it was awkward; he often seemed unable to finish a sentence: the same obstacle which kept him from writing kept him from talking as he might have talked. What made his talk unique was its reality, the fact that it was never trite and never secondhand, but always concerned with real things. He could be amusing, and he loved witty conversation, but this was his distinguishing quality. His benevolence came out very strongly in his talk. it was as if were looking at things with a fraternal eye and helping them to find themselves. But he had a keen enjoyment of the second-rate too, I remember him reciting T.E. Brown's poem:

> A garden is a lovesome thing, God wot,

with sardonic gusto, his voice rising with a pained incredulity in the line,

> Not *God*, in GARDENS, when the eve is COOL?

to assume a fine gentlemanly condescension in

> Nay, but I have a *sign*.
> 'Tis very sure He walks in *mine*.

Like Hugh Kingsmill I always had a strong sense of his goodness, although he was not good by his own standards. He gave me more strongly than anyone else I have known, a feeling of the reality of goodness as a simple almost concrete thing. Sometimes he seemed to breathe a goodness so natural and original that one felt the Fall had not happened yet, and the world was still waiting for the coming of evil. These 'good' times always brought with them a feeling of abundance, of fat herds, rich fields, full streams, endless food and drink, and all things gladly following the law of their nature. He had the capacity for simple enjoyment which Yeats says goes with goodness,

> Except by an evil chance,

a line which would have made him smile. He had an equally strong sense of evil, and a profound conviction of sin; but he had no trace of Puritanism, and I think his guilt came finally from his feeling that he was an immortal soul caught in the snares of the world, and both liking and loathing the bondage. His inability to express what was in him may have been partly due to the intensity of this feeling, but that in turn greatly deepened his sense of guilt, which grew with his failure to write.

In the spring, John and I motored all through Brittany with Pegeen and the maid, Doris being on her yearly holiday. It either rained all the time, or seemed to, for the country was covered with mist. We never saw the sun. Brittany had a certain ferocity and wild beauty with its savage cliffs and red earth. There were many pleasant beaches, but without sun they were forbidding. We saw wonderful old Celtic churches and passed on the roadside many early sculptures of Christ. These *calvaires* were unpretentious and astoundingly beautiful.

We wanted to rent a house for the summer but after looking for one in every corner of the peninsula, we gave up the idea. We had not found the ideal spot. John would never make a compromise about where he lived. He would spend months looking for a place that he would only be living in for a short period. We usually wasted half of the summer in search of a residence, but he always ended by finding the perfect place. After Brittany we went all over Normandy and then gave up the idea of living there also. Finally, in desperation, I suggested we go down to the Basque country to St. Jean de Luz where Helen and Giorgio Joyce were spending the summer. As we were leaving, Emily showed up and we took her with us as far as Poitiers. We drove through the Loire country, and visited all the châteaux again. We had exquisite meals and wonderful wine—John was a gourmet and connoisseur of vintages—in all the provincial towns we drove through. We always did ourselves well.

When we arrived in St. Jean de Luz, we again began looking at houses. Helen and Giorgio lived in the center of town and wanted us near them, but of course John rebelled. Finally he found the most beautiful house, a few miles away from St. Jean de Luz out in the country at the foot of the Pyrenees. It was situated high on a hill and was completely isolated. It was called Bettiri Baita and belonged to a painter called Monsieur de Bonnechose, who was the tallest man I have even seen. Even John looked like a dwarf next to him. He himself had built this house out of stone that had been found on the premises. M. de Bonnechose really wanted to sell the house and all the land, but he rented it to us for a minute sum. We spent the most wonderful summer, when we finally got around to it.

At last I was to have Sindbad stay with me for a fortnight. Laurence suggested that he come and live nearby during this visit; I think he was still afraid I was going to run away with Sindbad. In order to allay his fears, I said he could have Pegeen as a hostage, provided Doris went with her. When he consented, we crossed southern France by train to Sainte-Maxime, where we exchanged children. Laurence was then living at Cavalaire near Pramousquier. The exchange was effected and I took Sindbad to

Emma Goldman's house for the day and then home with me. Laurence had filled him with the most extraordinary stories and had warned him not to let me run away with him. Sindbad told me that he had come to visit me because Laurence said that if he didn't I could send the police after him. Evidently he had also promised Laurence he would not set foot in Spain (we lived only a few miles away) for he refused to walk on a bridge which connected the frontiers. When we visited some underground grottoes that were partially under Spanish soil, Sindbad insisted on coming out. We went on a little trip up to Gavarnie and walked on a glacier and drove around the Pyrenees. Emily was with us and that made things easier. I sat behind in the rumble seat of the car with Sindbad and by degrees renewed my acquaintance with him. I resumed telling him the exciting stories I had always invented for him. He adored them.

John was a wonderful athlete. When he was drunk he used to climb chimney stacks and walls of houses with the agility of a cat. He could dive from terrific heights like a bird and he swam like a fish. He was also a fine tennis player and because of his height he was expert at the net. His whole body was so agile and elastic that he could do anything with it. He climbed rocks like a mountain goat and used to make the most dangerous trips along the coast. I was terrified of rock climbing, and Emily went with him instead. He also took Sindbad, and they became very good friends after Sindbad thawed out. When the fortnight was over I had to take him back to Laurence. It was agonizing to be without him again, especially since I wasn't to see him until Christmas.

After I returned with Pegeen and Doris, John took Emily and me on a little trip to Spain, high up in the Pyrenees. We lived practically on the border and the country was filled with smugglers who brought back fire water and cigars on foot and hid them in the bushes around our house. We drove to Pamplona, the city Hemingway had immortalized in *The Sun Also Rises*. I was so miserable at being separated from Sindbad again that this trip did not make much of an impression on me. All I remember is seeing the bulls being driven through the town into the corrals.

Emily and John always spent hours discussing literary matters. I used to leave them and go to bed early. All day I retired into my shell and read Dreiser's *An American Tragedy*. Once I had a dream that I walked into the bathroom and found Emily and John in the bathtub reading poetry. I both loved and hated having Emily with us. She had so much life that, in spite of my jealousy, I always sent for her when I got bored. She was determined to squeeze every drop of knowledge she could from John and was at him all the time. Once, when she was angry with him, she burst out in a fury, saying, "I wish I would never see you again." I was sitting calmly writing to Sindbad and I replied nonchalantly, "It could be arranged," but of course it never was, and our lives got more and more tied up. Emily was always staying with us or going on trips with us. She was like our child. She was passionately interested in writing and she used to send John pages and pages of her poems when she was not with us. Sometimes he groaned and moaned in despair; sometimes he thought they were good.

During this summer my divorce was finally granted, after two years.

In the fall we went back to Paris and lived in the Royal Condé Hôtel, near the Odéon. We began hunting madly for a house, and John as usual refused to live in anything we found. At the last minute, while I was trying to bully him into a very nice apartment that he didn't want, he found the ideal house. It might have been built for us, it was so perfect in every respect. Georges Braque, the painter, had built it for himself. It was like a little skyscraper with one or two rooms on each of its five floors. It was in a working class quarter, way out of the center of Paris, on the Avenue Reille, almost at the Porte d'Orléans; but opposite us was the reservoir and behind us was a garden. Our neighbors were artists. On one side Amédée Ozefant had his school of painting. The view from the top floor was miraculous for Paris. In front of us stretched a whole field of grass which grew on the reservoir. In summer, the haycocks were neatly piled, we thought we were living away from the city. On the roof we had a terrace and a little pool, which we did not discover until years later when we lent Gabrielle Picabia the house and she unearthed it. We slept on the top floor, and it was like a nest in the tree-tops. John had a study here too. It was cold and uncomfortable and certainly the last place he would ever have worked in, even if he had been able to write, as it overlooked the reservoir. On the next floor below we had one room the whole depth of the house, which served as library, living room, dining room and guest room when necessary; also as a music room, where we played the phonograph all day. In the second year we bought an English handmade gramophone with an enormous papier maché horn. This room was like a large studio. It had windows front and back that reached to the ceiling. Underneath, Pegeen and Doris had a floor to themselves with two rooms, and below that was the kitchen and cook's room, and on the street floor was the garage, where we kept our Peugeot.

We lived in this house three years, but of course we always went on trips and never seemed to be stuck there. Before we had rented it we had signed a lease for three small apartments in an enormous building not far from the Avenue d'Orléans. It was built for artists, and each flat had a studio. The whole place was cheaply constructed and consequently the walls were thin. John, who could not bear any noise, insisted on having cork walls put into his apartments. This building was owned by a company that went broke, and it took years before they completed it. By that time we were living in our skyscraper house. We tried to recover all the money we had put into that place, but the French are good at holding on to anything they actually have in hand. Our lawyer was unsuccessful in recovering any part of the two thousand dollars we had invested in advance for rent, alterations, etc. But little did I dream what service I was rendering a future husband. When years later I met the tenant who eventually occupied the flat he told me that a mad American woman had much improved his studio by inserting cork walls like those which Proust had. (That tenant was Max Ernst.)

John drove me to Antwerp to visit Emily, in a new Delage we had just bought. These were the last six months she was to spend with her husband, who was manager of an advertising agency. It was the worst possible time of the year to go north, and the whole trip was made through fog. We did not remain long, and the best thing we did was to hear Mozart's opera, *Don Giovanni,* sung in Flemish. It was heavenly. On the way back I stuffed the car with Belgian-made Player cigarettes, for they were so much cheaper than in France. At the frontier the car was searched and the cigarettes dragged out from all their hiding places. Every time the customs official asked if there were others I insisted that he had found them all. It became more and more embarrassing as he kept finding new ones. At last he found all and fined us heavily, saying that he could confiscate the car, but would not go to such limits.

He took every cent we had and all the cigarettes, and we had to drive home penniless.

During this winter we saw quite a lot of Harold Loeb, my cousin, formerly editor of *Broom* magazine. Both he and John were very fond of Jean Gorman whose husband, Herbert Gorman, was writing a book on James Joyce. Gorman used to bring out of his pocket the most insulting replies from people he had written letters to about Joyce. But Gorman was so delighted with the letters that he did not seem to realize how insulting they were to him.

John never wanted to go to bed. He liked to sit up conversing and drinking very late. Evidently Jean Gorman, whom we saw nearly every day, complained to James Joyce because she brought us this little poem he had written for her about us:

> To Mrs. Herbert Gorman who complains that her visitors kept late hours:
>
> Go ca'canny with the cognac and of the wine fight shy
> Keep a watch upon the hourglass but leave the beaker dry
> Guest friendliness to callers is your surest thief of time
> They're so much at Holms when with you, they can't dream of
> Guggenheim.

I was quite jealous of Jean Gorman; John liked her so much. I liked her too; she was a vital, proud little thing. She looked like a lizard. She was unhappy with her husband, and although she was breaking up with him, she had the pride and character to maintain a deep silence about her affairs, even when drinking. Finally she left for America, got her divorce and married Carl Van Doren.

At this time Pegeen was in Marie Jolas' bilingual day school in Neuilly and was very happy. Doris drove her there every morning in a new little Peugeot car I had bought to run around Paris in, and either Doris or John and I went to fetch her every evening. That was about the only hour I saw her for she was already in school by the time we woke up.

John got up late as he slept so badly. He read most of the day and went out every night to night clubs in Montmartre or to cafés in Montparnasse or to friends' houses, or we had people at home.

John always liked society after six in the evening, so when Pegeen went down to have her supper and go to bed, we usually went out in search of people. Sometimes we brought home for dinner lots of unexpected guests for whom there always seemed to be enough food. We had a marvelous cook. If John stayed out very late, which he often did, I got so bored I went home without him. I hardly ever drank in those days and I could not keep up with him. Sometimes he spent the whole day in bed with a hangover and got up only for the evening. This used to make me extremely angry because I felt cheated of his company. He never wanted me to leave him, and was just as unhappy without me as I was without him. He was extremely dependent on me and never wanted me out of his sight.

In May we took Mary Reynolds with us and went to Italy, first to Florence and then to Assisi where Emily was spending a few months for her health. John wanted to go to the Abruzzi, a part of Italy I had never visited. We drove down the Adriatic coast which was different from the other coast of Italy that I knew so well. John drove the Delage as if it were an airplane. I always felt we were in the air, not on the earth.

Going over a high mountain pass to Aquila we struck a blizzard, though it was in May, and the wires of the car froze. We had stopped on a very slippery road covered with snow to see the scenery a few feet before the peak. On our right was a drop of thousands of feet. John insisted before we died of the cold we turn the car around and go back. We could start it by rolling downhill, but the danger of pushing it over the cliff while we turned it around was terrifying. We had to calculate it to an inch, and it was almost impossible because the car kept slipping on the ice. I really don't know how we ever did it; it must have been the fear of dying in the cold that egged us on.

Emily, who was with us, refused to help in any way; she disliked the blizzard, and she just sat in the Delage while Mary and John and I, by sheer force of will, managed to get it turned around without its going over the side. John put his scarf under the front wheel to stop it from skidding and then we rocked the car back and forth, fearing any moment it might fall over the precipice. Even this did not make Emily budge. We pushed and pulled and made tracks in the snow for the wheels to be free. Finally we got to an inn at Norcia in the valley below where we were treated regally. It was the most primitive place I had ever been in. A whole baby goat was brought on the table for us and gallons of Abruzzi wine. Our beds were warmed with copper warming pans. The innkeepers were so sweet to us that we were happy we had not perished in the blizzard. We were thrilled to be in the country of D. H. Lawrence's *Lost Girl*. John and I were great admirers of Lawrence's books.

We left Emily in Assisi and went to Venice. For the first time since I had been with John he let me down—he did not share my passion for this miracle city. I got up early and walked miles alone every morning before he awoke. He complained about it all afternoon and made me so unhappy that finally I decided to leave. I think it is the feeling of death that permeates Venice which upset him. I can't explain in any other way his taking a dislike to a place that has so much beauty to offer in every form and from so many ages. We drove down the Brenta and saw the strange summer palaces of the Venetian nobles, so varying in type but all built within a hundred years of each other.

In June we began again to travel all over France to find a house for the summer. My relations with Laurence had reached a more friendly state, and Sindbad came to me regularly Christmas and Easter and for one month in the summer. Pegeen went to Laurence for an equal length of time. This made things easier. We took a beautiful trip through the part of France that lies between Marseilles and the Spanish frontier. It resembled the country of the Var, but was even wilder and covered with grapevines. The few small towns, Port-Vendres, Banyuls, Cerbère, were filled with artists, and the life there must have been much like that of St. Tropez. After that we paid a visit to our friends, the Neagoes, at Mirmande, in the Drôme near Valence. They had bought three old houses in the one-street village and lived a peaceful life, he writing and she painting, in this strange medieval town perched high up on a hill with its ancient crumbling structures. John did not want to leave but I egged him on as I was anxious to find a home for Sindbad, whose visit I was so much looking forward to. We went next to the Haute-Savoie and looked all around the Lac d'Annecy, but ended up in Paris, where fortunately we were able to contact M. de Bonnechose and rented his house again.

This year the Joyces, Helen and Giorgio, were not at St. Jean de Luz. They had been married in the spring and had gone off with his parents, James and Nora Joyce, to the north for the summer. We missed them and our wonderful tennis parties. Emily joined us for part of the summer bringing with her an unpleasant little Italian who had followed us each separately around the streets of Assisi, even into the church, while we gazed at Giotto's masterpieces. He was so unbelievably unattractive and uninteresting in every way that John was horrified and began to work on Emily to disillusion her. It took many months. I said that at least I might as well benefit by his presence and use the occasion to refresh my Italian, since he could not speak French or English. That saved John a lot of unnecessary conversation. He could not speak Italian.

During this visit of Sindbad's he and Pegeen began fighting like cat and dog. I think there was a terrible jealousy between them because of the divorce. The first few days of Sindbad's stay were always rather a strain because he came from Laurence and Kay full of hatred for John. Sindbad used to say we led such easy rich lives while Laurence and Kay had to work hard. Kay was a second-rate novelist, but not quite bad enough in those days to make the large sums of money she did later, when she frankly became a pot-boiler writer. They did translations. I gave Laurence and Kay a large income, which they kept secret, and Sindbad could not believe it when finally, after years of my being taunted, Djuna came to my rescue and told him the facts. Sindbad really was fond of John, who was marvelous with children and fed them spiritually and mentally, as well as taking them rock climbing, swimming and playing rough-house games with them.

One day John drove Emily, her Italian and me to Spain for the weekend. We were so excited by the country we remained ten days with no other clothes except what we were wearing. For the first time in my life I went to bullfights and became more and more fascinated. We saw every type of bullfight, from little intimate country ones to Madrid's best. After I was satisfied that I had witnessed every variety, my curiosity died out and I never saw another one until fourteen years later, in Portugal. My most vivid memory of this trip was the desert we drove through from Burgos to Madrid, for every time the road curved we found ourselves in a different scene. The variety was unending, and the road was excellent. It had been built by King Alphonso for his personal benefit. In Madrid we met Jay Allen, an old friend of Emily's. They had worked together on the Chicago *Tribune* in Paris.

Once when the car broke down, John tried to explain, in a few broken words of Spanish, to a mechanic what was wrong with it. The mechanic politely told John not to exert himself so much, because the engine spoke much better Castilian than John did. At Avila, where we arrived at four in the morning, we found sheep grazing on the cathedral lawns, and at Toledo we spent the whole day searching for El Greco's painting of that city, not knowing it was in the Metropolitan Museum in New York.

We had to put up with Emily's Italian friend all winter, and finally one day she sent for John and told him that it was all over. I was greatly relieved and could now come out with a few of the things I had been repressing. In fact, I was so nasty about him that she finally gave me a black eye, and had even worse intentions, but John saved me by removing her. She was in a dangerous state. Of course my mother thought that John had given me the black eye. I did not see Emily again for many months as I really was annoyed with her.

At Easter time I had arranged to fetch Sindbad and take him somewhere in the south for ten days. Laurence and Kay were then living in Nice and were on the verge of getting married. For some morbid reason Laurence decided he would like to have John and me attend this ceremony and the wedding party that was to follow. He therefore forced our hand by choosing for the great event the week we arrived in Nice. We did not want to go to the wedding, but we had to, so as not to offend the children. Emily and her son were with us and we all drove from Le Rayol, where we were staying, to Nice. It gave the impression to the outside world that we were all excessively friendly.

Peter Neagoe, who always called me "Lady Peggy," had come down especially for the wedding, and he asked us to drive him back to Paris with us. We were delighted, except for the lack of space. We had Sindbad, Pegeen and Johnnie Coleman as well as Emily and innumerable suitcases. I don't know how we all got crammed into the Delage. Only John was comfortable—he was in the driver's seat. To make matters worse, Peter said we had to go to Mirmande to fetch some mysterious packages that he had to take to his wife. After Mirmande one of these packages suddenly flew out of the car. We were forced to stop and retrieve what turned out to be his wife's corsets.

After we got back to Paris we went to London for a few days, and suddenly John got the idea that it would be nice to remain in England all summer. He hadn't lived there for years, and he felt it would be the ideal place to find a country house to live in for several months. We rented a car and drove all through Dorset, Devonshire and Cornwall. We were tempted by Dorset, but of course John would not make up his mind about any of the houses we had seen. Only after we got back to Paris did he consent to write to the owner of a magnificent place we had found on the edge of Dartmoor. We took this house for two months.

The children were with Laurence in Austria. I flew to Zurich, which was half-way, to meet them, and brought them back to Paris. Of all the trips I had ever made in a plane, this was by far the most beautiful. We flew over the eastern part of France which is dotted with farmlands of every color, and then over the Jura.

After I had collected the children, we started out for England in both our cars with Djuna Barnes, our cook, the maid and Doris, who drove the Peugeot. We took a night boat from Le Havre and in the morning landed at Southampton. From there we drove down to Devonshire.

Chapter 6

Hayford Hall

The house we had rented was called Hayford Hall. It was a spacious, simply built, graystone structure about a hundred years old. The rooms centered around a large hall with a fireplace. This hall was well proportioned, but its paneling was of an ugly new-looking wood and its furniture, though comfortable, was not attractive. The walls were covered with the usual ancestral portraits, shipbuilders from the Clyde. At the end of this room was a big cathedral-like window. All one could see through it were vast trees that kept out the sun. Apart from the eleven bedrooms, we never used any of the other rooms, except a very dreary dining room, in which we ate our meals, adjourning immediately after to the hall. I am sure so much conversation was never made in this hall before or since.

The children had their own wing which consisted of several bedrooms and a large schoolroom downstairs where Doris reigned supreme. This was an ideal arrangement, but I was torn between the brilliant conversation in the hall and my children's company. They ate lunch with us and they rode with us and swam with us and played tennis with us, but they were not admitted to the hall except on rare occasions. The bedrooms were simple and adequate, except for the beds which were as hard as army cots. One bedroom, however, was rather dressed up in rococo style, and it looked so much like Djuna that we gave it to her. It was in this room, in bed, that she wrote most of *Nightwood*. Later she did not agree, and said we gave her this room because nobody wanted it.

We never used the respectable-looking sitting room armed with chintz-covered furniture, or the little writing room supplied with a library of the world's worst books, a fox's brush and an elephant's foot waste-paper basket. The house, one may gather, was not the main attraction. It was the situation and the surroundings that were beautiful beyond belief. Hayford Hall's back door gave out on to Dartmoor. Its front entrance was approached by a driveway of monkey-puzzle trees. In the early morning we were awakened by rooks, who inhabited a tree outside our window.

Although situated on the edge of Dartmoor, Hayford Hall had its own vast gardens which were half cultivated and half wild. There was one garden, a quarter of a mile long, with herbaceous borders. There were beautiful lawns, a well kept grass tennis-court and two ponds covered with lilies where we swam, but on the whole one had the impression nature had not been tampered with, and that this place was still part of the moor. At nightfall thousands of rabbits scurried over the grounds in all directions. We also had some woodland with a stream going through it; and another stream ran by the house.

The moor is hard to describe; it was so varied and so vast. It was hundreds of miles square and completely uninhabited except by wild ponies. The ground was strewn with bones and skeletons. The only plants that grew were bracken and heather. In the parts that were swamps, as if to warn one, there grew a little feathery white flower. The moor was covered with streams and enormous boulders. It was hilly but there were magnificent stretches for riding. Far on the other side was Dartmoor prison, but it was so far away that it meant a whole day's riding to get there and back. The wild ponies were rounded up once a year and tamed. We rented them for rides and though they were ridiculously inade-quate, the children learned to ride them in a paddock. After a few weeks we took them on the moors. We had one real horse. When the ponies bolted after throwing the children, this horse, gener-ally ridden by John, went in chase of the ponies.

The ponies belonged to a one-armed epileptic, who was sweet and patient with the children. He never tired or complained, and brought us as many as eight ponies at a time. Their bridles and saddles were forever slipping off or breaking, and it was impossible to get one's stirrups even. I remember one saddle whose girths would not hold, and I ended up by slipping more and more forward until I found myself on my pony's neck. The first year we had no serious accident. The second year was fatal, but that will come later.

Of course Emily spent the summer with us and she was always trying to get the best horse (there was really only one good one). It was called Katie and was a hunter. The other pathetic creatures were called Starlight, Mollie, Trixie, Polly, Ronie, etc.

One day Sindbad was thrown by Starlight, the children's favorite. He stood in the middle of the paddock crying, "Starlight, Starlight, come back!" But Starlight ran away and had to be chased for hours before he was caught. The great danger was the swamps, and we were generally guided by our one-armed groom who knew all the tracks over the moors. But often we left him with the children and went off with John, sometimes galloping for miles, getting lost, and escaping bogs by the skin of our teeth. Once John rode into a bog. Emily and I screamed at him to get off his horse, and he did so, just in time to pull the animal out.

Our life at Hayford Hall was completely cut off from the world. Apart from the visitors who came we saw nobody. Djuna and Emily and Emily's son were with us all the time, and we asked other friends down for the week-ends.

Emily's father, a puritanical gentleman from New England, came the first summer. Of course, he thought I was married to John and called me Mrs. Holms, as did the two maids who were left in the house to guard it, in case we turned out to be barbarians. Emily's father was fascinated by our life and especially by John. He told Emily that he thought John was a superman who lived in another world. Emily's father was terrified by Djuna. She called him Papa, which he didn't like.

Emily's father was shocked by his daughter's behavior, as she was greedy at table, and made scenes if she were not allowed to ride Katie, which was really John's horse. Emily said one day, after her father had scolded her about her table manners, "I don't want to be a pig." I replied, "What are you going to do instead?"

Djuna was annoyed because Emily tried to monopolize John and wanted to talk to him by the hour. They used to sit up until the early hours of the morning, John drinking but not Emily. She seldom drank. She did not have to; in fact she was overstimulated all the time. Djuna once told her she would be marvelous company slightly stunned.

Milton Waldman came down for a few days. He was having a nervous breakdown and, although he was greatly impressed by Hayford Hall, I doubt that he enjoyed it. My mother came but would never stay in my house, because I was not married to John. She was surprised when she saw in what style we were living, as she considered me a wild Bohemian on the edge of the gutter. William Gerhardi came with Vera Boyse. Antonia White and her husband, Tom Hopkinson. All these people made life amusing, but we really had a better time when we were alone with our little foursome, even if we fought and it all got intense. We somehow spurred each other on. We liked to insult each other. Once John asked Sindbad to fetch a pair of scissors. Sindbad was busy and refused. John was indignant. He said, "That boy is ten years old and can't even fetch a pair of scissors." I replied, "You are thirty-five and you can't fetch anything." When I was complaining that John never wrote, he said to Emily, "Peggy would like to be the wife of Stravinsky." I replied, "Which one?" Once Djuna said to John, "Why, I wouldn't touch you with a ten-foot pole." I replied for him that he could easily touch *her* with one, a gentle compliment meant for John, not Djuna. One night Djuna appeared looking quite different. She had just washed her hair. I called her "cutie redcock." Later I fell asleep, as was my habit when fatigued by Emily's conversations with John, and when I woke up, John was playing with Djuna's soft fluffy hair. I looked at them and said to John, "If you rise, the dollar will fall." Djuna said to John, "You smug little red melon of a Shakespeare. Busy old fool, unruly son."

Djuna was writing *Nightwood*. She stayed indoors all day, except for ten minutes when she went for a daily walk in the rose garden and brought me back a rose. Emily had threatened to burn *Nightwood* if Djuna repeated something Emily had confided to her by mistake. As a result Djuna was afraid to leave the house. She felt it necessary to guard her manuscript. She had no suitable clothes for the country, but in the evening she wore one of two very beautiful French gowns. Emily always wore a dirty sweater. She even rode in it. I usually wore riding pants and so did John. He looked handsome in them.

All our food came from Buckfastleigh, a little town miles below, where an abbey was being built. Doris drove down to shop every day with Marie, our French cook. On Thursdays she took Marie and Madeleine, the maid, to the coast for their day off. We were about twenty miles from Torquay, a gay seaside resort. On Thursdays we ate steak and kidney pie and cottage pie cooked by the English maid, who had been left there to oversee us.

John often drove us down to the sea and discovered wild coves where we could bathe in peace and quiet. We also went to local horse races, where our ponies were entered, so you can imagine what kind of racing was involved. It was all very crooked anyhow. We soon learned that the winners were controlled by the local butcher.

At the end of the summer Djuna took Sindbad back to Paris, where he met Laurence. She wrote me they met in a clinching embrace. We let Pegeen and Doris go to visit Peggy and her children, and we went to Bath and Glastonbury cathedral and through Somerset with Emily and her father. After they left us, we went to Cheltenham where John was to visit his family. Of course I could not meet them as we were not married, but his sister came to the hotel to see me. She must have been shocked by the whole affair because she had heard such wild tales from Dorothy about me. John tried to impress her with our domestic life, led with the children at Hayford Hall, so that she would realize how different it all was from what she imagined. When she said goodbye she told me to look after John. I was surprised because he always looked after me. I never dreamed of looking after him, as future events will show.

In January we went up to Austria to Gargellen to ski with the children. While we were away, Laurence and Kay lived in our house in Paris. Sindbad was a good skier and even Pegeen by now had had some practice with Laurence and could stand up. Emily came with us and asked her friend, Samuel Hoare, to join us. He was a dark little Scotsman, a frustrated writer, who in desperation had buried himself in the Foreign Office. Emily had been on his trail for four years already. He loved her, but he would not marry her, and only someone with her intense belief in performing miracles could have persevered so long. She had given it up temporarily, when she had gone away to Italy, but had gone back to it again. John liked Hoare because he was so intelligent and he could talk to him. I liked him too, but at first he was very shocked by my frankness. I tried for years to restrain myself in front of him, so as not to horrify him. I succeeded so well that I finally gained his confidence and friendship. Hoare was a very good skier and took Johnnie, Emily's son, and Sindbad on long trips. We could not have chosen a worse place for skiing, as Gargellen was on the wrong side of the valley. All the time we were there we were waiting for snow that never came. I don't know how John stood the strain of trying to ski for the first time in his life on these slippery frozen slopes. I never skied, of course, but went on a sled. At the end Johnnie got the chicken-pox, but we did not realize it and went on skiing. Afterward Pegeen and Sindbad came down with it.

During this winter Sindbad, who had been madly in love with Marlene Dietrich for over a year, wrote her a very touching letter. He told her he liked beer and skiing and added, "I hate Greta Garbo. Don't you?" He asked her to send him a signed photograph. After several months he received a letter from one of her secretaries saying he could have one for a dollar.

In the middle of March we went to London. Dorothy seemed to want to end her hostilities against me. Astrology was her new hobby and she cast my horoscope—some fifty pages. We took her on a motor trip through the Cotswolds and Wye valley. We made our headquarters in a place called Morton-in-the-Marsh, where John and I slept in a feather bed. Emily was living on a farm somewhere nearby, and we motored all over the place together, ending up in Wales. It was very pleasant except for one evening when Dorothy made a dreadful scene. I think it was when she discovered that Emily had been at Hayford Hall. Dorothy was no longer jealous of me; she had transferred all her feeling of hatred to Emily.

John wanted to help Djuna publish her novel, *Ryder,* in England, as it had been published only in New York. He wrote a note to an old friend of his, Douglas Garman, who was a publisher in an avant-garde publishing house. He met us in the Chandos pub. Some immediate combustion must have occurred. Garman took a great fancy to me and leaped into the rumble seat of the car, where I had installed myself after we left the pub. He asked if he could lend me five pounds. This was because a moratorium had been declared in England and all American banks were closed. My mother had had the bright idea at this moment to wire me not to sell my capital. I could not even get a penny out of the bank. Garman never published *Ryder*. I believe he did not like it, but he asked us if he could come to stay with us in Paris at Easter time. When he came, I fell in love with him. I did not tell John. I was very surprised and perturbed by the whole thing. I imagine I felt Garman was a real man and John was more like Christ or a ghost. I needed someone human to make me feel like a woman again. John was indifferent to the worldly aspects of life and did not care how I looked or what I wore. Garman, on the contrary, noticed everything and commented on my clothes, which I found very pleasant. One day he discovered me with a broom in my hand. The maid was sick and I was trying to clean the house. He took the broom and insisted on cleaning for me because he said I was doing it so badly. We soon found that we had the same recurring dream of encountering in the middle of the Atlantic an unknown island with three smokestacks. John got jealous, and after a dinner-party I had to be put to bed drunk. Garman came up and tried to look after me and this caused more trouble. He went back to England and we did not see him again for several months. But I had a strange premonition that in one year I would be his mistress.

In the spring Milton Waldman offered us a house in London he had borrowed, so we went to live in Trevor Square. We gave lots of parties and got quite settled and felt we should remain in England. We sent for Pegeen and Doris and the cook as we had decided to go back to Hayford Hall. Pegeen arrived at Folkestone with her hair so wild and fluffy that John named her Flossy, which name she kept for many years.

Garman was separated from his wife. He had a daughter, Debbie, about Flossy's age. We invited them to tea one day. They looked so much alike it was unbelievable. They both had a sort of stolid quality and resembled two oxen in harness. Garman was exceedingly handsome. He was taller than John and had brown hair and eyes, one of which was damaged, and a beautiful nose, slightly tilted. He was pale. He was another frustrated poet. Garman had produced a book of poems and John was embarrassed because Garman wanted to discuss them with him. However, John found one line he liked and, with his usual tact and hypocrisy, coped with the situation. He did not much relish Garman's conversation.

In Paris that spring we had met Eugene Jolas, the editor of *transition*. John liked him very much and they used to sit up very late drinking and reciting Hölderlin's poetry, which Jolas knew by heart. Jolas's wife, Maria, used to sing duets with Giorgio Joyce. She had a lovely voice, too.

In July we went back to Hayford Hall. It seemed all the more wonderful the second year, for nothing had changed, and we felt we owned it. The only difference was that we were trusted, and the formidable housekeeper-maid and her assistant were not there to guard us. To replace them we brought two more servants of our own who had been working for us in Trevor Square: Albert, a miraculous cockney who played at being butler, and his wife, a sad Belgian called Louise. We still had Marie, our cook, but Madeleine, our maid, had remained in France. Albert now took over the catering and went with Doris every morning to shop for food. He took everything in hand and saw to it that we were well supplied with liquor, which seemed to be his weakness. He also saw that other people were supplied at the back door. I told him to sell all the empty bottles but he said no one would buy them. However, one morning at six, he disturbed us by wheeling this fantastic assemblage past our windows and thus got caught red-handed. He made great friends with the butcher and did a lot of dirty deals with him at the pony races. I don't doubt that he sold or gave him all the empties. On Thursdays, when Doris took the servants for their outing, she had great trouble in bringing Albert back, he got so tight. He also served as a witness against Mrs. Boyse whose husband divorced her soon after her visit to Hayford Hall.

The second summer we seemed to have many more guests than the first. Of course Emily, who behaved worse than ever, and Johnnie and Djuna were with us, and Samuel Hoare came several times. My new friend Wyn Henderson, who was later to become so closely associated with me, dropped in on her way to Cornwall. My mother came again and at the same time Djuna's friends, the American-French painter Louis Bouché and his wife and daugh-

ter. He was an enormous man of some six feet or more with the
width of a giant. His wife was a little dainty creature with a very
young face and white hair. He had a beautiful daughter Sindbad's
age and Sindbad fell in love with her. The Bouchés drank as much
as John did, or even more, and had to go to bed after a few days,
they were so sick.

In late August the children flew to Munich with Doris.
Laurence was to meet them there. I accompanied them to
London, where we spent the night with my mother. I had written
Garman that I should like to see him. He had tried to come to
Hayford Hall and had phoned us somewhere on his route to
Cornwall but never found us. When I wrote to him my intentions
were very clear to me, but not in the least so to him. He was in
Cornwall when he got the letter and never suspected why I was
writing to him. He thought that I was alone in London and
wanted to be friendly.

Soon after I returned to Hayford Hall, John met with the
accident that was to cause his death five months later. It was due
to a series of mishaps, all completely unnecessary.

One afternoon in late August we went horseback riding in a
typical Dartmoor rain. The rain wasn't bad enough to be
uncomfortable but it was enough to cloud over John's glasses.
Half-blinded, he allowed Katie, his horse, to stumble into a rabbit
hole and throw him. His wrist was entirely dislocated. For some
strange reason I felt a kind of pleasure when I saw he was
helpless, but I soon recovered. John walked home leading Katie,
and Emily galloped back to get a doctor. Our local doctor came up
from Totnes, a few miles away. I helped him to administer
chloroform and he set the wrist very badly. John was in terrible
pain and I was quite insistent that we get some morphine for him.
The next day he was still in agony and we drove him over rough
roads to the hospital where he was X-rayed. It was necessary to
have his wrist in a plaster cast for six weeks, during which time I
had to dress and undress him like a baby.

Finally, at the end of the summer, I decided Emily had gone too
far. When she was about to leave in a few days she said to me, "I
had such a happy summer." I replied, "You're the only one who
has." She was so insulted she rushed upstairs and began to pack
her bags. She intended to leave at once. Everyone hoped that I

would ask her to remain. I didn't and not even at the station did I relent. John begged me to change my mind, but I would not; I was adamant.

As soon as we got to Paris I took John to the American Hospital, where he was examined and again X-rayed. They said he had a little piece chipped out of his wrist and recommended hot salt baths and a masseur. The masseur was blind. He was supposed to break down the extra muscle tissue which had grown in the wrist and was preventing its being used freely. The agony John went through every time this blind man treated him was terrible to witness. Sweat streamed down his face and all over his body. Finally the masseur dismissed John saying he could do no more for him.

We had decided by this time to live in London. John had written only one poem in all the years he had been with me. I had done nothing but complain about his indolent life, never dreaming how unhappy he was about it. He thought that maybe in London, surrounded by stimulating people who spoke his own language, he might be able to start writing again. He spoke French so badly that he never could have intellectual conversations with the French.

When he drank a lot he always complained saying, "I'm so bored, so bored," as though this cry came from his very depths and caused him great pain.

We sublet our house in the Avenue Reille and put Pegeen in a *pension* with Doris, near Mrs. Jolas' school, with the idea of their joining us as soon as we were settled in London. By this time John's wrist allowed him to drive, but he still could not use it freely.

Chapter 7

Death of John Holms

We were invited by Milton Waldman and Peggy to stay with them at Orchard Poyle until we had found a house. We motored into London every day where we saw every kind of unsuitable house and motored back to Buckinghamshire at night. Once when we went out on our tour Emily was with us and suddenly I got confidential and told her secretly about my attempt on Garman. She was horrified and told me that I was completely irresponsible and mad and that I risked losing John. She frightened me so much that I then and there decided never to see Garman again and lived up to my resolution until after John was dead.

We finally found a house through Wyn Henderson. It was in Woburn Square and, though very English eighteenth-century, it was really quite nice by the time we made it a little less formal. John was to live here only six weeks as he died in this house. Of course he never got around to writing, but he did have many people to talk to in London, including Hugh Kingsmill, who came back into his life a short time before his death, and Edwin Muir whom he loved, and Gerhardi who amused him frightfully, and Hoare and other people.

Shortly after we were living in the house I got drunk one night and became very bitchy and taunted John about Garman. I told him of my letter and my desire for Garman. John nearly killed me. He made me stand for ages naked in front of the open window (in December) and threw whiskey into my eyes. He said, "I would like to beat your face so that no man will ever look at it again." I was so frightened that I made Emily stay all night to protect me.

John had always sent Dorothy all the money that he received from his father. It was very little, only two hundred pounds a year. On one of his visits to England he succeeded in getting an extra forty pounds a year. This was still not sufficient for Dorothy to live on and she wanted some assurance of security. She would have preferred a settlement but, since all my money was in trust, all I could do was to sign a legal document engaging myself to give her, for the rest of her life—even if I died first—the sum of three hundred and sixty pounds a year. Shortly after this John's father gave him outright five thousand pounds, in order to avoid death duties. He invested it in some safe government stock. I made him make out a will in my favor. Dorothy, having forced the marriage, was his legal heir, and I felt that in all fairness as she was now protected, I should be the heir. The strange thing was that I thought so much about death and seemed to have a premonition that John would die. I was always worrying that because I was not his wife, I would have no right to bury him if he died and would have to get Dorothy's permission or his family's. Of course I wanted to marry him but the thought of going through a divorce from Dorothy was too much for John and I was too proud to insist. He was practically paralyzed by this time in his will power and could not even write a note. Finally, when we were settled in Woburn Square, he decided he would get a divorce and intended to speak to Dorothy about it, but of course it was never to be.

At Christmas, Sindbad came to London. Pegeen was with us and I had a hectic time trying to amuse them. They got so spoiled that they did not want to go any place except to cinemas, circuses and pantomimes.

All the time we were in Buckinghamshire John had been taking more massages from a person recommended by Milton Waldman. This came to an end when the masseur dismissed the case, claiming he could do no more. He said that if John wanted to be completely cured, he would have to undergo an operation. This was confirmed by a Harley Street doctor. It was a matter of taking an anesthetic and having the extra growth in his wrist broken. It would take three minutes. John decided to have this done. The operation was arranged for, but had to be called off at the last minute as John had the flu.

At the end of the Christmas holidays, I myself took Sindbad all the way to Zurich to meet Laurence who was then living in Austria. The parting was extremely painful. When he left, Sindbad cried as he did not want me to spend the whole day alone in the station waiting for a return train, which I was forced to do. I too started crying and couldn't stop. I cried the whole way back to Paris where I went to see Mary Reynolds. She begged me to stay with her, but some strange thing was pulling me back to John and I left by the next train. When I got back to Victoria Station I thought of Sindbad and mentally blamed John for all the years of agony that my separation from Sindbad had caused me. I swore a terrible oath that I never wanted to see John again. In less than thirty-six hours he was dead.

He met me at the station and took me home. Our house was full of people. He suddenly announced that, during my absence, Emily had arranged for him to have the operation and it was to take place the next morning. All his friends were worried. They seemed to have a premonition that it was bad. Gerhardi, who was writing a book about the Astral, warned John that he would surely leave his body under the anesthetic. John replied, "What if I never come back?" He stayed up drinking very late and the next morning woke up with a hangover. If I had had any sense of responsibility I would not have allowed the operation to take place. I can't imagine now why I was ashamed to tell the doctors, who had already postponed the operation once because John had the flu, that it would have to be called off again. Anyhow I allowed the doctors to come. John wanted me to remain with him, and there was no reason why I shouldn't. I held his hand until he was asleep, but then the doctors firmly and politely waved me out of the room and I went downstairs to wait. The whole thing should not have lasted more than half an hour. When that time elapsed I got nervous and went upstairs to listen outside the bedroom door. There was no sound, so I went below again. Shortly afterward one of the doctors went to get a little bag from the front hall. This made me feel that something had gone wrong and I was terrified, but I did not know what to do. After what seemed hours they came down all together—our doctor, who was a general practitioner, the surgeon, and the anesthetist, who was anesthetist to the king. The minute they came into the room I knew what had happened. John's heart had given out under the anesthetic.

After the operation all three had gone over to the other side of the room and had left him to his fate. Suddenly the physician noticed that John was failing, and then they had tried, too late, to revive him. They had cut open his chest and injected adrenalin into his heart and massaged it, but to no avail. They had killed him and they knew it. They were frightened. Everything they said made them seem more horrible to me. They had the insolence to apologize for the embarrassment of having this occur in my house. Then they told me stories of people dropping dead on the street from heart failure. They were worried because they knew there would be an inquest and they wanted to save themselves. Our physician, who was Milton's doctor, phoned to Buckinghamshire and asked him and Peggy to come and look after me. Knowing that it would be hours before they could arrive, the doctors departed and left me completely alone. I went up and looked at John. He was so far away it was hopeless. I knew that I would never be happy again.

The strange thing was that I had, for a second, felt a sense of relief when the doctors told me he was dead. It was as though I were suddenly released from a prison. I had been John's slave for years and I imagined for a moment I wanted to be free, but I didn't at all. I did not have the slightest idea how to live or what to do. I was absolutely bankrupt. Peggy and Milton arrived. None of us acted in the least solemnly or artificially. I was calm and there was no fuss. They sent for Emily. Peggy, who was practical, asked Emily to live with me as she herself had to go back to her children in a few days.

For years I had told Emily that if John were to die, I would never see her again. Now I was only too happy to allow her to give up her own life and stay with me. She slept in our room and we talked about John for nearly two months and that saved me. I can't think of anything else that would have been better. All my feelings of jealousy vanished when we wept together and shared our grief. I said to her, "Now that John is dead, we are running into eternal danger." We were.

In the afternoon the undertaker came to take away John's body.

I asked to have his watch and his dressing gown removed and I put them on at once and felt nearer to him and slightly safer. But as his body was being taken down the stairs, I suddenly remembered the oath I had made at Victoria Station wishing never to see him again, and I let out a terrible scream, because I felt I had killed him.

I wanted to have John cremated and we sent for his sister Beatrix and Dorothy. John died on January 19, 1934, at the age of thirty-seven. The next day was Dorothy's birthday, and he was cremated on Emily's birthday, January 21st. There had to be an autopsy and an inquest. Edwin Muir insisted that I have a lawyer present at the inquest in case any trouble arose. I was questioned by the coroner, and gave a report of the history of John's accident and of its consequences. The coroner was very polite and human. To my great surprise, he said to me more as a statement than as a question, "And you lived with him." And I replied, "Yes, for five years." Then a report was read on the autopsy. It seemed that all of John's organs were very much affected by alcohol and he was in rather bad shape. The doctors were exonerated.

After that we had the cremation. I didn't have the courage to go. Muir and Hugh Kingsmill and Dorothy and John's sister and Emily and Milton were present. I would not allow anyone else to be there. I went, during this hour, to a Catholic church in Soho with Peggy and we lit a candle. After that I came home and sat on the floor in our bedroom, where John had died, and listened to Beethoven's Tenth Quartet on the phonograph. While I sitting there in my extreme agony, John's sister came up to say goodbye to me. She had caught me completely unaware and for the first time she realized what John had meant to me. She said, "Whatever your life is to be, I hope it will be happy." It seemed strange at that moment to think of the future.

Emily spent a lot of time with Dorothy and tried to look after Pegeen. We didn't want to tell her that John was dead. She loved him very much. One day, when we were in a bookshop, she asked me when he would come back from the nursing home where she believed he was staying. I said, "Never. He is in heaven with the angels." A few days later she came home early from her school in Bloomsbury and refused ever to go back. Emily and I tried to find a new one in Bloomsbury. In the middle of my misery I endeavored to talk to the principal about Pegeen. The strange thing was that the principal of the school, whom I met again years later, told me that the day in which I had come to her was the worst day of her life. It certainly was one of mine. Doris had just been married and, although she was willing to come back, I was so jealous of her that I used her marriage as an excuse to look after Pegeen myself. But, in my awful state of misery, I wasn't very good at the task. Pegeen got the flu and was in bed for weeks because the doctor thought she had a higher temperature than she really had, as I did not take it by mouth. I finally found a good school for her in Hampstead where she was happy.

By the time Dorothy left we had come to some new agreement about her future. I gave her all of John's money and books and promised to give her another one hundred and sixty pounds a year. This time she trusted me and tore up our legal contract.

After John died I was in perpetual terror of losing my soul. Every day I looked in the mirror and watched my mouth sag more and more. That was a symbol of what I feared was happening to me. I did lose my soul and I knew it. If I found it again, how could I cope with it without John to guard it? I believe that in the future life some day I will find John again and my soul will be safe.

Edwin Muir and Hugh Kingsmill came often to my house. They felt that by sitting there they could in some way be closer to John. We were all most unhappy. I felt perpetually like seizing someone's hand and begging them to say something emotional. William Gerhardi was offended that I had not allowed him to go to the cremation, and had even wept about it, but we soon had a reconciliation. I received many letters of condolence. They were comforting. All John's friends saw him in a different light.

One day I received a letter in Garman's handwriting. I nearly fainted, for I had completely forgotten him. He wanted to know if he could do anything for me. He wanted to help with the usual things, thinking I was a foreigner in England. But it was too late, as they had all been attended to. As for the rest, it was too soon. But I began to think about him again, and by degrees I realized that I would use him to save me from my misery.

In February the lease of our house in the Avenue Reille expired, and I was forced to go to Paris to see the landlord and come to some terms with him, as we had made several alterations on the ground floor.

We had sublet the house to a sweet little couple, Charlotte and Ronnie Morris. I had taken a liking to her at once because she so much resembled my friend Peggy. They could not afford the house but we let them have it at their price. When I went to Paris it was at the time of the Stavisky scandal and I had just received a cable from my mother saying, "Avoid Paris dangerous." It certainly was. A maid had been shot on a balcony at the Crillon Hôtel and there had been a sort of revolution and lots of street fighting. It was over when I arrived. When I went to the Avenue Reille to remove my furniture I found a little bunch of roses Charlotte Morris had placed for me on the table of our living room. I was touched at what I assumed to be her understanding of how I felt about returning to this house where I had been so happy with John. I hated the thought of their having lived in it, but I was glad at least that they were such nice people. I had all the furniture removed and put into storage. When the house was empty I felt better—nothing remained there of my life with John for other people to be connected with.

Chapter 8

My Life with Garman

Besides John's friends, who came to our house as though to be nearer him, I saw very few people. Wyn Henderson was our neighbor in Woburn Square, and she kept sending her son Ion to see me. I allowed him to sit and play our E.M.G. gramophone but I barely noticed his presence in my house. I began to think more and more about Garman. It became an obsession, and I finally realized nothing else would save me from my misery. I told Emily that I wanted him, and then said I didn't mean it. Soon I made her write to him and meet him in order to see how he felt about me. They had a drink in the Café Royal. When she came back she told me that he had spoken nicely about me and that at least he was free, being separated from his wife. I invited him to dinner, and Emily invited Hoare. I must have made my intentions very clear this time because Garman took me home with him. He thought I was a wonderfully brave woman, prepared to start a new life. I had fooled him completely, and when I burst out crying he realized his error and wrote this poem for me which he produced the following day.

> Doubting I lay, but you too brought
> Tears from a world I had not shared,

Till in accord our bodies stirred
And broke the tyranny of thought
Finding again what treasure lies
In secret hushed between your thighs.
And stillness in the blood confirms
The age-old act we thus rehearse
An uncontracted universe
Swing in the circuit of our arms,
For the wild gift between your thighs
Drove out the terror from my eyes.

Garman fell very much in love with me and thought I was like Cleopatra, and quoted Shakespeare to me. "I found you as a morsel, cold upon dead Caesar's trencher." I imagine he thought of himself as Antony and of John as Caesar. He also said that I reminded him of the following very flattering lines, "Age cannot wither her, nor custom stale her infinite variety /Other women cloy the appetites they feed; but she makes hungry where most she satisfies/ For vilest things become themselves in her; that the holy priests bless her, when she is riggish." However, it was all very painful because of my unhappiness about John. I had been completely dependent on him; I was incapable of thinking for myself. He had always decided everything and as he was so brilliant it was much simpler to accept his judgments than make my own. He had told me that when I tried to think I looked like a puzzled monkey. No wonder I avoided it whenever I could! Apart from this I had a bad conscience about being untrue to him only seven weeks after his death. I tried therefore to hide Garman. I did not want anyone to know about the affair, and I always managed to get home before dawn.

Soon after John's death Mary Reynolds came to London on some business and she stayed with me in Woburn Square. I gave a big party for her and in the middle of it I retired to my room and wept. I was not prepared to face the world.

Wherever Garman took me I had memories of John and often burst out crying in public. Poor Garman always hoped that I would get over my grief and that we would eventually be happy together. He told me much later that I cried on his shoulder every day for a year and a half. Garman deserved a better fate, especially since he had been unhappy with his wife for a long time and had ended up with a nervous breakdown. He had been married for nine years, but had not lived with his wife all that time. They were uncongenial. They had been to Russia together after the revolution and Garman, who was a revolutionist at heart, had fallen in love with a Bolshevik woman. He remained with her for six months after his wife had returned to England, only to have to return home himself in the end as his passport expired. After that Garman went to Brazil to his brother's ranch to recover his lost health. He had been sick for years.

Garman was the son of a family doctor who had had a large practice outside Birmingham. There he had lived in a big house with a garden, completely removed from the world, with his one brother and seven sisters. His father died while Garman was still at Cambridge, and Garman felt his loss very much and his early responsibilities of being head of the family. His mother was a gentle English lady living in retirement and great modesty. She was supposed to be the illegitimate daughter of Earl Grey, and indeed she looked aristocratic. She was so feminine and so ladylike she had always done exactly what her husband had wanted, and now, although she rarely saw Garman, she adored him and treated him in the same way. He had just bought a little house for her in Sussex near the downs and he intended to go down there for weekends.

Garman was working in an avant-garde publishing house that belonged to one of his brothers-in-law, a millionaire who wanted to spend some of his money usefully.

Soon after I was with Garman I had to leave him to go and spend Easter with Sindbad. I had promised Sindbad in the station at Zurich, when he had cried so much, that I would. I did not want to go at all because I considered Laurence John's worst enemy, and it would be unpleasant for me to be with him and Kay at this time. In the end I decided I could bear it, because Nina, an Irish friend of Kay and Laurence and strangely enough also of John, was there, and I knew she would make things easier for me.

I took Pegeen with me and we spent about ten days in Kitzbühl. It was extremely painful to go back to the Austrian Tyrol where I had been so happy with John. But I was glad to be with Sindbad, and Laurence was very kind and made a great effort to get closer to me again. I suddenly realized that all my troubles with him about Sindbad were over. A few years before, a fortune-teller had told me, "You will get your child back through someone's death." It had never occurred to me it would be through John Holms's death. I had thought of everybody else's.

Laurence came up to my room and put me to bed every night. He wasn't satisfied until he made me cry. He forced me to talk about John. I didn't want to. I finally accused him of being very happy about John's death, but obvious as it was, I never got him to admit it. He said I should have another man. Of course I did not tell him about Garman, but he suspected I had somebody when I returned to London so soon. I went home leaving Pegeen with Laurence as it was her Easter holiday.

When I got back to London Garman met me and told me that he had been very sick during my absence, and that we had to go away to the country at once. We drove down to Surrey and stayed a few days at an inn. I had a new Delage by now, because after John's death I could not bear to see the old one any more or drive in it without him. My mother had made me a present of another car. I got rid of the Peugeot also and bought one that I could drive myself.

Garman drove me to Sussex to show me the house he had bought for his mother. It was in a little English village called South Harting, just under the downs. The village was absolutely dead, like all such places in England, but it was in the midst of the most lovely country. Naturally, it had a fine pub. Garman also took me to see his sister Lorna and his brother-in-law, the publisher Ernest Wishart, whom he called Wish. They had a lovely home. Garman and Wish seemed to be the very best of friends, having been to Cambridge together. Wish's wife Lorna was the most beautiful creature I had ever seen. She had enormous blue eyes, long lashes and auburn hair. She was very young, still in her early twenties, having been married at the age of sixteen. Out of seven sisters, she was Garman's favorite. They were all extraordinary girls. One of them was married to a fisherman in Martigues, and another one had three children by a world-famous sculptor. Another lived in Herefordshire with her illegitimate child, while a fourth spent half the year as a maidservant in order to be able to live in peace the other six months in a cottage she had bought on Thomas Hardy's favorite heath. Later she adopted a little boy and was reported to have had a love affair with Lawrence of Arabia, whom she met on the heath, but when I knew her she was most virginal. Another one was married to the famous South African poet Roy Campbell. They were Catholic and later became Fascist and lived in Spain. One very normal one married a garage owner and led a happy life with two children. In his youth Garman must have been overwhelmed by so many women, and preferred not to see most of them any more. However, I was fascinated by them and eventually managed to meet them all. Garman had a younger brother whom he liked. He had returned from Brazil and was now farming in Hampshire.

Garman was a straightforward, honest person with a wonderful sense of humor, and a fine mimic. He was simple, and disapproved of all snobbishness and chi-chi. He was a puritan and a frustrated poet. He was a revolutionary at heart, but all his habits and tastes belonged to the class in which he was born. He spoke beautiful English as well as excellent Russian, French and Italian. He was well educated. His tempo was quite different from mine. I moved about ten times faster than he did, and almost went mad waiting for him to finish sentences. He was five years younger than I which made me self-conscious. He found me very sloppy and would have liked me to dress much better than I did. He did not like me to have any gray hair.

After six months the lease of my house in Woburn Square expired and I moved to Hampstead with the greatest of delight. I could not bear to have Garman come to the house where John had died. It was a relief to be in a place where Garman could visit me freely, and even stay at night. Of course I continued to hide him.

Pegeen's school was near this house which was why I rented it. For the first time since Doris left she was very happy.

In summer Garman helped me find a house in the country for the children. I fussed nearly as much as if I had been John Holms, and Garman got very annoyed with me and made me rent a lovely place that was a few miles away from his mother's, in South Harting. He was editing a book and wanted to live at home, where he could work easily and yet be able to come and visit me.

The house I rented was called Warblington Castle. It was a pretty farm house with nice gardens and a tennis court, and was supposed to be an historic sight, since it could boast of a twelfth-century tower, still standing on its grounds and forming part of a wall with a moat. It was a public monument and open to the public who visited it on occasions.

Emily and Johnnie Coleman came down with us and Sindbad, who for the first time had traveled all alone across Europe. I invited Garman's daughter Debbie, who lived with his mother, as well as one of his nieces, to stay with Pegeen. Emily's friend Phyllis Jones adored our children and I persuaded her to come and look after them. Pegeen learned to ride a bicycle and I was in fits and trembling all summer over this fact. I have never been able to do this simple little thing myself.

We could not swim very much at Warblington as it was on a muddy inlet. We had to motor over to Hayling Island, ten miles away, in order to reach the sea.

Warblington Castle was very large, so we could invite quite a few guests. Garman came and went, and when he was with me I hid him in the tower bedroom I had chosen, away from everyone else. One day when Antonia White came into my room there was a pair of Garman's gray flannels on my bed. In order to keep my secret I wore the trousers myself, although they were several sizes too big for me. At breakfast Garman and I would arrive separately and greet each other politely. Even Sindbad did not suspect, but finally had to be told, because he resented Garman's correcting him. We managed to get horses and went for wonderful rides. The whole time I was bemoaning Dartmoor but Warblington Castle was a perfect place for the children.

Once when Garman was away working on his book we sent for Samuel Hoare, telling him to come and join the women and children. Emily was always begging me to invite Hoare, because she had so much trouble making him do what he really wanted to do. He resisted her with all his strength. He adored the life she gave him, but he made her fight for every gram that she forced on him, knowing all the time he would die without it. Of course he came to Warblington.

When Antonia White visited us she was rather worried by my vagueness, and Emily told me that I should behave more like the sort of hostess that Antonia expected. I rushed out and bought her a croquet set and various other things which I thought might please her. Emily said, "You mustn't overdo it," and I replied, "Oh, but I must."

Milton Waldman had given us a sweet little Sealyham dog. He wasn't quite a thoroughbred but he was nice-looking in his funny way. When John had died the dog was unhappy for he felt he had no master anymore. Our butler Blisset took charge of him and brought him everywhere. He even took him to the cinema where Robin, as the dog was called, barked wildly at his counterpart on the screen.

During the summer I bought a wife for Robin. She was a thoroughbred Sealyham, and Sindbad, with his great passion for tennis stars, named her Borotra. When I got her home, I discovered she had one bad eye and realized then why she had been sold to me so cheaply.

We had various guests, among them were Milton and Peggy, and Mary and Willard Loeb who arrived from New York with two daughters. Willard was one of my favorite cousins. He was a great music lover and owned ten thousand phonograph records. He played tennis like a champion. Mary had been Benita's best friend and this was the first time I had seen her since Benita died. John's death seemed to have wiped out the agony of Benita's, but I was happy to be able to talk about her to Mary. As usual I hid my relations with Garman from all these people, or thought I did. After five weeks our lease was up and the children had to go to Kitzbühl to stay with Laurence. Garman and I drove them down to Dover and put them on a boat. They went alone together, right across Europe. Sindbad was eleven years old and Pegeen was nine. They were a wonderful little pair. Sindbad wore Tyrolian pants with a dagger thrust in his belt.

After they had left, Garman took me to live in his house at South Harting. His mother was away on her summer holiday with one of her daughters and allowed me to stay there. Garman was finishing his book and I had very little to do all day. I lay in bed late reading *The Possessed* by Dostoevsky. It is the only one of his novels I have never grasped, even after reading it twice. It is so confusing, none of the characters stand out. The only part I like is the scene of the childbirth, which takes place in an adjoining room while all the political drama is going on next door.

When Garman finished editing his book we drove to Wales. Lorna and Wish had been to Pembrokeshire and had sung its praises, so we went there too. It is the only place in the British

Isles that looks anything like the Continent. The houses were all painted bright colors, as in Italy. There were beaches miles long with enormous boulders and there were no people to be seen anywhere. The coast was rocky and wild.

We took long walks over fields and moors covered in heather, and visited manor houses. The Welsh gentry had had an eighteenth-century social life like that of the Irish.

We lived in a little boarding-house on a river which was owned by a half-mad ex-sea-captain and his wife, who had formerly been the Duchess of Manchester's maid. She gave us a bedroom and a sitting room and wonderful five-course meals, with three choices for each, all for the modest sum of fifteen shillings a week per person. (Fifteen shillings was equivalent to three dollars and seventy-five cents.) It was unbelievable. Her husband, the captain, had built this house to resemble a boat, and it was surrounded by his derelict fleet in which he had once sailed up and down the coast. He had been an important shipping agent in former days. Now he was as finished as his boats, and although he always talked of mending them we knew he never would.

Opposite this house, on the other side of the river, lived a mad family. It seems they had two daughters whom they had kept under the table sewn up in bags for years and never allowed out until the authorities intervened.

I was still very unhappy about John all the time I was in Wales.

On the way back Garman took me to the Black Country where he was born and raised. He took me to see his family home which had been sold, and in return I took him to Warwick Castle where one of my uncles had lived with a mistress. I don't think Garman believed me until the guide, who was taking us over the Castle, mentioned their names.

When we got back to South Harting I tried to rent a house near Mrs. Garman so that Pegeen could go to day school with Debbie, Garman's daughter, and his niece Kitty. There were no houses to be rented, but there was one little Elizabethan cottage for sale and Garman made me buy it. Soon after I took this step I decided to commit suicide, I was still so unhappy about John. I therefore put the house in Garman's name as I intended to die. Of course I didn't and I went to live in the house instead.

It took some time to get my furniture over from Paris and settle the house. In the meantime Pegeen came back from Kitzbühl and lived with Mrs. Garman. Mrs. Garman had about thirteen grandchildren. She lived entirely for them and for her own children, but she immediately accepted Pegeen and was very kind to us both.

Chapter 9

Yew Tree Cottage

Yew Tree Cottage was my new home. It was named from a tree which must have been over five hundred years old, and which grew in front of the house, towering over its roof. It was a beautiful cottage because of its exposed rafters and beams. In the sitting room was an enormous fireplace, so spacious people could have sat in it. The windows of the house were small and from the sitting room you could see cows grazing in meadows a few feet away. It was a small house with two living rooms and four bedrooms, one bathroom, a kitchen and larder. The great attraction was the grounds. There was about an acre of land belonging to this property, but the whole countryside seemed to be a part of it. It was at the foot of the downs, but we were actually in a valley and we had a stream running through our garden, which was all sloping.

The real reason I wanted this house was because it was on the bus line between Harting and Petersfield, where Pegeen wanted to attend school with Garman's daughter Debbie and his niece Kitty. It was one hundred yards from a little road that was not a main road, but which I always insisted on calling so, as a result of summers spent on the moors. I felt upset by the thought of the world being at my gate, but I later appreciated the convenience of the bus and the deliveries it made for us from the shops.

Garman immediately engaged a gardener for me and began laying out the most lovely lawns and flower beds. He was a very good gardener himself and did a lot of the work. He had what is called a "green thumb."

Pegeen and I lived alone in this cottage with a darling little Italian maid we had had since London in Woburn Square. Garman came to visit me but he would not live with me, and I was unhappy every time he left.

At Christmas I was to visit Sindbad again in Kitzbühl. I wanted Garman to accompany me but he thought he wouldn't. However, at the last minute he decided to come. I had Pegeen with me and I got an extra berth for Garman in another stateroom. He happened to share this stateroom with Ira Morris, whom none of us knew at that time, but who had contributed years before to *The Calendar of Modern Letters,* a review edited by Edgell Rickword with Garman's assistance. He was traveling with his beautiful Swedish wife, Edita, and their child, Ivan. Ira was my Aunt Irene's nephew and though I had heard a lot about him I had not met him. His father I knew quite well. He was the eccentric millionaire meat packer who had been American Minister to Sweden. Both Edita and Ira were very ambitious writers.

Garman, who had never skied before, was much too venturesome and had a bad accident the first day. He broke several fingers and had to have his hand put into a horrid apparatus that pulled his fingers back into shape. This apparatus was about one foot long and as it stuck out in front of him it preceded Garman wherever he went. Every day he had to go to the doctor to have a heat treatment. This whole business upset me for it reminded me of all the agonies John had been through just before he died. I am afraid I was not nearly as sympathetic to Garman as I should have been.

I spent many hours reading to Sindbad, who had just recovered from pleurisy and was still in bed. Kay acted the efficient nurse, and made me feel *de trop* as much as she could. Garman was badly neglected and besides he felt quite out of our family life. He liked Edita very much and got on quite well with Kay, who had had her first story published in his review—he no longer liked her books, as she wrote worse and worse novels.

Myself with Sindbad and Pegeen, 1934

Pegeen, 1937

Emma Goldman was very
vain and it took me years to
see through her. She was a
Jewish *cordon bleu* and her
gefilte fish was her *pièce de
résistance*.

She had for her secretary a
mad American girl called
Emily Coleman who shared
with Blake the persuasion
that all things are possible if
you have faith. In the
summer of 1928 she was in
love with John Holms, an
Englishman whom she had
met in St. Tropez.

John Holms was very tall and had
a magnificent physique. He wore a
small red beard and looked very
much like Jesus Christ In World
War I he had killed four Germans
for which, to his great shame, he
was given the Military Cross.
Drink made him talk and he
talked like Socrates. He held
people spellbound for hours.

John Holms and
myself, 1931

Douglas Garman was a straightforward, honest person with a wonderful sense of humor, and a fine mimic. He was a revolutionary at heart, but all his habits and tastes belonged to the class in which he was born.

Myself with my mother, 1938

Myself with Yves Tanguy, 1938

Peggy was my oldest friend. She was the only really intelligent woman I have ever met. After divorcing my cousin Edwin Loeb she married a man named Deutschbine, on whom Djuna Barnes based one of the principal characters in *Nightwood*. (She is seen here in her wedding dress.) Later Peggy married my sister Hazel's former husband, Milton Waldman, with whom she appears.

John Tunnard looked a little like Groucho Marx and was as animated as a jazz-band leader, which he turned out to be. His gouaches were as musical as Kandinsky's, as delicate as Klee's, and as gay as Miró's.

Humphrey Jennings was dynamic and always bursting with a new idea; but, as he had too many, he never got much accomplished. He was a sort of genius, and he looked like Donald Duck.

E. L. T. Mesens (*left*), the Surrealist poet and art dealer, was a gay little Flamand, quite vulgar, but really very nice and warm. Henry Moore (*right*) was a very direct simple man from Yorkshire whose wonderful Surrealist drawings I liked better than his sculpture.

Samuel Beckett (whom I called Oblomov) and his friend Geer van Velde at Petersfield, where they visited me one weekend in 1938

Herbert Read looked like a prime minister and was reserved, dignified and quiet. He became a sort of father in my life and behind his back I called him Papa. He treated me the way Disraeli treated Queen Victoria. I suppose I was rather in love with him, spiritually.

Constantin Brancusi, Marcel Duchamp and Mary Reynolds in 1929. Mary was tall and elegant and had soft eyes. One night she lost her key and she went home with Duchamp. That started what one might designate as the Hundred Years' War. Mary was much too beautiful for him, but in the end she managed to get him anyhow. It took years, but that probably made it more exciting. Brancusi was half astute peasant and half real god. He made you very happy to be with him. Unfortunately he got too possessive, and wanted all of my time. He loved me very much, but I never could get anything out of him.

Jacqueline, André Breton's blonde, Surrealist-looking wife, had been an underwater dancer but came from a bourgeois family. She is seen here, in 1940, with Victor Brauner, who had lost an eye in 1938, after which he made great progress in painting, as though he had been freed from some impending evil.

Against his better judgment Garman decided, because of my insistence, to come and live with me in Yew Tree Cottage and bring his daughter Debbie with him. When we told this to Kay she had the impudence to ask me how I could take the responsibility of looking after Debbie. It was rather strange considering she had brought up Sindbad for over five years. I told her Debbie was so responsible she would look after all of us. Kay basked in the idea of my being an incompetent mother in order to prove her superiority.

When we got home Garman and Debbie moved into Yew Tree Cottage, and I found myself once again the mother of two children. I loved Debbie. She was just the opposite of any child I had ever known. She was so mature, calm, sensible, self contained and well behaved, and so little trouble. She was intellectual like her father and loved to read and to be read to. She had a wonderful influence over Pegeen, and Pegeen over her. She became less priggish in our home. They got on marvelously and were soon like sisters. They used to dress up in a strange collection of old clothes and costumes we kept in a chest, and gave charades, plays and all sorts of performances. Kitty, Garman's niece, was the third actress. Their only audience was Garman's mother, her lady companion and myself, and occasionally Garman, when he could be torn away from his intense intellectual life. In the evening I read to Debbie and Pegeen while they ate their supper.

Garman was wonderful to the children. They adored him. But one day Debbie said to him, "Pa, you look so monotonous." When we asked her what she meant, she replied, "You know, sort of going on and on." Garman wanted to instruct the children in the facts of life and procreation. He drew all kinds of diagrams for them, which meant nothing to Pegeen. Finally we reminded her of the times when she had seen dogs mating. She was so horrified that she turned to me and said, "Mama, you mean to say that you did that?" and then as an afterthought she added, to put everything right, "Of course, only twice to make me and Sindbad."

Soon after Garman moved into Yew Tree Cottage I made him give up his job as director of his brother-in-law's publishing firm. At the end of our garden he built himself a little one-room house in which to write. His health was bad and he needed a quiet life in the country with exercise and little drinking. He wrote a lot and became interested in a new review which he helped to edit. He soon began to read Karl Marx's *Das Kapital* and was immersed in it for months.

During this time I read Proust. I sat in bed under the Tudor rose which adorned my wall wearing fur gloves and shivering from cold. Dreadful drafts circulated from the holes in the ceiling where the beams were located. My room was so big it was impossible to heat it. I had a few little oil burners which I carried around with me when I got up and dressed and retired into the bathroom. Garman disapproved of my reading Proust. He wanted me to read Karl Marx.

Downstairs the sitting room with the enormous fireplace was filled with smoke. Garman did everything he could to alter this catastrophic state of affairs. Finally two local builders called Peacock and Waller, who had built Garman's little house, overcame the smoke problem by raising our chimney a few feet and cutting some branches off the yew tree. After that Garman, who loved building and remodeling houses, completely did over the second sitting room. Here he had already installed a stove that burned day and night. At least we had one warm room to come down to in the morning, which was a great blessing. By tearing down walls and closing up the formal ugly entrance door he made a really beautiful room. He had wonderful taste and chose perfect furniture and glazed chintz hangings. Then he had lovely bookshelves made for my records. The room gave out onto the garden, and in summer the sweet smell of tobacco plants wafted in through the windows.

Garman had foreseen everything except one thing. In rebuilding the house he had accidentally imprisoned my old Venetian oak chest and we realized it could never come out of the house again. In fact it is still there, though the house is sold, and I shall have to go back and tear down a wall if I want to get it back again.

Besides making such a beautiful home for me, Garman had a gravel tennis court built, and a little swimming pool and a cricket pitch for Sindbad. He sowed grass seeds to make lawns. He completely transformed the grounds and made the most lovely gardens by collecting every variety of plant he could find.

We had an amiable gardener called Jack, who played on the local cricket team in Petersfield. He worked very hard as he had to keep two engines going to feed us light and water. About a quarter of a mile from the house, down by a lake which belonged to our neighbor, we had a little house with a gasoline engine to pump water up to us. Our tank was small and the water problem was a daily affair. The engine was perpetually out of order but Jack knew how to cope with it. When he went on his yearly holiday I was very nervous, and once we had to carry buckets of water for three days.

The engine that generated electricity was in the garage just in front of our house. It made a terrible chuck-chuck noise and gave us feeble light. Only after I had lived in the house for four years was I able to connect up with the main electric line and thus end all our troubles.

The first winter we lived in Yew Tree, Garman and I rented a flat in London in the Adelphi quarter with Phyllis Jones, She had just returned from America where I had sent her for a little trip as she badly needed a change of thought.

However, I rarely went to London with Garman, for I still felt ashamed of my faithlessness to John's memory and preferred to hide in Yew Tree Cottage. In any case, I was very busy trying to retype all of John's manuscripts that I had fallen heir to. I wanted to have them published. Hugh Kingsmill had a whole collection of letters he had conserved and Dorothy had the replies that Hugh Kingsmill had written to John. We decided to do a book of these. I did not want Garman to know how much I was still preoccupied with John, and I tried to work without his knowing it.

Garman and I were really not at all congenial and the situation got more and more obvious and painful. We did not like the same people and we did not like the same things. He hated me to drink and for some perverse reason I now found it necessary to do so, though when I had lived with Laurence and John, who drank so much, I had indulged very seldom. I was all the time comparing Garman with John and even went as far as to tell Garman that he had bored John and that John had only gone to find him in London because he wanted to publish Djuna's book.

Garman's writing did not go very well and he was unhappy. He began to spend more and more time on Karl Marx.

In the spring Sindbad came to stay with us for two months. Laurence decided to put him in an English school and in order to be with him the first year, he also decided to stay in England, though he disliked it heartily. Garman taught Sindbad Latin and I taught him English grammar.

When Laurence and Kay came they left all their many little daughters in the pub at South Harting and went down to Devon to find a house. Sindbad had to live in a warm climate because of the touch of pleurisy he had recently recovered from. So they settled at Seaton and spent a year there, frankly hating it.

Sindbad became great friends with Jack, the gardener, and went with him to watch him play cricket. This must have started his great passion for that exceedingly dull game, because Sindbad thought of nothing else for years to come. He soon knew the scores and the names of all the famous players and became a great authority on the subject. He also played on his school team. I could not share this enthusiasm, and in fact have never even understood the game. Sindbad was a good tennis player and swimmer, and Yew Tree Cottage was an ideal home for him with the court and the little pool and the cricket pitch.

After I had been with Garman about a year and a half I began to get the idea of running away from him. I tried it on various occasions, but he always got me back. I didn't want to live with him and I didn't want to live without him. He still loved me very much, though I did everything to destroy it. I don't see how he could have endured me so long. Once I was so awful to him that he slapped me hard in the face and then was so ashamed of himself that he burst into tears.

In the summer we went back to the same place in Wales and the following Christmas we flew to Paris and went to Martigues to visit Garman's sister who had married the fisherman. I took to her at once. She was beautiful, like all Garman's sisters, but she was not at all happy. She seemed to have got herself into an awful jam. I think she wanted to leave her husband. He was a big, rough, handsome, Swedish-looking fisherman who had an inferiority complex as a result of marrying into another class. Helen, his wife, couldn't leave him because of their child. They both adored it. They lived a very simple life and she had to work hard at some job because his fishing did not bring in enough for them to live on.

We stopped in Paris on the way back. Garman wanted to see Dorothy Dudley who was translating a book about Mussolini for his firm, of which he was still adviser. We also met Gala Dali for the first time. She was a friend of Mary's and, though she was handsome, she was too artificial to be sympathetic. Garman was very much impressed by Mary's wonderful taste and found her new house in Montsouris exquisite. I had taken it for granted, but of course he was perfectly right.

My life in Yew Tree Cottage was so domestic I seemed to do nothing but look after Pegeen and Debbie. They were always having colds and flu. No wonder, as our house was so cold, and the temperature of the rooms so uneven. I seemed to spend weeks administering inhalations and medicines, taking temperatures and reading to sick children. All this made me desire to have a child by Garman. After his long illness he seemed incapable of giving me one, and I wanted to find out if it was really his fault or mine. It was, I discovered, his.

My mother adored her grandchildren with such fervor that Pegeen could not do otherwise than be touched by her affection and reciprocate it. Sindbad was not grateful. Once when my mother arrived from America, after a long absence due to her bad health and several operations, Pegeen said to her, "Oh, grandma, how striped you look." My poor mother certainly had grown older.

When she arrived at Yew Tree Cottage she met Emily. My mother had traveled on the *Ile de France* and asked Emily, who had just come on a ten-day boat, if she had ever been on the *Ile de France,* adding, "The vibration is terrible, terrible, terrible." Once when I told my mother how frightened Laurence was of Kay and how she kept him in order, my mother replied, "Too bad he wasn't frightened of you, frightened of you, frightened of you."

The third summer Garman took me on a sailing trip on the Norfolk broads. We invited Edgell Rickword and his wife Jackie to accompany us. Rickword was Garman's oldest friend. They had been co-editors of *The Calendar* and both had been directors of Wish's publishing house. Rickword was a good poet and critic. He was painfully introverted and very shy unless he was drunk. Jackie I had known for years. She was a good-natured, lively girl who helped make Rickword more comfortable in the world by being natural, if not hearty. I don't know how she ever got into the Bohemian world, but once there she stuck fast.

They were very agreeable on this trip and we had a good time, except that I hate sailing more than anything I can think of. It makes me restless, nervous and unpleasant. I probably ruined everyone else's fun. In fact, I think Jackie and I finally left the men to sail alone and walked down the shore.

We all went to Woodbridge, a miraculous eighteenth-century town, famous for its sheepskin industry, with at least a hundred pubs and an old market place with a beautiful building. All the houses were over two hundred years old. I bought a pair of beautiful gloves and soon after this Yew Tree Cottage was filled with natural sheepskin rugs that I kept ordering by mail.

Not long after our Woodbridge trip. Garman's wife wanted to marry again. For years she had been in love with a young actor and finally decided she wanted a divorce. Garman said I would have to be co-respondent. I protested violently because Mrs. Garman had left Garman long before I met him, and I considered this most unfair. But Garman said I was living with him, and there was no other way to do it, since he would not divorce his wife. The whole thing was very silly. We had to be found in a room together, Garman in a dressing gown and I in bed. A detective came down from London early in the morning, so that the children would not know about it. After that he wanted to come again, but Garman said he would not go through it a second time, it must suffice. The divorce was granted on the "humble petition of Mrs. Saddie Garman." It read that Garman and I had sinned not once, but many times. I often wondered how they knew. The only place this fact was ever recorded was in my diary, where I had written, "fighting all day, f——all night."

We had very few guests at Yew Tree Cottage and I led an extremely lonely life, getting more and more depressed. I was almost melancholic. The long winters with nothing to do but remain indoors, or take walks in the mud, or play tennis and freeze kept me inactive most of the time. My only joy was reading. I reread *Anna Karenina*, my favorite book, *War and Peace*, *Wuthering Heights*, Henry James's novels, all the novels of Defoe, given to me by Garman, *Pepys' Diary*, and the Countess Tolstoy's life of her husband. I started to ape her fiendishness and found myself behaving more and more like her. In the evenings I read *Robinson Crusoe* and *The Last Days of Pompeii* aloud to the children. But I wasted a lot of time buying our food myself and, as I always forgot something, I used to drive into town several times a day. Emily came down on a few occasions, but she never felt that Garman liked to have her there, though he said to her, "Emily, you make me feel like a welcome guest."

Emily, who passionately disliked playing tennis, one day when I asked her to have a set broke out into a fury and threatened to smash every racquet in the house if I ever invited her to play again. As I had several tennis racquets on approval from a shop in Petersfield I became terrified and immediately rushed them back. But Emily loved the children and they adored her. She seemed to fit in with people of every age.

Jackie and Rickword came several times, When Laurence and Kay first came to England they paid us a visit, but then Garman decided he was not going to see them any more, since he disbelieved in all this false friendship. Kay and I really hated each other. Djuna came down once, and Dorothy Holms several times. The Morrises came, but they were not in England often. Once we had a visit from the Muirs with their strange child, who was an infant prodigy and at the age of eight played the piano like a virtuoso. Mary came once, Phyllis came once, caught the flu and didn't come for ages. On the whole I lived alone, except for Garman's family whom we saw quite a bit of. I liked Lorna and her husband and also Garman's brother, the farmer. Garman had one friend called Wilson Plant, who was in the British Colonial Service and was stationed on the west coast of Africa in the bush. Out there he read Joyce and Djuna Barnes's books and seemed to be *au courant* of everything. He came to see us whenever he was home on leave.

Whatever else I found inferior to my former life, I certainly could not include the downs. They were just as fine as the moors and much safer to walk on. One was in less danger of getting lost or drowned in a bog. They extended for miles and although the scenery was not so varied as Dartmoor, it was equally beautiful and its vegetation and wild flowers far surpassed what grew in Devon. We constantly took walks on the downs and at a certain time we rode there. One could drive right up to the top and then park the car and walk for hours

Bertrand Russell had a house up there. I think he lived with a new wife and a young baby. One night he gave a lecture in Petersfield about the horrors of the next war and everything he foretold was not far from the actual truth as most of it occurred. It was a good prophecy but in no way helped to save the world from its doom.

The whole countryside abounded in pheasants which were shot down during the season in the woods that belonged to our neighbor, a general. He was an unpleasant bowlegged man who owned the biggest estate in the vicinity with a false Elizabethan house. We used to take long walks and we had a right of way through his estate. One day when I was with Debbie and Pegeen, Robin, the Sealyham, began chasing pheasants and the general, meeting us in his fields, screamed and swore at me because Robin was not on a lead. He was so extremely rude that Garman wanted to write him demanding an apology, but we were handicapped by Garman's not being able to think of the correct title for me. Debbie suggested that Garman should refer to me as his darling Peggy. In the end we had to give it up.

As we were not married the gentry did not call on us, thank God, and we did not frequent our neighbors.

At the edge of our property were beautiful woods. In the early spring they were filled with wild garlic and later with bluebells, campion and irises, and a strange flower that resembled an orchid. This was in contrast to all the flower beds and rock gardens that Garman had planted. The children loved to find bird nests and we had the heavenly cry of the cuckoo and at night there were nightingales. What the children loved most was wandering around in our garden without clothes and swimming in our little pool.

Our food was very bad since Jack, the gardener, had introduced into the household as cook his fiancée Kitty. She really knew only how to make Yorkshire pudding and roast pheasant. I decided to have her taught cooking and I invited Wahab, John's old friend and a schoolmate of Dorothy's, to teach Kitty. Wahab consented to give her a course. We had a real fiesta. It lasted over a week and we cooked about four dishes a day. I learned them all as well, to spur Kitty on, and that was how I began to cook. Never before had I tried to do anything except scramble eggs.

We made the most marvelous meals and tried them all on Garman. He loved them but he said he didn't care who made them. At the end of the ten days, I turned out to be a real cook instead of Kitty. I finally succeeded in getting her to put salt and pepper in our food which I felt was a great feat. After that we had the most delicious *paellas* and *boeuf en daubes* and Spanish omelettes, onion soups, *coq au vin* and chicken in sherry. I used to collect recipes for Kitty on the rare occasions when I went anywhere.

Soon after that, Kitty and Jack were married in the Petersfield church. It was an impressive affair, with Debbie and Pegeen as bridesmaids. Poor Kitty was terrified as she did not quite know what to expect, and Jack even more so, since he did know. They went off on a honeymoon and when they came back they talked as though they had done everything except what had worried them so much before. They were a happy couple and they created a lovely atmosphere in the cottage. Garman soon built them a new wing onto the kitchen. Fortunately they had no children till long after.

During the winter that Laurence lived in Devonshire he lost his uncle, his father and Clotilde. She died in the American Hospital at Neuilly, where John had been. She died, strangely enough, under the same circumstances as John. She had an operation and passed out under the anesthetic. Laurence was terribly upset, and when I saw him shortly after, he was bitterly armed against my sympathy, for he knew how much I had hated Clotilde.

Laurence had come up to Petersfield to see Pegeen act in a school performance of *The Pied Piper of Hamelin*. She had the leading rôle and I had made the most marvelous costume for her, half yellow and half red. Pegeen attended a little dame school in Petersfield with Debbie and her cousin Kitty who still lived with Mrs. Garman. I felt guilty about separating Debbie and Kitty when Debbie came to live with us, but Mrs. Garman said it was natural for Debbie to live with her father, and indeed it seemed to do her a lot of good.

Pegeen was embarrassed by the fact that I did not have the same name that she had. She wanted me to use hers, Vail, but I thought I ought to use Garman's. He sent me to the principal of the school, a very respectable old maid, and told me to ask her what to do. We walked up and down the garden for ages before I had the courage to approach this delicate subject. Finally when I did, she asked me if I were going to marry Garman. When I said no, she told me that I should keep my own name, since it was really mine. That ended the problem, but I never forgave Garman for making me have this idiotic interview.

In the spring of 1936 the French Surrealists gave a huge

exhibition at Burlington House. It was their first showing in London and it had a great success. Garman was excited about it and tried to get Djuna and me to go. We were both blasé and refused, saying Surrealism was over long ago, and that we had had enough of it in the twenties. In view of future events this was a most strange coincidence.

Chapter 10

Communism

By degrees Garman got more and more interested in Karl Marx and fell more and more under his spell. He began applying Marx's theories to everything. He gave a course of lectures to prove that all the great writers were revolutionary. He lost all sense of proportion and criticism and saw everything in one light. I went to these lectures and asked questions to embarrass and confuse him. After John's brilliant mind and detachment, all this was too silly for me to endure.

Garman got more and more involved and finally joined the Communist Party. All the money I gave him, which formerly went to paying for the building he had done on the house and on other things, now went to the Communist Party. I had no objection to that at all. I merely got bored listening to the latest orders from Moscow, which I was supposed to obey. Garman wanted me to join the Communist Party but he said that they would not accept me unless I did a job for them. I wrote a letter to Harry Pollitt, the head of the Party, and said that I wanted to join, but that I could not take a job as I lived in the country, took care of two little girls and had no free time. Of course I was accepted. Which was what I wanted to prove.

Garman went around the country in a second-hand car he had bought for the purpose, giving lectures and trying to recruit new members. I saw him less and less as he was so busy. I was more and more alone, and became more and more unhappy. It was during the period of the Spanish War and he was very excited about it. I was afraid he was going to join the International Brigade, but his health would not permit.

The only people he now wanted to invite to Yew Tree Cottage were Communists, and it didn't matter what other qualifications they had: if they were Communists they were welcome. I found myself entertaining the strangest guests. Any person from the working class became a sort of god to Garman. As I got more and more bored I fought more and more with Garman. Not that I was against Communism as a principle. I just found it difficult suddenly to have my whole life directed by Garman's new religion, for it had certainly become that. He was like Sir Galahad after he had seen the Holy Grail. During the time of the Moscow purges I was upset because I thought Stalin had gone rather far, but Garman explained it all away. He had a marvelous way of convincing me that everything the Communists did was right. I must say they are pretty clever.

At Yew Tree Cottage, Robin, our dog, became quite ferocious and suddenly turned into a wonderful watchdog, barking at everyone who passed on the road and biting everyone who wore a uniform. The postman delivered the mail in fear and trembling. Finally Garman had to tie up Robin in a barrel. He beat him so badly that I was horrified, but he did manage to cure him and we were able to let Robin loose once more. Robin finally married his fiancée Borotra and gave her a lot of puppies. After which he became so bored with Borotra and her offspring that we had to give her away. In the winter the house was filthy as a result of all the mud the dogs brought in from their long walks over the downs. It really was intolerable. Robin got sadder and sadder as he got older, but later he consoled himself by playing with cats.

Garman bought a Siamese cat which went around the house crying like a baby all day. One day we found it poisoned in the garden behind Garman's little house. We suspected the General.

Garman liked to ride and he bought himself a horse, but when his Communist activities became all-engrossing he gave the animal to his brother, so that he himself would be free and have more time to devote to the cause. He gave up everything for Communism and enjoyed his asceticism. Of course I found life worse and worse under these conditions.

If Garman didn't succeed in getting me to "go Communist," he was successful with his brother-in-law Wish, who soon drove Lorna crazy with the *Daily Worker* doctrines. Eventually Wish turned his publishing house into an organ for Moscow. Rickword became a staunch Communist and Jackie, being the ideal wife, swallowed Communism whole to ensure having a peaceful life. I made an honest attempt to be dishonest and I just couldn't make the grade. I became like a bull when it sees red. Only in my case I saw red every time I heard Communism mentioned. If Garman were angry with me, instead of calling me a whore, he would call me a Trotskyite.

When Garman's oldest sister and her husband, the South African poet, Roy Campbell, fled from Spain during the revolution we went to see them. They were living at Wish's house and behaving like refugees. They were so outrageously Fascist that Garman would never see them again.

Once when Garman was away on a Communist job, William Gerhardi came down to visit me at Yew Tree Cottage. He made me promise that he would not see Garman as they were so far apart intellectually and politically. Suddenly Garman returned without warning me and a most awkward situation arose. They got into terrible arguments and Gerhardi never would believe that I had not arranged it all on purpose.

We often had invasions of rats and, since there was no Pied Piper in the region, Garman had to take upon himself the job of exterminating them. He lured them all into hay piles to which he set fire, and as they ran out he killed them by knocking them with a big stick. To enable himself to do this horrid business he pretended the rats were Fascists and called them ugly names each time he hit one. The rats got into the house and died from a poison we left for them. They died in the most awkward places: under floor boards which had then to be taken up, and one rat even got into our water tank. This caused a fearful commotion, as its dead body stopped the flow of water and the whole tank had to be cleaned out

In the summer of 1936 I went alone to Venice for ten days. I had to take Sindbad back to Laurence, who was once more on the

Continent, so I stayed over and met Mary in Italy. The first few days I was with Sindbad and Mary, but after they left, when I was all alone, how happy I was. It had never occurred to me before that I could enjoy being alone, without talking to anyone except casual people for days on end. I kept the most peculiar hours and did anything that I felt like. I was unhampered by any influence or criticism and could enjoy Venice to my entire delight.

I walked miles all over the city at any time of the day or night and ate anywhere I happened to find myself. I revisited all my favorite churches and museums, and felt the same delight I always had in Carpaccio. I had only one temptation during these ten days, but I fled from it as though it were from the devil. It was a good-looking young man whom I kept meeting everywhere, but I was still in love with Garman.

On the way back I stopped over in Paris with my mother and bought some clothes. That always made her very happy. She had been down to Yew Tree Cottage a few times for the day and was very surprised by my new life and more disapproving than ever. She wanted to give me her pearl necklace but Garman told me if I took it I would have to sell it and give the money to the Communist Party. Of course my mother kept it.

When I returned to London Garman had found a three-room flat he wanted to take opposite the Foundling Estate. It was high up in the tree-tops and very small, but quite cozy. We had long since abandoned the place in the Adelphi, as it was too small for Garman amd Phyllis. Garman furnished this place with his usual good taste. I did not live in it very much for I stayed down in Petersfield.

Sindbad was now a boarder at Bedales boarding school. It was the first established co-educational school in England and was supposed to be progressive. Sindbad adored it because he played cricket on the school team and thought of nothing else. I was delighted Laurence had placed him in school so near me. It was only about six miles from Yew Tree. I fetched him every Sunday for the day, when he played tennis and swam and ate Kitty's *paellas* and English truffles.

Debbie had graduated from the dame school and was now in a progressive boarding school at Wimbledon. Pegeen wanted to be with her, so she went too. In the beginning both Pegeen and

Sindbad hated being in boarding school but they soon got to love it. Pegeen came home every weekend with Debbie.

In December 1936 the news of Mrs. Simpson and the King's intended marriage began leaking through to all the readers of American papers. No English people knew of it. *Time* magazine was censored and cut before it was sold, but Kay had given me a subscription which arrived straight from America; so I was one of the few people who knew about the affair. I told Garman and we made a bet that if it were true and the King married Mrs. Simpson, he would marry me.

One night when Emily and I were in Yew Tree, Garman sent me a telegram announcing "the great American victory" and congratulating me. Naturally I told him he had to keep his bet and marry me. But he knew it was too late and since we were getting on so badly about Communism there was no point in tying ourselves up. He had just made his last attempt on me by trying to recruit Emily, but he had failed.

I was so furious when he refused to marry me that I went out into the garden and tore up his best flower bed. It contained many rare plants and I took every one of these and hurled them over the fence into the field next door. It happened to be the coldest night of the year. The next day I was so ashamed that I collected all the plants and got Jack to assist me. He acted as though nothing unusual had occurred and helped me to place them in a wheelbarrow. We replanted them all with the exception of the few which had died of the frost overnight. This incident did not help to further my matrimonial aspirations. But I named the flower bed Mrs. Simpson's Bed.

During the week of the abdication we lived in the greatest state of excitement. Everything in England came to a standstill except the sale of extras. All the shops were empty, people just couldn't think of anything else. Finally we heard the King's abdication speech over the radio and even Garman cried.

Sindbad was staying with me during this exciting period as he was recovering from scarlet fever. He even forgot about cricket for a week in favor of the latest abdication bulletins.

Suddenly everything was over with Garman. He could endure no more. He said he had done all he could for me during the past three years and it was of no use, it wasn't what I wanted. I had killed his feelings for me and he was through. He really meant it. I don't see how he had stood it so long. The trouble was that I was still in love with him. He hated this because he said that I had never loved him, that I was only in love with him. It was true.

We had to separate, so Garman kept the flat in London and I retained the cottage. Garman asked if he could come down for weekends. He wanted to see Debbie and he loved Yew Tree, which was really his own creation. Of course, I said yes, he could come, for which I suffered greatly.

I lived alone all week for the children were in school and on weekends I looked forward to Garman's visits. When he came he insisted on sleeping with me. This caused great confusion. One weekend, when Phyllis Jones was with me, Garman and I had a row about Communism and I got so bitchy that he hit me. I slipped and fell. There was blood everywhere. Phyllis tried to stop me from sleeping with Garman but we always started again somehow.

At Eastertime I went to Paris and tried to forget Garman. I didn't. When I came back he told he was in love with a young Communist woman called Paddy, who used to work in a publishing house that amalgamated with his but who was now doing a Party job. She was very attractive and I had been the first one to remark on it. She looked rather American, with a tip-tilted nose and a smart little figure. I met her at Garman's flat one evening when she and Garman had been working late.

Garman had another staunch follower, Greta. She was in love with him and when I finally had to tell her about Paddy in order to clarify the situation, she became even more political and attended a summer school for Communism. She did this, however, only to get some life. The poor woman lived alone with three daughters on a hill the other side of Petersfield. Greta loved to have men around and thought of the summer school as a last resort to recruit them. She was right, because she found wounded soldiers from the International Brigade and invited them to her house to recuperate. Greta was a strange woman from the upper middle class, and she had led a peculiar life and was completely *déclassée*. When I first met her I thought she was a D. H. Lawrence heroine. But she became a good friend of mine and when Garman neglected her I consoled her by my friendship. Finally her eldest daughter married a truck driver and she didn't seem to mind, for she thought it was a sign of the times.

Garman was very upset about his new love affair because Paddy had a husband. They seemed to belong to the Communist Party to the extent of having no say about their private lives. Garman did not want to interfere and break up their marriage, and anyway Paddy wasn't quite ready to leave her husband, who was much older than she was, and whom she rarely saw. Also they had a child. They both belonged to the working class. Suddenly they were sent abroad on a mission together and Garman was very unhappy.

Garman and I took six months to really end our mutual life. As he came down to the cottage and insisted on sleeping with me the whole thing became very painful. I found myself being dragged into my life with him again and again instead of making a clean break. Once we even tried to live together in London. If I were in town, I stayed with Phyllis. But then Garman suddenly invited me. Of course it didn't work. We were too incompatible to live together anymore.

The one thing we had in common was the children. He adored them and that was what had kept us together. They loved him too.

In the summer Garman went down to Swanage to attend a Communist summer school. He wanted me to come too, with the children. I couldn't make up my mind but in the end I joined him. It would have been a wonderful holiday if only we hadn't been so at loggerheads. I loved Dorset ever since I had been there with John. Garman took us to beautiful places and we walked and swam and enjoyed the three children's company.

Garman was upset about Paddy and worried about what Harry Pollitt thought of this affair. I teased him unmercifully by telling him that Pollitt had sent for me to come and talk to him, and Garman believed me. The strange thing was that a year later Pollitt did send for me; so I lied only in so far as I set the date too soon.

My mother arrived in Europe that summer very ill and, although I knew she had had several operations. I got a fearful shock when her maid told me that she had only six months more to live. I stayed with her in London and later in the summer I joined her in Paris.

All the strength the poor woman had left she expended on the International Exposition that was held in Paris in the summer of 1937. She loved it and we spent hours there.

At this time I said to Emily, "I think my life is over." Emily replied, "If you feel that way, perhaps it is."

Chapter 11

Guggenheim Jeune

When the fact dawned on me that my life with Garman was over I was rather at a loss for an occupation, since I had never been anything but a wife for the last fifteen years. The problem was solved by my friend Peggy Waldman, who suggested that I start a publishing house or open an art gallery in London. I immediately renounced the idea of a publishing house, because I decided it would be too expensive. Little did I dream of the thousands of dollars I was about to sink into art.

The obvious person to help me was Emily's friend, Humphrey Jennings. He was a young Surrealist painter of thirty. He was also a photographer, a poet and a producer of films. He was dynamic and always bursting with a new idea; but, as he had too many, he never got much accomplished. He was a sort of genius, and he looked like Donald Duck. We began our collaboration by searching for a place for the gallery. Everything was vague on my part. My mother was dying, and I knew that I would never settle down to anything before she died. I expected to go to New York to spend Christmas with her, the last one of her life; and I was really only playing with the idea of a gallery.

Humphrey came down to Petersfield for the weekend. Emily

was there, and as she was finished with him, she offered him to me as though he were a sort of object she no longer required, and I went in his room and took him in the same spirit. He had strange ideas about pleasures in life, and one was to spend the weekend in a millionaire yacht club. He never achieved this ambition with me, since it was so far removed from my normal taste. But he did follow me to Paris where I was staying with my mother in the Hôtel Crillon. When Humphrey came I took a room in a small hotel on the Rive Gauche. It was filled with Napoleonic furniture and looked very formal.

Humphrey was very pleased with his ugly, emaciated body. He kept jumping all over the bed saying, "Look at me! Don't you like me? Don't you think I'm beautiful?" I had no desire to spend the weekend in bed. I insisted on going to the Paris Exposition every time I could manage to get him out of the hotel. He wanted to meet Marcel Duchamp, so I took him to see him, and in return he took me to meet André Breton in his little art gallery, Gradiva. Breton looked like a lion pacing up and down in a cage.

Humphrey came a second weekend, but then I refused to leave the Hôtel Crillon, and he had to take a room alone. I had Debbie with me, and used her as an excuse not to live with him. I really could not endure the thought of another weekend in bed with Humphrey. We went to see Yves Tanguy to ask him if we could exhibit his work in London. Humphrey had wild ideas about the way of presenting Tanguy's paintings. None of us understood these ideas, but Tanguy politely agreed. He must have been surprised by the strange trio we made.

Finally, I had to tell Humphrey that our affair was over, and that we could only be friends in the future. I put the blame on Garman, and said I was still in love with him. We were standing on one of the bridges of the Seine, and I remember how Humphrey wept. I think he had hopes of some kind of a wonderful life with me, surrounded by luxury, gaiety and Surrealism. After this was settled we had a good time at the Exposition, where I was able for the first time to study modern art.

After Humphrey left, Garman came to talk over our separation which really had to be settled. It was complicated because of the children, the house and the flat. We did not make much progress over these matters, since, to Garman's great surprise, I took a double room and we spent all our time making love and visiting the Exposition. He was very happy in Paris because of the *Front Populaire,* which was at its height.

Garman had come to talk over our separation, but I begged him not to leave me until I was settled in the gallery. He was adamant, however, and insisted on ending our life upon his return to London. I remember spending a whole day at the Exposition with tears streaming down my cheeks. But it did not alter things in any way. Garman expected soon to live with Paddy, but when he got back to London he wrote me of his great disappointment—she would not leave her husband. That did not alter his decision in any way about me.

My children came up from Mégève and we all lived at the Hôtel Crillon with my mother. Those were the last days we spent with her; she died in November in New York before I could reach her.

When I took the children back to England, Garman and I finally arranged our separation on a practical basis. He moved to Hampstead and I kept the flat. I gave him the furniture and rented Yew Tree Cottage from him. He now had a job with the Communist Party and this extra rent money came in very handy. He asked me to continue having Debbie for weekends with Pegeen. I was only too pleased, but her mother made a lot of trouble and the situation became almost as complicated as my divorce from Laurence. In the end it was decided that Debbie would come every third weekend.

After a while things petered out with Humphrey. He had so many other occupations that we gave up our collaboration. I finally rented a beautiful second floor in a building on Cork Street and engaged my friend Wyn Henderson as secretary. She was extremely clever and had the whole place decorated for me while I went off to Paris to try to arrange a Brancusi show. She named my gallery Guggenheim Jeune.

When I got to Paris, Brancusi was not there. But Marcel Duchamp and Mary introduced me to Cocteau and we decided to give him the opening exhibition.

At that time I couldn't distinguish one thing in art from another. Marcel tried to educate me. I don't know what I would have done without him. To begin with, he taught me the difference between Abstract and Surrealist art. Then he introduced me to all the artists. They all adored him, and I was well received wherever I went. He planned shows for me and gave me lots of advice. I have him to thank for my introduction to the modern art world.

Marcel first presented me to Jean Arp, the sculptor, who was an excellent poet and a most amusing man. He took me to Meudon to see the modern house he had built for himself and his wife Sophie. They each had a whole studio floor, and there was a garden full of Arp's work. Sophie was an abstract painter and a sculptress. His work was more Surrealist, but he managed to remain on both sides of the fence and exhibited with both groups. Sophie, a Swiss ex-school teacher, edited an interesting magazine called *Plastique*. Arp was always trying to further Sophie's career and, since her work was dull, it often became painful to be so bothered about nothing. They had done one good sculpture together called *Sculpture Conjugale*. Sophie was a wonderful wife. She did everything possible for Arp besides doing her own work and running the magazine. The first thing I bought for my collection was an Arp bronze. He took me to the foundry where it had been cast and I fell so in love with it that I asked to have it in my hands. The instant I felt it I wanted to own it.

I must have gone to Paris expecting something to occur but I never dreamed for an instant what was in store for me. In spite of the fact that I took every consolation which crossed my path, I was entirely obsessed for over a year by the strange creature, Samuel Beckett. He came into my life the day after Christmas, 1937. I had known him slightly. He had been to our house on the Avenue Reille. I knew that he was a friend of James Joyce, that he had been engaged to his daughter and had caused her great unhappiness. Beckett was not Joyce's secretary, as everyone has since claimed, though he was perpetually doing errands for him. Joyce had a Russian Jewish intellectual for secretary, called Paul Léon, who was later killed by the Germans.

Beckett was a tall, lanky Irishman of about thirty with enormous green eyes that never looked at you. He wore spectacles, and always seemed to be far away solving some intellectual problem; he spoke very seldom and never said anything stupid. He was excessively polite, but rather awkward. He dressed badly in tight-fitting French clothes and had no vanity about his appearance. Beckett accepted life fatalistically, as he never seemed to think he could alter anything. He was a frustrated writer, a pure intellectual. I met him again at Helen Joyce's.

That evening we dined at Fouquet's, where James Joyce gave us an excellent dinner. Joyce inquired a lot about my gallery in London, and as usual was charming and very attractive. He wore a beautiful Irish waistcoat which had belonged to his grandfather.

After dinner we went back to Helen's and then Beckett asked if he could take me home. I was surprised when he took my arm and walked me all the way to the Rue de Lille, where I was living in a borrowed apartment. He did not make his intentions clear but in an awkward way asked me to lie down on the sofa next to him. We soon found ourselves in bed, where we remained until the next evening at dinner time. We might be there still, but I had to go to dine with Arp, who unfortunately had no telephone. I don't know why, but I mentioned champagne, and Beckett rushed out and bought several bottles which we drank in bed. When Beckett left, he said very simply and fatalistically, as though we were never going to meet again, "Thank you. It was nice while it lasted." During his short disappearance Joyce, to whom he was a sort of slave, got very worried. Helen guessed he must be with me, so our secret was public. After that I moved to Mary Reynolds's house as she was in the hospital and I did not see Beckett for some time. One night I met him on a traffic island in the Boulevard Montparnasse. I must have been looking for him without realizing it, as I was not at all surprised when I found him. It was as though we had both come to a rendezvous.

We went home to Mary's house where we lived for twelve days. We were destined to be happy together only for this short period. Out of all the thirteen months I was in love with him, I remember this time with great emotion. To begin with he was in love with me as well, and we were both excited intellectually. Since John's death I had not talked my own, or rather his, language. And now I suddenly was free again to say what I thought and felt.

In spite of the fact that I was opening a modern art gallery in London I much preferred old masters. Beckett told me one had to accept the art of our day as it was a living thing. He had two passions besides James Joyce. One was Jack Yeats and the other a Dutch painter, Geer van Velde, a man of nearly forty, who seemed to be completely dominated by Picasso, and he wanted me to give them both exhibitions. I could not refuse him anything, so it was agreed. Jack Yeats luckily realized that his painting was not at all in line with my gallery and let me off. But I agreed and gave the Van Velde show. In fact, I bought some of the pictures which were rather like Picasso's, secretly under various names in order to please Beckett, but even after this Van Velde, not knowing I had done so, asked me for five hundred dollars, which I could not refuse him.

Beckett was a writer and brought me his works to read. I thought his poems were bad. They were so childish. But one of his books, *Murphy,* which had just been published, was rather extraordinary, and his previous study on Proust was excellent. I suppose he was much influenced by Joyce, but he did have certain strange and morbid ideas which were quite original and a wonderfully sardonic sense of humor.

The thing I liked best about our life together was that I never knew at what hour of the night or day he might return to me. His comings and goings were completely unpredictable, and I found that exciting. He was drunk all of the time and seemed to wander around in a dream. I had a lot of work to do because of my gallery and often I had to get up in the afternoon to see Cocteau, who was to have the opening show. Beckett objected to this; he wanted me to remain in bed with him.

It seemed ironic that I should create a new existence for myself because I had no personal life, and now that I had a personal life, it had to be sacrificed. On the tenth day of our amours Beckett was untrue to me. He allowed a friend of his from Dublin to creep into his bed. I don't know how I found it out, but he admitted it saying that he simply had not put her out when she came to him, and that making love without being in love was like taking coffee without brandy. From this I inferred I was the brandy in his life, but nevertheless I was furious, and said that I was finished with him. The next night he phoned me, but I was so angry that I refused to speak to him. A few minutes later he was stabbed in the ribs by an unknown maniac on the Avenue d'Orléans and taken to a hospital. I had no idea of this and as I was leaving for London I wanted to say goodbye to him. When I called his hotel the proprieter told me what had happened. I nearly went mad. I rushed to all the hospitals in Paris but could not find him. Finally I phoned Nora Joyce, who told me where he was. I went to him at once, and left some flowers and a note telling him how much I loved him and that I forgave him everything. The next day James Joyce went to see Beckett in the hospital and I went with him. As he was semi-blind, it took Joyce a long time to be conducted by his secretary to the right ward. But by a sort of instinct I rushed in and without any help found Beckett. He was surprised to see me, as he thought I had left for London. He was very happy. I said goodbye to him. I knew he was in good hands because Joyce was looking after him, and that he would be laid up for a long time. I had to go back to London to open my gallery, but I meant to return to Paris as soon as I could.

The arrangements for the Cocteau show were rather difficult. To speak to Cocteau one had to go to his hotel in the rue de Cambon and try to talk to him while he lay in bed, smoking opium. The odor was extremely pleasant, though this seemed a rather odd way of doing our business. One night he decided to invite me to dinner. He sat opposite a mirror, which was behind me, and so fascinated was he by himself that he could not keep his eyes off it. He was so beautiful, with his long oriental face and his exquisite hands and tapering fingers, that I do not blame him for the delight he took in his image.

His conversation was as fascinating as his face and hands, and I longed for him to come to London for the show, but he was not well enough. However, he wrote the introduction for his catalogue and Beckett translated it.

My life in London was hectic. There was so much work to be done, I don't know how I survived. To begin with I had to refurnish my flat, since I had given Garman all the furniture. Then I had to open the gallery, and obtain the names of hundreds of people to invite to the opening, and have a catalogue and invitations printed and sent out. Luckily Mary Reynolds and Marcel Duchamp flew over for the opening and Marcel hung the show and made it look beautiful.

Cocteau sent me about thirty original drawings he had made for the décor of his play *Les Chevaliers de la Table Ronde.* I had also borrowed the furniture which he had designed for it, and he especially made some dinner plates which were in the same spirit. He also made some drawings in ink in the same spirit as the

others, and two on linen bed sheets that were especially done for
the show. One was an allegorical subject called *La Peur donnant
ailes au Courage,* which included a portrait of the actor Jean
Marais. He and two very decadent looking figures appeared with
pubic hairs. Cocteau had pinned leaves over these, but the
drawing caused a great scandal with the British Customs, who
held it up at Croydon. Marcel and I rushed down to release it. I
asked why they objected to the nude in art, and they replied it was
not the nude but the pubic hairs which worried them. On
promising not to exhibit this sheet to the general public, but only
to a few friends in my private office, I was permitted to take it. In
fact, I liked it so much that in the end I bought it.

Jean Cocteau, *La Peur donnant ailes au Courage*

This was before I was thinking of collecting. But gradually I
bought one work of art from every show I gave, so as not to
disappoint the artists if I were unsuccessful in selling anything.
In those days, as I had no idea how to sell and had never bought
pictures, this seemed to be the best solution and the least I could
do to please the artists.

The opening of Guggenheim Jeune in January 1938 was a great
success, but what pleased me most was receiving a wire of *auguri*
signed "Oblomov."

I called Beckett Oblomov from the book by Goncharov that
Djuna Barnes had given me to read so long before. When I met

him I was surprised to find a living Oblomov. I made him read the book and of course he immediately saw the resemblance between himself and the strange inactive hero who finally did not even have the will power to get out of bed.

Conversation with Beckett was difficult. He was never very animated, and it took hours and lots of drink to warm him up before he finally unraveled himself. If he ever said anything to me which made me think he loved me, as soon as I taxed him with it he took it back by saying he had been drunk at the time. When I asked him what he was going to do about our life he invariably replied, "Nothing."

As soon as we could leave London, Mary, Marcel Duchamp and I went back to Paris. Beckett was now out of the hospital and was convalescing in his hotel. I took a room there but I don't think that pleased him at all. My sister Hazel had a wonderful flat on the Ile Saint-Louis which I was able to borrow. It had no furniture, only a big bed and lots of her own paintings (she was a good primitive painter). I tried to take Beckett to live with me on the island, but he refused to remain there all the time. He came and went and always brought champagne to bed.

Beckett had a friend called Brian Coffey. He was a little dark man, a sort of dried-up intellectual and a Thomist. He tried hard to attach himself to me, and I used to tease Beckett about him with great tactlessness. I often said I wanted to sleep with him. Beckett had an inferiority complex, and as I had talked to him so passionately about John Holms, and also made fun of Humphrey Jennings to him, he conceived the idea that he really was not at all the man I wanted. One day he announced that he was never going to sleep with me again and told me to have Brian, for then at least I might be satisfied. I was so infuriated by this proposition (though I now realize it was entirely my stupidity that made Beckett suggest it) that I went and slept with Brian. Beckett looked dignified and sad as he walked away from us, knowing what was going to happen. The next day Beckett asked me if I liked Brian, but I must have said "No," because Beckett came back to me. We were very happy together for twenty-four hours, and then everything was ruined. We met Brian for lunch and he asked Beckett if he were interfering in his life, as he had only just realized that I really belonged to Beckett. To my great surprise

Beckett gave me to Brian. I was so horrified I rushed out of the café and walked all over Paris in despair. I went to Beckett's hotel and made a terrible scene, but it did no good. He said he was no longer in love with me.

Even if our sex life was over nothing else was. Our relationship continued unchanged in every other respect. We were perpetually together, and I felt the same ecstasy in his society as I had previously. At night he walked me home over the bridge behind Notre Dame. When we reached my front door Beckett went through the most terrible agonies trying to decide what to do. But he always ended up by pulling himself together and running away. This caused me incalculable misery and I spent nights lying awake, longing for his return.

Beckett had little vitality and always believed in following the path of least resistance. However, he was prepared to do anything for Joyce, and he was always leaving me to see his great idol. I was very jealous of Joyce. I think Joyce loved Beckett as a son.

In February 1938 Joyce had his fifty-sixth birthday. Maria Jolas gave him a dinner party at Helen Joyce's. Beckett was in a state of great excitement about suitable presents. He went with me and made me buy a blackthorn stick. God knows why. As for his own gift he very much wanted to find some Swiss wine, Joyce's favorite beverage. I remembered that John Holms and I once years before had dined in a Swiss restaurant with Joyce, and I went back to the Rue Ste. Anne, found the place and asked them if they would sell some wine. Of course they consented when I told them whom it was for. Beckett went to get it and was very happy. At the dinner party Joyce offered a hundred francs to anyone who could guess the title of his new book (*Finnegans Wake*), which was just about to be published. Beckett I am sure won the bet. At the party were present only Joyce's sycophants. I met again Herbert Gorman, whom I had not seen for years. The table was decorated with a plaster model of Dublin through which ran a green ribbon representing Joyce's beloved Liffey. Joyce got very tight and did a little jig by himself in the middle of the room.

Marcel sent me to see Kandinsky. He was a wonderful old man of seventy, so jolly and charming, with a horrid wife some thirty years younger called Nina. Everybody adored him and detested her. I asked him if he wanted to have an exhibition in London,

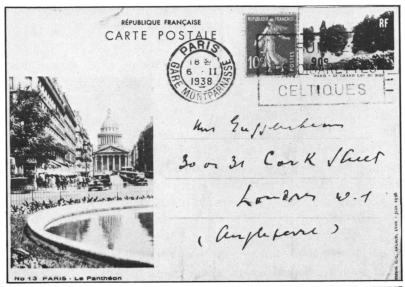

IMPRIM. GÉN., ARNAUD, LYON - JUIN 1936

Postcard from James Joyce thanking me for my gift of a blackthorn stick

and as he had never shown there he was delighted. He had a friend in England who owned a lot of his pictures, Sir Michael Sadleir.

Kandinsky, who was upset by my uncle Solomon Guggenheim's supplanting him by Rudolf Bauer, his third-rate imitator, claimed that though he had encouraged my uncle to buy Bauer's paintings now that Bauer had taken his place he never told my uncle to buy Kandinsky's paintings. He wanted me to get my uncle to buy one of his early works. It seems that it was one my uncle had wanted for a long time. I promised to do my best, never dreaming of the result.

Kandinsky and his wife arranged the whole London show themselves. It included paintings from 1910 to 1937. I merely sent them a plan of the gallery and they even decided where each picture was to be hung. They were very businesslike. No one looked less like an artist than Kandinsky, who resembled a Wall Street broker. Mrs. Kandinsky behaved horribly and I am surprised they ever sold any pictures: she was so grasping. At the end of the show, I bought one of the 1937 period and none of the marvelous early ones. Later in New York I bought many others, but I wish I now had several that were in my show.

One day, during the exhibition, an art teacher from a public school in the north of England came to the gallery and begged me to allow him to show ten Kandinskys to his pupils at the school. I was delighted with the idea and wrote to Kandinsky for his permission. He wrote back that he was very much pleased but with his usual businesslike attitude added that the pictures should be insured. When the show was over my schoolmaster came and strapped ten canvases on to his car and drove away with them. I am certain Kandinsky had never been so informally treated before. When the schoolmaster brought back the paintings he told me how much they had meant to the school.

As I had promised Kandinsky, I wrote to my uncle asking him if he still wanted to buy the painting that he had so long desired. I received a friendly answer saying that he had turned the letter over to the Baroness Rebay, the curator of his museum, and that she would reply herself. In due time I received this extraordinary document:

> Dear Mrs. Guggenheim "jeune"
>   Your request to sell us a Kandinsky picture was given to me, to answer.
>   First of all we do not ever buy from any dealer, as long as great artists offer their work for sale themselves & secondly will be your gallery the last one for our foundation to use, if ever the need to get a historically important picture, should force us to use a sales gallery.

doing "extra" for the artist ←

It is extremely distasteful at this moment, when the name of Guggenheim stands for an ideal in art, to see it used for commerce so as to give the wrong impression, as if this great philanthropic work was intended to be a useful boost to some small shop. Non-objective art, you will soon find out, does not come by the dozen, to make a shop of this art profitable. Commerce with real art cannot exist for that reason. You will soon find you are propagating mediocrity; if not thrash. If you are interested in non-objective art you can well afford to buy it and start a collection. This way you can get into useful contact with artists, and you can leave a fine collection to your country if you know how to chose. If you don't you will soon find yourself in trouble also in commerce.

Due to the foresight of an important man since many years collecting and protecting real art, through my work and experience, the name of Guggenheim became known for great art and it is very poor taste indeed to make use of it, of our work and fame, to cheapen it to a profit.

Yours very truly,
H. R.

P.S. Now, our newest publication will not be sent to England for some time to come.

During the Kandinsky show Brian came to visit me in London. We did nothing but talk about Beckett, whom we both adored. I think Brian wanted to marry me, but I had no such desire. It was a great relief when he returned to Paris after a week.

Cedric Morris, one of my oldest friends, was a painter of flowers who had an iris farm and a school of painting in Suffolk. He wanted to have a show in my gallery, but he did not want to exhibit his beautiful flower pictures for which he was famous. Instead he wished to exhibit some fifty portraits he had done of London celebrities. The portraits were in most cases nearly caricatures, all of them on the unpleasant side. There was no reason for showing them in any Surrealist and Abstract gallery, but Wyn and I loved Cedric so much that we could not refuse. He covered the walls three rows deep. I think he must have hung nearly one hundred of them. One evening during the exhibition we gave a party to stir up a little trade. The result was most unexpected. All we stirred up was a terrible row. One of the guests, an architect I shall call Mr. Silvertoe, so much disliked the portraits that in order to show his disapproval he started burning the catalogues. Cedric Morris, naturally infuriated, hit

Mr. Silvertoe and a bloody battle took place. The walls of the gallery were spattered with blood. The next day Cedric phoned to apologize and offered to remove his paintings. Of course we did not let him.

A few months later Arp came to visit me. Marcel Duchamp had helped me arrange a show of contemporary sculpture, and Arp who was one of the exhibitors came over to further it himself. Arp was very domestic about the house. He got up early and waited impatiently for me to wake up. He served me breakfast every mornng and washed all the dishes. We had so much fun together and were so gay that it really was a delightful week. We went to Petersfield. Arp was enthusiastic about the English countryside and loved the little Sussex churches. He went back to Paris with a porkpie hat and a bread box under his arm. He knew only one word of English, "candlesticks." His vocabulary did not increase during his stay.

During Arp's visit I was invited by Jacob Epstein to go and see his work. Of course I took Arp with me. This greatly enraged Epstein who barely wished to admit Arp until we protested that he was a great admirer. Epstein hated the Surrealists and thought Arp should not be interested in his work. But on the contrary Arp was fascinated by the strange things we saw, among them the enormous figure of Christ lying entombed. Epstein's portraits are miraculous. They certainly are as good as anything done in the Italian Renaissance; but I hate his other concoctions.

I soon got into trouble again with the British Customs. Marcel Duchamp had sent me from Paris a sculpture show, consisting of works by Brancusi, Raymond Duchamp-Villon, Antoine Pevsner, Arp, his wife, Henri Laurens and Alexander Calder. Henry Moore was to represent England. But the Customs would not admit the show into England as an art exhibition. J. B. Manson, the director of the Tate Gallery, had not passed on it, and therefore it could enter the country only if the exhibits were admitted as separate pieces of bronze, marble, wood, etc. This would have meant my having to pay heavy duty on them, which I would have done had it come to the worst. This was because of a stupid old law which existed to protect English stonecutters from foreign competition. It rested with the director of the Tate Gallery to decide in such cases what was art and what wasn't. Mr. Manson, the director, abused his privilege and refused to pass my

GUGGENHEIM

EXHIBITION
OF CONTEMPORARY
SCULPTURE

Brancusi
Laurens
Hans Arp
Duchamp-Villon
Henry Moore
Pevsner
Calder
Tauber-Arp

April 11 — May 2

30 CORK STREET (BOND STREET) W.1

JEUNE

Printed at The Curwen Press Ltd. for the Proprietors, The London Gallery Ltd.

show, which he declared was not art. This was really so scandalous that Wyn Henderson got all the art critics to sign a protest against this verdict. As a result, my case was brought up in the House of Commons and we won it. Mr. Manson not only lost his case, but pretty soon his job as well. I thus rendered a great service to foreign artists and to England.

All the papers immediately took up the story and the exhibition became famous. Brancusi's Sculpture for the Blind was re-produced in Tom Driberg's column in the *Daily Express.*

At this moment what I had told Garman a year before to tease him actually came true. Harry Pollitt, having read so much about my success in my battle against Mr. Manson, decided that I was much too important a person to have lost. He sent for me, telling me that he was certain he could fix up all my difficulties about Communism in ten minutes. I wrote back and said I was much too busy to go to him but that he "should come up and see me some time." He never did. By this time Garman was living with Paddy. Later he married her.

One day Edgell Rickword invited me for dinner and asked me if I would render a great service to the Communist Party. They wanted to borrow my flat for Louis Aragon and a whole convention of Communist writers who were coming to London. They needed a very chic apartment, as when the English writers had been invited to Paris they had been royally received at a hotel on the Avenue de l'Opéra. I protested, saying my flat was not nearly grand enough as it was on the third floor without a lift and was a modest little affair in Bloomsbury without servants. The Com-munists had to look elsewhere.

Wyn Henderson was a most remarkable woman. I don't know what I would have done without her. She made everything go like clockwork in the gallery, though she had had no previous experience of this kind. She was a typographer by profession and had run several modern presses. Therefore, we had the most beautiful invitations and catalogues printed. She had a lot of common sense, extraordinary tact and social grace, remembering the faces of all the people who came to the gallery whom I never recognized. She had a great zest for life. One day I made her count up her love affairs. When she came to a hundred she stopped. At this period she was very fat, although she must have resembled a Venetian beauty in her former years. To her great sorrow she now had much less success with men than before, but she was never jealous of anyone else's happiness. In fact she was always egging me on to enjoy myself. Years before she had pushed her favorite son Ion in my way, and now she tried it with Nigel, the younger one. He was a darling but I really only regarded him as a sweet baby, but I loved his soul and felt we were made of the same clay. When this did not work and she discovered that I was still in love with Beckett, Wyn sent me back to Paris. Beckett was flattered by my visit and by my constancy. He was in a strange state, and told me that our life would be all right one day. Ever since his birth he had retained a terrible memory of life in his mother's womb. He was constantly suffering from this and had awful crises, when he felt he was suffocating. He never seemed to be able to make up his mind whether or not he was going to have me, but he did not want to give me up. (To replace our sex life, we used to drink wildly and then walk all over Paris until the early morning.)

My passion for Beckett was inspired by the fact that I really believed he was capable of great intensity, and that I could bring it out. He, on the other hand, always denied it, saying he was dead and had no feelings that were human and that was why he had not been able to fall in love with Joyce's daughter.*

I asked Helen Joyce what to do about Beckett and she suggested that I rape him. So one night, when he was very indecisive and seemed to be yearning toward me and floating into me in spite of himself, I went home with him thinking how much less I should really like him if I ever had him. In fact, as he took my arm, I had the illusion of everything being settled and I thought, "How boring." Nevertheless I went home with him and insisted on remaining all night. He suddenly became terrified and rushed away and left me in his apartment alone. I was so upset that I got up at four in the morning and wrote a poem which I left on his desk, and then went back to England.

*A poem written by Beckett: They come
                          Different and the same
                          With each it is different and the same
                          With each the absence of love is different
                          With each the absence of life is the same

A woman storming at my gate—
Is this inevitable fate?
From far away the hammer fell:
Was that my life or death's last knell?

To my void she came much wanting
Shall I chance this fear unending?
Shall I face the pain of rupture?
Shall I execute the future?

Every step I take she battles,
Every inch the death-knell rattles.
Shall I kill her Holy passion?
Destroying life, not taking action.

So once again I had to renounce Beckett. I was, however, destined to see him soon in London, where he came for the opening of his dearly beloved Van Velde's show. When the paintings were hung in my gallery, they looked more Picasso than ever. All the critics seemed to think so and they gave Van Velde little publicity. However, Van Velde was very happy, as I kept buying all his paintings under different names, or as gifts for my friends. This was all because I loved Beckett so much and he loved Van Velde.

I took the Van Veldes down to Petersfield for the weekend and filled the house with Van Velde gouaches. Beckett followed us after much deliberation. We had quite a nice house party, since the George Reaveys came too. When I had gone to bed in the dining room, having given my bedroom to the Reaveys, Beckett came and talked to me. He told me he had a mistress and asked me if I minded. Of course I said no. She sounded to me more like a mother than a mistress. She had found him a flat and made him curtains and looked after him generally. He was not in love with her and she did not make scenes, as I did. I had met her once in his room before she was his mistress, when I was, and I could not be jealous of her; she was not attractive enough. She was about my age, and we were both older than Beckett. After he told me all this, I was even more keen than I had been to get off with Mesens.

E. L. T. Mesens was a Surrealist poet and the director of the London Gallery, my neighbor in Cork Street. We had a united

GUGGENHEIM JEUNE

30 CORK STREET, LONDON W.1

GEER VAN VELDE

CATALOGUE

1. Promenade des Anglais
2. L'anniversaire
3. Minuit 36-37
4. Femme
5. Paysage
6. Nature Morte
7. Rencontre dans la ville
8. Femme
9. Nature Morte
10. A la fenêtre
11. Fête foraine
12. Dans le midi
13. Aventure
14. Diseuse de bonne aventure
15. Couple
16. Mme. L. de la S.
17. Femme
18. Composition
19. Corbeille de fleurs
20. Eclairs à l'horizon
21. L'imprévu
    collection S.B.
22. Le Musicien
23. Hiob
24. Nature Morte, meridionale
25. La Dame au Balcon
26. La Silencieuse
    collection B.C.
27. Composition
28. Composition
29. Etrange visite
30. Masse
31. Des fleurs au clair de la Lune
32. Composition figurale
33. Concentration feminine
34. Jazz Band
35. Silence
36. L'Invitation
37. La Ville Lumière
38. Kermesse
39. l'Hiver
40. Portrait de Mr. M. H.
41. Portrait de Mr. E. K.
42. Coup de vent
43. Chartres
44. Méditation
45. Aprés le diner

GEER VAN VELDE

Born the third of four April 5th 1898 at Lisse near Leyden. Tulips and Rembrandt. 1911 apprenticed to a house-painter. Wandcrings in Holland and Brabant, rubbing colours in order to buy them. Since 1925 in Paris. 1927 South of France. 1931 Britanny. Exhibitions; 1925 at the Hague, 1926-30 in Paris with Independants. 1933 with his brother Bram Van Velde at the Hague, 1937 at the Hague, Pictures in Amsterdam in the Stedelijk and the Regnault collection, at the Hague in the Stedelijk and the Kramers collection, in private collections in Brabant, France, Germany, U.S.A. and even England.

Believes painting should mind its own business, *i.e.* colour. *I.e.* no more say Picasso than Fabritius, Vermeer. Or inversely.

Samuel BECKETT

15

front and we were very careful not to interfere with each other's exhibitions. I bought paintings from Mesens. He was a gay little Flamand, quite vulgar, but really very nice and warm. He now wanted me as his mistress, so we were to have dinner together. Before Beckett went back to Paris I went off with Mesens and took a diabolical pleasure in doing so.

The affair with Mesens did not last long. I told him how much I loved Beckett, and then I ran away and went to Paris again to see him. Mesens was the editor of the *London Bulletin,* a Surrealist paper which was rather good, but, like Mesens himself, a little too commercial. The paper advertised everything Mesens sold in his gallery, and he produced my catalogues free of charge in exchange for an advertisement that I paid for. I wanted to get control of this paper and improve it, but Mesens was jealous and would have no other collaborator besides Humphrey Jennings. This time I went to Paris and took my car with me for Beckett. I wired him I was coming, but he did not meet me at Calais as I had hoped. He merely waited for me listlessly in his apartment and seemed bored with me.

One afternoon at his flat, when the Van Veldes were there, Beckett and Van Velde began to exchange clothes. It was a rather homosexual performance, disguised, of course, by the most normal gestures. I accused Beckett of being in love with Van Velde. After that we went to a dancing place and an awful scene followed; Beckett went away leaving me with the Van Veldes.

Beckett and I did not get on well after this and I did not see much of him. I was living in Mary's house and one day I said to her, "There's no point in my being here, as a I never see Beckett." I decided to go back to London. Before leaving I wrote him a letter telling him I would like to say goodbye. This seemed to bring him back to life, as we then arranged to drive the Van Veldes to the Midi where they were going to live.

It was difficult to leave because Beckett always spent the weekends with his mistress and he could not suddenly change his habits. He managed to get off at two o'clock on Sunday, and we all departed in my Delage. Beckett drove us to Marseilles and then we went to Cassis for the day. The Van Veldes were surprised by all this, as they never could make head or tail of our relationship. They had seen Beckett and me fight so often that they never dreamt we could always begin all over again where we left off.

We deposited them in Marseilles and started off for the north. I had wasted so much time waiting around Paris for Beckett that now I really was in a hurry to get back, as I had to drive Yves Tanguy to London in time for his exhibition. On the way back we stopped at Dijon. I had many memories of this sad town; I did not think I would ever add any more. Beckett's behavior was so strange that I can never forget what happened this time. By mistake we had a dreary dinner in a depressing restaurant, which was stupid, considering Dijon is famous for its excellent food. Beckett had no flair for the right places, and his Protestant upbringing made him automatically shun the pleasant things in life. When we went to a hotel he took a double room. This I thought strange, but then all his behavior was most peculiar. We got into separate beds. I soon crept into his, and Beckett jumped out and got into the other bed saying I had cheated. When I asked him why he had taken a double room he said it was thirty francs cheaper than two singles.

The next morning we walked all over Dijon. I was happy to be with Beckett, who really was an ideal companion as he loved to see beautiful things. It was a pleasure to visit the museums with him. We really got on marvelously well, and I told him how much nicer he now was than he had been. He said I was much easier to get on with, since I no longer made scenes. This trip ended all too soon because of Tanguy. We parted with sorrow, Beckett as usual regretting he relinquished me.

Early the next morning I left for England. For some unknown reason the car would not start, and I wasted an hour before I could get off. This made me late for Tanguy and his wife. Our whole trip consequently was a mad rush to Boulogne and we nearly missed the boat. The Tanguys had never been to England and this was an exciting adventure for them. They were unspoiled and so different from all the blasé people I knew that it was a pleasure to be with them. When we arrived in London I turned them over to Peter Dawson, an English Surrealist who had invited them to live with him. He was frantic with joy about their being in London and felt he owned them, although he barely knew them, having met them only once in Paris.

I had to go down to Petersfield to see Pegeen, whom I had abandoned for five weeks. Peter and Tanguy were to hang the show over the weekend. Hazel was living in my house and Pegeen spent weekends with her. We unpacked an enormous trunk containing my mother's silver, which had arrived from America. Hazel and I divided it up while a friend took the rôle of referee. Neither of us really wanted any of it, it was ugly and Victorian. There was the enormous tea set I have already referred to. We both refused to accept it and decided to sell it. Later, when Djuna saw it, she said we should give it to Nora Joyce: it was just her style. Too bad I did not follow her advice, because I left it to be sold in a jeweler's shop in Petersfield and have no idea what has happened to it even today. After the weekend I went up to town leaving Pegeen at her school in Wimbledon.

The Tanguy exhibition was beautifully hung and looked wonderful. It was a retrospective show, and some of the earlier paintings were entirely different in feeling from the later ones. There were two of this early period I wanted very much. One called *Palais Promontoire* belonged to Mrs. Tanguy and she would not sell it. It had almost no color, which made the drawing show to greater advantage. The other one was a yellow canvas that Peter Dawson owned. Instead, I acquired *Toilette de l'Air,* which was full of color, and produced a strange rainbow effect when you looked at it upside down. Mesens insisted on giving me a small painting as a present for bargaining with Tanguy, which annoyed us all. There was also a wonderful painting called *Le Soleil dans son écrin.* This picture frightened me for a long time, but I knew it was the best one in the show, and I finally got over my fear and now I own it.

We had lots of parties all the time; Mesens gave a wild one in Roland Penrose's home where he lived. Penrose, the owner of the gallery Mesens ran, had a lovely house in Hampstead. He was not in London at this time. He was rich and was always traveling. Everybody was tight at this party and the next day the neighbors complained about the goings-on in the garden. Peter Dawson had a girl who kept appearing in a different costume every hour with the most silly excuses.

Finally Tanguy and I decided to leave together and go to my flat. We must have warned Wyn, for she facilitated our departure, but a man called Charles Ratton, who had come to London specially for the show, insisted on following us. He suddenly remembered, when we were in the cab, that he had forgotten his braces and wanted to go back. We wouldn't hear of it and we got

Yves Tanguy, *Palais Promontoire* (*Promontory Palace*)

rid of him as soon as we could and went to my flat where we spent the night. After that it was difficult to see Tanguy alone because of his wife. Wyn came to our rescue and invited Mrs. Tanguy to lunch and kept her occupied all one afternoon.

The Tanguys soon got bored with the Dawson ménage and came to live with me. Tanguy had a bad ulcer, and he suddenly had a severe attack. I ran all over London trying to find him a medicine called Tulane. When I obtained it he revived, and we went to Petersfield for the weekend. Tanguy got on very well with Hazel, whom he named *La Noisette*. The house was full of so many people, including Hazel's friends, that no one knew where to sleep. Finally Hazel left, or rather I packed up her things and sent them to London where she had gone for a few days. Hazel didn't at all mind this barbarity.

The Tanguys and I remained alone with Pegeen and Debbie. We left the gallery to Wyn. The Tanguys adored the children— Mrs. Tanguy particularly, as she had never had any of her own. The girls really were like creatures in a fairy tale. They dressed in wonderful clothes and had long flowing manes, Debbie very dark and Pegeen very blond. They painted in Garman's little house. Tanguy and Pegeen exchanged paintings.

Mrs. Tanguy was not very happy, as she was jealous of my being with Tanguy all the time. One day she disappeared, and we got a phone call from the pub in South Harting asking us if we knew her, and should they lend her money to come home in the bus. They thought she was the children's governess, as she was French. She must have been exceedingly tight for a governess.

Our enormous fireplace had a very strange effect on me; for years I wanted to jump into it. I had to hold myself together not to do so. One night when Tanguy was with me I nearly achieved my purpose, but this time by mistake. We were having a heated argument and in my animation I slipped and was rescued by Tanguy just in time or I would have been where I had wanted to be for so long, among the flames.

Before we left London Wyn conceived the marvelous idea of renting a motorboat and giving a party on the Thames. We took lots of people and drinks with us, and at midnight found ourselves at Greenwich. The party was wild and drunk, and many scenes occurred from various jealousies. This was supposed to replace the publicity parties we usually gave in the gallery in the evenings, but it certainly did not result in selling any pictures.

Suddenly Tanguy found himself rich for the first time in his life. As Surrealism was just becoming known in London his show had been a great success. He was a simple man from Brittany, who had been in the *Marine Marchande* for years. His father had once had a position in one of the *Ministères*, and Tanguy said he was born in a building on the Place de la Concorde. This did not make him pompous. On the contrary, he was completely unpretentious. He had come to André Breton in 1926 and joined the Surrealists, painting in their style. Yves had been mad at one time, and of course was exempted from the French army. He had a lovely personality, modest and shy and as adorable as a child. He had little hair (what he had stood straight up from his head when he was drunk, which was quite often) and beautiful little feet of which he was very proud. Tanguy was about thirty-nine years old. He adored Breton the way Beckett adored Joyce, and seemed to think his whole life depended on his being a Surrealist. It was worse than having a religion, and it governed all his actions, like Garman's Communism. He left a Manx cat in Paris with a friend and every few days sent him a pound note in a letter. The pound was really destined for the maintenance of the friend, Victor Brauner, a Romanian painter, more than for the cat. After a few weeks I drove the Tanguys down to Newhaven and they went back to France. I was sad and Mrs. Tanguy cried, but I knew I would be seeing Tanguy again before long.

Soon after, Pegeen had to go to Mégève to spend her summer holidays with Laurence. Sindbad was staying with me for his vacation. My mother's maid had just arrived in Paris with my mother's string of pearls, which she was bringing to me. This was a small part of my inheritance.

I wanted to see Tanguy. I had to maneuver quickly and cleverly. I sent Sindbad to Garman's for the weekend, took Pegeen in my car down to Newhaven where we caught the afternoon boat, and wired Laurence's mother to meet us. She was delighted to take Pegeen in charge and keep her till the train left for Mégève. I then went to see my mother's maid and got the pearls. She was in an awful state about them and was delighted to get rid of them. They were the least of my concerns. I was to meet Tanguy in a café at six.

While we sat plotting our elopement so many people saw us together that we had to move to a less known café, and even then we decided it would be safer to leave Paris at once. Tanguy had no baggage of any kind. I had only a little bag. We took a train for Rouen, where we arrived at three in the morning. It was almost impossible to get a room and we went to at least ten hotels before we found one. The next day we wandered around Rouen and took a train for Dieppe, where it was pouring rain. We had missed the last boat so we spent the night at Dieppe in a chic hotel on the port. So far no one had seen us except Nancy Cunard, who tactfully pretended she had not. We were worried for fear Mrs. Tanguy would discover our whereabouts. When we arrived in

Newhaven and got into the car, we felt safe and drove home in great style.

Sindbad liked Tanguy very much but had no idea why he was there without his wife and kept asking for her. While Tanguy was with us he did a lot of drawings in green ink, which was the color he always used. There was one drawing that looked so much like me I made him give it to me. It had a little feather in place of a tail, and eyes that looked like the china eyes of a doll when its head is broken and you can see inside. Tanguy read Proust, which I think must have bored him, and we took long walks and went to a cricket match and were very happy. But he got restless and wanted to go back to Paris to do things for Breton who was soon returning from Mexico. Sindbad and I motored him down to Newhaven and then we went to visit Hazel in Kent. We went up to London for a few days as Sindbad wanted to go to a cricket match.

Suddenly Beckett appeared. He was on his way to Ireland. I put him up in my flat. When Beckett saw a photo of me and Tanguy on the mantelpiece looking happy together, he became curious and could not help showing it. I was leaving the next day for Paris and offered him my flat in London. He wanted me to remain with him until the next day, when he was going to Dublin. I refused. I suppose he wanted me because he knew that I had somebody else. I told him I was forced to have all my other lovers in order to keep him as a friend, and I blamed him for my double life. He offered me his apartment in Paris. It was on the Rue des Favorites, which made everyone laugh when I gave them the address. It was in a workmen's building, but it had a nice studio, bedroom and kitchen and bath. There was no telephone and it was far away, in the fifteenth *arrondisement,* but I accepted it as I knew Mrs. Tanguy would never find me there.

I drove Sindbad to Paris and put him on the train, which we made by one minute. It was a mad race through Paris. I don't know how we ever did it. Little did Sindbad suspect Tanguy was waiting for me in the station when I said goodbye. Tanguy and I spent the first night in Beckett's apartment and then he disappeared for forty-eight hours. As neither of us had a phone I was rather worried and thought all sorts of awful things had occurred. Finally he came back and told me what had happened. There had been a row at a Surrealist party, and it had ended up with poor

Yves Tanguy,
Portrait of Peggy Guggenheim

Brauner, the painter, losing an eye. He had had nothing to do with the row, in fact he was an innocent onlooker. Dominguez, a Surrealist painter, an awful brute, had seized a bottle and hurled it at someone else, and it had broken and rebounded in Brauner's eye, which fell out. Tanguy had taken him to the hospital, where an operation was performed to remove the pieces of glass and replace his eye. Tanguy promised Breton he would go to see Brauner every day. As Brauner was a Surrealist, Breton felt responsible for him. Tanguy and I now had to give up our project of going on our holiday to Brittany and I remained in hiding from Mrs. Tanguy in Paris. I was careful what cafés I frequented so as not to meet her.

One day, when I was having lunch with Mary Reynolds, Tanguy and Mrs. Tanguy came into our restaurant. I was very embarrassed and didn't know what to do. Mary told me to go and say *bonjour* to her. Her reception was not cordial, but it was definite. She didn't utter a word. She just picked up her knife and fork and hurled three pieces of fish at me. Tanguy took her home soon after, but the owners of the restaurant were not very pleased. It happened to be the restaurant where I always went with Beckett. The owners were old friends of ours. They had once allowed us to go up into their private apartment to hear Giorgio Joyce sing on the radio. We had been making a futile search for a radio and at the last minute they had come to our rescue.

Now that Mrs. Tanguy knew I was in Paris, life became more difficult. Tanguy was afraid she would follow him or find us together. Of course she did not know where I lived, but she was a woman with a mystic sense and often knew things for no obvious reason. I really liked her and did not want to make her unhappy. I never meant to take her husband away from her, and he had had many other affairs. Tanguy told me that she stayed home and wept. I must say this upset me. One day when he was in the hospital with Brauner, where he told me not to come for fear of meeting his wife, I waited for him next door in a café. We were supposed to go and see a doctor for Tanguy's ulcer. Mrs. Tanguy followed him to the café and made an awful scene. He had to take her away in a taxi. This was most unfortunate, as it meant giving up the doctor. Tanguy was sick and neglected his health badly, and Mrs. Tanguy was incapable of looking after him. She was just like a child. They both drank too much and had fearful rows, but

in some way were very much attached to each other. Sometimes when they had rows she disappeared for days.

Every morning Tanguy came to my house to fetch me. We spent the whole day together, then he went home to his wife. I was living in Beckett's apartment. He had gone to Brittany with his mistress in my car. I was still terribly in love with him. Tanguy once said to me, "You don't come to Paris to see me, you come to see Beckett."

We were all upset by Brauner's accident. The poor thing had to have a second operation on his eye, as the doctor had not removed all of the glass. After that we bought him a glass eye. He had enormous pride and courage and began to paint very well once he was readjusted to life. I went to see him with Tanguy and bought one of his paintings. He showed me the painting he had done of himself the year before with one eye falling out of its socket. He seemed to have prophesied this catastrophe, and after it occurred his paintings made great progress, as though he had been freed from some impending evil.

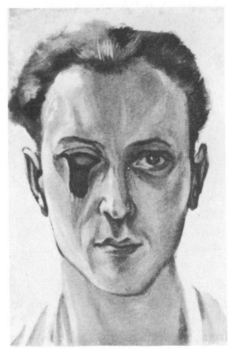

Victor Brauner, *Self-Portrait*

If Mrs. Tanguy and Brauner had a mystic sense, I don't think I
fell far behind them. One day Tanguy took me to a bookshop to
find a volume called *Huon de Bordeaux* by Gaston Paris and
illustrated by Orazi. This was a book Tanguy had received as a
prize in his schooldays. I paid little attention to what he was
doing, in fact I didn't even know what he was searching for. I
went next door to look at a Larousse Encyclopedia which I wanted
to buy for Tanguy. When I came back I walked absent-mindedly
up to the bookshelves and the first book I pulled out was the one
Tanguy had been seeking for half an hour. I think this pleased
him more than anything I ever did for him. Tanguy really loved
me, and if he had been less of a baby I would have married him
though the subject was never mentioned. He always told me
reproachfully that I could have had anything I wanted from him.
Laurence and my children were all for the marriage, but I needed
a father and not another son.

I went back to London just in time for the Munich crisis. I
must admit I have never been so scared in my life. I completely
lost my head. When the war came a year later I felt no personal
fear of any kind; but this time I was panicky. I began by having all
the paintings from the gallery moved to Petersfield. They did not
belong to me and I felt a great responsibility about leaving them in
London. As for myself and the children I thought we ought to get
away. I was going to Ireland with them and Djuna. She sat at the
bottom of my bed wrapped in my marabou cover and said, "We'll
be bombed in feathers." Sindbad refused to leave his school, and
Laurence phoned from Mégève and said that if I went to Ireland
he would never be able to see us again, so we decided to remain. I
was also worried about Tanguy and wired him to leave Paris. I had
a fixed idea that London and Paris would be bombed the first day
of the war. The evening Chamberlain came back from Munich I
spent with Ira and Edita Morris. They took me to Edward
O'Brien's house, where we heard Chamberlain on the radio.
Then we realized it was over. "Peace in our time," or one year.

When Breton came back from Mexico he brought with him a
collection of extraordinary nineteenth-century portraits and all
sorts of popular peasant art. I wanted to exhibit this collection,
but as most of it was very fragile it turned out to be impossible to
transport to England without paying a high insurance rate for
breakage. It was shown in Paris, however. Breton had a studio

apartment in Montmartre full of paintings and objects he had been collecting for years. The best things he never wanted to sell, but when he needed money he was willing to part with a minor object. As this was now the case, Tanguy took me there and I bought a beautiful pair of plaster hand-painted Mexican candelabra. They were so delicate they were perpetually breaking and finally had to be abandoned.

Breton was a marvelous talker, he seemed more like an actor or a preacher than a poet. He sat in a café surrounded by his disciples. Sometimes there were as many as forty. When the war was declared it was funny to see him appear in the uniform of a medical officer. In the last war he had served in the Army as a psychiatrist and this time they made him a doctor, though he had forgotten everything he ever knew about medicine. He went around with medical books in his pockets. Breton was a handsome man of about forty, with a head like a lion and a big shock of hair. He had a kingly appearance, but his manners were so formal and so perfect that it was difficult to get used to being treated so courteously. He was pompous, and I always felt he had no sense of humor. He had a blonde, artificial, Surrealist-looking wife called Jacqueline. She had been an underwater dancer but came from a bourgeois family. They had a child called Aube. Both Jacqueline and Aube followed Breton everywhere and the child was a pest in cafés. Tanguy adored the whole Breton family.

At this time there was a terrible feud among the Surrealists and they were split into two camps. Paul Éluard had taken away half or more of Breton's followers. They were both too strong to be leaders of the same party, and as one or the other had to give in, and as neither of them would, the party broke in two. Breton must have given orders to his disciples not to speak to any of the rebels, because Tanguy would not permit himself to remain in the room with any of the other group. The whole thing was ridiculous. All this complicated my life even more, because, while I could never go anywhere with Tanguy, fearing I might meet Mrs. Tanguy, he could never go anywhere with me where he might meet the rebels.

After bringing back all the paintings from Petersfield to the London gallery, we opened the season with an exhibition of children's paintings. I had been to Pegeen's school to speak to the art master there. He was an ideal teacher and gave the children

complete freedom. As a result they did the most beautiful work. I
borrowed a lot of his star pupils' work, and Laurence sent me
some his children had done. I also received a batch from Paris
from Maria Jolas' school. Dora Russell sent me some from her
school as did the schoolmaster who was the admirer of Kandinsky.
Peter Dawson who taught art sent me a lot done by his pupils, but
everyone said he did them himself. At the last minute Freud's
daughter-in-law brought in some paintings done by Freud's
grandchild, Lucien. One was of three naked men running
upstairs. I think it was a portrait of Freud. We sold a lot of these
paintings. All of Pegeen's were sold, and my dentist ordered a
duplicate of one. Roy Campbell's daughter had made a very pretty
little watercolor. One of her grandmothers brought it in and her
other grandmother who bought it took it back to South Africa.
Mesens bought a gouache that he thought was very Surrealist,
done by one of Laurence's children, and Roland Penrose purchased another.

One day a marvelous man in a highly elaborate tweed coat
walked into the gallery. He looked a little like Groucho Marx. He
was as animated as a jazz-band leader, which he turned out to be.
He showed us his gouaches, which were as musical as Kandinsky's, as delicate as Klee's, and as gay as Miró's. His color was
exquisite and his construction magnificent. His name was John
Tunnard. He asked me very modestly if I thought I could give him
a show, and then and there I fixed a date. (Later he told me he
couldn't believe it, he was so used to being turned down.) During
his exhibition, which was a great success from every point of
view, a woman came into the gallery and said, "Who is this John
Tunnard?" Turning three somersaults, he landed at her feet
saying, "I am John Tunnard." At the end of the show I bought
one of his best paintings, one with the extraordinary title *PSI* in
green letters. Alfred Barr, director of the Museum of Modern Art
in New York, admired it so much when he saw it years later that
he wanted to buy it for the Museum, but I would not part with it,
and he had to find another one instead. I was happy to think that I
had discovered a genius.

Another day Piet Mondrian, the famous Dutch abstract
painter, walked into Guggenheim Jeune and instead of talking
about art asked me if I could recommend night clubs where he
could dance. As he was sixty-six years old I was rather astonished,

but when I danced with him I realized how he could still enjoy himself so much. He was a very fine dancer with his military bearing and full of life and spirits, although it was impossible to talk to him in any language. Possibly his own, Dutch, would have been more satisfactory than his very odd French and English, but I somehow doubted that he even spoke his own native tongue.

I still had many paintings by Tanguy in London and I kept selling them all the time. There was one I wanted Roland Penrose to buy as he had the best collection of Surrealist painting in England. When he came to the gallery to see this Tanguy, he immediately appreciated it and bought it though he already owned several other Tanguys. It was in this way, in trying to render him a service, that I rendered Tanguy a great disservice, because I got friendly with Penrose at the same time. Penrose had a pretty little house in Hampstead and gave wonderful parties and entertained a lot. If he had no passion, he replaced it by charm and good taste. He certainly was capable of love. All his walls were covered with Surrealist paintings. He was the great promoter of Surrealism in England, and had arranged and brought over the big Surrealist show in 1936 which had been such a success. Penrose was extremely attractive, quite good-looking, had great success with women and was always having affairs. He had one eccentricity: when he slept with women he tied up their wrists with anything that was handy. Once he used my belt, but another time in his house he brought out a pair of ivory bracelets from the Sudan. They were attached with a chain and Penrose had a key to lock them. It was extremely uncomfortable to spend the night this way, but if you spent it with Penrose it was the only way. In his house he had beautiful paintings by the romantic Belgian Surrealist Paul Delvaux whom Mesens had discovered and was furthering. Once we slept under my favorite Delvaux painting, *The Call of Night*. I was so thrilled; I felt as though I were one of the women. I own one of these paintings which I bought from Mesens. It represents four women growing out of trees. Their legs are replaced by the bark of the trees. They are always the same women, as Delvaux's model was his wife, whom he adored. It is strange how different she can appear from different sides. In the paintings she is very handsome but her breasts are too big.

After a few months Tanguy finally got to London, where he had been meaning to visit me for ages. I met him at the station and the minute he saw me he knew something was wrong. I did not admit it for days, but in the end I told him I was caught in a trap and had to extricate myself, and that I was unhappy. I knew Penrose was in love with an American girl in Egypt. I did not tell Tanguy who it was that was causing me all this trouble, but Penrose gave a party and, as we sat holding hands all evening, Tanguy must have guessed. He was sad all the time he was in London, even though we went about a lot and lived together quite happily. We went to a cocktail party where the host asked if I were Mrs. Tanguy. We decided that I would be Mme Tanguy de Londres.

Tanguy felt rich as he was selling so many pictures. He had already spent, given or thrown away all the money he had made from the show. When he returned to Paris he used to take pound notes, roll them into a ball and throw them to people in cafés. I think he even burnt them. How I wished I had kept the money for him. He told me I should not have given it to him all at once. Now he bought us all presents. He gave me an orchid every day, and he gave me a painting. He gave Sindbad a wonderful stopwatch full of gadgets, Pegeen a miniature paintbox, and bought himself some English clothes. He soon went back to Paris as he was unhappy about Penrose. On the way back he made friends with the captain and was allowed to steer the boat into the harbor.

Henry Moore was a very direct simple man from Yorkshire, about forty years old, and he taught art to earn a living. He was having great success selling his things in London and exhibited in all the galleries. He did wonderful Surrealist drawings also. I liked them better than his sculpture. He lent us a very large wooden reclining figure, which looked beautiful in the center of the gallery. I would have liked to have bought it, but it was much too large for my home. While Tanguy was in London we were invited with Penrose to Moore's for dinner. Moore's wife, a Russian, cooked us a wonderful meal. Afterward Moore showed us his new sculptures. They were minute. I think I had given him the idea of making smaller things by writing him, at the time of my sculpture show, how much I admired his work, but how sorry I was that I had no room in my house for any of it. Now I could easily have one. One day, months later, he arrived at the gallery like a traveling salesman, carrying a little handbag. From this he brought out two elegant reclining figures, one in bronze and one in lead, and asked me to choose one. I infinitely preferred the bronze, which I acquired.

During this period I gave a collage show. Half of it was sent from Paris by Arp, who had gone to great pains to collect it. The rest I found in London. I borrowed some from Penrose and other people, and I got all the artists to make amusing new ones. As there was no limitation to the material used, we received every kind of object. Benno made one with a kitchen grater on it. Penrose hung the show for me. We put the old Picassos, Braques, Arps, and Massons in one room and all the less restrained works together in another room. Laurence sent some very obscene collages which we had to hide. Penrose lent me a few by Max Ernst, who was certainly the master of collages. As he was not mentioned by the critics in the reviews, Penrose was disgusted by their ignorance. After the opening I gave a large party at the Café Royal, as was my habit. I remember suddenly, in the middle of dinner, urging Penrose to go to Egypt to get his ladylove. He was surprised and asked me why I took such an interest in his affairs. I said, "Because I like you so much I want you to be happy, and if you don't go and storm her gates she will never come." He was touched by my interest in his affairs and followed my advice and brought back the lady he had been pining for so long.

In January 1939 I went to Paris and finally got over my passion for Beckett. I remember saying to him one day, "Oh, dear, I forgot that I was no longer in love with you." I think it was as a result of consulting a fortune teller. She seemed to think it was the moment to marry him or give him up. She said he was an awful autocrat. When I told this to Beckett he said, "Have you decided not to marry me?" I was relieved to say "Yes." After thirteen months of frustration it was about time it was over.

I was still friendly with Tanguy and saw him constantly. He painted a little pair of earrings for me. I was so excited I couldn't wait for them to dry and ruined one by wearing it too soon. I then made him paint me a second one. The first two were pink, but I thought it would be more fun if they were different colors, so he now made one blue. They were beautiful little miniature paintings and Herbert Read said they were the best Tanguys he had ever seen. Tanguy also designed a little phallic drawing for my cigarette lighter which he had Dunhill engrave. It was the smallest Tanguy drawing in the world, but unfortunately I left it later on in a taxi.

The earrings that Tanguy made for me

I came back to London giving up the idea of both Beckett and Tanguy. But I soon was in worse trouble. I got involved with an English artist called Llewellyn. The affair was very vague, but the consequences were disastrous. The pleasure gained from it was hardly worth the trouble it cost me. It all started because he was at rather loose ends, his wife being sick, and I took him home with me one night, which caused him great remorse, because of his wife. He had to be discreet and could see me only secretly or on business. We worked hard together on a Spanish Relief Committee which he organized. He collected paintings donated by all our artists from Paris and London. He wanted to borrow my gallery in order to hold an auction sale of these pictures, but in the end he found a house in Regent's Park that was more suitable. We held three auction sales on three successive nights, and sold the pictures for ridiculously low prices; most of the people, taking advantage of the artists' generosity, came for bargains. The whole thing was run in a state of great confusion and the auctioneers were ignorant of art. We had a nice drawing of Joyce done by Augustus John and a handsome 1937 Picasso, which raised good prices. I bought my first Ernst and a Llewellyn for normal prices, but most of the things were underbid, and we had to put a minimum on them. We raised a few hundred pounds, but we should have done much better considering the quality of the work and the cause involved.

Llewellyn had a wonderful house where he and his wife both worked and gave parties to which it was considered quite an honor to be invited. They were snobbish and both belonged to old English families.

All my troubles arose from the fact that John Davenport invited us to France for a weekend, I mean Llewellyn and me and another couple. No one knew of my connection with Llewellyn; in fact he sketched most of the day with John's wife and I spent all my time talking to John, who was a delightful companion. He took us to marvelous restaurants, and we had a most enjoyable two days, and then the others went on to Paris and I returned to Sindbad, who was spending his Easter holiday with me. When I departed Llewellyn brought me a little bottle of brandy to the boat, and I am sure he was delighted I left before we were found out. After that I spent three months in a state of great uncertainty, not knowing whether or not I was pregnant.

Every time I thought I was, I decided I wasn't, and vice versa. I had a stupid female doctor who spoke to me over the telephone and refused to see me. She was convinced I had had a miscarriage. I seemed to have had three. As time went on I got more and more ill and remained in bed for days. John Davenport invited me for the weekend to his beautiful home in the Cotswolds. I spent a whole afternoon weeding the gardens and pushing a heavy wheelbarrow, hoping it would have some effect, but it didn't alter matters.

One afternoon Llewellyn asked me out to his house to see his wife's work. The minute I entered the room and saw her I knew we were both pregnant. Shortly after this she had a miscarriage. She was taken to a hospital in the middle of the night in a dangerous condition. The irony of the situation was that they wanted a child. I offered mine to Llewellyn, but he refused it on the grounds that he could make a lot more.

After weeks of uncertainty I went down to Petersfield and consulted my local physician. I took an awful chance, but I must say he stood the shock very well. He had a test made on a mouse in Edinburgh, and after several days told me that it had proved positive. I then asked him to help me out of my troubles, but he said he could not take the risk. I protested on the grounds of being so ill, but he said that would doubtless pass in a few weeks time. I then went up to London and finally consulted a German refugee doctor. He said a blind man could see that I was pregnant and that I was much too old to have a child especially after not having had one for fourteen years. I was greatly relieved to find someone to end my troubles.

While I was in the nursing home John Davenport came to see me, bringing armfuls of flowers. He had no idea what ailed me, and little did he suspect the dangers I had incurred in France. Another visitor to the nursing home was Herbert Read. He looked so paternal. I am sure all the nurses thought he was the father of my child. He was even less suspicious than Davenport of my illness. He came to talk about our museum project, which by this time was well under way.

In March 1939 I had had the idea of opening a modern museum in London. It seemed stupid to go on with the gallery, which was suffering a loss of about six hundred pounds a year although it appeared to be a successful commercial venture. I felt that if I was losing that money I might as well lose a lot more and do something worthwhile. I approached Herbert Read, who was trying very hard to promote modern art in England. I liked him immensely and felt we could work well together. I made him give up his position as editor of the stuffy *Burlington Magazine,* and in exchange gave him a five-year contract as director of the new museum which we were to open in the fall. Wyn Henderson chose the title of "registrar" for herself. God knows what my position was to be. Herbert Read offered to help me for six months without accepting any money until we started; but he borrowed one year's salary in advance as he wanted to become a partner in Routledge's publishing house and buy some shares in it.

We spent weeks trying to find a suitable place for the museum but did not succeed until summer. I tried to think of ways to cut down my own personal expenses, in order to have sufficient money for the project. In fact, I had decided to live a monastic life in order to be able to produce the necessary funds. Actually I did not have nearly enough money for this venture as I had commitments of about ten thousand dollars a year to various old friends and artists whom I had been supporting for years. I could not suddenly let them down for the museum, much as I wanted to. I intended to buy no more clothes, sold my Delage car and bought a cheap little Talbot. Every penny that I could raise was to be used for the museum. As we had no money to buy paintings, we decided to borrow them or try to get people to give them to us. I went to my aunt, Irene Guggenheim, asking her if she thought I could get my uncle Solomon to give me something, but all she said was that the Baroness Rebay would have to be consulted and then maybe I would get a Bauer. I thanked her very much and left. Mr. Read did better—he got promises from lots of people. We had a marvelous press. Mr. Read's photo appeared in all the papers. The *Evening Standard* came out with a hideous photo of me with Pegeen. I really looked horrible, although I am generally photogenic. Djuna Barnes's comment was wonderful. She said, "The only chance you had, you muffed."

One day a young woman came into the gallery. She looked very masculine and said she had been sent by Marcel Duchamp, so we treated her well. She wanted to photograph Read and me in color. She had a large collection of celebrities she had already photographed, and was doing more in London, where she had succeeded in making everyone in the intellectual world pose for her. I thought it would be amusing to give her a chance to show her slides in my gallery. I combined this with a farewell party. Hundreds of people came, mostly gate crashers. Gisèle Freund showed her slides. Everybody was delighted to see celebrities in color, even more so than in black and white. We also had an enormous bar, so the party was a success. I was so ill at the last minute that I nearly did not appear. Llewellyn's wife, who had just recovered from her miscarriage and had no idea I was pregnant, told Llewellyn to throw me over his shoulder and take me to the next party. When I said I could not stand up, she asked me what ailed me and I said I had a sprained ankle.

After that Miss Freund photographed Mr. Read and me in my little flat. We couldn't get the camera far enough away, so I sat at Read's feet, while he showed me a book of Duchamp's. Behind us was a painting by Tanguy. We had to choose whether to cut this or ourselves in half. We decided to favor ourselves. Later Miss Freund gave me two photographs of Read's head. She had done a wonderful job. You could even see his closely shaven beard getting ready to grow again.

Mr. Read was a distinguished-looking man. He looked like a

prime minister, and seemed to be very well bred, though he boasted of being the son of a Yorkshire farmer. He had gray hair and blue eyes, and was reserved, dignified and quiet. He was learned and had written innumerable books, which I made him autograph as I had copies of all of them. He soon became a sort of father in my life and behind his back I called him Papa. He treated me the way Disraeli treated Queen Victoria. I suppose I was rather in love with him, spiritually. We had many meals together and we got very friendly; we talked a lot about John Holms and I made Mr. Read promise he would finally have the book of John's letters published for me. He told me how much he thought of John's criticism. I found an old article of John's about Read which was only moderately flattering, so I did not show it to him. It had appeared years before in *The Calendar,* the quarterly journal of modern letters that Garman had edited. Mr. Read and I had planned a wonderful future for ourselves. We were going to New York after the opening of the museum to raise money and to study the workings of the Museum of Modern Art. I blush now to think of our innocence.

Djuna was very much against the whole project and was extremely nasty about it all. She told me that I would soon find myself in the rôle of signing checks for Mr. Read, who would be running the whole show. Mr. Read had been rather nervous about staking his future with me. He wanted some kind of a reference, and as I could not give him one he went to T. S. Eliot, his best friend, and asked him what to do. Mr. Eliot, whom I had never met, reassured Mr. Read by saying, "I have never heard Mrs. Guggenheim spoken of in any but the highest terms." That settled it, I guess, for Mr. Read.

Mr. Read could hardly believe his good fortune. He must have thought I had tumbled from heaven. He had been curator of several museums, and could easily have been one again, and was eventually knighted; but all his life he had dreamt of making an ideal modern museum, and he showed me an article he had written on the subject. His first idea was to have an opening show in which we would exhibit borrowed paintings of the whole field of art we were to cover. Most of these were to be brought from Paris. This list, which was later revised by Marcel Duchamp, Nellie van Doesburg and myself because it contained so many mistakes, became the basis of my present collection. He wanted to start with the first Abstract and Cubist paintings from 1910, but every now and then he would relapse into Cézanne, Matisse or Rousseau and other painters whom I thought we ought to omit.

When Mr. Read came to visit me in the nursing home he brought a specific proposition from Mesens and Penrose, who wanted to be in on the project. It seems that they had been offered free a whole floor in a building of a famous dressmaker's in Berkeley Square. If we accepted this gift and Mesens with it on a small salary, Penrose promised to lend several of his best Picassos. All this seemed unnecessary to me, as Mesens and Penrose were my avowed enemies by then. We had had a terrible fight about an Abstract show which I had given in my gallery. You can therefore imagine my surprise when Mr. Read brought me this offer. I categorically refused it, but I think Mr. Read wanted to accept it.

Phyllis Jones came and took me out of the nursing home and brought me to Petersfield to recover from the operation. I was in a state of collapse and spent most of my time in bed rereading Proust and making budgets to find enough money for Mr. Read.

One day Mr. Read phoned me to say that he had been offered the ideal spot for the museum. It was Sir Kenneth Clark's house in Portland Place. I made a great effort and came up to town to look at it. I was still very feeble. In fact I did not recover for another three months—in all, six months of my life were ruined by this illness.

Lady Clark showed me all over her beautiful house. It really was the perfect place for the museum, even though it was Regency and not modern. Lady Clark, who had been a gym teacher, was particularly pleased with an air-raid shelter she had made in the basement. She told me she was going to live in the country to please her children. I was so silly I did not realize that she was preparing for the fast approaching war, and I thought I was very lucky to acquire her house. The only trouble with it was that it was too large, so I conceived the idea of living on one of the upper floors. But to my dismay Mrs. Read conceived the idea of living on another. We soon began arguing about which floor we would occupy.

We actually took the house, but as our lawyers were away on a holiday I never signed the lease, and when war was declared, I had no legal obligation toward Sir Kenneth Clark. He, however, thought that I had a moral one, and told Mr. Read he expected an indemnity as he could have let the house to someone else. He suggested that I give the indemnity to a committee he had formed for artists in distress, to which he had by then sacrificed his house. Mr. Read considered Sir Kenneth Clark was richer than I. Therefore I concentrated on Mr. Read to whom I felt not only legally but morally obligated.

After all this I began to think about a summer holiday. I needed a good rest and I wanted to go abroad before the museum opened. I was also to meet Mr. Read in Paris in the fall and have all the pictures lined up for him by then. For months I had been trying to get down to Chemaillere in the Ain, where Gordon Onslow Ford had a château for entertaining the Surrealists. I hoped he would give us some paintings out of his collection for our museum. Tanguy expected me to come there, but because of my health I had put it off. I wrote to Tanguy, but his replies got more and more vague, and I finally realized that I could not join him and that he must have a new girl friend.

I then accepted the invitation of Nellie van Doesburg to go to the Midi. Nellie was my newest friend and I did not know her very well at this period. About a year before she had walked into my gallery and given me a long lecture on who her husband had been and who she was. I was not in the least impressed and thought she was funny. I allowed her little by little to force her way into my life. I don't like women very much, and usually prefer to be with homosexuals if not with men. Women are so boring. Anyhow I asked Nellie to live in my flat, or most likely she asked herself, and as I had a guest room I let her come.

Nellie was a well-groomed woman of my age with a neat little figure, blue eyes, and red hair which was sparse and dyed. She dressed carefully, looked very attractive but made up too much. Because of her excessive vitality even I envied her. Her passion for abstract art was fanatical, which was why she had come to me. For ten years she had been the widow of Theo van Doesburg, the co-editor, with Mondrian, of the magazine *De Stijl*. He was also a painter, architect and theoretician. He was a sort of twentieth-century da Vinci, and Nellie worshippped his memory, which fact touched me very much.

One night in Paris Carl Nierendorf took us out to dinner, and we all got tight, Nellie and I weeping on his shoulder about our dead husbands. He never got over it. As a sentimental German he thought it was wonderful, which it was. When Nellie came to London I always put her up in my flat, and when I was in Paris she did her best to make me stay with her in her home in Meudon that her husband had built before his death. I always refused to live in Meudon because of Tanguy, but I never told her why. I once brought Nellie down to Petersfield and she made great friends with my children. She was so young and vital that they loved her.

In August I started out for France in my little Talbot car, never dreaming I was saying goodbye to Yew Tree Cottage forever. I let Sindbad drive through Normandy. It was also the last time I saw Normandy. Now I can't bear to think of the devastation and ruin that war brought to that beautiful country.

When I arrived in Paris I got Sindbad a sleeper to Mégève and then collapsed. My health was still fragile. As soon as we could Nellie and I started out for the Midi. We decided to go to Mégève and stop on the way, if possible, to see Onslow Ford. For some reason we never got there, but we did get to Mégève. The children had been begging me to come to visit their new home for years. Laurence had bought a house there in 1936. With Nellie as an excuse I could easily live in the hotel and leave in a few days. So we spent a week in this little skiing village, which by now was quite fashionable in winter. I did not like the place and never have, but the children adored it. Laurence and Kay were very hospitable; they had a beautiful home and the children were happy to have us there.

After that we motored to Grasse where we were to be the guests of Mr. Sides, Nellie's friend. He was a cordial businessman of Armenian extraction, a sort of adventurer who couldn't bear to feel money near him without getting at it somehow or other. He suggested every possible combine to me in order to attach some of my money, but as he was not nearly crooked or clever enough, none of his propositions came to a head. His latest interest was modern art, about which he knew nothing, but for which he was prepared to do anything. He was even ready to replace Mr. Read though he had no qualifications to do so.

Sides and Nellie had just put on three exhibitions of Abstract art in Paris. The artists told me they were awful, but artists are never satisfied, and I did not believe it was as bad as they made out. Nellie really knew her job. She had wonderful judgment, and I never saw her make a mistake.

Mr. Sides had rented a house and Nellie and I shared it with him. There were two floors; he lived downstairs, and Nellie and I lived upstairs. There was one bathroom for us all. It could be reached only through our bedrooms, which it connected, so I named it the Polish Corridor.

Mr. Sides saw to it that we had wonderful meals and lots of drinks. We really had a nice life in this funny little house lost up in the hills of Grasse. Sides had great vitality and although he was still going around on two canes, as a result of a train accident which had nearly cost him his life, he rushed around the country in my car and bought a chapel in La Tourelle which he started to transform into a house. He was very ambitious and was a *chevalier de la légion d'honneur*. Nellie and I saw him as the future mayor of La Tourelle. He was over fifty-five.

Every day Nellie and I drove down to the sea. We were always trying to get away from Mr. Sides and go on trips. We managed to escape to Le Canadel to Mme Octobon, where we spent a few days with this old friend, the innkeeper. I wanted to see my home at Pramousquier. It had been sold to bourgeois people and was completely transformed into a conventional Midi home. I hated to see it like that.

While we were at Le Canadel we went to see the Kandinskys. They were living in the stuffiest hotel of the whole coast, the Kensington at La Croix. I am sure Kandinsky's wife chose it. We drove them around, and when we showed them where we lived in Mme Octobon's café they nearly fainted. It was so unchic. I think they thought we were joking. During our visit a general mobilization was declared, and we rushed back to Mr. Sides.

Mr. Sides was the most optimistic man I have ever known. Of course he didn't believe there was going to be a war. When it was declared, he thought it would be over in a few weeks. The more he listened to the radio, the more encouraged he felt. God knows why. I certainly was rather worried and had no idea what to do next. Mr. Sides said, *"Elle cherche les enfers."* He thought I was looking for trouble.

At the beginning of the war I was a pacifist and was afraid Sindbad would join up. Nothing could have been further from his thoughts at that time. He was only sixteen. I did not know what to do about the future, but Laurence kept very calm and decided everything for me. He wrote me reassuring letters and I took no steps for the time being.

In Grasse we were surrounded by the army. Soldiers seemed to be everywhere. They were billeted all around our house and looked completely unprepared for war, which they turned out to be. Whole regiments passed by our house at night, and even in the daytime. We never knew where they were going. The mobilization went on for days and there seemed to be no equipment or organization. It all looked hopeless. There was a lot of time to be gained while Poland was being taken, but no one went to her rescue.

One day when I was down in Cannes waiting in line to send one of my many wires to Laurence or to Kitty to move everything from London to Petersfield, a strange incident occurred. We were all terribly tense, as people are in the first stages of a war, and no one felt like joking, especially in that rather fatiguing business of getting off long wires. A homosexual who was a few steps ahead of me suddenly came out with the wonderful remark, "Dear me, the way everyone is acting one would think France was at war!" If we hadn't been so upset I think we would have all burst out laughing, but I am afraid he missed his shot. One day we were told that Cannes would be bombed in two hours. It didn't seem to make much impression on anyone.

We had great trouble in getting gasoline, but always managed somehow. Sides did not want us to use what we had, but I was so excited about being in my beloved Midi again that I couldn't bear to stay still; I perpetually wanted to drive and revisit all the places that had meant so much to me during the four years I had lived in that region. I was in a state of excitement every minute and had to show Nellie all the places where things had happened to me in that very emotional period of my life.

I soon gave up the idea of going back to England, as Laurence decided the children should remain in France. We could not all be scattered about in different places, and the war would soon make travel impossible. I therefore had to relinquish the museum, which would have been impossible anyhow, since we could not have borrowed paintings and exposed them to the bombings of London.

I conceived a wonderful scheme of forming an artists' colony for the duration of the war, and inviting all the artists who wanted to join us to be my guests, and to receive a small allowance. In return they would give me paintings for the future museum. Nellie and I began looking all over the south of France for suitable accommodations for our colony. We looked at hotels, châteaux, houses. This gave me a good excuse for traveling, and as I really believed in the project it became a sort of mission. At one moment we thought Les Baux would be the ideal place, but it was not available, as the French Government was going to requisition it.

Had I known more about artists at that time I never would have dreamt of anything so mad as trying to live with them in any kind of harmony or peace. Nellie really should have known better. As soon as I got back to Paris and met a few of the people we had thought of inviting, I realized what a hell life would have been. They not only could not have lived together, but did not even want to come to dinner with each other. There were so many little feuds and jealousies, it was unbelievable.

While we were in the south we went to visit Albert Gleizes and his wife. They had several homes, one at Calvaire, and one at St. Rémy, and another across the Rhone. The first was a comparatively simple house near the sea, but at St. Rémy they had an enormous estate which they had been trying unsuccessfully to farm for years. At the outbreak of the war Mrs. Gleizes had been lent a donkey by the *commune,* and with it and a couple of Spaniards she had serious intentions of raising enough food to help save France from starvation. She wanted me to join her in her efforts, but vague as my project was, I felt hers was even more so. They had had a beautiful house built in the real Provençal style, and received us in a delightful manner. They were vegeterians, but produced exquisite meals which they served at the most peculiar hours, having no sense of time. Gleizes was an intellectual and was as much a writer as he was a painter. They were very charming people, and like most married couples provided great mirth for the public in their personal relations. Mrs. Gleizes interrupted him every time he tried to speak, which was really a pity as he was a very interesting man.

When we finally got back to Paris I went to live with Nellie in her home at Meudon. Her house was so constructed that in order

Antoine Pevsner was a timid little man who reminded me of Al Jolson's joke, "Are you man or mouse?" He conceived a great passion for me, but as he was mouse, not man, I did not in the least reciprocate this feeling. He behaved like a schoolboy in the spring, and we became great friends.

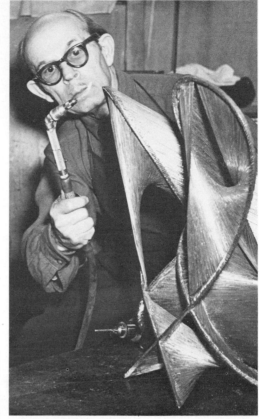

Arp had been born in Alsace, but he was now a Frenchman with the name of Jean instead of Hans. He was madly anti-German and would not let us listen to any German music. He served my breakfast every morning and washed all the dishes. He went back to Paris with a porkpie hat and a bread box under his arm. He knew only one word of English, "candlesticks."

Max Ernst had a terrific reputation
for his beauty, charm, and success
with women. He had white hair and
big blue eyes and a handsome beak-
like nose resembling a bird's. He was
exquisitely made.

Jimmy Ernst looked so sweet with his
wonderful, big blue eyes. He longed
to be friends with Max but Max felt
uncomfortable in his presence and did
not know how to talk to him. I
immediately took Jimmy to my heart
and became a sort of stepmother to
him.

Leonora Carrington was a young pupil of Max Ernst and not well known but very good and full of imagination in the best Surrealist manner. Her skin was like alabaster and her hair was rich in its black waviness. She had enormous, mad, dark eyes with thick black brows and a tip-tilted nose.

Djuna Barnes was handsome with her white skin, magnificent red hair and beautiful body. She wrote most of *Nightwood* in a rococo-style bedroom in Hayford Hall that looked so much like Djuna that we gave it to her.

One evening I went to Piet Mondrian's studio to see his new paintings and hear his boogie-woogie records. He kissed me and I was surprised to discover how young he still was at seventy-two.

Marcel Duchamp was a handsome Norman and looked like a crusader. Every woman in Paris wanted to sleep with him. He hadn't painted since 1911. Now he only played chess. I have him to thank for my introduction to the modern art world.

Yves Tanguy was a simple man from Brittany. He had a lovely personality, modest and shy and as adorable as a child. His hair stood straight up from his head when he was drunk, which was quite often.

Myself at Art of This Century seated before a picture by my daughter Pegeen

Frederick Kiesler was a man about five feet tall with a Napoleon complex. He told me that I would not be known to posterity for my collection of paintings, but for the way he presented them to the world in his revolutionary setting.

Art of This Century's Surrealist Gallery had curved walls made of gum wood. The unframed paintings, mounted on baseball bats, protruded about a foot from the walls. Each one had its own spotlight. The lights went on and off every three seconds, to everybody's dismay.

In the Abstract and Cubist Gallery the paintings were clustered in triangles, hanging on strings as if they were floating in space. At the right is Kandinsky's *White Cross*.

Kenneth McPherson came
into my life when I most
needed him and when he
most needed me. He
immediately gave me a sense
of peace, and when I sat
with his arm around me I
was perfectly happy,
happier than I had been for
years.

I can't say I like the music
of John Cage, but I went to
every concert of his in
Japan. He was not
interested in sightseeing and
would not let us out of his
sight. Everything we saw
we had to do by stealing
away from him.

to make a new room all you had to do was to move a rolling door. It was very convenient.

I found Tanguy again. He was living alone in a beautiful apartment owned by Kay Sage, an American princess. I had once sent him to see this lady, as I hoped she would buy a picture. The description he had given me of her the next day would never have made me suppose she would be his future wife. She had just left for America, and he was to follow her if he could get his papers. She had done everything she could to help him, and then went ahead trusting he would follow. If not, he was to join my colony.

I ran around Paris with Tanguy while he got his final papers and then he suddenly disappeared. He was spending the last days with his wife. A touching thought. She and I now became good friends again, as I was no longer her enemy. She sold me the painting I had wanted for so many months, *Palais Promontoire,* and I promised Tanguy I would pay her monthly installments for it. So in a way I inherited her after Tanguy's departure.

I put Djuna on the same boat that Tanguy sailed on. She was in a complete state of collapse, and I told Tanguy to look after her. Of course he didn't. I saw them off at the Gare d'Austerlitz late one night. It was very dramatic, and really gave one a feeling that we were at war. There was a terrible tension in the air, and the station was almost in darkness. I did not have the slightest desire to leave, and was not in the least afraid.

Laurence wrote me he was thinking of putting Sindbad in an English school near Pau. I decided to go to see the school and look for houses for my colony, as I had not yet found the ideal place. We drove from Mégève right across France in two cars, which seemed ridiculous. Sindbad and I drove the little Talbot, and Kay and Laurence had their Renault. As we were to part company at Pau we found it necessary to have both autos. The trip was beautiful through Dordogne and the Massif Central with the late autumn reds and browns. We visited wonderful old churches and ate magnificent meals in the old French tradition. Pau is a very dull town but the war seemed to have livened it up. The school was a silly little place compared with Bedales, and Sindbad frankly hated it. He was very unhappy to renounce cricket and not be allowed to return to Petersfield.

I stayed on a few days after Kay and Laurence left, hoping

Sindbad would get settled. In the meantime I began looking
around for a château again. I got hold of an agent and went all
over the countryside with her. By this time my project had
assumed an official character, as I found myself using the name of
M. de Monzie, the Minister of Education, who the agent thought
had sent me to find a château. It was a complete error, but I let it
go at that as I thought it sounded better. In France such things
are useful. I had some vague connection with M. de Monzie,
whom I had never met. As a result of this I was royally received
everywhere, and was shown the most beautiful châteaux, which
of course I never took.

In my absence Nellie, who was by now the secretary of the new
scheme, went around to see all the artists to find out if they were
interested in our project. There was little enthusiasm shown
except by certain artists who were on the rocks. To everybody's
relief we finally gave up the idea.

I then had to face a settlement with Mr. Read. I tried to get a
visa to England, as I wanted to go and talk to him. This was
refused me, but I was told that I could apply for one for the
duration of the war, if I were prepared to go back with my
children, and remain there. As this was out of the question I gave
up the idea. It was a good excuse to give Mr. Read, as I really did
not want to go on with the thing. Mrs. Read's resolution to live in
the museum rather terrified me. Some time later my friend
Hoare, in the Foreign Office, said he could get me a visa. By then
I had arranged everything by correspondence. Our lawyers broke
our contract, and Mr. Read accepted half of five years' salary,
minus what he had already received. He bore me no ill will, but
he was very much disappointed, as he thought London would have
been the ideal place for the museum during the war. I felt I had
rendered him a great service in freeing him from his dull job on
the *Burlington Magazine,* and as he was two thousand five hundred
pounds the richer for our brief association, and as a result of this,
a partner in Routledge, I had no qualms. He soon decided to write
a book about his life and dedicate it to me. He wrote the book, but
his wife may have objected to the dedication, as he omitted it.
When all this was over he decided to call me Peggy, and thereafter
we remained the best of friends and continued to correspond.

Chapter 12

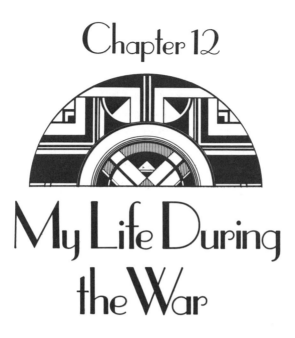

My Life During the War

Giorgio Joyce was in great trouble. His wife Helen had gone mad and was rushing around Paris with two blue Persian kittens which she took everywhere in order to attract attention. She was having an affair with a house painter in the country, and also tried to seduce every man she met. Giorgio had retired to Paris and was living with our friend Ponisovsky. He came to get me hoping I would console him and give him some advice. He was very worried about his child, and wanted to get it away from his wife. One night, when we were in a restaurant his wife came in with the nurse who was supposed to guard her. She made an awful scene and I left at once. The whole thing was painful and Ponisovsky and I were terrified that Giorgio was going to have her locked up. We did not realize how ill she was and we tried to prevail upon Giorgio to leave her in freedom. She was going about incurring debts with all the dressmakers, as she had the *folie de grandeur*. She went to the police and denounced as spies her friends Elsa Schiaparelli, James Joyce and some other people. She really was getting dangerous, but I hated the thought of her being locked up. This she finally brought on herself by becoming violent. Giorgio had removed the child, and this was too much for her. The police finally took her to a horrible *maison d'aliénés,* but Giorgio had her moved to a sanatorium where she was supposed to be looked after, but of course wasn't. We cabled her brother Robert Kastor to come to take her back to America, and he arrived by Clipper. He was not surprised, as she had already been in a sanatorium for over a year in Switzerland. Giorgio had remained with her there, and had looked after her, but now he felt he had come to his end. Her brother could not remove Helen, as she was too ill, but he arranged to have her go as soon as she was calmer. He wanted Giorgio to take her to New York, but Giorgio refused. He said he could not leave as he was subject to induction into the French Army. In the middle of all this I had a bad accident.

One night after dining with Brancusi I came home and received a visit from Beckett and Giorgio. I was living in Mary's house, which she had lent me as she had gone to Arcachon with Marcel and the Dalis. She did not want to leave Paris, but Marcel was so afraid of being bombed that he could not remain, and she followed him unwillingly. Beckett got very tight, and Giorgio and I put him to bed. We sat up drinking. The next morning Beckett was still in the house, so I decided to take him with me to meet Kandinsky, to whom I was going for tea. I had always wanted him to see Kandinsky's studio out in Neuilly-sur-Seine, in a modern apartment house. Beckett had translated the preface to the catalogue for Kandinsky's exhibition, and, as he was an authority on German art, I thought he ought to see Kandinsky's paintings.

We were not destined to see Kandinsky that day. When we went down the marble steps to the door we passed Fanny, Mary's maid. I caught her eye, and it occurred to me that she recognized Beckett, to whom she had served breakfast in bed when we lived in Mary's other house. (She had moved again to a bigger one next door.) The memory of all this was so upsetting that I missed my footing and fell down the stairs. I landed on my right knee and completely put it out of its socket. Fortunately Nellie was with us as Beckett stood by quite helplessly in his usual paralyzed state. Nellie made him carry me to a sofa, and sent for her doctor. He put the knee back into position, but I already had water on it. The next day, Nellie took me to the American Hospital in an ambulance where I was X-rayed and sent home, nothing being broken. I had to remain in bed, as I couldn't move, so I got used to lying quietly and peacefully during air-raid warnings. We never were bombed at this time, so I did not mind the sirens.

In a few weeks after a great deal of massage I was able to walk again. I had to find a place to live because Mary and Marcel were returning to Paris since it seemed so safe. Giorgio wanted me to take a room in the hotel where he was living with his family. I certainly did not want to get so much involved with him, so I went to another hotel.

At Christmastime I returned to Mégève to see the children, but the slippery winter weather made it almost impossible for me to get about with my bad leg, and I did not enjoy it. On my way home I went down to the Lac d'Annecy to see a new school that Sindbad was entering. Pau had not proved a success.

When I got back to Paris I started very seriously to buy paintings and sculptures. I had all the museum funds at my disposal, now that the problem of Mr. Read was settled, and lots of free time and energy on my hands. My motto was "Buy a picture a day" and I lived up to it.

I rented Kay Sage's apartment which I had found Tanguy living in. It was the most beautiful place I had ever seen. It was on the Ile St. Louis behind Notre-Dame on the Quai d'Orléans, on the seventh floor, having been retrieved from the attic, and under the eaves. It had a terrace, where you arrived in the lift, and across which you walked in order to enter the flat. There was a big studio with three exposures and a little silver-papered bedroom and dressing room and an elegant bathroom. The Seine played the most lovely reflections on the ceiling of my bedroom; I always lay in bed Sundays watching this. I was happy as all my life I had wanted to live by a river.

Here I gave a lot of dinner parties. I cooked the dinners myself with the help of Fanny, Mary's maid, who came to me daily. Nellie hated my home; she said there was no place to hang pictures. Nevertheless I managed to place all the smaller ones. The big ones had to remain in storage, where I could see them whenever I wanted.

Giorgio's wife stayed all winter in that dreadful nursing home, and they would never have relinquished her, and all the money she brought them, if I had not again insisted that her brother send for her. Finally, with the help of two nurses, a doctor and lots of drugs, she was put on a train for Genoa and caught a boat to New York. I went with Giorgio to a storage house and packed all her clothes. I then inherited her two Persian cats, who were no longer the darling little kittens they had been. One so much resembled Giorgio that I named it after him, and the other one I called *Sans Lendemain*.

Before Tanguy had left, he had taken me to see Brauner. Brauner had by now quite recovered from his accident and was painting very well. (He was living with a Jewish girl, who worked in one of the *Ministères,* to support him.) Nellie and I went to see him and I bought another of his paintings. It was so much admired by my doctor that I gave it to him to settle part of my bill. Brauner's paintings always had a great success. I remember giving another one in England to a schoolteacher who could not afford to buy it.

All winter I went to artists' studios and to art dealers to see what I could buy. Everyone knew that I was in the market for anything that I could lay my hands on. They chased after me, and came to my house with pictures. They even brought them to me in bed, in the morning before I was up.

For years I had wanted to buy a Brancusi bronze, but had not been able to afford one. Now the moment seemed to have arrived for this great acquisition. I spent months becoming more and more involved with Brancusi before this sale was actually consummated. I had known him for sixteen years, but never dreamed I was to get into such complications with him. It was very difficult to talk prices to Brancusi, and if you ever had the courage to do so, you had to expect him to ask you some monstrous sum. I was aware of this and hoped my excessive friendship with him would make things easier. But in spite of all this we ended up in a terrible row, when he asked four thousand dollars for the *Bird in Space*.

Brancusi's studio was in a *cul de sac*. It was a huge workshop filled with his enormous sculptures, and looked like a cemetery except that the sculptures were much too big to be on graves. Next to this big room was a little room where he actually worked. The walls were covered with every conceivable instrument necessary for his work. In the center was a furnace in which he heated instruments and melted bronze. In this furnace he cooked his delicious meals, burning them on purpose only to pretend that it had been an error. He ate at a counter and served lovely drinks made very carefully. Between this little room and the big room, which was so cold it was quite unusable in winter, there was a little recess, where Brancusi played Oriental music on a phonograph he had made himself. Upstairs was his bedroom, a very modest affair. The whole place was covered in white dust from the sculptures.

Brancusi was a marvelous little man with a beard and piercing dark eyes. He was half astute peasant and half real god. He made you very happy to be with him. It was a privilege to know him; unfortunately he got too possessive, and wanted all of my time. He called me Pegitza.

Brancusi told me he liked going on long trips. He had been to India with the Maharajah of Indore in whose garden he had placed three *Birds in Space*. One was white marble, one black, and the third one bronze. He also liked to go to very elegant hotels in France and arrive dressed like a peasant, and then order the most expensive things possible. Formerly he had taken beautiful young girls traveling with him. He now wanted to take me, but I would not go. He had been back to Romania, his own country, where the government had asked him to build public monuments. He was very proud of this. Most of his life had been very austere and devoted entirely to his work. He had sacrificed everything to this, and had given up women for the most part to the point of anguish. In his old age he felt it very much and was very lonely. Brancusi used to dress up and take me out to dinner when he did not cook for me. He had a persecution complex and always thought people were spying on him. He loved me very much, but I never could get anything out of him. (I wanted him to give Giorgio Joyce a portrait in crayon which he had done of his father, James Joyce, but I could not make him do so.) Laurence suggested jokingly that I should marry Brancusi in order to inherit all his sculptures. I investigated the possibilities, but soon suspected that he had other ideas, and did not desire to have me as an heir. He would have preferred to sell me everything and then hide all the money in his wooden shoes.

After the row, I vanished from Brancusi's life for several months, during which time I bought for one thousand dollars a much earlier work of his, *Maiastra*, from Paul Poiret's sister. It was the very first bird he did in 1912. It was a beautiful bird with

an enormous stomach, but I still hankered after the *Bird in Space.*
So Nellie (whom he called Nellitska) went to see Brancusi and
tried to patch up the row. I finally went back to his studio and we
began all over again to discuss the sale. This time we fixed the
price in francs, and by buying them in New York I saved a
thousand dollars on the exchange. Brancusi felt cheated but he
accepted the money.

One day I was having lunch with him in his studio workshop
and he was telling me about his adventures in the last war. He
said he would never leave Paris this time. In the last war he had
gone away and as a result he had broken his leg. Of course he did
not wish to leave his studio and all his enormous sculptures. They
could not possibly be removed. At this point of our conversation a
terrific bombardment of the outer boulevards of Paris took place.
He knew at once that it was the real thing, but I did not believe it,
as we had had so many false air-raid warnings. We were only a
few blocks from the Porte de Vaugirard, where some bombs were
falling, and the noise was infernal. He made me move from under
the glass roof into the other room, but I paid no attention at all
and kept going back to fetch wine and food from our lunch table.
Afterward we emerged into Paris, where the news was confirmed.
All the factories of the outer boulevards had been bombed, and a
lot of school children killed.

Brancusi polished all his sculptures by hand. I think that is the
main reason they are so beautiful. This *Bird in Space* was to give
him several weeks' work. By the time he had finished the
Germans were near Paris, and I went to fetch it in my little car to
have it packed and shipped away. Tears were streaming down
Brancusi's face, and I was genuinely touched. I never knew why
he was so upset, but assumed it was because he was parting with
his favorite bird.

I wanted to buy a painting by Jean Hélion, and heard that he
was in the Army, stationed near Paris. Nellie wrote to him and he
came in on a flying trip to sell me one. As he had been in the Army
and deprived of the company of women he was delighted to be
with Nellie and me. We appeared very feminine and brilliant to
him with all our make-up, and he said we were the first paintings
he had seen for a long time. We rushed all over Paris to find his
works that were stored in various places and I bought an
enormous canvas that we found in the attic of a friend's house. I

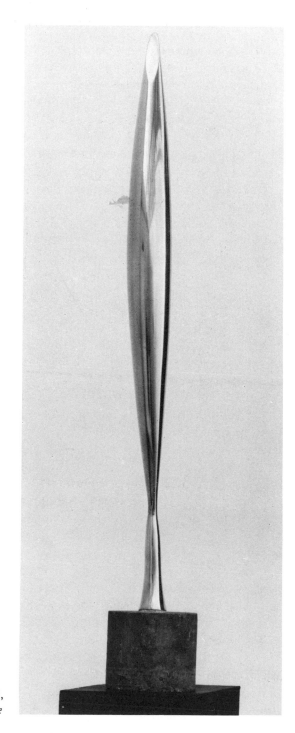

Constantin Brancusi,
Bird in Space

gave Hélion Herbert Read's anthology, *The Knapsack*, especially compiled for soldiers, and I felt at the time that I would never see him again. Little did I imagine that he would one day by my son-in-law. (Later, when he escaped from the German prison camp where he had been interned for nearly two years, he found the money for his painting still available in a French bank and it saved his life.) We had a wonderful dinner opposite the Gare Montparnasse and he rushed back to join his regiment.

One day I found a funny little picture at a dealer called Poissonnière, who claimed it was a Dali. It was extremely fascinating and very cheap, but it was most unlike Dali. I said I would buy it if he would get it signed by Dali. So poor M. Poissonnière, who was waiting to be transferred from Paris any minute, being in the Army, rushed down to Arcachon with the painting. He brought it back duly signed.

After that I still wanted a real Dali, by that I mean one that would be recognized by the public, and one of his best period, 1930 or thereabouts. A handsome little one was brought to me in bed early in the morning and I bought it at once, from a lady dealer. But it was very small and I still wanted to buy a big important one. Much as I objected to Dali and his goings-on, I still thought it necessary to represent him in my collection, which was supposed to be historical and unprejudiced. Mary was a great friend of the Dalis, so the first time Gala came to Paris she invited us to dinner together. We got into terrible arguments about my life, of which Gala did not approve. She thought I was mad to sacrifice it to art, and that I should marry one artist and concentrate on him as she did. The next day she dragged me all around Paris to find a Dali painting. We went to a storage house and to their mad apartment which was empty while they lived in Arcachon. I found a good painting, which she thought more appropriate than the first over-sexual one I had chosen quite innocently, not noticing what it represented. The one she chose certainly is sexual enough. It is called *The Birth of Liquid Desires* and is horribly Dali.

I also wanted to buy a sculpture by Giacometti, whose studio was in a tiny street off the Avenue du Maine and was so small I don't see how he could have worked in it. He looked like an imprisoned lion, with his lionesque head and an enormous shock of hair. His conversation and behavior were extremely Surrealist and whimsical, like a divertimento of Mozart. One day I found a badly damaged plaster of his in an art gallery. I went to see Giacometti and asked him if he would mend it for me if I bought it, as I wanted to have it cast in bronze. He told me he had a much better one in his studio. As it proved to be just as good I bought this one, and he promised to see to the casting of it.

This took several weeks, and one day, after he had the bronze cast, he arrived on my terrace with what resembled a strange medieval animal. He looked exactly like a painting by Carpaccio I had seen in Venice of St. George leading in the captive dragon. Giacometti was extremely excited, which surprised me because I thought he had lost interest in these early abstractions, which he had long since renounced in order to carve little Greek heads, which he carried in his pocket. He had refused to exhibit in my modern sculpture show because I would not exhibit one of these. He said all art was alike, but I did not agree. I saw no reason for his little Greek heads and much preferred my bronze, which certainly was far from classic. It was called *Woman with a Cut Throat* and was the first of Giacometti's works ever to be cast, and when, years later, I returned to Europe after the war, to my great horror I seemed to see it everywhere, though I suppose the number of casts must have been limited to about six.

May I here introduce Howard Putzel. He was nearly my twin in age, a man of great force of character. Since I got to know him I did everything he wanted, or resisted him with all my strength. The latter weakened me so much that I had no energy left for more important matters. He first became known to me in the winter of 1938, when he wrote me from Hollywood to wish me good luck on the opening of my gallery and to announce the closing of his. At the time, he sent me some Tanguy paintings that he had exhibited out there and that were to be included in my forthcoming show. I met him a few months later at Mary's in Paris and was surprised to discover he was the opposite, physically, of what I had imagined he was going to be. I had expected to meet a little black hunchback. Instead of this he turned out to be a big, fat blond. At first he was nearly incoherent, but little by little I realized the great passion for modern art that lurked behind his incomprehensible conversation and behavior. He immediately took me in hand and escorted me, or rather forced me to

accompany him, to all the artists' studios in Paris. He also made
me buy innumerable things that I didn't want; but he found me
many paintings I did need, and that balanced our account. He
used to arrive in the morning with several things under his arm
for my approval and was hurt when I did not buy them. If I found
and bought paintings "behind his back," as he must surely have
considered any independent action on my part, he was even more
offended. He and Nellie disliked each other only as rivals of
extreme passions can.

In the winter of '38–'39 Putzel decided he would take me to
meet Max Ernst. I resisted futilely as usual. I knew Ernst's work
well, and really wanted to buy a painting. He had had an
exhibition in London in Mesens' gallery and Penrose owned a
great number of his best works. Ernst knew who I was and I
suppose he assumed I came to buy a painting. Ernst had a terrific
reputation for his beauty, his charm, and his success with
women, besides being so well known for his paintings and his
collages. He certainly was still very good looking in spite of his
age. He was nearly fifty. He had white hair and big blue eyes and
a handsome beak-like nose resembling a bird's. He was exquisitely
made. He talked very little, so I was forced to carry on a
continuous chatter about Mesens and their gallery and mine. At
the feet of Ernst sat Leonora Carrington, his ladylove. I had seen
them around Paris and thought how intriguing they appeared
together. She was so much younger than Ernst; they looked
exactly like Nell and her grandfather in *The Old Curiosity Shop*. I
tried to buy a painting of Ernst's, but the one I wanted belonged to
Leonora, and another I liked was declared by Putzel, for some
unknown reason, to be too cheap. I ended up instead by buying
one of Leonora's. She was a young pupil of Ernst and not well
known but very good and full of imagination in the best Surrealist
manner and always painted animals and birds. This canvas, which
was called *The Horses of Lord Candlestick,* portrayed four horses of
four different colors in a tree. Everyone was delighted by this
purchase and I never thought about Ernst again until the winter
of the war, when I found some marvelous paintings of his at a
dealer's and bought three at once. At this time he was in a
concentration camp.

Nellie took me to meet Antoine Pevsner, the Russian Con-
structivist. I had known his work in London, and knew his

brother Naum Gabo quite well. Pevsner was a timid little man who reminded me of Al Jolson's joke, "Are you man or mouse?" I think he was mouse. His constructions were beautiful, and I bought one which must have been inspired by a mathematical object. Pevsner was an old friend of Marcel Duchamp, but had never met Mary Reynolds. We took her to Pevsner's for dinner, and when she told him she had been Marcel's mistress for over twenty years he just could not believe it. He did not even know of her existence, and he had seen Marcel every week of his life for as many years. Pevsner conceived a great passion for me, but as he was mouse, not man, I did not in the least reciprocate this feeling. He behaved like a schoolboy in the spring. We became great friends. When he could not get his wife to leave Paris during the German occupation, I sent him money, and looked after him all during the war.

At Eastertime I went down to Mégève to fetch Sindbad and Pegeen and took them to the Col da Voza to ski. I brought with me Jacqueline Ventadour, a friend of theirs. We drove in my little Talbot singing old southern ballads, which she taught me on the way. We all enjoyed the holiday very much except Pegeen, who was unhappy to leave Mégève. Sindbad and Jacqueline had a fine time and so did I, as I became enamored of a little Italian in the hotel. He was perfectly horrible, an impossible creature, but very handsome in a flashy way. This occupied most of my thoughts as I was left alone all day, not being a skier. On the way home I drove Sindbad back to Mégève with my new acquaintance. After the Italian had left by train I stayed the night with Kay and Laurence. The next morning, just as I was leaving, I slipped on the stair and sprained my ankle and cut open my elbow. Kay and I, as usual, were not getting on well, so I insisted on leaving after I had had two clips put in my arm. I don't know how I ever got back alone in my car to Paris in this state, as I couldn't walk and couldn't use my right arm.

During the winter I spent much time with Virgil Thomson. He and Putzel and I used to eat a lot of our meals together. Virgil was going to help me arrange concerts in my museum if I ever had one. He gave charming Friday evening parties at which he kept open house. He did a musical portrait of me which was not in the least resembling, but for which I posed quietly for several hours, reading his book, *The State of Music,* which is very smart. I

thought it would be nice to marry Virgil to have a musical
background, but I never got far with the project.

One night at Mary's there was an awful row about my saving
my paintings. Mary said it was indecent to think of anything
except the refugees. She intimated that if we managed to get a
camion we would run down the refugees with the paintings. Virgil
was very sweet to me and I remember weeping in his arms in my
little car afterward while he tried to console me for what I
considered my oldest friend's unnecessary tongue-lashing.

Virgil left Paris before I did, and when I got to America he was
one of the first people I looked up. By then he was the most
famous music critic in New York, and was so well known he told
me he no longer did anything he didn't enjoy. He was quite
independent. When I told him I had brought Max Ernst to
America and was living with him he made a prize remark. He
said, "Lots of ladies seem to have enjoyed that before." But I am
getting way ahead of events.

The day Hitler walked into Norway, I walked into Léger's
studio and bought a wonderful 1919 painting from him for one
thousand dollars. He never got over the fact that I should be
buying paintings on such a day. Léger was a terrifically vital man,
who looked like a butcher. During his stay in New York, where
he finally got after the German occupation of France, he became a
sort of guide and took us all to foreign restaurants in every quarter
of the city. He seemed to know every inch of New York, which he
had discovered on foot.

The next day I bought from Man Ray one of his early works, a
1916 painting and several Rayograms.

I tried to rent a suitable place to show my paintings, but the
Germans were advancing so quickly that I finally had to rescue my
collection and ship it out of Paris. I had actually rented a beautiful
apartment in the Place Vendôme. This apartment was not only
the place where Chopin had died but also had been the
establishment of O'Rossin the tailor. The first day I saw it was the
fatal day Hitler marched on Norway. The owner of the building
did everything in his power to discourage me, but when I insisted,
he said, "Think it over and come back tomorrow." I went back
and told him I had not changed my mind, so he had to give in. I
gave him my lawyer's name, who turned out to be an old friend of

his, and this greatly facilitated matters. I then got the architect Georges Vantongerloo to draw up plans for the remodeling of this spacious place so that I might live in it as well as make a museum there. It was much overdecorated in the *fin de siècle* style, and I insisted on having all the angels removed from the ceiling and scraped off the walls before we started painting it. At this point, however, it was so obviously impossible to continue with the scheme that I finally realized the only thing to do was to ship the pictures out of Paris before it was too late. At the last minute I made an attempt to use the cellars for the museum. However this was not allowed as they were being reserved for air-raid shelters. The extraordinary thing was that I neither signed a lease nor paid a cent deposit on this apartment, and in spite of that the owner removed all the *fin de siècle* décor without any guarantees from me. After I left Paris, I had a bad conscience and sent him twenty thousand francs indemnity. I have never known such a landlord.

The only thing to do with the paintings was to pack them and get them out of Paris before it was too late or store them in an underground vault. Léger told me he thought the Musée du Louvre would give me one cubic meter of space somewhere secret in the country where their pictures were being sent, so I had my pictures taken off their stretchers and packed when, to my dismay, the Louvre decided the pictures were too modern and not worth saving. What they considered not worth saving were a Kandinsky, several Klees and Picabias, a Cubist Braque, a Gris, a Léger, a Gleizes, a Marcoussis, a Delaunay, two Futurists, a Severini, a Balla, a Van Doesburg, and a "De Stijl" Mondrian. Among the Surrealist paintings were those of Miró, Max Ernst, Chirico, Tanguy, Dali, Magritte and Brauner. The sculpture they had not even considered, though it comprised works by Brancusi, Lipchitz, Laurens, Pevsner, Giacometti, Moore, and Arp. Finally my friend Maria Jolas, who had rented a château at St-Gerand-le-puy near Vichy to evacuate her bilingual school of children, said she would keep my collection in her barn. So I sent them there.

This was a most fortunate choice, as things turned out, since the Germans were there for only a short period and were quite unaware of the presence of my cases in the barn.

After that I really should have left Paris myself. The Germans were advancing so quickly, but I could not tear myself away from my new friend Bill. For two months I had been with him every afternoon. We used to sit in cafés and drink champagne. It is really incomprehensible now to think of our idiotic life, when there was so much misery surrounding us. Trains kept pouring into Paris with refugees in the direst misery and with bodies that had been machine-gunned en route. I can't imagine why I didn't go to the aid of all these unfortunate people. But I just didn't; instead I drank champagne with Bill. At the last minute my traveling permit expired, and when I tried to renew it I was refused a new one. I had a dream that I was trapped in Paris. When I found that I could not leave, I remembered my dream and was very scared. The Germans were getting nearer every minute. All my friends had left. Bill decided to stay, as his wife was too ill to be moved.

Finally I fled with Nellie and my two Persian cats three days before the Germans entered Paris. I took the Talbot, as I had plenty of gasoline. I had been saving it up for weeks in *bidons* which I kept on my terrace. We left for Mégève just as the Italians declared war. By then I did not need any papers, as there was a general exodus of about two million people. It was terrific. The main road to Fontainebleau was jammed with cars four abreast, all creeping along in first gear. They were laden down with every conceivable household object and advanced at the rate of one mile an hour. Everything was enveloped in a cloud of black smoke let loose by the Germans or by the French, I never found out which or why. We were covered with soot. I managed to get off the main roads finally and followed little side-paths. But after the first few hours it was much easier to advance, as nobody was going east. Everyone was trying to get to Bordeaux. Several times I was warned not to go east or I would meet the Italian army. In fact I was afraid I would be sent back by the police if I insisted. But we were allowed to continue and, needless to say, did not meet the Italian army, which never got far into France. On the way we learned the dreadful news of the fall of Paris and a few days later came the tragic armistice terms. There wasn't much left of France, but what there was we clung to desperately.

I found Laurence and the children resolved not to move. He did not want to add to the miseries of the road. As the Germans advanced everyone went on the road hoping to escape them. The confusion and misery and hunger and bombings that they suffered were unbelievable. After the armistice no one seemed to realize what had happened to France. The people all seemed to be in a daze as though they had been hit on the head with a hammer. It was very sad to see France like this. We still had plenty of food, but we realized how much was being sent to Germany. We were quite cut off from occupied France and had great difficulty in getting letters across the border. We soon discovered that for five francs letters were carried at many points, so we did not lose touch with our friends.

My children were happy to see me, and I decided to take a house for them for the summer at Le Veyrier on the Lac d'Annecy. Pegeen and Sindbad, at the tender ages of fifteen and seventeen, were terribly in love with a brother and sister called Edgar and Yvonne Kuhn. My son especially was suffering all the pangs of a first love affair which was unfortunately one-sided. In order to please them I took a house practically next door to their friends, and as a result I never saw them. They spent all their time with this strange half-American, half-French family. They played tennis and they swam and they went on picnics and they went to Annecy on motorbikes. They returned reluctantly for meals, and then went down to the Kuhns again. This was all quite natural, as they were so in love, and I had neither a tennis court nor a lake to offer them. Sometimes I joined them, but on the whole I preferred to keep away from this mad family, as they later proved themselves to be.

For company I had Arp and his wife and Nellie, who lived with me. They were worried about the future, as they could not go back to Meudon in occupied France. They were Hitler's avowed enemies, besides which they had left all their possessions in Meudon. Arp wanted to go to America and start a new sort of Bauhaus. He was very nervous about the war as all his predictions had come true and he foresaw the future in very gloomy terms. He was madly anti-German and would not let us listen to any German music. If Mozart or Beethoven came over the air he immediately turned off the radio. Arp had been born in Alsace, but was now a Frenchman with the name of Jean instead of Hans, which he had dropped.

During the summer I got rather bored and started having my hair dyed a different color every few weeks to amuse muself. First it was chestnut, which certainly was the nearest to nature, but then I got the wild idea of having it bleached bright orange, which made me look like Dorothy Holms. When I came home from the hairdresser's Sindbad laughed, but Pegeen burst into tears and made me have it changed to black, which way it remained thereafter. As a result of all the time I spent in the beauty parlor I conceived a sort of weakness for the little hairdresser who worked so hard on my beauty. From re-reading D. H. Lawrence I also got a romantic idea that I should have a man who belonged to a lower class. Therefore, on the coiffeur's free days I used to fetch him in my car and we drove off into the country together. He took me to a marvelous bistro where we danced. Later I took Laurence there and we gave a birthday party, but we did not invite the coiffeur. In fact, I was ashamed of him and kept him hidden. I spent hours sitting with Pegeen in the beauty salon, as my own hair didn't take up enough time. She never suspected anything, but she considered him a bad hairdresser and regretted that I had made her get a permanent wave from him.

Soon this got boring and I needed a change. There was not much choice. The only other man about was an old fisherman, who looked like Brancusi and took a great fancy to me. He let Nellie and me swim off his raft, which was a great privilege. It was very nice because in that way we could avoid the Kuhns. There was also a very amusing pansy who lived on the top of our hill. One day, seeing "G B" on the back of my car, he left a note in it, inviting us to his house as he claimed to be a friend of the English. He proved to be a good neighbor and gave us wonderful meals and sold us delicious wine which he made from his vineyard.

There was no one else except Mr. Kuhn or his brother-in-law, who suddenly came home as an escaped prisoner. It was a touching scene to witness, as the whole family got hysterical, especially Mrs. Kuhn, who nearly went off her head with joy. Laurence was down from Mégève visiting us at the time, and we retired discreetly in the middle of the family emotions. One night I went down to the Kuhns, where I was always welcome, with the idea of finding the brother-in-law, or *l'oncle,* as Nellie and I called him. I brought him back to our house for dinner. The next night, just when he was leaving, in came Mrs. Kuhn, his sister. She asked for her brother. I was rather surprised and realizing I must be careful said he had gone home long ago. At this moment he heard her loud voice claiming him, and he jumped out of the window into the garden before she could find him. She then searched the whole house saying she could not sleep unless he came home. She made a terrible noise, and not only the Arps, but the children and the cook were awakened. The next day, when we were swimming off the fisherman's raft *l'oncle* came and told me that he could never see me again. I insisted on getting in his boat and trying to talk to him but he looked nervous and soon brought me back. I never saw him again, though Sindbad did everything to bring him to me. Instead I had a visit from Mrs. Kuhn, who came, she said, to warn me that her brother was a *maquereau* and that she would not allow me to be imposed on by him. I said I was old enough to look after myself, and later I heard from Mr. Kuhn that she had done the same thing before on a similar occasion.

Mr. and Mrs. Kuhn hated each other and lived together separately. She was his housekeeper and they both adored their children. Mr. Kuhn had an old mother of eighty, who made great friends with me. The old lady supported them all. Not knowing about the *histoire* I had had with *l'oncle,* she told me that her daughter-in-law had suddenly become very ill and nearly died. I gathered this was a way of recapturing her brother when she thought she had lost him. She must have extracted a promise from him never to see me again. Mr. Kuhn was quite amusing and Laurence and Arp made friends with him. He was very entertaining. He thought I should go to Africa with him and try to wipe out syphilis among the natives. I never took this proposition seriously. When Nellie's twenty-five-year-old African friend arrived to visit her, the whole Kuhn family was horrified. Mr. Kuhn came up for dinner to meet him, and the young man spent the evening trying to inform Mr. Kuhn about the Negroes' position in Europe and Africa. He was an intellectual and talked very well. Later he became president of Dahomey.

By the end of the summer I got my pictures sent from the château by Giorgio Joyce who was living nearby. They were at the Gare d'Annecy for weeks before we realized it, and then when we found out, we had no idea where to put them. Every day Nellie and I went to see if they were safe. We covered the cases with tarpaulins and tried to keep the rain off them by moving them away from the part of the ceiling that was leaking. They remained on the *quai de petite vitesse* for months.

Being Jewish, I could not go back to Paris, but I wanted to

exhibit the pictures somewhere. Nellie was a friend of M. André Farcy, the director of the Musée de Grenoble. He liked modern art, so I sent her to see him and ask him to help us. She came back with no definite promise but with an invitation to me to send my pictures to the Musée, where he would at least shelter them. That was better than the *quai de petite vitesse*. We immediately dispatched them and followed them ourselves.

M. Farcy was in a very bad jam himself at this time and nearly lost his museum directorship and finally ended up in prison. Because of the Vichy government he couldn't do much for me. He did want to give an exhibition of my paintings, but he was so scared that he kept putting it off. The museum's collection of modern art he hid carefully in the cellar, as he was expecting Pétain's visit to Grenoble. He gave me perfect freedom in the museum, where I unpacked my paintings and had them photographed. I could bring my friends to see them; in fact I could do anything except hang them. I had a room to myself where they were all stacked against the wall. M. Farcy would never fix a date for the show, claiming that he must pave the way with Vichy first. He did not want me to remove the paintings, but after six months I lost my patience and told him that I was going to America. He begged me to leave the paintings with him. I hadn't the slightest intention of leaving them with him and I also had no idea how I could send them to America, but I knew that I would never go without them.

M. Farcy was a funny fat little man in his fifties. He liked to get away from home and from his adoring wife. Whenever we invited them for dinner he came alone, giving some excuse about his wife's inability to accompany him. Later I discovered he never conveyed my invitation to her. He was very gay when he was with Nellie and me, and told us wonderful stories. In his youth he had been a cyclist and had done the *tour de France*. You could hardly believe it from his present appearance. One evening after six, when we were sitting in the museum, he took my hand and began caressing my palm. Then, in a low voice, he asked me if I did not feel anything. I insisted that I did not feel the slightest tremor, as it suddenly occurred to me that his great weakness for ladies probably led him to make love to them in the museum after closing hours. He was forever running all over France giving lectures, and as he often stayed away a longer time than his wife expected we wondered what he was up to. He loved modern art, but he didn't know one thing from another. He often asked me who painted my paintings, and invariably when we came round to Marcoussis he said, "What, Brancusi?" I had one painting by Vieira da Sylva he liked, because he thought it was a Klee. When I left Grenoble, I offered him this painting or a Tanguy as a present. But when he asked me for the hundredth time if it were a Klee and I said "No," he chose the Tanguy. In spite of this he had managed to collect quite a nice number of modern paintings for the museum without any funds to back him. That probably was why he was not very well in with the Vichy government, which nearly dismissed him.

Through Nellie I had met Robert Delaunay and his wife Sonia. He had been an important and good painter about thirty years before. I wanted to buy one of his paintings of that period, as his contemporary ones were horrible. But he was foolish enough to ask me eighty thousand francs for it, so of course the deal did not come off. Putzel had found one at Leonce Rosenberg's of the same year for ten thousand. When I was in Grenoble the Delaunays were exiled from their home, which was in occupied territory, and they were living in the south of France. They had rescued a few paintings, and they began again to try to sell me one. They wrote and phoned Nellie every minute to make her get me to take the painting which I had not bought in Paris. Finally I got so bored that I offered to buy it for forty thousand francs.

Delaunay came up to Grenoble and he really was charming. I think most artists are better without their wives. He brought his painting with him. He very kindly restored for me a Gleizes I had bought in Paris, from the widow of Raymond Duchamp-Villon, Marcel's brother who had died in World War I. When Delaunay left, I gave him my darling cat Anthony as I could no longer endure living in one room with these two foul-smelling creatures. Delaunay loved cats, and this one took to him at once. Soon after this Delaunay got very sick and wrote me many letters about his own illness and about the cat. I had no idea Delaunay was dying and I was sad when I got the news.

Laurence had decided it would be safer for us to go to America in the spring, as we were being perpetually threatened with

German occupation of all of France, and we knew that the United States would be involved in the war sooner or later. The American consul had been urging us to leave for over a year and a half, and we had difficulty in renewing our passports. We had the children to consider and the possibility of being cut off from America with no money. Worse still was the prospect of being put in a concentration camp. I was determined to go to Vichy to see our ambassador and try to get him to help me with the shipment of the paintings. But we were more or less snowbound all winter and could not travel. Just at this time, as though he had fallen from heaven, René Lefèvre Foinet arrived in Grenoble.

When René came to Grenoble I had been having terrible rows with Nellie, and I more or less insisted that she should go to live in Lyons. Her African friend was working there in the university. After we were separated we got on much better. In fact there was no reason for our fights, but I was happier working alone on the catalogue of my collection. I typed for hours every day, but my room was so cold that I had to retire to a little office which the manager of the hotel lent me. Arp had written a preface for the catalogue and I was trying to get Breton to do one as well. Laurence could not make head or tail of these quarrels, which I explained to him passionately every time he came down to Grenoble. He called it all the Battle of Grenoble and we let it go at that.

René was one of the partners of the firm in Paris which had handled for me all shipping of paintings from Paris to London, when I had the gallery there. I told him my troubles, and to my great surprise he said nothing could be easier than to ship my collection from Grenoble to America as household objects, provided I could send some personal belongings too. He suggested sending my little car which I had left in a garage six months before, as I was not permitted to drive it because of gas shortage. The trouble was I forgot which garage I had left it in. So we wandered around to all the garages of Grenoble and finally came across it. M. Farcy had to give us his authority to remove the paintings, and then René and I set to work and together we packed them up in five cases with my linens and blankets. This, of course, was a great favor René conferred on me, but by this time we were having an affair, so he was very happy to render me any service. All this lasted for two months and it was very enjoyable. So there was really no hurry about getting the cases packed.

At the end of two months I ran away from René and went to Marseilles. This was my second trip there that winter. I will explain the other one first.

During my stay in Grenoble I received a cable from Tanguy's new wife Kay Sage asking me to help rescue and finance the passage to America of five distinguished European artists. When I cabled to inquire who they might be I received the reply, "André Breton, Jacqueline Breton, his wife, and his daughter Aube, Max Ernst and Dr. Mabille, the doctor of the Surrealists." I must say I protested that Dr. Mabille was not a distinguished artist, nor were Jacqueline and Aube, but nevertheless I did accept the charge of the entire Breton family and of Max Ernst. I was also trying to rescue Victor Brauner who had written me to ask if I could save him. He was hiding in the mountains near Marseilles living as a shepherd, and since he was a Jew I felt he might eventually get in great trouble. Breton was in Marseilles. I now combined my efforts and went down to Marseilles to see the Emergency Rescue Committee.

Varian Fry, the head of the committee, raised and distributed a lot of money among stranded refugees, many of whom were in hiding from the Gestapo. He worked underground to get them into Spain and Portugal or Africa and from there to America or Cuba. He also helped to repatriate the British soldiers who were still in France after Dunkerque and who wanted to join de Gaulle. Fry's right hand man was Daniel Bénedité, who had previously worked in the office of the prefect of police in Paris. They were assisted by Bénedité's English wife, Theo, and various other efficient people. With them was a handsome American girl, Mary Jayne Gold, who gave them vast sums of money for their noble work, in which she also took a hand. They all lived in an enormous dilapidated château called Belle Air outside of Marseilles. At the moment, Breton and his family were their guests. Here Breton held court and surrounded himself with Surrealists. Before I arrived Breton and Fry and Mary Jayne Gold and Bénedité had been arrested and held incommunicado on a boat for days during Pétain's visit to Marseilles. They had finally managed to get a secret note through to the American consul who rescued them.

Fry asked me to come and work with the committee. He wanted me to take his place while he returned to the States for a brief visit. I was so frightened by the fact that they had been arrested and by the general black-market atmosphere of Marseilles and all the strange goings-on that I went to the American consul for advice. I wanted to know what the committee really represented. The consul warned me to keep out of it. He did not tell me why, and at the time I had no idea what a dangerous job Fry was doing. The American government was perpetually trying to get him to go back to America to avoid difficulties with the Vichy government. However, he stuck it out to the bitter end. Living in Grenoble and thinking only about art I was completely unconscious of the underground and had no idea what all this was about.

The whole atmosphere of Marseilles was dominated by the black market and everyone was engaged in some illegal deal to get a visa, a passport, or some food or money. Later I got used to it, but in the beginning I was terrified. I went back to Grenoble after giving Breton and Fry some money.

After I had promised to pay Ernst's passage to America, Laurence and René suggested that I ask him to give me a painting in exchange. I wrote to him and he wrote back and said he would be delighted and sent me the photograph of one he considered suitable. It was a lovely painting, but from the photo did not appear to be very much, so I wrote back and said I thought it was a nice little picture, but perhaps I would prefer another one.

In the meantime Ernst had written asking me to send him six thousand francs and a letter for a lawyer, testifying that I had seen the sculptures in his house, and that they were worth at least a hundred and seventy-five thousand francs. It seems Leonora Carrington had gone mad and made over their house to a Frenchman in order to save it from the Germans, not knowing he would take advantage of the situation and seize the property. When Ernst emerged from the concentration camp and discovered what had happened, he thought he might at least try to recover the sculptures with which he had decorated his house. He was able to get his paintings out at night. I had seen his sculptures reproduced in *Cahiers d'Art,* and was glad to do this for him. Max Ernst had a reputation of liking very young girls, and one day

René said to me, "What would you do if Ernst ran away with your daughter?" I said, "I would rather run away with him myself." Ernst had also written to tell me how Leonora had disappeared and that he thought she was in Spain and had gone mad. It all sounded very coldblooded. Later I was to discover how passionately he still felt about her.

Chapter 13

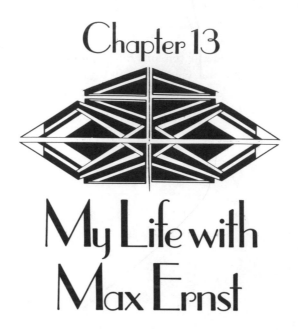

My Life with Max Ernst

When I arrived in Marseilles the second time the whole atmosphere of the château had changed. It was no longer dominated by Breton, who had finally managed to get all his papers, and had gone to America with his family. The Surrealist court had disappeared, but Max Ernst was living there, hoping to get away soon. Brauner met me at the station.

The very first night we met Ernst in a café and made a date with him for the next day to see his paintings at the château. This was the first time I had seen Ernst since I had been to his studio with Putzel two years before, and he certainly appeared much older after all his experience in concentration camps. He looked very romantic wrapped in a black cape. He seemed happy to see me and delighted at the prospect of showing me his new paintings. The next day Brauner and I went out to the château, and Ernst made a mervelous display of all his new works. I think that he was upset because I was so much more excited about the old ones, and tried to buy them all, instead of the new ones which I frankly did not yet like. I didn't manage to conceal my feelings. We soon came to some agreement, by which I was to give Ernst two thousand dollars minus the money he already owed me, in return for which

I was to get innumerable paintings. Brauner kept rushing around finding collages of historic interest, and Ernst said that I could have all these too. He was very generous. In the end we celebrated with a bottle of wine that Ernst had brought from his vineyard in St. Martin d'Ardèche. As the next day was his fiftieth birthday, we decided to have a party.

In the morning I met René on the Canebière and asked him to come and see Ernst. I then tried to persuade him to go and rescue some of Ernst's paintings that were left behind in his village, but René balked at this. Ernst invited us all to celebrate his birthday by eating seafood with him in the *vieux port.* Afterward we went to a black-market restaurant with Fry and had a wonderful dinner. René, who was with us, was supposed to return to Grenoble. But I took compassion on him as he had stood up in the train all the night before, and I said that he could spend the night with me and should leave next morning.

By this time I was very attracted to Ernst, and when he asked, "When, where, and why shall I meet you?" I replied, "Tomorrow at four in the Café de la Paix and you know why." As Brauner followed me everywhere (he was always with us) I had to slip my key to Ernst, and pretend to say goodnight to him, in order to fool Brauner.

When I began my affair with Max Ernst it was not serious but soon I discovered that I was in love with him. After ten days I had to leave him, because I had told Laurence that I would come and spend Easter with him and the children at Mégève.

At this time Laurence was having a sort of crisis in his affairs with Kay. They had been breaking up for a year, and he was unhappy. When Max put me on the train he cried, and he promised he would follow me to Mégève. So I felt pretty sure this was not the end of my life with him. He had given me all his books in Marseilles and even one that he had previously inscribed to Leonora in no uncertain terms. "To Leonora real, beautiful, and naked." He also gave me her books, which he had illustrated. I read them on the train, and wrote him from Valence how much I liked them; then from habit I wired René to meet me at Grenoble where I had to spend the night on my way to Mégève. I tried to explain to René that I was in love with Max. The next day I left for Mégève.

I didn't hear a word from Ernst and was very unhappy. Finally

Laurence and I went down to Lyons to obtain visas for Spain and Portugal, as we hoped to be able to leave for America in about a month with all six children and Kay. We were to meet Marcel Duchamp in Lyons and I had planned to go back to Marseilles with him to try to find Max again. The minute we arrived in the hotel in Lyons Max phoned that he was in Mégève. Of course I decided to go back. Marcel was surprised and annoyed at my sudden change of plans. As soon as we had obtained the visas, which we did with great ease since we were Americans, Laurence and I returned to Mégève.

Max had arrived at Mégève wearing his black cape, and the children thought he was a very romantic figure. Pegeen knew his books, so she welcomed him warmly. It seems he spent the whole evening telling them tales about himself and Leonora, about her departure and his troubles. They were most sympathetic, and he held them spellbound for hours.

After a week Max and I went back to Marseilles. We sat up all night in the train and it shocked me to see how old he looked when he was asleep and snoring. We had great difficulty in getting a room in Marseilles as the population had tripled since the fall of France. He took me to the château. Afterward I got a room in my old hotel and Max stayed with me at night.

We were all busy trying to get to America. Kay had reserved ten places on a Clipper for us, hoping to include her new friend whom she was rescuing from a concentration camp. But Laurence, though he behaved like an angel to her all through this period, refused to travel with this gentleman. I must say I didn't blame him. That left us one extra seat on the Clipper, and of course Max hoped to get it. Brauner also wanted this seat, but his papers were not yet in order and in the end the poor man was denied a visa as the Romanian quota was filled for two years. We had a third candidate, Jacqueline Ventadour, the friend of Pegeen and Sindbad. She had a very insistent mother who succeeded in forcing us to take her daughter with us. She did pay the girl's passage, however, which was a great relief, as I had to pay all the others.

Kay finally bought her friend a place on the *Winnipeg*, a boat which sailed from Marseilles. When he was out of danger, that is, out of France, she began to concentrate on our departure, which until then was more or less of secondary importance to her. She was living in Cassis at this time with her friend and some of her babies, who were ill, and came down to Marseilles to see the children, whom he adored.

Our papers were not exactly what one might call in order. I had forged a false date on my traveling permit in order to prolong it, and Laurence didn't have one at all. Max's visa to America had expired and we spent days getting it renewed. All the foreigners had to queue up in the streets outside the American Consulate, but Americans showing their passports were admitted at once. I used to accompany Max and wave my passport at the officials, so he never had to wait in the street. He had not only been in three concentration camps, but he was Hitler's avowed enemy and he was therefore to travel on an emergency visa. In order to leave the station at Marseilles, you had to show your traveling permit to the police, but we knew an exit through the *buffet de la gare* where there were no police. When Laurence arrived we took him out that way. Kay came into Marseilles to meet him, and though we frankly detested each other she tried to be friendly, as I was taking her and her whole family to America.

I had dinner with Max and Kay, Laurence and Marcel, and René who turned up in Marseilles again, this time with a whore from Grenoble. During dinner Kay, who was always dramatic, told me that the boat on which I had shipped all my paintings to America had been sunk. She loved to imagine things like this. Then she and Laurence got into a terrible row, because she refused to go to Mégève to pack before she had dispatched her friend to America. Laurence began throwing things around the café. Max was rather surprised, but Marcel and I were used to this. René quieted him down and then Kay wept; I offered Kay and Laurence my room for the night although they were no longer living together, and went to the château with Max.

Max had many friends from concentration camps. He was perpetually meeting these people. They seemed more like ghosts than anything else, but to him they must have been real and brought back many memories. To me they represented a new, strange society. He always mentioned the name of the camp where he had met them, as casually as if he were referring to St. Moritz or Deauville or Kitzbühl or some other equally well-known resort.

At this time all Jews were being combed out of the hotels in Marseilles and were being sent to live in special places. Max told me not to admit that I was Jewish if the police came to question me, but that I should insist I was an American. It was a good thing he had warned me, because early one morning after he had left and the breakfast cups were still on the table, one of the police arrived in plain clothes. I was absolutely terrified, but I insisted that I was an American and said I was leaving soon for America. He examined my papers and saw that I had changed the date on my traveling permit. I swore the officials of Grenoble had done this. Then he complained because I had not registered in Marseilles. I was frightened not only for myself, but for Max and Laurence. The former had no right to sleep in Marseilles and the latter was traveling without a permit. I also had a large sum of money on me from the black market, for which I wouldn't be able to account if I were searched. When the detective asked me to whom Laurence's valise and beret belonged I said they were my husband's, who was in Cassis. That made him all the more certain I was Jewish, as that was the spot where the Jews were segregated. He asked me if my name were not Jewish and I said my grandfather was a Swiss, from St. Gallen. He had never heard of it. Then he began looking around the room and under the bed to see if I were concealing any Jews. Finally he asked me what was in the cupboard. I told him to look and that he would find no Jews in there. In the end he said, "Come with me to the police. Your papers are not in order." I refused to get dressed in front of him, and I did not want to let him take my papers away with him, so I told him to wait outside the door. He took my papers and went outside. I followed him as soon as I could. I was worried that I might disappear and that Laurence and Max would not be able to find me. I wanted to leave a note for them and hide all my money, but I did not know how to do either. When I came out of my room the detective was not in the hall. He was with his chief in the lobby. When his chief saw me he apologized and told his underling to leave me alone. At this time Americans were popular in France, as we had just sent the French a big shipload of food. I was then politely asked to go and register with the police in Marseilles, where I actually intended to go that day in any case, and the chief told me how to get there. He seemed happy to be able to direct me. Later on when I complained to the hotel manageress about this visit, she said. "Oh, that is nothing, madam. They were just rounding up the Jews."

Leonor Fini was a great pet of Max's. She came to see us in Marseilles and arrived just after I had got rid of the police. I always accused Max of having two Sophies instead of one, like Arp. He had Leonora Carrington and Leonor Fini, and was perpetually trying to further their careers. Fini was a very handsome girl with a free manner. She came from Monte Carlo, where she was refuged and was painting portraits in order to live. She wanted to see Max's new paintings and brought me a little one of hers which I had previously bought after having seen a photograph of it. Laurence, Marcel and I did not like her spoiled vedette manner. Max adored her and wanted me to. He always seemed to require my approval of everything. He introduced me to Fini as a patron of the arts, not as his mistress. I am certain that he wanted to hide this fact. The painting Fini brought with her was a charming little affair that looked like a picture postcard. Later, in New York, Breton very much objected to its being in my collection, but because of Max he couldn't do anything about it. Max thought it was wonderful because Fini painted it, but then he liked the work of any beautiful young girl who admired him. With male painters he was not so indulgent.

Soon after this, Max got all his papers in order and wanted to leave for Spain. He needed fifty dollars in bills in order to travel through Spain and arrive in Lisbon with some money. It was forbidden to export any francs. In order to obtain this money he should have applied to the Banque de France for a permit, but he did not have time. The only other way was the black market which was then not available. Fry had told me that the painter Chagall had the large sum of eight thousand dollars he wanted to transfer to America before he sailed. He made Fry ask me if I would not take this money from him and give it to the committee for their relief work and reimburse Chagall in New York. Naturally I could not afford to do this, but I did take one thousand dollars, which I gave Fry for his fine work. Knowing how much Chagall had, Max and I went to him and asked him to lend us fifty dollars. When we asked Chagall for the money, Chagall hemmed and hawed and said he knew nothing about money, but added that his daughter arranged all his affairs for him. He said we could come back and talk to her in the afternoon, but when we came back she was not there. By this time we were quite desperate. We happened to meet Fry in the street and told him our troubles. He immediately took sixty dollars out of his pocket and handed it to Max.

The next day Max left with all his canvases rolled up in a suitcase. I had to remain in Marseilles in order to arrange to withdraw from the Banque de France the five hundred and fifty dollars each that we were entitled to for our Clipper passages. Application had to be made to the Banque de France and the money registered on our various passports. All this took about three weeks, much longer than I had expected. I had bad bronchitis and retired to bed reading Rousseau's *Confessions.*

One day, when I was walking to a restaurant, I met my old friend Jacques Schiffrin. He was surprised to see me, and happy too, if anything could have made him so at this stage of his collapse. I have never seen anyone so demoralized and frightened of the Nazis. Of course, he was right to realize what his fate would be if he remained in Europe: concentration camps, torture and death. But he hardly had the strength left to get out of France. I think all his papers had expired one by one while he was waiting for a boat. I did everything I could for him, but it was difficult to get him passage. Finally at the last minute, Fry managed to find room for him on a boat and he got off, only to be seized en route and taken to Lisbon, where at least he was safe; eventually he reached New York.

Nellie came down to Marseilles to stay with me until I left. We were reconciled, and I tried to do everything I could to get papers for her to come to New York. Unfortunately it all had to be done from the other side, and I left her behind, with only faint hope of her following me. The Banque de France business took so long that I grew impatient, as I wanted to join Max. I had had one letter from him from the frontier and also a note asking me to save the tenth place on the Clipper for him. All the time I was trying to get Brauner to America, but his case soon became hopeless. At the last minute I had to wait for Jacqueline, who was to go with me. Laurence and all the children got off before I did, to my great joy, as I did not want to travel with so many babies and suitcases.

Jacqueline and I had a lovely trip by ourselves. It was strange getting out of France, and at the frontier I was searched from head to foot, naked. It was wonderful to be free of the Gestapo and to enjoy life again. We had marvelous meals in Spain. The

markets overflowed with food. It seemed almost wicked after
France, where I had lost about ten pounds from under-nourish-
ment. I am sure there was terrible poverty in Spain: the people
looked miserable, as though they were still close to all they had
been through.

When I arrived at the station in Lisbon I was met by Laurence,
Pegeen, Sindbad and Max. Max looked strange and, taking me by
the arm, he said, "I have something awful to tell you." He walked
me down the platform and surprised me by saying, "I have found
Leonora. She is in Lisbon." I felt a dagger go through my heart,
but I pulled myself together and said, "I am very happy for you."
By this time I knew how much he loved her. Max was overcome
by my reply. My children were very much upset by this, and my
son thought I was getting a dirty deal.

We all went to the hotel and tried to be natural, and had a drink
out of a bottle I had brought. Max took me for a walk all over
Lisbon and told me the whole story of how he had managed to
discover Leonora's whereabouts. I felt as though I had been
stunned and wandered around in an agonized daze. Finally he
took me to meet Leonora at the home of an English girl. There
was a lot of talk about a Mexican, whom Leonora was about to
marry in order to get a passport to go to America. She said he was
very sensitive, and she did not want him to know that we knew
about it. They asked me to join them for dinner, but I refused.
Before she left she kissed Max goodbye and pinned a carnation on
him.

I went back to the hotel and sat through a painful meal,
consisting of some ten courses, with Laurence, Kay and the
children. The next day we all moved to different hotels. Jacqueline, Sindbad and I went to the Frankfort-Rocio Hotel, and
Laurence, Kay and all their children moved into a *pension* where
Max was living. Pegeen soon left them and joined us. We
remained here for two weeks.

I was so unhappy I wanted to go back to England and get a war
job, and I began trying for a British visa. This, of course, was
practically impossible, so I got the idea of marrying an Englishman
whom we had met on the train and with whom we had become
very friendly. In this way I could have re-entered England.
Fortunately, my Englishman disappeared, but anyhow Laurence

told me I had no right to abandon my children and that it was my duty to take them to America. I therefore gave up this mad project.

I saw very little of Max at this time and tried to put him out of my mind, but I soon had a definite feeling that my life with him was not yet over. He seemed to spend all his days with Leonora and at night was alone and used to wander around Lisbon with Laurence. This I found painful, as they rarely took me with them. I couldn't make head or tail out of all the complications with the Mexican. I did not realize Leonora was living with him. (Max carefully hid this fact from me.) One night we all had a crazy party together, Leonora, Max, Laurence, Kay and the Mexican. He turned out to be very nice but possessive about Leonora and took her home and locked her up in their apartment. This made me realize that she was living with him. It was a mad evening, full of terrible scenes. Kay left early and the rest of us went and danced in a night club where Sindbad hoped to lose his virginity. He was ashamed to arrive in America with it. We all tried to dissuade him from losing it in a country that was so rampant with venereal disease as Portugal.

After this party I told Max it was a *charmante soirée*, and from then on we called such wild, fighting parties *charmantes soirées.* There was a wonderful café called the Leão d'Ouro where we all went to eat seafood. Sometimes we met Max and Leonora there. She was not very friendly toward me, so I was rather astonished one day when she brought Max to my room and seemed in some strange way to be giving him to me.

Soon after this, Leonora went to a hospital to have an operation on her breast. Max spent the whole day with her and only left her in the evening, when the Mexican, who was by then her husband, came to see her. I went to visit her and realized more than ever how much Max loved her. They spent the whole day reading and doing drawings together and seemed to be in perfect harmony. He was completely happy when he was with her, and miserable the rest of the time. She had become great friends with Kay, who was in the same nursing-home for sinus. Leonora could not make up her mind whether to go back to Max or remain with her husband. She never knew what she wanted in life, and seemed to be perpetually waiting for someone to hypnotize her in order to make her decide. She was a pure medium and could be easily influenced. In the end it was Kay who persuaded her to remain with the Mexican. As he had originally been a friend of Max, Max felt bitter about this and thought it was a dirty trick. He despised the Mexican and always made fun of him, calling him an *homme inférieur*. The three of them were often together and must have had an unpleasant time. I don't think Leonora really wanted either of them. There was a moment when she preferred a certain toreador she had met to both of them. She felt that her life with Max was over because she could no longer be his slave, and that was the only way she could live with him. Leonora was beautiful; I realized it more than ever in the hospital when I saw her in bed. Her skin was like alabaster and her hair was rich in its black waviness; it swept all over her shoulders. She had enormous, mad, dark eyes with thick black brows and a tip-tilted nose. Her figure was lovely but she always dressed very badly, on purpose. It was connected with her madness. She had just come out of an asylum, where she had been confined for months, long after she was well. She had written about all her adventures and they were really terrifying. God knows how she ever got out of the place, but after she did she met the Mexican in Lisbon, and he looked after her. He was like a father to her. Max was always like a baby and couldn't be anyone's father. I think she felt she needed a father more than anything else, so as to give her some stability and prevent her from going mad again.

When Leonora left the hospital Max begged her not to go back to live with the Mexican, but she said she must remain with him until she left for America. Max had reserved another place for her on the Clipper and when she told Max this, he was so upset that he decided to leave Lisbon and go out to Monte Estoril with Laurence where he had taken rooms for himself and the children. Of course I went along too. As we were waiting for the Clipper, we had no idea how much longer we would have to stay in Portugal. The seaside was a much better place for the children than Lisbon.

On the first night at Monte Estoril my life with Max began all over again. I was looking for Laurence to say good night to him when I met Max in the hall. I asked him the number of Laurence's room. He told me the number was twenty-six, which was actually his own. Of course I never said good night to Laurence.

This only started a new round of trouble. Max was constantly waiting for Leonora to phone him. She often came and spent the day with him and I felt so let down that I wouldn't speak to him for days. But as we were at Monte Estoril for five weeks there were plenty of variations.

One night when I went to Lisbon with Laurence for dinner I met Leonora at the Leão d'Ouro. We had a terrible scene and I told her either to go back to Max, as he wanted nothing more than that, or to leave him in peace with me. She said that she saw him only out of pity and had no idea he was with me, and that she certainly would leave him alone. In the train on the way back I begged Laurence to save me from Max, but he said Kay had told him not to interfere, that I would only hold it against him afterward if he did. I was so upset that I rushed into another compartment of the train and got off at the next station and went back to Lisbon where I took a room at the Frankfort-Rocio. The next day I phoned Laurence to tell him where I was. He was greatly relieved.

Laurence had dragged Max out of bed when he discovered I was not on the train, and made him come down to the station and wait with him for the last train. He said to Max, "This is your business. You wait for the train." When I told Max about my scene with Leonora he was so upset that I wrote her a letter asking her please not to end her visits. But she never came again. I think her husband preferred it that way.

All the time we were in Portugal Laurence behaved like an angel . to Kay. When she was sick in the hospital she was perpetually making him send telegrams to her friend. These cost hundreds of *escudos,* and not only did he send them, but paid for them even when all our funds were getting low. Kay was worried that her friend would not get into the States. He had several adventures en route, his boat being captured and, in the end, would not have been admitted to the United States without a five hundred dollar bail. Kay asked Laurence if I would lend the money, and when I said I couldn't, she made him cable his mother for it. Not knowing anything about their separation, Mrs. Vail lent them a part of the money. I was so enraged to see Laurence behave so angelically to Kay, when she had made him act so fiendishly to me in our divorce, that I quarreled with him. Max, who hated the Mexican with a ferocious hatred, disapproved of

Laurence's superhuman behavior, and lectured him on the sweetness of revenge.

Our life in the hotel was rather strange. The children were looked after by Laurence, by Pegeen and by Kay's oldest daughter, as Kay remained in Lisbon and came for the day only on Sundays. We had a long table in the middle of the hotel dining-room. I sat at the head between Laurence and Max. On either side of them were long rows of children consisting of Sindbad aged eighteen, Pegeen aged sixteen, Jacqueline aged sixteen, Bobby (otherwise known as Sharon) aged fourteen, Apple aged eleven, Kathe aged seven and Clover aged two. No one knew whose wife I was or what connection Kay and Leonora had with us. We were always being asked the most embarrassing questions. There was a porter in the hotel whom Laurence named Edward the Seventh, because of his resemblance to the King. His tact was so great that on one occasion, when I phoned from Lisbon to say what train I was arriving by, he guessed my dilemma and, not knowing to whom I wanted the message delivered, went to the dining room and facing both Laurence and Max, said impersonally, "Madam arrives on the nine o'clock train."

The children were also leading a terrific life of their own. They too had many problems. Jacqueline was in love with Sindbad and Sindbad was in love with Miss Kuhn. He was also very worried about his virginity. One evening when Laurence was in Lisbon, Max and the children and I got into a terrific argument about who was the greatest genius in the world, living or dead. Sindbad claimed it was Napoleon, and Max and I claimed Max was a much greater person than Napoleon. No one could prove his case, and I am sure the children thought I had gone mad from being so much in love.

Portugal's chief source of income undoubtedly comes from its fishing industry. Next to Monte Estoril was a little fishing village called Cascais, which was a quarter of an hour's walk from our hotel. For a change we sometimes went there to swim, as we spent most of the day on our own beach. But it was after dinner that we liked best to stroll there. The fishing boats came in at night, and we went down to the beach to watch them unload. Millions of silver creatures were carried in baskets on the heads of the peasant women to the market a few hundred yards away, and at midnight the fish were all sold. One could buy marvelous

lobsters for almost nothing. Apart from these women and a few
whores, no other women appeared in Cascais. When the men
danced in the streets or did running-jumps over bonfires, it was
without female companions. The people had a great dignity but
looked sad. Cascais appeared to be more like an African village
than a European one. There was something rather mysterious
about it and you never knew what was going on inside the houses.
They seemed to be hermetically sealed, their walls closing up the
lives of all the women, who were not allowed on the streets.

One night, when Max and I were wandering around, we saw
two beautiful girls in a window combing their hair. They
beckoned us to come into the house. We did so with much
difficulty, forcing our way through closed doors and a courtyard;
and when we finally reached the first floor, our beautiful girls had
entirely disappeared and in their place was a Trappist monk lying
on a bed praying.

There were many little wine shops which offered indifferent
Portuguese wine for a few *milreis*. You could sit on wooden
benches and talk or make signs to the fishermen. They were
friendly and were always asking us to go fishing with them. They
never went far out to sea. In fact, they usually clustered together
in the port within swimming distance. One day I swam out to
them and when I got close they wanted me to come on board their
boats, but I was frightened and swam back.

One evening at Cascais I went swimming naked. It was pretty
dark, but Max was terrified. The Portuguese are Catholic and we
were always being taken up by the police for wearing what they
considered indecent bathing-suits. As they could not speak
French or English they used to measure the outstanding parts of
our bodies, make scenes, and then proceed to fine us. We
protested violently and went back to the shops which had sold us
the suits. They exchanged them for others, but the police were
never satisfied. Men were not allowed to wear trunks alone and
women were supposed to wear skirts. It was a great pity because
Max had such a beautiful body. The evening I swam naked Max
was also terrified that I would drown. He kept wailing from the
beach, "What will become of me if you drown?" I think he was
afraid he would never get to America without me, because when
he arrived in Lisbon he could not get the passage which
presumably the Museum of Modern Art had reserved for him and

had even paid a deposit on. After this wonderful midnight bath I dried myself with my chemise and we made love on the rocks. We soon discovered our error, as it turned out to be the town's chief latrine. Fortunately we were lying on a raincoat which we had borrowed and we had to scrub it for hours before returning it. On the way home we stopped in the bar of the chi-chi hotel next door, and I hung my chemise on the bar railing to dry. Max loved my unconventionalities.

One night I sprained my ankle when we were walking home. Again I fell into some *merde*. It seemed to be my fate. For days I could not walk, and Max carried me around on his back. It gave him an occupation and took his mind off his troubles. He seemed to enjoy looking after me. One night when we were sitting in a café in Cascais the fireman from the fire-station opposite came to get us and insisted on showing us all his wonderful fire engines. He saw that I could not walk and offered, in spite of Max's presence, to take me home in one of the vehicles. Naturally I declined.

There was a riding stable very near our hotel and Laurence made the children ride every day. Max had bought a lot of riding tickets and rode with Leonora in the country for hours. Her husband joined them on occasions. But when she no longer came to see Max he took me instead. The country was wonderful in its tropical luxuriousness. The further inland we went the richer it became.

One night, when we were all out for a stroll, Laurence picked up a strange-looking girl in a salmon satin dress. She had a dark face and a little black mustache. We could not talk to her, but we took her along with us to our café in Estoril and gave her some ice cream. After that she became so devoted to us that we were never rid of her. We had great difficulty in finding out what she did. She said that she sewed, but when we asked her to to make some dresses for the children she took us to a friend in Cascais who was a real dressmaker. Laurence's girl, who wrote her name on the sand as Jesus Concepção, became devoted to me. She insisted on drying me when I came out of the sea and when I sprained my ankle carried me on her back, to Max's great annoyance. She had a sister, and between them they owned two dresses and one bathing-suit. This caused great complications when they came to the beach together. We took Concepção everywhere with us. But she was not welcome in the English Bar or in our hotel, where Edward the Seventh frowned on her, and practically refused her admittance. By degrees we gathered what her real occupation must have been. But to us she was just a friend, and Laurence swore he never gave her a penny, even when he was alone with her on the beach at night. She taught us to speak Portuguese. Every morning we found her waiting for us on the beach. The same in the afternoon when we came out after our siesta. She was our only native friend.

We often went to Cintra, a wonderful palace built high up on a hill and surrounded by incredible boulders, which looked as if they had been brought there on purpose. The gardens had tropical flowers and trees of every description. The castle itself was more like a dream than a reality. It had a Surrealist quality, as it was all covered with fantastic sculptures. Apart from this it had terraces and ramparts like Elsinore. Hamlet's ghost might well have walked there and felt quite at home. The interior was not so exciting: there were a great many Victorian bedrooms and an enormous reception room with many sofas and chairs arranged in little groups. When Max saw this he said it would be an ideal place for a *charmante soirée*. The Portuguese royal family had lived here fifty years ago. I think the sculptured walls reminded Max of the work he had done in his home at St. Martin d'Ardèche and made him very miserable. But it also must have stimulated him, for I am sure they had an influence on his future painting.

Max had a very strange gift of foreseeing the future, or rather of "forepainting" it. He always painted countries before he got to them. He painted the Far East long before he ever saw it, and he did the same thing with America. Everyone thought he painted the Petrified Forest while in the west, but he painted it while he was in the concentration camps of France.

All the time we were in Portugal Max was very miserable about Leonora, and Laurence was very miserable about Kay. We used to sit for hours in the little English café that overlooked the sea wondering if we would ever leave. The extreme unhappiness of these two men saddened me and I was pretty wretched myself. It all seemed so silly that we could not help each other out of our miseries.

One day, in broad daylight, the spirit of John Holms appeared to me and burning two holes in my neck warned me to give up Max, saying that I would never be happy with him. This was like a vision or stigmata. If only I had accepted his warning! But it is my fate to go through with the impossible. Whatever form I find it in, it fascinates me, while I flee from all the easy things in life.

Max could not get a visa for Trinidad, and the Pan-American Airways could not sell him a ticket until he obtained one. I sent many cables to England and Herbert Read saw to it that he got the visa at once.

Finally on the thirteenth of July, 1941, the Pan-American Airways sent us all off together on the American Clipper. We were eleven people: one husband, two ex-wives, one future husband and seven children.

The Clipper trip was very dull except for one hour spent in the Azores, where I bought a gigantic hat, in which the reporters insisted on photographing me upon my arrival in New York. The worst part of the whole trip was half a broiling day spent in the Bermudas. Here our luggage was gone through and all our books and letters read by the censors. We were examined separately by the British Intelligence about conditions in France. We all told them completely different things, which must have left them confused. The children were air-sick and kept vomiting into paper bags and losing the braces which they were wearing for the purpose of straightening their teeth. Max had a terrible fight with Pegeen while our beds were being made, because he thought he was being cheated out of one. To settle the matter I took Pegeen in with me, and she gave him hers. Early in the morning there was a magnificent sky that looked like a Tanguy painting. For the rest of the trip we saw nothing but sea. At one moment we passed over the American boat that was carrying Leonora and her husband to New York. During the voyage we sat in comfortable chairs and walked in and out of the Clipper's three rooms and drank whiskey.

Before we landed, Max asked me to leave the family and take a room with him. Laurence's mother had reserved a large suite at the Great Northern Hotel, and we were all invited there as her guests. As soon as we arrived she reimbursed me for the Clipper passages of Laurence, Kay and their children.

The first sight we had of America was Jones Beach. It looked very beautiful from that height. There were about forty people on the Clipper when it started out, but thirty more came on at the

Bermudas. We seemed to be the only ones the press seized upon. We were all photographed over and over and asked a million stupid questions. Lots of our friends met us, including Jimmy, Max's son, who had been in America for four years, and of course Putzel. He told me that my collection had arrived safely. Jimmy had enormous blue eyes like Max and was so delicately made that he looked like a miniature. Just as Max was about to greet Jimmy he was seized by the officials, and not allowed to talk to him. This made a marvelous photograph for the Press and appeared in the papers. It seems the Pan-American Airways could not accept the responsibility of admitting a German into the United States without a hearing. I offered bail, but to no avail. Poor Max was whisked away. I gathered from the officials that the last boat had left for Ellis Island, so Max would have to spend the night in a hotel as a guest of the Pan-American Airways, guarded by a detective. He was not supposed to talk to anyone, but they said they would let me know where he was being taken, and the rest was up to me.

I followed Max to the Belmont-Plaza and took a room there. Then I began phoning him every half-hour. About the third time he told me the detective gave him permission to meet me in the hotel bar, otherwise known as the Glass Hat. I went there with Putzel and we met Max and had a drink. Then the detective, who called me Max's sister, suggested we all have dinner in Max's room. We said we preferred to go out, and he gave his consent. He followed us through the streets at a respectful distance and refused to join us at dinner, but remained alone at the bar of the little restaurant.

It was very strange to arrive in New York on the fourteenth of July after an absence of fourteen years and have to be followed by a detective. The first person we saw in the restaurant was Katherine Yarrow, a girlfriend of Leonora's who had been instrumental in helping her to escape from France. In fact, she had taken her to Portugal. Max was so upset by this that he refused to shake hands with this girl, and we almost had a dreadful scene. After dinner the detective said he wanted to take us to Chinatown, but we preferred Pierre's bar. He told us we were wasting our money and tried to prevent us from going there. Suddenly he chucked me under the chin and said, "Peggy is a marvelous girl." When we went back to the Belmont-Plaza he asked Max if he didn't want his sister to sleep with him, saying it was perfectly safe, as he would be sitting outside the door all night with a gun in his pocket, guarding not only Max but a G-man in a room opposite. I declined his offer, as I was scared, and the next morning he phoned me early to say it was time to go to Ellis Island. He apologized for not having known who I was the night before, but I never understood what he meant by this. He so much admired a five-cent straw hat and walking-stick that Max had bought in the Azores that he accepted them as a parting gift. At the ferry he handed us over to an official of the Pan-American Airways.

We were accompanied by Julien Levy, Max's dealer in America, who was prepared to testify at the hearing if necessary. The minute we landed Max was whisked away and imprisoned. I spent the next three days from nine until five on the Island waiting to be called as a witness in Max's hearing. I was almost out of my head, fearing he would be sent back to Europe. I could not speak to him on the phone, because I was at Ellis Island, but he was free to phone me if he wanted to. I went to all the relief societies working there and sent him reassuring little notes. Julien tried to get his uncle, a borough president of New York City, to help, but there really was nothing to do except to wait patiently. Unfortunately a Spanish boat had docked half an hour before the Clipper and there were fifty people on that boat, who had to pass before Max. Luckily Julien came out the first two days and helped me while away the dreary hours. I had not seen him for years and he had very much changed during that time. He was quite fascinating and wonderful company. He had greatly improved since the days when, as a young man in Paris, he had married Mina Loy's oldest daughter. From him I found out all about America. On the third day his business prevented him from coming, so I was forced to be alone. Julien wanted to know if he should find a girl for Max. This was almost prophetic as things turned out, but at the time I said it was too late. He did not seem to know I was in love with Max, or maybe he was trying to find out what our relationship was.

Luckily Jimmy turned up on the island on the third day. He had been sent by the Museum of Modern Art with letters of recommendation. He looked so sweet with his wonderful, big blue eyes. I knew Max was saved when Jimmy was called as a witness.

Suddenly a guard said, "Your case has been heard. Your friends are waiting for you outside." I nearly fainted. Max was free.

Jimmy had a job with the Museum of Modern Art at fifteen dollars a week. I don't know how he managed to live on it. His health had suffered greatly from it, and he used to have attacks of nervous cramps. I think they came from his being underfed for so long, but they were also brought on by any emotional strain. Our arrival in America and all the excitement that it entailed gave Jimmy cause for quite a few of these attacks. The minute Max got out of Ellis Island Jimmy asked him if he could leave the Museum. His job was not only very badly paid but it was also of a menial order; so of course Max said, "Yes." He promised to give Jimmy double what he had received at the Museum.

Jimmy longed to be friends with Max but Max felt uncomfortable in his presence and did not know how to talk to him. I immediately took Jimmy to my heart and became a sort of stepmother to him. In a way I always felt like Max's mother too. It seemed to me he was a baby deposited on my doorstep and that I had to look after him. That was why I was so frantic every time he was in trouble. I always felt that when I would no longer be useful to Max he would have no further use for me. This spurred me on to doing the most difficult things for him. I not only tried to obtain everything he needed, but also everything he wanted. It was the first time in my life that I had felt maternal toward a man. When I told Max that he was a baby deposited on my doorstep, he said, "You are a lost girl." I knew he was right and was surprised that he realized it.

Max, like all other babies, always wanted to be the center of attention. He tried to bring all conversations around to himself, no matter what they were about. He loved beautiful clothes and was jealous when I bought new dresses, because he would have loved to wear them himself instead of drab, male garments. In his paintings he portrayed himself and other men in marvelous Renaissance costumes. Once in Marseilles, when I bought myself a little sheepskin coat, Max was with me and he was so envious that I ordered him one too. No man had ever bought anything in this shop before, and the shopkeeper was rather surprised. However, the coat was made to order for Max, and when he wore it he looked like a Slavic prince.

We decided not to go back to the Belmont-Plaze and chose the

Shelton instead. Jimmy said we should take separate rooms. They were adjoining but not connecting. Then a very strange life began, and I suddenly felt married again. I had lived alone for four years.

Now I acquired a stepson. I felt much more at home with Jimmy than with Max. He was awfully happy to have a step-mother and we got on wonderfully well. Everything I didn't do with Max I did with Jimmy. I took him to shops, while I replenished my wardrobe (I had given away all my clothes in France). But if I took Jimmy to buy clothes with me, Max couldn't go shopping without me. He made me choose everything he ordered. I encouraged him to buy a trousseau. He looked so beautiful in American clothes, for he had a perfect figure and was extremely elegant by nature. I gave him the diamond and platinum lorgnon with the watch that had belonged to my mother, and he used it instead of glasses. It suited him perfectly, making him look English and aristocratic.

While Max was on Ellis Island I went to see Breton. He was installed in an apartment Kay Sage had rented for him for six months in the Village. It was very comfortable, but looked unlike his usual surroundings. He seemed worried about his future, yet in spite of this he was determined not to learn a word of English. He wanted to hear all about Max and our life in Lisbon and what had occurred between Leonora and Max. The report had gone around New York that Max would not leave Leonora in Lisbon, and that that was why we had remained there so long. Breton did not gather that I was in love with Max. We talked a lot about Leonora and Max, and Breton confirmed my opinion that she was the only woman Max had ever loved.

This was the first opportunity I had to thank Breton for his poem *Fata Morgana,* which he had sent me before leaving France. The Vichy government refused to allow its publication, but in America he soon found a publisher and it was translated into English. Breton had had many adventures on his way to America and had spent weeks in Cuba waiting for a boat. I think he was depressed and did not know what to do next.

As soon as Max was free he went to see Breton and asked him to dinner. Breton was anxious to get Max back into his group again. After all, Max was his biggest star and Breton had lost him during the Eluard crisis. The Surrealists were always playing at cat and mouse, and it was comparatively easy for Max to be seduced again. As soon as I arrived at the Brevoort Hotel, where I joined them for dinner, Max rushed up to me and kissed me, so that Breton would know what our relationship was. I think he was terribly surprised.

At the request of Kay Sage I soon put Breton's mind at rest and promised to give him two hundred dollars a month for a year. That would give him time to find out what he would do in New York, without worrying.

The first thing we did was to go down to Long Island for a weekend with Louis and Marian Bouché. They came to see me and said that they would be glad to have us visit them some time near Oyster Bay. I asked them to take us at once out of the terrible heat of New York. Bouché, though he was not an Abstract or Surrealist painter, had long been an admirer of Max's work and seemed to know all about it. They were very sweet to us and gave us a lovely weekend. The last time I had seen them was at Yew Tree Cottage in 1938.

When we arrived in New York the Museum of Modern Art was having a Picasso show. Penrose had sent all his paintings to New York for the duration, and some of the ones I knew best were in this exhibition. The Museum owned a lot of Max's paintings and collages, since Alfred Barr had bought fourteen. Most of them were in the cellar, however, as was the custom of the Museum of Modern Art. I remember going down into the depths there and finding Brancusi's sculpture *The Miracle*. It was a miracle to find it there. Upstairs they did show a *Bird in Space* very much like mine but made twenty years earlier. The collection of the Museum was pretty fine. They had wonderful Picassos, Braques, Légers, Dalis, Rousseaus, Arps, Tanguys and Calders, but not one Kandinsky. In the garden they showed sculpture. The atmosphere of the whole place was that of a girl's college. Yet at the same time it looked rather like a millionaire yacht club. I am sure Humphrey Jennings would have adored it.

We went to see my uncle's museum. It really was a joke. There were about a hundred paintings by Bauer in enormous silver frames which overshadowed the twenty Kandinskys. There was one marvelous Léger of 1919, a Juan Gris, a lot of Domelas, a John Ferren, a Calder, a Delaunay and a few other less interesting painters, whose names I can't remember. From the walls boomed forth music by Bach—a rather weird contrast. The museum was a beautiful little building completely wasted in this atrocious manner. Max called it the Bauer House; the Museum of Modern Art he called the Barr House; and Gallatin's collection in the New York University building was the Bore House. It really was boring because, although Mr. Gallatin had some nice abstract paintings, the surroundings were so dull that one had no pleasure in looking at them. Max was annoyed because Mr. Gallatin, no longer considering his painting sufficiently abstract, had removed it. This collection is now in a museum in Philadelphia.

What Max liked best in New York was the Museum of Natural History. He was delighted by the mathematical objects, which he claimed were much better than Pevsner's constructions. Another museum Max adored was the Museum of the American Indian, the Heye Foundation, where Breton took us. It had the best collection of British Columbian, Alaskan, Pre-Columbian, South Sea, Indian and Mayan art.

In contrast to the Bauer House there existed in the Plaza Hotel a really fine collection of modern paintings owned by my uncle, Solomon Guggenheim, but accessible to the public only by special invitation. Aunt Irene lived there with my uncle surrounded by the most beautiful Picassos, Seurats, Braques, Klees, Kandinskys, Gleizeses, Delaunays, Chagalls and a Lissitzky. I took Max there and Aunt Irene was delighted to meet him, but being rather confused, she thought he had replaced Herbert Read in my life. I told my Aunt Irene to burn all the Bauers and move these paintings to the Museum. She said, "Shush! Don't let your uncle hear that. He has invested a fortune in Bauer." Next time I saw her was when she came to my house, and, meeting Laurence whom she hadn't seen for seventeen years, she mistook him for Max. When I put her right she said, "I thought something was wrong because Ernst looks so much older." As a matter of fact they were born the same year, but Max certainly looked ten years older than he was. Max and Laurence were often mistaken for each other. One day when Laurence invited us all to lunch to meet Bob Coates, Bob first met Max and asked him if he were Laurence, whom he had not seen for fourteen years. Max took him along and presented him to his long-lost friend.

One night Jimmy met Leonora in a drugstore in Columbus Circle, and was in a terrific state of excitement about it. He hadn't seen her for years. He had been alternately in love with her and jealous of her because of his abnormal attachment to Max. Max couldn't wait until he saw Leonora. She had brought all his paintings with her. When he got them, he hung them up in Julien Levy's gallery and invited Breton, Putzel, Laurence and a few other people to see them. They were greatly admired. Max saw a lot of Leonora and, just when I told Jimmy I couldn't stand it any longer and I was going to leave Max, we were all invited to California by my sister Hazel.

Max was delighted to be invited anywhere, and I was pleased to see my sister again and to get out of the heat of New York. I also wanted to see Arenberg's famous collection of paintings in Hollywood. Sindbad, to whom I had just given my little Talbot automobile, went up to Rhode Island with Laurence and all his children. Pegeen and Jimmy came with us. Just when we were leaving by airplane, Hazel wired that she was getting a new nose and could we postpone our visit for a few days? It was too late to change our plans, so we went to San Francisco. From then on we called Hazel *le nouveau nez*.

The trip over America was incredibly beautiful. Max and I were thrilled every minute, but Jimmy and Pegeen were very sick. We flew so high poor Pegeen nearly died, and had to be given oxygen. At Reno I took her out, thinking the air would help her but she nearly collapsed in the ladies' room. She therefore missed all the marvelous scenery over Salt Lake, miles and miles of land covered with salt, where the sea had receded, and then stretches of blue and purple water. It was better than any painting, the colors were so delicate and the expanse so vast.

At San Francisco is was very exciting to see the Bay and all the bridges from above. It is a beautiful city and from the air the approach is ten times better. We enjoyed the Chinese restaurants and theatres and the modern art museums. We went to the Courvoisier Gallery and bought two paintings by Charles Howard. It was so nice to come into contact with his work again after all this time and he had made great progress since I had given him a show in London in 1939. It was very pleasant seeing him again. He was working in a shipyard and I think was rather sad.

We went to Dr. Grace McCann Morley's fine San Francisco Museum. I asked if I could see her but her secretary said she was too busy. I was very much offended. However, I was not prevented from meeting her, as Sidney Janis, the art dealer, was in the Museum, where he was showing a large exhibition of his primitives. When he told Dr. Morley that Max was there she took us out to a wonderful fish dinner, in what seemed to be America's Marseilles, and drove us all over the countryside showing us the sights. She was hospitable and charming and full of life. I asked her if I could send her exhibitions when I got my museum going, and she replied she would like it very much. She told me she gave a hundred and twenty exhibitions a year.

Max thought the primitive paintings quite remarkable. There happened to be a reporter in the Museum at the time, who interviewed him, and quoted his enthusiasm for this show. A scandal ensued as *The Art Digest* refused to take Max seriously, and said he was making fun of the American public. I had to write a letter to *The Art Digest* telling them that he really meant it, and admired this painting more than any other produced by Americans.

Before we left San Francisco we got into awful rows with Pegeen about Kay. Max hated Kay because she had induced Leonora to go off with the Mexican, and I too had always found Kay objectionable. Poor Pegeen had lived with Kay for two years because of the war, and was fond of her. She tried hard, but with no success, to justify Kay's behavior to Laurence. The fight became so fierce that Pegeen refused to come with us to Los Angeles. We nearly missed the plane, but at the last minute she gave in, and came along, because she was afraid to remain alone and penniless in San Francisco.

When we arrived in Los Angeles we found Hazel with a beautiful young husband. He seemed such a contrast to Max who looked so old. He was studying to be a pilot, as he wanted to be in the air force (in which he was to lose his life) as soon as America joined the war. They seemed very happy together, in fact it was the only time I ever found Hazel happily married. She painted a lot and one day asked Max if he could teach her to paint a jungle. He was amused and gave her a lesson, but afterward he claimed she had not paid much attention to what he had told her.

Max and I had no idea where to live, or where to establish the museum. We began to look at houses all over California. The place we came nearest to buying was a fifty-room castle at Malibu, built high on a hill. An American woman had conceived the idea of this extraordinary establishment but her funds had given out, and she had been forced to abandon the place There were thousands of tiles, made by Spanish workmen, who were brought to America especially for that purpose. The tiles had never been incorporated in the castle, however, and were stacked on the floor. We thought the whole place in its unfinished state was like a Surrealist dream. In Marseilles I had invited Breton to live in my museum in America and hold his Surrealist court there, and this place seemed to be the ideal spot for all these activities. Of course no one ever would have come out here. The distance made it impracticable. Another disadvantage was that the road to the castle disappeared in the rainy season.

There was one other house that tempted us very much, but it was situated on a steep incline overlooking the sea. The drawback was that the land was gradually slipping away at the cliff end of the garden. One tree was already lost and we did not know how long the house could remain, since it was so perilously near the edge.

Pegeen's one idea at this time was to meet or at least see movie stars. Hazel took her to a cocktail party where she met Charlie Chaplin. On her sixteenth birthday I gave her a dinner party at Ciro's, the restaurant most frequented by the movie people. Unfortunately it was the worst night of the week and there wasn't one star present. Pegeen burst into tears in the car going home. But to compensate for this I sent her to a Red Cross ball given by the Royal Air Force, where she could be sure to have her heart's desire and see all the movie people. She went quite alone, dressed in a long white evening dress and little white fur cape, looking like Cinderella dressed for the ball. She swept in majestically and had a most wonderful evening. Only long afterward did she admit she had not recognized the stars.

Hazel had a secretary, Albert Bush, who was a poet. He conducted a poet's hour on the radio. He wanted Max to give a little talk about France and what was happening there and why he had been forced to leave, and what his impressions of America were. I interviewed Max and translated what he said, and taught him to pronounce and read it in English which he couldn't speak at all. Jimmy and I sat in our newly acquired Buick listening to Max's interview on the radio. He did very well and made only one funny error in pronunciation. That was when he came to the word "hospitable," which he spat out with the accent on "pit." Jimmy had a pronounced father complex and adored Max as much as I did. We were always trying to do everything we could to make Max feel important in America. Jimmy was very good at publicity and Max was happy when he appeared in the public eye. He didn't seem to exist unless people noticed him. However, he was always very dignified and never made a fool of himself.

In Hazel's house we had a bedroom, a sleeping porch and a nursery at our disposal. I was supposed to share the nursery with Pegeen, but I slept with Max in his room, or we slept on the sleeping porch. Sometimes I changed my room three times a night to fool the maids. Over our bed was a family motto in Latin saying, "Never too much." It was Hazel's husband's room.

Max painted on the sleeping porch, and I was particularly thrilled when I woke up there to find opposite me, on his easel, his latest paintings. It was like being present at their birth.

I think my brother-in-law must have found it very trying to have us all descend upon him in this way, especially as Max didn't speak English and he couldn't speak French or German.

At one of Hazel's parties we met George Biddle, who considered himself America's greatest painter. He made a great effort to be nice to Max and talked about Surrealism, which I am sure he must have hated. Not knowing who he was, I naively said to him, "Do you paint too, Mr. Biddle?"

On my birthday Max and I cooked dinner for fourteen people. He made a wonderful fish soup, from fish which he had caught himself early that morning, and I made a *paella*. At this party we met Hazel's friends, the Gonzaleses, both painters, who lived in New Orleans. He was Spanish and she was a charming American girl. Albert Bush drank to my health saying, "Only Peggy knows 'The Importance of Being Ernst.'" In Hollywood we found Man Ray (with a new young wife) and Bob McAlmon and Caresse Crosby. It was nice to see old friends from France again. Bob tried to help me find a college for Pegeen, but all she wanted was to go to dramatic school and become a star in the movies, so I finally decided to leave this demoralizing atmosphere.

One reason I had come west was to visit Arensberg's collection of modern art. It was probably one of the finest in the world. Every room of his funny old Victorian house was crammed with magnificent paintings. Even the corridors and the bathrooms were

like the best rooms of a museum. Apart from owning practically all
the works of Marcel Duchamp, he had many fine Brancusis, a
wonderful Rousseau, a Chirico, Kandinskys, Klees, Mirós, lots of
Picassos, a few Ernsts, Tanguys, Dalis, Gleizeses, Delaunays.
His Cubist collection made me very jealous, but his later things
were not nearly up to mine. In fact where he left off, I began.
Lately he had been collecting mostly Pre-Columbian sculpture.
He was a sad man, who by now had a much greater interest in
proving Bacon wrote Shakespeare than in anything else. In spite
of this, he had a great passion for Duchamp. In his house I met
the painter John Ferren and his wife Inez. Ferren had lived in
Paris for years and wore a red beard. Later I bought two of his
paintings in New York and his wife brought out my catalogue (to
say nothing of typing the manuscript of this book).

After we had been with Hazel for three weeks, we motored to
the Grand Canyon where I was to meet Emily Coleman. She was
now married to a cowboy and living on a ranch. At this time Max
was showing some pictures in San Francisco where Julien Levy
had rented a gallery and I told Max to go there if he wanted to,
and join me later, but I think he was afraid of losing me so he
came along. When we got to the Grand Canyon I left Max with
Jimmy and went to Holbrook with Pegeen to fetch Emily. When I
kissed Max goodbye he said very pathetically, like a baby, "Are
you ever coming back?" For two days he wandered around alone,
as he never could speak to Jimmy, and found a shop with
wonderful Indian masks, totem poles and Kachina dolls. He
wanted to buy them all. He was like a child, and having found
himself suddenly in the position of being rich he wanted to buy
everything he fell in love with. I put him off as much as I could,
but in the end he always got what he wanted.

Emily and Max got along very well. She told me how much I
showed my insecurity with him, and that pained me. I had hoped
to hide it. After a few days we took Emily back to her sordid home
on the ranch. I could not understand how she could live in such
unspeakable squalor. I never saw her husband.

From there we drove on to Sante Fe. We passed Albuquerque
and Gallup, where there were beautiful shows of Indian art. We
were supposed to go to the Indian reservation to see the Hopi
dances. That was one of the reasons Max had come west. But
Jimmy told us we had passed the road miles after we were beyond

it, and we were so furious we never went back. When you have to drive hundreds of miles a day, you do not want to add to the number. Max did all the driving, which made me angry, but I let him and made terrible scenes afterward. We spent several days in Santa Fe and played with the idea of living there, but much as we loved the scenery, we knew life there would be deadly.

While we were motoring through the Texas desert, Pegeen developed a bad sore throat and a high fever. We were forced to remain four days in the most extraordinary place I have ever been in. Wichita Falls was like an oasis, an oasis for cockroaches. They came in from the desert at night, attracted by the lights of the town. When you walked in the streets, you felt them scrunch under your feet four layers deep. They climbed up the walls of the houses and managed to get in, despite the screens. At the movies they got into my low-necked dress and into my hair. When we came home we found Pegeen and a bellboy on all fours searching under the bed for one of these creatures. Pegeen could never endure any bugs, and these were too much for her. In the daytime they all vanished. Apart from this, Wichita Falls was a very dull place. The heat was unbelievable. You just couldn't go out until after sunset and then there was no place to go. If you drove half a mile in any direction you were in the desert. You had to buy your drinks in a drugstore and carry them with you to the hotel restaurant. That was a Texas law. We had stolen from some hotel a book telling us about the state liquor laws. As they varied so much, it was just as well to be prepared beforehand.

I was also much interested in the state marriage laws, because I wanted to marry Max. Every time we came to a new state, I sent Jimmy to find out what were our chances of marrying at once. Pegeen, however, soon put an end to all this by making Max admit that marriage was too bourgeois for him to go through with. She was jealous of my feeling for him and was clever at putting in her oar.

Our next stop was New Orleans, where the heat was terrific, although it was September. When we asked for a mint julep we were told that summer was over and there was no more mint. The same thing happened when we wanted bananas. Hazel's friends, the Gonzaleses, were charming to us and showed us everything, including plantation houses and swamps. They introduced us to all their friends. Dr. Marion Suchon showed us his paintings in his office, where he painted between patients' visits. We had wonderful meals in the French quarter and felt more at home there than anywhere in America.

Max had a long interview with a local paper and was photographed in our bedroom with one of his paintings that the Museum of Modern Art later acquired. The next day the social editor came to interview me and took my picture with Pegeen and Jacqueline, who lived in New Orleans. I hid everything that belonged to Max that was in our room, thinking it more proper. But to my dismay in walked the same photographer who had been there for Max the day before. Max was jealous that we were having publicity and Jacqueline's grandmother, a Southern lady of the old school, had the evening edition of the paper omit our photograph.

After New Orleans we motored back to New York. Of all the states we went through, I liked Tennessee the best. It had the most wonderful scenery and red earth. But we were destined to live in New York.

When we arrived in New York we went to the Great Northern Hotel. The first thing to do was to put Pegeen in school. I chose the Lenox High School, a preparatory to Finch Junior College. She boarded at Finch and came home weekends. Nothing could have been less appropriate than this stuffy school. She managed to survive it for two years, when she was graduated. Snobbish Finch Boarding School was too much for her to endure even during the week, and as soon as we had a house she insisted on living with us.

I started to look for a place for my museum. Laurence, who was living in Connecticut, tried to get us to be his neighbors. There were two houses we almost bought, one of which particularly fascinated Max because thirteen suicides had taken place there. The other house was sold ten minutes before we saw it.

In New York we looked everywhere. Finally we found a dream of a house on Beekman Place overlooking the river. We thought it would be the ideal place for the museum, except that it was too far away from the center of town. But we couldn't resist it. We intended to sleep in the servants' rooms when we were there, and to live in the country. However, we were not allowed to open a museum in this section. We had to take the house for ourselves, to live in instead. It was the most beautiful house in New York. It was a remodeled brownstone mansion called Hale House on the East River and Fifty-first Street. It had a big living room or chapel with an old fireplace that might well have been a baronial hall in Hungary. The chapel was two stories high and the whole front of the room gave on to the river, where we had a terrace. There was a balcony above with five little windows overlooking the chapel. Here five choirboys might well have sung Gregorian chants. On the third floor we had our bedroom in the back of the house, and in the front Max had a beautiful studio with another terrace. Pegeen had the second floor to herself. Out of the servants' rooms we made a guest suite. We had a big kitchen and, since we both cooked a lot, we ate many meals in there. Max was a marvelous cook and made especially fine curries.

It had been the Museum of Modern Art, at the request of Jimmy, which had started the machinery in motion to bring Max to America. When we arrived we expected a warm reception from the Museum, which we did not get. Alfred Barr was in Vermont and sent Max a telegram of welcome. He made a little show in the Museum of Max's and other people's collages, but we did not see him until the fall. Collage was undoubtedly Max's greatest contribution to art.

I had heard a great deal about Barr from Nellie van Doesburg and other people. His books on modern art had been my Bible for years, so I was naturally longing to meet him. We went to see him one day, and I was surprised to find someone who looked like Abraham Lincoln. His conversation was serious and learned. He was shy but very charming, and I liked him at once. Later, when I knew him better, I hated his cagey quality, and never knew what he was driving at; but he was one of the people whom I respected in the world who had done a pioneering job and done it well. When we were in the Great Northern Hotel he came to see Max's paintings. He was crazy about them, but he never could get the Museum to buy what he wanted. He always had to fuss and fuss and bargain, and drove me crazy with his indecision. Just before he arrived a sparrow flew in at the window. Barr was delighted to find Max, the King of Birds, harboring this little creature. Finally Barr gave me a Malevich, of which he had thirteen in the cellar, for an Ernst. Everyone was delighted, and Barr was impressed by my genuine passion for art. I gave Max the money that was not involved in this exchange.

When we moved into our house we gave a huge house-warming party. Leonora came, looking most ravishing, for once marvelously dressed in a sort of impromptu costume with a white mantilla. There was a terrible fight between enormous Nicolas Calas and little Charles Henri Ford, and in the middle of it Jimmy rushed to take down the Kandinskys from the walls before they were splattered with blood. Barr thought that was real devotion on Jimmy's part, to rescue my paintings before Max's. Jimmy was already my secretary. He was efficient and bright and knew everything, and I loved him and we got on marvelously. The house was entirely warmed by the blood of these two intellectuals. Maybe that started us off badly because we never had a moment's peace in that wonderful place. Peace was the one thing that Max needed in order to paint, and love was one thing I needed in order to live. As neither of us gave the other what he most desired, our union was doomed to failure.

When I finally got my paintings out of storage and hung in the house, I asked Alfred Barr to come to see them. I was in a state of great excitement to know what he would think of them. We invited him and his wife to dinner. I had already been to their house for cocktails, when Daisy Barr had embarrassed me terribly by asking what had occurred between Max and Leonora in Lisbon. I began by hating her, but the more I saw of her the better I liked her. She was a very attractive woman and delightfully un-American. Daisy Barr seemed Irish, but she was half Italian. They came for dinner and brought Jim Soby and his wife. At this time Soby was being broken-in to take Alfred Barr's place in the Museum of Modern Art, but I did not then realize all the machinations of that institution and never will. They were much interested in my collection and thought I had some very fine things. Soby bought a painting of Max's, a sort of portrait of Leonora sitting on a rock. It was called *Arizona*. He had painted it in Europe and finished it in California.

After Julien Levy came back from California he took a small gallery on Fifty-seventh Street. He had not been very successful in the west. We were annoyed with him because he had sold one of Max's paintings much too cheaply. Max did not want to exhibit in his gallery in New York as it was too small, so he decided to show with Dudensing's instead. This was my idea; I had talked Max into accepting Dudensing's offer.

When I first lived with Max I had no idea how famous he was, but little by little I realized it. People were always coming up to him and treating him with reverence and respect, like a great master. He took his adulation very well. He was perpetually being photographed for the press. He loved this, and he hated to have me included. Once, however, he had to succumb and we appeared in *Vogue* with our little dog Kachina, a Tibetan Lhasa terrier, who was all overgrown with white hair and looked like Max. Max bought an enormous chair about ten feet high. It was a Victorian theatrical prop. He sat in it as though it were his throne, and no one else ever dared use it, except Pegeen. He was always photographed in this chair.

The paintings Max had done in France between periods in concentration camps, or while he was actually in them, started a completely new phase of his work. The backgrounds of these paintings greatly resembled the desert land of Arizona and the swamps of Louisiana which he was soon to visit. It is unbelievable that he had this foresight. It seems to have been his special gift to forepaint the future. As his painting was completely unconscious and came from some deep hidden source, nothing he ever did surprised me. At one time, when he was alone in France after Leonora had left, he painted her portrait over and over in all the landscapes that he was so soon to discover in America. I was jealous that he never painted me. In fact it was a cause of great unhappiness to me and proof that he did not love me.

One day when I went into his studio I had a great shock. There on his easel was a little painting I had never seen before. In it was portrayed a strange figure with the head of a horse, which was Max's own head, and the body of a man dressed in shining armor. Facing this strange creature, and with her hand between his legs, was a portrait of me. Not of me as Max had ever known me, but of me as my face appeared as a child of eight. I have photographs of myself at this age and the likeness is unquestionable. I burst into tears the minute I recognized it and rushed to tell Max that he had at last painted my portrait. He was rather surprised as he had never seen the photos. Because my hand was placed where it was and because it was between two spears, I named the picture *The Mystic Marriage*. I asked for it as a present, telling Max that now he need never marry me, as this sufficed. I have still to describe the rest of the painting, as this was only one-third of it. In the

center was a figure which Max admitted to be Pegeen's back, and
on the left hand side was a terrifying sort of monster. It portrayed
a woman in a red dress with her stomach exposed. This was
undoubtedly my stomach, but the figure had two heads which
resembled nobody. They were animal heads and one looked like a
skeleton. Sidney Janis claimed I was this monster, which he
considered very strong, but that was later, when Max took this for
a theme and made an enormous canvas of it. In this new painting
my beautiful girl's head disappeared completely and gave way to a
portrait of a strange unknown person accompanied by Pegeen.
The original Pegeen in this painting gave way to a totem pole with
a head made of a substance resembling brains. Much later I
showed these photos to Alfred Barr because I wanted him to
corroborate my theory, and he was much impressed by the
resemblance.

I don't think Emily really liked Max's paintings but she did
appreciate his collages. She gave him long lectures about them
which he did not in the least understand. However, to hide his
ignorance and show his appreciation he always replied, *"Oui, oui,
oui."* I once said to Emily, "There are three reasons why I love
Max: because he is so beautiful, because he is such a good painter
and because he is so famous."

At this time I was still trying to complete my collection and buy
all the pictures that Mr. Read and I had meant to exhibit in
London, in our opening show, as a survey of modern art from 1910
to 1939. There were many paintings that I had not been able to
obtain in France because of the war. These I now bought in
America. Breton and Max helped me a great deal in my choice. I
was finishing the catalogue, and every time I bought another
painting I rushed a new photograph and biography over to Mrs.
Ferren, the publisher. Max did a beautiful cover for the
catalogue. I was rather worried about the book, however, and
decided it was very dull. I asked Breton to save it. He was always
telling me it was *catastrophique*. It probably would have been if it
had not been for him. He spent hours of research and found
statements made by each artist; we included these and photographs of their eyes. Breton's preface was excellent, containing a
whole history of Surrealism. I got Mondrian to do another preface
for me, which Charmian Wiegand put into English, and I
included the one Arp had done for me in Europe. Besides that,

Breton told me to add the manifestos of the different movements in art of the last thirty years, and then we included statements by Picasso, Max, Chirico and others. In the end the book turned out exceedingly well, being an anthology of modern art rather than a catalogue. We called it *Art of This Century*.

As Max sold more and more paintings he bought more and more Indian, Pre-Columbian, Alaskan and New Guinea art. We had practically no furniture and all these things made the house look very beautiful. Max got hold of a little man called Carlebach, or rather Carlebach got hold of Max. He let him have his collection on credit and Max paid him whenever he sold a painting. I was very much annoyed that Max refused to contribute to the household expenses. I think he based his refusal on the grounds that I still supported Laurence. Finally, Max reached the point where he would not even put aside money to pay his income tax. Carlebach used to phone Max almost every day to come around to his shop on Third Avenue to see some new things that he had found for him. He was perpetually scurrying around and finding things with which to tempt Max. There was no end to his ingeniousness and his activities. He even made deals with museums and got them to cede things to Max. Once he found out that I collected earrings and immediately got together a large quantity and began to work on me. But I did not succumb. Of course Max did, and bought me a beautiful pair with Spanish baroque pearls. But I resisted any further efforts on Mr. Carlebach's part, as I considered him sufficiently dangerous with his totem poles and masks. One day Max bought a beautiful, wooden painted animal that looked like a burial object. He said he had bought a little table, but it certainly was more like a cradle. At one time Max had had a passion for wooden horses and the house was full of these. He also bought a British Columbian totem pole twenty feet high. It was a terrifying object and I hated to have it in the house.

After Pearl Harbor the question of marriage came up again. I did not like the idea of living in sin with an enemy alien, and I insisted that we legalize our situation. In order to avoid publicity and the taking of a blood test, we decided to go down to Washington to visit my cousin Harold Loeb, and get the thing done quickly in Maryland. The night before we left we had an awful row, and when Pegeen came home Max was still looking unhappy. Pegeen, who was against my marrying, said, "Mama, how can you force the poor thing to marry you? Look how miserable he is." Max and I both said he looked this way because of our row, but Pegeen would not believe it, and convinced me she was right. I was so upset the next morning that I ran to Putzel and told him all my troubles. He said that I should get married if I wanted. I phoned Max and asked him how he felt. He said he wished to go to Washington, so we drove down there.

In Maryland they refused to marry us. We only had divorce papers in foreign languages which they could not translate. Besides, Max could not prove his first divorce, and they would not accept his second as proof of his first. They told us to go to Virginia. In Virginia you had to be a resident, over eighteen years of age and have a blood test taken. We did not have much difficulty in proving that we were of age; the Loebs gave us the residence. As to the blood test we managed to survive it. Compared with being a blood donor, it was nothing. When we got our marriage license we were asked when we wanted to marry. We said, "At once." They telephoned a judge who lived around the corner and he said we could come immediately. However, he did not admit us for some time but kept us waiting on his doorstep. We were accompanied by Harold's wife, who was doing everything to help us. When the judge finally admitted us, we found he had a girl with him. He said, "This poor little thing's husband, a doctor in the Navy, has just gone to sea and I am consoling her." We understood why he had kept us waiting so long. Max could not speak English and when he was asked to *wed* me, he understood *wet*, which he repeated. The ceremony was very simple and I did not have to promise to obey. When it was over we did not know how much to give the judge. Vera Loeb thought five dollars, but Max only had ten which he offered. The judge and his girl friend were so delighted that she tickled the palm of Max's hand. I think that partially consoled him for being no longer free. Afterward we went back to Washington and Max invited my cousins to a wonderful dinner to celebrate.

The marriage gave me a feeling of safety, but did not stop our rows, as I had hoped. They were awful and often lasted forty-eight hours, during which time we would not speak to each other. The fights were about nothing of importance. We fought if Max took my scissors without asking my permission. This annoyed me because they were the scissors John Holms had used to cut his beard. We fought if Max would not let me drive the car because he preferred to drive himself. We fought when he got bored because I had the flu and took too long to convalesce. We fought about the layout of my catalogue, after we had both worked peacefully on it together for hours. We fought most of all about his buying too many totem poles. It was all ridiculous and childish. The quarrels upset him terribly. He could not work and wandered around New York for days. I was also very unhappy and was always the first one to make up. He was too proud to do so himself. The worst of it all was that we fought in public. We fought anywhere we happened to be.

During the winter we made great friends with Amédée Ozenfant, a most fascinating man. For three years he had been my neighbor in the Avenue Reille, where I lived in Paris with John Holms, During all that period I had not known him. Now he lived on Twentieth Street, and we often went there to delicious dinners cooked by Marthe, his wife. I wanted to buy one of Ozenfant's Purist paintings, as I considered it of historic interest. All my advisers were against it, but I bought it all the same. I am very glad, because the Museum of Modern Art neglected him badly and bought a Jeanneret instead. There was no reason to consider Jeanneret superior to Ozenfant. They worked together in 1920 and it was unfair not to realize their equal value.

I was very busy all winter working on my catalogue, and postponed renting a place for the museum until this was finished. People came to the house to see the paintings and ended up on the top floor in Max's studio. Putzel brought customers and Max sold a lot of paintings and bought more and more totem poles and Kachina dolls and masks. It took me all winter to get my catalogue ready, as Breton took so long to do his article, which turned out to be about sixteen pages, and then Laurence had to translate it. By then the spring had come and the art season was over.

One of the things from which I suffered most was the fact that Max was never intimate with me. He considered me a sort of lady whom he was slightly afraid of, and never addressed me as *tu;* because of this I never felt he really loved me. Once, when I asked him to write something in the books he had given me, he merely wrote, "For Peggy Guggenheim from Max Ernst." This was upsetting, as I remembered what he had written for Leonora. He always made me feel that he would have liked me much better if I had been young and vulgar. He admitted that he liked stupid, vulgar girls.

Leonora used to phone Max to come and take her to lunch. Sometimes he would spend the whole day with her and they would wander around New York, something he never did with me. It made me wildly jealous and I suffered agonies. In the morning he always worked after we had breakfast, so he never bothered to wear street clothes. If I found he was dressed to go out my heart sank, because I knew he was going to dedicate the day to Leonora. On these occasions I used to lunch with other people. Sometimes with Alfred Barr, but more often with Jimmy Stern, whom I invited to our house. He was a fascinating Irishman, a friend of Beckett and Laurence. I had quite a *béguin* for him, but as our conversation was restricted to intellectual matters and to long talks about John Holms, whom he had never met, he did not suspect my feelings. He is a very good writer and surprisingly little known for one so talented.

Max was so insane about Leonora that he really could not hide it. Once I made him bring her back to lunch and asked Djuna Barnes to come and meet her. Djuna said it was the only time that Max seemed human or showed any emotion. Normally he was as cold as a snake. He always protested and said he was no longer in love with Leonora, and that I was the person he wanted to live with and sleep with. But I was never reassured and I was very happy when she went to Mexico.

We went to lots of parties at various houses, but the best ones were given by Mrs. Bernard Reis. She was a wonderful hostess and served marvelous meals. She loved to fill her home with Surrealists and then give them a free hand to do what they liked. Of course Breton took advantage of this to make us all play his favorite game, *Le jeu de la vérité*. We sat around in a circle while Breton lorded it over us in a true schoolmasterly spirit. The object of the game was to dig out people's most intimate sexual feelings and expose them. It was like a form of psychoanalysis done in public. The worse the things that we exposed, the happier everyone was. I remember once, when it was my turn, asking Max if he had preferred making love at the age of twenty, thirty, forty or fifty. Other people asked you what you would do about sex if your husband went to war or how long you could go without it, or what your favorite occupation was. It was ridiculous and childish, but the funniest part was the seriousness with which Breton took it. He got mortally offended if anyone spoke a word out of turn; part of the game was to inflict punishment on those who did so. You had to pay a forfeit. Breton ruled us with an iron hand, screaming *"Gage!"* at every moment. In the end the forfeits were redeemed in the most fantastic manner. You were punished by being brought blindfolded into a room on all fours and forced to guess who kissed you or something equally foolish.

In the spring Max had his exhibition at Dudensing's. I gave a big party for him after the opening. It was one of the best parties I have ever given. It went right off from the start with no effort.

The show had a great *succès d'estime,* but the pictures were not sold as they were priced too high and Dudensing had the wrong clientele for them. The same week the Hartford Atheneum bought one that was not in the show. After that Putzel and I sold the paintings, all to different people who came to the house. I loved being a painter's wife and by this time was insane about the new paintings. Charles Henri Ford devoted a whole number of his magazine *View* to Max. It was an amusing issue and good for Ford as well as for Max. Max appeared in it photographed on his throne by Berenice Abbott, and on our terrace with his Kachina dolls photographed by James Soby. Breton, Calas, Sidney Janis, Henry Miller, Julien Levy and Leonora wrote articles about him for this issue, and he wrote his own biography. A lot of paintings were reproduced with the catalogue of the exhibition.

After that Max went to Chicago where he was to have a show. I did not want to accompany him. My catalogue was finally coming out and I was extremely excited. He had a good time while all I thought about was my book. Several bookshops made window displays for me and it was thrilling to see my first production so well received. It began to sell at once, thanks to Jimmy's foresight in advance publicity.

I could not sleep all winter until Clifford Odets left for California. He occupied the two top floors of our house and his study was over our bedroom. Every night he rehearsed his plays until four in the morning. I have never heard such noise. One night his bath ran over and began leaking through my ceiling, and dripping on to my dressing-table. To make amends he gave his friend, J. B. Neumann, two seats to take me to see *Clash by Night.*

I much preferred it to *Waiting for Lefty,* which Garman had taken me to see in London in a Communist theatre which had benches without backs.

Shortly after Max came back he became infatuated with a very wild and crazy girl, who was either pereptually drunk or under the effects of benzedrine. She was very funny, quite pretty and full of life; but she was terribly American, and at the time seemed to be nearly off her head. One could always tell if Max were excited about a woman: his eyes would nearly pop out of his head with desire, like Harpo Marx's. Nothing much occurred with this girl, however, and we left New York to spend the summer on the Cape. As soon as we were gone, Jimmy fell madly in love with her. Because of unforeseen circumstances we were only away a fortnight, but when we came back Jimmy had clinched the affair. He did not want Max to know anything about it, and I suspected the whole thing was caused by his father complex.

Our summer was curtailed because Max had trouble with the FBI. It was my fault. I was forced to go down to Washington for a hearing on Nellie van Doesburg's case. I had been trying to get her to America, but it was not easy. When I finally got the affidavit through, the State Department refused it; but with the help of Summer Welles, who was a friend of Helen Joyce's brother, I obtained a hearing in Washington and the visa was granted. It was too late, however. I could no longer get Nellie out of France.

I sent Pegeen up to Wellfleet, Massachusetts, with Max in the car to Matta's, where they stayed for a week to look for a house. When I arrived they thought they had found one. It was a horrid little affair in the wilderness with a kerosene stove and a gasoline pump. This reminded me of our Yew Tree Cottage pump and of all our efforts to keep it going when the gardener was on holiday. I decided not to take it and we looked for others all over the vicinity. We ended up by taking a dreary affair belonging to a lady painter in Provincetown. She lived below us. There was a studio and some living rooms and lots of bedrooms. Max got the studio and as usual wanted everything else too. Pegeen had to fight for her rights to get a place where she could paint.

I then made Max leave Matta's, in spite of the fact that he told me he ought to get permission from the Board of Enemy Alien

Yves Tanguy, *Le Soleil dans son écrin (The Sun in its Casket)*, 1937

John Tunnard, *PSI*, 1938

Jean Hélion, *Large Volumes*, 193

Salvador Dali, *The Birth of Liquid Desires*, 1932

Max Ernst, *The Anti-Pope*
(2 versions), 1941-42

Morris Hirshfield, *Two Women in Front of a Mirror,* 1943

Paul Delvaux, *The Break of Day,* 1937

Jackson Pollock, Mural, 1943

Pegeen, one of a series of oils and pastels

Myself on my marble chair

Registration. It seemed silly to bother, when we moved only fifteen miles away.

The first day we were in Provincetown the FBI drove up alongside us as we were walking in the street and seized Max by the wrist. They said they wanted to see him. We told them to come at two o'clock. When they arrived they searched the whole house, asked us where we all slept, looked in our suitcases, and went off with Max and a box of matches with a Free French sign on it. They said, "We are taking your husband for a ride." I was terrified and did not know what to expect. They kept him for hours and he returned in an awful state. It seems they had tried to terrorize him into denouncing Matta as a spy. They wanted to know how many *ladders* Matta had on his roof. Max misunderstood them to say *letters* in his name, and answered five. They had already been to Matta's house before I arrived in Welfleet and had questioned Max.

They complained because the radio was too loud and, when Max turned it off, they said he had no right to touch it as it was a short-wave set. They now used that against him and made a report which they sent to Boston. They told him that if he didn't tell everything he knew about Matta they would hold him until his gray hair was much grayer than it already was. From then on, every time we sat down to a meal, they walked in and bothered us some more. Finally they came one day and took Max off to sign the report they had made, warning us that it was no longer in their hands to judge the case. We waited in fear and then one day, at lunchtime, they came and said Max would have to go to Boston to have a hearing with the district attorney. I insisted on going too, and as I was his wife they could not refuse. At last I could prove to Pegeen that marriage was useful. We left her with some friends and told her we had no idea when we would be back.

It took hours to get to Boston in their car and, when we arrived, it was almost too late for a hearing. The district attorney was very nice and allowed us to explain who Max was and who I was. He had once had some job with the Guggenheims. Unfortunately he could not discharge Max without first submitting him to a hearing before the jury, and that meant he would have to keep him in custody overnight. In order to spare Max this unpleasantness, he decided to phone the New York Bureau of Enemy Aliens and see

what they had to say. Luckily for us they accepted full responsibility, claiming Max was their case, and asking to have him sent
back. We got a pass to travel and were given seventy-two hours in
which to return, which was better than having Max imprisoned in
Boston. So we went back to Provincetown.

The next day we met Varian Fry, who happened to be in
Provincetown, and having lots of connections there he tried to
arrange matters for us. But it was no use. We had to go back to
New York. Once we were home again we phoned our friend,
Bernard Reis, who knew about everything and always helped
everyone in difficulties. He made contact with someone in the
Bureau of Enemy Aliens and explained the case. When we went
down there we were well received and Max was set free at once.
He was allowed to go back to Provincetown, but was advised to
keep away from the coast.

We remained all summer in New York in our lovely house on
the East River. This was very bad luck for three people. One was
Marcel Duchamp, to whom we had lent the house; the second was
Jimmy, who was having his holiday and liked to bring his new love
to breakfast on our terrace; and the third was Sindbad, who had a
key to the house and often brought his girl-friend there, having no
other suitable place to take her. Marcel Duchamp remained with
us and moved into the little guest suite, but our sons were out of
luck.

Meanwhile I had been trying to get my museum started, and
finally I found a top story at 30 West Fifty-seventh Street, but I
didn't know how to decorate it. Putzel said to me one day, "Why
don't you get Kiesler to give you a few ideas about decorating your
gallery?" Frederick Kiesler was the most advanced architect of the
century, so I thought this was a good suggestion, never dreaming
that the few ideas would little by little end up in my spending
seven thousand dollars for the construction of the gallery. He was
a little man about five feet tall with a Napoleon complex. He was
an unrecognized genius, and I gave him a chance, after he had
been in America fifteen years, to create something really sensational. He told me that I would not be known to posterity for my
collection of paintings, but for the way he presented them to the
world in his revolutionary setting.

We had lots of parties at night in our house on the river. It was
the coolest place in New York. One night very late after a party

Max, Marcel Duchamp and John Cage, a composer of percussion music, and his wife Zenia all got undressed while Kiseler and his wife and I looked on with contempt. The object was to show how detached one could be. But Max entirely failed to attain this object, as Zenia's presence in the nude had an immediate and obvious effect on him. I am afraid Zenia took it all rather too seriously, as she wept copious tears in a bus one night soon after this, Kiesler told me, because she decided Max was not the angel she had suspected him to be.

One night after a party in our house when, having drunk quite a bit, I rushed out in search of adventure, I went to a bar on Third Avenue just as it was closing and forced my way in. Some people at a table asked me to join them and gave me drinks. I had only ten dollars on me, but I insisted on paying. One of the men said it would be safer if he kept the money for me for the rest of the night. About five o'clock we all went to Chinatown to eat. I told these people I was a governess and lived in New Rochelle. I did not ask them what they were, but it dawned on me pretty soon that they must be gangsters and up to something. They had parked their car in a dead-end street near the East River and they were arguing about something that was hidden in the rumble seat. In spite of my drunken condition I realized it was high time to leave. They wanted to drive me to New Rochelle but I declined, and I asked for my ten dollars, or at least part of it. I tried in vain to retrieve enough for a taxi or carfare, but in the end I was forced to walk home over a mile at seven in the morning. The next time I passed the bar where I had met the gangsters I went in with Max and Marcel and asked for my money back. The bartender, who I was certain had been to Chinatown with us, disclaimed all connection with these people and said he did not know them. Max's chief worry about all this was the trouble he might get into as an enemy alien if I got mixed up with gangsters.

Another night when we were having a big party for my birthday, Gypsy Rose Lee announced her engagement to an actor called Alexander Kirkland. He was very charming and handsome, but seemed hardly suitable as a husband. William Saroyan was present too. In fact there were entirely too many stars about, and there were great jealousies. Putzel took Gypsy upstairs to buy another painting of Max's. She already owned one. Jean Gorman, who was then Mrs. Carl Van Doren, went upstairs also. If I had not been so occupied with Marcel, who suddenly kissed me for the first time after knowing me for twenty years, I would have gone upstairs too and seen to it that the sale was not ruined. Jean was very tight and confused everything, and Max gave Gypsy the picture for a very modest price, and threw in another one as a wedding present. When they came down again Gypsy knew that I was annoyed and said it wasn't fair that she should get a present on my birthday. A few weeks later we motored up to Gypsy's country house, where she was to have a midnight wedding. It was a very theatrical performance and the newspaper reporters were so much in evidence, and so welcome, that they did everything short of interrupting the ceremony, which was performed by a sort of musical-comedy clergyman. Gypsy did the blushing bride stunt very well and her husband, like all bridegrooms, seemed terrified. I never knew what the marriage was about, but it did not last long, and several months later Gypsy told me it was all off. At the wedding Max was photographed by *Life* magazine sipping champagne with a South American heiress. *Life* made a dirty crack about his having married into the Guggenheim fortune, and how he was now seen drinking with another heiress, as though money were his chief preoccupation in the world. Gypsy's mother and Kirkland's mother were both present at the wedding. They took it all very seriously. Mrs. Kirkland told me she was honored to have her son enter such a distinguished family.

After Marcel kissed me I began to think we might finally consummate our suppressed desire for each other, which had been hanging fire for twenty years. One night, when Max and Marcel and I were dining together, I got terribly tight and I undressed and put on a green transparent silk rain coat and ran around the house egging Marcel on. Max asked Marcel if he wanted me and of course he had to say no. To make matters worse I said the most terrible and insulting things to Max. Max began beating me violently, and Marcel looked on with his usual detached air, not interfering in any way.

Over Labor Day we were invited to Southampton to Geoffrey and Daphne Hellman's. They were a charming couple, and I looked forward to the visit. This time Max got permission to travel. I started off well by telling Max that now that I felt he no longer desired me he could have someone else. But I am afraid I failed to maintain this self-sacrificing attitude. There was a pretty girl there called Peggy Reilly who began to flirt with Max. She played up to him as a *grand maître*, which was just what he adored. One afternoon, when we were coming home from the beach, they went ahead on bicycles and disappeared for a short time, just long enough to arouse my suspicions. I made a terrible scene. Max protested violently, saying I really went too far to think that he could make love on a bicycle. This, at any rate, completely spoiled my weekend, and I would not talk to Max for days.

I was perpetually running away from Max and going to Laurence. On one of these occasions, Max rushed downstairs and seized our dog Kachina from my arms as though she were the child in a divorce. It was a terrific anticlimax, as we were all expecting him to beat me up. Max was a great believer in revenge. He was always thinking about it. He might have walked straight out of the Old Testament. But he had a wonderful sense of humor, turning everything into a joke, and if he were hurt he never showed it. He was quite jealous of Laurence and called him "Your husband." I perpetually complained about Max to Laurence in Max's presence. It must have been very humiliating for him.

About this time Elsa Schiaparelli, whom I had known for twenty years since the days when she wore black taffeta *robes de style* and wanted to go into the antique business to make her fortune, never dreaming that she was to set the fashions for the entire western world, came to ask me to help her arrange a Surrealist show for a charity called the Coordinating Council of French Relief Societies. I sent her to Breton. With the help of Max and Marcel Duchamp, Breton organized a big exhibition, which was held in the Whitelaw Reid Mansion, an ugly, old-fashioned building. Marcel decided to cover the ceiling with strings that he criss-crossed the entire length of the room and which extended from wall to wall. It was difficult to see the paintings, but the general effect was extraordinary. At the opening I made a scene because the pictures I had lent did not have my name on them, and every other lender was acknowledged. Max's photograph was taken at this moment and, as he was standing next to beautiful Daphne Hellman, I must have appeared in the role of a jealous wife.

Kiesler did not want the Surrealist show to open before our gallery—which was nearly ready by October—but everything was late and we had to let the Surrealists get ahead of us. It made no difference, however, because ours was so special and wonderful: It was called Art of This Century, after my catalogue, and had been awaited with such curiosity that we had no rivals. Absolutely nobody knew what Kiesler had invented for my gallery. Even Max was not admitted until two days before the opening. At first he balked at having all the frames removed from his paintings, but when he saw how well all the others looked he decided not to be different. Kiesler had done a wonderful job. The publicity we got was overwhelming. Photographs appeared in all the papers and, even if the press didn't unanimously approve of Kiesler's ultra-revolutionary method of showing paintings, at least they talked about it sufficiently to bring hundreds of people a day to the gallery.

Kiesler had really created a wonderful gallery—very theatrical and extremely original. Nothing like it had ever existed before. If the pictures suffered from the fact that their setting was too spectacular and took away people's attention from them, it was at least a marvelous décor and created a terrific stir.

The only condition I had made was that the pictures should be unframed. Otherwise Kiesler had *carte blanche*. I had expected that he would insert the pictures into the walls. I was quite wrong: his ideas were much more original. The Surrealist Gallery had curved walls made of gum wood. The unframed paintings, mounted on baseball bats, which could be tilted, at any angle, protruded about a foot from the walls. Each one had its own spotlight. The lights went on and off every three seconds, to everybody's dismay, first lighting one half of the gallery and then the other. People complained and said that if they were looking at one painting on their own side of the room, they would suddenly have to stop and look at a different one in another part of the room. Putzel finally made me abandon this lighting system and keep all the lights on at the same time.

In the Abstract and Cubist Gallery, where I had my desk next to the entrance door, I was perpetually flooded in a strong fluorescent light. Two walls consisted of an ultramarine curtain which curved around the room with a wonderful sweep and resembled a circus tent. The paintings hung at right angles to it from strings. In the center of the room the paintings were clustered in triangles, hanging on strings as if they were floating in space. Little triangular wooden platforms holding sculptures were also suspended in this manner.

Kiesler had designed a chair that could be adapted for seven different purposes. It was covered in varicolored linoleum with plywood at the ends, and could serve as a rocking chair, with support for the back and was restful; or it could be turned over and used as a stand for paintings and sculpture; or as a table or a bench. You could combine it with planks of wood and make other furniture out of it. The gallery was supposed to seat ninety people, so there were also little folding chairs of blue canvas to match the wall. The floors were turquoise. Kiesler also designed an ingenious rolling storage stand, both to store paintings and to exhibit them so that you could bring them in and out when you wished to look at them. This was very ingenious and saved much space which I needed to show my large collection.

There was a beautiful daylight gallery that skirted the front on Fifty-seventh Street, and was used for current monthly shows. Here pictures could be shown in frames on plain white walls. In order to temper the light, Kiesler had put up all along the window a transparent screen made of ninon. In one corridor he placed a revolving wheel on which to show seven works of Klee. The wheel automatically went into motion when the public stepped across a beam of light. In order to view the works of Marcel Duchamp in reproduction, you looked through a hole in the wall and turned by hand a very beautiful spidery wheel. The press named this part of the gallery Coney Island.

Behind the blue canvas I had an office, which I never used, as I wanted to be in the gallery all the time to see what was going on.

My first secretary in the gallery was Jimmy Ernst. Later, when he left me, Putzel came to work with me. The first show was dedicated to my collection. Fourteen of Max's paintings and collages were on exhibition, more than those of any other painter; naturally, as I owned so many.

The opening night, October 20, 1942, was dedicated to the American Red Cross, and tickets were sold for a dollar each. Many of the invitations were lost in the mail, but hundreds of people came anyhow. It was a real gala opening. I had had a white evening dress made for the occasion, and wore one of my Tanguy earrings and one made by Calder, in order to show my impartiality between Surrealist and abstract art. The last days we worked day and night to get the gallery ready in time, but in fact workmen were still in the place when the press arrived in the afternoon before the opening.

We had great money difficulties. More and more bills kept coming in. Finally, when I realized how much Kiesler's total cost exceeded his estimate, I practically broke with him and refused to let him come to my house, but I maintained a formal museum façade. He was keen on publicity and wrote a threatening letter to one woman reporter who had given me a long interview to be syndicated all over the United States of America, insisting that his name appear too. He said he did this to protect himself as his former inventions had been stolen. She was so frightened by the letter that she would have dropped the whole article if I hadn't managed to patch up her difficulties with Kiesler just as the gallery was opening.

All this was exciting and new, and I was delighted to get away from home, where I always felt Max did not love me. He looked very happy at the opening. He was a cross between the prince regent and the museum's biggest star.

A few days after the opening he went to New Orleans, where the Gonzaleses had arranged a show for him. In New Orleans he had a much smaller audience than we did, and he was jealous of the success the museum was having.

While Max was away I was untrue to him for the first time, with Marcel, at last after twenty years. It was really too late and was almost like incest. When Max came back I was so engrossed in the gallery that I neglected him completely. He was left alone all day in our enormous house, with no lunch, as the maid came only to make dinner and there was never any food in the icebox. I would come home in the evening about six-thirty, and he was always happy to see me and made me a drink. He would open the door with a charming smile. Then we might have enjoyed what was left of the day if I had not been so boring, with my endless talking about the museum, how many people came and how many catalogues I had sold. At that time I used to sit at the desk and collect the entrance fees I had made up my mind to charge, and for which everyone hated me. Finally Putzel put a stop to this, but not before six months had gone by.

In the mornings, as I had to get up early, Max was annoyed and refused to have breakfast with me. He never came downstairs until I had left the house, although he often appeared the minute after, when I could see him through the window from the street.

Before the opening of the gallery I had decided it would also have to be a gallery where I could sell paintings for Max and young unknown artists. However a great confusion arose in the minds of the public as to what was and was not for sale, as I consistently refused to sell most of my private collection.

Soon after the gallery opened, Sindbad, Emily's son Johnnie, and Jimmy, my secretary with whom I always worked happily, all came up for the draft. Sindbad had volunteered for the E.R.C. at Columbia but had been turned down and was waiting to be drafted. Suddenly Jimmy left me, as he thought he would be in the Army soon and wanted a fortnight's holiday first. To replace him he found a friend who had once worked with him in the Museum of Modern Art. Emily's son was turned down by the Draft Board and so was Jimmy, and in the end only Sindbad was accepted. Laurence and I were terribly upset, but Sindbad took it very well. We all went down to Pennsylvania Station to see him off and suddenly he was swallowed up in a sea of unknown, tough-looking boys and disappeared. We were without news for days. Finally we had a letter saying he was in Atlantic City, and Laurence, Pegeen and I went down to see him. He looked such a baby in his uniform with his GI haircut. It nearly broke my heart to leave him.

Chapter 14

End of My Life with Max Ernst

One night when I had a rendezvous I told Max I was going to a concert with Putzel. He often really took me to concerts on Sunday afternoons. This particular evening Max must have suspected that I was not with Putzel because he suddenly phoned him to ask how much money he could get for a Chirico drawing that he wanted to sell. I had warned Putzel, but he had fallen asleep. When the phone rang he woke up with a start and answered it, and to his horror it was Max. Of course it was too late to do anything about it, but he pulled himself together and hung up, saying, "I will phone you later." He phoned Max back and said he had left me at the opera to go home and turn off an electric stove he had left on by mistake. When I got home I found Putzel at my streetcorner waiting for me in pajamas over which he had hastily thrown an overcoat. It was snowing. He told me what had happened, and when we got to the house Max opened the door for us and I burst out laughing. There was nothing else to do. Putzel fled.

On January 19, 1943, John Holms had been dead nine years. His anniversary still upset me very much. I generally managed to spend it with Emily if possible. But this time Edita and Ira Morris gave us a party. Late in the evening I got up and ran out in an awful state of hysteria. Ira followed, rather worried, but I told him I was going to see Emily. Once I was with her I burst out crying and told her everything between Max and me was over, and that I would never go back to him. I said I knew he was incapable of any real emotion and had nothing to do with my inner life, and that I had married him because he was a baby deposited on my doorstep. But now he no longer needed me. In the morning I went home to tell Max my decision. He was worried, as it was the first time I had been out all night. He phoned Jimmy at once to tell him I had come home. His emotion upset me and I was immediately sucked back into the family life again.

The next show of Art of This Century was an exhibition for three artists' works: Laurence Vail's decorated bottles, Joseph Cornell's Surrealist objects, and Marcel Duchamp's valise, a little pigskin suitcase he had invented to contain all the reproductions of his works. I often thought how amusing it would have been to have gone off on a weekend and brought this along, instead of the usual bag one thought one needed.

The third show was an exhibition of works by thirty-one women painters. This was an idea Marcel Duchamp had given me in Paris. The paintings submitted were judged by a jury consisting of Max, Breton, Marcel, James Sweeney, James Soby, Putzel, myself and Jimmy, who left in the middle of the session, when his girl friend came to get him. Fearing her painting would be turned down, which it was, he withdrew. Gypsy Rose Lee had done a self-portrait in collage which was very clever and which we exhibited in this show.

When Edward Alden Jewell, the art critic of *The New York Times*, came to see the show he wrote a long article in *The Times* in which he said: "The elevator man, who is tremendously interested in 'Art of This Century,' told me on the way up that he had given the place an extra-thorough cleaning (and indeed it did appear immaculate) because Gypsy Rose Lee was expected in the afternoon." The superintendent, who was very jealous, fired the elevator boy for getting this publicity. When I told Mr. Jewell what had happened he was considerably upset because he thought the boy had lost his job through him. I became very friendly with Mr. Jewell, and translating his name into French I later called him *"Mon Bijou de l'Epoque."* This was his comment on the

Surrealist gallery in *The New York Times*: ". . . it looks faintly menacing—as if in the end it might prove that the spectator would be fixed to the wall and the art would stroll around making comments, sweet or sour as the case might be."

I made Max work hard for this show. He had to go around to all the women, choose their paintings and carry them in the car to the gallery. He adored this, as he loved women, and some of them were very attractive. He was always interested in women who painted. There was one called Dorothea Tanning, a pretty girl from the Middle West. She was pretentious, boring, stupid, vulgar and dressed in the worst possible taste but was quite talented and imitated Max's painting, which flattered him immensely. She was so much on the make and pushed so hard that it was embarrassing. She wanted to be on the jury and I had to refuse her. We had met her at Julien Levy's the year before and Max had fallen for her at once. Now he became friendly with her, and as I was in the gallery all day he was happy to have a companion. She also played chess with him, which was something I could not do. He took a great interest in her painting but I was surprised that he gave her so much thought since she was vastly inferior to Leonora, who really was a creature of genius. I couldn't understand his infatuation. Max protested and said in the most pathetic manner that she was not the *fille de rien* which I accused her of being.

One night I opened a special delivery from Miss Tanning addressed to Max. It was a very silly letter written in bad French, and enclosed in it was a piece of blue silk, which she claimed to be her hair. It made me quite wild with jealousy, as she assumed that Max must be as unhappy without her as she was without him. She was somewhere in the Middle West. After reading the letter I hit Max's face several times as hard as I could. Max could not have taken this letter very seriously, because he later read it aloud to Emily and me to prove it was not a love letter. He thought it was funny.

One night Alexander Calder invited us to one of his *bals musette* in a bistro on First Avenue and Ninetieth Street. Max insisted on bringing along Miss Tanning. I was annoyed and didn't really want to go myself, because I wasn't feeling well. Max said he would go without me. I knew Calder didn't like Max, and I didn't think Miss Tanning would be an asset; anyhow I was furiously jealous and felt humiliated. I phoned Max at Miss Tanning's to tell him not to take her to the *bal musette*, threatening him that if he did I would lock him out of the house. She insisted on speaking to me herself, and told me she did not wish to make trouble between Max and me and would send him home at once. He came home, but I did not talk to him and I went out.

Another night Max was invited to a party without me and, though he had declined, I forced him to accept, as I wanted a night off to spend with Marcel. Max afterward claimed this was what broke up our marriage; since I had given him complete liberty, and for the first time he spent the whole night with Miss Tanning, as a result of which he fell in love with her. All this was for nothing, because I could not even make contact with Marcel, and went to the theatre with Pegeen instead. The next day we went to Sidney Janis' for cocktails and suddenly Max got very scared and asked if I was going to make a scene, as Miss Tanning had arrived unexpectedly. I said, "Of course not," and ignored her, as I have done ever since.

A few days later there was a Surrealist gathering at Kurt Seligmann's and Marcel Duchamp phoned Max to come. Max did everything in his power to stop me from accompanying him as Miss Tanning was to be there. I was so enraged that I left him at the door and asked him to give me the key of our house. Naturally, he went to live with Miss Tanning. But a few days later her husband came back from the Navy on furlough, and she and Max both had to flee. Max had great trouble finding a room in New York and was scared to go to any of our friends, as it would cause trouble with me.

In desperation I went to Breton. He was very much surprised by my suffering and said I must see Max and at least talk things over with him. He promised to send Max to me. He scolded me for taking the house key away from Max, and said it was a terrible thing to do to an enemy alien. I said that it was Max's fault for refusing to let me go with him to the Surrealist gathering, and that he had humiliated me too much. In the end Jimmy sent Max to see me.

When Max came I was nearly off my head and I told him that I would commit suicide if he didn't come back to me. He said it was hardly the moment for us to try to live together, and that we should both calm down first. He asked me if I would let him take

Miss Tanning to Arizona, and come back to me afterward. I nearly had a fit.

At this period I was in such a state of nerves that Pegeen had to follow me everywhere. She was worried about me, as I crossed streets without paying any attention to the traffic. One night we invited Breton to dinner and, although we hoped to make things better, everything got worse. Max, Mary and Marcel were there and some other people. We got into arguments about VVV magazine, which Marcel, Breton and Max were publishing. Max had promised me a free ad in it for my gallery and now Breton refused to let me have it. I wanted it on principle, as I felt I had done so much for the Surrealists. But Breton maintained that all his life he had sacrificed to truth, beauty and art, and he expected everyone else to do as much. Pegeen said all the Surrealists were *mesquin* because they quarreled so much. Breton was very much offended that a little girl should insult him, and he held me responsible for my daughter's doing so in my house. Max took this as an excuse to join Miss Tanning, who had been phoning him all evening. This ended our relations with Max, who disappeared for days. Pegeen did her best to patch things up between us, but she didn't suceed. The next time I saw Max I offered to give up Marcel if he would give up Miss Tanning, but he said it was too easy for me if I were tired of Marcel to ask him to give up Miss Tanning. One night he accompanied me to a dinner party and told me all about the gay life he led with her. He acted in every way as though he meant to stay with me, but after dinner he left me at home and went off to Miss Tanning. I think he merely wanted to make a public sortie with me to fool people. During all this time I spent nights with Marcel, who was sweet to me and behaved more like a nurse than a lover. I was nearly off my head and could not sleep without drugs.

Max came every day to paint in his studio. One Sunday afternoon, while Emily was with me in the house, we had tea with Max and then he went upstairs to paint again. I asked Emily to go up and talk to him for me. For some strange reason I was terrified of living alone. I asked her to tell Max that I knew the whole thing was my fault, that I didn't want to break up our marriage, and that I would wait for him to get over his affair. She began by asking him what I thought of a new painting he was doing. He said he didn't know, as I was no longer interested in his work, and that he never saw me; that I was a destructive person who had broken up our life, and that I had been in love with Marcel for twenty years. She then gave him my message and came downstairs, saying he looked impressed by it. Earlier in the winter Max had tried to get me to go to Arizona with him, but I had refused to leave the gallery, and told Emily I would rather risk breaking my marriage than give up Art of this Century.

When Max talked about Miss Tanning he was very contradictory. Sometimes he said he was not in love with her and that it was just a physical attraction. At other times he said he was like a cat who wanted to run away. Once he told me that we had had no luck, because, though he had been in love with me in Marseilles, as soon as he found Leonora again it was all over with me.

At one moment he said I should wait for him to get over his love affair, at another that it was no use because he would always want a new one. He also said I made too many scenes for him to endure our life together.

Jimmy thought I ought to be psychoanalyzed in order to straighten myself out. The only person I wanted to have for a psychoanalyst was Breton, who had been a psychiatrist in the last war. I invited him to lunch and told him all my troubles. When he heard about Marcel he said Max would never come back to me because of his pride. Breton thought I had really gone too far and had done things to Max that he himself would never endure and he wanted to know why I did not live with Marcel instead of fussing about Max. I told him Marcel had Mary Reynolds and that we could never have a serious affair. Breton said he would do anything in the world for me, but that he couldn't analyze me as he was not qualified, and that under those circumstances it would be dangerous. He told me to go away to the country and rest my nerves.

In February, 1943, Jean Hélion, who had escaped from a German prison camp and written an excellent book about his adventures, *They Shall Not Have Me*, consented to hold a retrospective show in my gallery and to come up from Virginia where he was living to give a lecture relating to some of his experiences. The show was beautiful. I bought a handsome 1934 painting and sold some others. James Johnson Sweeney wrote the preface for the catalogue and Hélion gave a very moving lecture. Over a hundred people crowded into the gallery and we turned over the proceeds to the Free French. After the opening I gave a big party in my house on the river for Hélion. He met Pegeen who was only seventeen and immediately fell in love with her. I realized it at once but Pegeen was unaware of this fact for over a year and a half; later she married him.

It was a great strain to keep the gallery going when my private life was so horrible and causing me so much misery. I was like a little girl who had torn the house down on her head, and then sat surprised among the ruins. I couldn't sleep without drugs and felt worse each day. Every morning Max came to paint in his studio. It gave him intense joy to see how awful I looked and he taunted me for getting up so late. The worst of all was that, as a result of my fighting about VVV magazine, the show I was to have had of all the originals of this review was called off, and I was left at the last moment without anything to replace it. I had to think up a new show and organize it in forty-eight hours. I used a suggestion of Jimmy's and arranged an exhibition consisting of two works each by twenty well-known painters showing what they had done twenty or thirty years before and what they were doing now. The contrast was extraordinary. I was very nerve-wracked and longed for some peace, which I soon found.

One afternoon when I came back from the gallery to get Sindbad's new address, I found Max painting in his studio. We got into an argument about pride and he said that was all women thought about. I asked him what he would do in my place. He replied he would wait until the storm blew over, which was actually what I was tryng to do. But he really took advantage of my patience as he merely used the studio to paint in, and being in the gallery all day, I never laid eyes on him. Anyhow that very afternoon I went to an opening at Julien Levy's, where I saw Miss Tanning with her hair dyed turquoise. Inserted in her blouse, which was specially cut for this purpose, were little photographs of Max. This really was too much for me. I was so disgusted that I decided I had had enough of the whole affair and, as you will see, I finally put an end to it.

In London, in 1939, Herbert Read had conceived the idea of holding a spring salon. I decided to try it in New York. I appointed a jury consisting of Alfred Barr, James Sweeney, James Soby, Piet Mondrian, Marcel Duchamp, Putzel and myself. The first year it worked exceedingly well. Out of the pickings we had a very fine show of about forty paintings. The stars who emerged were Jackson Pollock, Robert Motherwell and William Baziotes. They had all three already exhibited their work the previous month in a show of collage and *papier collé* I had organized. We all realized that they were the three best artists we had found. Soon thereafter, David Hare came to me. He had formerly been a commercial photographer but now he was entirely absorbed by his beautiful plaster sculptures. He had been very much influenced by the Surrealists and seemed to be the best sculptor since Giacometti, Calder and Moore. I promised to give him a show.

Funny things were always occurring in the gallery. Once when Putzel was there a man came and complained that one of the Cubist paintings did not resemble a man. Putzel was indignant and told him that if he wanted to see a man he should go and look at one.

Kiesler had installed a wonderful box into which you could look by raising a handle that operated the eye of a camera. Inside the box was placed a magnificent Klee painted on plaster. A woman peering in said, "I do love a peepshow, even if it's on batik."

One day a girl came from a college and said, "Will you please sign a paper for me so that I can prove to my Professor Mason that I have been here? He said I was either to get the signature of Miss Guggenheim or the Duchess." I presume she was referring to the Baroness Rebay, with whom I certainly did not like to be confused. People were forever asking me what connection I had with the Museum of Non-Objective Art. I always replied, "Not the slightest, though Mr. Guggenheim is my uncle."

On another occasion we had a visit from Mrs. Roosevelt. Unfortunately this honor was not due to her desire to see modern art. She was brought by a friend and Justine Wise Polier to view a photographic exhibition of the Negro in American Life, arranged by John Becker. Mrs. Roosevelt was extremely cordial and wrote enthusiastically about the exhibit in her column, but unfortunately in print the gallery was called "Art of This Country." Before she left I did my best to make her go into the Surrealist gallery, but she retired through the door sideways, like a crab, pleading her ignorance of modern art. My English friend, Jack Barker, had come up in the elevator with the ladies. Following them into the gallery, he mimicked the gracious high falsettos with which they greeted me. Mrs. Roosevelt, evidently amused by his behavior, turned to him smiling and bowed. The embarrassed Barker, unable to recall how well he knew this lady, whose face was so familiar, was uncertain whether to fling himself into her arms, clasp her warmly by the hand or bow back in a reserved manner. In such a dilemma he decided to ignore the whole thing and failed to return the gracious salutation.

One evening I went to Mondrian's studio to see his ·new paintings and hear his boogie-woogie records on the phonograph. He kept moving strips of paper with which he was planning a new canvas and asked me just how I thought it would look best. He kissed me and I was surprised to discover how young he still was at seventy-two. The last party he went to was in my gallery. He loved parties and never missed an opening. One day my cousin, Colonel Guggenheim, came to Art of This Century and when I asked him which painting he disliked least of those in my collection he said, if offered, he would accept a Mondrian. Needless to say, I did not give him one.

Chapter 15

Peace

I often wonder (and never found out) why this man was destined to cause such a commotion in my life, why he occupied my entire thoughts for a year, and why I bore him no grudge after all we had been through. To begin with he entered my consciousness as a myth—the sort of myth that only a very rich, irresponsible, vague and spoiled person can be; the sort of person who is so attractive and so much sought after that he never bothers to do anything he is supposed to do; who loses addresses, and never goes anywhere on time, or arrives on the wrong day, or sends telegrams full of lies and apologies. Finally I met him and he appeared to be just the opposite of what I had expected. He visited my house to buy some of Max's paintings. He had given Max an affidavit to come to America, when Mrs. Barr had asked him, so we were very curious to meet him and Max wanted to thank him. He was so handsome, so charming, so modest, so shy, that I was overcome with surprise.

The next time I saw him I sat next to him at Mozart's opera, *Don Giovanni,* and a peculiar current seemed to pass between us. He often referred to it afterward. He took me home in a taxi. Later I told Putzel that if I weren't afraid he would give me a terrible runaround I would fall in love with Kenneth. I was quite right to beware of him. Not that he meant to be evasive, he just couldn't help it. And when the time arrived and I did fall in love with him, my prophecy proved true, but in quite an unexpected way.

He came into my life when I most needed him and when he most needed me. I know now that it was inevitable. He came to me when I was very unhappy, and that was why he offered me his friendship and why I seized it, with no thought of the consequences. He immediately became my friend, and because he was over six feet tall he assumed a domination over me. The first thing he made me do was break with Max. It was so obvious that it had to be done; I don't know why I waited for Kenneth to tell me. I couldn't go on in my ridiculous situation any longer. He merely said, "The situation is absurd. It's neither one thing nor the other." I made it the other. He didn't do this from any self-interest. He just gave me the advice any sensible friend would have given me. Then he suggested I go to a lawyer and have a legal separation drawn up. Because he was used to thinking about property in a practical way, he convinced me this was necessary, and I accepted his advice.

But I am running ahead of my story. It all started this way. Everything he did was extremely practical and kind and, because he knew I was unhappy, he invited me to his house and gave a little cocktail party for me. I had been there before to large impersonal parties, but this one was quite different. At the last minute I decided to bring Max with me, and I am sure my host must have been very surprised to see us arrive together; but he did not show it, and he showed no surprise when Max left the party to join Miss Tanning. However, that was exactly what we all wanted him to do. When he left we felt much freer.

I don't know why, but Kenneth McPherson immediately gave me a sense of peace, and when I sat with his arm around me I was perfectly happy, happier than I had been for years. It is most unfortunate that I could not have been satisfied with this. If only I had been able to accept the peace and ecstasy I felt when I lay in his arms listening to music, everything would have been different. But then I am not the kind of person to accept anything as it is. I always think I can change the situation. The incredible thing is that I never believe in failure, and no one can convince me that I cannot move mountains or stop the tide until I have proved to myself that I can't. I therefore immediately set out to achieve what I was destined never to accomplish. Of course I got many other things instead, things that I hadn't dreamed of.

We went to dinner with his sister and Putzel, and then came back to my house on the river. We spent a long time on a couch behaving like undergraduates. I seem to have covered Kenneth with my lipstick, and he said he enjoyed it so much that, when his sister and Putzel returned to the room after discreetly wandering around the house, Kenneth folded his legs, saying, "Oh, dear, this seems to be very necessary." I never found out whether it was or not. Before Kenneth left he said he would take me to dinner very soon. I wanted to go home with him but his sister was staying with him and his flat was very small.

A few days later Jean Connolly was giving a big birthday party for her sister's friend Lila. I couldn't make up my mind whether or not to go. Max refused to come with me, saying, *"Je ne connais pas cette dame."* Gypsy Rose Lee telephoned to ask if she could bring a friend to our house to meet Max and to see his books and paintings. I couldn't refuse her but I felt very uncomfortable and thought I ought to explain our situation to her, it was so ambiguous. I called her back and said that I had invited Max to meet her in my house, but that we were not living together, and that I didn't know whether or not I would be home. However I hoped she would enjoy herself without me, and excuse me for not being there if I couldn't make it. I lay in bed dithering between the two possibilities for the evening. Suddenly I remembered Kenneth was a friend of Jean's. That decided me. I leaped out of bed, and got dressed and rushed to the party before Gypsy arrived.

I had a very wild and wonderful evening, a sort of independence celebration. At last I felt free of Max and spent the whole time dancing wild dances with Kenneth. I embraced him in the bathroom, where we went to wash away the smell of pickled onions that we had secretly inserted in the birthday cake. It was this night that Kenneth told me to break with Max. The next morning I phoned Max asking him to find himself a studio and not to come to the house any more. He was so outraged that he came and took Kachina without warning me, leaving our two Persian kittens Romeo and Gypsy. Kenneth had the flu at this party and couldn't tear himself away from me, but he should have been in bed. Finally a motherly soul, an old English warhorse, forced him to go home. Before leaving he invited me to dinner the following Thursday.

I was in a state of great excitement all week about my next *rencontre* with Kenneth, wondering whether or not he would forget about it. Thursday afternoon he telephoned to me and said, "Do you remember, you're having dinner with me this evening?" It would have been impossible for me to forget, but I merely replied, "Yes, I do." He came to fetch me at my house very late. I was extremely perturbed about what to wear, as I knew how much stress Kenneth laid on the appearance of anyone he was seen with in public. Of course I had nothing suitable, but I did my best and did not feel too self-conscious. I wore green gloves and a green scarf. "Now let me see, where would you like to go?" Kenneth began, and I chose a restaurant Max used to take me to. This was the only time Kenneth ever took me to a place where I had been with Max. From then on he always chose where we would eat.

Getting to know somebody suddenly is an exciting, strange and alarming factor in life, but it is even more exciting when it is something one has desired for a long time. The full impact of Kenneth's Englishness came upon me. It delighted me, even though at first I felt it was a rather conventional Englishness. He talked so much I realized at once I was merely supposed to listen. I liked that. It was easier, and it couldn't cause trouble. The only thing I remember saying was that I had been to Curzon Street (as he referred to the home of his parents-in-law in London) the day before Sindbad was born and well recollected the extreme solicitude of his mother-in-law. It gave me a pleasant feeling to be thus connected with Kenneth even so remotely. It immediately made a sort of bridge between us and, as I knew, like all the English he was very snobbish, I felt pleased to think I had been to Curzon Street.

After dinner he took me to his flat. We lay on the sofa for hours, wrapped in each other's arms, while his automatic phonograph played Mozart, Bach and Beethoven. Later in bed he told me that he was apt to get claustrophobia as his mother had made him sleep in her bed when he was a child. Therefore I took the precaution of going home as soon as he went to sleep.

Little did I know that a few hours after I had left, all this was to give him a terrible heart attack. I only learned it some days later, when he suddenly announced to me, in the middle of dinner, that he had been terribly ill and that the doctor had told him he must not drink or have a love affair. "It happened a few hours after you left, and I couldn't move, not even to get to the bathroom. But it's horrible to be ill. I don't want to talk about it." I don't know whether he realized the full psychological import of what had happened, but I felt responsible and decided we must not try to make love any more. After dinner he took my arm and walked me to his flat. We lay on the sofa in a gentle embrace for a long time, and then we went to bed and took sleeping draughts, but I lay awake all night terrified lest I disturb him. In the morning he gave me a glass of milk in just the same way he had given me the sleeping potion. He offered it the way a child offers a gift. Then he kissed me goodbye in the sweetest way. On the steps, as I went out, I met Anaminta, his little colored maid. She looked surprised to see me emerging from his flat so early in the morning.

A few days later I gave a party. Kenneth came surrounded by a lot of little young men. They were charming. Kenneth showed them my house and suddenly said it would be nice to share a big house like this with some one. He asked me how I would like to rent half of it to him, or suggested that we take another one and have a trap door between our floors. Every time, even jokingly, that he dropped a word of this kind I would seize upon it and use it to build my future.

From that day on I knew I must live with him, and indeed I never rested until I had achieved my purpose. This was comparatively easy because he was very lonely. That was why he allowed me to become a part of his life. He needed to be admired and to be loved. Partially his mentality was that of a college boy; intrigues were an important pastime to him. He liked to have a lot of people in love with him. Not that this brought him any real satisfaction, because his life was fundamentally unhappy.

Kenneth had a job with the British Intelligence Service but it never seemed to involve any work. In fact he seemed to spend most of his time listening to music. His phonograph played all day. He wasted a lot of time eating and drinking. He drank more than anyone I have ever known, except John Holms. Kenneth belonged to the eighteenth century. His surroundings, his background, his taste, his behavior were all reminiscent of a great *seigneur* of that epoch. He was so subtle and sensitive that he never missed any *finesse* or *bon mot.* Nothing escaped him, and it was a pleasure to converse with him. He would not permit me to use the word fairy. In its place he insisted on Athenian. He claimed fairy was as vulgar as the terms wop or kike. He was civilized, therefore an oasis in the American desert. However, he was much too good for himself. In a sense he never lived up to the best in him. He was dragged down to the level of his friends, who were all inferior. Possibly out of politeness, so as not to make them feel uncomfortable, he aped their inferiority. He needed someone strong to bring out his qualities. He had many friends and among them were many women. He was an ideal friend. He always made you feel that he belonged to you.

As he lived entirely for pleasure he was always anxiously awaiting the opening of the opera, concert or ballet season. He spent fortunes in the best restaurants, for he loved good food and wine; they were an essential part of his life. He wore the most elegant clothes. His suits were usually blue to match his eyes, and he had dozens of them. They were always immaculate. He was well groomed and very much made up with Max Factor's cosmetics, and his hair was bleached too blond. In his bathroom, which was more like a star's dressing room than anything else, were every kind of makeup and the most expensive perfumes from Paris. He showed me how to fix my hair. He knew how to do it much better than I did.

Because of his health Kenneth went away to the country and I was miserable and lonely. Laurence came to live in my house because he had a broken leg and could not climb the stairs to his flat. I gave a party every night for him, so that he would not have to rush around with his bad leg.

One day when I thought Kenneth was still in the country Putzel brought him to the gallery. I was just going out to lunch, although it was four o'clock, so Kenneth took me to a bar and fed me. He was very sweet, but his evasive and escapist manner became more and more noticeable. He made me feel as if he never wanted to be pinned down to anything, or counted on in any way. I think that the only reason I went on with this affair was the fact that John Holms's spirit encouraged me to, by promising me great peace from Kenneth. John himself never promised me more. The rest was left ambiguous.

Soon after this Kenneth had a thirty-ninth birthday. Jimmy Stern, not knowing I was in love with Kenneth, took me to a birthday party that was given for him by a friend. Jimmy thought he was introducing me to a new world. It was funny. Kenneth was extremely artificial and polite, the way I always hated him most.

A few days before, I had sent him a beautiful Cornell object, chosen by Putzel, as a birthday gift. My secretary, John, delivered it and came back thrilled by the glimpse of Kenneth's real life, wafted through the door to him on an aroma of whiskey. I was jealous and felt shut out of Kenneth's intimate life.

When John went into the Army, Putzel insisted on taking his job. I had resisted this catastrophe for two winters, but now I weakened, in view of the fact that this move would bring me nearer to Kenneth. They were such good friends.

I was still having a vague affair with Marcel. This never meant very much to either of us; we were almost like brother and sister, having known each other so long. I used to phone him if the spirit so moved me, or he would come to the gallery and make a rendezvous with me and take me to lunch. He was at the same time my father-confessor, and he knew all about my affair with Kenneth. It was often difficult to tear myself away from Kenneth to join Marcel, and once I phoned from a bar excusing myself on the pretext of being drunk, which I certainly was. Marcel always pretended not to care about anything. He didn't believe in emotion and certainly not in love, but he felt more than he admitted. Being with Kenneth always meant one was drinking much too much. I think Marcel understood how I felt about Kenneth and soon after broke up our affair saying his wife would hear about it because I was so indiscreet. I agreed as it was all getting to be dangerous and I was relieved when it ended, so as to be able to concentrate on Kenneth. When I didn't go to see Marcel, Kenneth asked me if I wouldn't regret it, meaning he wouldn't be able to give me what I had missed by remaining with him. But of course I didn't mind.

For the birth of the second number of VVV magazine Kiesler gave a big party. Of course I was not invited, as I would not let him come to my house since our trouble about the gallery bills. However, I was determined to go at any price, and when I could not get an invitation upon Laurence's suggestion, I dressed up as a boy and wore some of Sindbad's clothes which were left in my house. I found a beautiful blue suit and a cap, into which I stuffed my hair. I made myself up with burnt cork giving myself sideburns and a little goatee. Then I phoned Kenneth to tell him what I had done and to ask him if he would escort me. He was amused at the idea until he saw the dirty-looking little Greek boy I turned out to be. Kenneth added to my makeup, but he was ashamed to be seen with me and left me at the door and went into the party alone. He said he did not know Kiesler and therefore felt shy about bringing me. As for me, I made a great hit and no one recognized me except Max, who fled with Miss Tanning from the party the minute I arrived, as though I were the devil in person. Georges Duthuit was there and asked Jean, *"Qui est ce garçon? Il a l'air très intéressant."* Jean said, *"C'est un Grec." "Ah oui, je comprends,"* Duthuit replied. When Kiesler discovered who I was, he was so delighted that we made up then and there and were friendly thereafter. I thought that if ever I built a house in America Kiesler must design it.

Soon after the party our period of house hunting began. We were both looking for a place to move to in October. My house had been sold over my head and Kenneth's flat was much too small for him. It was easy for me to get lists of apartments from my old friend the agent, Warren Mark, and then share them with Kenneth. After we had visited all the places on the lists we retired to bars and spent the rest of the afternoon drinking. The gallery was abandoned to Putzel who, whenever he saw me going off to lunch with Kenneth, remarked, "I suppose you will be back by five."

I was absolutely determined to share a place with Kenneth. He wanted to live in an accessible neighborhood, so I soon realized I would have to give up the river, which was what I really preferred. Every day we were given a new list. We looked at many flats, and they were all hopeless except one duplex apartment. This was so perfect in every respect (except that it had only one kitchen) that we decided to take it. Everyone was horrified at the prospect, and all our friends warned us of the terrible dangers we would incur in the common kitchen. But, since Kenneth never ate at home except on rare occasions, we thought our friends were silly. Putzel nearly went off his head with jealousy. We had to tear down three walls to make an extra room out of four servants' rooms that were useless. When Putzel heard the conversations on the telephone about this he got all mixed up and thought we were building a wall to separate our different abodes. He did not realize what we were doing, and went quite mad when he learned that we were taking down walls instead of putting them up. He was always pushing me into Kenneth's arms and then getting furious if we became too intimate.

Our new apartment was beautiful. It consisted of two floors in two brownstone houses, so that we had twelve windows in front and twelve windows in the back overlooking terraces and gardens. The top floor, which Kenneth was to have, had a big bedroom, a sitting room, and an enormous sort of ball-room. There was a kitchen and a pantry on this floor. Below this, to which you descended by a magnificent Regency staircase, I was to live in three rooms, and the extra room I was to build out of the servants' rooms. It was inconvenient to walk upstairs to the kitchen, but on the other hand I had four bathrooms and Kenneth had only one. I made him sign the lease because he was so unreliable. I felt safer that way.

After the lease was signed we spent hours in bars thinking about the décor of our new home. There was a large entrance hall from which an elevator took you upstairs. There was no staircase up to the apartment, only the Regency one between our two floors, so we were more or less at the mercy of the elevator. The emergency staircase was not supposed to be used, except in case of fire when you had to break a door which automatically set off a fire alarm. We were preoccupied for weeks trying to think of fantastic ways of decorating the entrance hall. I was horrified by Kenneth's ideas, which were so frivolous and prewar that I really would have found it difficult to agree with them. In spite of the fact that he was politically left wing, he didn't seem to realize that a certain highly luxurious pleasure-seeking life was over and no longer fits in with our times. Fortunately he wasn't serious about anything he suggested for the hall. So instead, and with his permission, I got Jackson Pollock to paint a mural twenty-three feet wide and six feet high. Marcel Duchamp said he should put it on a canvas, otherwise it would have to be abandoned when I left the apartment. This was a splendid idea, and—for the University of Iowa—a most fortunate one, as I gave it to them when I left America. It now hangs there in the students' dining hall.

Pollock obtained a big canvas and tore down a wall in his

apartment in order to make room to hang it up. He sat in front of it, completely uninspired for days, getting more and more depressed. He then sent his wife Lee Krasner away to the country, hoping to feel more free, and that when alone he might get a fresh idea. Lee came back and found him still sitting brooding, no progress made and nothing even attempted. Then suddenly one day, after weeks of hesitation, he began wildly splashing on paint and finished the whole thing in three hours.

The mural was more abstract than Pollock's previous work. It consisted of a continuous band of abstract figures in a rhythmic dance painted in blue and white and yellow, and over this black paint was splashed in drip fashion. Max Ernst had once invented, or set up, a very primitive machine to cover his canvases with drip paint. It had shocked me terribly at the time, but now I accepted this manner of painting unhesitatingly.

We had great trouble in installing this enormous mural, which was bigger than the wall it was destined for. Pollock tried to do it himself, but not succeeding, he became quite hysterical and went up to my flat and began drinking from all the bottles I had purposely hidden, knowing his great weakness. He not only telephoned me at the gallery every few minutes to come home at once and help place the painting, but he got so drunk that he undressed and walked quite naked into a party that Jean Connolly, who was living with me, was giving in the sitting room. Finally, Marcel Duchamp and a workman came to the rescue and placed the mural. It looked very fine, but I am sure it needed much bigger space, which it has today in Iowa.

I liked the mural but Kenneth couldn't bear it. He never allowed me to light it, saying the light I had installed especially for it blew out all the fuses, so it could only be seen in the daytime or when I went down and put the lights on surreptitiously. Everybody wanted to see the mural. One rainy night James Soby stopped in on his way home from the Museum. He arrived absolutely drenched as he was not able to get a cab. I borrowed a shirt from Kenneth, fearing Soby would get a bad cold if he remained in his wet garments. However, all he accepted was a stiff highball, which he claimed saved him. Of course he loved the mural.

One day at lunch Kenneth told Putzel and me he would take a

house on Long Island and invite us. The next day he forgot all about it, but I didn't. I immediately seized upon the plan of renting a house with him in the country for the summer. I tempted him with a beautiful camp in the Adirondacks, but this turned out to be impractical, though we both wanted very much to go there. Then I took a friend's camp in Maine, but we decided this was too far away and gave it up. In the end we decided to go to Connecticut to live next to Laurence on one side and Jean Connolly on the other. (This place was on a lake where Jews were not supposed to bathe.) I wanted Kenneth to go to see the landlord and take the house in his name, but he rebelled and said he couldn't talk to such a man, and finally I had to send my friend. Paul Bowles, to take the house for me.

Before going to Connecticut I wired Sindbad to get a three-day pass, and I flew down to Florida to see him on the Fourth of July. He was stationed at Drew Field near Tampa. The heat was terrific but we had a wonderful time together anyway and spent most of it in Spanish restaurants and on beaches. I hadn't seen Sindbad since the winter, when he was first inducted into the Army, and it was wonderful to be with him again. We loved each other very much and were happy to be together. After his pass was over, I remained a few days longer, as he managed to get off in the evening, but he was so exhausted from the heat and his long day that it was quite a strain on him.

In the daytime I had nothing to do and a lot of time on my hands. Kenneth had asked me to go and see an old friend of his in the hospital at Drew Field, who had broken his hip and was waiting for a discharge from the Army. I had met him once at a party at Kenneth's but was afraid that he would not recognize me, so I sent him a message that I was coming. I got lost at Drew Field and entered the hospital by the back entrance, after wading through hot swamps. Private Larkins, the nurse told me, was in the tenth bed. I found him easily, but he looked very strange. Because of his accident he was connected to contraptions, much like Kiesler's strings in my gallery, and was half suspended from the ceiling. He was asleep when I arrived and, not wishing to disturb him, I sat down and waited for him to wake up. After a long time I poked him gently with my finger. The heat was horrible and the ward was full of the most pathetic cases of soldiers in plaster casts with broken necks and other things. One man was not allowed to move his head and he had his eyes focused on a ball that hung from the ceiling.

Larkins seemed pleased to see me, but I felt I was bringing him out of another world and I was not certain that this was a good idea. He gave me a strange feeling that he had lain there for months with the patience of Buddha and didn't mind. I told him, in the most garrulous way, all about the duplex and our summer plans, never dreaming how he was to be the instrument of evil and destruction in my life, and that I was merely playing into his hands. Unfortunately, he too was secretly in love with Kenneth. He pretended he thought all our plans were wonderful, and he accepted my invitation to spend the summer with us if he got out of the Army in time. I went to see him twice and brought him books. Later I wrote to him from Connecticut, never dreaming what harm he was about to do me.

After I got the lease of the house in Connecticut all fixed up, Kenneth decided he wouldn't come up for the first ten days, and since we had taken it for a month, that meant he would only be there for three weeks. But there was no use in fussing. I was glad he was coming even for a short time. He helped me by going with me to buy food and lending me linen, mine being in storage; and he gave me some oil and other things I needed, and packed me in the car. I took with me an old friend, a Russian, who wanted to get out of New York for a few days, so when Kenneth arrived ten days later the whole house was in order. Maybe that was what he anticipated.

By this time I was known in the neighborhood as Mrs. Bowles, since that was the name the house was taken in. The house was horrid, but the non-Jewish lake was nice and just in front of our door. I loved sharing my life with Kenneth, and especially the feeling of sharing the responsibilities and the expenses, which made it all so domestic. He did most of the cooking, because he was so much better at it than I was. Besides being an excellent cook he was a very particular housekeeper, and fussed a lot about keeping the refrigerator clean. I washed the dishes and occasionally cooked a meal. We went shopping in my car, listened to the radio, also in the car, and did a lot of swimming and sun bathing, entertaining our neighbors and looking after my cats. I really felt as though I were married to Kenneth and was perfectly happy and peaceful for a change. Putzel came up to visit us several times as did Paul Bowles and his wife, the real Mrs. Bowles. I think Kenneth was very happy, and got restless only once and insisted on going to New York. Strangely enough, he wanted me to come along. Paul was returning to town that night, so we all went together. At this time Kenneth was quite jealous of my friendship with Paul.

When we arrived in New York, as Kenneth had a date, I asked Paul if he would put me up overnight in the big apartment he had borrowed for the summer from Virgil Thomson. We had a lovely evening. I lay on the floor on an air-mattress, wearing his African robes, while he played his compositions for me. We even made love. He is a very good modern composer. He had dozens of bottles filled with exotic perfumes which he had mixed himself, and he gave me some amber which he put on my wrists. The next day Mary, Marcel, Kenneth, Putzel, Paul and I had lunch together. Paul came in a white suit looking like a doll. He was very dainty and immaculate.

After lunch Kenneth and I went off to his flat and played the phonograph. He sat with his arm around me and, as usual under such circumstances, I was in heaven. Then we missed the train for Connecticut and spent hours drinking and eating in the bar of the Grand Central Station. We finally got home.

I lived with Kenneth during these three weeks as a wife in every respect but one. I never slept with him. One night he said I should share his bed because I was so frightened. We had come across a corpse or a crouching figure of some kind in Jean's garden. It was after a party and we were walking home. By the time we went back to fetch a light the corpse had disappeared, but not its terrifying memory.

During this period we got on so well we made all sorts of wonderful plans for the future. We decided to go to Cuba in February and leave the gallery to Putzel. Kenneth also promised to take me to Greece after the war, as I had never been there and he loved it so much.

Chapter 16

Life in the Duplex

On the first of September, as previously arranged, Kenneth insisted on going back to New York, although we could have remained over Labor Day. He wanted me to drive him back. It was more convenient for him, so of course I did. I then moved into the duplex alone, because Kenneth had to wait for some furniture he had in another house, which he had sublet. I think in the beginning I must have been very lonely in this enormous place, for I invited the strangest people.

Soon Jean Connolly moved into my flat for a few weeks, and stayed all winter. She was in love with Laurence and would have made him a wonderful wife, and it certainly would have been more sensible if she had lived with him rather than with me. She had been in England for years, where she had been married to Cyril Connolly, a leading English literary light. She was twenty years younger than Laurence, a handsome brunette and extremely intelligent, with a very sweet character. She was a great friend of Kenneth's but soon, without meaning to, she caused a great deal of trouble in our *ménage*.

While Kenneth was getting settled he spent all his free time in my flat. He liked to be able to escape from the confusion that existed upstairs. His ballroom floor was littered with every conceivable object, and looked more like a junk shop than anything else. It took days to put it in order. He had a lot of elaborate furniture, and spent a fortune redecorating his new apartment. I felt a strong contrast between his way of living and mine. In the beginning he loved the coziness of my home, but of course his own surroundings were what he wanted. In fact our tastes were so different that we never approved of each other's flats.

Once he got settled he instituted the closed door *régime*. He had his life with his friends. I was always made to feel most unwelcome when they were about.

Our domestic arrangements were very simple. We each had our own refrigerator. Kenneth's was in the pantry, which he considered his domain, while he gave me the kitchen where there was a larger refrigerator. I had to walk through his pantry to get to my kitchen, and he had to cook in my kitchen. I always used the back stairs to go up there, and made a lot of noise about getting ice, hoping to draw Kenneth out into the pantry. The door to his flat was sometimes mysteriously closed, or I would be invited to have a drink. He nearly always came into the pantry when he heard me there.

As he was very changeable, one never knew what to expect. Jean was very indiscreet and helped herself to everything Kenneth left about. One night she even took a bottle of Scotch. It was the only one in the house and a terrible scene followed. When Kenneth came home he came rushing downstairs to find it and bawled her out. In the mornings he would ask her to have a drink with him. He called it his first, but it was more likely his third by that time, as it was round midday. Very soon she formed the habit of going upstairs when she heard the ice rattling; she thought it was an invitation. I was in the gallery at that hour and did not partake of their little daily party. Soon Kenneth got tired of Jean's coming up uninvited every day and complained to me about it. I warned her and she stopped going. Then he missed her. Whatever he had always displeased him, and he invariably preferred what he didn't have. If a lot of people were living in my apartment he hated it, but if he were alone in the whole building he felt lonely. When Jean stopped coming up for drinks he was annoyed. He had to have a grievance of some kind in life to be happy.

At this time I became sort of a slave to Kenneth's dog, a Boxer called Imperator. The animal, neglected by his master, became greatly attached to me, and Jean named him Mr. Guggenheim. He slept on a rug next to my bed and spent all his spare time with my Persian cats, Gypsy and Romeo, whom he adored. Kenneth was very jealous of Imperator's love for me and my cats. This tremendous dog was perpetually rushing downstairs, which I must say was perfectly natural, considering how lonely and abandoned he felt upstairs, for Kenneth went out so much. I used to take Imperator to the gallery with me every day, and as he could not go in the bus I became his slave, walking him everywhere, and bringing him home for his dinner every night at six. In a way he replaced my darling Kachina. Kenneth was delighted to have found a nursemaid for Imperator, and I was delighted to be seen in public with Kenneth's dog. Kenneth certainly liked that aspect of the situation, too. Every night when he came home he called Imperator to take him out for his last walk. I always took this opportunity to ask Kenneth down for a drink. So we got in the habit of sitting up till four in the morning.

Pegeen was still in Mexico in October, where she had gone to spend her summer holiday. It was her second visit there, as she had gone the summer before with two girl friends after we were sent back from the Cape—but this time she was alone. Suddenly I got a letter of warning sent by Leonora to Mrs. Bernard Reis, telling me that Pegeen was in the most dangerous company and that I should come at once or send some one to look after her. I tried to get a reservation on an airplane but couldn't manage one for a week. In the meantime Laurence and I tried to phone Pegeen. We put in calls which were constantly delayed, and when they did get through Pegeen wouldn't come to the phone. I finally got Leonora on the phone in Mexico City and asked her if she could go to Pegeen's rescue. She said she couldn't, as it would involve too much responsibility, authority, and money to get Pegeen out of the bad hands she had fallen into. It all sounded terrifying and unreal, and we were in a state of complete hysteria. Even Kenneth tried to find out from his lawyer if he could get a visa and go with me to Mexico. (Laurence having been born abroad had to wait six weeks for one.) Suddenly we got a wire and several letters from Pegeen, saying she was fine and would be back as soon as she could get a reservation, and then a letter from

Leonora apologizing for all the trouble she had made. It was just one of her mad ideas.

I canceled my airplane reservation and was glad not to have left, as Sindbad suddenly appeared on furlough. He was surprised by my strange connection with Kenneth. Though he had to admit that he was exceedingly handsome, he could not understand what pleasure I got from this peculiar situation. Being open and free with my children, I tried to explain, and managed somehow to convey what I felt, but Sindbad thought it was very silly and inappropriate. We had a nice time while Sindbad was with us, but it was all too short. I was completely absorbed by his presence and one day when the airlines phoned me and said, "You have a reservation for Mexico City tonight" I felt as though I had fallen out of the sky, but told them it had been canceled for days. When Sindbad left he flew back to Florida. We saw him off at seven in the morning and he left by the same airline Pegeen had taken to Mexico. When my children disappeared through that cavernous door before taking a bus to La Guardia Airport I always felt as though they were being swallowed up by some dreadful monster, and that I would never see them again.

I opened the gallery in October 1943 with a wonderful show of Chirico's early works. There were about sixteen in all, borrowed from museums and private collections. Kenneth and I fell in love with *The Melancholy and Mystery of a Street* owned by Captain Resor, son of Mrs. Stanley Resor. We wanted to buy it, but he wouldn't part with it at any price. It is a most extraordinary painting. In it a little girl is rolling a hoop down a dark, deserted, north Italian street. The empty arcades and an abandoned circus wagon add to the peculiar poetic gloom of the scene.

Next came Jackson Pollock's show. The paintings were handsome and exciting and justified all my hopes. James Johnson Sweeney wrote a preface which gave the public confidence. Sweeney did so much to help me make Pollock known that I felt as though Pollock were our spiritual offspring. In a way Sweeney replaced Mr. Read in my life. He was forever giving me advice and helping me. I hate men who criticize me without dominating me. Sweeney dominated me without criticizing me. Therefore we were in perfect accord. Kenneth came and helped us hang the show and bought the best drawing. He had an incredible eye, and always knew just what he wanted. We sold quite a few Pollocks during the year and even sold one to the Museum of Modern Art. After deliberating for six months, which was their habit, they bought it. But what is certainly an unheard-of thing on their part, they bought this one without bargaining, due to Barr and Sweeney's efforts. After the opening I gave Pollock a party and we all ended up in Kenneth's apartment. He pretended to be very much annoyed, but I think he liked it.

About two in the morning I slipped on the floor and broke my ankle. I had no idea it was broken, but I would allow no one to come near me except Djuna and Kenneth, who put me to bed. I couldn't walk the next day, and I thought this was merely a repetition of what had occurred so often to me in my life. Laurence insisted on taking me to his Austrian doctor, who immediately diagnosed a broken ankle. I had an X-ray taken, and then he told me I must have broken it in the same place two months before, when I was alone in the flat, and hopped around all unsuspectingly. Dr. Kraus was a wonderful little man, and he put my foot in a plaster cast with a stirrup, which took all the weight off my ankle and permitted me to hobble around. I was therefore never laid up and was able to go to the gallery every day. I wore a blue knitted sock over my foot in place of a shoe, and everyone thought I was trying to be Surrealist and admired my color scheme. The treatment and exercises which followed upon removal of the cast entirely cured my ankle. During the treatment I could no longer exercise Imperator.

It was impossible to do anything secret in the flat, because of Imperator. I had to leave all the doors ajar for him and the cats. There was a complicated arrangement for them to go to their box through many open doors, and for Imperator to go upstairs to Kenneth when he came home. Kenneth and I were very domestic at this period, fussing about the two Persian cats and Imperator. Our life was not only boringly domestic, but it became distinctly unpleasant. To begin with the cats had their box in a little back room which was consecrated to them. It smelled rather like a jungle, in spite of the fact that the box was cleaned out every day. This awful smell used to permeate my whole flat, and even mount to the kitchen and to Kenneth's rooms. But the worst of all was the fact that Imperator, who never was sufficiently exercised by Kenneth as he was used to having lots of servants look after the dog and could no longer depend on me, became filthy. I think

Imperator was demoralized by the cats' having the privilege of using the little back room instead of having to go out-of-doors; he began to dirty the floor around the box, and from there he went further and further and finally messed up my whole apartment. In the beginning I didn't mind cleaning up after Imperator, especially as it made Kenneth actually vomit if he did it himself. But Imperator got worse and worse, and what irritated me most of all was that he never made a mess upstairs—he was too terrified Kenneth would beat him. I didn't dare beat him, as Kenneth warned me it would be dangerous. I spent all this period rushing around with a little shovel like a man between circus acts. Every time I came home I trembled at the thought of what would greet me on my exit from the elevator.

Finally we gave Gypsy to a friend of Kenneth's, and I promised Romeo to Pollock's brother. I did this partly to please Kenneth and partly because the jungle odor got me down. But giving away Romeo was too much for me. I loved him. So, after deciding to send him to the country, I wired Pollock's brother at a little country post office saying, "Cannot part with Romeo after all. Many regrets."

I then sent Romeo away to the pet shop, hoping that if he were mated he would smell less foul. For weeks he had tried to mate with Gypsy and I had done all I could to assist him, but it never came off. There was a beautiful little Persian female in the pet shop window next door, and when she came in heat the pet shop sent for Romeo, as we prearranged. This however was a great fiasco, Romeo proving to be not at all what his name implied, and he came back in disgrace. Worst of all, his habits were all changed and he now messed up my bedroom three times a night. This finally decided me to give him up.

Then only Imperator remained to torment me, but this was a much more difficult problem to solve. All Kenneth's friends said that I should not clean up after Imperator, but make him do it. I used to send him little notes informing him how often Imperator misbehaved and finally, long after, Kenneth sent him away to the country.

Kenneth wanted so much to have people think I was his mistress that he nearly convinced me of it on many occasions. When I was in his flat on Sundays (he always cooked lunch for me on that day) and my telephone rang he used to rush down and answer it for me. He wanted people not only to know that I was upstairs with him, but that he had a proprietory right to answer my phone. He often brought his friends down to my flat and acted as though he felt as at home there, as I really longed for him to be. He wanted everyone to think I belonged to him. He was very sweet to people in trouble and was always being sent for by them and going to their rescue. That was the reason he had become so friendly with me in the beginning; though I did not need his financial help, I certainly needed his spiritual aid.

Because of Kenneth's very strong influence over me I suddenly completely changed my style of dress. I tried to stop looking like a slut and bought some expensive clothes, among them a little stonemarten coat that cost a fortune. He loved it and, as he always took good care of things, he made me raise it before I sat down. Once when I said it was a good idea, that I probably would never have another such coat in my life, he replied, "If you hang around long enough you may." He hated red so much that though it was my favorite color I entirely gave up wearing anything that approached it. I bought a little blue suit with buttons, which he adored, because he said I looked like a little boy in it. He loved what he called my *gamin* quality.

At this time Kenneth and I were very happy together. He depended on me and would have been quite lost without me. If he ever felt he was losing me, he turned on all his charm to get me back. Putzel called this putting another log on the fire. I really think that at this time Kenneth half considered me his wife.

Jean slept in my bed, and one night I made her invite Kenneth to sleep with us. The next time we tried this I realized that Jean's presence was no asset, so I asked her to sleep in the room I had had made for Pegeen. I don't think Kenneth liked my having Jean there all the time. I knew I should have sent her away. One night she was in my bed when he walked in unexpectedly to talk to me. I tried to hide her. Even though he must have known that our relationship was perfectly innocent, I felt he objected to her being there.

Our wonderful Regency staircase we never used. Jean and I always went up the back staircase into the kitchen. As most of our life seemed to depend on whether or not we met in the kitchen, Kenneth and I became sort of backstairs people. We often used to sit on the steps like servants. It was very funny, when we had this enormous and beautiful apartment, to find ourselves sitting on the backstairs.

One day I asked Max to come to the flat to take away his last remaining objects. There was practically nothing left; he had removed, one by one, his whole collection of primitive artifacts, leaving the house on the river as bare as a hospital. I also wanted to show him Kenneth's paintings. Besides several of Max's he had bought my *Toilette de l'Air* by Tanguy, a marvelous Klee, an incredible Miró, and a Picasso and a Braque. Putzel was always urging him to buy more.

When I arrived home with Max, to my great surprise I found Marcel Duchamp playing chess with Laurence Vail in my sitting room. I hadn't expected them to be there, so I burst out laughing for more reasons than one. As usual, Marcel was the detached outsider while my past, present and future were about to be assembled. I brought down Kenneth, who looked very self-conscious in the rôle of reigning prince, and made many excuses about his house costume. Max never knew exactly what my connection with Kenneth was. Probably a lot of other people didn't either—I certainly was asked enough indiscreet questions by my friends.

What Kenneth really wanted from me, and what would have made our life successful, would have been a very one-sided arrangement. He really would have liked me to live alone in my apartment and have me entirely at his disposal when it was convenient for him, and not when it wasn't. Before I had time to arrange it this way, it was all over. One weekend when Joan went away I was quite convinced of this, and I should have sent her away, but Pegeen came back from Mexico then and that complicated our life still more.

The weekend we spent alone in the flat was a very happy one. It began at lunch time when Kenneth came to fetch me at the gallery and gave me a wonderful new name, which he inscribed in the guest book. It was a combination of Max's name and his, and by changing only one letter he used both names. After lunch we went to buy a rug for our entrance hall. Then he waited for me in a bar, while I went to a necessary but boring opening of a friend's exhibition and bought a little sculpture which I soon gave to Kenneth. After that we went home. He had fo finish a quarterly article he did for an art paper. We had dinner together and went to see *For Whom the Bell Tolls*. Afterward we went home and read some poetry and I asked him to spend the night with me and to my great surprise he did. The next day we had lunch together. That night I went up and slept with him in his flat. The next day Jean came back and everything was different.

One night at midnight, when I was in bed (resting my broken ankle) and Kenneth was sitting talking to me, we heard the bell ring. Kenneth was determined not to admit anyone, but finally put his head out of the window to see who persisted so violently in ringing. It turned out to be Pegeen, home from Mexico at last. She wore a raincoat and carried a little bag, having lost everything else at the frontier. She looked like such a baby, it really was pathetic. We showed her the duplex, which she had so much encouraged us to take in the spring, and the room which I had built for her. She was glad to be home but quite lost in this new setting. Complications arose at once. She was jealous of Kenneth and he was jealous of her. That night when I went upstairs to sleep with him he sent me back saying, "You can't do that the first night Pegeen comes home," and when I came down, Pegeen said, "You've been making love with Kenneth." I was caught between two opposing forces. When I went upstairs to Kenneth's apartment Pegeen used to follow me, which was quite natural as I provided no home life for her downstairs, being perpetually with Kenneth in his flat at this time. When she followed me upstairs, I invited her into Kenneth's flat, and he was annoyed that I should take such liberties. Poor Pegeen had accepted Kenneth as a sort of stepfather, and jokingly called him "Father," which he liked very much. Pegeen wore high heels. They resounded mercilessly on my uncarpeted floors, and she had a very loud voice which could be heard all over the duplex. Added to Jean's presence, it was too much for Kenneth to endure.

To add to the very feminine atmosphere we created, our maid, who did our laundry, insisted on drying it in the kitchen. I must say it was a revolting sight to see brassieres, panties, and blouses all hanging overhead. Now that we were three females living there, I realized it was too much for Kenneth and had the laundry removed to one of my bathrooms.

Jean and I tried to make a home life for Pegeen. She was miserable in New York and wanted to go back to the Mexican family she had lived with and marry their son. Laurence and I were against this for many reasons and we thought if she were happier in New York she would change her mind.

Jean used to cook dinner for us. She was very sweet to me when I broke my ankle and behaved like my wife. She was a good cook. Both Pegeen and Kenneth liked eating home.

A very short time after this David Larkins, whom Kenneth had been expecting for weeks, suddenly announced his arrival. The night before he came I went up to Kenneth's apartment and tried to remain all night. He had a perfect fit and turned me out saying, "How can you think of such a thing when David is coming tomorrow?" There certainly was no connection that I could see between these two facts. However it must have been an omen of the future. The next morning when I was on my way to the gallery Kenneth called me upstairs and said, "David is here. Come up and greet him." We were all pleased to see each other or pretended to be. We talked about our various broken bones, and had a drink to celebrate his arrival, and then I went off to the gallery.

David, exhausted by his trip, got a sort of relapse and went to bed for a few days. After that we all saw a lot of each other. Kenneth took us to the opera and, as usual, he and I held hands all evening. I couldn't walk very well because of the stirrup I was still wearing, and Kenneth helped me up and down the steps of the Metropolitan Opera House with great affection and care. After a few days Kenneth gave a party for David.

I had bought yards of rose taffeta with which to cover an old chair. I now decided to turn it into a dress. Kenneth cut it for me, and I got a dressmaker to sew it up. It made me look like some one in a Mozart opera. The party was not much fun. Kenneth didn't know how to mix people and the atmosphere of his flat was too formal. I invited Gypsy Rose Lee and spent most of the evening talking to her. She was extremely handsome and wore a wonderful John Fredericks costume, and all the women were jealous and rather nasty to her. Kenneth seemed to expect me to act as hostess; he assumed a possessive attitude toward me, patting the costume he had invented for me in a most intimate way.

A few days later we had our first quarrel. Kenneth went out to dinner and David came down and told me I was to get the superintendent to take Imperator out for a walk. When Kenneth returned he came to my room, where I was lying in bed and resting my ankle, surrounded by some of his friends. I asked him why he had sent me such a crazy message about the superintendent and Imperator. The superintendent had never taken the dog out in his life. Kenneth got furious and said he had not sent me such a message. Then I got boring and domestic and began nagging him about blown-out fuses and other stupid things. He suddenly turned on me and, in front of his friends, said that I had made him sign the lease in order to avoid all responsibility, that he wished he had never taken the flat, and that he hated his life in it. After he went upstairs, his best friend, Polo, apologized for him, explaining that he was drunk. This was too much for me to bear. I told Polo he need not apologize for Kenneth, that it was my affair and that he must understand I wouldn't be in such a situation if my intimacy and relationship with Kenneth didn't warrant it.

I am sure Kenneth never told his friends about his life with me. When they were around he always denied me. He was terribly hypocritical and it was often difficult for me to know what he meant. He wanted to please everyone, so he had many sides.

The next day I was very unhappy. All my peace had vanished and I felt as though I ought to leave the duplex. I had had no apology from Kenneth when I left in the morning for the gallery. Djuna came to see me and I told her what had happehed and sent her to Kenneth. He liked her very much and was always pleased to have her visit him. When I got home I found a note on my mantelpiece from Kenneth apologizing and telling me how badly he would feel if I were to leave the duplex. I rushed upstairs and fell into Kenneth's arms and we kissed and made up. Afterward Djuna told me that he had been in a bad state of nerves. I attributed it to our row, but I think I was wrong. It was already the beginning of the end.

Kenneth and I had always meant to share a big house-warming party. So far we had each given a small one. But now, suddenly, he decided to give the house-warming party on his own. I was surprised and disappointed. He said it would be compromising to put my name on the invitation because he was married. Anyhow, he wanted to give an elaborate party, not at all the kind I would have chosen, so I let it go at that. I helped him make a list of guests. We thought of all the people of importance in the art world, and of course Kenneth knew lots of other people too. He had invitations printed. Unfortunately when the evening arrived he and David had the flu. In the meantime we had sworn never to fight again but to remain real friends, with emphasis on the "friends." Kenneth always insisted that I must never expect more than that from him. If I got more, it was either in my imagination or because I wrung it out of him. What he most wanted was affection.

Because Kenneth had the flu, and David was no good socially, and I had nothing to do with the party, and because it was very formal, and had millions of different elements and lots of Negro performers and God knows what else, it was awful. Also the elevator broke down under the strain and kept going to all the wrong floors. A lot of people came down to my flat, the Sweeneys, the Barrs, and the Sobys, and forgot, Kenneth claimed, to say good-night to him, which upset him. He had a high fever and felt extremely ill.

The worst of all was that, at the end of the evening, David suddenly took it into his head to make love to me. He told me he had fallen in love with me in the hospital at Drew Field when I came to see him. I was very tight by this time and believed him, and made a scene, telling Kenneth that I was sick of everything and was going off with David. I must say Kenneth took it very well and merely treated me like a spoiled child. David and I didn't get very far, but we did get to bed that night and the next. After that he told me he really couldn't feel anything about a woman, that what he really liked was choirboys. Of course what he wanted was Kenneth. We were both in love with him. We knew it was that which drew us together. I am furious when I think of all the men who have slept with me while thinking of other men who have slept with me before.

It was bitchy of me to do this to Kenneth, though he had always talked about it before David came and expected it to happen. I was in my favorite rôle and making the most of it, a thorn between two roses. I told David how much I loved Kenneth, and that I would never leave him and that he gave me a sense of security and peace. Never dreaming how things would turn out, I told David he would get the worst of all this in the end. I think all my confidence about how I felt toward Kenneth made David decide to break up our friendship. He was jealous and afraid that I was going to marry Kenneth. He plotted and planned very carefully to get me out of the flat. All this time Kenneth never dreamed David was in love with him. Fate played into David's hands and, from every point of view, I was doomed. Kenneth was already tired of having so many women around and did not like to have us come up so freely to his flat.

Suddenly Kenneth got sick, and when I took his temperature and saw that it was 104, I sent for my doctor, who told me I had called him in the nick of time. He gave him some sulfa and saved his life. Two days later Kenneth got news from England that his mother had died, while he himself had been so near death. From then on he was completely under David's control. He collapsed and wouldn't see anyone else. When I finally did see him again he was very far away from me and I realized that I had lost him.

We ended with a dreadful explosion. We were in the kitchen, where I had cooked dinner for him and David, when suddenly he told me I was a dangerous woman and accused me of opening one of his letters. David had seen me open a bill from our windowcleaner which was lying on Kenneth's desk, and had reported it to make trouble. I wanted to see that the horrid little man I had engaged to do all our windows hadn't cheated Kenneth, so I had opened the bill to verify the price. The real catastrophe came when I complained about the closed-door attitude. I was playing straight into David's hands, because then Kenneth burst out and said he could not live any other way, and that if I wanted to preserve his friendship, I should leave the duplex. David egged him on and we both got more and more furious. Of course Kenneth was not in his right mind. He had been completely abnormal ever since his mother died and really had no idea what he was doing. I refused to leave the duplex and offered to take it over. David said it was more suitable for Kenneth to remain, as the lease was in his name. I said that was merely chance; anyhow, I had found the flat, had urged Kenneth to take half of it, and I really considered myself responsible for his being there. Then David said that the flat was too big for me, as I was not used to running a large establishment. This made me angry when I thought of my beautiful house on the river. David then suggested that I remain and buy all Kenneth's furniture. The more he interfered the worse things got. Naturally neither of us wanted to leave and we both felt we had a right to remain. No one left, but from then on the whole thing was over. David ruled supreme upstairs and tried to get Putzel to help him in his further efforts to have me ousted, but of course Putzel was disgusted with him. In the end David himself left, as Kenneth finally had enough of him.

Subsequently Kenneth and I became the best of friends, but that is another story. We only arrived at this, I suppose, by going through all the rest. If only we could have started where we ended, even David could not have come between us. But one lives and learns, or maybe one lives too much to learn.

Chapter 17

Art of This Century

As it was noncommercial, Art of This Century soon became a center for all avant-garde activities. The young American artists, much inspired by the European abstract and Surrealist artists who had taken refuge in New York, started an entirely *new* school of painting, which Robert Coates, art critic for *The New Yorker,* named Abstract Expressionism.

We had the great joy of discovering and giving first one-man shows not only to Pollock, Motherwell and Baziotes, but also to Hans Hofmann, Clyfford Still, Mark Rothko and David Hare. The group shows included Adolph Gottlieb, Hedda Sterne and Ad Reinhardt.

We also gave one-man shows to Chirico, Arp, Giacometti, Hélion, Hans Richter, Hirshfield, Theo van Doesburg, Pegeen and Laurence Vail and I. Rice Pereira. We also held several spring salons, gave another woman's show, two collage shows, and exhibited the work of various unknown artists.

After the first spring salon it became evident that Pollock was the best painter. Both Matta, the painter who was a friend of mine, and Putzel urged me to help him, as at the time he was working in my uncle's museum as a carpenter. He had once been a pupil of the well-known academic painter Thomas Hart Benton and through his terrific efforts to throw off Benton's influence had, in reaction, become what he was when I met him. From 1938 to 1942 he had worked on the WPA Federal Art Project for artists, which was part of the scheme originated by President Roosevelt for reducing unemployment.

When I first exhibited Pollock he was very much under the influence of the Surrealists and of Picasso. But he very soon overcame this influence, to become, strangely enough, the greatest painter since Picasso. As he required a fixed monthly sum in order to work in peace, I gave him a contract for one year. I promised him a hundred and fifty dollars a month and a settlement at the end of the year, if I sold more than two thousand seven hundred dollars' worth, allowing one-third to the gallery. If I lost I was to get pictures in return.

Pollock immediately became the central point of Art of This Century. From then on, 1943, until I left America in 1947, I dedicated myself to Pollock. He was very fortunate, because his wife Lee Krasner, a painter, did the same, and even gave up painting at one period, as he required her complete devotion. I welcomed a new protégé, as I had lost Max. My relationship with Pollock was purely that of artist and patron, and Lee was the intermediary. Pollock himself was rather difficult; he drank too much and became so unpleasant, one might say devilish, on these occasions. But as Lee pointed out when I complained, "He also has an angelic side," and that was true. He was like a trapped animal who never should have left Wyoming, where he was born.

As I had to find a hundred and fifty dollars a month for the Pollocks, I concentrated all my efforts on selling his pictures and neglected all the other painters in the gallery, many of whom soon left me, as Sam Kootz, the art dealer, gave them contracts, which I could not afford to do.

I felt Pollock had a deep feeling for West American-Indian sculpture, as it came out a lot in his earlier paintings, and in some of those that were to be in his first exhibition. This was held in November 1943. The introduction to the catalogue was written by James Johnson Sweeney, who helped a lot to further Pollock's career. In fact, I always referred to Pollock as our spiritual offspring. Clement Greenberg, the critic, also came to the fore and championed Pollock as the greatest painter of our time. Alfred

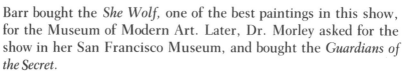

Barr bought the *She Wolf,* one of the best paintings in this show, for the Museum of Modern Art. Later, Dr. Morley asked for the show in her San Francisco Museum, and bought the *Guardians of the Secret.*

We did not sell many Pollock paintings, but when he gave us gouaches it was much easier. A lot of these I gave away as wedding presents to my friends. I worked hard to interest people in his work and never tired doing so, even when it involved dragging in and out his enormous canvases. One day Mrs. Harry Winston, the famous Detroit collector, came to the gallery to buy a Masson. I persuaded her to buy a Pollock instead.

In 1945, Bill Davis, the collector, who was also a fan of Pollock's, advised me to raise my contract with him to three hundred dollars a month, and in exchange, to take all Pollock's works. Pollock was very generous in giving me presents. At this time I had acute infectious mononucleosis, and during the annual Pollock show had to stay in bed. This distressed Lee Pollock very much, as she said no one could sell anything in the gallery except me, and Putzel had left to set up his own gallery in New York. Poor man, this proved to be a great tragedy, as it ended in his suicide.

Lee was so dedicated to Pollock that when I was sick in bed, she came every morning to try to persuade me to lend them two thousand dollars to buy a house on Long Island. She thought that if Pollock got out of New York he would stop drinking. Though I did not see how I could produce any extra funds I finally agreed to do so as it was the only way to get rid of Lee. Now it all makes me laugh. I had no idea then what Pollock paintings would be worth. I never sold one for more than a thousand dollars and when I left America in 1947, not one gallery would take over my contract. I offered it to them all, and in the end Betty, of the Betty Parsons Gallery, said she would give Pollock a show, but that was all she could do. Pollock himself paid the expenses of it out of one painting Bill Davis bought. All the rest were sent to me, according to the contract, at Venice, where I had gone to live. Of course, Lee had her pick of one painting a year. When the pictures got to Venice, I gave them away one by one to various museums, and now only have two of this collection left, though I also have nine earlier ones dating from 1943 to 1946. And so now Lee is a millionaire, and I think what a fool I was.

In my struggles for Pollock I also had to contend with such things as Dorothy Miller absolutely refusing to include him in an exhibition of twelve young American artists—artists who were obviously what she considered the best we had—which she did in 1946, as a traveling show for the Museum of Modern Art. I complained to Alfred Barr, but he said it was Dorothy Miller's show and nothing could be done about it. I also had great money difficulties to keep both Pollock and the gallery going, and often found myself in the position of having to sell what I called an old master. Thus, I was once forced to part with a marvelous Delaunay of 1912, called *Disks*, which I had bought from him in Grenoble, when he was a refugee from occupied Paris. This picture later turned up in the Museum of Modern Art. Its loss is one of the seven tragedies of my life as a collector.

The second was my stupidity in not availing myself of the opportunity of buying *La Terre Labourée*, by Miró, in London in 1939 for fifteen hundred dollars. Now, if it were for sale, it would be worth well over fifty thousand.

The third tragedy was selling a 1936 Kandinsky, called *Dominant Curve*, in New York during the war, because I listened to people saying it was a Fascist picture. To my great sorrow I later found it in my uncle's collection in an exhibition in Rome.

The fourth was not buying Picasso's *Pêche de Nuit à Antibes*, because I had no cash on hand, and did not have enough sense to sell some capital, which my friend and financial adviser Bernard Reis told me to do when the picture was offered to me in 1950; and now that, too, is in the Museum of Modern Art.

The fifth was having to sell a Henri Laurens sculpture and a beautiful Klee water color in order to pay Nellie van Doesburg's passage to New York; and the sixth, to have all but two of my last remaining Klees stolen from Art of This Century. But the worst mistake of all was giving away eighteen Pollocks. However, I comfort myself by thinking how terribly lucky I was to have been able to buy all my wonderful collection at a time when prices were still normal, before the whole picture world turned into an investment market.

As the gallery was a center where all the artists were welcome, they treated it as a sort of club. Mondrian was a frequent visitor, and always brought his paintings carefully wrapped up in white paper. I had bought two of his beautiful large charcoal Cubist drawings from a gallery in New York, and these I much preferred to his later works, of which I also had one. When I once asked him to clean one of his own paintings, which always had to be immaculate, he arrived with a little bag and cleaned not only his picture, but also an Arp and a Ben Nicholson relief. He admired Max's and Dali's paintings very much and said, "They are great artists. Dali stands a little apart from the others, he is great in the old tradition. I prefer the true Surrealists, especially Max Ernst. They do not belong to the old tradition, they are sometimes naturalists in their own way, but free from tradition. I feel nearer in spirit to the Surrealists, except for the literary part, than to any other kind of painting."

In the winter of 1946, I asked Alexander Calder to make me a bedhead, which I thought would be a marvelously refreshing change from our grandmothers' old brass ones. He said he would, but never got around to it. One day I met him at a party and said, "Sandy, why haven't you made my bed?" At this strange question, Louisa, his wife, a beautiful niece of Henry James, pricked up her ears and urged Sandy to get to work. Because of the war, the only available material was silver, which cost more than all the work Sandy did on it. It was not mobile, except for the fact that it had a fish and a butterfly that swung in space from the background, which resembled undersea plants and flowers. I am not only the only woman in the world who sleeps in a Calder bed, but the only one who wears his enormous mobile earrings. Every woman in New York who is fortunate enough to be decorated by a Calder jewel, has a brooch or a bracelet, or a necklace.

After Morris Hirshfield's death, Sidney Janis, the dealer, asked me to give him a memorial show. It was very beautiful, and I acquired what I consider his best painting, *Two Women in Front of a Mirror*. It portrays the women perfuming themselves, combing and brushing their hair and putting on lipstick. It is unrealistically presented, with the women seen back to front in the mirror. They also have four bottoms, which, when the painting was hung in my entrance hall, received many pinpricks from sensuous admirers who were passing through the hall.

In the summer of 1945 my great friend Emily Coleman came to see me, and brought with her a fantastic creature called Marius Bewley. I have never met anyone like him in my life. He looked like a priest, which he had once intended to be, and spoke with a strange false English accent. I took to him at once, and immediately asked him to come and be my secretary in the gallery. He accepted just as readily, as he thought the idea very pleasant. Our collaboration was a great success. We became tremendous friends and remained so ever since, though Marius left me after a year to go to take a PH.D. at Columbia University. He was extremely learned and a brilliant writer, and everything he said was brilliant too. He had a marvelous sense of life and of humor. He loved modern pictures, and though he sold very few, he bought a lot from my gallery.

After Marius left me, he sent in his place a very strange young man who couldn't type and who never appeared on time—in fact, some days not at all. I was kept very busy answering the telephone for him, as his friends never stopped phoning him. The only thing he liked to do was to take my Lhasa terriers for walks, as they served as introductions to other fascinating Lhasa terriers who belonged to such distinguished people as Lily Pons, John Carradine, and Philip Barry. The original Lhasa had been given to Max Ernst, but when we were divorced he had taken it away with him. I had wanted very much to retain this darling dog, Kachina, for half the year, and wished to have this put in the divorce contract, but it was too complicated and I had to content myself, years later, with two of her puppies, which Max sold me at birth.

Much as I loved Art of This Century, I loved Europe more than America, and when the war ended I couldn't wait to go back. Also, I was exhausted by all my work in the gallery, where I had become a sort of slave. I had even given up going out to lunch. If I ever left for an hour to go to a dentist, oculist or hairdresser, some very important museum director would be sure to come in and say, "Miss Guggenheim is never here." It was not only necessary for me to sell Pollocks and other pictures from current shows, but I also had to get the paintings circulated in traveling exhibitions. The last year was the worst, when my secretary couldn't even type, and this extra burden was added to my chores. I had become a sort of prisoner and could no longer stand the strain. Levi Straus, the French cultural attaché, gave me a letter to the French consul, saying I had to go abroad to see French and European art, and with this excuse I got to Paris and then to Venice, where Mary McCarthy and her husband, Bowden Broadwater, insisted that I accompany them.

On my way there, I decided Venice would be my future home. I had always loved it more than any place on earth and felt I would be happy alone there. I set about trying to find a palace that would house my collection and provide a garden for my dogs. This was to take several years; in the meantime I had to go back to New York to close the gallery. We ended it with a retrospective show of Theo van Doesburg, which I arranged to have circulated all over the United States. Nellie van Doesburg came to New York from France as my guest, with all the pictures. I had been trying to arrange this during the war, but had not succeeded until it was too late for her to leave France.

I sold all Kiesler's fantastic furniture and inventions. There was terrific bidding for them, and to avoid complications I let them be removed by the cash and carry system. Poor Kiesler never even got one thing as a souvenir, they disappeared so quickly.

Betty Parsons fell heir to my work, spiritually, and as I said, promised Pollock a show. Happy to think that she was there to help the unknown artists, I left my collection in storage and flew to Europe with my two dogs, not to return for twelve years.

Interlude

In 1945 the Dial Press of New York had asked me write my memoirs for publication. After I finished my manuscript Laurence Vail read it and suggested various changes and Inez Ferren typed it for me. My editor at Dial insisted on making many changes. In fact, she practically rewrote the book, and I had to put most things back the way I had originally written them. Finally the book, which was called *Out of This Century*, was published in March 1946.

Many years later John H. Davis, the author of a book called *The Guggenheims*, claimed that some of my relatives were so scandalized they sent "hordes of messengers and clerks out to the major bookstores with orders to buy up every available copy," so that in the end the only people who got a look at the book were my friends, people who bought it outside of Manhattan, "the gentle ladies who borrow from their local library; and the critics"—by which presumably he meant the book reviewers.

He was right about the reviewers, if not about much else. Many of them took the opportunity to display their own cleverness by attacking me.

Time was typical:

Stylistically her book is as flat and witless as a harmonica rendition
of the *Liebestod,* but it does furnish a few peeks—between boudoir
blackouts—at some of the men who make art a mystery.

The well-known reviewer Harry Hansen was more serious:

Sometimes her remarks are amusing, but gradually the reader feels
that this book is a social document: a testimony of reckless
Bohemianism, irresponsible conduct on the part of wealthy young
Americans let loose in Paris and further evidence why artists shock
conventional people—like ourselves. . . . The complete absence of
any moral responsibility is the trademark of this sort of sophistication. Conventions, in behavior or painting, do not seem valid for
the generation between-the-wars. Conduct is dictated, apparently,
by caprice. Is this written for our amusement or does publicizing
this life mean a catharsis for the author? The more I read this type
of writing, the more I begin to understand the social and artistic
usefulness of restraint.

Another approach was taken by the art reviewer Katharine
Kuh:

Because Peggy Guggenheim has a distinguished and discriminating
collection of contemporary art, her vulgar autobiography, "Out of
this Century," is doubly offensive. For several years she has been
known in art circles as a generous patron of the most advanced
experimental art, especially Surrealism, and also as the founder
and director of a somewhat "chi-chi" but none-the-less provocative
New York gallery called Art of This Century. . . . I have no
quarrel with a writer who is impelled to "tell all," if a well written
book is the result, but Miss Guggenheim, unfortunately not a
gifted literata, has done the cause of modern art no kindness by
mixing it irrevocably with a compulsive recital of her own decadent
life.

Miss Kuh concluded:

A supreme masochist, she is as relentlessly honest about herself as
she is about her "friends." She leaves us with a picture of a lonely
woman, too hard, too hurt, to have retained normal sensitivities.

out of this century

century

peggy guggenheim

peggy guggenheim

out of this century

dial

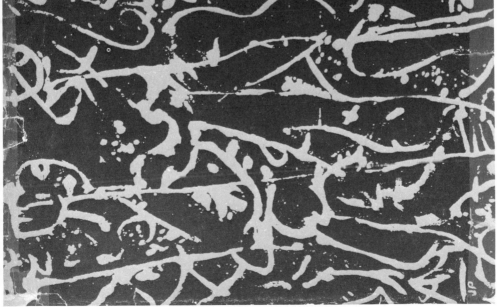

But in *View* magazine, Everett McManus wrote more positively:

> The book convinces us the way Flaubert convinces of Madame Bovary, because it is about the feelings of a woman—not necessarily of a particular woman but of a *modern* woman. . . . Miss Guggenheim should be praised for taking positive advantage of everything money could buy for her. One might criticize the author's taste, among other points, but she is never ridiculous. Most of her dignity, I would hazard, lies in her apparent awareness of the established tenet that money can not buy happiness if happiness be based, as we suppose on love. . . . Some of Miss Guggenheim's relentless critics are guilty of esthetic snobbery where her slate is clean. . . . Her book is not the autobiography of an art connoisseur or critic but of a human being. From this viewpoint, Miss Guggenheim reveals her progressive spiritualization. She passed through respective stages of infatuation with a lusty bohemian, a temperamental idealist, an enthusiastic Communist, a more or less carnal and calculating painter, and finally to a platonically minded "Athenian"; that is, in a descending scale so far as the male's carnal reaction to her went. She was always earnestly in love and regularly plunged into the despair of which she was capable. It is significant that her most frequently applied adjective for the moods of her own friends is "sad." It recurs with striking force. . . . But she has not been saddened.

In 1959, at the suggestion of Nicolas Bentley, the English editor and illustrator, I condensed *Out of This Century* into fewer than a hundred pages and added material about my life during the intervening period. As *Confessions of an Art Addict* it was published in 1960 by André Deutsch in London and the Macmillan Company in New York. The following pages (through Chapter 21) are reprinted from the latter half of that book. I seem to have written the first book as an uninhibited woman and the second one as a lady who was trying to establish her place in the history of modern art. That is perhaps why the two books read so differently. And since the Conclusion of this third book was written when I was almost 80 years old, it reads differently from the first two.

Chapter 18

Venice and the Biennale

One of the first people I met in Venice in 1946 was an artist called Vedova. I was in the Café Angelo at the Rialto. Not knowing anyone in Venice, I inquired of the *patron* where I might meet some modern artists. He said, "Go to the other Angelo restaurant at San Marco and ask for Vedova." I wrote this name on a matchbox and proceeded to the other Angelo. Here I received a wonderful welcome from Vedova and another Venetian artist, Santomaso, who both became my friends. They were very much interested in modern art, and knew about my uncle's collection, which surprised me. In fact, they even had the catalogue. As they spoke Venetian dialect together, I spent painful hours in their company, not understanding a word they said. But when I was alone with either of them it was better, as I could speak a little Italian.

Vedova, who painted abstractions, was an enormously tall man with a beard. He was a Communist and during the war had been a partisan. He was very young and mad about lovely young girls. Santomaso was less tall and rounder. He also had a roving eye, and a wife and child as well. He was extremely well versed in Venetian history and recounted the most fascinating things of his great city's past. Of the two, he was the more cultivated. The Angelo restaurant was filled with their paintings and a great many other people's. This is a Venetian custom: painters are allowed to eat free and give their works in return.

It was through Santomaso that I was invited to show my entire collection at the XXIVth Biennale of Venice. He had suggested to Rodolfo Pallucchini, the secretary-general of the Biennale, that the collection should be exhibited, and it was agreed that it should be shown in the Greek pavilion, which was free because of the Greeks being at war.

The Biennale, which was started in 1895, is an international exhibition of contemporary art, which is held every other year in the Public Gardens at the end of Venice, on the lagoon near the Lido. A lot of very ugly buildings put up in the time of Mussolini give it a distinct character. The trees and the gardens are wonderfully looked after and make a beautiful background for the various pavilions. In the middle of June, when the Biennale opens, the lime trees are flowering and the perfume they exhale is overpowering. I often feel this must compete strongly with the exhibition, as it is so much pleasanter to sit in the gardens than to go into the terribly hot and unventilated pavilions.

The foreign countries that exhibit are each responsible for the shows in their own pavilions, which are run under the auspices of their various governments. In the main Italian pavilion there are miles and miles of very boring paintings, though occasionally something good is shown. There are also innumerable large and small one-man shows which are supposed to be devoted to contemporary painters, though sometimes earlier artists, such as Delacroix, Courbet, Constable, Turner, and even Goya have slipped in. No one knows why. Most of the Italians who exhibit go on doing so year after year out of habit. There have also been one-man shows of Picasso, Braque, Miró, Ernst, Arp, Giacometti, Marini, Klee, Mondrian, Douanier Rousseau, as well as shows of the Fauves and the Futurists. Before 1948, only Picasso and Klee were known in Italy, apart from the Italian Futurists.

The Biennale is opened by the president of Italy, who comes in full pomp and regalia to inaugurate it, and the Venetian state boats of the past are brought out for the procession from the Prefettura, the prefect's palace, to the Public Gardens.

In 1948, after so many years of disuse, the pavilions were in a bad state and there was an awful lot of repairing going on up to the last minute. My pavilion was being done over by Scarpa, who was the most modern architect in Venice. Pallucchini, the secretary-general, was not at all conversant with modern art. He was a great student of the Italian Renaissance, and it must have been very difficult for him, as well as very brave, to do his task. When he gave a lecture in my pavilion he asked me to help him distinguish the various schools; he was even unfamiliar with the painters. Unfortunately I had to go to the dentist, but he claimed that he had managed without me.

Pallucchini was very strict and tyrannical. He reminded me of an Episcopalian minister. He would not allow me into the Gardens until my pavilion was finished. I was very upset, as everyone else in Venice who was interested in modern art seemed to be getting passes. Finally I was invited to come, and was taken all over by Pallucchini's aide-de-camp, a lovely man called Umbro Apollonio. I don't know how, but while talking to him I sensed that this was the first time in his life that he was doing a job that he enjoyed, and my recognition of the fact touched him so much that we immediately became friends. Like Pallucchini, he knew nothing about modern art. In Italy, the Surrealists, Brancusi, Arp, Giacometti, Pevsner and Malevich had never been heard of. If Santomaso was conversant with what was going on outside Italy, it was only because he had been to Paris in 1945. Also, he and Vedova had both seen copies of *Minotaur* and *Cahiers d'Art*, brought clandestinely into Italy.

In 1948 the foreign pavilions were, naturally, *à la page*. But some were still very much behind the Iron Curtain, I was allowed to hang my collection three days before the Biennale opened. Actually, I wanted to go to Ravenna with Dr. Sandberg, the director of the Stedelijk Museum in Amsterdam, who had already finished his work in the Dutch pavilion. But this was out of the question, so I buckled down to work. Fortunately I was given a free hand and a lot of efficient workmen, who did not mind my perpetual changes. We managed to get the show finished in time, and though it was terribly crowded it looked gay and attractive, all on white walls—so different from Kiesler's décor for Art of This Century.

The opening of the Biennale was very formal, but, as usual, I had no hat, stockings or gloves and was in quite a dilemma. I

borrowed stocking and a girdle from a friend, and instead of a hat
wore enormous marguerite-flowered earrings made out of Venetian glass beads. Count Elio Zorzi, the head of the press office and
the ambassador of the Biennale, who had actually extended to me
the Biennale invitation, gave me strict instructions that when
President Einaudi came to my pavilion I should try to explain to
him as much as I could about modern art in the five minutes he
would remain with me. I received exactly contrary orders from
Pallucchini, who said the president was lame and would be
terribly tired after visiting the whole Biennale, my pavilion being
his last effort.

When His Excellency arrived he greeted me by saying, "Where
is your collection?" I said, "Here," and he corrected himself and
asked where it had been before. I tried to obey Count Zorzi rather
than Pallucchini, and put in a few words, but luckily the
photographers intervened and the entire official party was photographed with Gonella, the minister of education, the president
and me under my lovely Calder mobile.

The same morning I had a visit from the American ambassador
and the consular staff. The United States pavilion was not open,
as the pictures had not arrived in time, and James Dunn, our
ambassador, was very pleased that at least I represented the
United States. Looking at one of my abstract Picassos, he seemed
rather happy to note that it was "almost normal."

The introduction to the Biennale catalogue for my show was
written by Professor Argan. It was very confusing, as he was all
mixed up about the different trends in modern art. Upon the
insistence of Bruno Alfieri, the owner of a bookshop, I had made a
little catalogue of my own to sell in my pavilion, although I was
included in the Biennale one. I wrote a short introduction for my
own catalogue, but it was so badly translated that I became quite
hysterical and even wept. I could not speak Italian well enough to
cope with the situation and begged Marga Barr, Alfred's wife,
who was half Italian, and who was then in Venice, to help me.
But the moment I chose was on board a vaporetto and she had to
get off before she could finish her task.

The two most unfortunate things that occurred at the Biennale
were the theft of a little piece of bronze from a David Hare
sculpture representing a baby; it must have been taken as a
souvenir. And the other was Pallucchini's decision (as some

priests were coming to visit my pavilion) to take down a very sexual Matta drawing of centaurs and nymphs. The drawing itself was so annoyed that it fell on the ground and the glass broke into smithereens, thus obviating its insulting removal.

A third catastrophe was avoided by Bruno Alfieri, who saved a dismantled Calder mobile from being thrown away by the workmen, who thought that it was bits of iron bands which had come off the packing cases.

My exhibition had enormous publicity and the pavilion was one of the most popular of the Biennale. I was terribly excited by all this, but what I enjoyed most was seeing the name of Guggenheim appearing on the maps in the Public Gardens next to the names of Great Britain, France, Holland, Austria, Switzerland, Poland, Palestine, Denmark, Belgium, Egypt, Czechoslovakia, Hungary, Romania. I felt as though I were a new European country.

My next illustrious visitor was Bernard Berenson. I greeted him as he came up my steps and told him how much I had studied his books and how much they had meant to me. His reply was, "Then why do you go in for this?" I knew beforehand how much he hated modern art and said, "I couldn't afford old masters, and anyhow I consider it one's duty to protect the art of one's time." He replied, "You should have come to me, my dear, I would have found you bargains." He liked best the works of Max Ernst and Pollock. Nevertheless, he said Max's were too sexual and that he did not like sex in art; the Pollocks, to him, were like tapestries. He was horrified by a little bronze Moore, a reclining figure of a woman, which he said was distorted.

The next time I saw Berenson was at I Tatti, his own home near Florence, and I was more polite to him than he had been to me as I admired his collection. I thought it very sad that so little was left of all the marvelous paintings that had passed through his hands. I begged him to visit me in Venice and promised to put sheets over all my paintings, if that would be an inducement for him to come. He asked me to whom I was going to leave my collection when I died, and though he was already eighty-five at that time, he looked at me with horror when I replied, "To you, Mr. Berenson."

As a result of all the publicity, I was plagued by everyone who wanted to sell me something and I couldn't come down into the lobby of the hotel where I was staying without being accosted by innumerable people. I asked Vittorio Carrain, a young friend, who was one of the owners of the Angelo restaurant, to protect me. As a result, he became my secretary and worked with me for years. He was intellectual, musical and very knowledgeable, and also served me as a key to the life of Venice, as I never read any newspapers. He loved the atmosphere I lived in and was exceedingly kind and a devoted friend, and a great help when we made exhibitions and catalogues.

I requested Ingeborg Eichmann, a Sudeten art historian, to give a lecture in my pavilion to explain the various trends in art. So many people came to the first lecture, on Cubism and abstract art, that we had to call off the second lecture, on Surrealism, in order to save the pictures from damage. They had all just been marvelously cleaned and refreshed by a Venetian painter called Celeghin, a charming man with enormous mustachios.

I used to go myself to the Biennale every few days and take my dogs with me. They were very well treated by a restaurant at the entrance called the Paradiso, and always given ice cream on their way in. Therefore whenever I asked them if they wished to accompany me to the Biennale, they wagged their tails and jumped with joy. They were the only dogs admitted to the exhibition, and when they were lost in this labyrinth I always found them in the Picasso exhibition; which proves how valuable their education had been at Art of This Century, where they had accompanied me every day.

At the end of the Biennale, the question arose of what to do with the pictures. I had taken it for granted that if the Biennale had brought them to Europe, paying all the expenses, at least they would be allowed to remain in Italy. But this was not the case. They had been brought in on a temporary permit and had to go out again. For several months I hesitated about what to do. I was expected to pay three per cent duty for importing them permanently into Italy. So I decided they would have to be taken out and brought back again at a lower valuation.

In the meantime the museum of Turin asked me to exhibit them there. I was delighted, but at the last minute, the day before the collection was to leave for Turin, the authorities of that city decided against showing anything so modern. A well known critic, Dr. Carlo Ragghianti, then asked me if I would show the collection in Florence, in the Strozzina, the cellar of the Strozzi Palace, which he was about to turn into a modern art gallery. He wanted to have my collection to inaugurate it, and made an excellent catalogue, which has been the basis ever since for my Italian one.

When I arrived in Florence I was shocked by the lack of space in the Strozzina and by some dreadful screens that resembled shower curtains, which had been set up to make more space. Dr. Ragghianti was very agreeable about removing these horrors, and accepted my proposal to give three different expositions. The first one was of Cubist and abstract art, the second Surrealist and the third dedicated to the young painters. This idea was very successful and permitted me to make three visits to Florence, all of which I enjoyed immensely, staying with my friend Roloff Beny. We had a very social life, and here I met a charming lady poetess from Dublin, New Hampshire, called Elise Cabbot. She was amazed by the number of my paintings shown in Florence and said, "How did Peggy ever have time to paint them all?"

After this, I was invited to exhibit in Milan in the Palazzo Reale. Here there was no space problem. I have never had so many rooms at my disposal before or since. This show was such a great success that the catalogues had to be hired out while new ones were being printed. Francesco Flora wrote the preface to the catalogue and the show was given for the benefit of the Associazione Artisti d'Italia, as a result of which all the debts of this association were paid off.

When the collection came back from Florence the problem again arose of what to do with it. I had reached no settlement with the authorities in Rome, though I had offered the whole collection to Venice on my death, if the Italian government would waive the duty they were claiming. But the old fogies in the Ministry of Foreign Affairs were adamant and would not let me off. The pictures in the meantime were housed in the Museum of Modern Art in Venice, the Cà Pesaro, a beautiful seventeenth-century building designed by Longhena, where Dr. Guido Perrocco, its curator, kept them for me. I was allowed to borrow a few at a time, but not too many.

A year after the Biennale exhibition Dr. Giulio Lorenzetti, the director of the Cà Pesaro, had asked me to make an American exhibition in two small rooms. Poor man, I am sure he was only doing his duty, as he must have hated modern art a thousand times more even than Pallucchini did.

At this same time, at the request of Michael Combe Martin, who was director of the British Institute, which was in the beautiful Palazzo Sagredo, I made a show of British painters there, so the pictures did manage to be seen.

The Palazzo Venier dei Leoni has the widest space of any palace on the Grand Canal, and at the back one of the largest gardens in Venice, with very old trees. Everyone stops in the street to look at the entrance gate, which Claire Falkenstein welded by hand and into which she inserted pieces of glass from Murano.

The view from
my roof

With Pevsner's
construction

With my Lhasa terriers and Alexander Calder's bedhead, 1956

With Vittorio Carrain, c. 1954

In my gondola

The two Sir Herberts
and Raoul Gregorich

With Edmondo Bacci
and Tancredi in my
garden

The celebration of my 80th birthday, August 26, 1978

Myself in the center hall of my palazzo, 1978. On the wall is Picasso's *Girls with a Toy Boat;* on the table is Giacometti's *Piazza* (or *The Square);* Calder's *Mobile* is hung overhead.

Myself in 1978

Chapter 19

Palazzo Venier dei Leoni

Finally, in 1949, Flavia Paulon, secretary of Count Zorzi, found me a lovely abode. It was an unfinished palace on the Grand Canal, started in 1748 by the Veniers, a famous Venetian family who had given two doges to Venice and who were alleged to have kept lions in their garden. The front of the palace bore eighteen lions' heads, which may be the reason for the name given to it: Venier dei Leoni. It stands opposite the Prefettura, the palace of the prefect of the Veneto.

The palace was all built in white stone and covered with vines; "All" is saying a lot, as the building never exceeded one floor, and in Venice is called the *"palazzo non compiuto,"* the "unfinished palace." It had the widest space of any palace on the Grand Canal, and also had the advantage of not being regarded as a national monument, which things are sacred in Venice and cannot be altered. It was therefore perfect for the pictures. At the front entrance there was a lovely courtyard with steps going down to the Grand Canal, and at the back one of the largest gardens in Venice, with very old trees. The top of the palace formed a flat roof, perfect for sunbathing. I naturally took advantage of this, but was rather worried about the reaction of the prefect, my *vis-à-*

vis. However, he merely said, "When I see Mrs. Guggenheim sunbathing on the roof, I know the spring has come."

Signora Paulon got her husband to do up the place for me. Actually, it was not in very bad shape, though it had changed tenants very often since 1938. Before that, in 1910, Luisa, Marchesa Casati, a poetess, had lived in one of the wings, giving fantastic Diaghilev parties and keeping leopards instead of lions in the garden. In 1938, the Viscountess Castlerosse bought the house and spent a fortune doing over what was then practically a ruin. (I believe the Marchesa Casati barely had a roof over her head.) Lady Castlerosse installed six marble bathrooms and beautiful mosaic floors. Her taste was not the same as mine, and I had to scrape off all the Liberty stucchi from the walls. After the first year Lady Castlerosse lent the palace to Douglas Fairbanks, Jr., and then three armies of occupation, German, British and American, lived in it in turn.

In the autumn of 1949, I made an exhibition of more or less recent sculpture in the garden, and Professor Giuseppe Marchíori, a well-known critic, wrote the introduction to the catalogue. We exhibited an Arp, a Brancusi, a Calder mobile, three Giacomettis, a Lipchitz, a Moore, a Pevsner, a David Hare, from my collection, and a Mirko, a Consagra, a Salvatore and two Vianis, which we borrowed from the artists. There was also a Marino Marini, which I bought from him in Milan. I went to borrow one for the sculpture show, but ended up by buying the only thing available. It was a statue of a horse and rider, the latter with his arms spread way out in ecstasy, and to emphasize this, Marini had added a phallus in full erection. But when he had it cast in bronze for me he had the phallus made separately, so that it could be screwed in and out at leisure. Marini placed the sculpture in my courtyard on the Grand Canal, opposite the Prefettura, and named it *The Angel of the Citadel*. Herbert Read said the statue was a challenge to the prefect. The best view of it was to be seen in profile from my sitting room window. Often, peeking through it, I watched the visitors' reaction to the statue.

When the nuns came to be blessed by the Patriarch, who on special holy days, went by my house in a motorboat, I detached the phallus of the horseman and hid it in a drawer. I also did this on certain days when I had to receive stuffy visitors, but occasionally I forgot, and when confronted with this phallus

Marino Marini, *The Angel of the Citadel*

found myself in great embarrassment. The only thing to do in such cases was to ignore it. In Venice a legend spread that I had several phalluses of different sizes, like spare parts, which I used on different occasions.

The sculpture show was supposed to be held in the garden, but because Viani had brought two works in plaster they had to be exhibited in the house. So many people came wandering into all our bedrooms that we had to cordon off the exhibition. I had a house guest, Philip Lasalle, staying with me at the time, who perpetually forgot that there was an exhibition and often found himself in the midst of strangers in his pajamas in the garden.

One of my Giacometti statues that I wanted to place in this show got stopped in the customs at Padua on its way from Milan. We went to fetch it in my open car. It was a beautiful thin figure without a head. We brought her back to Venice along the autostrada at great speed. Everyone who saw her must have thought she was a decapitated corpse. She was in very bad condition, so with the help of Pietro Consagra, a sculptor whom I knew, I got her back to her normal state and had her cast in bronze. But when the original one saw her new bronze sister, she was so scornful of her, and rightly so, as her own beauty far exceeded the other, that she remained intact ever since.

In 1950, I was asked if I would lend all my Pollocks (there were still twenty-three) to an art organization to give a show. They were supposed to get a room from the local authorities, but as they did not succeed, I came to their rescue and got old Dr. Lorenzetti to lend us the Sala Napoleonica in the Correr Museum, opposite San Marco cathedral. All that the organization did was to make a catalogue, for which I wrote an introduction and Bruno Alfieri a preface. When it came to fetching the pictures and hanging them, Vittorio Carrain and I had to do everything. The climax came when a terrible Greenwich Village-looking poster was put up, and when the catalogues gave out, they refused to print any more. I was so enraged that I took over the show, which really was mine, by all rights, and made a new catalogue, omitting Alfieri's article on Pollock. Thousands of people saw this exhibition, as it was in a room through which one had to pass in order to get into the Correr Museum. It was always lit at night, and I remember the extreme joy I had sitting in the Piazza San Marco beholding the Pollocks glowing through the open windows of the museum, and then going out on the balcony of the gallery to see San Marco in front of me, knowing that the Pollocks were behind me. It seemed to place Pollock historically where he belonged as one of the greatest painters of our time, who had every right to be exhibited in this wonderful setting. All the young painters were very much influenced by this show.

A Giacometti statue in my open car

Encouraged by the Pollock exhibition, I got Dr. Lorenzetti to lend me the Sala degli Specchi in the Palazzo Giustinian, the headquarters of the Biennale, for an exhibition I wanted to give Jean Hélion, my son-in-law. Everything went wrong from beginning to end. It was an ill-fated show. First of all, Christian Zervos, who edits *Cahiers d'Art,* took ages to write the introduction to the catalogue. When it arrived, it was much too long and I had to cut it and have it translated, and then Hélion was displeased by my cutting it. The pictures got stuck in the customs, as always happens in Italy, and we nearly had to call the show off. Finally, Vittorio Carrain overcame all these difficulties, only to find new ones creeping up. Two days before the show was to open, the brocade that covered the walls of the Sala degli Specchi was removed by the person who owned it, and we were forced to replace it with some sacking. Then, as though the gods were against us, a terrible storm came and rain dripped from the crimson banner we had placed in the street to announce the show and ruined the dress of a girl passing beneath it. After that, the wind blew down the banner altogether. It really was a triumph that we held the exhibition at all.

Hélion showed three periods of his work, his early naturalistic paintings, his abstract period, and his new period, which began in 1943, portraying men with umbrellas, nudes, men with news-papers, and *natures mortes* with bread. People were very much interested to see these various transitions and how he was getting around to complete realism, which he now does.

As a result of all our troubles in connection with this show, I decided never again to do anything with works from abroad, or ever again to ask the authorities for a gallery. My own troubles with the customs had not been solved, and Dr. Sandberg, of the Stedelijk museum, suggested taking my collection to Amsterdam for an exhibition, and then sending it on to the Brussels Palais des Beaux-Arts and to the Zurich Kunsthaus, thus giving me a proper excuse to reintroduce it into Italy. This was done very suc-cessfully. After the three shows, the pictures were brought back from Zurich and finally I was allowed to pay the least possible amount of duty.

I was so happy to have my collection back again, and at last to be able to hang it in my palazzo; but the next problem was one of space. I got three architects in Milan, Belgioioso, Peressutti and Rogers, to draw up plans to make a penthouse on my roof. They were very much under the influence of Le Corbusier, and thought of an arrangement that reminded one of him, namely a two-story gallery elevated from my roof on pillars twenty feet high. The front was to resemble the Doge's Palace, and in their minds they conceived something that they thought would be a link between the past and the present. I found it very ugly and I was certain the Belle Arti of Venice, the authority that controls all rebuilding in the city, would never have allowed it to be built. It would have cost sixty thousand dollars, only a bit less than I paid for the whole *palazzo,* and I could not afford it. In fact, I was only able to buy the *palazzo* because Bernard Reis broke one of my trusts for me. Peressutti was terribly disappointed, and asked me if I could not sell a picture in order to find the money. Had I liked the scheme, and had prices been what they are today. I could easily have parted with one painting to have built this museum.

Finally, in order to create space, I began turning all the downstairs rooms, where the servants lived and the laundry was done, into galleries. Some of these rooms had been used as studios, which I had lent to various artists. Matta helped me transform the enormous laundry into a beautiful gallery, and then one by one the other rooms followed suit, till finally the servants got pushed into smaller quarters and the laundry had to be done in a basin at the entrance to the waterfront.

Since 1952, I had been sponsoring a young Italian painter from Feltre, whom Bill Congdon had asked me to help. His name was Tancredi Parmeggiani, but he used only his Christian name, dropping the one that so much resembled the cheese. I promised him seventy-five dollars a month in exchange for two gouaches. His first ones were very geometrical and resembled Theo van Doesburg's (which greatly pleased Nellie, his widow), but gradually he evoked a Pollock style, and then finally his own. He was what is called in Italy a *spazialista,* a spatial artist. His gouaches soon filled my house. They were so delicate and airy, and were very easy to sell after the first year, when I had given them away as presents. As there was no room other than a guest room to show and sell them in, they had to be piled up on a bed. When James Sweeney came to Venice and saw them, he at once said, "Get that boy canvas and paints and let him expand, he needs space." I did as I was told, and then my spatial problem grew to such an extent that I no longer knew where to show the canvases. Tancredi had one of the studios in the cellar for several years, but it was a great relief when he finally left, as he used to drive the servants crazy by walking all over the house with his feet covered in paint of every conceivable color. When at last he left, it took four days to remove this mess from the floor of his studio. This room has now become a Pollock museum, and for a time Tancredi's paintings were sold in the room that used to be the laundry.

My second protégé was Edmondo Bacci, a very lyrical painter in his mid-forties, whose work was inspired by Kandinsky. He had a very organized way of life and with him everything went calmly and successfully. Tancredi, on the other hand, who was in his early thirties, was madly temperamental and perpetually made rows. Often he removed all his paintings, only to bring them back in a few days. As I gave him the money (keeping no commission other than the pictures he gave me, which in turn I gave to museums) he threw it all away, only to come back for more. When I tried to give him a weekly allowance he went around Venice saying he would sue me for having ruined his career. Bacci and Tancredi were the two painters in Italy whose works gave me most pleasure, and I had my private apartments filled with them. I also admire Vedova's work and own two of his paintings.

Apart from this, and opening my house to the public three afternoons a week, I have not done much in Italy. Santomaso was madly disappointed, as he thought I was about to become a new dynamic and cultural center for Italian art. But I was so uninspired by what I found in Italy that little by little I lost interest. The painting in the Biennale gets worse every year. Everybody just copies the people who did interesting things forty years ago, and so it goes on down the line, getting more and more stereotyped and more and more boring. I have continued buying whenever possible, but infinitely prefer contemporary sculpture to painting.

Since my collection has been opened to the public, people come from all over the world to see it, and as I also hold a salon for intellectuals, a great confusion arises. Anyone is welcome to visit the gallery on public days, but some people, not understanding this, think that I should be included as a sight. I get phone calls from many persons whom I do not know, who begin by saying, "You don't know me, but I once met your sister Hazel in California." or "Your friend Paul Bowles told me to phone you," or "We have just arrived in Venice and have a letter of introduction to you, and would like to invite you to lunch or dinner or a drink." On one occasion a young American, in Italy on a Guggenheim musical fellowship, even wrote and asked if I had a piano, as he would like to come and practice on it. I was happy to be able to say I hadn't got one. I would never dare phone a stranger on such flimsy pretenses. If I had a letter of introduction,

I would send it round and wait to be invited. People don't know how to behave any more. Oh, for the good old days, when they still had manners!

My salon is most informal, provided you have been invited, but my museum days are strictly for art lovers. All my personal guests are requested to write in my guest-book, and if they are poets or artists they may add a poem or a drawing, which is more than welcome.

When Mrs. Clare Boothe Luce, whom I had met occasionally at consular parties, was the U.S. ambassador in Italy, I invited her to come and see my collection, which she did very late one night, followed by a train of people. I felt that none of them were much interested in art, but Mrs. Luce, as usual, was very polite and charming, and of course marvelously dressed, looking younger and more glamorous than ever. She seemed to like best my daughter Pegeen's paintings, though when I made the observation that the people in Pegeen's paintings, strangely enough, never seem to be engaged in any conversation with each other, all going their own ways, Mrs. Luce replied, "Maybe they have nothing to say." When Mrs. Luce went into my dining room she encountered three young Italian painters, Dova, Tancredi and Crippa. In her true ambassadorial manner, she asked them whom they considered the best painter in Italy. Each of the three at once answered, "I."

Mrs. Luce complained that my corridors were not sufficiently lit to view the paintings properly. I must admit she was quite right, and I afterward installed strong fluorescent lights for which idea I am very grateful to Mrs. Luce. This suggestion gave me occasion to make a good Italian pun, as "la Luce" (as Mrs. Luce was called in Italy) thus brought *"la luce"* to my house, *"luce"* in Italian meaning light.

Count Zorzi, who ran the Biennale review, and who now, to my sorrow, is dead, was one of the few remaining grand seigneurs of Venice. He was, quite fittingly, the descendent of a doge, and one of the few people in Venice with elegant manners and a sense of humor. The Biennale always consulted him about protocol. But that wasn't the only thing he knew about. He ran their bimonthly review extremely well, and always encouraged me to write for it. He wanted an article on Pollock, but I never felt up to it. But I did write one, which he also asked for, about how I became a collector. Then I wrote one on my painter-daughter, Pegeen, and one on Bill Congdon. In this article I claimed that he was the first painter since Turner who had understood the soul of Venice, and in the article on Pegeen I expounded Herbert Read's theory that she remained as fresh and pure in her painting, and still brought the same magical, innocent touch to her work, as she did at the age of eleven.

In the article on how I started to be a collector, I related a story about a woman who went around an art show grumbling bitterly all the time. I approached her and asked why she bothered to come and look at painting that seemed so much to displease her. She replied that she wished to learn what modern art was all about. I warned her how dangerous it was to do so, as she might become an addict.

After my show at the Biennale, they were perpetually asking me to lend them pictures for their successive exhibitions. In the beginning I complied with their requests, but later there were so many demands from everyone that when my house was opened to the public it became impossible to lend any more. Pallucchini took offense at this and wrote me a very unpleasant letter, scolding me and telling me how ungrateful I was for all the Biennale had done for me. I wrote back and said, on the contrary, they should be grateful to me for having lent them my collection, which turned out to be the most popular show in the Biennale of 1948, and that therefore we were quits. He was so infuriated by this that he had my name withdrawn from the list of people who were invited to the opening of the Biennale, and in 1952 I had to accept Santomaso's kind offer of his invitation in order to get into the opening.

When Count Zorzi died, Pallucchini wrote a beautiful obituary in the Biennale magazine. I was so moved by this that I felt it incumbent upon me to write to Pallucchini telling him so, and thanking him. This brought about our reconciliation, and my name was put back on the invitation list.

At one time I considered buying the United States pavilion at the Biennale, which belonged to the Grand Central Art Galleries, who wished to part with it for about twenty thousand dollars. But I felt it would have been an awful responsibility, and also one that I could not afford. It would have meant going to New York every two years to choose the shows, and then incurring all the expense of transport and insurance. It obviously was a museum's job, if not a government one. All the other foreign pavilions of the Biennale are under the auspices of organizations sponsored or supported by their governments. But we in the United States had no government subsidy for the Biennale. Luckily, in 1954, the Museum of Modern Art bought the pavilion, which was more fitting.

In 1950, Alfred Frankfurter, editor of *Art News,* arranged an American show in this pavilion, in which Pollock was represented by three paintings. By far the best in the whole Biennale was one of his called *N I 1948,* owned by the Museum of Modern Art. This magnificent painting, which several years later was one of the few to suffer in the museum fire, stood out beyond everything in the whole Biennale, even though there were shows of the Douanier Rousseau, Matisse and Kandinsky. I remember at the time my infinite surprise at having been convinced of this fact, because it was always difficult for me to accept Pollock's greatness.

In 1950 also, the Biennale made a very small mixed sculpture exhibition in a ridiculously inadequate space, not in the main hall of the Italian pavilion, where it should have been held, but in an outside one. The exhibitors were Arp, Zadkine and Laurens. Giacometti refused to exhibit because Laurens had such a bad *salle.* Arp had been warned that he was very badly shown, and when he arrived in the central hall, where there was a Viani show, he said with joy, "Oh, I haven't such a bad place at all."

In 1954 Arp had a beautiful show at the Biennale. So did Max Ernst. They each received the most important prize. On this occasion Max came to my home and wrote in my guest-book: "An old friend is come back forever and ever and ever." And so finally peace was made.

The prizes given at the Biennale always cause great excitement. A lot of politics are involved and no one is ever pleased. The four most important prizes, two for painting and two for sculpture, are given by the Presidenza del Consiglio dei Ministri, which gives two for two million lire each, and by the Commune of Venice, which gives two for one million five hundred thousand lire each. Innumerable other small prizes are given by all sorts of people and business firms, not only in Venice but all over Italy. Among these there is one given by the Angelo restaurant, which belongs to my ex-secretary, Vittorio Carrain. The Angelo is much frequented by artists and the walls are covered witn contemporary paintings, an idea started by Vittorio's brother, Renato, who died in a car accident. He also catered for rugby players as well as artists, and it was very odd to see these two completely different elements equally at home in this restaurant, which serves delicious food and where I ate daily for years before I found my *palazzo*.

In 1956, the Museum of Modern Art lent their Biennale pavilion to the Chicago Art Institute, and Katharine Kuh, who was then a curator of the Institute, made an exhibition called "The American Painters and the City." Katharine came to my house to buy a Bacci, and was very much impressed with my two maids, whom she called my curators, who helped drag enormous canvases in and out. These two Italian country girls acted as hostesses on Mondays, Wednesdays and Fridays, the days on which my house is open to the public. I usually hide on these occasions. Afterward, they often related to me what had happened during the course of the afternoon. Once they told me with great horror that a Cubist Braque had been pointed out to a group of students as a Picasso. I said, "Why didn't you correct this?" and they replied, "Oh no, we couldn't, because it was a professor." Besides making my maids into curators, I also taught my two gondoliers to be expert picture hangers.

One day, in 1948, when I was walking through the Campo Manin, I noticed a very exciting painting in the window of a little art gallery. My first reaction was to take it for a Pollock. I went in and met the artist, who turned out to be Alan Davie, a tall Scotsman with a red beard. He had a blonde, equally Scottish wife called Billie. I bought a painting at once and we became great friends. Later his father, a clergyman, wrote me the sweetest letter, thanking me for the interest I took in his son. Alan Davie developed his own style very quickly, and though his work was not bought by anyone except me for years, he is one of the best British painters. Now, like everyone else as good, he has finally been recognized in England and New York, where he has been a great success, though for years he had to support his wife and baby by making jewelry.

In 1950 I met Dr. Eugene Colp, the curator of the museum of Tel Aviv. He asked me to lend him a large number of pictures to show there. At that time, my basement was stacked with the overflow of my collection, and as the cellar was very damp, I began giving away pictures, including Pollocks, in all directions, which, as I have already said, I now very much regret. My friend Bernard Reis said that instead of lending Dr. Colp the pictures I should give them to him, so I gave him thirty-four, and later some more. Dr. Colp was very much infatuated by me, and one day when he asked me what there was between us I replied, "Nothing, except thirty-four paintings."

My cellar was also stacked with all the paintings I had bought during Art of This Century shows, such as those of Baziotes, Motherwell, Still, Virginia Admiral, Pousette-Dart, Laurence Vail, Pegeen, Kenneth Scott, Janet Sobel, Rothko, Hirshfield and Gorky. In 1953, Walter Shaw and Jean Guerin, old friends of mine, who lived in Bordighera, asked me to lend them all these paintings to make an American show there. It was under the auspices of the Commune, and therefore rather official. Cocteau wrote the introduction to the catalogue. I accepted, and went there with Laurence Vail and a friend of mine called Raoul. The luncheon that Walter and Jean gave for Cocteau and for us was very amusing, but the long-drawn-out official dinner party bored Raoul, and he left as soon as it was over. To my surprise, we were all three the guests of the city of Bordighera and were given three lovely rooms in a hotel. Raoul, who was interested only in motor cars (in one of which he was so soon after to meet his untimely death) never took much interest in art, but he was, as Herbert Read called him, quite a "philosopher." Raoul always maintained that I would go down in history, which statement, though quite exaggerated, I found very touching.

I had a dog named Sir Herbert, after Mr. Read (as he then was), though the dog was knighted by me long before Herbert. When I phoned Raoul to tell him about the real Herbert Read's knighthood he said, "Do you mean the dog?" The same thing always happened in my home when Sir Herbert was my guest. The servants invariably asked, "Do you mean the dog or the man?"

After I left New York, Pollock had a very unsuccessful show at Betty Parsons' gallery. A few months later my contract with Pollock expired, and he remained with Betty without a contract until 1952, when he went to Sidney Janis's gallery. Not being in New York, I had no idea what was happening, but soon I began to realize that little by little everything I had done for Pollock was being either minimized or completely forgotten. Catalogues and articles began to appear, ignoring me or speaking of me in inadequate terms, as in the case of Sam Hunter, later curator of the Minneapolis Museum, who referred to me in his introduction to a traveling Pollock show as Pollock's "first dealer." In the São Paulo catalogue and in the New York catalogue of the Museum of Modern Art, Sweeney's introduction to my first Pollock show was attributed to my uncle's museum (where I knew Pollock had merely worked as a carpenter). In the biographies in the São Paulo catalogue I was completely ignored. Everyone gave credit to the Fachetti studio in Paris for Pollock's first European show, ignoring the ones that were held in Venice by me, and one in Milan, for which I had lent my pictures. Worst of all was an article that appeared in *Time* magazine, accusing Pollock of having followed up his success at the Biennale by coming to Europe to further his career by showing in the Correr Museum in Venice, and in Milan. Pollock was furious and wrote a letter to deny this, saying he had never left the United States. My name was not mentioned in the article, nor in Pollock's reply, and my great friend Truman Capote, who was very indignant, said someone should have written another letter with the true facts, but no one did. I complained to Alfred Barr and to Sam Hunter, and Barr did his best to straighten things out, but I was taking no chances, and when Pollock's pictures were shown in Rome, I was very careful to write all the facts to Giovanni Carandente, assistant to the museum director. At least in Italy I wished to have things straight.

In 1956 Rudi Blesh, who had exhibited his paintings in Art of This Century, wrote a book about modern art called *Modern Art U.S.A.* He knew all about my gallery and wrote the truth as he saw it, and as it was. I believe this made the book very unpopular among those who were pretending to have discovered Pollock. Some of the facts I referred to occurred before Pollock's death and gave me reason to believe that Pollock had been very ungrateful, so when in the summer of 1956 Lee Pollock arrived in France and phoned to ask if I would find her a room in Venice, I said that Venice was absolutely full up. A few days later, I received a cable from Clement Greenberg telling me to break the news of Pollock's death in a car accident to Lee Pollock, who was supposed to have been with me. Imagine how I felt. Maybe it would have been a fitting end to the Pollock cycle if Lee and I had been together at this moment. But we were not, and that is why.

Actually, when I went to Rome for the Pollock show in the Museum of Modern Art in 1958, I was terribly moved, seeing all the early enormous canvases that for years I had dragged in and out and encouraged, if not forced, people to buy. It certainly had been the most interesting and important time of my life, since 1934, and I think by far my most honorable achievement.

At this point I must go back to certain events that occurred in 1948, in order to lead up to the Museum of Modern Art in Rome. After I accepted Count Zorzi's invitation to the Biennale, I went to Capri for the winter. In the spring, Italy was to have a general election, and everyone was terrified that it would go Communist and that Tito would immediately walk into Italy. The atmosphere in Capri was very hysterical and some of my friends made me so nervous that I began to regret my promise to the Biennale. I thought the collection was safer in storage in New York. However, I decided to consult the head of the United States Information Service (USIS) in Naples. He sent me on to Rome to Dr. Morey, who was the cultural attaché at the United States Embassy. What a charming and distinguished man he was! He immediately reassured me so much (being convinced himself that Italy would not go Communist) that I decided to let the Biennale have my pictures. Not only that, he also sent me to Dr. Palma Bucarelli, the director of the Museum of Modern Art in Rome, to arrange to show my collection there, under the auspices of the United States government, after the Biennale. Dr. Palma Bucarelli accepted with joy, as the United States was to pay all the expenses. Unfortunately when the time came the government had withdrawn a greater part of the funds from the new budget of USIS, and the project had to be relinquished.

Dr. Palma Bucarelli was a very beautiful woman. She had an aquiline nose, wavy chestnut hair, mauve eyes with superbly long eyelashes, and very white skin. She was petite and slim and very elegantly dressed, and had known many Fascists, thus acquiring this wonderful position. She knew nothing about modern art, but she worked very hard in later years to make her dreadful morgue of a museum give good exhibitions and buy pictures. She held Mondrian, Modigliani, Malevich, Kandinsky and Pollock shows, besides one of my uncle's collection. She did behave a little bit as though she had discovered modern art, but she must be excused as, with her assistant Carandente, she really did wonders for Italy.

My most famous house guests were Giacometti and Truman Capote. Giacometti, when he married Annette, came to spend his honeymoon in my house. Nancy Cunard was in Venice at that time and often came to visit me. Giacometti said she resembled a marvelous race horse. At that time or later Giacometti offered me his six Venetian statues for a million French francs. Of course I accepted. However I never got them, though he thought, being Venetian, they belonged in my collection. I think his dealer, Pierre Matisse, must have objected.

Truman Capote I first met in my entrance hall. A little man in carpet slippers huffling around. We became very good friends and later he spent two months as my house guest writing *The Muses Are Heard.* He was very keen on keeping his line and made me diet also. Every night he took me to Harry's Bar and made me eat fish. He only allowed me a very light lunch of eggs. He is always madly amusing and I loved having him stay with me.

Chapter 20

Ceylon, India and Venice Again

In the fall of 1954, after Raoul's death, I decided to get out of Italy and try to think of something else. Paul Bowles had invited me to Ceylon, where he had bought a little island. It was fantastically beautiful and luxuriant, with every conceivable flower and exotic plant from the east. The house resembled the Taj Mahal, as it was built in octagonal form. We all lived there together in separate rooms divided by curtains, we being Paul, his wife Jane, Ahmed, a young Arab primitive painter of great talent, and an Arab chauffeur, who seemed rather sad without the Jaguar car, which had been left behind in Tangiers, Paul's other home.

In order to get to the island one had to pick up one's skirts and wade through the Indian Ocean. There was no bridge or boat. The waves usually wet one's bottom, even though the distance one walked could be done in one minute and a half. It was terribly unpleasant to go about all day with a wet bottom, but there was no other way. The beauty of the surroundings made up for all the inconveniences, which were many. There was no water on the island and the servants had to carry it over on their heads. This made bathing, apart from sea-bathing, virtually impossible. But there was a raft just below the house and the swimming was superb. The beach opposite was skirted with coconut palms, and there were narrow fishing craft with beautiful Singhalese fishermen riding them astride. It was another dream world, so different from Venice.

As Ceylon was such a small island, I was received with enthusiasm and written up in the papers as a great art authority and asked to broadcast. I was even consulted by the wife of the chief of police, who begged me to tell her if her twelve-year-old son should be encouraged to paint. His father very much disapproved of his artistic child's pursuits, which were fostered by the adoring mother. Actually, the child was an infant prodigy, and I had to admit it to the father, with the reservation that often children who began painting well lose all their freshness when they grow up.

Reading from my diary I find the following entry:"Yesterday I was invited to go and see the paintings of a child genius, son of the chief of police. His father does not want him to paint, except as a hobby, the mother is fostering the child's genius. An angelic little creature of twelve, who showed me all his pets, dogs, puppies and white mice. His paintings are as mature as a man of twenty-five. He has an extraordinary talent amounting to genius. His style is not formed, sometimes it resembles Matisse or Bonnard, but he has great force and sense of color and design. A direct, simple and pure approach, and at the same time quite sophisticated. His mother was a beautifully dressed little elegant Singhalese, with oriental jewelry and wearing an occidentalized sari. The house was a little gem, all opening on to lovely cinnamon gardens. My infant prodigy had exquisite hands. He showed me all his art books, Egyptian, Japanese, Dufy, Picasso, etc. The child had wonderful taste and perception in pointing out details. The mother spends all her money on his paints and art books.

"There was another infant prodigy, a cellist, a protégé of Casals. He belonged to a very distinguished family and his uncle, Darangale, is one of the best painters of Ceylon, but I fear too much influenced by Tchelichef. This infant prodigy was much older, about sixteen, and already well known as a cellist. He also had an adoring mother, who lived only to further his career. But she seemed as worried as the wife of the chief of police. Neither of these ladies seemed to be entirely convinced that they were doing the right thing."

After five weeks in Ceylon, I set off alone for India. My trip was planned by Thakore Saheb, the Indian ambassador in Colombo. He had formerly been in Washington and was married to the sister of the Maharajah of Mysore. He must have had a very exaggerated idea about the speed of American travelers, which I grant can be rather racy, as the itinerary he prepared for me would have killed a far stronger person than I was. I had to cut out about half of it, though I managed to visit over twenty cities in forty-eight days. In Colombo I was told by a journalist not to miss the paintings of Jaminy Roy, in Calcutta. When I got to Mysore, where I went to visit the maharajah, I went to the art museum. Faced with a painting that resembled a Brauner, my mind began to wander and I tried to remember the name of the painter whom I was supposed to look up in Calcutta. I was very upset because I did not succeed. I thought I must send a wire to the person in Colombo who had told me about him. Suddenly I looked up at the painting I was standing in front of, and realized that it was a Jaminy Roy.

When I got to Calcutta the publicity agent of the West Bengal government, to whom I had a letter of introduction from the Indian ambassador, took me, upon my request, to visit Jaminy Roy, to whom he presented me as an art critic. In my diary I find the following entry: "Went to visit Jaminy Roy, a saintly man of sixty. Lives in a beautiful white modern house, where he shows his paintings. They are all mythological subjects, even the Christian ones. He has exhibited in New York and London, but has never left India."

Jaminy Roy painted a lot on a woven papyrus, but I bought a picture for seventy-five rupees which was on paper, as it was easier to pack. The picture depicts the abduction of Siva by Ravana. The demon King Jataya wanted to stop Ravana, a fight ensued and Jataya, the valiant bird, was killed. This is an episode from the Ramayana, the great Hindu mythology. Jaminy Roy had copied a few European painters from reproductions. One was Campigli and another was Van Gogh. His own work resembled Victor Brauner's, except that all his eyes are shaped like little boats or almonds. He had a primitive quality, like the Arab Ahmed. He did not approve of three-dimensional painting. His was quite flat. I felt he was a wise man and quite unspoilt.

When I got to New Delhi, exhausted by all my travels, trying to keep up with the itinerary of Thakore Saheb, I was rescued by Paxton Haddow, a lovely girl in the American Embassy, who worked for USIS. She invited me to live with her in a beautiful house, and thus for a while I forgot I was a tourist.

Pax drove me to Chandigarh, a city which took the place of Lahore, the former capital of the Punjab, which belongs to Pakistan, since the division of India. The following entry is in my diary: "Went . . . to Chandigarh, where we arrived a few hours after the Prime Minister had held the official opening of the supreme court, the masterpiece of Le Corbusier, a very fine monument, much resembling his apartment house in Marseilles, but of course much less domestic. The whole town of Chandigarh, laid out by Le Corbusier, is an amazing example of modern town planning, all built within his theory of Man's proportions. The head, the body, the arms must all be represented approximately. It was amazing to see Chandigarh after seeing Fatehpur-Sikri, the dead city near Agra. There are twenty-six sectors in all, with huge highways for fast traffic and roads for pedestrians . . . Few sectors are finished, but those which are contain houses all alike, in straight rows, to be rented by government officials at ten per cent of their salaries. So everybody knows by your house-rent what your salary is. All the people who are judges live in one row, etc., down to the coolies, who have their own houses. As a venture, this is stupendous, but the other buildings, designed by Maxwell Fry and Jane Drew, are not so nice. Le Corbusier designed some of the official buildings, engineering college, schools (each sector is to have one), hospital, printing office, etc. There are few trees, and the whole effect so far is very desert-like and monotonous. In ten or twenty years it will be interesting to see. Now, everything is makeshift, the schools being used for assembly halls, local dispensaries for hospitals, etc.

"A very charming woman, wife of a judge, accompanied us, and though she knew much less than Pax, who had been there once before, she knew more of the practical side of living in Chandigarh. She had chosen a house that she already regretted, as a huge building was going up opposite, though she had especially chosen the house for its privacy. She lamented her dining-room, which served as a corridor. There was no portico over the entrance to protect her from the rain, which is devastating in Chandigarh. Her garage was behind the house, as were the servant's quarters; all very bad for the monsoon time, which causes floods. Her house, being one of the first to be built, was already out of date. The new ones had benefited by all the mistakes made in building the others, and were much nicer, as we saw for ourselves. '

"We stayed in a Le Corbusier hotel. It was quite comfortable. Le Corbusier had made lattice-work cement walls everywhere to keep out the sun and let in the wind. This idea, though seemingly his invention, is an old Indian custom, so everyone is happy. The city is not beautiful, and never will be, because the houses are too regular, similar and uninspired. Anyhow, the idea is to raise the standard of living of the poor. It is quite socialistic. We saw one cinema in one sector that is finished. This sector resembled a town in the United States . . . The whole enterprise must give great satisfaction to Le Corbusier, who is the only person in the whole world ever entrusted with such a commission. In his office there is a plan on the wall, which you are supposed to view before you see the town. The workmen of Chandigarh have been honored by having the streets lined with poles bearing the colorful bowls which carry earth and cement, the symbols of their work. The worst houses looked like women's knitting or embroidery. There were one or two rows of very handsome houses, but nothing really wonderful or stately. However, the enterprise was not supposed to be anything else. Too bad. It could have been much better, even within these limits."

Modern art in India was very disappointing, as it was in Ceylon, where George Keytes was considered the best modern painter. He decorated temples in semi-realistic style with Buddhist myths as subjects. I could find nothing to buy besides my Jaminy Roy, except one very lovely primitive painting I saw in an all-Indian show in New Delhi. This depicted a village scene of peasants seated at night around a table. It had tremendous atmosphere and, though it was not at all realistic, gave one a great sense of Indian life. I wished to buy it, but when Pax went with the money she was just too late, as Nehru had given it as a present to Nasser.

What I lost in painting I made up for in earrings, coming home with a great many bought all over India, and even some from Tibet. These I found in Darjeeling, where I went to look for Lhasa terriers, endeavoring to put an end to the inbreeding of my numerous dog family. I went to visit Tenzing Norkay, the sherpa who climbed Mount Everest with Hillary. Tenzing had six Lhasas who walked with him daily in the Himalayas, but he would not part with any of them.

Princess Pignatelli once said to me, "If you would only throw all those awful pictures into the Grand Canal, you would have the most beautiful house in Venice." And so it was considered. But no Venetian approved of my modern décor. However, I had to have a suitable modern décor for the collection, which was exhibited all over the house for lack of space. In place of a Venetian glass chandelier, I hung a Calder mobile, made out of broken glass and china that might have come out of a garbage pail. I had sofas and chairs covered in white plastic that could be washed every morning, as my large family of dogs felt most at home in the best seats. (My two darling Lhasa terriers had mated with a gentleman dog specially brought for this purpose from America by Mrs. Bernard Reis, and had produced fifty-seven puppies in my home. About six usually remained in residence.) Over the sofas I placed black-and-white striped fur rugs, which the dogs adored to lick. This was also un-Venetian.

Most Venetian, and at the same time un-Venetian, is a *forcole*, or gondolier's oar-rest, which Alfred Barr presented me with for my garden. Those who don't know what it is admire it as a wonderful piece of modern sculpture, which is just what Alfred intended.

Originally the entire house was open to the public on museum days. My poor guests—how they suffered! I remember once the painter Matta locking himself up in his room in order to take a siesta. The lock was so seldom used that we had to get a locksmith to release him. I did not even have the privacy of my own bedroom, as it contained my Calder bed, which, strangely enough, against my turquoise walls looked as though it had been made for its ultimate destination—Venice. There is also a painting by Francis Bacon, the only one of his I have ever seen that didn't frighten me. It depicts a very sympathetic ape seated on a chest, guarding a treasure; the background is all done in fuchsia-colored pastel, which goes admirably with my turquoise walls, and with a curtain made out of an Indian sari and a marabou bedcover of the same color. The rest of the walls are decorated by my collection of earrings, a hundred pairs or more, collected from all over the world. In addition to this, the room has Venetian mirrors and Laurence Vail's decorated bottles and Cornell's Surrealist "objects." Everything combined makes a fantastic atmosphere.

It was difficult to exclude the public from all this, but in the end I had to. Now, only friends, or visitors who specially ask to see it, are allowed to. My dining room, hung with Cubist paintings, has to be open to the public. This room has fifteenth-century Venetian furniture which I bought in Venice years ago, and brought back to its original home, after having lived with it in the South of France, Paris and Sussex, my previous homes. The Cubist pictures look admirable with the old furniture.

When all the spatial possibilities of the *palazzo* were exhausted I decided to build a pavilion in the garden. At least there was plenty of room. Next came the tree problem. In Venice no one is allowed to cut down trees, not even their own. I therefore decided to build along a wall which I shared with my neighbors, the American Consulate, the State Department having bought this property a few years previously. (This turned out to be a blessing in disguise, as I was guarded by soldiers night and day for many years thereafter.) This was the only part of the garden where there were no trees. I now required the permission of the State Department. It seemed very odd, living in Italy, to need this. However, it was no problem. Permission was soon granted. After that, I had to have the permission of the Belle Arti. My architect submitted our plans to the Commune of Venice who, thinking they were pleasing the American consul, never presented the plans, but hid them in a drawer and hung me up all winter. In the end I had to write to the mayor of Venice to have them released. Finally the commission of the Belle Arti came to inspect my garden and passed the project.

During this time I had changed my plans several times. At first, I had wished to build a pavilion that would have resembled a painting by Giorgio de Chirico, called *Melancholy and Mystery of a Street,* but Vittorio Carrain warned me that my building with all its arches might turn out to look too Fascist. My friend Martyn Coleman, who always gave me the best advice in matters of taste, told me to make a loggia outside the building. I copied as closely as possible the wing of the Palladian villa Emo at Fanzole. However, my loggia had to be much smaller, as there was room for only six arches, instead of eleven. The Belle Arti consented to this plan, with the exception of one vital point: a lady architect called Renata Trincanato insisted on preserving intact a little lost corner of the garden and would not allow this very necessary space to be used. Therefore I could not join up the new wing with my house, which I should have done in order to make a real *barchessa* (as such wings were called in Veneto, where they were and still are used for storing grain and hay). So my architect, Vincenzo Passero, had to modify the plans. There was no time to waste. The Biennale was to open in two months, and my *barchessa* had to be finished by then.

The opening of the Biennale is of great importance in Venice. The entire art world comes for a week—not only all the organizers of the different exhibitions, and the architects of the new pavilions, but all the artists who are invited, or failing that, the ones who can afford to, as well as many others. It is a big fair, and a tremendous amount of salesmanship goes on. All the art critics come too, and all the gallery owners who have any exhibition on. As I am a collector, and as I made a point, as long as I could, of buying something at the Biennale, everyone focuses their attention on me. Also the art collectors come, and all this means innumerable parties continuously for a whole week. I usually give a very big cocktail party in my garden, so the *barchessa* had to be finished in time, and it was. But not only had the *barchessa* to be finished, but the whole garden, which I had let grow wild for ten years, had to be put in order. However, this was finally accomplished too, and the garden looked larger than before, which surprised everyone. In the *barchessa* I made an exhibition of all the younger artists' work that I had bought in the last few years. It really looked lovely, and I called it "my Biennale."

In the fall the builder, against the wishes of the architect, took matters in his own hands and said we could finish the *barchessa* as it had been originally planned without getting the permission of the Belle Arti. We persuaded the architect to proceed, and then disregarding Renata Trincanato's admonition, built the second half of the pavilion, which was much prettier than the first, on her sacred spot, leaving just a fragment of the garden in the very background. This time we connected the *barchessa* with the *palazzo,* and it was an immense improvement.

The workmen had been very nice all the time they worked in

the garden, in spite of the fact that they had completely upset our life. We were in perpetual danger of falling into pits, being covered in dust, or being deafened by the noise of machines. A fifteenth-century well came to light during the excavations, as did also part of a house of the last century. Wanting to show my appreciation of the workmen, I asked the builder what I should do for them, and he said that at the termination of the building operations I should give them what is called a *granzega*, meaning a dinner party. It was a great success, held in June in the garden of my favorite restaurant near the Accademia. We were eighteen to twenty people, and the architect's wife and I were the only women present. We drank a lot and got very gay. I moved from one guest to another in order to talk to them all. They sang songs and one played a mandolin. Suddenly I remembered my guest-book, and sent home for it. When it came, they all signed their names, and the partner of the builder turned out to be a poet and wrote a lovely poem for me, in which he called me the Lioness, in honor of the name of my *palazzo*. The architect, Passero, made a lovely drawing of the *barchessa*. The next morning, when I woke and looked in my guest-book, I found my addition to all my guests' signatures. The following words were written in a very wobbly handwriting: "The nicest night of my life in Venice, 1948–58, Peggy G."

I gave a second *granzega* in the fall, at the termination of the second building. It was held in the same restaurant but because of the season was not in the garden. Maybe for this reason it was not so pleasant. In fact, it was a complete letdown. I presume one cannot repeat such a marvelous soirée. But if the second party was not such a success, the second building definitely was. The *barchessa* was now large enough to permit me to place all my Surrealist paintings and sculptures in it. I removed them from a very overcrowded corridor in my *palazzo,* and also took this occasion to rehang everything in my home, as well as finally deciding not to admit the public to my library and sitting room any more. I painted both rooms white, instead of the dirty dark blue I had suffered for ten years, and felt that a new life was commencing.

Chapter 21

New York Revisited

I had many times put off returning to America, where I had not been for twelve years. Instead I had been to Sicily, Malta, Cyprus, India, Ceylon, Lebanon, Syria, Greece, Corfu, Turkey, Ireland, England, Holland, Belgium, Yugoslavia, Austria, France, Switzerland, Germany, Spain and Tangiers. I had always said I would return to New York for the opening of my Uncle Solomon's museum. When my uncle died, several years later, his nephew, Harry Guggenheim, took over the museum and the Baroness Rebay, the former curator, was replaced by my great friend James Johnson Sweeney. This was a great blessing for the museum. I had been expecting it to open sometime in the winter of 1959, and was prepared to go to New York at any moment. However, at Christmas my friends, the Cardiffs, invited me to visit them in Mexico, where Maurice Cardiff was stationed as cultural attaché to the British Embassy. I had met them in Italy, in 1948, when he was posted in Milan, and once followed them to Cyprus. I now was delighted to go to see them in Mexico, which was much more exciting than New York, though I intended to go there on my way home.

It was a most marvelous trip. Maurice and I went to Yucatan, where we saw the most fantastic ruins at Palenque, which is set deep in the jungle and really seems to be out of this world. It was so inaccessible we could go there only by helicopter, which took us forty minutes. Then we had to make an enormous climb up many steep steps. Of everything that.I saw in this one month, Palenque was by far the most exciting. The setting was wild and beautiful and the sculpture and the architecture thrilling. In fact, the ruins were more beautiful than any I have seen anywhere. After this, I went to Oaxaca, Puebla, Acapulco, Taxco, Cuernavaca and many other places. However, this is not the place to write about my trip, as I must confine myself to modern art.

Let me first of all say how much I hate the enormous frescoes of Diego Rivera, Orozco and Siqueiros that one sees in all official buildings in Mexico—and how much I like Tamayo, but even better, two remarkable women painters, Frida Kahlo, Diego Rivera's wife, and Leonora Carrington, who lived in Mexico City. She was still very beautiful, and was married to a Hungarian photographer and had two lovely little sons. She was by now quite a well-established painter and her work had greatly developed. She still painted animals and birds rather resembling Bosch's, but nevertheless her work was very personal. There were no other painters of interest, though all the galleries in Mexico seemed to be flourishing.

Frida Kahlo was dead and her home had been turned into a museum. I was familiar with her work, having included her in my women's shows, realizing how gifted she was in the true Surrealist tradition. Her museum was very touching and very sad. One felt how much she must have suffered in this home, where she was to die in 1954 from a spinal injury caused in a motor accident in her youth, which had practically invalided her for life. Many of her pictures dealt with physical sufferings and her various operations to cure her spinal condition, none of which were successful. We felt an atmosphere of tragedy on another plane. We saw her invalid's chair, in which she painted to the end. There could have been no love between Diego Rivera and Frida at the end of her life.

Diego Rivera, at his death, left no money to his children, who nevertheless continued to adore him. Instead, he left a fortune to be used to build a monument to himself designed by himself. It was in the suburbs of Mexico City, in a forlorn spot surrounded by houses of poor squatters. In this pyramid, which was a bad imitation of a Mayan ruin, were to be placed not only Rivera's bones, but also many of his paintings and his collection of pre-Columbian art.

When I got to New York, it was still too soon for the opening of the Guggenheim Museum. Sweeney had warned me of this, but I decided to go anyway, on my way back to Venice. Sweeney asked my cousin Harry Guggenheim to show me over the museum. I had not seen him for thirty-five years and was delighted to have this occasion to do so. I was also delighted, when I got back from Venice, to receive a letter in which he said:

> Before your arrival, and before we had a chance to become reacquainted after all these years, I had the general feeling that perhaps some day you might want to leave your collection to the Foundation to be housed in the new Frank Lloyd Wright Museum. However, after thinking the matter through, I most sincerely believe that your Foundation and your palace, which has, thanks to your initiative, become world-renowned, should, after your death, be bequeathed, as you have planned, to Italy. I think that is the appropriate place for it, and I think from the family point of view—which I confess is always uppermost in my mind, this plan would be the most beneficial. I do hope while you were over here you were able to make progress with your plans.
>
> May you continue, in great success, in your life dedicated to the progress of art, and also get lots of pleasure and fun from it.

Harry seemed to take his responsibilities very seriously and obviously had had great difficulties as a buffer between what he referred to as "two egotistical geniuses," Sweeney and Wright, the latter then a very old man. I did not envy Harry his position, but I completely sided with Sweeney against Wright who, I am certain, like Kiesler, was not interested in the pictures, but only in his architecture.

Two people could not have been more at loggerheads than Sweeney and Wright. Poor Sweeney, who inherited this millstone along with his job as director of the museum, was an absolute purist about display—in fact, he was a fanatic. The interior of his home resembled a Mondrian painting. Luckily Wright died while I was in New York, and I presume this cleared the air and left Sweeney with fewer difficulties.

The museum resembles a huge garage. It is built on a site that is inadequate for its size and looks very cramped, suffering from its nearness to adjacent buildings. It should have been placed on a hill in the Park; instead it is on the wrong side of Fifth Avenue. Around an enormous space intended for sculpture displays, the rising ramp, Wright's famous invention, coils like an evil serpent. The walls bend backward, and a cement platform keeps one at a respectful distance from the pictures. Nothing could be more difficult than viewing them at this angle. Eventually they were to be placed on brackets extending from the walls. It is amazing how Kiesler's ideas have been copied. The colors were very ugly, beige in some places, white in others. But I felt, somehow, that Sweeney with his genius would eventually overcome all the difficulties and the museum would be all right. Nevertheless, I much preferred my modest *barchessa* in Venice, and for the first time I did not regret the enormous fortune I had lost when my father left his brothers to go into his own business, a few years before he was drowned on the *Titanic*.

My best day in America was spent visiting the Barnes collection and the Philadelphia Museum, ending up for cocktails in the modern apartment of Ben Heller, the art collector. Rather a heavy program for one day, which also included a midnight party.

I was escorted to the Barnes Foundation by my friend Robert Brady, who had once been a pupil there. He obtained a special invitation for me, as I was leaving in a few days. He was not admitted with me, as his invitation was for a fortnight later. It was the first time that I had asked to visit the collection. The house, situated in a lovely park, is not very large or modern, but this marvelous collection is unbelievable. The place is not in any way considered as a museum. The pictures are intended to be shown only to art students and are taken down from the walls when being studied. Miss Violette de Mazia presided as hostess and teacher. She was very kind and hospitable, but when I asked her for a catalogue she seemed very shocked. It took half an hour to get used to the arrangement of the pictures. I have never seen so many masterpieces assembled in such confusion, at times five rows deep. There were about twenty small rooms, apart from the large hall. Here, in a gallery above, there was a large series of paintings by Matisse, done specially for the space. One had to concentrate with all one's will power to look at each picture in turn, as the surrounding ones were so close. There were about two hundred and forty Renoirs, one hundred and twenty Cézannes, forty-three Matisses, thirty Picassos, twenty Douanier Rousseaus, twelve Seurats, twenty-five Soutines, as well as paintings by Modigliani, Manet, Monet, Daumier, Van Gogh, Courbet, Klee, Vlaminck, Degas, Jean Hugo, Laurens, Utrillo, Braque and Derain. There were also some old masters, like Titian, Tintoretto, Cranach, Van de Velde and Franz Hals. Another room contained old American furniture, and another was filled with pre-Columbian sculpture and jewelry. The walls were dotted everywhere with early-American wrought-iron arabesques. I was permitted to remain two hours, though I could have stayed a month. I went around two or three times, and at the end Robert Brady slipped in unnoticed.

Completely exhausted and overwhelmed by what I had seen, I nevertheless proceeded to the Philadelphia Museum to see the Arensberg and Gallatin collections in their new setting. I was enormously impressed by Henry Clifford's installation. Apart from this, the museum had innumerable other treasures and I wandered around through a part of the Indian temple of Madura, a Chinese palace hall, a Japanese teahouse, a Japanese scholar's study, the cloister of St. Michel de Cuxa, from Toulouse, the fountain of St. Genis des Fontaines, as well as Italian, French and English interiors, all brought to America like the Scottish castle in the Robert Donat movie, *The Ghost Goes West*.

After such a day, it seemed a fitting climax to take cocktails surrounded by Pollocks, Philip Gustons, Stamoses, Rothkos, in the home of Mr. and Mrs. Ben Heller and in the company of Mr. and Mrs. Bernard Reis, outstanding collectors themselves, and with Lee Pollock. The Hellers' apartment was dedicated to their collection. They had taken down walls in order to make space for Pollock's fabulous painting called *Blue Poles*. In fact, they moved from a lovelier place, because here, on Central Park West, they had more room. The flat was so bare that it looked halfway between a sanctuary and a hospital. This is the prescribed way of life for those who dedicate themselves to modern art, and the Hellers were not the only victims.

In the twelve years I had been away from New York everything had changed. I was thunderstruck, the entire art movement had become an enormous business venture. Only a few persons really cared for paintings. The rest bought them from snobbishness or to avoid taxation, presenting pictures to museums and being allowed to keep them until their death, a way of having your cake and eating it. Some painters could not afford to sell more than a few paintings a year, as now they were the people to be taxed. Prices were unheard of. People only bought what was the most expensive, having no faith in anything else. Some bought merely for investment, placing pictures in storage without even seeing them, phoning their gallery every day for the latest quotation, as though they were waiting to sell stock at the most advantageous moment. Painters whose work I had sold with difficulty for six hundred dollars now received twelve thousand. Someone even tried to sell me a Brancusi head for forty-five thousand dollars. Lee Pollock kept all Pollock's paintings in storage and did not even want to sell to museums.

I could not afford to buy anything that I wanted, so I turned to another field, that is, after a few artists were very kind to me and made me special prices. I began buying pre-Columbian and primitive art. In the next few weeks I found myself the proud possessor of twelve fantastic artifacts, consisting of masks and sculptures from New Guinea, the Belgian Congo, the French Sudan, Peru, Brazil, Mexico, and New Ireland. It reminded me, in reverse, of the days after Max had left our home, when he came back in the afternoons, while I was in the gallery, and removed his treasures one by one from the walls. Now they all seemed to be returning. I even succumbed to the dangerous little Mr. Carlebach, who had formerly sold so many things to Max in New York, and who now had a magnificent gallery on Madison Avenue. His prices had doubled, but at least they were still possible.

For several years Clement Greenberg had said that when I came back to New York he would like to make a show called "Hommage à Peggy," to include all my "war babies," as I called the painters I had discovered during the war. It was to have been a huge exhibition launched with a champagne party. But I had to decline. Greenberg had become artistic adviser to French and Company, where it would have to have been held, but I did not like what they exhibited in their galleries, nor what most of my "war babies" were now painting. In fact, I do not like art today. I think it has gone to hell, as a result of the financial attitude. People blame me for what is painted today because I had encouraged and helped this new movement to be born. I am not responsible. In the early 1940s there was a pure pioneering spirit in America. A new art had to be born—Abstract Expressionism. I fostered it. I do not regret it. It produced Pollock, or rather, Pollock produced it. This alone justifies my efforts. As to the others, I don't know what got into them. Some people say that I got stuck. Maybe it is true. I think this century has seen many great movements, but the one which undoubtedly stands out way beyond all the others is the Cubist movement. The face of art has been transformed. It is natural that this should have come about, as a result of the industrial revolution. Art mirrors its age, therefore it had to change completely, as the world changed so vastly and so quickly. One cannot expect every decade to produce genius. The twentieth century has already produced enough. We should not expect any more. A field must lie fallow every now and then. Artists try too hard to be original. That is why we have all this painting that isn't painting any more. For the moment we should content ourselves with what the twentieth century has produced—Picasso, Matisse, Mondrian, Kandinsky, Klee, Léger, Braque, Gris, Ernst, Miró, Brancusi, Arp, Giacometti, Lipchitz, Calder, Pevsner, Moore and Pollock. Today is the age of collecting, not of creation. Let us at least preserve and present to the masses all the great treasures we have.

Conclusion

In 1956, Carlo Cardazzo asked me to write a short and amusing book of anecdotes, one of a series. Laurence Vail named it *Una Collezionista Ricorda* (which the publisher rendered on the copyright page as *A Collectioner Remembers*). On the cover was a fabulous photograph of me under by Calder bedhead with my eight Lhasa terriers.

In 1960, an Italian publisher called Ugo Mursia asked me to write an introduction to a book called *Invitation to Venice*. The photographs were by Ugo Mulas and the text by Michelangelo Murare. I never thought I could do it, but Mursia insisted so much that I finally did. The introduction turned out to be quite full of fantasy and very unlike *Out of This Century*, which I thought was the only way I could write, and the text is reprinted as an appendix to this book.

That same year, I went to Japan with John Cage. He was invited by the Master of Flowers to give concerts in different cities. I followed him everywhere. I can't say I like his music, but I went to every concert. Yoko Ono was our guide and translator and also took part in one of the performances. She was terribly efficient and nice and we became great friends. She was followed

everywhere by an American boy called Tony Cox who had come to
Japan to find her, never having met her. He came on all our trips,
even though her husband, a fine composer, was also with us. We
were a large party and had our own private photographer. I
allowed this Tony to come and sleep in the room I shared with
Yoko. The result was a beautiful half-Japanese half-American
baby whom Tony later stole when Yoko was married to John
Lennon, having meanwhile married and divorced Tony.

What I liked best in Japan was Kyoto, but I never managed to
see enough temples as John Cage was not interested in sightseeing
and would not let us out of his sight. He spent a whole afternoon
looking for a special tie he had had made in Japan years before.
Everything we saw we had to do by stealing away from him. I
managed to get away and went along to Bangkok, Hong Kong and
Angkor Wat. At last I was free to see everything I wanted. I could
remain in Angkor Wat only forty-eight hours but managed to visit
nearly all the temples. The combination of the jungle and the
ruins is a most impressive sight and reminded me of Palenque. It
certainly is one of the most marvelous places I have ever seen.

In 1960, or about then, André Malraux came to Venice. The
French consul brought him to visit me and the collection.
Malraux was quite fascinated by Pegeen and insisted on explaining her own paintings to her. She did not understand a word of
what he said but was very pleased to have his attention. Several
days later he sent me photographs of two masks that he owned.
They were very beautiful, but I never knew why he sent them to
me unless he might have thought I would be interested in case he
wanted to sell them. Later on, Pegeen made use of his friendship
to ask his help to get two of her fairy photographer friends out of
trouble. Of course Malraux thought one of these men was her
lover. At the same time I asked his advice about whether or not I
should allow my pictures to be shown in Paris in the Ville de Patis
side of the Musée de l'Art Moderne where I had been invited.
Nellie van Doesburg said it was not at all a suitable place for me as
it was not important enough. Malraux said if I would show there
they would make it just as nice as the other side of the Museum,
which was the national side. However, I did not take his advice
and luckily waited until my collection was shown in the Orangerie
years later. During the time my show was at the Orangerie, I
happened to meet Malraux at a luncheon in the country near

Paris and wondered if he remembered all this and maybe was vexed, because he did not talk to me very much on this occasion. I did not know him at all well, but when he died I really felt very sad.

In 1961, I had a visit from a man called Egidio Constantini, who sought my help to execute glass sculptures from the many designs he had from all the most famous artists. He had no money to produce the glass and was quite desperate. He even wept. As I cannot bear to see a man cry, I promised to help him. Anyhow, I thought it a very good project and was always looking for someone to help. He made the most beautiful glass sculptures from designs by Picasso, Arp, Max Ernst, Cocteau, Calder, Le Corbusier, Chagall, Matta, Kokoschka and many others. Cocteau named the enterprise *La Fucina degli Angelli*. My house is now filled with these sculptures and I have given a great many to museums in America. I launched this man, sold a lot of his works and even obtained an exhibition for him at the Museum of Modern Art in New York. Constantini has been eternally grateful to me, which is more than I can say of a great many other artists.

Also in 1961, I asked Claire Falkenstein to make me new gates for the entrance to my palace. I had seen photographs of beautiful ones she had made for somebody on the Adriatic Coast and admired them so much I thought she would be just the person to do this. With bands of iron, which she personally welded by hand, a tremendous job for a woman, she inserted discarded pieces of glass from Murano. The result was stunning. Everyone stops in the street to look at the gates. Herbert Read was afraid they would not be strong enough, but they were. Perry Rathbone, director of the Boston Museum of Fine Arts, was all for them. I used to say to Claire, "Now go home and do your knitting," referring to her welding. When she had a show, I wrote in the catalogue: "Claire presented herself at the Gates of Heaven. St. Peter said, 'What are you doing here, my child? You may not be admitted.' And Claire replied, 'But I made these gates myself.' 'In that case,' said St. Peter, 'you may come in.'"

Alan Ansen, an American poet, wrote and produced two lovely masques in my garden, acted by all our friends. After he left Venice and went to live in Athens, he came back on a short visit every year on his way to Auden in Austria. On one of these occasions when I was giving Ansen his usual cocktail party,

Norton Simon phoned that he was in Venice and wanted to come at once. We said we could not receive him then as we were having a party for a Greek poet. Norton Simon insisted, saying that the appointment had been made by the American Embassy. I, too, insisted that he had come one day too soon, but finally we gave in. He turned out to be charming, not a bit like a millionaire, and fitted very well into our Bohemian party. The next day he came to lunch alone and asked me if I would leave my collection to the University of California, Berkeley. I said I would on one condition, that he would save Venice, and that, I am afraid, was the end of it.

I was at last made an honorary citizen of Venice in 1962. My dear friend Count Elio Zorzi wrote a speech for me to make. The mayor made a speech also written by someone else, and so did a third person. Thus all our speeches were not our own. This occurred in the Town Hall. I was presented with a beautiful bouquet and a parchment. Drinks were served and later all my artist friends gave me a luncheon at the Angelo restaurant.

About this time Joseph Losey asked me if I would act in the film *Eve* he was making with Jeanne Moreau. Actually, all I had to do was to sit at a gambling table and play baccarat. I had no idea how to play baccarat, but a very nice man who sat next to me, whom I suspected of being a gondolier dressed up in very fashionable cheap clothes, showed me how to play or played for me. I don't really see what I was paid for—some enormous sum—except that I had to get up very early in the morning to get to the Casino in time.

One of the worst gaffes since I have been in Venice was when I met Prince Philip, who was telling us how he attended a ball in my house given by Lady Castlerosse, and he had a great flirt with a young woman, who since then had married and become the mother of four children. At this time Princess Elizabeth and Prince Philip had only two children. I perked up and replied, "Ah, she did better than you, then." Everybody surrounding us was silent with horror.

My other bad gaffe occurred when I first met Tennessee Williams. I did not know which was he and which was his boy friend. After talking to him for quite a while I decided he must be a writer and I said to him, "You don't write, by any chance, do you?"

One day I had a visit from Amilcare Fanfani, the president of the Italian Senate. He came with two detectives and his wife and Giovanni Carandente, who gave him a lecture tour of my collection. He seemed not at all interested in what he saw and made no comments. Signora Fanfani was very charming and told me her husband was a painter and invited me to Rome to lunch to see his work. I imagine that Signor Fanfani thus had hopes of being in my collection and that was the purpose of his visit.

In 1965, I was invited to show nearly my entire collection at the Tate Gallery in London. A tremendous fuss was made over this. The Tate's chief restorer came to prepare the paintings to travel. I felt very guilty to think how much I had neglected them and how badly they were in need of restoration. The Tate Gallery hoped to inherit the collection. They gave a big dinner party for me in one of the galleries, borrowing old silver for the occasion. I was allowed to hang the pictures; this was the last time I ever did so. We had a very impressive opening. I went around on the arm of the new director, Norman Reed, receiving the guests. The show was a terrific success, with people queuing up all the way down the steps of the Tate and along the Embankment. My only rival was Churchill's funeral. After the show, which was prolonged two weeks, they restored lots of paintings for me.

In 1966, we had a most terrible flood in Venice. The city was completely under water for twenty-four hours and when the tide receded, it left behind the most filthy brown oil which covered everything and even got on the faces of my lions' heads. For the second time my basement was flooded, but the pictures were safe as they were all packed ready to go to Stockholm, and were outside in the *barchessa*, which was too high for the water to penetrate. Actually, my house is on the highest land in Venice, called Dorso Duro, so the flood reached only the basement.

So much damage was done by this flood that it was necessary to think of restoring Venice. Many committees were formed, CRIA being the first. But that was mostly to help Florence, and was started by Fred Licht, who was then director of the Florida State University Center in Florence and later became director of the Princeton University Art Museum. Soon after, many different countries formed their own committees. First was the United States and then came Great Britain, France, Germany and Australia. They have all done wonders of restoration, which

Venice so badly needed even before the flood, and certainly much more after. I myself became an honorary member of Save Venice and have given lots of money every year to John MacAndrew, its former chairman. There is, of course, the possibility of Venice sinking, which would make all this useless, but we all hope that some solution will be found to prevent this terrible catastrophe from occurring.

One year after the Tate Gallery show, I was asked by Pontus Hulten to show in his gallery, the Modern Museum of Stockholm. King Gustaf Adolf opened the exhibition, and I had to show him around. I fear he was much more interested in excavations and Chinese art than in modern art.

While I was in Stockholm, Knud Jensen came from Louisiana, the beautiful museum outside of Copenhagen, to ask me if I would allow the collection to go there after the show in Stockholm ended. He invited me and Pegeen to come and visit in Copenhagen so that we could see Louisiana. Even before seeing it I had decided I would show there, but we had three lovely days in Denmark, almost my happiest and last days with Pegeen, who was to die a few months later. Sam Kaner, who runs the Royal Gallery in Copenhagen and who is a painter, showed us around and took great care of us. Copenhagen is a delightful city. I had not thought so when I visited it before. I did not go to my show, as I went to visit Robert Brady in Mexico, and that is where I was when I got the tragic news of Pegeen's death. My darling Pegeen, who was not only a daughter, but also a mother, a friend and a sister to me. We seemed also to have had a perpetual love affair. Her untimely and mysterious death left me quite desolate. There was no one in the world I loved so much. I felt all the light had gone out of my life. Pegeen was a most talented primitive painter. For years I had fostered her talent and sold her paintings. She was just beginning to have a real success, having shows that winter in Canada, Stockholm and Philadelphia.

In 1967, I decided to enlarge my museum. I had so many new paintings and sculptures, in spite of the fact that I had given a vast amount to museums in America, that I found it necessary to have more space. This, of course, was all accomplished in my basement. Some old caretakers had left, which left me their apartments free, so I added four more rooms. This was just after Pegeen's death, so having started the work before, I consecrated one room to Pegeen. As I was no longer to sell her paintings, I closed my sales gallery. Pegeen's room was very lovely, with about twelve of her paintings from all ages, beginning with one done when she was twelve. Constantini gave me a present of a lovely glass she had executed with him. This was the high spot of the room. It was in twelve parts and looked just like her paintings. He said he would never repeat it for anyone else so that I should have the only one in existence. I also placed in the room a photograph of Pegeen sitting in my Byzantine throne in the garden and her biography on a beautiful parchment. To me this was Pegeen's tomb.

Also in 1967, I was made a commendatore of the Italian Republic, which deserved another ceremony. But because of Pegeen's death I did not wish to have one. This time I was given a parchment and a medal, which I never wear but which I expose on a glass shelf. It makes me feel like the old lady shows her medals. There are, I believe, only two other lady commendatores in Italy.

In 1968, I accompanied Roloff Beny, the photographer, to India. He was a state guest, as he was doing a book on that country. We went everywhere, driving over a thousand miles. I went almost mad waiting for Roloff to photograph everything in sight. His photographs are all works of art, each one looks like a painting. We went to the most marvelous places quite off the beaten track where I felt no one had ever been before. This was quite unlike my previous trip to India which was quite touristy. We stayed almost every night in a different place, and what places they were. Terrible government hostels with practically no conveniences. But it was marvelously worthwhile considering all the fantastic things we saw.

In 1969, the Guggenheim Museum of New York invited me to give a show. A great fuss was made over this, as they wanted to inherit my collection. I had had the same idea, so I was like someone who was longing to be proposed to by someone who was longing to marry her. Harry Guggenheim, my cousin, the president of the museum in New York, was in hospital where I went to visit him, and we drew up an agreement. The terms were that the collection remain in Venice intact in my name to be administered by them. Nothing was to be removed.

The museum gave wonderful parties for me in New York, and

so did everyone else. It was an exhausting time. I was put in charge of Robin Greene, their publicity manager, who took wonderful care of me and my publicity, so the show was a great success. I became devoted to Robin as he was to me. I never dreamt, after all the rows I had with my uncle Solomon, that I would one day see my collection descending the ramp of the Guggenheim Museum like Marcel Duchamp's nude descending the stairs. It was a great relief to have the collection's future settled.

While I was in America I stayed with my friends Bernard and Rebecca Reis and with darling Marius Bewley in Staten Island, Jim Moon in North Carolina, Barbara Obroe, my cousin, in South Carolina, and John Goodwin in Santa Fe. I also visited Perry Rathbone in Boston, where I was robbed on the Common—not mugged, thank goodness. When I came back to New York I stayed with my friends the Garnetts next door to the Museum. I have never liked the museum and called it my uncle's garage. I did not think my collection looked well there, especially seen across the ramp, where the paintings looked like postage stamps. One day, when passing the museum in a bus, I had forgotten the collection was there and had such a shock to find it there.

Since I have been back in Venice, I have given first the *palazzo* and after that the entire collection to the Guggenheim Museum with the condition that I can live here until I die and administer the collection myself until then.

In 1971, Virginia Dorazio asked me if I would allow her to write a book about me. I accepted gladly and helped her as much as I could, putting at her disposal all my library of documents, catalogues, newspaper clippings, photographs etc. She obtained a contract with the Viking Press, but the book is still not finished.

In 1973, John Hohnsbeen, an old friend, whom I asked to help me with the gallery as it was all getting too much for me alone, came to stay with me every summer as a house guest. He took charge of selling the catalogues. The entrance is free, but the catalogues are for sale. He also does all my errands for me in the morning and writes my letters, but spends all the rest of the day at Cipriani's pool. He is the most social person I have ever met and the telephone rings for him all day long. He adores going to parties, but always comes home disillusioned. Besides the new friends he makes at the pool, he seems to know everybody. He never stays with me, but goes out for all his meals. I don't think he can bear being at home, but he is very kind and helpful and when I broke my wrist was an angel of kindness. I depend on him very much.

In recent years the kindness and devotion of Jane Rylands and her husband Philip have been beyond all I could imagine.

In the winter of 1972 fifteen of my very valuable small paintings were stolen. They were taken out of my house by the front and probably deposited next door in an empty house. The thieves broke through a window in the Pollock galleries. The chief of police here is a very active man, who makes friends with the underworld to help his work. After two weeks he recovered all of the paintings where they were, rolled up and buried in the mud near Mestre. An insurance agent had come from Milan to offer his services to help me find the paintings. The very next day the chief of police found them. He could brook no rival. The next robbery occurred ten months later. The Guggenheim Museum in New York had been promising to send someone to see about installing an alarm system. They delayed so long that I wrote them that if they did not hurry, it would be too late. And so it was. That very night thieves broke through the thick iron grill on one of the windows of my sitting room on the Grand Canal and stole sixteen small paintings. It was a very foggy night when the visibility was practically nil. This time I was in the house and the dogs barked like mad, but I thought they were barking at a cat. There was no trace of the paintings for months and I was beginning to get very worried. Finally, I pretended that the insurance agent from Milan had come back to offer his services. The next day all the pictures were returned. Now I have an alarm system that goes off often without any provocation.

Downstairs in a long corridor of my *palazzo* there are many drawings and gouaches. One day a visitor held out a bag to someone next to him, and said, "Hold this." Whereupon he took a Tanguy gouache off the wall and put it in the bag, departing with it. Luckily, this was observed by another visitor who came up to John Hohnsbeen and told him. He rushed after the thief and got back the Tanguy without any trouble. The man neither resisted nor fled. In fact, he docilely came back to the house with John and waited for the police to come and take him away. He must have been drugged.

In 1975, I was invited to show my collection in the Orangerie of the Louvre. This was a great honor and also my revenge for the time when the Louvre had refused to save it in 1940. The newspapers made a great point of this, so I was rather pleased. Unfortunately, Jean Leymarie, who did the show, placed my two Brancusis in front of the windows, where you could not see them because of the light. I asked to have them moved and never have I been treated with so little courtesy at any of my shows. Leymarie said he had placed them there because there were trees outside and he felt my birds belonged in the trees. Everyone else was terribly disagreeable and treated me as though I had no right to make this modest demand. They all knew much better than I did. However, in the end I won my battle by sheer force of will. This show was prolonged because of its popularity, as the one in the Tate Gallery had been. There were 120,000 visitors.

In 1976, Dr. Ezio Gribaudo, the publisher of my catalogue and of the book on my collection by Nicolas and Elena Calas, asked me to show my collection in Turin in the Modern Museum where he was a trustee. In 1949, the city of Turin had invited me to have a show there, but at the very last minute called it off for no reason except that my collection was too modern for them at the time. This was another revenge for me. This time they had two modern architects to set up the collection. However, their idea of being modern was to place all the sculptures helter-skelter on tables covered with turquoise linoleum, large and small all mixed up. They even placed the two tall Giacomettis on these tables. I did succeed in having them put on the ground. They were very polite and nice to me—not like the Orangerie. Turin is a very Communist city and the mayor, who is a Communist, received me most charmingly, giving me caviar and smoked salmon sandwiches and a big box of orchids and a book on the art treasures of the Piedmont. I told him I was so happy that the Communists had gotten in with the recent regional elections. He looked rather surprised to hear this from an American, but understood that I preferred the Communists to the Christian Democrats, who have ruined Italy. All the time I was in Turin I was escorted everywhere by the Communist cultural *assessore,* Giorgio Balmas, and followed everywhere by two policemen in a car. Dr. Balmas explained that this was not the kind of show that the new government planned to give, but that it was too good to refuse, and that they wanted to make it very polemic, in order, I suppose, to be more Communist. The show had 80,000 visitors and was also prolonged two weeks. In 1967, Madame Agnelli had asked me to lend her my Surrealist paintings for a show she was giving there in the Modern Museum. At the time she wrote me that my paintings had made the show. So this was the second time they were exhibited in Turin. In the entrance they put a photo enlargement of my Marino Marini sculpture, which was too big to travel, and also an enormous photograph of me by Man Ray, taken in the early twenties, wearing a Poiret dress and a headdress by Vera Stravinsky. They also made a vitrine of photographs and documents from my life.

When I was in Turin I was the guest of the city and was invited back again for the end of the show. Unfortunately, I did not accept, as I could not bear to see the blue linoleum again. Instead I remained in Venice, where, without knowing it, I had a blood pressure of 300 and fainted, breaking eight ribs and remaining in the Ospedale Civile seventeen days. The nurses were terribly nice and kind, but as there were only two of them to forty patients, it was almost impossible to be bathed. The bed pan, to my horror, was brought by male orderlies. I seem to have survived all this, being overwhelmed by visitors and flowers, fruits, wines and sweets.

I used to have a lovely Fiat car with a beautiful Ghia body, a motorboat, which I had made to order by the famous Oscar, and a gondola. I gave up everything except the gondola, my last remaining joy. My gondola was made to order and is beautifully carved with lions. The *cavalli* are Golden Lions. First I used it to go to parties and to do errands in and to shop, like a car. Then I had it at my disposal all day and sometimes at night. After that I used it only four hours a day, and now I am reduced to two, which is really quite enough and very expensive, as the price of a gondolier is now excessive. When I had the motorboat the chauffeur served as a second gondolier, but now I am reduced to one. So every afternoon during the warmer months, at sunset time I go for a two-hour ride which is sacred and with which nothing must interfere. Sometimes I take friends to see churches, if they do it briefly enough, as every hour is so precious that I can't bear to interrupt the ride. Mine is the last private gondola in Venice, as all the Venetians, and there were about twenty, have given up their gondolas in favor of motorboats. Having a car was really unnecessary and worried me a lot, as I never used it and I felt I had to exercise it like a horse at least once a week. The motorboat I gave up when my darling Guido, whom I had for twelve years, left me with one day's notice, as he was given a taxi to drive. This is the great ambition of every driver in Venice and Guido was extremely lucky to get it. I have seen him only once in all these years and he is very happy.

In May 1977, Giovanni Carandente gave a lecture about me and the collection at the Athenee. It was very comprehensive and complete with slides, nearly all of which were shown upside down. Then he gave two lectures in my house for the Friends of the Museum. After the lecture, Countess Zavagli gave a big dinner party in my honor. While we were at dinner, we suddenly saw everything swinging from the curtains to the chandeliers. It was very exciting but did not in the least frighten me, as I did not believe that Venice could suffer a real earthquake. This was the tail end of the Friuli earthquake and frightened most people so much that they spent the night in the street. Not me, however, as I went peacefully to bed and to sleep.

In 1978, Jacqueline Bograd wrote me that Holt, Rinehart and Winston had asked her to write my biography. She came to Venice and was a charming girl and we got on beautifully. I was so pleased that she could then put right all the awful things John Davis had written about me in his book *The Guggenheims: An American Epic*. He wrote, for example, that I had given a garage to Raoul Gregorich. In fact, I gave him exactly three cars. Raoul did not murder a man; the man died long after. Davis wrote that Tancredi was my lover. In fact, he was strictly a protégé. Davis wrote that Pegeen was deprived of seeing her children after her divorce from Jean Hélion. That is not true. She saw them constantly. I gave a large regular allowance to Pegeen and Sindbad and sold many paintings for Pegeen in my gallery. If she was short of money it was because her husband Ralph Rumney provided nothing and spent fortunes. Sindbad did not trudge the streets for his insurance company. He had two cars which he could use. There is no proof that Pegeen committed suicide. The doctor who performed the autopsy said that she died from her lungs. I think she must have suffocated from her vomit. When married to Kay

Boyle, Laurence Vail did not lead a promiscuous life but a very domestic one. Finally, I resent particularly Mr. Davis's question, "What to do after fifteen years in and out of various, ultimately worthless beds?" since at that time I had had only one husband and two lovers.

After writing *Confessions of an Art Addict* and the introduction to *Invitation to Venice*, I stopped writing altogether for sixteen years. A few years ago, Fred Licht had an offer from his publisher Louis Barron of Universe Books for me to combine *Out of This Century* and *Confessions of an Art Addict*, bringing my memoirs up to date. At the time I did not feel like it, but now several years later I came round to thinking of it. It came about in this way: The French consul, André Tronc, wanted to do a best-selling book of my memoirs with me on a tape-recording machine. It turned out to be a complete fiasco. He had a very good publisher, who wanted to give me $15,000, but luckily I hesitated about signing the contract. Nothing ever came of this. I disappointed Mr. Tronc thoroughly. I could not produce anything he wanted, I was so much in love with *Out of This Century*. He said I should read it again to get new ideas, but I got only old ones. Mr. Tronc said the French would not like *Out of This Century;* it was for an English public, and anyhow he could not give them a translation, it would not be fair. I got hold of Mrs. Jenny Bradley in Paris and asked her to be my agent. But in the meantime, I was worried about what the French consul would produce, so I went and told her I could not sign the contract until I saw his version. She quite agreed with me, which was terribly nice of her, considering all the money she was about to lose. Anyhow, I came back to Venice with the idea of doing my own book. The French consul also wanted to get rid of me, but he never said so. We just drifted apart and this book is the result of the failed Franco-American effort.

To end my memoirs I think it appropriate to add that on August 26, 1978, to celebrate my eightieth birthday, Dr. Passante, the director of the Gritti Hotel, gave a dinner party for me and twenty-two of my chosen guests. My son Sindbad made an impromptu speech, and other speeches were made by the British consul Ray Jacques, by the film director Joseph Losey, and by Dr. Guido Perocco, director of the Museum of Modern Art of Venice. There was a banner with my name on it and "To the Ultima

Dogaressa," wishing me a happy birthday, and a beautiful sugar model of my *palazzo*, an exact replica lit from the inside. The American and Italian flags on the wall and millions of photographers greeted me as I descended from my gondola. The evening ended with all of us watching me on television. Altogether a memorable occasion.

Appendix
Venice

It is always assumed that Venice is the ideal place for a honeymoon. This is a grave error. To live in Venice or even to visit it means that you fall in love with the city itself. There is nothing left over in your heart for anyone else. After your first visit you are destined to return at every possible chance or with every possible excuse. There is no staying away for long. You are inevitably drawn back as though by magic. As to the Venetians themselves, they are all in love with Venice. With sighs they recount their undying passion for their beloved city. With the rising tide their love mounts and with the receding tide it gently diminishes only to surge forth again when the sea pours back its waters. When Venice is flooded it is even more truly beloved. Then a new ecstasy comes over the inhabitants, as they sweep out the waters from their ground floors, in order to be able to proceed with their daily lives and normal existence. Normal existence is a *façon de parler*. There is no normal life in Venice. Here everything and everyone floats. Not only the gondolas, launches, barges, vaporettos and *sandolos* but also the buildings and the people float.

Reprinted, with permission, from *Invito a Venezia,* wih a text by Michelangelo Muraro and photographs by Ugo Mulas, published by Ugo Mursia Editore, Milan, 1962.

One floats in and out of restaurants, shops, cinemas, theaters, museums, churches and hotels. One floats luxuriously with such a sense of freedom, never tormented by traffic or even disturbed by the sound of a klaxon. It is this floatingness which is the essential quality of Venice. As the tide rises and recedes twice a day one has the impression of the entire city being in perpetual motion. The buildings seem to rise and sink with the tide. Sometimes Venice partly disappears under the sea for a few hours. In very high tides it can be submerged a whole meter. But this does not greatly alter its character. It merely makes one even more conscious of how much it is a city sprung from the sea and living in it.

Here no sense of time exists. One is barely aware of the passing of the hours. The only thing that makes one realize time is the change of the light.

Church bells ring all day long, but one becomes so accustomed to them that one does not relate the chimes to time. The only hour of the day of which one is definitely conscious is noon. Then all the church bells of the entire city ring out at once in chorus, with an extra force, and added to this, a mysterious cannon goes off.

Every hour of the day is a miracle of light. In summer with daybreak the rising sun produces such a tender magic on the water that it nearly breaks one's heart. As the hours progress the light becomes more and more violet until it envelops the city with a diamond-like haze. Then it commences slowly to sink into the magic sunset, the *capolavoro* of the day. This is the moment to be on the water. It is imperative. The canals lure you, call you, cry to you to come and embrace them from a gondola. More pity to those who cannot afford this poetic luxury. In this brief hour all of Venice's intoxicating charm is poured forth on its waters. It is an experience never to be forgotten. Day after day one is drawn from *terraferma* to float in the lagoon, to watch the sunset, or to go gently past the palaces seeing their images reflected in the canal. The reflections are like paintings more beautiful than any painted by the greatest masters. The striped *pali,* when seen in the water, deny their functional use and appear like colored snakes. If anything can rival Venice in its beauty, it must be its reflection at sunset in the Grand Canal.

Though this is the irresistible hour to be in a gondola the nights also have their own special fascination and mystery. The people look quite different in the dimly lit city. One can barely distinguish their modern costumes. One can imagine these semi-invisible figures, as they were once dressed in all their splendor and glory, in their velvets and brocades and sables with their swords and jewels and even masqued in carnival time. To go out in a gondola at night is to reconstruct in one's imagination the true Venice, the Venice of the past alive with romance, elopements, abductions, revenged passions, intrigues, adulteries, denouncements, unaccountable deaths, gambling, lute playing and singing.

To evoke the Venice of the past one must keep away from the Grand Canal with its trumped-up tourist serenades, sheer mockeries of the past, and float through small dark canals, past dimly lit crumbling palaces, under bridges, where lovers nightly plight their troth, past gondolas with Japanese lanterns and harmonica players, past *fondamentas* with *bistros,* where gondoliers assemble to drink wine, past warehouses and closed shops and rats and floating garbage.

I have never been in a city that gave me the same sense of freedom as Venice. The extraordinary enjoyment experienced from walking about without being tormented by the dangers of traffic is only rivaled by the sense of freedom one enjoys in choosing one's attire. Here one can wear almost anything and not appear ridiculous. On the contrary, the more exaggerated one's clothes, the more suitable they appear in this city, where carnival once reigned supreme.

The bourgeois ladies, who go about donned in suits, small hats with veils, gloves and handbags seem ridiculously out of place. In this fantastic city only fantastic clothes should be worn.

Venice is not only the city of freedom and fantasy but it is also the city of pleasure and joy. I have never seen anyone cry here except at a funeral. But to a Venetian a funeral without tears would not be a real funeral. A Venetian funeral is still a completely medieval spectacle. The large black barge with four gondoliers in ancient black costumes, the coffin buried under a mass of gigantic wreaths, is one of the most impressive sights on the Grand Canal. But apart from death there is no sorrow here. One notices great patience and a sort of resignation in the people, who take all unpleasant things for granted. They do not worry. They have a *dolce far niente* attitude.

One spends most of one's life in Venice waiting for things that either do or do not occur. One accepts this, as part of the Venetian tempo. No Venetian has any sense of time. He is never on time, comes to appointments late or appears days after he was expected, showing no sense of guilt. One waits hours, days, weeks, even months for the most trivial or even the most important things. And so one drifts along barely aware of anything new happening or of any changes of the seasons.

A book was once published called *Venice Without Water*. This was a great surprise to many people, who believed that Venice is a city without streets and that one circulates only by boat. This is completely false. To get about with haste one must walk. If you know your way through this labyrinth you can, by making short cuts, get on foot from any given point of the city to any other in twenty minutes. This might involve crossing the Grand Canal two or three times as it winds its serpentine route through the city.

If you go on foot you discover quite a different Venice to the one you have seen from a gondola. The entrances to the houses are from the streets and not from the canals, often through gardens with big trees and lovely flowers enlivened by the sweet songs of birds. The gardens are enclosed by brick walls and one is amazed by their quantity.

Apart from the gardens one sees flowers everywhere in window boxes. They mostly are various shades of pink and red geraniums. This is a great relief from the austerity of the city. Wherever one walks, one's eye is confronted with sculptures and carvings, not only of lions, but also of camels and dwarfs and madonnas with Christs, crusaders, people in boats and numerous other subjects. One's eyes can never rest. There is at every point some fascinating surprise.

On one's strolls one passes from campo to campo each with its own church and café, and often with a market. One winds in and out of narrow *calles* so narrow that two umbrellas cannot be held at the same level. One comes to dead ends either in mysterious courtyards or at a canal. If there are a great many gardens in Venice there are even more courtyards with wells and beautiful gothic staircases with balustrades ornamented by carved lions. There are innumerable cloisters which bring one back to the Middle Ages. One passes buildings of every century in the last thousand years, all so harmonious that there appears no difference in the times when they were built. Venice is the most oriental of European cities, not only in architecture but also in its tempo. The people unexpectedly are very blond, the result of their having intermarried with the Germans and Austrians. One rather would expect to find dark Turkish visages. One finds here everywhere *altanas,* little pergolas on the top floors of houses, where ladies used to bleach their hair. This combined with the beautiful chimney pots and the lovely crooked old tiled roofs cause one to be looking upward continuously. One is perpetually walking up and down bridges. In fact there are so many that they are used as landmarks to give directions; one says *over the next bridge to the left,* or *at the foot of the bridge* or *three bridges away!* People stand for hours on the bridges watching the traffic go by. Women also are forever gazing out of their windows, as though they were expecting some important event to take place, though they know only too well that nothing will occur. Maybe they are looking for a fiancé or for some charming young man to pass by. But I think more likely they go to mass for this purpose.

The Venetian nobles used to keep horses and not only rode over the city and its bridges but also up the winding staircases to their high palaces. The steps were built especially for the horses to mount with perfect ease. Gone are the days of the horses and sadly enough now we find only lions, and stone ones at that. As the lion was the symbol of Venice one finds him everywhere. My own palace has eight lion heads on the front. They look as though they were about to spout water into the Grand Canal. Most of the lions of Venice look very fierce and most of them have a certain resemblance to each other. Many have wings. But there is one little creature at the Arsenale, who was brought here from Delos, who bears no resemblance to the other nine which adorn this beautiful building. In fact he looks quite melancholy, rather lost and extremely pathetic, as though he were longing to go home to his Greek isle and leave all the other lions to roar here without him.

There are no other animals here today except thousands of cats and a few dogs. Most of the cats are homeless and are fed in the *calles* by so-called charitable people, who bring filthy little packages of leftovers, which they leave about in the streets and which they even have the effrontery to toss into private gardens, where the cats come to eat. It is amazing that the cats have survived this poisonous form of charity. During the war all the cats were eaten as rabbits, but now they seem to have been reborn. Dogs, in Venice, are supposed to be muzzled or kept on a lead. A few years ago, failing this, they were seized and carried off to the stockyards, or more often their owners were merely fined. Now the authorities are more indulgent, and there seems to be no more control exerted over the happy creatures, who are so fortunate as to live in a trafficless city. At least they should be allowed to benefit by this blessing. The best *maison de coiffeur* in Venice is called Casa del Cane. They perform such miracles of hairstyling that I often with I were a dog myself to benefit from their services.

Venice has become so popular lately that in the summer months it is almost impossible to walk in the streets or to ride on a vaporetto or even to circulate in a gondola. In November everyone has gone home again and left the city to its loneliness and poverty. The summers are rich with tourists. Money pours in. The glass business thrives. The gondoliers overcharge in order to make enough money to last during the winter months, when people huddle together around brasiers, their throats wrapped in woollen scarves, their only protection against cold. The city is covered in a deep fog until January, when the weather becomes crisper and colder. In February it snows once, which transforms the city into a complete fairyland. The outer lagoons freeze but the canals never, as there is a perpetual movement of the water from the tides. There is plenty of sun in January and February, and in March suddenly the spring appears. But November and December are cast in gloom. Saint Mark's is barely recognizable. It rises through the fog like a ghost with no resemblance to itself, or rather completely distinguishable from its summer sister. Possibly a much more beautiful San Marco than the real one, which is over-gaudy, ornamented by hideous 19th-century mosaics on its front. Piazza San Marco, Napoleon's ballroom, is no longer a ballroom. Gone are the open-air cafés with their music, each band rivaling one opposite. Gone are the open-air concerts playing beautiful Wagnerian operas. Gone are postcard vendors and photographers and the grain merchants leaving the starved pigeons to the inadequate public feedings of the Commune. One walks under the arcades, not daring to face the rain and the slippery wet stones underfoot.

There are practically no gondolas in circulation except the public ones at the traghettos, and a very few that are hired with their *felze,* the winter cabin, which protects one from the wind and cold but which must give the passengers claustrophobia. On the other hand, the *felze* has the advantage of affording a certain privacy, which is entirely lacking in summer when everyone stares at you and takes your photograph.

Many people prefer Venice in winter. Not only the Venetians themselves but also some of the foreigners, who live here permanently. They say, at last we have it to ourselves. But to me the poor city seems to be reduced to the lowest level of gloom, cold, ice, fog and rain. Most of all one misses the society of stimulating visitors, who come from all corners of the earth. This is very important, as they serve as a link with the rest of the world, which one is so prone to forget when one lives in this island of lotus eaters.

If the summer tourists ruin Venice, at least they serve to keep it alive. Without them it could not exist. Its life is in the past and its beauties, like those of a museum, are preserved for those who care to come and admire them. Venice is kept alive only by this means and would perish entirely were the tourists to cease their pilgrimages. Ten centuries of magnificent architecture must be maintained. A city as beautiful, as unique as Venice must not die. The paintings of Vivarini, Mantegna, Crivelli, Bellini, Antonello, Carpaccio, Cima, Giorgione, Sebastiano, Lotto, Tiziano, Palma, Pordenone, Bassano, Tintoretto, Veronese, Tiepolo, Canaletto and Guardi belong here and must be preserved as part of this miraculous city, Venice, which must be eternal.

Index

An asterisk before a name indicates that the person or work of art is illustrated in this book. Page references for illustrations are in italics.